About the author

JAMES HALLIDAY is Australia's most respected wine writer. Over the past 30-plus years he has worn many hats: lawyer, winemaker and grape grower, wine judge, wine consultant, journalist and author. He has discarded his legal hat, but actively continues in his other roles, incessantly travelling, researching and tasting wines in all the major wine-producing countries. He judges regularly at wine shows in Australia, Europe, the US, South Africa and New Zealand.

James Halliday has written or contributed to more than 50 books on wine since he began writing in 1979 (notable contributions include those to the *Oxford Companion to Wine* and the *Larousse Encyclopedia of Wine*). His books have been translated into Japanese, French, German, Danish and Icelandic, and have been published in the UK and the US as well as Australia.

His works include *Varietal Wines*, *Classic Wines of Australia and New Zealand* (3rd edition) and *Wine Odyssey: A Year of Wine, Food and Travel*.

The 2006 edition of the *Australian Wine Companion* earned James Halliday the prestigious 2005 Saltram Australian Wine Communicator Award.

James Halliday
Australian Wine
Companion
2007 Edition

Collins

Collins
An imprint of HarperCollins*Publishers*

First published as *Australia and New Zealand Wine Companion* in Australia in 1997
This edition published in Australia in 2006
by HarperCollins*Publishers* Australia Pty Limited
ABN 36 009 913 517
www.harpercollins.com.au

Published in the United Kingdom in 2006
by Collins
Collins is a registered trademark of HarperCollinsPublishers Ltd
The Collins website address is www.collins.co.uk

HarperCollins*Publishers*
25 Ryde Road, Pymble, Sydney, NSW 2073, Australia
31 View Road, Glenfield, Auckland 10, New Zealand
77–85 Fulham Palace Road, London W6 8JB, United Kingdom
2 Bloor Street East, 20th floor, Toronto, Ontario M4W 1A8, Canada
10 East 53rd Street, New York NY 10022, USA

ISBN 0 7322 8369 8 (Australia)
ISBN 0 00 724078 3 (UK)
ISSN 1448-3564

A catalogue record for this book is available from the British Library.

Cover design by Mark Gowing Design
Internal design modified from original by de Luxe & Associates
Preliminary pages typeset by Katy Wright, HarperCollins Design Studio
Body text typeset by Kirby Jones in Miller Text 9/10
Printed and bound in Australia by Griffin Press on 60gsm Bulky Paperback White

5 4 3 2 1   06 07

Contents

Introduction

It may seem trite to say it, but the focus of this book is on the wineries of Australia, and the wines they produce. So this is where I start this introduction before I move on to briefly examine the big picture of an industry working in troubled waters after two decades of plain sailing.

Last year's *Companion* detailed 2001 wineries, with 172 making their appearance for the first time (down from 377 new entries the previous year). While all the portents suggested the flow would continue to diminish, the opposite has happened: 230 new wineries join the band. But on the opposite side of the ledger, 46 producers have decided it is all too difficult. I know from previous experience that 'out there' are yet more new arrivals, and yet more — perhaps very many more — deaths.

The tastings for this *Companion* were as exhausting as they were exhaustive, with a tsunami wave of wines coming in just prior to and well after the tasting deadline. At one stage Australia Post (which offers a wine delivery service far better than the freight companies) was sending a dedicated van each morning to disgorge dozens upon dozens of wine boxes of every size, shape and description. To say there were logistical problems at my end is an understatement, some wines disappearing into the ether.

In the outcome, a little over 6400 wines were tasted and rated (last year 5950), with tasting notes for 5200 wines (last year 4440). As a space-saving exercise, the use of symbols for food (ranging from platters, café lunches to à la carte restaurants), accommodation and music events has been introduced; you will find these, along with a glass symbol for those wineries which have a cellar door, in the regional index (on page 765). Other new features include the systematic recording of alcohol and the type of closure used for each wine (further details on page 54 'A note on corks and closures'). Another innovation has been the choice of 'Winery of the year' (page 39).

Turning to the bigger picture, the table (opposite page) tells a goodly part of the story, while also proving that statistics can be damned lies. The mad rush of plantings between 1996 (77,682 ha) and 2002 has more or less come to a halt. The 2004 and 2005 production figures are almost identical; estimates for 2006 are in the range of 1.96 million tonnes. What is not yet known is the number of (additional) tonnes left unharvested.

Beneath the picture of continuing success, there are a host of rather more sinister undercurrents, continuing past the end of the 2005 financial year to March 2006 and beyond. The average price per litre of overall exports has continued its two-year-long decline. While bottled wines account for 70% of total volume, bulk wines have provided 70% of the growth in volume, growing by 40% (i.e. their total litres), while bottled wine shipments grew by just 3%.

This is the inevitable outcome of the much publicised grape surplus, and the concomitant excess in wine stocks. Emptying tanks to make way for the 2006 vintage

	1998	1999	2000	2001	2002	2003	2004	2005
Hectares	98,612	122,915	139,861	148,257	158,594	157,492	164,181	166,665
Tonnes	975,669	1,125,840	1,145,238	1,423,950	1,605,846	1,398,528	1,917,238	1,925,490
Production (million L)	695.2	811.4	824.4	1052.9	1195.2	1059.4	1424.2	1433.8
Domestic* Sales ($m)	—	—	—	1830.9	1946.3	2097.9	1970.9	2097.4
Exports ($m)	873.7	1068.0	1372.7	1751.8	2105.2	2423.5	2494.0	2715.3
Exports (million L)	192.4	200.8	284.9	338.2	418.3	518.6	584.4	669.7

* Figures for domestic sales in dollar terms for the years 1998 to 2000 are not available.

became a priority for companies such as McGuigan Simeon; partial success meant partial failure, leading to the termination of grape purchase contracts, and to a sharp reduction in grape prices across the board.

Those to experience the worst pain were — and are — grape growers. The outlook for the medium-to-big companies with strong brands is a great deal better. The ensuing lower production costs help to offset the dampening effect of the strong Australian dollar; moreover, the key UK market (still keeping its nose in front of the US) is showing signs of recognising that the profitless prosperity of holding retail price points the same year after year after year — despite rises in duty each year — simply can't continue.

Within Australia, the power of Woolworths and Coles Myer continues to grow, exerting pressure on the big companies to reduce their prices (and hence margins), and denying the small producers meaningful access to their shelves. Specialist fine wine retailers offer opportunities to the best-known boutique makers, leaving the rest to writhe in the wilderness.

For these, cellar door sales and websites become ever more critical. The growth in the number of websites — some incomplete or moribund, it is true — over the past few years has been dramatic, and has been the rationale for the shortening of many winery summaries in the *Companion*: what is the point of talking about mail order, cellar door sales, retailers, local distribution and so forth if the website covers such matters (and more).

Finally, wine has become a more significant global commodity. Fine Australian wine can be found from Moscow to Beijing, Paris to Tokyo. But the same is true of fine wine from other New World and Old World producers alike. The internet is cutting through the tryanny of distance at the same time as lifestyle tourism is growing exponentially. Australia's offering of this is second to none.

Wine regions of Australia

Key to regions

Adelaide Hills (SA) **45**
Adelaide Plains (SA) **47**
Alpine Valleys (Vic) **27**
Ballarat (Vic) **19**
Barossa Valley (SA) **48**
Beechworth (Vic) **27**
Bendigo (Vic) **20**
Blackwood Valley (WA) **54**
Canberra District (NSW) **12**
Clare Valley (SA) **50**
Coonawarra (SA) **37**
Cowra (NSW) **6**
Eden Valley (SA) **46**
Geelong (Vic) **31**
Geographe (WA) **56**
Gippsland (Vic) **28**
Glenrowan (Vic) **25**
Goulburn Valley (Vic) **22**
Grampians (Vic) **17**
Granite Belt (Qld) **62**
Great Southern (WA) **52**
Gundagai (NSW) **13**
Hastings River (NSW) **3**
Heathcote (Vic) **21**
Henty (Vic) **16**
Hilltops (NSW) **11**
Hunter Valley, Lower (NSW) **1**
Hunter Valley, Upper (NSW) **2**
Kangaroo Island (SA) **43**
King Valley (Vic) **26**
Langhorne Creek (SA) **41**
Macedon Ranges (Vic) **33**
McLaren Vale (SA) **42**
Manjimup (WA) **53**
Margaret River (WA) **55**
Mornington Peninsula (Vic) **29**
Mount Benson (SA) **39**
Mount Gambier (SA) **36**
Mudgee (NSW) **4**
Murray Darling (NSW/Vic) **8**
Nagambie Lakes (Vic) **23**
Orange (NSW) **5**
Padthaway (SA) **40**
Peel (WA) **57**
Pemberton (WA) **53**
Perricoota (NSW) **10**
Perth Hills (WA) **58**
Pyrenees (Vic) **18**
Queensland Coastal **61**
Riverina (NSW) **9**

Riverland (SA) **49**
Rutherglen (Vic) **25**
Shoalhaven (NSW) **15**
South Burnett (Qld) **60**
Southern Eyre Peninsula (SA) **51**
Southern Fleurieu (SA) **44**
Sunbury (Vic) **32**
Swan District (WA) **59**
Swan Hill (Vic/NSW) **7**
Tasmania, Northern **34**
Tasmania, Southern **35**
Tumbarumba (NSW) **14**
Upper Goulburn (Vic) **24**
Wrattonbully (SA) **38**
Yarra Valley (Vic) **30**

WA

59 ● **Perth**
58
57
56
54
55   53   52

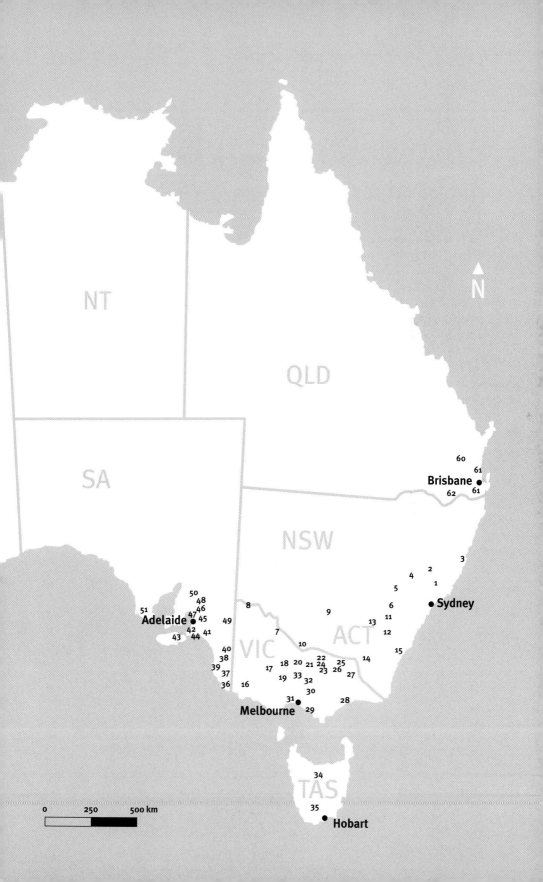

Australia's geographical indications

The process of formally mapping Australia's wine regions continues to ever-so-slowly inch forward. The table following shows the division into states, zones, regions and subregions; those regions or subregions marked with an asterisk are variously in an early or late stage of determination. In two instances I have gone beyond the likely finalisation: it makes no sense to me that the Hunter Valley should be a zone, the region Hunter, and then subregions which are all in the Lower Hunter Valley. I have elected to stick with the traditional division between the Upper Hunter Valley on the one hand, and the Lower on the other.

I am also in front of the game with Tasmania, dividing it into Northern, Southern and East Coast, and, to a lesser degree, have anticipated that the Coastal Hinterland Region of Queensland will seek recognition under this or some similar name. Those regions and subregions marked with an asterisk have taken, or are likely to take, steps to secure registration; they may or may not persevere.

Zone	Region	Subregion
VICTORIA		
Central Victoria	Bendigo Goulburn Valley Heathcote Strathbogie Ranges Upper Goulburn	Nagambie Lakes
Gippsland		
North East Victoria	Alpine Valleys	Kiewa Valley* Ovens Valley*
	Beechworth Glenrowan King Valley* Rutherglen	Myrrhee* Whitlands* Wahgunyah*
North West Victoria	Murray Darling Swan Hill	
Port Phillip	Geelong Macedon Ranges Mornington Peninsula Sunbury Yarra Valley	
Western Victoria	Grampians Henty Pyrenees	

Zone	Region	Subregion
NEW SOUTH WALES		
Big Rivers	Murray Darling Perricoota Riverina Swan Hill	
Central Ranges	Cowra Mudgee Orange	
Hunter Valley	Hunter	Allandale* Belford* Broke Fordwich Dalwood* Pokolbin* Rothbury*
Northern Rivers	Hastings River	
Northern Slopes		
South Coast	Shoalhaven Coast Southern Highlands New England*	
Southern NSW	Canberra District Gundagai Hilltops Tumbarumba	
Western Plains		
WESTERN AUSTRALIA		
Central Western Australia		
Eastern Plains, Inland and North of WA		
Greater Perth	Peel Perth Hills Swan District	Swan Valley
South West Australia	Blackwood Valley Geographe Great Southern	Albany Denmark Frankland River Mount Barker Porongurup
	Manjimup Margaret River Pemberton	
WA South East Coastal	Esperance*	

Zone	Region	Subregion
SOUTH AUSTRALIA		
Adelaide (Super Zone, includes Mount Lofty Ranges, Fleurieu and Barossa)		
Barossa	Barossa Valley	
	Eden Valley	High Eden
		Springton*
Far North	Southern Flinders Ranges	
Fleurieu	Currency Creek	
	Kangaroo Island	
	Langhorne Creek	
	McLaren Vale	Clarendon*
	Southern Fleurieu Peninsula	
Limestone Coast	Coonawarra	
	Mount Benson	
	Penola*	
	Padthaway	
	Robe	
	Wrattonbully	
Lower Murray	Riverland	
Mount Lofty Ranges	Adelaide Hills	Gumeracha*
		Lenswood
		Piccadilly Valley
	Adelaide Plains	
	Clare Valley	Auburn*
		Clare*
		Hill River*
		Polish Hill River*
		Sevenhill*
		Watervale*
The Peninsulas	Southern Eyre Peninsula*	
QUEENSLAND		
Queensland	Granite Belt	
	Coastal Hinterland*	
	South Burnett	
TASMANIA		
Tasmania	Northern Tasmania*	
	Southern Tasmania*	
	East Coast Tasmania*	
AUSTRALIAN CAPTIAL TERRITORY		
NORTHERN TERRITORY		

Grape variety plantings

(See table on following pages.)

The seven-year decline in the share of white wine production, from 61.85% in 1998 to 41.48% in 2004, has been halted, with a rise to 44.46% in 2005. The unlikely hero (in some people's eyes) is chardonnay, which continues its long march, up from 311 000 tonnes in 2004 to 378 000 tonnes in 2005. (I am deliberately using rounded figures.) If you look back to 1998, the chardonnay crush was only 148 000 tonnes. Whatever café talk may be, the ABC of chardonnay is 'always bring cash', not 'anything but chardonnay'.

On the other side of the ledger, the decline in cabernet sauvignon from 320 000 in 2004 to 284 000 tonnes in 2005 comes as no surprise. With both chardonnay and cabernet sauvignon, the change in tonnage is also reflected in the hectares planted. Shiraz is the unexpected odd man out: its tonnage fell (a surprise in itself) from 437 000 tonnes in 2004 to 415 000 tonnes in 2005, while plantings continued their steady increase since 2000 (prior to that time the increase was tumultuous).

So did any major red variety hold the line? Yes, merlot did; although new plantings have come to a halt, yield from plantings made between 2001 and 2004 lifted total tonnage from 124 000 in 2004 to 133 000 tonnes in 2005. Merlot has well and truly fallen from favour as a varietal wine with wine judges and (some) winemakers, although it is very useful as a blend component with cabernet sauvignon. It is also true to say it has been planted in areas where the climate is too warm, and there is an element of shooting the messenger when it comes to regions to which it is in fact suited.

The question is whether ABM will mean 'anything but merlot', or 'always buy merlot'. The pundits have been wrong about chardonnay, and it is possible the same will apply here. Nonetheless, I think we will see merlot drift downwards in the years ahead. On the other hand, petit verdot, the only statistically important variety captured in the 'other red' category, will likely see its 2005 crush of 25 000 tonnes increase.

	1998	1999	2000
CHARDONNAY hectares tonnes	14,662 148,515	16,855 210,770	18,526 201,248
RIESLING hectares tonnes	3,345 33,811	3,347 30,144	3,658 26,800
SAUVIGNON BLANC hectares tonnes	1,904 18,405	2,413 22,834	2,706 21,487
SEMILLON hectares tonnes	5,287 57,112	6,044 80,191	6,832 77,506
OTHER WHITE hectares tonnes	25,566 271,620	26,331 282,459	27,873 265,196
TOTAL WHITE **hectares** **tonnes**	**50,764** **529,463**	**54,990** **626,398**	**59,595** **592,237**
CABERNET SAUVIGNON hectares tonnes	14,695 91,876	21,169 127,494	26,674 159,358
GRENACHE hectares tonnes	1,988 23,842	2,255 24,196	2,756 23,998
MERLOT hectares tonnes	3,802 13,881	6,387 31,801	8,575 51,269
MOURVEDRE hectares tonnes	696 8,238	866 9,217	1,147 10,496
PINOT NOIR hectares tonnes	2,192 19,123	2,996 19,668	3,756 19,578
SHIRAZ hectares tonnes	17,930 131,427	25,596 192,330	32,327 224,394
OTHER RED hectares tonnes	6,372 38,224	8,656 45,103	11,347 57,255
TOTAL RED **hectares** **tonnes**	**47,675** **326,611**	**67,925** **449,809**	**86,582** **546,348**
TOTAL GRAPES **hectares** **tonnes**	**98,439** **856,074**	**122,915** **1,076,207**	**146,177** **1,138,585**
PERCENTAGE (TONNES) **White** **Red**	**61.85%** **38.15%**	**59.21%** **41.79%**	**52.02%** **47.98%**

2001	2002	2003	2004	2005
18,434 245,199	21,724 256,328	24,138 233,747	28,008 311,273	30,507 378,287
3,558 26,980	3,962 27,838	3,987 28,994	4,255 36,404	4,326 41,237
2,766 25,326	2,914 28,567	2,953 21,028	3,425 39,774	4,152 38,355
6,803 88,427	6,610 100,785	6,283 77,096	6,278 99,237	6,282 96,727
25,781 232,334	26,215 255,253	24,700 196,209	23,925 266,794	23,365 253,837
57,342 **618,266**	**61,425** **666,771**	**62,051** **557,074**	**65,891** **753,482**	**68,632** **808,443**
28,609 249,288	29,573 257,223	28,171 225,723	29,313 319,955	28,621 284,062
2,427 22,563	2,528 26,260	2,322 19,866	2,292 24,987	2,097 25,418
9,330 80,142	10,101 104,423	10,352 92,865	10,804 123,944	10,816 132,586
1,128 11,624	1,238 12,452	1,092 11,822	1,040 13,992	963 10,149
4,142 29,514	4,414 21,341	4,270 27,949	4,424 41,690	4,231 36,887
33,676 311,045	37,031 326,564	37,106 309,000	39,182 436,691	40,508 415,421
11,621 68,640	12,284 99,467	12,268 85,297	11,235 101,816	10,797 105,460
90,933 **772,816**	**97,169** **847,730**	**95,491** **772,522**	**98,290** **1,063,075**	**98,033** **1,009,983**
148,275 **1,391,082**	**158,594** **1,514,501**	**157,492** **1,329,596**	**164,181** **1,816,556**	**166,665** **1,818,426**
44.45% **55.55%**	**44.02%** **55.98%**	**41.90%** **58.10%**	**41.48%** **58.52%**	**44.46%** **55.54%**

Australian vintage 2006: a snapshot

The April 2006 forecast for the vintage from the Australian Wine & Brandy Corporation was a total of 1.96 million tonnes. While yields were down 5% on 2005, they were still above average, the crush augmented by new plantings coming on-stream. The defining point of the vintage was the widespread and perfectly timed spring rains in October and November 2005, which resulted in accelerated vine growth and an unusually early vintage. The only month to threaten quality was the hot January; thereafter nigh-on perfect conditions through to the end of harvest should produce good to excellent wine from most regions in the eastern half of the country.

New South Wales

The **HUNTER VALLEY** had its usual mixed bag, with minimal winter rain but good spring/summer rainfall. Then came the furnace of Christmas Day and New Year's Day (at 45°C the hottest for over 50 years) followed by a further 7–10 days over 40°C. Nonetheless, low shiraz yields are being compared with 2003, and there is (contrarily) much confidence about semillon. Overall, the vintage was 2–3 weeks early. The **SHOALHAVEN RIVER** had very similar weather, and similar pleasing outcomes.

The western side of the Great Dividing Range enjoyed a very good growing season, sharing with many parts of South Eastern Australia flavour ripeness coming at lower alcohol levels than usual, and an early, at times hectic, vintage. **ORANGE** had a near to ideal vintage, the higher vineyards experiencing lower temperatures and early-to-normal harvest dates for disease-free grapes with excellent varietal character (especially chardonnay). **HILLTOPS** provided more of the same, with cooler weather in March in the lead up to picking cabernet sauvignon resulting in wine with outstanding colour and intense flavour. **TUMBARUMBA**, like Hilltops, had an early (by 2 weeks) trouble-free vintage, warmer than usual, with rich chardonnay the star.

COWRA had the agony of a 50% fall in prices plus many tonnes left on the vine, and the (ironic) ecstasy of excellent quality chardonnay and shiraz. **RIVERINA** had first-class growing conditions, with few very hot days, the vintage starting early, but the small-berry, thick-skinned shiraz and cabernet sauvignon ripening more slowly. Tonnage was up 20% (chardonnay, semillon and shiraz), due in large measure to increase in winery capacity courtesy of Casella's yellow tail.

The **SOUTHERN HIGHLANDS** had a wet spring and January, giving rise to mildew pressure in the warm conditions, but with an Indian summer thereafter helping combat the mildew. The cool climate varieties of riesling, chardonnay and pinot noir were the high points of a very good year. **HASTINGS RIVER** experienced searing Christmas Day and New Year's Day temperatures, but overall the season was mild, the heat spikes much less severe. Shiraz is likely to shine in a good vintage.

In the **CANBERRA DISTRICT** generous spring rain was followed by one of the three hottest summers on record (1983 and '98 were the others). The absence of rain led to disease-free fruit; in the warmer, lower vineyards shiraz (and viognier) was superb, riesling likewise. In the higher, cooler vineyards riesling, chardonnay and pinot noir are the standouts.

Victoria

For most of the state, the 2006 vintage in Victoria will be remembered as one of the earliest and most compressed ever.

In the traditionally warm regions of **BENDIGO** and **HEATHCOTE**, an absence of frost early on and regular rainfall through the growing season combined with a hot and dry finish to produce a year well suited to the red varieties which predominate. Harvest dates were on par with the (early) 2005 vintage and expectations are for wines which are at least the equal of the 2005s.

However, throughout the cooler regions, one of the most benign seasons on record led to unprecedented early harvest dates and the extraordinary situation of all regions harvesting concurrently. In the **YARRA VALLEY**, **MORNINGTON PENINSULA**, **GEELONG**, **BALLARAT**, **HENTY** and **MACEDON RANGES**, mild day and night temperatures and regular rainfall throughout spring led to lush vine growth and plenty of ripening capacity. The unusually warm conditions continued into summer, with January delivering a couple of bursts of extreme heat. There was a return to normality in February (lower than average temperatures and cool nights) but, by then, the accumulated heat over the growing season meant that many vignerons were scrambling to harvest up to 4 weeks earlier than normal. The low to moderate crops should produce some very good results, particularly for chardonnay and the late season red varieties.

The pattern of high temperatures and early harvest was repeated in the **ALPINE VALLEYS**, **GRAMPIANS** and **PYRENEES**, where there were some concerns that flavours and tannins had insufficient time to develop to maximum potential. This was in direct contrast to regions such as the Yarra Valley, Ballarat and **BEECHWORTH** (the last with tiny yields) where flavour development outpaced sugar accumulation, resulting in wines with great natural acidity and vibrant flavours.

Finally, **RUTHERGLEN** enjoyed a perfect season for fortifieds. There, the early season meant ample time for both muscat and tokay to attain the highest baume levels well before the threat of late autumn rain and rot.

South Australia

The **BAROSSA VALLEY** had a year which will be divided into two sections: those who picked before the rain (which started shortly prior to Easter) and those who picked during and after the rain. All agree cabernet sauvignon is the standout (the best since 2002) in a vintage which started a week late but then became a mad scramble as every variety ripened quickly and simultaneously. The **EDEN VALLEY** produced gloriously delicate and fragrant riesling and high-quality, spicy shiraz; the rain and cold conditions of mid to late April may prove to have impacted on the quality of cabernet sauvignon. Pinot gris did well, likewise chardonnay. The conditions in the **CLARE VALLEY** remained warm from start to finish, with little rain of consequence. Well-managed vineyards produced grapes with perfect natural balance of flavour, sugar and acidity, shiraz and cabernet sauvignon excellent, riesling a tad behind.

ADELAIDE HILLS, with abundant spring rain and a perfect 4-week run up to vintage, has produced excellent sauvignon blanc, pinot gris, chardonnay (low yields) and pinot noir, all ripening together. The **ADELAIDE PLAINS** produced very good colombard, and — if picked before the late March rains — even better shiraz.

McLAREN VALE had heavy spring rains followed by a hot December, then cooler conditions in January/February with small rain events requiring vigilant control of mildew. The red varieties developed flavour at lower baume levels than usual, and all except grenache will produce high-quality wines. **LANGHORNE CREEK** had similar conditions; the whites have zesty flavour and acidity, the reds (down 30% in yield) deep colour, great fruit and alcohol at or below 14°. The nearby **FLEURIEU PENINSULA** followed suit, sauvignon blanc and cabernet sauvignon doing best.

COONAWARRA, like the Barossa, had a vintage in two halves, but with a big difference: red grapes harvested after the rain had similar baume but better fruit depth and riper tannins. Overall, a very early vintage (some finished by end March), due in part to extremely low yields of the region's star turn, cabernet sauvignon. **MOUNT BENSON** had low yields across the board, flavour ripeness (yet again) developing early with excellent alcohol, pH and acid balance.

The all-important **RIVERLAND** shared the major weather patterns of South East Australia, resulting in good quality across all the major varieties. The fly in the ointment was excess grapes: in the outcome, around 10% of the potential crop was left unharvested.

Western Australia

The 2006 vintage was the direct opposite to that of the eastern half of Australia: an extremely cool and frequently wet growing season resulted in a vintage up to 4 weeks later than usual. Moreover, the conditions from the **SWAN VALLEY** in the north to **ALBANY** in the extreme south were freakishly similar. The Swan Valley shivered through December and January, with heat summations little more than those of Melbourne.

It is thus not surprising that the varieties to do best in all regions (**PERTH HILLS**, **SWAN VALLEY**, **PEEL**, **GEOGRAPHE**, **MARGARET RIVER**, **MANJIMUP**, **PEMBERTON** and **GREAT SOUTHERN**) were the whites and (south of Margaret River) pinot noir. The saving grace for shiraz and cabernet sauvignon may hinge more on elegance and great flavour intensity than the alcohol levels would suggest. A cruel twist came in the form of smoke taint in some areas from bushfires started by the Department of Conservation and Land Management.

Tasmania

All three main regions — **NORTHERN TASMANIA**, **SOUTHERN TASMANIA** and the **EAST COAST** — had one of their best ever vintages. The dynamics were similar to southern Victoria, with lavish growing conditions in spring and ideal ripening weather thereafter. Despite generous yields, vintage was up to six weeks early (March instead of May for some blocks), fortunate given the frigid conditions which arrived mid-April. The whites will be superb, pinot noir very good, though not with quite the same depth as the great 2005 pinots.

Queensland

As with the rest of the east coast the vintage commenced very early due to the record hot summer temperatures of 2005. The first grapes harvested were in Kenilworth (**SUNSHINE COAST HINTERLAND**) on 8 January, next 11 January on the **DARLING DOWNS**, and the last in the **GRANITE BELT** in late April; up to 4 weeks earlier than 2005 in some regions. The South Burnett producers started in the second week of January with verdelho and experienced their longest vintage ever, with the last cabernet grapes off in the second week of March. As with the rest of the country not all grapes were harvested; up to 10% were left on the vine.

Wine quality has been high all round in the Darling Downs, **SOUTH BURNETT** and the Granite Belt. The shiraz and cabernet look equal to the great wines of 2002 and 2005, so there ought to be many happy Granite Belt producers, particularly those who picked late. The best white varietals are chardonnay, semillon, verdelho and viognier.

Australian vintage chart

Each number represents a mark out of 10 for the quality of vintages in each region.

■ RED   ▨ WHITE

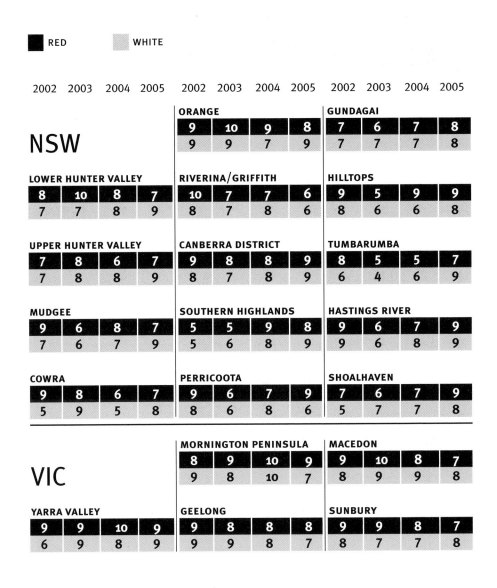

	2002	2003	2004	2005		2002	2003	2004	2005		2002	2003	2004	2005
NSW					**ORANGE**					**GUNDAGAI**				
					Red	9	10	9	8	Red	7	6	7	8
					White	9	9	7	9	White	7	7	7	8
LOWER HUNTER VALLEY					**RIVERINA/GRIFFITH**					**HILLTOPS**				
Red	8	10	8	7	Red	10	7	7	6	Red	9	5	9	9
White	7	7	8	9	White	8	7	8	6	White	8	6	6	8
UPPER HUNTER VALLEY					**CANBERRA DISTRICT**					**TUMBARUMBA**				
Red	7	8	6	7	Red	9	8	8	9	Red	8	5	5	7
White	7	8	8	9	White	8	7	8	9	White	6	4	6	9
MUDGEE					**SOUTHERN HIGHLANDS**					**HASTINGS RIVER**				
Red	9	6	8	7	Red	5	5	9	8	Red	9	6	7	9
White	7	6	7	9	White	5	6	8	9	White	9	6	8	9
COWRA					**PERRICOOTA**					**SHOALHAVEN**				
Red	9	8	6	7	Red	9	6	7	9	Red	7	6	7	9
White	5	9	5	8	White	8	6	8	6	White	5	7	7	8
VIC					**MORNINGTON PENINSULA**					**MACEDON**				
					Red	8	9	10	9	Red	9	10	8	7
					White	9	8	10	7	White	8	9	9	8
YARRA VALLEY					**GEELONG**					**SUNBURY**				
Red	9	9	10	9	Red	9	8	8	8	Red	9	9	8	7
White	6	9	8	9	White	9	9	8	7	White	8	7	7	8

	2002	2003	2004	2005
GRAMPIANS	7	9	10	10
	7	8	6	9
PYRENEES	8	8	10	10
	8	6	9	9
HENTY	8	7	9	9
	8	10	9	8
BENDIGO	9	7	9	8
	7	6	9	7
HEATHCOTE	9	8	10	8
	8	6	9	9

	2002	2003	2004	2005
GOULBURN VALLEY	9	8	9	8
	8	6	7	8
UPPER GOULBURN	9	7	7	9
	7	6	7	9
STRATHBOGIE RANGES	8	8	8	9
	8	7	8	8
GLENROWAN & RUTHERGLEN	10	9	9	7
	9	7	6	7
KING VALLEY	10	7	8	7
	9	8	9	9

	2002	2003	2004	2005
ALPINE VALLEYS	9	4	9	8
	8	4	9	10
BEECHWORTH	8	8	10	8
	7	6	8	8
GIPPSLAND	5	7	10	9
	5	6	9	9
MURRAY DARLING	9	7	7	8
	8	6	7	8

SA

	2002	2003	2004	2005
BAROSSA VALLEY	10	7	9	7
	8	7	7	8
EDEN VALLEY	9	7	8	8
	10	9	9	9

	2002	2003	2004	2005
CLARE VALLEY	10	8	9	9
	10	10	8	9
ADELAIDE HILLS	9	8	8	7
	9	8	7	8
ADELAIDE PLAINS	9	6	8	8
	8	7	7	9

	2002	2003	2004	2005
COONAWARRA	9	9	7	8
	8	8	6	7
PADTHAWAY	9	8	7	8
	9	9	7	7
MOUNT BENSON & ROBE	9	8	7	8
	9	9	8	9

WRATTONBULLY

2002	2003	2004	2005
8	7	4	8
7	8	7	8

SOUTHERN FLEURIEU

2002	2003	2004	2005
8	7	7	8
8	7	8	8

KANGAROO ISLAND

2002	2003	2004	2005
7	7	8	8
6	7	7	8

McLAREN VALE

2002	2003	2004	2005
9	8	9	8
8	7	7	8

LANGHORNE CREEK

2002	2003	2004	2005
9	8	8	9
7	7	7	8

RIVERLAND

2002	2003	2004	2005
10	8	8	8
9	9	8	9

WA

MANJIMUP

2002	2003	2004	2005
7	6	9	7
8	6	5	9

SWAN DISTRICT

2002	2003	2004	2005
10	7	9	9
9	6	7	8

MARGARET RIVER

2002	2003	2004	2005
8	8	9	9
8	8	8	9

PEMBERTON

2002	2003	2004	2005
7	6	8	9
8	7	8	9

PEEL

2002	2003	2004	2005
8	8	8	10
9	8	7	10

GREAT SOUTHERN

2002	2003	2004	2005
8	7	7	9
8	6	8	9

GEOGRAPHE

2002	2003	2004	2005
7	8	9	7
9	8	9	8

PERTH HILLS

2002	2003	2004	2005
9	7	9	10
8	8	7	9

QLD

GRANITE BELT

2002	2003	2004	2005
9	8	7	9
8	7	9	9

SOUTH BURNETT

2002	2003	2004	2005
8	8	6	9
8	8	6	10

TAS

NORTHERN TASMANIA

2002	2003	2004	2005
9	7	6	10
9	7	8	9

SOUTHERN TASMANIA

2002	2003	2004	2005
9	8	7	10
9	7	8	9

Best of the best of
Australian wine 2007

I make my usual disclaimer: while there are two periods of intense tasting activity in the 12 months during which the tasting notes for this edition are made, and while some wines are tasted more than once, an over-arching comparative tasting of all the best wines is simply not possible, however desirable it might be.

So the points for the individual wines scoring 94 or above stand uncorrected by the wisdom of hindsight. Nonetheless, the link between variety and region (or, if you prefer, between variety and *terroir*) is, in most instances, strikingly evident. It is for this reason that I have shown the region for each of the best wines. While the short-term focus of the export industry is the paramount necessity of reducing stock either in bulk or under the generic bottling of BOB (buyer own brand), medium and longer term prosperity will depend on a sense of place, of regional identity.

Brand Australia has been the foundation upon which the success of the past 20 years has been built, but all recognise it is time to move on. While some naysayers may regard this as marketing rhetoric, the truth is that Australia is blessed with an unmatched range of *terroir* (including climate in that deceptively simple term), enabling it to make wines ranging from the uniquely complex fortified wines of Rutherglen (fashioned from frontignac and muscadelle, known locally as muscat and tokay), to the 100-year-old Para Liqueur of Seppelt in the Barossa Valley, all the way through to the exceptional sparkling wines of Tasmania, grown in a climate every bit as cool as that of Champagne.

This is one of the principal reasons for the index to be arranged by region, even though the text is alpha-ordered. I should also point out that the cut-off for listing the wines of each variety differs considerably, depending on the strength of the class concerned.

Best of the best by variety

Riesling

There are 88 Rieslings scoring 94 points or more, reflecting — if you like — Jancis Robinson's assertion in the *Oxford Companion to Wine* that this is the noblest of all white grapes, most faithfully reproducing its essential character without the active intervention of the winemaker. Thus well over half of the 36 wines at 95 points and above come from the Eden Valley (11) and the Clare Valley (10). The remainder all come from the cool, moderately to strongly continental climates, with maritime regions conspicuous by their absence.

97	**2005 Seppelt Drumborg Riesling** (Grampians)
96	**2001 Peter Lehmann Reserve Riesling** (Barossa Valley)
96	**2004 Annie's Lane Copper Trail Valley Riesling** (Clare Valley)
96	**2005 Wilson Vineyard DJW Riesling** (Clare Valley)
96	**2001 Heggies Vineyard Museum Reserve Riesling** (Eden Valley)
96	**2005 Leo Buring Leonay DW117 Riesling** (Eden Valley)
96	**2005 Crawford River Reserve Riesling** (Henty)
96	**2004 Crawford River Reserve Riesling** (Henty)
96	**2005 Forest Hill Vineyard Block 1 Riesling** (Great Southern)
96	**2005 Howard Park Riesling** (Great Southern)
96	**2005 Granite Hills Riesling** (Macedon Ranges)
96	**2004 Pooley Coal River Riesling** (Southern Tasmania)
95	**2005 Coobara Riesling** (Adelaide Hills)
95	**2005 Shaw & Smith Riesling** (Adelaide Hills)
95	**2005 Orlando Steingarten Riesling** (Barossa Valley)
95	**2005 St John's Road Peace of Eden Riesling** (Barossa Valley)
95	**2005 Annie's Lane Copper Trail Riesling** (Clare Valley)
95	**2005 Kilikanoon Mort's Block Reserve Riesling** (Clare Valley)
95	**2005 Leasingham Bin 7 Riesling** (Clare Valley)
95	**2005 Leasingham Classic Clare Riesling** (Clare Valley)
95	**2005 O'Leary Walker Polish Hill River Riesling** (Clare Valley)
95	**2005 Olssens of Watervale Riesling** (Clare Valley)
95	**2005 Pikes The Merle Riesling** (Clare Valley)
95	**2005 Wilson Vineyard Polish Hill River Riesling** (Clare Valley)
95	**2005 Cascabel Riesling** (Eden Valley)
95	**2005 Henschke Julius Riesling** (Eden Valley)
95	**2005 Leo Buring Riesling** (Eden Valley)
95	**1999 Leo Buring Maturation Reserve Riesling** (Eden Valley)

95   **1997 Leo Buring Maturation Reserve Riesling** (Eden Valley)
95   **2004 McWilliam's Regional Collection Riesling** (Eden Valley)
95   **2001 Pewsey Vale The Contours Riesling** (Eden Valley)
95   **2005 Radford Dale Riesling** (Eden Valley)
95   **2003 Radford Dale Riesling** (Eden Valley)
95   **2005 Ferngrove Vineyards Cossack Riesling** (Frankland River)
95   **2005 Frankland Estate Isolation Ridge Vineyard Riesling** (Frankland River)
95   **2004 Bream Creek Riesling** (Southern Tasmania)

Chardonnay

With 174 wines scoring 94 points or more, this is the most prolific varietal, and rather spoils the Riesling story. It is still work in progress: while the best Chardonnays of today are more complex yet less ostentatious (and oaky) than the wines of yesteryear, and while the Adelaide Hills, Margaret River and Yarra Valley set the cool climate tone for these top wines, many makers are locked in an arm wrestle with undesired alcohol levels of 14° or more, against a preferred level of 13° or so. Whether the answer lies in the vineyard (earlier picking) or the winery (reverse osmosis) remains to be seen. The sheer weight of numbers has forced a cut-off at 96 points.

97   **2004 Chardonnay by Farr** (Geelong)
97   **2002 Leeuwin Estate Art Series Chardonnay** (Margaret River)
96   **2004 Ashton Hills Chardonnay** (Adelaide Hills)
96   **2004 Grosset Piccadilly Chardonnay** (Adelaide Hills)
96   **2003 Penfolds Yattarna Chardonnay** (Adelaide Hills)
96   **2004 Shaw & Smith M3 Vineyard Chardonnay** (Adelaide Hills)
96   **2003 Hardys Eileen Hardy Chardonnay** (cool climate blend)
96   **2004 Shadowfax Chardonnay** (Geelong)
96   **2004 Howard Park Chardonnay** (Great Southern)
96   **2004 Tarrington Vineyards Chardonnay** (Henty)
96   **2004 Lake's Folly Hunter Valley Chardonnay** (Lower Hunter Valley)
96   **2004 Cape Mentelle Chardonnay** (Margaret River)
96   **2003 Cullen Chardonnay** (Margaret River)
96   **2004 Eldridge Estate of Red Hill Chardonnay** (Mornington Peninsula)
96   **2004 Red Hill Estate Chardonnay** (Mornington Peninsula)
96   **2004 Mount Mary Chardonnay** (Yarra Valley)
96   **2003 Tarrawarra Estate Chardonnay** (Yarra Valley)
96   **2004 Toolangi Vineyards Reserve Chardonnay** (Yarra Valley)
96   **2000 Yarra Burn Bastard Hill Chardonnay** (Yarra Valley)
96   **2004 YarraLoch Stephanie's Dream Chardonnay** (Yarra Valley)

Semillon

Varietal Semillons are sparingly made in other parts of the world, and none in a climate remotely approaching that of the Hunter Valley. This lack of an international currency is the only explanation for the lack of interest in these magical wines by export markets. There are 47 wines with 94 points or more, and of the top 23 (95 points or more), 20 are from the Lower Hunter Valley. While they range in age from 1994 to 2005, rest assured the latter is a great vintage, the best since 1979.

97	**1999 Tyrrell's Vat 1 Semillon** (Lower Hunter Valley)
97	**1994 Tyrrell's Museum Release Vat 1 Semillon** (Lower Hunter Valley)
96	**2003 Alkoomi Wandoo Semillon** (Frankland River)
96	**1999 Brokenwood ILR Reserve Semillon** (Lower Hunter Valley)
96	**2005 Chatto Semillon** (Lower Hunter Valley)
96	**1998 McWilliam's Mount Pleasant Museum Release Elizabeth Semillon** (Lower Hunter Valley)
95	**2005 McLeish Estate Semillon** (Lower Hunter Valley)
95	**2005 Brokenwood Semillon** (Lower Hunter Valley)
95	**2001 Capercaillie Semillon** (Lower Hunter Valley)
95	**2000 McWilliam's Mount Pleasant Lovedale Semillon** (Lower Hunter Valley)
95	**1999 Pepper Tree Grand Reserve Semillon** (Lower Hunter Valley)
95	**2005 Piggs Peake Sows Ear Semillon** (Lower Hunter Valley)
95	**2005 Cockfighter's Ghost Semillon** (Lower Hunter Valley)
95	**2005 Thomas Braemore Semillon** (Lower Hunter Valley)
95	**2005 Tower Estate Semillon** (Lower Hunter Valley)
95	**2005 Tulloch JYT Julia Semillon** (Lower Hunter Valley)
95	**2004 Tulloch JYT Julia Semillon** (Lower Hunter Valley)
95	**1999 Tyrrell's Belford Reserve Semillon** (Lower Hunter Valley)
95	**2005 Tyrrell's Lost Block Semillon** (Lower Hunter Valley)
95	**2005 Warraroong Estate Semillon** (Lower Hunter Valley)
95	**2005 Ashbrook Estate Semillon** (Margaret River)
95	**2005 Vasse Felix Semillon** (Margaret River)
95	**2005 Coolangatta Estate Semillon** (Shoalhaven Coast)

Sauvignon Blanc

The Sauvignon Blanc success story flies in the face of all reason, and — in particular — in defiance of the otherwise apparent invincibility of Marlborough Sauvignon Blanc. That said, the quality of Adelaide Hills and Margaret River Sauvignon Blancs (responsible for half the 35 wines) cannot be gainsaid, and the remainder, while of diverse origin, all come from cool climates.

95   **2005 Kirrihill Sauvignon Blanc** (Adelaide Hills)
95   **2005 Shaw & Smith Sauvignon Blanc** (Adelaide Hills)
95   **2005 Tower Estate Adelaide Hills Sauvignon Blanc** (Lower Hunter Valley)
95   **2005 Ashbrook Estate Sauvignon Blanc** (Margaret River)
95   **2005 Stella Bella Sauvignon Blanc** (Margaret River)
95   **2005 Word of Mouth Sauvignon Blanc** (Orange)
94   **2005 Aldgate Ridge Sauvignon Blanc** (Adelaide Hills)
94   **2005 Bird in Hand Sauvignon Blanc** (Adelaide Hills)
94   **2005 Brindabella Hills Sauvignon Blanc** (Canberra District)
94   **2005 Brookland Valley Sauvignon Blanc** (Margaret River)
94   **2005 Brown Brothers Whitlands Sauvignon Blanc** (King Valley)
94   **2005 Hanging Rock The Jim Jim Sauvignon Blanc** (Macedon Ranges)
94   **2005 Hill Smith Estate Sauvignon Blanc** (Eden Valley)
94   **2005 Lenton Brae Sauvignon Blanc** (Margaret River)
94   **2005 Limbic Sauvignon Blanc** (Port Phillip Zone)
94   **2005 Lowe Family Tinja Sauvignon Blanc** (Orange)
94   **2005 Matilda's Estate Sauvignon Blanc** (Denmark)
94   **2005 McGuigan Genus 4 Sauvignon Blanc** (Adelaide Hills)
94   **2005 O'Leary Walker Sauvignon Blanc** (Adelaide Hills)
94   **2005 Parri Estate Sauvignon Blanc** (Southern Fleurieu)
94   **2005 Rosily Vineyard Sauvignon Blanc** (Margaret River)
94   **2005 Shadowfax Sauvignon Blanc** (Adelaide Hills)
94   **2004 Stefano Lubiana Sauvignon Blanc** (Southern Tasmania)
94   **2005 Stumpy Gully Sauvignon Blanc** (Mornington Peninsula)
94   **2005 Taltarni Victoria/Tasmania Sauvignon Blanc** (Pyrenees)
94   **2005 Tamar Ridge Sauvignon Blanc** (Northern Tasmania)
94   **2005 Tassell Park Sauvignon Blanc** (Margaret River)
94   **2005 Taylors Sauvignon Blanc** (Adelaide Hills)
94   **2005 TK Sauvignon Blanc** (Adelaide Hills)
94   **2005 Voyager Estate Sauvignon Blanc** (Margaret River)
94   **2005 Wangolina Station Sauvignon Blanc** (Mount Benson)
94   **2005 Watershed Awakening Sauvignon Blanc** (Margaret River)
94   **2005 Wellington Sauvignon Blanc** (Southern Tasmania)
94   **2005 Will Taylor Sauvignon Blanc** (Adelaide Hills)
94   **2005 Willow Bridge Estate Family Reserve Sauvignon Blanc** (Pemberton)

Sauvignon Semillon blends

More than 50% of the wines come from the Margaret River; taken with its dominance of the Cabernet Merlot sector, this maritime region is Australia's version of Bordeaux (sans sauternes).

96   2005 Grosset Semillon Sauvignon Blanc (Clare Valley)
95   2005 Harewood Estate Sauvignon Blanc Semillon (Denmark)
95   2005 Brookland Valley Verse 1 Semillon Sauvignon Blanc (Margaret River)
95   2004 Cape Mentelle Wallcliffe Sauvignon Blanc Semillon (Margaret River)
95   2003 Cape Mentelle Wallcliffe Sauvignon Blanc Semillon (Margaret River)
95   2005 Stella Bella Semillon Sauvignon Blanc (Margaret River)
95   2004 Suckfizzle Sauvignon Blanc Semillon (Margaret River)
95   2005 Voyager Estate Sauvignon Blanc Semillon (Margaret River)
95   2005 Watershed Sauvignon Blanc Semillon (Margaret River)
94   2005 Alexandra Bridge Semillon Sauvignon Blanc (Margaret River)
94   2005 Crawford River Sauvignon Blanc Semillon (Henty)
94   2005 Cullen Sauvignon Blanc Semillon (Margaret River)
94   2005 De Bortoli Gulf Station Sauvignon Blanc Semillon (Yarra Valley)
94   2004 Gibraltar Rock Semillon Sauvignon Blanc (Porongurup)
94   2005 Hamelin Bay Five Ashes Vineyard Semillon Sauvignon Blanc (Margaret River)
94   2005 Henschke Eleanor's Cottage Sauvignon Blanc Semillon (Eden Valley)
94   2005 Littles Semillon Sauvignon Blanc (Lower Hunter Valley)
94   2005 Longview Vineyard My Fat Goose Semillon Sauvignon Blanc (Adelaide Hills)
94   2005 Mt Jagged Semillon Sauvignon Blanc (Southern Fleurieu)
94   2004 Mount Mary Triolet (Yarra Valley)
94   2005 Pierro Semillon Sauvignon Blanc LTC (Margaret River)
94   2005 Redgate Sauvignon Blanc Semillon (Margaret River)
94   2005 Rosabrook Estate Semillon Sauvignon Blanc (Margaret River)
94   2005 Sienna Estate Momentum of Passion Semillon
       Sauvignon Blanc (Margaret River)
94   2005 We're Estate Semillon Sauvignon Blanc (Margaret River)
94   2005 West Cape Howe Semillon Sauvignon Blanc (Denmark)
94   2005 Willow Bridge Estate Sauvignon Blanc Semillon (Geographe)
94   2005 Xanadu Secession Semillon Sauvignon Blanc (Margaret River)

Other white wines

A new category for this edition, reflecting the growth in the number of quality Viogniers (primarily) and Pinot Gris.

96   2004 Yalumba The Virgilius Viognier (Barossa Valley)
96   2005 Penfolds Cellar Reserve Gewurztraminer (Eden Valley)
95   2005 Haan Viognier Prestige (Barossa Valley)
95   2005 Clonakilla Viognier (Canberra District)
95   2004 T'Gallant Tribute Pinot Gris (Mornington Peninsula)

94   **2005 Bay of Fires Pinot Gris** (Northern Tasmania)
94   **2004 Brokenwood Pinot Gris** (Beechworth)
94   **2004 by Farr Viognier** (Geelong)
94   **2005 Deviation Road Pinot Gris** (Adelaide Hills)
94   **2004 Lyre Bird Hill Gewurztraminer** (Gippsland)
94   **2005 Millbrook Limited Release Viognier** (Perth Hills)
94   **2005 Mr Riggs Wine Company Viognier** (Adelaide)
94   **2005 Shelmerdine Vineyards Viognier** (Heathcote)
94   **2004 Spring Vale Vineyards Gewurztraminer** (East Coast Tasmania)
94   **2004 Stella Bella Viognier** (Margaret River)
94   **2005 Stonehaven Hidden Sea Viognier** (Padthaway)
94   **2005 Tahbilk Viognier** (Nagambie Lakes)
94   **1998 Tahbilk 1927 Vines Marsanne** (Nagambie Lakes)
94   **2004 Yalumba Viognier** (Eden Valley)

Sparkling, Sweet and Rose

A marriage of convenience, if ever there was one. Tasmania leads the cool climate charge with the sparkling wines; those from the mainland come from high altitude vineyards, or from the coolest sites in regions such as the Yarra Valley.

96   **NV Hanging Rock Cuvee XI** (Macedon Ranges)
96   **NV Hanging Rock Macedon Cuvee Six** (Macedon Ranges)
96   **2000 Bay of Fires Arras** (Northern Tasmania)
96   **1999 Kreglinger** (Northern Tasmania)
95   **1999 Freycinet Radenti Pinot Noir Chardonnay** (East Coast Tasmania)
95   **2002 Domaine Chandon Tasmanian Cuvee** (Tasmania)
95   **2002 Domaine Chandon Vintage Brut** (Yarra Valley)
95   **2002 Domaine Chandon Blanc de Blancs** (Yarra Valley)
95   **2000 Yarrabank Cuvee** (Yarra Valley)

The sparkling red category mirrors that of rose; these (plus Seppelt, missing this time around due to timing) are the real article. Behind them come an unholy mess of failed red wines of inappropriate varieties and the wrong region.

95   **NV Rockford Black Shiraz** (Barossa Valley)
94   **1998 Ashton Hills Sparkling Red** (Adelaide Hills)
94   **NV Primo Estate Joseph Sparkling Red** (Adelaide Plains)
94   **NV Turkey Flat Barossa Valley Sparkling Shiraz** (Barossa Valley)

The sweet wines are split equally between Riesling and Semillon, all but one (Charles Melton) with high levels of botrytis.

95	**2004 Craigow Botrytis Riesling** (Southern Tasmania)
95	**2004 De Bortoli Noble One** (Riverina)
95	**2004 Freycinet Botrytis** (East Coast Tasmania)
94	**2001 Charles Melton Sotto di Ferro** (Barossa Valley)
94	**2003 De Bortoli Noble One** (Riverina)
94	**2004 Keith Tulloch Wine Botrytis Semillon** (Lower Hunter Valley)
94	**2005 Laurel Bank Dessert Riesling** (Southern Tasmania)
94	**2004 McWilliam's Limited Release Botrytis Semillon** (Riverina)
95	**2005 Oakridge 864 Riesling** (Yarra Valley)
94	**2004 Phillip Island Vineyard The Pinnacles Botrytis Riesling** (Gippsland)

Not so long ago, the three roses bloomed in the wilderness; now, with the curious worldwide surge of interest in the style, they are the generals commanding a vast army, albeit largely foot soldiers of common birth.

94	**2005 Charles Melton Rose Of Virginia** (Barossa Valley)
94	**2005 Turkey Flat Barossa Valley Rose** (Barossa Valley)
94	**2005 Yering Station Pinot Noir ED Rose** (Yarra Valley)

Pinot Noir

Yes, I love Pinot Noir beyond all other red wines, which can be seen as a contributing factor to 82 wines scoring 94 or more points. I would like to think, however, that I am a hard taskmaster, with no tolerance of 'dry red' versions of Pinot Noir grown in the wrong (i.e. too warm) regions. I would also plead my objectivity by pointing to the fact that 11 of the 25 wines scoring 95 or more come not from the Yarra Valley but from the Mornington Peninsula, the remainder from eight of the coolest regions. Next year, with the 2005 Tasmanian Pinot Noirs on-stream, may tell a different story. Here the cut-off comes at 95 points.

96	**2002 Bannockburn Vineyards Stuart Pinot Noir** (Geelong)
96	**2004 Tarrington Vineyards Pinot Noir** (Henty)
96	**2004 Bindi Wine Growers Block 5 Pinot Noir** (Macedon Ranges)
96	**2003 Kooyong Single Vineyard Meres Pinot Noir** (Mornington Peninsula)
96	**2004 Paringa Estate Pinot Noir** (Mornington Peninsula)
96	**2004 Paringa Estate Reserve Special Barrel Selection Pinot Noir** (Mornington Peninsula)
96	**2005 Dalrymple Special Bin Reserve Pinot Noir** (Northern Tasmania)

96   **2004 De Bortoli Reserve Pinot Noir** (Yarra Valley)
95   **2004 Grosset Pinot Noir** (Clare Valley)
95   **2004 Old Kent River Burls Reserve Pinot Noir** (Frankland River)
95   **2004 Austin's Pinot Noir** (Geelong)
95   **2004 St Regis Wild Reserve Pinot Noir** (Geelong)
95   **2004 Bellvale Pinot Noir** (Gippsland)
95   **2004 Bindi Wine Growers Original Vineyard Pinot Noir** (Macedon Ranges)
95   **2004 Eldridge Estate of Red Hill Single Clone Pinot Noir** (Mornington Peninsula)
95   **2004 Eldridge Estate of Red Hill Single Clone Pinot Noir** (Mornington Peninsula)
95   **2004 Farr Rising Mornington Pinot Noir** (Mornington Peninsula)
95   **2003 Hurley Vineyard Homage Pinot Noir** (Mornington Peninsula)
95   **2004 Kooyong Estate Pinot Noir** (Mornington Peninsula)
95   **2004 Merricks Creek Nick Farr Pinot Noir** (Mornington Peninsula)
95   **2004 Moorooduc Estate The Moorooduc Pinot Noir** (Mornington Peninsula)
95   **2004 Tuck's Ridge Buckle Vineyard Pinot Noir** (Mornington Peninsula)
95   **2004 Pirie Estate Pinot Noir** (Northern Tasmania)
95   **2005 Chatto Tasmania Pinot Noir** (Tasmania)

Shiraz

Pinot Noir notwithstanding, Shiraz is the jewel in Australia's crown, partly a priceless inheritance, but also with a lusty new generation of regional styles. The former is represented by the Barossa Valley, the latter by Heathcote. Segmenting the wines by points, 193 scored 94 points, 57 scored 95 points, and 41 received 96 or more. The dynamics are the remaining 2002 vintage wines, and the flood of 2004s. For obvious reasons, the cut-off is at 96 points.

97   **2002 Wolf Blass Platinum Label Shiraz** (Adelaide Hills)
97   **2002 The Willows Vineyard Bonesetter Shiraz** (Barossa Valley)
97   **2002 Trevor Jones Wild Witch Reserve Shiraz** (Barossa Valley)
97   **2002 Wirra Wirra Chook Block Shiraz** (McLaren Vale)
96   **2002 Chain of Ponds Ledge Shiraz** (Adelaide Hills)
96   **2003 Wolf Blass Platinum Label Shiraz** (Adelaide Hills)
96   **2004 Glaetzer Shiraz** (Barossa Valley)
96   **2002 Kilikanoon Greens Vineyard Shiraz** (Barossa Valley)
96   **2003 Langmeil The Freedom Shiraz** (Barossa Valley)
96   **2002 Laughing Jack Shiraz** (Barossa Valley)
96   **2002 Mount Toolleen Ebenezer Vineyard Shiraz** (Barossa Valley)
96   **2002 Penfolds St Henri Shiraz** (Barossa Valley)
96   **2001 Penfolds Grange** (Barossa Valley)
96   **2002 St Hallett Old Block Shiraz** (Barossa Valley)

96   **2003 Torbreck Vintners The Factor** (Barossa Valley)
96   **2003 Torbreck Vintners The RunRig** (Barossa Valley)
96   **2003 Turkey Flat Shiraz** (Barossa Valley)
96   **2001 Yalumba Octavius Shiraz** (Barossa Valley)
96   **2002 Annie's Lane Copper Trail Shiraz** (Clare Valley)
96   **2002 Jim Barry The Armagh** (Clare Valley)
96   **2002 Katnook Estate Prodigy Shiraz** (Coonawarra)
96   **2002 Henschke Mount Edelstone** (Eden Valley)
96   **2001 Henschke Hill Of Grace** (Eden Valley)
96   **2002 Best's Bin O Shiraz** (Grampians)
96   **2003 Howard Park Scotsdale Shiraz** (Great Southern)
96   **2004 Domaines Tatiarra Trademark Shiraz** (Heathcote)
96   **2004 Domaines Tatiarra Caravan of Dreams Shiraz Pressings** (Heathcote)
96   **2003 Eppalock Ridge Kylix Shiraz** (Heathcote)
96   **2004 Jasper Hill Georgia's Paddock Shiraz** (Heathcote)
96   **2004 Munari Lady's Pass Shiraz** (Heathcote)
96   **2004 Red Edge Shiraz** (Heathcote)
96   **2002 Shadowfax One Eye Shiraz** (Heathcote)
96   **2004 Taltarni Shiraz** (Heathcote)
96   **2003 Brokenwood Graveyard Shiraz** (Lower Hunter Valley)
96   **2004 Brini Estate Limited Release Sebastian Shiraz** (McLaren Vale)
96   **2004 Mitolo Savitar Shiraz** (McLaren Vale)
96   **2004 Mr Riggs Wine Company Shiraz** (McLaren Vale)
96   **2004 Paringa Estate Reserve Shiraz** (Mornington Peninsula)
96   **2004 Paringa Estate Shiraz** (Mornington Peninsula)
96   **2003 Shays Flat Vineyard Shiraz** (Pyrenees)

Shiraz Viognier

In best Australian Tall Poppy Syndrome style it has already become fashionable in some quarters to challenge the remarkable synergy obtained by co-fermenting around 5% of Viognier with Shiraz. The enhancement of colour, aroma and flavour is remarkable, as is the softening and smoothing of texture. Yes, it is not a panacea for lesser quality grapes, and yes, it is, and should remain, a subtext to the thrust of Shiraz simplicity. Nonetheless, the 30 wines in this group offer hedonistic pleasure second to none.

96   **2004 Clonakilla Shiraz Viognier** (Canberra District)
96   **2004 Spinifex Shiraz Viognier** (Eden Valley)
96   **2004 Torbreck Vintners The Descendant** (Barossa Valley)
95   **2004 d'Arenberg The Laughing Magpie Shiraz Viognier** (McLaren Vale)
95   **2004 De Bortoli Estate Shiraz Viognier** (Yarra Valley)

95   2004 **Pondalowie Vineyards Shiraz Viognier** (Bendigo)
95   2004 **Turner's Crossing Vineyard Shiraz Viognier** (Bendigo)
94   2004 **Armstrong Vineyards Shiraz Viognier** (Grampians)
94   2004 **Boireann Shiraz Viognier** (Granite Belt)
94   2004 **Centennial Vineyards Reserve Limited Release Shiraz Viognier** (Hilltops)
94   2004 **Diamond Valley Vineyards Shiraz Viognier** (Yarra Valley)
94   2003 **Eden Hall Shiraz Viognier** (Eden Valley)
94   2004 **Hardys Starvedog Lane Shiraz Viognier** (Adelaide Hills)
94   2004 **Hugh Hamilton Jekyll & Hyde Shiraz Viognier** (McLaren Vale)
94   2004 **Kamberra Shiraz Viognier** (Canberra District)
94   2003 **Millbrook Shiraz Viognier** (Perth Hills)
94   2003 **Mitchelton Parish Shiraz Viognier** (Nagambie Lakes)
94   2003 **Mount Torrens Vineyards Solstice Shiraz Viognier** (Adelaide Hills)
94   2004 **Mr Riggs Wine Company Shiraz Viognier** (McLaren Vale)
94   2004 **Robert Johnson Vineyards Eden Valley Shiraz Viognier** (Eden Valley)
94   2004 **Saltram Pepperjack Shiraz Viognier** (Barossa Valley)
94   2004 **SpringLane Shiraz Viognier** (Yarra Valley)
94   2002 **The Standish Wine Company The Relic Single Vineyard Shiraz Viognier** (Barossa Valley)
94   2004 **West Cape Howe Shiraz Viognier** (Denmark)
94   2004 **Wolf Blass Gold Label Shiraz Viognier** (Adelaide Hills)
94   2003 **Yarra Burn Shiraz Viognier** (Yarra Valley)
94   2004 **Yering Station Shiraz Viognier** (Yarra Valley)

Cabernet Sauvignon

The 77 wines scoring 94 points or more come from a mix of continental and maritime climates, the majority moderately cool, with heat summations similar to that of Bordeaux. Unsurprisingly, Coonawarra and Margaret River lead the way, the cut-off at 95 points.

96   2003 **Turkey Flat Cabernet Sauvignon** (Barossa Valley)
96   2004 **Balnaves The Tally Reserve Cabernet Sauvignon** (Coonawarra)
96   2001 **Jamiesons Run Winemakers Reserve Cabernet Sauvignon** (Coonawarra)
96   2001 **Katnook Estate Odyssey Cabernet Sauvignon** (Coonawarra)
96   2002 **Henschke Cyril Henschke Cabernet** (Eden Valley)
96   2002 **Bremerton Reserve Cabernet Sauvignon** (Langhorne Creek)
96   2001 **Bremerton Reserve Cabernet Sauvignon** (Langhorne Creek)
96   2003 **Howard Park Leston Cabernet Sauvignon** (Margaret River)
96   2003 **Suckfizzle Cabernet Sauvignon** (Margaret River)
95   2004 **Setanta Black Sanglain Cabernet Sauvignon** (Adelaide Hills)
95   2002 **Barossa Valley Estate Ebenezer Cabernet Sauvignon** (Barossa Valley)

95   **2002 Leasingham Classic Clare Cabernet Sauvignon** (Clare Valley)
95   **2003 Jamiesons Run Rothwell Cabernet Sauvignon** (Coonawarra)
95   **2000 Best's Great Western Cabernet Sauvignon** (Grampians)
95   **2003 Howard Park Scotsdale Cabernet Sauvignon** (Great Southern)
95   **2004 Chalkers Crossing Cabernet Sauvignon** (Hilltops)
95   **2004 Gralyn Estate Cabernet Sauvignon** (Margaret River)
95   **2002 Sandalford Prendiville Reserve Cabernet Sauvignon** (Margaret River)
95   **2002 Geoff Merrill Reserve Cabernet Sauvignon** (McLaren Vale)
95   **2004 Dalwhinnie Moonambel Cabernet Sauvignon** (Pyrenees)
95   **2004 Taltarni Cabernet Sauvignon** (Pyrenees)

Cabernet blends

It is with Cabernet Merlot blends that Margaret River really flexes its muscles, accounting for 14 of the 32 wines scoring 94 and above, and (in racing parlance) daylight second. I have treated Cabernet Shiraz and Shiraz Cabernet blends (and such) as a separate subgroup; here the regional base is more widespread. The cut-off comes at 95 points.

96   **2002 Voyager Estate Cabernet Sauvignon Merlot** (Margaret River)
95   **2003 Primo Estate Joseph Moda Cabernet Merlot** (Adelaide Plains)
95   **2003 Haan Wilhelmus** (Barossa Valley)
95   **2002 Alkoomi Blackbutt** (Frankland River)
95   **2004 Piggs Peake House of Bricks Cabernet Merlot** (Lower Hunter Valley)
95   **2004 Cullen Diana Madeline Cabernet Sauvignon Merlot** (Margaret River)
95   **2003 Happs Three Hills Charles Andreas** (Margaret River)
95   **2003 Stella Bella Cabernet Sauvignon Merlot** (Margaret River)
95   **2003 Vasse Felix Heytesbury** (Margaret River)
95   **2003 Voyager Estate Cabernet Sauvignon Merlot** (Margaret River)
95   **2004 Woodlands Margaret Reserve Cabernet Merlot** (Margaret River)
95   **2003 Houghton Crofters Cabernet Merlot** (Swan Valley)
96   **2002 Wolf Blass Black Label Cabernet Sauvignon Shiraz** (Barossa Valley)
95   **2004 Murdock The Merger** (Coonawarra)
95   **2002 Stonehaven Rat & Bull Cabernet Shiraz** (Padthaway)
95   **2004 Tapanappa Whalebone Vineyard Cabernet Shiraz** (Wrattonbully)
95   **2003 Tapanappa Whalebone Vineyard Cabernet Shiraz** (Wrattonbully)

Bordeaux varietals

A smallish group of Merlots and lesser Bordeaux varieties, the majority — once again — from Margaret River and nearby WA regions.

95   2002 Irvine Grand Merlot (Eden Valley)
95   2004 Hackersley Merlot (Geographe)
95   2004 Woodlands Reserve du Cave Malbec (Margaret River)
94   2004 Eighteen Forty-Seven Home Block Petit Verdot (Barossa Valley)
94   2003 Picardy Merlot Cabernet Sauvignon Cabernet Franc (Pemberton)
94   2004 Tahbilk Cabernet Franc (Nagambie Lakes)
94   2004 Woodlands Reserve du Cave Cabernet Franc (Margaret River)
94   2003 Brookland Valley Verse 1 Merlot (Margaret River)
94   2004 Cape Naturaliste Vineyard Torpedo Rocks Merlot (Margaret River)
94   2003 Chestnut Grove Estate Merlot (Manjimup)
94   2003 Haan Merlot Prestige (Barossa Valley)
94   2004 Happs Three Hills Merlot (Margaret River)
94   2004 Murdock Merlot (Coonawarra)
94   2004 YarraLoch Stephanie's Dream Merlot (Yarra Valley)

Rhone blends and varieties

Almost, but not quite, the back gardens of the Barossa Valley and McLaren Vale, with the Barossa providing most of the Shiraz-dominant blends, McLaren Vale most of the Grenache-dominant blends.

95   2004 John Duval Plexus Shiraz Grenache Mourvedre (Barossa Valley)
95   2003 Soul Growers Shiraz Grenache Mourvedre (Barossa Valley)
95   2002 Soul Growers Shiraz Grenache Mourvedre (Barossa Valley)
95   2004 Spinifex Esprit (Barossa Valley)
95   2004 Spinifex Indigene (Barossa Valley)
94   2004 Boireann Mourvedre Shiraz Grenache (Granite Belt)
94   2003 d'Arenberg The Ironstone Pressings Grenache Shiraz Mourvedre (McLaren Vale)
94   2004 Five Geese Grenache Shiraz (McLaren Vale)
94   2002 Grant Burge The Holy Trinity Grenache Shiraz Mourvedre (Barossa Valley)
94   2004 Hardys Reynell Grenache (McLaren Vale)
94   2004 Henschke Johann's Garden Grenache Mourvedre Shiraz (Barossa Valley)
94   2004 Hewitson Old Garden Mourvedre (Barossa Valley)
94   2004 Jasper Hill Cornella Vineyard Grenache (Heathcote)
94   2004 Rolf Binder Heinrich Shiraz Grenache Mataro (Barossa Valley)
94   2001 Soul Growers Shiraz Grenache Mourvedre (Barossa Valley)
94   2004 Spinifex Grenache (Barossa Valley)
94   2005 Spinifex Papillon (Barossa Valley)
94   2004 The Islander Estate Vineyards Old Rowley Bush Vine
       Grenache (Kangaroo Island)

Fortified wines

A relatively small but immensely impressive group of wines, as quintessentially Australian as a Drizabone.

98   **1906 Seppelt 100 Year Old Para Liqueur** (Barossa Valley)

97   **NV Seppelt Rare Tawny DP90** (Barossa Valley)

95   **NV John Kosovich Liqueur Shiraz** (Swan Valley)

95   **NV Penfolds Great Grandfather Port** (Barossa Valley)

95   **NV Seppelt Oloroso DP38** (Barossa Valley)

95   **1985 Seppelt Para Liqueur** (Barossa Valley)

95   **2001 Stanton & Killeen Vintage Port** (Rutherglen)

Special value wines

As always, these are lists of 10 of the best value wines, not the 10 best wines in each price category. There are literally dozens of wines with similar points and prices, and the choice is necessarily an arbitrary one. I have, however, attempted to give as much varietal and style choice as the limited numbers allow.

Ten of the best value whites under $10

87	**2005 De Bortoli Sacred Hill Colombard Chardonnay**	$6
86	**2005 Angove's Butterfly Ridge Riesling**	$6.99
88	**2005 Yalumba Oxford Landing Sauvignon Blanc**	$7.95
88	**2005 McPherson Murray Darling Chardonnay**	$9
89	**2005 McWilliam's Inheritance Semillon Sauvignon Blanc**	$9
93	**2004 Barwite Vineyards Upper Goulburn Riesling**	$9.20
88	**2005 Paul Bettio King Valley Sauvignon Blanc Chardonnay**	$9.90
88	**2005 Casella yellow tail Semillon Sauvignon Blanc**	$9.99
87	**2005 Zilzie Buloke Sauvignon Blanc**	$9.99
90	**2005 Orlando Jacob's Creek Chardonnay**	$9.99

Ten of the best value reds under $10

87	**2005 De Bortoli Sacred Hill Cabernet Merlot**	$6
87	**2003 Macaw Creek 3 Valley Shiraz Cabernet**	$6
87	**2004 Jindalee Estate Shiraz**	$7
89	**2003 Angove's Stonegate Cabernet Sauvignon**	$7.99
89	**2004 Hardys Nottage Hill Cabernet Sauvignon**	$8
88	**2004 McPherson Murray Darling Shiraz Cabernet**	$8.99
87	**2005 Beelgara Estate Shiraz Cabernet**	$9
89	**2004 Hardys Four Emus Shiraz**	$9.95
87	**2004 Deakin Estate Shiraz**	$9.99
87	**2004 Poet's Corner Shiraz Cabernet Sauvignon**	$9.99

Ten of the best value whites $10–$15

94   **2005 Peter Lehmann Barossa Riesling** $12
94   **2005 Charles Sturt University Orange Chardonnay** $13
92   **2005 Minot Vineyard Margaret River Semillon Sauvignon Blanc** $13
94   **2005 De Iuliis Semillon** $14
93   **2005 Tahbilk Marsanne** $14.25
94   **2005 Willow Bridge Geographe Sauvignon Blanc Semillon** $14.50
94   **2005 Jamiesons Run Chardonnay** $14.99
95   **2005 Tyrrell's Lost Block Semillon** $14.99
94   **2005 Bellarmine Pemberton Chardonnay** $15
94   **2005 Brindabella Hills Canberra Sauvignon Blanc** $15

Ten of the best value reds $10–$15

93   **2004 Heartland Vineyard Shiraz Viognier** $10
93   **2004 Scaffidi Wines One Tree Hill Shiraz** $10
93   **2004 Leasingham Bastion Shiraz Cabernet** $12
94   **2004 Hardys Oomoo McLaren Vale Shiraz** $12.95
94   **2003 Bleasdale Vineyards Langhorne Creek Shiraz Cabernet Sauvignon** $13
93   **2004 Thorn-Clark Sandpiper The Blend** $13
93   **2004 Hare's Chase Barossa Red Blend** $14
94   **2004 Xabregas Shiraz** $14
93   **2003 David Hook The Gorge Hunter Valley Shiraz** $15
94   **2004 Wirra Wirra Scrubby Rise Red** $15

Winery of the year

It is with a degree of trepidation that I introduce this accolade. There are many great wineries in Australia, and they come in all shapes and sizes. A few, however, excel themselves in a given year (and longer, perhaps, but once selected, these cannot qualify for the next year — union rules) with a series of outstanding wines.

The first award goes to the magician, **LINDSAY McCALL** of **PARINGA ESTATE**. A quick look at the tasting notes (page 501) will almost say it all. Almost, because Paringa Estate is arguably best known for its Pinot Noirs, typically released under three labels of ascending price and quality, the lowest equal to many others' best.

Paringa also makes superb Chardonnay (again under several labels), which has the style and complexity to match the best from this country. If all this were not enough, Lindsay McCall was one of two pioneers of Shiraz in the Mornington Peninsula, the 2004 Shiraz taking an unprecedented number of trophies at the Royal Sydney Wine Show 2006, including the trophy for Best Wine of Show.

This former school teacher/self-taught winemaker has vinous green thumbs. He has an instinctive feel for all parts of the passage from grapes on the vine to wine in the bottle, coupled with the near-obsessive attention to detail which all great winemakers must have.

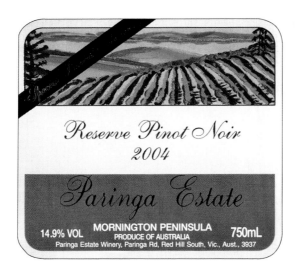

Reserve Pinot Noir
2004

Paringa Estate

14.9% VOL   MORNINGTON PENINSULA   750mL
PRODUCE OF AUSTRALIA
Paringa Estate Winery, Paringa Rd, Red Hill South, Vic., Aust., 3937

Ten of the best new wineries

Confronted with 16 new 5-star wineries, I selected those with the most 5-glass/94 points or above wines, which worked well for the first nine, but left me with a tie for tenth spot between wineries with two such wines. The back-up wines of Sedona Estate got it over the line.

Bellarmine Wines PEMBERTON page 102

The owners are German residents Dr Willi and Gudrun Schumacher, long-term wine connoisseurs who decided to expand their wine interests in a stable socio-economic country. The winemaking team headed by Mike Bewsher is making a series of supremely elegant wines from 20 ha of estate vineyards.

Mount Toolleen BAROSSA VALLEY/HEATHCOTE page 466

An investor-owned, near virtual winery which gained immediate prominence when its 2002 Ebenezer Shiraz won the George Mackey Award for the best wine exported in 2004–2005. Shiraz from the Barossa Valley and Heathcote regions (and nothing else) is a canny plan, skilled contract winemaking the icing on the cake.

Prancing Horse Estate MORNINGTON PENINSULA page 537

Good things can come in small packages when new owners (Anthony and Catherine Hancy) acquire a vineyard planted in 1990, upgrade the viticulture (bravely embarking on an organic path) and retain Sergio Carlei as winemaker — and then become partners with Sergio in Carlei Wines.

Radford Dale EDEN VALLEY page 546

Former Flying Winemaker Ben Radford — with a several-year stint in South Africa — and wife Gillian purchased a 4-ha vineyard with riesling planted in 1930 (1.2 ha) and 1970 (1.1. ha) plus a more recent planting of 1.7 ha of shiraz. As well as contract winemaking for others, Ben has made four faultless wines.

Sedona Estate UPPER GOULBURN page 594

Former Oakridge Estate winemaker Paul Evans and wife Sonja looked long and hard before they purchased their Murrindindi property, planting 4 ha of shiraz, cabernet sauvignon, merlot and sangiovese on north-facing, gently undulating slopes with gravelly black soils. Graceful red wines of impeccable quality have vindicated their search.

Soul Growers BAROSSA VALLEY page 615

Fifth-generation Barossan James Lindner moved straight from school into the wine industry, and had ample experience before planting shiraz (1.6 ha), grenache (0.8 ha) and mourvedre (0.3 ha) on the hills of Seppeltsfield. The grapes are separately open-fermented and the wines are barrel-aged for two years before being blended and bottled without fining or filtration.

Spinifex BAROSSA VALLEY page 617

Wow, what an impressive newcomer this is, owned by New Zealand-born Peter Schell and French-born wife Magali Gely. After graduation from Roseworthy they worked for four vintages in the south of France, and when they established Spinifex, it was only natural to focus on Mourvedre, Grenache, Shiraz and Cinsaut. Great wine and immaculate packaging is a heady mixture.

Turner's Crossing Vineyard BENDIGO page 686

Former corporate executive, business school lecturer and self-taught viticulturist Paul Jenkins planted this 40-ha vineyard (his second) in 1999, selling grapes to various wineries before Sergio Carlei (that man again) joined with Phil Bennet to form a partnership with Jenkins, and make increasing quantities of infinitely stylish red wines under the Turner's Crossing label.

Twofold CLARE VALLEY/HEATHCOTE page 689

This is the virtual winery business of brothers Nick and Tim Stock, whose excellent palates and varied experience in restaurants, retail and wholesale led them to the very smart idea of (vicariously) making Clare Valley Riesling via Neil Pike and Heathcote Shiraz via Sergio Carlei.

YarraLoch YARRA VALLEY page 753

Wealthy investment banker Stephen Wood has set out to make every post a winner with a carefully thought out and brilliantly executed business plan to suck the best out of the Yarra Valley's varied meso-climates, marrying site and variety, appointing Sergio Carlei as winemaker, and packaging the wines with imagination and flair.

Best wineries of the regions

I have explained the rationale for the ratings in the 'How to use the *Companion*' section (page 49). For the record, 12.5% of wineries received 5 stars.

ADELAIDE HILLS
Ashton Hills
Mount Torrens Vineyards
Setanta Wines
Shaw & Smith
TK Wines

ADELAIDE PLAINS
Primo Estate

ADELAIDE ZONE
Uleybury Wines

BALLARAT
Tomboy Hill

BAROSSA VALLEY
Barossa Valley Estate
Charles Melton
Craneford
Dutschke Wines
Gibson Barossavale
Glaetzer Wines
Grant Burge
Haan Wines
John Duval Wines
Kaesler Wines
Langmeil Winery
Laughing Jack
Leo Buring
Liebich Wein
Mount Toolleen
Orlando
Penfolds
Peter Lehmann
Rockford
Saltram
Seppelt
Soul Growers
Spinifex
St Hallet
St John's Road
Thorn-Clarke Wines
Torbreck Vintners
Trevor Jones/
    Kellermeister

Turkey Flat
Wolf Blass
Yalumba

BEECHWORTH
battely wines
Smiths Vineyard

BENDIGO
Balgownie
Pondalowie Vineyards
Turner's Crossing Vineyard

BIG RIVERS ZONE
Charles Sturt University
    Winery

CANBERRA DISTRICT
Brindabella Hills
Clonakilla
Kamberra
Lark Hill

CLARE VALLEY
Annie's Lane
Grosset
Kilikanoon
Kirrihill Wines
Leasingham
Little Brampton Wines
Mitchell
Neagles Rock Vineyards
O'Leary Walker Wines
Paulett
Taylors
Twofold
Wendouree
Wilson Vineyard

COONAWARRA
Balnaves of Coonawarra
Jamiesons Run
Katnook Estate
Murdock
Penley Estate
Punters Corner

DENMARK
Harewood Estate
Moombaki Wines
West Cape Howe Wines

EAST COAST TASMANIA
Freycinet

EDEN VALLEY
Eden Hall
Henschke
Hill Smith Estate
Hutton Vale Vineyard
Irvine
Pewsey Vale
Radford Dale

FRANKLAND RIVER
Alkoomi
Ferngrove Vineyards
Frankland Estate
Old Kent River

GEELONG
Bannockburn Vineyards
by Farr
Clyde Park Vineyard
Curlewis Winery
Farr Rising
Scotchmans Hill
Shadowfax

GEOGRAPHE
Willow Bridge Estate

GIPPSLAND
Bass Phillip
Bellvale Wines
Caledonia Australis
Jinks Creek Winery
Narkoojee
Phillip Island Vineyard

GLENROWAN
Baileys of Glenrowan

GRAMPIANS
Armstrong Vineyards
Best's Wines
Grampians Estate
Michael Unwin Wines
Mount Langi Ghiran
  Vineyards
Seppelt
Westgate Vineyard

GRANITE BELT
Boireann

GREAT SOUTHERN
Forest Hill Vineyard
Howard Park
Trevelen Farm

HEATHCOTE
Coliban Valley Wines
Dead Horse Hill
Domaines Tatiarra
Downing Estate Vineyard
Eppalock Ridge
Heathcote Estate
Jasper Hill
La Pleiade
Munari Wines
Red Edge
Shelmerdine Vineyards

HENTY
Crawford River Wines
Tarrington Vineyards

HILLTOPS
Chalkers Crossing
Grove Estate Wines

KANGAROO ISLAND
The Islander Estate
  Vineyards

KING VALLEY
Brown Brothers

LANGHORNE CREEK
Bleasdale Vineyards
Bremerton Wines
John's Blend

LOWER HUNTER VALLEY
Brokenwood
Capercaillie
Chatto Wines
Glenguin
McLeish Estate
McWilliam's Mount
  Pleasant
Meerea Park
Mistletoe Wines
Mt Vincent Estate
Pepper Tree Wines
Peter Howland Wines
Piggs Peake
Thomas Wines
Tower Estate
Tulloch
Tyrrell's

MACEDON RANGES
Bindi Wine Growers
Cope-Williams
Curly Flat
Hanging Rock Winery

MARGARET RIVER
Alexandra Bridge Wines
Artamus
Ashbrook Estate
Brookland Valley
Cape Mentelle
Chalice Bridge Estate
Cullen Wines
Deep Woods Estate
Gralyn Estate
Hamelin Bay
Happs
Howard Park
Leeuwin Estate
Lenton Brae Wines
Moss Wood
Pierro
Redgate
Rosabrook Estate
Sandalford
Suckfizzle/Stella Bella
Vasse Felix
Voyager Estate
Watershed Wines
We're Estate
Woodlands
Woodside Valley Estate

McLAREN VALE
Arakoon
Brini Estate Wines
Coriole
d'Arenberg
Foggo Wines
Fox Creek Wines
Geoff Merrill Wines
Hugh Hamilton
Ingoldby
Mitolo Wines
Mr Riggs Wine Company
Tapestry
Wirra Wirra

MORNINGTON PENINSULA
Darling Park
Eldridge Estate of Red Hill
Hurley Vineyard
Kooyong
Merricks Creek Wines
Moorooduc Estate
Paringa Estate
Port Phillip Estate
Prancing Horse Estate
Red Hill Estate
Stonier Wines
Stumpy Gully
Ten Minutes by Tractor
  Wine Co
Tuck's Ridge
Willow Creek
Yabby Lake Vineyard

MOUNT BARKER
Xabregas

NAGAMBIE LAKES
Mitchelton
Tahbilk

NORTHERN TASMANIA
Bay of Fires
Dalrymple
Humbug Reach Vineyard
Lake Barrington Estate
Pipers Brook Vineyard
Tamar Ridge

ORANGE
Bloodwood

PADTHAWAY
Stonehaven

PEMBERTON
Bellarmine Wines
Merum
Picardy

PERTH HILLS
Millbrook Winery

PORONGURUP
Gibraltar Rock

PORT PHILLIP ZONE
Three Wise Men

PYRENEES
Dalwhinnie
Kara Kara Vineyard
Landsborough Valley
  Estate
Pyrenees Ridge Vineyard
Shays Flat Vineyard
Taltarni

RIVERINA
McWilliam's

RUTHERGLEN
All Saints Estate
Bullers Calliope
Campbells
Chambers Rosewood
Morris
Stanton & Killeen Wines
Warrabilla

SOUTHEAST AUSTRALIA
Hewitson

SOUTHERN HIGHLANDS
Centennial Vineyards

SOUTHERN TASMANIA
Craigow
Domaine A
Pooley Wines
Wellington

STRATHBOGIE RANGES
Plunkett Wines

SUNBURY
Craiglee
Witchmount Estate

SWAN VALLEY
Faber Vineyard
Houghton
John Kosovich Wines

UPPER GOULBURN
Sedona Estate

WESTERN VICTORIA ZONE
Norton Estate

WRATTONBULLY
Tapanappa

YARRA VALLEY
Carlei Estate & Green
  Vineyards
De Bortoli
Diamond Valley Vineyards
Domaine Chandon
Dominique Portet
Giant Steps
Labyrinth
Lillydale Estate
Metier Wines
Mount Mary
Oakridge
Punch
Rochford Wines
Tarrawarra Estate
Toolangi Vineyards
Wantirna Estate
Yarra Burn
Yarra Yering
Yarrabank
YarraLoch
Yering Station
Yeringberg

Ten dark horses

The same idea as last year, though (of course) not the same wineries: 10 producers which have excelled themselves over the past 12 months.

Arakoon MCLAREN VALE page 73
A once zany business has turned serious with ever better wines and elegant packaging.

Charles Sturt University Winery BIG RIVERS ZONE page 170
The idea of a teaching winery is often beset with problems; Charles Sturt is making light of it with excellent wines at bargain prices.

Forest Hill Vineyard GREAT SOUTHERN page 257
Out of the blue, as it were, come four very special wines made from the oldest (up to 40 years old) blocks in the vineyard.

Harewood Estate DENMARK page 304
Five-star wines have come fast and furious from James Kellie: Shiraz, Sauvignon Blanc Semillon, Riesling and Chardonnay.

Mistletoe Wines LOWER HUNTER VALLEY page 442
Has come and gone periodically since 1909, now very much here; Shiraz, Semillon and Chardonnay leading the way.

Mount Torrens Vineyards ADELAIDE HILLS page 467
Export market blues have allowed tiny quantities of these marvellous wines to be purchased by mail order.

Mount Vincent Estate LOWER HUNTER VALLEY page 468
Arguably the darkest horse of all, suddenly producing a stellar array of wines from here, there and everywhere.

Munari Wines HEATHCOTE page 471
Never far off the pace, but the Munaris have blitzed the field with their outstanding 2004 reds.

Oakridge YARRA VALLEY page 488
Whoever buys Oakridge from Evans & Tate would be well advised to retain the services of winemaker David Bicknell, who seems to have flourished in adversity.

Thorn-Clarke Wines BAROSSA VALLEY page 664
Major trophy successes with the 2004 wines have underlined the viticultural resources (270 ha) and winemaking skills of this family-owned business.

Wine and food or food and wine?

It all depends on your starting point: there are conventional matches for overseas classics such as caviar (Champagne), fresh foie gras (Sauternes, Riesling or Rose), and new-season Italian white truffles (any medium-bodied red). Here the food flavour is all important, the wine incidental.

At the other extreme come 50-year-old classic red wines: Grange, Grand Cru Burgundy, First Growth Bordeaux, or a Maurice O'Shea Mount Pleasant Shiraz. Here the food is — or should be — a low-key foil, but at the same time must be of high quality.

In the Australian context I believe not enough attention is paid to the time of year, which — particularly in the southern states — is or should be a major determinant in the choice of both food and wine. And so I thus present my suggestions, always bearing in mind how many ways there are to skin a cat.

Spring

SPARKLING
Oysters, cold crustacea, tapas, any cold hors d'oeuvres

YOUNG RIESLING
Cold salads, sashimi

GEWURZTRAMINER
Asian

YOUNG SEMILLON
Antipasto, vegetable terrine

PINOT GRIS, COLOMBARD
Crab cakes, whitebait

VERDELHO, CHENIN BLANC
Cold smoked chicken, gravlax

MATURE CHARDONNAY
Grilled chicken, chicken pasta, turkey, pheasant

ROSE
Caesar salad, trout mousse

YOUNG PINOT NOIR
Seared kangaroo fillet, grilled quail

MERLOT
Pastrami, warm smoked chicken

YOUNG MEDIUM-BODIED CABERNET SAUVIGNON
Rack of baby lamb

LIGHT TO MEDIUM-BODIED COOL CLIMATE SHIRAZ
Rare eye fillet of beef

YOUNG BOTRYTISED WINES
Fresh fruits, cake

Summer

CHILLED FINO
Cold consommé

2–3-YEAR-OLD SEMILLON
Gazpacho

2–3-YEAR-OLD RIESLING
Seared tuna

**YOUNG BARREL-FERMENTED
SEMILLON SAUVIGNON BLANC**
Seafood or vegetable tempura

YOUNG OFF-DRY RIESLING
Prosciutto and melon/pear

COOL CLIMATE CHARDONNAY
Abalone, lobster, Chinese-style prawns

10-YEAR-OLD SEMILLON OR RIESLING
Braised pork neck

MATURE CHARDONNAY
Smoked eel, smoked roe

OFF-DRY ROSE
Chilled fresh fruit

YOUNG LIGHT-BODIED PINOT NOIR
Grilled salmon

AGED PINOT NOIR (5+ YEARS)
Coq au vin, wild duck

YOUNG GRENACHE/SANGIOVESE
Osso bucco

MATURE CHARDONNAY (5+ YEARS)
Braised rabbit

HUNTER VALLEY SHIRAZ (5–10 YEARS)
Beef spare ribs

MERLOT
Saltimbocca, roast pheasant

**MEDIUM-BODIED CABERNET
SAUVIGNON (5 YEARS)**
Barbequed butterfly leg of lamb

ALL WINES
Parmigiana

Autumn

AMONTILLADO
Warm consommé

BARREL-FERMENTED MATURE WHITES
Smoked roe, bouillabaisse

COMPLEX MATURE CHARDONNAY
Sweetbreads, brains

FULLY AGED RIESLING
Char-grilled eggplant, stuffed capsicum

AGED MARSANNE
Seafood risotto, Lebanese

YOUNG MUSCAT
Plum pudding

AGED PINOT NOIR
Grilled calf's liver, roast kid, lamb or
pig's kidneys

**MATURE MARGARET RIVER
CABERNET MERLOT**
Lamb fillet, roast leg of lamb with
garlic and herbs

SOUTHERN VICTORIAN PINOT NOIR
Peking duck

COOL CLIMATE MERLOT
Lamb loin chops

MATURE GRENACHE/RHONE BLENDS
Moroccan lamb

RICH, FULL-BODIED HEATHCOTE SHIRAZ
Beef casserole

Winter

DRY OLOROSO SHERRY
Full-flavoured hors d'oeuvres

SPARKLING BURGUNDY
Borscht

VIOGNIER
Pea and ham soup

AGED SEMILLON (10+ YEARS)
Vichyssoise (hot)

SAUVIGNON BLANC
Coquilles St Jacques, pan-fried scallops

MATURE CHARDONNAY
Quiche Lorraine

CHARDONNAY (10+ YEARS)
Cassoulet

MATURE SEMILLON SAUVIGNON BLANC
Seafood pasta

YOUNG TASMANIAN PINOT NOIR
Squab, duck breast

MATURE PINOT NOIR
Mushroom ragout, ravioli

MATURE MERLOT
Pot au feu

10-YEAR-OLD HEATHCOTE SHIRAZ
Char-grilled rump steak

15–20-YEAR-OLD FULL-BODIED BAROSSA SHIRAZ
Venison, kangaroo fillet

COONAWARRA CABERNET SAUVIGNON
Braised lamb shanks/shoulder

MUSCAT (OLD)
Chocolate-based desserts

TOKAY (OLD)
Crème brûlée

VINTAGE PORT
Dried fruits, salty cheese

How to use the *Companion*

The *Australian Wine Companion* is arranged with wineries in alphabetical order; the index at the back lists the wineries by region, which adds a search facility. The entries should be self-explanatory, but here I will briefly take you through the information for each entry, using Paringa Estate as an example.

Winery entries

Paringa Estate ★★★★★

44 Paringa Road, Red Hill South, Vic 3937 **REGION** Mornington Peninsula
T (03) 5989 2669 **F** (03) 5931 0135 **WWW**.paringaestate.com.au **OPEN** 7 days 11–5
WINEMAKER Lindsay McCall **EST.** 1985 **CASES** 9500
Schoolteacher-turned-winemaker Lindsay McCall has shown an absolutely exceptional gift for winemaking across a range of styles, but with immensely complex Pinot Noir and Shiraz leading the way. The wines have an unmatched level of success in the wine shows and competitions Paringa Estate is able to enter, the limitation being the relatively small size of the production. His skills are no less evident in contract winemaking for others. The restaurant is open 7 days.

WINERY NAME Paringa Estate

Although it might seem that stating the winery name is straightforward, this is not necessarily so. To avoid confusion, wherever possible I use the name that appears most prominently on the wine label, and do not refer to any associated trading name.

RATINGS ★★★★★

The winery star system may be interpreted as follows:

★★★★★	Outstanding winery capable of producing wines of the highest calibre.
★★★★☆	Excellent producer of very high quality wines.
★★★★	Very good producer of wines with class and character.
★★★☆	A solid, usually reliable, maker of good to very good wines.
★★★	A typically good winery, but may have some lesser wines.
★★☆	Adequate; usually aspires to improve.
NR	Normally ascribed where I have not tasted any current release wines.

Each year I agonise over the means by which I arrive at the rating to be ascribed for each winery. For this edition I adopted a stringent approach: if I did not taste any wines from a winery in the 12-month period, it automatically received an NR classification, regardless of its reputation. In the outcome, just under 39% fell into this category.

At the other end of the scale, if a winery had at least two wines in the 5-glass/94 points or above category, it received a 5-star rating, regardless of the other wines in its portfolio. The reasons for this are numerous: all large producers have a wide price range, and should not be denied recognition just because they have cheap wines in their portfolio which will necessarily score less. Likewise, a small producer might have a rose or an unwooded chardonnay priced well below their best — and so on: the tail should not wag the dog. Thus 12.5% of wineries received the maximum rating.

Fractionally under 40% ranked between 3.5 to 4.5 stars. It is here that the ratings were more subjective as I endeavoured to take into account both the glass ratings and the points spread within those ratings. I am attracted to the idea of some kind of algorithm, but would have to test drive it first. In the meantime, I can only say that I have done my best to be fair.

Finally, I should make it clear that, consistently with the NR approach, the star ratings are all derived from tastings during the 12-month period. Some wineries will be displeased to find their ratings have fallen; others will be happy to find theirs have been raised. I simply cannot have a 'carry forward' credit or debit system.

CONTACT DETAILS 44 Paringa Road, Red Hill South, Vic 3937 **T** (03) 5989 2669 **F** (03) 5931 0135

The details are usually those of the winery and cellar door, but in a few instances may simply be of the winery; this occurs when the wine is made under contract at another winery and is sold only through retail.

REGION Mornington Peninsula

The mapping of Australia into Zones and Regions with legally defined boundaries is now well underway. This edition sees radical changes (and additions) to the regional names and boundaries. Wherever possible the official 'Geographic Indication' name has been adopted, and where the registration process is incomplete, I have used the most likely name. Occasionally you will see 'Warehouse' as the region. This means the wine is made from purchased grapes, in someone else's winery. In other words, it does not have a vineyard or winery in the ordinary way.

WWW.paringaestate.com.au

An increasingly important reference point for the reasons I have covered in the Introduction.

OPEN 7 days 11–5

Although a winery might be listed as not open or only open on weekends, some may in fact be prepared to open by appointment. Many will, some won't; a telephone call will establish whether it is possible or not. Also, virtually every winery that is shown as being open only for weekends is in fact open on public holidays as well. Once again, a telephone call will confirm this.

WINEMAKER Lindsay McCall

In the large companies the winemaker is simply the head of a team; there may be many executive winemakers actually responsible for specific wines.

EST. 1985

A more or less self-explanatory item, but keep in mind that some makers consider the year in which they purchased the land to be the year of establishment, others the year in which they first planted grapes, others the year they first made wine, others the year they first offered wine for sale, and so on. There may also be minor complications where there has been a change of ownership or a break in production.

CASES 9500

This figure (representing the number of cases produced each year) is merely an indication of the size of the operation. Some winery entries do not feature a production figure: this is either because the winery (principally, but not exclusively, the large companies) regards this information as confidential or because the information was not available at the time of going to press.

SUMMARY Schoolteacher-turned-winemaker Lindsay McCall has shown an absolutely exceptional gift for winemaking across a range of styles, but with immensely complex Pinot Noir and Shiraz leading the way. The wines have an unmatched level of success in the wine shows and competitions Paringa Estate is able to enter, the limitation being the relatively small size of the production. His skills are no less evident in contract winemaking for others. The restaurant is open 7 days.

My summary of the winery. Little needs to be said, except that I have tried to vary the subjects I discuss in this part of the winery entry.

🍃 The vine leaf symbol indicates the 230 wineries that are new entries in this year's listing.

Note: For an explanation of the symbols used in the regional index, see page 53.

Tasting notes

RATINGS

94–100   Outstanding. Wines of the highest quality, usually with a distinguished pedigree.

90–93   Highly recommended. Wines of great quality, style and character, worthy of a place in any cellar.

87–89   Recommended. Wines of above average quality, fault-free, and with clear varietal expression.

84–86   Fair to good. Wines with plenty of flavour (usually varietal) and good balance; free of technical faults.

80–83   Everyday wines: price is particularly relevant; under $10 will represent good value.

75–79   Also tasted: usually wines with some deficiency, technical or otherwise.

I should emphasise that the ratings are for the vintage(s) specified in the notes. Thus in outstanding vintages, such as 2004, many of the red wines in particular have higher points than normal. I also freely acknowledge that the 100-point scale is effectively a 20-point scale, with 0.1 increments if viewed as being out of 20. In international usage the same holds true.

> **Estate Pinot Noir 2004** Powerful black cherry fruit aromas and flavours backed by perfectly balanced and integrated French oak; fine tannins. Screwcap. 14.9° alc. **RATING** 96 **DRINK** 2010 $ 55

The tasting note opens with the vintage of the wine tasted. With the exception of a very occasional classic wine, this tasting note will have been made within the 12 months prior to publication. Even that is a long time, and during the life of this book the wine will almost certainly change. More than this, remember that tasting is a highly subjective and imperfect art. NV = non-vintage. The price of the wine is listed where information is available. Another innovation is the frequent comment, at the end of the tasting note, on the closure used.

DRINK 2010

Rather than give a span of drinking years, I have simply provided a (conservative) 'best by' date. Modern winemaking is such that, even if a wine has 10 or 20 years' future during which it will gain much greater complexity, it can be enjoyed at any time over the intervening months and years.

Index of wineries by region

A new feature of this edition is the inclusion of symbols in the index which allow the reader to see, at a glance, facilities/activities provided by the winery. Details should be checked with each winery.

♟ Cellar door sales

⊗ Food — lunch platters to à la carte restaurants

⛸ Accommodation — B&B cottages to luxury vineyard apartments

♪ Music events — monthly jazz in the vineyard to spectacular yearly concerts

Refer to regional index on page 765.

A note on corks and closures

I wrote at length on this subject in last year's *Wine Companion*, and won't repeat all I said then. Instead, I will start with the statistics which come from this year's database. More than half (51.5% or 3302 wines) were sealed with screwcaps, less than one-third (31.5% or 2025) with cork. The only other significant closure was Diam, with 2.75% (177) of the total — a total, incidentally, of those wines where the closure was recorded. Wine shows and other circumstances prevented a record of every closure on every wine, but there is no reason to suppose the omissions would have any impact on the relative percentages.

The 2006 Macquarie Bank Sydney Royal Wine Show keeps a record of every wine entered. The figures were very similar: 52.5% of all wines entered were under screwcap. In the white wine category the screwcap total was 72.76%, red wine with 38.74%. The combined screwcap totals were 14.95% at the 2004 show, 32.9% in 2005, and (as above) 52.5% in 2006. Where it will be in three years time is anyone's guess, but to say the Australian wine industry as a whole has made up its mind on the subject is a statement of the obvious.

Incidentally, Diam is the most interesting alternative to conventional cork. It is made by grinding cork pieces to the consistency of flour, then treating it to super-critical CO_2 at high pressure and freezing temperature which removes all taints and moulds; the flour is then compressed (with non-tainting glue) into the finished cork. Its short-term performance (five years or so) cannot be faulted; what is unknown is whether it will retain its shape and prevent oxygen transfer over a longer term (say 20 years).

As a tailpiece, the percentage of cork-finished wines with TCA (trichloranisole) taint at the Sydney show has decreased significantly over the past three years: 8.45% in 2004, 5.44% in 2005, and 4.06% in 2006. The trend is encouraging, but most in the industry would say anything above 1% is unacceptable. Moreover, the major issue confronting cork is not TCA, but random (or sporadic) bottle oxidation.

Australian Wineries and Wines 2007

A note on alphabetical order

Wineries beginning with 'The' are listed under 'T'.
For example 'The Blok Estate'. Winery names that
include a numeral are treated as if the numeral is
spelled out. For example '5 Corners Wines' is listed
under 'F'.

Abbey Creek Vineyard ★★★★☆

Porongurup Road, Porongurup, WA 6324 **REGION** Porongurup
T (08) 9853 1044 **F** (08) 9454 5501 **OPEN** By appt
WINEMAKER Castle Rock Estate (Robert Diletti) **EST.** 1990 **CASES** 850
This is the family business of Mike and Mary Dilworth, the name coming from a winter creek running alongside the vineyard, and a view of The Abbey in the Stirling Range. The vineyard is only 1.5 ha, equally split between riesling, pinot noir and cabernet sauvignon, the pinot noir and riesling planted in 1990, the remainder in 1993. Another 0.5 ha of riesling may follow in the near future. The rieslings, in particular, have had significant show success.

ŸŸŸŸŸ **Porongurup Riesling 2005** Very lively and crisp, some CO_2 still lingering; elegant citrus blossom, green apple and lime fruit; long finish. Screwcap. 12.5° alc. **RATING** 94 **DRINK** 2015 $18

ŸŸŸŸŸ **Late Harvest Riesling 2004** Attractive wine; much better balance and intensity than the '05; lemon/lemon zest/lime aromas and flavours. Screwcap. 11° alc. **RATING** 90 **DRINK** 2010 $16

ŸŸŸŸ **Porongurup Pinot Noir 2004** **RATING** 86 **DRINK** Now $22
Late Harvest Riesling 2005 A pleasant wine; just off-dry; less alcohol and higher residual sugar would have been even better; will grow with time in bottle. Screwcap. 12° alc.
RATING 86 **DRINK** 2010 $16
Porongurup Cabernet Sauvignon 2003 **RATING** 85 **DRINK** 2008 $22

Abbey Rock NR

1 Onkaparinga Valley Road, Balhannah, SA 5242 **REGION** Mount Lofty Ranges Zones
T (08) 8398 0192 **F** (08) 8398 0188 **WWW**.abbeyrock.com.au **OPEN** 7 days 9–5
WINEMAKER Les Sampson **EST.** 2001 **CASES** 10 000
A recent but expanding business with wines sourced from a number of regions spread across SA. The premium wines will be made from pinot noir (2.2 ha) and chardonnay (3.5 ha) near Hahndorf in the Adelaide Hills, and from chardonnay (2 ha), semillon (6.5 ha), shiraz (8 ha) and grenache (2 ha) in the Clare Valley. Plans are afoot to increase both the Adelaide Hills and the Clare Valley plantings.

AbbeyVale NR

392 Wildwood Road, Yallingup, WA 6282 **REGION** Margaret River
T (08) 9755 2121 **F** (08) 9755 2121 **WWW**.abbeyvale.com.au **OPEN** 7 days 10–5
WINEMAKER Philip May **EST.** 1986 **CASES** 10 000
This AbbeyVale is a completely different business from that which operated prior to May 2003, when a 19-member grower group contributed $1.25 million for start-up capital, coupled with grape supply agreements. Well-known and highly-skilled vigneron Philip May heads the operation (indeed he is the only director) and the services of two equally skilled and experienced winemaking consultants, Richard Rowe and Bruce Dukes, have been secured.

Abercorn ★★★☆

Cassilis Road, Mudgee, NSW 2850 **REGION** Mudgee
T 1800 000 959 **F** (02) 6373 3108 **WWW**.abercornwine.com.au **OPEN** Thurs–Mon 10.30–4.30
WINEMAKER Tim Stevens **EST.** 1996 **CASES** 8000
Tim and Connie Stevens acquired the 25-year-old Abercorn Vineyard in 1996. The quality of the red wines has improved over the years to the point where two-thirds of the production is released under the 'A Reserve' banner, led by A Reserve Shiraz and A Reserve Shiraz Cabernet Merlot. These now rank among the best of the region, selling out prior to the next release. A few hundred cases of white wines continue to be made for cellar door release only. In late 2005 the Stevens acquired neighbour Huntington Estate, which they will run as a separate entity.

ŸŸŸŸŸ **Reserve Vintage Port 2004** Spicy, almost cedary, fruit married with clean spirit; excellent balance with an appealing, near-dry finish. Screwcap. 19° alc. **RATING** 90 **DRINK** 2014 $30

♈♈♈♈ **Shiraz 2002** Good colour; sweet blackberry fruit on the medium-bodied palate, with good line and length; balanced tannins and oak. Has transformed over the past 3 years. **RATING** 89 **DRINK** 2011

♈♈♈♉ **Mudgee Cabernet Merlot 2004** Light- to medium-bodied; a pleasant core of sweet fruit, but just a few green tinges to the moderate tannin structure. Screwcap. **RATING** 86 **DRINK** 2009 $ 20

Acacia Ridge   NR

169 Gulf Road, Yarra Glen, Vic 3775 **REGION** Yarra Valley
T (03) 9730 1492 **F** (03) 9730 2292 **WWW**.acaciaridgeyarravalley.com **OPEN** By appt
WINEMAKER Various contract **EST.** 1996 **CASES** 500
Tricia and Gavan Oakley began the establishment of 4 ha each of pinot noir, shiraz and cabernet sauvignon in 1996. Most of the grapes are sold to three other Yarra Valley winemakers, and when the Oakleys decided to have part of the production vinified for them under the Acacia Ridge label, they and some other small vignerons set up a marketing and grape-sharing co-operative known as Yarra Valley Micromasters. It was through this structure that the Oakleys obtained their Chardonnay, which complements the Cabernet Merlot and Shiraz made from their own plantings.

🦡 Acreage Vineyard & Winery   ★★★

Gardner and Holman Roads, Drouin South, Vic 3818 **REGION** Gippsland
T (03) 5627 6383 **F** (03) 5627 6135 **OPEN** W'ends 10–5, or by appt
WINEMAKER Terry Blundell **EST.** 1997 **CASES** NFP
Terry and Jan Blundell commenced the planting of their vineyard in September 1997 with chardonnay and pinot noir. In 2003 shiraz, merlot and cabernet sauvignon were added, taking the total plantings to 2.5 ha. Former school principal Terry says 'I am under threat of further pain from Jan if I plant any more of what she calls "your little weeds".' He also points out that the cellar door, with views to the Baw Baw Ranges, is only 65 mins from the Melbourne CBD.

♈♈♈♈ **Pinot Noir 2003** A solid wine with plenty of depth and power; dark plum, small black berries and spice; slightly dry tannins, should develop. Cork. **RATING** 88 **DRINK** 2009 $ 19

♈♈♈♉ **Chardonnay 2003** **RATING** 84 **DRINK** Now $ 17

♈♈♈ **Unwooded Chardonnay 2003** **RATING** 83 $ 16
Rose 2003 **RATING** 81 $ 15

Across the Lake   ★★★★☆

Box 66, Lake Grace, WA 6353 **REGION** Central Western Australia Zone
T (08) 9864 9026 **OPEN** By appt
WINEMAKER Diane Miller (Contract) **EST.** 1999 **CASES** 380
The Taylor family has been farming (wheat and sheep) for over 40 years at Lake Grace; a small diversification into grapegrowing started as a hobby, but has developed into a little more than that with 1.6 ha of shiraz. They were also motivated to support their friend Bill (WJ) Walker, who had started growing shiraz 3 years previously, and has since produced a gold medal-winning wine. Having learnt the hard way which soils are suitable, and which are not, the Taylors intend to increase their plantings.

♈♈♈♈♉ **Shiraz 2004** Dark red-purple; powerful, complex black fruits, spice and licorice; very good texture and structure. Another great success from this far-flung outpost. Screwcap. 14.5° alc. **RATING** 93 **DRINK** 2015 $ 17

Ada River   ★★★★☆

2330 Main Road, Neerim South, Vic 3831 **REGION** Gippsland
T (03) 5628 1661 **F** (03) 5628 1661 **OPEN** W'ends & public hols 10–6
WINEMAKER Peter Kelliher **EST.** 1983 **CASES** 1500
The Kelliher family first planted vines on their dairy farm at Neerim South in 1983, extending the

original Millstream Vineyard in 1989 and increasing plantings further by establishing the nearby Manilla Vineyard in 1994. Until 2000, Ada River leased a Yarra Valley vineyard; it has relinquished that lease and in its place established a vineyard at Heathcote in conjunction with a local grower.

ΥΥΥΥΥ **Reserve Heathcote Shiraz 2004** Very different style in both flavour and structure to the varietal; more mocha oak and softer tannins to go with the rounded blackberry fruit. **RATING** 93 **DRINK** 2019 $ 32

Heathcote Shiraz 2004 Strong colour; a faintly reductive bouquet, then powerful, savoury black fruits, licorice and spice on the palate; long, fractionally angular finish. Screwcap. **RATING** 92 **DRINK** 2019 $ 27

Heathcote Merlot 2004 Medium-bodied; moderately sweet red fruits, fine, soft tannins and balanced oak. Nice wine, though not particularly varietal. Screwcap. **RATING** 90 **DRINK** 2014 $ 24

Heathcote Cabernet Sauvignon 2004 Purple-red; a substantial palate with blackcurrant, earth, licorice and balanced tannins; subtle oak. Screwcap. **RATING** 90 **DRINK** 2015 $ 24

ΥΥΥΥ **Gippsland Chardonnay 2004** **RATING** 85 **DRINK** 2009 $ 16

ΥΥΥ **Non Vintage Gewurztraminer NV** **RATING** 83 $ 16

Adelina Wines

PO Box 75, Sevenhill, SA 5453 **REGION** Clare Valley
T (08) 8842 1549 **F** (08) 8842 2909 **WWW.**adelina.com.au **OPEN** Not
WINEMAKER Colin McBryde, Jennie Gardner **EST.** 2000 **CASES** 400
When the Gardner family acquired Spring Farm Estate, it had 0.5 ha of shiraz and 0.3 ha of grenache planted around 1910, and a further 0.3 ha of cabernet sauvignon and pinot noir planted in 1970. In 2000 it was decided to cease selling the grapes and establish Adelina Wines. Winemakers Jennie Gardner and Colin McBryde have a broad background, from winemaking and cellar experience to medical research and hospitality, both having worked in numerous regions in New and Old World wineries over the past 10 years. Both are currently completing their doctorates in oenological science at the Adelaide University (Waite Campus), studying yeast metabolism.

Adinfern Estate ★★★★

Bussell Highway, Cowaramup, WA 6284 **REGION** Margaret River
T (08) 9755 5272 **F** (08) 9755 5206 **WWW.**adinfern.com **OPEN** 7 days 11–5.30
WINEMAKER Merv Smith, Transview Pty Ltd (Kevin McKay, Michael Langridge) **EST.** 1996 **CASES** 3500
Merv and Jan Smith have farmed their property as a fine wool and lamb producer for over 30 years, but in 1996 diversified by the development of a 25-ha vineyard planted to sauvignon blanc, semillon, chardonnay, pinot noir, merlot, shiraz, cabernet sauvignon and malbec. One hundred tonnes of grapes are sold to other makers, 25 retained for Adinfern Estate. They also built 2 self-contained rammed earth cottages. Exports to the UK and Singapore.

ΥΥΥΥΥ **Shiraz 2004** Deep colour; medium- to full-bodied; plum, blackberry, spice, licorice and chocolate all intermingle on both bouquet and palate; more structure than most shirazes from the region. Cork. 14.5° alc. **RATING** 94 **DRINK** 2015 $ 23

ΥΥΥΥΥ **Cabernet Sauvignon 2003** Good varietal character firms both the flavour and structure; medium-bodied, blackcurrant fruit; fine, slightly earthy, tannins. Cork. 14° alc. **RATING** 90 **DRINK** 2013 $ 23

ΥΥΥΥ **Shepherd's Rhapsody Semillon Sauvignon Blanc 2005** Sweet tropical/gooseberry/ citrus melange on the bouquet, moving more to white peach on the palate, then lemony/grassy acidity on the finish. Screwcap. 12.9° alc. **RATING** 89 **DRINK** 2008 $ 17

Merlot 2004 Good fruit weight and depth; distinctly sweet, ripe red berries; better picked earlier. Cork. 14° alc. **RATING** 89 **DRINK** 2010 $ 20

ΥΥΥ **Shepherd's Harmony Autumn Harvest Cabernet Shiraz 2004** **RATING** 83 $ 20

Affleck

NR

154 Millynn Road off Bungendore Road, Bungendore, NSW 2621 **REGION** Canberra District
T (02) 6236 9276 **F** (02) 6236 9090 **www**.affleck.com.au **OPEN** Fri–Wed 9–5
WINEMAKER Ian Hendry **EST.** 1976 **CASES** 500
The cellar door and mail order price list says that the wines are 'grown, produced and bottled on the estate by Ian and Susie Hendry with much dedicated help from family and friends'. The original 2.5-ha vineyard has been expanded to 7 ha, and a tasting room (offering light lunches) opened.

Ainsworth & Snelson

★★★★☆

22 Gourlay Street, St Kilda East, Vic 3183 **REGION** Warehouse
T (03) 9530 3333 **F** (03) 9530 3446 **www**.ainsworthandsnelson.com **OPEN** Not
WINEMAKER Brett Snelson **EST.** 2002 **CASES** NFP
Brett Snelson and Gregg Ainsworth take a handcrafted regional approach to the production of their wines. They use traditional techniques which allow the emphasis to remain on *terroir*, sourcing grapes from the Clare Valley, Yarra Valley, Barossa and Coonawarra. Brett Snelson keeps his winemaking skills sharp with an annual vintage in Rousillon. Exports to the UK, France, Denmark and Singapore.

♥♥♥♥♡ **Watervale Riesling 2005** Flowery perfumed blossom aromas; the palate opens with generous lime and passionfruit, then moves to delicious lemony acidity on the finish. Screwcap. 13° alc. **RATING** 93 **DRINK** 2012 $ 22

Yarra Valley Chardonnay 2004 Elegant style; bracing minerally acidity runs through the palate from start to finish; a touch of French oak adds to complexity. Cork. 13.5° alc. **RATING** 93 **DRINK** 2012 $ 27

Yarra Valley Chardonnay 2003 Very well-made; a fusion of ripe melon, fig, nectarine and subtle French oak; good length; developing nicely. Quality cork. **RATING** 91 **DRINK** 2008 $ 29

Barossa Valley Shiraz 2002 Light- to medium-bodied; savoury, spicy style; good length; well controlled extract and oak; needs a little more concentration. Cork. **RATING** 90 **DRINK** 2010 $ 29

Coonawarra Cabernet Sauvignon 2003 Light- to medium-bodied; pleasantly soft and spicy fruit, aided by silky tannins, provides very good mouthfeel. Screwcap. 14° alc. **RATING** 90 **DRINK** 2011 $ 27

Coonawarra Cabernet Sauvignon 2002 Savoury, earthy blackcurrant fruit typical of the region (and vintage); neatly sweetened by oak and ripe tannins. Cork. **RATING** 90 **DRINK** 2012 $ 29

♥♥♥♥ **Barossa Valley Shiraz 2003** Medium-bodied, showing some signs of development; spicy, earthy edges to plum and blackberry fruit; integrated French oak. Cork. 14.5° alc. **RATING** 88 **DRINK** 2009 $ 27

Ainsworth Estate

NR

110 Ducks Lane, Seville, Vic 3139 **REGION** Yarra Valley
T (03) 5964 4711 **F** (03) 5964 4311 **www**.ainsworth-estate.com.au **OPEN** Thurs–Mon 10.30–5
WINEMAKER Denis Craig **EST.** 1994 **CASES** 3000
Denis Craig and wife Kerri planted their first 2 ha of chardonnay and shiraz near Healesville in 1994, establishing a second vineyard at Ducks Lane, Seville, with another 2 ha of vines, planted to shiraz and pinot noir. They have also turned from selling to purchasing chardonnay, shiraz and cabernet sauvignon. For the time being, at least, Denis Craig and Al Fencaros make the wines at Fencaros' Allinda Winery in Dixons Creek.

Albert River Wines

★★★

869 Mundoolun Connection Road, Tamborine, Qld 4270 **REGION** Queensland Coastal
T (07) 5543 6622 **F** (07) 5543 6627 **www**.albertriverwines.com.au **OPEN** Wed–Sun 10–4
WINEMAKER Peter Scudamore-Smith MW (Consultant) **EST.** 1998 **CASES** 3000

Albert River is one of the high-profile wineries on the Gold Coast hinterland. All of its distribution is through cellar door, mail order and local restaurants. The proprietors are David and Janette Bladin, with a combined 30 years' experience in tourism and hospitality, who have acquired and relocated two of Qld's most historic buildings, Tamborine House and Auchenflower House. The winery itself is housed in a newly constructed annex to Auchenflower House; the Bladins have established 4 ha of vineyards on the property, and have another 50 ha under contract. Exports to Japan.

ŸŸŸŸ **Estate Shiraz Viognier 2002** Developed colour; light- to medium-bodied; spicy, savoury red and black fruits, fine tannins. Pleasantly developed, though minimal viognier impact. Cork. 13.5° alc. **RATING** 87 **DRINK** Now $29

ŸŸŸŸ **Cabernet Shiraz Merlot 2002 RATING** 86 **DRINK** Now $25
Red Belly Black Tawny Port NV RATING 84 **DRINK** Now $20

Aldgate Ridge ★★★☆

23 Nation Ridge Road, Aldgate, SA 5154 **REGION** Adelaide Hills
T (08) 8388 5225 **F** (08) 8388 5856 **WWW.**aldgateridge.com.au **OPEN** By appt
WINEMAKER Torbreck Vintners **EST.** 1992 **CASES** 500
Jill and Chris Whisson acquired their vineyard property in 1988, when the land was still being used as a market garden. The first vines were planted in 1992 and 1997, the first block with some of the first of the new Burgundian clones to be propagated in Australia. Further plantings of pinot noir and a block of sauvignon blanc have been added, taking the total plantings to 1 ha of each variety. The vineyard is typical of the Adelaide Hills region, on a rolling to steep southeast-facing hillside at the 440m altitude line.

ŸŸŸŸŸ **Sauvignon Blanc 2005** Powerful and intense; given the benefit of doubt on faintly sweaty edges to the bouquet; passionfruit, gooseberry, herb and grass drive and extremely long and stylish palate. Screwcap. 12.5° alc. **RATING** 94 **DRINK** Now $22

ŸŸŸŸ **Pinot Noir 2003 RATING** 86 **DRINK** Now $33

Aldinga Bay Winery NR

Main South Road, Aldinga, SA 5173 **REGION** McLaren Vale
T (08) 8556 3179 **F** (08) 8556 3350 **OPEN** 7 days 10–5
WINEMAKER Nick Girolamo **EST.** 1979 **CASES** 8000
The former Donolga Winery has had a name and image change since Nick Girolamo, the son of founders Don and Olga Girolamo, returned from Roseworthy College with a degree in oenology. Nick has taken over both the winemaking and marketing; prices remain modest, though not as low as they once were, reflecting an increase in the quality and an upgrade in packaging. Aldinga Bay also has some very interesting varietal plantings, 16 varieties in all, including petit verdot, nebbiolo, barbera and sangiovese.

Alexandra Bridge Wines ★★★★★

101 Brockman Highway, Karridale, WA 6288 **REGION** Margaret River
T (08) 9758 5999 **F** (08) 9758 5988 **WWW.**alexandrabridgewines.com.au **OPEN** 7 days 10–4.30
WINEMAKER Virginia Willcock **EST.** 1999 **CASES** 3500
Alexandra Bridge has become the operating arm of Australian Wine Holdings. The 800-tonne winery, commissioned in February 2000, was the first built in the Karridale area at the southern end of the Margaret River. The Brockman Vineyard, planted in three stages commencing in 1995, is estate-owned and has a total of 30.5 ha of semillon, sauvignon blanc, chardonnay, shiraz and cabernet sauvignon. The grapes coming from the Brockman Vineyard are supplemented by long-term supply agreements with other Margaret River growers. Exports to Europe and South-East Asia.

ŸŸŸŸŸ **Margaret River Semillon Sauvignon Blanc 2005** Spotlessly clean and fresh bouquet; excellent palate, with seamless, long and lingering lemon, grass and passionfruit flavours. Screwcap. 12.5° alc. **RATING** 94 **DRINK** 2009 $18
Margaret River Chardonnay 2004 An elegant, fine, understated style; melon, citrus and stone fruit; sophisticated barrel ferment French oak handling. Screwcap. 14° alc.
RATING 94 **DRINK** 2012 $19

ᵀᵀᵀᵀᵞ **Margaret River Cabernet Merlot 2003** Medium-bodied; attractive mix of cassis, blackcurrant and olive; fine tannins, very nice wine. Screwcap. 13.4° alc. **RATING** 91 **DRINK** 2013 $ 18

ᵀᵀᵀᵀ **Margaret River Shiraz 2003** Clean; light- to medium-bodied; licorice, spice, pepper, mint and green leaf notes throughout; struggled for full ripeness. Screwcap. **RATING** 87 **DRINK** 2009 $ 18.85

Alkoomi ★★★★★

Wingebellup Road, Frankland, WA 6396 **REGION** Frankland River
T (08) 9855 2229 **F** (08) 9855 2284 **www**.alkoomiwines.com.au **OPEN** 7 days 10–5
WINEMAKER Michael Staniford, Merv Lange, Darren Burke **EST**. 1971 **CASES** 90 000
For those who see the wineries of WA as suffering from the tyranny of distance, this most remote of all wineries shows there is no tyranny after all. It is a story of unqualified success due to sheer hard work, and no doubt to Merv and Judy Lange's aversion to borrowing a single dollar from the bank. The substantial production is entirely drawn from the ever-expanding estate vineyards — now over 100 ha. Wine quality across the range is impeccable, always with precisely defined varietal character. Exports to all major markets.

ᵀᵀᵀᵀᵀ **Wandoo Frankland River Semillon 2003** Lovely wine; partial barrel fermentation adds to complexity of both the bouquet and entry to the mouth; then citrus/gooseberry appears and wonderful squeaky acidity on the long, lingering finish and aftertaste. Cork. 11° alc.
RATING 96 **DRINK** 2012 $ 31
Blackbutt 2002 Aristocratic finesse and style; a mix of spice, cedar, cigar box and black fruits in a perfectly balanced, medium-bodied palate; very long finish. Cork. 14° alc.
RATING 95 **DRINK** 2017 $ 59
Frankland River Riesling 2005 Very fragrant blossom, herb and lime; abundant flavour tightened by slatey minerality; harmonious. Screwcap. 13° alc. **RATING** 94 **DRINK** 2015 $ 20
Jarrah Frankland River Shiraz 2003 Medium-bodied; a woven tapestry moves across the palate; blackberry, plum, licorice and lingering spicy notes; minimal tannin and oak. Cork. 14.5° alc. **RATING** 94 **DRINK** 2017 $ 40
Frankland River Cabernet Sauvignon 2004 Medium-bodied; fragrant cedary/spicy/ earthy overtones to blackcurrant fruit; quality oak; overall sweetness without the least bit of residual sugar. Cork. 14° alc. **RATING** 94 **DRINK** 2015 $ 20

ᵀᵀᵀᵀᵞ **Frankland River Sauvignon Blanc 2005** Light straw-green; in winery fashion, spotlessly clean; tightly wound and sprung; gooseberry, herb and minerally acidity; long finish. Screwcap. 12.5° alc. **RATING** 93 **DRINK** 2008 $ 20
Frankland River Chardonnay 2004 A nice touch of smoky, spicy barrel ferment oak on the bouquet leads into a complex, fruit-driven palate; nectarine, grapefruit and melon; long finish. Screwcap. 13.5° alc. **RATING** 93 **DRINK** 2012 $ 20
Frankland River Shiraz Viognier 2004 Medium red-purple; fragrant, elegant, spicy black fruit aromas; the medium-bodied palate continues with the theme of fine, spicy fruit; curiously, seems almost diluted by viognier, rather than lifted/intensified. Cork. 13.5° alc.
RATING 91 **DRINK** 2014 $ 20

All Saints Estate ★★★★★

All Saints Road, Wahgunyah, Vic 3687 **REGION** Rutherglen
T (02) 6035 2222 **F** (02) 6035 2200 **www**.allsaintswine.com.au **OPEN** Mon–Sat 9–5.30, Sun 10–5.30
WINEMAKER Dan Crane **EST**. 1864 **CASES** 40 000
The winery rating reflects the fortified wines, but the table wines are more than adequate. The Terrace restaurant (open 7 days for lunch and Saturday night for dinner) makes this a most enjoyable stop for any visitor to the northeast. The faux castle, modelled on a Scottish castle beloved of the founder, is classified by the Historic Buildings Council. All Saints and St Leonards were wholly owned by Peter Brown, tragically killed in a road accident in late 2005. Ownership has passed to Peter Brown's three children, Eliza, Angela and Nicholas, and it is the intention to keep the business in the family. Exports to the US.

ΥΥΥΥΥ **Rare Rutherglen Tokay Museum Release NV** Dark olive-brown; the extreme age shows most clearly in the incredible length, finish and aftertaste of the wine; not a trace of staleness. **RATING** 97 **DRINK** Now $434

Rare Rutherglen Muscat Museum Release NV An exceedingly complex wine, yet retains elegance, and, like the Museum Tokay, there is no hint of staleness. The description of flavours is endless, as is the lingering finish. **RATING** 97 **DRINK** Now $434

Rare Rutherglen Tokay NV Far, far deeper colour than the Grand; layer-upon-layer of lusciously rich varietal fruit, moving beyond tea leaf into the Christmas cake/Christmas pudding spectrum. **RATING** 96 **DRINK** Now $107

Rare Rutherglen Muscat NV Deep, dark brown, dark olive rim; very complex, with a balance of aged raisiny material and a touch of youthful freshness; the equally complex, powerful palate has a strong nutty, rancio framework yet has great balance and suppleness, then a cleansing, dry finish. **RATING** 96 **DRINK** Now $107

Grand Rutherglen Tokay NV Lusciously rich and complex, with Christmas cake and dried fruit flavours, along with the hallmark echoes of tea leaf and butterscotch, and a lovely skein of sweet fruit running through the mid-palate, the structure fine and intense. **RATING** 94 **DRINK** Now $55

Grand Rutherglen Muscat NV Deep, olive-rimmed brown; a very complex, extremely rich bouquet with intense rancio and some volatile lift. An ultra-rich and dense palate with abundant raisin and plum pudding flavours, the twist of volatility on the finish well within bounds. **RATING** 94 **DRINK** Now $55

ΥΥΥΥΥ **Classic Rutherglen Tokay NV** Tea leaf, smoke, toffee and butterscotch aromas lead into an intense, long and lingering palate, with abundant weight. Future releases might well see a little more fresh, younger material in the blend. **RATING** 91 **DRINK** Now $30

Rutherglen Shiraz 2004 Brilliant, bright red-purple; the fresh, medium-bodied black cherry and plum palate belies the alcohol; oak neatly controlled. Cork. 14.4° alc. **RATING** 90 **DRINK** 2012 $22

Rutherglen Cabernet Sauvignon 2004 In medium-bodied house style; fresh cassis/blackcurrant fruit; light tannins and extract. Cork. 13.8° alc. **RATING** 90 **DRINK** 2011 $22

Classic Rutherglen Muscat NV Distinct olive hints to the full tawny colour; the bouquet and palate show considerable rancio, complexity and depth. Just a suggestion of the pendulum swinging a little too far towards aged material. **RATING** 90 **DRINK** Now $30

ΥΥΥΥ **Rutherglen Riesling 2005** Fragrant apple blossom aromas; light, soft and clean flavours moving more to lime juice. Impressive for the region. Screwcap. 11.8° alc. **RATING** 89 **DRINK** 2010 $17.50

Pierre Limited Release Cabernet Sauvignon Merlot Cabernet Franc Malbec 2004 Again, in very consistent style; light, fresh red fruits; minimal oak and tannins. Cork. 13.8° alc. **RATING** 89 **DRINK** 2011 $24

ΥΥΥΥ **Late Harvest Rutherglen Muscat 2005 RATING** 86 **DRINK** Now $20.50

Allandale   ★★★☆

132 Lovedale Road, Lovedale, NSW 2321 **REGION** Lower Hunter Valley
T (02) 4990 4526 **F** (02) 4990 1714 **WWW**.allandalewinery.com.au **OPEN** Mon–Sat 9–5, Sun 10–5
WINEMAKER Bill Sneddon, Rod Russell **EST.** 1978 **CASES** 15 000
Owners Wally and Judith Atallah have overseen the growth of Allandale from a small, cellar door operation to a business with sales in all the eastern states, and export markets in five countries. Allandale has developed a reputation for its Chardonnay, but offers a broad range of wines of consistently good quality, including red wines variously sourced from the Hilltops, Orange and Mudgee regions. Exports to the UK, the US and other major markets.

ΥΥΥΥ **Hunter Valley Semillon 2001** Glowing light yellow-green; tasted after a series of wines with Stelvin closures, the difference quite remarkable, with a pseudo-oak aroma coming from the cork. The palate is fresh and long, but ... Cork. **RATING** 89 **DRINK** 2010 $17

ΥΥΥΥ **Hunter Valley Semillon 2005 RATING** 86 **DRINK** 2010 $17

Hunter Valley Verdelho 2005 Full fruit salad; lots of flavour for the addicts (of which I am not one). Screwcap. 14° alc. **RATING** 86 **DRINK** 2008 $17

Allinda ★★★★

119 Lorimers Lane, Dixons Creek, Vic 3775 **REGION** Yarra Valley
T(03) 5965 2450 **F**(03) 5965 2467 **OPEN** W'ends & public hols 11–5
WINEMAKER Al Fencaros **EST.** 1991 **CASES** 2500
Winemaker Al Fencaros has a Bachelor of Wine Science (Charles Sturt University) and was formerly employed by De Bortoli in the Yarra Valley. All of the Allinda wines are produced onsite; all except the Shiraz (from Heathcote) are estate-grown from a little over 3 ha of vineyards. Limited retail distribution in Melbourne and Sydney.

TTTTY **Riesling 2005** Perfumed, flowery aromas; a delicate, but intense, palate with tangy citrus and spice; lingering finish. Exceptional for the Yarra Valley. Screwcap. 12.5° alc. **RATING** 91 **DRINK** 2012 $ 17
Chardonnay 2005 Light straw-green; strong citrus overtones to stone fruit and melon; subtle French oak inputs; a long finish typical of Yarra chardonnay. Screwcap. 14° alc. **RATING** 90 **DRINK** 2010 $ 22
Pinot Noir 2004 Bright red-purple; light-bodied, spicy red cherry and plum varietal fruit; good balance and length in a lighter style. Screwcap. 14° alc. **RATING** 90 **DRINK** 2009

TTTT **Double Picked Riesling 2005** Exotically rich lime, mandarin, cumquat and honey, the fortifying spirit curiously more obvious on the bouquet than the palate; an adventurous and largely successful blend of Amarone technique (sun-dried grapes) and fortification into a quasi-white port style. Twin top. 15° alc. **RATING** 89 **DRINK** Now $ 22

Allison Valley Wines ★★★☆

RSM 457 North Jindong Road, Busselton, WA 6280 (postal) **REGION** Margaret River
T(08) 9368 6370 **F**(08) 9474 1804 **WWW**.allisonvalley.com.au **OPEN** Not
WINEMAKER Harmans Ridge Estate (Paul Green) **EST.** 1997 **CASES** 3000
The Porter family planted 10 ha of semillon, sauvignon blanc, shiraz and cabernet sauvignon with the sole intention of selling the grapes to other winemakers in the region. However, as has been the case with hundreds of other such ventures, the family has decided to have some of the production vinified under the Allison Valley label. Exports to Taiwan.

TTTTY **Cabernet Merlot 2003** Bright, clear colour; light- to medium-bodied, fresh and lively red and black fruits; elegant wine, good length and balance. Twin top. 13° alc. **RATING** 90 **DRINK** 2011 $ 12

TTTT **Semillon Sauvignon Blanc 2004** Spotlessly clean; flavoursome tropical fruit, but a little too sweet on the finish. Screwcap. 12.5° alc. **RATING** 87 **DRINK** Now $ 12
Cabernet Sauvignon 2003 Similar to the Cabernet Merlot, but doesn't quite click in the same way; light, fresh red fruits need more conviction (much the same as the '03 Shiraz). Cork. 13° alc. **RATING** 87 **DRINK** 2010 $ 12

TTTY **Shiraz 2003** **RATING** 86 **DRINK** 2008 $ 12

Allusion Wines NR

Smith Hill Road, Yankalilla, SA 5203 **REGION** Southern Fleurieu
T(08) 8558 3333 **F**(08) 8558 3333 **OPEN** Thurs–Sun 11–5
WINEMAKER Contract **EST.** 1996 **CASES** 750
Steve and Wendy Taylor purchased the property on which Allusion Wines is established in 1980, since planting 4 ha of vines and 35 000 trees. Steve Taylor's 20 years as a chef has strongly influenced both the varietal plantings and the wine styles made: not altogether surprisingly, they are designed to be consumed with good food. The wine is fermented offsite, then matured onsite before being contract-bottled.

Allyn River Wines

NR

Torryburn Road, East Gresford, NSW 2311 **REGION** Upper Hunter Valley
T (02) 4938 9279 **F** (02) 4938 9279 **OPEN** Fri–Mon & public hols 9–5, or by appt
WINEMAKER David Hook (Contract) **EST.** 1996 **CASES** 650
Allyn River is situated on the alluvial soils on the banks of the stream which has given the vineyard its
name. The plantings of 1.5 ha each of semillon and chambourcin were in part inspired by the
knowledge that Dr Henry Lindeman had established his famous Cawarra Vineyard in the locality.

Alta Wines

★★★★

PO Box 63, Mount Torrens, SA 5244 **REGION** Adelaide Hills
T 0434 077 059 **F** (08) 8389 9587 **OPEN** Not
WINEMAKER Sarah Fletcher **EST.** NA **CASES** NA
Sarah Fletcher comes to Alta with an impressive winemaking background, starting with 4 years at
the Roseworthy campus of Adelaide University culminating in a degree in oenology, and thereafter 7
years working for Orlando Wyndham as both red and white winemaker. In this time she came face to
face with grapes from all over Australia, and developed a particular regard for those coming from the
Adelaide Hills. She became financially involved with Alta in February 2005, leading to the making of
the 2005 Sauvignon Blanc, her first under the Alta brand. The range will be extended with varieties
suited to the cool climate of the Adelaide Hills, with Pinot Noir an obvious candidate.

▼▼▼▼▼ **Adelaide Hills Sauvignon Blanc 2005** Clean, fresh and crisp; mineral, grass, touches of
lime, gooseberry and asparagus; all this with overall delicacy; has length. Screwcap.
12.6° alc. **RATING** 92 **DRINK** Now $18

Amarillo Vines

NR

27 Marlock Place, Karnup, WA 6176 **REGION** Peel
T (08) 9537 1800 **F** (08) 9537 1800 **OPEN** 7 days 10–5
WINEMAKER Phil Franzone (Contract) **EST.** 1995 **CASES** 700
The Ashby family have market garden and landscaping backgrounds, and the establishment of a
small vineyard on the block of land in which their house sits seemed a natural thing to do. What is
unusual is the density of the planting, the utilisation of a lyre trellis, and the permanent netting
erected around the vineyard — this means they do not speak of acres or ha, but of the 2500 vines
planted, and of the production as 8400 bottles.

Amarok Estate

NR

Lot 547 Caves Road, Wilyabrup, WA 6284 (postal) **REGION** Margaret River
T (08) 9756 6888 **F** (08) 9756 6555 **OPEN** Not
WINEMAKER Kevin McKay (Contract) **EST.** 1999 **CASES** 5000
John and Libby Staley, with their youngest daughter, Megan, her husband, Shane, and youngest
grandson, Lewis, have all had hands-on involvement in the establishment of 20 ha of vineyards —
clearing bushland, ripping, rock picking, stick picking and planting, etc. The soils are gravelly loam
over a clay granite base; the vineyard has a western aspect and is 5 km from the Indian Ocean.

Amberley Estate

★★★★

Thornton Road, Yallingup, WA 6282 **REGION** Margaret River
T (08) 9755 2288 **F** (08) 9755 2171 **WWW**.amberleyestate.com.au **OPEN** 7 days 10–4.30
WINEMAKER Paul Dunnewyk **EST.** 1986 **CASES** 120 000
Based its initial growth on its ultra-commercial, fairly sweet Chenin Blanc, which continues to provide
the volume for the brand, selling out well before the following release. However, the quality of all the
other wines has risen markedly over recent years as the 31 ha of estate plantings have become fully
mature. Purchased by Canadian company Vincor in early 2004. Exports to the UK and the US.

▼▼▼▼▼ **Margaret River Semillon Sauvignon Blanc 2005** Pleasant light- to medium-bodied;
gentle herb and grass aromas and flavours; has good length. Screwcap. 13° alc. **RATING** 90
DRINK 2008 $21.99

▼▼▼▼ **Margaret River Sauvignon Blanc 2005** Clean, light-bodied passionfruit and gooseberry; balance rather than length. Screwcap. 13° alc. **RATING** 89 **DRINK** Now $ 21.99
Chimney Brush Margaret River Chardonnay 2005 Fresh, lively, well-balanced nectarine and grapefruit plus subtle twist of oak. Screwcap. 13° alc. **RATING** 89 **DRINK** 2008 $ 16.99

Ambrook Wines ★★★☆

114 George Street, West Swan, WA 6055 **REGION** Swan Valley
T (08) 9274 1003 **F** (08) 9379 0334 **WWW**.ambrookwines.2ya.com **OPEN** Wed–Fri 12–5, w'ends & public hols 10–5
WINEMAKER Rob Marshal **EST.** 1990 **CASES** 1500
Michele Amonini has established 4 ha of chenin blanc, semillon, verdelho, shiraz, cabernet sauvignon and merlot and quietly gone about producing a solid range of varietal, estate-based wines which have had their fair share of success at the various West Australian regional wine shows. Modest pricing increases the appeal.

▼▼▼▼ **Swan Valley Shiraz 2003** Solid blackberry and plum with touches of earth and chocolate; well constructed. Cork. 13.5° alc. **RATING** 88 **DRINK** 2009 $ 18
Swan Valley Semillon 2005 Water white; firm mineral, slate, grass and lemon fruit; a refreshingly dry finish. Cork. 11.2° alc. **RATING** 87 **DRINK** 2009 $ 14
Swan Valley Merlot 2003 Light- to medium-bodied; bright red fruits and crisp acidity; curious pricing. Cork. 13.4° alc. **RATING** 87 **DRINK** 2008 $ 35

▼▼▼▽ **Swan Valley Verdelho 2004** **RATING** 85 **DRINK** Now $ 15
Swan Valley Semillon 2004 **RATING** 84 **DRINK** Now $ 14

▼▼▼ **Swan Valley Cabernet Sauvignon 2003** **RATING** 83 $ 16

Amherst Winery ★★★★☆

Talbot-Avoca Road, Amherst, Vic 3371 **REGION** Pyrenees
T (03) 5463 2105 **F** (03) 5463 2502 **WWW**.amherstwinery.com **OPEN** W'ends & public hols 10–5
WINEMAKER Graham Jukes (Red), Paul Lesock (White) **EST.** 1991 **CASES** 1000
Norman and Elizabeth Jones have planted 4 ha of vines on a property with an extraordinarily rich history, a shorthand reflection of which is seen in the name Dunn's Paddock Shiraz. This variety dominates the planting, with 3.4 ha; the rest is cabernet sauvignon and chardonnay. Samuel Knowles was a convict who arrived in Van Diemen's Land in 1838. He endured continuous punishment before fleeing to SA in 1846 and changing his name to Dunn. When, at the end of 1851, he married 18-year-old Mary Therese Taaffe in Adelaide, they walked from Adelaide to Amherst pushing a wheelbarrow carrying their belongings. They had 14 children, and Samuel Dunn died in 1898, a highly respected citizen; his widow lived until 1923.

▼▼▼▼▼ **Dunn's Paddock Pyrenees Shiraz 2004** Deep, dense red-purple; a powerful, multifaceted array of plum, blackberry and licorice fruits; substantial but fine-grained tannins; long finish. Screwcap. 13.8° alc. **RATING** 94 **DRINK** 2019 $ 25

▼▼▼▼▽ **Chinese Garden Pyrenees Cabernet Sauvignon 2004** Good hue; a substantial wine; lots of tannin structure underneath the savoury blackcurrant cabernet fruit. Needs time. Screwcap. 14.2° alc. **RATING** 91 **DRINK** 2019 $ 25

Amietta Vineyard ★★★★☆

30 Steddy Road, Lethbridge, Vic 3332 **REGION** Geelong
T (03) 5281 7407 **F** (03) 5281 7427 **WWW**.amietta.com.au **OPEN** By appt
WINEMAKER Nicholas Clark, Janet Cockbill **EST.** 1995 **CASES** 450
Janet Cockbill and Nicholas Clark are multitalented. Both are archaeologists, but Janet manages to combine part-time archaeology, part-time radiography at Geelong Hospital and part-time organic viticulture. Nicholas Clark has nearly completed a viticulture degree at Charles Sturt University, and both he and Janet worked vintage in France at Michel Chapoutier's biodynamic Domaine de Beates in Provence in 2001. Amietta is producing cameo wines of some beauty.

ŢŢŢŢŢ **Angels' Share Shiraz Cabernet 2004** Good purple-red; extremely rich and concentrated, with great blackberry fruit and ripe tannins in abundance. Trophy 2005 Geelong Wine Show. Screwcap. 13° alc. **RATING** 94 **DRINK** 2012 $ 30

ŢŢŢŢŢ **Geelong Rose 2005** Bright, light fuchsia; clean and fresh cherry fruit; modern Australian style. Screwcap. 13.8° alc. **RATING** 91 **DRINK** Now $ 20

ŢŢŢŢ **Geelong Shiraz 2004** Big, very ripe, slightly confit blackberry fruit; certainly has presence. Screwcap. 13.8° alc. **RATING** 89 **DRINK** 2014 $ 35

Geelong Riesling 2005 Pale straw-green; clean, crisp and spicy, finishing with attractive lemony acidity. Screwcap. 12.5° alc. **RATING** 87 **DRINK** 2010 $ 20

Amulet Vineyard   NR

Wangaratta Road, Beechworth, Vic 3747 **REGION** Beechworth
T (03) 5727 0420 **F** (03) 5727 0421 **OPEN** Fri–Mon, public & school hols 10–5, or by appt
WINEMAKER Sue Thornton, Ben Clifton **EST.** 1998 **CASES** 2000
Sue and Eric Thornton have planted a patchwork quilt 4-ha vineyard, with sangiovese taking 1 ha, the other varieties 0.5 ha or less, and in descending order of magnitude are barbera, shiraz, cabernet sauvignon, merlot, nebbiolo, orange muscat, pinot gris and pinot blanc. The vineyard (and cellar door) is 11 km west of Beechworth on the road to Wangaratta, the vines planted on gentle slopes at an elevation of 350m. Co-winemaker and son Ben Clifton is studying wine science at Charles Sturt University. The cellar door enjoys panoramic views, and wine sales are both by the glass and by the bottle.

🍇 Anakie Ridge Vineyard   ★★★☆

2290 Ballan Road, Anakie, Vic 3221 **REGION** Geelong
T 0409 418 175 **F** (03) 5222 3157 **OPEN** W'ends 11–5
WINEMAKER Ernesto Vellucci **EST.** 1998 **CASES** NFP
Leo and Isobel Gold planted 2 ha of cabernet sauvignon and 0.8 ha of chardonnay in the spring of 1998, leading to the first vintage in 2001. The winemaking techniques are described as traditional, using small vat fermentation, minimum time in oak and minimal filtration. The Pinot Noir comes from the Quarry Vineyard at Waurn Ponds, the Shiraz from Sutherlands Creek Vineyard, both in the Geelong region.

ŢŢŢŢ **Barrel Fermented Chardonnay 2003** Light- to medium-bodied; well-balanced and integrated oak; gently creamy notes under melon and white peach fruit. Cork. 14° alc. **RATING** 89 **DRINK** Now $ 18

Shiraz 2003 Medium-bodied; black fruits with touches of spice; gentle extract of oak and tannins. Cork. 14° alc. **RATING** 87 **DRINK** 2008 $ 21

ŢŢŢŢ **Pinot Noir 2002** Very spicy/savoury/earthy/herbal characters; crisp finish. Cork. 13.5° alc. **RATING** 86 **DRINK** Now $ 18

Cabernet Sauvignon 2001 RATING 85 **DRINK** 2009 $ 21

Anderson   ★★★★

Lot 12 Chiltern Road, Rutherglen, Vic 3685 **REGION** Rutherglen
T (02) 6032 8111 **F** (02) 6032 9028 **WWW.**andersonwinery.com.au **OPEN** 7 days 10–5
WINEMAKER Howard Anderson **EST.** 1992 **CASES** 1700
Having notched up a winemaking career spanning over 30 years, including a stint at Seppelt Great Western, Howard Anderson and family started their own winery, initially with a particular focus on sparkling wine but now extending across all table wine styles. There are 4 ha of estate shiraz, and 1 ha each of durif and petit verdot, with yields controlled at a very low 2.5 tonnes per ha (or, in the old money, 1 tonne per acre).

ŢŢŢŢŢ **Shiraz Methode Champenoise 1998** Excellent mousse; as expected, richly flavoured, lush, blackberry and plum fruit; dosage expertly handled, though why Howard Anderson should recommend drinking within 12 months I don't understand. **RATING** 90 **DRINK** 2010 $ 27

???? **Cellar Block Shiraz 2001** Deep colour; full-bodied, ultra-ripe prune and blackberry fruit; controlled extract, but 15.5° alcohol strips the mid-palate. Quality cork. 15.5° alc. **RATING** 89 **DRINK** 2011 $ 25
Basket Press Cabernet Sauvignon 2000 Ripe, rich chocolate, earth, blackberry and blackcurrant fruit; ripe tannins, and a twist of acidity on the finish. High-quality cork. 14.2° alc. **RATING** 89 **DRINK** 2010 $ 18.50
Merlot 2004 Clear savoury/olive varietal aromas; at the ripe end of the spectrum; unusually, no malolactic fermentation. Screwcap. **RATING** 87 **DRINK** 2008 $ 14.50
Basket Press Sangiovese 2002 Good colour; very fragrant, ripe red fruit aromas; a very rich palate, the variety entombed in 14.9° alcohol. Cork. 14.9° alc. **RATING** 87 **DRINK** 2010 $ 20

???? **Unoaked Chardonnay 2002** Rich, ripe peaches and cream style, which looks as if it may have been held in tank for a long time before being bottled. Screwcap. 13.5° alc. **RATING** 86 **DRINK** Now $ 14.50

Andraos Bros   NR

Winilba Vineyard, 150 Vineyard Road, Sunbury, Vic 3429 **REGION** Sunbury
T (03) 9740 9703 **F** (03) 9740 9795 **OPEN** Fri–Sun & public hols 11–5, or by appt
WINEMAKER Fred Andraos, Mario Marson (Consultant) **EST.** 1989 **CASES** 2500
The original Winilba Vineyard was first planted in 1863 and remained in production until 1889. Exactly 100 years later the Andraos brothers began replanting the vineyard on the property they had purchased 5 years earlier. Over the following years they built a winery from the ruins of the original bluestone cellar, making the inaugural vintage in 1996.

Andrew Garrett   NR

Ingoldby Road, McLaren Flat, SA 5171 **REGION** McLaren Vale
T (08) 8383 0005 **F** (08) 8383 0790 **WWW.**andrewgarret.com.au **OPEN** 7 days 10–4
WINEMAKER Charles Hargrave **EST.** 1983 **CASES** 170 000
Andrew Garrett has long been owned by the FWE group, with many of the wines now not having a sole McLaren Vale source but instead being drawn from regions across southeastern Australia. Over the years, winemaker Charles Hargrave has produced some excellent wines which provide great value for money.

Andrew Harris Vineyards   NR

Sydney Road, Mudgee, NSW 2850 **REGION** Mudgee
T (02) 6373 1213 **F** (02) 6373 1296 **WWW.**andrewharris.com.au **OPEN** 7 days 9–5
WINEMAKER Damian Grindley **EST.** 1991 **CASES** 65 000
Andrew and Deb Harris got away to a flying start after purchasing a 300-ha sheep station and planting it with 106 ha of vines. The early red wine releases had considerable show success, but these days the accent seems to be on relatively low prices, rather than on quality.

Andrew Peace Wines   ★★★☆

Murray Valley Highway, Piangil, Vic 3597 **REGION** Swan Hill
T (03) 5030 5291 **F** (03) 5030 5605 **WWW.**apwines.com **OPEN** Mon–Fri 8–5, Sat 12–4, Sun by appt
WINEMAKER Andrew Peace, Nina Viergutz **EST.** 1995 **CASES** 400 000
The Peace family has been a major Swan Hill grapegrower since 1980, with 100 ha of vineyards. They moved into winemaking with the opening of a $3 million winery in 1996. The modestly priced wines are aimed at supermarket-type outlets in Australia and exports to all major markets.

???? **Signature Shiraz 2004** Light- to medium-bodied; good balance and texture to the red and black fruits, and a gentle touch of vanilla oak. Screwcap. 14° alc. **RATING** 88 **DRINK** 2012 $ 12.99
Masterpeace Vintage Port 2005 Nicely framed and balanced; fresh red berry fruits; clean, spicy fruit; quite dry. Cork. 18° alc. **RATING** 88 **DRINK** 2010 $ 19

Angas Plains Estate ★★★

Lot 1 Angas Plains Road, Langhorne Creek, SA 5255 **REGION** Langhorne Creek
T (08) 8537 3159 **F** (08) 8537 3353 **WWW**.angasplainswines.com.au **OPEN** W'ends & public hols 10–5
WINEMAKER Judy Cross (Contract) **EST.** 2000 **CASES** 2500
Angas Plains Estate is situated 10 mins' drive south from the historic town of Strathalbyn, on the banks of the Angas River. Owners Phillip and Judy Cross employ organic measures to tend their 14 ha of shiraz, 11 ha of cabernet sauvignon and 1 ha of chardonnay. Exports to the US, China and Thailand.

♥♥♥♡ **PJ's Langhorne Creek Unwooded Chardonnay 2005 RATING** 85 **DRINK** Now $15

Angas Vineyards NR

PO Box 53, Langhorne Creek, SA 5255 **REGION** Langhorne Creek
T (08) 8537 3337 **F** (08) 8537 3231 **OPEN** Not
WINEMAKER Ben Glaetzer (Contract) **EST.** 1997 **CASES** NA
Angas Vineyards is the umbrella organisation for a number of separately marketed brands. Its principal viticultural resource is 222 ha of vineyards, with multiple examples of ultra-trendy varietals. Most of the wine is exported under either the Angas Vineyards or Bushy Road Vineyard brands.

Angove's ★★★★

Bookmark Avenue, Renmark, SA 5341 **REGION** Riverland
T (08) 8580 3100 **F** (08) 8580 3155 **WWW**.angoves.com.au **OPEN** Mon–Fri 9–5
WINEMAKER Warrick Billings, Shane Clohesy, Tony Ingle **EST.** 1886 **CASES** 1.8 million
Exemplifies the economies of scale achievable in the Australian Riverland without compromising potential quality. Very good technology provides wines which are never poor and which sometimes exceed their theoretical station in life; the white varietals are best. Angove's expansion into Padthaway has resulted in estate-grown premium wines at the top of the range. Angove's also acts as a distributor for several small Australian wineries. Exports to all major markets.

♥♥♥♥♡ **Vineyard Select Clare Valley Riesling 2004** Powerful tropical/pineapple aromas and flavours; rich and mouthfilling, but not flabby. Early maturing. Screwcap. **RATING** 90 **DRINK** 2009 $14.99
Vineyard Select McLaren Vale Shiraz 2003 Medium-bodied; a pleasing regional overlay to the Shiraz given freedom of expression by controlled alcohol, which also invests the palate with lively red fruit flavours. Cork. 14° alc. **RATING** 90 **DRINK** 2010 $18.99
Vineyard Select Coonawarra Cabernet Sauvignon 2003 Good colour; significantly better than most of the prior vintages of this wine; more concentration and focus to the medium-bodied blackcurrant fruit and gentle tannins. Cork. 14° alc. **RATING** 90 **DRINK** 2012 $18.99

♥♥♥♥ **Stonegate Cabernet Sauvignon 2003** Very impressive wine at the price; clear-cut blackcurrant fruit is the driver. Cork. **RATING** 89 **DRINK** 2008 $7.99
Nine Vines Grenache Shiraz Rose 2005 Vivid, light fuchsia red; intense cherry/soda pop aromas; crisp and clean; lively, dry finish. Grenache/Shiraz. Screwcap. **RATING** 88 **DRINK** Now $14.99
Stonegate Verdelho 2005 Has well above-average fruit weight and interest; fruit salad with some structure. Great value. Screwcap. 13.5° alc. **RATING** 87 **DRINK** Now $7.99

♥♥♥♡ **Butterfly Ridge Riesling 2005** Light straw-green; generous tropical fruit aromas and mouthfilling, soft, but not flabby, flavours with a hint of sweetness. Excellent value. Screwcap. **RATING** 86 **DRINK** Now $6.99
Butterfly Ridge Shiraz Cabernet 2005 A quite substantial wine; red and black fruits, perhaps slightly jammy, but great value nonetheless. Screwcap. 14° alc. **RATING** 86 **DRINK** 2008 $6.99
Stonegate Petit Verdot 2004 Youthful purple-red; ripe black fruits; plenty of structure, but does dip on the mid-palate; at the price, who's complaining? Cork. 13.5° alc. **RATING** 86 **DRINK** 2008 $7.99

Long Row Sauvignon Blanc 2005 RATING 85 DRINK Now $9.99
Long Row Chardonnay 2004 RATING 85 DRINK Now $9.99
Butterfly Ridge Colombard Chardonnay 2005 RATING 85 DRINK Now $6.99
Butterfly Ridge Merlot Cabernet 2005 RATING 85 DRINK Now $7
Sarnia Farm Cabernet Sauvignon 2000 RATING 85 DRINK 2008 $13.99
Long Row Shiraz 2003 RATING 84 DRINK Now $9.99
Long Row Cabernet Sauvignon 2003 RATING 84 DRINK Now $9.99

ΨΨΨ **Butterfly Ridge Rose 2005** RATING 83 $7

Angullong Wines

NR

Four Mile Creek Road, Orange, NSW 2800 (postal) REGION Orange
T (02) 6366 4300 F (02) 6466 4399 WWW.angullong.com.au OPEN Not
WINEMAKER Bimbadgen Estate (Simon Thistlewood) EST. 1998 CASES 3000
The Crossing family (Bill and Hatty Crossing, and third generation James and Ben Crossing) have
owned a 2000 ha sheep and cattle station for over half a century. Located 40 km south of Orange on
the lower slopes of the Orange region, overlooking the Belubula Valley, 217 ha of vines have been
planted since 1998. In all, there are 13 varieties, with shiraz, cabernet sauvignon and merlot leading
the way. Most of the production is sold to Hunter Valley wineries.

Angus the Bull

PO Box 3016, South Yarra, Vic 3141 REGION Southeast Australia
T (03) 9820 4077 F (03) 9820 4677 WWW.angusthebull.com OPEN Not
WINEMAKER Hamish MacGowan EST. 2002 CASES 20 000
Hamish McGowan, who describes himself as 'a young Australian wine industry professional', has
taken the virtual winery idea to its ultimate conclusion, with a single wine (Cabernet Sauvignon)
designed to be drunk with premium red meat, or, more particularly, a perfectly cooked steak.

ΨΨΨΨ **Cabernet Sauvignon 2004** Well put together blackcurrant fruit, tannins and oak; good
texture and mouthfeel; better again than the 2003. Twin top. RATING 89 DRINK 2008 $19

Angus Wines

Captain Sturt Road, Hindmarsh Island, SA 5214 REGION Southern Fleurieu
T (08) 8555 2320 F (08) 8555 2323 WWW.anguswines.com.au OPEN W'ends & public hols 11–5
WINEMAKER Boar's Rock (Mike Farmilo), Angas Buchanan EST. 1995 CASES 3000
Susan and Alistair Angus are the pioneer viticulturists on Hindmarsh Island. They have established
3.75 ha of shiraz, and 1.25 ha of semillon; the wine is contract-made. Part is bottled under the Angus
Wines label, some is sold in bulk to other wineries. Every aspect of packaging and marketing the wine
has a sophisticated touch. Exports to the UK, the US and other major markets.

ΨΨΨΨΨ **A3 Shiraz 2004** Strong purple-red; rich, opulent, ripe blackberry and plum fruit and a
touch of chocolate; fruit has consumed the oak; my original tasting read 'style shift?', and
there is; 80 dozen made by son Angas Buchanan. Screwcap. 15° alc. RATING 93 DRINK 2015
$35

ΨΨΨΨΨ **Sturt Ridge Shiraz 2003** Elegant, medium-bodied wine; quite complex bouquet and
palate; a nice contrast between sweet blackberry fruit and more spicy, savoury nuances.
Screwcap. 14.5° alc. RATING 91 DRINK 2012 $24
Sturt Ridge Semillon 2005 Spotlessly clean; the high alcohol gives more body and weight
but inevitably slightly blurs focus. No shortage of flavour, of course. Screwcap. 14° alc.
RATING 90 DRINK 2010 $17

Annapurna Estate

Simmonds Creek Road, Mount Beauty, Vic 3698 REGION Alpine Valleys
T (03) 5754 1356 F (03) 5754 4517 WWW.annapurnaestate.com.au
OPEN Wed–Sun, public & school hols 10–5
WINEMAKER Ezio Minutello EST. 1989 CASES 25 000

Ezio and Wendy Minutello began the establishment of the 21-ha vineyard at 550m on Mt Beauty in 1989, planted to pinot noir, chardonnay, pinot gris and merlot. Finally, in 1999, the first wines were released. Annapurna, the second highest mountain after Mt Everest, is Nepalese for 'goddess of bountiful harvest and fertility'.

ŸŸŸŸ **Mt Beauty Pinot Gris 2005** Has some pear, musk and apple flavours; good balance and length within the limitations of the variety. Screwcap. 13.5° alc. **RATING** 87 **DRINK** Now $18

ŸŸŸŸ **Mt Beauty Merlot 2005** Youthful purple; despite the alcohol, not heavy, although there is a skein of sweetness through to the finish and aftertaste; guaranteed to charm cellar door visitors. Screwcap. 14.5° alc. **RATING** 86 **DRINK** 2008 $20
Sparkling White 2005 **RATING** 85 **DRINK** Now $22
Methode Classique Pinot Noir Chardonnay 2004 **RATING** 85 **DRINK** Now $34
Sparkling Red 2005 **RATING** 85 **DRINK** Now $26

Annie's Lane ★★★★★

Quelltaler Road, Watervale, SA 5452 **REGION** Clare Valley
T (08) 8843 0003 **F** (08) 8843 0096 **WWW**.annieslane.com.au **OPEN** Mon–Fri 8.30–5, w'ends 11–4
WINEMAKER Mark Robertson **EST.** 1851 **CASES** 120 000
The Clare Valley portfolio of Beringer Blass, formerly made at the historic Quelltaler winery, is sold under the Annie's Lane label, the name coming from Annie Weyman, a turn-of-the-century local identity. Since 1996, a series of outstanding wines have appeared under the Annie's Lane label, Copper Trail the flagship release. Exports to the UK, the US, Canada and NZ.

ŸŸŸŸŸ **Copper Trail Clare Valley Riesling 2004** Remarkable wine; early-picked, yet abundant flavour and character to a perfectly balanced long, linear palate. Bert Bear Trophy Best 1-Year-Old White Sydney Wine Show '06. Screwcap. 11° alc. **RATING** 96 **DRINK** 2019
Copper Trail Shiraz 2002 Hyper-rich, luscious, dense fruit with great tannin structure and extreme length; oak is there, but the fruit is the fat lady's song. Will live for a very long time. Cork. **RATING** 96 **DRINK** 2027
Copper Trail Clare Valley Riesling 2005 Light straw-green; fine, intense citrus, lime and mineral; very good balance and length. Screwcap. 12° alc. **RATING** 95 **DRINK** 2015 $35
Copper Trail Shiraz 2001 Largely belies its alcohol; ripe, luscious red and black fruits; fine tannin and oak balance and integration from 22 months in barrel. Winner Shiraz Challenge 2005. Cork. 15° alc. **RATING** 95 **DRINK** 2016 $49.99

ŸŸŸŸŸ **Clare Valley Riesling 2005** Glowing yellow-green; rich, forward, mouthfilling style; ripe tropical/lime mix. Screwcap. 12° alc. **RATING** 93 **DRINK** 2010 $17.99
Clare Valley Shiraz 2003 Strong red-purple; medium-bodied blackberry, spice and plum; very good tannin and oak control. Screwcap. 14.5° alc. **RATING** 93 **DRINK** 2015
Clare Valley Cabernet Merlot 2004 Strong purple-red; medium- to full-bodied, flooded with blackcurrant, cassis and a touch of licorice; good tannins and oak. Screwcap. 14.5° alc. **RATING** 93 **DRINK** 2019
Clare Valley Cabernet Merlot 2003 Deep colour; dense, dark, black fruit aromas; rich and concentrated, with the oak contribution evident throughout. Screwcap. **RATING** 92 **DRINK** 2013 $16.99
Copper Trail Clare Valley Cabernet Sauvignon 2002 Deep colour; clean, powerful blackcurrant and earth varietal fruit; lingering tannins. Screwcap. 14.5° alc. **RATING** 92 **DRINK** 2022 $35
Clare Valley Semillon 2005 Bright green-yellow; attractive, full-bodied style; ripe lemon and pear fruit; good balance. Screwcap. 12.5° alc. **RATING** 90 **DRINK** 2008 $17.99
Clare Valley Semillon 2004 Glowing yellow-green; a rich wine with complex texture and structure to the lemon/preserved lemon fruit; nice balance. Screwcap. 12.5° alc. **RATING** 90 **DRINK** 2009 $16.99

ŸŸŸŸ **Copper Trail Shiraz Grenache Mourvedre 2001** In the mainstream of Clare Valley style for this blend, which simply doesn't catch my imagination; jammy, weakly structured wines seem to be the order of the day. Screwcap. 13° alc. **RATING** 89 **DRINK** 2010

Clare Valley Chardonnay 2005 Some well-handled barrel ferment inputs on ripe peach and melon fruit; soft finish. Screwcap. 13.5° alc. **RATING** 88 **DRINK** 2009 $17.99

Clare Valley Rose 2005 Light- to medium-bodied; crisp and clean; light red fruits, balanced finish. Screwcap. 13° alc. **RATING** 87 **DRINK** Now $17.99

Antcliff's Chase   NR

RMB 4510, Caveat via Seymour, Vic 3660 **REGION** Strathbogie Ranges
T (03) 5790 4333 **F** (03) 5790 4333 **OPEN** W'ends 10–5
WINEMAKER Chris Bennett, Ian Leamon **EST.** 1982 **CASES** 800
A small family enterprise which began planting the vineyards at an elevation of 600m in the Strathbogie Ranges in 1982; wine production from the 4-ha vineyard began in the early 1990s. After an uncertain start, wine quality has picked up considerably.

Anvers Wines

Lot 11 Main Road, McLaren Vale, SA 5171 **REGION** Adelaide Hills
T (08) 8323 9603 **F** (08) 8323 9502 **WWW.**anvers.com.au **OPEN** 7 days 10–5
WINEMAKER Duane Coates **EST.** 1998 **CASES** 7000
Myriam and Wayne Keoghan established Anvers Wines with the emphasis on quality rather than quantity. The first Cabernet Sauvignon was made in 1998, and volume has increased markedly since then. The quality of the wines is exemplary, no doubt underwriting the increase in production and expansion of markets both across Australia and in most major export markets.

🍷🍷🍷🍷🍷 **Adelaide Hills Chardonnay 2004** Elegant, light- to medium-bodied; melon and quality oak interwoven; very good balance, line and length, developing slowly. Wild yeast. Great value. Cork. 13.2° alc. **RATING** 93 **DRINK** 2010 $20

🍷🍷🍷🍷 **The Warrior Shiraz 2003** Medium-bodied; quite savoury, and showing elements of bottle development; not the expected concentration for an icon wine, particularly on the mid- to back-palate. Cork. 14.9° alc. **RATING** 89 **DRINK** 2010 $45

Razorback Road Shiraz Cabernet 2004 Bright red-purple; medium-bodied, nicely balanced, red and black fruits; appropriately firm tannins and controlled oak; good length. Cork. **RATING** 89 **DRINK** 2012 $18

🍷🍷🍷🍷 **Brabo Shiraz Cabernet 2004 RATING** 85 **DRINK** Now $9

Apsley Gorge Vineyard   NR

The Gulch, Bicheno, Tas 7215 **REGION** East Coast Tasmania
T (03) 6375 1221 **F** (03) 6375 1589 **OPEN** By appt
WINEMAKER Brian Franklin **EST.** 1988 **CASES** 3000
While nominally situated at Bicheno on the east coast, Apsley Gorge is in fact some distance inland, taking its name from a mountain pass. Clearly, it shares with the other east coast wineries the capacity to produce Chardonnay and Pinot Noir of excellent quality. Brian Franklin travels to Burgundy each year for the vintage, putting into practice at Apsley Gorge what he learns in Burgundy.

Apthorpe Estate   NR

475 Lovedale Road, Lovedale, NSW 2321 **REGION** Lower Hunter Valley
T (02) 4930 9177 **F** (02) 4930 9088 **WWW.**apthorpe.com.au **OPEN** By appt
WINEMAKER Mark Apthorpe **EST.** 1996 **CASES** NFP
Samuel Apthorpe was given 14 years' imprisonment as a convict in Australia for stealing a few teaspoons. In the mid-1850s, after he had completed his sentence, he established a vineyard in the Hunter Valley at Bishops Bridge. In 1996 his great-great-great-grandson Mark Apthorpe continued the tradition when he planted 1 ha each of cabernet franc and chambourcin at nearby Lovedale.

Arakoon

★★★★★

229 Main Road, McLaren Vale, SA 5171 **REGION** McLaren Vale
T (08) 8323 7339 **F** (02) 6566 6288 **OPEN** Fri–Sun 10–5, or by appt
WINEMAKER Raymond Jones **EST.** 1999 **CASES** 3500
Ray and Patrik (sic) Jones' first venture into wine came to nothing: a 1990 proposal for a film about the Australian wine industry with myself as anchorman. Five years too early, say the Joneses. In 1999 they took the plunge into making their own wine, and exporting it as well as the wines of others. As the quality of the wines has increased, so has the originally zany labelling been replaced with simple, but elegant, labels. Exports to the US, Germany, Denmark, Belgium and Sweden.

ŸŸŸŸŸ **Sellicks Beach Shiraz 2004** Strong purple-red; a different fruit register on the medium-bodied palate; dark chocolate and spice lead into vibrant black fruits and fine, lingering tannins to close. Screwcap. 14.5° alc. **RATING** 95 **DRINK** 2019 $ 20
Clarendon Shiraz 2004 Full-bodied; brighter fruit than the Blewitt Springs, with more spice and touches of plum to go with the blackberry and chocolate; well-integrated and balanced oak. Screwcap. 15° alc. **RATING** 94 **DRINK** 2024 $ 32
Blewitt Springs Shiraz 2004 Deep purple-red; full-bodied, rich, dense, velvety blackberry and dark chocolate fruit literally shrieks its regional origin; soft tannins. Screwcap. 15° alc. **RATING** 94 **DRINK** 2024 $ 32

Aramis Vineyards

NR

PO Box 208, Marleston, SA 5033 **REGION** McLaren Vale
T (08) 8238 0000 **F** (08) 8234 0485 **WWW.**aramisvineyards.com **OPEN** Not
WINEMAKER Scott Rawlinson **EST.** 1998 **CASES** 4000
The estate vineyards have been planted to just 2 varieties: shiraz (18 ha) and cabernet sauvignon (8 ha). Viticulturist David Mills is a third-generation McLaren Vale resident and has been involved in the establishment of the vineyards from the very beginning. Winemaker Scott Rawlinson was with Mildara Blass for 8 years before joining the Aramis team under the direction of owner Lee Flourentzou. Exports to the UK, the US, Canada, Singapore and Hong Kong.

Archer Falls Vineyard

NR

1253 Newrum Road, Kilcoy via Woodford, Qld 4514 **REGION** Queensland Coastal
T (07) 5496 3507 **F** (07) 5496 3507 **OPEN** W'ends & public hols 10–5
WINEMAKER Contract **EST.** 1995 **CASES** NA
Ronald Field has a small vineyard of chardonnay and shiraz. The wine is sold through the cellar door and by mail order; there are the usual cellar door facilities, including barbecue and picnics.

Arlewood Estate

★★★★☆

Harmans Road South, Wilyabrup, WA 6284 **REGION** Margaret River
T (08) 9755 6267 **F** (08) 9755 6267 **WWW.**arlewood.com.au **OPEN** W'ends 11–5
WINEMAKER Ian Bell, Mark Messenger **EST.** 1988 **CASES** 6000
The Heydon and Gosatti families acquired Arlewood Estate in October 1999, having previously established a small vineyard in Cowaramup in 1995, and have expanded the vineyard to 15 ha. George Heydon is a Perth dentist whose passion for wine has led him to study viticulture at the University of Western Australia; Garry Gosatti has been involved in the boutique brewing and hospitality industries for many years. Exports to the UK and the US.

ŸŸŸŸŸ **Cabernet Sauvignon 2002** Firm, savoury blackcurrant/blackberry/cedary/earthy flavours; firm but fine tannins on a long palate. Screwcap. 14.5° alc. **RATING** 92 **DRINK** 2012 $ 33
2003 Complex, full-blown wine with ripe stone fruit and barrel ferment/malolactic ferment inputs; layers of flavour; 490 cases made. Cork. 13.8° alc. **RATING** 91 **DRINK** 2009 $ 33
Single Vineyard Semillon 2004 Typical rich barrel-fermented Margaret River style; structural and flavour complexity, but a slightly congested finish Screwcap. 13° alc. **RATING** 90 **DRINK** Now $ 27

♥♥♥♥ **Single Vineyard Sauvignon Blanc Semillon 2005** Sotto voce wine; a complex but subtle interplay of 60% sauvignon blanc, 40% semillon and partial barrel ferment. Screwcap. 13.5° alc. **RATING** 89 **DRINK** 2008 $ 22

♥♥♥♡ **Cabernet Merlot 2003** **RATING** 86 **DRINK** 2009 $ 27

Armstrong Vineyards ★★★★★

Lot 1 Military Road, Armstrong, Vic 3381 (postal) **REGION** Grampians
T (08) 8277 6073 **F** (08) 8277 6035 **WWW**.winesource.com.au **OPEN** Not
WINEMAKER Tony Royal **EST.** 1989 **CASES** 1000
Armstrong Vineyards is the brain- or love-child of Tony Royal, former Seppelt (Great Western) winemaker, former CEO of Seguin Moreau Australia, and now CEO and joint owner of Portavin Integrated Wine Services which provides packaging, oenological and logistics services for SA wineries. Armstrong Vineyards has 6.7 ha of shiraz, the first 2 ha planted in 1989, the remainder in 1995–96. Low yields (4.5–5.5 tonnes per ha) mean the wine will always be produced in limited quantities. Exports to the UK.

♥♥♥♥♥ **Great Western Shiraz Viognier 2004** Very deep, dark colour; medium- to full-bodied; powerful, rich, luscious blackberry aromas and flavours, with that unmistakable twist of citrus from the viognier. Screwcap. **RATING** 94 **DRINK** 2015 $ 32

Arranmore Vineyard ★★★☆

Rangeview Road, Carey Gully, SA 5144 **REGION** Adelaide Hills
T (08) 8390 3034 **F** (08) 8390 0005 **WWW**.arranmore.com.au **OPEN** By appt
WINEMAKER John Venus **EST.** 1998 **CASES** 700
One of the tiny operations which dot the landscape of the beautiful Adelaide Hills. At an altitude of around 550m, the 2-ha vineyard is planted to clonally selected pinot noir, chardonnay and sauvignon blanc. Exports to the UK.

♥♥♥♥♡ **Black Pinot 2004** Deep colour; spiced plummy fruit; good mouthfeel and length; delicate, crisp red fruits; not phenolic, but halfway between rose and red wine; has good texture. Screwcap. 13.2° alc. **RATING** 90 **DRINK** 2009 $ 29

♥♥♥♡ **Adelaide Hills Pinot Noir 2004** **RATING** 86 **DRINK** Now $ 19
Adelaide Hills Sauvignon Blanc 2005 **RATING** 84 **DRINK** Now $ 19

Arrivo NR

22 Kanmantoo Road, Aldgate, SA 5154 (postal) **REGION** Adelaide Hills
T (08) 8370 8072 **F** (08) 8303 6621 **OPEN** Not
WINEMAKER Peter Godden, Sally McGill **EST.** 1998 **CASES** 100
While the establishment date of Arrivo is 1998, when Peter Godden and partner Sally McGill established a nursery block of 35 vines of nebbiolo, the inspiration goes back to 1990, while Peter was still at Roseworthy College/Adelaide University, heading the following year to become assistant winemaker to Joe Grilli at Primo Estate. In 1995 and 1996 Peter spent much time in Barolo, Italy, working the 1996 vintage at leading producer Vietti. In the meantime, Sally had become a leading Italian wine exporter and importer/distributor with Red+White. By 2001 they had propagated sufficient vines from the original 35 to plant 1 ha of vineyard, using a unique trellis and training system derived from Barolo, but with an Australian twist. Not only is the trellis complicated and unique, but so are the amazingly complicated fermentation techniques being used by Peter Godden, best known these days for his work with the Australian Wine Research Institute. Arrivo means 'arrival' in Italian, the first 100 cases (from 2004) released in August 2006.

Arrowfield Estate ★★★★

Golden Highway, Jerrys Plains, NSW 2330 **REGION** Upper Hunter Valley
T (02) 6576 4041 **F** (02) 6576 4144 **WWW**.arrowfieldestate.com.au **OPEN** 7 days 10–5
WINEMAKER Barry Kooij, Adrianna Mansueto **EST.** 1968 **CASES** 80 000
Arrowfield continues in the ownership of the Inagaki family, which has been involved in the Japanese
liquor industry for over a century. It has boosted its management team under the direction of new
managing director, Michael Goundrey. It has 52 ha of low-yielding, old vines in the Upper Hunter
Valley, and also buys grapes from other parts of the Australia, making varietal wines appropriate to
those regions. Exports to all major markets.

ΨΨΨΨΨ **JOT Chapter Two Margaret River Semillon Sauvignon Blanc 2004** Good varietal
synergy typical of the region; a mix of asparagus, gooseberry and citrus; very long finish.
Screwcap. **RATING** 90 **DRINK** Now $ 16.99

ΨΨΨΨ **JOT Chapter Two Alpine & King Valley Merlot 2004** Super-elegant; strongly varietal;
fruit-driven and long. Gold medal Sydney Wine Show '06. **RATING** 88 **DRINK** 2008 $ 17
JOT Chapter Two Alpine & King Valley Merlot 2003 Spicy, savoury, leafy, berry aromas; a
nice touch of black olive to the light-bodied palate; has length. Screwcap. **RATING** 87
DRINK 2008 $ 16.99

ΨΨΨΨ **JOT Chapter Two Hunter Valley Chardonnay 2004 RATING** 86 **DRINK** Now $ 16.99
JOT Chapter Two Frankland River Shiraz 2003 RATING 86 **DRINK** 2008 $ 16.99

Artamus ★★★★★

PO Box 489, Margaret River, WA 6285 **REGION** Margaret River
T (08) 9757 8131 **F** (08) 9757 8131 **WWW**.artamus.com.au **OPEN** Not
WINEMAKER Michael Gadd **EST.** 1994 **CASES** 280
Ann Dewar and Ian Parmenter (the celebrated television food presenter) planted 1 ha of chardonnay
cuttings (from Cape Mentelle) at their property on the north bank of the Margaret River. Their first
wine was produced in 1998, and the style of each succeeding vintage has been remarkably consistent.

ΨΨΨΨΨ **Margaret River Chardonnay 2003** Pale green-straw; intense tangy, citrussy melon and
nectarine fruit; oak a pure support role; has great length and will be long lived. Screwcap.
13° alc. **RATING** 94 **DRINK** 2015 $ 32.50

Arthurs Creek Estate NR

Strathewen Road, Arthurs Creek, Vic 3099 (postal) **REGION** Yarra Valley
T (03) 9714 8202 **F** (03) 9824 0252 **WWW**.arthurscreekestate.com **OPEN** Not
WINEMAKER Yering Station (Tom Carson), Gary Baldwin (Consultant) **EST.** 1975 **CASES** 1500
A latter-day folly of leading Melbourne QC SEK Hulme. He began the planting of 3 ha of
chardonnay, 4.3 ha of cabernet sauvignon and 0.7 ha of merlot at Arthurs Creek in the mid-1970s,
and had wine made by various people for 15 years before deciding to sell any of it. The back vintages,
sadly, are long since gone. Exports to the UK, the US, Denmark and Japan.

Arundel ★★★★☆

Arundel Farm Estate, PO Box 136, Keilor, Vic 3036 **REGION** Sunbury
T (03) 9335 3422 **F** (03) 9335 4912 **WWW**.arundel.com.au **OPEN** Not
WINEMAKER Bianca Hayes **EST.** 1995 **CASES** 600
Arundel was built around an acre of cabernet and shiraz planted in the 1970s, but abandoned. When the
Conwell family purchased the property in the early 1990s, the vineyard was resurrected, and the first
vintage made by Rick Kinzbrunner in 1995. Thereafter the cabernet was grafted over to shiraz, the block
slowly increased to 1.6 ha, and an additional 4 ha of shiraz and 1.6 ha of viognier and marsanne planted.

ΨΨΨΨ **Viognier 2005** The bouquet is still developing, but the palate is crammed with varietal
apricot, musk and lychee; fully ripe, but not hot. Cork. **RATING** 91 **DRINK** 2009 $ 28
Shiraz 2004 Bright colour; soft mouthfeel/profile to the medium-bodied palate; spicy
flavours and nice mocha oak; is there viognier at work? Cork. **RATING** 90 **DRINK** 2012 $ 28

Ashbrook Estate ★★★★★

Harmans Road South, Wilyabrup via Cowaramup, WA 6284 **REGION** Margaret River
T (08) 9755 6262 **F** (08) 9755 6290 **OPEN** 7 days 11–5
WINEMAKER Tony Devitt, Brian Devitt **EST.** 1975 **CASES** 8000
A fastidious maker of consistently excellent estate-grown table wines which shuns publicity and the wine show system alike and is less well-known than it deserves to be, selling much of its wine through the cellar door and by an understandably very loyal mailing list clientele. All of the white wines are of the highest quality, year in, year out. Exports to the UK, Canada, Japan, Singapore and Hong Kong.

🍷🍷🍷🍷🍷 **Margaret River Semillon 2005** Spotlessly clean; extremely rich and powerful, with ripe, sweet, citrussy fruit. Substantial mouthfeel from 14˚ alcohol, but not hot. Gold medal Sheraton Wine Awards 2005. Screwcap. 14° alc. **RATING** 95 **DRINK** 2010 $17
Sauvignon Blanc 2005 Super-intense and powerful; very strong varietal character, flooded with ripe gooseberry and passionfruit; not phenolic. Screwcap. **RATING** 95 **DRINK** 2008 $19
Margaret River Chardonnay 2004 Controlled barrel ferment and oak maturation support the ripe nectarine and peach fruit of both bouquet and palate; supple and mouthfilling. Screwcap. 14.5° alc. **RATING** 94 **DRINK** 2014 $27
Margaret River Shiraz 2003 Spotlessly clean and fragrant mix of cherry, raspberry, blackberry and spice; medium-bodied with fine tannins and well-integrated oak. Screwcap. 14.5° alc. **RATING** 94 **DRINK** 2015 $27

Ashley Estate NR

284 Aldersyde Road, Bickley, WA 6076 **REGION** Perth Hills
T (08) 9257 2313 **F** (08) 9257 3403 **OPEN** Sunday & public hols by appt
WINEMAKER John Griffiths (Contract) **EST.** 1988 **CASES** NA
Ashley Estate (formerly Ashley Park) has 8 ha of vines planted exclusively to pinot noir by proprietor John Ashley. Highly experienced winemaker John Griffiths is responsible for winemaking, and the wine is sold through the cellar door.

Ashton Hills ★★★★★

Tregarthen Road, Ashton, SA 5137 **REGION** Adelaide Hills
T (08) 8390 1243 **F** (08) 8390 1243 **OPEN** Fri–Mon 11.30–5
WINEMAKER Stephen George **EST.** 1982 **CASES** 1500
Stephen George wears three winemaker hats: one for Ashton Hills, drawing upon a 3.5-ha estate vineyard high in the Adelaide Hills; one for Galah Wines; and one for Wendouree. It would be hard to imagine three wineries with more diverse styles, from the elegance and finesse of Ashton Hills to the awesome power of Wendouree. The Riesling, Chardonnay and Pinot Noir have moved into the highest echelon. Exports to the UK and the US.

🍷🍷🍷🍷🍷 **Chardonnay 2004** Elegant and fine, proclaiming its quality from the first sniff; a complex and seamless texture and line; nectarine, melon, creamy/nutty oak and malolactic influences. Screwcap. 13.5° alc. **RATING** 96 **DRINK** 2012 $31
Reserve Pinot Noir 2004 Slightly deeper in colour than the Estate; more plum and French oak aromas; a fine and elegant palate, silky and supple, having swallowed up the 100% new French oak. French clone selection. Screwcap. **RATING** 94 **DRINK** 2011 $58.50
Sparkling Red 1998 Very complex, but nowhere near as phenolic or ripe as I had expected; serious sparkling red, with masses of spicy flavour and excellent balance. Base wine kept in old oak for 5 years (presumably Wendouree), re-fermented and dosed with fortified shiraz. 13° alc. **RATING** 94 **DRINK** 2015 $44

🍷🍷🍷🍷🍷 **Estate Pinot Noir 2004** Fine, light- to medium-bodied, black cherry and spice aromas and flavours; scores more for elegance than concentration; good length. No new oak. Screwcap. **RATING** 93 **DRINK** 2009 $43.75
Piccadilly Valley Pinot Noir 2004 Good colour; light- to medium-bodied; elegant spicy, savoury, foresty surrounds to the core of blackberry and plum fruit. Screwcap. 14° alc. **RATING** 92 **DRINK** 2010 $31

Five 2002 Spicy, cedary, savoury nuances run through the cassis and blackcurrant fruit; fine tannins and oak integration; good length. Merlot/Cabernet Sauvignon/Malbec/Cabernet Franc/Petit Verdot. Screwcap. 13.5° alc. **RATING** 92 **DRINK** 2015 $ 29

Three 2005 Lively, fresh, tangy citrus, apple and spice aromas; a light-bodied palate with crisp texture and a lingering, dry finish. Gewurztraminer/Pinot Gris/Riesling. Screwcap. 13.5° alc. **RATING** 91 **DRINK** 2008 $ 24

Riesling 2005 The closed bouquet, with subliminal reduction, leads into a surprisingly soft and fruit-forward palate, with ripe apple, tropical and lime nuances. Screwcap. 13° alc. **RATING** 90 **DRINK** 2009 $ 24

Audrey Wilkinson Vineyard ★★☆

Oakdale, De Beyers Road, Pokolbin, NSW 2320 **REGION** Lower Hunter Valley
T (02) 4998 7411 **F** (02) 4998 7824 **WWW**.audreywilkinson.com.au **OPEN** Mon–Fri 9–5, w'ends & public hols 9.30–5
WINEMAKER Mark Woods **EST.** 1999 **CASES** 12 500
One of the most historic properties in the Hunter Valley, set in a particularly beautiful location, and with a very attractive cellar door. In 2004 it was acquired by Brian Agnew and family, and hence is no longer part of the Pepper Tree/James Fairfax wine group. The wines are made from estate-grown grapes; the vines were planted between the 1970s and 1990s.

TTT **Pioneer Series Verdelho 2005 RATING** 79 $ 20

Auldstone NR

Booths Road, Taminick via Glenrowan, Vic 3675 **REGION** Glenrowan
T (03) 5766 2237 **F** (03) 5766 2131 **WWW**.auldstone.com.au **OPEN** Thurs–Sat & school hols 9–5, Sun 10–5
WINEMAKER Michael Reid **EST.** 1987 **CASES** 2000
Michael and Nancy Reid have restored a century-old stone winery and have replanted the largely abandoned 26-ha vineyard around it. All the Auldstone varietal and fortified wines have won medals (usually bronze) in Australian wine shows.

Austin's Wines ★★★★☆

870 Steiglitz Road, Sutherlands Creek, Vic 3331 **REGION** Geelong
T (03) 5281 1799 **F** (03) 5281 1673 **WWW**.austinswines.com.au **OPEN** By appt
WINEMAKER Scott Ireland, Richard Austin **EST.** 1982 **CASES** 25 000
Pamela and Richard Austin have quietly built their business from a tiny base, and it has flourished. The vineyard has been progressively extended to 56 ha, and production has soared from 700 cases in 1998 to 25 000 cases in 2005. Scott Ireland is now full-time resident winemaker in the new and capacious onsite winery, and the quality of the wines is admirable.

TTTTT **Pinot Noir 2004** Light- to medium-bodied; a complex mix of black and red fruits and a touch of whole bunch/stem; has very good length and finish. Trophy 2005 Geelong Wine Show. **RATING** 95 **DRINK** 2010 $ 25

TTTTT **Geelong Sauvignon Blanc 2005** Spotlessly clean; an intense and very long palate of citrus, gooseberry and kiwifruit; the faintest touch of sweetness of the finish adds, rather than detracts. Screwcap. 12.5° alc. **RATING** 93 **DRINK** Now $ 20

Chardonnay 2004 Light green-yellow; clean and fresh, with elegant citrussy fruit; long and balanced. **RATING** 92 **DRINK** 2009 $ 25

Ellyse Chardonnay 2004 Smokey/charry oak off-set by quite intense fruit; a big, rich style. **RATING** 90 **DRINK** 2008 $ 28

Shiraz 2003 Rich, ripe and luscious but not too jammy; excellent mouthfeel, notwithstanding a touch of adjusted acidity. **RATING** 90 **DRINK** 2009 $ 25

Reserve Geelong Shiraz 2002 Fine, smoky, briary, foresty aromas; a long palate with almost lemony overtones, lingering finish; pronounced cool climate style. Cork. **RATING** 90 **DRINK** 2012 $ 40

ΥΥΥΥ **Geelong Riesling 2005** Bright green-yellow; a solid wine with strong lime juice and incipient kerosene; slightly thick finish. All in all, shows the maritime influence. Screwcap. 12.5° alc. **RATING** 89 **DRINK** 2010 $ 20

Australian Domaine Wines

NR

PO Box 166, Walkerville, SA 5081 **REGION** Various
T (08) 8342 3395 **F** (08) 8269 4008 **OPEN** By appt
WINEMAKER Pikes (Neil Pike), Andrew Braithwaite **EST.** 1998 **CASES** 5000
Australian Domaine Wines is the reincarnation of Barletta Bros, who started their own brand business for leading Adelaide retailer Walkerville Cellars, which they then owned. The wines are made at Pikes using tanks and barrels owned by the Barlettas. Grapes are sourced from the Clare Valley, McLaren Vale and the Barossa Valley. Exports to the UK, the US and other major markets.

Australian Old Vine Wine

NR

Farm 271, Rossetto Road, Beelbangera, NSW 2680 **REGION** Riverina
T (02) 6963 5239 **F** (02) 6963 5239 **WWW**.ausoldvine.com.au **OPEN** 7 days 10–4
WINEMAKER Piromit Wines (Dom Piromalli) **EST.** 2002 **CASES** 2000
Elio and Marie Alban have registered the name Australian Old Vine Wine Pty Ltd for their business. It is designed to draw attention to their 7.6 ha of 50-year-old shiraz and 2.4 ha of 40-year-old cabernet sauvignon. The younger wines, coming from chardonnay, colombard, semillon, merlot and chambourcin plantings, are released under the Australian Sovereign label. The plan is ultimately to buy grapes from old vines in the Barossa Valley and McLaren Vale for an Old Vine blend.

Avalon Vineyard

★★★☆

1605 Bailey Road, Glen Forrest, WA 6071 **REGION** Perth Hills
T (08) 9298 8049 **F** (08) 9298 8049 **WWW**.avalonvineyard.com.au **OPEN** By appt
WINEMAKER Rob Marshall (Contract) **EST.** 1986 **CASES** 500
One of the smaller wineries in the Perth Hills, drawing upon 0.75 ha each of chardonnay, semillon and cabernet sauvignon. Plans to open a cellar door sales and tasting area in 2006/07. Exports to Malaysia.

ΥΥΥΥ **Perth Hills Semillon 2004** Quite soft and rounded, already showing some honeyed characters; good balance, ready now. Diam. 11.9° alc. **RATING** 88 **DRINK** Now $ 14
Perth Hills Classic Dry White 2004 Still very delicate and fresh in Feb '06; gentle fruit salad and stone fruit flavours; good length. Chardonnay/Chenin Blanc/Verdelho. Cork. 13.4° alc. **RATING** 88 **DRINK** Now $ 12
Reserve Perth Hills Cabernet Merlot 2004 Light but bright colour; light- to medium-bodied, fresh red fruits are at the core, with some savoury/olive notes. Well-made. Cork. 13.8° alc. **RATING** 88 **DRINK** 2009 $ 17

ΥΥΥ **Perth Hills Cabernet Sauvignon 2003** **RATING** 86 **DRINK** 2008 $ 17
Perth Hills Unwooded Chardonnay 2005 **RATING** 84 **DRINK** Now $ 14

Avalon Wines

★★★☆

RMB 9556 Whitfield Road, Wangaratta, Vic 3678 **REGION** King Valley
T (03) 5729 3629 **F** (03) 5729 3635 **WWW**.avalonwines.com.au **OPEN** 7 days 10–5
WINEMAKER Doug Groom **EST.** 1981 **CASES** 1000
Roseworthy graduate Doug Groom and wife Rosa established a 10-ha vineyard, selling part of the grapes, but making *inter alia* highly rated Shiraz. Non-interventionist winemaking is reflected in the use of indigenous yeasts and unfiltered wines.

ΥΥΥΥ **King Valley Shiraz 2004** Dark colour; concentrated, rich blackberry, licorice and chocolate fruit; balanced tannins; impressive. Cork. 14.4° alc. **RATING** 90 **DRINK** 2012 $ 20

ΥΥΥΥ **King Valley Tempranillo 2004** Unusually good colour; rich, ripe spicy fruit aromas and powerful prune and plum fruit. Patience may provide rich rewards. Cork. 14.2° alc. **RATING** 89 **DRINK** 2014 $ 25

ŶŶŶŸ **King Valley Riesling 2005** Clean; relatively subdued aromas and flavours, but balance and length OK. Screwcap. 12.8° alc. **RATING** 86 **DRINK** 2008 $14
Late Harvest King Valley Verdelho 2005 RATING 86 **DRINK** Now $20

Avenel Park/Hart Wines   NR

24/25 Ewings Road, Avenel, Vic 3664 **REGION** Goulburn Valley
T (03) 9347 5444 **F** (03) 9349 3278 **WWW**.avenelpark.com.au **OPEN** Sunday 11–4, or by appt.
WINEMAKER David Traeger, Plunkett Wines (Sam Plunkett) **EST.** 1994 **CASES** 1000
Jed and Sue Hart have, in their words, 'turned the rocky, ironstone soils of Lovers Hill into a 22-acre vineyard over some back-breaking years'. Seven of the 10 ha are planted to shiraz and cabernet sauvignon, with a small amount each of merlot, semillon and chardonnay. Most of the grapes have been and will continue to be sold to Southcorp, but since 2000 the equivalent of 1000 cases of wine have been retained and contract-made. Nonetheless, the Harts' main viticultural business (Jed Hart is in aviation) will be grapegrowing.

Aventine Wines   NR

86 Watters Road, Ballandean, Qld, 4382 **REGION** Granite Belt
T 0409 270 389 **F** (07) 3001 9299 **WWW**.aventinewines.com.au **OPEN** W'ends & public hols 9–6
WINEMAKER Jim Barnes **EST.** 1995 **CASES** NA
The 9-ha Aventine vineyard is situated at an elevation of 1000m, on a north-facing hill high above the Ballandean Valley. The highest portions of the site are planted to nebbiolo and sangiovese, the soils shallow, weathered granite; shiraz, cabernet sauvignon and muscat are also planted. All wines are estate-grown.

Avonbrook Wines   NR

7 Benrua Road, Clackline, WA 6564 **REGION** Central Western Australia Zone
T (08) 9574 1276 **F** (08) 9574 1070 **OPEN** W'ends & public hols 10–5
WINEMAKER Peter Murfit **EST.** 1993 **CASES** NA
Avonbrook Wines is loosely based on 2.3 ha of vineyards planted to chenin blanc, chardonnay, verdelho, merlot and shiraz by winemaker/viticulturist Peter Murfit. The wines are exported to the UK and the US under various brands.

Avonmore Estate   NR

Mayreef-Avonmore Road, Avonmore, Vic 3558 **REGION** Bendigo
T (03) 5432 6291 **F** (03) 5432 6291 **WWW**.avonmoreestatewine.com **OPEN** Wed–Sun & public hols 11–5, or by appt
WINEMAKER Shaun Bryans, Rob Bryans **EST.** 1996 **CASES** 1500
Rob and Pauline Bryans own and operate a Grade A-certified biodynamic farm, producing and selling beef, lamb and cereals as well as establishing 9 ha of viognier, sangiovese, cabernet sauvignon, cabernet franc and shiraz which produced its first crop in 2000. The winery is also biodynamic-certified and the wines are sold with the worldwide Demeter logo. Exports to Canada and Thailand.

B'darra Estate   NR

1415 Stumpy Gully Road, Moorooduc, Vic 3933 **REGION** Mornington Peninsula
T 0418 310 638 **OPEN** W'ends 10–5
WINEMAKER Gavin Perry **EST.** 1998 **CASES** 2000
Gavin and Linda Perry fell in love with Bedarra Island (off the north Queensland coast) when they stayed there, hence the name of their property, which they acquired in 1998. They planted just under 5 ha of vines in 1999, and are progressively developing the 21-ha holding. A revegetation and wetland, of which a lake and two big dams form part, are planned. Gavin Perry made his first wine in 1993 from grapes grown in the Peninsula while completing a Winery Supplies course. He has won numerous trophies and gold medals, including Most Successful Exhibitor in 1997, 1999 and 2000 in the amateur section of the Victorian Wines Show.

Baarrooka Vineyard

NR

Coach Road, Strathbogie, Vic 3666 **REGION** Strathbogie Ranges
T (03) 5790 5288 **F** (03) 5790 5205 **WWW**.baarrooka.com.au **OPEN** W'ends & public hols 11–5
Sept–May, or by appt
WINEMAKER Paul Evans, Travis Bush, Russell Synnot **EST.** 1996 **CASES** 1200
The establishment of the 32-ha Baarrooka Vineyard began in 1996, on a north-facing slope at an elevation of 550m. Plantings consist of riesling, sauvignon blanc, chardonnay, pinot noir, cabernet sauvignon, shiraz, merlot, zinfandel and small blocks of petit verdot, cabernet franc and malbec. The majority of the grapes are sold under contract into the Yarra Valley, but a small quantity is released under the Baarrooka label, the quantities and varieties varying according to the vintage.

Bacchanalia Estate

NR

160 Taverner Street, Bacchus Marsh, Vic 3340 **REGION** Sunbury
T (03) 5367 6416 **F** (03) 5367 6416 **OPEN** Most w'ends & public hols
WINEMAKER Peter Dredge (Contract), John Reid **EST.** 1994 **CASES** 1000
Noted ABC broadcaster and journalist John Reid, and wife Val, established Bacchanalia Estate in 1994 on the fertile black soils of Bacchus Marsh, adjacent to the Werribee River. The 3.2-ha vineyard is planted to shiraz, semillon, cabernet sauvignon and viognier.

Bacchus Hill

NR

100 O'Connell Road, Bacchus Marsh, Vic 3340 **REGION** Sunbury
T (03) 5367 8176 **F** (03) 5367 8176 **OPEN** Wed–Sun 10–5
WINEMAKER Bruno Tassone **EST.** 2000 **CASES** 2200
Lawyer Bruno Tassone migrated from Italy when he was 8 years old, and watched his father carry on the Italian tradition of making wine for home consumption. Tassone followed the same path before purchasing a 35-ha property at Bacchus Marsh with his wife, Jennifer. Here they have planted 2 ha each of riesling, semillon, sauvignon blanc, chardonnay, pinot noir, merlot, shiraz and cabernet sauvignon, plus 1 ha each of chenin blanc and nebbiolo. The massively powerful, and extremely rustic Le Repaire de Bacchus Cabernet Sauvignon is a striking wine.

🐦 Baddaginnie Run

★★★★

PO Box 579, North Melbourne, Vic 3051 **REGION** Strathbogie Ranges
T (03) 9348 9310 **F** (03) 9348 9370 **WWW**.baddaginnierun.net.au **OPEN** Not
WINEMAKER Toby Barlow **EST.** 1996 **CASES** 1250
Winsome McCaughey and Professor Snow Barlow (Professor of Horticulture and Viticulture at the University of Melbourne) spend part of their week in the Strathbogie Ranges, part in Melbourne, both having high-profile careers. The business name, Seven Sisters Vineyard, reflects the 7 generations of the McCaughey family associated with the land for over 135 years; Baddaginnie is the name of the nearby township. The vineyard is one element in a restored valley landscape, 100 000 indigenous trees having been replanted over the last 2 decades. The wines are made by son Toby Barlow, winemaker at Mitchelton.

▼▼▼▼▽ **Merlot 2004** Powerful and rich wine; densely structured; atypical for the variety, but impressive nonetheless. **RATING** 92 **DRINK** 2012 $ 23
Shiraz 2004 Nice wine; blackberry and plum fruit; good structure and length. **RATING** 90 **DRINK** 2010 $ 23

▼▼▼▽ **Verdelho 2005 RATING** 85 **DRINK** Now $ 17

Badger's Brook

NR

874 Maroondah Highway, Coldstream, Vic 3770 **REGION** Yarra Valley
T (03) 5962 4130 **F** (03) 5962 4238 **WWW**.badgersbrook.com.au **OPEN** Wed–Mon 11–5
WINEMAKER Contract **EST.** 1993 **CASES** 5000
Situated next door to the well-known Rochford, it has a total of 10 ha of vineyard, planted mainly to chardonnay, sauvignon blanc, pinot noir, shiraz and cabernet sauvignon, with a few rows each of

viognier, roussanne, marsanne and tempranillo. All of the wines are Yarra Valley-sourced, including the second Storm Ridge label. Now houses a smart brasserie restaurant with well-known chef Gary Cooper in charge. Exports to Asia.

Bago Vineyards NR

Milligans Road, off Bago Road, Wauchope, NSW 2446 **REGION** Hastings River
T (02) 6585 7099 **F** (02) 6585 7099 **WWW.**bagovineyards.com.au **OPEN** 7 days 11–5
WINEMAKER Jim Mobbs, John Cassegrain (Consultant) **EST.** 1985 **CASES** 6000
Jim and Kay Mobbs began planting the Broken Bago Vineyards in 1985 with 1 ha of chardonnay, with total plantings now 12.5 ha. Regional specialist John Cassegrain is consultant winemaker.

Baileys of Glenrowan

Cnr Taminick Gap Road/Upper Taminick Road, Glenrowan, Vic 3675 **REGION** Glenrowan
T (03) 5766 2392 **F** (03) 5766 2596 **WWW.**baileysofglenrowan.com.au **OPEN** Mon–Fri 9–5, w'ends 10–5
WINEMAKER Paul Dahlenburg **EST.** 1870 **CASES** 15 000
Just when it seemed that Baileys would remain one of the forgotten outposts of the Bering Blass empire, the reverse has occurred. Since 1998 Paul Dahlenburg has been in charge of Baileys, and has overseen an expansion in the vineyard to 143 ha and the construction of a totally new 2000-tonne winery. The cellar door has a heritage museum, winery viewing deck, contemporary art gallery and landscaped grounds; much of the heritage value of Baileys has been preserved. Baileys has also picked up the pace with its Muscat and Tokay, reintroducing the Winemaker's Selection at the top of the tree, while continuing the larger-volume Founder series. Exports to the UK and NZ.

1904 Block Shiraz 2003 Bright purple-red; medium-bodied, exemplary handling of old vine grapes from the picking decision onwards; seamless blackberry, plum, fine tannins and controlled oak. Cork. 14° alc. **RATING** 95 **DRINK** 2015
Winemaker's Selection Old Tokay NV Obvious age from the mahogany, olive-rimmed colour; toffee, malt and tea varietal characters are very complex, yet retain freshness. Excellent balance. Trophy Best Fortified Wine 2005 National Wine Show. **RATING** 95 **DRINK** Now $ 30
Shiraz 2004 Deep, dense red-purple; rich, yet supple and fresh medium-bodied blackberry fruit; good tannins and structure. Cork. 14.5° alc. **RATING** 94 **DRINK** 2013
1920's Block Shiraz 2003 Rich but controlled fruit; medium-bodied, rather than Leviathan; fully ripe, but not jammy flavours, with appropriate tannins and oak. Cork. **RATING** 94 **DRINK** 2018 $ 35

Founder Liqueur Tokay NV Moderate age showing in the colour; very good varietal character ranging through tea leaf, malt, butterscotch and Christmas cake; good balance; clean finish. **RATING** 93 **DRINK** Now $ 17
Founder Liqueur Muscat NV Rich, intense, dried raisin, Christmas pudding and spice; varietal character again bell-clear; good balance, moderate age. **RATING** 93 **DRINK** Now $ 17
Shiraz 2003 Clean dark berry fruit aromas; a powerful palate engorged with black fruits, dark chocolate and positive but ripe tannins. Cork. **RATING** 92 **DRINK** 2013 $ 19.99
Founder Tawny Port NV Tawny as it is made in Northeast Victoria, more luscious and raisined than classic South Australian Tawnys. Clean, modern packaging a feature for the fortified range. **RATING** 92 **DRINK** Now $ 17
Cabernet Sauvignon 2004 Purple-red; medium-bodied cassis fruit; well-handled oak; soft, almost milky tannins. Treading softly in Northeast Victoria. Cork. 14.5° alc. **RATING** 90 **DRINK** 2015

Bainton Family Wines NR

390 Milbrodale Road, Bulga, NSW 2330 (postal) **REGION** Lower Hunter Valley
T (02) 9968 1764 **F** (02) 9960 3454 **WWW.**bainton.com.au **OPEN** Not
WINEMAKER Tony Bainton **EST.** 1998 **CASES** 3500
The Bainton family, headed by eminent Sydney QC Russell Bainton, has 48 ha of vineyard, with the oldest semillon planted over 80 years ago (1923), most in 1940. The major part of the shiraz, too, dates back to plantings in 1950 and 1955.

Bald Mountain

41 Hickling Lane, via Wallangarra, Qld 4383 **REGION** Granite Belt
T (07) 4684 3186 **F** (07) 4684 3433 **OPEN** 7 days 10–5
WINEMAKER Monarch Winemaking Services **EST.** 1985 **CASES** 3500
Denis Parsons is a self-taught but exceptionally competent vigneron who has turned Bald Mountain into one of the viticultural showpieces of the Granite Belt. The Sauvignon Blanc-based wines, Classic Queenslander and Late Harvest Sauvignon Blanc, are interesting alternatives to the mainstream wines. Future production will also see grapes coming from new vineyards near Tenterfield just across the border in NSW. Significant exports to The Netherlands.

ŸŸŸŸ **Classic Queenslander Sauvignon Blanc 2004** Light straw-green; a clean, herbaceous entry, then tropical fruit on the mid-palate, and a slightly sweet finish for the cellar door. Estate-grown. Screwcap. 11.1° alc. **RATING** 87 **DRINK** Now **$** 15
Reserve Chardonnay 2004 Light straw-green; very understated style; fruit and oak balanced, but neither assertive; for those who are reticent about heavy fruit flavour. Screwcap. 13.1° alc. **RATING** 87 **DRINK** 2008 **$** 20

Bald Rock Vineyard

Alexandersons Road, Locksley, Vic 3665 (postal) **REGION** Strathbogie Ranges
T (03) 5798 5277 **F** (03) 5798 5277 **OPEN** Not
WINEMAKER Travis Bush (Contract) **EST.** 1999 **CASES** 350
John and Judy Thomson began the establishment of their vineyard in 1999, the first commercial bottling following in March 2005. They have 2.4 ha pinot noir, 1.4 ha shiraz and 0.6 ha chardonnay, established under monitored drip irrigation to control berry size. The wines are available through King & Godfrey, Lygon Street, Carlton.

ŸŸŸŸ **Strathbogie Ranges Pinot Noir 2004** **RATING** 84 **DRINK** Now **$** 14.50

Balgownie Estate

Hermitage Road, Maiden Gully, Vic 3551 **REGION** Bendigo
T (03) 5449 6222 **F** (03) 5449 6506 **WWW**.balgownieestate.com.au **OPEN** 7 days 11–5
WINEMAKER Tobias Ansted **EST.** 1969 **CASES** 5000
Balgownie Estate continues to grow in the wake of its acquisition by the Forrester family. A $3 million upgrade of the winery coincided with a doubling of the size of the vineyard to 35 ha, and in 2003 Balgownie Estate opened a separate cellar door in the Yarra Valley (see separate entry). Exports to the UK, the US and other major markets.

ŸŸŸŸŸ **Bendigo Shiraz 2004** Deep, bright red-purple; rich black fruits and licorice; great structure and mouthfeel; power with finesse. Screwcap. 14° alc. **RATING** 95 **DRINK** 2019 **$** 19

Balgownie Estate (Yarra Valley)

Cnr Melba Highway/Gulf Road, Yarra Glen, Vic 3775 **REGION** Yarra Valley
T (03) 9730 0700 **F** (03) 9730 2647 **WWW**.balgownieestate.com.au **OPEN** 7 days 10–5
WINEMAKER Tobias Ansted **EST.** 2004 **CASES** NA
Balgownie Estate opened a very attractive rammed-earth cellar door in 2004, offering the full range of Balgownie wines. The Yarra Valley range of Chardonnay, Pinot Noir, Shiraz and Cabernet Sauvignon are 100% Yarra Valley, using contract-grown grapes from several vineyards.

ŸŸŸŸ **Chardonnay 2004** Elegant, light-bodied, understated style; melon and nectarine fruit, minimal oak influence. Screwcap. 13.5° alc. **RATING** 89 **DRINK** 2008 **$** 19
Pinot Noir 2004 Good colour; powerful plummy fruit, but even more powerful tannins; patience may or may not reward. Screwcap. 13.5° alc. **RATING** 87 **DRINK** 2009 **$** 19

Balhannah Vineyards

Lot 100, Johnson Road, Balhannah, SA 5242 **REGION** Adelaide Hills
T (08) 8398 0698 **F** (08) 8398 0698 **OPEN** By appt
WINEMAKER Rod Short, Rachel Short **EST.** 1997 **CASES** 500
Rod and Rachel Short began the planting of 3 ha of shiraz, 2 ha of chardonnay, 1.5 ha of merlot and 1 ha of pinot noir in 1997. The first vintage was in 2002, made from 100% estate-grown grapes. Yields are limited to 1.5 to 2 tonnes per acre for the red wines, and 2 to 3 tonnes for the chardonnay. Most of the grapes are sold; the limited production is sold by mail order.

ŸŸŸŸŸ **Adelaide Hills Pinot Noir 2003** Light- to medium-bodied; fresh spice, plum and black cherry; persistent finish and aftertaste. Massive variation between two bottles tasted, one with brettanomyces. Cork. **RATING** 90 **DRINK** 2009 **$** 38

ŸŸŸŸ **Adelaide Hills Shiraz 2003** Lively, fresh, spicy, peppery red and black cherry fruits; elegant style, with a crisp finish. Cork. **RATING** 89 **DRINK** 2010 **$** 24
Adelaide Hills Merlot 2003 Savoury, earthy, olive, spice and game; fine tannins on a long aftertaste. Cork. **RATING** 89 **DRINK** 2009 **$** 19

Ballabourneen Wines

Talga Road, Rothbury, NSW 2320 **REGION** Lower Hunter Valley
T (02) 4930 7027 **F** (02) 4930 9180 **WWW**.ballabourneenwines.com.au **OPEN** Thurs–Sun 10–5, or by appt
WINEMAKER Alasdair Sutherland, Andrew Thomas **EST.** 1994 **CASES** 900
Between 1994 and 1998 Alex and Di Stuart established 2 ha of chardonnay, 1.5 ha of verdelho and 1 ha of shiraz. The viticulture uses natural sprays, fertilisers, mulches and compost, with a permanent sward maintained between the rows.

ŸŸŸŸŸ **The Stuart Hunter Valley Chardonnay 2004** Bright yellow-green; a very stylish wine, combining complexity (ex barrel fermentation) and finesse; has intriguing notes more often associated with cool-climate Chardonnay. Ageworthy. Screwcap. 13.5° alc. **RATING** 91 **DRINK** 2009 **$** 25
Hunter Valley Verdelho 2004 Light green-yellow; above-average intensity and length; complex multi-fruit flavours, with bracing acidity. Screwcap. 13.5° alc. **RATING** 90 **DRINK** Now **$** 20

Ballandean Estate NR

Sundown Road, Ballandean, Qld 4382 **REGION** Granite Belt
T (07) 4684 1226 **F** (07) 4684 1288 **WWW**.ballandeanestate.com **OPEN** 7 days 9–5
WINEMAKER Dylan Rhymer, Angelo Puglisi **EST.** 1970 **CASES** 12 000
The senior winery of the Granite Belt and by far the largest. The white wines are of diverse but interesting styles, the red wines smooth and usually well-made. The estate specialty, Sylvaner Late Harvest, is a particularly interesting wine of great character and flavour if given 10 years bottle age, but it isn't made every year.

Ballast Stone Estate Wines NR

Myrtle Grove Road, Currency Creek, SA 5214 **REGION** Currency Creek
T (08) 8555 4215 **F** (08) 8555 4216 **WWW**.ballaststone.com.au **OPEN** 7 days 10.30–4.30
WINEMAKER John Loxton **EST.** 2001 **CASES** 15 000
The Shaw family had been grapegrowers in McLaren Vale for 25 years before deciding to establish a large vineyard (250 ha) in Currency Creek in 1994. The vineyard is planted mainly to cabernet sauvignon and shiraz, with much smaller quantities of other trendy varieties. Only a small part of the production is sold under the Ballast Stone Estate label, most is sold in bulk. Exports to the UK and Germany.

Balnaves of Coonawarra ★★★★★

Main Road, Coonawarra, SA 5263 REGION Coonawarra
T (08) 8737 2946 F (08) 8737 2945 WWW.balnaves.com.au OPEN Mon–Fri 9–5, w'ends 12–5
WINEMAKER Peter Bissell EST. 1975 CASES 7500
Grapegrower, viticultural consultant and vigneron Doug Balnaves has 52 ha of high-quality estate vineyards. The pick of the crop is made by the immensely talented Pete Bissell in the winery built in 1996. The wines are invariably excellent, often outstanding. The wines are notable for their supple mouthfeel, varietal integrity, balance and length; the tannins are always fine and ripe, the oak subtle and perfectly integrated. Coonawarra at its best. Exports to all major markets.

ŸŸŸŸŸ **The Tally Reserve Cabernet Sauvignon 2004** An extra degree of fragrance above others of the year; while full-bodied, also has a dimension of elegance the others don't have; very sophisticated oak handling, long finish. Cork. 14.5° alc. RATING 96 DRINK 2025 $ 80
Shiraz 2004 Deep colour; complex wine; spice, pepper, blackberry, plum and quality oak all coalesce on both bouquet and palate; touches of chocolate too; fine, ripe tannins. Screwcap. 14.5° alc. RATING 94 DRINK 2014 $ 24
Cabernet Merlot 2004 Very deep colour; full-bodied, dense and powerful; layers of cassis, blackcurrant and blackberry fruit, and balanced but positive tannins. Cork. RATING 94 DRINK 2018 $ 24
Cabernet Sauvignon 2004 Typical colour of the Balnaves '04 reds; very concentrated, dense, full-bodied blackcurrant/blackberry fruit, with long, lingering tannins; high-quality oak in restrained support. Cork. RATING 94 DRINK 2024 $ 31

ŸŸŸŸ♡ **Chardonnay 2004** Typically polished Balnaves style; whole bunch-pressed; stone fruit interwoven with quality French oak and partial malolactic inputs. Screwcap. 13° alc. RATING 92 DRINK 2010 $ 28
Sparkling Cabernet NV Good mousse; a surprisingly fine and elegant palate; cedar, cassis and spice flavours, with no hint of phenolics requiring a high dosage to compensate; perfect balance. Lovely wine. RATING 91 DRINK 2008 $ 28

ŸŸŸŸ **The Blend 2004** Medium-bodied; bright berry fruits, although the tannins do stick to the gums more than usual for this wine. Screwcap. 14.5° alc. RATING 89 DRINK 2012 $ 19

Balthazar of the Barossa ★★★★☆

PO Box 675, Nuriootpa, SA 5355 REGION Barossa Valley
T (08) 8562 2949 F (08) 8562 2949 WWW.balthazarbarossa.com OPEN At the Small Winemakers Centre, Chateau Tanunda
WINEMAKER Anita Bowen EST. 1999 CASES 870
Anita Bowen announces her occupation as 'a 40-something sex therapist with a 17-year involvement in the wine industry': she is also the wife of a high-ranked executive with FWE. She undertook her first vintage at Mudgee, then McLaren Vale, and ultimately the Barossa; worked at St Hallet while studying at Roseworthy College. A versatile lady, indeed. As to her wine, she says, 'Anyway, prepare a feast, pour yourself a glass (no chalices, please) of Balthazar and share it with your concubines. Who knows? It may help to lubricate thoughts, firm up ideas and get the creative juices flowing!' Exports to all major markets.

ŸŸŸŸ♡ **Shiraz 2003** Elegant, medium-bodied wine; blackberry, plum, mocha and spice with a fluid line and fine tannins. Cork. 14.5° alc. RATING 93 DRINK 2010 $ 38

Bamajura NR

775 Woodbridge Hill Road, Gardners Bay, Tas 7112 REGION Southern Tasmania
T (03) 6295 0294 F (03) 6295 0294 OPEN By appt
WINEMAKER Scott Polley EST. 1987 CASES NA
Bamajura's name is derived from the first two letters of the names of the late Ray Polley and his sisters Barbara, Margaret and Judy. The vineyard was planted by Ray Polley, and son Scott took over in the early 1990s, assuming the winemaking mantle from Michael Vishacki.

🐿 Banca Ridge ★★★

2 McGlew Street, Stanthorpe, Qld 4380 **REGION** Granite Belt
T (07) 4681 5833 **F** (07) 4681 3416 **WWW**.bancaridge.eq.edu.au **OPEN** Mon–Fri 9–3
WINEMAKER Ravens Croft Wines **EST.** 2001 **CASES** 500
Banca Ridge is an initiative of the Stanthorpe State High School, which has established the first commercial school winery in Qld. It has 0.5 ha each of marsanne and merlot, and students are involved in all stages of the grape growing and winemaking process under the direction of Mark Ravenscroft (of Ravens Croft Wines and Robert Channon). It is designed to train students in the wine, hospitality and tourism industry, and the 3 wines produced are a credit to the school and the program.

ΨΨΨΨ **Granite Belt Marsanne 2003** Still remarkably fresh; gentle chalky/honeysuckle flavours; good balance. Cork. 11.5° alc. **RATING** 88 **DRINK** Now $16

ΨΨΨΨ **Granite Belt Merlot 2004** **RATING** 84 **DRINK** Now $16

ΨΨΨ **Tin Miner's Red NV** **RATING** 83 $12

Banks Road ★★★★

600 Banks Road, Marcus Hill, Vic 3222 **REGION** Geelong
T (03) 9822 6587 **F** (03) 9822 5077 **WWW**.banksroadwine.com.au **OPEN** By appt
WINEMAKER Justyn Baker, William Derham **EST.** 2001 **CASES** 1500
Banks Road, owned and operated by William Derham, has 2 vineyards: the first, 2.5 ha, is on the Bellarine Peninsula at Marcus Hill, planted to pinot noir and chardonnay; the second is at Harcourt in the Bendigo region, planted to 3 ha of shiraz and cabernet sauvignon, the vines ranging from 8 to 12 years of age. Winemaker Justyn Baker has dual degrees from Charles Sturt University, and has worked in the Hunter Valley, France and the Mornington Peninsula. There is a consistent theme of elegance to the Bendigo wines, perhaps reflecting Justyn Baker's winemaking experience in France.

ΨΨΨΨΨ **Bellarine Pinot Noir 2004** Complex but well-balanced wine; full of dark plum fruit; good length, structure and oak. **RATING** 92 **DRINK** 2011 $25
Bendigo Merlot 2003 Surprisingly elegant and distinctly varietal red berry fruits; fine tannins, subtle oak. Screwcap. 13° alc. **RATING** 90 **DRINK** 2011 $22
Bendigo Cabernet 2003 Good colour; here the cabernet sauvignon does work, with the fruit body to carry the tannins and extract; attractive cassis fruit and a balanced finish. Screwcap. 13.9° alc. **RATING** 90 **DRINK** 2013 $26

ΨΨΨΨ **Bendigo Shiraz 2003** Light- to medium red-purple; medium-bodied, with distinctly earthy/savoury edges to the blackberry fruit; softened by 20 months in oak. Screwcap. 13.8° alc. **RATING** 89 **DRINK** 2012 $26
Bendigo Cabernet Merlot 2003 Does not work as well as the varietal Merlot; slightly astringent tannins in the context of what is a light- to medium-bodied wine, taking the edge off the fruit. Screwcap. 13.5° alc. **RATING** 88 **DRINK** 2011 $26

Banks Thargo Wines ★★★☆

Racecourse Road, Penola, SA 5277 (postal) **REGION** Coonawarra
T (08) 8737 2338 **F** (08) 8737 3369 **OPEN** Not
WINEMAKER Banks Kidman, Jonathon Kidman **EST.** 1980 **CASES** 900
The unusual name comes directly from family history. One branch of the Kidman family moved to the Mt Gambier district in 1858, but Thomas Kidman (who had been in the foster care of the Banks family from the age of 2 to 13) moved to the Broken Hill/southwest Queensland region to work for the famous Kidman Bros pastoral interests. When he 'retired' from the outback, he bought this property, in 1919. His second son was named Banks Thargomindah Kidman, and it was he and wife Jenny who decided to diversify their grazing activities by planting vines in the 1980s: 16.5 ha are under contract, leaving 1.3 ha each of merlot and cabernet sauvignon for the Banks Thargo brand.

ΨΨΨΨ **Coonawarra Cabernet Sauvignon 2003** Elegant light- to medium-bodied wine; cassis blackcurrant fruit, positive oak, and fine-grained tannins. Cork. 14° alc. **RATING** 89 **DRINK** 2010 $18

ΨΨΨΨ **Coonawarra Merlot 2004** **RATING** 85 **DRINK** Now $15

Bannockburn Vineyards ★★★★★

Midland Highway, Bannockburn, Vic 3331 (postal) **REGION** Geelong
T (03) 5281 1363 **F** (03) 5281 1349 **WWW**.bannockburnvineyards.com **OPEN** Not
WINEMAKER Michael Glover **EST.** 1974 **CASES** 10 000
With the qualified exception of the Cabernet Merlot, which can be a little leafy and gamey, produces outstanding wines across the range, all with individuality, style, great complexity and depth of flavour. The low-yielding estate vineyards play their role. Incoming winemaker Michael Glover brings a wealth of experience to the job, and a determination to enhance the reputation of Bannockburn. Exports to the UK, Denmark, the US, Hong Kong, Singapore, NZ and Malaysia.

▼▼▼▼▼ Stuart Geelong Pinot Noir 2002 Typically rich, complex and intense; multiple layers of spice, forest, plum and black cherry flavours; excellent structure and mouthfeel; classic wine from a classic vintage. Cork. **RATING** 96 **DRINK** 2012 $ 47

Banrock Station ★★★

Holmes Road (off Sturt Highway), Kingston-on-Murray, SA 5331 **REGION** Riverland
T (08) 8583 0299 **F** (08) 8583 0288 **WWW**.banrockstation.com **OPEN** 7 days 10–5, except public hols
WINEMAKER Mark Zeppel, Paul Kassebaum **EST.** 1994 **CASES** 1.9 million
The $1 million visitor centre at Banrock Station was opened in February 1999. Owned by Hardys, the Banrock Station property covers over 1700 ha, with 240 ha of vineyard and the remainder being a major wildlife and wetland preservation area. The wines have consistently offered excellent value for money.

▼▼▼▼ The Reserve Shiraz 2003 Light- to medium-bodied; gentle black fruits and some extract; not complex, simply because at this price you can't expect that. Value. 13° alc. **RATING** 87 **DRINK** Now $ 12

▼▼▼▽ The Reserve Merlot 2003 RATING 86 **DRINK** Now $ 12
Shiraz Cabernet 2003 RATING 85 **DRINK** Now $ 7.20
Cabernet Merlot 2004 RATING 84 **DRINK** Now $ 12
The Reserve Pinot Noir Chardonnay NV RATING 84 $ 12

▼▼▼ White Shiraz 2005 RATING 83 $ 7.20
The Reserve Sparkling Shiraz NV RATING 83 $ 12
Crimson Cabernet 2005 RATING 82 $ 7.20

Baptista NR

c/- David Traeger, 139 High Street, Nagambie, Vic 3608 **REGION** Heathcote
T (03) 5794 2514 **F** (03) 5794 1776 **WWW**.baptista.com.au **OPEN** Mon–Fri 10–5, w'ends 12–5
WINEMAKER David Traeger **EST.** 1993 **CASES** 400
In 1993 David Traeger acquired a vineyard he had coveted for many years, and which had been planted by Baptista Governa in 1891. He has been buying grapes from the vineyard since 1988, but it was in a run-down condition, and required a number of years' rehabilitation before he felt the quality of the grapes was sufficient for a single-vineyard release. The business is jointly owned by David Traeger and the Wine Investment Fund, the latter a majority shareholder in Dromana Estate. Exports to the UK, Singapore and Japan.

Barak Estate NR

Barak Road, Moorooduc, Vic 3933 **REGION** Mornington Peninsula
T (03) 5978 8439 **F** (03) 5978 8439 **OPEN** W'ends & public hols 11–5
WINEMAKER James Williamson **EST.** 1996 **CASES** 500
When James Williamson decided to plant vines on his 4-ha Moorooduc property and establish a micro-winery, he already knew it was far cheaper to buy wine by the bottle than to make it. Undeterred, he ventured into grapegrowing and winemaking, picking the first grapes in 1993 and opening Barak Estate in 1996. Old telegraph poles, railway sleepers, old palings and timber shingles have all been used in the construction of the picturesque winery.

Barambah Ridge

NR

79 Goschnicks Road, Redgate via Murgon, Qld 4605 **REGION** South Burnett
T (07) 4168 4766 **F** (07) 4168 4770 **WWW**.barambahridge.com.au **OPEN** 7 days 10–5
WINEMAKER Winenet **EST.** 1995 **CASES** 10 000
Barambah Ridge, like Stuart Range, hit turbulent financial waters in 2005. Owned by an unlisted public company, it had an administrator appointed, and the 2005 vintage was made under the direction of leading wine consultancy business Winenet. Coupled with its high-quality 7 ha vineyard (some regard it as the best in South Burnett) top-quality wines were made, but attempts to sell the business as a going concern failed, with a break up of the assets likely.

Baratto's

NR

Farm 678, Hanwood, NSW 2680 **REGION** Riverina
T (02) 6963 0171 **F** (02) 6963 0171 **OPEN** 7 days 10–5
WINEMAKER Peter Baratto **EST.** 1975 **CASES** 6250
Baratto's is in many ways a throwback to the old days. Peter Baratto has 15 ha of vineyards and sells the wine in bulk or in 10 and 20 litre casks from the cellar door at old-time prices, from as little as a few dollars per litre.

Bare Rooted

NR

101 Broome Street, Cottesloe, WA 6011 (postal) **REGION** Margaret River
T (08) 9384 9764 **F** (08) 9385 3120 **OPEN** Not
WINEMAKER Contract **EST.** 1996 **CASES** 200
Ross and Jeannine Ashton planted 1 ha of sauvignon blanc in 1996, located on their 8-ha property surrounded by groves and avenues of poplars, cork oaks, deciduous trees, conifers, olives and eucalypts; a small frog-filled dam overlooks the vineyard. The quirky name comes from the fact that when vine rootlings are planted, they are devoid of any soil around their roots and are in a dormant phase.

Barfold Estate

★★★★☆

57 School Road, Barfold, Vic 3444 **REGION** Heathcote
T (03) 5423 4225 **F** (03) 5423 4225 **WWW**.barfoldestate.com.au **OPEN** 7 days 10–5
WINEMAKER Craig Aitken **EST.** 1998 **CASES** 900
Craig and Sandra Aitken acquired their farm property in the southwestern corner of the Heathcote wine region with the specific intention of growing premium grapes. They inspected more than 70 properties over the 18 months prior to purchasing Barfold, and are in fact only the second family to own the property since the 1850s. So far they have planted 3.8 ha of shiraz, and 0.4 ha of cabernet sauvignon; a small planting of viognier is planned for the future.

TTTTY **Heathcote Shiraz 2004** Medium- to full-bodied; velvety, rich blackberry, plum and spice, with restrained oak; has a certain elegance, though still in the shadow of the drought. Procork. 14.5° alc. **RATING** 93 **DRINK** 2014 $ 25
Heathcote Cabernet Sauvignon 2004 Massively powerful and concentrated brooding, black fruits, a touch of bitter chocolate, and powerful, rustic tannins. Time and prayer recommended. Cork. 14° alc. **RATING** 90 **DRINK** 2014 $ 25

TTTT **Heathcote Sparkling Shiraz 2004** A very big wine, but not overly oaky or sweet; 10 or so years cellaring well worth while. Cork. 13.1° alc. **RATING** 87 **DRINK** 2015 $ 20

🍇 Barmah Park Wines

★★★

945 Moorooduc Road, Moorooduc, Vic 3933 **REGION** Mornington Peninsula
T (03) 5978 8049 **F** (03) 5978 8088 **WWW**.barmahparkwines.com.au **OPEN** 7 days 10–5
WINEMAKER Ewan Campbell (Contract) **EST.** 2000 **CASES** 1800
Tony Williams planted 1 ha of pinot gris and 2 ha of pinot noir (using 2 clones, MV6 and G5V15), having the first vintage made in 2003. In December 2005 a substantial restaurant was opened,

offering breakfast in the vines up to 11.30am, and lunch from noon to 5pm. At this point, all of the production is sold through the cellar door and restaurant.

ΨΨΨΨ **Chardonnay 2004** Clean, fresh and direct; light- to medium-bodied stone fruit and a touch of citrus. Any oak is not obvious. Screwcap. 13.5° alc. **RATING** 89 **DRINK** 2008 $ 24

ΨΨΨΨ **Back Paddock Cabernet Sauvignon 2004** **RATING** 85 **DRINK** Now
Pinot Gris 2004 **RATING** 84 **DRINK** Now $ 25

Barnadown Run ★★★★

390 Cornella Road, Toolleen, Vic 3551 **REGION** Heathcote
T (03) 5433 6376 **F** (03) 5433 6386 **WWW.**barnadownrun.com.au **OPEN** 7 days 10–5
WINEMAKER Andrew Millis **EST.** 1995 **CASES** 1700
Named after the original pastoral lease of which the vineyard forms part, established on rich terra rossa soil for which Heathcote vineyards are famous. Owner Andrew Millis carries out both the viticulture and winemaking at the 5-ha vineyard. Exports to the US and the UK.

ΨΨΨΨΨ **Henry Bennett's Voluptuary 2003** Medium-bodied; nicely ripened juicy redcurrant, raspberry and cherry fruit; ripe tannins, minimal oak. Shiraz/Cabernet Sauvignon/Malbec. Cork. 15° alc. **RATING** 91 **DRINK** 2013 $ 45

ΨΨΨΨ **Heathcote Cabernet Sauvignon 2003** Firm, savoury overtones to the medium-bodied blackcurrant fruit; some colour development, likewise flavour. Cork. 14.5° alc. **RATING** 89 **DRINK** 2011 $ 29

ΨΨΨΨ **Heathcote Merlot 2003** **RATING** 86 **DRINK** 2010 $ 29

Barokes Wines ★★★

75 Cecil Street, South Melbourne, Vic 3205 (postal) **REGION** Warehouse
T (03) 9684 7121 **F** (03) 9690 8114 **WWW.**wineinacan.com **OPEN** Not
WINEMAKER Steve Barics **EST.** 1997 **CASES** 60 000
Barokes Wines packages its wines in aluminium cans. The filling process is patented, and has been in commercial production since 2003. The wines show normal maturation development, and none of the cans used since startup shows signs of corrosion. The wines are supplied in bulk by 7 large wineries in southeast Australia, with Peter Scudamore-Smith MW acting as consultant responsible for blending. The wines are perfectly adequate for the market they serve, and do not exhibit reduced characters and retail for $4.59 per can. Re-tasted 2006. Exports to all major markets.

Barossa Cottage Wines NR

Nuriootpa-Angaston Road, Angaston, SA 5353 **REGION** Eden Valley
T (08) 8562 3212 **F** (08) 8562 3243 **WWW.**barossawines.com.au **OPEN** Mon–Sat & public hols 10–4.30
WINEMAKER Rod Chapman **EST.** 1990 **CASES** NA
Heather and Ray Bartsch have been grapegrowers for over 20 years; they are descendants of Gottfried Harwig who settled in the Eden Valley in 1860, and have 26 ha of vines in the Eden Valley and 12 ha at Angaston. Most of the 300 tonnes of annual grape production is sold to others, but a small percentage is made into a modestly priced but wide range of wines.

Barossa Ridge Wine Estate ★★★☆

Light Pass Road, Tanunda, SA 5352 **REGION** Barossa Valley
T (08) 8563 2811 **F** (08) 8563 2811 **OPEN** By appt
WINEMAKER Marco Litterini **EST.** 1987 **CASES** 1500
A grapegrower turned winemaker with a small list of interesting red varietals, shunning the more common Rhone varietals and looking to Bordeaux. Increasing retail distribution in Australia; exports to Switzerland, Germany, Malaysia and Thailand.

ΨΨΨΨ **Rocky Valley Cabernet Sauvignon 2000** As might be expected, developed colour; mature, cedary/earthy cabernet characters; nicely balanced, and good length. Cork. 13.5° alc. **RATING** 90 **DRINK** 2010 $ 24.95

ΨΨΨΨ **Mardia's Vineyard Cabernet Franc 2003** Slightly dull colour; big, rich, dusty confit dark fruit, at the opposite end of the world to cabernet franc from the Great Southern, WA; flavour, not finesse. Cork. 14° alc. **RATING** 87 **DRINK** 2010 $24.95
Petit Verdot 2001 Savoury, earthy black fruits, and a tangy, fairly acidity, finish, possibly over acid-adjusted. Cork. 12° alc. **RATING** 87 **DRINK** 2011 $24.95

ΨΨΨ **Classic Barossa Valley Red 2003** **RATING** 85 **DRINK** Now $12

Barossa Settlers

NR

Trial Hill Road, Lyndoch, SA 5351 **REGION** Barossa Valley
T (08) 8524 4017 **F** (08) 8524 4519 **OPEN** 7 days 11–3
WINEMAKER Jane Haese **EST.** 1983 **CASES** 500
A superbly located cellar door (dating back to 1860) is the only outlet (other than mail order) for the wines from this excellent vineyard owned by the Haese family; the shiraz was planted in 1887. Most of the grapes from the 31-ha vineyard are sold to others.

Barossa Valley Estate

Seppeltsfield Road, Marananga, SA 5355 **REGION** Barossa Valley
T (08) 8562 3599 **F** (08) 8562 4255 **WWW**.bve.com.au **OPEN** 7 days 10–4.30
WINEMAKER Stuart Bourne **EST.** 1984 **CASES** 100 000
Barossa Valley Estate is owned by Hardys, marking the end of a period during which it was one of the last significant co-operative owned wineries in Australia. Across the board, the wines are full flavoured and honest. E&E Black Pepper Shiraz is an upmarket label with a strong reputation and following; the Ebenezer range likewise.

ΨΨΨΨΨ **E&E Black Pepper Shiraz 2002** Ripe black fruits with obvious mocha/vanilla oak; full-bodied blackberry and sweet chocolate flavours; good texture and weight; round, ripe tannins. Cork. 14.5° alc. **RATING** 95 **DRINK** 2017 $78
Ebenezer Shiraz 2002 Very well-integrated and balanced black fruits, oak and ripe tannins; an elegant, long finish. Cork. 14° alc. **RATING** 95 **DRINK** 2015 $28.50
Ebenezer Cabernet Sauvignon 2002 Holding red-purple hue well; an elegantly structured wine with classic blackcurrant varietal fruit and a touch of chocolate; long, fine, ripe tannins. Exceptional Barossa cabernet. Cork. 14° alc. **RATING** 95 **DRINK** 2017 $30

ΨΨΨΨ **Epiphany Chardonnay 2005** Light straw-green; altogether surprising elegance and intensity; melon/citrus fruit-driven through to an excellent finish; sensational value. Screwcap. 13.5° alc. **RATING** 90 **DRINK** 2008 $12
E&E Sparkling Shiraz 2002 Complex flavours of blackberry, earth, spice and some oak; long palate and finish; not too sweet. Cellaring recommended. 14.5° alc. **RATING** 90 **DRINK** 2012 $50

ΨΨΨΨ **Epiphany Shiraz 2002** Black cherry, spice, anise and bitter chocolate; good length, minimal oak. Cork. **RATING** 88 **DRINK** Now $13

ΨΨΨ **Epiphany Cabernet Merlot 2003** **RATING** 85 **DRINK** Now $13

Barratt

Uley Vineyard, Cornish Road, Summertown, SA 5141 **REGION** Adelaide Hills
T (08) 8390 1788 **F** (08) 8390 1788 **WWW**.barrattwines.com.au **OPEN** Mon, Wed–Fri 11.30–4, w'ends 11.30–5
WINEMAKER Lindsay Barratt **EST.** 1993 **CASES** 1800
Lindsay and Carolyn Barratt own 2 vineyards at Summertown: the Uley Vineyard and the Bonython Vineyard. They have 8.4 ha of vines; sauvignon blanc and merlot were added to the wine range from 2002. Part of the production from the vineyards is sold to other makers, with Jeffrey Grosset the maker of the Chardonnay and Reserve Pinot Noir. Arrangements were finalised for a winery facility at the Adelaide Hills Business and Tourism Centre at Lobethal in time for the 2003 vintage. Limited quantities are sold in the UK, Canada and Asia.

ŦŦŦŦŸ **The Reserve Pinot Noir 2004** Light red; plum and red fruit aromas; sweet though not heavy fruit; good texture and mouthfeel. Quality cork. 14° alc. **RATING** 93 **DRINK** 2009 $40

The Bonython Pinot Noir 2004 Shows considerable colour development; a light-bodied fragrant and perfumed cocktail of berries, forest and violets; super-fine tannins. Colour certainly suggests early consumption. Screwcap. 14° alc. **RATING** 92 **DRINK** 2009 $22

Piccadilly Valley Sauvignon Blanc 2005 Spotlessly clean; elegant, light passionfruit and gooseberry aromas; not intense, but perfectly balanced. Screwcap. 13.5° alc. **RATING** 90 **DRINK** Now $20

Piccadilly Valley Merlot 2003 Spicy savoury black olive aromas and flavours; appealingly soft in the mouth; finest imaginable tannins. Screwcap. 14.5° alc. **RATING** 90 **DRINK** 2008 $20

ŦŦŦŦ **Piccadilly Sunrise Rose 2005** Bright, light pink; gentle strawberry and rose petal aromas; very light-bodied, but has length and balance. Estate pinot noir. Screwcap. 13.5° alc. **RATING** 87 **DRINK** Now $19

Barrecas

South West Highway, Donnybrook, WA 6239 **REGION** Geographe
T (08) 9731 1716 **F** (08) 9731 1716 **OPEN** Fri–Mon 10–5 or by appt
WINEMAKER Iolanda Ratcliffe **EST.** 1994 **CASES** NA
Three generations of the Barreca family have been involved in winemaking, first in Italy and ultimately in Donnybrook. Third-generation Tony Barreca sold his orchard in 1994, using the proceeds to buy the site upon which he has since established 32 ha planted to a Joseph's Coat of 11 different varieties. Most of the grapes are sold under contract, but a small, modern winery onsite produces a limited amount of wine.

ŦŦŦŸ **Zinfandel 2005** Semi-conventional red wine with semi-conventional alcohol, especially for zinfandel; bright colour, bright red fruits; acidity dangerously high, but better than that of the Barbera which also carries an unbelievable 17.3° alcohol. Cork. 16.5° alc. **RATING** 86 **DRINK** 2012 $18

ŦŦŸ **Barbera 2005 RATING** 79 $14

Barretts Wines NR

Portland-Nelson Highway, Portland, Vic 3305 **REGION** Henty
T (03) 5526 5251 **OPEN** 7 days 11–5
WINEMAKER Rod Barrett **EST.** 1983 **CASES** 1000
Has a low profile, selling its wines locally, but deserves a far wider audience. The initial releases were made at Best's, but since 1992 all wines have been made (with increasing skill) on the property by Rod Barrett, emulating John Thomson at Crawford River Wines. The 5.5-ha vineyard is planted to riesling, pinot noir and cabernet sauvignon.

Barrgowan Vineyard

30 Pax Parade, Curlewis, Vic 3222 **REGION** Geelong
T (03) 5250 3861 **F** (03) 5250 3840 **OPEN** By appt
WINEMAKER Dick Simonsen **EST.** 1994 **CASES** 100
Dick and Dib (Elizabeth) Simonsen began the planting of their 0.5 ha of shiraz (with 5 clones) in 1994, intending to simply make wine for their own consumption. As all of the 5 clones are in full production, the Simonsens expect a maximum production of 200 cases, and have accordingly released small quantities of Shiraz, which sell out very quickly. The vines are hand-pruned, the grapes hand-picked, the must basket-pressed, and all wine movements are by gravity.

ŦŦŦŦŸ **Simonsen Shiraz 2004** Supple, smooth, medium-bodied wine, with red and black cherry fruit, and smooth oak and tannins. **RATING** 93 **DRINK** 2014 $30

Barringwood Park ★★★★

60 Gillams Road, Lower Barrington, Tas 7306 **REGION** Northern Tasmania
T (03) 6492 3140 **F** (03) 6492 3360 **www**.barringwoodpark.com.au **OPEN** Jan & Feb 7 days, March-Dec Wed–Sun & public hols 10–5
WINEMAKER Tamar Ridge **EST.** 1993 **CASES** 1600
Judy and Ian Robinson operate a sawmill at Lower Barrington, 15 mins south of Devonport on the main tourist trail to Cradle Mountain, and when they planted 500 vines in 1993 the aim was to do a bit of home winemaking. In a thoroughly familiar story, the urge to expand the vineyard and make wine on a commercial scale came almost immediately, and they embarked on a 6-year plan, planting 1 ha a year in the first 4 years (doing all the work themselves while also running their sawmill), and then built the cellar and tasting rooms during the following 2 years.

♀♀♀♀♀ **Mill Block Pinot Noir 2004** Concentrated and powerful plum and blackberry fruit, but not over-extracted, the fruit intensity from the vineyard. **RATING** 92 **DRINK** 2010 $ 24
North Bank Chardonnay 2004 A stylish wine, with good intensity, length and grip; fruit forward, but carried by that intensity. **RATING** 90 **DRINK** 2010 $ 20
Pinot Gris 2004 Rich, with full-on ripe fruit, but not too phenolic or sweet; has benefitted greatly from time in bottle. **RATING** 90 **DRINK** 2009 $ 22

♀♀♀♀ **Pinot Meunier 2004 RATING** 86 **DRINK** Now $ 18
Schonburger 2005 RATING 85 **DRINK** Now $ 22
Rose 2005 RATING 85 **DRINK** Now $ 17
Pinot Gris 2005 RATING 84 **DRINK** Now $ 22

♀♀♀ **IJ Pinot Noir Chardonnay 2002 RATING** 83 $ 28

Barrymore Estate NR

76 Tuerong Road, Tuerong, Vic 3933 **REGION** Mornington Peninsula
T (03) 5974 8999 **F** (03) 9789 0821 **www**.barrymore.com.au **OPEN** Not
WINEMAKER Peter Cotter **EST.** 1998 **CASES** 1500
Barrymore Estate is part of a much larger property first settled in the 1840s; the abundance of water and wetlands, with the confluence of the Devil Bend and Balcombe Creeks nearby, has sustained grazing and farming since the first settlement. Peter Cotter has planted 8.5 ha of pinot noir, 1 ha each of chardonnay and sauvignon blanc, and 0.5 ha of pinot gris, selling part of the grapes and making part under the Barrymore label.

Bartagunyah Estate NR

7 Survey Road, Melrose, SA 5483 **REGION** Southern Flinders Ranges
T (08) 8666 2136 **F** (08) 8666 2136 **www**.smartaqua.com.au/bartagunyah **OPEN** By appt
WINEMAKER Charles Melton, O'Leary Walker **EST.** 2000 **CASES** 2000
Rob and Christine Smart have established 3 ha of shiraz, 2 ha of cabernet sauvignon and 1 ha of viognier on a property adjoining the southern ridge of the beautiful and rugged Mt Remarkable. The Smarts offer 4-wheel drive and mountain bike tours to take in both the scenery and the abundant wildlife of the Flinders Ranges.

Barton Estate ★★★☆

45 Milford Street, Latham, ACT 2615 (postal) **REGION** Canberra District
T (02) 6254 6121 **F** (02) 6254 7606 **www**.bartonestate.com.au **OPEN** Not
WINEMAKER Brindabella Hills, Kyeema Estate **EST.** 1997 **CASES** 900
Bob Furbank and wife Julie Chitty are both CSIRO plant biologists, he is a biochemist (physiologist) and she a specialist in plant tissue culture. In 1997 they acquired the 120-ha property forming part of historic Jeir Station, and have since planted 8 ha to 15 varieties, the most substantial plantings to cabernet sauvignon, shiraz, merlot, riesling and chardonnay, the Joseph's Coat completed with micro quantities of other varieties. While involved to some degree in the winemaking, Roger Harris makes the unwooded white wine, Andrew McEwin the chardonnay and red wines.

ŸŸŸŸŸ **Riesling 2003** Glowing yellow-green; developed but intense lime juice and spice aromas and flavours; plenty of depth and richness. Screwcap. **RATING** 90 **DRINK** 2010

ŸŸŸŸ **Petit Verdot 2003** Attractive wine; clean, ripe, black and red fruit with a tangy edge; light tannins. Cork. **RATING** 89 **DRINK** 2010 $ 25
Semillon Sauvignon Blanc 2003 Soft, quite developed, toasty, honeyed overlay to sweet tropical fruit. Screwcap. **RATING** 88 **DRINK** Now $ 16
Chardonnay 2002 Light-bodied; well-balanced white peach and melon fruit with a touch of creamy malolactic influence; subtle oak. Cork. **RATING** 88 **DRINK** Now $ 10
Semillon Sauvignon Blanc 2004 Clean; while a 50/50 blend the herb, mineral and lanolin semillon component seems dominant; firm, dry finish. Screwcap. **RATING** 87 **DRINK** 2009 $ 16

ŸŸŸŸ **Shiraz 2002** **RATING** 86 **DRINK** Now $ 18
Merlot 2002 **RATING** 86 **DRINK** 2008 $ 18
Riesling 2004 **RATING** 85 **DRINK** 2008 $ 17
Sangiovese 2003 **RATING** 84 **DRINK** Now $ 15

Barwang Vineyard ★★★★☆

Barwang Road, Young, NSW 2594 (postal) **REGION** Hilltops
T (02) 6382 3594 **F** (02) 6382 2594 **www**.mcwilliams.com.au **OPEN** Not
WINEMAKER Jim Brayne, Martin Cooper, Russell Cody **EST.** 1969 **CASES** NFP
Peter Robertson pioneered viticulture in the Young region when he planted his first vines in 1969 as part of a diversification program for his 400-ha grazing property. When McWilliam's acquired Barwang in 1989, the vineyard amounted to 13 ha; today the plantings exceed 100 ha. Wine quality has been exemplary from the word go: always elegant, restrained and deliberately understated, repaying extended cellaring.

ŸŸŸŸŸ **Chardonnay 2005** In the typically tight, restrained style for which the wine is known; melon and stone fruit, subtle French oak; squeaky acidity. Screwcap. 13.5° alc. **RATING** 93 **DRINK** 2010 $ 19
Tumbarumba Chardonnay 2004 Super-fine, and super-elegant; light grapefruit and nectarine has absorbed the French oak in which it was matured; long and vibrant finish. **RATING** 93 **DRINK** 2014 $ 29
Cabernet Sauvignon 2001 Blackcurrant and blackberry fruit is supported by quality French oak on the bouquet; the palate has sweet, luscious fruit balanced by fine, savoury tannins. Has developed impressively in bottle. **RATING** 93 **DRINK** 2011 $ 24
Cabernet Sauvignon 2002 Holding hue well; typical savoury, earthy overtones to blackcurrant fruit; a certain austerity, but impressive nonetheless. Cork. **RATING** 91 **DRINK** 2015 $ 20

Barwick Wines

Yelverton North Road, Dunsborough, WA 6281 **REGION** Margaret River
T (08) 9755 7100 **F** (08) 9755 7133 **www**.barwickwines.com **OPEN** Wed–Mon & public hols 10.30–5
WINEMAKER Nigel Ludlow **EST.** 1997 **CASES** 120 000
The production gives some guide to the size of the operation. Since 1997 Barwick Wines has been supplying grapes and bulk wine to some of the best-known names in WA and the eastern states from three very large vineyards. The first is the 83-ha Dwalganup Vineyard in the Blackwood Valley region, the second the 38-ha St John's Brook Vineyard in the Margaret River, and the third the 73-ha Treenbrook Vineyard in Pemberton. Exports to the US and other major markets.

ŸŸŸŸŸ **Margaret River Sauvignon Blanc 2005** Clean bouquet; a rich mix of passionfruit and tropical fruits off-set by more herbal/mineral notes; nicely balanced. Screwcap. 12.5° alc. **RATING** 90 **DRINK** Now $ 18

ŸŸŸŸ **Margaret River Chardonnay 2005** Medium-bodied; complex but gentle barrel ferment/malolactic/lees inputs to soft nectarine and fig fruit. Screwcap. 13.5° alc. **RATING** 89 **DRINK** 2010 $ 18

Margaret River Shiraz 2004 Good colour; high-toned blackberry and raspberry fruit; the oak is a fraction edgy, but good all-up flavours. Screwcap. 14.5° alc. **RATING** 88 **DRINK** 2012 $18

Sauvignon Blanc Semillon 2005 Plenty of flavour from sweet sauvignon blanc tropical fruit and more reserved lemon and mineral characters from the semillon; sauvignon blanc is the flavour-driver. Screwcap. 12.5° alc. **RATING** 87 **DRINK** Now $15

Classic White 2005 Tangy, crisp, melon grass, and mineral; lively and fresh, good length. Chardonnay/Sauvignon Blanc/Semillon from southwest WA. Screwcap. 13° alc. **RATING** 87 **DRINK** Now $12

The Collectables Cabernet Sauvignon 2003 Similar mouthfeel to all of the Barwick red wines; has just a little more structure from savoury tannins; needs more flesh. Screwcap. 13.5° alc. **RATING** 87 **DRINK** 2009 $22

ŦŦŦ♀ The Collectables Shiraz 2003 Clean, bright red fruit and spice aromas; a very light-bodied palate, needing more flesh. Screwcap. 14° alc. **RATING** 86 **DRINK** 2010 $22

Margaret River Cabernet Sauvignon 2004 Clean, but very lightweight varietal redcurrant fruit; savoury tannins, minimal oak. Screwcap. 14° alc. **RATING** 86 **DRINK** Now $18

Chardonnay 2005 RATING 85 **DRINK** Now $15

Shiraz 2003 RATING 85 **DRINK** 2009 $15

Cabernet Sauvignon 2003 RATING 84 **DRINK** 2008 $15

ŦŦŦ Crush 2005 RATING 83 $12

Barwite Vineyards ★★★★

PO Box 542, Mansfield, Vic 3724 **REGION** Upper Goulburn
T 0408 525 135 **F** (03) 5776 9800 **WWW**.barwitevineyards.com.au **OPEN** Not
WINEMAKER Chrismont Wines (Warren Proft) **EST.** 1997 **CASES** 4000
David Ritchie and a group of fellow grape and wine enthusiasts established their substantial vineyard in 1997 on a slope facing the mouth of the Broken River and thereon to Mt Stirling. A little under 26 ha of pinot noir and 12 ha of chardonnay were planted for Orlando, to be used in sparkling wine. Given the reputation of the region for the production of aromatic white wines, 4.5 ha of riesling were also planted, the intention being to sell the grapes. However, since 2003 some of the best parcels have been kept aside for the Barwite label.

ŦŦŦŦ♀ Upper Goulburn Riesling 2004 Has developed magnificently over the past 12 months; fresh, lime blossom and mineral aromas; excellent balance, length and intensity; still very fine. **RATING** 93 **DRINK** 2010 $9.20

ŦŦŦŦ Upper Goulburn Riesling 2005 A mix of citrus, tropical and apple; the rich palate is fleshed out by a touch of residual sugar; could develop well with age. Screwcap. **RATING** 88 **DRINK** 2011 $14.60

Barwon Plains ★★★

61 Trebeck Court, Winchelsea, Vic 3241 **REGION** Geelong
T (03) 5267 2792 **F** (03) 5267 2792 **OPEN** By appt
WINEMAKER Phil Kelly **EST.** 1995 **CASES** 300
Phil and Merridee Kelly planted 1.5 ha of pinot noir, 1 ha of chardonnay and 0.2 ha of shiraz between 1995 and 1998. The Kellys personally carry out all of the vineyard and winery operations, selling most of the grape production to Shadowfax. The first commercial wine release under the Barwon Plains label was in 2000, and the wines have been medal winners at the Geelong Wine Show.

ŦŦŦŦ Geelong Chardonnay 2005 Crisp, clean and citrussy; headed towards Sauvignon Blanc in character; long, clean and linear. Screwcap. 13° alc. **RATING** 89 **DRINK** 2008 $14

ŦŦŦ♀ Geelong Rose 2005 RATING 85 **DRINK** Now $14

Geelong Pinot Noir 2004 RATING 85 **DRINK** Now $14

Geelong Shiraz 2004 RATING 84 **DRINK** 2008 $14

🐦 Barwon Ridge Wines   NR

50 McMullans Road, Barrabool, Vic 3221 **REGION** Geelong
T 0418 324 632 **F** (03) 9882 4587 **WWW**.barwonridge.com.au **OPEN** By appt
WINEMAKER Geoff Anson, Ken King **EST.** 1999 **CASES** 200
This is the venture of Geoff and Joan Anson, and Ken King (who also owns Kings of Kangaroo Ground and manages the Eltham post office out of his winery). The partners have established 3.6 ha of pinot noir, shiraz, chardonnay, marsanne and cabernet sauvignon on the northern side of a ridge above the Barwon River, overlooking the You Yangs and ultimately the plains towards Port Phillip. Drought conditions since 1999, and limited access to water, has meant that many vines had to be replaced, and the vineyard has grown slowly. In the meantime limited quantities of grapes sourced from Geelong vineyards are being purchased, and the wines made at the Kangaroo Ground winery by the partners.

Basedow   ★★★★

951 Bylong Valley Way, Baerami via Denman, NSW 2333 (postal) **REGION** Barossa Valley
T 1300 887 966 **F** (02) 6574 5164 **WWW**.basedow.com.au **OPEN** Not
WINEMAKER Peter Orr **EST.** 1896 **CASES** 20 000
An old and proud label, once particularly well known for its oak-matured Semillon, but which has changed hands on a number of occasions before passing into the ownership of James Estate in 2003. Continues making ultra-traditional styles, particularly the American-oaked Semillon which, while in no way reflecting the future direction for the variety in the Barossa, is a true-to-itself rock of ages. Exports to the UK and the US.

🍷🍷🍷🍷🍷 **Johannes Barossa Valley Shiraz 1999** Traditional Barossa Valley style; gentle black fruits and dark chocolate with lots of vanilla oak; soft tannins, and ready now. Diam. 14.5° alc. **RATING** 90 **DRINK** 2014 $ 70

🍷🍷🍷🍷 **Barossa Valley Semillon 2004** The traditional Basedow white burgundy style; while obvious, the oak is well-handled (partial barrel ferment and 4 months maturation); full-bodied, ready now, and not phenolic. Screwcap. 12.5° alc. **RATING** 89 **DRINK** 2008 $ 15

Basket Range Wines   NR

PO Box 65, Basket Range, SA 5138 **REGION** Adelaide Hills
T 0427 021 915 **F** (08) 8390 1515 **OPEN** Not
WINEMAKER Phillip Broderick **EST.** 1980 **CASES** 500
A tiny operation known to very few, run by civil and Aboriginal rights lawyer Phillip Broderick, a most engaging man with a disarmingly laid-back manner.

Bass Fine Wines   ★★★★☆

Upper McEwans Road, Rosevears, Tas 7270 **REGION** Northern Tasmania
T (03) 6331 0136 **F** (03) 6331 0136 **OPEN** Not
WINEMAKER Guy Wagner **EST.** 1999 **CASES** 4500
The business of Bass Fine Wines changed radically shortly prior to the 2006 vintage. Owner/winemaker Guy Wagner had been carrying on the business as a classic negociant (in Burgundian terms) originally buying wine from various vineyards in bottle and/or in barrel, but from 2000 also purchasing grapes, the wines made at other existing wineries. Prior to the 2006 vintage, he completed the construction of a new winery, at which he now makes his own wines, and offers contract winemaking services for others.

🍷🍷🍷🍷🍷 **Bass Strait Pinot Noir 2004** Good colour; sweet confit plum fruit; very generous and mouthfilling. Top gold medal Tasmanian Wine Show '06. **RATING** 94 **DRINK** 2010 $ 21

🍷🍷🍷🍷🍷 **Bass Strait Riesling 2005** Generous and intense lime/lemon/tropical fruit mix; good balance, length and focus. **RATING** 91 **DRINK** 2010 $ 21

🍷🍷🍷🍷 **Block 1 Pinot Noir 2004** Dense, inky over-the-top fruit and extract; a pinot noir for Parker. **RATING** 87 **DRINK** 2010 $ 32

Bass Phillip ★★★★★

Tosch's Road, Leongatha South, Vic 3953 **REGION** Gippsland
T (03) 5664 3341 **F** (03) 5664 3209 **OPEN** By appt
WINEMAKER Phillip Jones **EST.** 1979 **CASES** 1500
Phillip Jones has retired from the Melbourne rat-race to handcraft tiny quantities of superlative Pinot Noir which, at its best, has no equal in Australia. Painstaking site selection, ultra-close vine spacing and the very, very cool climate of South Gippsland are the keys to the magic of Bass Phillip and its eerily Burgundian Pinots.

ŶŶŶŶŶ **Premium Pinot Noir 2004** Good spicy aromas and a mix of predominantly red, and some black, fruits running through a particularly long, linear palate; definite echoes of Burgundy here. Cork. 12.9° alc. **RATING** 94 **DRINK** 2010 $ 110
Reserve Pinot Noir 2004 Developed colour; fragrant plums and spices, moving to dark fruits on the palate; selected (presumably) on the basis of structure, which is more evident, though still fine. Cork. 12.8° alc. **RATING** 94 **DRINK** 2012 $ 200

ŶŶŶŶŶ **Estate Pinot Noir 2004** Light- to medium-bodied, with supple and silky red fruits, minimal oak, and fine-grained tannins. **RATING** 92 **DRINK** 2012 $ 65

ŶŶŶŶ **Village Pinot Noir 2004** Light colour; a firm wine with spicy/savoury flavours, not especially complex, but is long in the mouth. **RATING** 89 **DRINK** 2009 $ 30

Bass Valley Estate Wines ★★☆

175 Nyora-St Helier Road, Loch, Vic 3945 **REGION** Gippsland
T (03) 5659 6321 **F** (03) 5659 0256 **OPEN** 7 days 10–6
WINEMAKER Robert Cutler, Roger Cutler **EST.** 1991 **CASES** NA
The Cutler family has established 3 ha of riesling, pinot noir, cabernet sauvignon and shiraz on the eastern slopes of the Bass River Valley. The cellar door has barbecue and picnic facilities which take full advantage of the expansive views over the Valley.

ŶŶŶŶ **Port NV** A surprise packet; good overall style, with an appropriately clean, dry finish; slightly raw spirit, but nonetheless in the direction of the best Australian examples of this style. **RATING** 88 **DRINK** Now

ŶŶŶŶ **Riesling 2004 RATING** 84 **DRINK** Now

ŶŶŶ **Chardonnay 2004 RATING** 82

Batista NR

Franklin Road, Middlesex, WA 6258 **REGION** Manjimup
T (08) 9772 3530 **F** (08) 9772 3530 **OPEN** By appt
WINEMAKER Bob Peruch **EST.** 1993 **CASES** 1200
Batista is in fact the baptismal name of owner Bob Peruch, a Pinot Noir devotee whose father planted 1 ha of vines back in the 1950s, although these have since gone. The estate has 2 vineyards, one for pinot noir and chardonnay, and the other (2 km away) for shiraz, cabernet sauvignon, cabernet franc and merlot. The well-drained soils are of quartz and ironstone gravel; yields are restricted to around 7 tonnes per ha.

battely wines ★★★★★

1375 Beechworth-Wangaratta Road, Beechworth, Vic 3747 **REGION** Beechworth
T (03) 5727 0505 **F** (03) 5727 0506 **WWW.**battelywines.com.au **OPEN** By appt
WINEMAKER Russell Bourne **EST.** 1998 **CASES** 450
Dr Russell Bourne is an anaesthetist and former GP at Mt Beauty, who has always loved the food, wine and skiing of northeast Victoria. He completed his oenology degree at Charles Sturt University in 2002 following his 1998 acquisition of the former Brown Brothers Everton Hills vineyard. He has since planted 1.6 ha of shiraz and viognier in the spring of 2001, with further Rhône Valley varietal plantings planned, including counoise. Since 2001 all wines made under the battely label have come from the estate vineyards, which have increased to 2.3 ha. Exports to the US, Denmark and Singapore.

ŦŦŦŦŦ **Beechworth Syrah 2004** Aromatic, complex spicy/earthy/savoury aromas; intense black cherry and plum fruit; long and powerful; fine tannins. Cork. 14.5° alc. **RATING** 94 **DRINK** 2017 $ 48

Battle of Bosworth

Edgehill Vineyards, Gaffney Road, Willunga, SA 5172 **REGION** McLaren Vale
T (08) 8556 2441 **F** (08) 8556 4881 **www**.battleofbosworth.com.au **OPEN** By appt
WINEMAKER Ben Riggs (Consultant) **EST.** 1996 **CASES** 2500
The 75-ha Edgehill Vineyard, established many years ago by Peter and Anthea Bosworth, was taken over by son Joch Bosworth in 1996. He set about converting 10 ha of shiraz, cabernet sauvignon and chardonnay to fully certified A-grade organic viticulture. The regime prohibits the use of herbicides and pesticides; the weeds are controlled by soursob, the pretty yellow flower considered a weed by many, which carpets the vineyards in winter, but dies off in early spring as surface moisture dries, forming a natural weed mat. But organic viticulture is never easy, and when Joch Bosworth moved to make the first wines from the vines, the Battle of Bosworth name was a neat take. Joch's partner, Louise Hemsley-Smith, runs the marketing and promotion side of the business. Exports to the UK, the US and other major markets.

ŦŦŦŦŦ **White Boar Shiraz 2004** Less purple than the McLaren Vale version; a much more spicy, savoury palate and less opulent fruit, with more regional chocolate, then fine tannins. Organically grown; more a style than quality choice. Cork. **RATING** 94 **DRINK** 2010 $ 45

ŦŦŦŦŦ **McLaren Vale Shiraz 2004** Strong purple-red, typical of the vintage; medium- to full-bodied succulent, opulent black fruits and a dash of chocolate and spice fill the mouth; well-controlled extract. Cork. 15° alc. **RATING** 93 **DRINK** 2011 $ 25
McLaren Vale Cabernet Sauvignon 2004 Strong colour; regional dark chocolate is the first aroma, then blackcurrant fruit switches on in abundance. Good structure, texture and balance. Cork. 14.5° alc. **RATING** 92 **DRINK** 2014 $ 25
McLaren Vale Shiraz 2003 Good colour; rich, medium- to full-bodied, archetypal McLaren Vale wine; ripe blackberry and chocolate and a touch of warmth. Cork. 14.5° alc.
RATING 91 **DRINK** 2012 $ 23.50

ŦŦŦŦ **McLaren Vale Chardonnay Viognier 2005** Generous fruit off-set by crisp acidity; well enough made but an androgynous blend. Screwcap. 13.5° alc. **RATING** 87 **DRINK** Now $ 19

Battunga Vineyards

NR

RSD 25A Tynan Road, Meadows, SA 5201 (postal) **REGION** Adelaide Hills
T (08) 8388 3866 **F** (08) 8388 3877 **OPEN** Not
WINEMAKER Robert Mann, Simon White **EST.** 1997 **CASES** A few
The development of this substantial vineyard venture began in 1997 under the direction of David Eckert. The plantings extend to pinot noir (7 ha), merlot (3.6 ha), sauvignon blanc (3.4 ha), chardonnay (2.3 ha), shiraz (2 ha), pinot gris (1.8 ha) and viognier (1.8 ha), but only a limited amount of wine is made and released under the Battunga Vineyards brand.

Baudin Rock Wines

NR

RSD 109, Kingston SE, SA 5275 (postal) **REGION** Mount Benson
T (08) 8768 6217 **F** (08) 8768 6217 **OPEN** Not
WINEMAKER Contract **EST.** 1997 **CASES** NA
The Ling family, headed by Robin Ling, began the development of Baudin Rock Wines in 1997, and now has 40 ha planted to sauvignon blanc, cabernet sauvignon, merlot and shiraz. Only a small amount of the wine is made under the Baudin Rock label, with most of the production sold.

Baxter Stokes Wines   NR

65 Memorial Avenue, Baskerville, WA 6065 **REGION** Swan Valley
T (08) 9296 4831 **F** (08) 9296 4831 **OPEN** 9.30–5 w'ends & public hols
WINEMAKER Greg Stokes **EST.** 1988 **CASES** 750
A weekend and holiday operation for Greg and Lucy Stokes, with the production sold by mail order
and through cellar door.

Bay of Fires

40 Baxters Road, Pipers River, Tas 7252 **REGION** Northern Tasmania
T (03) 6382 7622 **F** (03) 6382 7225 **WWW**.bayoffireswines.com.au **OPEN** 7 days 10–5
WINEMAKER Fran Austin **EST.** 2001 **CASES** 3000
In 1994 Hardys purchased its first grapes from Tas, with the aim of further developing and refining
its sparkling wines, a process which quickly gave birth to Arras. The next stage was the inclusion of
various parcels of chardonnay from Tas in the 1998 Eileen Hardy, then the development in 2001 of
the Bay of Fires brand, offering wines sourced from various parts of Tas. As one would expect, there is
great potential for the brand. The winery was originally that of Rochecombe, then Ninth Island, and
now, of course, Bay of Fires.

TTTTT Arras 2000 Pale green-straw, good mousse; intense aromas and an explosively intense
palate; mineral/nectarine/green apple/citrus flavours; a powerhouse, but with grace.
RATING 96 **DRINK** 2009 $ 49
Chardonnay 2004 Fresh, delicate, with an extremely long palate and finish, supported by
suitably restrained French oak. Cork. 13.1° alc. **RATING** 94 **DRINK** 2010 $ 27
Tigress Chardonnay 2004 A complex wine, with controlled barrel ferment inputs to
nectarine and peach fruit; balanced acidity. Cork. 12.9° alc. **RATING** 94 **DRINK** 2012 $ 21
Pinot Gris 2005 Rich and unusually complex, almost suggesting a touch of oak
somewhere in the process; the generosity does not lead either to heat or phenolics. Top
gold medal Tasmania Wine Show '06. Screwcap. 14° alc. **RATING** 94 **DRINK** 2008 $ 27

TTTTT Tigress Sauvignon Blanc 2005 Great length and intensity; a lovely mix of gooseberry,
grass and mineral flavours; good balance. Screwcap. 12.5° alc. **RATING** 93 **DRINK** Now
$ 21.50
Pinot Chardonnay 2001 Fine, pure; very good structure and focus; attractive pear, citrus
and stone fruit; lovely aftertaste. **RATING** 92 **DRINK** Now $ 28
Tigress Riesling 2005 Abundant intense lime fruit; good balance typical of the vintage.
Screwcap. 11.5° alc. **RATING** 91 **DRINK** 2011 $ 21.50
Non Vintage Pinot Noir Chardonnay NV Pale straw-green, good mousse; extremely fine,
delicate strawberry notes ex the pinot noir come through quite strongly; good length and
balance. **RATING** 91 **DRINK** Now $ 21.50
Riesling 2005 Ultimate manifestation of the vintage, with ultra-ripe and sweet tropical
fruit, partially balanced by lime-tingle acidity. Screwcap. 12° alc. **RATING** 90 **DRINK** 2009
$ 27
Gewurztraminer 2005 Pleasant mouthfeel; gentle spice and citrus, with good length and
balance; varietal character still a little subdued. Screwcap. 13° alc. **RATING** 90 **DRINK** 2009
$ 27
Tigress Rose 2005 Bright pale pink; strawberry and cherry fruit; delicious balance and
mouthfeel. Screwcap. 13.5° alc. **RATING** 90 **DRINK** Now $ 21.50
Tigress Pinot Noir 2004 Bright, clear colour; a pretty wine with gentle cherry and plum
fruit; fine, soft tannins, controlled oak. Screwcap. 13.3° alc. **RATING** 90 **DRINK** Now $ 25
Tigress Pinot Chardonnay NV Abundant, quite ripe and rich fruit, but avoids heaviness.
RATING 90 **DRINK** 2008 $ 21.50
Tigress Sparkling Rose NV Blush rose; well put together; crisp and lively, with small red
berry/strawberry nuances. **RATING** 90 **DRINK** Now $ 21.50

Bay of Shoals

NR

19 Flinders Avenue, Kingscote, Kangaroo Island, SA 5223 (postal) **REGION** Kangaroo Island
T (08) 8553 2229 **F** (08) 8553 2229 **OPEN** Not
WINEMAKER Bethany Wines **EST.** 1994 **CASES** 1000
John Willoughby's vineyard overlooks the Bay of Shoals, which is the northern boundary of Kingscote, Kangaroo Island's main town. Planting of the vineyard began in 1994, and has now reached 10 ha (riesling, chardonnay, sauvignon blanc, cabernet sauvignon and shiraz). In addition, 460 olive trees have been planted to produce table olives.

Bayview Estate

NR

365 Purves Road, Main Ridge, Vic 3928 **REGION** Mornington Peninsula
T (03) 5989 6130 **F** (03) 5989 6373 **WWW**.bayviewestate.com.au **OPEN** 7 days 11–7
WINEMAKER Dean Burford **EST.** 1980 **CASES** 10 000
Few enterprises have cast such a broad net over the tourist traffic in the Mornington Peninsula. The estate has The Pig and Whistle Tavern and cellar door, the 5-star Views Restaurant (which also serves 70 local and imported beers), an 80-seat beer garden, a produce store, fly fishing, antiques, and rose and lavender gardens. Almost incidental are the 7 ha of pinot gris, pinot noir and pinot grigio.

Beattie Wines

NR

53 Andrew Street, Windsor, Vic 3181 (postal) **REGION** Upper Goulburn
T 0411 187 871 **F** (03) 9682 3630 **OPEN** Not
WINEMAKER Brendon Beattie **EST.** 1998 **CASES** NA
Brendon Beattie has planted chardonnay, cabernet sauvignon and merlot at his Kanumbra vineyard. The small production is sold by mail order.

Beaumont Estate

★★★

Lot 20, 155 Milbrodale Road, Broke, NSW 2330 **REGION** Lower Hunter Valley
T 0419 616 461 **F** (07) 5474 3722 **OPEN** Not
WINEMAKER Scott Stephens (Contract) **EST.** 1999 **CASES** 1500
The estate vineyards were planted in September 1999 on the river flats of Parson Creek, nestled between the Yengo and Wollemi National Parks. The soils were enhanced with organic preparations; after 17 months the 2.2 ha of semillon and 1.3 ha of merlot produced a substantial crop, the vine growth, it is said, equivalent to 3 years under normal conditions. The intention is to continue the organic farming approach, and to eventually become certified biodynamic. Profits from wine sales will support a respite and natural therapies centre for limited life children that is currently being constructed on the property.

 Semillon 2005 Light straw-green; clean, fresh and gentle lemon and lemon rind and stoney flavours; not quite the impact expected of '05. Screwcap. **RATING** 88 **DRINK** 2010 $18

Rose 2005 RATING 85 **DRINK** Now $17
Merlot 2005 RATING 85 **DRINK** 2009 $19

Beckett's Flat

★★★★

Beckett Road, Metricup, WA 6280 **REGION** Margaret River
T (08) 9755 7402 **F** (08) 9755 7344 **WWW**.beckettsflat.com.au **OPEN** 7 days 10–6
WINEMAKER Belizar Ilic **EST.** 1992 **CASES** 8000
Bill and Noni Ilic opened Beckett's Flat in September 1997. Situated just off the Bussell Highway, midway between Busselton and the Margaret River, it draws upon 14 ha of estate vineyards, first planted in 1992. Since 1998 the wines have been made at the onsite winery. Exports to the UK, Singapore and Canada.

 Belizar's Sauvignon Blanc 2005 Light green-straw; a clean bouquet, the palate opening with gooseberry, passionfruit, tropical fruit then underpinned by crisp acidity. Screwcap. 13° alc. **RATING** 90 **DRINK** Now $16

Beckingham Wines

6–7/477 Warrigal Road, Moorabbin, Vic 3189 **REGION** Mornington Peninsula
T (03) 9258 7352 **F** (03) 9360 0713 **WWW**.beckinghamwines.com.au **OPEN** W'ends 10–5
WINEMAKER Peter Beckingham **EST.** 1998 **CASES** 3500
Peter Beckingham is a chemical engineer who has turned a hobby into a part-time business, moving operations from the driveway of his house to a warehouse in Moorabbin. The situation of the winery may not be romantic, but it is eminently practical, and more than a few winemakers in California have adopted the same solution. His friends grow the grapes, and he makes the wine.

TTTTT **Reserve Sunbury Shiraz 2003** Good colour, bright red-purple; a light- to medium-bodied palate, with gently sweet red fruits, touches of spice and soft tannins. Cork. 14° alc. **RATING** 90 **DRINK** 2010 $ 25

TTTT **Chardonnay Liqueur NV** Barely fermented; cleverly made, with good fortifying spirit; likewise, deliberate oxidation in the winemaking process adds complexity. **RATING** 88 **DRINK** Now $ 11
Edgehill Chardonnay 2004 Solid stone fruit flavours supported by prolonged lees contact but no oak; developing nicely. Cork. 14.5° alc. **RATING** 87 **DRINK** 2008 $ 18
Cornelia Creek Shiraz 2002 Light- to medium-bodied; strongly savoury/earthy-accented fruit with some oak sweetening; does reflect the good vintage. Swan Hill. Cork. 14° alc. **RATING** 87 **DRINK** 2009 $ 28
Strathbogie Shiraz 2000 Mature, savoury/spicy/cedary/chocolate/mocha overtones to medium-bodied blackberry fruit. Cork. **RATING** 87 **DRINK** 2008 $ 25
Pas de Deux Methode Champenoise 1999 The oak in the base wine gives rise to hay/straw aromas, but the palate is fine enough, and, overall, the wine is still youthful. 11.5° alc. **RATING** 87 **DRINK** Now $ 22

TTTT **Strathbogie Cabernet 1999** **RATING** 86 **DRINK** Now $ 20
Pas de Deux Methode Champenoise 2003 **RATING** 86 **DRINK** Now $ 22
Strathbogie Shiraz 2001 **RATING** 85 **DRINK** Now $ 25
Cornelia Creek Cabernet 2001 **RATING** 85 **DRINK** 2008 $ 18
Botrytis Affected Heathcote Riesling 2000 **RATING** 85 **DRINK** Now $ 20
White Pinot 2005 **RATING** 84 **DRINK** Now $ 15
Cornelia Creek Shiraz 2001 **RATING** 84 **DRINK** Now $ 18

Beechwood Wines   NR

PO Box 869, Echuca, Vic 3564 **REGION** Goulburn Valley
T (03) 5482 4276 **F** (03) 5482 1185 **OPEN** Not
WINEMAKER Gavin Beech **EST.** 1995 **CASES** NA
The Beech family (headed by Gavin and Keith) have planted 4.5 ha of verdelho, shiraz and cabernet sauvignon. There are no cellar door facilities; the wine is distributed by Brian Downie.

Beelgara Estate

Farm 576 Rossetto Road, Beelbangera, NSW 2680 **REGION** Riverina
T (02) 6966 0200 **F** (02) 6966 0298 **WWW**.beelgara.com.au **OPEN** Mon–Sat 10–5, Sun 11–3
WINEMAKER Belinda Morandin, Andrew Schulz, Danny Toaldo, Sean Hampel **EST.** 1930 **CASES** 700 000
Beelgara Estate was formed in 2001 after the purchase of the 60-year-old Rossetto family winery by a group of growers, distributors and investors. The name Beelgara is a contraction of Beelbangera. The new management is placing far greater emphasis on bottled table wine (albeit at low prices), spreading its wings to premium regions, but still maintaining excellent value for money.

TTTTT **Pepperton Estate Adelaide Hills Sauvignon Blanc 2004** Very pale straw-green; delicate, pure, still very fresh and clearly delineated grass, herb, passionfruit and gooseberry; bright finish. Screwcap. 12.5° alc. **RATING** 92 **DRINK** Now $ 20
Pepperton Estate Two Thumbs Sauvignon Blanc 2005 Spotlessly clean and well-balanced; gentle tropical, gooseberry, passionfruit and grass; way above its station. Fantastic value. Screwcap. 12° alc. **RATING** 91 **DRINK** Now $ 14

Bianca Sun Dried Botrytis Semillon 2004 Lusciously rich and sweet; a mix of apricot, cumquat, pineapple and citrus; the flavour due to botrytis, and not sundried fruit, despite the curious name. Cork. 11° alc. RATING 91 DRINK 2008 $20

The Gun Shearer Coonawarra Cabernet Sauvignon 2003 Earthy, cedary, savoury classic Coonawarra cabernet as it starts to move from its primary phase, though still with cassis fruit; good structure and length. Cork. 14° alc. RATING 90 DRINK 2015 $20

♥♥♥♥ **The Gun Shearer Margaret River Chardonnay 2004** Light- to medium-bodied; peach and nectarine fruit with a nice touch of lees and oak; well-balanced. Screwcap. 13.5° alc. RATING 89 DRINK 2008 $20

Pepperton Estate Coonawarra Cabernet Sauvignon 2003 Attractive, fresh, juicy berry cassis blackcurrant; a slight jab of what may be an element of volatile acidity. Cork. 14° alc. RATING 89 DRINK 2012 $20

Chardonnay 2004 Plenty of melon and stone fruit; good length, with minimal oak influence; a faint hint of sweetness driven by the market. Screwcap. 13.5° alc. RATING 88 DRINK 2008 $9

Rascal's Prayer Old Vine Shiraz 2004 Well-made; light- to medium-bodied plum, blackberry and chocolate; not complex but flavoursome, with a twitch of sweetness. Screwcap. 14° alc. RATING 87 DRINK Now $15

Shiraz 2004 Medium-bodied; a mix of red and black fruits carry the alcohol quite well; ripe tannins and a whisk of oak. Screwcap. 15° alc. RATING 87 DRINK 2010 $15

Shiraz Cabernet 2005 Bright, lively and fresh cassis, plum and cherry fruit; fine tannins, well-made. Screwcap. 14° alc. RATING 87 DRINK Now $9

Rascal's Prayer Cabernet Merlot 2004 Bright, clear red-purple; firm blackcurrant and cassis fruit; plenty of life. Screwcap. 14° alc. RATING 87 DRINK 2008 $14

Pepperton Estate Two Thumbs Cabernet Merlot 2004 Light- to medium-bodied; lively, clean, fresh red fruits; ready right now. Screwcap. 14° alc. RATING 87 DRINK 2008 $14

♥♥♥♡ **Unoaked Chardonnay 2004** Light, fresh nectarine and peach; unforced wine, the alcohol balanced. Screwcap. 13.5° alc. RATING 86 DRINK 2008 $12

Pepperton Estate Goodwyn Chardonnay 2004 RATING 86 DRINK Now

Cabernet Rose 2005 RATING 86 DRINK Now $15

Petit Verdot 2003 Powerful black fruits; lots of heavy duty tannins. Screwcap. 14.5° alc. RATING 86 DRINK Now $15

Pepperton Estate Goodwyn Semillon Sauvignon Blanc 2005 RATING 85 DRINK Now $15

Shiraz 2005 RATING 85 DRINK Now $9

Pepperton Estate Goodwyn Shiraz Cabernet 2004 RATING 85 DRINK 2008

Sun Dried Liqueur Muscat NV RATING 85 DRINK Now $20

Semillon Sauvignon Blanc 2005 RATING 84 DRINK Now $9

Rascal's Prayer Verdelho 2005 RATING 84 DRINK Now $15

Cabernet Merlot 2004 RATING 84 DRINK Now $12

♥♥♥ **Rascal's Prayer Sauvignon Blanc 2005** RATING 83 $14

Rascals Prayer Chardonnay 2004 RATING 83 $14

Merlot 2005 RATING 83 $9

Pepperton Estate Goodwyn Cabernet Merlot 2003 RATING 83

Beer Brothers

NR

Pheasant Farm Road, Nuriootpa, SA 5355 REGION Barossa Valley
T (08) 8562 4477 F (08) 8562 4757 www.maggiebeer.com.au OPEN 7 days 10–5
WINEMAKER Contract EST. 1997 CASES 500
Yes, they really are Beer brothers, and, yes, they grow grapes and make wine, not beer. The brothers in question are Colin Beer (brother of famed chef and author Maggie Beer) and Bruce, who became a partner in the grapegrowing business in 1987. Ten years later they decided to venture into winemaking, using the team at Yalumba (to whom they sell the lion's share of the grape production); after selling some of the 40-year-old Barossa shiraz to Rockford for inclusion in the Basket Press Red, they persuaded Dave Powell (of Torbreck) to make Old Vine Barossa Shiraz.

Belalie Bend ★★★

Mannanarie Road, Jamestown, SA 5491 **REGION** Southern Flinders Ranges
T (08) 8664 1323 **F** (08) 8664 1923 **www.**belaliebend.com.au **OPEN** Future opening
WINEMAKER Emma Bowley **EST.** 2001 **CASES** 350
Emma Bowley obtained her wine science degree from Charles Sturt University, and after a varied career working for large Australian wine companies, and thereafter in the US and Italy, decided to turn her attention to smaller wineries where she could have a hands-on winemaking role. Thus she works as a contract winemaker in the Clare Valley, while she and husband Guy have established a vineyard in Jamestown situated beneath Mount Remarkable at an elevation of over 400m. One ha each of shiraz, cabernet sauvignon and riesling were planted in 2001, followed by 1.5 ha each of mourvedre and shiraz the following year. Until these vines come into production, Emma Bowley is making wines from Clare Valley grapes for the Belalie Bend label. She and Guy are both working to develop tourism in this emerging region.

🍷🍷🍷🍷🍷 **Connection Clare Valley Shiraz Cabernet 2002** Attractive medium-bodied wine; a mix of ripe black fruits and more spicy/savoury/cedary notes; good tannin structure, likewise oak. **RATING** 90 **DRINK** 2012 $20

🍷🍷🍷🍷 **Jamestown Southern Flinders Ranges Riesling 2004** **RATING** 85 **DRINK** Now $16

🍷🍷🍷 **Jamestown Southern Flinders Ranges Sangiovese 2004** **RATING** 79 $18

Belgenny Vineyard NR

92 De Beyers Road, Pokolbin, NSW 2320 (postal) **REGION** Lower Hunter Valley
T (02) 9247 5300 **F** (02) 9247 7273 **www.**belgenny.com.au **OPEN** Not
WINEMAKER Monarch Winemaking Services **EST.** 1990 **CASES** 7000
In 1999 partners Norman Seckold and Dudley Leitch realised a long-held ambition to establish a vineyard in the Hunter Valley with the acquisition of their 17-ha site. Plantings have steadily increased and are presently chardonnay (5.7 ha), shiraz (4.9 ha), merlot (2 ha), semillon (1.2 ha) and a carefully thought out marketing strategy has been put in place. Exports to Hong Kong and Singapore.

Belgravia Vineyards ★★★★

84 Byng Street, Orange, NSW 2800 **REGION** Orange
T (02) 6361 4441 **F** (02) 6365 0646 **www.**belgravia.com.au **OPEN** Sun–Thurs 10–8, Fri–Sat 10-late
WINEMAKER David Lowe, Jane Wilson (Contract) **EST.** 1996 **CASES** 6000
Belgravia is an 1800-ha mixed farming property (sheep, cattle and vineyards) 20 km north of Orange. The first plantings took place in 1996, and there are now 190 ha with 10 ha devoted to the Belgravia brand. In 2006 Belgravia opened its cellar door at the heritage-listed former Union Bank building in Orange, which also operates as a wine bar with an all-day tapas menu. Exports to the UK and Denmark.

🍷🍷🍷🍷🍷 **Chardonnay 2004** Fragrant melon, stone fruit and grapefruit lead into an elegant and long, fruit-focused palate. Screwcap. **RATING** 92 **DRINK** 2009 $18

🍷🍷🍷🍷 **Merlot 2004** A spicy, savoury bouquet, then a palate with a mix of cassis and black fruits plus a touch of black olive; medium-bodied, but quite powerful. Screwcap. **RATING** 89 **DRINK** 2010 $18

Bell River Estate NR

Mitchell Highway, Neurea, NSW 2820 **REGION** Central Ranges Zone
T (02) 6846 7277 **F** (02) 6846 7277 **www.**bellriverestate.com.au **OPEN** 7 days 9–6
WINEMAKER Sandra Banks **EST.** 1974 **CASES** 500
Situated 15 km south of Wellington, Bell River Estate was formerly known as Markeita Cellars, the name change due to its purchase by Michael and Sandra Banks. They have 2.5 ha of grenache, cabernet sauvignon, shiraz and muscat, and as well as producing Bell River Estate wines, offer bottling, contract winemaking and viticultural services.

Bell's Lane Wines

NR

Mangoola Road, Denman, NSW 2328 **REGION** Upper Hunter Valley
T (02) 6547 1191 **F** (02) 6547 1191 **OPEN** W'ends 10–5, or by appt
WINEMAKER Hunter Wine Services (John Hordern) **EST.** 1998 **CASES** NA
In the words of Paul and Megan Melville, 'we were a typical hardworking Sydney couple, but we were tired of the daily slog of city life and conversations about real estate prices, so we uprooted the kids, sold the house, cleared the land and started planting the vines — 30 000 in all'. Thus was born Bell's Lane Vineyard, 3 km from Denman, in 1998. A dilapidated dairy on the property has been converted to a cellar door, which serves light lunches on weekends.

Bella Ridge Estate

★★★★

78 Campresic Road, Herne Hill, WA 6056 **REGION** Swan District
T (08) 9250 4962 **F** (08) 9246 0244 **OPEN** By appt
WINEMAKER Alon Arbel **EST.** 2003 **CASES** 2000
Alon Arbel came to WA from Israel in search of strong, easterly sea breezes to power his passion for windsurfing. Here he met wife-to-be, Jodi, and, after working overseas and travelling, they returned to Perth to live. A year out from completing a degree in engineering, Alon switched to Curtin University's oenology and viticulture course, which he duly completed. Entirely fortuitously, Jodi's parents, Frank and Lois, discovered a 10-ha property (8 ha under vine) on the foothills of the Darling Scarp, with plantings dating back to 1966. The July 2003 purchase of the property was a couple of months after the birth of their first child, and a couple of months before the commencement of the 2004 vintage, by which time they had managed to erect a 30-tonne winery, crushing 20 tonnes of fruit for their own label, and 10 tonnes for contract clients. Since then they have grafted the plantings to an ultra-eclectic mix, which includes 2 Japanese grapes, kyoho and madonna. Further grafting is underway, and they also buy a pinot noir sparkling base from Denmark, and in 2005 produced a Margaret River Chardonnay. Fast work.

ΨΨΨΨΨ **Shiraz 2004** Attractive medium-bodied black cherry and plum fruit; round and supple; good balance of oak and extract. Screwcap. 14.5° alc. **RATING** 90 **DRINK** 2012 **$** 26

ΨΨΨΨ **Cabernet Shiraz 2004** Well-balanced, medium-bodied mix of blackcurrant, blackberry and a touch of chocolate; good tannin structure. Screwcap. 14° alc. **RATING** 89 **DRINK** 2014 **$** 18

ΨΨΨΨ **Chenin Blanc 2004** **RATING** 85 **DRINK** Now **$** 18

Bellarine Estate

NR

2270 Portarlington Road, Bellarine, Vic 3222 **REGION** Geelong
T (03) 5259 3310 **F** (03) 5259 3393 **www.**bellarineestate.com.au **OPEN** 7 days 10–4
WINEMAKER Scotchmans Hill **EST.** 1995 **CASES** 7000
A substantial business, with 4 ha each of chardonnay and pinot noir, 3 ha of shiraz (producing an excellent wine with a dash of viognier), 1 ha of merlot and 0.5 ha each of pinot gris and viognier. The wines are made by Robin Brockett at Scotchmans Hill. Bella's restaurant is open for lunch 7 days and dinner on Friday and Saturday evenings.

Bellarmine Wines

★★★★★

PO Box 1450, Manjimup, WA 6258 **REGION** Pemberton
T (08) 9776 0667 **F** (08) 9776 0657 **www.**bellarmine.com.au **OPEN** Not
WINEMAKER Mike Bewsher, Tam Bewsher, Robert Paul (Consultant) **EST.** 2000 **CASES** 4000
This substantial operation is owned by German residents Dr Willi and Gudrun Schumacher. Long-term wine lovers, with a large personal wine cellar, the Schumachers decided to take the next step by establishing a vineyard and winery of their own, using Australia partly because of its stable political climate. The venture is managed by Mike and Tam Bewsher, both of whom have extensive knowledge of the wine industry in both Pemberton and Mudgee. There are 20 ha of chardonnay, riesling, sauvignon blanc, pinot noir, shiraz, merlot and petit verdot.

ΨΨΨΨΨ **Pemberton Riesling Dry 2005** As the name indicates, fermented to dryness; very good structure with lime and mineral; excellent length. Screwcap. 13.1° alc. **RATING** 94 **DRINK** 2015 **$** 15

Pemberton Riesling 2005 Delicious cool climate style with much of the lime juice flavour of Mosel spatlese; great aperitif or Chinese food match. Slightly lower alcohol would be even better again. Screwcap. 12.8° alc. **RATING** 94 **DRINK** 2010 $15

Pemberton Chardonnay 2005 A touch of spicy oak on the bouquet, but intense and lively nectarine and grapefruit then takes over on the very long palate; excellent finish and aftertaste. Fantastic value. Screwcap. 13.6° alc. **RATING** 94 **DRINK** 2011 $15

ŸŸŸŸŸ **Pemberton Riesling Dry 2004** Good wine; doesn't quite have the length and drive of the '05s but is still developing; similar lime, apple and mineral components. Screwcap. 12° alc. **RATING** 92 **DRINK** 2014 $15

Pemberton Pinot Noir 2005 Strong purple-red, bright and clear; powerful black cherry and plum; quite firm finish; needs and will repay cellaring. Great value. Screwcap. 14.5° alc. **RATING** 90 **DRINK** 2010 $15

ŸŸŸŸ **Pemberton Sauvignon Blanc 2005** Water white colour; delicate, fresh, crisp light-bodied wine; well-made, though lacks varietal intensity. Screwcap. 13.7° alc. **RATING** 87 **DRINK** Now $15

ŸŸŸŸ **Bellarmino Chardonnay Pinot 2005** **RATING** 86 **DRINK** Now $15

Bellbrae Estate ★★★★

520 Great Ocean Road, Bellbrae, Vic 3228 **REGION** Geelong
T (03) 5264 8480 **F** (03) 5222 6182 **WWW**.bellbraeestate.com.au **OPEN** W'ends 11–5 (winter), Thurs–Mon 11–5 (summer)
WINEMAKER Matthew di Sciascio, Peter Flewellyn **EST.** 1999 **CASES** 1800
Bellbrae Estate (and the Longboard Wines brand) is the venture of friends Richard Macdougall and Matthew di Sciascio, both with strong family connections to the nearby beach and surfing. Sharing a common love of wine, surf and coastal life, they decided to establish a vineyard and produce their own wine. In 1998 Richard Macdougall purchased a small sheep grazing property with 8 ha of fertile, sheltered north-facing slopes on the Great Ocean Road near Bellbrae, and with Matthew's help as business associate, Bellbrae Estate was born. Since 2003 all the wines have been Geelong-sourced, and include estate Shiraz and Pinot Noir.

ŸŸŸŸŸ **Longboard Shiraz 2004** Medium-bodied; ripe blackberry fruit with touches of licorice and chocolate; gently fleshy, very good silky mouthfeel. Screwcap. 14.5° alc. **RATING** 93 **DRINK** 2014 $25

Longboard Chardonnay 2004 Fine, elegant and intense; stone fruit, citrus and melon with gentle oak; long finish. Screwcap. 13° alc. **RATING** 91 **DRINK** 2010 $19

ŸŸŸŸ **Longboard Sauvignon Blanc Semillon 2005** Highly flowery blossom and spice; long, clean and crisp. **RATING** 88 **DRINK** 2009 $17

Longboard Shiraz 2004 Light- to medium-bodied; attractive spicy red cherry fruit with a touch of mint, in typical cool climate style. Screwcap. 14° alc. **RATING** 88 **DRINK** 2010 $19

Longboard Rose 2005 Quite fragrant; strawberry fruit with a cleverly balanced touch of sweetness which does not cloy. **RATING** 87 **DRINK** Now $17

ŸŸŸŸ **Longboard Pinot Noir 2004** Light- to medium-bodied; cherry, red plums and spice, but with stemmy/green characters suggesting the grapes were not entirely ripe. Screwcap. 13.5° alc. **RATING** 86 **DRINK** 2008 $19

Wally's Shiraz Roussanne 2004 **RATING** 85 **DRINK** Now $17

Bellvale Wines ★★★★★

Forresters Lane, Berrys Creek, Vic 3953 **REGION** Gippsland
T (03) 5668 8230 **F** (03) 5668 8230 **WWW**.bellvalewine.com.au **OPEN** By appt
WINEMAKER John Ellis **EST.** 1998 **CASES** 2000
John Ellis, in this instance, is the third under this name to be actively involved in the wine industry. His background as a former 747 pilot, and the knowledge he gained of Burgundy over many visits, sets him apart from the others. In 1998 he established 10 ha of pinot noir and 3 ha of chardonnay on the red soils of a north-facing slope on the property. He chose a density of 7150 vines per ha,

following as far as possible the precepts of Burgundy, but limited (as are so many) by tractor size, which precludes narrower row spacing and thus even higher plant density. Exports to the US, Singapore and Hong Kong.

🍷🍷🍷🍷🍷 **Gippsland Pinot Noir 2004** Typical strong colour; excellent dark plum, black cherry and spice aromas, the palate following down the same track; has the structure to age for longer than most. 12.6° alc. **RATING** 95 **DRINK** 2012 $ 33

🐌 Belvoir Park Estate ★★★☆

39 Belvoir Park Road, Big Hill, Vic 3453 **REGION** Bendigo
T (03) 5435 3075 **WWW**.belvoirparkwines.com.au **OPEN** W'ends & public hols 11–5
WINEMAKER Ian Hall, Achilles Kalanis **EST**. 1997 **CASES** 800
Ian Richard and Julie Ann Hall have established 2 ha of shiraz and 0.5 ha of cabernet sauvignon on deep, granite-based soils. As is common with small winery vineyards, the vines are hand-pruned and all the grapes hand-picked, followed by small batch processing in the winery via open fermenters and a basket press.

🍷🍷🍷🍷 **Bendigo Shiraz 2004** Spice, licorice, anise and herb components to the bouquet; not quite enough mid-palate fruit, and savoury tannins. Diam. 13° alc. **RATING** 89 **DRINK** 2012 $ 25

Bendigo Merlot 2004 Very ripe, luscious fruit, saying much more about the region and alcohol than the variety; a bit less would be much better. Diam. 14.3° alc. **RATING** 87 **DRINK** 2010 $ 22

The Symposiarch 2004 A complex array of aromas and flavours not all pulling in the same direction, but ultimately held together by the tannins on the finish. Like all the wines, work in progress. Shiraz/Merlot/Cabernet Sauvignon. Diam. 14° alc. **RATING** 87 **DRINK** 2011 $ 22

Ben Potts Wines ★★★★

Step Road, Langhorne Creek, SA 5255 (postal) **REGION** Langhorne Creek
T (08) 8537 3029 **F** (08) 8537 3284 **WWW**.benpottswines.com.au **OPEN** Not
WINEMAKER Ben Potts **EST**. 2002 **CASES** 1000
Ben Potts is the sixth generation to be involved in grapegrowing and winemaking in Langhorne Creek, the first being Frank Potts, founder of Bleasdale Vineyards. Ben completed the oenology degree at Charles Sturt University, and (aged 25) ventured into winemaking on a commercial scale in 2002. Fiddle's Block Shiraz is named after great-grandfather Fiddle; Lenny's Block Cabernet Sauvignon Malbec after grandfather Len; and Bill's Block Malbec after father Bill.

🍷🍷🍷🍷🍷 **Lenny's Block Langhorne Creek Cabernet Malbec 2003** Good red-purple colour; rich, velvety cabernet fruit flavours; nice tension between riper and more savoury elements; carries the alcohol. Cork. 15.3° alc. **RATING** 94 **DRINK** 2018 $ 32

🍷🍷🍷🍷 **Fiddle's Block Langhorne Creek Shiraz 2003** Unconvincing colour; spicy red and black fruits, then the alcohol catches on fire on the finish. Cork. 16.4° alc. **RATING** 86 **DRINK** 2010 $ 32

Ben's Run NR

PO Box 127, Broke, NSW 2330 **REGION** Lower Hunter Valley
T (02) 6579 1310 **F** (02) 6579 1370 **OPEN** Not
WINEMAKER Pooles Rock (Patrick Auld) **EST**. 1997 **CASES** 800
Ben's Run, say the owners, 'is named for our kelpie dog for graciously allowing part of his retirement run to be converted into a showpiece shiraz-only vineyard'. Patriarch Norman Marran was one of the pioneers of the Australian cotton industry, with a long and distinguished career as a former director of both the Australian Wheat Board and the Grains Research Corporation, and is currently chairman of a leading food research company.

Benarra Vineyards

NR

PO Box 1081, Mt Gambier, SA 5290 **REGION** Mount Gambier
T (08) 8738 9355 **F** (08) 8738 9355 **OPEN** Not
WINEMAKER Bochara Wines **EST.** 1998 **CASES** 150
Lisle Pudney has planted a substantial vineyard with the help of investors. In all there are over 26 ha
of pinot noir and 4 ha each of sauvignon blanc and chardonnay, with another 40 ha to be planted.
The vineyard is 20 km from the Southern Ocean on ancient flint beds; a million-year-old mollusc
found on the property is depicted on the label of the Pinot Noir. Most of the grapes are sold; a small
portion is contract-made for the Benarra label, and is of good quality and varietal character.

Bendigo Wine Estate

NR

682 Axedale-Goornong Road, Axedale, Vic 3551 **REGION** Bendigo
T (03) 5439 7444 **F** (03) 5439 7433 **OPEN** 7 days
WINEMAKER Contract **EST.** 2000 **CASES** NA
A quite substantial operation, with plantings of riesling, chardonnay, verdelho, pinot noir, cabernet
sauvignon, merlot, malbec, shiraz and mourvedre, producing both table and sparkling wines. The
wines are chiefly sold by mail order and through the cellar door, which has barbecue and picnic
facilities, and periodically stages events.

Bent Creek Vineyards

★★★★

Lot 10 Blewitt Springs Road, McLaren Flat, SA 5171 **REGION** McLaren Vale
T (08) 8383 0414 **F** (08) 8353 7777 **WWW**.bentcreekvineyards.com.au **OPEN** Sundays & public hols 11–5
WINEMAKER Michael Scarpantoni, Peter Polson **EST.** 2001 **CASES** 5000
Loretta and Peter Polson became wine drinkers and collectors a decade before they acquired 2.5 ha of
40-year-old dry-grown chardonnay and shiraz at McLaren Flat. Another 2.5 ha of cabernet
sauvignon and sauvignon blanc are leased.

ŶŶŶŶŶ **The Nude McLaren Vale Shiraz 2003** Deep red-purple; extremely ripe, luscious and very
sweet black fruits, together with some dark chocolate. Here the wine has swallowed up the 18
months spent in French and American oak. Screwcap. 15.5° alc. **RATING** 92 **DRINK** 2015 $30

ŶŶŶŶ **The Black Dog McLaren Vale Shiraz 2004** Good colour; a touch of reduction on the
bouquet; blackberry, mocha and dark chocolate with good tannins; the oak is less
convincing than with the '03. Screwcap. 14.5° alc. **RATING** 89 **DRINK** 2010 $21
McLaren Vale Unwooded Chardonnay 2005 A clean bouquet, without the reduction
evident in the Sauvignon Blanc; crisp, juicy, citrussy aromas and flavours; clean, bright
finish. Screwcap. 13.5° alc. **RATING** 87 **DRINK** 2008 $17
McLaren Vale Cabernet Merlot 2004 Good colour; a chunky style with lots of alcohol-
derived sweetness and softness; abundant flavour. Screwcap. 15.5° alc. **RATING** 87
DRINK 2010 $20

ŶŶŶŶ **Nero McLaren Vale Sparkling Shiraz 2003 RATING** 86 **DRINK** 2010 $24
Adelaide Hills Sauvignon Blanc 2005 RATING 85 **DRINK** Now $19

Benwarin Wines

★★★★

32 Kings Lane, Darlinghurst, NSW 2010 (postal) **REGION** Lower Hunter Valley
T (02) 8354 1375 **F** (02) 8354 1376 **WWW**.benwarin.com.au **OPEN** Not
WINEMAKER Monarch Winemaking Services (Jim Chatto) **EST.** 1999 **CASES** 7000
Allan Bagley and wife Janneke have planted a substantial vineyard with shiraz (9.7 ha), verdelho
(2.43 ha), sangiovese (1.95 ha), chambourcin (1.61 ha), semillon (1.6 ha) and chardonnay (1.28 ha).
Until 2004 most of the grapes were sold to other wineries, but since then all of the production has
gone to the Benwarin label. The yield is restricted to 2 tonnes per acre, and the wines have been
consistent medal winners. Exports to Canada.

ŶŶŶŶ **Hunter Valley Semillon 2005** Classic young semillon from a great vintage, stacked with
lemon/lemongrass flavour, yet retaining finesse; long palate; give it the time it deserves.
Screwcap. 10.9° alc. **RATING** 93 **DRINK** 2015 $14

Hunter Valley Verdelho 2005 Lively, clean and fresh; clearly expressed varietal fruit salad; also line and drive. Screwcap. 14° alc. **RATING** 91 **DRINK** 2008 $15

Hunter Valley Chardonnay 2004 Very well-made; gentle stone fruit with a drizzle of citrus; particularly good length and balance. Screwcap. 13.5° alc. **RATING** 90 **DRINK** 2008 $16

ŸŸŸŸ Hunter Valley Shiraz 2003 Distinctly regional earthy, leathery overtones to light- to medium-bodied red fruits; not forced to be something it isn't. Cork. 13.4° alc. **RATING** 89 **DRINK** 2008 $18

ŸŸŸŸ Hunter Valley Rose 2005 **RATING** 86 **DRINK** Now $14

Beresford Wines

26 Kangarilla Road, McLaren Vale, SA 5171 **REGION** McLaren Vale
T (08) 8323 8899 **F** (08) 8323 7911 **WWW**.beresfordwines.com.au **OPEN** Mon–Fri 9–5, w'ends 10–5
WINEMAKER Scott McIntosh, Rob Dundon **EST.** 1985 **CASES** 130 000
The Beresford brand sits at the top of a range of labels primarily and successfully aimed at export markets in the UK, the US, Hong Kong and China. The intention is that ultimately most, if not all, the wines will be sourced from grapes grown in McLaren Vale. The cellar door and boutique winery are run as an entirely separate operation to its sister winery, Step Road in Langhorne Creek.

ŸŸŸŸŸ McLaren Vale Shiraz 2003 A powerful mix of black fruits, dark chocolate, licorice and earth; very distinctive McLaren Vale style. **RATING** 93 **DRINK** 2013 $24

McLaren Vale Cabernet Sauvignon 2002 Light- to medium-bodied, skipping past the alcohol; cedary, earthy black fruits and dark chocolate; good tannins. Overall distinctly stylish. Screwcap. 14.5° alc. **RATING** 90 **DRINK** 2010 $20

ŸŸŸŸ Highwood McLaren Vale Shiraz 2004 Soft plum and blackberry fruit; quite supple and generous mouthfeel; micro-oxygenation? Screwcap. 14.5° alc. **RATING** 87 **DRINK** 2008 $15

Highwood Merlot 2004 Light- to medium-bodied; bright, fresh red fruits; not especially varietal, but easy on the gums. Screwcap. 14° alc. **RATING** 87 **DRINK** 2008 $15

ŸŸŸŸ Highwood Sauvignon Blanc 2005 **RATING** 85 **DRINK** Now $15

🍃 Bergamin Wines   NR

511 Upper King River Road, Cheshunt, Vic 3678 **REGION** King Valley
T (03) 5729 8172 **F** (03) 5729 8173 **WWW**.bergamin.com.au **OPEN** By appt
WINEMAKER Steven Bergamin **EST.** 1998 **CASES** 1200
John and Steven Bergamin have established a 23-ha vineyard, planted to 5 ha each of pinot gris, chardonnay, merlot and shiraz, 3 ha of sauvignon blanc. These supply both the three varietal releases (Sauvignon Blanc, Merlot and Shiraz) but also the production of Grappa (using merlot, shiraz and purchased nebbiolo). They also produce Vinocotto, a slow reduction of sauvignon blanc juice to the point of syrup. Something different, indeed.

Berrys Bridge ★★★☆

633 Carapooee Road, Carapooee, Vic 3478 **REGION** Pyrenees
T (03) 5496 3220 **F** (03) 5496 3322 **WWW**.berrysbridge.com.au **OPEN** W'ends 10.30–4.30, or by appt
WINEMAKER Jane Holt **EST.** 1990 **CASES** 1500
While the date of establishment is 1990, Roger Milner purchased the property in 1975, intending to plant a vineyard. In the mid-1980s he returned with Jane Holt, and together they began the construction of the stone house-cum-winery. Planting of the existing 7 ha of vineyard commenced in 1990, around the time that Jane began viticulture and oenology studies at Charles Sturt University. Until 1997 the grapes were sold to others; the first vintage (from 1997) was released in November 1998. Exports to the US, Germany and Switzerland.

ŸŸŸŸ 2002 Berrys Bridge Pyrenees Merlot **RATING** 86 **DRINK** 2012

Berton Vineyard ★★★☆

Boehm Springs Road, Eden Valley, SA 5235 (postal) **REGION** Eden Valley
T (02) 6962 9455 **F** (02) 6962 9755 **OPEN** Not
WINEMAKER James Ceccato **EST.** 2001 **CASES** 15 000
The Berton Vineyard partners — Bob and Cherie Berton, Paul Bartholomaeus, James Ceccato and Jamie Bennett — have almost 100 years cumulative experience in winemaking, viticulture, finance, production and marketing. The venture began in May 1996 with the acquisition of a 30-ha property and the planting of the first vines. It took 2 years for the dam to fill, and until irrigation became available the vines struggled on the white rock soil, looking like little bonsais — hence the names of the estate-grown Bonsai Shiraz and White Rock varietals. The business also offers (in descending order of price) the cleverly labelled Head Over Heels range, the Hay Plains range, and Odd Socks range. Exports to the UK and Europe.

TTTT **High Eden Bonsai Shiraz 2003** Intense wild herb, spice, pepper and leather aromas; a fine, elegant palate, with a trace of herbal notes on the finish; fine tannins. Cork. **RATING** 89 **DRINK** 2013 $ 45

TTTY **Head Over Heels Sauvignon Blanc Semillon 2004 RATING** 85 **DRINK** Now $ 11
Head Over Heels Eden Valley Pinot Noir 2004 RATING 85 **DRINK** Now $ 11
Head Over Heels Cabernet Merlot 2004 RATING 85 $ 11

Best's Wines ★★★★★

111 Best's Road, Great Western, Vic 3377 **REGION** Grampians
T (03) 5356 2250 **F** (03) 5356 2430 **WWW.**bestswines.com **OPEN** Mon–Sat 10–5, Sun 11–4
WINEMAKER Viv Thomson, Adam Wadewitz **EST.** 1866 **CASES** 30 000
Best's Great Western winery and vineyards are among the best-kept secrets of Australia. Indeed the vineyards, with vines dating back to 1867, have secrets which may never be revealed: for example, certain vines planted in the Nursery Block have defied identification and are thought to exist nowhere else in the world. The cellars, too, go back to the same era, constructed by butcher-turned-winemaker Joseph Best and his family. Since 1920, the Thomson family has owned the property, with father Viv and sons Ben, Bart and Marcus representing the fourth and fifth generations. Consistently producing elegant, supple wines which deserve far greater recognition than they receive. The Shiraz is a classic, the Thomson Family Shiraz magnificent. Exports to all major markets.

TTTTT **Bin O Shiraz 2002** Black cherry, plum, spice and a hint of mint; a delicious, classic medium-bodied wine; long and fine, subtle oak. Cork. 13.5° alc. **RATING** 96 **DRINK** 2017 $ 42.50
Bin O Shiraz 2003 Full-bodied; super-intense blackberry, licorice and plum, way beyond the normal Best's laid-back style; perhaps drought influenced, but none the worse for that. **RATING** 95 **DRINK** 2015 $ 42
Great Western Cabernet Sauvignon 2000 Fragrant cassis and red fruit aromas; lovely, unforced medium-bodied palate; gentle oak, fine tannins, lingering finish; aging surely; 5% Merlot. Cork. 13° alc. **RATING** 95 **DRINK** 2012 $ 26.50
Great Western Riesling 2005 An excellent core of minerally acidity for the tight apple and lime juice flavour. Delicious wine; great future. Screwcap. 12.5° alc. **RATING** 94 **DRINK** 2012 $ 21

TTTTY **Shiraz 2003** Very good hue; medium-bodied spicy, earthy plum and black cherry fruit; fine tannins, controlled oak. Screwcap. 13.5° alc. **RATING** 90 **DRINK** 2012 $ 15

TTTT **Riesling 2005** Herb, mineral, spice and leaf; soft, slightly broad/sweet palate; fair fruit depth. **RATING** 88 **DRINK** 2008 $ 13
Cabernet Sauvignon 2003 Light- to medium-bodied; spicy/leafy/minty notes to the red fruits at the core. **RATING** 87 **DRINK** 2010 $ 15

TTTY **Chardonnay 2005 RATING** 86 **DRINK** Now $ 15

Bethany Wines

Bethany Road, Bethany via Tanunda, SA 5352 **REGION** Barossa Valley
T (08) 8563 2086 **F** (08) 8563 0046 **WWW**.bethany.com.au **OPEN** Mon–Sat 10–5, Sun 1–5
WINEMAKER Geoff Schrapel, Robert Schrapel **EST.** 1977 **CASES** 25 000
The Schrapel family has been growing grapes in the Barossa Valley for over 140 years, but the winery has only been in operation since 1977. Nestled high on a hillside in the site of an old quarry, it is run by Geoff and Rob Schrapel, who produce a range of consistently well-made and attractively packaged wines. They have 36 ha of vineyards in the Barossa Valley, 8 ha in the Eden Valley and (recently and interestingly) 2 ha each of chardonnay and cabernet sauvignon on Kangaroo Island. Exports to the UK, Europe and Asia.

ΨΨΨΨ **Barossa Semillon 2004** This is a surprise packet, the best barrel-fermented semillon for a long time from the Barossa Valley; French, not American, oak is part of the story, matched with lemon/lemongrass fruit, and perfectly integrated. Screwcap. 12.5° alc.
RATING 92 **DRINK** 2010 $14
Select Late Harvest Riesling 2005 Quite intense lemon/lemon tart/lime aromas and flavours; excellent acidity and length. Screwcap. 11° alc. **RATING** 90 **DRINK** 2009 $22

ΨΨΨΨ **Barossa Chardonnay 2004** Flavoursome peach and nectarine; simple, unpretentious, but reasonably well-balanced. Screwcap. 13° alc. **RATING** 87 **DRINK** 2008 $16
Barossa Cabernet Merlot 2003 Savoury/spicy/cedary/earthy mix; does have length and fair balance. Cork. 14° alc. **RATING** 87 **DRINK** 2010 $23

ΨΨΨ **Steinbruch Riesling 2005** Full, soft, tropical fruit; unashamed sweetness for the cellar door. Screwcap. 11.5° alc. **RATING** 86 **DRINK** 2008 $14
Manse Semillon Riesling Chardonnay 2004 There's no law against it (the blend, that is) and the controlled alcohol assists the tangy freshness. Screwcap. 12° alc. **RATING** 86 **DRINK** Now $13
Barossa Cabernet Franc Rose 2005 Aromatic red fruits just a little too sweet, though nice acidity on the finish pulls it back to a certain degree. Screwcap. 13.5° alc. **RATING** 86 **DRINK** Now $18
Barossa Grenache 2004 **RATING** 86 **DRINK** 2008 $16

Bettenay's

NR

Cnr Harmans South Road/Miamup Road, Wilyabrup, WA 6284 **REGION** Margaret River
T (08) 9755 5539 **F** (08) 9755 5539 **WWW**.bettenaysmargaretriver.com.au **OPEN** 7 days 10–5
WINEMAKER Greg Bettenay, Peter Stanlake (Consultant) **EST.** 1989 **CASES** 1500
Greg Bettenay began the development of 10 ha of vineyards in 1989, planted to sauvignon blanc, semillon, chardonnay, cabernet sauvignon, merlot and shiraz. The development now extends to two farm vineyard cottages and a luxury tree-top spa apartment known as The Leafy Loft.

Beyond Broke Vineyard

NR

Cobcroft Road, Broke, NSW 2330 **REGION** Lower Hunter Valley
T (02) 6026 2043 **F** (02) 6026 2043 **WWW**.wine2go.com.au **OPEN** At Broke Village Store 10–4
WINEMAKER Pete Howland (Contract) **EST.** 1996 **CASES** 4000
Beyond Broke Vineyard is the reincarnation of a former Lindemans vineyard, purchased by Bob and Terry Kennedy in 1996. In a more than slightly ironic twist, the 1997 Beyond Broke Semillon won 2 trophies at the Hunter Valley Wine Show of that year.

Bianchet

★★★☆

187 Victoria Road, Lilydale, Vic 3140 **REGION** Yarra Valley
T (03) 9739 1779 **F** (03) 9739 1277 **OPEN** Thurs–Fri 10–4, w'ends 10–5
WINEMAKER Contract **EST.** 1976 **CASES** 2500
Owned by a small Melbourne-based syndicate which acquired the business from the founding Bianchet family. One of the most unusual wines from the winery is Verduzzo Gold, a late-harvest sweet white wine made from the Italian grape variety. The wines are still basically sold through the cellar door.

ҮҮҮҮҮ **Yarra Valley Chardonnay 2001** Green-gold; has prospered over the 3 years since first tasted; still holding structure and length, with appealing nectarine fruit. **RATING** 90 **DRINK** 2008
Yarra Valley Pinot Noir 2003 Good red-purple; a well-made wine, with soft, supple plummy fruit on the palate; good length and balance. Cork. 14° alc. **RATING** 90 **DRINK** 2008 $ 23

ҮҮҮҮ **Yarra Valley Cabernet Sauvignon 2000** Light colour, though the hue is still good; fresh cassis and raspberry fruit; low pH from the low alcohol has helped preserve the wine. Cork. 12.9° alc. **RATING** 87 **DRINK** 2008 $ 22

ҮҮҮҮ **Yarra Valley Verduzzo 2001** Yellow-gold; spicy, soft honeyed fruit, rapidly reaching its use-by date. Cork. 14° alc. **RATING** 86 **DRINK** Now $ 25
Yarra Valley Shiraz 2001 Probably didn't have enough in the first place, though there is some length to the savoury fruit. Cork. 12.5° alc. **RATING** 86 **DRINK** Now $ 22
Duet (375 ml) NV **RATING** 85 **DRINK** Now $ 15

Bidgeebong Wines ★★★★☆

352 Byrnes Road, Wagga Wagga, NSW 2650 **REGION** Gundagai
T (02) 6931 9955 **F** (02) 6931 9966 **www**.bidgeebong.com **OPEN** Mon–Fri 9–4
WINEMAKER Andrew Birks, Keiran Spencer **EST.** 2000 **CASES** 12 000
Encompasses what the founders refer to as the Bidgeebong triangle — between Young, Wagga Wagga, Tumbarumba and Gundagai — which provides grapes for the Bidgeebong brand. Two of the partners are Andrew Birks, lecturer and educator at Charles Sturt University, and Simon Robertson, with a substantial viticultural management business in the area. A winery was completed for the 2002 vintage, and will eventually be capable of handling 2000 tonnes of grapes: for Bidgeebong's own needs, and those of other local growers and larger producers who purchase grapes from the region. Exports to the UK and the US.

ҮҮҮҮҮ **Tumbarumba Chardonnay 2005** Highly aromatic, almost floral bouquet; intense grapefruit, white peach and nectarine, a subtle glow of French oak in the background; seriously nice wine. Screwcap. 13.5° alc. **RATING** 93 **DRINK** 2012 $ 17
Tumbarumba Chardonnay 2004 Fragrant, cool-grown nectarine and citrus bouquet; unexpectedly sweet and supple fruit on entry to the palate, tightened up by acidity on the finish; subtle oak throughout. Screwcap. 13.5° alc. **RATING** 91 **DRINK** 2010 $ 17
Triangle Chardonnay 2005 Straw-green; light- to medium-bodied, with good mouthfeel and line; stone fruit, melon and citrus; attractive finish and aftertaste. Screwcap. 13.5° alc. **RATING** 90 **DRINK** 2009 $ 13
Gundagai Shiraz 2004 Deep purple-red; a fragrant, lifted bouquet, then a savoury, blackberry-accented palate; plenty of tannin backbone. Screwcap. 14° alc. **RATING** 90 **DRINK** 2015 $ 22
Triangle Shiraz 2004 Complex black fruits; notes of sweet leather and spice; soft tannins, subtle oak. Screwcap. 13.5° alc. **RATING** 90 **DRINK** 2013 $ 13
Tumbarumba Tempranillo 2004 Fascinating fragrant and flowery red fruits; light- to medium-bodied, finely structured and balanced; early maturing. Screwcap. 13° alc. **RATING** 90 **DRINK** 2010 $ 22

ҮҮҮҮ **Tumbarumba Sauvignon Blanc 2005** A spotlessly clean, very restrained style; crisp, mineral notes run through the bouquet and nicely balanced palate; may emerge fully with another year in bottle. Screwcap. 13° alc. **RATING** 89 **DRINK** 2008 $ 17

ҮҮҮҮ **Triangle Semillon Sauvignon Blanc 2005** **RATING** 86 **DRINK** Now $ 14

Big Barrel Vineyard & Winery NR

787 Landsborough Road, Maleny, Qld 4551 **REGION** Queensland Coastal
T (07) 5429 6300 **F** (07) 5429 6331 **OPEN** 7 days 10–5
WINEMAKER Stuart Pierce **EST.** 2000 **CASES** 1280
The Pagano family's forebears made wine on the foothills of Mt Etna for many generations, and the family has been involved in the Australian wine industry for over 40 years. But it was not until 12

years ago that father Sebastian and wife Maria Pagano saw the Maleny area with its Glasshouse Mountain and surrounding Blackall Range, reminiscent of a scaled-down Mt Etna. They have now planted 4 ha of chambourcin, and opened a tasting room (in the shape of a giant barrel) which sells a wide range of wines sourced from elsewhere in Australia. In best Qld tradition, there are plenty of attractions for tourists, including vineyard tours, light foccacia lunches Mon–Sat, and a continental buffet lunch on Sunday.

Big Hill Vineyard NR

Cnr Calder Highway/Belvoir Park Road, Big Hill, Bendigo, Vic 3550 **REGION** Bendigo
T (03) 5435 3366 **F** (03) 5435 3311 **www.**bighillvineyard.com **OPEN** 7 days 10–5
WINEMAKER Stuart Auld (Contract) **EST.** 1998 **CASES** 1200
A partnership headed by Nick Cugura began the re-establishment of Big Hill Vineyard on a site which was first planted to grapes almost 150 years ago. That was in the height of the gold rush, and there was even a long-disappeared pub, the Granite Rock Hotel. The modern-day plantings began with 2 ha of shiraz in 1998, followed by 1 ha each of merlot and cabernet sauvignon.

big shed wines ★★★☆

1289 Malmsbury Road, Glenlyon, Vic 3461 **REGION** Macedon Ranges
T (03) 5348 7825 **F** (03) 5348 7825 **www.**bigshedwines.com.au **OPEN** 7 days, winter 10–6, summer 10–7
WINEMAKER Ken Jones **EST.** 1999 **CASES** 1400
Founder and winemaker Ken Jones was formerly a geneticist and molecular biologist at Edinburgh University, and the chemistry of winemaking comes easily. The estate-based wine comes from the 2 ha of pinot noir; the other wines are made from purchased grapes grown in various parts of Central Victoria.

▼▼▼▼▽ **Reserve Shiraz 2003** Strong red-purple; medium- to full-bodied licorice, spice, leather, game and blackberry; powerful cool-grown style. Cork. 14.9° alc. **RATING** 90 **DRINK** 2023 **$** 25

▼▼▼▼ **Cabernet Merlot 2003** Full-bodied assertive black fruits, earth and olive; slightly rustic tannins. Cork. 14.5° alc. **RATING** 87 **DRINK** 2015 **$** 22

Bimbadgen Estate ★★★★☆

790 McDonalds Road, Pokolbin, NSW 2321 **REGION** Lower Hunter Valley
T (02) 4998 7585 **F** (02) 4998 7732 **www.**bimbadgen.com.au **OPEN** 7 days 9.30–5
WINEMAKER Simon Thistlewood, Jane Turner **EST.** 1968 **CASES** 60 000
Established as McPherson Wines, then successively Tamalee, Sobels, Parker Wines and now Bimbadgen, this substantial winery had what might be politely termed a turbulent history. It has 109 ha of estate plantings, mostly with relatively old vines, supplemented by a separate estate vineyard at Yenda for the lower-priced Ridge series, and purchased grapes from various premium regions. Exports to the UK, Hong Kong and Japan.

▼▼▼▼▼ **Signature Semillon 2002** A year ago the wine needed more time; having had that it now offers a marriage of youth and complexity, with considerable depth and finesse. Gold medal Sydney Wine Show '06. **RATING** 94 **DRINK** 2012 **$** 25

▼▼▼▼▽ **Semillon 2005** Lime, lemon and mineral aromas; an extra burst of flavour typical of the vintage; perfect mouthfeel. Screwcap. **RATING** 93 **DRINK** 2015 **$** 17.50

▼▼▼▼ **Hunter Valley Verdelho 2005** Unexpected length and flavour; a tangy, citrus cast with a faint flick of residual sugar. Screwcap. **RATING** 87 **DRINK** Now **$** 17.50

Bindaree Estate NR

Fish Fossil Drive, Canowindra, NSW 2804 **REGION** Cowra
T (02) 6344 1214 **F** (02) 6344 3217 **www.**bindareeestate.com.au **OPEN** Wed–Fri 11–5, w'ends 10–5
WINEMAKER Contract **EST.** 1998 **CASES** 2000
The Workman family have established their property in the foothills of the Belubula River Valley, near Canowindra. They have planted 1 ha of chardonnay, and 3 ha each of cabernet sauvignon and shiraz.

Bindi Wine Growers

343 Melton Road, Gisborne, Vic 3437 (postal) **REGION** Macedon Ranges
T (03) 5428 2564 **F** (03) 5428 2564 **OPEN** Not
WINEMAKER Michael Dhillon, Stuart Anderson (Consultant) **EST.** 1988 **CASES** 1500
One of the icons of Macedon, indeed Vic. The Chardonnay is top-shelf, the Pinot Noir as remarkable (albeit in a very different idiom) as Bass Phillip, Giaconda or any of the other tiny-production, icon wines. The addition of the Heathcote-sourced Shiraz under the Bundaleer label simply confirms Bindi as one of the greatest small producers in Australia. Notwithstanding the tiny production, the wines are exported (in small quantities, of course) to the UK, the US and other major markets.

ＹＹＹＹＹ **Block 5 Pinot Noir 2004** A potent wine, with luscious red fruits, almost into confit, off-set by fine, spicy, persistent tannins, and an undertone of earthy forest floor. Diam. **RATING** 96 **DRINK** 2014 $ 75
Quartz Chardonnay 2004 Shows an enormous increase in power, concentration and complexity, yet retains finesse thanks to its mineral core; here, too, the oak plays a pure support role. Diam. **RATING** 95 **DRINK** 2016 $ 60
Original Vineyard Pinot Noir 2004 Typically aromatic, with a mix of plum and small berry fruits; a powerful but pure palate, with spicy notes and great length. Diam. **RATING** 95 **DRINK** 2012 $ 55
Composition Chardonnay 2004 Vibrant and fragrant citrus and melon aromas and flavours; hints of cream and nut, the oak an invisible support behind the fruit. Diam. **RATING** 94 **DRINK** 2014 $ 35

ＹＹＹＹＹ **Composition Pinot Noir 2004** Fine and elegant, with a mix of savoury, spicy notes and cherry fruit; silky and harmonious. Diam. **RATING** 93 **DRINK** 2010 $ 35

Bird in Hand

Bird in Hand Road, Woodside, SA 5244 **REGION** Adelaide Hills
T (08) 8232 9033 **F** (08) 8232 9066 **WWW**.birdinhand.com.au **OPEN** Not
WINEMAKER Andrew Nugent, Kym Milne **EST.** 1997 **CASES** 15 000
This substantial wine and olive oil property is situated on the Bird in Hand Road at Woodside, which in turn took its name from a 19th century gold mine called Bird in Hand. It is the venture of the Nugent family, headed by Dr Michael Nugent. Son Andrew Nugent is a Roseworthy graduate, and his wife, Susie, manages the olive oil side of the business. The family also has properties on the Fleurieu Peninsula and in the Clare Valley, the latter providing both riesling and shiraz (and olives from 100-year-old wild olive trees). National distribution and exports to the UK, the US and other major markets.

ＹＹＹＹＹ **Adelaide Hills Sauvignon Blanc 2005** Spotlessly clean; the touch of oak, as usual, restrains the exuberance of the aroma, but is handsomely repaid on the extremely fine and long palate; great structure and texture. Screwcap. 12.5° alc. **RATING** 94 **DRINK** Now $ 25

ＹＹＹＹＹ **Clare Valley Riesling 2005** A very attractive wine, with a mix of apple, passionfruit and minerally acidity; delicacy comes from the restrained alcohol, which emphasises the long, lingering finish. Screwcap. 12° alc. **RATING** 93 **DRINK** 2012 $ 25
Two in the Bush Adelaide Hills Semillon Sauvignon Blanc 2005 Another spotlessly clean wine, driven (to advantage) by the Semillon, introducing some more herbal notes to the citrus background; fluid mouthfeel and good acidity. Screwcap. 12° alc. **RATING** 93 **DRINK** 2009 $ 20
Adelaide Hills Shiraz 2004 Strong colour; the hallmark clean bouquet, then a supple palate ranging through plum, dark chocolate and blackberry, with seamless oak and tannins. Cork. 14° alc. **RATING** 92 **DRINK** 2012 $ 30
Two in the Bush Adelaide Hills Cabernet Merlot 2004 The wine seems to carry the alcohol better than the Merlot, with sweet cassis, blackcurrant and raspberry. Screwcap. 15.5° alc. **RATING** 90 **DRINK** 2012 $ 25

ＹＹＹＹ **Adelaide Hills Pinot Noir Rose 2005** Delicate but clear-cut spicy/strawberry aromas and flavours, followed by a near-dry finish. Classy rose. Screwcap. 12.5° alc. **RATING** 89 **DRINK** Now $ 20

Adelaide Hills Merlot 2004 The high alcohol does invest the wine with sweetness which is a little distracting; this apart, the texture and weight are good. Cork. 15.5° alc. **RATING** 89
DRINK 2010 $ 30

Adelaide Hills Cabernet Sauvignon 2004 Despite the alcohol, is in a savoury mould, the blackcurrant fruit with tangy, verging lemony, tannins. Cork. 15° alc. **RATING** 88
DRINK 2009 $ 30

Joy Sparkling Pinot Noir NV Similar to the vintage sparkling, the strawberry sweetness balanced by acidity, and just a little more fruit. **RATING** 88 **DRINK** Now $ 45

Adelaide Hills Sparkling Pinot Noir 2004 Pale blush-pink; appealing strawberry fruit with a touch of sweetness; does not have to be taken too seriously. 12° alc. **RATING** 87
DRINK Now $ 25

Birdwood Estate

NR

Mannum Road, Birdwood, SA 5234 (postal) **REGION** Adelaide Hills
T (08) 8263 0986 **F** (08) 8263 0986 **OPEN** Not
WINEMAKER Oli Cucchiarelli **EST.** 1990 **CASES** 700
Birdwood Estate draws upon 7 ha of estate vineyards progressively established since 1990. The quality of the white wines, and in particular the Chardonnay, has generally been good. The tiny production is principally sold through retail in Adelaide.

Birnam Wood Wines

NR

Turanville Road, Scone, NSW 2337 **REGION** Upper Hunter Valley
T (02) 6545 3286 **F** (02) 6545 3431 **OPEN** W'ends & public hols 11–4
WINEMAKER Monarch Winemaking Services **EST.** 1994 **CASES** 4000
Former Sydney car dealer Mike Eagan and wife Min moved to Scone to establish a horse stud; the vineyard came later (in 1994) but is now a major part of the business, with 32 ha of vines. Most of the grapes are sold; part only is vinified for Birnam Wood. Son Matthew has now joined the business after working for 5 years for Tyrrell's in its export department. Exports to Switzerland, Canada and China.

Birrarung Estate

NR

PO Box 116, Eltham, Vic 3095 **REGION** Yarra Valley
T 0412 324 510 **F** (03) 9431 4815 **www.**birrarung.com.au **OPEN** Not
WINEMAKER Chris Seidler **EST.** 1994 **CASES** 2000
One ha each of chardonnay and sauvignon blanc, and 4 ha of pinot noir, have been established using sustainable agriculture headed towards organic grower accreditation. The first vintage was 2001, and owners Chris and Joanne Seidler are planning an eco 5-star resort with restaurant, health spa and conference facilities. Early experiments with a revolutionary glass closure have been terminated.

Birthday Villa Vineyard

★★★★

PO Box 10, Malmsbury, Vic 3446 **REGION** Macedon Ranges
T (03) 5423 2789 **F** (03) 5423 2789 **OPEN** Not
WINEMAKER Greg Dedman (Contract) **EST.** 1966 **CASES** 350
The Birthday Villa name comes from the 19th century Birthday Mine at nearby Drummond, discovered on Queen Victoria's birthday. The 1.5 ha of traminer was planted in 1962, the 0.5 ha of cabernet sauvignon following at a later date. The quality of the Gewurztraminer comes as no surprise; the very cool climate is suited to the variety. On the other hand, the Cabernet Sauvignon comes as a major surprise although there are likely to be vintages where the variety will provide a major challenge as it struggles for ripeness.

 Malmsbury Cabernet Sauvignon 2004 Good purple-red; clean, firm, fresh blackcurrant fruit, fine tannins and good length. Impressive for the region. Screwcap. 12.1° alc.
RATING 90 **DRINK** 2011 $ 25

Malmsbury Gewurztraminer 2004 Significantly more sweetness than the '03, aimed for the cellar door, one assumes; lots of flavour and well-made. Screwcap. 11° alc. **RATING** 88
DRINK Now $ 22

Malmsbury Auslese Traminer 2004 Very interesting wine; extremely rich and sweet spicy/nutmeg flavours; freeze concentration possibly used; more acidity needed. Cork. 12° alc. **RATING** 88 **DRINK** 2008 $ 15

Malmsbury Gewurztraminer 2003 A rich, full style, slightly phenolic, but the flavour is there, as is the spicy varietal character. Cork. 12.2° alc. **RATING** 87 **DRINK** 2008 $ 22

Bishop Grove Wines
NR

Lot 136 Old Maitland Road, Bishops Bridge, NSW 2326 **REGION** Lower Hunter Valley
T (02) 4930 4698 **F** (02) 4930 4698 **www**.bishopgrove.com.au **OPEN** By appt
WINEMAKER Monarch Winemaking Services (Greg Silkman) **EST.** 1990 **CASES** NA
Retired engineer Harry Wells began planting the vineyard in 1990, choosing chardonnay, verdelho and shiraz. Initially the grapes were sold, but Harry's daughter Beth and son-in-law Peter Parkinson began producing wines under the Bishop Grove Label. Thanks to skilled contract-winemaking and mature vines, Bishop Grove has had significant show success.

Bishops Rock
★★★☆

RSD Melrose, Cranbrook, Tas 7190 **REGION** East Coast Tasmania
T (03) 6257 8531 **F** (03) 6257 8531 **OPEN** 7 days 10–4
WINEMAKER Winemaking Tasmania (Julian Alcorso) **EST.** 1998 **CASES** 1350
Bob and Annie Browning have been progressively establishing 3 ha of pinot noir, 1 ha of sauvigon blanc, a little over 1 ha of riesling and 0.5 ha of chardonnay since 1998. The name comes from a famous lighthouse 4 miles west of the Scilly Isles which the Brownings felt was similar to the Oyster Bay area near their vineyard site.

♆♆♆♆♆ **Unwooded Chardonnay 2005** Good length and citrus/stone fruit flavours; likewise, good balance. **RATING** 90 **DRINK** 2008 $ 19

♆♆♆♆ **Pinot Noir 2004** **RATING** 86 **DRINK** 2009 $ 28
Sauvignon Blanc 2005 **RATING** 85 **DRINK** Now $ 23

Black George
NR

Black Georges Road, Manjimup, WA 6258 **REGION** Manjimup
T (08) 9772 3569 **F** (08) 9772 3102 **www**.blackgeorge.com **OPEN** 7 days 10.30–4.45
WINEMAKER Gregory Chinery **EST.** 1991 **CASES** 3750
Black George arrived with aspirations to make high-quality Pinot Noir. As with so much of the Manjimup region, it remains to be seen whether the combination of soil and climate will permit this; the quality of the Black George Merlot Cabernet Franc once again points in a different direction. Exports to the UK and The Netherlands.

Black Swan Wines
★★★☆

8600 West Swan Road, Henley Brook, WA 6055 **REGION** Swan Valley
T (08) 9296 6090 **www**.blackswanwines.com.au **OPEN** 7 days 10–5
WINEMAKER Rob Marshall (Contract) **EST.** NA **CASES** 3000
Barry Scrivener and Robyn Meloury have established a little over 3 ha of chardonnay, cabernet sauvignon, cabernet franc and merlot, all made as easy drinking styles with the emphasis on fresh fruit. The vines are mostly unirrigated, and managed by John Corich, who has over 50 years vineyard experience.

♆♆♆♆ **Unwooded Chardonnay 2005** Elegant, attractive citrus/melon/stone fruit; nice acidity. Screwcap. 13.2° alc. **RATING** 88 **DRINK** Now $ 19

Cabernet Franc 2004 Light- to medium-bodied; sweet berry fruit allied with clever use of oak; fine tannins. Screwcap. 13.8° alc. **RATING** 87 **DRINK** 2008 $ 25

♆♆♆ **Cabernet Merlot 2004** **RATING** 83 $ 25

Blackbilly Wines ★★★☆

Main Street, McLaren Vale, SA 5171 **REGION** McLaren Vale
T 0419 383 907 **F** (08) 8323 9747 **www**.blackbilly.com **OPEN** By appt
WINEMAKER Nick Haselgrove, Warren Randall **EST.** 2005 **CASES** 5000
Blackbilly has emerged from the numerous changes in the Haselgrove wine interests. It has 600 ha of vines, but only a small portion of the estate fruit is vinified under the Blackbilly label. Exports to the UK and the US.

ŸŸŸŸŸ **McLaren Vale Shiraz 2004** Deep, dense but bright purple-red; extremely rich, ripe and concentrated, but avoids jammy/dead fruit; does need time to shed some of the puppy fat, and well worth the wait. Screwcap. 14° alc. **RATING** 92 **DRINK** 2018 $ 22

ŸŸŸŸ **McLaren Vale Sparkling Shiraz NV** While not especially complex, has appealing shiraz fruit without excess dosage or evident oak; will develop on cork. Bottling no. SD2.
RATING 88 **DRINK** 2009 $ 28

ŸŸŸŸ **Fleurieu Pinot Gris 2005 RATING** 86 **DRINK** Now $ 22

Blackboy Ridge Estate ★★★☆

PO Box 554, Donnybrook, WA 6239 **REGION** Geographe
T (08) 9731 2233 **www**.blackboyridge.com.au **OPEN** Not
WINEMAKER David Crawford (Contract) **EST.** 2003 **CASES** 730
The 22-ha property on which Blackboy Ridge Estate is established was partly cleared and planted to 2.5 ha of semillon, chenin blanc, shiraz and cabernet sauvignon in 1978. When current owners Adrian Jones and Jackie Barton purchased the property in 2000 the vines were already some of the oldest in the region. The vineyard and the owners' house is on gentle north-facing slopes, with extensive views out over the Donnybrook area.

ŸŸŸŸ **Geographe Shiraz 2004** A fragrant mix of red and black fruits, and some oak on the bouquet; medium-bodied, the plummy fruit well-integrated with oak. Cork. 13.5° alc.
RATING 89 **DRINK** 2011 $ 18
Geographe Semillon 2004 Despite a touch of reduction, offers a flavoursome mix of tropical and lemon fruit, with hints of oak and a touch of sweetness. Good value, and doubtless has much appeal at cellar door. Screwcap. **RATING** 87 **DRINK** 2009 $ 13
Geographe Cabernet Sauvignon 2004 Light- to medium-bodied; spicy, leafy notes to blackcurrant fruit; slightly high, peaky, acidity. Cork. **RATING** 87 **DRINK** 2010 $ 16.50

ŸŸŸŸ **Geographe Shiraz 2003 RATING** 86 **DRINK** Now $ 18

BlackJack Vineyards ★★★★

Cnr Blackjack Road/Calder Highway, Harcourt, Vic 3453 **REGION** Bendigo
T (03) 5474 2355 **F** (03) 5474 2355 **www**.blackjackwines.com.au **OPEN** W'ends & public hols 11–5, when stock available
WINEMAKER Ian McKenzie, Ken Pollock **EST.** 1987 **CASES** 2500
Established by the McKenzie and Pollock families on the site of an old apple and pear orchard in the Harcourt Valley, best known for some very good Shirazes. Ian McKenzie, incidentally, is not to be confused with Ian McKenzie formerly of Seppelt Great Western. Exports to NZ.

ŸŸŸŸ **Bendigo Cabernet Merlot 2003** A mix of savoury, minty, blackcurrant fruit, with splashes of red fruits and olives into the bargain. Cork. **RATING** 89 **DRINK** 2011 $ 25

Blackwood Crest Wines NR

RMB 404A, Boyup Brook, WA 6244 **REGION** Blackwood Valley
T (08) 9767 3029 **F** (08) 9767 3029 **OPEN** 7 days 10–6
WINEMAKER Max Fairbrass **EST.** 1976 **CASES** 1500
Blackwood Crest is holding a low profile while developing its vineyards and a new 100-tonne winery. It is hoped that developments will be complete in 2008 when the family will celebrate its centenary (Max Fairbrass's grandparents took up the property as virgin bush in 1908).

Blackwood Wines ★★☆

Kearney Street, Nannup, WA 6275 **REGION** Blackwood Valley
T (08) 9756 0077 **F** (08) 9756 0089 **WWW**.blackwoodwines.com.au **OPEN** 7 days 10–4
WINEMAKER Peter Nicholas **EST.** 1996 **CASES** 15 000
Blackwood Wines draws upon 1 ha each of chardonnay, merlot and chenin blanc and 0.5 ha of pinot noir, supplemented by contract-grown fruit which significantly broadens the product range. Redevelopment of the cellar door and winery is designed to see production increase to 50 000 cases by 2009. Exports to Ireland, Singapore and The Netherlands.

ŸŸŸŸ **Fishbone Merlot 2004 RATING** 85 **DRINK** Now $15
Fishbone Unwooded Chardonnay 2005 RATING 84 **DRINK** Now $15

ŸŸŸ **Fishbone Classic White 2005 RATING** 83 $15

Blanche Barkly Wines ★★★★

14 Kingower-Brenanah Road, Kingower, Vic 3517 **REGION** Bendigo
T (03) 5438 8223 **F** (03) 5438 8223 **WWW**.bendigowine.org.au/blanchebarkly **OPEN** W'ends & public hols 10–5, or by appt
WINEMAKER David Reimers, Arleen Reimers **EST.** 1972 **CASES** 500
The Reimers are happy with their relatively low profile; yields from the 30⁺-year-old, dry-grown vines are low, and the quality of the wines is reward in itself. Limited availability makes the mailing list the best way of securing the wines.

ŸŸŸŸŸ **Mary Eileen Shiraz 2003** Medium-bodied; spicy/earthy/savoury overtones to the blackberry fruit; subtle oak and tannins; well-balanced. Cork. 13.5° alc. **RATING** 90 **DRINK** 2015 $25
Mary Eileen Shiraz 1984 Clear colour; still sound, with medium-bodied cedary, earthy flavours; in excellent condition after 22 years. The odd bottle is being sold at cellar door. **RATING** 90 **DRINK** 2008

ŸŸŸŸ **Johann Cabernet Sauvignon 2003** A firm, slightly austere style, with a mix of earthy/leafy/minty edges to the fruit suggesting a lack of full ripeness. Cork. 13.5° alc. **RATING** 86 **DRINK** 2010 $25

Bleasdale Vineyards ★★★★★

Wellington Road, Langhorne Creek, SA 5255 **REGION** Langhorne Creek
T (08) 8537 3001 **F** (08) 8537 3224 **WWW**.bleasdale.com.au **OPEN** Mon–Sun 10–5
WINEMAKER Michael Potts, Renae Hirsch **EST.** 1850 **CASES** 100 000
One of the most historic wineries in Australia, drawing upon 63.5 ha of vineyards that are flooded every winter by diversion of the Bremer River, which provides moisture throughout the dry, cool, growing season. The wines offer excellent value for money, all showing that particular softness which is the hallmark of the Langhorne Creek region. Production has soared; export markets established in the UK, the US, NZ, Switzerland and Germany.

ŸŸŸŸŸ **Generations Langhorne Creek Shiraz 2002** Good hue; a highly polished, elegant style; seamless black fruits, vanillan oak and tannins; very good length, controlled alcohol. Cork. 14° alc. **RATING** 94 **DRINK** 2017 $38
Langhorne Creek Shiraz Cabernet Sauvignon 2003 A medium-bodied, attractive mix of black fruits, ripe tannins and vanilla oak; very good value. Screwcap. 14° alc. **RATING** 94 **DRINK** 2017 $13

ŸŸŸŸŸ **Frank Potts 2003** Bright colour; medium-bodied, bursting with cassis, raspberry and blackcurrant fruit; fine, ripe tannins; good length. Cabernet Sauvignon/Malbec/Petit Verdot. Cork. 14° alc. **RATING** 93 **DRINK** 2018 $28

ŸŸŸŸ **Langhorne Creek Verdelho 2005** Plenty of fruit salad dressed with zingy, lemony acidity; long experience with the variety produces a particularly good example. Value-plus. Screwcap. 13° alc. **RATING** 89 **DRINK** Now $13

ŸŸŸŸ **Mulberry Tree Cabernet Sauvignon 2003 RATING** 84 **DRINK** Now $9

✿ Blickling Estate ★★★★

Green Valley Road, Bendemeer, NSW 2355 **REGION** Northern Slopes Zone
T (02) 6769 6786 **F** (02) 6769 6740 **www**.blickling.com.au **OPEN** 7 days 9–5
WINEMAKER Monarch Winemaking Services **EST.** 1999 **CASES** 6500
Rolf Blickling has established his 10-ha vineyard, planted to riesling, chardonnay, sauvignon blanc, pinot noir, cabernet sauvignon and shiraz, at an elevation of 950m. Frosts in spring and April underline how cool the climate is, necessitating careful site selection. The cellar door also operates a lavender and eucalyptus oil distillery.

ŢŢŢŢŢ **Sauvignon Blanc 2005** An attractive mix of tropical, passionfruit, gooseberry and stone fruit aromas and flavours; excellent acidity; well-made. Screwcap. 12° alc. **RATING** 91 **DRINK** Now **$** 20
Wooded Chardonnay 2005 Subtle oak balance and integration; in the opposite direction to the unwooded version, seemingly with lower alcohol (it's higher) with elegant stone fruit and some cashew. Screwcap. 13.5° alc. **RATING** 90 **DRINK** 2010 **$** 20

ŢŢŢŢ **Riesling 2005** Generous, sweet lime juice; open and inviting; good finish. Screwcap. 11.7° alc. **RATING** 89 **DRINK** 2008 **$** 18
Pinot Noir 2004 Firm, savoury, briary, foresty flavours; undoubted varietal character, but seems to have been picked too early. Much promise. Screwcap. 12.5° alc. **RATING** 89 **DRINK** 2010 **$** 22
Unwooded Chardonnay 2005 Riper flavours than the restrained bouquet would suggest, with yellow peach and fig fruit. Screwcap. 12.3° alc. **RATING** 87 **DRINK** 2008 **$** 18

Blind Man's Bluff Vineyard NR

Lot 15 Bluff Road, Kenilworth, Qld 4574 **REGION** Queensland Coastal
T (07) 5472 3168 **F** (07) 5472 3168 **OPEN** W'ends & school hols 10–5
WINEMAKER Peter Scudamore-Smith (Contract) **EST.** 2001 **CASES** 450
Noel Evans and Tricia Toussaint have planted 1 ha of chardonnay and 1.3 ha of shiraz on their property. Wines are available both by the glass and bottle, and can be purchased with a local cheese platter.

Bloodwood ★★★★★

4 Griffin Road, Orange, NSW 2800 **REGION** Orange
T (02) 6362 5631 **F** (02) 6361 1173 **www**.bloodwood.com.au **OPEN** By appt
WINEMAKER Stephen Doyle **EST.** 1983 **CASES** 4000
Rhonda and Stephen Doyle are 2 of the pioneers of the burgeoning Orange district. The wines are sold mainly through the cellar door and by an energetically and informatively run mailing list; the principal retail outlet is Ian Cook's Fiveways Cellar, Paddington, Sydney. Bloodwood has done best with elegant but intense Chardonnay and the intermittent releases of super-late-harvest Ice Riesling. Exports to the UK.

ŢŢŢŢŢ **Chardonnay 2004** A complex bouquet with obvious barrel ferment inputs; powerful nectarine and white peach fruit drives the long palate, oak playing second fiddle. Screwcap. 13.5° alc. **RATING** 94 **DRINK** 2010 **$** 22
Chirac 2001 Fine, fragrant and elegant; delicate stone fruit, citrus and apple flavours; excellent length and balance; 48 months on lees; disgorged March 2005. Cork. 11.5° alc. **RATING** 94 **DRINK** 2008 **$** 30

ŢŢŢŢŢ **Riesling 2005** Very floral herb, spice and blossom; intensely focused and long; excellent balance. Screwcap. 12° alc. **RATING** 93 **DRINK** 2012 **$** 18
Schubert 2003 Rich, ripe stone fruit and melon, and a touch of honey balanced by good acidity; attractive mouthfeel. Cork. 13.5° alc. **RATING** 93 **DRINK** 2008 **$** 25
Noble Riesling 2005 Some SO_2 still settling down; a long, intense palate, with lingering, lime juice flavours; will richly reward patience however good it tastes now. Screwcap. 11.5° alc. **RATING** 92 **DRINK** 2012 **$** 20

ŸŸŸŸ **Big Men in Tights 2005** Vivid purple-red; long expertise in handling the malbec and cabernet franc components results in bright strawberry and raspberry fruit with a twist of lemon; relatively dry finish. Rose. Screwcap. 13° alc. RATING 89 DRINK Now $15
Shiraz 2003 Relatively developed colour; light- to medium-bodied spice, licorice and red fruits; nicely balanced within its limitations. Screwcap. 14° alc. RATING 89 DRINK 2008 $22
Pinot Noir 2004 Very good colour; intense herb, spice and dried leaf; high acidity adds to the wild ride. Demands time. Cork. 13.5° alc. RATING 88 DRINK 2010 $32

Blown Away   ★★★

PO Box 108, Willunga, SA 5172 REGION McLaren Vale
T (08) 8557 4554 F (08) 8557 4554 OPEN Not
WINEMAKER Trevor Tucker (Contract) EST. 2001 CASES 500
Dave and Sue Watson purchased their property, situated on the corner of Plains Road and Rogers Road at the base of Sellicks Hill, in 1993. It had 0.8 ha of old shiraz, cabernet sauvignon, a few rows of grenache, and a little over 3 ha of almond trees. In 1995 they removed the trees and planted 3 ha to shiraz and grenache. The grapes from the new plantings are sold, the production for Blown Away coming entirely from the old block.

ŸŸŸŸ **Summer of 2003 Cabernet Sauvignon 2003** Ripe, savoury berry fruit; chocolate and mocha nuances; good tannins. Screwcap. 13° alc. RATING 88 DRINK 2010 $25

ŸŸŸŸ **Silver Sands Grenache Cabernet 2004** RATING 86 DRINK 2008 $20

Blue Metal Vineyard   ★★★★

Lot 18 Compton Park Road, Berrima, NSW 2025 REGION Southern Highlands
T 0438 377 727 F (02) 9327 2753 WWW.bluemetalvineyard.com OPEN Thurs–Sun 10–5 or by appt
WINEMAKER Nick Spencer EST. 1999 CASES 1300
The 10.74-ha Blue Metal Vineyard is situated on part of a cattle station at an elevation of 790m; the name comes from the rich red soil that overlies the cap of basalt rock. A wide range of grape varieties are planted, including sauvignon blanc, pinot gris, merlot, cabernet sauvignon, sangiovese and petit verdot. The wines have been very competently made. Exports to the UK.

ŸŸŸŸ **Southern Highlands Sauvignon Blanc 2005** Clean herb, mineral and grass, with just a hint of gooseberry; pleasing length and balance. Screwcap. 12° alc. RATING 90 DRINK Now $19

ŸŸŸŸ **Single Estate Southern Highlands Pinot Gris Sauvignon Blanc 2005** Crisp, clean, fresh, minerally light-bodied wine; dry finish. Screwcap. 13.5° alc. RATING 89 DRINK Now $24
Single Estate Southern Highlands Sangiovese Cabernet Sauvignon 2004 Light-bodied, but does have some varietal dusty/earthy nuances; the texture and silky mouthfeel is pleasantly at odds with the austere but authentic flavours. Screwcap. 13° alc. RATING 88 DRINK 2008 $25
Single Estate Southern Highlands Merlot 2004 Lively, fresh, tangy mint, leaf and berry fruit; bracing acidity; entirely fruit-driven. Cork. 12° alc. RATING 87 DRINK 2009 $25

ŸŸŸŸ **Southern Highlands Cabernet Merlot Petit Verdot 2004** RATING 85 DRINK 2008 $20

Blue Pyrenees Estate   ★★★★

Vinoca Road, Avoca, Vic 3467 REGION Pyrenees
T (03) 5465 3202 F (03) 5465 3529 WWW.bluepyrenees.com.au OPEN Mon–Fri 10–4.30, w'ends & public hols 10–5
WINEMAKER Andrew Koerner EST. 1963 CASES 100 000
Forty years after Remy Cointreau established Blue Pyrenees Estate (then known as Chateau Remy), it sold the business to a small group of Sydney businessmen led by John Ellis (no relation to the John Ellis of Hanging Rock). The winemaking and marketing teams remain in place, although John Ellis has become involved in all areas of the business. The core of the business is the 180-ha estate vineyard, much of it fully mature. Exports to all major markets.

ᵱᵱᵱᵱᵱ **Brut 2000** Apple, citrus, spice and strawberry aromas; in the mouth there is a slight break in the line between acidity and dosage, albeit for no obvious reason. Cork. 12° alc.
RATING 91 **DRINK** Now $ 23
Cabernet Sauvignon 2002 Strong red-purple hues; blackcurrant, dark chocolate and earth on a powerful palate with incisive tannins; lots of character. Cork. **RATING** 90 **DRINK** 2012 $ 18

ᵱᵱᵱᵱ **Shiraz Viognier 2003** Medium-bodied; some Viognier lift to the fresh red fruits, but needs more structure. Cork. 13.5° alc. **RATING** 89 **DRINK** 2009 $ 32

ᵱᵱᵱᵱ **Summer Rose 2004** **RATING** 86 **DRINK** Now $ 18
Fiddlers Creek Victoria Cabernet Merlot 2001 **RATING** 84 **DRINK** Now $ 10

Blue Wren   NR

433 Cassilis Road, Mudgee, NSW 2850 **REGION** Mudgee
T (02) 6372 6205 **F** (02) 6372 6206 **www.**bluewrenwines.com.au **OPEN** 7 days 10.30–4.30
WINEMAKER Various contract **EST.** 1985 **CASES** 2000
James and Diana Anderson have 2 vineyards. The first is Stoney Creek, 20 km north of Mudgee, which was planted in 1985 and has 2 ha each of dry-grown chardonnay and semillon, 1.5 ha of cabernet and 0.5 ha of merlot. The Bombira Vineyard, adjacent to the old Augustine vineyards, has been planted to 3.8 ha of shiraz and verdelho, leaving more than 20 ha unplanted.

Blueberry Hill Vineyard   NR

Cnr McDonalds Road/Coulson Road, Pokolbin, NSW 2320 **REGION** Lower Hunter Valley
T (02) 4998 7295 **F** (02) 4998 7296 **www.**blueberryhill.com.au **OPEN** 7 days 10–5,
until 6.30 Fri–Sat in summer
WINEMAKER Monarch Winemaking Services (Greg Silkman) **EST.** 1973 **CASES** 2000
Blueberry Hill Vineyard is part of the old McPherson Estate, with fully mature plantings of chardonnay, sauvignon blanc, shiraz, pinot noir, merlot and cabernet sauvignon. Until 2000 the grapes were sold to other winemakers, but since then part of the crush goes towards the extensive Blueberry Hill range.

Bluebush Estate   NR

Wilderness Road, Cessnock, NSW 2325 (postal) **REGION** Lower Hunter Valley
T (02) 4930 7177 **F** (02) 4930 7666 **www.**bluebush.com.au **OPEN** Not
WINEMAKER Contract **EST.** 1991 **CASES** 200
Robyn and David McGain have established 2 ha of vineyards (half chardonnay, half shiraz); the wines are contract-made and sold by mail order, and B&B and self-contained accommodation (Bluebush Cottage and Bridstowe Barn) overlooks the vineyard.

Boat O'Craigo   NR

458 Maroondah Highway, Healesville, Vic 3777 **REGION** Yarra Valley
T (03) 9899 9986 **F** (03) 9987 1442 **www.**boatocraigo.com.au **OPEN** Thurs–Sun 10–5
WINEMAKER Rob Dolan, Kate Goodman, Al Fencaros (Contract) **EST.** 1998 **CASES** 7000
The 13.6-ha hillside vineyard is one of the highest sites in the Yarra Valley, bounded on the south by the Little Grace Burn River. It was acquired by Steve Graham in 2003, who changed the name to Boat O'Craigo, a tiny place in a Scottish valley where his ancestors lived. Plans are afoot to graft the 4.6 ha of cabernet sauvignon and shiraz to chardonnay and sauvignon blanc, a sensible move given the very cool site.

Boatshed Vineyard   ★★☆

703 Milbrodale Road, Broke, NSW 2330 (postal) **REGION** Lower Hunter Valley
T (02) 9876 5761 **F** (02) 9876 5761 **OPEN** Not
WINEMAKER Tamburlaine **EST.** 1989 **CASES** 3500
Mark Hill and wife Helen acquired their property in June 1998. At that time it had 5 ha of chardonnay, and in the spring of 1999 the plantings were extended with 2 ha each of verdelho,

merlot, chambourcin, shiraz and cabernet sauvignon. Sustainable viticultural practices are used, and no insecticides have been applied for the past 17 years.

YYY   **Verdelho 2005** RATING 82 $ 18

Bochara Wines   ★★★★☆

1099 Glenelg Highway, Hamilton, Vic 3300 REGION Henty
T (03) 5571 9309 F (03) 5570 8334 WWW.bocharawine.com.au OPEN Fri–Sun 11–5, or by appt
WINEMAKER Martin Slocombe EST. 1998 CASES 1500
This is the small husband and wife business of experienced winemaker Martin Slocombe and former Yalumba viticulturist Kylie McIntyre. They have established 1 ha each of pinot noir and sauvignon blanc, together with 1.6 ha of shiraz and cabernet sauvignon, and 0.5 ha of pinot meunier, supplemented by grapes purchased from local grapegrowers. The modestly priced, but well-made wines are principally sold through the cellar door sales cottage on the property, which has been transformed from a decrepit weatherboard shanty with one cold tap to a fully functional 2-room tasting area, and through a number of local restaurants and bottle shops. The label design, incidentally, comes from a 1901 poster advertising the subdivision of the original Bochara property into smaller farms.

YYYYY   **Melville Forest Shiraz 2004** Good colour; attractively sweet, rich and juicy mix of black fruits, spices, nicely tempered oak and ripe tannins. From the northern part of the region. Screwcap. 13.5° alc. RATING 94 DRINK 2014 $ 20

YYYYY   **Pinot Noir 2004** Complex, spicy plum aromas; light- to medium-bodied, the sweet fruit balanced by attractive super-fine, ripe tannins; nice flick of oak. Screwcap. 13.1° alc. RATING 93 DRINK 2010 $ 20

Henty Sauvignon Blanc 2004 Vibrant and crisp; minerally acidity runs through the gooseberry asparagus and grassy fruit; lovely dry finish. Screwcap. 12° alc. RATING 91 DRINK Now $ 15

Drumborg Chardonnay 2004 Very light, crisp and fresh; developing extremely slowly with minerally stone fruit; cries out for more time. Screwcap. RATING 90 DRINK 2014 $ 20

Boggy Creek Vineyards   ★★★★

1657 Boggy Creek Road, Myrrhee, Vic 3732 REGION King Valley
T (03) 5729 7587 F (03) 5729 7600 WWW.boggycreek.com.au OPEN 7 days 10–5
WINEMAKER Graeme Ray EST. 1978 CASES 15 000
Graeme and Maggie Ray started their vineyard in 1978, planting small quantities of riesling and chardonnay. Since then the vineyard has grown to over 40 ha with the addition of cabernet sauvignon, shiraz, barbera, pinot gris and other experimental lots. It is situated on northeast-facing slopes at an altitude of 350m, with warm summer days and cool nights. Exports to the US, Malaysia and Hong Kong.

YYYYY   **King Valley Shiraz 2004** Good colour; medium-bodied; attractive plum and blackberry fruit does the talking; good length to a seriously nice wine. RATING 90 DRINK 2010 $ 20

YYYY   **King Valley Shiraz Cabernet Sauvignon 2003** More powerful and more savoury than the '04 Shiraz; while the herb and olive components are obvious, the wine has compelling length. RATING 88 DRINK 2009 $ 20

Bogie Man Wines   NR

160 Gum Road, Caveat, Vic 3660 (postal) REGION Strathbogie Ranges
T (03) 5790 4024 F (03) 5790 4025 WWW.bogiemanwines.com OPEN Not
WINEMAKER Plunkett Wines (Sam Plunkett) EST. 2001 CASES 600
Andrew Smythe and family have planted a little under 4 ha of chardonnay, and 0.7 ha of the rare Italian grape lagrein. Plantings began in 2001, and supplemented by chardonnay from 18-year-old vines on a nearby vineyard, and shiraz from 25-year-old vines near Murchison in the Goulburn Valley. Plans are in place to expand the vineyard to 18 ha, with varieties including tempranillo and prosecco as well as more mainstream grapes being considered.

Bogong Estate

NR

Cnr Mountain Creek Road/Damms Road, Mount Beauty, Vic 3699 **REGION** Alpine Valleys
T 0419 567 588 **F** (03) 5754 4946 **WWW**.pinotnoir.com.au **OPEN** 7 days 10–5
WINEMAKER Bill Tynan **EST.** 1997 **CASES** 2500

In the flesh, Bill Tynan looks exactly as a tax partner for a large accounting firm should look: slim, quietly spoken and self-deprecating. His business card, featuring the imprint in vivid pink of an impression of Marilyn Monroe's lips, tells you all is not what it seems. He has in fact given up accounting practice, and planted 10 ha of pinot noir in the upper reaches of Kiewa River Valley, with no near neighbours to keep him company. Winemaking is all about fermenting pinot noir in large plastic bags with gas valves, a system developed by the Hickinbotham family.

Boireann

★★★★★

Donnellys Castle Road, The Summit, Qld, 4377 **REGION** Granite Belt
T (07) 4683 2194 **OPEN** 7 days 10–4.30
WINEMAKER Peter Stark **EST.** 1998 **CASES** 900

Peter and Therese Stark have a 10-ha property set amongst the great granite boulders and trees which are so much part of the Granite Belt. They have established 1.5 ha of vines planted to no less than 11 varieties, including the four Bordeaux varieties which go to make a Bordeaux-blend; shiraz and viognier; grenache and mourvedre provide a Rhône blend, and there will also be a straight merlot. Tannat (French) and barbera and nebbiolo (Italian) make up the viticultural League of Nations. Peter Stark is a winemaker of exceptional talent, making cameo amounts of red wines which are quite beautifully made and of a quality equal to Australia's best.

TTTTT **Shiraz Viognier 2004** Very good colour; super-elegant supple, silk and velvet palate; blackberry and plum fruit; ripe tannins and controlled oak. Cork. 14° alc. **RATING** 94 **DRINK** 2014 $ 45

Mourvedre Shiraz Grenache 2004 Similar bright, clear purple-red; a finely sculptured and balanced wine in hallmark elegant Boireann style; walks a fine but composed line between the 3 varieties. Cork. 13° alc. **RATING** 94 **DRINK** 2013 $ 26

TTTTY **Merlot 2004** Rich plum fruit with nuances of spice and olive; ripe tannins and integrated oak; not especially varietal, though well-made. Cork. 13° alc. **RATING** 90 **DRINK** 2012 $ 22

TTTT **Cabernet Sauvignon 2004** Light- to medium-bodied; cassis berry fruit with touches of leaf and mint; fine tannins, subtle oak. Cork. 13° alc. **RATING** 89 **DRINK** 2010 $ 24

Boneo Plains

NR

RMB 1400, Browns Road, South Rosebud, Vic 3939 **REGION** Mornington Peninsula
T (03) 5988 6208 **F** (03) 5988 6208 **OPEN** By appt
WINEMAKER R D Tallarida **EST.** 1988 **CASES** 2500

A 9-ha vineyard and winery established by the Tallarida family, well known as manufacturers and suppliers of winemaking equipment to the industry. Chardonnay is the best of the wines so far Tasted.

Bonneyview

NR

Sturt Highway, Barmera, SA 5345 **REGION** Riverland
T (08) 8588 2279 **OPEN** 7 days 9–5.30
WINEMAKER Robert Minns **EST.** 1975 **CASES** 2500

The smallest Riverland winery selling exclusively via cellar door, with an ex-Kent cricketer and Oxford University graduate as its owner/winemaker. The Shiraz Petit Verdot (unique to Bonneyview) and Cabernet Petit Verdot add a particular dimension of interest to the wine portfolio.

Boora Estate

NR

'Boora', Warrie Road, Dubbo, NSW 2830 **REGION** Western Plains Zone
T (02) 6884 2600 **F** (02) 6884 2600 **WWW**.boora-estate.com **OPEN** 7 days 2–5
WINEMAKER Frank Ramsay **EST.** 1984 **CASES** 500

The wheel comes full circle with Boora Estate, where Frank Ramsay has established approximately 0.5 ha each of chardonnay, semillon, cabernet franc, cabernet sauvignon, merlot, tempranillo and shiraz. In the 1870s and 1880s Dubbo supported a significant winemaking industry, with Eumalga Estate (owned and run by French-born JE Serisier) said (by the local newspaper of the time) to have the second-largest winery in Australia (which I doubt). Another highly successful winery was established by German-born Frederich Kurtz; Mount Olive won a number of awards in international exhibitions in the 1880s. That achievement was matched 120 years later by Boora Estate winning a silver medal at the 2001 Brisbane Wine Show with its 2000 Shiraz, competing against wines from all parts of Australia.

Booroolite Wines ★★☆

PO Box 542, Mansfield, Vic 3724 **REGION** Upper Goulburn
T (03) 5775 2195 **F** (03) 5779 1636 **WWW**.booroolitewines.com.au **OPEN** Not
WINEMAKER King Valley Wines **EST.** 2004 **CASES** 1000
David and Catherine Ritchie (of Delatite fame) set up Booroolite Wines in 2004 to salvage locally grown, high-quality grapes which could not find an owner. They have started with an Unoaked Chardonnay and a Cabernet Merlot blend, and the product range will vary according to grape supply and pricing. The aim is to provide wines from small vineyards which are competitive price-wise with wines from the big companies.

ΨΨΨΨ **Chardonnay 2004** Light-bodied; clean, direct stone fruit and citrus, with some minerality. Screwcap. 13° alc. **RATING** 86 **DRINK** 2008 $14
Cabernet Merlot 2004 **RATING** 85 **DRINK** 2008 $14

Borambola Wines NR

Sturt Highway, Wagga Wagga, NSW 2650 **REGION** Gundagai
T (02) 6928 4210 **F** (02) 6928 4210 **WWW**.borambola.com **OPEN** 7 days 11-4
WINEMAKER Charles Sturt University **EST.** 1995 **CASES** 6000
Borambola Homestead was built in the 1880s, and in the latter part of that century was the centre of a pastoral empire of 1.4 million ha, ownership of which passed to the McMullen family in 1992. It is situated in rolling foothills 25 km east of Wagga Wagga in the Gundagai region. Just under 10 ha of vines surround the homestead (4 ha shiraz, 3.5 ha cabernet sauvignon, 2.2. ha chardonnay).

Borrodell on the Mount ★★★★☆

Lake Canobolas Road, Orange, NSW 2800 **REGION** Orange
T (02) 6365 3425 **F** (02) 6365 3588 **WWW**.borrodell.com.au **OPEN** 7 days 10-5
WINEMAKER Chris Durrez, Lucy Maddox **EST.** 1995 **CASES** 1300
Barry Gartrell and Gaye Stuart-Williams have planted 4 ha of pinot noir, sauvignon blanc, pinot meunier, traminer and chardonnay adjacent to a cherry, plum and heritage apple orchard and trufferie. It is 10 mins' drive from Orange, and adjacent to Lake Canobolas, at an altitude of 1000m. The wines have been consistent medal winners at regional and small winemaker shows.

ΨΨΨΨΨ **Orange Sauvignon Blanc 2005** Lovely juicy wine; clear-cut tropical gooseberry/redcurrant varietal character on both bouquet and palate; excellent balance, though half a gramme more acidity might have been even better. Screwcap. 12.8° alc. **RATING** 93 **DRINK** 2008 $20
Opus Cabernet Sauvignon 2004 Strong purple-red; powerful, linear, incisive blackberry, mulberry/cassis fruit; lingering fine tannins, oak in the back seat. Bred to stay. Screwcap. 13.8° alc. **RATING** 93 **DRINK** 2017 $20
Orange Pinot Noir 2004 Fragrant spicy plum and black cherry aromas; a light-bodied, supple palate with good pinot varietal character throughout. Impressive outcome for the region. Screwcap. 13.5° alc. **RATING** 90 **DRINK** 2012 $24

ΨΨΨΨ **Sister's Rock 2000** Extremely bright, fresh, crisp and long; a slightly higher dosage would have been justified. Chardonnay/Pinot Noir/Pinot Meunier. 12° alc. **RATING** 89 **DRINK** 2008 $28

Boston Bay Wines

NR

Lincoln Highway, Port Lincoln, SA 5606 **REGION** Southern Eyre Peninsula
T (08) 8684 3600 **F** (08) 8684 3637 **WWW**.bostonbaywines.com.au **OPEN** W'ends, school/public hols
11.30–4.30
WINEMAKER David O'Leary, Nick Walker **EST.** 1984 **CASES** 3000
A strongly tourist-oriented operation which has extended the viticultural map in SA. It is situated at
the same latitude as Adelaide, overlooking the Spencer Gulf at the southern tip of the Eyre Peninsula.
Say proprietors Graham and Mary Ford, 'It is the only vineyard in the world to offer frequent
sightings of whales at play in the waters at its foot.'

Botobolar

NR

89 Botobolar Road, Mudgee, NSW 2850 **REGION** Mudgee
T (02) 6373 3840 **F** (02) 6373 3789 **OPEN** Mon–Sat 10–5, Sun 10–3
WINEMAKER Kevin Karstrom **EST.** 1971 **CASES** 4000
One of the first organic vineyards in Australia, with present owner Kevin Karstrom continuing the
practices established by founder Gil Wahlquist. Preservative Free Dry White and Dry Red extend the
organic practice of the vineyard to the winery. Shiraz is consistently the best wine to appear under the
Botobolar label. Exports to the UK, Denmark and Germany.

Bowen Estate

★★★

Riddoch Highway, Coonawarra, SA 5263 **REGION** Coonawarra
T (08) 8737 2229 **F** (08) 8737 2173 **OPEN** 7 days 10–5
WINEMAKER Doug Bowen, Emma Bowen **EST.** 1972 **CASES** 12 000
Bluff-faced regional veteran Doug Bowen, now with daughter Emma at his side in the winery,
presides over one of the Coonawarra landmarks. For reasons I do not begin to understand, the wines
no longer have the edge they once possessed.

 Coonawarra Shiraz 2003 **RATING** 83 **$** 26.50

🍇 Bowman's Run

★★★

1305 Beechworth-Wodonga Road, Wooragee, Vic 3747 **REGION** Beechworth
T (03) 5728 7318 **OPEN** Most w'ends, or by appt
WINEMAKER Fran Robertson, Andrew Doyle **EST.** 1989 **CASES** 250
Struan and Fran Robertson have 1 ha of cabernet sauvignon, 0.5 ha of riesling and small plots of
shiraz and traminer dating back to 1989. The tiny winery came onstream in 2000, part of a larger
general agricultural holding.

 Seven Springs Beechworth Riesling 2003 A pleasant wine with a gentle citrus/mineral
mix; lacks the drive and line of the best examples of the variety. Screwcap. 12.5° alc.
RATING 87 **DRINK** 2010 **$** 20

Granite Rise Beechworth Cabernet Sauvignon 2002 Quite developed, with tawny
aspects; savoury, earthy, olive aromas and flavours; despite the substantial alcohol, didn't
achieve full flavour ripeness. Cork. 13.9° alc. **RATING** 86 **DRINK** 2009 **$** 25

Box Stallion

NR

64 Turrarubba Road, Merricks North, Vic 3926 **REGION** Mornington Peninsula
T (03) 5989 7444 **F** (03) 5989 7688 **WWW**.boxstallion.com.au **OPEN** 7 days 11–5
WINEMAKER Alex White **EST.** 2001 **CASES** 9000
Box Stallion is the joint venture of Stephen Wharton, John Gillies and Garry Zerbe, who have linked
2 vineyards, one at Bittern and one at Merricks North, with 20 ha of vines planted between 1997 and
2003. What once was a thoroughbred stud has now become a vineyard, with the Red Barn (in their
words) 'now home to a stable of fine wines'. Those wines are made at the jointly owned winery with
Alex White as winemaker. Exports to the US and Canada.

Boynton's   ★★★☆

Great Alpine Road, Porepunkah, Vic 3741 **REGION** Alpine Valleys
T (03) 5756 2356 **F** (03) 5756 2610 **WWW**.boynton.com.au **OPEN** 7 days 10–5
WINEMAKER Kel Boynton **EST.** 1987 **CASES** 20 000
Kel Boynton has a beautiful 16-ha vineyard, framed by Feathertop Mountain rising into the skies above it. Overall, the red wines have always outshone the whites. The initial very strong American oak input has been softened in more recent vintages to give a better fruit/oak balance. The wines are released under the Boyton Reserve, Feathertop and Paiko labels. The Paiko label is for wines grown near Mildura by business partner and famed nurseryman Bruce Chalmers. Exports to Germany, Austria and the US.

ŸŸŸŸ♀ **Feathertop Shiraz Viognier 2002** Holding excellent hue; a very appealing medium-bodied silky wine with seductive red fruits; fine, almost sweet, tannins. Dry-grown. Screwcap. 13.5° alc. **RATING** 91 **DRINK** 2012 **$** 20

ŸŸŸŸ **Feathertop Riesling 2005** Delicate lemon and apple blossom aromas; a pleasing palate, though not particularly intense. Cork. 12.5° alc. **RATING** 89 **DRINK** 2008 **$** 20
Feathertop Pinot Gris 2005 Abundant flavour with a tropical fruit peak, then nice lemony acidity on the finish; well above average. Screwcap. 13° alc. **RATING** 89 **DRINK** Now **$** 20
Feathertop Merlot 2003 Light- to medium-bodied sweet berry/cassis fruit; negligible tannins, silky mouthfeel. Screwcap. 14° alc. **RATING** 88 **DRINK** 2008 **$** 20

ŸŸŸ♀ **Feathertop Sauvignon Blanc 2005** **RATING** 86 **DRINK** Now **$** 20
Feathertop Cabernet Sauvignon 2002 **RATING** 86 **DRINK** 2009 **$** 20

Bracken Hill   NR

81 Tinderbox Road, Tinderbox, Tas 7052 **REGION** Southern Tasmania
T (03) 6229 6475 **OPEN** Annual open w'ends in March & October
WINEMAKER Contract **EST.** 1993 **CASES** 120
Max Thalmann came from Switzerland in 1961, retiring 30 years later, and took the decision to plant his 0.4-ha vineyard entirely to gewurztraminer. As Tasmanian writer Phil Laing has pointed out, it is probably the only specialist gewurztraminer producer in the southern hemisphere. The label, incidentally, comes from a painting by Max Thalmann, which proves he is a man of many talents.

Braewattie   NR

351 Rochford Road, Rochford, Vic 3442 **REGION** Macedon Ranges
T (03) 9818 5742 **F** (03) 9818 8361 **OPEN** By appt
WINEMAKER Hanging Rock Winery **EST.** 1993 **CASES** 300
Des and Maggi Ryan bought Braewattie in 1990; Maggi's great-grandfather, James McCarthy, had acquired the property in the 1880s, and it remained in the family until 1971. When the property came back on the market the Ryans seized the opportunity to reclaim it, complete with a small existing planting of 300 pinot noir and chardonnay vines. Those plantings now extend to 5 ha; part of the production is sold as grapes, and a small amount is contract-made. The Macedon Brut is a particularly good wine.

Bramley Wood   NR

RMB 205 Rosa Brook Road, Margaret River, WA 6285 (postal) **REGION** Margaret River
T (08) 9757 9291 **F** (08) 9757 9291 **WWW**.bramleywood.com.au **OPEN** Not
WINEMAKER Cliff Royle **EST.** 1994 **CASES** 200
David and Rebecca McInerney planted 2 ha of cabernet sauvignon in 1994, with an inaugural vintage in 1998. Encouraged by the quality of that wine and, in particular, the 1999 which followed, the McInerneys intend to increase their plantings.

Brand's of Coonawarra

Riddoch Highway, Coonawarra, SA 5263 **REGION** Coonawarra
T (08) 8736 3260 **F** (08) 8736 3208 **WWW**.mcwilliams.com.au **OPEN** Mon–Fri 8–5, w'ends 10–4
WINEMAKER Jim Brayne, Peter Weinberg **EST.** 1966 **CASES** NFP
Part of a very substantial investment in Coonawarra by McWilliam's, which first acquired a 50%
interest from the founding Brand family then moved to 100%, and followed this with the purchase of
100 ha of additional vineyard land. Significantly increased production of the smooth wines for which
Brand's is known has followed. The estate plantings include the 100-year-old Stentiford block.

TTTTT **Shiraz 2003** Fresh red fruits in an elegant and lively frame; clean finish. Cork. **RATING** 90
DRINK 2009 $23

TTTT **Cabernet Sauvignon 2003** Good bright red-purple; pretty austere and savoury; distinct
sweet and sour cassis and green bean flavours; does have presence. Cork. 14° alc.
RATING 88 **DRINK** 2011 $20

TTTT **Chardonnay 2004** **RATING** 86 **DRINK** 2008 $19

Brandy Creek Wines

570 Buln Buln Road, Drouin East, Vic 3818 **REGION** Gippsland
T (03) 5625 4498 **F** (03) 5623 5102 **WWW**.brandycreekwines.com.au **OPEN** W'ends & public hols 10–5
WINEMAKER Peter Beckingham, Ben Tyler (Contract) **EST.** 1999 **CASES** 1200
Marie McDonald and Rick Stockdale purchased the property on which they have since established
their vineyard, cellar door and café restaurant in 1997. One ha each of pinot gris and tempranillo
were progressively planted over the 1999, 2001 and 2002 vintages, with other varieties purchased
from local growers in the region. The café (and surrounding vineyard) is situated on a northeast-
facing slope with spectacular views out to the Baw Baw Ranges, and the vine covered open-air terrace
and gazebo have been thoughtfully built.

TTTT **Reserve Tempranillo 2004** Slightly deeper and brighter colour than the varietal;
appreciably more substance and tannins, though these remain in balance; good length;
likely new oak. **RATING** 89 **DRINK** 2011 $33
Gippsland Pinot Gris 2004 Well-made; citrus, pear and apple; low alcohol a real plus;
good length, and does not rely on sweetness. Screwcap. 12.8° alc. **RATING** 87 **DRINK** Now
$24
Tempranillo 2004 Light, bright colour; light- to medium-bodied, sweet black cherry fruit
and fine tannins; quite good length. Older oak maturation? **RATING** 87 **DRINK** 2009 $28
Sparkling Pinot Gris 2004 An excellent effort with good balance and length; a faint touch
of sweetness in balance. **RATING** 87 **DRINK** Now $33

TTTT **Pinot Noir Chardonnay 2004** Pale straw-green, with good mousse; an abundance of
citrussy fruit; slightly sweet finish. **RATING** 86 **DRINK** Now $28
Gippsland Pinot Gris 2005 **RATING** 85 **DRINK** Now $24

Brangayne of Orange

49 Pinnacle Road, Orange, NSW 2800 **REGION** Orange
T (02) 6365 3229 **F** (02) 6365 3170 **WWW**.brangayne.com **OPEN** Sat 10–4.30 or by appt
WINEMAKER Simon Gilbert Wines **EST.** 1994 **CASES** 3000
Orchardists Don and Pamela Hoskins decided to diversify into grapegrowing in 1994 and have
progressively established 25 ha of high-quality vineyards. Brangayne made an auspicious debut,
underlining the potential of the Orange region. Pamela has now taken over responsibility for the day-
to-day management of the business and marketing. Exports to the UK, Canada and Singapore.

TTTTT **Isolde Reserve Chardonnay 2004** Light straw-green; very much in Isolde style, intense
and complex; nectarine and grapefruit in a seamless marriage with barrel ferment oak and
lees. Screwcap. 13.5° alc. **RATING** 94 **DRINK** 2012 $24

TTTTT **Sauvignon Blanc 2005** Flavoursome tropical, passionfruit, gooseberry; big and rich style,
though balanced by acidity. Screwcap. 13° alc. **RATING** 91 **DRINK** Now $23

Pinot Noir 2004 A complex mix of dark plums and black fruits; avoids dry red, but is at the full-bodied end of the pinot spectrum. Should age well. Screwcap. 13.5° alc. **RATING** 90 **DRINK** 2011 $ 23

Pinot Noir 2003 Firm, savoury, spicy black cherry, long palate; sustained tannins keep just within bounds; aging impressively. Screwcap. 13.3° alc. **RATING** 90 **DRINK** 2010 $ 26

Brave Goose Vineyard

PO Box 633, Seymour, Vic 3660 **REGION** Goulburn Valley
T (03) 9593 9421 **F** (03) 9493 9431 **OPEN** By appt
WINEMAKER John Stocker, Joanne Stocker **EST.** 1988 **CASES** 500

Dr John Stocker and wife Joanne must be among the most highly qualified boutique vineyard and winery operators in Australia. John Stocker is the former chief executive of CSIRO and chairman of the Grape and Wine Research & Development Corporation for 7 years, and daughter Nina has completed the Roseworthy postgraduate oenology course. Moreover, they established their first vineyard (while living in Switzerland) on the French/Swiss border in the village of Flueh, working in conjunction with friends. On returning to Australia in 1987 they finally found a property on the inside of the Great Dividing Range with north-facing slopes and shallow, weathered ironstone soils. Here they have established 2.5 ha each of shiraz and cabernet sauvignon, and 0.5 ha each of merlot and gamay, selling the majority of grapes from the 18-year-old vines, but making small quantities of Cabernet Merlot, Merlot and Gamay, principally sold through the mailing list.

Braydon Estate

40 Londons Road, Lovedale, NSW 2325 (postal) **REGION** Lower Hunter Valley
T (02) 4990 9122 **F** (02) 4990 9133 **OPEN** Not
WINEMAKER Pothana (David Hook) **EST.** 1998 **CASES** 500

Peter and Lesley Giles have established 1.25 ha of vines, split equally between semillon and shiraz. The vine count is 1500 of each variety, which the Giles' describe as 'truly boutique'. The vineyard is looked after by Keith Holder of Pokolbin Viticultural Services, who has a 35-year track record, and the winemaking by the highly skilled David Hook.

TTTTT Home Paddock Hunter Valley Shiraz 2004 Very good colour; has significantly more depth and structure than the shy bouquet suggests; blackberry and plum; soft tannins, minimal oak. Screwcap. 12° alc. **RATING** 90 **DRINK** 2014 $ 18

Braydun Hill Vineyard

38–40 Hepenstal Road, Hackham, SA 5163 **REGION** McLaren Vale
T (08) 8382 3023 **F** (08) 8326 0033 **WWW**.braydunhill.com.au **OPEN** By appt
WINEMAKER Rebecca Kennedy **EST.** 2001 **CASES** 1500

It is hard to imagine there would be such an interesting (and inspiring) story behind a 4-ha vineyard planted between 1998 and 1999 by the husband and wife team of Tony Dunn and Carol Bradley, wishing to get out of growing angora goats and into grapegrowing. The extension of the business into winemaking was totally unplanned, forced on them by the liquidation of Normans in late 2001. With humour, courage and perseverance, they have met obstacles and setbacks which would have caused many to give up, and produced wines since 2001 which have had very significant show success, including a gold medal at the Royal Adelaide Wine Show with their first wine show entry.

TTTTT McLaren Vale Shiraz 2003 Well-made; carries its 14.8° alcohol with relative ease; blackberry, licorice and dark chocolate fruit; well-balanced oak; fine tannins. Cork. 14.8° alc. **RATING** 90 **DRINK** 2010 $ 26.99

Bream Creek ★★★★☆

Marion Bay Road, Bream Creek, Tas 7175 **REGION** Southern Tasmania
T (03) 6231 4646 **F** (03) 6231 4646 **OPEN** At Potters Croft, Dunally, tel (03) 6253 5469
WINEMAKER Winemaking Tasmania (Julian Alcorso) **EST.** 1975 **CASES** 3500

Until 1990 the Bream Creek fruit was sold to Moorilla Estate, but since then the winery has been independently owned and managed under the control of Fred Peacock, legendary for the care he bestows on the vines under his direction. Peacock's skills have seen both an increase in production and also a vast lift in wine quality across the range, headed by the Pinot Noir. The 1996 acquisition of a second vineyard in the Tamar Valley has significantly strengthened the business base of the venture.

ŸŸŸŸŸ **Riesling 2004** Has literally blossomed over the last 12 months. Fine, delicate and pure apple and citrus blossom aromas, then a long, fine and very intense palate. **RATING** 95 **DRINK** 2014 $ 18

ŸŸŸŸŸ **Cabernet Sauvignon 2003** Excellent colour; quite intense and varietal fruit expression in a cassis/currant spectrum; just a ghost of green tannins. **RATING** 93 **DRINK** 2013 $ 23
Chardonnay 2004 Nectarine, stone fruit and citrus, with more intensity and length than many from the vintage; subtle oak. **RATING** 92 **DRINK** 2011 $ 20
Pinot Noir 2004 Luscious, sweet red and black confit fruit; very typical of the vintage; late-picked notes. **RATING** 92 **DRINK** 2010 $ 26
Gewurztraminer 2004 Quite rich and spicy fruit, lime-accented; good palate length and depth; has developed very well over the past year. **RATING** 91 **DRINK** 2008 $ 20

ŸŸŸŸ **Chardonnay 2005** Love it or hate it style, some finding the feral characters too strong, others (myself included) enjoying the tangy complexity. **RATING** 89 **DRINK** Now $ 20

ŸŸŸ **Riesling 2005** **RATING** 83 $ 19

Bremerton Wines ★★★★★

Strathalbyn Road, Langhorne Creek, SA 5255 **REGION** Langhorne Creek
T (08) 8537 3093 **F** (08) 8537 3109 **www.**bremerton.com.au **OPEN** 7 days 10–5
WINEMAKER Rebecca Willson **EST.** 1988 **CASES** 25 000
The Willsons have been grapegrowers in the Langhorne Creek region for some considerable time but their dual business as grapegrowers and winemakers has expanded significantly. Their vineyards have more than doubled to over 100 ha (predominantly cabernet sauvignon, shiraz and merlot), as has their production of wine under the Bremerton label. In February 2004 sisters Rebecca and Lucy (marketing) took control of the business, marking the event with (guess what) revamped label designs. Exports to the UK, the US and other major markets.

ŸŸŸŸŸ **Reserve Cabernet Sauvignon 2002** Excellent colour; supple and smooth; blackcurrant, chocolate and quality oak seamlessly flow across the tongue; great finish and aftertaste. Cork. **RATING** 96 **DRINK** 2017 $ 40
Reserve Cabernet Sauvignon 2001 Very good hue; a fragrant and pure varietal aroma of mulberry, cassis, blackcurrant and earth, and an equally pure expression on the elegant palate; fine tannins, good oak and great length. Cork. 14° alc. **RATING** 96 **DRINK** 2015 $ 40
BOV Shiraz Cabernet 2003 Medium red-purple; a complex array of soft, plush fruit swathed in a cocoon of mocha, vanilla oak. Totally seductive. Cork. **RATING** 94 **DRINK** 2015 $ 75

ŸŸŸŸŸ **Selkirk Shiraz 2003** Strong colour; a rich, full-bodied wine with good balance, the oak obvious but not over the top. Gold medal Sydney Wine Show '06. **RATING** 93 **DRINK** 2013 $ 20
Old Adam Shiraz 2003 Layered and textured black fruits, chocolate and mocha; ripe tannins; looking very good, especially for an '03. Cork. **RATING** 93 **DRINK** 2015 $ 36
Rebecca Willson Sauvignon Blanc 2005 Light, fresh, clean bouquet; progressively lengthens in the mouth; tangy, citrussy acidity on the finish. Screwcap. 12° alc. **RATING** 91 **DRINK** Now $ 17.50
Langhorne Creek Verdelho 2003 Very well-made; quite intense fruit salad; long palate, and amazingly fresh. Screwcap. 13.5° alc. **RATING** 90 **DRINK** 2008 $ 16
Langhorne Creek Malbec 2004 As expected, excellent colour; an interesting wine, with abundant black fruits and a touch of licorice; far better structure than normal with the variety. Screwcap. 13.5° alc. **RATING** 90 **DRINK** 2012 $ 24

ŸŸŸŸ **Langhorne Creek Verdelho 2005** Typical fruit salad flavours, but extended and improved by appealing lemony acidity. Screwcap. 13.5° alc. **RATING** 87 **DRINK** Now $ 17
Racy Rose 2005 Bright, fresh and crisp; small red fruit flavours; dry finish. Screwcap. 14° alc. **RATING** 87 **DRINK** Now $ 15

Tamblyn 2003 Bright, fresh, sweet fruit-driven; medium-bodied; easy access. Value as always. Screwcap. **RATING** 87 **DRINK** 2009 $ 15

▼▼▼▽ **Rebecca Willson Verdelho 2005** **RATING** 85 **DRINK** Now $ 16

Bress ★★★★☆

3894 Calder Highway, Harcourt, Vic 3453 **REGION** Bendigo
T (03) 5474 2262 **F** (03) 5474 2553 **WWW**.bress.com.au **OPEN** W'ends & public hols 11–5, or by appt
WINEMAKER Adam Marks **EST.** 2001 **CASES** 4000
Adam Marks has made wine in all parts of the world since 1991, and made the brave decision (during his honeymoon in 2000) to start his own business. He has selected Margaret River semillon and sauvignon blanc as the best source of white Bordeaux-style wine in Australia; Yarra Valley as the best pinot noir region; and shiraz from Heathcote for precisely the same reason. In early 2005 the Marks family acquired the former Mt Alexander Vineyard and cellar door, expanding the business overnight.

▼▼▼▼▼ **Gold Label Unfiltered Heathcote Shiraz 2004** Superb purple-red; laden with black cherry, blackberry and spice; no viognier mentioned, though it is of that style; tannins fine, alcohol likewise. Screwcap. 14.5° alc. **RATING** 95 **DRINK** 2017 $ 38

▼▼▼▼▽ **Harcourt Valley OD Riesling 2005** Delicate floral, spice and lime aromas; in true Mosel style, balancing sweetness and acidity. One of a growing band making this lovely style. Screwcap. 10.5° alc. **RATING** 93 **DRINK** 2009 $ 20
Margaret River Semillon Sauvignon Blanc 2005 A clean but quiet bouquet; flavours of lemon, green apple and mineral; good structure and length. Screwcap. **RATING** 93 **DRINK** 2008 $ 20
Silver Label Yarra Valley Pinot Noir 2005 Bright light red; elegant but positive cherry, plum and spice mix; fine tannins; long, balanced finish. Screwcap. 13° alc. **RATING** 92 **DRINK** 2012 $ 18

▼▼▼▼ **Heathcote Bendigo Shiraz 2004** Vibrant purple-red; strong, blackberry fruit, still very tightly wound up, needing time to soften. Screwcap. **RATING** 89 **DRINK** 2012 $ 20
Harcourt Valley Cabernets Rose 2005 Salmon-pink; more to European in style; spicy, dry finish. Screwcap. **RATING** 87 **DRINK** Now $ 20

Briagolong Estate ★★★☆

Valencia–Briagolong Road, Briagolong, Vic 3860 **REGION** Gippsland
T (03) 5147 2322 **F** (03) 5147 2400 **WWW**.briagolongestate.com.au **OPEN** By appt
WINEMAKER Gordon McIntosh **EST.** 1979 **CASES** 400
This is very much a weekend hobby for medical practitioner Gordon McIntosh, who invests his chardonnay and pinot noir with Burgundian complexity, battling the climatic elements to do so. He has made several decisions since 2003. First, having had his best vintage in the 1990s (1998) destroyed by TCA cork taint, he has moved to screwcaps. Next, he has introduced the Foothills of Gippsland range at a lower price point (but still estate-grown). Third, he has increased the price of the Estate Chardonnay and Pinot Noir, limited to exceptional barrels, which will not be released every year.

▼▼▼▼▽ **Chardonnay 2003** A complex, rich, nutty wine with many winemaking inputs; honeyed notes and touches of creme brulee; drink sooner rather than later. Cork. 12.8° alc.
RATING 90 **DRINK** 2008 $ 35

▼▼▼▽ **Foothills of Gippsland Chardonnay 2004** **RATING** 86 **DRINK** 2008 $ 22
Foothills of Gippsland Pinot Noir 2004 **RATING** 85 **DRINK** Now $ 22

Brian Barry Wines

PO Box 128, Stepney, SA 5069 **REGION** Clare Valley
T (08) 8363 6211 **F** (08) 8362 0498 **WWW**.brianbarrywines.com **OPEN** Not
WINEMAKER Brian Barry, Judson Barry **EST.** 1977 **CASES** 6000

Brian Barry is an industry veteran with a wealth of winemaking and show-judging experience. His is nonetheless in reality a vineyard-only operation, with a substantial part of the output sold as grapes to other wineries and the wines made under contract at various wineries, albeit under his supervision. As one would expect, the quality is reliably good. Exports to the UK and the US.

ŢŢŢŢŢ Jud's Hill Cabernet Sauvignon 2004 Ultra-ripe, luscious, concentrated cassis and blackcurrant fruit; French oak adds to the impact; so, unfortunately, does the alcohol. Screwcap. 16° alc. **RATING** 91 **DRINK** 2012 $ 22

Briar Ridge ★★★★

Mount View Road, Mount View, NSW 2325 **REGION** Lower Hunter Valley
T (02) 4990 3670 **F** (02) 4990 7802 **WWW**.briarridge.com.au **OPEN** 7 days 10–5
WINEMAKER Karl Stockhausen, Mark Woods **EST.** 1972 **CASES** 25 000
Semillon and Shiraz, each in various guises, have been the most consistent performers, underlying the suitability of these varieties to the Hunter Valley. The Semillon, in particular, invariably shows intense fruit and cellars well. Briar Ridge has been a model of stability, and has the comfort of over 48 ha of estate vineyards, from which it is able to select the best grapes. Exports to the US and Canada.

ŢŢŢŢŢ Signature Mark Woods Chardonnay 2005 Obvious barrel ferment inputs on the bouquet; a tight, focused palate driven by nectarine and melon fruit; long, zesty finish. Cork. 13.5° alc. **RATING** 94 **DRINK** 2009 $ 26

ŢŢŢŢŢ Old Vines Shiraz 2004 Masses of full-bodied black fruit and oak aromas and flavour; allspice, vanilla and leather overtones to the black fruit; strongly regional; 25-year-old vines. Cork. 13.5° alc. **RATING** 92 **DRINK** 2014 $ 23

ŢŢŢŢ Cabernet Rose 2005 Bright colour; quite firm and uncompromisingly dry, but has nice cassis fruit and good balance. Screwcap. 13° alc. **RATING** 88 **DRINK** Now $ 23
Cold Soaked Cabernet Sauvignon 2004 An unusual mix of fruit and oak flavours; firm blackcurrant and earth; lean finish. Cork. 13.5° alc. **RATING** 88 **DRINK** 2012 $ 23
Pinot Noir Chardonnay 2004 Well-balanced; gently sweet citrus, and a crisp finish. No regional status claimed. 10.5° alc. **RATING** 87 **DRINK** Now $ 25

ŢŢŢŢ Early Harvest Semillon 2005 RATING 86 **DRINK** 2010 $ 21
Rock Pile Chardonnay 2005 RATING 86 **DRINK** Now $ 21
Stockhausen Semillon 2005 RATING 84 **DRINK** 2010 $ 26

ŢŢŢ Verdelho 2005 RATING 83 $ 21

Briarose Estate ★★★★

Bussell Highway, Augusta, WA 6290 **REGION** Margaret River
T (08) 9758 4160 **F** (08) 9758 4161 **WWW**.briarose.com.au **OPEN** 7 days 10–4.30
WINEMAKER Cath Oates **EST.** 1998 **CASES** 10 000
Brian and Rosemary Webster began the development of the estate plantings in 1998, which now comprise sauvignon blanc (2.33 ha), semillon (1.33 ha), cabernet sauvignon (6.6 ha), merlot (2.2 ha) and cabernet franc (1.1 ha). The winery is situated at the southern end of the Margaret River region, 6 km north of Augusta, where the climate is distinctly cooler than that of northern Margaret River.

ŢŢŢŢŢ Margaret River Semillon 2004 Amazingly, has soaked up fermentation and 10 months maturation in new French oak without turning a hair; very well-balanced and developing slowly; interesting future. Screwcap. 13° alc. **RATING** 93 **DRINK** 2012 $ 23
Margaret River Sauvignon Blanc 2005 A spotlessly clean bouquet; quite sweet gooseberry, passionfruit, tropical mix, but no sweetness on the finish. Screwcap. 13° alc. **RATING** 91 **DRINK** Now $ 25

ŢŢŢŢ Margaret River Rose 2005 An attractive mix of sweet strawberry and cherry fruit; good balance and length; stylish. Screwcap. 13° alc. **RATING** 88 **DRINK** Now $ 20

Reserve Margaret River Cabernet Sauvignon 2003 Light- to medium-bodied; again, very savoury earthy characters; easier for merlot to get away with it; like an old-time Bordeaux from a lesser vintage. Cork. 13.5° alc. **RATING** 87 **DRINK** 2011 $ 32

Blackwood Cove 2003 Spicy/leafy/minty/savoury/earthy nuances; light- to medium-bodied; in very typical style. The climate simply seems that little bit too cool for the later ripening varietals. Cabernet Sauvignon/Merlot/Cabernet Franc. Cork. 13.5° alc. **RATING** 87 **DRINK** 2010 $ 36

Brick Kiln ★★★★

PO Box 56, Glen Osmond, SA 5064 **REGION** McLaren Vale
T (08) 8379 9314 **F** (08) 8338 6652 **www**.brickiln.com.au **OPEN** Not
WINEMAKER Branson Coach House Winery **EST.** 2001 **CASES** 1500
This is the venture of Malcolm and Alison Mackinnon, Garry and Nancy Watson, and Ian and Pene Davey. They purchased the 8-ha Nine Gums Vineyard, which had been planted to shiraz in 1995/96, in January 2001. The majority of the grapes are sold with a lesser portion contract-made for the partners under the Brick Kiln label, which takes its name from the Brick Kiln Bridge adjacent to the vineyard. Exports to the UK.

TTTTT **McLaren Vale Shiraz 2004** A voluptuous, rich array of dark chocolate and bright red plum and blackberry fruit; fruit-driven; minimal oak. Screwcap. 15° alc. **RATING** 92 **DRINK** 2014 $ 22

Bridgeman Downs NR

Barambah Road, Moffatdale via Murgon, Qld 4605 **REGION** South Burnett
T (07) 4168 4784 **F** (07) 4168 4767 **OPEN** Thurs–Mon 10–4
WINEMAKER Bruce Humphery-Smith **EST.** NA **CASES** NA
A substantial, albeit new, vineyard with 4 ha of vines, the major plantings being verdelho, chardonnay and shiraz and lesser amounts of merlot and cabernet sauvignon.

Briery Estate NR

Lot 16 Briar Lane, Bindoon, WA 6502 **REGION** Perth Hills
T (08) 9576 1417 **F** (08) 9576 1417 **www**.brieryestatewines.com **OPEN** Wed–Mon 10–6, Tuesday by appt
WINEMAKER Ron Waterhouse **EST.** 1994 **CASES** 500
Ron Waterhouse and Christine Smart run Briery Estate (formerly Jacaranda Homestead) in the hills of Bindoon. They have 9 ha of verdelho, pinot noir, grenache, shiraz, cabernet sauvignon, muscat, furmint and harslevelu, although they steer away from varietal naming of their wines.

Brindabella Hills ★★★★★

Woodgrove Close, via Hall, ACT 2618 **REGION** Canberra District
T (02) 6230 2583 **F** (02) 6230 2023 **OPEN** W'ends & public hols 10–5
WINEMAKER Dr Roger Harris **EST.** 1986 **CASES** 2000
Distinguished research scientist Dr Roger Harris presides over Brindabella Hills, which increasingly relies on estate-produced grapes, with small plantings of cabernet sauvignon, cabernet franc, merlot, shiraz, chardonnay, sauvignon blanc, semillon and riesling, and a new planting of sangiovese and brunello. Wine quality has been consistently impressive.

TTTTT **Canberra Sauvignon Blanc 2005** A spotless, ripe, gooseberry/tropical bouquet; gentle passionfruit comes swirling through on a gloriously focused palate, which has great mouthfeel. Phenomenal value. Screwcap. 11.7° alc. **RATING** 94 **DRINK** 2008 $ 15

Canberra Shiraz 2004 Strong red-purple; firm spice, blackberry and dark plum fruit; flavour without undue alcohol; fine tannins. Screwcap. 14° alc. **RATING** 94 **DRINK** 2015 $ 25

TTTTT **Canberra Chardonnay 2005** Clean, tightly structured melon and stone fruit, with oak very much in the background; overall elegance; 25% barrel-fermented. Screwcap. 12.3° alc. **RATING** 91 **DRINK** 2012 $ 20

Canberra Riesling 2005 Light straw-green; floral lime blossom and spice aromas; smooth mouthfeel; clean finish. Screwcap. 12° alc. **RATING** 90 **DRINK** 2012 $ 20

Canberra Merlot 2004 Medium-bodied; attractive cedar, spice, olive and blackcurrant varietal fruit; soft, fine tannins. Screwcap. 14° alc. **RATING** 90 **DRINK** 2010 $ 18

Canberra Cabernet Sauvignon 2004 Light- to medium-bodied; sweet and lively cassis, mulberry, raspberry and blackcurrant fruit; fine tannins, good oak. Screwcap. 14° alc. **RATING** 90 **DRINK** 2014 $ 20

Brini Estate Wines   ★★★★★

RSD 600 Blewitt Springs Road, McLaren Vale, SA 5171 (postal) **REGION** McLaren Vale
T (08) 8383 0080 **F** (08) 8383 0104 **OPEN** Not
WINEMAKER Brian Light (Contract) **EST.** 2000 **CASES** 3000
The Brini family has been growing grapes in the Blewitt Springs area of McLaren Vale since 1953. In 2000 brothers John and Marcello Brini established Brini Estate Wines to vinify a portion of the grape production; up to that time it had been exclusively sold to companies such as Penfolds, Rosemount Estate and d'Arenberg. The flagship Sebastian Shiraz is produced from dry-grown vines planted in 1947, the Shiraz Grenache from dry-grown vines planted in 1964. Skilled winemaking, coupled with impeccable fruit sources, has resulted in a new star in the McLaren Vale firmament.

ŸŸŸŸŸ **Limited Release Sebastian Shiraz 2004** Dense colour; incredibly concentrated and luscious; deep, velvety black fruits, high-quality French oak, and rippling, ripe tannins. Amazing stuff. Not jammy or porty. Cork. 14.5° alc. **RATING** 96 **DRINK** 2029

Sebastian McLaren Vale Shiraz 2004 Another dimension of depth and power; luscious, perfectly ripened blackberry, licorice and dark chocolate; positive French/American oak support, but does not threaten the fruit. Screwcap. 14.5° alc. **RATING** 95 **DRINK** 2024 $ 25

ŸŸŸŸŸ **Blewitt Springs Shiraz 2004** A mix of blackberry, plum and quintessential regional dark chocolate; ripe but soft tannins. Screwcap. 14.5° alc. **RATING** 93 **DRINK** 2014 $ 17

McLaren Vale Shiraz Grenache 2004 Plum, blackberry and dark chocolate; mouthfilling juicy fruit, with very good structure and balance, long finish. Screwcap. 14.5° alc. **RATING** 92 **DRINK** 2013 $ 17

Brischetto Wines   NR

106 Hughes Road, Bargara, Qld 4670 **REGION** Queensland Coastal
T (07) 4159 0862 **F** (07) 4159 0860 **OPEN** 7 days 8–5
WINEMAKER Angelo Puglisi (Contract), Joe Brischetto **EST.** 1996 **CASES** NA
Joe and Elizabeth Brischetto planted the first vines in 1996, expanding the vineyard to its present size of 12 000 vines (around 8 ha) the following year. The winery is at the coastal town of Bargara, 12 km from Bundaberg, and offers views of the sea and vineyards from the outdoor tasting area.

Bristol Farm   NR

59 Bellingham Road, Main Ridge, Vic 3928 **REGION** Mornington Peninsula
T (03) 9830 1453 **F** (03) 9888 6794 **www**.bristolfarm.com.au **OPEN** By appt
WINEMAKER Contract **EST.** 1997 **CASES** 250
Bristol Farm is a pinot noir specialist; Wayne Condon has established slightly over 1 ha of multiple clones of the variety and, for good measure, has not used irrigation in their establishment or ongoing grapegrowing. Monty's Paddock is the premium release, made only in the best vintages; Lionheart is the normal label.

Britannia Creek Wines   NR

75 Britannia Creek Road, Wesburn, Vic 3799 **REGION** Yarra Valley
T (03) 5967 1006 **F** (03) 5780 1426 **OPEN** W'ends 10–6
WINEMAKER Charlie Brydon **EST.** 1982 **CASES** 1600
The wines are made under the Britannia Falls label from 4 ha of estate-grown grapes. A range of vintages are available from the cellar door, with some interesting, full-flavoured Semillon.

Broadview Estate NR

Rowbottoms Road, Granton, Tas 7030 **REGION** Southern Tasmania
T (03) 6263 6882 **F** (03) 6263 6840 **OPEN** Tues–Sun 10–5
WINEMAKER Andrew Hood (Contract) **EST.** 1996 **CASES** 250
David and Kaye O'Neil planted 0.5 ha of chardonnay and 0.25 ha each of riesling and pinot noir in
the spring of 1996, and produce limited quantities of normally very good Riesling and Chardonnay.

Brocks View Estate ★★★★

PO Box 396, Yankalilla, SA 5203 **REGION** Southern Fleurieu
T (08) 8558 2233 **OPEN** Not
WINEMAKER Phillip Christiansen (Contract) **EST.** 1998 **CASES** 250
Peter and Julie Brocksopp have planted a single ha of shiraz at Carrickalinga, with coastal views out
over Yankalilla Bay, giving rise to the slogan 'from vines with a view'. The close density planting on
gravel loam over red clay soils is managed organically, with minimal irrigation, the vines hand-
pruned and hand-picked.

ŸŸŸŸŸ **Southern Fleurieu Shiraz 2003** A richly robed and structured mix of blackberry, spice
and licorice; subtle oak and fine, firm tannins. Cork. **RATING** 90 **DRINK** 2013 $18.50

Brockville Wines NR

15th Street Ext, Irymple South, Vic 3498 **REGION** Murray Darling
T (03) 5024 5143 **WWW.**brockvillewines.com.au **OPEN** 7 days 10–4
WINEMAKER Contract **EST.** 1999 **CASES** 800
Mark Bowring, a great-grandson of WB Chaffey (responsible for the design and implementation of
the irrigation scheme in the Sunraysia district in the 1880s), and wife Leigh have been growing
grapes since 1975. They have 10 ha of chardonnay, 4.4 ha of cabernet sauvignon and 1 ha of shiraz. In
1999 the Bowrings decided to have some cabernet sauvignon vinified for their own label, choosing
Brockville as the name, as it is (or was) the Canadian hometown of WB Chaffey. More recently (in
2003) they acquired an additional 23 ha of vineyard directly across the road from their original
plantings, and have opened a cellar door.

Broke Estate/Ryan Family Wines ★★★☆

Wollombi Road, Broke, NSW 2330 **REGION** Lower Hunter Valley
T (02) 6579 1065 **F** (02) 6574 5199 **WWW.**ryanwines.com.au **OPEN** W'ends & public hols 11–5
WINEMAKER Matthew Ryan **EST.** 1988 **CASES** 2000
This is the flagship operation of the Ryan family, with 25 ha of largely mature vineyards, the lion's
share to chardonnay, but also including meaningful plantings of semillon, sauvignon blanc, shiraz,
merlot, barbera, tempranillo, cabernet sauvignon and cabernet franc.

ŸŸŸŸŸ **Broke Estate Semillon 2001** Very good colour; lively and fresh, but starting to show some
bottle-developed honeyed touches to the aroma; lively grassy/lemony/herbal fruit
flavours. Cork. **RATING** 91 **DRINK** 2010 $22

ŸŸŸŸ **Broke Estate Cabernet Sauvignon 2003** Light- to medium-bodied; firm, earthy/briary
cabernet fruit on both bouquet and palate, but does tail off towards the finish. Cork.
14° alc. **RATING** 87 **DRINK** 2009 $30

ŸŸŸŸ **Broke Estate Lacrima Angelorum 2001 RATING** 86 **DRINK** Now $28

Broke's Promise Wines ★★★☆

725 Milbrodale Road, Broke, NSW 2330 **REGION** Lower Hunter Valley
T (02) 6579 1165 **F** (02) 9972 1619 **WWW.**brokespromise.com.au **OPEN** Mon–Fri by appt, w'ends 10–4
WINEMAKER Margan Family **EST.** 1996 **CASES** 4000
Joe and Carol Re purchased Broke's Promise in 2005 from Jane Marquard and Dennis Karp, and have
continued the winemaking arrangements with Andrew Margan. A new cellar door opened at Easter
2006. The 3.3-ha vineyard is complemented by 1800 olive trees. Exports to the UK and Hong Kong.

♈♈♈♈♈ **The Dance of Anna Chardonnay 2003** Glorious green-yellow; a lovely wine, with melon, nectarine and citrus; pure and penetrating, the touch of barrel ferment merely a note. Screwcap. 13.5° alc. **RATING** 94 **DRINK** 2010 $16

♈♈♈♈ **Hunter Valley Verdelho 2005** Clean, fresh, aromatic fruit salad aromas and flavours, with a twist of citrus; a very good example of the variety. Screwcap. 13.5° alc. **RATING** 89 **DRINK** Now $16
Hunter Valley Chardonnay 2005 Very developed colour; likewise bouquet; the palate, however, is much better, with soft peachy fruit and touches of honey and cream. Screwcap. 13° alc. **RATING** 87 **DRINK** Now $16

♈♈♈ **Hunter Valley Barbera 2004** **RATING** 82 $16
Hunter Valley Barbera 2003 **RATING** 80 $16

Broken Gate Wines ★★★★

101 Munster Terrace, North Melbourne, Vic 3051 (postal) **REGION** Southeast Australia
T (03) 9348 9333 **F** (03) 9348 9688 **WWW.**brokengate.com.au **OPEN** Not
WINEMAKER Contract **EST.** 2001 **CASES** 4000
Broken Gate is a partnership between Brendan Chapman and Joseph Orbach. Chapman has an extensive liquor retailing background, and is presently bulk wine buyer for Swords Wines, responsible for the purchase of 160 000 litres of wine across Australia. Joseph Orbach lived and worked in the Clare Valley from 1994 to 1998 at Leasingham Wines, while also leading the restoration of the Clarevale Winery Co-op building.

♈♈♈♈♈ **Sunbury Shiraz 2004** Medium purple-red; an attractive, supple, medium-bodied wine, easily carrying its alcohol; black cherry and plum fruit caresses the mouth; controlled oak. Screwcap. 14.5° alc. **RATING** 93 **DRINK** 2014 $20
Adelaide Hills Sauvignon Blanc 2005 Clean tropical/gooseberry fruit with minerally notes; gathers power on the back-palate and finish. Screwcap. 13.5° alc. **RATING** 90 **DRINK** Now $18

♈♈♈♈ **Heathcote Sangiovese 2004** Well into the savoury, briary, earthy spectrum of flavours; the tannins not too lean, but nonetheless a food style, pure and simple. Cork. 14.6° alc. **RATING** 89 **DRINK** 2008 $17

Brokenwood ★★★★★

401–427 McDonalds Road, Pokolbin, NSW 2321 **REGION** Lower Hunter Valley
T (02) 4998 7559 **F** (02) 4998 7893 **WWW.**brokenwood.com.au **OPEN** Sun–Fri 10–5, Sat 9.30–5
WINEMAKER Iain Riggs, PJ Charteris **EST.** 1970 **CASES** 100 000
Deservedly fashionable winery producing consistently excellent wines. Has kept Graveyard Shiraz as its ultimate flagship wine, while extending its reach through many of the best eastern regions for its broad selection of varietal wine styles. Its big-selling Hunter Semillon remains alongside Graveyard, and there is then a range of wines coming from regions including Orange, Central NSW Ranges, Beechworth, McLaren Vale, Cowra and elsewhere. A newly built 2-storey tasting facility named the Albert Room (in honour of the late Tony Albert, one of the founders) was opened in April 2006. Exports to all major markets.

♈♈♈♈♈ **ILR Reserve Semillon 1999** Fine, delightfully tight and crisp; an absolute definition of Hunter Valley Semillon style, the finish going on forever. Cork is the only threat. Cork. 11.5° alc. **RATING** 96 **DRINK** 2014 $35
Graveyard Shiraz 2003 Very good colour; blackberry and cherry with touches of chocolate and spicy oak; restrained power to a wine of immaculate balance and length. Happily, only 13.5° alcohol. Screwcap. 13.5° alc. **RATING** 96 **DRINK** 2023 $100
Hunter Valley Semillon 2005 Vibrantly fresh and crisp; spotlessly clean; lemony, grassy, minerally flavours; citrussy acidity; dry finish. Spot on the money. Screwcap. **RATING** 95 **DRINK** 2010 $17
Hunter Valley Semillon 2004 Spotlessly clean; precisely balanced and structured lime, lemon and talc/mineral acidity. Screwcap. **RATING** 94 **DRINK** 2016 $17

Beechworth Pinot Gris 2004 Very good, highly scented, flowery bouquet; a lovely palate; neatly juxtaposed sweet fruit and grainy acidity. Screwcap. 14° alc. **RATING** 94 **DRINK** Now $ 25

Wade Block 2 McLaren Vale Shiraz 2004 Ultra McLaren Vale style, black fruits and dark chocolate; stuffed full of everything, yet retains balance. **RATING** 94 **DRINK** 2019 $ 39

Wade Block 2 McLaren Vale Shiraz 2003 A rich and sweet mix of blackberry, plum, chocolate and vanilla/mocha oak; soft, almost plush, tannins; 60-year-old vines. Screwcap. **RATING** 94 **DRINK** 2018 $ 35

ΨΨΨΨΨ Indigo Vineyard Chardonnay 2004 Bright green-yellow; subdued though clean (no reduction) bouquet; a seamless palate of ripe melon, fig and stone fruit with subtle barrel ferment inputs; lovely wine. Screwcap. **RATING** 93 **DRINK** 2009 $ 30

Rayner Vineyard McLaren Vale Shiraz 2003 Supple, mouthfilling, medium- to full-bodied wine; dark fruits with splashes of chocolate and mocha; ripe tannins. Screwcap. 14° alc. **RATING** 92 **DRINK** 2013 $ 69

Cricket Pitch Sauvignon Blanc Semillon 2004 Still fresh and lively; a mix of lemon juice, gooseberry and herb; excellent crisp, citrussy acidity; a hint of barrel ferment lurks in one corner. Screwcap. **RATING** 90 **DRINK** Now $ 17

ΨΨΨΨ Beechworth Pinot Noir 2004 The strong colour heralds a strong pinot, with black cherry, plum and powerful, savoury tannins; may soften, but in the meantime will satisfy cabernet drinkers. Screwcap. **RATING** 89 **DRINK** 2009 $ 24

Cabernet Sauvignon Merlot 2003 Clean, fresh, lively aromas; medium-bodied, with juicy red berry fruits; fine-grained tannins; subtle oak. Beechworth/King Valley/McLaren Vale. Screwcap. **RATING** 89 **DRINK** 2012 $ 28

Brook Eden Vineyard ★★★☆

Adams Road, Lebrina, Tas 7254 **REGION** Northern Tasmania
T (03) 6395 6244 **F** (03) 6395 6211 **WWW**.brookeden.com.au **OPEN** 7 days 10–5 Aug–June
WINEMAKER Tamar Ridge **EST.** 1988 **CASES** 750
In September 2004 Peter McIntosh and Sue Stuart purchased Brook Eden from Sheila Bezemer. At 41° south and at an altitude of 160m it is one of the coolest sites in Tas, and (in the words of the new owners) 'represents viticulture on the edge'. While the plantings remain the same (1 ha pinot noir, 0.75 ha chardonnay and 0.25 ha riesling) yield has been significantly reduced, resulting in earlier picking and better quality grapes.

ΨΨΨΨ Pinot Noir 2004 Bright colour; fresh red and black fruits; light- to medium-bodied, with a slightly firm mouthfeel needing to soften. **RATING** 89 **DRINK** 2010 $ 25

Chardonnay 2004 Pleasant, although not particularly intense, sweet stone fruit; well-handled in the winery. **RATING** 87 **DRINK** 2009 $ 25

ΨΨΨΨ Riesling 2005 RATING 84 **DRINK** 2008 $ 23

Brookhampton Estate NR

South Western Highway, Donnybrook, WA 6239 **REGION** Geographe
T (08) 9731 0400 **F** (08) 9731 0500 **WWW**.brookhamptonestate.com.au **OPEN** Wed–Sun 10–4
WINEMAKER Contract **EST.** 1998 **CASES** 4000
Brookhampton Estate, situated 3 km south of Donnybrook, has wasted no time since its establishment in 1998: 127 ha of vines have been established with three fashionable red varietals to the fore — cabernet sauvignon (34 ha), shiraz (29 ha) and merlot (22 ha); 1 ha of tempranillo and 3 ha of grenache can safely be classed as experimental. The three white varieties planted are chardonnay, sauvignon blanc and semillon.

Brookland Valley ★★★★★

Caves Road, Wilyabrup, WA 6280 **REGION** Margaret River
T (08) 9755 6042 **F** (08) 9755 6214 **WWW**.brooklandvalley.com.au **OPEN** 7 days 10–5
WINEMAKER Ross Pamment **EST.** 1984 **CASES** 2800

Brookland Valley has an idyllic setting, plus its much enlarged Flutes Café (one of the best winery restaurants in the Margaret River region) and its Gallery of Wine Arts, which houses an eclectic collection of wine and food-related art and wine accessories. After acquiring a 50% share of Brookland Valley in 1997, Hardys moved to full ownership in September 2004. Exports to the UK, Germany, Switzerland, Japan and Hong Kong.

🍷🍷🍷🍷🍷 **Verse 1 Semillon Sauvignon Blanc 2005** A clean, zesty, vibrant mix of herbaceous and tropical fruit; crunchy, lemony acidity on the finish; very good length. Screwcap. **RATING** 95 **DRINK** 2009 $ 19

Sauvignon Blanc 2005 A spotlessly clean bouquet; rich tropical gooseberry fruit; good length and balance. Gold medal Sydney Wine Show '06. Screwcap. **RATING** 94 **DRINK** Now $ 24

Chardonnay 2003 Fine, long and tightly focused; gentle white peach and nectarine; good balance, refined oak use. Cork. 14° alc. **RATING** 94 **DRINK** 2008 $ 25

Verse 1 Margaret River Merlot 2003 Generous plum, black olive and earth fruit; good structure and balance; controlled oak. Gold medal Sydney Wine Show '06. Cork. 14° alc. **RATING** 94 **DRINK** 2010 $ 21.50

Cabernet Sauvignon Merlot 2002 Light- to medium-bodied; very pure and clear cool-grown cabernet supported by fine tannins. Gold medal National Wine Show '05. **RATING** 94 **DRINK** 2012 $ 37

🍷🍷🍷🍷🍷 **Verse 1 Margaret River Shiraz 2003** Very elegant, fresh and lively; medium-bodied, well-balanced red and black fruits; good tannin and oak extract. Cork. 14° alc. **RATING** 92 **DRINK** 2010 $ 21.50

🍷🍷🍷🍷 **Verse 1 Rose 2005** Bright, light fuchsia; fragrant cherry and strawberry fruits on a lively and fresh palate; near-dry finish. Screwcap. **RATING** 89 **DRINK** Now $ 15.90

Verse 1 Cabernet Sauvignon Merlot 2003 Aromatic notes of spice, berry and mint; medium-bodied, with good balance and fine, savoury tannins. Cork. **RATING** 89 **DRINK** 2010 $ 21.50

Brookside Vineyard   NR

5 Loaring Road, Bickley Valley, WA 6076 **REGION** Perth Hills
T (08) 9291 8705 **F** (08) 9291 5316 **WWW**.geocities.com/brooksidevineyard **OPEN** W'ends & public hols 11–5
WINEMAKER Darlington Estate **EST.** 1984 **CASES** 400
Brookside is one of the many doll's house-scale vineyard operations which dot the Perth Hills. It has 0.25 ha each of chardonnay and cabernet sauvignon, and sells the wine through a mailing list. B&B accommodation has attractive views of the Bickley Valley.

Brookwood Estate   ★★★★

Treeton Road, Cowaramup, WA 6284 **REGION** Margaret River
T (08) 9755 5604 **F** (08) 9755 5870 **WWW**.brookwood.com.au **OPEN** 7 days 10–5
WINEMAKER Lyn Mann **EST.** 1996 **CASES** 2000
Trevor and Lyn Mann began the development of their 50-ha property in 1996, and now have 1.1 ha each of shiraz, semillon, sauvignon blanc and chenin blanc, and 1 ha of cabernet sauvignon. An onsite winery was constructed in 1999 to accommodate the first vintage. Viticultural consultants advise on management in the vineyard; the Manns are aiming to establish export markets.

🍷🍷🍷🍷🍷 **Margaret River Sauvignon Blanc 2005** Spotlessly clean; fine, delicate passionfruit and gooseberry, finishing with lemony acidity; delicious lighter style. Screwcap. 13° alc. **RATING** 92 **DRINK** Now $ 22

Margaret River Cabernet Sauvignon 2004 Lovely cassis blackcurrant fruit drives the medium-bodied palate; balanced, fine tannins. Cork. 14.5° alc. **RATING** 91 **DRINK** 2015 $ 35

Margaret River Shiraz 2004 Elegant, light- to medium-bodied; black cherry, plum and spice fruit; fine tannins and good oak handling. Cork. 14.5° alc. **RATING** 90 **DRINK** 2014 $ 28

🍷🍷🍷🍷 **Margaret River Semillon Autumn Harvest 2005** Only slightly off-dry; while aimed at the cellar door and those with a sweet tooth, will age well, but likely be given little chance to do so. Screwcap. 12.5° alc. **RATING** 87 **DRINK** 2012 $ 20

🍷🍷🍷 **Margaret River Chenin Blanc 2005** **RATING** 83 $ 18

Broomstick Estate

4 Frances Street, Mount Lawley, WA 6050 (postal) **REGION** Margaret River
T (08) 9271 9594 **F** (08) 9271 9741 **WWW**.broomstick.com.au **OPEN** Not
WINEMAKER Rockfield Estate (Andrew Gaman) **EST.** 1997 **CASES** 1000
Robert Holloway and family purchased the property on which the vineyard is now established in 1993 as an operating dairy farm. In 1997, 5.5 ha of shiraz was planted. Over the following years 3.8 ha of merlot and then (in 2004) 5.3 ha of chardonnay and 2 ha of sauvignon blanc were added. The Holloways see themselves as grapegrowers first and foremost, but make a small amount of wine under the Broomstick Estate label.

ŸŸŸŸ **Margaret River Petit Verdot 2004** Almost inevitably has more structure than the Cabernet; dark berry fruits, then typical varietal tannins on the finish. A blend of the 2 wines beckons. Screwcap. 13.5° alc. **RATING** 88 **DRINK** 2011 $ 27
Margaret River Cabernet Sauvignon 2004 Indifferent colour; leafy, minty, red berry fruit with some cassis; lost the battle for full ripeness. Screwcap. 13.5° alc. **RATING** 87 **DRINK** 2009 $ 17

Brothers in Arms

PO Box 840, Langhorne Creek, SA 5255 **REGION** Langhorne Creek
T (08) 8537 3070 **F** (08) 8537 3415 **WWW**.brothersinarms.com.au **OPEN** Not
WINEMAKER David Freschi **EST.** 1998 **CASES** 18 000
The Adams family has been growing grapes at Langhorne Creek since 1891, when the first vines at the famed Metala vineyards were planted. Tom and Guy Adams are the fifth generation to own and work the vineyard, and over the past 20 years have both improved the viticulture and expanded the plantings to the present 40 ha (shiraz and cabernet sauvignon). It was not until 1998 that they decided to hold back a small proportion of the production for vinification under the Brothers in Arms label. Exports to the UK, US, Canada and Singapore.

ŸŸŸŸŸ **Langhorne Creek Shiraz 2002** Deep, dense, red-purple; layer-upon-layer of black cherry, plum, bitter chocolate, ripe tannins and oak; carries 15° alcohol very well. Cork. 15° alc. **RATING** 95 **DRINK** 2017 $ 40

ŸŸŸŸ **No. 6 Shiraz Cabernet 2003** **RATING** 86 **DRINK** 2008 $ 20

Brown Brothers

Milawa-Bobinawarrah Road, Milawa, Vic 3678 **REGION** King Valley
T (03) 5720 5500 **F** (03) 5720 5511 **WWW**.brownbrothers.com.au **OPEN** 7 days 9–5
WINEMAKER Wendy Cameron, Marc Scalzo, Hamish Seabrook, Joel Tilbrook, Catherine Looney **EST.** 1885 **CASES** 1.1 million
Brown Brothers draws upon a considerable number of vineyards spread throughout a range of site climates, ranging from very warm to very cool. It is also known for the diversity of varieties with which it works, and the wines represent good value for money. Deservedly one of the most successful family wineries in Australia. Exports to all major markets.

ŸŸŸŸŸ **Whitlands Sauvignon Blanc 2005** Spotless passionfruit and gooseberry aromas; great line, length and balance, the vibrant gooseberry fruit lengthened with lemony acidity. Screwcap. 12.5° alc. **RATING** 94 **DRINK** Now $ 16
Patricia Pinot Noir Chardonnay 1999 Aromatic pear, apple and spice bouquet; crisp, clean, lively and fresh; good length and intensity; dry finish. **RATING** 94 **DRINK** Now $ 39
Liqueur Muscat NV Dark olive-brown; super-rich raisin varietal character; Christmas pudding richness; excellent length and balance. **RATING** 94 **DRINK** Now $ 30

ŸŸŸŸŸ **Very Old Tokay NV** Obvious age from the olive rim colour; retains good varietal character; toffee, cold tea and brandy snap; good spirit. **RATING** 93 **DRINK** Now $ 27.90
Patricia Pinot Noir Chardonnay 2003 Intense citrus, nectarine and strawberry mix with nutty, bready lees complexity; good length. **RATING** 92 **DRINK** 2010 $ 39
Patricia Chardonnay 2003 Rich yellow peach, fig and melon fruit; the oak balanced and integrated; full-bodied chardonnay style. Cork. **RATING** 90 **DRINK** 2009 $ 31

Sparkling Shiraz 2002 A generous array of spicy black fruit flavour; neither oaky nor sweet; a serious example, worthy of cellaring. 14.5° alc. RATING 90 DRINK 2010 $ 24

▼▼▼▼ **Victoria Riesling 2005** Clean and crisp, with good structure and balance; minerally/slatey mouthfeel, with a touch of citrus. Screwcap. 13° alc. RATING 89 DRINK 2012 $ 16
King Valley Pinot Rose 2005 Very pale blush; attractive rose petal/strawberry/citrus aromas, and a dry, crisp palate. Great summer wine. Screwcap. 12.5° alc. RATING 89 DRINK Now $ 19
Patricia Chardonnay 2002 Solid, ripe, rich yellow peach fruit; some sweetness, as much from the alcohol as anything else; subtle oak. RATING 88 DRINK 2009 $ 30.80
Cellar Door Release Pinot Gris 2005 Apple, pear and a flick of musk; late picking adds flavour, without diminishing the fresh, bright finish. Screwcap. 15° alc. RATING 88 DRINK Now $ 17
Cellar Door Release Arneis 2005 Often shares the anonymity of its countryman pinot grigio; light, dry, green apple and pear fruit; bright finish. Screwcap. 13° alc. RATING 87 DRINK Now $ 16
Cellar Door Release Vermentino 2005 Quite fresh, fragrant and fruity, with notes of orange and mandarin; good acidity. The first release of this Italian variety for Brown Brothers. Screwcap. 14.5° alc. RATING 87 DRINK Now $ 16
Pinot Noir Chardonnay Pinot Meunier NV Fine, elegant, crisp and fresh; not complex, however. 12.5° alc. RATING 87 DRINK 2008 $ 19
Orange Muscat & Flora 2005 Friendly fruit salad sweetness, with some blossom aromas; a long-standing Brown Brothers' special. Cork. 10.5° alc. RATING 87 DRINK Now $ 10

▼▼▼▽ **Victoria Pinot Grigio 2005** RATING 86 DRINK Now $ 16
Moscato 2005 RATING 86 DRINK Now $ 14
Limited Release Merlot 2002 RATING 86 DRINK 2008 $ 27

▼▼▼ **Victoria Cienna 2005** RATING 83 $ 12
Victoria Dolcetto & Syrah 2005 RATING 83 $ 14

Brown Hill Estate ★★★★

Cnr Rosa Brook Road/Barrett Road, Rosa Brook, WA 6285 REGION Margaret River
T (08) 9757 4003 F (08) 9757 4004 www.brownhillestate.com.au OPEN 7 days 10–5
WINEMAKER Nathan Bailey EST. 1995 CASES 3000
The Bailey family's stated aim is to produce top-quality wines at affordable prices, via uncompromising viticultural practices emphasising low yields per ha, in conjunction with the family being involved in all stages of production with minimum outside help. They have established 7 ha each of shiraz and cabernet sauvignon, 4 ha of semillon and 2 ha each of sauvignon blanc and merlot, and by the standards of the Margaret River, the prices are indeed affordable.

▼▼▼▼▽ **Finniston Reserve Shiraz 2004** Dense red-purple; rich, powerful and intense black fruits with firm tannins and controlled oak. Stained cork. 14.8° alc. RATING 91 DRINK 2012 $ 25
Croesus Reserve Merlot 2004 Bright red-purple; an attractive varietal mix of redcurrant, black olive and snow peas; the tannins just a little abrasive for the style. Cork. 14.8° alc. RATING 90 DRINK 2011 $ 25

▼▼▼▼ **Chaffers Shiraz 2004** Medium-bodied; blackberry and plum, with a touch of mint; soft tannins and fair length. Screwcap. 14.5° alc. RATING 88 DRINK 2010 $ 18
Ivanhoe Reserve Cabernet Sauvignon 2004 Strong red-purple; blackcurrant/cassis opens the medium-bodied palate; the tannins needed taming, however, and may not come back into balance. Cork. 14.8° alc. RATING 88 DRINK 2011 $ 25

▼▼▼▽ **Hannans Cabernet Sauvignon 2004** RATING 86 DRINK 2008 $ 18

Brown Magpie Wines ★★★★

125 Larcombes Road, Moriac, Vic 3249 REGION Geelong
T (03) 5261 3875 F (03) 5261 3875 www.brownmagpiewines.com OPEN 7 days 12–3
WINEMAKER Loretta Breheny, Shane Breheny, Karen Coulston (Consultant) EST. 2000 CASES 3000

Shane and Loretta Breheny own a 20-ha property predominantly situated on a gentle, north-facing slope, with cypress trees on the western and southern borders providing protection against the wind. Over 2001 and 2002, 9 ha of vines were planted, with pinot noir (5 ha) taking the lion's share, followed by pinot gris (2 ha), shiraz (1.5 ha) and 0.25 ha each of chardonnay and sauvignon blanc. Viticulture is Loretta Breheny's love; winemaking (and wine) is Shane's.

ㅇㅇㅇㅇㅇ **Geelong Shiraz 2004** Dense purple-red; medium-bodied, silky texture; cool black fruits and spice; good French oak balance and integration. Screwcap. 14° alc. **RATING** 94 **DRINK** 2012 $ 22

ㅇㅇㅇㅇ **Breheny Vineyards Geelong Pinot Gris 2005** Strongly varietal spice, musk and pear aromas and flavours; helped by brisk acidity and a subliminal hint of sugar. Screwcap. 14° alc. **RATING** 89 **DRINK** Now $ 20
Pinot Gris 2005 Quite floral and fragrant blossom aromas; long palate; good acidity; just a twitch of alcohol. **RATING** 89 **DRINK** Now $ 20

ㅇㅇㅇㅇ **Breheny Vineyards Thomsons Creek Pinot Noir 2004** **RATING** 84 **DRINK** Now $ 15

Brown's Farm Winery ★★★

3675 Great North Road, Laguna, NSW 2325 (postal) **REGION** Lower Hunter Valley
T (02) 4998 8273 **F** (02) 4998 8273 **www**.wollombivalley.com **OPEN** Not
WINEMAKER Frank Geisler, Jarmila Geisler **EST.** 1998 **CASES** 250
Frank and Jarmila Geisler established their 1-ha vineyard with the simple belief that 'the best wine is made in the smallest vineyard'. It is principally planted to cabernet sauvignon and merlot, with a small quantity of chardonnay and pinot gris. It is managed on quasi-organic principles, and both the viticulture and winemaking are carried out by the Geislers 'without too much outside help'.

ㅇㅇㅇㅇ **Cabernet Sauvignon 2004** Firm, fresh, crisp blackcurrant varietal fruit; nervous acidity. Cork. 12° alc. **RATING** 87 **DRINK** 2010 $ 12

ㅇㅇㅇㅇ **Merlot 2004** **RATING** 85 **DRINK** Now $ 12

Browns of Padthaway ★★★★

Keith Road, Padthaway, SA 5271 **REGION** Padthaway
T (08) 8765 6063 **F** (08) 8765 6083 **www**.browns-of-padthaway.com **OPEN** At Padthaway Estate
WINEMAKER Contract **EST.** 1993 **CASES** 35 000
The Brown family has for many years been the largest independent grapegrower in Padthaway, a district in which most of the vineyards were established and owned by Wynns, Seppelt, Lindemans and Hardys, respectively. After a slow start, has produced excellent wines since 1998, and wine production has increased accordingly.

ㅇㅇㅇㅇㅇ **Cabernet Sauvignon 2002** Supple, smooth, round and ripe; very good balance and oak integration. **RATING** 92 **DRINK** 2015 $ 24

ㅇㅇㅇㅇ **Ernest Family Reserve Shiraz 2003** Big, ripe style; sweet black fruits; lots of mocha and vanilla. **RATING** 88 **DRINK** 2010 $ 24

ㅇㅇㅇㅇ **Riesling 2005** **RATING** 84 **DRINK** Now $ 16

Brumby Wines ★★★

Sandyanna, 24 Cannon Lane, Wood Wood, Vic 3596 **REGION** Swan Hill
T 0438 305 364 **F** (03) 5030 5366 **www**.brumbywines.com.au **OPEN** Mon–Fri 9–5
WINEMAKER Neil Robb, John Ellis, Glen Olsen (Contract) **EST.** 2001 **CASES** 2000
The derivation of the name is even more direct and simple than you might imagine: the owners are Stuart and Liz Brumby, who decided to plant grapes for supply to others before moving to having an increasing portion of their production from the 13.5 ha of chardonnay, cabernet sauvignon, shiraz and durif vinified under their own label.

ㅇㅇㅇㅇ **Chardonnay 2004** A pleasant, fruit-driven wine; nectarine and stone fruit with subliminal oak; good finish. Screwcap. 13.5° alc. **RATING** 89 **DRINK** 2008 $ 14

Durif 2004 Typical depth, concentration and power; dark fruits, licorice, prune and plum; a vinous black hole in space. Cork. 14° alc. **RATING** 89 **DRINK** 2015 **$** 22

🍷🍷🍷 **Cabernet Sauvignon 2003** **RATING** 79 **$** 15

Brunswick Hill Wines NR

34 Breese Street, Brunswick, Vic 3056 **REGION** Port Phillip Zone
T (03) 9383 4681 **OPEN** By appt
WINEMAKER Peter Atkins, Graeme Rojo **EST.** 1999 **CASES** NA
Peter Atkins owns the Brunswick Hill Wines venture, which claims to be Melbourne's only urban winery, situated in the heart of urban Brunswick, 15 mins from the CBD. Studley Park Vineyard is even closer, but its grapes are sent to Granite Hills for winemaking. A member of the Eltham and District Winemakers Guild, Atkins moved to commercial winemaking after 10 years as an amateur. Brunswick Hill Wines takes grapes from a number of Victorian regions, ranging from cool to warm.

Brushwood Wines ★★★☆

Suite 3, 49 Ord Street, West Perth, WA 6005 (postal) **REGION** Margaret River
T (08) 9426 6300 **F** (08) 9322 6954 **www**.brushwoodwines.com.au **OPEN** Not
WINEMAKER Peter Stanlake (Contract) **EST.** 2000 **CASES** 2100
This is very much a part-time occupation for owners David van der Walt and Stephen Vaughan. They have planted 6 ha of cabernet sauvignon, 2 ha of chardonnay and 1 ha of shiraz, limiting the make of each variety to 700 cases a year and selling the surplus grapes.

🍷🍷🍷🍷🍷 **Margaret River Shiraz 2004** Strong colour; potent blackberry, dark plum and spice, the alcohol thrusting through a little; will develop. Screwcap. **RATING** 90 **DRINK** 2012 **$** 12

🍷🍷🍷🍷 **Margaret River Chardonnay 2005** A complex, rich wine with strong barrel ferment/oak maturation influences on the peach and nectarine fruit. Screwcap. 14.1° alc. **RATING** 89 **DRINK** 2009 **$** 10

Margaret River Chardonnay 2004 Fragrant, light-bodied style; melon, nectarine and citrus aromas and flavours; possibly young vines. Screwcap. **RATING** 87 **DRINK** Now **$** 10

🍷🍷🍷🍷 **Limited Release Margaret River Cabernet Sauvignon 2003** **RATING** 86 **DRINK** 2009 **$** 15

Bulga Wine Estates NR

Bulga Road, Swan Hill, Vic 3585 **REGION** Swan Hill
T (03) 5037 6685 **F** (03) 5037 6992 **OPEN** By appt
WINEMAKER Rod Bouchier **EST.** 1999 **CASES** NA
Bulga Wine Estates draws on a little over 50 ha altogether: chardonnay (10 ha), cabernet sauvignon (10 ha), the remainder shiraz and a little colombard. Only part of the wine is vinified under the Bulga Wine Estates label, and handsomely so.

Bullers Beverford NR

Murray Valley Highway, Beverford, Vic 3590 **REGION** Swan Hill
T (03) 5037 6305 **F** (03) 5037 6803 **www**.buller.com.au **OPEN** Mon–Sat 9–5
WINEMAKER Richard Buller (Jnr) **EST.** 1951 **CASES** 120 000
This is a parallel operation to the Calliope winery at Rutherglen, similarly owned and operated by third-generation Richard and Andrew Buller. It offers traditional wines which in the final analysis reflect both their Riverland origin and a fairly low-key approach to style in the winery.

Bullers Calliope ★★★★★

Three Chain Road, Rutherglen, Vic 3685 **REGION** Rutherglen
T (02) 6032 9660 **F** (02) 6032 8005 **www**.buller.com.au **OPEN** Mon–Sat 9–5, Sun 10–5
WINEMAKER Andrew Buller **EST.** 1921 **CASES** 4000
The Buller family is very well known and highly regarded in Northeast Victoria, and the business benefits from vines that are now 80 years old. The rating is for the superb releases of Museum

fortified wines. Limited releases of Calliope Shiraz and Shiraz Mondeuse can also be very good. Exports to the UK and the US.

ỸỸỸỸỸ **Rare Rutherglen Liqueur Muscat NV** Deep brown with a touch of olive on the rim; full and deep, almost into chocolate, with intense raisined fruit; richly textured, with great structure to the raisined/plum pudding fruit flavours, and obvious rancio age. Clean finish and aftertaste. **RATING** 95 **DRINK** Now

Rare Rutherglen Liqueur Tokay NV Medium deep golden-brown; a mix of sweet tea leaf and Christmas cake is a highly aromatic entry point for the bouquet; the palate has a sweet core of muscadelle fruit, and rancio, tea leaf, nutty and cake elements surrounding the core. **RATING** 94 **DRINK** Now

🐌 Bullerview Wines ★★★

PO Box 457, Reservoir, Vic 3073 **REGION** Upper Goulburn
T (03) 9355 7070 **F** (03) 9355 7353 **WWW**.bullerviewwines.com.au **OPEN** Not
WINEMAKER George Apted (Contract) **EST.** 1996 **CASES** 1750
Pasquale 'Charlie' Orrico migrated from his native Calabria in 1956, establishing a successful commercial building enterprise in Melbourne. Childhood memories of winemaking on his grandfather's vineyard remained with Charlie, and in 1982 he and his wife, Maria, purchased land near Mansfield with the intention of establishing a vineyard. This eventuated in 1996, with the planting of 2 ha of merlot and 0.8 ha of cabernet sauvignon. From 2002 the estate-grown fruit has been processed onsite. It has to be said that Charlie Orrico has gone where angels fear to tread by choosing to plant merlot and cabernet sauvignon, rather than earlier ripening varieties. The cool climate is very evident in all of the wines.

ỸỸỸỸ **Mansfield Merlot 2003** Firm, medium-bodied redcurrant fruit supported by fine tannins, then crisp acid on the finish. The oak influence is restrained throughout. Cork. 14° alc. **RATING** 87 **DRINK** Now $ 12.50

ỸỸỸỸ **Mansfield Merlot 2002** **RATING** 86 **DRINK** 2008 $ 12.50
Mansfield Chardonnay 2004 **RATING** 84 **DRINK** Now $ 12.50
Mansfield Cabernet Sauvignon Merlot 2004 **RATING** 84 **DRINK** 2009 $ 12.50

Bulong Estate ★★★☆

70 Summerhill Road, Yarra Junction, Vic 3797 (postal) **REGION** Yarra Valley
T (03) 5967 1358 **F** (03) 5967 2487 **WWW**.bulongestate.com **OPEN** Mon–Fri 10–4, w'ends 10–5
WINEMAKER Matt Carter, MasterWineMakers **EST.** 1994 **CASES** 2000
Judy and Howard Carter purchased their beautifully situated 45-ha property in 1994, looking down into the valley below and across to the nearby ranges with Mt Donna Buang at their peak. Most of the grapes from the immaculately tended vineyard are sold, with limited quantities made for the Bulong Estate label. Exports to the UK.

ỸỸỸỸ **Yarra Valley Cabernet Sauvignon 2003** Good colour; medium-bodied, a centre of sweet cassis fruit; neat use of quality oak off-sets slightly savoury/green tannins. Cork. 13° alc. **RATING** 89 **DRINK** 2009 $ 21

Yarra Valley Sauvignon Blanc 2004 Bright, light straw-green; clean, crisp mineral, apple and a whisper of tropical fruit; not in the least confrontational. Cork. 12.5° alc. **RATING** 88 **DRINK** Now $ 16

Yarra Valley Cabernet Franc 2003 Interesting wine, not dissimilar to cabernet franc made in the Loire Valley. Fresh red fruits, with virtually no tannins or oak influence; lightly chilled summer red. Cork. 13.5° alc. **RATING** 87 **DRINK** 2009 $ 21

Bundaleer Wines ★★★☆

41 King Street, Brighton, SA 5048 (postal) **REGION** Southern Flinders Ranges
T (08) 8296 1231 **F** (08) 8296 2484 **WWW**.bundaleerwines.com.au **OPEN** Not
WINEMAKER Angela Meaney **EST.** 1998 **CASES** 600
Bundaleer is a joint venture between third-generation farmer Des Meaney and manufacturing industry executive Graham Spurling (whose family originally came from the Southern Flinders).

Planting of the 8-ha vineyard began in 1998, the first vintage in 2001. It is situated in a region known as the Bundaleer Gardens, on the edge of the Bundaleer Forest, 200 km north of Adelaide, at an altitude of 500m. This should not be confused with the Bundaleer Shiraz brand made by Bindi.

TTTT **Southern Flinders Ranges Shiraz 2003** Distinctly earthy/savoury nuances to medium-bodied black fruit flavours; fine tannins, subtle oak. Screwcap. 14° alc. **RATING** 89 **DRINK** 2009 $ 18
Southern Flinders Ranges Shiraz Cabernet 2002 A mix of red and black fruits, with a twist of sweetness before a more savoury finish. Again, minimal oak influence. Screwcap. 13.5° alc. **RATING** 89 **DRINK** 2010 $ 18
Southern Flinders Ranges Cabernet Sauvignon 2003 Shades of mint and leaf to light-to medium-bodied blackberry fruit; firm acidity lengthens the finish. Screwcap. 13° alc. **RATING** 88 **DRINK** 2009 $ 18

Bundaleera Vineyard

449 Glenwood Road, Relbia, Tas 7258 (postal) **REGION** Northern Tasmania
T (03) 6343 1231 **F** (03) 6343 1250 **OPEN** W'ends 10–5
WINEMAKER Pirie Consulting (Andrew Pirie) **EST.** 1996 **CASES** 1000
David (a consultant metallurgist in the mining industry) and Jan Jenkinson have established 2.5 ha of vines on a sunny, sheltered north to northeast slope in the North Esk Valley. The 12-ha property on which their house and vineyard are established give them some protection from the urban sprawl of Launceston; Jan is the full-time viticulturist and gardener for the immaculately tended property.

TTTT **Pinot Noir 2004** Substantial wine; medium-bodied, with quite chewy dark plum flavours; slightly heavy oak and extract. 13.4° alc. **RATING** 88 **DRINK** 2009 $ 27

TTTY **Riesling 2005** **RATING** 85 **DRINK** 2009 $ 16
Rose 2005 **RATING** 85 **DRINK** Now $ 18

Bungawarra

Bents Road, Ballandean, Qld 4382 **REGION** Granite Belt
T (07) 4684 1128 **F** (07) 4684 1128 **WWW**.bungawarrawines.com.au **OPEN** 7 days 10–4.30
WINEMAKER Jeff Harden **EST.** 1975 **CASES** 2000
Now owned by Jeff Harden, Bungawarra draws upon 5 ha of mature vineyards which over the years have shown themselves capable of producing red wines of considerable character.

TTTTY **2005 Bungawarra Shiraz** Vivid, deep purple-red; solid earthy/savoury edges to blackberry and plum flavours; spicy tannins and a touch of mocha oak. Well-made. Cork. **RATING** 90 **DRINK** 2013 $ 24

TTTY **2005 Bungawarra Reserve Chardonnay** Glowing yellow-green; considerable development to the peach and honey fruit; old-fashioned style, albeit flavoursome. Twin top. **RATING** 86 **DRINK** Now $ 15

Bunnamagoo Estate

Bunnamagoo, Rockley, NSW 2795 (postal) **REGION** Central Ranges Zone
T 1300 304 707 **F** (02) 6377 5231 **WWW**.bunnamagoowines.com.au **OPEN** Not
WINEMAKER Printhie Wines (Robert Black) **EST.** 1995 **CASES** 3700
Bunnamagoo Estate (on one of the first land grants in the region) is situated near the historic town of Rockley, itself equidistant south of Bathurst and west of Oberon. Here a 6-ha vineyard planted to chardonnay, merlot and cabernet sauvignon has been established by Paspaley Pearls, a famous name in the pearl industry.

TTTT **Semillon 2005** A very complex wine, reflecting multiple-winemaker inputs (barrel ferment and malolactic ferment;) all this work softens and slightly shortens the finish. Screwcap. 13° alc. **RATING** 89 **DRINK** 2010 $ 18
Chardonnay 2004 Opulent, rich and ripe peachy fruit; a big style, slightly old-fashioned perhaps, not quite carrying the alcohol. Cork. 13.8° alc. **RATING** 88 **DRINK** 2009

Kids Earth Fun Autumn Semillon 2005 Smooth and supple; nicely balanced, neither intense nor complex, but well-made. From Bunnamagoo's Mudgee vineyard, harvested in June. Cork. **RATING** 87 **DRINK** 2008 $ 20

ŦŦŦŶ **Cabernet Sauvignon 2003 RATING** 86 **DRINK** 2008 $ 20
Pinot Noir Chardonnay 2003 RATING 86 **DRINK** Now

Burge Family Winemakers ★★★★☆

Barossa Way, Lyndoch, SA 5351 **REGION** Barossa Valley
T (08) 8524 4644 **F** (08) 8524 4444 **WWW**.burgefamily.com.au **OPEN** Mon & Thurs–Sat 10–5
WINEMAKER Rick Burge **EST.** 1928 **CASES** 3500
Rick Burge and Burge Family Winemakers (not to be confused with Grant Burge, although the families are related) has established itself as an icon producer of exceptionally rich, lush and concentrated Barossa red wines. Rick Burge's sense of humour was evident with the Nice Red (a Merlot/Cabernet blend made for those who come to cellar door and ask 'Do you have a nice red?').

ŦŦŦŦŦ **Draycott Shiraz 2004** Bright purple-red, moderately deep; much more restrained and elegant than most prior releases; sweet (not dead or jammy) blackberry and raspberry fruit; very good oak and tannins. Cork. 14° alc. **RATING** 94 **DRINK** 2015 $ 36

ŦŦŦŦŶ **Olive Hill Shiraz Grenache Mourvedre 2004** Bright red-purple; floods the mouth with a sweet array of red and black fruits, mocha and gentle tannins; the French oak is appropriately subtle. Cork. 14.5° alc. **RATING** 93 **DRINK** 2012 $ 28
Olive Hill Semillon 2005 Powerful, rich and mouthfilling; sweet, tropical fruits; good balance and length; ready now. Screwcap. **RATING** 90 **DRINK** Now $ 18
D & OH Shiraz Grenache 2004 Juicy raspberry, dark plum and black cherry fruit; minimal oak input; good length. Screwcap. **RATING** 90 **DRINK** 2009 $ 22

ŦŦŦŦ **Garnacha Dry Grown Grenache 2004** Despite old, dry-grown vines (planted in the 1920s) is in the lighter style so common in the Barossa Valley, with juicy, jammy fruit and not a lot of structure. Cork. 15° alc. **RATING** 89 **DRINK** 2008 $ 25
The Homestead Blend Cabernet Shiraz 2004 Very rich, ripe and sweet, seemingly more so than the alcohol might suggest; a nice backdrop of dark chocolate and ripe tannins. Cork. 14.5° alc. **RATING** 89 **DRINK** 2014 $ 25

Burgi Hill Vineyard ★★★☆

290 Victoria Road, Wandin North, Vic 3139 **REGION** Yarra Valley
T (03) 5964 3568 **F** (03) 5964 3568 **WWW**.burgihill.com.au **OPEN** By appt
WINEMAKER Christopher Sargeant, Dominique Portet **EST.** 1974 **CASES** 500
The 4.5-ha vineyard now operated by Christopher Sargeant and family was established 30 years ago and is planted to chardonnay, sauvignon blanc, pinot noir, merlot and cabernet sauvignon. For many years the grapes were sold, but now some are vinified for the Burgi Hill label.

ŦŦŦŦŶ **Yarra Valley Chardonnay 2003** Elegant, creamy/nutty overtones to gentle melon fruit; harmonious flavours, good balance and aftertaste. Cork. 13.5° alc. **RATING** 92 **DRINK** 2009 $ 21

ŦŦŦŦ **Yarra Valley Sauvignon Blanc 2005** Bright, light straw-green; a faint touch of reduction on the bouquet, then a light- to medium-bodied apple and gooseberry palate, a little down in intensity. Screwcap. 12° alc. **RATING** 87 **DRINK** Now $ 18
Yarra Valley Cabernet Merlot 2003 A light- to medium-bodied core of sweet red and black fruits, with traces of mint and leaf; fractionally green tannins. Cork. 13° alc. **RATING** 87 **DRINK** 2009 $ 23

ŦŦŦŶ **Yarra Valley Pinot Noir 2003 RATING** 85 **DRINK** 2008 $ 21

Burk Salter Wines ★★★

Lot 5, Paisley Road, Blanchetown, SA 5357 **REGION** Riverland
T (08) 8540 5023 **F** (08) 8540 5023 **WWW**.burksalterwines.com.au **OPEN** Fri–Sun & public hols
11–4.30, 7 days during school hols
WINEMAKER Various contract **EST.** 2002 **CASES** 3000
The husband and wife team of Gregory Burk Salter and Jane Vivienne Salter is the third generation of the Salter family to grow grapes at their Blanchetown property. They have a little over 20 ha of chardonnay, semillon, colombard, ruby cabernet, shiraz, merlot, cabernet sauvignon and muscat gordo blanco; 450 tonnes are sold each year, the remaining 50 tonnes contract-made at various small Barossa Valley wineries. The cellar door and a self-contained B&B adjoin the vineyard, which has a Murray River frontage.

ΥΥΥΥ **Semillon Chardonnay 2005** Semillon adds a flavour dimension; tangy, zesty, lemony notes above peachy fruit; good length. Screwcap. 12.5° alc. **RATING** 88 **DRINK** 2009 $ 10

ΥΥΥϒ **Chardonnay 2005** **RATING** 86 **DRINK** Now $ 10

Burke & Hills NR

Cargo Road, Lidster, NSW 2800 **REGION** Orange
T (02) 6365 3456 **F** (02) 6365 3456 **OPEN** Fri–Mon 11–5 at Lakeside Café, Lake Canobolas
WINEMAKER Christophe Derrez, Lucy Maddox **EST.** 1999 **CASES** 3500
In response to my standard request for insight into motives and goals, founder Doug Burke wrote, 'I guess you would scream if you heard another new small vineyard/winery prattling on about small volumes, low yields, best practice ... in a quest for great quality, subtlety and complexity.' Very likely, but here the facts speak for themselves: the selection of a steeply sloping, frost-free, north-facing slope rising to an altitude of 940m on Mt Lidster; the planting of 10 ha of classic varieties, but including a mix of the best clones of pinot noir; the appointment of Brett Wilkins as viticulturist and former Gevrey Chambertin-cum-Flying Winemaker Christophe Derrez; the erection of a 200 tonne capacity winery to supplement cash flow by undertaking contract winemaking; and the running of the Lakeside Café at Lake Canobolas, 2 km from the winery ... All of these things point to a business plan with one objective: in Burke's words, 'Don't go broke.'

Burke & Wills Winery ★★★★☆

3155 Burke & Wills Track, Mia Mia, Vic 3444 **REGION** Heathcote
T (03) 5425 5400 **F** (03) 5425 5401 **WWW**.wineandmusic.net **OPEN** By appt
WINEMAKER Andrew Pattison **EST.** 2003 **CASES** 1500
Andrew Pattison established Burke & Wills Winery in 2003, after selling Lancefield Winery. He is in the course of establishing 1 ha of shiraz, 0.5 ha of gewurztraminer, and has 1 ha each of chardonnay and cabernets at Malmsbury, plus 0.5 ha of pinot noir, supplemented by contract-grown grapes from a Macedon Ranges vineyard supplying chardonnay, pinot noir and cabernets. Not to be confused with Burke & Hills.

ΥΥΥΥϒ **Heathcote Shiraz 2004** Medium-bodied; attractive black cherry, plum and blackberry fruit; alcohol, tannins and oak in the back seat. Diam. 14° alc. **RATING** 92 **DRINK** 2014 $ 24
Pattison Family Reserve Macedon Ranges Shiraz 2004 Light- to medium-bodied; bright, spicy, herbal red fruits; fine tannins and good length; elegant, but won't live forever. Diam. 12.8° alc. **RATING** 92 **DRINK** 2009 $ 35
Dig Tree Merlot 2004 Attractive, spicy red fruits; good texture and balance, the blend of regions synergistic; fine, sweet tannins. Good value. Central Victoria/Macedon Ranges. Screwcap. 14° alc. **RATING** 90 **DRINK** 2009 $ 17

ΥΥΥΥ **Macedon Ranges Unwooded Chardonnay 2005** Abundant peach and nectarine fruit; round, supple and mouthfilling; unusually generous, especially at low alcohol. Screwcap. 12.5° alc. **RATING** 89 **DRINK** 2008 $ 17
Dig Tree Macedon Ranges Chardonnay 2004 Powerful wine with ripe peach fruit; oak woven throughout, though never dominant. Screwcap. 13.5° alc. **RATING** 89 **DRINK** 2009 $ 17

Dig Tree Unwooded Chardonnay 2004 Attractive, elegant cool-grown style; nectarine fruit; nice line. Screwcap. **RATING** 88 **DRINK** Now $17.95

Pattison Family Reserve Macedon Ranges Cabernet Merlot 2004 Light-bodied; not too green, but not much structure, either; pretty, sweet berry, fruits; clean finish. Diam. 13° alc. **RATING** 87 **DRINK** 2009 $25

Burnbrae

NR

Hill End Road, Erudgere via Mudgee, NSW 2850 **REGION** Mudgee
T (02) 6373 3504 **F** (02) 6373 3435 **WWW**.burnbraewines.com.au **OPEN** Mon–Sat 9–5, Sun 9–4
WINEMAKER Frank Newman **EST.** 1976 **CASES** 4500
In 2005 Burnbrae was acquired by Tony Bryant and veteran winemaker Frank Newman, then with 37 vintages (half with Penfolds) under his belt. The aim is to maximise the potential of the 23 ha of old-vine vineyards, and also provide contract winemaking services for makers in the Gulgong/Mudgee/Rylstone subregions.

Burrundulla Vineyards

Sydney Road, Mudgee, NSW 2850 **REGION** Mudgee
T (02) 6372 1620 **F** (02) 6372 4058 **WWW**.burrundulla.com **OPEN** 7 days 10–4
WINEMAKER Contract **EST.** 1996 **CASES** 3000
A substantial venture; the Cox family (Chris, Michael and Ted) have established 60 ha of shiraz, cabernet sauvignon, chardonnay, merlot and semillon, selling much of the production, and having part made in two ranges: Heritage at the top, then GX.

ƳƳƳƳƳ **Heritage Mudgee Semillon 2005** Light straw-green; a clean bouquet, and much more flavour than usual; lemon/lemon tart fruit, good balance and length. Drink sooner rather than later. Cork. 11° alc. **RATING** 91 **DRINK** 2009 $15

ƳƳƳƳ **GX Mudgee Chardonnay Semillon 2005** A tried and true blend, opening with soft yellow peach fruit, then grassy, lively semillon kicks in on the finish. Cork. 12° alc. **RATING** 87 **DRINK** Now $13

ƳƳƳƳ **GX Mudgee Merlot Rose 2005** Bright cherry red; full red berry/cassis fruit; needlessly sweet, a pity. Screwcap. 12.5° alc. **RATING** 86 **DRINK** Now $13
Heritage Mudgee Cabernet Sauvignon 2004 **RATING** 86 **DRINK** 2009 $19
Heritage Mudgee Shiraz 2004 **RATING** 85 **DRINK** 2008 $19

Burton Premium Wines

NR

PO Box 242 Killara, NSW 2071 **REGION** Southeast Australia
T (02) 9416 6631 **F** (02) 9416 6681 **WWW**.burtonpremiumwines.com **OPEN** Not
WINEMAKER Boar's Rock (Mike Farmilo), Pat Tocaciu (Contract) **EST.** 1998 **CASES** 5000
Burton Premium Wines has neither vineyards nor winery, purchasing its grapes from the Limestone Coast (including Coonawarra) and McLaren Vale, and having the wines made in various locations by contract winemakers. It brings together the marketing and financial skills of managing director Nigel Burton, and the extensive wine experience (as a senior judge) of Dr Ray Healy, who is director in charge of winemaking. Exports to the UK, the US, Canada, Finland, Sweden, Taiwan and Japan.

Bush Piper Vineyard

NR

Badenoch, Horspool Way via Molon Road, Orange, NSW 2800 **REGION** Orange
T (02) 6361 8280 **F** (02) 6361 8432 **OPEN** By appt
WINEMAKER Tamburlaine (Mark Davidson) **EST.** 1996 **CASES** 3000
Shortly after Jo and Richard Cummins moved to Orange, they realised their property was ideal viticultural land. Planting began in 1996 with cabernet sauvignon, followed the next year by further blocks of cabernet and shiraz. The wines are sold by mail order and through select restaurants.

by Farr ★★★★★

PO Box 72, Bannockburn, Vic 3331 **REGION** Geelong
T (03) 5281 1979 **F** (03) 5281 1433 **OPEN** Not
WINEMAKER Gary Farr, Nick Farr **EST.** 1999 **CASES** 3000
In 1994 Gary Farr and family planted 12 ha of clonally-selected viognier, chardonnay, pinot noir and shiraz at a density of 7000 per ha on a north-facing hill which is directly opposite the Bannockburn Winery. The quality of the wines is exemplary, their character subtly different from those of Bannockburn itself due, in Farr's view, to the interaction of the *terroir* of the hill and the clonal selection. Exports to the UK, the US, Canada, Singapore, Russia and Japan.

🍷🍷🍷🍷🍷 **Chardonnay by Farr 2004** A beautiful wine in every respect; elegant but intense, superb mouthfeel and length; the winemaker inputs are so seamlessly interwoven through the fruit there is nothing more to say. Cork. 13° alc. **RATING** 97 **DRINK** 2011 $ 50

Shiraz by Farr 2004 Utterly distinctive, highly aromatic (whole bunch component) and the suggestion of a touch of viognier; the palate is complex yet elegant, with great texture from intense black fruits and cashmere tannins. Cork. 14° alc. **RATING** 95 **DRINK** 2014 $ 50

Viognier by Farr 2004 An unusually open and aromatic bouquet, with apricot blossom, spice and what may or may not be a touch of barrel ferment; an elegant palate with no phenolics or heat. Viogniers don't come much better than this. Cork. 12.5° alc. **RATING** 94 **DRINK** 2009 $ 55

Sangreal by Farr 2004 A very complex, perfumed bouquet of ripe, spiced plums; a more restrained palate, but with great texture, the plum flavours supported by high-quality oak. Cork. 13° alc. **RATING** 94 **DRINK** 2011 $ 60

Byramgou Park NR

Wade Road, Brookhampton, WA 6239 **REGION** Geographe
T (08) 9731 8248 **F** (08) 9731 8248 **WWW**.byramgou.com.au **OPEN** 7 days 10–6
WINEMAKER Siobhan Lynch **EST.** 1997 **CASES** 700
The unusual name comes courtesy of the great-great-grandfather of Richard Knox, who is, with Geraldine Knox, the proprietor of the business. Byramgou was the name of the ship which his forebear sailed to Arabia in 1821; he received a gold cup, depicted on the label, for his deeds. These details to one side, there are 5 ha of chardonnay, grenache, shiraz and cabernet sauvignon, and the wine is made by Siobhan Lynch, a district veteran.

Byrne & Smith Wines ★★★☆

PO Box 640, Unley, SA 5061 **REGION** South Australia
T (08) 8272 1911 **F** (08) 8272 1944 **WWW**.byrneandsmith.com.au **OPEN** Not
WINEMAKER Duane Coates (Contract) **EST.** 1999 **CASES** 40 000
Byrne & Smith is a substantial business with 2 vineyards totalling 53 ha at Stanley Flat in the northern Clare Valley, and a third vineyard of 106 ha near Waikerie in the Riverland. The major part of the grapes are sold, and the wines being marketed also use purchased grapes from regions as far away as the Margaret River.

🍷🍷🍷🍷🍷 **Antiquarian McLaren Vale Shiraz 2001** Sweet, ripe red and black fruits woven through mocha/spice French oak; soft, ripe tannins. Cork. 14° alc. **RATING** 90 **DRINK** 2011 $ 40

🍷🍷🍷🍷 **Ardent Estates Artisan Chardonnay 2005** Light-bodied; clean, nectarine/white peach; unoaked, but has good flavour and length; better than many. Screwcap. 12.9° alc. **RATING** 88 **DRINK** 2008 $ 10

Antiquarian McLaren Vale Cabernet Sauvignon 2001 Good colour; strong, bright cassis fruit and a touch of regional chocolate; overly firm acidity on the finish. Cork. 13.5° alc. **RATING** 88 **DRINK** 2009 $ 40

🍷🍷🍷🍷 **Devlin's Ghost Semillon Chardonnay 2004** **RATING** 86 **DRINK** 2008 $ 8

Ardent Estates Limestone Coast Cabernet Sauvignon 2001 **RATING** 84 **DRINK** Now $ 13

Calais Estate

NR

Palmers Lane, Pokolbin, NSW 2321 **REGION** Lower Hunter Valley
T (02) 4998 7654 **F** (02) 4998 7813 **WWW**.calaiswines.com.au **OPEN** 7 days 9–5
WINEMAKER Adrian Sheridan **EST.** 1987 **CASES** 10 000
Richard and Susan Bradley purchased the substantial Calais Estate in 2000. Long-serving winemaker Adrian Sheridan continues his role, and the estate offers a wide range of facilities for visitors, ranging from private function rooms, to picnic spots, to an undercover outdoor entertaining area.

Caledonia Australis

PO Box 626, North Melbourne, Vic 3051 **REGION** Gippsland
T (03) 9416 4156 **F** (03) 9416 4157 **WWW**.caledoniaaustralis.com **OPEN** Not
WINEMAKER MasterWineMakers **EST.** 1995 **CASES** 6000
The reclusive Caledonia Australis is a Pinot Noir and Chardonnay specialist, with a total of 18 ha in three separate vineyard locations. All of the vineyards are in the Leongatha area, on red, free-draining, high-ironstone soils, on a limestone or marl base, and the slopes are east to northeast-facing. Small-batch winemaking by Martin Williams MW (MasterWineMakers) has resulted in consistently high-quality wines.

ŸŸŸŸŸ **Reserve Chardonnay 2003** Very good green-yellow; a richer, bigger, bolder style with nectarine, melon and fig; some Burgundian funk; excellent balance and length. Screwcap. 14° alc. **RATING** 95 **DRINK** 2012 $50
Chardonnay 2003 Bright green-yellow; citrus and nectarine fruit, with long, lingering, racy acidity. Trophy Best Wine of Show Gippsland Wine Show '06. Screwcap. 13.5° alc. **RATING** 94 **DRINK** 2011 $25

ŸŸŸŸŸ **Mount Macleod Chardonnay 2003** Has a distinctly offbeat bouquet, high-toned, almost floral; rich, sweet peachy fruit, then zingy acidity. Screwcap. 13.6° alc. **RATING** 92 **DRINK** 2011 $19

ŸŸŸŸ **Rose 2004** A pleasant wine; good balance and length, with spicy fruit nuances; holding in there. Screwcap. 12.5° alc. **RATING** 86 **DRINK** Now $19

Calem Blue/Shelton Wines

NR

PO Box 4132, Wembley, WA 6913 **REGION** Margaret River
T (08) 6380 1511 **F** (08) 6380 1522 **WWW**.sheltonwines.com **OPEN** Not
WINEMAKER Flying Fish Cove, Bill Crappsley (Contract) **EST.** 1996 **CASES** NA
David and Nicky Shelton are vineyard holders within the 80-ha Margaret River Vineyards Estate in Clews Road, Cowaramup. The Estate is a relatively rare example of so-called *clos* farming being an unqualified success, with a generally high level of viticulture throughout (under the control of Ian Davies). The name Calem is a combination of the Sheltons' children's names, Cal and Emma. The vineyard was planted in 1996, and the first vintage was 2000.

Callipari Wine

★★★

Cureton Avenue, Nichols Point, Vic 3501 **REGION** Murray Darling
T (03) 5023 4477 **F** (03) 5021 0988 **WWW**.callipari.com **OPEN** W'ends & public hols 10–4
WINEMAKER Michael Callipari **EST.** 1999 **CASES** 2000
Michael Callipari is among the third generation of the Callipari family, the first members of which left Calabria, Sicily in May 1951. Various members of the family have developed vineyards over the years, with over 25 ha of vines on 2 properties. Mother Giuseppa Callipari makes food products (from produce grown on the family farm) that are sold through the cellar door and at tourism outlets and shops in the district. Ned's Red, incidentally, is described as a 'premium red wine with a dash of orange and lemon'.

ŸŸŸŸ **Nichols Point Shiraz 2001** Light colour, but good hue; holding on remarkably well, with gentle earth and leather flavours akin to an aged Hunter Shiraz. Cork. 14° alc. **RATING** 87 **DRINK** 2008 $18

ᵧᵧᵧᵧ **Karkarooc Chardonnay 2005** Warm, ripe, tropical fruit; old-fashioned style, but abundant flavour. Screwcap. 13° alc. **RATING** 86 **DRINK** Now $13
Nichols Point Cabernet Merlot 2001 RATING 86 **DRINK** Now $18
Nichols Point Grenache Cabernet Franc Shiraz 2001 RATING 84 **DRINK** Now $13
Nichols Point Cabernet Sauvignon 2001 RATING 84 **DRINK** Now $18

Cambewarra Estate   NR

520 Illaroo Road, Cambewarra, NSW 2540 **REGION** Shoalhaven Coast
T(02) 4446 0170 **F**(02) 4446 0170 **WWW**.cambewarraestate.com.au **OPEN** Thurs–Sun 10–5 & public & school hols
WINEMAKER Tamburlaine **EST.** 1991 **CASES** 3500
Louise Cole owns and runs Cambewarra Estate, near the Shoalhaven River on the central southern coast of New South Wales, the wines made at Tamburlaine in the Hunter Valley. Cambewarra continues to produce attractive wines which have had significant success in wine shows.

🐚 Campania Hills   ★★★

447 Native Corners Road, Campania, Tas 7026 **REGION** Southern Tasmania
T(03) 6260 4387 **OPEN** By appt
WINEMAKER Winemaking Tasmania (Julian Alcorso) **EST.** 1994 **CASES** 350
This is the former Colmaur, purchased by Jeanette and Lindsay Kingston in 2005. They had just sold a business they had built up over 22 years and thought they were returning to country life and relaxation when they purchased the property with 1.5 ha of vines equally split between pinot noir and chardonnay (plus 700 olive trees). Says Lindsay Kingston, somewhat wryly, 'We welcome visitors. The last lot stayed 3 hours.'

ᵧᵧᵧᵧ **Unwooded Chardonnay 2005** Fractionally sweaty, though fragrant and complex; noticeable fruit sweetness. **RATING** 87 **DRINK** Now $18

Campbells   ★★★★★

Murray Valley Highway, Rutherglen, Vic 3685 **REGION** Rutherglen
T(02) 6032 9458 **F**(02) 6032 9870 **WWW**.campbellswines.com.au **OPEN** Mon–Sat 9–5, Sun 10–5
WINEMAKER Colin Campbell **EST.** 1870 **CASES** 40 000
A wide range of table and fortified wines of ascending quality and price, which are always honest. As so often happens in this part of the world, the fortified wines are the best, with the extremely elegant Isabella Rare Tokay and Merchant Prince Rare Muscat at the top of the tree; the winery rating is for the fortified wines. A feature of the Vintage Room at the cellar door is an extensive range of back vintage releases of small parcels of wine not available through any other outlet, other than the Cellar Club members. The wines are critically assessed before being re-released. Exports to the UK, the US, Canada and NZ.

ᵧᵧᵧᵧᵧ **Isabella Rare Rutherglen Tokay NV** Very deep olive-brown; broodingly complex, deep and concentrated aromas, then layer upon layer of flavour in the mouth. Incredibly intense and complex, with varietal tea leaf/muscadelle fruit continuity. **RATING** 97 **DRINK** Now $94
Grand Rutherglen Tokay NV Deep mahogany, olive rim. An intensely complex bouquet, with hints of smoke, abundant rancio. Glorious malty, tea leaf flavours linger long in the mouth; great style and balance. **RATING** 95 **DRINK** Now
Merchant Prince Rare Rutherglen Muscat NV Dark brown, with olive-green on the rim; particularly fragrant, with essencey, raisiny fruit; supple, smooth and intense wine floods every corner of the mouth, but yet retains elegance, and continues the house style to perfection. **RATING** 95 **DRINK** Now $94

ᵧᵧᵧᵧᵧ **Classic Rutherglen Tokay NV** Medium brown; a complex bouquet with dried muscadelle fruit; deliciously idiosyncratic. The faintly smoky palate has power and depth, again with dried muscadelle grapes reflecting the bouquet. **RATING** 93 **DRINK** Now $35
Grand Rutherglen Muscat NV Full olive-brown; highly aromatic; a rich and complex palate is silky smooth, supple and long, the raisiny fruit perfectly balanced by the clean, lingering acid (and spirit) cut on the finish. **RATING** 93 **DRINK** Now

Classic Rutherglen Muscat NV Spicy/raisiny complexity starting to build; in typical Campbells style, lively, clearly articulated, with good balance and length. **RATING** 92 **DRINK** Now $35

Rutherglen Tokay NV Bright, light golden-brown; classic mix of tea leaf and butterscotch aromas lead into an elegant wine which dances in the mouth; has balance and length. **RATING** 92 **DRINK** Now $16.70

The Barkly Durif 2002 A mix of black fruits, licorice, chocolate and spice; good balance and texture, especially the tannins; an alcohol twitch is inevitable. Cork. 15° alc. **RATING** 91 **DRINK** 2012 $39

Rutherglen Muscat NV Bright, clear tawny-gold; a highly aromatic bouquet, spicy and grapey, is mirrored precisely on the palate, which has nigh-on perfect balance. Trophy at 2005 International Wine Challenge, London. **RATING** 91 **DRINK** Now $16.70

ΨΨΨΨ   **Limited Release Roussanne 2004** Clean and well-made; haunting touches of nutmeg and baked apple; good finish, cellar-worthy. Classy packaging. Cork. 12.5° alc. **RATING** 89 **DRINK** 2010 $17

Bobbie Burns Shiraz 2003 A complex bouquet and palate, with a mix of prune, chocolate, mint and blackberry in a medium- to full-bodied frame; the alcohol pokes through slightly. Cork. 14.5° alc. **RATING** 89 **DRINK** 2010 $21.10

Limited Release Cabernets 2003 Sweet cassis and blackcurrant fruit, with tannins lurking at the back door. Rump steak the answer. Cork. 14.5° alc. **RATING** 87 **DRINK** 2010 $21

ΨΨΨΨ   **Riesling 2005** Solid wine with plenty of tropical fruit flavour; soft finish. Cork. 11.5° alc. **RATING** 86 **DRINK** Now $15

Rutherglen Shiraz Durif 2003 **RATING** 85 **DRINK** Now $15.50

Chardonnay 2005 **RATING** 84 **DRINK** Now $14

Trebbiano 2005 **RATING** 84 **DRINK** Now $15

Camyr Allyn Wines ★★★

Camyr Allyn North, Allyn River Road, East Gresford, NSW 2311 **REGION** Upper Hunter Valley
T (02) 4938 9576 **F** (02) 4938 9576 **WWW**.camyrallynwines.com.au **OPEN** 7 days 10–5
WINEMAKER James Evers **EST.** 1999 **CASES** 2500
John and Judy Evers purchased the Camyr Allyn North property in 1997, and immediately set about planting 1.7 ha of verdelho, 1.2 ha of merlot and 1.5 ha of shiraz. The wines are made at the new Northern Hunter winery at East Gresford by James Evers, who worked for Mildara Blass in Coonawarra for some time. The promotion and packaging of the wines is innovative and stylish.

ΨΨΨΨ   **Hunter Valley Shiraz 2004** Very regional earthy aromas, perhaps augmented by the screwcap; light- to medium-bodied red fruit flavours; soft tannins. Screwcap. 13° alc. **RATING** 87 **DRINK** 2009 $18

ΨΨΨΨ   **Hunter Valley Rose 2005** Pale, bright fuchsia; lively, fresh, zesty small red fruit flavours. Screwcap. 12° alc. **RATING** 86 **DRINK** Now $16

Hunter Valley Verdelho 2005 **RATING** 85 **DRINK** Now $18

Hunter Valley Sparkling Merlot Shiraz 2003 **RATING** 85 **DRINK** Now $24

Hunter Valley Merlot 2004 **RATING** 84 **DRINK** Now $18

Candlebark Hill ★★★★

Fordes Lane, Kyneton, Vic 3444 **REGION** Macedon Ranges
T (03) 9836 2712 **F** (03) 9836 2712 **WWW**.users.bigpond.com/candlebarkhillwines.htm **OPEN** By appt
WINEMAKER David Forster, Vincent Lakey, Llew Knight (Consultant) **EST.** 1987 **CASES** 600
Candlebark Hill, established by David Forster at the northern end of the Macedon Ranges, has magnificent views over the Central Victoria countryside north of the Great Dividing Range. The 3.5 ha vineyard is planted to pinot noir (1.5 ha), 1 ha each of chardonnay and the three main Bordeaux varieties, and 0.5 ha of shiraz and malbec. The Reserve Pinot Noir is especially meritorious.

YYYYY **Reserve Cabernet Sauvignon 2001** Good colour; balanced but obvious oak around cassis and blackcurrant fruit. Shows the warm vintage to advantage. Cork. **RATING** 90 **DRINK** 2008 $ 35

Cannibal Creek Vineyard ★★★★

260 Tynong North Road, Tynong North, Vic 3813 **REGION** Gippsland
T (03) 5942 8380 **F** (03) 5942 8202 **www**.cannibalcreek.com.au **OPEN** 7 days 11–5
WINEMAKER Patrick Hardiker **EST.** 1997 **CASES** 2000
The Hardiker family moved to Tynong North in 1988, initially only grazing beef cattle, but aware of the viticultural potential of the sandy clay loam and bleached sub-surface soils weathered from the granite foothills of the Black Snake Ranges. Plantings began in 1997, using organically based cultivation methods. The family decided to make their own wine, and a heritage-style shed built from locally milled timber has been converted into a winery and small cellar door facility. Exports to the UK.

YYYYY **Sauvignon Blanc 2005** Light straw-green; well-made; good balance, line and length to the mix of tropical and citrus fruit on the light-bodied palate; good finish. None of the sweaty characters of the '04. Cork. 13° alc. **RATING** 90 **DRINK** Now $ 24
Chardonnay 2004 Pale straw-green; tightly wound, with Chablis-like minerally, green-tinged fruit. **RATING** 90 **DRINK** 2010 $ 24

Canobolas-Smith ★★★★

Boree Lane, off Cargo Road, Lidster via Orange, NSW 2800 **REGION** Orange
T (02) 6365 6113 **F** (02) 6365 6113 **OPEN** W'ends, public hols 11–5
WINEMAKER Murray Smith **EST.** 1986 **CASES** 2000
Canobolas-Smith has established itself as one of the leading Orange district wineries, and has distinctive blue wraparound labels. Much of the wine is sold from the cellar door, which is well worth a visit. Exports to the US and Asia.

YYYY **Alchemy 2002** A medium-bodied mix of spice, cedar and gentle black fruits; good mouthfeel and balance. Cabernet Sauvignon/Cabernet Franc/Shiraz. Screwcap. 14.5° alc. **RATING** 89 **DRINK** 2011 $ 35

Canonbah Bridge ★★★

Merryanbone Station, Warren, NSW 2824 (postal) **REGION** Western Plains Zone
T (02) 6833 9966 **F** (02) 6833 9980 **www**.canonbahbridge.com **OPEN** Not
WINEMAKER Hunter Wine Services (John Hordern) **EST.** 1999 **CASES** 20 000
The 29-ha vineyard has been established by Shane McLaughlin on the very large Merryanbone Station, a Merino sheep stud which has been in the family for four generations. The wines are at three price points: at the bottom is Bottle Treen, from southeast Australia, then Ram's Leap, specific regional blends, and at the top, Canonbah Bridge, either estate or estate/regional blends. Exports to the US, the UK, Canada, Malaysia and Hong Kong.

YYYYY **Shiraz Grenache Mourvedre 2003** Light- to medium-bodied; savoury, dusty, chocolatey black fruits; lingering tannins. Not up to the '02. Western Plains/McLaren Vale. Cork. 14° alc. **RATING** 86 **DRINK** 2010 $ 20

Canungra Valley Vineyards NR

Lamington National Park Road, Canungra Valley, Qld 4275 **REGION** Queensland Coastal
T (07) 5543 4011 **F** (07) 5543 4162 **www**.canungravineyards.com.au **OPEN** 7 days 10–5
WINEMAKER John Hislop, Mark Davidson (Contract) **EST.** 1997 **CASES** 5000
Canungra Valley Vineyards has been established in the hinterland of the Gold Coast with a clear focus on broad-based tourism. Vines (8 ha) have been established around the 19th century homestead (relocated to the site from its original location in Warwick), but these provide only a small part of the wine offered for sale. In deference to the climate, 70% of the estate planting is chambourcin, the rain and mildew-resistant hybrid; the remainder is semillon.

Cape Barren Wines ★★★★

Lot 20, Little Road, Willunga, SA 5172 **REGION** McLaren Vale
T (08) 8556 4374 **F** (08) 8556 4364 **OPEN** By appt
WINEMAKER Brian Light (Contract) **EST.** 1999 **CASES** 3000
Lifelong friends and vignerons Peter Matthews and Brian Ledgard joined forces in 1999 to create Cape Barren Wines. In all they have 62 ha of vineyards throughout the McLaren Vale region, the jewel in the crown being 4 ha of 70-year-old shiraz at Blewitt Springs, which provides the grapes for the Old Vine Shiraz. The McLaren Vale Grenache Shiraz Mourvedre and McLaren Vale Shiraz come from their other vineyards; most of the grapes are sold. Exports to the US, Canada, NZ, Malaysia, Singapore, Dubai, Germany and Switzerland.

ŸŸŸŸỲ **McLaren Vale Shiraz 2004** Good colour; rich, ripe plum/plum cake/mocha/chocolate flavours; soft tannins and good balance. Screwcap. 14.5° alc. **RATING** 92 **DRINK** 2014 **$** 21

ŸŸŸŸ **Grenache Shiraz Mourvedre 2004** Aromas of red and black fruits, touches of regional chocolate and a whisper of vanillan oak, exactly what one would expect of a blend of grenache (46%) and shiraz (41%) from McLaren Vale. Flavours in the black fruit spectrum, with relatively firm tannins from the mourvedre (13%). Screwcap. **RATING** 89 **DRINK** 2014 **$** 22.50
McLaren Vale Shiraz 2003 Light- to medium-bodied; savoury spicy, plummy fruit aromas and flavours; controlled oak, fine tannins; 14.2° alcohol. Screwcap. **RATING** 88 **DRINK** 2009 **$** 21

Cape Bernier Vineyard ★★★★

GPO Box 1743, Hobart, Tas 7001 **REGION** Southern Tasmania
T (03) 6253 5443 **F** (03) 6253 6087 **WWW**.capebernier.com.au **OPEN** Not
WINEMAKER Winemaking Tasmania (Julian Alcorso) **EST.** 1999 **CASES** 750
Alastair Christie (and family) has established 2 ha of Dijon clone pinot noir, another 1.5 ha of chardonnay and 0.5 ha of pinot gris on a north-facing slope overlooking historic Marion Bay. The property is not far from the Bream Creek vineyard, and is one of several developments in the region changing the land use from dairy and beef cattle to wine production and tourism.

ŸŸŸŸỲ **Pinot Noir 2004** Powerful; very savoury, very long; the question is whether the stemmy/capsicum nuance is over the top; exceptional length. Controversial wine. Screwcap. 13.9° alc. **RATING** 92 **DRINK** 2011 **$** 24

ŸŸŸŸ **Unwooded Chardonnay 2005** Big winemaking inputs; lots of wild ferment and lees contact; fractionally sweaty characters. Screwcap. 14.3° alc. **RATING** 89 **DRINK** 2009 **$** 22

Cape Bouvard NR

Mount John Road, Mandurah, WA 6210 **REGION** Peel
T (08) 9739 1360 **F** (08) 9739 1360 **OPEN** 7 days 10–5
WINEMAKER NA **EST.** 1990 **CASES** 2000
While it continues in operation after its sale in 2003, there have been recent changes, the details of which are still unavailable.

Cape d'Estaing NR

PO Box 214, Kingscote, Kangaroo Island, SA 5223 **REGION** Kangaroo Island
T (08) 8383 6299 **F** (08) 8383 6299 **WWW**.capedestaingwines.com **OPEN** Not
WINEMAKER Boar's Rock (Mike Farmilo), Robin Moody **EST.** 1994 **CASES** 4000
Graham and Jude Allison, Alan and Ann Byers, Marg and Wayne Conaghty and Robin and Heather Moody have established 10 ha of cabernet sauvignon and shiraz near Wisanger on Kangaroo Island. Robin Moody was a long-serving senior employee of Southcorp and has a broad knowledge of all aspects of grapegrowing and winemaking. Exports to the US.

Cape Grace ★★★★

Fifty One Road, Cowaramup, WA 6284 **REGION** Margaret River
T (08) 9755 5669 **F** (08) 9755 5668 **WWW**.capegracewines.com.au **OPEN** 7 days 10–5
WINEMAKER Robert Karri-Davies, Mark Messenger (Consultant) **EST.** 1996 **CASES** 2000
Cape Grace Wines can trace its history back to 1875, when timber baron MC Davies settled at Karridale, building the Leeuwin lighthouse and founding the township of Margaret River; 120 years later, Robert and Karen Karri-Davies planted just under 6 ha of vineyard to chardonnay, shiraz and cabernet sauvignon, with smaller amounts of merlot, semillon and chenin blanc. Robert is a self-taught viticulturist; Karen has over 15 years of international sales and marketing experience in the hospitality industry. Winemaking is carried out on the property; consultant Mark Messenger, a veteran of the Margaret River region, has over 9 years' experience at Cape Mentelle and 3 at Juniper Estate. Exports to Singapore.

🍷🍷🍷🍷🍷 **Margaret River Chardonnay 2004** A complex bouquet; positive, à la mode, slightly funky barrel ferment aromas; a rich palate, but not over the top, with ripe nectarine and grapefruit; good finish. Screwcap. 14° alc. **RATING** 94 **DRINK** 2010 $ 24

🍷🍷🍷🍷 **Margaret River Shiraz 2004** Not particularly deep colour; an elegant light- to medium-bodied wine with raspberry and blackberry fruit; has balance, but not the power of the first few vintages. Screwcap. 14.5° alc. **RATING** 89 **DRINK** 2010 $ 29
Margaret River Cabernet Sauvignon 2004 Like the Shiraz, medium-bodied with cassis berry fruit and slightly earthy/briary tannins. Screwcap. 14.5° alc. **RATING** 88 **DRINK** 2010 $ 39

Cape Horn Vineyard NR

Echuca-Picola Road, Kanyapella, Vic 3564 **REGION** Goulburn Valley
T (03) 5480 6013 **F** (03) 5480 6013 **WWW**.capehornvineyard.com.au **OPEN** 7 days 11–5
WINEMAKER John Ellis (Contract) **EST.** 1993 **CASES** 1800
The unusual name comes from a bend in the Murray River which was considered by riverboat owners of the 19th century to resemble Cape Horn: this is now on the wine label. The property was acquired by Echuca GP Dr Sue Harrison and her schoolteacher husband Ian in 1993. Ian Harrison has progressively planted their 9-ha vineyard to chardonnay, shiraz, zinfandel, cabernet sauvignon, marsanne and durif.

Cape Jaffa Wines ★★★☆

Limestone Coast Road, Cape Jaffa, SA 5276 **REGION** Mount Benson
T (08) 8768 5053 **F** (08) 8768 5040 **WWW**.capejaffawines.com.au **OPEN** 7 days 10–5
WINEMAKER Derek Hooper **EST.** 1993 **CASES** 30 000
Cape Jaffa is the first of the Mount Benson wineries and all of the production now comes from the substantial estate plantings of 16.4 ha, which include the four major Bordeaux red varieties, plus shiraz, chardonnay, sauvignon blanc and semillon. The winery (built of local paddock rock) has been designed to allow eventual expansion to 1000 tonnes, or 70 000 cases. Exports to the UK, Philippines, Hong Kong, Singapore and China.

🍷🍷🍷🍷 **Chardonnay 2004** Light, clean and fresh stone fruit and melon; subtle oak infusion despite spending 16 weeks in new French oak from fermentation onwards; quite delicate, modern style. High-quality cork. **RATING** 89 **DRINK** Now $ 21

Cape Landing ★★★☆

PO Box 1441, Margaret River, WA 6285 **REGION** Margaret River
T (08) 9757 6418 **F** (08) 9757 6148 **OPEN** Not
WINEMAKER Rockfield Estate (Andrew Gaman) **EST.** 1998 **CASES** 650
Larry and Cheryl de Jong planted a total of 12.8 ha of shiraz, cabernet sauvignon, chardonnay, semillon and sauvignon blanc in 1998, adding another 2 ha (chardonnay) in 2003, lifting the total to 14.8 ha. The intention was to simply be grapegrowers, but in 2003, concerned about the uncertain nature of the industry, they decided to have part of the grapes contract-made. For once Murphy's Law worked favourably; with 3 wineries competing for the grapes, a long-term contract was entered into

with one winemaker, allowing the de Jongs to pursue their other aim of making small quantities of wines for sale primarily to friends and through Cheryl's boutique guest house in Subiaco.

ΨΨΨΨ♀ **Margaret River Sauvignon Blanc Semillon 2005** Faintly fuzzy aromas; then a very powerful, intense and long palate with tangy grapefruit, gooseberry and lemon flavours. Screwcap. 12.5° alc. **RATING** 93 **DRINK** 2008 $14

ΨΨΨΨ **Margaret River Cabernet Shiraz 2004** Light- to medium-bodied; spicy, earthy, licorice nuances surround the black fruits; neat tannin and oak management. Screwcap. 13.5° alc. **RATING** 87 **DRINK** 2011 $17

ΨΨΨ♀ **Margaret River Shiraz 2003** Light but bright colour; light- to medium-bodied, showing apparent young vine character; spicy blackberry fruits; light tannins. Screwcap. 13° alc. **RATING** 86 **DRINK** 2009 $17

Cape Lavender ★★★☆

4 Carter Road, Metricup, WA 6280 **REGION** Margaret River
T (08) 9755 7552 **F** (08) 9755 7556 **WWW.**capelavender.com.au **OPEN** 7 days 10–5
WINEMAKER Peter Stanlake, Eion Lindsay **EST.** 1999 **CASES** 3500
With 11.5 ha of vines, a much-awarded winery restaurant, and lavender fields which help make unique wines, this is a business with something extra. There are 7 Lavender wines, moving from sparkling through table to port, which have been infused with *Lavandula angustifolia*; the impact isn't overwhelming, but is nonetheless evident, and far from unpleasant. Whether it is a legal additive to wine, I do not know. There is also a conventional estate range of Semillon, Sauvignon Blanc, Chardonnay, Merlot, Shiraz and Cabernet Sauvignon, made without lavender.

ΨΨΨΨ♀ **Moss Penny Margaret River Chardonnay 2002** Stone fruit and a hint of French oak on the bouquet; a medium-bodied, smooth and supple palate; well-integrated and balanced fruit and oak; long, clean finish. Ageing impressively. Well-made. Cork. **RATING** 90 **DRINK** 2009 $25

ΨΨΨΨ **Moss Penny Margaret River Shiraz 2004** An attractive mix of spice, blackberry, plum and licorice aromas and flavours; medium-bodied, the oak and tannin extract well-controlled. Fully ripe. Cork. **RATING** 89 **DRINK** 2011 $35

ΨΨΨ♀ **JC's Sparkling Lavender Shiraz 2004 RATING** 85 **DRINK** Now $28.50
Rosea Sparkling Rose 2004 RATING 84 **DRINK** Now $25

Cape Lodge Wines ★★★★

Caves Road, Yallingup, WA 6282 (postal) **REGION** Margaret River
T (08) 9755 6311 **F** (08) 9755 6322 **WWW.**capelodge.com.au **OPEN** Not
WINEMAKER Jan Macintosh **EST.** 1998 **CASES** 1000
Cape Lodge has evolved from a protea farm in the early 1980s, through a small luxury B&B operation in 1993, and now to the point where multi-million dollar investments has propelled it to the top 100 hotels of the world in the Condé Nast *Traveler* magazine gold list of 2005, the fourth-best restaurant in the world for food by the same publication, and the best 5-star resort in Australia and Asia Pacific by a conference of its peers. Since 2001 it has been owned by Malaysians Seng and So Ong, who were responsible for the major expansion to 22 rooms, a new restaurant and a 14,000-bottle wine cellar. In 1998, 1.6 ha each of sauvignon blanc and shiraz were planted, the wine sold exclusively through the Cape Lodge resort.

ΨΨΨΨ♀ **Margaret River Sauvignon Blanc 2004** Still pale straw-green; a clean bouquet, then obviously ripe grass, herb and gooseberry fruit; has length. Screwcap. 14.1° alc. **RATING** 90 **DRINK** Now $28
Margaret River Shiraz 2002 Good colour; medium-bodied; ripe blackberry, plum and spice; good tannins, controlled oak. Cork. 13.9° alc. **RATING** 90 **DRINK** 2012 $38

ΨΨΨΨ **Margaret River Shiraz 2003** Light- to medium-bodied; savoury/earthy nuances to herb, mint and leaf fruit, seemingly struggling for complete ripeness. Cork. 13.1° alc. **RATING** 87 **DRINK** 2008 $28

Cape Mentelle ★★★★★

Wallcliffe Road, Margaret River, WA 6285 **REGION** Margaret River
T (08) 9757 0888 **F** (08) 9757 3233 **WWW**.capementelle.com.au **OPEN** 7 days 10–4.30
WINEMAKER Robert Mann, Simon Burnell, Lara Bray **EST.** 1970 **CASES** NFP
Part of the LVMH (Louis Vuitton Möet Hennessy) group. Since the advent of Dr Tony Jordan as
Australasian CEO there has been a concerted and successful campaign to rid the winery of the
brettanomyces infection which particularly affected the Cabernet Sauvignon. The Chardonnay and
Semillon Sauvignon Blanc are among Australia's best, the potent Shiraz usually superb, and the
berry/spicy Zinfandel makes one wonder why this grape is not as widespread in Australia as it is in
California. Exports to all major markets.

YYYYY **Chardonnay 2004** A potent, powerful and complex wine, with a lovely touch of mineral to
hold the nectarine/melon fruit and barrel ferment inputs together; likewise acidity.
Screwcap. 14° alc. **RATING** 96 **DRINK** 2014 $ 40
Wallcliffe Sauvignon Blanc Semillon 2004 As always, a very complex wine
unambiguously headed towards white Bordeaux in style; fleshy, citrus fruit with barrel
ferment and malolactic inputs woven throughout; great drive and length. Screwcap.
RATING 95 **DRINK** 2009 $ 36
Wallcliffe Sauvignon Blanc Semillon 2003 A gloriously complex yet smooth bouquet
with ripe fruit and spicy oak; elegant, supple and mouthfilling, yet not heavy; again into
ripe flavours. Screwcap. 13.5° alc. **RATING** 95 **DRINK** 2011 $ 35
Wallcliffe Shiraz 2004 Excellent colour, very deep; strongly structured, with complex
texture, the black fruits having absorbed the French oak; long palate, finish and aftertaste.
Screwcap. 14.5° alc. **RATING** 94 **DRINK** 2020 $ 56

YYYY⅃ **Margaret River Semillon Sauvignon Blanc 2005** High-toned, intensely aromatic fruit,
with the faintest touch of sweatiness; follows up in the mouth with appropriate length and
power. Screwcap. 13.5° alc. **RATING** 93 **DRINK** 2008 $ 24
Margaret River Shiraz 2004 Very good purple-red; an excellent expression of medium-
to full-bodied cool-grown shiraz; highly focused but elegant, with pure red and black
cherry, spice and blackberry fruit. Screwcap. **RATING** 93 **DRINK** 2015 $ 36
Margaret River Cabernet Sauvignon 2002 Some development in colour; an elegant,
medium-bodied wine, with cedary, spicy fruit and no hint of brett; silky tannins. Cork.
RATING 92 **DRINK** 2012 $ 69
Trinders Margaret River Cabernet Merlot 2004 Trademark '04 colour; a powerful,
medium- to full-bodied wine, with layers of blackcurrant, spice and ripe tannins; good
structure and finish. Screwcap. 14.5° alc. **RATING** 91 **DRINK** 2012 $ 29
Marmaduke 2004 Bright purple-red; medium-bodied, with good texture consistent with
the other '04 releases; fresh fruit, subtle oak, fine tannins. Screwcap. 14° alc. **RATING** 90
DRINK 2012 $ 17
Margaret River Zinfandel 2004 Good colour; a distinctly savoury, spicy version with red
and black fruits; the tannins are fine but persistent, oak a mere backdrop. Screwcap.
16° alc. **RATING** 90 **DRINK** 2009 $ 48

YYYY **Georgiana 2005** Some of the faintly sweaty characters evident on the Semillon Sauvignon
Blanc, but abundant tropical fruit and peach aromas ranging into pineapple, passionfruit
and gooseberry on the palate. Screwcap. 13° alc. **RATING** 89 **DRINK** 2008 $ 17

🐌 Cape Naturaliste Vineyard ★★★★☆

Lot 77, Caves Road, Yallingup, WA 6282 **REGION** Margaret River
T (08) 9755 2538 **F** (08) 9755 2538 **WWW**.capenaturalistevineyard.com.au **OPEN** Wed–Mon 10.30–5
WINEMAKER David Moss, Barney Mitchell, Craig Brent-White **EST.** 1997 **CASES** 4000
Cape Naturaliste Vineyard has a long and varied history, going back 150 years when it was a coach inn for
travellers journeying between Perth and the Margaret River. Later it became a dairy farm, and in 1970
was purchased by a mining company intending to extract the mineral sands. The government stepped in
and declared it a national park, whereafter (in 1980) Craig Brent-White purchased the property. It was
not until 1997 that the 9-ha vineyard was planted to cabernet sauvignon, shiraz, merlot, semillon and
sauvignon blanc. The vineyard is run on an organic/biodynamic basis, designed to improve soil health.
The consistently high quality of the wines would suggest the effort is well worthwhile.

ŸŸŸŸŸ **Torpedo Rocks Margaret River Merlot 2004** Perfect varietal definition; gently spicy/savoury/olivaceous edges to the red fruit core; ripe, fine tannins and good oak. Shows what a light- to medium-bodied wine can achieve. Cork. 14.4° alc. **RATING** 94 **DRINK** 2013 $ 27

ŸŸŸŸŸ **Torpedo Rocks Margaret River Shiraz 2004** Excellent purple-red; very attractive, medium-bodied black and red cherry fruit meshed with supple, ripe tannins; oak just a touch overdone. Cork. 14.6° alc. **RATING** 93 **DRINK** 2015 $ 19
Margaret River Sauvignon Blanc 2005 Light straw-green; clean, and has the powerful and focused drive of good Margaret River sauvignon blanc, pure and uncompromising; long finish and aftertaste. Screwcap. 12.6° alc. **RATING** 92 **DRINK** Now $ 18
Torpedo Rocks Margaret River Cabernet Merlot 2003 Much deeper colour, more purple hue; a tightly focused array of predominantly blackcurrant/black fruits; good length and balance; very different style. Cork. 13.8° alc. **RATING** 92 **DRINK** 2017 $ 27
Margaret River Semillon Sauvignon Blanc 2005 A similar style, emphasising the closeness of Margaret River semillon and sauvignon blanc in terms of flavour; crisp grass, asparagus, lemon and mineral. Screwcap. 12.6° alc. **RATING** 91 **DRINK** 2008 $ 18
Torpedo Rocks Margaret River Cabernet Merlot 2004 Good purple-red; more cassis/red fruits on entry and the mid-palate, then the merlot influence starts to express itself in the savoury notes of the finish. Cork. 14.4° alc. **RATING** 90 **DRINK** 2014 $ 27

ŸŸŸŸ **Torpedo Rocks Margaret River Semillon 2004** Big, generous flavour, texture and structure; light oak; food wine. Cork. 12.5° alc. **RATING** 89 **DRINK** 2008 $ 23
Torpedo Rocks Margaret River Cabernet Sauvignon 2004 Light- to medium-bodied; savoury/earthy/leafy/minty aromas and flavours; notwithstanding the alcohol, didn't achieve full flavour ripeness. Cork. 14.4° alc. **RATING** 88 **DRINK** 2010 $ 27

Capel Vale ★★★★☆

Lot 5 Stirling Estate, Mallokup Road, Capel, WA 6271 **REGION** Geographe
T (08) 9702 1012 **F** (08) 9727 1904 **WWW**.capelvale.com **OPEN** Cellar door & restaurant 7 days 10–4
WINEMAKER Rebecca Catlin, Justin Hearn, Peter Pratten **EST.** 1974 **CASES** 100 000
Dr Peter Pratten's Capel Vale has expanded its viticultural empire to the point where it is entirely an estate-run business, with 220 ha of vineyards spread through Mt Barker, Pemberton, Margaret River and Geographe. Its wines cross every price point and style from fighting varietal to ultra-premium; always known for its Riesling, powerful red wines are now very much part of the portfolio. Exports to all major markets.

ŸŸŸŸŸ **Sauvignon Blanc Semillon 2005** Clean, fresh and crisp; lively grassy/lemony/passionfruit flavours; long, clean finish; slippery acidity. Screwcap. **RATING** 91 **DRINK** 2010 $ 18
CV Sauvignon Blanc 2005 Lively, crisp and crunchy; a lemony tang to gooseberry fruit; drives through on the finish. Screwcap. **RATING** 90 **DRINK** Now $ 15
Geographe Chardonnay 2003 Light straw-green; a tight, restrained style; nectarine and grapefruit drives the flavours, French oak barrel ferment influences tightly controlled. Screwcap. 13.5° alc. **RATING** 90 **DRINK** 2010 $ 21
Cabernet Sauvignon 2002 Good colour; medium-bodied, supple and elegant, the fruit framed by attractive tannins and gentle oak; touches of merlot, cabernet franc and malbec. Frankland/Pemberton/Geographe. Cork. 14.5° alc. **RATING** 90 **DRINK** 2012 $ 23

ŸŸŸŸ **Seven Day Road Sauvignon Blanc 2005** Doesn't really have enough concentration of varietal fruit, though no obvious fault; somewhat expensive given the quality. Screwcap. **RATING** 87 **DRINK** Now $ 25
CV Unwooded Chardonnay 2005 Has the tangy citrussy grapefruit edge common to many of the better unwooded chardonnays; a virtual crossover from sauvignon blanc. Screwcap. 14° alc. **RATING** 87 **DRINK** 2008 $ 15

ŸŸŸŸ **CV Shiraz 2003 RATING** 86 **DRINK** 2008 $ 15
Verdelho 2005 RATING 85 **DRINK** Now $ 17
CV Pinot Noir 2002 RATING 85 **DRINK** Now $ 15
Viognier 2005 RATING 84 **DRINK** Now $ 18

Capercaillie ★★★★★

Londons Road, Lovedale, NSW 2325 **REGION** Lower Hunter Valley
T (02) 4990 2904 **F** (02) 4991 1886 **WWW**.capercailliewine.com.au **OPEN** Mon–Sat 9–5, Sun 10–5
WINEMAKER Alasdair Sutherland, Daniel Binet **EST.** 1995 **CASES** 6000
The former Dawson Estate, now run by Hunter Valley veteran Alasdair Sutherland. The Capercaillie wines are particularly well-made, with generous flavour. Following the example of Brokenwood, its fruit sources are spread across southeastern Australia. Exports to the UK, NZ, Japan and Singapore.

▼▼▼▼▼ **Hunter Valley Semillon 2001** A beautifully balanced and focused wine, still very fresh and youthful, but with superb lemony fruit and a lingering, haunting finish. From cygnet to swan since first tasted 3 years ago. Quality cork. 10.5° alc. **RATING** 95 **DRINK** 2010 **$** 23
The Clan 2004 Vivid colour; a perfumed array of black and red fruits; the palate opens with fresh fruit, and just when you think there are no tannins, they appear in balance; 40% Cabernet Sauvignon (SA)/40% Petit Verdot (McLaren Vale)/20% Merlot (Orange). Screwcap. 14° alc. **RATING** 94 **DRINK** 2014 **$** 28

▼▼▼▼▽ **Orange Highlands Merlot 2004** Good colour; fresh, vibrant small red fruits; fine but sweet tannins, balanced oak. Screwcap. 14.8° alc. **RATING** 93 **DRINK** 2010 **$** 27
Ceilidh Shiraz 2004 An interesting blend; while quite powerful (McLaren Vale 65%) it also has elegance (Hunter Valley). Plum, blackberry and chocolate in the mouth, with good balance and soft tannins. Screwcap. 14.5° alc. **RATING** 92 **DRINK** 2014 **$** 28
Cullin Chardonnay 2005 Smart wine; melon, nectarine and fig fruit-driven, flavour with finesse; good balance and length. Screwcap. 14° alc. **RATING** 91 **DRINK** 2010 **$** 21

▼▼▼▼ **Hunter Valley Rose 2005** Brilliant purple-red; a cellar door special with small, sweet berry fruits; some acidity and length. Cork. 12.5° alc. **RATING** 87 **DRINK** Now **$** 19

▼▼▼▽ **Hunter Valley Gewurztraminer 2005** Old vines, but really is the effort worth it? Gewurztraminer by elimination; well-made, of course. Screwcap. 12° alc. **RATING** 86 **DRINK** Now **$** 19
The Creel Semillon 2005 **RATING** 86 **DRINK** 2009 **$** 19

Capogreco Winery Estate NR

3078 Riverside Avenue, South Mildura, Vic 3500 **REGION** Murray Darling
T (03) 5022 1431 **F** (03) 5022 1431 **OPEN** Mon–Sat 10–5
WINEMAKER Bruno Capogreco, Domenico Capogreco **EST.** 1976 **CASES** NFP
Italian-owned and run, the wines are a blend of Italian and Australian Riverland influences. The estate has 13 ha of chardonnay, 14 ha of shiraz and 6 ha of cabernet sauvignon, but also purchases other varieties.

Captain's Paddock NR

18 Millers Road, Kingaroy, Qld 4610 **REGION** South Burnett
T (07) 4162 4534 **F** (07) 4162 4502 **WWW**.captainspaddock.com.au **OPEN** 7 days 10–5
WINEMAKER Luke Fitzpatrick **EST.** 1995 **CASES** 1000
Don and Judy McCallum planted the first ha of vineyard in 1995, followed by a further 3.5 ha in 1996, focusing on shiraz and chardonnay. Their son Stuart built many unusual but practicable objects dotted around the property. In April 2002 Maryanne Pidcock and Peter Eaton purchased the property, with business as usual thereafter.

Captains Creek Organic Wines ★★★

160 Mays Road, Blampied, Vic 3364 **REGION** Ballarat
T (03) 5345 7408 **F** (03) 5345 7408 **WWW**.captainscreek.com **OPEN** By appt
WINEMAKER Norman Latta, Kilchurn Wines (David Cowburn) **EST.** 1994 **CASES** 1000
Doug and Carolyn May are the third generation of farmers at the Captains Creek property, and have been conducting the business for over 20 years without using any chemicals. When they began establishing the vineyard in 1994, with 1.5 ha chardonnay and 0.5 ha pinot noir, they resolved to go down the same path: they use preventive spray programs of copper and sulphur, thermal flame weeding, and beneficial predatory insects to control weeds and mites.

▼▼▼▼ **Organic Pinot Noir Chardonnay 2004** Fine, crisp, clean and fresh; while well-balanced is inevitably not complex, but that's not the point. Minimum SO_2 added. 12° alc. **RATING** 87 **DRINK** 2008 $ 27

▼▼▼▽ **Organic Chardonnay 2003 RATING** 84 **DRINK** Now $ 23

Carbunup Crest Vineyard   ★★★☆

PO Box 235, Busselton, WA 6280 **REGION** Margaret River
T (08) 9754 2618 **F** (08) 9754 2618 **WWW**.carbunupcrestwines.com.au **OPEN** Not
WINEMAKER Flying Fish Cove **EST.** 1998 **CASES** 2000
Carbunup Crest is operated by 3 local families, with Kris Meares managing the business. Initially it operated as a grapevine rootling nursery, but it has gradually converted to grapegrowing and winemaking. There are 6 ha of vineyard, all of which are all now in production, and plans to extend the plantings to 20 ha (the property is 53 ha in total). The contract-made wines are great value.

▼▼▼▼ **Beach Head Semillon Sauvignon Blanc 2005** Bright green-yellow; semillon does most of the talking with herb, spice, mineral and stone providing appreciable texture. Screwcap. 12.8° alc. **RATING** 89 **DRINK** 2009 $ 13
Beach Head Shiraz 2001 Remarkable hue and freshness given a heavily stained cork; fresh and lively, light- to medium-bodied cherry and blackberry fruit; balanced extract and (as is usual), great value. Cork. 13.9° alc. **RATING** 89 **DRINK** 2010 $ 12.95
Beach Head Cabernet Merlot 2001 Light- to medium-bodied; a positive varietal mix of blackcurrant, cassis, olive and spice backed by gentle tannins; aging very well and offering outstanding value. Cork. 13.7° alc. **RATING** 89 **DRINK** 2010 $ 13

▼▼▼▽ **Beach Head Sunset Rose 2001 RATING** 85 **DRINK** Now $ 12.95

Cardinham Estate   ★★★

Main North Road, Stanley Flat, SA 5453 **REGION** Clare Valley
T (08) 8842 1944 **F** (08) 8842 1955 **WWW**.cardinham.com **OPEN** 7 days 10–5
WINEMAKER Scott Smith, Emma Bowley **EST.** 1981 **CASES** 4500
The Smith family has progressively increased the vineyard size up to its present level of 60 ha, the largest plantings being of cabernet sauvignon, shiraz and riesling. It entered into a grape supply contract with Wolf Blass, which led to an association with then Quelltaler winemaker Stephen John. The joint venture then formed has now terminated, and Cardinham is locating its 500-tonne winery on its Emerald Vineyard and using only estate-grown grapes. This has seen production rise, with the 3 staples of Riesling, Cabernet Merlot and Stradbroke Shiraz available from the winery and through retail distribution, and additional wines made in small volume available only at the cellar door and by mail order. Exports to Singapore.

▼▼▼▼ **Smith Family Vineyards Clare Valley Riesling 2005** Generous, tropical flavours tending soft and somewhat broad. Screwcap. 11.9° alc. **RATING** 87 **DRINK** 2009 $ 18

▼▼▼▽ **True Colours Semillon Sauvignon Blanc 2005** Fresh gooseberry, grass and mineral aromas; a light-bodied, crisp palate, pleasantly dry, but does shorten off somewhat on the finish. Screwcap. **RATING** 86 **DRINK** Now $ 12.50
True Colours Rose 2005 Bright pink; perfumed strawberry and plum aromas, then an uncompromisingly sweet and fruity palate; should be served either well-chilled as an aperitif, or possibly with cake or fruit to off-set the sweetness. Malbec. Screwcap. **RATING** 86 **DRINK** Now $ 12.50
True Colours Cabernet Shiraz 2003 Complex, earthy/gamey/spicy aromas and flavours; medium-bodied, the tannins and extract controlled, likewise the oak influence. Cork. **RATING** 86 **DRINK** Now $ 12.50

Cargo Road Wines ★★★★

Cargo Road, Orange, NSW 2800 **REGION** Orange
T(02) 6365 6100 **F**(02) 6365 6001 **WWW**.cargoroadwines.com.au **OPEN** W'ends & public hols 11–5, or by appt
WINEMAKER James Sweetapple **EST.** 1983 **CASES** 3000
Originally called The Midas Tree, the vineyard was planted in 1984 by Roseworthy graduate John Swanson. He established a 2.5-ha vineyard that included zinfandel: he was 15 years ahead of his time. The property was acquired in 1997 by Charles Lane, James Sweetapple and Brian Walters. Since then they have rejuvenated the original vineyard and planted more zinfandel, sauvignon blanc and cabernet. They are all actively involved in the Orange region community, and have opened the Pippin Bistro.

ТТТТ️ **Orange Riesling 2005** Bright, lively lime and apple blossom aromas; a crisp palate, with a touch of sweetness balanced by acidity. Screwcap. 12.4° alc. **RATING** 90 **DRINK** 2011 $18
Orange Sauvignon Blanc 2005 Fresh and clean; delicious varietal passionfruit and gooseberry flavours neatly balanced by lemony acidity. Screwcap. 14° alc. **RATING** 90 **DRINK** Now $18
Orange Merlot 2004 Vibrant, light- to medium-bodied wine; spice, olive and redcurrant flavours; fine tannins. Cork. 14.5° alc. **RATING** 90 **DRINK** 2010 $22

ТТТТ **Orange Cabernet Merlot 2004** Light- to medium-bodied; blackcurrant/cassis/olive fruit, and sweet vanillan oak. Cork. 14.5° alc. **RATING** 89 **DRINK** 2011 $22
Dessert Zinfandel (500ml) 2005 Rich, spicy prune/plum jam/pudding flavours balanced by good acidity; works surprisingly well. Dehydrated grapes picked in May; not fortified; specialised yeast. Cork. 14.5° alc. **RATING** 89 **DRINK** Now $35
Orange Cabernet Sauvignon 2004 Follows in the light- to medium-bodied pattern of the winery; leafy, minty, spicy edges to firm black fruits. Austere. Cork. 14.5° alc. **RATING** 88 **DRINK** 2012 $22

ТТТ️ **Orange Zinfandel 2004** Slightly cloudy; you can't get away from the alcohol; an altogether weird wine even by Californian standards. Cork. 16.5° alc. **RATING** 86 **DRINK** Now $30

Carilley Estate ★★★

Lot 23 Hyem Road, Herne Hill, WA 6056 **REGION** Swan Valley
T(08) 9296 6190 **F**(08) 9296 6190 **WWW**.carilleyestate.com.au **OPEN** 7 days 10.30–5
WINEMAKER Rob Marshall **EST.** 1985 **CASES** 2000
The Carija family has owned and operated vineyards in the Swan Valley since 1957, culminating in the establishment of Carilley Estate in 1985 by doctors Laura and Isavel Carija. They have an 8-ha vineyard planted to chardonnay, chenin blanc, vigonier, sharaz, malbec, merlot and grenache. Most of the grapes are sold, with a small proportion made under the Carilley Estate label.

ТТТТ **Verdi Viognier Chenin Blanc 2004** Light straw-green; clean musk, apricot and herb mix; firm, dry finish. Screwcap. **RATING** 87 **DRINK** 2009 $21
Mozart Reserve Merlot 2003 Savoury, leafy style; light- to medium-bodied; despite the challenges of the climate, has kept some varietal character; silky tannins. Stained, creased cork. **RATING** 87 **DRINK** 2009 $39

ТТТ️ **Sanguinea Shiraz 2003** Savoury aromas and flavours; pleasant balance and mouthfeel, but lacks fruit intensity. Nonetheless, well-made. Cork. **RATING** 86 **DRINK** 2008 $17
Unwooded Chardonnay 2004 **RATING** 84 **DRINK** Now $16

ТТТ **Fortuniana Chenin Blanc 2004** **RATING** 83 $14

Carindale Wines NR

Palmers Lane, Pokolbin, NSW 2321 **REGION** Lower Hunter Valley
T(02) 4998 7665 **F**(02) 4998 7065 **WWW**.carindalewines.com.au **OPEN** Fri–Mon 10–5
WINEMAKER Brian Walsh (Contract) **EST.** 1996 **CASES** 1500
Carindale draws upon 2 ha of chardonnay, 1.2 ha of cabernet franc and 0.2 ha of merlot (together with few muscat vines). Exports to the US, Canada, Singapore and China.

🐚 Carlaminda Estate

NR

59 Richards Road, Ferguson, WA 6236 **REGION** Geographe
T (08) 9728 3002 **F** (08) 9728 3002 **WWW**.carlaminda.com **OPEN** To open in 2006
WINEMAKER Siobhan Lynch **EST.** 2003 **CASES** 800
Quirinus Olsthoorn is primarily a cattle breeder, but has established 2 ha each of semillon and shiraz, and 1 ha each of viognier and tempranillo on his property, the first plantings dating back to 1994. Until 2003 the grapes were sold, but since then district veteran Siobhan Lynch has made the wine for Carlaminda Estate.

Carlei Estate & Green Vineyards

★★★★★

1 Albert Road, Upper Beaconsfield, Vic 3808 **REGION** Yarra Valley
T (03) 5944 4599 **F** (03) 5944 4599 **WWW**.carlei.com.au **OPEN** W'ends by appt
WINEMAKER Sergio Carlei **EST.** 1994 **CASES** 10 000
Carlei Estate has come a long way in a little time, with Sergio Carlei graduating from home winemaking in a suburban garage to his own (commercial) winery in Upper Beaconsfield, which happens to fall just within the boundaries of the Yarra Valley. Along the way Carlei acquired a Bachelor of Wine Science from Charles Sturt University, and has established a 2.25-ha vineyard with organic and biodynamic accreditation adjacent to the Upper Beaconsfield winery. His contract winemaking servies are now a major part of the business, and are a showcase for his extremely impressive winemaking talents.

🍷🍷🍷🍷🍷 **Green Vineyards Yarra Valley Chardonnay 2004** Fine and elegant citrus and nutty barrel ferment aromas, then a long, precisely focused palate; nectarine and grapefruit; bracing and crisp finish. Diam. 13.5° alc. **RATING** 94 **DRINK** 2014 $ 29
Carlei Estate Tre Bianchi 2004 Light straw-green; elegant and complex; the barrel ferment and oak maturation has had more impact on texture than flavour; lovely acidity and length; 80% Sauvignon Blanc/12% Semillon/8% Chardonnay. Screwcap. 12° alc. **RATING** 94 **DRINK** 2009 $ 26

🍷🍷🍷🍷🍸 **Green Vineyards Central Victoria Shiraz 2003** Very fragrant and vibrant juciy berry style; not at all typical of Heathcote; medium-bodied, silky and supple with a touch of spice. Diam. 14.2° alc. **RATING** 93 **DRINK** 2013 $ 29

Carn Estate

NR

Eleventh Street, Nichols Point, Vic 3501 **REGION** Murray Darling
T (03) 5024 7393 **F** (03) 5021 2929 **OPEN** 7 days
WINEMAKER Contract **EST.** 1997 **CASES** NA
Richard Carn has established 9 ha of colombard, cabernet sauvignon, merlot and shiraz on 2 vineyard sites, and has the wine contract-made. In a relatively short time, exports to England have been established, and the cellar door offers light meals, barbecue and picnic facilities.

Carosa

★★★☆

310 Houston Street, Mount Helena, WA 6082 **REGION** Perth Hills
T (08) 9572 1603 **WWW**.carosavineyard.com **OPEN** W'ends & hols 11–5, or by appt
WINEMAKER James Elson **EST.** 1984 **CASES** 500
Very limited production and small-scale winemaking result in wines which sell readily enough into the local market. Winemaker Jim Elson has extensive eastern Australia winemaking experience (with Seppelt).

🍷🍷🍷🍷 **Perth Hills Cabernet Sauvignon 2003** Attractive, sweet, almost juicy fruit, along with dark chocolate and vanilla; comes together well. Diam. **RATING** 89 **DRINK** 2010 $ 17
Hannah Perth Hills Shiraz 2003 Medium-bodied; an array of blackberry, spice, earth and vanilla on the bouquet and palate; slightly dusty tannins. Diam. **RATING** 87 **DRINK** 2009 $ 17

Carpinteri Vineyards

NR

PO Box 61, Nyah, Vic 3594 **REGION** Swan Hill
T (03) 5030 2569 **F** (03) 5030 2680 **OPEN** Not
WINEMAKER Michael Kyberd (Contract) **EST.** 1945 **CASES** 900
Vince and Con Carpinteri are primarily grapegrowers, with 30 ha planted to chardonnay, grenache, malbec, shiraz, mourvedre, black muscat and sultana. A small amount of wine is made under contract by Michael Kyberd at Red Hill Estate in the Mornington Peninsula.

Casa Freschi

PO Box 45, Summertown, SA 5141 **REGION** Langhorne Creek
T 0409 364 569 **F** (08) 8390 3232 **www**.casafreschi.com.au **OPEN** Not
WINEMAKER David Freschi **EST.** 1998 **CASES** 1000
David Freschi graduated with a degree in Oenology from Roseworthy College in 1991 and spent most of the decade working overseas in California, Italy and NZ. In 1998 he and his wife decided to trade in the corporate world for a small family-owned winemaking business, with a core of 2.5 ha of vines established by his parents in 1972; an additional 2 ha of nebbiolo have now been planted adjacent to the original vineyard. Says David, 'The names of the wines were chosen to best express the personality of the wines grown in our vineyard, as well as to express our heritage.' The establishment of a 3-ha vineyard in the Adelaide Hills began in 2004, with further plantings in 2005. Exports to the US and Canada.

YYYYY **Profondo Grand 2003** Good colour; powerful wine, with abundant blackberry, spice and licorice; quality French oak well-integrated; balanced tannins. Shiraz (69%)/Cabernet Sauvignon/Malbec. Cork. 14.5° alc. **RATING** 94 **DRINK** 2015 $ 58

YYYYY **La Signora 2003** Medium red-purple; an assemblage of predominantly black fruits; sinewy strength, and finely honed tannins. Nebbiolo (48%)/Cabernet Sauvignon/Shiraz/Malbec. Cork. 14° alc. **RATING** 90 **DRINK** 2013 $ 38

Casas Wines

NR

RMB 236D Rosa Brook Road, Margaret River, WA 6285 **REGION** Margaret River
T (08) 9757 4542 **F** (08) 9757 4006 **www**.casas.com.au **OPEN** By appt
WINEMAKER Janice MacDonald **EST.** 1992 **CASES** 2000
John Casas has established 5 ha of shiraz, 4 ha of cabernet sauvignon and 1 ha each of chardonnay and sauvignon blanc. The vineyard is managed to produce low yields of 1–2 tonnes per acre, with the aim of making a wine of sufficient power and density to merit barrel maturation of 1.5–2.5 years. Domestic distribution by the quirkily named Medicinal Purposes Wine Co (tel 0438 250 372) supplements website sales. Exports to the UK and the US.

Cascabel

Rogers Road, Willunga, SA 5172 (postal) **REGION** McLaren Vale
T (08) 8557 4434 **F** (08) 8557 4435 **OPEN** Not
WINEMAKER Susana Fernandez, Duncan Ferguson **EST.** 1997 **CASES** 2500
Cascabel's proprietors, Duncan Ferguson and Susana Fernandez, planted a 5 ha mosaic of southern Rhône and Spanish varieties. The choice of grapes reflects the winemaking experience of the proprietors in Australia, the Rhône Valley, Bordeaux, Italy, Germany and NZ — and also Susana Fernandez's birthplace, Spain. Production has moved steadily towards the style of the Rhône Valley, Rioja and other parts of Spain. Exports to the UK, the US, Switzerland, Japan and Spain.

YYYYY **Eden Valley Riesling 2005** Light straw-green; fragrant spice, citrus and apple aromas; a crisp and crunchy palate, with excellent acidity and length; very pure. Screwcap. 12.5° alc. **RATING** 95 **DRINK** 2015 $ 23

Casella Wines ★★★★

Wakely Road, Yenda, NSW 2681 **REGION** Riverina
T (02) 6961 3000 **F** (02) 6961 3099 **WWW**.casellawines.com.au **OPEN** Not
WINEMAKER Alan Kennett, Phillip Casella **EST.** 1969 **CASES** 25 million
One of the modern-day fairytale success stories, transformed overnight from a substantial, successful but non-charismatic business shown as making 650 000 cases in 2000. Its opportunity came when the American distribution of Lindemans Bin 65 Chardonnay was taken away from WJ Deutsch & Sons, leaving a massive gap in its portfolio, which was filled by yellow tail. It has built its US presence at a faster rate than any other wine or brand in history. The only problem was the weakening US dollar; all the financial and marketing skills of Casella and WJ Deutsch will be needed to keep sales growing. A major plus in 2004 was Casella's capture of 2 most important trophies in Australia, Brisbane's Stoddart and Melbourne's Jimmy Watson (both with unbottled wines, however).

ΥΥΥΥΥ **Icon Shiraz 2003** Rich and full with a mix of dark chocolate and blackberry; powerful tannins but in balance. Gold medal Sydney Wine Show '06. Cork. **RATING** 94 **DRINK** 2010 $ 50

ΥΥΥΥΥ **yellow tail Premium Wrattonbully Cabernet Sauvignon 2003** Medium purple-red; clean cassis/blackcurrant fruit aromas; a medium-bodied wine with distinctly herbal/savoury edges to black fruits at the core; cerebral elegance. Jimmy Watson Trophy winner 2004. Cork. 13.5° alc. **RATING** 92 **DRINK** 2013 $ 50
yellow tail Premium Shiraz 2003 A powerful and condensed array of blackberry and dark chocolate; slightly raw tannins needing to soften. McLaren Vale. **RATING** 90 **DRINK** 2015 $ 50

ΥΥΥΥ **yellow tail Merlot 2004** Attractive medium-bodied wine; good varietal character and structure; small, sweet berry fruit. Silver National Wine Show '05. Synthetic. 13.5° alc. **RATING** 89 **DRINK** Now $ 10
yellow tail Semillon Sauvignon Blanc 2005 Spotlessly clean and fresh; grass, lemon and mineral flavours; not sweet; good length; very well-made. Screwcap. **RATING** 88 **DRINK** 2009 $ 9.99

ΥΥΥΥ **yellow tail Chardonnay 2005** Ripe, quite complex texture and structure, with peaches and cream; does finish short. Synthetic. **RATING** 86 **DRINK** Now $ 9.99
yellow tail Cabernet Sauvignon 2004 **RATING** 86 **DRINK** Now $ 9.99
yellow tail Merlot 2005 **RATING** 85 **DRINK** Now $ 9.99
King Valley Alpine Valleys Sauvignon Blanc 2004 **RATING** 84 **DRINK** Now $ 14.99

Casley Mount Hutton Winery NR

'Mount Hutton', Texas Road, via Stanthorpe, Qld 4380 **REGION** Granite Belt
T (07) 4683 6316 **F** (07) 4683 6345 **OPEN** Fri–Sun 10–5
WINEMAKER Grant Casley **EST.** 1999 **CASES** NA
Grant and Sonya Casley have established 9 ha of sauvignon blanc, chenin blanc, semillon, chardonnay, cabernet sauvignon, merlot and shiraz, making the wine onsite. The chief wine sales are by mail order and through the cellar door, which offers all the usual facilities, and meals by prior arrangement.

Cassegrain ★★★★☆

764, Fernbank Creek Road, Port Macquarie, NSW 2444 **REGION** Hastings River
T (02) 6582 8377 **F** (02) 6582 8378 **WWW**.cassegrainwines.com.au **OPEN** 7 days 9–5
WINEMAKER Simon Gilbert Wines **EST.** 1980 **CASES** 60 000
In late 2005 Cassegrain and Simon Gilbert Wines merged their businesses. In the outcome, Simon Gilbert holds 70% of Cassegrain, the remainder held by John Cassegrain and associates. Winemaking will shift to Simon Gilbert, but the Cassegrain restaurant and cellar door will continue as before.

ΥΥΥΥΥ **Hastings River Reserve Semillon 2000** Glowing yellow-green; excellent varietal fruit; intense lemon and honey mix; great length; near its peak. Cork. **RATING** 94 **DRINK** Now $ 26.95

ŸŸŸŸŸ **Limited Release Sauvignon Blanc 2005** Spotlessly clean; tightly wound up mineral, gooseberry, lemongrass and herb mix; a lively, light, bone-dry finish. Tumbarumba. Screwcap. 11.5° alc. **RATING** 92 **DRINK** Now $ 18

Reserve Chardonnay 2004 A complex wine with the full bag of winemaking techniques; creamy, supple texture to the nectarine and melon fruit; integrated oak. Cork. **RATING** 92 **DRINK** 2010 $ 27

Limited Release Gewurztraminer 2005 The clearest possible varietal expression of lychees, musk and rose petals on the bouquet, tracking through with precision to the palate. Alcohol heat almost inevitable. From a single New England vineyard at 900m. Screwcap. 14.8° alc. **RATING** 90 **DRINK** 2008 $ 17.95

Unwooded Chardonnay 2005 Crisp, lively and very fresh; tangy fruit, headed almost in the direction of Sauvignon Blanc; a strange regional ménage à trois: South Coast/ Tumbarumba/Northern Slopes. Screwcap. 12.5° alc. **RATING** 90 **DRINK** 2008 $ 16.95

ŸŸŸŸ **Limited Release Riesling 2005** Well-made; spicy, minerally, tangy fruit, with citrussy acidity. Adelaide Hills. Screwcap. 13.5° alc. **RATING** 89 **DRINK** 2011 $ 18

Reserve Chardonnay 2003 Medium-bodied; soft peach and fig fruit; well-integrated oak; full of flavour, though not particularly long. Hunter Valley/metropolitan Sydney/ Tumbarumba. Cork. **RATING** 89 **DRINK** 2008 $ 26.95

Verdelho 2005 Light-bodied, but clean and fresh, with nice length and line running through varietal fruit. **RATING** 87 **DRINK** 2008 $ 16.95

Limited Release Tempranillo 2005 Light-bodied; pleasant, spicy cherry/berry fruit; reasonably representative of cool-grown tempranillo. Northern Slopes, NSW. Cork. 14° alc. **RATING** 87 **DRINK** 2009 $ 18

ŸŸŸŸ **Chardonnay 2005 RATING** 86 **DRINK** 2008 $ 19
Shiraz 2003 RATING 86 **DRINK** 2008 $ 16.95

Castagna
★★★★☆

88 Ressom Lane, Beechworth, Vic 3747 **REGION** Beechworth
T (03) 5728 2888 **F** (03) 5728 2898 **WWW**.castagna.com.au **OPEN** By appt
WINEMAKER Julian Castagna **EST.** 1997 **CASES** 2000
The elegantly labelled wines of Castagna will ultimately come from 4 ha of biodynamically managed estate shiraz and viognier being established (the latter making up 15% of the total). Winemaker Julian Castagna is intent on making wines which reflect the *terroir* as closely as possible, and declines to use cultured yeast or filtration. Genesis Syrah deserves its icon status.

ŸŸŸŸŸ **Ingenue 2004** An unusually minerally and structurally complex wine, suggesting wild yeast, and ambient fermentation temperatures in old oak; good length. Diam. 14° alc.
RATING 92 **DRINK** 2009 $ 55

Castle Glen Vineyard
NR

Amiens Road, The Summit, Qld, 4377 **REGION** Granite Belt
T (07) 4683 2363 **F** (07) 4683 2169 **OPEN** 7 days 10–5
WINEMAKER Cedric Millar **EST.** 1990 **CASES** NA
Unashamedly caters for the general tourist, with a large castle boasting an open fire set in 40 ha, and specialising in 27 liqueur-style fruit wines, but with Chardonnay, Shiraz, Merlot, Cabernet Sauvignon, Semillon and White Muscat also available.

Castle Rock Estate
NR

Porongurup Road, Porongurup, WA 6324 **REGION** Porongurup
T (08) 9853 1035 **F** (08) 9853 1010 **WWW**.castlerockestate.com.au **OPEN** Mon–Fri 10–4, w'ends & public hols 10–5
WINEMAKER Robert Diletti **EST.** 1983 **CASES** 5000
An exceptionally beautifully sited vineyard, winery and cellar door sales area on a 55-ha property with sweeping vistas from the Porongurups, operated by the Diletti family. The standard of viticulture is very high, and the site itself ideally situated (quite apart from its beauty). The 2-level

winery, set on the natural slope, maximises gravity flow, in particular for crushed must feeding into the press. The Rieslings have always been elegant and have handsomely repaid time in bottle; the Pinot Noir is the most consistent performer in the region.

Cathcart Ridge Estate

NR

Moyston Road, Cathcart via Ararat, Vic 3377 **REGION** Grampians
T (03) 5352 1997 **F** (03) 5352 1558 **WWW.**cathcartwines.com.au **OPEN** 7 days 11–5
WINEMAKER David Farnhill **EST.** 1977 **CASES** 10 000
In recent years has raised capital to fund a significant expansion program of both vineyards and the winery, but is still little known in the wider retail trade. Mount Ararat Estate is a parallel operation to Cathcart Ridge, David Farnhill being the Chief Executive of both. There are 8 ha of vineyard in the Grampians region providing cabernet sauvignon, merlot, chardonnay and shiraz. Exports to Ireland.

Cathedral Lane Wines

NR

228 Cathedral Lane, Taggerty, Vic 3714 **REGION** Upper Goulburn
T (03) 5774 7305 **F** (03) 5774 7696 **WWW.**cathedrallanewines.com **OPEN** By appt
WINEMAKER MasterWineMakers **EST.** 1997 **CASES** 450
Rod Needham and Heather Campbell planted their 3.2-ha vineyard on the lower slopes of Mt Cathedral, at a height of 280m using a variant of the Scott Henry trellis system, with high-density 1m spacing between the vines, alternately trained up or down. The vineyard planning was supervised by former Coldstream Hills viticulturist Bill Christophersen.

Catherine Vale Vineyard

656 Milbrodale Road, Bulga, NSW 2330 **REGION** Lower Hunter Valley
T (02) 6579 1334 **F** (02) 6579 1299 **WWW.**catherinevale.com.au **OPEN** W'ends & public hols 10–5, or by appt
WINEMAKER Hunter Wine Services (John Hordern) **EST.** 1994 **CASES** 1200
Former schoolteachers Bill and Wendy Lawson have established Catherine Vale as a not-so-idle retirement venture. Part of the production from the 5.8-ha vineyard is sold to contract winemaker John Hordern; the remainder is vinified for the Catherine Vale label. A new cellar door opened in May 2004. Exports to Germany.

ŸŸŸŸŸ **Hunter Valley Semillon 2004** Strong green-yellow; good depth and structure; ripe style with citrus moving even into stone fruit, then minerally acidity to close. Screwcap. 11.5° alc. **RATING** 92 **DRINK** 2010 $14

ŸŸŸŸ **Hunter Valley Verdelho 2004** Faintly sweaty/reduced aromas; however, a powerful and complex palate with a citrus/tropical mix; good length. Screwcap. 13.5° alc. **RATING** 88 **DRINK** Now $14

ŸŸŸŸ **Hunter Valley Chardonnay 2004** **RATING** 85 **DRINK** Now $16

Catherine's Ridge

NR

Fish Fossil Drive, Canowindra, NSW 2804 **REGION** Cowra
T (02) 6344 3212 **F** (02) 6344 3242 **OPEN** By appt
WINEMAKER Contract **EST.** 1999 **CASES** NFP
Kay and David Warren have 18 ha of chardonnay, verdelho, shiraz and cabernet sauvignon. The wine is made under contract from part of the annual grape production.

Catspaw Farm

NR

Texas Road, Stanthorpe, Qld 4380 **REGION** Granite Belt
T (07) 4683 6229 **F** (07) 4683 6386 **WWW.**catspaw.cjb.net **OPEN** Thurs–Sun & public hols 10–5,
7 days Easter, June & September school hols
WINEMAKER Christopher Whitfort **EST.** 1989 **CASES** 300
The foundations for Catspaw Farm were laid back in 1989 when planting of the vineyard began with chardonnay, riesling, cabernet franc, cabernet sauvignon, merlot, chambourcin and shiraz, totalling 4.6 ha, followed by roussanne, semillon, barbera and sangiovese, lifting total plantings to just under 8 ha.

Cavalier Crest   NR

Davis Road, Rosa Glen, WA 6285 **REGION** Margaret River
T (08) 9757 5091 **F** (08) 9757 5091 **OPEN** 7 days 10–5 by appt
WINEMAKER Andrew Gaman (Contract) **EST.** 1978 **CASES** 4500
The Halcyon Vineyard, as it is known locally, was established in 1978 with the planting of little under 5 ha of cabernet sauvignon, merlot, pinot noir, chardonnay and semillon. Graham and Sue Connell purchased the property in 1991, increasing the plantings to 8 ha with more pinot noir, cabernet sauvignon and merlot. Until 2003 they sold the grapes, but in that year small batches of Cabernet Sauvignon, Merlot, Pinot Noir and Semillon were contract-made by Andrew Gaman.

Cawdor Wines   NR

Old Mount Barker Road, Echunga, SA 5153 **REGION** Adelaide Hills
T (08) 8388 8456 **F** (08) 8388 8807 **WWW**.cawdorwines.com.au **OPEN** By appt
WINEMAKER Contract **EST.** 1999 **CASES** 350
Jock Calder and his family began the establishment of Cawdor Wines with the purchase of 22 ha near the township of Echunga; 5 ha of sauvignon blanc were planted in 1999, with a further 2.6 ha of sauvignon blanc, 7.9 ha of shiraz and 2.7 ha of riesling the following year. The major part of the production is sold to Nepenthe Wines, but Cawdor nominates how much it wishes to have vinified under its own label each year. It has followed a softly, softly approach, with only small amounts being made.

Ceccanti Kiewa Valley Wines   ★★★☆

Bay Creek Lane, Mongans Bridge, Vic 3691 **REGION** Alpine Valleys
T (03) 5754 5236 **F** (03) 5754 5353 **WWW**.ceccanti.com.au **OPEN** 7 days 11–5
WINEMAKER Angelo Ceccanti, Moya Ceccanti, Danny Ceccanti **EST.** 1988 **CASES** NA
Angelo and Moya Ceccanti, with son Danny, have established 16 ha of vines, and now use all the production for their wines, which are made onsite by the family. Angelo, raised in Tuscany, had extensive exposure to viticulture and winemaking, but it is Moya and Danny who have the technical knowledge.

ΥΥΥΥ   **Riesling 2004** The bouquet has a fragrant mix of lime, herb and passionfruit; the generous flavours track the bouquet. A touch of CO_2 is not distracting, and, together with the screwcap, should give it a long life. Screwcap. **RATING** 89 **DRINK** 2012 $ 13.90
The Reserve 2002 Good colour; light- to medium-bodied, cool-climate style; spice, pepper and blackcurrant run through a savoury palate, which finishes with fine tannins. Cabernet/Merlot/Shiraz blend works well. Cork. **RATING** 88 **DRINK** 2009 $ 18

Cedar Creek Estate   NR

104–144 Hartley Road, Mt Tamborine, Qld 4272 **REGION** Queensland Coastal
T (07) 5545 1666 **F** (07) 5545 4762 **WWW**.cedarcreekestate.com.au **OPEN** 7 days 10–5
WINEMAKER Contract **EST.** 2000 **CASES** 1500
Opened in November 2000, Cedar Creek Estate takes its name from the creek which flows through the property at an altitude of 550m on Tamborine Mountain. A 3.7-ha vineyard has been planted to chambourcin and verdelho, and is supplemented by grapes grown elsewhere. The focus will always be on general tourism, with a host of facilities for visitors, including a restaurant; it also offers wines from Ballandean Estate.

🐚 Celestial Bay   ★★★★☆

33 Welwyn Avenue, Manning, WA 6152 (postal) **REGION** Margaret River
T (08) 9450 4191 **F** (08) 9313 1544 **WWW**.celestialbay.com.au **OPEN** Not
WINEMAKER Bernard Abbott **EST.** 1999 **CASES** 6000
Michael and Kim O'Brien had a background of farming in the Chittering Valley when they purchased the 104-ha property now known as Celestial Bay. It is very much a family enterprise, with son Aaron studying viticulture and oenology at Curtin University, and daughter Daneka involved in the winery's

marketing and sales. Under the direction of vineyard manager Sam Juniper, 50 ha of vines have been rapidly planted. The plantings are totally logical: semillon and sauvignon blanc (13 ha in all); chardonnay (13 ha); shiraz (6 ha) and cabernet sauvignon, merlot, malbec and petit verdot (18 ha in all). A winery has been built with winemaker Bernard Abbott celebrating his 21st Margaret River vintage in 2006. Unfortunately a computer gremlin has prevented tasting notes from appearing in this edition.

Cellarmasters ★★★★

Cnr Barossa Valley Way/Siegersdorf Road, Tanunda, SA 5352 **REGION** Barossa Valley
T(08) 8561 2200 **F**(08) 8561 2299 **WWW**.cellarmasters.com.au **OPEN** Not
WINEMAKER Nick Badrice, John Schwartzkopff, Sally Blackwell, Neil Doddridge, Mark Starick **EST.** 1982 **CASES** 800 000
The Cellarmaster Group was acquired by FWE in 1997. Dorrien Estate is the physical base of the vast Cellarmaster network which, wearing its retailer's hat, is by far the largest direct-sale outlet in Australia. It buys substantial quantities of wine from other makers either in bulk or as cleanskin (unlabelled bottles), or with recognisable but subtly different labels of the producers concerned. It also makes wine on its own account at Dorrien Estate, many of which are quite excellent, and of trophy quality. Chateau Dorrien is an entirely unrelated business.

▼▼▼▼▼ **Storton Vineyards Riesling 2005** A lovely, highly aromatic bouquet, and ripe lime juice flavours. Screwcap. **RATING** 94 **DRINK** 2012 $ 17

▼▼▼▼ **Black Wattle Vineyard Mount Benson Chardonnay 2004** A complex wine, with a nice touch of wild barrel ferment aromas; good length; dodgy, wet cork. 13° alc. **RATING** 89 **DRINK** Now $ 24.99
The Ridge Coonawarra Cabernet Sauvignon 2004 Medium-bodied; supple blackcurrant fruit with good tannin and oak management. **RATING** 88 **DRINK** 2012 $ 19.50
Dorrien Estate Bin 7 Cabernet Shiraz 2003 Has weight and substance; nice blackberry, blackcurrant and plum fruit mix; ripe tannins. **RATING** 88 **DRINK** 2009 $ 15.99
Lysander Mount Benson Chardonnay 2005 Fragrant, fresh, citrus and stone fruit; light-bodied, but good balance and length. Screwcap. **RATING** 87 **DRINK** Now $ 14.50

▼▼▼▽ **Dorrien Estate Barossa Valley Shiraz 2002** **RATING** 86 **DRINK** 2008 $ 17.99
Mum's Block Barossa Valley Shiraz 2002 **RATING** 86 **DRINK** 2008 $ 32.99
Dorrien Estate Organic Semillon 2004 **RATING** 85 **DRINK** Now $ 19.99
Dorrien Estate Bin 6 Semillon Chardonnay 2004 **RATING** 84 **DRINK** Now $ 15.99

Celtic Farm NR

39 Sweyn Street, North Balwyn, Vic 3104 (postal) **REGION** Southeast Australia
T(03) 9857 3600 **F**(03) 9857 3601 **OPEN** Not
WINEMAKER Gerry Taggert **EST.** 1997 **CASES** 4000
Yet another warehouse winery, these days owned and run by co-founder Gerry Taggert, joined by long-time friends Mark McNeill and Mike Shields — all fine Celts, according to Taggert. Taggert says, 'Celtic Farm is produced from classic varieties selected from Australia's premium wine regions and made with a total commitment to quality. While we have a desire to pay homage to our Celtic (drinking) heritage we are also acutely aware that wine should be about enjoyment, fun and not taking yourself too seriously.'

Centennial Vineyards ★★★★★

'Woodside', Centennial Road, Bowral, NSW 2576 **REGION** Southern Highlands
T(02) 4861 8700 **F**(02) 4681 8777 **WWW**.centennial.net.au **OPEN** 7 days 10–5
WINEMAKER Tony Cosgriff **EST.** 2002 **CASES** 10 000
Centennial Vineyards is a substantial development jointly owned by wine professional John Large and investor Mark Dowling, covering 133 ha of beautiful grazing land, with 31 ha planted to sauvignon blanc, riesling, verdelho, chardonnay, albarino, pinot gris, pinot noir, pinot meunier, cabernet sauvignon and tempranillo. Production from the estate vineyards is supplemented by purchases of grapes from other regions, including Orange. The winery fully utilises its 120-tonne capacity. Exports to the US, China and Korea.

ŢŢŢŢŢ **Reserve Orange Chardonnay 2004** Fine, elegant and intense; nectarine/stone fruit/citrus fruit mix; touch of creamy malolactic cashew; subtle oak, long finish. Screwcap. RATING 94 DRINK 2010 $ 27

Reserve Limited Release Hilltops Shiraz Viognier 2004 Vivid red-purple; luscious plum, spice and black cherry; the viognier at work without being overly obvious; medium-bodied, good length and balance. Lovely wine. Cork. 14.8° alc. RATING 94 DRINK 2014 $ 27

ŢŢŢŢŢ **Woodside Single Vineyard Riesling 2005** Apple, lime and blossom aromas; a tangy, zesty and lively palate with touches of minerally acidity. Very well-made. Estate-grown. Screwcap. 11.5° alc. RATING 92 DRINK 2010 $ 19

Woodside Single Vineyard Sauvignon Blanc 2005 Fine, elegant with very good balance and mouthfeel; slightly subdued but spotlessly clean varietal fruit (gooseberry and passionfruit) and a compelling finish. Estate-grown. Screwcap. 12.9° alc. RATING 92 DRINK Now $ 20

Reserve Orange Merlot 2004 Good colour; medium-bodied red fruits, with touches of leaf, mint, spice and olive; perfect weight and tannins for the variety. Cork. 14.5° alc. RATING 92 DRINK 2014 $ 28

Reserve Cabernet Merlot 2004 Clear, bright red-purple; fresh, bright red fruits and blackcurrant on entry to the mouth; tannins just a little firm and needing time to soften, which they will. Hilltops Cabernet/Orange Merlot. Cork. 14.6° alc. RATING 92 DRINK 2014 $ 27

Woodside Single Vineyard Chardonnay 2004 Bright yellow-green; a stylish wine, again with excellent length; white and yellow clingstone peach; gently nutty finish. Screwcap. RATING 91 DRINK 2009 $ 22

Woodside Single Vineyard Verdelho 2005 Manages to invest verdelho with far more character and style than usual; a mix of citrus, apple and tropical fruit; has length. Estate-grown. Screwcap. 13.5° alc. RATING 90 DRINK 2008 $ 19

Reserve Single Vineyard Orange Pinot Noir 2004 Sweet preserved cherry and spice aromas; light- to medium-bodied; good length and balance, moving more to savoury characters; fine, silky tannins. Screwcap. RATING 90 DRINK 2009 $ 29

Methode Champenoise NV While not particularly complex has length and finesse; light stone fruit flavours; 70% Pinot Noir/30% Chardonnay. 11.5° alc. RATING 90 DRINK 2010 $ 25

ŢŢŢŢ **Reserve Limited Release Rondinella Corvina 2004** A radically different wine, made in Amarone style; high spice and alcohol components; distinctive flavour and texture; 57% rondinella; Hilltops. Cork. 15.2° alc. RATING 89 DRINK 2015 $ 30

Woodside Single Vineyard Tempranillo 2004 Medium red-purple; fresh, clean, lively, juicy berry fruit; brisk acidity and clean finish; well-made. Screwcap. RATING 89 DRINK 2009 $ 20

Bong Bong White 2005 Driven by the Sauvignon Blanc component (86%), the remaining Chardonnay fitting in without disruption; plenty of depth, and just a touch of sweetness. Screwcap. 13° alc. RATING 87 DRINK Now $ 17

Rose 2005 Vivid fuchsia; a mix of cherry, strawberry with a dusting of spice; good balance, neither sweet nor dry. Cabernet Sauvignon. Screwcap. 12° alc. RATING 87 DRINK Now $ 17

ŢŢŢŢ **Woodside Single Vineyard Pinot Noir 2004** RATING 86 DRINK Now $ 20

Ceravolo Wines NR

Suite 16, 172 Glynburn Road, Tranmere, SA 5073 (postal) REGION Adelaide Plains
T (08) 8336 4522 F (08) 8365 0538 WWW.ceravolo.com.au OPEN Not
WINEMAKER Colin Glaetzer, Ben Glaetzer (Contract) EST. 1985 CASES 20 000
Joe Ceravolo, dental surgeon-turned-vigneron, and wife Heather have been producing single-vineyard wines from their family-owned estate since 1999, centred around Shiraz, but with Chardonnay and Merlot in support. Conspicuous success at the London International Wine Challenge led both to exports and the registration of the Adelaide Plains region under the GI legislation. Wines are released under the Ceravolo, St Andrews Estate and Red Earth labels. Exports to the UK, Denmark and Asia.

Chain of Ponds

Adelaide Road, Gumeracha, SA 5233 **REGION** Adelaide Hills
T (08) 8389 1415 **F** (08) 8389 1877 **WWW**.chainofponds.com.au **OPEN** Mon–Fri 9.30–4.30, w'ends &
public hols 10.30–4.30
WINEMAKER Neville Falkenberg **EST.** 1993 **CASES** 30 000
Chain of Ponds is the largest grower in the Adelaide Hills, with 100 ha of vines at Gumeracha and
120 ha at Kersbrook, producing 1000 tonnes of grapes a year. Almost all are sold to other wineries,
but a significant amount of wine is made under the Chain of Ponds label; these enjoy consistent show
success. Exports to the UK, the US and Singapore.

ＹＹＹＹＹ **Ledge Shiraz 2002** Elegant, fine, cool-grown style, with a mix of spice, black cherry and
plum on the medium-bodied, well-balanced palate. Fine tannins and nice oak on a long
finish. Cork. **RATING** 96 **DRINK** 2015 $ 29.95

ＹＹＹＹ **Novello Rosso 2004** More to light dry red; abundant fruit in a delicate frame runs
through well to a long, quite dry finish. Grenache/Mourvedre/Sangiovese. Screwcap.
RATING 89 **DRINK** Now $ 14.95
Novello Nero 2004 Strongly spicy red fruit aromas; beguiling mouthfeel; gently sweet red
fruits and a touch of sweetness on the finish; an alternative midpoint between rose and dry
red; 67% Sangiovese, 22% Grenache, 11% Barbera. Screwcap. 13.5° alc. **RATING** 89
DRINK Now $ 14.90
Section 400 Pinot Noir 2001 Some curious aromas, but then a fully mature savoury, *sous
bois* palate with good length; a surprise in more ways than one. Cork. 14.5° alc. **RATING** 88
DRINK Now $ 24.95

Chalice Bridge Estate

796 Rosa Glen Road, Margaret River, WA 6285 **REGION** Margaret River
T (08) 9388 6088 **F** (08) 9382 1887 **WWW**.chalicebridge.com.au **OPEN** By appt
WINEMAKER Bob Cartwright **EST.** 1998 **CASES** 14 000
Planting of the vineyard began in 1998; there are now 28 ha each of cabernet sauvignon and shiraz,
27 ha of chardonnay, 12.5 ha of semillon, 18 ha sauvignon blanc and 7 ha merlot making up the total
plantings of 122 ha; it is the second-largest single vineyard in the Margaret River region. The January
2006 appointment of former Leeuwin Estate senior winemaker Bob Cartwright was major news,
adding thrust to a growing business. Exports to the UK, the US and other major markets.

ＹＹＹＹＹ **Shiraz 2004** A perfumed array of black fruits; lovely mouthfeel; fine but persistent
tannins; quality oak. Screwcap. **RATING** 94 **DRINK** 2015 $ 21.50
Cabernet Merlot 2004 Good colour; spotlessly clean and bright fruit aromas; fresh
raspberry and blackcurrant; fine, ripe tannins; nice oak. Screwcap. **RATING** 94 **DRINK** 2014
$ 21.50

ＹＹＹＹＹ **Margaret River Chardonnay 2004** Elegant and lively thanks to its moderate alcohol and
crisp acidity; melon and grapefruit flavours plus subtle oak. Screwcap. 13.5° alc. **RATING** 93
DRINK 2012 $ 21.50
Margaret River Chardonnay 2005 Fruit-driven, stone fruit, grapefruit and melon in a
direct, light- to medium-bodied, nicely balanced, frame. Screwcap. 13.5° alc. **RATING** 91
DRINK 2009 $ 21.50
Shiraz Cabernet Sauvignon 2004 Clean, fresh, pure red and black fruit aromas and
flavours; fine ripe tannins; utterly seductive; ready now. Screwcap. **RATING** 91 **DRINK** 2009
$ 21.50
Margaret River Semillon Sauvignon Blanc 2005 Grass, apple and lemon aromas and
flavours; crisp and lively. Screwcap. 13.5° alc. **RATING** 90 **DRINK** 2008 $ 16
Merlot 2004 Attractive medium-bodied wine; black olive, dark cherry and spice;
controlled oak and tannins. Screwcap. **RATING** 90 **DRINK** 2009 $ 21.50
Calamus Red 2004 Rich black fruits and dark chocolate; good tannins and controlled
oak; silver medal Qantas WA Wine Show '05. No varieties specified. Screwcap. 13.5° alc.
RATING 90 **DRINK** 2014 $ 16

ТТТТ **Sauvignon Blanc 2005** Subdued aromas, with a touch of passionfruit, lead on to delicate fruit on the palate, redeemed by good balance and mouthfeel. Screwcap. 12.5° alc. **RATING** 89 **DRINK** Now $ 21.50

Margaret River Wild Rose 2005 Vivid purple-red; intense rose petal and strawberry bouquet; neatly balanced palate; subliminal sweetness. Screwcap. 13.5° alc. **RATING** 89 **DRINK** Now $ 16

Chalk Hill ★★★★☆

PO Box 205, McLaren Vale, SA 5171 **REGION** McLaren Vale
T (08) 8556 2121 **F** (08) 8556 2221 **WWW**.chalkhill.com.au **OPEN** Not
WINEMAKER Emmanuelle Requin-Bekkers **EST.** 1973 **CASES** 5000
Chalk Hill is in full flight again, drawing upon the 3 vineyards (Slate Creek, Wits End and Chalk Hill) of grapegrowing owners John and Di Harvey, who acquired Chalk Hill in 1995. There has been considerable work on the Chalk Hill home vineyard since its acquisition: part has been retrellised, and riesling has been replaced by new plantings of shiraz and cabernet sauvignon, plus small amounts of barbera and sangiovese. Exports to all major markets; exports to the US and Canada under the Wits End label.

ТТТТТ **The Procrastinator 2005** Excellent colour; one of the very best cabernet francs in Australia; bright, berry fruits, fragrant and beguiling. Screwcap. **RATING** 93 **DRINK** 2010 $ 13

McLaren Vale Shiraz 2003 Strong colour; medium-bodied black fruits, licorice, spice and dark chocolate; ripe tannins. Excellent '03. Cork. **RATING** 92 **DRINK** 2013 $ 25

Barbera 2004 Strong colour; medium- to full-bodied, rich, ripe black fruits and some chocolate; a barbera with lots of attitude. Screwcap. **RATING** 92 **DRINK** 2015 $ 20

Sangiovese 2004 Medium red; light- to medium-bodied; spicy, savoury cherry fruit; fine tannins. Screwcap. **RATING** 90 **DRINK** 2010 $ 20

ТТТТ **Sidetrack 2004** Juicy fruit-driven style; lovely flavour uninhibited by tannins or more than a touch of French oak. Shiraz/Cabernet Sauvignon; great value. Screwcap. **RATING** 89 **DRINK** Now $ 13

McLaren Vale Cabernet Sauvignon 2003 Slightly dull colour; savoury black fruits and the inevitable chocolate; fine tannins. Cork. **RATING** 89 **DRINK** 2010 $ 25

Chalkers Crossing ★★★★★

387 Grenfell Road, Young, NSW 2594 **REGION** Hilltops
T (02) 6382 6900 **F** (02) 6382 5068 **WWW**.chalkerscrossing.com.au **OPEN** 7 days 10–4
WINEMAKER Celine Rousseau **EST.** 2000 **CASES** 9000
Owned and operated by Ted and Wendy Ambler, Chalkers Crossing is based near Young, where the first vines were planted at the Rockleigh vineyard in late 1997, with follow-up plantings in 1998 lifting the total to 10 ha. It also purchases grapes from Tumbarumba and Gundagai. A winery was opened for the 2000 vintage, with Celine Rousseau as winemaker. Born in France's Loire Valley and trained in Bordeaux, Celine has worked in Bordeaux, Champagne, Languedoc, Margaret River and the Perth Hills, an eclectic mix of climates if ever there was one. This Flying Winemaker (now an Australian citizen) has exceptional skills and dedication. Exports to France, Hong Kong and the UK.

ТТТТТ **Hilltops Cabernet Sauvignon 2004** Great colour; absolutely classic cool-grown cabernet sauvignon characters; a perfect balance of cassis, blackcurrant, cedar and fine, ripe tannins. Screwcap. **RATING** 95 **DRINK** 2018 $ 24

Tumbarumba Chardonnay 2004 Typical Rousseau style; spotlessly clean, with intense grapefruit and melon; very long palate and finish; barrel ferment/12 months oak maturation absorbed by the fruit. Cork. 14° alc. **RATING** 94 **DRINK** 2011 $ 21.75

ТТТТТ **Hilltops Semillon 2004** Has developed distinct White Bordeaux elements, richness on the back-palate and aftertaste; continued development of a sophisticated, barrel-fermented Semillon **RATING** 93 **DRINK** 2012 $ 16

Tumbarumba Sauvignon Blanc 2005 Pale straw-green; clean, crisp aromas; a firm, minerally palate built around citrus and gooseberry fruit. Screwcap. **RATING** 92 **DRINK** 2008 $ 18.30

Tumbarumba Pinot Noir 2004 Light- to medium-bodied; silky smooth plum and black cherry fruit; beautifully made, but lacks the fruit intensity for maximum points. Twin top. 12.5° alc. **RATING** 91 **DRINK** 2010 $ 22.75

Hilltops Shiraz 2004 Clean, firm, spicy background to tightly wound black cherry and blackberry fruit; good balance, but needs time. Cork. **RATING** 90 **DRINK** 2014 $ 24

Kingsvale Shiraz 2002 High-toned, lifted, spicy anise fruit on the bouquet; persistent savoury tannins on a long palate; evident oak. Dodgy cork. **RATING** 90 **DRINK** 2008 $ 20

Chambers Rosewood ★★★★★

Barkly Street, Rutherglen, Vic 3685 **REGION** Rutherglen
T (02) 6032 8641 **F** (02) 6032 8101 **WWW**.rutherglenvic.com **OPEN** Mon–Sat 9–5, Sun 11–5
WINEMAKER Bill Chambers, Stephen Chambers **EST.** 1858 **CASES** 15 000
The winery rating is given for the Grand and Rare Muscat and Tokay wines, which are on a level all their own, somewhere higher than five stars. The chief virtue of the table wines is that they are cheap. Exports to all major markets.

ΨΨΨΨΨ **Rare Rutherglen Muscat NV** Very deep mahogany-brown, olive rim; the bouquet comes on like a blitzkrieg, so powerful and complex it very nearly imprisons the senses. The palate is a magical combination of extreme rancio, driving the length and finish, but seamlessly filled out by essence-like raisin fruit. **RATING** 97 **DRINK** Now
Grand Rutherglen Muscat NV Full olive-brown; ultra-complex aromas, with a piercing strand of rancio; layer upon layer of flavour, balanced and integrated, no one flavour is dominant. **RATING** 94 **DRINK** Now $ 50

ΨΨΨΨ **Rutherglen Light Muscat 2005** Crisp, clean and lively, a rose by any other name; gentle red fruits and tingling, lemony, acidity. Screwcap. 7° alc. **RATING** 88 **DRINK** Now $ 20
Rutherglen Roussanne 2005 Clean, fresh gently floral aromas; light-bodied, with a nice twist of lemony acidity. Value plus. Screwcap. 11° alc. **RATING** 87 **DRINK** 2008 $ 10
Rutherglen Gouais 2002 Brassy-green; fragrant blossom aromas; the palate doesn't quite deliver, but is interesting, with touches of preserved lemon rind. A threatened species of grape variety. Cork. 11.8° alc. **RATING** 87 **DRINK** Now $ 12
Rutherglen Tokay NV Glowing orange-gold; very young, strongly varietal in tea leaf and malt biscuit primary phase. No bottle-development possible, of course. **RATING** 87 **DRINK** Now $ 15

ΨΨΨΨ **Rutherglen Muscat NV** **RATING** 86 **DRINK** Now $ 15
Rutherglen Cabernet Sauvignon 2003 **RATING** 84 **DRINK** 2010 $ 12

ΨΨΨ **Rutherglen Palomino NV** **RATING** 83 $ 5
Merlot 2003 **RATING** 83 $ 8
Mt Carmel Liqueur Port NV **RATING** 81 $ 13

Channybearup Vineyard NR

Lot 4, Channybearup Road, Pemberton, WA 6260 (postal) **REGION** Pemberton
T (08) 9776 0042 **F** (08) 9776 0043 **WWW**.channybearup.com.au **OPEN** Not
WINEMAKER Larry Cherubino (Contract) **EST.** 1999 **CASES** 13 500
Channybearup has been established by a small group of Perth businessmen who have been responsible for the establishment of 62 ha of vineyards. The leading varieties are chardonnay, merlot, shiraz, cabernet sauvignon and pinot noir, with lesser amounts of verdelho and sauvignon blanc. While principally established as a grape supplier to other makers, the amount of wine being vinified for Channybearup has increased significantly. Exports to the US.

Chanters Ridge ★★★

440 Chanters Lane, Tylden, Vic 3444 **REGION** Macedon Ranges
T 0427 511 341 **F** (03) 9509 2484 **WWW**.chantersridge.com.au **OPEN** W'ends 10–4, or by appt
WINEMAKER Hanging Rock Winery **EST.** 1995 **CASES** 700
Orthopaedic surgeon Barry Elliott, as well as running the surgery unit at Melbourne's Alfred Hospital, became involved with the Kyneton Hospital 6 years ago. Through a convoluted series of

events, he and his wife acquired the 24-ha property without any clear idea of what they might do with it; later his lifelong interest in wine steered him towards the idea of establishing a vineyard. He retained John Ellis as his consultant, and this led to the planting of 2 ha of pinot noir, and the first tiny make in 2000.

ȲȲȲȲ Back Paddock Pinot Noir 2004 A light-bodied, bright, fresh and lively wine halfway between rose and table wine; crisp acidity. **RATING** 87 **DRINK** Now $ 15

Chapel Hill ★★★☆

Chapel Hill Road, McLaren Vale, SA 5171 **REGION** McLaren Vale
T (08) 8323 8429 **F** (08) 8323 9245 **WWW**.chapelhillwine.com.au **OPEN** 7 days 12–5
WINEMAKER Michael Fragos **EST.** 1979 **CASES** 50 000
A leading medium-sized winery in the region; in the second half of 2000 Chapel Hill was sold to the diversified Swiss Thomas Schmidheiny group, which owns the respected Cuvaison winery in California as well as vineyards in Switzerland and Argentina. Wine quality is as good, if not better, than ever. Exports to the UK, the US, Canada, Switzerland, Germany, Belgium, NZ and Hong Kong.

ȲȲȲȲȲ Il Vescovo 2004 Attractive flavour and texture; bright red and black cherry fruits given structural support by the cabernet component. Sangiovese/Cabernet Sauvignon. Screwcap. 14° alc. **RATING** 90 **DRINK** 2008 $ 20

ȲȲȲȲ Unwooded Chardonnay 2005 Some quite appealing grapefruit/citrus nuances to the core of stone fruit; not complex, but lively. Screwcap. 13° alc. **RATING** 87 **DRINK** Now $ 14
McLaren Vale Verdelho 2005 Typical tropical fruit salad with notes of citrus and passionfruit; acidity on the finish lifts it from the ruck. Screwcap. 13.5° alc. **RATING** 87 **DRINK** Now $ 16

Chaperon Wines ★★★☆

'Grange Hill', Gallaghers Lane, Maldon, Vic 3463 **REGION** Bendigo
T (03) 5435 7427 **OPEN** W'ends & public hols 10–5, or by appt
WINEMAKER Graeme Leith **EST.** 1994 **CASES** 800
In 1856 English immigrant Edward Bond purchased land in the Maldon area, followed by an adjoining property in 1871. Here he established the 'Grange Hill' winery and vineyard, which flourished in the 1880s, leading to the establishment of a second winery and second vineyard. It disappeared in the 20th century, but in 1994 Russell Clarke and Angelina Chaperon bought the property and began replanting the vineyard and restoring the old winery buildings. They have chosen to bypass irrigation and practise organic viticulture in growing 1.2 ha of bush vine grenache and mourvedre, and 1.8 ha of trellised shiraz.

ȲȲȲȲȲ Shiraz 2003 Full-bodied, super-concentrated and rich; blackberry confit, licorice and spice and massive alcohol, all products of the drought, and over the top. Cork. 16.1° alc. **RATING** 90 **DRINK** 2013

ȲȲȲȲ Grenache Mourvedre 2002 Light- to medium-bodied; spicy, savoury, chocolatey flavours; ripe tannins; carries the higher alcohol better than the Shiraz. Cork. 15.7° alc. **RATING** 87 **DRINK** 2009 $ 23

ȲȲȲȲ Shiraz 2002 RATING 86 **DRINK** Now $ 25
Grenache Mourvedre Shiraz 2003 Light- to medium red; not surprisingly quite sweet, though there is also a hint of green tannin. Stress? Screwcap. 15.5° alc. **RATING** 86 **DRINK** 2008

Chapman Valley Wines NR

Lot 14 Howatharra Road, Nanson, Chapman Valley via Geraldton, WA 6530 **REGION** Central Western Australia Zone
T (08) 9920 5148 **F** (08) 9920 5206 **WWW**.chapmanvalleywines.com.au **OPEN** 7 days 10–5
WINEMAKER Lilac Hill Estate **EST.** 1995 **CASES** 5500
Chapman Valley Wines is WA's most northern winery, situated 30 km northeast of Geraldton in the picturesque valley which gives the business its name. A hobby vineyard on a nearby property led to the

establishment of 5 ha of vines in 1995, followed by a further 3 ha in 1999 comprising of semillon, chenin blanc, chardonnay, verdelho, sauvignon blanc, shiraz, merlot, cabernet sauvignon and zinfandel.

Chapman's Creek Vineyard NR

RMS 447 Yelverton Road, Wilyabrup, WA 6280 **REGION** Margaret River
T (08) 9755 7545 **F** (08) 9755 7571 **WWW**.chapmanscreek.com.au **OPEN** Mon–Sat 10.30–4.30
WINEMAKER Various contract **EST.** 1989 **CASES** 5000
Chapman's Creek was founded by the late Tony Lord, an extremely experienced wine journalist who for many years was editor and part-owner of *Decanter* magazine of the UK, one of the leaders in the field. Notwithstanding this, he was always reticent about seeking any publicity for Chapman's Creek; why, I do not know. Regrettably, it is now too late to find out, as he died in February 2002. Chapman's Creek continues to be managed by his long-term pal, Chris Leach, who kept an eye on him throughout his prolonged illness. The property is currently being offered for sale.

Charles Cimicky ★★★★

Gomersal Road, Lyndoch, SA 5351 **REGION** Barossa Valley
T (08) 8524 4025 **F** (08) 8524 4772 **OPEN** Tues–Sat 10.30–4.30
WINEMAKER Charles Cimicky **EST.** 1972 **CASES** 15 000
These wines are of very good quality, thanks to the sophisticated use of new oak in tandem with high-quality grapes. The intense, long-flavoured Sauvignon Blanc has been a particularly consistent performer, as has the rich, voluptuous Signature Shiraz. Exports to the UK, the US, Switzerland, Canada, Malaysia and Hong Kong.

ŶŶŶŶŶ **Trumps Shiraz 2004** Dense colour; a rich wine with layers of black fruits; controlled oak and extract; good length. Twin top. **RATING** 92 **DRINK** 2015 $ 17

Charles Melton ★★★★★

Krondorf Road, Tanunda, SA 5352 **REGION** Barossa Valley
T (08) 8563 3606 **F** (08) 8563 3422 **WWW**.charlesmeltonwines.com.au **OPEN** 7 days 11–5
WINEMAKER Charlie Melton, Nicola Ormond **EST.** 1984 **CASES** 18 000
Charlie Melton, one of the Barossa Valley's great characters, with wife Virginia by his side, makes some of the most eagerly sought à la mode wines in Australia. Inevitably, the Melton empire grew in response to the insatiable demand, with a doubling of estate vineyards to 13 ha (and the exclusive management and offtake of a further 10 ha) and the erection of a new barrel store in 1996. The expanded volume has had no adverse effect on the wonderfully rich, sweet and well-made wines. Exports to all major markets.

ŶŶŶŶŶ **Rose Of Virginia 2005** Vivid, deep fuchsia; has real depth to the plum and raspberry fruit, yet is not heavy or sweet; a rose with attitude. Screwcap. **RATING** 94 **DRINK** Now $ 19.90
Sotto di Ferro 2001 Intense, complex, powerful and multi-layered nougat, caramel and cumquat jam; sweeter than Italian Vin Santo but made using similar methods. Cork. 10.5° alc. **RATING** 94 **DRINK** 2008 $ 55

ŶŶŶŶŶ **Nine Popes 2003** Complex, ripe, but not jammy; very good structure to the medium-bodied, multi-fruit and spice flavours; good extract and oak. Cork. 14.5° alc. **RATING** 92 **DRINK** 2011 $ 51
Sparkling Red NV Has all the basic requirements for the style: some age to the base wine which is neither too oaky nor too sweet. Will improve with further extended cellaring. **RATING** 92 **DRINK** 2015 $ 60
Cabernet Sauvignon 2003 Smooth, supple and ripe blackcurrant fruit; ripe tannins and restrained oak; great outcome for the vintage. Screwcap & cork. 14.5° alc. **RATING** 91 **DRINK** 2013 $ 42
Shiraz 2003 Inauspicious colour; earthy, savoury fruit with some spicy notes; medium-bodied, soft tannins. Qualtiy cork. 14.5° alc. **RATING** 90 **DRINK** 2009 $ 45

ŶŶŶŶ **The Father In Law Shiraz 2003** Medium-bodied; spiced plums, blackberries and mocha/vanilla oak; fine tannins. Brilliant front and back labels. Screwcap. 14.5° alc. **RATING** 89 **DRINK** 2008 $ 23.90

Charles Reuben Estate — NR

777 Middle Tea Tree Road, Tea Tree, Tas 7017 **REGION** Southern Tasmania
T (03) 6268 1702 **F** (03) 6231 3571 **OPEN** Wed–Sun 10–5
WINEMAKER Tim Krushka **EST.** 1990 **CASES** 350
Charles Reuben Estate has 1.5 ha of pinot noir, 0.5 ha of chardonnay and a few rows of riesling in production. It has also planted 1.2 ha of the four Bordeaux varieties, headed by cabernet sauvignon, with a little cabernet franc, merlot and petit verdot, and 0.6 ha of sauvignon blanc plus a few rows of semillon.

Charles Sturt University Winery — ★★★★★

McKeown Drive (off Coolamon Road) Wagga Wagga, NSW 2650 **REGION** Big Rivers Zone
T (02) 6933 2435 **F** (02) 6933 4072 **WWW**.csu.edu.au/winery/ **OPEN** Mon–Fri 11–5, w'ends 11–4
WINEMAKER Andrew Drumm **EST.** 1977 **CASES** 15 000
A totally new $2.5 million commercial winery (replacing the 1977 winery) was opened in 2002, complementing the $1 million experimental winery opened in June 2001. The commercial winery has been funded through the sale of wines produced under the Charles Sturt University brand, which always offer the consumer good value. Interestingly, this teaching facility is using screwcaps for all its wines, white and red, recalling its pioneering use in 1977.

Orange Chardonnay 2005 Light straw-green; perfumed, elegant peach and citrus blossom; lively, long and fresh melon and nectarine; very good finish, a small percentage of barrel ferment. Sensational value. Screwcap. 13.2° alc. **RATING** 94 **DRINK** 2009 $ 13
Limited Release Orange Chardonnay 2005 More rounded, soft and rich flavours; barrel ferment in larger oak much to do with the texture; I prefer the cheaper wine. Screwcap. 13.5° alc. **RATING** 94 **DRINK** 2010 $ 20

Sauvignon Blanc 2005 Clean, but muted, passionfruit and gooseberry aromas; builds flavour on the back-palate and long finish. Great value. Orange/Yarra Valley. Screwcap. 13° alc. **RATING** 90 **DRINK** Now $ 13
Limited Release Pinot Noir Chardonnay 2001 Well-made; crisp and delicate, minerally, dry style; great aperitif on a hot day. Tumbarumba/Orange/Canberra. 12.5° alc. **RATING** 90 **DRINK** 2009 $ 20

Cellar Reserve Shiraz Cabernet 2004 Light- to medium-bodied; fresh red and black fruits; soft, fine tannins and an airbrush of oak in balance. Selection of the best barrels. Screwcap. 14° alc. **RATING** 89 **DRINK** 2009 $ 20
Shiraz 2004 Plenty of sweet fruit flavour in a black fruit spectrum, oak a minor player in the orchestra. Big Rivers/Gundagai. Screwcap. 14.6° alc. **RATING** 88 **DRINK** 2009 $ 13
Cabernet Sauvignon Merlot 2004 Medium-bodied; considerable power and length to blackcurrant, cassis and mulberry fruit. Big Rivers/Cowra/Hilltops. Screwcap. 14.6° alc. **RATING** 88 **DRINK** 2010 $ 13

Limited Release Pinot Gris 2004 From estate plantings (planted 1978) which may well have been the first of this variety in Australia. However, shows even old vines can't triumph over climate; semitropical fruit and a slightly short finish. Screwcap. 13.2° alc. **RATING** 86 **DRINK** Now $ 18
Limited Release Cabernet Sauvignon 2003 RATING 86 **DRINK** 2008 $ 20
Limited Release Sparkling Shiraz NV A crowd pleaser, with rich plummy, spicy shiraz and a quite sweet finish. 14° alc. **RATING** 86 **DRINK** Now $ 20

🐂 Charlies Estate Wines — NR

38 Swan Street, Henley Brook, WA 6055 **REGION** Swan Valley
T (08) 9296 3100 **F** (08) 9396 3099 **WWW**.charliesestatewines.com.au **OPEN** 7 days 10–4.30
WINEMAKER Mark Sheppard **EST.** 1998 **CASES** 30 000
Charlies Estate is the new name and face for a long-established 50-ha vineyard and winery site, originally Evans & Tate Gnangara and thereafter Swanbrook Estate. It is the venture of Carmelo Salpietro, and offers wines at 4 price levels: at the bottom the Untamed Land range (simply labelled Wine of Australia); then the Origins range of wines; next the Eight series of Sauvignon Blanc, Merlot

and Shiraz; and finally Reserve Tempranillo and Reserve Marsanne Viognier. The Origins, Eight and Reserve range wines are all sourced from various regions in WA, including, of course, the Swan Valley.

Charlotte Plains

RMB 3180, Dooleys Road, Maryborough, Vic 3465 **REGION** Bendigo
T (03) 5361 3137 **OPEN** By appt
WINEMAKER Graeme Jukes **EST.** 1990 **CASES** 80
Charlotte Plains is a classic example of miniaturism. Production comes from a close-planted vineyard which is only 1.6 ha, part being shiraz, the remainder sauvignon blanc. The minuscule production is sold solely via the mailing list and by phone.

ŸŸŸŸŸ **Maryborough Shiraz 2004** Good hue and depth; powerful blackberry fruit, the strong structure aided by firm acidity. Needs to loosen up; will do so. Screwcap. 14° alc.
RATING 90 **DRINK** 2015 $ 18

Chartley Estate ★★★☆

38 Blackwood Hills Road, Rowella, Tas 7270 **REGION** Northern Tasmania
T (03) 6394 7198 **F** (03) 6394 7598 **WWW**.chartleyestatevineyard.com.au **OPEN** 7 days 10–5
WINEMAKER Winemaking Tasmania (Julian Alcorso) **EST.** 2000 **CASES** 800
The Kossman family began the establishment of 2 ha each of pinot gris, sauvignon blanc and pinot noir, and 1 ha of riesling in 2000. Although the vines are still young, some attractive wines from each variety have been made.

ŸŸŸŸ **Black Crow Pinot Noir 2004** From the big end of town, with slurpy, luscious plum and cherry fruit providing obvious and immediate satisfaction. Diam. **RATING** 89 **DRINK** 2009 $ 27.95
Riesling 2005 Big, ripe, generous tropical fruit in vintage mould; slightly loose overall.
RATING 88 **DRINK** 2009 $ 20

ŸŸŸŸ **Pinot Gris 2005 RATING** 86 **DRINK** 2008 $ 23
Sauvignon Blanc 2005 RATING 84 **DRINK** Now $ 19

Chateau Champsaur NR

Wandang Lane, Forbes, NSW 2871 **REGION** Central Ranges Zone
T (02) 6852 3908 **F** (02) 6852 3902 **OPEN** Saturday 10–5, or by appt
WINEMAKER Pierre Dalle, Andrew McEwin **EST.** 1866 **CASES** 200
Yes, the establishment date of 1866 is correct. In that year Frenchmen Joseph Bernard Raymond and Auguste Nicolas took up a 130-ha selection and erected a large wooden winery and cellar, with production ranging up to 360 000 litres in a year in its heyday. They named it Champsaur after Raymond's native valley in France, and it is said to be the oldest French winery in the southern hemisphere. In recent years it traded as Lachlan Valley Wines, but under the ownership of Pierre Dalle it has reverted to its traditional name and French ownership.

Chateau Dore NR

303 Mandurang Road, Mandurang, Vic 3551 **REGION** Bendigo
T (03) 5439 5278 **OPEN** 7 days 10–5
WINEMAKER Ivan Grose **EST.** 1860 **CASES** 1000
Has been in the ownership of the Grose family since 1860, with the winery buildings dating back to 1860 and 1893. All wine is sold through the cellar door and function centre.

Chateau Dorrien

Cnr Seppeltsfield Road/Barossa Valley Way, Dorrien, SA 5352 **REGION** Barossa Valley
T (08) 8562 2850 **F** (08) 8562 1416 **OPEN** 7 days 10–5
WINEMAKER Fernando Martin, Ramon Martin **EST.** 1985 **CASES** 2000
The Martin family, headed by Fernando and Jeanette, purchased the old Dorrien winery from the Seppelt family in 1984; in 1990 the family purchased Twin Valley Estate, and moved the winemaking

operations of Chateau Dorrien to the Twin Valley site. All the Chateau Dorrien group wines are sold at Chateau Dorrien; Twin Valley is simply a production facility. In March 2006 the Martin family purchased a 32-ha property at Myponga, with over 15 ha of mature vineyards which will now provide the grapes for San Fernando Estate, as the vineyard has been renamed. Exports to Singapore and the US.

TTTT **Barossa Valley Shiraz 2002** Good colour; medium-bodied, quite intense and long, reflecting the cool vintage; blackberry and a touch of spice; clean finish. Cork. 14.4° alc. **RATING** 89 **DRINK** 2010 $ 20

San Fernando Estate Cloud Catcher Sauvignon Blanc 2005 A clean, firm, minerally framework for green apple and gooseberry fruit; good length and finish. Screwcap. 11.5° alc. **RATING** 88 **DRINK** Now $ 15

Barossa Valley Shiraz 2000 Pleasantly developed, traditional, earthy style; a light- to medium-bodied palate with touches of mocha and vanilla, and a dash of acidity to lift the finish. Cork. 13.3° alc. **RATING** 87 **DRINK** 2008 $ 20

TTTY **San Fernando Estate Weeping Willow Verdelho 2005** Given a little more interest than usual by citrus/minerally acidity. Screwcap. 13.5° alc. **RATING** 86 **DRINK** Now $ 15

Matries Barossa Valley Rose 2005 Pale salmon; a blend of mataro (mourvedre) and riesling, hence the name. Pleasant enough, and not too sweet. Cork. 13.5° alc. **RATING** 86 **DRINK** Now $ 12

Chateau Francois   NR

Broke Road, Pokolbin, NSW 2321 **REGION** Lower Hunter Valley
T (02) 4998 7548 **F** (02) 4998 7805 **OPEN** W'ends 9–5, or by appt
WINEMAKER Don Francois **EST.** 1969 **CASES** 300
Former NSW Director of Fisheries Don Francois makes soft-flavoured and structured wines which are modestly priced and are sold through the cellar door and by the mailing list to a loyal following. The tasting room is available for private dinners for 12–16 people. Don Francois sailed through a quadruple bypass followed by a mild stroke with his sense of humour intact, if not enhanced. A subsequent newsletter said (*inter alia*) '… my brush with destiny has changed my grizzly personality and I am now sweetness and light … Can you believe? Well, almost!' He even promises comfortable tasting facilities.

Chateau Leamon

5528 Calder Highway, Bendigo, Vic 3550 **REGION** Bendigo
T (03) 5447 7995 **F** (03) 5447 0855 **WWW**.chateauleamon.com.au **OPEN** Wed–Mon 10–5
WINEMAKER Ian Leamon **EST.** 1973 **CASES** 2500
One of the longest-established wineries in the region, with estate and locally grown shiraz and cabernet family grapes providing the excellent red wines. Exports to the UK, Asia and Canada

TTTTY **Reserve Bendigo Shiraz 2004** Slightly deeper colour than the varietal; full-bodied blackberry, dark plum and chocolate; savoury/spicy tannins, good oak. Screwcap. **RATING** 93 **DRINK** 2020 $ 38

Bendigo Shiraz 2004 Faintly hazy colour; a medium- to full-bodied mix of blackberry and blood plum, along with touches of spice. Screwcap. 15° alc. **RATING** 92 **DRINK** 2015 $ 22

Strathbogie Ranges Riesling 2005 A powerful, rich, intense citrus and tropical mix of flavours, the fruit and a touch of residual sweetness balanced by acidity. Early developing. Screwcap. 13.4° alc. **RATING** 91 **DRINK** 2010 $ 17

Reserve Bendigo Cabernet Sauvignon 2004 Good colour; medium- to full-bodied; clear-cut cabernet varietal fruit; blackcurrant, cassis, earth, leaf and mint; typical mid-Victorian style. Screwcap. **RATING** 91 **DRINK** 2014 $ 38

TTTT **Bendigo Cabernet Sauvignon Cabernet Franc Merlot 2004** Strongly savoury/herbal/woody nuances to the core of blackcurrant fruit; notwithstanding the alcohol, doesn't appear entirely ripe. Screwcap. 15° alc. **RATING** 89 **DRINK** 2012 $ 22

🐌 Chateau Mildura ★★★

191 Belar Avenue, Irymple, Vic 3498 **REGION** Murray Darling
T (03) 5024 5901 **F** (03) 5024 5763 **WWW**.chateaumildura.com.au **OPEN** 7 days 10–4
WINEMAKER Neville Hudson **EST.** 1888 **CASES** 5000

The history of Chateau Mildura is inextricably bound up with that of winemaking along the Murray River in the northwest corner of Victoria, and Mildara Wines in particular. The fathers of irrigation, the founders of Mildura and Renmark (across the border in SA), were the Chaffey Brothers, who built the triple gable brick winery in 1892. The story of the Chaffeys is an epic one, marked by as many failures as successes. In the outcome, table wine production ceased in 1910, whereafter it was used for the production of brandy until the 1950s, and then for the maturation of sherry until 1997. In 2002 the building was sold by Beringer Blass to Lance Milne, a local fourth-generation horticulturist. He has incorporated a boutique winery in a small area of the building, the remainder of which will be opened as a museum for the Chaffeys and their pioneering work. The 2005 vintage has 3 ranges: Heritage, Psyche Smuggler and Psyche Reserve.

🍷🍷🍷🍷 **Psyche Reserve Shiraz Viognier 2005** Attractive, light- to medium-bodied wine, showing viognier to advantage without going over the top. Screwcap. 14.5° alc. **RATING** 89 **DRINK** 2008 **$** 17

Psyche Smuggler Shiraz 2005 Plum and blackberry fruit; good mouthfeel, suggesting the use of micro-oxygenation; attractive fruit flavours. Screwcap. 14.5° alc. **RATING** 88 **DRINK** 2009 **$** 12

🍷🍷🍷🍷 **Psyche Reserve Viognier 2005** Highly aromatic and full of varietal fruit; sabotaged by residual sugar, even if cellar door customers want it. Screwcap. 14° alc. **RATING** 86 **DRINK** Now **$** 17

Psyche Smuggler Chardonnay 2005 **RATING** 84 **DRINK** Now **$** 12

🍷🍷🍷 **Psyche Steam White 2005** **RATING** 83 **$** 10
Psyche Riverboat Rose 2005 **RATING** 83 **$** 10

Chateau Pâto ★★★★☆

Thompsons Road, Pokolbin, NSW 2321 **REGION** Lower Hunter Valley
T (02) 4998 7634 **F** (02) 4998 7860 **OPEN** By appt
WINEMAKER Nicholas Paterson **EST.** 1980 **CASES** 350

Nicholas Paterson took over responsibility for this tiny winery following the death of father David Paterson during the 1993 vintage. The winery has 2.5 ha of shiraz, 1 ha of chardonnay and 0.5 ha of pinot noir; most of the grapes are sold, with a tiny quantity of shiraz being made into a marvellous wine. David Paterson's inheritance is being handsomely guarded.

🍷🍷🍷🍷 **Hunter Valley DJP Shiraz 2004** Light- to medium-bodied; earthy/leathery regional characters; the black fruits on the palate are fresh, the finish clean and firm. Screwcap. 14.5° alc. **RATING** 91 **DRINK** 2015 **$** 40

Chateau Tanunda ★★★☆

9 Basedow Road, Tanunda, SA 5352 **REGION** Barossa Valley
T (08) 8563 3888 **F** (08) 8563 1422 **WWW**.chateautanunda.com **OPEN** 7 days 10–5
WINEMAKER Ralph Fowler **EST.** 1890 **CASES** 8000

This is one of the most imposing winery buildings in the Barossa Valley, built from stone quarried at nearby Bethany in the late 1880s. It started life as a winery, then became a specialist brandy distillery until the death of the Australian brandy industry, whereafter it was simply used as storage cellars. It has now been completely restored, and converted to a major convention facility catering for groups of up to 400. The large complex also houses a cellar door where the Chateau Tanunda wines are sold; Chateau Bistro, gardens and a croquet lawn; the Barossa Small Winemakers Centre, offering wines made by small independent winemakers in the region; and specialist support services for tour operators. It is a sister winery to Cowra Estate, as both are owned by the Geber family. Prior to the 2005 vintage Ralph Fowler joined the business as full-time chief winemaker, leaving Ralph Fowler Wines in the care of his daughter, Sarah Squires.

TTTTY **Grand Barossa Shiraz 2004** Good colour; ripe, supple, sweet blackberry and mocha aromas and flavours; controlled alcohol a plus. Cork. 14° alc. **RATING** 90 **DRINK** 2010 $ 33

TTTT **Barossa Tower Moscato 2005** Fresh, lively, gently grapey fruit flavours rather than outright sweetness; doesn't even hint at 13° alcohol; well-made; for immediate, light-hearted consumption. First wine released from the 2005 vintage. Screwcap. **RATING** 87 **DRINK** Now $ 15

Chatsfield ★★★★

O'Neil Road, Mount Barker, WA 6324 **REGION** Mount Barker
T (08) 9851 1704 **F** (08) 9851 2660 **www.chatsfield.com.au** **OPEN** By appt
WINEMAKER Diane Miller **EST.** 1976 **CASES** 6000
Irish-born medical practitioner Ken Lynch can be proud of his achievements at Chatsfield, as can most of the various contract winemakers who have taken the high-quality estate-grown material and made some impressive wines, notably the Riesling and spicy, licorice Shiraz. Exports to the US, Ireland and Japan.

TTTTY **Mount Barker Shiraz 2004** Medium red-purple; attractive black cherry, licorice and spice; medium-bodied, good texture and structure. Cork. 14.5° alc. **RATING** 92 **DRINK** 2014 $ 20

Chatto Wines ★★★★★

McDonalds Road, Pokolbin, NSW 2325 **REGION** Lower Hunter Valley
T 0417 109 794 **F** (02) 4998 7294 **www.chattowines.com.au** **OPEN** 7 days 9–5
WINEMAKER Jim Chatto **EST.** 2000 **CASES** 5000
Jim Chatto spent several years in Tas as the first winemaker at Rosevears Estate, and helped design the Rosevears winery. He has since moved to the Hunter Valley to work for Monarch Winemaking Services, but has used his Tasmanian contacts to buy small parcels of riesling and pinot noir. Possessed of a particularly good palate, he has made wines of excellent quality under the Chatto label. He was a star Len Evans Tutorial scholar and is an up-and-coming wine show judge. Exports to Canada and Denmark.

TTTTT **Hunter Valley Semillon 2005** Unusually fragrant for a young semillon, though not so unusual for '05; lemon blossom aromas, then a palate with marvellous finesse, perfect ripeness, balance and length; lingering, lemony acidity. Screwcap. 10.5° alc. **RATING** 96 **DRINK** 2020 $ 17

Tasmania Pinot Noir 2005 Vivid purple-red; waves of plum, black cherry and spice fruit are supported by nigh-on perfect tannins, quality oak in the background. Coal River/Tamar Valley. Screwcap. 13° alc. **RATING** 95 **DRINK** 2012 $ 35

Canberra District Riesling 2005 Spotlessly clean; lime aroma and flavour define the taste boundaries; rich but not heavy; a riesling with attitude. Screwcap. 12.5° alc. **RATING** 94 **DRINK** 2015 $ 17

TTTTY **Hunter Valley Shiraz 2004** A refined, elegant, medium-bodied wine; black fruits with silky tannins and mouthfeel; good length, the oak restrained. Still evolving. Screwcap. 13.5° alc. **RATING** 93 **DRINK** 2019 $ 35

Chepstowe Vineyard NR

178 Fitzpatricks Lane, Carngham, Vic 3351 **REGION** Ballarat
T (03) 5344 9412 **www.chepstowevineyard.com** **OPEN** W'ends 10–5, or by appt
WINEMAKER Matt Thain, Sally Thain **EST.** 1994 **CASES** 1500
One ha each of pinot noir and chardonnay were planted in November 1994 on a block of steeply sloping grazing land on the side of the Chepstowe Hill, looking northeast across to the Grampians, followed by an additional ha of pinot noir in 1996. In the warmest of vintages it is possible to obtain full ripeness for table wines, but in normal years I suspect sparkling wine (of potentially high quality) might be the best option.

Chestnut Grove ★★★★

Chestnut Grove Road, Manjimup, WA 6258 **REGION** Manjimup
T (08) 9755 6046 **F** (08) 9755 6083 **WWW**.chestnutgrove.com.au **OPEN** Not
WINEMAKER Virginia Willcock **EST.** 1988 **CASES** 15 000
A substantial vineyard (18 ha) which is now mature, and the erection of an onsite winery are the most obvious signs of change, but ownership, too, has been passed on from the late founder Vic Kordic to his sons Paul (a Perth lawyer) and Mark (the general manager of the wine business) and thence (in 2002) to Mike Calneggia's Australian Wine Holdings Limited group. Exports to Canada, Denmark, Germany, Hong Kong, Singapore and the UK.

TTTTT **Estate Merlot 2003** An elegant, sculpted wine; gentle redcurrant fruit, fine tannins and good oak; an exercise in restraint, deserving of its exalted reputation. Cork. 13.2° alc. **RATING** 94 **DRINK** 2013 $ 55

TTTT **Pinot Noir Chardonnay 2003** Crisp, lively, crunchy green apple, pear and strawberry flavours; dry finish. Cork. 12.8° alc. **RATING** 88 **DRINK** Now $ 35

TTTY **Verdelho 2005** Has abundant sweet tropical fruit salad, but rather less finesse. Friendly enough. Screwcap. 13.8° alc. **RATING** 86 **DRINK** Now $ 20

Chestnut Hill Vineyard NR

1280 Pakenham Road, Mount Burnett, Vic 3781 **REGION** Gippsland
T (03) 5942 7314 **F** (03) 5942 7314 **WWW**.chestnuthillvineyard.com.au **OPEN** W'ends & public hols 10.30–5.30, or by appt
WINEMAKER Charlie Javor **EST.** 1995 **CASES** 1200
Charlie and Ivka Javor started Chestnut Hill with small plantings of chardonnay, sauvignon blanc and pinot noir in 1985 and have slowly increased the vineyards to their present total of a little over 3 ha. Less than one hour's drive from Melbourne, the picturesque vineyard is situated among the rolling hills in the southeast Dandenongs near Mt Burnett. The label explains, 'Liberty is a gift we had never experienced in our homeland', which was Croatia, from which they emigrated in the late 1960s.

Cheviot Bridge/Long Flat ★★★★

10/499 St Kilda Road, Melbourne, Vic 3004 (postal) **REGION** Upper Goulburn
T (03) 9820 9080 **F** (03) 9820 9070 **WWW**.cheviotbridge.com.au **OPEN** Not
WINEMAKER Hugh Cuthbertson **EST.** 1998 **CASES** NFP
Cheviot Bridge/Long Flat brings together a highly experienced team of wine industry professionals and investors who provided the $10 million-plus required to purchase the Long Flat range of wines from Tyrrell's; the purchase took place in the second half of 2003. In November 2004 the group acquired the listed vehicle Winepros Limited, changing its name to Cheviot Bridge Limited. The bulk of the business activity is that of virtual winery, acquiring bulk and/or bottled wine from various third party suppliers. The brands include Cheviot Bridge Yea Valley, Cheviot Bridge CB, Kissing Bridge, Thirsty Lizard, Long Flat, The Long Flat Wine Co and Terrace Vale. Exports to all major markets.

TTTTY **The Long Flat Wine Co Eden Valley Riesling 2005** Spotless lime, lemon, herb and spice aromas; the delicate palate delivers more of the same, with good acidity and balance; subliminal sweetness. Screwcap. **RATING** 92 **DRINK** 2012 $ 13.99

The Long Flat Wine Co Adelaide Hills Sauvignon Blanc 2005 Spotless aromatic, flowery bouquet; a delicate passionfruit and green apple mix; excellent balance and length. Screwcap. **RATING** 91 **DRINK** Now $ 13.99

TTTT **Cheviot Bridge CB Semillon Sauvignon Blanc 2005** Surprising colour development; solid tropical fruit; good depth and length. Screwcap. **RATING** 88 **DRINK** Now $ 13.99

The Long Flat Wine Co Yarra Valley Pinot Noir 2004 Plum and cherry with savoury notes; has varietal character but some dead fruit nuances. Screwcap. **RATING** 87 **DRINK** Now $ 13.99

The Long Flat Wine Co Coonawarra Cabernet Sauvignon 2003 Light- to medium-bodied; well-made, fresh, light cassis and red fruits; not much structure, but fairly priced. Twin top. **RATING** 87 **DRINK** Now $ 13.99

🍷🍷🍷🍷 **Long Flat White 2005** RATING 86 DRINK Now $ 8.99
Cheviot Bridge CB Adelaide Hills Pinot Grigio 2004 RATING 86 DRINK Now $ 13.99
Cheviot Bridge CB Cabernet Shiraz 2003 RATING 84 DRINK Now $ 13.50

🍷🍷🍷 **Long Flat Red 2003** RATING 83 $ 8

Chidlow's Well Estate NR

PO Box 84, Chidlow, WA 6556 REGION Perth Hills
T (08) 9572 3770 F (08) 9572 3750 OPEN By appt
WINEMAKER Rob Marshall EST. 2002 CASES 500

Chidlow is around 60 km east of Perth and was originally known as Chidlows Well; its railway station was a hub for train services to the interior of the State. While within the Perth Hills region, it is some way distant from the majority of the wineries in the region. Rod and Marilyn Lange have 3 ha of chardonnay, chenin blanc and shiraz, using the experience and skill of Rob Marshall as contract winemaker. The sales are by word-of-mouth, mail order and through the cellar door (by appointment).

Chittering Valley Winery/Nesci Estate Wines NR

Lot 12 Great Northern Highway, Chittering, WA 6084 REGION Perth Hills
T (08) 9571 4102 F (08) 9571 4288 OPEN Not
WINEMAKER Kevin Nesci EST. 1948 CASES NA

The roots of this business go back well over 50 years. Kevin Nesci has 25 ha of sauvignon blanc, chenin blanc, semillon, chardonnay, pinot noir, grenache, merlot, shiraz, cabernet sauvignon, zinfandel and pedro ximinez. Most of the grape production is sold; a lesser amount is made onsite and sold by mail order.

Chiverton NR

605 Mid Western Highway, Cowra, NSW 2794 REGION Cowra
T (02) 6342 9308 F (02) 6342 9314 OPEN W'ends & public hols 10–4
WINEMAKER Simon Gilbert Wines EST. 1994 CASES NA

Greg Thompson began the development of Chiverton in 1994; in 1998 a cellar door and small tasting room attached to the Chiverton Homestead were opened. The wines are sold under the Chiverton, Billygoat Hill and Nude Estate labels. Much of the production from the 107 ha of semillon, chardonnay, verdelho, cabernet sauvignon, merlot and shiraz is sold to other wineries. Exports to the UK.

Chocolate Hills NR

87 Hill Street, Muswellbrook, NSW 2333 REGION Upper Hunter Valley
T (02) 6541 4211 F (02) 6541 4611 www.chocolatehills.com.au OPEN Mon & Wed–Sat 9–5
WINEMAKER Contract EST. 2002 CASES NFP

The quaintly named Chocolate Hills is a virtual wine business operated by Craig and Margaret Benjamin, who own and operate the Upper Hunter Wine Centre, with shops in Musswellbrook and Scone also selling horse riding products under the Australian Thoroughbred Racing Shop banner. The wines are purchased from Upper Hunter winemakers and labelled for Chocolate Hills.

Chrismont Wines ★★★★☆

251 Upper King River Road, Cheshunt, Vic 3678 REGION King Valley
T (03) 5729 8220 F (03) 5729 8253 www.chrismont.com.au OPEN 7 days 11–5
WINEMAKER Warren Proft EST. 1980 CASES 7500

Arnold (Arnie) and Jo Pizzini have established 86 ha of vineyards in the Whitfield area of the Upper King Valley. They have planted riesling, sauvignon blanc, chardonnay, pinot gris, cabernet sauvignon, merlot, shiraz, barbera, marzemino and arneis. The La Zona range ties in the Italian heritage of the Pizzinis and is part of the intense interest in all things Italian.

ŸŸŸŸŸ **La Zona Marzemino 2002** Spotlessly clean; bright red and black cherry and raspberry fruit; excellent tannin structure and balance. Impressive. Cork. **RATING** 93 **DRINK** 2010 $ 19
King Valley Chardonnay 2003 Very well-made; medium-bodied; nectarine and cashew/creamy mix; good length and balance; major surprise. Cork. **RATING** 92 **DRINK** 2008 $ 18
La Zona Barbera 2002 Medium-bodied; attractive spicy plum and blackberry fruit; fine, ripe tannins; good oak; another surprise. Cork. **RATING** 91 **DRINK** 2010 $ 19
King Valley Riesling 2004 Pale straw-green; floral apple blossom aromas flowing through to spice and apple palate; excellent acidity. Screwcap. **RATING** 90 **DRINK** 2012 $ 14

ŸŸŸŸ **La Zona Marzemino 2004** Good colour; firm, fruit-driven wine with plum and black cherry fruit; long palate, needs to soften a bit. Screwcap. 12.5° alc. **RATING** 89 **DRINK** 2010 $ 22
King Valley Shiraz 2004 Good colour; clean, firm, clear varietal fruit expression; subtle oak. **RATING** 88 **DRINK** 2010
La Zona Marzemino Frizzante NV The sweetness (35 grammes per litre) is more evident than the CO_2 spritz, but in the end result the balance is good, the jam/coulis flavours not too high. Not everyone's cup of tea, perhaps. Screwcap. 12.5° alc. **RATING** 88 **DRINK** 2008 $ 19
La Zona Pinot Grigio 2004 Clean, fresh, gentle fruit, with touches of musk and apricot; well-balanced, and developing slowly. Screwcap. **RATING** 87 **DRINK** 2009 $ 23

ŸŸŸŸ **King Valley Sauvignon Blanc 2003** **RATING** 86 **DRINK** Now $ 17

Christmas Hill ★★★★☆

RSD 25C, Meadows, SA 5201 (postal) **REGION** Adelaide Hills
T (08) 8388 3779 **F** (08) 8388 3759 **OPEN** Not
WINEMAKER Nepenthe Vineyards **EST.** 2000 **CASES** 1000
Christmas Hill is primarily a grapegrower, selling most of its production from the 13 ha of chardonnay, sauvignon blanc, shiraz, cabernet sauvignon and pinot noir, but keeping back the equivalent of around 1000 cases of Sauvignon Blanc. It is primarily sold to two leading Adelaide clubs and by the case through Christmas Hill's mailing list, with a dribble finding its way onto the Adelaide retail market.

ŸŸŸŸŸ **Adelaide Hills Sauvignon Blanc 2005** A clean bouquet; soft passionfruit and gooseberry on entry to the mouth, then tightens up nicely on the finish with lemony acidity. A virtual carbon copy of the '04. Screwcap. 13° alc. **RATING** 92 **DRINK** Now $ 14

Churchview Estate ★★★★☆

Cnr Bussell Highway/Gale Road, Metricup, WA 6280 **REGION** Margaret River
T (08) 9755 7200 **F** (08) 9755 7300 **WWW.**churchview.com.au **OPEN** Mon–Sat 9.30–5.30
WINEMAKER Paul Green **EST.** 1998 **CASES** 20 000
The Fokkema family, headed by Spike Fokkema, immigrated from The Netherlands in the 1950s. Their business success in the following decades led to the acquisition of the 100-ha Churchview Estate property in 1997, and to the progressive establishment of 56 ha of vineyards, with another 14 ha scheduled for planting by 2007. This will result in production rising. Exports to Asia and The Netherlands.

ŸŸŸŸŸ **The Bartondale Reserve Chardonnay 2005** A complex wine with skilful use of the full range of making techniques; melon, stone fruit and cream mix; good French oak, then magical squeaky acidity to close. Screwcap. 14.5° alc. **RATING** 94 **DRINK** 2012 $ 29

ŸŸŸŸŸ **Premium Range Cabernet Merlot 2004** Medium- to full-bodied; an attractive array of blackcurrant, blackberry, cassis and dark chocolate fruit supported by positive tannins and good oak. Cork. 14° alc. **RATING** 93 **DRINK** 2014 $ 24
Premium Range Cabernet Sauvignon 2004 Medium-bodied; classic cabernet sauvignon blackcurrant, earth and spice; fine, ripe tannins, plus an injection of quality French oak. Cork. 14° alc. **RATING** 92 **DRINK** 2017 $ 26

ҮҮҮҮ **Premium Range Riesling 2005** Light straw-green; clean, floral, some lime blossom; soft, tropical/lime fruit; easy style. Screwcap. 12.5° alc. **RATING** 88 **DRINK** 2009 $ 18

Premium Range Marsanne 2005 Tangy, flowery honeysuckle aromas; good mouthfeel, length and varietal definition; good value for this variety. Screwcap. 13.5° alc. **RATING** 88 **DRINK** 2010 $ 14

The Bartondale Reserve Shiraz 2003 Good colour; medium-bodied blackberry, black cherry fruit with distinctly riper flavours, balanced tannins and extract. Cork. 14.5° alc. **RATING** 88 **DRINK** 2008 $ 36

Premium Range Unwooded Chardonnay 2005 Light-bodied stone fruit and melon; crisp, clean; good length. Screwcap. 14.5° alc. **RATING** 87 **DRINK** 2008 $ 18

Premium Range Shiraz 2003 Light red-purple; light- to medium-bodied spicy, black and red fruits; appropriate extract for fruit weight. Cork. 14° alc. **RATING** 87 **DRINK** 2008 $ 22

ҮҮҮҮ **Premium Range Rose 2005** **RATING** 84 **DRINK** Now $ 14

Ciavarella ★★★

Evans Lane, Oxley, Vic 3678 **REGION** King Valley
T (03) 5727 3384 **F** (03) 5727 3384 **OPEN** Mon–Sat 9–6, Sun 10–6
WINEMAKER Cyril Ciavarella, Tony Ciavarella **EST.** 1978 **CASES** 3000
Cyril and Jan Ciavarella both entered the wine industry from other professions, and have been producing wine since 1992. The vineyard was planted in 1978, with plantings and varieties being extended over the years. One variety, aucerot, was first produced by Maurice O'Shea of McWilliam's Mount Pleasant 60 or more years ago; the Ciavarella vines have been grown from cuttings collected from an old Glenrowan vineyard before the parent plants were removed in the mid-1980s. A purpose-built tasting room has been added to the winery. Tony Ciavarella left a career in agricultural research in mid-2003 to join his parents at Ciavarella.

ҮҮҮҮ **Late Harvest Semillon Aucerot 2002** Not especially complex, but nicely balanced, with touches of orange and lime. One of only 2 or 3 growers of the rare French grape aucerot. Cork. 9° alc. **RATING** 87 **DRINK** 2008 $ 25

ҮҮҮҮ **White Port NV** Made from verdelho and aucerot, the main interest lying in the varietal base, although the juxtaposition of sugar and acidity works well enough. In Portugal it might be served on the rocks in summer, with tonic water a possible addition. Cork. 18.3° alc. **RATING** 86 **DRINK** 2009 $ 18

Oxley Estate Chenin Blanc 2005 **RATING** 85 **DRINK** Now $ 18
Oxley Estate Verdelho 2005 **RATING** 85 **DRINK** Now $ 18
Chardonnay 2004 **RATING** 84 **DRINK** Now $ 19

🐚 Clair de Lune Vineyard ★★★

Lot 8805 South Gippsland Highway, Kardella South, Vic 3951 **REGION** Gippsland
T (03) 5655 1032 **WWW**.clairdelune.com.au **OPEN** 7 days 11.30–5.30
WINEMAKER Brian Gaffy **EST.** 1997 **CASES** 500
Brian Gaffy married a successful 20-year career in civil engineering with a long-term involvement in the Bundaburra Wine & Food Club in Melbourne. His interest in wine grew, leading to studies at the Dookie Agricultural College, with particular input from Martin Williams MW and Denise Miller. He has now planted a total of 4 ha on the rolling hills of the Strzelecki Range to sauvignon blanc, chardonnay, pinot noir and a mixed block of shiraz/merlot/cabernet. The vineyard utilises the Scott Henry trellising system.

ҮҮҮҮ **Pinot Rose 2005** Bright red-purple; lots of CO_2, just acceptable in the context of the style; fresh fruit and good acidity. Trophy (Best of Class) Gippsland Wine Show '06. **RATING** 89 **DRINK** Now $ 15

South Gippsland Pinot Noir 2004 Good colour; sweet cherry/plum fruit; a touch of CO_2 suggests it may have been bottled cold, but this will disappear with further time in bottle. Cork. 11° alc. **RATING** 87 **DRINK** 2009 $ 18

ҮҮҮҮ **South Gippsland Unoaked Chardonnay 2004** **RATING** 84 **DRINK** Now $ 17

ҮҮҮ **Moonlight Brut Chardonnay Pinot Noir 2001** **RATING** 83 $ 17

Clairault ★★★★☆

Caves Road, Wilyabrup, WA 6280 REGION Margaret River
T (08) 9755 6225 F (08) 9755 6229 WWW.clairaultwines.com.au OPEN 7 days 10–5
WINEMAKER Will Shields EST. 1976 CASES 35 000
Bill and Ena Martin, with sons Conor, Brian and Shane, acquired Clairault several years ago. This has
led to a major expansion of the vineyards on the 120-ha property. The 12 ha of vines established by
the former owners (these are up to 30 years old) are being supplemented by another 70 ha of vines,
with an end-point ratio of 70% red varieties to 30% white. Brian Martin is moving the vineyard to a
100% chemical-free management, with biodynamic management at the end of the process. Exports
to the UK, the US and other major markets.

ΥΥΥΥΥ **Reserve 1999** Aging slowly but surely; starting to build secondary aromas and flavours;
exemplary oak handling, fine tannins and very good length. Cabernet
Sauvignon/Merlot/Cabernet Franc. Cork. 14° alc. RATING 94 DRINK 2012 $58

ΥΥΥΥΥ **Estate Chardonnay 2003** Rich stone fruit/peach with well-balanced and integrated oak;
complex and powerful. Cork. 14° alc. RATING 93 DRINK 2010 $29
Margaret River Semillon Sauvignon Blanc 2005 Similar smoky aroma to that of the
Sauvignon Blanc; the semillon tightens and lengthens the palate without compromising
overall flavour. Screwcap. 13.5° alc. RATING 92 DRINK 2011 $19

ΥΥΥΥ **Margaret River Sauvignon Blanc 2005** Faintly smoky aroma; a complex palate, with a
hint of sweetness from the alcohol; abundant flavour and length. Screwcap. 13.5° alc.
RATING 89 DRINK Now $19
Estate Riesling 2005 Pale straw-green; apple, spice and a touch of passionfruit; soft,
clean and well-made. Screwcap. 12° alc. RATING 87 DRINK 2008 $21

ΥΥΥΥ **Cape Pink Rose 2005** RATING 85 DRINK Now $19

🐎 Clancy Fuller ★★★★☆

PO Box 34, Tanunda, SA 5352 REGION Barossa Valley
T (08) 8563 0080 F (08) 8563 0080 OPEN Not
WINEMAKER Chris Ringland EST. 1996 CASES 550
This is the venture of 2 industry veterans who should know better: Paul Clancy, for long responsible
for the Wine Industry Directory which sits in every winery office in Australia; and Peter Fuller, who
has built up by far the largest public relations business for all sectors of the wine industry. They own
2 ha of 120-year-old shiraz at Bethany, another 1.5 ha of shiraz at Jacob's Creek, and 0.5 ha of
grenache, also at Jacob's Creek. All are dry-grown.

ΥΥΥΥΥ **Silesian Barossa Shiraz 2002** Excellent hue; a stylish wine reflecting the cool vintage
and winemaking skills; supple, smooth black cherry, plum and blackberry fruit; ripe
tannins and oak in the back seat. Cork. 15° alc. RATING 94 DRINK 2017 $30

ΥΥΥΥΥ **Scribblers Barossa Grenache Shiraz 2002** Retains good hue; a medium-bodied wine,
the components judiciously balanced; the shiraz structure underpins the dominant juicy
red berry fruit of the grenache. Lovely old vine wine. Cork. 15.5° alc. RATING 93 DRINK
2012 $20

Clancy's of Conargo NR

Killone Park, Conargo Road, Deniliquin, NSW 2710 REGION Riverina
T (03) 5884 6684 F (03) 5884 6779 OPEN 7 days 10–6
WINEMAKER Bernard Clancy, Jason Clancy EST. 1999 CASES 1000
The Clancy family has been carrying on a mixed farming enterprise (lucerne growing, cropping and
sheep production) on their property north of Deniliquin for over 25 years. A tiny planting of taminga
was made in 1988, but it was not until 6 ha were planted in 1997 that the Clancys ventured into
commercial grapegrowing and winemaking. The predominant varieties are shiraz and semillon, and
the production is sold through the cellar door.

Clarence Hill   NR

PO Box 530, McLaren Vale, SA 5171 **REGION** McLaren Vale
T (08) 8323 8946 **F** (08) 8323 9644 **WWW**.clarencehillwines.com.au **OPEN** Not
WINEMAKER Claudio Curtis, Brian Light (Contract) **EST.** 1990 **CASES** 50 000
In 1956 the Curtis family emigrated from Italy to Australia, and purchased its first vineyard land
from one Clarence William Torrens Rivers. They renamed it Clarence Hill. Further land was
acquired in the 1980s and 1990s, establishing the Landcross Farm and California Rise vineyards,
which, together with Clarence Hill, now have over 100 ha in production. Claudio Curtis (who has a
science degree from the Adelaide University) manages wine production and sales. A new winery
adjacent to the company's vineyards is called Landcross Estate Winery. Exports to the UK, the US
and other major markets.

Clarendon Hills   NR

Brookmans Road, Blewitt Springs, SA 5171 **REGION** McLaren Vale
T (08) 8364 1484 **F** (08) 8364 1484 **OPEN** By appt
WINEMAKER Roman Bratasiuk **EST.** 1989 **CASES** 12 000
Age and experience, it would seem, have mellowed Roman Bratasiuk — and the style of his wines.
Once formidable and often rustic, they are now far more sculpted and smooth, at times bordering on
downright elegance. Exports to the UK, the US and other major markets.

Classic McLaren Wines

Lot B, Coppermine Road, McLaren Vale, SA 5171 **REGION** McLaren Vale
T (08) 8323 0115 **F** (08) 8323 9242 **WWW**.classicmclarenwines.com.au **OPEN** By appt
WINEMAKER Andrew Braithwaite **EST.** 1996 **CASES** 7100
Classic McLaren Wines is a substantial business, with 57 ha of vines planted to shiraz, merlot, cabernet
sauvignon, semillon and chardonnay, and they are building a new winery and underground cellar
storage for wine in barrel and packaged wine. Exports to the UK, the US and other major markets.

TTTTT **La Testa Shiraz 2002** Deep colour, good hue; velvety, supple blackberry, plum and dark
chocolate; good oak and tannins; a slight kick on the finish from alcohol. Cork. **RATING** 94
DRINK 2017 $ 45

TTTTY **La Testa Chardonnay 2002** Outstanding green-yellow; packed with nectarine and white
peach fruit with a twist of citrus; very good oak handling; long and powerful. Cork.
14.5° alc. **RATING** 93 **DRINK** 2010 $ 22
La Testa Cabernet Sauvignon 2002 Medium red-purple; powerful, focused
blackcurrant, earth and chocolate; a long palate, sustained by good tannins. Cork.
RATING 93 **DRINK** 2015 $ 36
La Testa Grenache 2002 Medium red; savoury, earthy aromas, the palate like a cherry-
centred chocolate: first you taste the chocolate, then the cherry. Cork. **RATING** 92
DRINK 2009 $ 25
La Testa Blend 2002 Big, bold McLaren Vale red with layers of fruit alternating with
layers of chocolate; ripe tannins, good length. Shiraz/Grenache/Cabernet Sauvignon.
Cork. **RATING** 92 **DRINK** 2018 $ 25
La Testa Blend 2001 Complex flavours, each of the varietal components adding to the
whole; appealing sweetness from the Grenache, balanced tannins from the Cabernet,
Shiraz providing the mainframe. **RATING** 90 **DRINK** 2011 $ 25

TTTT **Quarryman Semillon Sauvignon Blanc 2005** Dry, austere, flinty style; herb, grass and
asparagus flavours; appropriately dry finish. Screwcap. 13° alc. **RATING** 89 **DRINK** 2008 $ 13
Quarryman Shiraz 2003 Archetypal regional style; dark chocolate envelopes the spicy,
savoury blackberry fruit; controlled French oak. Screwcap. 14.5° alc. **RATING** 89
DRINK 2013 $ 16
La Testa Merlot 2002 Marked colour change to towards brown; strongly cedary, savoury
aromas, then that regional chocolate allied with mocha oak comes over the top on the
palate; will have undoubted appeal, for weight and texture are good. Cork. **RATING** 89
DRINK 2015 $ 36

Quarryman Cabernet Merlot 2003 Medium-bodied mix of blackcurrant, chocolate and briary fruit; persistent, but ripe, tannins. Screwcap. 14.5° alc. **RATING** 88 **DRINK** 2009 $16

ΨΨΨΨ **Quarryman Grenache 2003 RATING** 85 **DRINK** Now $16

Clayfield Wines ★★★★☆

Wilde Lane, Moyston, Vic 3377 **REGION** Grampians
T (03) 5354 2689 **www.**clayfieldwines.com **OPEN** Mon–Sat 10–5, Sun 11–4
WINEMAKER Simon Clayfield **EST.** 1997 **CASES** 500
Former long-serving Best's winemaker Simon Clayfield and wife Kaye are now doing their own thing. They planted 2 ha of shiraz between 1997 and 1999. Production is modest, but the quality is high. Currently one-third of the production is exported to the US.

ΨΨΨΨΨ **2004 Clayfield Massif Shiraz** Super-elegant, light- to medium-bodied wine, reflecting the modest alcohol level; cherry, raspberry and blackberry flavours; balanced tannins and oak. Screwcap. **RATING** 91 **DRINK** 2014 $24

ΨΨΨΨΨ **2003 Clayfield Grampians Shiraz** Strong purple-red; an absolute contrast in style to the Massif, perhaps part the drought vintage; super-ripe, confit fruit; boldly ripe and luscious, yet not absolutely convincing. Cork. **RATING** 93 **DRINK** 2015 $45

Claymore Wines NR

Leasingham Road, Leasingham, SA 5452 **REGION** Clare Valley
T (08) 8244 8932 **F** (08) 8347 7865 **www.**claymorewines.com.au **OPEN** W'ends & public hols 10–5
WINEMAKER David Mavor **EST.** 1998 **CASES** 8000
Claymore Wines draws on various vineyards, some situated in the Clare Valley, others in McLaren Vale. The Kupu-Kupu Vineyard at Penwortham has 9 ha of shiraz and 2 ha of merlot planted in 1997; the Nocturne series of wines come from the Wilpena and Moray Park vineyards owned by the Trott family; the well-regarded Joshua Tree Watervale Riesling comes from old vines on the Leasingham-Mintaro Road which are not estate-owned. Exports to Denmark, Sweden and Philippines.

Clearview Estate Mudgee ★★★

Cnr Sydney Road/Rocky Water Hole Road, Mudgee, NSW 2850 **REGION** Mudgee
T (02) 6372 4546 **F** (02) 6372 7577 **OPEN** Mon–Fri 10–3 (March–December), w'ends 10–4, or by appt
WINEMAKER Robert Stein Vineyard **EST.** 1995 **CASES** 1500
In February 2006 Paul and Michelle Baguley acquired the 11-ha vineyard from the founding Hickey family. Paul brings 10 years experience as a viticulturist, and Paul and Michelle have already introduced new wine styles to Clearview.

ΨΨΨΨ **Church Creek Unwooded Chardonnay 2005** Quite attractive, light-bodied wine; nectarine and citrus flavours; bright, zesty finish; low alcohol a plus. Screwcap. 12° alc. **RATING** 87 **DRINK** 2008
Sparkling Shiraz NV Light- to medium-bodied, and not too sweet; fresh cherry fruit, simple but enjoyable. 12.5° alc. **RATING** 87 **DRINK** Now

ΨΨΨ **Liqueur Shiraz NV RATING** 84 **DRINK** Now

ΨΨΨ **Pink Cabernet NV RATING** 83

Cleggett Wines ★★★☆

'Shalistin', Langhorne Creek, SA 5255 (postal) **REGION** Langhorne Creek
T (08) 8537 3133 **F** (08) 8537 3102 **www.**cleggettwines.com.au **OPEN** At Bremer Place, Wellington Road, Langhorne Creek
WINEMAKER Ballast Stone Estate (John Loxton), Bleasdale (Duane Coates) **EST.** 2000 **CASES** 1500
The Cleggett family first planted grape vines at Langhorne Creek in 1911. In 1977 a sport (a natural mutation) of cabernet sauvignon produced bronze-coloured grapes; cuttings were taken and increasing quantities of the vine were gradually established, and called malian. Ten years later one of the malian vines itself mutated to yield golden-white bunches, and this in turn was propagated with

the name shalistin. There are now 4 ha of shalistin and 2 ha of malian in bearing. Shalistin is made as a full-bodied but unoaked white wine; malian produces both an early and a late harvest wine, the former in a rose style, the latter with significant residual sugar, but again in a rose style. Exports to the UK.

▼▼▼▼▽ **Legend Series Cabernet Sauvignon 2002** Medium-bodied; an attractive mix of blackberry, mocha, leather and dark chocolate; ripe fine tannins; shows cool vintage to advantage. Cork. 14.5° alc. **RATING** 90 **DRINK** 2012 $ 18

▼▼▼▽ **Malian Bronze Cabernet Sauvignon 2005** **RATING** 85 **DRINK** Now $ 14

▼▼▼ **Sparkling Malian Bronze Cabernet 2005** **RATING** 83 $ 15
Sweet Shalistin 2005 **RATING** 83 $ 14

Clemens Hill ★★★☆

686 Richmond Road, Cambridge, TAS 7170 **REGION** Southern Tasmania
T (03) 6248 5985 **F** (03) 6248 5985 **OPEN** By appt
WINEMAKER Winemaking Tasmania **EST.** 1994 **CASES** 600
The Shepherd family acquired Clemens Hill in June 2001 after selling their Rosabrook winery in the Margaret River. They also have a shareholding in Winemaking Tasmania, the newly established contract winemaking facility run by Julian Alcorso, who makes the Clemens Hill wines. The estate vineyards have now been increased to 2.1 ha.

▼▼▼▼▽ **Sauvignon Blanc 2005** Lively, fresh passionfruit and gooseberry aromas and flavours; good length. **RATING** 90 **DRINK** Now $ 20

▼▼▼▽ **Pinot Noir 2004** **RATING** 86 **DRINK** 2008 $ 27

Cleveland ★★★☆

Shannons Road, Lancefield, Vic 3435 **REGION** Macedon Ranges
T (03) 5429 9000 **F** (03) 5429 2143 **WWW**.clevelandwinery.com.au **OPEN** 7 days 9–5
WINEMAKER Kilchurn Wines (David Cowburn) **EST.** 1985 **CASES** 2500
The Cleveland homestead was built in 1889 in the style of a Gothic Revival manor house, but had been abandoned for 40 years when purchased by the Briens in 1983. It has since been painstakingly restored and 3.8 ha of surrounding vineyard established. In January 2002 the new owner, Grange Group of Conference Centres, initiated fast-track development of The Grange at Cleveland Winery, with 22 suites, plus a large conference room and facilities alongside a new winery and warehouse.

▼▼▼▼▽ **Pinot Gris 2005** Considerable mouthfeel and power; semi-Alsace in style and texture, with predominantly pear-flavoured fruit. **RATING** 90 **DRINK** Now

▼▼▼▽ **Macedon Chardonnay 2003** **RATING** 86 **DRINK** 2008

Cliff House NR

57 Camms Road, Kayena, Tas 7270 **REGION** Northern Tasmania
T (03) 6394 7454 **F** (03) 6394 7454 **OPEN** By appt
WINEMAKER Winemaking Tasmania (Julian Alcorso) **EST.** 1983 **CASES** 2500
Cliff House has undergone a metamorphosis. In 1999 Geoff and Cheryl Hewitt sold the 4-ha vineyard they established in the Tamar Valley area in 1983. They have now turned a 2-hole golf course around their house into a second, new vineyard, planted to riesling and pinot noir.

Clonakilla ★★★★★

Crisps Lane, Murrumbateman, NSW 2582 **REGION** Canberra District
T (02) 6227 5877 **F** (02) 6227 5871 **WWW**.clonakilla.com.au **OPEN** 7 days 10–5
WINEMAKER Tim Kirk **EST.** 1971 **CASES** 6500
The indefatigable Tim Kirk, with an inexhaustible thirst for knowledge, is the winemaker and manager of this family winery founded by father, scientist Dr John Kirk. It is not at all surprising that the quality of the wines is excellent, especially the highly regarded Shiraz Viognier, which sells out quickly every year. Exports to all major markets.

ΥΥΥΥΥ Canberra District Shiraz Viognier 2004 Spotlessly clean, lifted black cherry/blackberry and spice aromas, together with the unmistakable tang of Viognier; silky soft tannins, very good balance and length. Screwcap. 14° alc. **RATING** 96 **DRINK** 2015 $ 78

Canberra District Viognier 2005 Glowing green-yellow; rich and mouthfilling, and has amazingly absorbed the 100% barrel fermentation. Apricot, lychee and pear; no alcohol heat whatsoever. Australia's response to Guigal La Doriane. Screwcap. 14° alc. **RATING** 95 **DRINK** 2010 $ 50

Hilltops Shiraz 2005 Deep, bright purple-red; medium- to full-bodied, but in a beautifully controlled mode. Black fruits, spice and licorice; fine-grained tannins, long finish. Screwcap. 14° alc. **RATING** 94 **DRINK** 2015 $ 28

Ballinderry Canberra District Cabernet Sauvignon Cabernet Franc Merlot 2004 Medium- to full-bodied; perfectly ripened fruit, bordering on luscious, but in no way jammy; masses of blackcurrant and wisps of chocolate; good oak and tannins; wonderfully harmonious. Cork. 14° alc. **RATING** 94 **DRINK** 2015 $ 30

ΥΥΥΥΥ Canberra District Riesling 2005 A powerful, rich wine; Alsace without the phenolics; solid, citrus fruit; good length. Screwcap. 12° alc. **RATING** 90 **DRINK** 2010 $ 24

Clos Clare ★★★☆

Old Road, Watervale, SA 5452 **REGION** Clare Valley
T (08) 8843 0161 **F** (08) 8843 0161 **OPEN** W'ends & public hols 10–5
WINEMAKER Various contract **EST.** 1993 **CASES** 1200
Clos Clare is based on a small (2 ha), unirrigated section of the original Florita Vineyard once owned by Leo Buring; it produces Riesling of extraordinary concentration and power. Exports to the US, Singapore and Ireland.

ΥΥΥΥΥ Riesling 2005 Light green-straw; powerful mineral/slate/lime aromas; strongly structured, masculine style. Will repay cellaring. Screwcap. 12° alc. **RATING** 90 **DRINK** 2012 $ 20

ΥΥΥΥ Shiraz 2003 RATING 86 **DRINK** 2009 $ 24

Clovely Estate ★★★☆

Steinhardts Road, Moffatdale via Murgon, Qld 4605 **REGION** South Burnett
T (07) 3216 1088 **F** (07) 3216 1050 **www.**clovely.com.au **OPEN** Wed–Sun 10–5
WINEMAKER Luke Fitzpatrick **EST.** 1998 **CASES** 25 000
Although new-born, Clovely Estate has the largest vineyards in Qld, having established 173 ha of immaculately maintained vines at two locations just to the east of Murgon in the Burnett Valley. There are 127 ha of red grapes (including 74 ha of shiraz) and 47 ha of white grapes. The attractively packaged wines are sold in four tiers: Clovely Estate at the top end (it will not be produced every year); Left Field, strongly fruity and designed to age; Fifth Row, for early drinking; and Qld, primarily designed for the export market.

ΥΥΥΥΥ South Burnett Verdelho 2005 Clean, tangy and fresh; fruit salad/grapefruit flavours, with particularly good length and balance; restrained alcohol a plus. Screwcap. 12.1° alc. **RATING** 90 **DRINK** Now $ 10

ΥΥΥΥ South Burnett Semillon 2003 Mineral, herb, grass and citrus rind, still very youthful; the finish is slightly hard. Give it another year or two. Screwcap. 12.5° alc. **RATING** 88 **DRINK** 2009 $ 15

Queensland Chardonnay 2004 Peachy fruit off-set by subtle oak, and balanced by good acidity. Not complex. Screwcap. 13° alc. **RATING** 87 **DRINK** 2008 $ 10

ΥΥΥΥ First Picked Queensland Chardonnay 2005 RATING 85 **DRINK** Now $ 7
Queensland Rose 2005 RATING 85 **DRINK** Now $ 10
First Picked Rubicon Cabernet Sauvignon 2004 RATING 85 **DRINK** 2009 $ 18

ΥΥΥ First Picked Queensland Shiraz 2003 RATING 83 $ 7

Clover Hill

★★★★☆

60 Clover Hill Road, Lebrina, Tas 7254 **REGION** Northern Tasmania
T (03) 6395 6114 **F** (03) 6395 6257 **WWW**.taltarni.com.au **OPEN** 7 days 10–5, by appt in winter
WINEMAKER Leigh Clarnette, Loic Le Calvez, Louella McPhan **EST.** 1986 **CASES** 10 000
Clover Hill was established by Taltarni in 1986 with the sole purpose of making a premium sparkling
wine. Its 21 ha of vineyards, comprising 13 ha of chardonnay, 6.76 of pinot noir and 1.24 of pinot
meunier, are now all in bearing, although extensive retrellising took place in 2002. The sparkling
wine quality is excellent, combining finesse with power and length.

ŢŢŢŢŢ **2001** Pale straw-bronze; spice and some strawberry aromas lead into a stylish, light- to
medium-bodied palate, with attractive multi-fruit flavours, though not quite the focus and
intensity of the very best. **RATING** 93 **DRINK** Now $ 40.99

Clyde Park Vineyard

★★★★★

2490 Midland Highway, Bannockburn, Vic 3331 **REGION** Geelong
T (03) 5281 7274 **F** (03) 5281 7274 **WWW**.clydepark.com.au **OPEN** W'ends & public hols 11–4
WINEMAKER Simon Black **EST.** 1979 **CASES** 5000
Clyde Park Vineyard was established by Gary Farr, but sold by him many years ago, and has passed
through several changes of ownership. It is now owned by Terry Jongebloed and Sue Jongebloed-
Dixon. It has significant mature plantings of pinot noir (3.4 ha), chardonnay (3.1 ha), sauvignon
blanc (1.5 ha), shiraz (1.2 ha) and pinot gris (0.9 ha).

ŢŢŢŢŢ **Shiraz 2004** A spotless array of black fruit aromas to a medium-bodied, pure and focused
palate crammed with black cherry, plum, spice and licorice; excellent oak. Screwcap.
14° alc. **RATING** 95 **DRINK** 2019 $ 27
Pinot Noir 2004 Clear and bright colour; a powerful wine in the context of the 2004
vintage, with ripe plum and redcurrant fruit; long finish, long future. Screwcap. 14° alc.
RATING 94 **DRINK** 2010 $ 27

ŢŢŢŢ **Sauvignon Blanc 2005** Very pale straw; clean, crisp, minerally style needing a bit more
sweet fruit. **RATING** 87 **DRINK** Now $ 20
Pinot Gris 2005 Bright, pale straw-green; tangy and citrussy, with line and length; does
have a touch of volatile acidity. **RATING** 87 **DRINK** Now $ 24

ŢŢŢ **Chardonnay 2004** **RATING** 83 $ 24

Coal Valley Vineyard

★★★

257 Richmond Road, Cambridge, Tas 7170 **REGION** Southern Tasmania
T (03) 6248 5367 **F** (03) 6248 4175 **WWW**.coalvalley.com.au **OPEN** Wed–Mon 10–4
WINEMAKER Andrew Hood (Contract) **EST.** 1991 **CASES** 600
Coal Valley Vineyard is the new name for Treehouse Vineyard & Wine Centre, the change brought
about by the fact that Treehouse had been trademarked by the Pemberton winery, Salitage. The
vineyard was purchased by Todd Goebel and wife Gillian Christian in 1999. They have set about
doubling the size of the riesling vineyard and establishing 1.5 ha of another vineyard planted to pinot
noir, with a few vines of cabernet. The Wine Centre now incorporates a full commercial kitchen and
overlooks the existing vineyard and the Coal River Valley.

ŢŢŢŢ **Cabernet Merlot 2004** Clean and fresh, with cassis/blackcurrant fruit; good line and
length; just a tinge green, but not aggressively so. **RATING** 89 **DRINK** 2009 $ 30

ŢŢŢŢ **Riesling 2005** **RATING** 86 **DRINK** 2008 $ 27

Coalville Vineyard

NR

RMB 4750 Moe South Road, Moe South, Vic 3825 **REGION** Gippsland
T (03) 5127 4229 **F** (03) 5127 4229 **OPEN** 7 days 10–5
WINEMAKER Peter Beasley **EST.** 1985 **CASES** 3000
This is the new name for Mair's Coalville, following the sale of the property by Dr Stewart Mair to
Peter Beasley, who has significantly increased not only the volume but the range of wines available.

🐚 Coates Wines

PO Box 859, McLaren Vale, SA 5171 **REGION** McLaren Vale
T 0417 882 557 **F** (08) 8363 9925 **WWW**.coates-wines.com **OPEN** Not
WINEMAKER Duane Coates **EST.** 2003 **CASES** 800
Duane Coates has Bachelor of Science, Master of Business Administration and Master of Oenology degrees from Adelaide University; for good measure he completed the theory component of the Masters of Wine degree in 2005. Having made wine in various parts of the world, and in SA for a number of important brands, he is more than qualified to make and market the Coates Wines. Nonetheless, his original intention was to simply make a single barrel of wine employing various philosophies and practices outside the mainstream, and with no intention of moving to commercial production. In fact the single barrel in 2003 became 11, 15 barrels in 2004 and 30 in 2005. The key is organically grown grapes and the refusal to use additives and fining agents. A deliberately low level of new oak (20%) is also part of the picture.

🍷🍷🍷🍷 **Organically Grown McLaren Vale Shiraz 2003** Impressive wine, highly focused and intense; a long palate flooded with black fruits; well-integrated oak. Great outcome for the vintage. Cork. 14.5° alc. **RATING** 94 **DRINK** 2013 $ 35

🍷🍷🍷🍷🍷 **Organically Grown McLaren Vale Shiraz 2004** Very powerful, savoury, earthy style with the usual McLaren Vale chocolate and plenty of oak; long finish, needs time. Cork. 14.5° alc. **RATING** 92 **DRINK** 2015 $ 35

🍷🍷🍷🍷 **McLaren Vale Fortified Shiraz 2005** Classic Australian/McLaren Vale style; super-intense; when to drink? Now, 5, 10 or 20 years? Cork. 20° alc. **RATING** 89 **DRINK** 2030 $ 25

Cobaw Ridge

31 Perc Boyer's Lane, East Pastoria via Kyneton, Vic 3444 **REGION** Macedon Ranges
T (03) 5423 5227 **F** (03) 5423 5227 **WWW**.cobawridge.com.au **OPEN** Mon–Fri 10–5, w'ends 12–5.30
WINEMAKER Alan Cooper **EST.** 1985 **CASES** 1500
Nelly and Alan Cooper established Cobaw Ridge's 6-ha vineyard at an altitude of 610m in the hills above Kyneton, complete with pole-framed mudbrick house and winery. The plantings of cabernet sauvignon have been removed and partially replaced by lagrein, a variety which sent me scuttling to Jancis Robinson's seminal book on grape varieties: it is a northeast Italian variety typically used to make delicate Rose, but at Cobaw Ridge it is made into an impressive full-bodied dry red. This success has prompted Alan Cooper to remove 0.5 ha of chardonnay and plant vermentino in its place. Exports to the UK and the US.

🍷🍷🍷🍷 **Chardonnay 2004** Complex barrel ferment/malolactic inputs work very well; mouthfilling, long and racy — and classy. Diam. **RATING** 94 **DRINK** 2010 $ 32

🍷🍷🍷🍷 **Shiraz Viognier 2004** Strongly scented and spicy; a lively medium-bodied palate with black fruits, spice and tangy viognier; crisp acid. Diam. **RATING** 92 **DRINK** 2012 $ 42
Pinot Noir 2004 Strong red-purple; clean, fresh, pure bouquet; light- to medium-bodied palate with small red fruits; still linear and needs to grow complexity. Diam. **RATING** 90 **DRINK** 2009 $ 38
Lagrein 2004 Aromas of freshly baked fruit cake; a long palate with off-setting lemony acidity, and overall freshness. Diam. **RATING** 90 **DRINK** 2011 $ 60

Cobb's Hill

NR

Oakwood Road, Oakbank, SA 5243 **REGION** Adelaide Hills
T (08) 8388 4054 **F** (08) 8388 4820 **WWW**.cobbshillwine.com.au **OPEN** Not
WINEMAKER Shaw & Smith **EST.** 1997 **CASES** 400
Sally and Roger Cook have a 140-ha property in the Adelaide Hills that takes its name from Cobb & Co, which used it as a staging post and resting place for 1000 horses. The Cooks now use the property to raise Angus cattle, grow cherries and, more recently, grow grapes. Three different sites on the property, amounting to just over 10 ha, were planted to selected clones of sauvignon blanc, chardonnay, semillon, riesling and merlot. Part of the production is sold to Shaw & Smith, who vinify the remainder for Cobb's Hill. The Sauvignon Blanc has been most successful.

Cobbitty Wines
NR

Cobbitty Road, Cobbitty, NSW 2570 **REGION** South Coast Zone
T (02) 4651 2281 **F** (02) 4651 2671 **OPEN** Mon–Sat 9.30–5.30, Sun 11–5.30
WINEMAKER Giovanni Cogno **EST.** 1964 **CASES** 5000
Draws upon 10 ha of estate plantings of muscat, barbera, grenache and trebbiano, relying very much on local and ethnic custom.

Cockatoo Ridge
NR

PO Box 855, Nuriootpa, SA 5355 **REGION** Riverland
T (08) 8563 6400 **F** (08) 8563 1117 **WWW**.cockatooridge.com.au **OPEN** Not
WINEMAKER Stephen Obst **EST.** 1990 **CASES** NFP
Cockatoo Ridge was established by Geoff Merrill, and rapidly built volume by sales through the large retail chains, the extremely colourful label standing out on the shelf. The business was already a large one when it was acquired by a company headed by ex-Orlando winemaker Ivan Limb. The large production is based on estate plantings of 98 ha at Waikerie on the Murray River, supplemented by grapes grown under contract in the Barossa Valley. Exports to all major markets.

Cody's
NR

New England Highway, Ballandean, Qld 4382 **REGION** Granite Belt
T (07) 4684 1309 **F** (07) 5572 6500 **OPEN** 7 days 10–5
WINEMAKER Sirromet **EST.** 1995 **CASES** 500
John Cody has established 2.5 ha of cabernet sauvignon, merlot and shiraz at his Ballandean vineyard. The wines are contract-made by Adam Chapman at Sirromet, and are sold by mail order and through the cellar door, which offers the usual facilities.

Cofield Wines
★★★★

Distillery Road, Wahgunyah, Vic 3687 **REGION** Rutherglen
T (02) 6033 3798 **F** (02) 6033 0798 **WWW**.cofieldwines.com.au **OPEN** Mon–Sat 9–5, Sun 10–5
WINEMAKER Max Cofield, Damien Cofield **EST.** 1990 **CASES** 8000
District veteran Max Cofield, together with wife Karen and sons Damien (winery) and Andrew (vineyard), is developing a strong cellar door sales base, and also providing a large barbecue and picnic area. The Pickled Sisters Café is open for lunch Wed–Mon (phone 02 6033 2377). The influence of Damien Cofield in developing an impressively broad-based product range is quite evident.

🍷🍷🍷🍷🍷 **Sauvignon Blanc 2005** Clean, fresh bouquet; a light-bodied mix of tropical, citrus and grassy fruit; good length. Exceptional for the region. Screwcap. 12.5° alc. **RATING** 90 **DRINK** Now $16
Rutherglen Cabernet Sauvignon 2003 Generous, sweet cassis/blackcurrant fruit, not the least bit jammy. Fruit-driven; a real surprise packet. Cork. 13.9° alc. **RATING** 90 **DRINK** 2010 $20
Durif 2004 Good colour; rich, ample black fruits, prunes and plums, the tannin and extract controlled. Impressive. Diam. **RATING** 90 **DRINK** 2012 $20
QVP Vintage Port 2005 Good modern style; spicy plum cake fruit and a relatively dry finish, with good spirit. Intelligent winemaking. Cork. **RATING** 90 **DRINK** 2015 $26

🍷🍷🍷🍷 **Rutherglen Sauvignon Blanc Semillon 2005** Pale straw-green; a powerful palate with some citrus and a touch of barrel ferment complexity for texture and structure. Well-made. Screwcap. 13° alc. **RATING** 89 **DRINK** 2008 $16
The Fifth Son 2003 Light- to medium-bodied, with good mouthfeel; gentle cassis, mulberry and cedar flavours are in no way jammy; finishes with fine tannins. Made from the 5 Bordeaux varieties. Cork. 14.4° alc. **RATING** 89 **DRINK** 2012 $20
Malbec 2004 An interesting wine showing the typical slightly jammy/confection varietal character of malbec; has unexpected length. Diam. **RATING** 88 **DRINK** 2010 $20
Chardonnay 2005 Light- to medium-bodied; clean, correct melon fruit and a touch of citrus; simple but pleasant. Screwcap. 13° alc. **RATING** 87 **DRINK** 2008 $17

Rutherglen Sangiovese 2004 A wine in 2 parts; initially, sweet red cherry fruit, then distinctly Italianate tannins. Cork. 13.7° alc. **RATING** 87 **DRINK** 2008 $ 20

T XIII Sparkling Shiraz NV Far more elegant than expected, the elegance meaning the dosage sweetness can be and is controlled. Just a little simple, perhaps. Cork. 14.5° alc. **RATING** 87 **DRINK** Now $ 29

Late Harvest Muscadelle 2005 Rich, poached peach and honey flavours; good balance, although inevitably lacking complexity. Cork. 9.1° alc. **RATING** 87 **DRINK** 2010 $ 20

ΥΥΥΥ **T XII Pinot Noir Chardonnay NV** **RATING** 86 **DRINK** Now $ 22

Reserve Rutherglen Muscat NV Still predominantly red hues; young, raisiny varietal fruit; needs more age and rancio to cut back the sweetness. **RATING** 86 **DRINK** Now $ 26

ΥΥΥ **T V Kristalee Chenin Blanc NV** **RATING** 83 $ 20

Coldstream Hills   NR

31 Maddens Lane, Coldstream, Vic 3770 **REGION** Yarra Valley
T (03) 5964 9410 **F** (03) 5964 9389 **WWW**.coldstreamhills.com.au **OPEN** 7 days 10–5
WINEMAKER Andrew Fleming, Greg Jarratt, James Halliday (Consultant) **EST.** 1985 **CASES** 55 000
Founded by the author, who continues to be involved with the winemaking, but acquired by Southcorp in mid-1996, thus now a small part of FWE. Expansion plans already then underway have been maintained, with well in excess of 100 ha of owned or managed estate vineyards as the base. Chardonnay and Pinot Noir continue to be the principal focus; Merlot came on-stream in 1997, Sauvignon Blanc around the same time. Vintage conditions permitting, these wines are made in both varietal and Reserve form, the latter in restricted quantities. Tasting notes are written by Andrew Fleming. Exports to the UK and other major markets.

Sauvignon Blanc 2005 Vibrant straw with pale-green hues. The bouquet has attractive varietal characters of lychee, passionfruit and gooseberry. A well-balanced wine that finishes with lingering freshly squeezed lemon acidity. Screwcap. 13° alc. **RATING** NR **DRINK** Now $ 25.90

Chardonnay 2004 An elegant style of chardonnay, with distinctive Upper Yarra characters of citrus and nectarine and Lower Yarra white peach; excellent barrel ferment, cashew nut flavours and texture, and finishes with fine, minerally acid and flinty, slate tones. Screwcap. 13.5° alc. **RATING** NR **DRINK** 2014 $ 25.90

Pinot Noir 2005 Attractive varietal aromas of dark cherries, plums and spice; has great structure, fine tannins, fruit concentration and length, exhibiting fruit characters of cherries and plums, with underlying hints of gaminess and spice; toasty integrated oak is evident. Screwcap. 13.5° alc. **RATING** NR **DRINK** 2012 $ 26.90

Reserve Pinot Noir 2004 The bouquet is restrained, yet concentrated, with characters of dark cherry, plum and blueberries supported by attractive toasty oak. The palate is rich and focused, with seamless tannins and length. An elegant wine from the cool '04 vintage. Screwcap. 14° alc. **RATING** NR **DRINK** 2014 $ 75

Merlot 2003 Attractive aromas of ripe cherry and red plum, blackcurrant and underlying spice. Round and supple, exhibiting attractive cherry/plum characters with licorice and spice. French oak will integrate with maturation. Screwcap. 13.5° alc. **RATING** NR **DRINK** 2012 $ 28.50

Coldstream Hills Reserve Chardonnay 2004 Classic cool climate aromas and flavours of white peach and citrus with toasty oak and slatey/mineral notes. Barrel ferment characters of grilled nuts provide additional complexity. Screwcap. 13.5° alc. **RATING** NR **DRINK** 2015 $ 46

2004 Coldstream Hills Limited Release Shiraz Attractive cool climate shiraz aromas ad flavours of dark cherry, plum and rose petal, with underlying pepper and spice. Toasty oak is evident but does not dominate. Screwcap. 14° alc. **RATING** NR **DRINK** 2012 $ 35

2003 Coldstream Hills Reserve Cabernet Sauvignon Aromas of dark chocolate, blueberry and French oak; blackcurrant and dark cherry fruit flavours; fine and persistent tannins provide a seamless backbone. Screwcap. 14° alc. **RATING** NR **DRINK** 2015 $ 50

Coliban Valley Wines ★★★★★

Metcalfe-Redesdale Road, Metcalfe, Vic 3448 **REGION** Heathcote
T 0417 312 098 **F** (03) 9813 3895 **www**.heathcotewinegrowers.com.au **OPEN** W'ends 10–5
WINEMAKER Helen Miles **EST.** 1997 **CASES** 400
Helen Miles (with a degree in science) and partner, Greg Miles, have planted 2.8 ha of shiraz, 1.2 ha of cabernet and 0.4 ha of merlot near Metcalfe, at the cooler southwest corner of the Heathcote wine region. The granitic soils and warm climate allow organic principles to be used successfully. The shiraz is dry-grown, while the cabernet sauvignon and merlot receive minimal irrigation. Some grapes are sold, but most of the production is used for the Coliban Valley label.

▼▼▼▼▼ **Heathcote Shiraz 2004** Opaque purple-red; full-bodied, dense blackberry, licorice and dark chocolate fruit, all achieved without excess tannins or extract; carries the alcohol with ease, and oak is a bystander. Diam. 15° alc. **RATING** 94 **DRINK** 2017 **$** 25
Heathcote Cabernet Sauvignon 2004 Very good purple-red; powerful, dense blackcurrant, blackberry and cassis fruit; lingering, fine, emery board tannins. Diam. 15° alc. **RATING** 94 **DRINK** 2014 **$** 20

▼▼▼▼▽ **Heathcote Merlot 2004** Light- to medium-bodied; fragrant red fruits and spices; has rightly backed off both the alcohol and extraction; light tannins, pretty wine. Diam. 13° alc. **RATING** 90 **DRINK** 2010 **$** 20

🐌 Collina del Re NR

PO Box 349, Paddington, NSW 2021 **REGION** King Valley
T (02) 9332 1623 **F** (02) 9380 8810 **OPEN** Not
WINEMAKER Various contract **EST.** 1995 **CASES** 200
This is the venture of John and Pam Love and Andrew and Susie Wright, who have established 3 ha each of pinot noir, pinot meunier and chardonnay at an elevation of 820–850m at Whitlands, high in the King Valley. The primary purpose is to supply Domaine Chandon with grapes for sparkling wine, but a small amount is made for sale by phone, the prices for the Chardonnay and Pinot ranging between $10-$15 per bottle.

Colvin Wines ★★★★

19 Boyle Street, Mosman, NSW 2088 (postal) **REGION** Lower Hunter Valley
T (02) 9908 7886 **F** (02) 9908 7885 **www**.colvinwines.com.au **OPEN** Not
WINEMAKER Andrew Spinaze, Trevor Drayton (Contract) **EST.** 1999 **CASES** 500
Sydney lawyer John Colvin and wife and Robyn purchased the De Beyers Vineyard in 1990, which has a history going back to the second half of the 19th century. By 1967, when a syndicate headed by Douglas McGregor purchased 35 ha of the original vineyard site, no vines remained. The syndicate planted semillon on the alluvial soil of the creek flats and shiraz on the red clay hillsides. When the Colvins acquired the property the vineyard was in need of attention. Up to 1998 all the grapes were sold to Tyrrell's, but since 1999 quantities have been made for the Colvin Wines label. These include Sangiovese, from a little over 1 ha of vines planted by John Colvin in 1996 because of his love of the wines of Tuscany.

▼▼▼▼▽ **2005 Colvin De Beyers Vineyard Hunter Valley Semillon** Very pale straw-green; a vibrant, racy, minerally palate intensified by a touch of CO_2; lemony acidity on a prolonged finish. Screwcap. **RATING** 92 **DRINK** 2015

Connor Park Winery NR

59 Connors Road, Leichardt, Vic 3516 **REGION** Bendigo
T (03) 5437 5234 **F** (03) 5437 5204 **www**.connorparkwinery.com.au **OPEN** 7 days 10–6
WINEMAKER Ross Lougoon **EST.** 1994 **CASES** 7000
The original planting of 2 ha of vineyard dates back to the mid-1960s and to the uncle of the present owners, who had plans for designing an automatic grape harvester. The plans came to nothing, and when the present owners purchased the property in 1985 the vineyard had run wild. They resuscitated the vineyard (which formed part of a much larger mixed farming operation) and until 1994 were content to sell the grapes to other winemakers. Since then the vineyard has been expanded to 10 ha. Exports to the US, Canada and Singapore.

Constable & Hershon

NR

205 Gillards Road, Pokolbin, NSW 2320 **REGION** Lower Hunter Valley
T (02) 4998 7887 **F** (02) 4998 6555 **WWW**.constablehershon.com.au **OPEN** 7 days 10–5
WINEMAKER Neil McGuigan (Contract) **EST.** 1981 **CASES** 3000
Features 4 spectacular formal gardens: the Rose, Knot and Herb, Secret and Sculpture; a free 30-minute garden tour is conducted Mon–Fri at 10.30 am. The 7-ha vineyard is spectacularly situated under the backdrop of the Brokenback Range. Offers a range of several vintages of each variety.

Coobara Wines

★★★★☆

PO Box 231, Birdwood, SA 5234 **REGION** Adelaide Hills
T (08) 8568 5375 **F** (08) 8568 5375 **WWW**.coobarawines.com.au **OPEN** By appt
WINEMAKER David Cook **EST.** 1992 **CASES** 700
David Cook has worked in the wine industry for over 18 years, principally with Orlando, but also with Jim Irvine, John Glaetzer and the late Neil Ashmead. As well as working full-time for Orlando, he undertook oenology, viticulture and cellar procedure courses, and — with support from his parents — planted 4 ha of cabernet sauvignon and merlot on the family property at Birdwood. In 1993 they purchased the adjoining property, planting 2 ha of riesling, and thereafter lifting the plantings of merlot and cabernet sauvignon to 4 ha each, plus 0.4 ha of shiraz. In 2003 David decided to commence wine production, a fortuitous decision given that the following year their long-term grape purchase contracts were not renewed, thus upcoming releases will see the production rise from 700 to 2500 cases. Coobara means 'place of birds' (Aboriginal).

🍷🍷🍷🍷🍷 **Adelaide Hills Riesling 2005** Delicate, flowery apple and passionfruit; lovely palate, beautifully balanced with great acidity. What a joy at 10% alcohol. Screwcap. 10° alc. **RATING** 95 **DRINK** 2010 $18

🍷🍷🍷🍷🍷 **Adelaide Hills Shiraz 2004** Fresh, clean, lively zesty red cherry with some spice; fruit-driven style, with very clear-cut varietal fruit. Screwcap. 14° alc. **RATING** 92 **DRINK** 2013 $18
Adelaide Hills Cabernet Merlot 2004 Very good colour; has more stuffing than the Merlot without going over the top; attractive blackcurrant and cassis fruit; fine tannins. Screwcap. 14° alc. **RATING** 90 **DRINK** 2012 $18

🍷🍷🍷🍷 **Adelaide Hills Merlot 2004** In keeping with the winery style; elegant and fresh; however, so light-bodied it needs more fruit intensity and/or structure. Screwcap. 14° alc. **RATING** 88 **DRINK** 2009 $18

Coolangatta Estate

★★★★

1335 Bolong Road, Shoalhaven Heads, NSW 2535 **REGION** Shoalhaven Coast
T (02) 4448 7131 **F** (02) 4448 7997 **WWW**.coolangattaestate.com.au **OPEN** 7 days 10–5
WINEMAKER Tyrrell's **EST.** 1988 **CASES** 5000
Coolangatta Estate is part of a 150-ha resort with accommodation, restaurants, golf course, etc; some of the oldest buildings were convict-built in 1822. It might be thought that the wines are tailored purely for the tourist market, but in fact the standard of viticulture is exceptionally high (immaculate Scott Henry trellising), and the contract winemaking is wholly professional. Has a habit of bobbing up with gold medals at Sydney and Canberra wine shows.

🍷🍷🍷🍷🍷 **Estate Grown Semillon 2005** Delicious wine; tangy, vibrant, lemon/grass/herb fruit; excellent acidity, long finish. Screwcap. 10.5° alc. **RATING** 95 **DRINK** 2012 $18

🍷🍷🍷🍷 **Alexander Berry Chardonnay 2004** Gentle stone fruit and melon; nice touch of oak; well-balanced. Screwcap. 13° alc. **RATING** 88 **DRINK** Now $22
Estate Grown Verdelho 2005 Classic fruit salad; nicely balanced; good expression of the variety. Screwcap. 14.1° alc. **RATING** 87 **DRINK** Now $18

Coombe Farm Vineyard   NR

11 St Huberts Road, Coldstream, Vic 3770 **REGION** Yarra Valley
T (03) 9739 1136 **F** (03) 9739 1136 **www**.coombefarm.com.au **OPEN** Not
WINEMAKER Wine Network **EST.** 1999 **CASES** 2000
Coombe Farm Vineyard is owned by Pamela, Lady Vestey (Dame Nellie Melba's grand-daughter), Lord
Samuel Vestey and The Right Honourable Mark Vestey. After a small initial planting, the decision was
taken in 1999 to very significantly extend the vineyard: there are now 25 ha of pinot noir, 18 ha of
chardonnay, 7.4 ha of merlot, 5.4 ha of cabernet sauvignon, 1.9 ha of marsanne and 0.7 ha of arneis. The
vast majority of the fruit is sold; a small amount is made for the Coombe Farm Vineyard label.

Coombend Estate   ★★★☆

Coombend via Swansea, Tas 7190 **REGION** East Coast Tasmania
T (03) 6257 8881 **F** (03) 6257 8884 **OPEN** 7 days 10–5
WINEMAKER Tamar Ridge **EST.** 1985 **CASES** 4000
In 2005 Tamar Ridge acquired Coombend Estate, including all the assets and the business name,
Tamar Ridge has immediately commenced the establishment of a large vineyard which will dwarf the
existing 1.75 ha of cabernet sauvignon, 2.25 ha of sauvignon blanc, 0.5 ha of pinot noir and 0.3 ha of
riesling.

▼▼▼▼♡ **Cabernet Sauvignon 2004** Medium-bodied; quite attractive blackcurrant fruit to a tight,
firm palate; good oak handling. **RATING** 90 **DRINK** 2010 **$** 28

▼▼▼▼ **Sauvignon Blanc 2005** Pleasant wine; soft texture and minimal oak. **RATING** 88
DRINK Now **$** 22

🐚 Cooper Burns   ★★★★☆

1 Golden Way, Nuriootpa, SA 5353 (postal) **REGION** Barossa Valley
T (08) 8562 2271 **F** (08) 8562 2271 **www**.cooperburns.com.au **OPEN** Not
WINEMAKER Troy Kalleske **EST.** 2004 **CASES** 200
This is a virtual winery, focusing on small batch, hand-made winemaking. Presently grapes come
from the Kalleske vineyard near Greenock and winemaking is handled by Troy Kalleske. As from the
2006 vintage, the business has more tangible substance, with the establishment of a micro-winery
and barrel store. The aim is to gradually increase production, with a primary focus on shiraz, but
wines from other traditional and non-traditional Barossa varieties will be made when opportunities
arise.

▼▼▼▼♡ **Barossa Valley Shiraz 2004** An elegant wine, with spicy black and red fruits; bright
acidity, the oak just a little assertive; silky, spicy finish. Screwcap. 14.5° alc. **RATING** 92
DRINK 2015 **$** 30

Cooper Wines   ★★☆

Lovedale Road, Lovedale, NSW 2321 **REGION** Lower Hunter Valley
T (02) 4930 7387 **F** (02) 4930 7900 **www**.cooperwines.com.au **OPEN** Mon–Fri 10–5, w'ends 9.30–5
WINEMAKER Max Cooper **EST.** 2001 **CASES** 3000
Max Cooper is a Qantas pilot who purchased the former Allanmere Winery & Vineyard. The chardonnay
is estate-grown; the other wines are made onsite from grapes purchased by growers in the region.

▼▼▼ **Verdelho 2005 RATING** 83 **$** 15

🐚 Cooralook Wines   ★★★★

Garden Street, South Yarra, Vic 3141 (postal) **REGION** Mornington Peninsula
T (03) 9251 5375 **F** 03 9639 1540 **www**.cooralook.com.au **OPEN** Not
WINEMAKER Tod Dexter **EST.** 2002 **CASES** 6000
Cooralook Wines, owned by Robert and Mem Kirby, has substantial vineyards in the Mornington
Peninsula, Heathcote and Strathbogie Ranges, each vineyard focusing on the varieties most suited to
each region. The wines represent great value. Exports to the US.

ŸŸŸŸ♀ **Mornington Peninsula Chardonnay 2004** Green-straw; light- to medium-bodied, elegant nectarine, grapefruit and melon; just a hint of oak; has precision. Screwcap. 13.5° alc. **RATING** 91 **DRINK** 2012 $ 18
Heathcote Shiraz 2004 Bright purple-red; clean, pure black cherry, plum and spice; supple tannins, good balance and length; well priced. Screwcap. 14° alc. **RATING** 90 **DRINK** 2012 $ 20

ŸŸŸŸ **Mornington Peninsula Pinot Noir 2004** A ghost of reduction behind fragrant, red fruits on the bouquet; lively, cherry, berry fruit with little distraction from oak or tannins; attractive luncheon style. Screwcap. 13.5° alc. **RATING** 89 **DRINK** 2008 $ 20
Heathcote Grenache Shiraz 2004 Light- to medium-bodied cherry fruit on entry, then hijacked by tannins; a curious wine. Screwcap. 14.5° alc. **RATING** 88 **DRINK** 2010 $ 20
Mornington Peninsula Unwooded Chardonnay 2005 White peach and lemon/citrus mix; has some character and length. Screwcap. 14° alc. **RATING** 87 **DRINK** 2008 $ 17

Coorinja NR

Toodyay Road, Toodyay, WA 6566 **REGION** Greater Perth Zone
T (08) 9574 2280 **OPEN** Mon–Sat 10–5
WINEMAKER Michael Wood **EST.** 1870 **CASES** 3200
An evocative and historic winery nestling in a small gully which seems to be in a time warp, begging to be used as a set for a movie. A revamp of the packaging accompanied a more than respectable 'Hermitage', with lots of dark chocolate and sweet berry flavour, finishing with soft tannins.

Cooyal Grove

Lot 9 Stoney Creek Road, Mudgee, NSW 2850 **REGION** Mudgee
T (02) 6373 5337 **F** (02) 6373 5337 **OPEN** 7 days by appt
WINEMAKER Moore Haszard (Contract) **EST.** 1990 **CASES** 1000
In late 2002 the 10-ha Cooyal Grove property of vines, pistachio nut trees and olives was purchased by Sydney publican John Lenard, and Paul and Lydele Walker, a local Mudgee vigneron and his wife. The partners say, 'We have worked almost every weekend in the vineyard and grove, undertaking every task from planting new blocks, pruning, training, harvesting, bottling and labelling. Given that all of the partners are only 30 years old and not yet financially able to employ outside labour, we seem to call on every friend, relative and friend's relatives to assist in the production of the crops. This has made for a feeling of building something from scratch which we are proud of.' The vineyards are now 4.5 ha in total, with chardonnay, semillon, sauvignon blanc, merlot, shiraz and cabernet sauvignon.

ŸŸŸ♀ **Mudgee Chardonnay 2005 RATING** 86 **DRINK** 2008 $ 15
Mudgee Cabernet Sauvignon 2004 Light- to medium-bodied; some cassis/blackcurrant fruit; tannin-free zone. Screwcap. **RATING** 86 **DRINK** 2008 $ 15
Mudgee Shiraz 2004 RATING 85 **DRINK** 2009 $ 20

Cope-Williams

Glenfern Road, Romsey, Vic 3434 **REGION** Macedon Ranges
T (03) 5429 5428 **F** (03) 5429 5655 **OPEN** 7 days 11–5
WINEMAKER David Cowburn **EST.** 1977 **CASES** 7000
One of Macedon's pioneers, specialising in sparkling wines which are full flavoured but also producing excellent Chardonnay and Pinot Noir table wines in warmer vintages. A traditional 'English Green'-type cricket ground is available for hire and booked out most days from spring through till autumn

ŸŸŸŸŸ **Chardonnay 2003** Strong oak inputs on a tight, intense palate of grapefruit and stone fruit; has admirable length and acidity. Screwcap. **RATING** 94 **DRINK** 2012 $ 24
R.O.M.S.E.Y. Brut NV 96 Cuvee. Rich, complex, full-bodied fruit sweetness almost into the tropical; chardonnay component obvious. **RATING** 94 **DRINK** 2008 $ 28
R.O.M.S.E.Y. Brut NV 98 Cuvee. Lemony fruit combines with biscuity/bready characters, in turn supported by good acidity; well balanced and plenty of depth. **RATING** 92 **DRINK** Now $ 28

ŸŸŸŸ **Cabernet Blanc 2005 RATING** 86 **DRINK** Now $ 21

Copper Bull Wines   NR

19 Uplands Road, Chirnside Park, Vic 3116 **REGION** Yarra Valley
T (03) 9726 7111 **OPEN** Wed–Sun 11–6
WINEMAKER David Schliefert **EST.** 1982 **CASES** 800
Copper Bull is the reincarnation of Halcyon Daze. The Rackleys, having gone into semi-retirement, have leased the vineyard, winery and cellar door to David and Janie Schliefert, who produced the first wines under the Copper Bull label in 2003. David Schliefert spent 19 years at Lindemans Karadoc winery, becoming a cellar supervisor in the process, while wife Janie worked in quality management at Lindemans. The small production is sold from the cellar door.

Copper Country   NR

Lot 6 Kingaroy Road, Nanango, Qld 4615 **REGION** South Burnett
T (07) 4163 1011 **F** (07) 4163 1122 **OPEN** 7 days 9–5
WINEMAKER Contract **EST.** 1995 **CASES** 1000
The Winter family (Derek, Helena, Stephen and Justyne) were restaurateurs before venturing into grapegrowing and winemaking. The name of the vineyard and the restaurant recognises that copper was the first mineral mined in the region. The Winters also make cheese; the principal outlet for their products is their restaurant and cellar door.

Coriole   ★★★★★

Chaffeys Road, McLaren Vale, SA 5171 **REGION** McLaren Vale
T (08) 8323 8305 **F** (08) 8323 9136 **WWW**.coriole.com **OPEN** Mon–Fri 10–5, w'ends & public hols 11–5
WINEMAKER Grant Harrison **EST.** 1967 **CASES** 34 000
Justifiably best known for its Shiraz, which — in both the rare Lloyd Reserve and standard forms — is extremely impressive. One of the first wineries to catch on to the Italian fashion with its Sangiovese, but its white varietal wines lose nothing by comparison. It is also a producer of high-quality olive oil distributed commercially through all states.

▼▼▼▼▼ **McLaren Vale Shiraz 2004** Strong, deep red-purple; rich, dark plum, blackberry, bitter chocolate and spice; oak well-handled; brighter than most on the finish. Cork. 14.5° alc. **RATING** 94 **DRINK** 2014 $ 25
Mary Kathleen Reserve McLaren Vale Cabernet Merlot 2003 Complex flavours and texture; blackcurrant, spice and a touch of bitter chocolate; sweet, silky tannins; lovely, supple and smooth wine. Cork. 14° alc. **RATING** 94 **DRINK** 2013 $ 39
McLaren Vale Cabernet Sauvignon 2004 Deep colour; clean, ripe, luscious blackcurrant and touches of dark chocolate; silky mouthfeel and perfect alcohol. Cork. 13.5° alc. **RATING** 94 **DRINK** 2014 $ 25

▼▼▼▼▽ **Semillon 2005** Spotlessly clean; has that typical extra touch of elegance of Coriole; green apple fruit with touches of mineral and lemon; bright finish. Screwcap. **RATING** 91 **DRINK** 2010 $ 16
The Old Barn Cabernet Shiraz 2003 A neat corollary to The Old Barn Chardonnay; medium-bodied, bright, fresh fruits run through the length of the palate; enough structure to support the wine for a decade; 586 dozen made. 14° alc. **RATING** 91 **DRINK** 2016 $ 30
Poet Series Jude Aquilina Cabernet Barbera 2004 Appropriately seductive mouthfeel (read the back label poem); dark, deep black fruit flavours; good tannin and oak management. **RATING** 91 **DRINK** 2014 $ 30
McLaren Vale Sangiovese 2004 Bright purple-red; clean and clear black cherry aromas; plenty of black cherry and raspberry fruit depth; nice tannins, best yet for Coriole. Screwcap. 14° alc. **RATING** 91 **DRINK** 2009 $ 17
The Old Barn Adelaide Hills Chardonnay 2004 Elegant, lively and fresh; light- to medium-bodied, well-balanced, citrus, stone fruit and a nice veneer of oak; wild yeast; 350 dozen made. Screwcap. 13.5° alc. **RATING** 90 **DRINK** 2009 $ 19

▼▼▼▼ **Lalla Rookh Grenache Shiraz 2003** Clear, bright colour; a clean, fruit-driven light- to medium-bodied array of red fruits and spices; light oak. Cork. **RATING** 89 **DRINK** 2008 $ 24

Chenin Blanc 2005 Fine, elegant gentle fruit salad and pear; a light touch of citrus. Screwcap. **RATING** 88 **DRINK** Now $ 13

Semillon Sauvignon Blanc 2005 Solid, flavoursome mix of herb, grass and mineral, largely from the semillon; slightly broader finish. McLaren Vale/Adelaide Hills. Screwcap. 13.5° alc. **RATING** 87 **DRINK** Now $ 15

Contour 4 Sangiovese Shiraz 2003 Typical light colour; gently fragrant and savoury, cedary flavours; fine tannins. Screwcap. 13.5° alc. **RATING** 87 **DRINK** 2008 $ 24

ŸŸŸŸ **Redstone 2003 RATING** 86 **DRINK** Now $ 18.50

Adelaide Hills Nebbiolo Rose 2005 RATING 85 **DRINK** Now $ 16

Cosham ★★★☆

101 Union Road, Carmel via Kalamunda, WA 6076 **REGION** Perth Hills
T (08) 9293 5424 **F** (08) 9293 5062 **WWW**.coshamwines.com.au **OPEN** W'ends & public hols 10–5
WINEMAKER Julie Smith (Contract) **EST.** 1989 **CASES** 1000
Has grown significantly from its small base in recent years. The vineyard is planted on an old orchard, and consists of 2 ha of cabernet sauvignon, merlot, shiraz, pinot noir, cabernet franc, chardonnay and petit verdot, established between 1990 and 1995. They grow in gravelly loam with some clay, but overall in a well-drained soil with good rainfall.

ŸŸŸŸ **Chardonnay 2004** Appealing stone fruit, melon and a touch of citrus supported by grainy minerally acidity. Screwcap. **RATING** 89 **DRINK** 2008 $ 18

Methode Champenoise Pinot Noir Brut 2003 Pale straw; pleasant strawberry and citrus on the mid-palate and finish; consistent show success is not surprising. 11.8° alc. **RATING** 88 **DRINK** 2008 $ 25

Cow Hill NR

PO Box 533, Beechworth, Vic 3747 **REGION** Beechworth
T 0411 249 704 **OPEN** Not
WINEMAKER Andrew Doyle **EST.** 2001 **CASES** NA
Andrew Doyle began the development of Cow Hill with the planting of 1.5 ha each of viognier and nebbiolo on very steep mudstone, slate and shale soils. Tempranillo and muscat, and possibly shiraz, are to follow, taking the plantings to a total of 10 ha. In the meantime, Doyle purchases grapes from others in the Beechworth region to produce his wines.

Cowra Estate NR

Boorowa Road, Cowra, NSW 2794 **REGION** Cowra
T (02) 9907 7735 **F** (02) 9907 7734 **OPEN** At The Quarry Restaurant Tues–Sun 10–4
WINEMAKER Ralph Fowler **EST.** 1973 **CASES** 6000
Cowra Estate was purchased from the family of founder Tony Gray by South African-born food and beverage entrepreneur John Geber in 1995. A vigorous promotional campaign has gained a higher domestic profile for the once export-oriented brand. John Geber is actively involved in the promotional effort and rightly proud of the wines. The Quarry Wine Cellars and Restaurant offer visitors a full range of Cowra Estate's wines, plus wines from other producers in the region. The Geber family, incidentally, also owns Chateau Tanunda in the Barossa Valley.

Crabtree Watervale Wines ★★★★

North Terrace, Watervale SA 5452 **REGION** Clare Valley
T (08) 8843 0069 **F** (08) 8843 0144 **WWW**.crabtreewines.com.au **OPEN** Mon–Sat 11–5
WINEMAKER Robert Crabtree **EST.** 1979 **CASES** 5000
Robert Crabtree and wife Elizabeth are the drivers of the business, making full-flavoured, classic Clare Valley styles with great success in some recent vintages. Exports to Canada and Malaysia.

ŸŸŸŸŸ **Riesling 2005** A solid wine with plenty of ripe fruit depth in a citrus spectrum; moderately long finish. Screwcap. 12.5° alc. **RATING** 90 **DRINK** 2009 $ 20

Picnic Hill Vineyard Shiraz 2003 Medium- to full-bodied; ripe plum and blackberry with a touch of chocolate; mouthfilling but not too hot or heavy. Screwcap. 14° alc. **RATING** 90 **DRINK** 2013 $ 20

Centinas Gaze Tempranillo 2005 A clean, fresh and bright array of cherry, raspberry and plum fruits; oak merely a handmaiden; delicious; 300 cases made. Screwcap. 13° alc. **RATING** 90 **DRINK** 2009 $ 20

ΨΨΨΨ **Robert Crabtree's Three Sixty Shiraz Cabernet 2004** Good colour; clean, fresh and lively; light- to medium-bodied, driven by a mix of red and black fruits. Screwcap. 14.5° alc. **RATING** 89 **DRINK** 2010 $ 17

ΨΨΨΨ **Bay of Biscay Rose 2005** Vivid fuchsia; vibrant red fruits with distinct but balanced sweetness. Screwcap. 12.5° alc. **RATING** 86 **DRINK** Now $ 20

Windmill Vineyard Cabernet Sauvignon 2002 Good colour; light- to medium-bodied with small, bright, berry fruits, albeit not a lot of structure. Screwcap. **RATING** 86 **DRINK** 2008 $ 20

Clare Valley Muscat NV **RATING** 86 **DRINK** Now $ 20

Zibibbo 2005 **RATING** 85 **DRINK** Now $ 20

Windmill Tawny NV **RATING** 85 **DRINK** Now $ 20

Craig Avon Vineyard NR

Craig Avon Lane, Merricks North, Vic 3926 **REGION** Mornington Peninsula
T (03) 5989 7465 **F** (03) 5989 7615 **OPEN** By appt
WINEMAKER Ken Lang **EST.** 1986 **CASES** 1000
The estate-grown wines are produced from 0.9 ha of chardonnay, 0.5 ha of pinot noir and 0.4 ha of cabernet sauvignon. They are competently made, clean, and with pleasant fruit flavour. All the wines are sold through the cellar door and by mailing list.

Craiglee ★★★★★

Sunbury Road, Sunbury, Vic 3429 **REGION** Sunbury
T (03) 9744 4489 **F** (03) 9744 4489 **WWW**.craiglee.com.au **OPEN** Sun, public hols 10–5, or by appt
WINEMAKER Patrick Carmody **EST.** 1976 **CASES** 3000
A winery with a proud 19th-century record which recommenced winemaking in 1976 after a prolonged hiatus. Produces one of the finest cool-climate Shirazes in Australia, redolent of cherry, licorice and spice in the better (warmer) vintages, lighter-bodied in the cooler ones. Mature vines and improved viticulture have made the wines more consistent (and even better) over the past 10 years or so. Exports to the UK, the US and NZ.

ΨΨΨΨΨ **Chardonnay 2005** Elegantly fashioned; melon and stone fruit, quality oak and nutty/creamy notes all intertwined; harmonious and balanced. Diam. 14.5° alc. **RATING** 94 **DRINK** 2012 $ 27

Shiraz 2005 Good colour; classic blackberry and plum fruit, crushed black pepper and licorice; immaculate balance and French oak inputs. Diam. 14.5° alc. **RATING** 94 **DRINK** 2020 $ 41

ΨΨΨΨΨ **Cabernet Sauvignon 2005** Archetypal cool-grown savoury, earthy nuances to the varietal expression; blackcurrant at the core, long and fine tannins to finish. Diam. 14.5° alc. **RATING** 92 **DRINK** 2015 $ 28

Craigow ★★★★★

528 Richmond Road, Cambridge, Tas 7170 **REGION** Southern Tasmania
T (03) 6248 5379 **WWW**.craigow.com.au **OPEN** 7 days Christmas to Easter (except public hols), or by appt
WINEMAKER Winemaking Tasmania (Julian Alcorso) **EST.** 1989 **CASES** 1500
Craigow has substantial vineyards, with 5 ha of pinot noir and another 5 ha (in total) of riesling, chardonnay and gewurztraminer. Barry and Cathy Edwards have moved from being grapegrowers with only one wine made for sale to a portfolio of 5 wines, while continuing to sell most of their

grapes. Craigow has an impressive museum release program; the best are outstanding, others show the impact of sporadic bottle oxidation. Exports to the UK.

YYYYY Botrytis Riesling 2004 Very powerful, intense and long; massive botrytis impact; long, lingering acidity; glorious overall flavour. Screwcap. **RATING** 95 **DRINK** 2010 $ 23.95
Pinot Noir 2000 Some colour development, but still remarkable hue; from a great Tasmanian vintage for pinot; spice, cherry and plum with some forest floor notes. Has time to go yet. **RATING** 94 **DRINK** 2010 $ 45

YYYYY Easy Pinot Noir 2004 Light- to medium-bodied, supple spicy fruits with good balance and length; ripe tannins. **RATING** 92 **DRINK** 2010 $ 18
Pinot Noir 2003 Amazing hue retention, still bright, light purple; a similarly fresh and vibrant palate with cherry/raspberry fruit; the tannins have subsided markedly; nonetheless intense and long. **RATING** 92 **DRINK** 2011 $ 28
Unwooded Chardonnay 2004 Potent, powerful wine driven by linear Tasmanian acidity running through grapefruit and nectarine flavours. Screwcap. 14° alc. **RATING** 91 **DRINK** 2013 $ 19
Chardonnay 2003 Glorious straw-green; has developed slowly but surely over the past 2 years; high natural acidity is the steely structure around which the wine has been built; very Chablis-like. **RATING** 91 **DRINK** 2012 $ 22.50
Sauvignon Blanc 2005 Citrussy overtones to a core of passionfruit and gooseberry; crisp, clean and tangy. **RATING** 90 **DRINK** Now $ 19

YYYY Riesling 2005 A lime sherbet tingle to the intense, tight and long palate. Unready as at Jan '06. Will evolve. **RATING** 89 **DRINK** 2010 $ 19

YYYY Gewurztraminer 2005 RATING 86 **DRINK** 2008 $ 22

Crane Winery ★★★☆

Haydens Road, Kingaroy, Qld 4610 **REGION** South Burnett
T (07) 4162 7647 **F** (07) 4162 8381 **WWW.**cranewines.com.au **OPEN** 7 days 10–4
WINEMAKER John Crane, Bernie Cooper **EST.** 1996 **CASES** 900
Founded by John and Sue Crane, has 8 ha of estate plantings but also purchases grapes from 20 other growers in the region. Sue Crane's great-grandfather established a vineyard planted to shiraz 100 years ago (in 1898) and which remained in production until 1970. The vineyard was sold to Bernard and Judy Cooper on condition that John Crane made the 2005-07 vintages.

YYYYY Late Harvest Frontignac NV Extremely rich and luscious Christmas cake/plum pudding/brandysnap flavours. A big fish in a tiny pond, with 4 Qld Wine Show trophies for Best Qld Fortified Wine. Cork. 17.8° alc. **RATING** 90 **DRINK** 2008 $ 20

YYYY Shiraz 2005 Clean, rich, sweet blackberry and plum fruit; has development potential. Twin top. 13.5° alc. **RATING** 88 **DRINK** 2009 $ 16

Craneford ★★★★★

Moorundie Street, Truro, SA 5356 **REGION** Barossa Valley
T (08) 8564 0003 **F** (08) 8564 0008 **WWW.**cranefordwines.com **OPEN** Mon–Fri 10–5
WINEMAKER John Zilm, Carol Riebcke **EST.** 1978 **CASES** 25 000
The purchase of Craneford by owner/winemaker John Zilm wrought many changes. It has moved to a new winery and is supported by contract-grown grapes, with the purchase price paid per ha, not per tonne, giving Craneford total control over yield and (hopefully) quality. Exports to all major markets.

YYYYY John Zilm Barossa Valley Shiraz 2004 Intense and elegant, with silky mouthfeel and great length; plum, spice, blackberry and even blackcurrant; seamless oak and tannins. Screwcap. 14° alc. **RATING** 95 **DRINK** 2019 $ 30
Allyson Parsons Barossa Valley Shiraz 2004 Dense red-purple; rich blackberry, blood plum, dark chocolate and spice; medium-bodied, moderate alcohol a pleasure; fine, ripe tannins. Screwcap. 14° alc. **RATING** 94 **DRINK** 2016 $ 16

TTTTT **John Zilm Barossa Valley Merlot 2004** Strong colour; medium- to full-bodied; generous cassis/plum fruit, supple and smooth, but alcohol takes away from the varietal profile. So may the addition of a little cabernet sauvignon and petit verdot. Screwcap. 15° alc. **RATING** 92 **DRINK** 2012 $ 35

John Zilm Barossa Valley Merlot 2002 The cool vintage is to the advantage of the variety; olive, blackcurrant and spice; long, fine palate and finish. Cork. 14.5° alc. **RATING** 92 **DRINK** 2012 $ 45

Barossa Valley Cabernet Sauvignon 2004 Extremely powerful, concentrated full-bodied wine; black fruits and dark chocolate, the tannins still very assertive; probably enough fruit to carry the tannins, but don't touch for 5, better still, 10 years. Screwcap. 14.5° alc. **RATING** 91 **DRINK** 2024 $ 25

Barossa Valley Grenache 2004 Super-ripe, ultra-juicy grenache floods the mouth with fruit. Screwcap. 15° alc. **RATING** 90 **DRINK** 2010 $ 23

Barossa Valley Petit Verdot 2002 Blackberry, prune and licorice in a sweet wrapping of chocolate and ripe tannins. A seemingly impossible variety to subvert in moderate climates. Cork. 14° alc. **RATING** 90 **DRINK** 2012 $ 45

TTTT **Adelaide Hills Viognier 2005** Abundant apricot and peach varietal flavour; medium-bodied, good balance and acidity. Screwcap. 14.5° alc. **RATING** 89 **DRINK** 2008 $ 15

Crawford River Wines   ★★★★★

741 Hotspur Upper Road, Condah, Vic 3303 **REGION** Henty
T (03) 5578 2267 **F** (03) 5578 2240 **WWW**.crawfordriverwines.com **OPEN** By appt
WINEMAKER John Thomson **EST.** 1975 **CASES** 5000
Time flies, and it seems incredible that Crawford River has celebrated its 30th birthday. Once a tiny outpost in a little-known wine region, Crawford River has now established itself as one of the foremost producers of Riesling (and other excellent wines) thanks to the unremitting attention to detail and skill of its founder and winemaker, John Thomson. Exports to the UK and Denmark.

TTTTT **Reserve Riesling 2005** Spotlessly clean; more immediately floral and aromatic than the varietal; distilled lime juice and passionfruit; great length, perfect acidity. Screwcap. 13.5° alc. **RATING** 96 **DRINK** 2018 $ 37

Reserve Riesling 2004 Delicate, yet intense, mineral, apple and citrus aromas; light as a feather, fine, long and crisp, with touches of passionfruit and citrus; 29-year-old vines. Screwcap. 12° alc. **RATING** 96 **DRINK** 2020 $ 39.50

Riesling 2005 Spotless; lime, herb, apple and spice; super-intense flavours and mouthfeel, veering slightly towards the tropical. Screwcap. 14° alc. **RATING** 94 **DRINK** 2015 $ 29

Sauvignon Blanc Semillon 2005 Light straw-green; immaculately balanced and constructed gooseberry and passionfruit; lemony/citrus acidity; long, clean finish. Screwcap. 13.5° alc. **RATING** 94 **DRINK** 2008 $ 23

TTTT **Cabernet Sauvignon 2003** Cedary, spicy, leafy, minty aromas and flavours; supple mouthfeel, fine tannins. Cork. 13° alc. **RATING** 88 **DRINK** 2011 $ 39

Creeks Edge Wines   NR

Creeks Edge Vineyard, Lue Road, Mudgee, NSW 2850 **REGION** Mudgee
T (02) 6372 6186 **F** (02) 6372 6182 **WWW**.creeksedge.com.au **OPEN** Thurs–Mon 9.30–5
WINEMAKER Simon Gilbert Wines, Andrew Harris Vineyards **EST.** 2003 **CASES** 5000
Creeks Edge Wines is a redevelopment of an old 43-ha vineyard purchased from Orlando Wyndham by a partnership of American and Australian wine enthusiasts. The oldest vines were planted in 1976, with follow-on plantings in 1988 and a final block of semillon in 1994. The red wines are brought to the onsite barrel store for maturation, with small quantities of super-premium Shiraz and Cabernet made onsite since the 2005 vintage.

Crisford Winery

NR

556 Hermitage Road, Pokolbin, NSW 2022 **REGION** Lower Hunter Valley
T (02) 9387 1100 **F** (02) 9387 6688 **OPEN** Not
WINEMAKER Steve Dodd **EST.** 1990 **CASES** 340
Carol and Neal Crisford have established 2.6 ha of merlot and cabernet franc which go to produce a single wine — Synergy. Neal Crisford produces educational videos on wine used in TAFE colleges and by the Australian Society of Wine Education. The wine is sold through the Hunter Valley Wine Society.

Crittenden at Dromana

★★★☆

25 Harrisons Road, Dromana, Vic 3936 **REGION** Mornington Peninsula
T (03) 5981 8322 **F** (03) 5981 8366 **WWW**.geppettowines.com.au **OPEN** Dec–Mar 7 days 11–4, Apr–Nov w'ends & public hols 11–4
WINEMAKER Garry Crittenden **EST.** 2003 **CASES** 6000
Like a phoenix from the ashes, Garry Crittenden has risen again, soon after his formal ties with Dromana Estate were severed (son Rollo remains chief winemaker at Dromana Estate). He took with him the Schinus range; has Sangiovese and Arneis due for progressive release under the Pinocchio label; and, under the premium Crittenden at Dromana label, wines made from the 22-year-old 5-ha vineyard surrounding the family house and cellar door. Exports to the UK, Malaysia and Singapore.

ᵞᵞᵞᵞᵞ **Pinocchio Arneis 2005** Bracingly fresh and crisp, but with real fruit presence; nashi pear and a drizzle of lemon juice; long finish. King Valley/Mornington Peninsula. Screwcap. 13.5° alc. **RATING** 90 **DRINK** Now $ 23

ᵞᵞᵞᵞ **Mornington Peninsula Sauvignon Blanc Semillon 2005** Clean; a quite robust style with plenty of mid-palate fruit, though slightly unfocused. Screwcap. 13.5° alc. **RATING** 88 **DRINK** Now $ 23
Mornington Peninsula Pinot Grigio 2005 Very typical Grigio; food-friendly texture and structure, but not much to say in varietal fruit terms (which comes as no surprise). Screwcap. 13.5° alc. **RATING** 88 **DRINK** Now $ 28
Mornington Peninsula Cabernet 2004 Spotlessly clean and clear blackcurrant and cassis run through a light- to medium-bodied palate with minimal tannins. The old argument about Mornington Peninsula and Cabernet goes on. Screwcap. 13.5° alc. **RATING** 88 **DRINK** 2011 $ 30
Geppetto Sauvignon Blanc Semillon 2005 A soft, tropical fruit entry moving through to a slightly talcy/stoney finish. The synergy works. Screwcap. 12.5° alc. **RATING** 87 **DRINK** Now $ 15

ᵞᵞᵞᵞ **Pinocchio Rosato 2005** Pale salmon; crisp, firm, drier food style; faintly spicy flavours run throughout. Screwcap. 13.5° alc. **RATING** 86 **DRINK** Now $ 19
Pinocchio Barbera 2004 RATING 86 **DRINK** Now $ 24
Pinocchio Dolcetto 2005 RATING 86 **DRINK** Now $ 20
Geppetto Merlot 2004 RATING 85 **DRINK** 2008 $ 15
Geppetto Sangiovese 2004 RATING 84 **DRINK** Now $ 19

Crooked River Wines

★★★

11 Willow Vale Road, Gerringong, NSW 2534 **REGION** Shoalhaven Coast
T (02) 4234 0975 **F** (02) 4234 4477 **WWW**.crookedriverwines.com **OPEN** 7 days 10.30–4.30
WINEMAKER Bevan Wilson **EST.** 1998 **CASES** 10 000
With 14 ha of vineyard planted to riesling, traminer, semillon, sauvignon blanc, chardonnay, verdelho, viognier, arneis, shiraz, cabernet sauvignon, sangiovese and chambourcin, Crooked River Wines has the largest vineyard on the south coast.

ᵞᵞᵞᵞ **Softly Wooded Chardonnay 2005** Softly wooded, and also softly fruited, with gentle stone fruit and citrus flavours. Screwcap. 12.3° alc. **RATING** 86 **DRINK** Now $ 22
Romance Rose 2005 Pale, bright fuchsia; a fresh bouquet, well-constructed for the cellar door, the low alcohol off-set by a touch of residual sugar. Screwcap. 10° alc. **RATING** 86 **DRINK** Now $ 22

Illawarra Flame 2004 RATING 85 DRINK Now $22
Premium Shiraz 2004 RATING 84 DRINK Now $22

▼▼▼ Romance Shiraz 2004 RATING 83 $22
Romance Cabernet Sauvignon 2004 RATING 83 $22

Crosswinds Vineyard ★★☆

10 Vineyard Drive, Tea Tree, Tas 7017 REGION Southern Tasmania
T (03) 6268 1091 F (03) 6268 1091 OPEN Mon–Fri 10–5
WINEMAKER Andrew Vasiljuk EST. 1990 CASES NA
Crosswinds is in a wind-down phase; Andrew Vasiljuk has decided to concentrate on grape-growing and consulting for others, but it will be some time before all of the Crosswinds stocks are sold.

▼▼▼▽ Vintage Sparkling 2001 RATING 85 DRINK Now $25

Cruickshank Callatoota Estate ★★★☆

2656 Wybong Road, Wybong, NSW 2333 REGION Upper Hunter Valley
T (02) 6547 8149 F (02) 6547 8144 WWW.cruickshank.com.au OPEN 7 days 9–5
WINEMAKER John Cruickshank, Laurie Nicholls EST. 1973 CASES 4000
Owned by Sydney management consultant John Cruickshank and family. An improvement in wine quality and style followed a period of consultancy with Andrew Thomas, although winemaking is now back in the hands of John Cruickshank and Laurie Nicholls. The Rose continues its good form, but it is with the younger Cabernet Franc and Cabernet Sauvignon wines that the greatest show success is being achieved (mainly in the Hunter Valley Boutique Winemakers Show).

▼▼▼▼▽ Shiraz 2003 Deep colour; solid black fruits; touches of regional leather and earth in the background; good balance and length. Gold medal Hunter Valley Wine Show '04.
RATING 91 DRINK 2012 $25

▼▼▼▼ Rose 2005 Bright, light red-purple; a crossover between rose and light dry red, fruit-sweet as much as sugar-sweet, and not so much of that. Plenty of red fruit flavours and good length. Cork. 13.5° alc. RATING 88 DRINK Now $12

▼▼▼▽ Cabernet Shiraz NV RATING 85 DRINK 2010

Cullen Wines ★★★★★

Caves Road, Cowaramup, WA 6284 REGION Margaret River
T (08) 9755 5277 F (08) 9755 5550 WWW.cullenwines.com.au OPEN 7 days 10–4
WINEMAKER Vanya Cullen, Trevor Kent EST. 1971 CASES 20 000
One of the pioneers of Margaret River which has always produced long-lived wines of highly individual style from the substantial and mature estate vineyards. Since the 2003 vintage, the vineyard has received 'A grade' certification from the Biological Farmers Association, and received the award as runner-up for best organic producer (all crops) with less than 5 years' certification. Winemaking is now in the hands of Vanya Cullen, daughter of the founders; she is possessed of an extraordinarily good palate. It is impossible to single out any particular wine from the top echelon; all three are superb. Exports to all major markets.

▼▼▼▼▼ Chardonnay 2003 A beautifully crafted, perfect marriage of barrel ferment inputs, fruit and controlled oak; rich but not heavy, developing very well. Screwcap. 14° alc. RATING 96 DRINK 2013 $58
Chardonnay 2004 The usual complexity, but here there is an extra degree of finesse thanks to the (relatively) low alcohol; cashew, fig and melon, with seamless oak and very good acidity; 70% barrel-fermented in new French oak; 70% malolactic fermentation. Screwcap. 14° alc. RATING 95 DRINK 2014 $55
Diana Madeline Cabernet Sauvignon Merlot 2004 Excellent hue and depth; a complex, medium- to full-bodied web of texture and flavour; perfectly balanced oak and tannins supporting blackcurrant fruit; long finish. Screwcap. 14° alc. RATING 95 DRINK 2019 $90

Sauvignon Blanc Semillon 2005 As always, a very complex wine, with layers of flavour, but ultimately driven by the gooseberry and herb fruit; very long finish. Screwcap. 14.5° alc. **RATING** 94 **DRINK** 2010 $ 35

Mangan Malbec Petit Verdot Merlot 2004 Medium-bodied, bright, highly expressive juicy red fruits of the malbec given structure by the petit verdot; fine tannins, delicious now or in 10 years. Screwcap. 14° alc. **RATING** 94 **DRINK** 2014 $ 43

ΨΨΨΨ **Ellen Bussell White 2005** Very attractive, entirely fruit-driven style, the fruit sweetness tinged by citrussy acidity. Long, clean finish; restaurant wine list special. Semillon/Sauvignon Blanc. Screwcap. 13.5° alc. **RATING** 90 **DRINK** 2009 $ 19

ΨΨΨΨ **Ellen Bussell Red 2004** A soft array of black and red fruits with splashes of spice and minimal tannins. Cabernet Franc/Merlot. Screwcap. 13.5° alc. **RATING** 89 **DRINK** 2008 $ 19

Cumulus Wines ★★★★

PO Box 41, Cudal, NSW 2864 **REGION** Orange
T (02) 6390 7900 **F** (02) 6364 2388 **WWW**.cumuluswines.com.au **OPEN** Not
WINEMAKER Philip Shaw, Nic Millichip **EST.** 1995 **CASES** 550 000
Cumulus Wines is the reborn Reynolds Wines, purchased by Assetinsure in 2003, with Philip Shaw, previously head of winemaking for Rosemount and Southcorp, as Chief Executive Officer. This is an asset-rich business, with over 500 ha of vineyards planted to all the mainstream varieties, the lion's share going to shiraz, cabernet sauvignon, chardonnay and merlot. The wines are released under 3 brands: Rolling, from the Central Ranges region; Climbing, solely from Orange fruit, and a third, yet to be named, super-premium from the best of the estate vineyard blocks. Exports to the UK and the US.

ΨΨΨΨ **Climbing Shiraz 2004** Attractive medium-bodied wine; fresh black cherry and plum fruit, plus touches of spice and licorice; well-controlled tannins and oak. Screwcap. 13.9° alc. **RATING** 91 **DRINK** 2012 $ 19

Rolling Sauvignon Blanc Semillon 2005 A clean though not especially fragrant bouquet; the wine creeps up on you on the palate, gaining power through to the finish and aftertaste. Very good value. Screwcap. 13.5° alc. **RATING** 90 **DRINK** Now $ 14

Climbing Chardonnay 2005 A reserved but complex wine; elegant, seamless creamy malolactic inputs along with controlled oak. Screwcap. 13.5° alc. **RATING** 90 **DRINK** 2009 $ 19

ΨΨΨΨ **Rolling Chardonnay 2005** Rich, traditional style with ripe peachy fruit and good oak; not the future for chardonnay style, but an honest wine. Screwcap. 13.5° alc. **RATING** 89 **DRINK** Now $ 14

Rolling Shiraz 2004 Light- to medium-bodied; bright, fresh spice/black cherry/ blackberry fruit; minimal oak. Screwcap. 13.5° alc. **RATING** 87 **DRINK** 2008 $ 14

Climbing Merlot 2004 Clean, fresh and elegant; light-bodied, needing more flesh on the bones. Screwcap. 14° alc. **RATING** 87 **DRINK** 2008 $ 19

Rolling Cabernet Merlot 2004 Light- to medium-bodied; a pretty wine with light red and black small berry fruits. Screwcap. 13.9° alc. **RATING** 87 **DRINK** 2008 $ 14

Climbing Cabernet Sauvignon 2004 Powerful, with distinctly savoury/briary edges to the black fruits; fractionally green tannins. Screwcap. 13.5° alc. **RATING** 87 **DRINK** 2009 $ 19

Curlewis Winery ★★★★★

55 Navarre Road, Curlewis, Vic 3222 **REGION** Geelong
T (03) 5250 4567 **F** (03) 5250 4567 **WWW**.curlewiswinery.com.au **OPEN** By appt
WINEMAKER Rainer Breit **EST.** 1998 **CASES** 2700
Rainer Breit and partner Wendy Oliver have achieved a great deal in a remarkably short period of time. In 1996 they purchased their property at Curlewis with 1.6 ha of what were then 11-year-old pinot noir vines. They set to and established an onsite winery; Rainer Breit, a self-taught winemaker, uses the full bag of pinot noir winemaking tricks: cold-soaking, hot-fermentation, post-ferment

maceration, part inoculated and partly wild yeast use, prolonged lees contact, and bottling the wine neither fined nor filtered. While Breit and Oliver are self-confessed 'pinotphiles', they have planted a little chardonnay and buy a little locally grown shiraz and chardonnay. Exports to Asia.

ŸŸŸŸŸ **Geelong Chardonnay 2004** If anything, even more complex than Bel Sel, and certainly has more intensity and weight, even though the alcohol is slightly lower. French oak absorbed, and acidity gives great length. Cork. 13° alc. RATING 95 DRINK 2012 $ 39

Bel Sel Chardonnay 2004 Bright yellow-green; complex aromas, flavours and texture; white peach, nectarine and hazelnut with perfectly integrated oak; glides across the tongue. Diam. 13.5° alc. RATING 94 DRINK 2011 $ 25

Reserve Geelong Pinot Noir 2003 Slightly brighter colour than the Bel Sel; distinctly more plum and cherry fruit, though still with nice spicy/foresty complexity; elegant, well-balanced and has a lovely finish. Diam. 13° alc. RATING 94 DRINK 2012 $ 75

ŸŸŸŸŸ **Bellarine Selection Pinot Noir 2004** Light colour showing obvious development; the wine follows on with savoury/foresty aromas and flavours; does have length. Diam. 13.5° alc. RATING 91 DRINK 2010 $ 25

Curly Flat ★★★★★

Collivers Road, Lancefield, Vic 3435 REGION Macedon Ranges
T (03) 5429 1956 F (03) 5429 2256 WWW.curlyflat.com OPEN Sun, or by appt
WINEMAKER Phillip Moraghan, Jillian Ryan EST. 1991 CASES 5000
Phillip and Jeni Moraghan began the development of Curly Flat in 1992, drawing in part upon Phillip's working experience in Switzerland in the late 1980s, and with a passing nod to Michael Leunig. With ceaseless help and guidance from the late Laurie Williams (and others) the Moraghans have painstakingly established 8.5 ha of pinot noir, 3.4 ha of chardonnay and 0.6 ha of pinot gris, and a multilevel, gravity-flow winery. The wines included in the 2006 Wine Companion swept all before them at the Macedon Wine Show '05, and justify the 5-star rating pending new releases. Exports to the UK.

ŸŸŸŸŸ **2004 Curly Flat Macedon Ranges Chardonnay** Good colour; a very complex, funky/savoury bouquet leads into a powerful palate, again complex, and driving through to a long, haunting finish. Screwcap. RATING 95 DRINK 2015 $ 35

ŸŸŸŸŸ **2004 Curly Flat Williams Crossing Pinot Noir** Bright red-purple; fresh and lively red cherry, strawberry and plum flavours; long, fruit-driven finish. Delicious. Screwcap. RATING 93 DRINK 2010 $ 20

Currans Family Wines NR

PO Box 271 SM, Mildura South, Vic 3501 REGION Murray Darling
T (03) 5025 7154 F (03) 5025 7154 WWW.curransfamilywines.com.au OPEN Not
WINEMAKER Olsen Wines (Glenn Olsen) EST. 1997 CASES 1500
The Currans' story is a familiar one. In 1997 Chris and Sue Curran planted 4 ha of shiraz for sale to large wineries, but after 2 years of production (2000 and 2001) their grapes were suddenly no longer required, notwithstanding the great vintage. The only solution was to find a winemaker who was in tune with their organic approach to viticulture; and duly retained Glenn Olsen. Their success has encouraged the Currans to plant an additional 0.25 ha of durif and 1 ha of viognier. Exports to the US.

Currency Creek Estate NR

Winery Road, Currency Creek, SA 5214 REGION Currency Creek
T (08) 8555 4069 F (08) 8555 4100 WWW.currencycreekwines.com.au OPEN 7 days 10–5
WINEMAKER John Loxton EST. 1969 CASES 9000
For over 35 years this relatively low-profile winery has produced some outstanding wood-matured whites and pleasant, soft reds selling at attractive prices. Exports to the US and Canada.

Cuttaway Hill Estate ★★★★

PO Box 2034, Bowral, NSW 2576 **REGION** Southern Highlands
T (02) 4871 1004 **F** (02) 4871 1005 **WWW**.cuttawayhillwines.com.au **OPEN** Not
WINEMAKER Monarch Winemaking Services (Jim Chatto, Mark Bourne) **EST.** 1998 **CASES** 10 000
Owned by the O'Neil family, Cuttaway Hill Estate is one of the largest vineyard properties in the
Southern Highlands, with a total of 38 ha on 3 vineyard sites. The original Cuttaway Hill vineyard at
Mittagong has 17 ha of chardonnay, merlot, cabernet sauvignon and shiraz. The Allambie vineyard of
6.9 ha, on the light sandy loam soils of Ninety Acre Hill, is planted to sauvignon blanc, pinot gris and
pinot noir. The third and newest vineyard is 14.2 ha at Maytree, west of Moss Vale in a relatively drier
and warmer meso-climate. Here cabernet sauvignon, merlot and pinot noir (and a small amount of
chardonnay) have been planted. The standard of both viticulture and contract winemaking is evident
in the quality of the wines, not to mention the growth in production and sales. Exports to the US,
Canada and Ireland.

ΥΥΥΥΫ **Southern Highlands Semillon Sauvignon Blanc 2005** A very clean and lively mix of
herb/grass, green pea, apple and ripe pear; pleasingly delicate finish and aftertaste.
Screwcap. **RATING** 91 **DRINK** 2008 $ 14.99
Southern Highlands Sauvignon Blanc 2005 Spotlessly clean and correct; tropical
gooseberry and passionfruit mix on a long, lingering palate. Screwcap. **RATING** 90
DRINK Now $ 14.99
Southern Highlands Pinot Gris 2005 Blush pink; high-toned, precise musk and pear
varietal aromas; lots of soft and fleshy mid-palate fruit; balanced acidity. Screwcap.
RATING 90 **DRINK** Now $ 19.99

ΥΥΥΥ **Southern Highlands Chardonnay 2004** Fragrant nectarine and white peach aromas;
subtle oak; the overall sweetness just within bounds. Screwcap. 12.5° alc. **RATING** 89
DRINK 2010 $ 14.99
Southern Highlands Merlot 2004 Clearcut varietal character throughout; light- to
medium-bodied; spicy, savoury, black olive, mulberry and blueberry; fine, soft tannins.
Screwcap. **RATING** 89 **DRINK** 2008 $ 14.99

ΥΥΥΫ **Southern Highlands Cabernet Sauvignon 2004** **RATING** 86 **DRINK** 2009 $ 14.99
Southern Highlands Rose 2005 **RATING** 84 **DRINK** Now $ 14.99

d'Arenberg ★★★★★

Osborn Road, McLaren Vale, SA 5171 **REGION** McLaren Vale
T (08) 8323 8206 **F** (08) 8323 8423 **WWW**.darenberg.com.au **OPEN** 7 days 10–5
WINEMAKER Chester Osborn, Phillip Dean **EST.** 1912 **CASES** 250 000
Originally a conservative, traditional business (albeit successful), d'Arenberg adopted a much higher
profile in the second half of the 1990s, with a cascade of volubly worded labels and the opening of a
spectacularly situated and high-quality restaurant, d'Arry's Verandah. Happily, wine quality has
more than kept pace with the label uplifts. The winery has over 100 ha of estate vineyards dating
back to the 1890s, 1920 and 1950s, and a Joseph's Coat of trendy new varieties planted in the 1990s.
Exports to all major markets.

ΥΥΥΥΥ **The Laughing Magpie Shiraz Viognier 2004** Deeply coloured; strong black fruit aromas
are lifted by the Viognier component; a rich tapestry of dense, dark fruits has swallowed
up the oak. Cork. 14.5° alc. **RATING** 95 **DRINK** 2014 $ 30
d'Arry's Original Shiraz Grenache 2003 Clear colour; a fragrant bouquet; bursts into life
on the medium-bodied palate with a glorious mix of spice, raspberry and blackberry fruit;
long finish. Outstanding for a difficult vintage. Cork. **RATING** 94 **DRINK** 2013 $ 19.95
The Ironstone Pressings Grenache Shiraz Mourvedre 2003 Sturdy red and black fruits,
chocolate and savoury tannins, all on a scale the Barossa doesn't deliver; seamlessly
integrated tannins and oak ex barrel ferment. Screwcap. 14.5° alc. **RATING** 94 **DRINK** 2015
$ 65
The Coppermine Road Cabernet Sauvignon 2003 No doubting the region; black
chocolate surrounds the blackcurrant fruit centre; good tannin and oak management.
Cork. 14.5° alc. **RATING** 94 **DRINK** 2012 $ 65

PPPPP **The Dead Arm Shiraz 2003** Deep colour; typically massively rich and concentrated; black fruits, chocolate, tannins and oak are all fighting each other for top spot. Hopefully, a truce will be declared in 5 or so years. Cork. 15° alc. **RATING** 93 **DRINK** 2018 $ 65

The Cadenzia Grenache Shiraz Mourvedre 2004 Good colour; substantial structure and texture; attractive spicy black fruits; persistent but fine tannins. Zork. **RATING** 93 **DRINK** 2009 $ 25

Twentyeight Road Mourvedre 2004 Very ripe, almost scented, fruit aromas; as befits the variety, a substantial palate, but the tannins are not too aggressive, the oak incidental. Cork. 14.5° alc. **RATING** 93 **DRINK** 2012 $ 35

The Galvo Garage 2003 Abundant blackcurrant/blackberry fruit; good texture and mouthfeel, the Adelaide Hills component a blessing; quite silky texture. Cabernet Sauvignon/Merlot/Petit Verdot/Cabernet Franc. Cork. 14.5° alc. **RATING** 92 **DRINK** 2013 $ 35

The Derelict Vineyard Grenache 2003 In inimitable McLaren Vale style, avoids the vapid/jammy notes found in many (not all) Barossa Valley Grenaches; however, the multifaceted red fruit flavours do border on the delicate. 14.5° alc. **RATING** 91 **DRINK** 2009 $ 30

The Lucky Lizard Chardonnay 2004 Complex, slightly funky barrel ferment aromas; rich, mouthfilling, ripe stone fruit, peach and citrus; big impact style. Cork. **RATING** 90 **DRINK** Now $ 25

The Noble Riesling 2002 Brassy gold; extremely intense and rich, with a huge botrytis impact; sugar on a stick, yet still ends up with 14° alcohol. Amazing. Cork. 14° alc. **RATING** 90 **DRINK** Now $ 25

The Noble Riesling 2001 Golden colour; an extremely intense and complex bouquet of crystallised ginger; less sweet on the palate than expected, but has character. Drink soon. Cork. **RATING** 90 **DRINK** Now $ 25

PPPP **The Last Ditch Viognier 2004** Abundant varietal character in an apricot, rose petal, musk spectrum; slightly high alcohol, but avoids phenolics. Well priced. Screwcap. **RATING** 89 **DRINK** Now $ 14.20

The Hermit Crab Viognier Marsanne 2004 Marsanne pulls back the opulence of the viognier to good effect; more obvious food style; plenty of flavour and length. Screwcap. **RATING** 89 **DRINK** Now $ 11.80

The Feral Fox Pinot Noir 2004 Light-bodied; bright, brisk, cherry, plum and spice; acid tweaked a little too much. Cork. 14.5° alc. **RATING** 89 **DRINK** 2008 $ 30

The High Trellis Cabernet Sauvignon 2003 A ripe mix of dark chocolate, blackcurrant and earth; overall sweet fruit. Cork. **RATING** 89 **DRINK** 2008 $ 19.95

Sticks & Stones 2003 A fragrant mix of spice, berry, leaf and mint; fine tannins; most excitement on the label. Tempranillo/Grenache/Souzao. Cork. 14.5° alc. **RATING** 89 **DRINK** 2010 $ 37

The Broken Fishplate Sauvignon Blanc 2005 Gently tropical, faintly smoky, bouquet; plenty of flavour in a soft style. Screwcap. **RATING** 88 **DRINK** Now $ 19.95

The Footbolt Old Vine Shiraz 2003 Medium red-purple; red and black fruits in a medium-bodied frame; pleasant flavours, but not much structure. Screwcap. **RATING** 88 **DRINK** 2009 $ 19.95

The Custodian Grenache 2004 Spicy, juicy, jammy berry varietal character on both bouquet and palate; tannins and oak in restraint. Cork. **RATING** 88 **DRINK** 2009 $ 19.95

The Olive Grove Chardonnay 2004 Bright yellow-green; solid commercial wine with plenty of peachy fruit; subtle oak influence. Screwcap. **RATING** 87 **DRINK** 2008 $ 11.80

PPPP **The Stump Jump Grenache Shiraz Mourvedre 2004** Offers rather more than most in this price range; light- to medium-bodied; sweet red fruits braced by a touch of tannins. Twin top. **RATING** 86 **DRINK** Now $ 8.50

Dal Zotto Estate

1944 Edi Road, Cheshunt, Vic 3678 **REGION** King Valley
T (03) 5729 8321 **F** (03) 5729 8490 **WWW**.dalzottoestatewines.com.au **OPEN** 7 days 11–5
WINEMAKER Otto Dal Zotto, Michael Dal Zotto **EST.** 1987 **CASES** 10 000
Dal Zotto remains primarily a contract grapegrower, with 48 ha of vineyards (predominantly chardonnay, cabernet sauvignon and merlot, with smaller plantings of riesling, pinot gris, shiraz,

sangiovese, barbera, marzemino and prosecco), however increasing amounts of impressive and always interesting wines are made. Exports to the UK, Canada, Hong Kong and China.

ΤΤΤΤΤ **King Valley Cabernet Sauvignon 2002** Good purple-red colour; spotlessly clean, with clear-cut varietal cabernet fruit; excellent structure, and particularly good tannins for the King Valley. Long finish. Gold medal Adelaide Wine Show. **RATING** 94 **DRINK** 2012 $ 19

ΤΤΤΤΨ **King Valley Riesling 2005** Passionfruit and apple blossom aromas; a lively, crisp palate with a touch of spritz; quite intense fruit and a long finish. Screwcap. 12.5° alc. **RATING** 92 **DRINK** 2010 $ 15

King Valley Cabernet Merlot 2002 Powerful though medium-bodied, driven by cabernet blackcurrant fruit; good texture and balance; way above average for the region. **RATING** 92 **DRINK** 2010 $ 19

King Valley Shiraz 2003 Bright red-purple; considerable power and structure, especially for the King Valley. Black fruits, bitter chocolate and savoury, but controlled, tannins. **RATING** 90 **DRINK** 2011 $ 29

King Valley Barbera 2003 A very attractive example; sweet berry fruit in a red spectrum; soft, fine tannins; good mouthfeel. Cork. 13.5° alc. **RATING** 90 **DRINK** 2010 $ 22

ΤΤΤΤ **King Valley Pinot Grigio 2005** Light blossom aromas; a cunningly balanced palate with just a touch of sweetness to add proportion and length. Screwcap. 13° alc. **RATING** 89 **DRINK** Now $ 19

King Valley Merlot 2002 Good colour; light- to medium-bodied; pure and elegant varietal expression; has considerable length, though not depth. Quality cork. **RATING** 89 **DRINK** 2009 $ 19

King Valley Arneis 2005 Water white; does have ripe apple and pear flavour augmented by a touch of residual sugar; good length, well-made. Screwcap. 13° alc. **RATING** 88 **DRINK** Now $ 19

King Valley Prosecco 2004 A clean, fresh, though essentially neutral bouquet; a faint lemony twist on the delightfully dry palate is the driver. Cork. **RATING** 87 **DRINK** Now $ 28

ΤΤΤΨ **King Valley Rosata 2005** **RATING** 86 **DRINK** Now $ 16

Dalfarras

NR

PO Box 123, Nagambie, Vic 3608 **REGION** Nagambie Lakes
T (03) 5794 2637 **F** (03) 5794 2360 **OPEN** Not
WINEMAKER Alister Purbrick, Alan George **EST.** 1991 **CASES** 15 000
The personal project of Alister Purbrick and artist wife Rosa (née Dalfarra), whose paintings adorn the labels of the wines. Alister, of course, is best known as winemaker at Tahbilk, the family winery and home, but this range of wines is intended to (in Alister's words) 'allow me to expand my winemaking horizons and mould wines in styles different from Tahbilk'. It now draws upon 23 ha of its own plantings in the Goulburn Valley. Its dedicated cellar door is the restaurant which forms part of the Tahbilk wetlands project.

Dalrymple

★★★★★

1337 Pipers Brook Road, Pipers Brook, Tas 7254 **REGION** Northern Tasmania
T (03) 6382 7222 **F** (03) 6382 7222 **WWW**.dalrymplevineyards.com.au **OPEN** 7 days 10–5
WINEMAKER Bertel Sundstrup **EST.** 1987 **CASES** 6000
A partnership between Jill Mitchell and her sister and brother-in-law, Anne and Bertel Sundstrup, inspired by father Bill Mitchell's establishment of the Tamarway Vineyard in the late 1960s. In 1991 Tamarway reverted to the Sundstrup and Mitchell families and it, too, will be producing wine in the future, probably under its own label but sold ex the Dalrymple cellar door. As production has grown (significantly), so has wine quality across the board, often led by its Sauvignon Blanc, and (more recently) Pinot Noir.

ΤΤΤΤΤ **Special Bin Reserve Pinot Noir 2005** Slightly lighter colour than the varietal; fragrant and scented; a glorious wine, long and intense, with oceans of varietal plum and black cherry fruit. Screwcap. **RATING** 96 **DRINK** 2014 $ 35

Pinot Noir 2005 Strong purple-red; rich, sumptuous plummy fruit, fleshy but in no way dead; excellent wine, but doesn't have the scintillating complexity of the Reserve. Screwcap. RATING 94 DRINK 2012 $25

TTTTY Chardonnay 2004 Medium-bodied; clean and fragrant mainstream nectarine flavours; good length, balance and acidity. RATING 92 DRINK 2012 $20
Unwooded Chardonnay 2005 Typical Tasmanian intensity; zesty grapefruit and nectarine backed by lingering acidity; ultimate seafood style, but will age well. Screwcap. RATING 90 DRINK 2008 $20

TTTT Sauvignon Blanc 2005 Clean and generous, with the tropical fruit of the vintage coming through. RATING 87 DRINK Now $25

TTTTY Special Bin Reserve Pinot Noir 2004 RATING 86 DRINK Now $35
Pinot Noir 2004 RATING 86 DRINK 2008 $25

Dalwhinnie ★★★★★

448 Taltarni Road, Moonambel, Vic 3478 REGION Pyrenees
T (03) 5467 2388 F (03) 5467 2237 WWW.dalwhinnie.com.au OPEN 7 days 10–5
WINEMAKER David Jones, Gary Baldwin (Consultant) EST. 1976 CASES 4500
David and Jenny Jones are making wines with tremendous depth of fruit flavour, reflecting the relatively low-yielding but very well-maintained vineyards. It is hard to say whether the Chardonnay, the Cabernet Sauvignon or the Shiraz is the more distinguished. A further 8 ha of shiraz (with a little viognier) were planted in the spring of 1999 on a newly acquired block on Taltarni Road. A 50-tonne contemporary high-tech winery now allows the Eagle Series Shiraz and Pinot Noir to be made onsite. Exports to the UK, Sweden, Switzerland, the US, Canada, NZ and Hong Kong.

TTTTT Moonambel Cabernet Sauvignon 2004 A delicious medium- to full-bodied, but silky smooth and supple, palate. Blackcurrant and cassis, high-quality oak, and fine, ripe tannins. Cork. 13.4° alc. RATING 95 DRINK 2019 $44
Moonambel Chardonnay 2003 An elegant, fine wine; stone fruit, subtle oak, and lingering, citrussy acidity seamlessly interwoven; good length. RATING 94 DRINK 2009 $34
Moonambel Shiraz 2004 Excellent bright colour; intense and powerful blackberry and plum fruit; long, lingering finish; subtle oak. Cork. 13.8° alc. RATING 94 DRINK 2015 $48
Southwest Rocks Shiraz 2003 Good colour; very full-bodied, ultra-concentrated and powerful; black fruits and tannins in hyper abundance. A 20-year drought-driven special. Cork. 13.8° alc. RATING 94 DRINK 2025 $52
Eagle Series Pyrenees Shiraz 2003 Splashes of spice run through the bouquet and full-bodied palate; concentrated black fruits, oak, and ripe Italianate tannins. Cork. 14.5° alc. RATING 94 DRINK 2020 $148

TTTT Pinot Noir 2004 Spicy, plummy varietal character, with a strong lemony/minty overlay, the acid high. The alcohol explains everything. Cork. 11.6° alc. RATING 87 DRINK Now $38

Dalyup River Estate NR

Murrays Road, Esperance, WA 6450 REGION West Australian South East Coastal Zone
T (08) 9076 5027 F (08) 9076 5027 OPEN W'ends 10–4 Oct–May
WINEMAKER Tom Murray EST. 1987 CASES 1000
Arguably the most remote winery in Australia, drawing upon 2.5 ha of estate vineyards. The quantities are as small as the cellar door prices are modest; this apart, the light but fragrant wines show the cool climate of this ocean-side vineyard. Came from out of the clouds to win the trophy for Best Wine of Show at the West Australian Show in 1999 with its Shiraz, but hasn't repeated that success.

Danbury Estate NR

Billimari, NSW 2794 (PO Box 605, Cowra, NSW 2794) REGION Cowra
T (02) 6341 2204 F (02) 6341 4690 OPEN Tues–Sun 10–4
WINEMAKER Hope Estate EST. 1996 CASES 6000
A specialist Chardonnay producer established by Jonathon Middleton, with 22 ha in production. The Quarry Restaurant at the winery is open Tues–Sun 10–4.

Dargo Valley Winery

NR

Lower Dargo Road, Dargo, Vic 3682 **REGION** Gippsland
T (03) 5140 1228 **F** (03) 5140 1388 **OPEN** Mon–Thurs 12–8, w'ends, hols 10–8
WINEMAKER Hermann Bila **EST.** 1985 **CASES** 1000
The winery's 2.5 ha are situated in mountain country north of Maffra looking towards the Bogong National Park. Hermann Bila comes from a family of European winemakers; the white wines tend to be rustic, the sappy/earthy/cherry Pinot Noir the pick of the red wines. There is a restaurant which serves Devonshire teas and ploughman's lunches — very useful given the remote locality. B&B accommodation is available.

Darling Estate

NR

Whitfield Road, Cheshunt, Vic 3678 **REGION** King Valley
T (03) 5729 8396 **F** (03) 5729 8396 **OPEN** By appt
WINEMAKER Guy Darling **EST.** 1990 **CASES** 500
Guy Darling was one of the pioneers of the King Valley when he planted his first vines in 1970. For many years the entire production was purchased by Brown Brothers for their well-known Koombahla Estate label. Much of the production from the 23 ha is still sold to Brown Brothers (and others), but since 1991 Guy Darling has made a small portion of the production into wine at the onsite winery — which was, in fact, his original aim. All wines on sale have considerable bottle age.

Darling Park

232 Red Hill Road, Red Hill, Vic 3937 **REGION** Mornington Peninsula
T (03) 5989 2324 **F** (03) 5989 2324 **WWW**.darlingparkwinery.com **OPEN** January 7 days 11–5, every weekend 11–5
WINEMAKER Judy Gifford **EST.** 1986 **CASES** 2500
Josh and Karen Liberman and David Coe purchased Darling Park before the 2002 vintage and the product range has been revamped to an impressive effect.

YYYYY **Reserve Mornington Peninsula Chardonnay 2004** Light- to medium-bodied; a very stylish wine of considerable length, built around nectarine and a touch of grapefruit. Whole bunch-pressed, wild ferment, lees contact. Screwcap. 13.5° alc. **RATING** 94 **DRINK** 2011 $ 24
Mornington Peninsula Syrah 2004 Great colour; spicy, peppery red fruit aromas; surprising power, extract and length, and will continue to develop. Screwcap. 13.9° alc. **RATING** 94 **DRINK** 2015 $ 28

YYYY **Mornington Peninsula Griognier 2005** Improbable, but the pinot gris certainly gives the viognier with which it is blended a bite; attractive apricot, musk, honeysuckle flavours. Off-putting name. Screwcap. 14° alc. **RATING** 88 **DRINK** 2009 $ 24

Darlington Estate

NR

Lot 39 Nelson Road, Darlington, WA 6070 **REGION** Perth Hills
T (08) 9299 6268 **F** (08) 9299 7107 **WWW**.darlingtonestate.com.au **OPEN** Thurs–Sun & hols 12–5
WINEMAKER Caspar van der Meer **EST.** 1983 **CASES** 3000
Established by the van der Meer family, it is one of the oldest wineries in the Perth Hills (once the largest), for a while setting the standard. After an intermission, Caspar van der Meer has returned to the winemaking role.

Darlington Vineyard

NR

Holkam Court, Orford, Tas 7190 **REGION** Southern Tasmania
T (03) 6257 1630 **F** (03) 6257 1630 **OPEN** Thurs–Mon 10–5
WINEMAKER Hood Wines (Andrew Hood) **EST.** 1993 **CASES** 600
Peter and Margaret Hyland planted a little under 2 ha of vineyard in 1993. The first wines were made from the 1999 vintage, forcing retired builder Peter Hyland to complete their home so that the small building in which they had been living could be converted into a cellar door. The vineyard looks out

over the settlement of Darlington on Maria Island, the site of Diego Bernacci's attempt to establish a vineyard and lure investors by attaching artificial bunches of grapes to his vines.

Date Brothers Wines ★★★☆

PO Box 1599, Swan Hill, Vic 3585 **REGION** Swan Hill
T (03) 5033 2325 **F** (03) 5033 2325 **www**.datebroswines.com.au **OPEN** Not
WINEMAKER Travis Bush (Contract) **EST.** 1997 **CASES** 1500
The brothers in question are Roy, Barry and Tony Date, who, with sister Kerry, run the 42-ha vineyard. They had a background in dryland cereal farming, and in their words 'decided to have a go' at the grape industry, which in turn led them into winemaking. There are 12 ha of shiraz, and 10 ha each of chardonnay, cabernet sauvignon and durif; part of the grape production is made for the Date Brothers Wines labels, the remainder sold. So far, sales have been within the local community, complemented by exports of Shiraz and Durif to Japan.

ⵖⵖⵖⵖ **Tony Date Shiraz Cabernet 2003** Bright red-purple; an attractive mix of sweet red and black fruits; fine tannins, controlled oak. Twin top. 14.5° alc. **RATING** 89 **DRINK** 2012 $ 14
Roy Date Durif 2003 Full red-purple; a relatively controlled version of the variety, with abundant black fruits. Twin top. 14.5° alc. **RATING** 88 **DRINK** 2011 $ 14

ⵖⵖⵖⵔ **Swan Hill Chardonnay 2004** Plenty of peachy fruit; oak evident, but balanced. Twin top. 13.5° alc. **RATING** 86 **DRINK** Now $ 14
Barry Date Shiraz 2003 Good colour for the vintage; an extra degree of depth and structure for the region, albeit at the cost of some slightly extractive characters. Twin top. 14.5° alc. **RATING** 86 **DRINK** 2009 $ 14

David Hook Wines ★★★★

Pothana Lane, Belford, NSW 2335 **REGION** Lower Hunter Valley
T (02) 4998 7121 **www**.davidhookwines.com.au **OPEN** 7 days 10–5
WINEMAKER David Hook **EST.** 1984 **CASES** 5000
David Hook has over 20 years' experience, as a winemaker for Tyrrell's and Lake's Folly, also doing the full Flying Winemaker bit, with jobs in Bordeaux, the Rhône Valley, Spain, the US and Georgia. He and his family began establishing the vineyard in 1984, the winery in 1990. In 2004 they moved the winery home to the former Peppers Creek Winery.

ⵖⵖⵖⵖⵔ **The Gorge Hunter Valley Shiraz 2003** Quite fragrant; marvelously rich and textured; abundant black fruits and ripe tannins. What a great Hunter vintage. Screwcap. 13.5° alc. **RATING** 93 **DRINK** 2013 $ 15

ⵖⵖⵖⵔ **The Gorge Hunter Valley Verdelho 2005** **RATING** 86 **DRINK** 2008 $ 14.40

David Traeger Wines

139 High Street, Nagambie, Vic 3608 **REGION** Nagambie Lakes
T (03) 5794 2514 **F** (03) 5794 1776 **www**.dromanaestate.com.au **OPEN** Mon–Fri 10–5, w'ends & public hols 12–5
WINEMAKER David Traeger **EST.** 1986 **CASES** 10 000
David Traeger learned much during his years as assistant winemaker at Mitchelton and knows Central Victoria well. The red wines are solidly crafted, the Verdelho interesting and surprisingly long-lived. In late 2002 the business was acquired by the Dromana Estate group, but David Traeger has stayed on as winemaker. See also Baptista entry. Exports to the UK, Japan, Italy and Canada.

Dawson Estate NR

Cnr Old Naracoorte Road/Kangaroo Hill Road, Robe, SA 5276 **REGION** Mount Benson
T (08) 8768 2427 **F** (08) 8768 2987 **OPEN** Not
WINEMAKER Derek Hooper (Contract) **EST.** 1998 **CASES** 500
Anthony Paul and Marian Dawson are busy people. In addition to establishing over 20 ha of chardonnay, pinot noir, shiraz and cabernet sauvignon, they are in the process of opening a wine bar/restaurant in Robe, and intend to continue extending the vineyard on a further 16 ha of plantable land. All of this is largely financed by the crayfishing boat which Anthony runs in the crayfish season.

Dawson's Patch

NR

71 Kallista-Emerald Road, The Patch, Vic 3792 (postal) **REGION** Yarra Valley
T 0419 521 080 **OPEN** Not
WINEMAKER Paul Evans (Contract) **EST.** 2000 **CASES** 500
In 1996 James and Jody Dawson planted 1.2 ha of chardonnay on their vineyard at the southern end of the Yarra Valley. The climate here is particularly cool, and the grapes do not normally ripen until late April. Jody Dawson manages the vineyards, and has completed a degree in viticulture through Charles Sturt University. The tiny production is sold through local restaurants and cellars in the Olinda/Emerald/Belgrave area. So far only a barrel-fermented (French oak) wine has been produced, but it may be that an unoaked version will join the roster sometime in the future.

De Bortoli

★★★★☆

De Bortoli Road, Bilbul, NSW 2680 **REGION** Riverina
T (02) 6966 0100 **F** (02) 6966 0199 **WWW**.debortoli.com.au **OPEN** Mon–Sat 9–5, Sun 9–4
WINEMAKER Julie Mortlock, John Coughlan, Frank Cotroneo, Sam Brewer **EST.** 1928 **CASES** 3 million
Famous among the cognoscenti for its superb Botrytis Semillon, which in fact accounts for only a minute part of its total production, this winery turns around low-priced varietal and generic wines which are invariably competently made and equally invariably provide value for money. These come in part from 250 ha of estate vineyards, but mostly from contract-grown grapes. The death of founder Deen De Bortoli in 2003 was widely mourned by the wine industry. Exports to all major markets.

ᵀᵀᵀᵀᵀ **Noble One 2004** Green-gold; intense citrus, cumquat, honey and peach on a long, lingering palate; perfect acidity. Screwcap. **RATING** 95 **DRINK** 2010 $25
Noble One 2003 Deliciously intense; perfect fruit, sugar and acid balance to cumquat, lime and lemon rind and peach fruit; interesting alcohol level. Cork. 10.5° alc. **RATING** 94 **DRINK** 2009 $29

ᵀᵀᵀᵀᵀ **Deen Vat 8 Shiraz 2004** Punches way above its price weight; plenty of black fruits and supporting oak; good structure. Quality cork. **RATING** 90 **DRINK** 2008 $10
Sero King Valley Syrah Tempranillo 2005 Sumptuous and rich, moving towards Amarone style; luscious red fruits give the impression of higher alcohol; both varieties had a percentage of dried fruit à la Amarone. Screwcap. 14.5° alc. **RATING** 90 **DRINK** 2013 $14

ᵀᵀᵀᵀ **Sero King Valley Chardonnay Pinot Grigio 2005** The blend works surprisingly well, even if the fruit characters are slightly anonymous; elegant and balanced, with good mouthfeel. Screwcap. 13.5° alc. **RATING** 88 **DRINK** Now $14
Deen De Bortoli Vat 9 Cabernet Sauvignon 2004 Has well above-average fruit structure and varietal character in its price category; good tannins, and a touch of oak. Great value. Cork. 13.5° alc. **RATING** 88 **DRINK** 2012 $10
Deen De Bortoli Vat 1 Durif 2003 Good colour; spiced plums and blackberry; good depth of sweet, but not jammy, fruit; a well-controlled hint of sweetness on the finish. Cork. 13.5° alc. **RATING** 88 **DRINK** Now $10
Deen Vat 2 Sauvignon Blanc 2005 Spotless; impressive gooseberry aromas, though much less intense on the palate; a faint touch of residual sugar. Screwcap. **RATING** 87 **DRINK** Now $10
Sacred Hill Semillon Chardonnay 2005 A well-balanced mix of peach and more tangy/citrussy fruit; has length; near-invisible oak. Twin top. **RATING** 87 **DRINK** Now $6
Sacred Hill Colombard Chardonnay 2005 Fresh, clean citrus and apple aromas; clean and fresh palate; a touch of stone fruit; good balance reflecting the synergistic blend. Screwcap. **RATING** 87 **DRINK** Now $6
Sacred Hill Cabernet Merlot 2005 Attractive, sweet juicy berry fruit has mouthfeel and an airbrush of oak. Twin top. **RATING** 87 **DRINK** Now $6
Sero King Valley Merlot Sangiovese 2005 Sweet cherry aromas and entry to the mouth; the texture and structure then wobble around somewhat. A percentage of the merlot was partially dried. Screwcap. 14.5° alc. **RATING** 87 **DRINK** Now $14

ŸŸŸŸ   **Sacred Hill Traminer Riesling 2005** Intense, spicy lychee; full-on sweetness, with masses of flavour; made to a successful formula. Screwcap. 11.5° alc. **RATING** 86 **DRINK** Now $6
Wild Vine Shiraz 2004 RATING 86 **DRINK** Now $9
Sacred Hill Shiraz Cabernet 2005 Attractive, light-bodied, fresh red fruits; not much structure, but not to be expected at this price; dry finish, great value. Cork. 13.5° alc. **RATING** 86 **DRINK** Now $6
Deen Vat 4 Petit Verdot 2003 RATING 86 **DRINK** Now $10
Deen De Bortoli Vat 1 Durif 2004 Very good colour; a powerful framework though not so much vinosity; some dark berry fruit flavours. Cork. 13.5° alc. **RATING** 86 **DRINK** 2009 $10
Deen Vat 3 Semillon 2002 RATING 84 **DRINK** Now $10
Montage Semillon Sauvignon Blanc 2005 RATING 84 **DRINK** Now $9
Deen De Bortoli Vat 9 Cabernet Sauvignon 2003 RATING 84 **DRINK** Now $11

ŸŸŸ   **Sacred Hill Rhine Riesling 2005 RATING** 83 $6
Wild Vine Chardonnay 2005 RATING 83 $7.50
Deen Vat 6 Verdelho 2005 RATING 83 **DRINK** Now $10
Sacred Hill Rose 2004 RATING 83 $6.50

De Bortoli (Hunter Valley) ★★★★

532 Wine Country Drive, Pokolbin, NSW 2320 **REGION** Lower Hunter Valley
T (02) 4993 8800 **F** (02) 4993 8899 **WWW**.debortoli.com.au **OPEN** 7 days 10–5
WINEMAKER Stephen Webber, Scott Harrington **EST.** 2002 **CASES** 35 000
De Bortoli extended its wine empire in 2002 with the purchase of the former Wilderness Estate, giving it an immediate and substantial presence in the Hunter Valley courtesy of the 26 ha of established vineyards; this was expanded significantly by the subsequent purchase of an adjoining 40-ha property.

ŸŸŸŸŸ   **Hunter Valley Semillon 2004** Youthful, tight, crisp, fine and long; its whole life in front of it. Gold medal Sydney Wine Show '06. **RATING** 94 **DRINK** 2014 $18

ŸŸŸŸŸ   **Wills Hill Shiraz 2003** Bright purple-red; another dimension of power, yet not at all over the top. Medium- to full-bodied palate, concentrated and powerful, with balanced tannins. Cork. **RATING** 93 **DRINK** 2018 $35
Hunter Valley Chardonnay 2004 A nice touch of slightly funky barrel ferment aromas; the palate has length and focus to the melon and stone fruit flavours; clean finish. Screwcap. 13.5° alc. **RATING** 92 **DRINK** 2009 $17

ŸŸŸŸ   **Hunter Valley Shiraz 2004** Reflects a low-yielding vintage; firm, medium-bodied black fruits with positive, ripe tannins; could develop well. Screwcap. 14° alc. **RATING** 89 **DRINK** 2012 $18
Hunter Valley Merlot 2004 At an unforced level is thoroughly enjoyable; small, gently sweet, red fruits; balanced tannins and acidity. Screwcap. 14° alc. **RATING** 87 **DRINK** 2008 $18

De Bortoli (Victoria) ★★★★★

Pinnacle Lane, Dixons Creek, Vic 3775 **REGION** Yarra Valley
T (03) 5965 2271 **F** (03) 5965 2464 **WWW**.debortoli.com.au **OPEN** 7 days 10–5
WINEMAKER Stephen Webber, David Slingsby-Smith, Paul Bridgeman, Bill Downie, Sarah Fagan
EST. 1987 **CASES** 400 000
The quality arm of the bustling De Bortoli group, run by Leanne De Bortoli and husband Stephen Webber, ex-Lindeman winemaker. The top label (De Bortoli), the second (Gulf Station) and the third label (Windy Peak) offer wines of consistently good quality and excellent value — the complex Chardonnay and the Pinot Noirs are usually of outstanding quality. The volume of production, by many times the largest in the Yarra Valley, simply underlines the quality/value for money ratio of the wines. Exports to all major markets.

ŸŸŸŸŸ   **Reserve Yarra Valley Pinot Noir 2004** Bright purple-red; exceptional mouthfeel, structure and complexity; silky plum fruit with hints of spice, great line and length. I cannot begin to understand the choice of closure. Cork. **RATING** 96 **DRINK** 2010 $40

Reserve Yarra Valley Syrah 2004 A beautifully made wine with absolutely perfect balance, structure and style; silky smooth and long black fruits, with splashes of spice. Cork. 14° alc. **RATING** 96 **DRINK** 2012 $40

Reserve Yarra Valley Chardonnay 2004 A deliberately complex wine, with lots of funky, Burgundian barrel ferment, lees and wild yeast characters; the fruit sustains the winemaker inputs very well; rich and profound. Gold medal Sydney Wine Show '06. Screwcap. 13° alc. **RATING** 95 **DRINK** 2013 $40

Estate Yarra Valley Shiraz Viognier 2004 Vivid purple-red; floods the mouth with red fruit and balanced flavours, but is elegant and medium-bodied thanks to the restrained alcohol; great texture, structure and harmony. Cork. 13.5° alc. **RATING** 95 **DRINK** 2014 $27

Gulf Station Sauvignon Blanc Semillon 2005 Delicate but intense; very fine and very long palate; graceful and compelling. Screwcap. **RATING** 94 **DRINK** Now $16

Estate Yarra Valley Chardonnay 2004 Still incredibly tight and youthful; a long palate with finesse and elegance; everything is in balance, simply needing time. Screwcap. 13° alc. **RATING** 94 **DRINK** 2014 $31.50

Estate Yarra Valley Pinot Noir 2004 Purple-red; complex, spicy, black cherry and plum fruit; very good balance and length; obvious development potential. Screwcap. **RATING** 94 **DRINK** 2011 $27

ϓϓϓϓϔ **Gulf Station Chardonnay 2004** A nice touch of funky barrel ferment inputs making it more expressive than the Estate early in its life; melon and grapefruit flavour; classy. Screwcap. 13° alc. **RATING** 93 **DRINK** 2009 $20

Estate Yarra Valley Pinot Noir 2003 Elegant, light- to medium-bodied style with fine, silky mouthfeel; savoury forest floor with spicy red fruits; good length and aftertaste. Cork. **RATING** 93 **DRINK** 2008 $30

Windy Peak Cabernet Shiraz Merlot 2003 Outstanding colour and clarity; light- to medium-bodied, sweet berry fruit; a long, lingering, supple palate; really is amazing. Components barrel-fermented in new and used barriques. What a bargain. Screwcap. 13.5° alc. **RATING** 92 **DRINK** 2009 $14

Gulf Station Pinot Noir 2005 Bright red-purple; well-balanced and structured medium-bodied wine, with supple black cherry and spice fruit; good balance and length. Screwcap. 13° alc. **RATING** 91 **DRINK** 2010 $18

Windy Peak King Valley Sangiovese 2005 Great purple-red colour, freakish for sangiovese; light- to medium-bodied, with clear-cut varietal cherry fruit; very fresh and long; good tannin balance. Pre-fermentation cold soak; a killer at this price. Screwcap. 14° alc. **RATING** 91 **DRINK** 2009 $14

Windy Peak Riesling 2005 Quality way above its price; lots of lime juice, and a no doubt deliberate tweak of sweetness on the finish; Chinese food special. King Valley/Yarra Valley. Screwcap. 12.5° alc. **RATING** 90 **DRINK** 2008 $14

ϓϓϓϓ **Gulf Station Riesling 2005** Floral apple blossom fruit; delicate balance is the crux, rather than intensity. Screwcap. 12.5° alc. **RATING** 89 **DRINK** 2008 $20

Windy Peak Pinot Grigio 2005 A seriously nice grigio, with unusually lively citrussy notes cutting through the oily flabbiness of many pinot gris; crisp and clean, good texture. Warm-fermented, lees contact. Screwcap. 13.5° alc. **RATING** 89 **DRINK** Now $14

Yarra Valley Cabernet Sauvignon 2003 Not star-bright; savoury, earthy edges to firm blackcurrant fruit; off the pace for this wine. Screwcap. **RATING** 89 **DRINK** 2011 $27

Windy Peak Sauvignon Blanc Semillon 2005 Clean, fresh and lively; light-bodied but lingering passionfruit and lemon; good balance. Screwcap. 12° alc. **RATING** 88 **DRINK** Now $14.99

Gulf Station Pinot Noir Rose 2005 Salmon colour; full-on into European style with dusty, spicy notes and a dry, fractionally grippy, finish. Screwcap. 13° alc. **RATING** 88 **DRINK** Now $16

Windy Peak Pinot Noir 2004 Light- to medium-bodied; stylish spicy, sappy style showing complex winemaking techniques; fine savoury tannins; not rich, but long. Yarra Valley/Geelong/Mornington Peninsula. Great value. Screwcap. **RATING** 88 **DRINK** Now $15

Windy Peak King Valley Sangiovese 2004 Good structure and mouthfeel; spice, black cherry, rose petal and cedar nuances; a fine web of tannins. Cork. **RATING** 88 **DRINK** Now $15

Windy Peak Chardonnay 2005 Light-bodied; pleasant nectarine and citrus fruit with an airbrush of oak; good balance. Screwcap. 13° alc. **RATING** 87 **DRINK** Now $ 14
Windy Peak Spaetlese Riesling 2005 Gentle lime/tropical fruit; balanced sweetness; could surprise with bottle age. Screwcap. 12° alc. **RATING** 87 **DRINK** 2010 $ 15

De Iuliis ★★★★☆

21 Broke Road, Pokolbin, NSW 2320 **REGION** Lower Hunter Valley
T (02) 4993 8000 **F** (02) 4998 7168 **WWW**.dewine.com.au **OPEN** 7 days 10–5
WINEMAKER Michael De Iuliis **EST.** 1990 **CASES** 10 000
Three generations of the De Iuliis family have been involved in the establishment of their 45-ha vineyard. The family acquired the property in 1986 and planted the first vines in 1990, selling the grapes from the first few vintages to Tyrrell's but retaining increasing amounts for release under the De Iuliis label. Winemaker Michael De Iuliis has completed postgraduate studies in oenology at the Roseworthy Campus of Adelaide University and was a Len Evans Tutorial scholar.

▼▼▼▼▼ **Semillon 2005** Medium- to full yellow-green, bright and clear; a powerful, wine with gently ripened lemon/lime fruit; excellent acidity and length. Perverse use of Zork. **RATING** 94 **DRINK** 2015 $ 14

▼▼▼▼▽ **Show Reserve Hunter Valley Shiraz 2004** Deep colour; generous blackberry and plum fruit with notes of spice and earth; controlled tannins. Screwcap. 13.5° alc. **RATING** 93 **DRINK** 2015 $ 20
Limited Release Hunter Valley Chardonnay 2005 Controlled complexity and integration of barrel ferment French oak with very ripe peach fruit. Impressive at the price. Screwcap. 13.9° alc. **RATING** 91 **DRINK** 2010 $ 20
Aged Release Hunter Valley Semillon 1999 Glowing yellow-green; abundant flavour, but reigned in around a core of acidity; good length and balance; ready right now. Well priced. Cork. 11° alc. **RATING** 90 **DRINK** 2009 $ 20

▼▼▼▽ **Show Reserve Hunter Valley Verdelho 2005** **RATING** 86 **DRINK** Now $ 16
Verdelho 2005 **RATING** 85 **DRINK** 2008 $ 16

Dead Horse Hill ★★★★★

Myola East Road, Toolleen, Vic 3551 **REGION** Heathcote
T (03) 5433 6214 **F** (03) 5433 6214 **OPEN** By appt
WINEMAKER Jencie McRobert **EST.** 1994 **CASES** 500
Jencie McRobert (and husband Russell) 'did a deal with Dad' for approximately 65 ha of her parents' large sheep and wheat farm at Toolleen, 20 km north of Heathcote. It took a number of years for the 4-ha dry-grown shiraz vines to achieve reasonable yields, but they are now yielding between 3.7 and 5 tonnes per ha of high-quality fruit. Jencie's introduction to wine came partly through the family dining table and partly from meeting Steve Webber, then working for Lindemans at Karadoc, when she was working in soil conservation and salinity management in the Mallee. She subsequently completed a course at Charles Sturt University, and makes the wine at De Bortoli in the Yarra Valley with the odd bit of assistance from Webber.

▼▼▼▼▼ **Heathcote Shiraz 2004** Inky, impenetrable purple colour; as rich and concentrated as the bouquet promises, still locked up, but with a cave of blackberry and licorice flavours to unleash. Not too tannic. A bargain for a wine of this style. Cork. 14.5° alc. **RATING** 94 **DRINK** 2019 $ 25

Deakin Estate ★★★

Kulkyne Way, via Red Cliffs, Vic 3496 **REGION** Murray Darling
T (03) 5029 1666 **F** (03) 5024 3316 **WWW**.deakinestate.com.au **OPEN** Not
WINEMAKER Phil Spillman **EST.** 1980 **CASES** 500 000
Part of the Katnook Estate, Riddoch and Deakin Estate triumvirate, which constitutes the Wingara Wine Group, now 60% owned by Freixenet of Spain. Sunnycliff is still used for export purposes but does not appear on the domestic market any more. Deakin Estate draws on over 300 ha of its own

vineyards, making it largely self-sufficient, and produces competitively priced wines of consistent quality and impressive value. Exports to the UK, the US, Canada, NZ and Asia.

ΨΨΨΨ **Shiraz 2004** Strong red-purple colour; light- to medium-bodied; good blackberry fruit and a flick of oak; excellent value. Screwcap. 14° alc. **RATING** 88 **DRINK** 2009 $9.99
Cabernet Sauvignon 2003 Very competently made; light- to medium-bodied redcurrant/raspberry/blackcurrant. Excellent value. Screwcap. 14° alc. **RATING** 87 **DRINK** 2008 $9.99

ΨΨΨΨ **Sauvignon Blanc 2005** Very respectable warm-grown Sauvignon Blanc à la Oxford Landing; light passionfruit and gooseberry supported by a touch of residual sugar. Screwcap. 12° alc. **RATING** 86 **DRINK** Now $10
Chardonnay 2005 RATING 86 **DRINK** Now $10
Shiraz 2003 RATING 85 **DRINK** Now $9.99

Deep Dene Vineyard

NR

36 Glenisla Road, Bickley, WA 6076 **REGION** Perth Hills
T (08) 9293 0077 **F** (08) 9293 0077 **OPEN** By appt
WINEMAKER Contract **EST.** 1994 **CASES** 4000
Improbably, was once one of the largest Perth Hills vineyards, but no more. It has 4 ha of pinot noir and 0.5 ha of shiraz, continuing the near obsession of the Perth Hills vignerons with pinot noir in a climate which, to put it mildly, is difficult for the variety, other than in sparkling wine.

Deep Woods Estate

Lot 10 Commonage Road, Yallingup, WA 6282 **REGION** Margaret River
T (08) 9756 6066 **F** (08) 9756 6366 **WWW**.deepwoods.com.au **OPEN** Tues–Sun 11–5, 7 days during hols
WINEMAKER Ben Gould **EST.** 1987 **CASES** 20 000
The Gould family acquired Deep Woods Estate in 1991, 4 years after the commencement of the estate plantings. There are 15 ha of estate vines planted to nine varieties, with the intake supplemented by grapes for the Ebony and Ivory wines. At the top of the tree are the occasional and tiny releases under the Boneyard label. A second vineyard at Cowaramup is being established: 7 ha of sauvignon blanc and 7 ha of semillon have been planted and another 32 ha of various varieties to follow. In 2005 the business was acquired by Peter Fogarty (owner of Millbrook and Lake's Folly) but Ben Gould is being retained as winemaker and (now) general manager. Exports to Switzerland.

ΨΨΨΨΨ **Block 7 Margaret River Shiraz 2004** Good colour; a most attractive fusion of red and black fruits, spicy French oak and gentle, ripe tannins; great balance and mouthfeel. Cork. 14.5° alc. **RATING** 94 **DRINK** 2014 $22
Margaret River Cabernet Merlot 2004 Very good colour; rich and powerful, largely driven by quality cabernet blackcurrant fruit and French oak; excellent tannins sustain the structure. Cork. 14.5° alc. **RATING** 94 **DRINK** 2017 $32

ΨΨΨΨ **Margaret River Semillon Sauvignon Blanc 2005** Spotlessly clean; a light-bodied, harmonious blend of grass, citrus and kiwifruit, and fruit sweetness on the back-palate. Screwcap. 13° alc. **RATING** 90 **DRINK** Now $18

ΨΨΨΨ **Margaret River Verdelho 2005 RATING** 86 **DRINK** Now $16

🐛 Deetswood Wines

Washpool Creek Road, Tenterfield, NSW 2372 **REGION** Northern Slopes Zone
T (02) 6736 1322 **F** (02) 6736 1322 **WWW**.deetswoodwines.com.au **OPEN** Fri–Mon 10–5, or by appt
WINEMAKER Contract **EST.** 1996 **CASES** 1500
Deanne Eaton and Tim Condrick began the establishment of their micro-vineyard in 1996, planting semillon, chardonnay, pinot noir, shiraz, merlot and cabernet sauvignon within the 2 ha of plantings. Back at the end of the 19th century a German immigrant (Joe Nicoll) planted vines and made wines for family use, and there is still one vine surviving on the site today from the original plantings. The wines are are strikingly consistent both in quality and style, offering further proof that this is a very interesting area.

ΥΥΥΥ♀ **Tenterfield Pinot Noir 2003** Good hue and colour for age; clear varietal character with gently savoury plum fruit; good length and balance. Great value. Screwcap. 13° alc. **RATING** 90 **DRINK** 2008 $ 15

ΥΥΥΥ **Tenterfield Chardonnay 2005** Light straw-green; medium-bodied peach and nectarine fruit with well-balanced and integrated oak. Screwcap. 13.5° alc. **RATING** 89 **DRINK** 2008 $ 14

Tenterfield Shiraz 2002 Retaining hue well; a medium-bodied and elegant wine, with spicy black fruits and fine-grained, light tannins. Cork. 13° alc. **RATING** 89 **DRINK** 2010 $ 15

Tenterfield Semillon 2005 Clean, crisp, well-made with gentle grassy fruit; light-bodied and well-balanced. Screwcap. 12° alc. **RATING** 88 **DRINK** 2009 $ 14

Tenterfield Cabernet Sauvignon 2002 Very much in winery style; light- to medium-bodied; savoury/spicy overtones, though still fresh. and some cassis lurking. Cork. 12.5° alc. **RATING** 88 **DRINK** 2010 $ 15

Tenterfield Chardonnay 2003 Crisp, clean and fresh; interesting low alcohol style, not too thin; nectarine and citrus in a simple, direct frame. Screwcap. 11.6° alc. **RATING** 87 **DRINK** 2009 $ 13

Tenterfield Merlot 2002 Similar to the '03, but with more concentration, albeit still in the earthy/savoury spectrum. Cork. 12.5° alc. **RATING** 87 **DRINK** 2010 $ 15

ΥΥΥΥ♀ **Tenterfield Merlot 2003** **RATING** 86 **DRINK** 2009 $ 15

del Rios of Mt Anakie ★★★☆

2320 Ballan Road, Anakie, Vic 3221 **REGION** Geelong
T (03) 9497 4644 **F** (03) 9499 9266 **www**.delrios.com.au **OPEN** W'ends 10–5
WINEMAKER Matthew Bowden **EST.** 1996 **CASES** 7000
German del Rio was born in northern Spain (in 1920) where his family owned vineyards. After 3 generations in Australia, his family has established 15 ha of vines on their 104-ha property on the slopes of Mt Anakie, the principal focus being chardonnay, pinot noir and cabernet sauvignon (4 ha each), then marsanne, sauvignon blanc, merlot and shiraz (1 ha each). Planting commenced in 1996, and vintage 2000 was the first commercial release; winemaking moved onsite in 2004.

ΥΥΥΥ♀ **Shiraz 2004** A style bound to split opinion; ripe licorice and blackberry fruit reminiscent of Côte Rôtie, but showing some alcohol heat. **RATING** 90 **DRINK** 2012 $ 23

ΥΥΥΥ **Sauvignon Blanc 2005** Easy access style, with underlying hints of sweetness to the tropical fruit. **RATING** 87 **DRINK** Now $ 18
Marsanne 2004 **RATING** 87 **DRINK** Now $ 18

ΥΥΥΥ♀ **Rose 2005** **RATING** 86 **DRINK** Now $ 16
Pinot Noir 2003 **RATING** 86 **DRINK** Now $ 19
Chardonnay 2004 **RATING** 85 **DRINK** 2009 $ 18
Cabernet Sauvignon 2003 **RATING** 84 **DRINK** Now $ 20

ΥΥΥ **Pinot Noir 2004** **RATING** 83 $ 19
Merlot 2004 **RATING** 83 $ 19

Delacolline Estate NR

Whillas Road, Port Lincoln, SA 5606 **REGION** Southern Eyre Peninsula
T (08) 8682 5277 **F** (08) 8682 4455 **OPEN** W'ends 9–5
WINEMAKER Mitchell (Contract) **EST.** 1984 **CASES** 650
Joins Boston Bay as the second Port Lincoln producer. The 3-ha vineyard, run under the direction of Tony Bassett, reflects the cool maritime influence, with ocean currents that sweep up from the Antarctic. The wines are made in the Clare Valley.

Delamere

NR

Bridport Road, Pipers Brook, Tas 7254 **REGION** Northern Tasmania
T (03) 6382 7190 **F** (03) 6382 7250 **OPEN** 7 days 10–5
WINEMAKER Richard Richardson **EST.** 1983 **CASES** 2000
Richie Richardson produces elegant, rather light-bodied wines that have a strong following. The Chardonnay has been most successful, with a textured, complex, malolactic-influenced wine with great, creamy feel in the mouth. The Pinots typically show pleasant varietal fruit, but seem to suffer from handling problems.

Delaney's Creek Winery

NR

70 Hennessey Road, Delaneys Creek, Qld 4514 **REGION** Queensland Coastal
T (07) 5496 4925 **F** (07) 5496 4926 **OPEN** Wed–Fri 11–4, w'ends & public hols 10–5
WINEMAKER Stuart Pearce (Contract) **EST.** 1997 **CASES** 3000
Barry and Judy Leverett established Delaney's Creek Winery in 1997 and thus expanded the vineyard map of Qld yet further. Delaney's Creek is near the town of Woodford, not far northwest of Caboolture. In 1998 they planted an exotic mix of 1 ha each of shiraz, chardonnay, sangiovese, touriga nacional and verdelho. In the meantime they are obtaining their grapes from 4 ha of contract-grown fruit, including cabernet sauvignon, cabernet franc, merlot, shiraz, chardonnay, marsanne and verdelho.

Delatite

★★★☆

Stoneys Road, Mansfield, Vic 3722 **REGION** Upper Goulburn
T (03) 5775 2922 **F** (03) 5775 2911 **WWW**.delatitewinery.com.au **OPEN** 7 days 10–5
WINEMAKER Jane Donat **EST.** 1982 **CASES** 16 000
With its sweeping views across to the snow-clad Alps, this is uncompromising cool-climate viticulture, and the wines naturally reflect that. Light but intense Riesling and spicy Traminer flower with a year or two in bottle, and in the warmer vintages the red wines achieve flavour and mouthfeel. In spring 2002 David Ritchie (the viticulturist in the family) embarked on a program to adopt biodynamics, commencing with the sauvignon blanc and gewurztraminer. He says, 'It will take time for us to convert the vineyard and change our mindset and practices, but I am fully convinced it will lead to healthier soil and vines.' Exports to Japan and Malaysia.

▼▼▼▼ **Dungeon Gully 2003** Youthful purple-red; light-bodied; direct red cherry and plum fruit, the oak in restraint; scores on its clean finish. Screwcap. **RATING** 88 **DRINK** Now $ 20

Dennis

★★★★

Kangarilla Road, McLaren Vale, SA 5171 **REGION** McLaren Vale
T (08) 8323 8665 **F** (08) 8323 9121 **OPEN** Mon–Fri 10–5, w'ends, hols 11–5
WINEMAKER Peter Dennis **EST.** 1970 **CASES** 5000
Egerton (Ege) was well-known in McLaren Vale, starting his vineyard at McLaren Flat in 1947 after serving in the RAAF during the war. Wine production under the Dennis label in 1971, and in 1979 winemaking and management passed to son Peter. The 36-ha vineyard is planted to cabernet sauvignon, shiraz, merlot, chardonnay and sauvignon blanc, most now fully mature. Exports to the UK, NZ and Canada.

Derwent Estate

★★★★

329 Lyell Highway, Granton, Tas 7070 **REGION** Southern Tasmania
T (03) 6263 5802 **F** (03) 6263 5802 **WWW**.derwentestate.com.au **OPEN** Mon–Fri 10–4 (closed winter)
WINEMAKER Winemaking Tasmania (Julian Alcorso) **EST.** 1993 **CASES** 1200
The Hanigan family established Derwent Estate as part of a diversification program for their 400-ha mixed farming property: 10 ha of vineyard have been planted, since 1993, to riesling, pinot noir, chardonnay, cabernet sauvignon and pinot gris.

♥♥♥♥♥ Riesling 2005 Lively, crisp, intense and long; fully ripe lime juice fruit finishing with lemony/grassy minerality. **RATING** 94 **DRINK** 2013 $ 20

♥♥♥♥ Rose 2005 Bright fuchsia pink; vibrant fruit, acid and residual sugar all in good balance. **RATING** 89 **DRINK** Now $ 15
Pinot Noir 2004 Confit jam and plum, but not excessively sweet; gently ripe tannins. **RATING** 88 **DRINK** 2009 $ 24

♥♥♥♥ Unwooded Chardonnay 2005 RATING 85 **DRINK** Now $ 20

🍷 Deviation Road ★★★★☆

Lobethal-Mount Torrens Road, Charleston, SA 5244 **REGION** Adelaide Hills
T (08) 8389 4455 **F** (08) 8389 4407 **WWW**.deviationroad.com **OPEN** 7 days 11–5
WINEMAKER Kate Laurie, Hamish Laurie **EST**. 1999 **CASES** 1000
Deviation Road was created in 1998 by Hamish Laurie, great-great grandson of Mary Laurie, SA's first female winemaker. He had joined with father Dr Chris Laurie in 1992 to help build the Hillstowe Wines business. The brand was sold to Banksia Wines in 2001, but the Laurie family retained the vineyard, which now supplies Deviation Road with its grapes. Wife Kate Laurie joined the business in 2001, having studied winemaking and viticulture in Champagne, then spending 4 years at her family's Stone Bridge winery in Manjimup. All the wines except the Sangiovese (WA) and Riesling (other Adelaide Hills growers) come from the 16-ha family vineyards, but only account for a small portion of the annual grape production of those vineyards.

♥♥♥♥♥ Adelaide Hills Pinot Gris 2005 Highly aromatic pear, apple, spice and musk; well above-average intensity and length; as good as they come with this variety. Screwcap. **RATING** 94 **DRINK** 2008 $ 22.95

♥♥♥♥♥ Adelaide Hills Sauvignon Blanc 2005 Crisp, spicy, minerally aromas; interesting mouthfeel (from partial barrel ferment) to the asparagus and citrus mix; long finish. Screwcap. **RATING** 90 **DRINK** Now $ 18.95

♥♥♥♥ Adelaide Hills Pinot Noir 2004 Light- to medium-bodied; savoury/foresty/earthy aromas; some dark plum joins on the palate; good varietal character. Cork. **RATING** 89 **DRINK** Now $ 22.95
Adelaide Hills Merlot 2003 Strong herb, olive, earth and varietal aromas and flavours, and a substrate of red fruits; just needed a touch more intensity. Cork. **RATING** 87 **DRINK** Now $ 24.95
Manjimup Sangiovese 2003 Authentic, light varietal indicators; red cherry, rose petal and small red fruits; dusty tannins. Screwcap. **RATING** 87 **DRINK** Now $ 22.95

Devil's Lair ★★★★☆

Rocky Road, Forest Grove via Margaret River, WA 6285 **REGION** Margaret River
T (08) 9757 7573 **F** (08) 9757 7533 **WWW**.devils-lair.com **OPEN** Not
WINEMAKER Stuart Pym **EST**. 1981 **CASES** 40 000
Having rapidly carved out a high reputation for itself through a combination of clever packaging and marketing and impressive wine quality, Devil's Lair was acquired by Southcorp Wines (Penfolds, etc) in December 1996. The estate vineyards have been substantially increased since then. Exports to the UK, the US and other major markets.

♥♥♥♥♥ Fifth Leg White 2002 Aromatic fruit salad bouquet and well-structured palate offering tropical fruit salad balanced by lemony acidity running through to a long, cleansing finish. **RATING** 93 **DRINK** Now $ 19
Fifth Leg Rose 2005 Aromatic spice and herbs; crisp, crunchy and lively herb and red fruits; long finish. Screwcap. **RATING** 92 **DRINK** Now $ 18.99

♥♥♥♥ Fifth Leg White 2005 Firm, clean and fresh; a mix of mineral, grass and melon; good balance and finish. Sauvignon Blanc/Semillon/Chardonnay. Screwcap. **RATING** 89 **DRINK** Now $ 18.99
Fifth Leg Dry Red 2004 Good depth to colour; bright, fresh raspberry, red berry, blackcurrant mix; medium-bodied; easy access. Cabernet Sauvignon/Merlot/Shiraz. Screwcap. **RATING** 89 **DRINK** 2008 $ 18

di Lusso Wines
NR

Eurunderee Lane, Mudgee, NSW 2850 **REGION** Mudgee
T (02) 6373 3125 **F** (02) 6373 3128 **WWW**.dilusso.com.au **OPEN** 7 days 10–5
WINEMAKER 21C Wine Company (Drew Tuckwell) **EST.** 1998 **CASES** 2700
Rob Fairall and partner Luanne Hill have brought to fruition their vision to establish an Italian 'enoteca' operation, offering Italian varietal wines and foods. The plantings of 2 ha each of barbera and sangiovese, 1 ha of nebbiolo and 0.5 ha of picolit, supplemented by the purchase of aleatico and sangiovese from the Mudgee region, and pinot grigio from Orange, set the tone for the wine, which is made by Drew Tuckwell, a specialist in Italian varieties. The estate also produces olives for olive oil and table olives, and the range of both wine and food will increase over the years. The decision to focus on Italian varieties has been a major success.

Di Stasio
NR

Range Road, Coldstream, Vic 3770 **REGION** Yarra Valley
T (03) 9525 3999 **F** (03) 9525 3815 **OPEN** By appt, or at Café Di Stasio, 31 Fitzroy Street, St Kilda
WINEMAKER Rob Dolan, Kate Goodman (Contract) **EST.** 1995 **CASES** 900
Famous Melbourne restaurateur Rinaldo (Ronnie) Di Stasio bought a virgin bushland 32-ha hillside block in the Yarra Valley, adjacent to the Warramate Flora and Fauna Reserve, in 1994. He has since established 2.8 ha of vineyards, equally split between pinot noir and chardonnay, put in roads and dams, built a substantial house, and also an Allan Powell Monastery, complete with art gallery and tree-filled courtyard sitting like a church on top of the hill. Production has never been large, but did commence in 1999, the wines of that and subsequent vintages being initially sold through Café Di Stasio in St Kilda, a Melbourne icon. Exports to the UK.

Diamond Valley Vineyards
★★★★★

PO Box 4255, Croydon Hills, Vic 3136 **REGION** Yarra Valley
T (03) 9722 0840 **F** (03) 9722 2373 **WWW**.diamondvalley.com.au **OPEN** Not
WINEMAKER James Lance **EST.** 1976 **CASES** 7000
One of the Yarra Valley's finest producers of Pinot Noir and an early pacesetter for the variety, making wines of tremendous style and crystal-clear varietal character. They are not Cabernet Sauvignon lookalikes but true Pinot Noir, fragrant and intense. The Chardonnays show the same marriage of finesse and intensity, and the Cabernet family wines shine in the warmer vintages. In early 2005 the brand and wine stocks were acquired by Graeme Rathbone (of SpringLane), the Lances continuing to own the vineyard and winery, and to make the wine.

ΨΨΨΨΨ **Yarra Valley Chardonnay 2004** Very fragrant nectarine and grapefruit aroma, almost into lime; a lively, fresh and very long palate, the barrel ferment inputs in the background. Screwcap. 13.5° alc. **RATING** 95 **DRINK** 2014 $ 22
Estate Chardonnay 2003 A very complex bouquet marrying ripe stone fruit and nutty barrel ferment inputs; powerful, long and intense. Cork. 14.5° alc. **RATING** 95 **DRINK** 2010 $ 32
Estate Chardonnay 2004 Immaculate winemaking; melon, stone fruit and fig with perfectly balanced and integrated quality French oak. Cork. 13° alc. **RATING** 94 **DRINK** 2011 $ 35
Estate Pinot Noir 2004 Good colour; spiced plum aromas, and more of the same on the palate plus sous bois nuances; good structure and texture. Cork. 13° alc. **RATING** 94 **DRINK** 2011 $ 64
Yarra Valley Shiraz Viognier 2004 Bright colour; once again, a compellingly synergistic blend; luscious black plum fruit with that lift ex viognier which is felt as much as tasted. Screwcap. 14.2° alc. **RATING** 94 **DRINK** 2014 $ 25

ΨΨΨΨ▽ **Yarra Valley Pinot Noir 2004** Fragrant spice and red berry aromas; a light- to medium-bodied supple and smooth palate; not forced. Screwcap. **RATING** 93 **DRINK** 2010 $ 24
Yarra Valley Sauvignon Blanc 2005 Bright green-straw; abundant varietal aromas and flavours in a kiwifruit/passionfruit/green apple spectrum; good length and finish. Screwcap. 13° alc. **RATING** 91 **DRINK** Now $ 19

Yarra Valley Cabernet Sauvignon Cabernet Franc 2001 Cedar, olive, spice and earth; overall rather lean and austere, but does have length; reminiscent of Bordeauxs of yesteryear. Cork. **RATING** 90 **DRINK** 2010 $ 35

▼▼▼▼ **Yarra Valley Cabernet Merlot 2003** A mix of sweet blackcurrant fruit and opposing savoury, almost bitter, earthy tannins and flavours. For the time being, the tannins are winning. Cork. 15° alc. **RATING** 89 **DRINK** 2011 $ 22

▼▼▼▽ **Yarra Valley Viognier 2005** Better off used in the Shiraz; this is Plain Jane stuff; vineyard, not winery, limitations. Screwcap. **RATING** 86 **DRINK** 2008 $ 26

Diggers Rest   NR

205 Old Vineyard Road, Sunbury, Vic 3429 **REGION** Sunbury
T (03) 9740 1660 **F** (03) 9740 1660 **OPEN** By appt
WINEMAKER Peter Dredge **EST.** 1987 **CASES** 1000
Diggers Rest was purchased from the founders Frank and Judith Hogan in July 1998; the new owners, Elias and Joseph Obeid, intend to expand the vineyard resources and, by that means, significantly increase production.

DiGiorgio Family Wines

Riddoch Highway, Coonawarra, SA 5263 **REGION** Coonawarra
T (08) 8736 3222 **F** (08) 8736 3233 **www**.digiorgio.com.au **OPEN** 7 days 10–5
WINEMAKER Peter Douglas **EST.** 1998 **CASES** 10 000
Stefano DiGiorgio emigrated from Abruzzi, Italy, arriving in Australia in July 1952. Over the years, he and his family gradually expanded their holdings at Lucindale. In 1989 he began planting cabernet sauvignon (99 ha), chardonnay (10 ha), merlot (9 ha), shiraz (6 ha) and pinot noir (2 ha). In 2002 the family purchased the historic Rouge Homme winery, capable of crushing 10 000 tonnes of grapes a year, and its surrounding 13.5 ha of vines, from Southcorp. The enterprise is offering full winemaking services to vignerons in the Limestone Coast Zone. Exports to Germany and The Netherlands.

▼▼▼▼ **Coonawarra Emporio 2002** Solid black fruits, with some oak push; plenty of overall flavour. Cork. **RATING** 88 **DRINK** 2010 $ 23

▼▼▼▽ **Francesco Cabernet Sauvignon 2002** **RATING** 86 **DRINK** 2009 $ 40

▼▼▼ **Coonawarra Cabernet Sauvignon 2002** **RATING** 82 $ 23

Diloreto Wines   NR

45 Wilpena Terrace, Kilkenny, SA 5009 (postal) **REGION** Adelaide Plains
T (08) 8345 0123 **OPEN** Not
WINEMAKER Tony Diloreto **EST.** 2001 **CASES** 250
The Diloreto family have been growing grapes since the 1960s, with 8 ha of shiraz, cabernet sauvignon, mourvedre and grenache. The vineyard was founded by father Gesue Diloreto and, like so many Adelaide Plains grapegrowers, the family sold the grapes to South Australian winemakers. However, at the end of the 1990s, son Tony and wife Gabriell (herself with a winemaking background from the Rhine Valley in Germany) decided they would jointly undertake a short winemaking course. In 2001 Tony Diloreto entered two wines in the Australian Amateur Wine Show, competing against 700 vignerons from around Australia. Both were Shiraz from the 2001 vintage, one with new oak, the other not. Both won gold medals, and the judges strongly recommended that the wines be made and sold commercially. Great oaks from little acorns indeed.

Dindima Wines   NR

Lot 22 Cargo Road, Orange, NSW 2800 **REGION** Orange
T (02) 6365 3388 **F** (02) 6365 3096 **www**.dindima.com.au **OPEN** W'ends & public hols 10–5, or by appt
WINEMAKER James Bell **EST.** 2002 **CASES** 440
David Bell and family acquired the property known as Osmond Wines in 2002, renaming it Dindima Wines, with the first vintage under the new ownership made in 2003 from the 4.5 ha plantings. It is a retirement occupation for Dave Bell and his wife, but both sons are becoming involved with grapegrowing and winemaking.

Dingo Creek Vineyard   NR

265 Tandur-Traveston Road, Traveston, Qld 4570 **REGION** Queensland Coastal
T (07) 5485 1731 **F** (07) 5485 0041 **WWW**.dingocreek.com.au **OPEN** W'ends 10–4, or by appt
WINEMAKER Bruce Humphery-Smith **EST.** 1997 **CASES** NA
Marg and David Gillespie both had agricultural or viticultural backgrounds before moving to Qld
(Marg worked with Bullers Wines). In 1994 they began a search for agriculturally viable land with
permanent water to start their own vineyard, and the property at Traveston provided the answer.
Planting began in 1997 with chardonnay and cabernet sauvignon, followed a year later by merlot and
sauvignon blanc; a total of 2 ha is now under vine.

Dinny Goonan Family Estate   ★★★☆

880 Winchelsea-Deans Marsh Road, Bambra, Vic 3241 **REGION** Geelong
T 0438 408 420 **WWW**.dinnygoonan.com.au **OPEN** By appt
WINEMAKER Dinny Goonan **EST.** 2004 **CASES** 1000
Although the establishment date is given as 2004, the estate dates back to the 1980s when Dinny and
Susan Goonan bought a 20-ha property near Bambra, on the hinterland of the Otway Coast. Dinny
had recently completed a viticulture diploma at Charles Sturt University, but, as he and Susan were
viticultural pioneers in the area, they were not sure what varieties would do well, and which wouldn't.
In the early 1990s they planted a wide range of varieties in what they now call their Nursery Block.
Dinny also headed back to Charles Sturt University to complete a wine science degree, and out of all
of this 2 ha of riesling and 2 ha of shiraz have been taken through to commercial production, leaving
0.6 ha of cabernet sauvignon, cabernet franc, merlot and malbec, plus smaller blocks of pinot noir
and chardonnay.

TTTT **Riesling 2005** Spicy, intense and lingering, with excellent focus and length. **RATING** 93
    DRINK 2010 $18

TTTT **Cabernets 2003** Medium-bodied; spicy, cedary notes through a well-balanced palate.
    RATING 87 **DRINK** 2009 $18

TTTT **Semillon Sauvignon Blanc 2004** **RATING** 86 **DRINK** 2008 $18
    Riesling 2003 **RATING** 85 **DRINK** Now $18

Dionysus Winery   ★★★★

1 Patemans Lane, Murrumbateman, NSW 2582 **REGION** Canberra District
T (02) 6227 0208 **F** (02) 6227 0209 **WWW**.dionysus-winery.com.au **OPEN** W'ends & public hols
10–5, or by appt
WINEMAKER Michael O'Dea **EST.** 1998 **CASES** 1000
Michael and Wendy O'Dea are both public servants in Canberra seeking weekend and holiday relief from
their everyday life at work. They purchased their property at Murrumbateman in 1996, and planted 4 ha
of chardonnay, sauvignon blanc riesling, pinot noir, cabernet sauvignon and shiraz between 1998 and
2001. Michael has completed an associate degree in winemaking at Charles Sturt University, and is
responsible for viticulture and winemaking; Wendy has completed various courses at the Canberra TAFE
and is responsible for wine marketing and (in their words) 'nagging Michael and being a general slushie'.

TTTT **Merlot 2004** Clear-cut varietal flavour and structure; olive nuances to plum and berry
    fruit; fine-grained, savoury tannins; austere but authentic. Cork. 14° alc. **RATING** 90
    DRINK 2011 $18

TTTT **Shiraz 2003** Complex spicy/cedary/leafy/savoury edges to the kernel of sweet fruit;
    touches of bitter chocolate, too. Cork. 13° alc. **RATING** 89 **DRINK** 2010 $18

Disaster Bay Wines   ★★★★

133 Oaklands Road, Pambula, NSW 2549 (postal) **REGION** South Coast Zone
T (02) 6495 6488 **WWW**.disasterbaywines.com **OPEN** Not
WINEMAKER Dean O'Reilly, Andrew McEwen **EST.** 2000 **CASES** 250
Dean O'Reilly has a 10-year background in the distribution of fine table wines, culminating in
employment by Fine Wine Partners. He has accumulated the UK-based WSET Intermediate and

Advanced Certificates, completed various other programs and competitions, and has been associate judge and judge and various Canberra district events. He has also travelled through the wine regions of NZ, Champagne, Bordeaux, Chablis, Piedmont and Tuscany. The wines are made at Kyeema with Andrew McEwen overseeing Dean's apprenticeship, coming from small parcels of fruit grown on some of the original vineyards of the Canberra District.

TTTTT **SS Ly-ee-Moon 1886 Semillon Sauvignon Blanc 2005** A complex, powerful wine, the varietal blend plus a touch of barrel ferment oak leading towards white Bordeaux style; has more texture and structure than most. Screwcap. 12.5° alc. **RATING** 92 **DRINK** 2010 $ 20

Deano's Vino Handpicked Riesling 2004 Light green-straw; bracingly fresh, crisp and lively; pure, lancing acidity runs through a lingering palate. Screwcap. 11° alc. **RATING** 91 **DRINK** 2014 $ 15

TTTT **Deano's Vino Handpicked Riesling 2005** Has made the most out of the grapes; clean, well-balanced apple and citrus fruit with a touch of spritz; fractionally hollow; more conventional than the '04. Screwcap. 12.5° alc. **RATING** 89 **DRINK** 2009 $ 15

SS City of Sydney 1862 Cabernet Merlot 2004 Light- to medium-bodied; cassis-accented fruit; fine tannins and controlled oak. Screwcap. 13.5° alc. **RATING** 88 **DRINK** 2009 $ 20

TTTT **Deano's Vino Shiraz Mourvedre 2004** **RATING** 86 **DRINK** 2008 $ 15

Deano's Vino Shiraz Mourvedre 2003 **RATING** 85 **DRINK** Now $ 15

Divers Luck Wines   NR

'Hellenvale', Nelson Bay Road, Bobs Farm, Port Stephens, NSW 2316 **REGION** Northern Rivers Zone **T** (02) 4982 2471 **F** (02) 4982 2726 **OPEN** 7 days 10–5 **WINEMAKER** Anthony Adams **EST.** 2000 **CASES** 2000 Anthony Adams and wife Hellen purchased their property in June 2000, after Anthony had spent 10 years as an abalone diver on the far south coast of New South Wales. He was struck down with a severe case of the bends in 1999, and after spending 4 days in the re-compression chamber at the Prince of Wales Hospital in Sydney, he wisely decided on a change of career. The Adams and their son Damien have a 3-ha vineyard planted to chambourcin, merlot, shiraz, verdelho and chardonnay, and built the onsite boutique winery. The wines are sold by mail order and through the cellar door.

Dixons Run   NR

5 Carrick St, Mont Albert, Vic 3127 (postal) **REGION** Yarra Valley **T** (08) 9898 7476 **F** (03) 9349 2434 **www**.dixonsrun.com **OPEN** Not **WINEMAKER** Contract **EST.** 2002 **CASES** 2000 Named after a Mr Dixon who grazed cattle on a squatter's run in the 1840s, the Dixons Creek subregion of the Yarra Valley is now home to a number of vineyards and wineries. The 18.5-ha vineyard is planted to chardonnay, sauvignon blanc, pinot noir and cabernet sauvignon, heralding further increases in production.

Djinta Djinta Winery   ★★★☆

10 Stevens Road, Kardella South, Vic 3951 **REGION** Gippsland **T** (03) 5658 1163 **F** (03) 5658 1163 **www**.winesofgippsland.com/Wineries/DjintaDjinta/ **OPEN** 7 days 10–6 **WINEMAKER** Peter Harley **EST.** 1991 **CASES** 600 One of a group of wineries situated between Leongatha and Korumburra, the most famous being Bass Phillip. Vines were first planted in 1986 but were largely neglected until Peter and Helen Harley acquired the property in 1991. They set about reviving the 2 ha of sauvignon blanc and a little cabernet sauvignon, and planted an additional 3 ha of merlot, cabernet franc, cabernet sauvignon, semillon, marsanne, roussanne and viognier. The first vintage was 1995, while Peter Harley was completing a Bachelor of Applied Science (Wine Science) at Charles Sturt University. They are deliberately adopting a low-technology approach to both vineyard and winery practices, using organic methods wherever possible.

ŦŦŦŦŶ **Sauvignon Blanc 2005** Light straw-green; clean, generous gooseberry, kiwifruit and passionfruit flavours; very good balance and length; 15% semillon. **RATING** 90 **DRINK** 2008 $ 21

Classique Marsanne Viognier Roussane 2005 Very well-made; a classic Rhone blend; has good length, and will develop well. **RATING** 90 **DRINK** 2012 $ 21

ŦŦŦŶ **Merlot 2003** Very light green olive, spice and earth aromas and flavours; unquestioned varietal character, simply needing more grunt for higher points. 13.2° alc. **RATING** 86 **DRINK** 2009 $ 25

Cabernet Merlot 2004 Similar weight and structure to the Merlot; has a touch of cassis from the cabernet component. 13.5° alc. **RATING** 86 **DRINK** 2010 $ 22

DogRidge Vineyard NR

RSD 195 Bagshaws Road, McLaren Flat, SA 5171 **REGION** McLaren Vale
T (08) 8383 0140 **F** (08) 8383 0430 **WWW**.dogridge.com.au **OPEN** By appt
WINEMAKER Dave Wright, Jen Wright, Fred Howard, Mike Brown (Consultant) **EST.** 1993 **CASES** 2500

Dave and Jen Wright had a combined background of dentistry, art and a Charles Sturt University viticultural degree when they moved from Adelaide to McLaren Flat to become vignerons. They inherited vines planted in the early 1940s as a source for Chateau Reynella fortified wines, and their viticultural empire now has 56 ha of vineyards, ranging from 2001 plantings to some of the oldest vines remaining in the immediate region today. At the McLaren Flat vineyards, DogRidge has 60+-year-old shiraz, as well as 60-year-old grenache. Only part of the grape production is retained; most is sold to other leading wineries. Exports to the UK, the US, Canada, Singapore and NZ.

🐾 DogRock Winery ★★★★

114 De Graves Road, Crowlands, Vic 3377 **REGION** Pyrenees
T (03) 5354 9201 **WWW**.dogrock.com.au **OPEN** From October 2006 w'ends 11–5
WINEMAKER Allen Hart **EST.** 1999 **CASES** 100

This is the micro-venture (but with inbuilt future growth to something slightly larger than micro) of Allen (winemaker) and Andrea (viticulturist) Hart. Having purchased the property in 1998, planting of 6.4 ha of riesling, chardonnay, shiraz, tempranillo and grenache began in 2000. Given Allen Hart's position as research scientist/winemaker with Fosters Wine Estates, the attitude taken to both viticulture and winemaking is utterly unexpected. Andrea's Vineyard (planted to riesling) is dry-grown, while Pedro's Vineyard (planted to tempranillo and shiraz) receives minimal irrigation from a small dam. The wines are made in an ultra low-tech fashion, without gas cover or filtration. The one concession to technology, say the Harts, is that 'all wine will be sealed with a screwcap and no DogRock wine will ever be released under natural cork bark'. They continue, 'prices are to remain at the lower end as we are intent on making the world's best wine, not the world's best profit'.

ŦŦŦŦŶ **Pyrenees Shiraz 2003** Medium-bodied, fresh mix of red and black fruits; a subtle touch of vanilla oak; firm but fine tannins; refreshing alcohol. Screwcap. 13° alc. **RATING** 91 **DRINK** 2015 $ 25

Pyrenees Riesling 2005 A firm bouquet with notes of herb and mineral; delicate, stoney/minerally entry, with more citrus on the finish. Screwcap. 13.5° alc. **RATING** 90 **DRINK** 2012 $ 17

ŦŦŦŦ **Pyrenees Shiraz Tempranillo 2004** Light- to medium-bodied with fairly brisk acidity to the fresh berry fruits; minimal oak. Screwcap. 13° alc. **RATING** 87 **DRINK** 2008 $ 19

Domain Day ★★★☆

24 Queen Street, Williamstown, SA 5351 **REGION** Barossa Valley
T (08) 8524 6224 **F** (08) 8524 6229 **WWW**.domaindaywines.com **OPEN** By appt
WINEMAKER Robin Day **EST.** 2000 **CASES** NA

This is a classic case of an old dog learning new tricks, and doing so with panache. Robin Day had a long and distinguished career as winemaker, then chief winemaker, then technical director of Orlando; participated in the management buy-out; and profited substantially from the on-sale to

Pernod Ricard. After the sale he remained as a director, but became a globe-trotting adviser, consultant and observer. He has hastened slowly with the establishment of Domain Day, but there is nothing conservative about his approach in establishing his 15-ha vineyard at Mt Crawford, high in the hills (at 450m) of the southeastern extremity of Australia's Barossa Valley wine region, bordering (on two sides of the vineyard) the Eden Valley. While the mainstream varieties are merlot, pinot noir and riesling, he has trawled Italy, France and Georgia for the other varieties: viognier, sangiovese, saperavi, lagrein, garganega and sagrantino.

▼▼▼▼ **Mt Crawford Garganega 2005** A nice wine, with gentle apple and pear aromas and flavours; well-balanced, the limitations lying in the vineyard rather than the winery. Domaine Day is the only producer of this variety in Australia. Screwcap. 12° alc. RATING 87 DRINK Now $ 19.95

▼▼▼▽ **Mt Crawford Viognier 2004** RATING 86 DRINK Now $ 26

Domaine A ★★★★★

Campania, Tas 7026 REGION Southern Tasmania
T (03) 6260 4174 F (03) 6260 4390 WWW.domaine-a.com.au OPEN Mon–Fri 9–4, w'ends by appt
WINEMAKER Peter Althaus, Vetten Tiemann EST. 1973 CASES 5000
The striking black label of the premium Domaine A wine, dominated by the single, multicoloured 'A', signified the change of ownership from George Park to Swiss businessman Peter Althaus many years ago. The wines are made without compromise, and reflect the low yields from the immaculately tended vineyards. They represent aspects of both Old World and New World philosophies, techniques and styles. Exports to the UK, Denmark, Switzerland, Germany, France, China and Singapore.

▼▼▼▼▼ **Lady A Fume Blanc 2004** A typically complex, intense and exceptionally long palate; herb, asparagus and gooseberry with seamless oak; another beautiful wine under this label. Cork. 13.5° alc. RATING 94 DRINK 2012 $ 55
Pinot Noir 2002 Exceptional depth and hue; no less exceptionally powerful and dense in the mouth, with dark plummy fruit the overall extract controlled. A rare pinot noir needing 5 years, and guaranteed for 10 years. Cork. 13.5° alc. RATING 94 DRINK 2012 $ 65
Cabernet Sauvignon 2001 Medium- to full red-purple; intense, relatively austere (in a good sense) black fruits, spice and the first signs of cedar; as always, good structure, the tannins and oak performing to the conductor's baton. Cork. 14.5° alc. RATING 94 DRINK 2016 $ 65

▼▼▼▼▽ **Stoney Vineyard Sauvignon Blanc 2005** Powerful structure and body, but does carry its alcohol well; predominantly mineral, with some citrus and herb; balanced finish, will age quite well. Cork. 13.5° alc. RATING 91 DRINK 2009 $ 35
Pinot Noir 2003 Bright, youthful purple-red; tight spicy, savoury, lingering — almost minerally — fine tannins support the briary varietal fruit. A wine all about structure rather than primary fruit flavour. Cork. 13.5° alc. RATING 91 DRINK 2009 $ 65

▼▼▼▽ **Stoney Vineyard Cabernet Sauvignon 2002** RATING 86 DRINK 2010 $ 26

Domaine Chandon ★★★★★

Green Point, Maroondah Highway, Coldstream, Vic 3770 REGION Yarra Valley
T (03) 9739 1110 F (03) 9739 1095 WWW.yarra-valley.net.au/domaine_chandon/ OPEN 7 days
10.30–4.30
WINEMAKER Dr Tony Jordan, Neville Rowe, James Gosper, John Harris EST. 1986 CASES 150 000
Wholly owned by Möet et Chandon, and one of the two most important wine facilities in the Yarra Valley, the Green Point tasting room has a national and international reputation, having won a number of major tourism awards in recent years. The sparkling wine product range has evolved, and there has been increasing emphasis placed on the table wines. The return of Dr Tony Jordan, the first CEO of Domaine Chandon, has further strengthened both the focus and quality of the brand. Exports to the UK, Asia and Japan.

▼▼▼▼▼ **Vintage Brut 2002** Bright, light straw-green; no hint of onion skin or pink; fine mousse; very crisp, fine and pure; a long and lively citrus/stone fruit palate and lingering finish. Best yet from Domaine Chandon. Cork. 12.5° alc. RATING 95 DRINK 2010 $ 33.95

Tasmanian Cuvee 2002 Potent apple, spice, pear, citrus and strawberry; highly focused; very good back-palate and finish. Cork. 12.5° alc. **RATING** 95 **DRINK** Now $ 33.95

Blanc de Blancs 2002 Light straw-green; good mousse; tight, fine and long citrussy fruit with nutty brioche nuances; perfect balance. Cork. 12.5° alc. **RATING** 95 **DRINK** Now $ 33.95

Green Point Reserve Chardonnay 2003 Sophisticated, elegant wine; tightly focused and structured nectarine/citrus fruit; exemplary oak. Cork. 13° alc. **RATING** 94 **DRINK** 2013 $ 41

Green Point Reserve Yarra Valley Shiraz 2003 Lush and rounded fruit provides great mouthfeel; ranges through raspberry to blackberry, with fine tannins and quality oak. **RATING** 94 **DRINK** 2015 $ 47

Z*D Blanc de Blancs 2002 Bright, lively, zesty mineral and citrus blossom; crisp mouthfeel, great finish. Cap. 12.5° alc. **RATING** 94 **DRINK** Now $ 33.95

Z*D Vintage Brut 2002 A new release which, while continuing the zero dosage approach of the Blanc de Blancs, is a mix of chardonnay and pinot. Unusual aromas of wet hay, pastry, citrus and spice; a fine, crisp and lively palate with abundant fruit expression; lingering finish; 49% Chardonnay/44% Pinot Noir/7% Pinot Meunier. 12.5° alc. **RATING** 94 **DRINK** 2008 $ 37

ŸŸŸŸŸ **Green Point Shiraz 2003** Powerful wine; blackberry and plum, with a touch of fruit lift ex viognier; fine but persistent tannins. Screwcap. **RATING** 92 **DRINK** 2013 $ 29.99

ŸŸŸŸ **Green Point Sauvignon Blanc Semillon 2004** Clean; light- to medium-bodied; gentle tropical fruit with some herb and lemon; soft finish. Cool southern Victorian regions. Screwcap. **RATING** 89 **DRINK** Now $ 20.95

Domaine Epis

NR

812 Black Forest Drive, Woodend, Vic 3442 **REGION** Macedon Ranges
T (03) 5427 1204 **F** (03) 5427 1204 **OPEN** By appt
WINEMAKER Stuart Anderson **EST.** 1990 **CASES** 900
Three legends are involved in the Domaine Epis and Epis & Williams wines, two of them in their own lifetime. They are long-term Essendon guru and former player Alec Epis, who owns the two quite separate vineyards and brands; Stuart Anderson, who directs winemaking, with Alec Epis doing all the hard work; and the late Laurie Williams, the father of viticulture in the Macedon region and the man who established the Flynn & Williams vineyard in 1976. Alec Epis purchased that vineyard from Laurie Williams in 1999, and as a mark of respect (and with Laurie Williams' approval) continued to use his name in conjunction with his own. The Cabernet Sauvignon comes from this vineyard, the Chardonnay and Pinot Noir from the vineyard at Woodend, where a small winery was built in 2002.

Domaines Tatiarra

★★★★★

2/102 Barkers Road, Hawthorn, Vic 3124 (postal) **REGION** Heathcote
T 0411 240 815 **F** (03) 9822 4108 **WWW**.cambrianshiraz.com **OPEN** Not
WINEMAKER Ben Riggs **EST.** 1991 **CASES** 2000
Domaines Tatiarra Limited is an unlisted public company, its core asset being a 60-ha property of Cambrian earth first identified and developed by Bill Hepburn, who sold the project to the company in 1991. It is intended to produce only one varietal wine: Shiraz. The majority of the wine will come from the Tatiarra (Aboriginal word meaning 'beautiful country') property, but the Trademark Shiraz is an equal blend of McLaren Vale and Heathcote wine. The wines are made at the Pettavel Winery in Geelong, with Ben Riggs commuting between McLaren Vale and the winery as required.

ŸŸŸŸŸ **Trademark Shiraz 2004** Slightly more developed colour than the pressings; full-bodied (again) but greater complexity in both flavour and structure, possibly because the McLaren Vale chocolate and blackberry is less dense than the Heathcote; tannins more evident. Cork. 15.5° alc. **RATING** 96 **DRINK** 2019 $ 67

Caravan of Dreams Heathcote Shiraz Pressings 2004 Deep, dark, opaque colour; full-bodied, with an extra degree of intensity and structure, the greater tannins (still ripe and in balance) from the pressings; another dimension to the licorice, blackberry and plum. Cork. 15.5° alc. **RATING** 96 **DRINK** 2024 $ 55

Cambrian Shiraz 2004 Deep purple-red; densely lush, luscious, sweet plum, prune, licorice and blackberry; sweetness from the high alcohol, presumably. Oak plays second fiddle. Cork. 15.5° alc. **RATING** 94 **DRINK** 2019 $ 44

ŢŢŢŢŢ **Culled Barrel Heathcote Shiraz 2004** Very good colour; full-bodied; slightly woodier, more savoury, but still an impressive wine on any terms at this price. Cork. 15.5° alc. **RATING** 90 **DRINK** 2012 $ 22

Dominic Versace Wines

NR

Lot 258 Heaslip Road, MacDonald Park, SA 5121 **REGION** Adelaide Plains
T (08) 8379 7132 **F** (08) 8338 0979 **WWW**.versacewines.com.au **OPEN** By appt
WINEMAKER Dominic Versace, Armando Verdiglione **EST**. 2000 **CASES** 1500
Dominic Versace and brother-in-law Armando Verdiglione have a long association with wine, through their families in Italy and in Australia since 1980. In that year Dominic Versace planted 4.5 ha of shiraz, grenache and sangiovese (one of the earliest such plantings in Australia), selling the grapes until 1999. Armando Verdiglione, with Caj Amadio and Michael von Berg, had in the meantime helped create the first commercial vineyard on Kangaroo Island. In 2000 the pair decided to pool their experience and resources, using the near-organically grown grapes from the Versace vineyard, and deliberately rustic winemaking techniques.

Dominion Wines

★★★☆

Upton Road, Strathbogie Ranges via Avenel, Vic 3664 **REGION** Strathbogie Ranges
T (03) 5796 2718 **F** (03) 5796 2719 **WWW**.dominionwines.com **OPEN** By appt
WINEMAKER Travis Bush, Michael Clayden **EST**. 1999 **CASES** 140 000
This is a substantial venture, with a winery capable of processing 7500 tonnes of grapes, and a 91-ha vineyard planted to a Joseph's Coat array of varieties. In late 2005 it was sold to a consortium including Sam Plunkett of Plunkett Wines, but will continue to provide high-scale contract winemaking for major wine companions, particularly those in SA wishing to access Victorian fruit. Phylloxera concerns mean that wines have to be fully fermented before they can be sent to SA.

ŢŢŢŢ **Vinus Cabernet Merlot 2004** Opens quietly on the bouquet, but builds on the medium-bodied palate with appealing red berry fruit and soft tannins. Screwcap. **RATING** 89 **DRINK** 2010 $ 10

ŢŢŢŢ **Alexander Park Cabernet Sauvignon 2003** **RATING** 84 **DRINK** 2008 $ 18

Dominique Portet

★★★★★

870–872 Maroondah Highway, Coldstream, Vic 3770 **REGION** Yarra Valley
T (03) 5962 5760 **F** (03) 5962 4938 **WWW**.dominiqueportet.com **OPEN** 7 days 10–5
WINEMAKER Dominique Portet, Scott Baker **EST**. 2000 **CASES** 7000
Dominique Portet was bred in the purple. He spent his early years at Chateau Lafite (where his father was regisseur) and was one of the very first Flying Winemakers, commuting to Clos du Val in the Napa Valley where his brother is winemaker. Since 1976 he has lived in Australia, spending more than 20 years as managing director of Taltarni, and also developing the Clover Hill Vineyard in Tas. After retiring from Taltarni, he moved to the Yarra Valley, a region he had been closely observing since the mid-1980s. In 2001 he found the site he had long looked for, and in a twinkling of an eye built his winery and cellar door, and planted a quixotic mix of viognier and merlot next to the winery; he also undertakes contract winemaking for others. Exports to the UK, the US and other major markets.

ŢŢŢŢŢ **Heathcote Shiraz 2004** Excellent purple-red; medium-bodied; supple, rich black fruits, spice, chocolate and high-quality oak seamlessly interwoven; fine tannins, long finish. Cork. 14.5° alc. **RATING** 94 **DRINK** 2017 $ 45
Heathcote Cabernet Sauvignon 2004 Ripe, luscious, cassis and blackcurrant fruit is the driving force, pulling oak and tannins behind; velvety smooth mouthfeel and controlled alcohol. Cork. 14° alc. **RATING** 94 **DRINK** 2019 $ 40

ŢŢŢŢŢ **Yarra Valley Sauvignon Blanc 2005** Crisp, lively, smokey blossom aromas; fresh, bright, vibrant, mineral, gooseberry and citrus flavours; clean, tingling finish. Screwcap. **RATING** 92 **DRINK** Now $ 24.50

Yarra Valley Merlot 2004 Rich and mouthfilling without sacrificing varietal character; blackcurrant/redcurrant with spice and black olive nuances; good oak and tannins. Cork. 14° alc. **RATING** 92 **DRINK** 2015 $28

Fontaine Rose 2005 Fragrant cherry/strawberry/red fruit aromas; delicious palate with very good balance and length. **RATING** 91 **DRINK** Now $18.50

Donnelly River Wines NR

Lot 159 Vasse Highway, Pemberton, WA 6260 **REGION** Pemberton
T (08) 9776 2052 **F** (08) 9776 2053 **OPEN** 7 days 9.30–4.30
WINEMAKER Blair Meiklejohn **EST.** 1986 **CASES** 15 000
Donnelly River Wines draws upon 16 ha of estate vineyards planted in 1986, and has performed consistently well with its Chardonnay. Exports to the UK, Denmark, Germany, Singapore, Malaysia and Japan.

Donnybrook Estate NR

Hacket Road, Donnybrook, WA 6239 **REGION** Geographe
T (08) 9731 0707 **F** (08) 9731 0707 **OPEN** 7 days 10–5.30
WINEMAKER Gary Greirson **EST.** 1997 **CASES** 5000
Gary Greirson and wife Sally have completed the long-planned move to Donnybrook Estate from Cape Bouvard. The new winery was completed during the 2003 vintage, and Gary Greirson contract-makes a small amount of wine for others in the Donnybrook area. The wines are estate-grown from 11 acres of vineyards.

Donovan Wines NR

RMB 2017 Pomonal Road, Stawell, Vic 3380 **REGION** Grampians
T (03) 5358 2727 **F** (03) 5358 2727 **OPEN** Mon–Sat 10–5, Sun 12–5
WINEMAKER Chris Peters **EST.** 1977 **CASES** 250
Donovan quietly makes some concentrated, powerful Shiraz, with several vintages of the latter typically on offer. Limited distribution in Melbourne; most of the wine is sold by mail order with some bottle age. Has 5 ha of estate plantings.

Dookie College Winery

Dookie-Nalinga Road, Dookie, Vic 3647 **REGION** Goulburn Valley
T (03) 5833 9296 **F** (03) 5833 9296 **WWW**.dookie.unimelb.edu.au **OPEN** Fri–Sun 11–5
WINEMAKER Tony Lacy **EST.** 1896 **CASES** 1000
Viticulture and winemaking have been taught at Dookie since 1883; in the 1880s the Dookie Hills produced a quarter of Australia's total vintage, and included Australia's largest winery, before being devastated by phylloxera. Exactly 100 years after the Dookie winery was built in 1896, it was reopened, and since 1996 has been producing campus wine, used in teaching and research, and providing contract winemaking for boutique winemakers. It has 21 ha of vineyards planted to cabernet sauvignon (7 ha), shiraz (6 ha), sauvignon blanc and semillon (3 ha each) and tarango (2 ha).

360° Shiraz 2002 Strong, bright colour; seductive blackberry, prune and dark chocolate; very good texture and structure. Bargain basement price. Twin top. 14° alc. **RATING** 93 **DRINK** 2015 $16

Shiraz 2004 Very good colour; full-bodied, with very good blackberry, prune, plum and some chocolate; fine tannins, good length. Twin top. **RATING** 92 **DRINK** 2019 $16

Shiraz 2003 Good colour; medium- to full-bodied, with abundant black fruits; similar to the '04 but with slightly less finesse. Twin top. **RATING** 90 **DRINK** 2013 $16

Cabernet 2004 Medium-bodied; clearly articulated sweet cassis blackcurrant and earth varietal fruit; controlled oak. Cork. **RATING** 88 **DRINK** 2011 $16

360° Sauvignon Blanc 2004 Tending soft and broad, but does have passionfruit/tropical varietal flavours; better younger. Screwcap. 14° alc. **RATING** 86 **DRINK** Now $16

Tarango 2000 **RATING** 85 **DRINK** Now $16

Doonkuna Estate

Barton Highway, Murrumbateman, NSW 2582 **REGION** Canberra District
T (02) 6227 5811 **F** (02) 6227 5085 **WWW**.doonkuna.com.au **OPEN** 7 days 11–4
WINEMAKER Malcolm Burdett **EST.** 1973 **CASES** 4000
Following the acquisition of Doonkuna by Barry and Maureen Moran in late 1996, the plantings have been increased from a little under 4 ha to 20 ha. The cellar door prices remain modest, and increased production has followed in the wake of the new plantings. A wide range of vintages of many of the wines are available at cellar door at modest prices.

▼▼▼▼ **Rising Ground Sauvignon Blanc Semillon 2003** Potent, intense, bottle-developed aromas and flavours held together by the 45% semillon component; at its best now (2006) and offers good value. Screwcap. 12.6° alc. **RATING** 88 **DRINK** Now $12

Cabernet Merlot 2000 Light- to medium-bodied; blackcurrant/redcurrant/mint aromas and flavours; early picking gives a certain freshness, although not depth. Cork. 12.4° alc. **RATING** 87 **DRINK** 2009 $25

▼▼▼▽ **Sauvignon Blanc Semillon 2002 RATING** 86 **DRINK** Now $16

Dos Rios ★★★☆

PO Box 343, Nyah, Vic 3594 **REGION** Swan Hill
T (03) 5030 3005 **F** (03) 5030 3006 **WWW**.dosrios.com.au **OPEN** 7 days 9–5
WINEMAKER Cobaw Ridge (Alan Cooper) **EST.** 2003 **CASES** 600
Bruce Hall entered the wine business as a small contract grower for McGuigan Simeon Wines. From this point on, the story goes in reverse: instead of McGuigan Simeon saying it no longer required the grapes, it purchased the vineyard outright in 2003. In the meantime, Hall had hand-picked the grapes left at the end of the rows after the mechanical harvester had passed through, and had the wines made by Alan Cooper of Cobaw Ridge. In 2004 he purchased a small property northwest of Swan Hill with plantings of 20-year-old shiraz, which has been extended by small areas of viognier, tempranillo, durif and merlot.

▼▼▼▼▽ **Shiraz 2004** Very good hue and depth; clean, plum, black cherry and blackberry fruit; fine tannins; way above its theoretical station in life. Diam. 13.5° alc. **RATING** 91 **DRINK** 2012 $15

▼▼▼▽ **Chardonnay 2004** Soft, medium-bodied, tropical, yellow peach fruit, with some French oak inputs; nice, but lacks length. Diam. 14° alc. **RATING** 86 **DRINK** Now $15

Merlot 2003 RATING 86 **DRINK** Now $15

Dowie Doole ★★★☆

Cnr McMurtrie Road/Main Road, McLaren Vale, SA 5171 **REGION** McLaren Vale
T (08) 8323 8875 **F** (08) 8323 8895 **WWW**.dowiedoole.com **OPEN** 7 days 10–5, closed Christmas Day & Good Friday
WINEMAKER Brian Light (Contract) **EST.** 1996 **CASES** 9000
The imaginatively packaged and interestingly named Dowie Doole was a joint venture between two McLaren Vale grapegrowers: architect Drew Dowie and one-time international banker Norm Doole. Between them they have 42 ha of vineyards, and only a small proportion of their grapes are used to produce the Dowie Doole wines. In 1999 the partnership was expanded to include industry marketing veteran Leigh Gilligan, who returned to his native McLaren Vale after 5 years in Coonawarra (Gilligan is also involved with Boar's Rock). Exports to Canada, Alaska, Germany, Denmark, Fiji, Singapore and Hong Kong.

▼▼▼▼ **Hooley Dooley 2004** Medium-bodied; good mouthfeel, with a mix of blackberry and blackcurrant and a nice skein of sweetness running throughout; fine tannins, good value. Cabernet Sauvignon/Merlot/Shiraz/Petit Verdot. Screwcap. 14.5° alc. **RATING** 89 **DRINK** 2011 $14.95

McLaren Vale Merlot 2004 Spicy, cedary, savoury overtones to sweet fruit; nice wine, although not particularly varietal. Diam. 14.5° alc. **RATING** 87 **DRINK** 2009 $21 ᵀᵀᵀ♡ **McLaren Vale Chenin Blanc 2005** At the end of the day, poor man's verdelho, a variety which struggles for character; here helped by some lemony acidity. Screwcap. 13° alc. **RATING** 86 **DRINK** Now $ 15

Fleurieu Rose 2005 **RATING** 86 **DRINK** Now $ 16

Downing Estate Vineyard ★★★★★

19 Drummonds Lane, Heathcote, Vic 3523 **REGION** Heathcote
T (03) 5433 3387 **F** (03) 5433 3389 **WWW**.downingestate.com.au **OPEN** W'ends 11–6, or by appt
WINEMAKER Don Lewis **EST.** 1994 **CASES** 1300
Bob and Joy Downing purchased 24 ha of undulating land in 1994, and have since established a 9.5-ha dry-grown vineyard planted to shiraz (75%), cabernet sauvignon and merlot. At any one time, a number of vintages of each wine are available for sale.

ᵀᵀᵀᵀᵀ **Heathcote Shiraz 2001** Star-bright colour; a very elegant wine; perfectly poised, silky black fruits and integrated, though evident, oak. Aging slowly and surely. Cork. 15° alc. **RATING** 94 **DRINK** 2013 $ 39

Heathcote Cabernet Sauvignon 2002 A powerful and long full-bodied palate; blackcurrant, with touches of sweet earth and spice; very good oak and tannin management. Cork. 14.5° alc. **RATING** 94 **DRINK** 2015 $ 39

ᵀᵀᵀᵀ♡ **Heathcote Shiraz 2003** Strong colour; complex aromas and flavours reflecting the drought vintage; blackberry, plum, prune and a touch of mint. No shortage of flavour. Cork. **RATING** 92 **DRINK** 2015 $ 39

Heathcote Shiraz 2002 Medium-bodied; blackberry, plum, licorice and spice; a curious talc-like sensation on entry to the mouth, presumably deriving from tannins, yet there is no grip on the finish. Cork. 14.5° alc. **RATING** 90 **DRINK** 2012 $ 39

ᵀᵀᵀᵀ **Heathcote Cabernet Sauvignon 2003** Lots of dark blackcurrant fruit, but fierce tannins may never loosen their grip on the wine. Cork. **RATING** 89 **DRINK** 2013 $ 39

Drakesbrook Wines NR

PO Box 284, Waroona, WA 6215 **REGION** Peel
T (08) 9446 1383 **F** (08) 9446 1383 **WWW**.drakesbrookwines.com.au **OPEN** Not
WINEMAKER Bernard Worthington **EST.** 1998 **CASES** NA
Bernard (Bernie) Worthington, a Perth-based property specialist, developed a serious interest in wine and spent 4 years looking for a site which met all his criteria: ample water, easy access to a major population, and supporting tourist attractions. During that time he also completed a winegrowing course at Charles Sturt University. All his interests coalesced when he found Drakesbrook, a 216-ha property taking its name from the Drakesbrook River which flows through it. An hour's drive from Perth, it has views out to the ocean and is adjacent to the Lake Navarino tourist resort. He has subdivided the property, retaining 121 ha. The 11.9-ha vineyard is planted to semillon, chardonnay, shiraz, merlot, petit verdot, cabernet franc and cabernet sauvignon.

Drayton's Family Wines

Oakey Creek Road, Cessnock, NSW 2321 **REGION** Lower Hunter Valley
T (02) 4998 7513 **F** (02) 4998 7743 **WWW**.draytonswines.com.au **OPEN** Mon–Fri 8–5, w'ends & public hols 10–5
WINEMAKER Trevor Drayton **EST.** 1853 **CASES** 90 000
A family-owned and run stalwart of the Hunter Valley, producing honest, full-flavoured wines which sometimes excel themselves and are invariably modestly priced. The size of the production will come as a surprise to many, but it is a clear indication of the good standing of the brand, notwithstanding the low profile of recent years. It is not to be confused with Reg Drayton Wines. Exports to NZ, the US, Japan, Singapore, Taiwan, Samoa and Switzerland.

ᵀᵀᵀ♡ **Hunter Valley Semillon 2005** Easy style, with plenty of ripe, flavoursome fruit. **RATING** 86 **DRINK** 2009 $ 16.50

ᵀᵀᵀ **Hunter Valley Verdelho 2005** **RATING** 83 $ 16.50

Drews Creek Wines

NR

558 Wollombi Road, Broke, NSW 2330 **REGION** Lower Hunter Valley
T(02) 6579 1062 **F**(02) 6579 1062 **OPEN** By appt
WINEMAKER David Lowe (Contract) **EST.** 1993 **CASES** 300
Graeme Gibson and his partners are developing Drews Creek step by step. The initial planting of 2 ha of chardonnay and 3 ha of merlot was in 1991, and the first grapes were produced in 1993. A further 2.5 ha of sangiovese were planted in September 1999. Most of the grapes are sold to contract winemaker David Lowe, but a small quantity of wine is made for sale to friends and through the mailing list.

Driftwood Estate

NR

Lot 13 Caves Road, Yallingup, WA 6282 **REGION** Margaret River
T(08) 9755 6323 **F**(08) 9755 6343 **OPEN** 7 days 11–4.30
WINEMAKER Barney Mitchell, Mark Pizzuto **EST.** 1989 **CASES** 15 000
Driftwood Estate is now a well-established landmark on the Margaret River scene. Quite apart from offering a brasserie restaurant capable of seating 200 people (open 7 days for lunch and dinner) and a mock Greek open-air theatre, its wines feature striking and stylish packaging (even if strongly reminiscent of that of Devil's Lair) and opulent flavours. The winery architecture is, it must be said, opulent rather than stylish. Exports to Singapore.

drinkmoor wines

All Saints Road, Wahgunyah, Vic 3687 **REGION** Rutherglen
T(02) 6033 5544 **F**(02) 6033 5645 **WWW**.drinkmoorwines.com.au **OPEN** 7 days 10–5
WINEMAKER Damien Cofield **EST.** 2002 **CASES** 2500
This is a separate venture of Max and Karen Cofield (who also own Cofield Wines) and son Damien, with a very clear vision and marketing plan. It is to encourage people to make wine their beverage of choice; in other words, don't drink beer or spirits, drink wine instead, or drink more wines. Thus the wines are made in an everyday, easy-drinking style, with the cost kept as low as possible. The labelling, too, is designed to take the pretentiousness out of wine drinking, and to provide a bit of fun. Although the Cofields don't say so, this is the heartland of Generation X.

ΥΥΥΥ **Shiraz NV** Strong colour; ripe blackberry, plum and spice aromas and flavours; plenty of depth, but not extractive. **RATING** 88 **DRINK** Now $ 13.80
Al Dente Red NV Rich, rose style with plenty of fruit, a touch of sweetness and mass appeal. Whether the name communicates the style is another matter. Screwcap. 13.5° alc. **RATING** 87 **DRINK** Now $ 14
Traveller NV A light but appealing tawny style; not so much rancio as the best wines, but the fortifying spirit is good; echoes of Portugal. **RATING** 87 **DRINK** 2012 $ 13.80

ΥΥΥΥ **Cabernet Merlot NV** Clean, light- to medium-bodied red fruits, forest and stem; entirely fruit-driven. **RATING** 86 **DRINK** Now $ 13.80
Cabernets NV **RATING** 86 **DRINK** Now $ 13.80
Sticky NV Nicely balanced, mid-weight dessert wine with undoubted mass appeal. **RATING** 86 **DRINK** Now $ 11.80
Petit Verdot NV **RATING** 85 **DRINK** Now $ 13.80
Chardonnay 2005 **RATING** 84 **DRINK** Now $ 12.50

ΥΥΥ **Chenin Blanc NV** **RATING** 83 $ 11.80

Dromana Estate

555 Old Moorooduc Road, Tuerong, Vic 3933 **REGION** Mornington Peninsula
T(03) 5974 4400 **F**(03) 5974 1155 **WWW**.dromanaestate.com.au **OPEN** Wed–Sun 11–5, 7 days in summer
WINEMAKER Rollo Crittenden **EST.** 1982 **CASES** 30 000
Since it was established, Dromana Estate has always been near or at the cutting edge, both in marketing terms and in terms of development of new varietals, most obviously the Italian range

under the 'i' label. Rollo Crittenden has taken over winemaking responsibilities after the departure of father Garry, and the business is now majority-owned by investors. The capital provided has resulted in the Yarra Valley Hills and Mornington Estate wines coming under the Dromana Estate umbrella. Exports to the UK.

ΤΤΤΤΥ **Mornington Peninsula Chardonnay 2003** Fine, elegant, light- to medium-bodied wine; barrel ferment and malolactic ferment inputs work well with restrained stone fruit and citrus flavours; long finish. Screwcap. 14° alc. **RATING** 93 **DRINK** 2011 $ 29
Gary Crittenden i Arneis 2004 Citrus, honeysuckle, pear and spice aromas; a very attractive palate, fresh and focused; particularly good balance and finish. King Valley/Mornington Peninsula. Screwcap. **RATING** 91 **DRINK** Now $ 20
Mornington Estate Pinot Noir 2004 Good colour; spicy plum and black cherry fruit with plenty of fruit intensity; firm finish. Screwcap. 13.5° alc. **RATING** 90 **DRINK** 2009 $ 20

ΤΤΤΤ **Mornington Peninsula Sauvignon Blanc Semillon 2005** Light, clean and fresh; a light-bodied, gentle interplay between passionfruit, citrus and tropical fruit; clean finish. Screwcap. 13° alc. **RATING** 89 **DRINK** Now $ 20
Mornington Estate Chardonnay 2003 Sweet, mouthfilling peachy fruit, and a controlled flick of oak. Pleasant bottle development. Screwcap. 14° alc. **RATING** 89 **DRINK** 2008 $ 20
Mornington Estate Pinot Gris 2005 Subtle, spicy pear aromas; fills the mouth; quite sweet, almost tropical; lower alcohol (13.5°) than expected. Screwcap. **RATING** 89 **DRINK** Now $ 20
Mornington Peninsula Shiraz 2003 Fresh, spicy, peppery cherry and blackberry fruit on a light- to medium-bodied palate; balanced oak. Cork. 14° alc. **RATING** 89 **DRINK** 2012 $ 29
i Pinot Grigio 2005 Crisp, clean, minerally lemony pear fruit; bright, crisp, typical grigio finish. Screwcap. 14° alc. **RATING** 88 **DRINK** Now $ 20
Mornington Estate Shiraz Viognier 2004 Distinctive apricot-tinged lift from viognier; vibrant, fresh red and black fruits; light- to medium-bodied, summer style. Screwcap. **RATING** 88 **DRINK** Now $ 20
Mornington Estate Sauvignon Blanc 2005 Clean, light, fresh and well-made; some tropical fruit but lacks intensity; vineyard, not winery, shortcoming. Screwcap. 13.5° alc. **RATING** 87 **DRINK** Now $ 18

ΤΤΤΥ **i Nebbiolo 2001 RATING** 85 **DRINK** Now $ 20

Dromana Valley Wines   NR

Cnr Nepean Highway/Pickings Lane, Dromana, Vic 3936 **REGION** Mornington Peninsula
T (03) 5987 2093 **F** (03) 5987 2093 **WWW**.dvwines.com.au **OPEN** W'ends & public hols 11–5
WINEMAKER Greg Ray **EST.** 1974 **CASES** NA
The Stavropoulos family established Dromana Valley Wines in 1974, planting a small block of shiraz. When the Hickinbotham family purchased the property across the road in 1988 it led to the first Dromana Valley wines being made by Andrew Hickinbotham, and to the extension of the vineyard in 1989, with further plantings in 1997. There is now a little under 2 ha of chardonnay, over 1 ha of pinot noir, the remaining 2 ha divided between shiraz and cabernet sauvignon. Winemaking is carried out onsite by Greg Ray.

Drummonds Corrina Vineyard   NR

85 Wintles Road, Leongatha South, Vic 3953 **REGION** Gippsland
T (03) 5664 3317 **OPEN** W'ends 12.30–4.30
WINEMAKER Bass Phillip **EST.** 1983 **CASES** NA
The Drummond family has 3 ha of vines (1 ha each of pinot noir and sauvignon blanc, and 0.5 ha each of cabernet sauvignon and merlot) which was slowly established without the aid of irrigation. The viticultural methods are those practised by Phillip Jones, who makes the wines for Drummonds: north–south row orientation, leaf plucking on the east side of the rows, low yields, and all fruit picked by hand. Similarly restrained winemaking methods (no pumping, no filters and low SO_2) follow in the winery.

🐚 Ducketts Mill

NR

RMB 816, Scotsdale Road, Denmark, WA 6333 **REGION** Denmark
T (08) 9840 9844 **WWW**.duckettsmillwines.com.au **OPEN** 7 days 11–5
WINEMAKER Harewood Estate **EST.** 1997 **CASES** 2000
Ducketts Mill is a twin operation with Denmark Farmhouse Cheese, both owned and operated by
Ross and Dallas Lewis. They have the only cheese factory in the Great Southern, and rely on James
Kellie (Harewood Estate) to make the wines from the extensive estate plantings. Riesling,
chardonnay, merlot, cabernet franc, ruby cabernet and cabernet sauvignon total 7 ha; part of the
grapes are sold, part made into Riesling, Late Harvest Riesling, Merlot and Three Cabernets under
the Ducketts Mill label. The 10 different cheeses make an even wider choice.

Dudley Partners

NR

Porky Flat Vineyard, Penneshaw, Kangaroo Island, SA 5222 (postal) **REGION** Kangaroo Island
T (08) 8553 1509 **F** (08) 8553 1509 **OPEN** Not
WINEMAKER Wine Wise Consultancy **EST.** 1994 **CASES** NA
Colin Hopkins, Jeff Howard, Alan Willson and Paul Mansfield have formed a partnership to bring
together 3 vineyards on Kangaroo Island's Dudley Peninsula: the Porky Flat Vineyard (5 ha), Hog
Bay River (2 ha) and Sawyers (4 ha). It is the quirky vineyard names which give the products their
distinctive identities. The partners not only look after viticulture, but also join in the winemaking
process. Most of the wines are sold through licensed outlets on Kangaroo Island.

Due South

NR

PO Box 72, Denmark, WA 6333 **REGION** Denmark
T (08) 9848 3399 **F** (08) 9848 1690 **OPEN** Not
WINEMAKER Harewood Estate (James Kellie) **EST.** 1999 **CASES** 1000
Another substantial new development in the Great Southern, with 100 ha of sauvignon blanc,
semillon, chardonnay, pinot noir, shiraz, merlot, cabernet franc and cabernet sauvignon. Part of the
grapes produced each year go to make wine under the Due South brand, which is stocked exclusively
by Vintage Cellars. The remainder is sold as grapes or processed wine to others. Exports to the UK.

Duke's Vineyard

NR

Porongurup Road, Porongurup, WA 6324 **REGION** Porongurup
T (08) 9853 1107 **F** (08) 9853 1107 **WWW**.dukesvineyard.com **OPEN** 7 days 10–4.30
WINEMAKER Mike Garland (Contract) **EST.** 1998 **CASES** 2500
When Hilde and Ian (Duke) Ranson sold their clothing manufacturing business in 1998 they were
able to fulfil a long-held dream of establishing a vineyard in the Porongurup subregion of Great
Southern. It took two abortive efforts before they became third-time-lucky with the acquisition of a
65-ha farm at the foot of the Porongurup Range. They planted 3 ha each of shiraz and cabernet
sauvignon and 4 ha of riesling. Hilde Ranson is a successful artist, and it was she who designed the
beautiful scalloped, glass-walled cellar door sale area with its mountain blue cladding. The 2002
Riesling was a trophy winner at the 2006 Sydney Royal Wine Show, adding to previous gold medal
success for this lovely mature Riesling.

Dulcinea

NR

Jubilee Road, Sulky, Ballarat, Vic 3352 **REGION** Ballarat
T (03) 5334 6440 **F** (03) 5334 6828 **WWW**.dulcinea.com.au **OPEN** 7 days 10–6
WINEMAKER Rod Stott **EST.** 1983 **CASES** 3000
Rod Stott is a passionate grapegrower and winemaker (with 6 ha of vineyard) who chose the name
Dulcinea from *The Man of La Mancha*, where only a fool fights windmills. With winemaking help
from various sources, he has produced a series of interesting and often complex wines. Exports to
Japan, Fiji and China.

Dumaresq Valley Vineyard

NR

Bruxner Highway, Tenterfield, NSW 2372 **REGION** Northern Slopes Zone
T (02) 6737 5281 **F** (02) 6737 5293 **www**.dumaresqvalleyvineyard.com.au **OPEN** 7 days 9–5
WINEMAKER Contract **EST.** 1997 **CASES** NA
Three generations of the Zappa family have been involved in the establishment of what is now a very large mixed farming property on 1600 ha, all beginning when the first generation arrived from Italy in the late 1940s to work as cane-cutters in Qld. Today, Martin and Amelia, with three of their sons and their wives, have a property sustaining 120 cattle, 5000 super-fine wool Merino sheep, 140 ha of fresh produce, 250 ha of cereal crops and a 25-ha vineyard. The vineyard was progressively established between 1997 and 2000, with plantings of chardonnay, semillon, sauvignon blanc, shiraz, merlot, cabernet sauvignon, barbera and tempranillo.

Dunelm Wines

Lot 509 Scotsdale Road, Denmark WA 6333 **REGION** Great Southern
T (08) 9840 9027 **F** (08) 9840 9027 **OPEN** W'ends, public and school hols 10–4, or by appt
WINEMAKER Harewood Estate (James Kellie) **EST.** 1999 **CASES** 350
After 35 years as a General Practitioner in Fremantle, Graeme Gargett (and wife Lesley) decided to 'semi-retire' and pursue a career in viticulture. They purchased their beautiful 35-ha property in the Scotsdale Valley, only a few kms from Denmark, in 1997. It had been used for mixed farming, but the north-facing slopes of well-drained karri loam soils were ideal for viticulture. In September 1999 they planted 2 ha of pinot noir, 1 ha of chardonnay and 0.5 ha each of shiraz and cabernet sauvignon. Most of the grapes are sold to Plantagenet, but small quantities have been made each year since 2002, some by Graeme Gargett without the use of preservatives. The Barking Dog label is in honour of the resident bird-scarer, the Gargett's dachshund Harley.

Barking Dog Chardonnay 2005 Bright, light green-straw; elegant, fine melon and citrus, the oak incidental; excellent length and finish. Screwcap. 13.5° alc. **RATING** 92 **DRINK** 2010 $ 22

Barking Dog Cabernet Sauvignon 2005 Light- to medium red-purple; juicy berry with some earthy/leafy/minty flavours; on the cusp of ripeness. Screwcap. 12.5° alc. **RATING** 86 **DRINK** 2008 $ 24
Barking Dog Pinot Noir 2004 **RATING** 85 **DRINK** Now $ 22

Dunns Creek Estate

137 McIlroys Road, Red Hill, Vic 3937 **REGION** Mornington Peninsula
T 0413 020 467 **F** (03) 5989 2011 **www**.dunnscreek.com.au **OPEN** By appt
WINEMAKER Sandro Mosele (Contract) **EST.** 2001 **CASES** 1270
This is the retirement venture of Roger and Hannah Stuart-Andrews, a former professional couple whose love of Italian and Spanish wines led them to their eclectic choice of varieties. Thus they have planted a total of 2.7 ha of tempranillo, albarino, arneis and barbera in more or less equal quantities. There seems no reason why these grapes should not produce wines of distinction.

Mornington Peninsula Arneis 2005 Some orange blossom aromas, the palate with a firm, stoney/minerally texture, followed by a nice touch of orange/citrus on the finish. Diam. 13.5° alc. **RATING** 88 **DRINK** 2009 $ 25
Mornington Peninsula Barbera 2004 Strong colour; lots of black fruits, but a slightly angular mouthfeel and the palate chops off on the finish; interesting to watch as the vines mature. Diam. 14.5° alc. **RATING** 87 **DRINK** 2010 $ 25

Dusty Hill Wines

Barambah Road, Moffatdale via Murgon, Qld 4605 **REGION** South Burnett
T (07) 4168 4700 **F** (07) 4168 4888 **www**.dustyhill.com.au **OPEN** 7 days 9.30–5
WINEMAKER Symphony Hill (Mike Hayes) **EST.** 1996 **CASES** 1500
Joe Prendergast and family have established 2 ha each of shiraz and cabernet sauvignon, 1 ha each of verdelho and semillon and 0.5 ha each of merlot and black muscat. The vines are crop-thinned to

obtain maximum ripeness in the fruit and to maximise tannin extract, although the winery's specialty is the Dusty Rose.

ΨΨΨΨ **South Burnett Semillon 2005** Plenty of aroma and flavour; intermediate alcohol works well, with a spread of grass/lemon into the tropical end of the spectrum; good length and finish. Screwcap. 12° alc. **RATING** 89 **DRINK** 2010 $17

ΨΨΨ **South Burnett Verdelho 2005** **RATING** 83 $17

Dutschke Wines ★★★★★

PO Box 107 Lyndoch, SA 5351 **REGION** Barossa Valley
T (08) 8524 5485 **F** (08) 8524 5489 **WWW**.dutschkewines.com **OPEN** Not
WINEMAKER Wayne Dutschke **EST.** 1998 **CASES** 6000
Wayne Dutschke had over 20 years working in Australia and overseas for companies large and small before joining his uncle (and estate grapegrower), Ken Semmler to form Dutschke Wines in 1990. In addition to outstanding table wines, he has a once-yearly release of fortified wines (doubtless drawing on his time at Baileys of Glenrowan); these sell out overnight, and have received the usual stratospheric points from Robert Parker. Exports to the UK, the US and other major markets.

ΨΨΨΨΨ **Single Barrel Barossa Valley Shiraz 2003** The wine is distinctly different from the other '03 reds; highly aromatic and spicy; vibrant fruit, luscious but not jammy, has absorbed the new French oak; long finish. Cork. **RATING** 95 **DRINK** 2015 $50
St Jakobi Shiraz 2003 Intense and focused mix of damson plum and black fruits, plus touches of chocolate and vanilla; a nice web of supporting tannins aid length. Cork. **RATING** 94 **DRINK** 2013 $30
Oscar Semmler Shiraz 2003 Good purple-red; nicely proportioned and balanced; plum and blackberry fruit with subtle oak; overall, surprising elegance. Cork. **RATING** 94 **DRINK** 2013 $48

ΨΨΨΨΨ **Willow Bend Merlot Shiraz Cabernet 2003** A quite fragrant and distinctly elegant mix of small red fruits (predominantly) and a twist of spicy blackberry. Cork. **RATING** 91 **DRINK** 2012 $22

ΨΨΨΨ **Barossa Valley Sun Dried Shiraz NV** **RATING** 86 **DRINK** 2009 $35

Dyson Wines NR

Sherriff Road, Maslin Beach, SA 5170 **REGION** McLaren Vale
T (08) 8386 1092 **F** (08) 8327 0066 **OPEN** 7 days 10–5
WINEMAKER Allan Dyson **EST.** 1976 **CASES** 2000
Allan Dyson, who described himself (a few years ago) as 'a young man of 50-odd years', has recently added to his 1.5 ha of viognier with 2.5 ha each of chardonnay and cabernet sauvignon, and has absolutely no thoughts of slowing down or retiring. All wines are estate-grown, made and bottled.

Eagle Vale ★★★★

51 Caves Road, Margaret River, WA 6285 **REGION** Margaret River
T (08) 9757 6477 **F** (08) 9757 6199 **WWW**.eaglevalewine.com **OPEN** 7 days 10–5
WINEMAKER Guy Gallienne **EST.** 1997 **CASES** 7500
Eagle Vale is a joint venture between the property owners, Steve and Wendy Jacobs, and the operator/winemaking team of Guy, Chantal and Karl Gallienne. It is a united nations team: Steve Jacobs was born in Colorado, and has business interests in Bali. The Galliennes come from the Loire Valley, although Guy secured his winemaking degree at Roseworthy College/Adelaide University. The vineyard, now 11.5 ha, is managed on a low-impact basis, without pesticides (guinea fowls do the work) and with minimal irrigation. All the wines are made from estate-grown grapes. Exports to the UK, Germany, The Netherlands, Indonesia, Singapore and the US.

ΨΨΨΨΨ **Margaret River Chardonnay 2003** Good colour; a complex bouquet leads into a powerful palate; stone fruit and nuts, with a streak of minerality running throughout. Cork. **RATING** 91 **DRINK** 2010 $39

TTTT **Margaret River Semillon Sauvignon Blanc 2005** Plenty of flavour richness and depth in the tropical spectrum, needing a little more acidity. Screwcap. 13.5° alc. **RATING** 87 **DRINK** Now $ 18

East Arm Vineyard ★★★★

111 Archers Road, Hillwood, Tas 7250 **REGION** Northern Tasmania
T (03) 6334 0266 **F** (03) 6334 1405 **OPEN** W'ends & public hols, or by appt
WINEMAKER Bert Sundstrup, Nicholas Butler (Contract) **EST.** 1993 **CASES** 1200
East Arm Vineyard was established by Launceston gastroenterologist Dr John Wettenhall and partner Anita James, who has completed the Charles Sturt University Diploma in Applied Science (winegrowing). The 2 ha of vineyard, which came into full production in 1998, are more or less equally divided among riesling, chardonnay and pinot noir. It is established on a historic block, part of a grant made to retired British soldiers of the Georgetown garrison in 1821, and slopes down to the Tamar River. The property is 25 ha, and there are plans for further planting and, somewhere down the track, a winery. The Riesling is usually excellent. The business is to be sold (health reasons), but as at April 2006 the sale process was incomplete.

TTTTY **Riesling 2005** Ripe, tropical and fleshy, with a juicy mid-palate; nice acidity. **RATING** 90 **DRINK** 2012

TTTT **Riesling 2004** Has plenty of lime/passionfruit flavour, but is also marked by slightly crumbly acidity. 11.5° alc. **RATING** 88 **DRINK** 2009 $ 20

Eastern Peake NR

Clunes Road, Coghills Creek, Vic 3364 **REGION** Ballarat
T (03) 5343 4245 **F** (03) 5343 4365 **OPEN** 7 days 10–5
WINEMAKER Norman Latta **EST.** 1983 **CASES** 3000
Norm Latta and Di Pym established Eastern Peake, 25 km northeast of Ballarat on a high plateau overlooking the Creswick Valley, over 20 years ago. In the early years the grapes were sold to Trevor Mast of Mount Chalambar and Mount Langi Ghiran, but the 5 ha of vines are now dedicated to the production of Eastern Peake wines. The Pinot Noir is on the minerally/stemmy side; earlier bottling might preserve more of the sweet fruit. Exports to the UK.

Eden Hall ★★★★★

36a Murray Street, Angaston, SA 5353 **REGION** Eden Valley
T (08) 8562 4590 **F** (08) 8342 3950 **WWW** .edenhall.com.au **OPEN** 7 days 10–5
WINEMAKER Wine Wise Consultancy **EST.** 2002 **CASES** 1820
David and Mardi Hall purchased the historic Avon Brae property in 1996. The 120-ha property has now been planted to 32 ha of cabernet sauvignon (the lion's share), shiraz, merlot, cabernet franc, riesling (over 9 ha), and viognier. The majority of the production is contracted to Yalumba, St Hallett and McGuigan Simeon, with 10% of the best grapes held back for the Eden Hall label. The Riesling, Shiraz Viognier and Cabernet Sauvignon are all excellent, the red wines outstanding. Exports to the UK, the US and Asia.

TTTTT **Riesling 2005** Classic, floral lime and apple blossom aromas; fine but generous lime/lemon fruit progressively builds on the long palate; good acid. Screwcap. 12° alc. **RATING** 94 **DRINK** 2015 $ 20
Shiraz Viognier 2003 Blackcurrant, spice and earth aromas and flavours; excellent tannins give very good texture and structure, almost Italianate; a very interesting wine clearly showing the Irvine touch. Screwcap. 14.5° alc. **RATING** 94 **DRINK** 2015 $ 32

TTTTY **CSV 2003** A highly fragrant bouquet, with blackcurrant, spice and mocha flowing through to the palate; quite firm tannins march along the palate from start to finish; not, perhaps, the usual Irvine style. Cabernet/Shiraz/Viognier. Screwcap. 14.5° alc. **RATING** 91 **DRINK** 2015 $ 32
Cabernet Sauvignon 2003 Somewhat austere blackcurrant fruit, the powerful structure driven by savoury tannins. A cabernet for traditionalists. Screwcap. 14.5° alc. **RATING** 90 **DRINK** 2013 $ 32

♥♥♥♥ **Ratafia Riesling 2004** Extremely interesting and complex; partially fermented then fortified, with the illusion of a dry finish. Screwcap. 16° alc. **RATING** 89 **DRINK** 2008 $ 25

Eden Springs

NR

Boehm Springs Road, Springton, SA 5235 **REGION** Eden Valley
T (08) 8564 1166 **F** (08) 8564 1265 **WWW**.edensprings.com.au **OPEN** Not
WINEMAKER Andrew Ewart (Contract) **EST.** 2000 **CASES** 1500
Richard Wiencke and Meredith Hodgson opened the Eden Springs wine doors on 1 July 2000. It is a remote vineyard (6 km by dirt road from Springton) and sells its wine through a high-quality newsletter to mailing list customers and the website. Exports to all major markets.

Edwards Vineyard

★★★★☆

Cnr Caves Road/Ellensbrook Road, Cowaramup, WA 6284 **REGION** Margaret River
T (08) 9755 5999 **F** (08) 9755 5988 **WWW**.edwardsvineyard.com.au **OPEN** 7 days 10.30–5
WINEMAKER Michael Edwards **EST.** 1994 **CASES** 7500
Edwards Vineyard is a family-owned and operated winery, with brothers Michael and Christo being the winemaker and viticulturist, respectively. Michael, formerly a winemaker at Voyager Estate, is now involved full-time with the business. There is 25 ha of chardonnay, semillon, sauvignon blanc, shiraz, cabernet sauvignon and merlot. Exports to the US, Canada, Denmark, Philippines, Indonesia, Singapore and Hong Kong.

♥♥♥♥♥ **Margaret River Chardonnay 2004** Excellent green-yellow; a high-quality wine skilfully using barrel ferment oak woven through elegant, intense melon/white peach/nectarine fruit finishing with citrussy acidity. Screwcap. 13.5° alc. **RATING** 94 **DRINK** 2014 $ 24

♥♥♥♥♀ **Margaret River Semillon Sauvignon Blanc 2005** Spotlessly clean; driven by herb and grass semillon varietal fruit and sophisticated, subtle oak inputs; good mouthfeel. Screwcap. 13° alc. **RATING** 92 **DRINK** 2010 $ 19
Margaret River Sauvignon Blanc 2005 Again, spotlessly clean; a light-bodied mix of mineral, passionfruit and gooseberry, the touch of oak adding as much to texture as to flavour; appealing lemony acidity. Screwcap. 13.5° alc. **RATING** 91 **DRINK** Now $ 19
Margaret River Cabernet Sauvignon 2004 Powerful blackcurrant fruit and equally powerful (but not dry or green) tannins; medium- to full-bodied; good future; in typical vineyard style. Screwcap. 14° alc. **RATING** 90 **DRINK** 2014 $ 29

♥♥♥♥ **Margaret River Shiraz 2004** Developed, albeit dark, colour; very powerful, but over-extracted, black fruits and dry tannins. Seems to have been picked a little too late. Not typical of the vineyard. Screwcap. 14.5° alc. **RATING** 87 **DRINK** Now $ 26

Eighteen Forty-Seven

★★★★☆

PO Box 918, Rowland Flat, SA 5352 **REGION** Barossa Valley
T (08) 8524 5328 **F** (08) 8524 5329 **WWW**.eighteenfortyseven.com **OPEN** Not
WINEMAKER Rod Chapman, Andrew Lindner **EST.** 1996 **CASES** 2000
A youthful John Curnow began his career over 30 years ago buying and selling wines from all over the world. He then moved to Coca-Cola, becoming a senior executive or CEO in Hungary, the Czech Republic, NZ, the US and Australia. In 1996 he and wife Sue began the development of Eighteen Forty-Seven, with 2 vineyards planted to a mix of old and new vines, the lion's share (8 ha) going to shiraz and semillon, with an additional ha planted predominantly to petit verdot and a little sauvignon blanc. The name has a dual source: the original land grant of the Rowland Flat property dates from 1847, and 1–8–47 is John Curnow's birthdate. Up until 2002 the grapes were sold to other Barossa Valley producers, but in that vintage the first wines were made, and have had much critical acclaim. Exports to Hungary, the Czech Republic and Canada.

♥♥♥♥♥ **Home Block Petit Verdot 2004** Deep, healthy colour; plenty of inky, dark fruits with good structure, ripe tannins and controlled oak. The variety is definitely suited to the Barossa Valley. Cork. 13.8° alc. **RATING** 94 **DRINK** 2017 $ 42

ΥΥΥΥ️ **Pappy's Paddock Shiraz 2004** Bright, dark red-purple; powerful blackberry, licorice and dark chocolate fruit; good handling of American oak; full-bodied, but not heavy. Cork. 14.4° alc. **RATING** 93 **DRINK** 2014 $ 42

Pappy's Paddock Shiraz 2002 An elegant, medium-bodied wine; a long, sustained palate with black fruits and licorice; good extract and oak. Cork. 14° alc. **RATING** 93 **DRINK** 2012 $ 41.90

Home Block Petit Verdot 2002 Good depth to the colour; powerful black fruits, dark chocolate and ripe tannins with some spicy notes. Cork. 14.1° alc. **RATING** 92 **DRINK** 2015 $ 41.90

ΥΥΥΥ **Pappy's Paddock Shiraz 2003** Good colour, quite dense; very ripe plum and prune flavours on a rich palate showing some slightly dead fruit notes. Cork. 14.5° alc. **RATING** 89 **DRINK** 2011 $ 41.90

High Patch Chardonnay 2004 A touch of French oak gives slightly more complexity and intensity than the unwooded '05; nectarine and peach fruit. Screwcap. 12.7° alc. **RATING** 87 **DRINK** Now $ 26.75

ΥΥΥΥ️ **Emma Lydia's Garden Semillon 2004** **RATING** 86 **DRINK** 2008 $ 26.75
Emma Lydia's Garden Semillon 2005 **RATING** 85 **DRINK** 2008 $ 26.75
Home Block Petit Verdot 2003 **RATING** 85 **DRINK** 2008 $ 42
High Patch Chardonnay 2005 **RATING** 84 **DRINK** Now $ 27

Elan Vineyard   ★★★☆

17 Turners Road, Bittern, Vic 3918 **REGION** Mornington Peninsula
T (03) 5983 1858 **F** (03) 5983 2821 **WWW**.elanvineyard.com.au **OPEN** First weekend of month, public hols 11–5, or by appt
WINEMAKER Selma Lowther **EST.** 1980 **CASES** 400
Selma Lowther, fresh from Charles Sturt University (as a mature-age student) made an impressive debut with her spicy, fresh, crisp Chardonnay, and has continued to make tiny quantities of appealing and sensibly priced wines. Most of the grapes from the 2.5 ha of estate vineyards are sold; production remains minuscule.

ΥΥΥΥ **Chardonnay 2004** A big wine, slightly heavy, bordering sweet fruit; some sulphide complexity. **RATING** 87 **DRINK** 2009 $ 16

Elderton   ★★★★☆

3 Tanunda Road, Nuriootpa, SA 5355 **REGION** Barossa Valley
T (08) 8568 7878 **F** (08) 8568 7879 **WWW**.eldertonwines.com.au **OPEN** Mon–Fri 8.30–5, w'ends, hols 11–4
WINEMAKER Richard Langford, James Irvine (Consultant) **EST.** 1984 **CASES** 32 000
The wines are based on old, high-quality Barossa floor estate vineyards, and most are driven to a lesser or greater degree by American oak; the Command Shiraz is at the baroque end of the spectrum and has to be given considerable respect within the parameters of its style. Exports to all major markets.

ΥΥΥΥΥ **Ashmead Single Vineyard Cabernet Sauvignon 2002** Dark, deep red-purple; medium- to full-bodied blackcurrant, earth, dark chocolate and bramble fruit; persistent, ripe tannins; good French oak. Screwcap. 14.5° alc. **RATING** 94 **DRINK** 2022 $ 85

ΥΥΥΥ️ **Estate Barossa Valley Merlot 2002** Has all the intensity expected of the vintage; dark, sombre fruit expression in keeping with the variety; good French oak. Cork. 14.5° alc. **RATING** 92 **DRINK** 2015 $ 30

Friends Cabernet Sauvignon 2003 Medium-bodied; attractive supple mouthfeel, flooded with juicy cassis/blackcurrant/black cherry fruit, the oak balanced and integrated. Cork. **RATING** 91 **DRINK** 2012 $ 16

ΥΥΥΥ **Friends Barossa Valley Shiraz 2003** Traditional Barossa style; softly sweet, warm and rich black fruits; mocha and vanilla; ripe tannins. Cork. 14.5° alc. **RATING** 89 **DRINK** 2010 $ 18

Sauvignon Blanc Verdelho 2005 A quixotic mix of varieties; actually works quite well; fresh, sweet gooseberry fruit; bright finish; 85% Sauvignon Blanc. Screwcap. **RATING** 88 **DRINK** Now $ 12.90

ŸŸŸ♀ **Friends Eden Valley Riesling 2005 RATING** 85 **DRINK** Now $ 18
Unwooded Chardonnay 2005 RATING 84 **DRINK** Now $ 12.90

Eldredge   ★★★★☆

Spring Gully Road, Clare, SA 5453 **REGION** Clare Valley
T (08) 8842 3086 **F** (08) 8842 3086 **OPEN** 7 days 11–5
WINEMAKER Leigh Eldredge **EST.** 1993 **CASES** 6000
Leigh and Karen Eldredge have established their winery and cellar door sales area in the Sevenhill Ranges at an altitude of 500m, above the town of Watervale. Both the Rieslings and red wines have had considerable success in recent years. Exports to the UK, the US, Canada and Hong Kong.

ŸŸŸŸŸ **Watervale Riesling 2005** Delicious passionfruit aromas and flavours; delicate, but perfectly balanced. Screwcap. **RATING** 94 **DRINK** 2015 $ 17

ŸŸŸŸ♀ **Blue Chip Shiraz 2004** Powerful blackberry, briar, earth and dark chocolate fruit; integrated oak, but the tannins are fractionally edgy, needing time to soften. Screwcap. 14.7° alc. **RATING** 90 **DRINK** 2010 $ 25
Boundary Sangiovese 2002 Strong colour; a powerful wine, with a rich and spicy array of red and black cherry fruits; medium- to full-bodied, ripe tannins; nice wine, not particularly varietal. Cork. 14° alc. **RATING** 90 **DRINK** 2012 $ 25

ŸŸŸŸ **Sangiovese Rose 2005** Vividly coloured; a high-flavoured mix of sundry red fruits and obvious sweetness on the finish. Mass appeal. Screwcap. **RATING** 88 **DRINK** Now $ 17

ŸŸŸ♀ **Sauvignon Blanc Semillon 2004 RATING** 86 **DRINK** Now $ 17

Eldridge Estate of Red Hill   ★★★★★

120 Arthurs Seat Road, Red Hill, Vic 3937 **REGION** Mornington Peninsula
T (03) 5989 2644 **WWW.**eldridge-estate.com.au **OPEN** Mon–Fri 12–4, w'ends & hols 11–5
WINEMAKER David Lloyd **EST.** 1985 **CASES** 800
The Eldridge Estate vineyard, with 7 varieties included in its 3.5 ha, was purchased by Wendy and David Lloyd in 1995. Major retrellising work has been undertaken, changing to Scott Henry, and all the wines will now be estate-grown and made. David Lloyd has also planted several Dijon-selected pinot noir clones (114, 115 and 777) which have made their contribution since 2004. A new cellar door opened in 2005.

ŸŸŸŸŸ **Chardonnay 2004** Intensely focused, fine and long; a seamless fusion of nectarine fruit and oak on both bouquet and palate; long, clean finish. Screwcap. 14° alc. **RATING** 96 **DRINK** 2010 $ 35
Single Clone Pinot Noir 2004 Clone MV6. Deeper colour than all except 777 Clone; red and black cherry aromas and flavours; excellent length, finish and aftertaste. Screwcap. **RATING** 95 **DRINK** 2011
Single Clone Pinot Noir 2004 Clone 777. Clean and aromatic with a faint hint of stem, far from unattractive; a range of black (plum and cherry) and red (cherry and strawberry) fruits; overall elegance and excellent length. Screwcap. 14° alc. **RATING** 95 **DRINK** 2010 $ 35
Single Clone Pinot Noir 2004 Clone 114. A mix of sweet and more savoury notes; red and black cherry and spice; silky palate; excellent length and style. Screwcap. **RATING** 94 **DRINK** 2010
West Patch Pinot Noir 2003 Has the lightest colour of the '04s, but unexpected length and persistence; similar to the varietal Pinot (main release). Screwcap. 13.5° alc. **RATING** 94 **DRINK** 2009 $ 30

ŸŸŸŸ♀ **Single Clone Pinot Noir 2004** Clone G5V15. Highly aromatic; very tangy, almost lemony edges to the spicy, forest fruit; long finish. Screwcap. **RATING** 92 **DRINK** 2009

Single Clone Pinot Noir 2004 Clone 115. Leather, spice and earth on black cherry fruit; reasonably firm tannins; powerful wine. Screwcap. **RATING** 92 **DRINK** 2010

Euroa Creek Reserve Shiraz 2004 An elegant wine; supple, smooth blackberry and black cherry fruit; fine tannins, controlled oak; 250 cases made chiefly for the US market. Avant garde labelling. Screwcap. 14° alc. **RATING** 92 **DRINK** 2015 $ 42

Clonal Blend Pinot Noir 2004 Stylish; light- to medium-bodied; spicy, savoury cherry fruits; clean finish; seems to be a blend of lesser barrels. Screwcap. **RATING** 91 **DRINK** 2009

🐢 Eleven Paddocks ★★★★

PO Box 829, Macleod, Vic 3084 **REGION** Pyrenees
T (03) 9458 4997 **F** (03) 9458 5075 **WWW**.elevenpaddocks.com.au **OPEN** Not
WINEMAKER Gabriel Horvat, Gary Mills **EST.** 2003 **CASES** 1000
Eleven partners, under the direction of managing partner Danny Gravell, purchased a small vineyard in 2002, in the foothills of the Pyrenees Ranges near Landsborough. The quality of the first vintage was sufficient to encourage the partners to increase planting to 4 ha of shiraz, 2 ha each of chardonnay and cabernet sauvignon and a dash of petit verdot.

ŦŦŦŦŶ **Shiraz 2004** Strong colour; attractive medium-bodied plum and blackberry flavours; controlled alcohol and extract, both to the wine's advantage; gently savoury, fine, tannins. Cork. 13.2° alc. **RATING** 91 **DRINK** 2012 $ 18

Cabernet Sauvignon 2004 Earthy/cedary/savoury/leafy notes; despite the alcohol, a fairly austere wine which may or may not soften with age. Cork. 13.6° alc. **RATING** 91 **DRINK** 2012 $ 18

ŦŦŦŶ **Rose 2005 RATING** 85 **DRINK** Now $ 15

Elgee Park ★★★★☆

RMB 5560 Wallaces Road, Merricks North, Vic 3926 **REGION** Mornington Peninsula
T (03) 5989 7338 **F** (03) 5989 7338 **WWW**.elgeeparkwines.com.au **OPEN** One day a year — Sunday of Queen's Birthday weekend
WINEMAKER Contract **EST.** 1972 **CASES** 1600
The pioneer of the Mornington Peninsula in its 20th century rebirth, owned by Baillieu Myer and family. The wines are now made at Stonier and T'Gallant, Elgee Park's own winery having been closed, and the overall level of activity decreased, although the quality has increased.

ŦŦŦŦŶ **Family Reserve Chardonnay 2004** Intense cool-grown fruit; stylish barrel ferment/malolactic/lees notes on grapefruit, melon and peach; perfect balance. Screwcap. 14° alc. **RATING** 93 **DRINK** 2010 $ 30

Family Reserve Pinot Gris 2004 Very fragrant and floral; good balance and faintly honeyed mouthfeel; doesn't show any alcohol heat. Screwcap. 14° alc. **RATING** 90 **DRINK** 2008 $ 25

Family Reserve Viognier 2004 A clean bouquet; a rich and textured palate with an interesting and unusual mix of flavours including apricot and a distinct touch of ginger. Pioneer of the variety in Australia. Screwcap. 14.4° alc. **RATING** 90 **DRINK** 2009 $ 40

Cuvee Brut 2001 A fine, elegant style, largely driven by chardonnay (60%) but with some complexity from the pinot noir (40%) and 3 years on lees. 12.5° alc. **RATING** 90 **DRINK** Now $ 30

ŦŦŦŦ **Family Reserve Pinot Noir 2004** Clear, light purple-red; a bright, clean, lively and fresh bouquet leading into a light-bodied, zesty, zippy palate with red fruits. Needs a touch more weight. Screwcap. 14° alc. **RATING** 89 **DRINK** 2009 $ 30

Family Reserve Riesling 2005 Cut grass, mineral and lime on both the bouquet and palate; firm finish, masculine style. Screwcap. 13.5° alc. **RATING** 88 **DRINK** 2009 $ 18

ŦŦŦŦ **Family Reserve Cabernet Merlot 2003 RATING** 86 **DRINK** 2008 $ 25

Elgo Estate

2038 Upton Road, Upton Hill, via Longwood, Vic 3665 **REGION** Strathbogie Ranges
T (03) 5798 5563 **F** (03) 5798 5524 **WWW.**elgoestate.com.au **OPEN** By appt
WINEMAKER Cameron Atkins, Dennis Clarke **EST.** 1999 **CASES** 12 000
The second Australian generation of the Taresch family has an 890-ha grazing property, with 55 ha of vines in 3 different vineyards: Tarcombe Valley Vineyard (the warmest, planted to shiraz and cabernet); Lakeside Vineyard (planted in the 1970s with chardonnay, merlot and riesling); and the highest at Upton Hill (pinot noir and sauvignon blanc), the last adjacent to the winery built in 2004. Most of the power for the winery comes from a 150 kW wind-powered turbine.

TTTTT **Strathbogie Ranges Chardonnay 2004** Very good wine; abundant nicely ripened nectarine and stone fruit flavour supported by good oak management. Trophy 2005 Strathbogie Wine Show. Screwcap. **RATING** 93 **DRINK** 2009 $ 21

TTTT **Allira Sauvignon Blanc 2005** Lively and long; tangy/citrussy overtones; good balance and length; clever touch of sweetness. Screwcap. **RATING** 88 **DRINK** Now $ 12

TTTT **Strathbogie Ranges Riesling 2005** **RATING** 86 **DRINK** 2008 $ 21
Allira Shiraz 2004 **RATING** 86 **DRINK** 2008 $ 12
Allira Cabernet Merlot 2004 **RATING** 86 **DRINK** 2009 $ 12
Strathbogie Ranges Pinot Noir Rose 2005 **RATING** 84 **DRINK** Now $ 18
Strathbogie Ranges Pinot Noir 2004 **RATING** 84 **DRINK** Now $ 21

Eling Forest Winery

Hume Highway, Sutton Forest, NSW 2577 **REGION** Southern Highlands
T (02) 4878 9155 **F** (02) 4878 9246 **WWW.**elingforest.com.au **OPEN** 7 days 10–5
WINEMAKER Michelle Crockett **EST.** 1987 **CASES** 6000
Eling Forest's mentally agile and innovative founder Leslie Fritz celebrated his 80th birthday not long after he planted the first vines here in 1987. He celebrated his 88th birthday by expanding the vineyards from 3 to 4 ha, primarily with additional plantings of Hungarian varieties. He also developed a Cherry Port using the spinning cone technology to produce various peach-based liqueurs, utilising second-class peach waste. The vineyard has since been expanded to 32 ha.

TTTTT **Hilltops Shiraz 2003** Good colour; medium-bodied sweet black and red fruits, and ripe tannins; good mouthfeel, structure and oak. Cork. 12.9° alc. **RATING** 91 **DRINK** 2013 $ 25

TTTT **Southern Highlands Chardonnay 2005** Plenty of peach/stone fruit flavour; good weight, texture and mouthfeel. Screwcap. 13.1° alc. **RATING** 89 **DRINK** 2008 $ 20
Hilltops Cabernet Sauvignon 2003 Good colour; medium-bodied savoury black fruits and firm tannins; just a hint of green; good oak. Cork. 13.2° alc. **RATING** 89 **DRINK** 2011 $ 22
Southern Highlands Semillon 2004 Brassy-green; an abundance of lemon, citrus and honey flavour; quick-developing style, the first from the Southern Highlands. Screwcap. 11.5° alc. **RATING** 88 **DRINK** 2009 $ 15
Southern Highlands Pinot Noir 2003 Light but good hue; touches of mint and leaf, but also attractive red fruits; clear varietal character, even if slightly underripe. Cork. 12.6° alc. **RATING** 87 **DRINK** 2008 $ 25

TTTT **Southern Highlands Riesling 2005** Some premature colour development, despite the screwcap; powerful, full but soft complex flavours; all pointing to some degree of botrytis at work. Screwcap. 12.3° alc. **RATING** 86 **DRINK** 2008 $ 15
Reserve Southern Highlands Cabernet Sauvignon 2002 Intense and focused but does proclaim its cool-grown origins, with leaf, mint and wintergreen surrounding the red fruits. Head for the Hilltops. Cork. 12.6° alc. **RATING** 86 **DRINK** 2012 $ 30
Southern Highlands Sauvignon Blanc 2004 **RATING** 85 **DRINK** Now $ 20
Southern Highlands Botrytis Semillon 2005 **RATING** 84 **DRINK** Now $ 25

TTT **Southern Highlands Rose 2005** **RATING** 83 $ 15
Reserve Merlot 2003 **RATING** 83 $ 20

Ellender Estate

Leura Glen, 260 Green Gully Road, Glenlyon, Vic 3461 **REGION** Macedon Ranges
T (03) 5348 7785 **F** (03) 5348 7784 **WWW**.ellenderwines.com **OPEN** W'ends & public hols 11–5, or by appt
WINEMAKER Graham Ellender **EST.** 1996 **CASES** 1200
The Ellenders have established 4 ha of pinot noir, chardonnay, sauvignon blanc and pinot gris. Wine style is now restricted to those varieties true to the ultra-cool climate of the Macedon Ranges: pinot noir, pinot rose, chardonnay and sparkling. Exports to Dubai.

ΥΥΥΥΥ **Red Nelle Shiraz 2002** Holding hue, flavour and freshness remarkably well given its Canowindra origin; smooth, supple, medium-bodied black fruits supported by ripe, balanced tannins and oak. Cork. 14.5° alc. **RATING** 90 **DRINK** 2010 $ 20

ΥΥΥΥ **Macedon Pinot Noir 2004** Clean and fresh red fruit flavours; fairly light, but not forced. Diam. **RATING** 87 **DRINK** 2008 $ 33

Elliot Rocke Estate

NR

Craigmoor Road, Mudgee, NSW 2850 **REGION** Mudgee
T (02) 6372 7722 **F** (02) 6372 0680 **WWW**.elliotrockeestate.com.au **OPEN** 7 days 9–4
WINEMAKER Monarch Winemaking Services **EST.** 1999 **CASES** 6000
Elliot Rocke Estate has 24.2 ha of vineyards dating back to 1987 when the property was known as Seldom Seen. Plantings are made up of around 9 ha of semillon, 4.3 ha of shiraz and chardonnay, 2.2 ha of merlot and 2 ha each of cabernet sauvignon and traminer, with 0.5 ha of doradillo. Exports to South Korea.

Elmslie

NR

Upper McEwans Road, Legana, Tas 7277 **REGION** Northern Tasmania
T (03) 6330 1225 **F** (03) 6330 2161 **OPEN** By appt
WINEMAKER Ralph Power **EST.** 1972 **CASES** 600
A small, specialist red winemaker, from time to time blending Pinot Noir with Cabernet. The fruit from the now fully mature vineyard (0.5 ha of pinot noir and 1.5 ha of cabernet sauvignon) has depth and character, but operational constraints mean that the style of the wine is often somewhat rustic.

Elmswood Estate

★★★★

75 Monbulk-Seville Road, Wandin East, Vic 3139 **REGION** Yarra Valley
T (03) 5964 3015 **F** (03) 5964 3405 **WWW**.elmswoodestate.com.au **OPEN** 7 days 10–5
WINEMAKER Paul Evans **EST.** 1981 **CASES** 2000
Elmswood Estate has 9.5 ha of vineyard, planted in 1981 on the red volcanic soils of the far-southern side of the Yarra Valley. The cellar door offers spectacular views across the Upper Yarra Valley to Mt Donna Buang and Warburton. Exports to China.

ΥΥΥΥΥ **Yarra Valley Cabernet Sauvignon 2004** Excellent colour; strong blackcurrant varietal fruit; fine, ripe and positive tannins; good oak. **RATING** 92 **DRINK** 2015 $ 30
Yarra Valley Chardonnay 2004 Attractive wine with similar stone fruit and melon to that of the '05 unoaked; well-controlled oak adding a flavour and structure dimension. Diam. 13.5° alc. **RATING** 91 **DRINK** 2010 $ 23
Yarra Valley Cabernet Merlot 2004 Good colour; plenty of weight and substance to the medium-bodied blackcurrant fruit; good tannins and length, controlled oak. Diam. **RATING** 90 **DRINK** 2013 $ 27

ΥΥΥΥ **Yarra Valley Unoaked Chardonnay 2005** Clean melon and stone fruit aromas; good structure for the style, a minerally substrate to the acidity helping. Diam. **RATING** 89 **DRINK** 2008 $ 20

ΥΥΥΥ **Yarra Valley Methode Champenoise 2004 RATING** 86 **DRINK** Now $ 25

Elsewhere Vineyard ★★★☆

42 Dillons Hill Road, Glaziers Bay, Tas 7109 **REGION** Southern Tasmania
T (03) 6295 1228 **F** (03) 6295 1591 **WWW**.elsewherevineyard.com **OPEN** Not
WINEMAKER Andrew Hood (Contract), Steve Lubiana (Contract) **EST.** 1984 **CASES** 4000
Kylie and Andrew Cameron's evocatively named Elsewhere Vineyard used to jostle for space with a commercial flower farm. The estate-produced range comes from the 6 ha of pinot noir, 3 ha of chardonnay and 1 ha of riesling which constitute the immaculately tended vineyard.

▼▼▼▼ **Riesling 2005** Tight citrus and lemon flavours, quite piercing and long; good balance, though does dip slightly. **RATING** 88 **DRINK** 2010 $ 25
Somewhere Else Unwooded Chardonnay 2005 Nice gentle wine with good balance, though not particularly complex. **RATING** 87 **DRINK** Now $ 17

Elsmore's Caprera Grove NR

657 Milbrodale Road, Broke, NSW 2330 **REGION** Lower Hunter Valley
T (02) 6579 1344 **F** (02) 6579 1355 **WWW**.elsmorewines.com.au **OPEN** W'ends & public hols 10–5, or by appt
WINEMAKER Monarch Winemaking Services (Jim Chatto), Gary Reid (Contract) **EST.** 1995 **CASES** 800
Bindy and Chris Elsmore purchased their 16-ha property at Broke in 1995, subsequently establishing a little over 4 ha of chardonnay, verdelho and shiraz, with chardonnay taking the lion's share of the plantings. Their interest in wine came not from their professional lives — Chris is a retired commodore of the RAN and Bindy had a career in advertising, marketing and personnel — but from numerous trips to the wine regions of France, Italy and Spain.

Eltham Vineyards NR

225 Shaws Road, Arthurs Creek, Vic 3099 **REGION** Yarra Valley
T (03) 9439 4144 **F** (03) 9439 5121 **OPEN** By appt
WINEMAKER George Apted, John Graves **EST.** 1990 **CASES** 600
Drawing upon vineyards at Arthurs Creek and Eltham, John Graves (brother of David Graves, of the illustrious Californian Pinot producer Saintsbury) produces tiny quantities of quite stylish Chardonnay and Pinot Noir, the former showing nice barrel ferment characters. The wines have been consistent medal winners in regional Victorian wine shows.

Elysium Vineyard ★★★

393 Milbrodale Road, Broke, NSW 2330 **REGION** Lower Hunter Valley
T 0417 282 746 **F** (02) 9664 2368 **WWW**.winecountry.com.au/accommodation/elysium **OPEN** W'ends 10–5, or by appt
WINEMAKER Tyrrell's (Nick Paterson) **EST.** 1990 **CASES** 500
Elysium was once part of a much larger vineyard established by John Tulloch. Tulloch (not part of the Tulloch operation previously owned by Southcorp) continues to look after the viticulture, with the 1 acre of verdelho being vinified at Tyrrell's. The Elysium Cottage, large enough to accommodate 14 people, has won a number of tourism awards. Proprietor Victoria Foster, in partnership with Ben Moechtar (Vice-President of the Australian Sommeliers Association), conduct wine education weekends on request, with meals prepared by a chef brought in for the occasion. Exports to the US, Canada and China.

▼▼▼▽ **Limited Release Broke Fordwich Verdelho 2005** **RATING** 86 **DRINK** Now $ 20

▼▼▼ **Broke Fordwich Verdelho 2005** **RATING** 82 $ 20

Emma's Cottage Vineyard NR

Wilderness Road, Lovedale, NSW, 2320 **REGION** Lower Hunter Valley
T (02) 4998 7734 **F** (02) 4998 7209 **WWW**.emmascottage.com.au **OPEN** Fri–Mon, public & school hols 10–5, or by appt
WINEMAKER David Hook (Contract) **EST.** 1987 **CASES** NA
Rob and Toni Powys run a combined boutique winery and accommodation business on their 12-ha property at Lovedale; 4 ha of semillon, chardonnay, verdelho, merlot, pinot noir and shiraz have been planted, and a range of varietals and vintages are on offer.

🐂 Emmetts Crossing Wines ★★★

PO Box 84, Dwellingup, WA 6213 **REGION** Peel
T (08) 9538 4110 **F** (08) 9538 4110 **OPEN** Not
WINEMAKER Frank Kittler **EST.** 1996 **CASES** 3000
The Ganfield family has established its 4.5 ha-vineyard and winery in a pristine area of the Darling Range. There is a 4-generation family history of farming, and the development has been planned with the maximum possible respect for the environment. Chardonnay, Verdelho, Shiraz, Cabernet Malbec and Cabernet Sauvignon are produced.

ΥΥΥΥ **Cabernet Sauvignon 2004 RATING** 85 **DRINK** Now $16
Chardonnay 2005 RATING 84 **DRINK** Now $16

Empress Vineyard NR

Drapers Road, Irrewarra, Vic 3250 (postal Amberley House, 391 Sandy Bay Road, Hobart, Tas 7005)
REGION Western Victoria Zone
T (03) 6225 1005 **F** (03) 6225 0639 **WWW**.empress.com.au **OPEN** By appt
WINEMAKER Robin Brockett, Cate Looney, Lisa Togni **EST.** 1998 **CASES** 1000
If the address of Empress and its Geographic Zone seem schizophrenic, don't be alarmed. Allistair Lindsay has moved to Hobart, but has decided to retain Empress Vineyard, and to 'ramp it up again' (his words) as the wines have found a ready market in Hobart.

England's Creek NR

PO Box 6, Murrumbateman, NSW 2582 **REGION** Canberra District
T (02) 6227 5550 **F** (02) 6227 5605 **WWW**.barrique.com.au **OPEN** At Barrique Café, Murrumbateman
WINEMAKER Ken Helm (Contract) **EST.** 1995 **CASES** 250
The diminutive England's Creek was established in 1995 by Stephen Carney and Virginia Rawling with the planting of 1 ha each of riesling and shiraz; both areas have subsequently been doubled. The wines are available at selected Canberra restaurants and Vintage Cellars, Manuka, or from the winery.

Ensay Winery NR

Great Alpine Road, Ensay, Vic 3895 **REGION** Gippsland
T (03) 5157 3203 **F** (03) 5157 3372 **OPEN** W'ends, public & school hols 11–5, or by appt
WINEMAKER David Coy **EST.** 1992 **CASES** 1500
A weekend and holiday business for the Coy family, headed by David Coy, with 2.5 ha of chardonnay, pinot noir, merlot, shiraz and cabernet sauvignon.

Eppalock Ridge ★★★★★

633 North Redesdale Road, Redesdale, Vic 3444 **REGION** Heathcote
T (03) 5443 7841 **WWW**.eppalockridge.com **OPEN** By appt
WINEMAKER Rod Hourigan **EST.** 1979 **CASES** 1500
In 1976 Sue and Rod Hourigan gave up their careers in fabric design and television production at the ABC to chase their passion for fine wine. This took them first to McLaren Vale in SA, Sue working in the celebrated Barn Restaurant, Rod starting at d'Arenberg, and over the next 3 years did vintages at Pirramimma and Coriole while undertaking the first short course for winemakers at what is now Charles Sturt University. After 3 hectic years they moved to Redesdale in 1979 and established Eppalock Ridge on a basalt hilltop overlooking Lake Eppalock. The 10 ha of shiraz, cabernet sauvignon, cabernet franc and merlot are capable of producing wines of high quality. Exports to the UK, the US, Canada, NZ, Singapore and Fiji.

ΥΥΥΥΥ **Kylix Shiraz 2003** Spotlessly clean and pure blackberry and dark plum fruit; fine, elegant, medium- to full-bodied; excellent oak handling; 140 cases made. Screwcap. 14.5° alc.
RATING 96 **DRINK** 2018
Heathcote Shiraz 2003 Dense colour; full-bodied, rich blackberry, dark chocolate and plum; ripe tannins, not extractive; carries the alcohol. Cork. 15° alc. **RATING** 94
DRINK 2013 $33

ΥΥΥΥΥ **Rocklands Cabernet Franc 2004** Inky purple-red; unusual depth and richness for Cabernet Franc; luscious black fruits and fine, supple tannins. Screwcap. 14° alc. **RATING** 92 **DRINK** 2014 $ 27

Heathcote Cabernet Merlot 2003 Full-bodied, powerful blackcurrant, blackberry and earth; strong structure; ripe tannins. Cork. 14.5° alc. **RATING** 91 **DRINK** 2015 $ 33

ΥΥΥΥ **Rocklands Cabernet Franc 2001** Earthy, savoury, medium-bodied wine; a much more conventional expression of Cabernet Franc than the '04. Cork. 14° alc. **RATING** 88 **DRINK** 2010 $ 27

Ermes Estate   NR

2 Godings Road, Moorooduc, Vic 3933 **REGION** Mornington Peninsula
T (03) 5978 8376 **F** (03) 5978 8396 **OPEN** W'ends & public hols 11–5
WINEMAKER Ermes Zucchet, Denise Zucchet **EST.** 1989 **CASES** 700
Ermes and Denise Zucchet commenced planting of the 2.5-ha estate in 1989 with chardonnay, riesling, cabernet sauvignon and merlot, adding pinot gris in 1991. In 1994 an existing piggery on the property was converted to a winery and cellar door area (in the Zucchets' words, 'the pigs having been evicted'). The wines are modestly priced.

Ernest Hill Wines   NR

307 Wine Country Drive, Nulkaba, NSW 2325 **REGION** Lower Hunter Valley
T (02) 4991 4418 **F** (02) 4991 7724 **WWW**.ernesthillwines.com.au **OPEN** 7 days 10–5
WINEMAKER Mark Woods **EST.** 1999 **CASES** 1400
The Wilson family has owned the Ernest Hill property since 1990; the vineyard has 3 ha of semillon, and 1 ha each of chardonnay, traminer and verdelho; an additional ha of shiraz is leased. The business has had show success with the wines so far released.

`ese Vineyards   ★★★★

1013 Tea Tree Road, Tea Tree, Tas 7017 **REGION** Southern Tasmania
T 0417 319 875 **OPEN** By appt
WINEMAKER Winemaking Tasmania (Julian Alcorso) **EST.** 1994 **CASES** 3000
Elvio and Natalie Brianese are an architect and graphic designer couple whose extended family have centuries-old viticultural roots in the Veneto region of northern Italy. They have 2.5 ha of bearing vineyard. The Pinot Noir can be outstanding.

ΥΥΥΥΥ **Chardonnay 2004** Intense, long nectarine and grapefruit palate; the oak perfectly balanced and integrated; developing slowly. Screwcap. **RATING** 93 **DRINK** 2012 $ 23

Pinot Noir 2004 Fragrant red fruits and spice, moving more to plum and cherry on the palate; good texture, weight and finesse. Cork. **RATING** 90 **DRINK** 2010 $ 30

ΥΥΥΥ **Unwooded Chardonnay 2005** Faint blossom aromas; delicate tropical, stone fruit and citrus cross with sauvignon blanc; typical Tasmanian acidity. Screwcap. 13.5° alc. **RATING** 87 **DRINK** 2008 $ 20

Pinot Rose 2005 Pale, bright colour; strawberry and cherry fruit, uncompromisingly sweet, though fresh acidity does provide some balance. Screwcap. **RATING** 87 **DRINK** Now $ 18

Eumundi Winery   NR

310 Memorial Drive, Eumundi, Qld 4562 **REGION** Queensland Coastal
T (07) 5442 7444 **F** (07) 5442 7455 **OPEN** 7 days 11–6
WINEMAKER Andrew Hickinbotham (Contract) **EST.** 1996 **CASES** 5000
Eumundi Vineyard is set on 21 ha of river-front land in the beautiful Eumundi Valley, 12 km from Noosa Heads. The climate is hot, wet, humid and maritime, the only saving grace being the regular afternoon northeast sea breeze. It is a challenging environment for growing grapes: the owners, Robyn and Gerry Humphrey, have trialled 14 different grape varieties and 3 different trellis systems. Currently they have tempranillo, shiraz, chambourcin, petit verdot, mourvedre and verdelho.

Plantings in 2001 included tannat, albarino and refosco, which gives some idea of their eclectic approach. The establishment of the vineyard was financed by the sale of a 19m charter yacht which used to sail the oceans around northern Australia. Quite a change in lifestyle!

Eurabbie Estate ★★★★

251 Dawson Road, Avoca, Vic 3467 **REGION** Pyrenees
T (03) 5465 3799 **OPEN** 7 days 10–5
WINEMAKER John Higgins **EST.** 2000 **CASES** 1500
John and Kerry Higgins have established Eurabbie Estate in an 80-ha forest property overlooking a 4-ha natural lake. Two separate blocks of cabernet sauvignon, shiraz and merlot, with a dash of pinot noir, give rise to the Eurabbie Estate range. From 2004, grapes have been purchased from three small Pyrenees growers to produce the Pyrenees Villages range: Percydale Chardonnay, Percydale Cabernet Franc, Amherst Shiraz, Stuart Mill Shiraz and Avoca Cabernet Sauvignon. The wines are made in a mud-brick winery powered by solar energy.

TTTTT **Stephen James Avoca Shiraz 2004** Light- to medium-bodied; almost swaps places with the Pinot; a mix of black and red fruits, supple mouthfeel and fine tannins; unusual elegance. Cork. 13.5° alc. **RATING** 92 **DRINK** 2014 $ 23

TTTT **Tracey Lynne Avoca Pinot Noir 2004** Powerful medium-bodied wine; John Higgins has worked hard in the winery, using the right oak, and control over-extract; the varietal character is inevitably diminished by the climate, but the wine could surprise with time in bottle. Cork. 13.5° alc. **RATING** 89 **DRINK** 2010 $ 23
Nicole Jayne Avoca Cabernet Sauvignon 2004 Good hue; medium-bodied blackcurrant and cassis fruit; the fine, supple tannins are in marked contrast to those of the Merlot; controlled oak. Cork. 13.5° alc. **RATING** 89 **DRINK** 2014 $ 20

TTTT **Matthew John Avoca Merlot 2004 RATING** 86 **DRINK** 2014 $ 20
Pyrenees Village Dalys Cottage Chardonnay 2005 RATING 85 **DRINK** 2008 $ 20

TTT **Cellar Door Release Avoca Riesling 2005 RATING** 83 $ 17

Evans & Tate ★★★★

Metricup Road, Wilyabrup, WA 6280 **REGION** Margaret River
T (08) 9755 2199 **F** (08) 9755 4362 **WWW**.evansandtate.com.au **OPEN** 7 days 10.30–5
WINEMAKER Richard Rowe **EST.** 1970 **CASES** NFP
From its Swan Valley base 30 years ago, Evans & Tate became the largest Margaret River winery and producer. Having increased its estate vineyard holdings with the establishment of a large planting in the Jindong area, it raised substantial capital by listing on the Stock Exchange. It then turned its attention eastwards, with the acquisition of Oakridge Estate in the Yarra Valley, followed by Cranswick Wines (since sold). It became a casualty of the downturn in the market in 2005, its future direction uncertain.

TTTTT **Margaret River Chardonnay 2005** Light straw-green; light- to medium-bodied with sweet nectarine and melon fruit on entry; oak restrained throughout. Screwcap. 14.5° alc. **RATING** 91 **DRINK** 2010 $ 22
Classic Margaret River Shiraz Cabernet 2004 Medium-bodied; attractive, round mix of blackberry and blackcurrant fruit; fine tannins, integrated oak. Screwcap. 14° alc. **RATING** 90 **DRINK** 2012 $ 20

TTTT **Margaret River Verdelho 2005** An attractive example of a variety with inherent limitations; citrus-tinged fruit salad; bright acidity, will age well in bottle. Screwcap. 13.5° alc. **RATING** 89 **DRINK** 2008 $ 22
Gnangara Sauvignon Blanc 2005 Herb, gooseberry and grassy aromas; the tight palate has length though not too much fruit. Screwcap. **RATING** 87 **DRINK** Now $ 13.99
Classic Margaret River Rose 2005 Bright pink; attractive, lively, tangy/lemony fruit balanced by an airbrush of residual sugar. Screwcap. 13° alc. **RATING** 87 **DRINK** Now $ 19.95
Gnangara Cabernet Sauvignon 2003 A pretty useful wine, especially for the vintage; light- to medium-bodied, but has length and persistence; spice overtones to black fruits. Predominantly from Margaret River. Screwcap. **RATING** 87 **DRINK** 2008 $ 13.99

ᵀᵀᵀᵞ **Gnangara Shiraz 2003** RATING 86 DRINK Now $14
Margaret River Classic White 2005 RATING 85 DRINK Now $19.99
Gnangara Cabernet Sauvignon 2004 RATING 85 DRINK Now $14

ᵀᵀᵀ **Gnangara Unwooded Chardonnay 2005** RATING 83 $14
Gnangara Brut NV RATING 83 $13

Evans & Tate Salisbury ★★★

Campbell Avenue, Irymple, Vic 3498 REGION Murray Darling
T (03) 5024 6800 F (03) 5024 6605 OPEN Mon–Sat 10–4.30, Sun 12–4
WINEMAKER Krister Jonsson, Donna Stephens, Tony Pla Bou EST. 1977 CASES NFP
This is the former Milburn Park winery; the positions of the Salisbury and Milburn brands have been reversed, with Salisbury now the senior and the relaunched Milburn Park label sold at cellar door and as export only. Mosaic is a new, alternative variety, label.

ᵀᵀᵀᵀ **Milburn Park Shiraz 2004** Well-made; medium-bodied, abundant plum and blackberry fruit; supple tannins, a hint of oak. Cork. 14° alc. RATING 88 DRINK 2009 $15
Mosaic Petit Verdot 2004 Typical dense colour; potent black fruit which retains its core of sweetness, yet isn't jammy. Great barbecue red. Screwcap. 14° alc. RATING 88 DRINK 2009 $13
Mosaic Viognier 2004 Glowing yellow-green; rich, developed, mouthfilling peach and apricot; avoids excess phenolics, though slightly hot. Screwcap. 14° alc. RATING 87 DRINK Now $13

ᵀᵀᵀᵞ **Semillon Sauvignon Blanc 2005** RATING 86 DRINK Now $11
Chardonnay 2005 RATING 86 DRINK 2008 $11
Cabernet Merlot 2004 RATING 86 DRINK Now $11
Milburn Park Chardonnay 2004 RATING 85 DRINK Now $15
Shiraz Cabernet 2004 RATING 84 DRINK Now $11
Mosaic Sangiovese Shiraz 2003 RATING 84 DRINK Now $13

ᵀᵀᵀ **Victorian Rose 2005** RATING 82 $10.60

Evans Family Wines ★★★★☆

97 Palmers Lane, Pokolbin, NSW 2320 REGION Lower Hunter Valley
T (02) 4998 7237 F (02) 4998 7201 OPEN Thurs–Mon 10–5
WINEMAKER Andrew Thomas, Michael De Iuliis EST. 1979 CASES 2500
In the wake of the acquisition of Rothbury by Mildara Blass, Len Evans' wine interests now focus on Evans Family (estate-grown and produced from vineyards around the family home), the Evans Wine Company (a quite different, part-maker, part-negociant business) and, most recently, Tower Estate. Exports to the US.

ᵀᵀᵀᵀᵀ **Reserve Hunter Valley Shiraz 2004** An elegant, medium-bodied palate with sweet blackberry and plum fruit supported by fine-grained tannins and controlled oak; excellent length and aftertaste; 250 cases made. Cork. 14° alc. RATING 94 DRINK 2014 $45

ᵀᵀᵀᵀᵞ **Hunter Valley Semillon 2001** Bright green-straw; developing slowly but well, the first signs of honey and toast emerging; good line and length. Twin top. 11° alc. RATING 92 DRINK 2009 $16.50
Hunter Valley Chardonnay 2002 Glowing yellow-green; rich, full honey, toast and stone fruit, oak simply a backdrop. Cork. 13.7° alc. RATING 90 DRINK 2008 $22.50
Hunter Valley Shiraz 2002 Light- to medium-bodied; more savoury/earthy regional characters have developed; appealing style, but not in the same class as the Reserve. Cork. 13.1° alc. RATING 90 DRINK 2010 $28.50

ᵀᵀᵀᵀ **Hunter Valley Rose 2005** Pale, bright fuchsia pink; has flavour and length; good balance, and doesn't pander to sweet teeth. Twin top. 12.5° alc. RATING 88 DRINK Now $16.50
Hunter Valley Gamay 2005 Would make an excellent rose; almost got there anyway with its light, bright red fruits. Cork. 12.6° alc. RATING 87 DRINK Now $16.50

Evelyn County Estate   NR

55 Eltham-Yarra Glen Road, Kangaroo Ground, Vic 3097 **REGION** Yarra Valley
T (03) 9437 2155 **F** (03) 9437 2188 **WWW**.evelyncountyestate.com.au **OPEN** Mon–Wed 11–5,
Thurs–Fri 11–10, Sat 11–midnight, Sun 9–6
WINEMAKER Robyn Male, Diamond Valley Vineyards (James Lance) **EST.** 1994 **CASES** 3000
The 8-ha Evelyn County Estate has been established by former Coopers & Lybrand managing
partner Roger Male and his wife Robyn, who has completed a degree in Applied Science (wine
science) at Charles Sturt University. An architect-designed cellar door, gallery and restaurant opened
in April 2001. As one would expect, the quality of the wines is very good. A small planting of
tempranillo bore its first crop in 2004 and this wine is made onsite by Robyn Male.

Excelsior Peak   NR

PO Box 269, Tumbarumba, NSW 2653 **REGION** Tumbarumba
T (02) 6948 5102 **F** (02) 6948 5102 **OPEN** Not
WINEMAKER Contract **EST.** 1980 **CASES** 700
Excelsior Peak proprietor Juliet Cullen established the first vineyard in Tumbarumba in 1980. That
vineyard was thereafter sold to Southcorp, and Juliet Cullen subsequently established another
vineyard, now releasing wines under the Excelsior Peak label. Plantings total over 10 ha, with most of
the grapes sold. Sales by mail order only.

Ey Estate   NR

Main Road, Coonawarra, SA 5263 **REGION** Coonawarra
T (08) 8739 3063 **F** (08) 8739 3069 **WWW**.eyestatewines.com **OPEN** Not
WINEMAKER Patrick T Wines **EST.** 1989 **CASES** 900
The Ey family arrived in Coonawarra in 1908, establishing a mixed farming business on terra rossa
soil just to the north of the Coonawarra township. Between 1988 and 1998, third generation Robin
Ey, and fourth generation son Peter Ey, have established 20 ha of cabernet sauvignon, 4 ha of
chardonnay and 2 ha of shiraz, planted in 5 separate blocks. Most of the grapes are sold to Southcorp
under contract, with a small amount made by Pat Tocaciu.

Eyre Creek   NR

PO Box 162, Auburn, SA 5451 **REGION** Clare Valley
T 0418 818 400 **F** (08) 8849 2266 **OPEN** Not
WINEMAKER Ashton Hills **EST.** 1999 **CASES** NA
John Osborne established Eyre Creek in 1999, with 2 ha of riesling, grenache, cabernet sauvignon
and shiraz. The tiny output is sold by mail order and through limited wholesale distribution.

Faber Vineyard   ★★★★★

233 Hadrill Road, Baskerville, WA 6056 (postal) **REGION** Swan Valley
T (08) 9296 0619 **F** (08) 9296 0681 **OPEN** Not
WINEMAKER John Griffiths **EST.** 1997 **CASES** 800
Former Houghton winemaker, and now university lecturer and consultant, John Griffiths has
teamed with his wife, Jane Micallef, to found Faber Vineyard. Since 1997 they have established 1 ha
of shiraz, and 0.5 ha each of chardonnay, verdelho, cabernet sauvignon, petit verdot and brown
muscat. Says John Griffiths, 'It may be somewhat quixotic, but I'm a great fan of traditional warm
area Australia wine styles — those found in areas such as Rutherglen and the Barossa. Wines made in
a relatively simple manner that reflect the concentrated ripe flavours one expects in these regions.
And when one searches, some of these gems can be found from the Swan Valley.' Possessed of an
excellent palate, and with an impeccable winemaking background, the quality of John Griffiths'
wines is guaranteed.

 Margaret River Chardonnay 2005 Light straw-green; crisp and elegant, with excellent
length to the nectarine, melon and citrus fruit; the oak well-balanced and integrated.
Screwcap. 13.5° alc. **RATING** 94 **DRINK** 2012 $19

Reserve Shiraz 2004 Very good colour; a skilfully structured wine, with very attractive black and red fruits; silky, smooth tannins and a whisk of quality oak. Cork. **RATING** 94 **DRINK** 2015 $ 40

TTTTY **Riche Shiraz 2005** Generous, ripe blackberry and plum fruit; restrained alcohol and oak; overall, medium-bodied and well-balanced. Cork. 14° alc. **RATING** 90 **DRINK** 2015 $ 16
Swan Valley Petit Verdot 2005 Strong purple-red; much more red fruit tones than is normally the case, also more to medium-bodied than full-bodied; all these are better things. Cork. 14° alc. **RATING** 90 **DRINK** 2013 $ 19

TTTT **Swan Valley Verdelho 2005** Well-made and clean; fruit salad/stone fruit/pear; good length and acidity. Screwcap. 13.5° alc. **RATING** 88 **DRINK** Now $ 12
Swan Valley Shiraz Cabernet 2004 Light- to medium-bodied; sweet cherry, plum and blackberry; controlled extract, though not especially complex. Cork. 13.5° alc. **RATING** 88 **DRINK** 2009 $ 12

Fairview Wines

422 Elderslie Road, Branxton, NSW 2335 **REGION** Lower Hunter Valley
T (02) 4938 1116 **F** (02) 9383 8609 **www**.fairviewwines.com.au **OPEN** By appt
WINEMAKER Rhys Eather (Contract) **EST.** 1997 **CASES** 500
Greg and Elaine Searles purchased the property on which they have established Fairview Wines in 1997. For the previous 90 years it had sustained an orchard, but since that time 2 ha of shiraz, 1 ha each of barbera and semillon and 0.5 ha of chambourcin and verdelho have been established, using organic procedures wherever possible.

TTTT **Hunter Valley Shiraz 2003** Light- to medium-bodied; earthy, spicy regional overtones to the plum and blackberry fruit, with a whisk of chocolate in the background. Screwcap. 13.5° alc. **RATING** 88 **DRINK** 2010 $ 20
Hunter Valley Barbera 2004 A surprise packet; medium-bodied, with solid, spicy black fruits/plums; ripe tannins. Diam. **RATING** 88 **DRINK** 2010 $ 18

TTTY **Hunter Valley Saignee 2004 RATING** 86 **DRINK** Now $ 16

Faisan Estate NR

Amaroo Road, Borenore, NSW 2800 **REGION** Orange
T (02) 6365 2380 **OPEN** Not
WINEMAKER Col Walker **EST.** 1992 **CASES** 500
Faisan Estate, within sight of Mt Canobolas and 20 km west of the city of Orange, has been established by Trish and Col Walker. They now have almost 10 ha of vineyards and also purchase grapes from other growers in the region.

Falls Wines NR

Belubula Way, Canowindra, NSW 2804 **REGION** Cowra
T (02) 6344 1293 **F** (02) 6344 1290 **www**.fallswines.com **OPEN** 7 days 10–4
WINEMAKER Jon Reynolds (Contract) **EST.** 1997 **CASES** 3200
Peter and Zoe Kennedy have established Falls Vineyard & Retreat (to give it its full name) on the outskirts of Canowindra. They have planted chardonnay, semillon, merlot, cabernet sauvignon and shiraz, with luxury B&B accommodation offering large spa baths, exercise facilities, fishing and a tennis court.

Faranda Wines NR

768 Wanneroo Road, Wanneroo, WA 6065 **REGION** Swan District
T (08) 9306 1174 **OPEN** Mon–Fri 9–5
WINEMAKER Basil Faranda **EST.** NA **CASES** NA
Basil Faranda has 3 ha of mixed wine and table grapes, planted to grenache, shiraz, muscat, chasselas, cardinal and italia. He makes the wine onsite, selling through local outlets and the cellar door.

Farmer's Daughter Wines ★★★★

791 Cassilis Road, Mudgee, NSW 2850 **REGION** Mudgee
T (02) 6373 3177 **F** (02) 6373 3759 **WWW**.farmersdaughterwines.com.au **OPEN** 7 days 9–5
WINEMAKER Joe Lesnik **EST.** 1995 **CASES** 6000
The intriguingly named Farmer's Daughter Wines is a family-owned vineyard, run by the daughters of a feed-lot farmer, with winemaking by Joe Lesnik. Much of the production from the substantial vineyard of 20 ha, planted to shiraz (7 ha), merlot (6 ha), chardonnay and cabernet sauvignon (3 ha each) and semillon (1 ha), is sold to other makers, but 6000 cases are made for the Farmer's Daughter label.

TTTTY **Mudgee Merlot 2003** Youthful, fresh red berry fruits; elegant mouthfeel, with clarity and length. Delicious now. Cork. **RATING** 90 **DRINK** Now $22

Farosa Estate NR

1157 Port Wakefield Road, Waterloo Corner, SA 5110 (postal) **REGION** Adelaide Plains
T 0412 674 655 **F** (08) 8280 6450 **OPEN** Not
WINEMAKER Frank Perre (Contract) **EST.** 2000 **CASES** 500
The family-owned Farosa Estate has 11 ha of shiraz and 3 ha of mataro (mourvedre) in production. The aim is to produce a full-bodied wine with as little preservative as possible, with open fermentation and oak maturation varying between 10 and 18 months. The first release of Farosa Estate Shiraz was in 2003. To date, winemaking has taken place in the Barossa Valley, but the family is contemplating building its own winery.

Farr Rising ★★★★★

27 Maddens Road, Bannockburn, Vic 3331 **REGION** Geelong
T (03) 5281 1733 **F** (03) 5281 1433 **WWW**.byfarr.com.au **OPEN** By appt
WINEMAKER Nicholas Farr **EST.** 2001 **CASES** 2000
Nicholas Farr is the son of Gary Farr, and with encouragement from his father has launched his own brand. He has learnt his winemaking in France and Australia, and has access to some excellent base material, hence the quality of the wines. Exports to Denmark, Hong Kong and Japan.

TTTTT **Geelong Chardonnay 2004** Complex but controlled barrel ferment aromas, with some pleasing touches of French funk; an elegant, highly focused and long palate, with excellent citrussy acidity to close. Cork. 13.5° alc. **RATING** 95 **DRINK** 2012 $25
Mornington Pinot Noir 2004 Very good purple-red; a supple, silk and velvet palate, offering black cherry and plum, seamless oak and tannins. Lovely wine. Cork. 14° alc. **RATING** 95 **DRINK** 2011 $33
Geelong Chardonnay 2003 Still very fresh and lively nectarine, white peach and grapefruit; excellent acidity drives the long, lingering palate. Cork. 14.5° alc. **RATING** 94 **DRINK** 2008 $25
Geelong Pinot Noir 2004 Very good texture and structure; long, evenly distributed tannins lie behind the plummy fruit and appropriate oak. Diam. **RATING** 94 **DRINK** 2008 $33

Farrawell Wines ★★★★

60 Whalans Track, Lancefield, Vic 3435 **REGION** Macedon Ranges
T (03) 5429 2020 **F** (03) 9817 7215 **WWW**.farrawellwines.com.au **OPEN** 4th Sat of each month 1–5, or by appt
WINEMAKER Mount Charlie Wines (Trefor Morgan), Kilchurn Wines (David Cowburn) **EST.** 2000 **CASES** 400
Farrawell had a dream start to its commercial life when its 2001 Chardonnay was awarded the trophy for Best Chardonnay at the 2003 Macedon Ranges Wine Exhibition. Given that slightly less than 1 ha each of chardonnay and pinot noir are the sole source of wines, production will always be limited. Trefor Morgan is the owner/winemaker of Mount Charlie Winery, but perhaps better known as a Professor of Physiology at Melbourne University.

ŢŢŢŢŶ **Macedon Ranges Chardonnay 2005** Well-made; gently complex nectarine, citrus and creamy malolactic mix; subtle oak, good length. Screwcap. 12.5° alc. **RATING** 90 **DRINK** 2010 $ 22
Macedon Ranges Pinot Noir 2004 Good hue; clear-cut varietal character in a light- to medium-bodied mode; plum, cherry, spice and bramble; good length, spicy finish. Cork. 13.5° alc. **RATING** 90 **DRINK** 2009 $ 25

ŢŢŢŢ **Macedon Ranges Chardonnay 2004** Excellent balance, line and length to a wine of great delicacy; melon and citrus fruit flavours. Screwcap. **RATING** 89 **DRINK** 2008 $ 22
Macedon Pinot Noir Chardonnay 2003 A young wine with plenty of character and good balance; further time on lees would make it even better. A 50/50 blend of Pinot Noir/Chardonnay. **RATING** 87 **DRINK** 2008 $ 30

Farrell's Limestone Creek

Mount View Road, Mount View, NSW 2325 **REGION** Lower Hunter Valley
T (02) 4991 2808 **F** (02) 4991 3414 **OPEN** 7 days 10–5
WINEMAKER Neil McGuigan (Contract) **EST.** 1980 **CASES** 3500
The Farrell family purchased 20 ha on Mt View in 1980 and gradually established 7.3 ha of vineyards planted to semillon, verdelho, chardonnay, shiraz, cabernet sauvignon and merlot. Most of the grapes are sold to McWilliam's.

Feehans Road Vineyard

★★★☆

50 Feehans Road, Mount Duneed, Vic 3216 **REGION** Geelong
T (03) 5264 1706 **F** (03) 5264 1307 **www**.feehansroad.com.au **OPEN** W'ends 10–5
WINEMAKER Ray Nadeson **EST.** 2000 **CASES** 350
Peter Logan's interest in viticulture dates back to a 10-week course run by Denise Miller (at Dixons Creek in the Yarra Valley) in the first half of the 1990s. This led to further formal studies, and the planting of a 'classroom' vineyard of 500 chardonnay and shiraz vines. A move from Melbourne suburbia to the slopes of Mount Duneed led to the planting of a 1.2 ha vineyard of shiraz in August 2000, and through long-term friend Nicholas Clark of Amietta, to the appointment of Ray Nadeson as winemaker. The cellar door opened in January 2006, and is easily accessed just off the Surfcoast Highway between Geelong and Torquay. Future plans include the planting of chardonnay and sauvignon blanc to extend the range.

ŢŢŢŢ **Geelong Shiraz 2004** A mix of earth, blackberry and dark chocolate; good balance and fine tannins. **RATING** 89 **DRINK** 2012 $ 23
Geelong Saignee Rose 2005 Salmon pink; good texture and length; some spice; very good dry finish. Shiraz fermented in old barrels. Screwcap. 13° alc. **RATING** 88 **DRINK** Now $ 16

Feet First Wines

★★★

32 Parkinson Lane, Kardinya, WA 6163 (postal) **REGION** Southeast Australia
T (08) 9314 7133 **F** (08) 9314 7134 **OPEN** Not
WINEMAKER Contract **EST.** 2004 **CASES** 5000
This is the business of Ross and Ronnie (Veronica) Lawrence, who have been fine wine wholesalers in Perth since 1987, handling top-shelf Australian and imported wines. It is a virtual winery, with both grapegrowing and winemaking provided by contract, the aim being to produce easy-drinking, good-value wines under $20; the deliberately limited portfolio includes Semillon Sauvignon Blanc, Cabernets Merlot and Cabernet Merlot.

ŢŢŢŢŶ **Semillon Sauvignon Blanc 2005** Clean, fresh and lively passionfruit and citrus mix; light, but quite intense; good finish. Value. Screwcap. 12.2° alc. **RATING** 90 **DRINK** Now $ 15

ŢŢŢŢ **Cabernet Merlot 2004** **RATING** 84 **DRINK** Now $ 15

Felsberg Winery ★★★

116 Townsends Road, Glen Aplin, Qld 4381 **REGION** Granite Belt
T (07) 4683 4332 **F** (07) 4683 4377 **OPEN** 7 days 9–5
WINEMAKER Otto Haag **EST.** 1983 **CASES** 2500
Felsberg has a spectacular site, high on a rocky slope, with the winery itself built on a single huge boulder. It has been offering wine for sale via the cellar door (and mailing list) made by former master brewer Otto Haag for many years; the red wines are usually its strength.

TTTT **Gewurztraminer 2004** Bright colour; fresh, clear-cut spice, lychee and musk varietal aromas; the palate doesn't quite deliver all the bouquet promises, but still has good flavour. Cork. 12.3° alc. **RATING** 89 **DRINK** 2008 $15

TTTP **Shiraz 2003** Caramel/vanilla oak dominates the bouquet and palate, though there are some sweet black fruits underneath. Bronze medal sticker improper, as it does not specify the show and class. Cork. 14.2° alc. **RATING** 86 **DRINK** 2010 $19
Merlot 2004 **RATING** 85 **DRINK** Now $19
Cabernet Sauvignon 2003 **RATING** 85 **DRINK** 2013 $19

Fenton Views Winery NR

182 Fenton Hill Road, Clarkefield, Vic 3430 **REGION** Sunbury
T (03) 5428 5429 **F** (03) 5428 5304 **OPEN** W'ends 11–5, or by appt
WINEMAKER David Spiteri **EST.** 1994 **CASES** 800
Situated on the north-facing slopes of Fenton Hill at Clarkefield, just northeast of Sunbury, the Hume and Macedon Ranges provide a spectacular and tranquil setting. It is a small family operation, with plantings of shiraz, chardonnay, pinot noir and cabernet sauvignon. Co-owner David Spiteri studied winemaking at Charles Sturt University, and has vintage experience in Australia and California.

Ferguson Falls Estate NR

Pile Road, Dardanup, WA 6236 **REGION** Geographe
T (08) 9728 1083 **F** (08) 9728 1616 **OPEN** W'ends & public hols 11–5, or by appt
WINEMAKER David Crawford (Contract) **EST.** 1983 **CASES** 1000
Peter Giumelli and family are dairy farmers in the lush Ferguson Valley, 180 km south of Perth. In 1983 they planted 3 ha of cabernet sauvignon, chardonnay and merlot, making their first wines for commercial release from the 1995 and 1996 vintages, which confirmed the suitability of the region for the production of premium wine. This led to a doubling of the plantings, including 1 ha of tempranillo and 0.6 ha of nebbiolo.

Ferguson Hart Estate NR

Cnr Pile Road/Garden Court Drive, Ferguson Valley, WA 6236 **REGION** Geographe
T (08) 9728 0144 **F** (08) 9728 0144 **OPEN** W'ends 11–5
WINEMAKER Contract **EST.** 1994 **CASES** 400
Merv Hart and family have established 2.7 ha of shiraz, sauvignon blanc and semillon on gravelly soils on north-facing slopes. State-of-the-art viticultural techniques are used to keep vigour and yield under control. An art gallery and coffee shop operate on weekends.

Fergusson

Wills Road, Yarra Glen, Vic 3775 **REGION** Yarra Valley
T (03) 5965 2237 **F** (03) 5965 2405 **WWW.**fergussonwinery.com.au **OPEN** 7 days 11–5
WINEMAKER Christopher Keyes, Peter Fergusson **EST.** 1968 **CASES** 5000
One of the very first Yarra wineries to announce the rebirth of the Valley, now best known as a favoured destination for tourist coaches, offering hearty fare in comfortable surroundings and wines of both Yarra and non-Yarra Valley origin. For this reason the limited quantities of its estate wines are often ignored, but they should not be. Exports to the UK.

▼▼▼▼▼ **Jeremy Shiraz 2003** A supple, smooth, medium-bodied palate with an array of licorice, blackberry and spicy fruit; good oak handling, and excellent overall structure. Screwcap. 15° alc. **RATING** 94 **DRINK** 2015 $ 25

▼▼▼▼ **Ned's Red 2004** Slightly blackish hues to the dark colour; attractively bright, sweet cassis and blackcurrant fruit flavours; not much structure, but no problem with an early drinking style. Cabernet Merlot. Screwcap. 13° alc. **RATING** 89 **DRINK** 2008 $ 15
Victoria Chardonnay 2005 Light-bodied stone fruit and melon, the oak absorbed; understated, and may develop in bottle. Screwcap. 14.5° alc. **RATING** 88 **DRINK** 2010 $ 25

▼▼▼▼ **Benjamyn Cabernet Sauvignon 2004** **RATING** 86 **DRINK** 2009 $ 25

Fermoy Estate   NR

Metricup Road, Wilyabrup, WA 6280 **REGION** Margaret River
T (08) 9755 6285 **F** (08) 9755 6251 **WWW**.fermoy.com.au **OPEN** 7 days 11–4.30
WINEMAKER Michael Kelly **EST.** 1985 **CASES** 25 000
A long-established estate-based winery with 14 ha of semillon, sauvignon blanc, chardonnay, cabernet sauvignon and merlot. Notwithstanding its substantial production, it is happy to keep a relatively low profile. Exports to the UK, Holland, Switzerland and the US.

Fern Gully Winery   NR

63 Princes Highway, Termeil, NSW 2539 **REGION** Shoalhaven Coast
T (02) 4457 1124 **WWW**.shoalhavencoast.com.au/wineries **OPEN** W'ends & hols 11–5.30 (except winter)
WINEMAKER Max Staniford **EST.** 1996 **CASES** 250
Glenda and Max Staniford planted 0.25 ha each of chardonnay, shiraz, cabernet sauvignon and chambourcin in 1996 and 1997, producing the first grapes in 1998. The wines are all estate-grown (hence the limited production) and all the winemaking takes place onsite. The vineyard is enclosed in permanent netting, and hand-picking the grapes ensures the exclusion of diseased fruit.

Fern Hill Estate   NR

2 Chalk Hill Road, McLaren Vale, SA 5171 **REGION** McLaren Vale
T (08) 8323 9666 **F** (08) 8323 9600 **OPEN** At Marienberg Limeburners Centre 7 days 10–5
WINEMAKER Peter Orr **EST.** 1975 **CASES** 5000
Fernhill Estate, along with Marienberg and Basedow, became part of the James Estate empire in 2003. The wines are made under the direction of Peter Orr and sold through the Marienberg cellar door. Exports to the UK and the US.

Fernbrook Estate Wines

Bolganup Dam Road, Porongurup, WA 6324 **REGION** Porongurup
T (08) 9853 1030 **F** (08) 9853 1030 **OPEN** By appt
WINEMAKER David McNamara (Consultant) **EST.** 1976 **CASES** 1000
Run by Danuta Faulkner and Michelle Faulkner-Pearce, Fernbrook Estate (formerly Bolganup Heritage Wines) has 4 ha of cabernet sauvignon and gamay, and makes table, sparkling and organic wines. Exports to the UK, Germany and Sweden are the primary outlet.

▼▼▼▼ **Cabernet Sauvignon 2002** Light- to medium-bodied; gently sweet cassis mulberry fruit; soft tannins, minimal oak. Cork. **RATING** 86 **DRINK** 2009

Ferngrove Vineyards

Ferngrove Road, Frankland, WA 6396 **REGION** Frankland River
T (08) 9855 2378 **F** (08) 9855 2368 **WWW**.ferngrove.com.au **OPEN** 7 days 10–4
WINEMAKER Kim Horton **EST.** 1997 **CASES** 50 000
After 90 years of family beef and dairy farming heritage, Murray Burton decided in 1997 to venture into premium grapegrowing and winemaking. Since that time he has moved with exceptional speed

(and equal success), establishing 414 ha of grapes on 3 vineyards in the Frankland River subregion, and a fourth at Mount Barker. The operation centres around the Ferngrove Vineyard, where a large rammed-earth winery and tourist complex was built in 2000. Part of the vineyard production is sold as grapes; part is sold as juice or must; part is sold as finished wine; and part is made under the Ferngrove Vineyards label. Exports to the UK and the US.

ᵀᵀᵀᵀᵀ Cossack Frankland River Riesling 2005 Spotlessly clean lime, lemon and apple aromas; fine, intense and long palate; great line drives through to the finish. Every bit as good as the '03. Screwcap. 13° alc. RATING 95 DRINK 2015 $21

Dragon Shiraz 2004 Good colour; powerful, concentrated blackberry, licorice and spice fruit supported by positive, balanced tannins. Good oak rounds off a top wine. High-quality cork. 14.5° alc. RATING 95 DRINK 2019 $25

Majestic Cabernet Sauvignon 2004 Very good colour; complex, rich blackcurrant fruit on the medium- to full-bodied palate; excellent tannin and structure; quality oak. Gold medal Sydney Wine Show '06. Cork. 14.5° alc. RATING 94 DRINK 2019 $25

Leaping Lizard Reserve Cabernet Sauvignon 2003 Elegant, medium-bodied, fruit-driven wine; flooded with cassis and blackcurrant; perfect alcohol. Cork. 13.5° alc. RATING 94 DRINK 2013 $25

The Stirlings 2003 Strong purple-red, holding hue very well; medium- to full-bodied; luscious blackcurrant and cassis with high-quality fine, ripe tannins. Cork. 14° alc. RATING 94 DRINK 2018 $40

ᵀᵀᵀᵀ▽ Leaping Lizard Semillon Sauvignon Blanc 2005 Brilliant light green-yellow; a powerful and clean bouquet; strong grass, herb and a touch of gooseberry fruit; considerable length. Screwcap. 13° alc. RATING 92 DRINK 2009 $14.99

King Malbec 2004 Unquestionably the best malbec in Australia, year in, year out; rich, juicy mulberry, blackberry and blood plum mix; good structure and length. Cork. 13.5° alc. RATING 92 DRINK 2015 $25

Frankland River Sauvignon Blanc 2005 Spotlessly clean; a light- to medium-bodied array of gooseberry, ripe apple and passionfruit flavours; good balance. Screwcap. 13° alc. RATING 90 DRINK Now $18

Sauvignon Blanc Semillon 2005 Powerful, ripe gooseberry tropical aromas; full-flavoured; sweet fruit on the finish, but not phenolic. Cork. RATING 90 DRINK 2009 $15.99

Symbols Sauvignon Blanc Semillon 2005 Attractive wine; vibrant citrussy/lemony/gooseberry fruit; very good acidity provides length. Value. Screwcap. 13° alc. RATING 90 DRINK Now $14.99

Leaping Lizard Reserve Chardonnay 2003 Rich and complex peach, nectarine and grapefruit; nice French oak. Cork. 13.5° alc. RATING 90 DRINK 2008 $22

Shiraz 2004 Medium purple-red; medium-bodied, nicely balanced and composed mix of red and black spicy fruits; fine tannins. Screwcap. 14° alc. RATING 90 DRINK 2012 $18

Merlot 2004 Bright colour; appealing mid-weight wine with red berries and some spicy, savoury edges, moderately varietal; good finish. Screwcap. 14° alc. RATING 90 DRINK 2012 $18

ᵀᵀᵀᵀ Diamond Frankland River Chardonnay 2004 Elegant, light- to medium-bodied style; neatly integrated smoky oak with stone fruit and melon; good length, though not intense; will undoubtedly improve and gain weight. Screwcap. RATING 89 DRINK 2008 $22.99

Symbols Cabernet Merlot 2004 Similar colour and style to the Merlot; bright, fresh blackcurrant fruit; restrained tannins and oak. Screwcap. 13.5° alc. RATING 89 DRINK 2013 $15

Symbols Chardonnay 2005 Medium-bodied melon, peach and nectarine with a touch of sweetness on the finish; apparently unoaked. Screwcap. 14° alc. RATING 87 DRINK Now $14.99

ᵀᵀᵀ▽ Leaping Lizard Unwooded Chardonnay 2005 RATING 86 DRINK 2008 $14.99
Leaping Lizard Cabernet Sauvignon Merlot 2004 RATING 86 DRINK 2009 $14.99

Fighting Gully Road

NR

RMB 1315, Whorouly South, Vic 3735 **REGION** Beechworth
T (03) 5727 1434 **F** (03) 5727 1434 **OPEN** By appt
WINEMAKER Mark Walpole **EST.** 1997 **CASES** 500

Mark Walpole (chief viticulturist for Brown Brothers) and partner Carolyn De Poi have begun the development of their Aquila Audax vineyard, planting the first vines in 1997. It is situated between 530 and 580m above sea level: the upper eastern slopes are planted to pinot noir and the warmer western slopes to cabernet sauvignon; there are also small quantities of tempranillo, sangiovese and merlot.

Finestra

★★★★

PO Box 120, Coldstream, Vic 3770 **REGION** Yarra Valley
T (03) 9739 1690 **WWW.**yarrandah.com.au **OPEN** Not
WINEMAKER Alan Johns, Bruce Lang **EST.** 1989 **CASES** 400

Owners Bruce and Jo-Anne Lang have combined professional careers and small-scale winemaking for over 30 years. In the early 1970s they gained vacation employment with Yarra Valley wineries, and at the end of that decade they joined with friends in acquiring the old Brown Brothers' Everton Hills vineyard near Beechworth, bringing them into contact with Rick Kinzbrunner. In 1987 they acquired their property adjacent to Yeringberg, overlooking Domaine Chandon, beginning the establishment of the vineyard in 1989, and extending it in 1996. With a total of 2.9 ha of pinot noir, chardonnay, shiraz and cabernet sauvignon it is small, and until 2002 all of the grapes were sold to 2 major Yarra Valley wineries. Since then 50% of the grapes have been used for the Finestra label, with considerable success.

TTTTY **Dalla Mia Yarra Valley Pinot Noir 2003** Good colour; generous plum and black cherry fruit; spice and a breath of oak, with some tannins for the longer term. Cork. 13.2° alc. **RATING** 91 **DRINK** 2009 $ 17

TTTT **Dalla Mia Yarra Valley Cabernet Sauvignon 2003** Tight, austere, savoury, earthy profile; some blackcurrant fruit, and fine, persistent tannins. Cork. 13.2° alc. **RATING** 89 **DRINK** 2013 $ 20

Finniss Hills Wines

★★★☆

RSD 455 Braeside Road, Finniss, SA 5255 (postal) **REGION** Southern Fleurieu
T (08) 8536 0061 **F** (08) 8536 0061 **OPEN** Not
WINEMAKER O'Leary Walker **EST.** 1996 **CASES** 1000

Owner Nigel Wood traces his interest in wine back to 1971, and the time he spent in Bordeaux that year. The germ took some time to hatch, but in 1996 he selected an outstanding 15-ha property in the southern Mount Lofty Ranges, looking out over the Finniss River, Lake Alexandrina and the coast of Goolwa. The focus is on cabernet sauvignon and shiraz, and a skilled contract winemaking team.

TTTT **Fleurieu Shiraz 2002** Strongly savoury, foresty, spicy aromas; an intense palate with a long finish and fine tannins. Cork. **RATING** 89 **DRINK** 2010 $ 15

Fleurieu Cabernet Sauvignon 2002 Black fruits, camphor, earth and vanilla aromas; some unexpected sweetness on the palate, with notes of beeswax. **RATING** 87 **DRINK** 2010 $ 15

Fire Gully

★★★★

Metricup Road, Wilyabrup, WA 6280 **REGION** Margaret River
T (08) 9755 6220 **F** (08) 9755 6308 **OPEN** By appt
WINEMAKER Dr Michael Peterkin **EST.** 1998 **CASES** 5000

The Fire Gully vineyard has been established on what was first a dairy and then a beef farm. A 6-ha lake created in a gully ravaged by bushfires gave the property its name, and is stocked with marron. The vineyard was planted in 1988. In 1998 Mike Peterkin, of Pierro, purchased the property and manages the vineyard in conjunction with former owners Ellis and Margaret Butcher. He regards the Fire Gully wines as entirely separate from those of Pierro, being estate-grown: just under 9 ha is planted to cabernet sauvignon, merlot, shiraz, semillon, sauvignon blanc, chardonnay and viognier. Exports to the US, Europe, Asia and Russia.

ҰҰҰҰ♀ Margaret River Chardonnay 2005 A wine of elegance and finesse; bright stone fruit aromas and flavours are complexed by just a touch of barrel ferment; very good length and drive. Screwcap. 13.5° alc. **RATING** 93 **DRINK** 2011 $ 24

Margaret River Shiraz 2003 Aromatic and flavoursome spices and black fruits intertwined through the medium-bodied palate; good length. Cork. 13.5° alc. **RATING** 91 **DRINK** 2012 $ 22

ҰҰҰҰ Margaret River Sauvignon Blanc Semillon 2005 Firm, clean grass/herb/mineral aromas; a softer palate moving into ripe apple and gooseberry fruit. Screwcap. 13.5° alc. **RATING** 89 **DRINK** 2008 $ 23

Fireblock

St Vincent Street, Watervale, SA 5452 **REGION** Clare Valley
T 0414 441 925 **F** (02) 9144 1925 **OPEN** Not
WINEMAKER O'Leary Walker Wines **EST.** 1926 **CASES** 3600
Fireblock (formerly Old Station Vineyard) is owned by Alastair Gillespie and Bill and Noel Ireland, who purchased the 6 ha, 70-year-old vineyard in 1995. Watervale Riesling, Old Vine Shiraz and Old Vine Grenache are skilfully contract-made, winning trophies and gold medals at capital city wine shows. Exports to the US.

ҰҰҰҰҰ Clare Valley Old Vine Shiraz 2004 Intense, deep purple-red; full-bodied; extremely powerful and dense blackberry, plum and dark chocolate fruit, the oak incidental, and alcohol adding more to sweetness than to heat. Parkeresque. Screwcap. 15.5° alc. **RATING** 94 **DRINK** 2024 $ 20

ҰҰҰҰ♀ Watervale Riesling 2005 Gently ripe, sweet tropical aromas; a generously flavoured palate, with good balance. Early drinking style. Screwcap. 13° alc. **RATING** 90 **DRINK** 2010 $ 17

Clare Valley Old Vine Shiraz 2003 Abundant, dense, chewy blackberry and dark chocolate fruit, full-bodied yet not over-extracted. Screwcap. **RATING** 90 **DRINK** 2013 $ 19.95

ҰҰҰҰ Clare Valley Old Vine Grenache 2003 Typical Clare Valley grenache, relatively light-bodied, with juicy, jammy varietal fruit. Screwcap. 15° alc. **RATING** 87 **DRINK** 2008 $ 17

First Creek Wines

Cnr McDonalds Road/Gillards Road, Pokolbin, NSW 2321 **REGION** Lower Hunter Valley
T (02) 4998 7293 **F** (02) 4998 7294 **WWW**.firstcreekwines.com.au **OPEN** 7 days 9.30–5
WINEMAKER Monarch Winemaking Services (Jim Chatto) **EST.** 1984 **CASES** 25 000
First Creek is the shopfront of Monarch Winemaking Services, which has acquired the former Allanmere wine business and offers a complex range of wines under both the First Creek and the Allanmere labels. The quality is very reliable.

ҰҰҰҰҰ Durham Hunter Valley Chardonnay 2005 Light straw-green; clean bouquet, and more finesse than most Hunter Valley chardonnays, with striking focus and length. Partial barrel ferment allows the fruit to shine on the long palate and lingering finish. Screwcap. 13.5° alc. **RATING** 94 **DRINK** 2013 $ 20

ҰҰҰҰ♀ Canberra District Shiraz Viognier 2004 Medium-bodied; lush, ripe black fruits tempered by the viognier influence; soft tannins, gentle oak; a farewell touch of spice. Screwcap. 13.5° alc. **RATING** 93 **DRINK** 2014 $ 30

Canberra District Viognier 2005 A complex, rich wine, again showing the controlled use of oak to complement, not subjugate, fruit; classic apricot/musk flavours and a whisper of oak. Screwcap. 13° alc. **RATING** 91 **DRINK** 2009 $ 20

Semillon 2005 Well-balanced; harmonious line and length; elegant and fresh. Screwcap. **RATING** 90 **DRINK** 2012 $ 14.50

Tumbarumba Sauvignon Blanc 2005 A clean but subdued bouquet; opens quietly on the palate, then intensifies all the way through to the finish and aftertaste; zesty and tangy, good acidity. Screwcap. **RATING** 90 **DRINK** Now $ 17.50

ҰҰҰ♀ Three Degrees Semillon Sauvignon Blanc 2005 RATING 86 **DRINK** Now $ 12

5 Corners Wines   NR

785 Henry Lawson Drive, Mudgee, NSW 2850 **REGION** Mudgee
T (02) 6373 3745 **F** (02) 6373 3749 **WWW**.5corners.biz **OPEN** Fri–Mon 10–5
WINEMAKER Contract **EST.** 2001 **CASES** NA
5 Corners Wines came together in a hurry. Grant and Suzie Leonard came to Mudgee in 2001 for an
overnight visit, and promptly fell in love with the region. They purchased a 40-ha property with 5 ha
of established vineyard and a small cottage. The property now includes the family's house (5 children
and 6 dogs come and go), the original cottage (occupied by the vineyard manager), and plantings
which have been increased by a further 3 ha.

Five Geese   ★★★★

RSD 587 Chapel Hill Road, Blewitt Springs, SA 5171 (postal) **REGION** McLaren Vale
T (08) 8383 0576 **F** (08) 8383 0629 **WWW**.fivegeese.com.au **OPEN** Not
WINEMAKER Boar's Rock (Mike Farmilo) **EST.** 1999 **CASES** 2600
Sue Trott is passionate about her Five Geese wine, which is produced by Hillgrove Wines, a company
established in 1999. The wines come from 32 ha of vines, 1 vineyard planted in 1927, the other in
1963. The grapes were sold for many years, but in 1999 Sue decided to create her own label and make
a strictly limited amount of wine from the pick of the vineyards. Exports to the UK, the US, Canada,
Singapore and NZ.

▼▼▼▼▼ **McLaren Vale Grenache Shiraz 2004** Good hue; serious grenache, in best Southern
Rhône style; medium-bodied black and red fruits; fine, spicy tannins; good oak. Diam.
14.5° alc. **RATING** 94 **DRINK** 2017 $ 20

Five Oaks Vineyard   ★★★★

60 Aitken Road, Seville, Vic 3139 **REGION** Yarra Valley
T (03) 5964 3704 **F** (03) 5964 3064 **WWW**.fiveoaks.com.au **OPEN** W'ends & public hols 10–5 & by appt
WINEMAKER Wally Zuk **EST.** 1997 **CASES** 2000
Wally Zuk and wife Judy run all aspects of Five Oaks — far removed from Wally's background in
nuclear physics. He has, however, completed his wine science degree at Charles Sturt University, and
is thus more than qualified to make the Five Oaks wines. Exports to Canada.

▼▼▼▼ **Yarra Valley Cabernet Sauvignon 2004** Light- to medium-bodied; gentle cassis and
blackcurrant, with fine tannins and subtle oak in support. Simply lacks concentration.
Screwcap. 12.7° alc. **RATING** 88 **DRINK** 2010 $ 24
Yarra Valley Riesling 2005 Potent herb and spice aromas, with a whisper of reduction; an
appreciably sweet palate and finish crafted for the cellar door. Screwcap. 11.9° alc.
RATING 87 **DRINK** 2010 $ 18

▼▼▼▽ **Yarra Valley Merlot 2004 RATING** 86 **DRINK** 2008 $ 20

572 Richmond Road   ★★★★

572 Richmond Road, Cambridge, Tas 7170 (postal) **REGION** Southern Tasmania
T 0418 889 477 **OPEN** Not
WINEMAKER Tony Scherer **EST.** 1994 **CASES** 450
John and Sue Carney have decided not to sell 572 Richmond Road, acknowledging they enjoyed the
masochism of owning a vineyard and winery more than they realised. Tony Scherer (of Frogmore
Creek) has taken over the day-to-day management allowing the Carneys some free time. The wines
are available for sale at Wellington cellar door.

▼▼▼▼▽ **Riesling 2005** Tight lime and passionfruit; excellent intensity and even better length.
RATING 93 **DRINK** 2010
Riesling 2004 Intense, penetrating and long with lime juice essence and tingling lemony
acidity. **RATING** 93 **DRINK** 2012

▼▼▼▼ **Gewurztraminer 2005** Very fine and crisp, with wisps of spice and lychee; scores more for
balance and mouthfeel than overt varietal character. **RATING** 89 **DRINK** Now

▼▼▼▽ **Gewurztraminer 2004 RATING** 86 **DRINK** 2008

Five Sons Estate ★★★★

85 Harrisons Road, Dromana, Vic 3936 **REGION** Mornington Peninsula
T (03) 5987 3137 **F** (03) 5981 0572 **WWW**.fivesonsestate.com.au **OPEN** W'ends & public hols 11–5,
7 days in Jan
WINEMAKER Rollo Crittenden (Contract) **EST.** 1998 **CASES** 2700
Bob and Sue Peime purchased the most historically significant viticultural holding in the
Mornington Peninsula in 1998. Development of the 68-ha property began in the early 1930s, and in
the 1940s it was sold to a member of the Seppelt family, who planted riesling in 1948. Two years later
the property was sold to the Broadhurst family, close relatives of Doug Seabrook, who persisted with
growing and making riesling until a 1967 bushfire destroyed the vines. Since 1998 approximately 19
ha of vines have been planted to (in descending order) pinot noir, chardonnay, shiraz, pinot gris and
cabernet sauvignon.

ŸŸŸŸŸ **Mornington Peninsula Chardonnay 2004** Good intensity, length and focus to the stone
fruit and citrus flavours and well-integrated, balanced oak. Cork. 13.5° alc. **RATING** 93
DRINK 2010 $26
Mornington Peninsula Shiraz 2004 Good colour; nicely ripened blackberry and black
cherry fruit; spicy nuances and ripe tannins. Elegant. Cork. 13.5° alc. **RATING** 92
DRINK 2012 $26
Mornington Peninsula Pinot Noir 2004 Light- to medium-bodied red cherry and black
plum fruits, with a savoury, spicy backdrop; well-balanced and integrated oak. Cork. 13.5°
alc. **RATING** 91 **DRINK** 2010 $24

ŸŸŸŸ **The Boyz Mornington Peninsula Pinot Noir 2004** Entirely fruit-driven by fresh and
lively plum and cherry flavours; shortens slightly on the finish. Cork. 13.5° alc. **RATING** 88
DRINK 2009 $18
The Boyz Mornington Peninsula Rose 2005 Bright, fresh strawberry aromas; a similarly
crisp, fresh and dry palate; well-made. Screwcap. 13.5° alc. **RATING** 87 **DRINK** Now $18

ŸŸŸŸ **The Boyz Mornington Peninsula Chardonnay 2005** **RATING** 86 **DRINK** Now $18

🐌 Flaxman Wines ★★★★☆

Lot 535 Flaxmans Valley Road, Angaston, SA 5353 **REGION** Eden Valley
T 0411 668 949 **F** (08) 8565 3299 **WWW**.flaxmanwines.com.au **OPEN** By appt
WINEMAKER Colin Sheppard, Tim Smith **EST.** 2005 **CASES** 500
After visiting the Barossa Valley over a decade, and working during vintage with Andrew Seppelt
at Murray Street Vineyards, Melbourne residents Colin and Fiona Sheppard decided on a
seachange, and found a small, old vineyard overlooking Flaxmans Valley. It consists of 1 ha of 40⁺-
year-old riesling, 1 ha of 50⁺-year-old shiraz and a small planting of 40⁺-year-old semillon. The
vines are all dry-grown, hand-pruned and hand-picked, and treated — say the Sheppards — as
their garden, right down to mowing the vine mid-rows with a ride-on mower to prevent soil
compaction. Yields are restricted to under 4 tonnes per ha, and small amounts of locally grown
grapes are also purchased.

ŸŸŸŸŸ **The Stranger Barossa Shiraz Cabernet 2004** Good colour; delicious, sweet red and
black fruits, supple and round; soft tannins and great mouthfeel; 32 cases made.
Screwcap. 14.5° alc. **RATING** 93 **DRINK** 2019 $35
Cordon Cut Eden Valley Semillon 2005 Extremely luscious and, while not especially
complex, has a very long and quite crisp finish; nicely balanced alcohol; 65 cases made.
Screwcap. 11° alc. **RATING** 90 **DRINK** 2009 $18

ŸŸŸŸ **Eden Valley Riesling 2005** Obvious regional lime blossom aromas and lime juice
flavours; slightly diffuse line and focus; 200 cases made. Screwcap. 12° alc. **RATING** 89
DRINK 2012 $25

Flinders Bay

★★★★☆

Bussell Highway, Metricup, WA 6280 **REGION** Margaret River
T (08) 9757 6281 **F** (08) 9757 6353 **OPEN** 7 days 10–4
WINEMAKER O'Leary Waker, Flying Fish Cove **EST.** 1995 **CASES** 10 000
A joint venture between Alastair Gillespie and Bill and Noel Ireland, the former a grapegrower and viticultural contractor in the Margaret River region for over 25 years, the latter two Sydney wine retailers for an even longer period. The wines are made from grapes grown on the 50-ha Karridale Vineyard (planted between 1995 and 1998), with the exception of a Verdelho, which is purchased from the northern Margaret River. Part of the grape production is sold, and part made under the Flinders Bay and Dunsborough Hills brands. Exports to the UK and the US.

▼▼▼▼▼ **Margaret River Sauvignon Blanc Semillon 2005** Clean, flowery, aromatic bouquet; an intense mix of grass, asparagus and mineral; plenty of length and impact. Screwcap. **RATING** 91 **DRINK** 2010 $ 17
Dunsborough Hills Shiraz 2004 The colour doesn't convince, but there is more concentration and structure than the colour might suggest; plum, spice, blackberry and a hint of chocolate make their presence felt. Screwcap. 14° alc. **RATING** 91 **DRINK** 2012 $ 16
Dunsborough Hills Chardonnay 2005 Has attractive nectarine and peach fruit, with hints of citrus and cream, but no oak; elegant, light- to medium-bodied wine. Screwcap. 13.5° alc. **RATING** 90 **DRINK** 2009 $ 16
Margaret River Shiraz 2003 Medium-bodied; a quite complex array of fruits from licorice and spice through to prune; gentle tannins. Screwcap. 14° alc. **RATING** 90 **DRINK** 2011 $ 16.99

▼▼▼▼ **Dunsborough Hills Semillon Sauvignon Blanc 2005** Aromatic, tropical gooseberry fruit on a solid core of semillon; powerful, but does shorten slightly. Screwcap. 13° alc. **RATING** 89 **DRINK** 2008 $ 16
Dunsborough Hills Verdelho 2005 A distinguished example of an undistinguished variety; length and elegance; fruit salad with a drizzle of lime juice. Classy packaging. Screwcap. **RATING** 89 **DRINK** Now $ 16

Flint's of Coonawarra

★★★☆

PO Box 8, Coonawarra, SA 5263 **REGION** Coonawarra
T (08) 8736 5046 **F** (08) 8736 5146 **WWW**.flintsofcoonawarra.com.au **OPEN** Not
WINEMAKER Majella **EST.** 2000 **CASES** 700
Six generations of the Flint family have lived and worked in Coonawarra since 1840. Damian Flint and his family began the development of 19.5 ha of cabernet sauvignon, shiraz and merlot in 1989, but it was not until 2000 that they decided to keep a small portion of cabernet sauvignon back and have it made at Majella, owned by their lifelong friends the Lynn brothers. Around 700 cases were vinified, and the wine had immediate show success in Melbourne; another 10 tonnes were diverted from the 2001 vintage, and the first wines were released in 2003.

▼▼▼▼ **Rostrevor Coonawarra Shiraz 2003** Firm, intense blackberry/black cherry fruit; still very tight, and showing brisk acidity. Needs time. Screwcap. **RATING** 89 **DRINK** 2013 $ 25
Gammon's Crossing Cabernet Sauvignon 2003 Unconvincing colour; earthy Coonawarra cabernet style, although the development has been quick; cedary French oak helps the flavours. Cork. 14° alc. **RATING** 87 **DRINK** 2011 $ 23

Fluted Cape Vineyard

★★★

28 Groombridge Road, Kettering, Tas 7155 **REGION** Southern Tasmania
T (03) 6267 4262 **OPEN** 7 days 10–5
WINEMAKER Hood Wines **EST.** 1993 **CASES** 170
For many years Val Dell was the senior wildlife ranger on the central plateau of Tasmania, his wife Jan running the information centre at Liawenee. I met them there on trout fishing expeditions, staying in one of the park huts. They have now retired to the Huon Valley region, having established 0.25 ha each of pinot noir and chardonnay overlooking Kettering and Bruny Island, said to be a

spectacularly beautiful site. The wines are made for them by Andrew Hood and are sold through the cellar door and Hartzview Cellars in Gardners Bay.

ΤΤΤΫ **Chardonnay 2005 RATING** 86 **DRINK** Now
Pinot Noir 2004 RATING 85 **DRINK** 2008

Flying Duck Estate ★★★

3838 Wangaratta–Whitfield Road, King Valley, Vic 3678 **REGION** King Valley
T (03) 9819 7787 **F** (03) 9819 7789 **www**.flyingduckestate.com.au **OPEN** By appt
WINEMAKER Trevor Knaggs, Paul Burgoyne **EST.** 1998 **CASES** 850
Wayne and Sally Burgoyne, with John and Karen Butler, purchased the 3-year-old vineyard in 2001, at which time there were 2 ha of shiraz which had been planted by Paul Burgoyne, who continues to be involved with the operation as assistant winemaker. In 2001 2.3 ha of merlot and 1 ha of viognier were planted, with Shiraz Viognier, Merlot and Viognier first made in 2005.

ΤΤΤΤ **Shiraz 2003** A clean, fresh light- to medium-bodied wine with clean, fresh plum, cherry and raspberry fruit; while the tannins are very light, the wine has good length. Cork. 13.8° alc. **RATING** 87 **DRINK** 2009 $ 19

Flying Fish Cove ★★★★☆

Caves Road, Wilyabrup, WA 6284 **REGION** Margaret River
T (08) 9755 6600 **F** (08) 9755 6788 **www**.flyingfishcove.com **OPEN** 7 days 11–5
WINEMAKER Damon Eastaugh **EST.** 2000 **CASES** 18 000
A group of 20 shareholders acquired the 130-ha property on which the Flying Fish Cove winery was subsequently built. It has two strings to its bow: contract winemaking for others, and the development of three product ranges (Upstream, Prize Catch and Margaret River varietals), partly based on 22 ha of estate plantings, with another 10 ha underway.

ΤΤΤΤΤ **Prize Catch Cabernet Sauvignon 2001** Plenty of weight and depth; ripe blackcurrant fruit with attractive cedar/mocha oak; ripe tannins. A very good vintage with the first signs of bottle development. Screwcap. 14.5° alc. **RATING** 94 **DRINK** 2015 $ 65

ΤΤΤΤΫ **Upstream Reserve Shiraz 2004** Deep but bright colour; spotlessly clean, ripe plum and blackberry aromas; typical Margaret River finesse on the palate; fine and persistent tannins. Screwcap. **RATING** 93 **DRINK** 2010 $ 34.99
Margaret River Semillon Sauvignon Blanc 2005 Spotlessly clean; excellent definition and length, with a mix of mineral, grass, herb and nettle flavours. Screwcap. **RATING** 92 **DRINK** 2010 $ 20
Upstream Reserve Cabernet Sauvignon 2003 A powerful mix of cassis, raspberry and blackcurrant, with persistent tannins needing time to soften; 12 months in French oak. Screwcap. 15° alc. **RATING** 92 **DRINK** 2019 $ 34.99
Chardonnay 2005 Very pale straw-green; lively, fresh melon and grapefruit flavours; has attitude and length; good balance. Screwcap. **RATING** 90 **DRINK** 2009 $ 18.99

ΤΤΤΤ **Pink Fish Rose 2005** Fresh red fruits; a flick of residual sugar makes the wine more off-dry than outright sweet; well-made. Screwcap. 13.5° alc. **RATING** 87 **DRINK** Now $ 20

ΤΤΤΫ **Chenin Blanc 2005 RATING** 86 **DRINK** 2008 $ 20
Cuttlefish Classic White 2005 RATING 84 **DRINK** Now $ 14
Cuttlefish Classic Red 2004 RATING 84 **DRINK** Now $ 14

Foate's Ridge NR

241 Fordwich Road, Broke, NSW 2330 (postal) **REGION** Lower Hunter Valley
T (02) 6579 1284 **F** (02) 9922 4397 **www**.foate.com.au **OPEN** By appt
WINEMAKER Steve Dodd (Contract) **EST.** 1992 **CASES** 1000
The Foate family, headed by Tony Foate, planted a total of 10 ha, chardonnay (4 ha) and verdelho, merlot and cabernet sauvignon (2 ha each), between 1992 and 2001 on the 36-ha property purchased in 1991. The soils are the typical light alluvial loam of the region, which promote vigorous vine growth and generous yields, yields which need to be controlled if quality is to be maximised. Using a

Scott Henry trellis, bunch thinning and fewer spur positions have reduced the 15 tonnes per ha yields to 10 tonnes per ha.

Foggo Wines ★★★★★

Lot 21 Foggos Road, McLaren Vale, SA 5171 **REGION** McLaren Vale
T (08) 8323 0131 **F** (08) 8323 7626 **WWW**.foggowines.com.au **OPEN** Mon–Fri 10.30–4.30, w'ends & public hols 11–5
WINEMAKER Herb Van De Wiel **EST.** 1999 **CASES** 3000

Herb and Sandie Van De Wiel have been grapegrowers in McLaren Vale for 16 years, and in 1999 they were able to purchase the former Curtis winery, which, after refurbishment, gave them the opportunity to establish Foggo Wines. They have 3 vineyards: the oldest (on Foggos Road) is 9 ha of shiraz dating back to 1915; their 80-year-old grenache, 45-year-old cinsaut and 20-year-old chardonnay and sauvignon blanc come from their other vineyards, totalling 25 ha in all. They have wasted no time in establishing a formidable reputation for a range of Shiraz, Grenache, Grenache Shiraz Cinsaut and Cabernet Sauvignon equal to the best. Exports to the US, Canada and Taiwan.

▼▼▼▼▼ **Old Vine Shiraz 2004** Good colour; slightly more savoury/spicy than the Hubertus, though shares the elegance; fine, silky tannins. Cork. **RATING** 94 **DRINK** 2017 $ 28
Hubertus Reserve Shiraz 2004 Very good bright purple-red; a medium-bodied, harmonious array of blackberry and plum fruit with some dark chocolate and seamless oak; very elegant, showing the vintage to full advantage. Cork. **RATING** 94 **DRINK** 2019 $ 45
McLaren Vale Cabernet Sauvignon 2004 Deep colour; rich blackberry, blackcurrant, licorice and dark chocolate fruit; abundant, ripe tannins; good oak. Cork. 14° alc. **RATING** 94 **DRINK** 2019 $ 28

▼▼▼▼▽ **Cadenzia Grenache 2004** Medium red-purple; has substance and structure to go with the sweetly vibrant, juicy varietal fruit of grenache. Cork. **RATING** 93 **DRINK** 2014 $ 22
Hubertus Reserve Shiraz 2003 Concentrated and dense blackberry jam, dark chocolate, plum and vanilla; extreme patience required, though very stained cork a concern. Cork. 15° alc. **RATING** 92 **DRINK** 2015 $ 45
Chardonnay 2004 Generous yellow peach and fig fruit; well-balanced and integrated oak; good acidity on the finish. Cork. **RATING** 90 **DRINK** 2008 $ 25
Old Bush Vine Grenache 2004 Vivid light colour; classic juicy jammy red fruits; fine tannins; best now. Cork. **RATING** 90 **DRINK** 2009 $ 28
Grenache Shiraz Cinsaut 2004 Light- to medium-bodied; smooth, silky/spicy red fruits; grenache with a little stiffening. Cork. **RATING** 90 **DRINK** 2010 $ 22

▼▼▼▼ **Sauvignon Blanc 2005** Super-rich, medium- to full-bodied; the varietal character is there, but carries a mountain of ripe, sweet fruit of less precise varietal profile. Radically different from the '04. Screwcap. **RATING** 89 **DRINK** Now $ 18
Commemorative Red Dodge Shiraz 2003 Notwithstanding the provenance of the grapes (all planted 1915) the vintage won the battle; fruit (and alcohol) is powerful, but not with the vibrancy of '04. Cork. 15° alc. **RATING** 89 **DRINK** 2010 $ 30

▼▼▼▽ **Unwooded Chardonnay 2005** **RATING** 86 **DRINK** Now $ 18
Cinsaut Rose 2004 **RATING** 86 **DRINK** Now $ 15

Fonty's Pool Vineyards ★★★★☆

Seven Day Road, Manjimup, WA 6258 **REGION** Manjimup
T (08) 9777 0777 **F** (08) 9777 0788 **WWW**.fontyspoolwines.com.au **OPEN** 7 days 10–4.30
WINEMAKER Eloise Jarvis, Mark Morton **EST.** 1989 **CASES** 30 000

This is a joint venture between Cape Mentelle (which makes the wine) and Fonty's Pool Farm. The Fonty's Pool vineyards are part of the original farm owned by pioneer settler Archie Fontanini, who was granted land by the government in 1907. In the early 1920s a large dam was created to provide water for the intensive vegetable farming which was part of the farming activities. The dam became known as Fonty's Pool, and to this day remains a famous local landmark and recreational facility. The first grapes were planted in 1989, and at 110 ha, the vineyard is now one of the region's largest, supplying grapes to a number of leading WA wineries. An increasing amount of the production is used for Fonty's Pool. Exports to the UK and Europe.

 TTTTY **Viognier 2004** Complex, rich and multi-layered; apricot and fig; spicy but subtle oak. Barrel-fermented, part wild yeast. Screwcap. 14.5° alc. RATING 91 DRINK 2009 $ 20
Chardonnay 2004 Gentle but sophisticated wine; melon, nectarine and a touch of grapefruit; sotto voce oak; good length. Screwcap. 13.5° alc. RATING 90 DRINK 2010 $ 20
Cabernet Merlot 2004 Supple, smooth, cassis/raspberry/blackcurrant; beguiling finish and aftertaste to the light- to medium-bodied palate. Drink sooner rather than later. Screwcap. 13.1° alc. RATING 90 DRINK 2008 $ 15.99
Black Granite Brut 2003 The strawberry pinot noir component quite obvious; likewise brioche/cream from extended lees contact. Attractive wine. Cork. 13.5° alc. RATING 90 DRINK 2008 $ 25

TTTT **Pinot Noir 2004** Light-bodied; foresty, savoury notes surround shy red fruits; drink asap. Screwcap. 14° alc. RATING 87 DRINK Now $ 20

TTTY **Merlot 2004** RATING 84 DRINK Now $ 20

Forest Hill Vineyard ★★★★★

South Coast Highway, Denmark, WA 6333 REGION Great Southern
T (08) 9381 2911 F (08) 9381 2955 WWW.foresthillwines.com.au OPEN 7 days 10–5
WINEMAKER Shane McKerrow, Liz Richardson EST. 1965 CASES 10 000
This is one of the oldest 'new' winemaking operations in WA, and was the site for the first grape plantings for the Great Southern region in 1965, on a farming property owned by the Pearse family. The Forest Hill brand became well known, aided by the fact that a 1975 Riesling made by Sandalford from Forest Hill grapes won 9 trophies in national wine shows. In 1997 the property was acquired by interests associated with Perth stockbroker Tim Lyons, and a program of renovation and expansion of the vineyards commenced. The 2006 release of tiny quantities of 4 wines made from the oldest vines on the property came as a bolt from the blue.

TTTTT **Block 1 Riesling 2005** Pale straw-green; extremely intense, yet fine and elegant; lime juice through the palate finishing with lingering acidity; 40-year-old vines. Screwcap. 12° alc. RATING 96 DRINK 2025 $ 35
Block 8 Chardonnay 2004 Elegant, intense and sophisticated, yet deliberately understated; melon, fig and citrus, the gentle acidity perfectly balanced in the context of the low alcohol. As with all the individual block wines, hand-pruned and hand-picked. Screwcap. 13° alc. RATING 95 DRINK 2014 $ 35
Block 9 Shiraz 2004 Super-refined, medium-bodied black cherry, blackberry, licorice and spice; careful oak management so as to simply provide a frame for the painting of the fruit. Screwcap. 14.5° alc. RATING 95 DRINK 2015 $ 45
Riesling 2005 Light straw-green; a very fine wine, partially living within the shadow of Block 1; by ordinary standards, high-quality lime and mineral flavours with great length. Screwcap. 13° alc. RATING 94 DRINK 2020 $ 19
Block 5 Cabernet Sauvignon 2004 Clear, deep purple-red; medium-bodied, with classic cedary/earthy/blackcurrant varietal fruit; fine-grained tannins, good length and likewise oak. Screwcap. 14.5° alc. RATING 94 DRINK 2016 $ 45

TTTTY **Mount Barker Shiraz 2004** Good colour; attractive medium-bodied wine, with lively plum, red cherry and blackberry fruit; fine, ripe tannins, good length. Screwcap. 14° alc. RATING 93 DRINK 2015 $ 22
Semillon Sauvignon Blanc 2005 Light straw-green; elegant and delicate style, but with no shortage of gently tropical/citrus flavours; clean bouquet, clean finish. Screwcap. 13° alc. RATING 91 DRINK Now $ 17
Mount Barker Chardonnay 2005 A tight, minerally substrate to the melon and citrus fruit; oak influence very subtle, needs time. Screwcap. 13° alc. RATING 90 DRINK 2012 $ 22
Mount Barker Cabernet Sauvignon 2004 Medium-bodied; attractive blackcurrant fruit with sweet, supple French oak inputs. Screwcap. 14° alc. RATING 90 DRINK 2013 $ 22

ΤΤΤΤ **Sauvignon Blanc 2005** Flawed by a touch of reduction (or sweaty varietal character) on the bouquet (take your pick); the palate is much better, long and crisp. Screwcap. 13° alc. **RATING** 89 **DRINK** Now $ 19

Mount Barker Cabernet Merlot 2004 A pleasant array of berry fruits, balanced extract and oak. Screwcap. 14° alc. **RATING** 88 **DRINK** 2009 $ 17

ΤΤΤΤ **Unwooded Chardonnay 2005** **RATING** 86 **DRINK** 2008 $ 17

Forester Estate ★★★★☆

Lot 11 Wildwood Road, Yallingup, WA 6282 **REGION** Margaret River
T (08) 9755 2788 **F** (08) 9755 2766 **WWW**.foresterestate.com.au **OPEN** By appt
WINEMAKER Kevin McKay, Michael Langridge **EST.** 2001 **CASES** 20 000
The Forester Estate business partners are Kevin McKay and Redmond Sweeny. Winemaker Michael Langridge has a Bachelor of Arts (Hons) in Psychology and a Bachelor of Applied Science (wine science, Charles Sturt). As Kevin McKay says, 'He is the most over-qualified forklift driver in Australia.' Langridge also has 6 vintages in the Margaret River region under his belt. Together they have built and designed a 500-tonne winery, half devoted to contract winemaking, the other half for the Forester label. Part of the intake comes from the 4.5-ha estate plantings of sauvignon blanc, cabernet and shiraz, the remainder from nearby growers, one of whom is the operating viticulturist at Forester Estate.

ΤΤΤΤΤ **Home Block Margaret River Shiraz 2003** Stylish wine; an elegant mix of red and black cherries and spice; seamless oak, fine tannins. Cork. **RATING** 94 **DRINK** 2010 $ 28

ΤΤΤΤΤ **Cellar Reserve Cabernet 2000** Smooth, supple, bottled-developed style; black fruits, mocha, spice and vanilla; fine tannins to close. High-quality cork. **RATING** 92 **DRINK** 2010 $ 46

Margaret River Chardonnay 2004 Elegant style, with gentle, floral citrus aromas; seamless citrus, nectarine and subtle oak on the palate. Diam. **RATING** 91 **DRINK** 2011 $ 24.99

Margaret River Cabernet Sauvignon 2003 Clean, cassis, blackcurrant and red capsicum aromas and flavours; substantial palate and tannins; a subtly integrated touch of French oak. Cork. **RATING** 91 **DRINK** 2018 $ 28

Margaret River Semillon Sauvignon Blanc 2005 Light-bodied; good balance; very precise and clean herb, lime and mineral; long finish. Screwcap. **RATING** 90 **DRINK** 2009 $ 16.99

Margaret River Shiraz 2003 Light- to medium-bodied; fresh and lively; vibrant, direct cherry fruit; has good length. Screwcap. **RATING** 90 **DRINK** 2009 $ 16.99

Margaret River Cabernet Merlot 2004 Plenty of cassis and blackcurrant fruit; the tannins seem a little underworked, but there is lots happening; long finish. Screwcap. **RATING** 90 **DRINK** 2014 $ 16.99

ΤΤΤΤ **Margaret River Sauvignon Blanc 2005** Diminished aromas, but plenty of flavour ranging through citrus to asparagus and redcurrant. Screwcap. **RATING** 89 **DRINK** Now $ 19.99

Fosters Wine Estates ★★★★☆

77 Southbank Boulevard, Southbank, Vic 3006
T 1300 651 650 **F** (03) 8626 3450 **WWW**.fosters.com.au **OPEN** Not
WINEMAKER Chris Hatcher **EST.** 2005 **CASES** NA
Fosters Wine Estates has 2 main streams of brands, those which it had prior to the amalgamation with Southcorp, and those that came with Southcorp. Alphabetically, in the former category are: Andrew Garrett, Annie's Lane, Baileys of Glenrowan, Cartwheel, Early Harvest, Eye Spy, Half Mile Creek, Ingoldby, Jamiesons Run, Maglieri of McLaren Vale, Maglieri Lambrusco, Metala, Mildara, Mount Ida, Pepperjack, Robertson's Well, Saltram, Shadowood, St Huberts, T'Gallant, The Rothbury Estate, Wolf Blass, Yarra Ridge and Yellowglen. The Southcorp originated brands are Blues Point, Coldstream Hills, Devil's Lair, Edwards & Chaffey, Fifth Leg, Fisher's Circle, Glass Mountain, Kaiser Stuhl, Killawarra, Kirralaa, Leo Buring, Lindemans, Matthew Lang, Minchinbury, Penfolds, Queen Adelaide, Rosemount Estate, Rouge Homme, Seaview, Seppelt, the Little Penguin, Tollana, and

Wynns Coonawarra. Those which have dedicated vineyards wholly or partially within their control and/or have separate winemaking facilities will be found under their separate entries. Those which are brands without, as it were, an independent existence are covered within this entry. Exports to all major markets.

▼▼▼▼▼ Shadowood Eden Valley Cabernet Sauvignon 2004 Strong red-purple; an elegant yet formidable wine, perfectly delineating Eden Valley cabernet sauvignon; slightly sombre blackcurrant fruit, precise tannins and quality French oak. Screwcap. 14.5° alc. **RATING** 94 **DRINK** 2024

▼▼▼▼▽ Shadowood Eden Valley Chardonnay 2004 Elegant, finely crafted style; light citrus and melon fruit, with harmonious oak. Screwcap. 13.5° alc. **RATING** 90 **DRINK** 2010
Cartwheel Margaret River Chardonnay 2004 Soft barrel ferment/malolactic/lees inputs; gently complex nectarine, cashew and cream flavours; developing slowly. Screwcap. 13.5° alc. **RATING** 90 **DRINK** 2008
Shadowood Eden Valley Shiraz 2003 Interestingly, a trace of reduction on the bouquet and palate; medium-bodied, savoury/spicy black fruits, very typical of the Eden Valley; good length and balance. Screwcap. 14.5° alc. **RATING** 90 **DRINK** 2013

▼▼▼▼ Cartwheel Western Australia Semillon Sauvignon Blanc 2005 Clean, lively and pure; light-bodied, but well-balanced in both flavour and structure terms. Screwcap. 13° alc. **RATING** 88 **DRINK** Now
Cartwheel Margaret River Cabernet Merlot 2004 Medium-bodied; attractive red and black fruits; more body than the sister Sauvignon Blanc Semillon; good length. Screwcap. 14.5° alc. **RATING** 88 **DRINK** 2011

▼▼▼▽ Cartwheel Margaret River Semillon Sauvignon Blanc 2004 RATING 86 **DRINK** Now
Early Harvest Semillon Sauvignon Blanc 2005 An interesting wine; fresh and tight; slightly off-dry to add to mouthfeel and flavour. Only 9.5° alcohol. Screwcap. **RATING** 86 **DRINK** Now $ 17
Fishers Circle Chardonnay 2005 RATING 86 **DRINK** Now $ 12.99
Fishers Circle Classic Dry White 2005 RATING 86 **DRINK** Now $ 12.99
The Little Penguin Merlot 2005 RATING 86 **DRINK** Now $ 10.99
Early Harvest Chardonnay 2005 RATING 85 **DRINK** Now $ 17

Four Winds Vineyard   NR

PO Box 131, Murrumbateman, NSW 2582 **REGION** Canberra District
T (02) 6226 8182 **F** (02) 6226 8257 **WWW**.fourwindsvineyard.com.au **OPEN** Not
WINEMAKER Graeme Lunney **EST.** 1998 **CASES** NA
Graeme and Suzanne Lunney conceived the idea for Four Winds in 1997, planting the first vines in 1998, moving to the property full-time in 1999, and making the first vintage in 2000. Son Tom manages the day-to-day operations of the vineyard; daughter Sarah looks after events and promotions; and youngest daughter Jaime, complete with a degree in Forensic Biology, joins the party at the most busy times of the year. Graeme Lunney makes the wine, and Suzanne tends the gardens and the 100 rose bushes at the end of the vine rows.

Fox Creek Wines   ★★★★★

Malpas Road, Willunga, SA 5172 **REGION** McLaren Vale
T (08) 8556 2403 **F** (08) 8556 2104 **WWW**.foxcreekwines.com **OPEN** 7 days 10–5
WINEMAKER Chris Dix, Scott Zrna **EST.** 1995 **CASES** 35 000
Fox Creek has made a major impact since coming on-stream late in 1995. It is the venture of the Watts family: Jim (retired surgeon) and wife Helen and son Paul Watts (viticulturist); and the Roberts family: John (retired anaesthetist) and wife Lyn. Kristin McLarty (nee Watts) is marketing manager and Paul Rogers (married to Georgy, nee Watts) is general manager. The wines have enjoyed considerable show success. Exports to the UK, the US and other major markets.

▼▼▼▼▼ Short Row McLaren Vale Shiraz 2004 Dense stygian colour; top example of a full-bodied McLaren Vale loaded with blackberry fruit and dark chocolate, yet not hot or heavy; good extract and oak. Screwcap. 14.5° alc. **RATING** 94 **DRINK** 2019 $ 28

Reserve McLaren Vale Cabernet Sauvignon 2004 Good colour; a potent mix of blackcurrant, blackberry and bitter chocolate supported by ripe tannins and controlled oak. Screwcap. 14.5° alc. **RATING** 94 **DRINK** 2024 $ 36

ŸŸŸŸŸ **Reserve McLaren Vale Shiraz 2004** Dark colour; opulent, rich and mouthfilling; chocolate, vanilla and mocha provide much of the energy, though there is plenty of blackberry/licorice fruit. Screwcap. 14.5° alc. **RATING** 93 **DRINK** 2019 $ 70

Duet McLaren Vale Cabernet Merlot 2004 Deeply coloured; medium- to full-bodied, with massively concentrated black fruits and that ever-present touch of bitter chocolate; a serious long haul wine. Screwcap. 14.5° alc. **RATING** 92 **DRINK** 2024 $ 19

McLaren Vale Shiraz Grenache 2004 Very spicy and rich with a momentary hot spot on the tongue balanced by bitter chocolate and pleasantly dry tannins; a bigger style of this blend. Screwcap. 14.5° alc. **RATING** 90 **DRINK** 2009 $ 17

ŸŸŸŸ **Shadow's Run Shiraz Cabernet Sauvignon 2004** Deep red-purple; succulent and smooth blackberry, dark chocolate and blackcurrant; ripe tannins, good oak. Exceptional value. Screwcap. 14.5° alc. **RATING** 89 **DRINK** 2012 $ 12

McLaren Vale Semillon Sauvignon Blanc 2005 Texturally complex; largely driven by the partially barrel-fermented semillon, with herb and lemongrass off-set against some slightly sweet fruit notes from the sauvignon blanc. Screwcap. 12.5° alc. **RATING** 88 **DRINK** 2008 $ 16

McLaren Vale Chardonnay 2005 Light green-straw; a clean bouquet, the palate with soft stone fruit, the proportion barrel-fermented providing texture as much as flavour. Screwcap. 13.5° alc. **RATING** 88 **DRINK** 2010 $ 16

ŸŸŸŸ **McLaren Vale Sauvignon Blanc 2005** **RATING** 86 **DRINK** Now $ 16
Shadow's Run The White 2005 **RATING** 86 **DRINK** Now $ 12
McLaren Vale Verdelho 2005 **RATING** 85 **DRINK** Now $ 16

🦊 Fox Gordon ★★★★☆

PO Box 178, Williamstown, SA 5351 **REGION** Barossa Valley
T (08) 8269 4343 **F** (08) 8269 4343 **WWW**.foxgordon.com.au **OPEN** Not
WINEMAKER Natasha Mooney **EST**. 2000 **CASES** 3000
This is the venture of 3 very well known figures in the wine industry, Jane Gordon, Rachel Atkins (nee Fox) and Natasha Mooney. Natasha Mooney (Tash) has had first class experience in the Barossa Valley, particularly during her time as chief winemaker at Barossa Valley Estate. She and her partners wanted to produce small quantities of high-quality wine which would allow them time to look after their children, the venture planned in the shade of the wisteria tree in Tash's back garden. The grapes come from dry-grown vineyards on the western side of the Barossa Valley, and in the warmer, northern end. All are farmed under bio-diversity principles which, says Mooney, makes the winemaker's job easy.

ŸŸŸŸŸ **Hannah's Swing Shiraz 2003** Deep colour; rich, luscious blackberry and plum fruit; densely packed, but not extractive; good tannins and oak. Diam. **RATING** 94 **DRINK** 2018 $ 49

ŸŸŸŸ **King Louis Cabernet Sauvignon 2003** Very potent, powerful and slightly extractive, in-your-face style; plenty of black fruits, black olives, and tannins needing to soften. Diam. **RATING** 89 **DRINK** 2013 $ 49

Eight Uncles Shiraz 2003 Complex, savoury/earthy style; blackberry, spice and briar; lingering tannins; apparently unfiltered. Diam. **RATING** 88 **DRINK** 2011 $ 29

Foxeys Hangout ★★★★☆

795 White Hill Road, Red Hill, Vic 3937 **REGION** Mornington Peninsula
T (03) 5989 2022 **F** (03) 9809 0495 **WWW**.foxeys-hangout.com.au **OPEN** W'ends & public hols 11–5
WINEMAKER Tony Lee **EST**. 1998 **CASES** 3000
Brothers Michael and Tony Lee spent 20 years in the hospitality business, acquiring a considerable knowledge of wine through the selection of wine lists for two decades, opting for a change of lifestyle and occupation when they planted 2.2 ha of pinot noir, 2 ha of chardonnay and 0.5 ha of pinot gris on

the northeast-facing slopes of an old farm. The name (and the catchy label) stems from the true tale of two Mornington Peninsula fox-hunters who began a competition with each other in 1936, hanging their kills on the branches of an ancient eucalypt tree to keep count. The corpses have gone, but not the nickname for the area.

ŸŸŸŸŸ Reserve Pinot Noir 2003 Slightly hazy colour; a complex, powerful wine with ripe, dark plum fruit and touches of forest; strong structure underpins the flavours. Diam. 13.5° alc. RATING 94 DRINK 2013 $ 35

ŸŸŸŸŸ Mornington Peninsula Chardonnay 2004 Elegant citrus and stone fruit; excellent balance and mouthfeel, the oak in modulated support. Screwcap. 13.5° alc. RATING 92 DRINK 2010 $ 20
Reserve Chardonnay 2003 Bright, light green-yellow; an elegant wine with ripe melon and stone fruit; well-managed, positive, oak inputs. Cork. 13° alc. RATING 92 DRINK 2010 $ 35
Mornington Peninsula Late Harvest Pinot Gris 2005 Made using the cordon cut method, resulting in extreme shrivel of the grapes and concentration of the juice; acidity balances the luscious sweetness. Cork. 11.5° alc. RATING 90 DRINK 2008 $ 20

ŸŸŸŸ Mornington Peninsula Pinot Noir 2004 Light but good hue; spiced red fruits; cherry and a touch of damson plum; good length and balance. Diam. 13.5° alc. RATING 89 DRINK 2009 $ 25
Mornington Peninsula Shiraz 2004 Good colour; a mix of spice, leaf, bramble and blackberry fruit; has length and tannins. Cork. 14.5° alc. RATING 89 DRINK 2010 $ 20
Vintage Port (500ml) 2004 Very much in the modern, drier style. A pretty nice young vintage port, but is this the best use for Mornington Peninsula shiraz? Cork. 18.5° alc. RATING 89 DRINK 2012 $ 20
Mornington Peninsula Pinot Gris 2005 Mainstream pinot gris; faint pear and apple, alcohol the principal driver, giving the impression of a touch of sweetness. Screwcap. 13.5° alc. RATING 87 DRINK Now $ 20
Mornington Peninsula Rose 2005 Attractive red fruits with a light slash of leaf/grass; dry-ish finish. Screwcap. 13° alc. RATING 87 DRINK Now $ 15
Blanc de Noirs 2003 Pale onion skin colour; a delicate yet firm palate attesting to the pinot noir; a flick of sweet fruit (not sugar) before a crisp finish. 12.5° alc. RATING 87 DRINK 2009 $ 25

ŸŸŸŸ Sparkling Shiraz 2004 RATING 86 DRINK 2010 $ 25

Francois Jacquard   NR

14 Neil Street, Osborne Park, WA 6017 REGION Perth Hills
T (08) 9380 9199 F (08) 9380 9199 OPEN Not
WINEMAKER Francois Jacquard EST. 1997 CASES 2000
Francois (Franky) Jacquard graduated from Dijon University in 1983. He worked that vintage as a cellar hand at Domaine Dujac, and came to Australia for Bannockburn in 1985. Between then and 1992 he worked in both the northern and southern hemispheres, before moving back to Australia to become chief winemaker at Chittering Estate in the Perth Hills in 1992, a position he held until 1997 when he established his own brand. He has since kept a consistently low profile.

Frankland Estate   ★★★★★

Frankland Road, Frankland, WA 6396 REGION Frankland River
T (08) 9855 1544 F (08) 9855 1549 OPEN Mon–Fri 10–4, public hols & w'ends by appt
WINEMAKER Barrie Smith, Judi Cullam EST. 1988 CASES 15 000
A significant Frankland River operation, situated on a large sheep property owned by Barrie Smith and Judi Cullam. The 29-ha vineyard has been established progressively since 1988, and a winery was built in 1993. The recent introduction of an array of single-vineyard Rieslings has been a highlight. All the wines are energetically promoted and marketed by Judi Cullam, especially the Riesling. Frankland Estate has held several important International Riesling tastings and seminars over recent years. Exports to the UK, the US and other major markets.

ŸŸŸŸŸ **Isolation Ridge Vineyard Riesling 2005** Stacked with sweet citrus fruit on the mid-palate, with strong structure; the most intense of the Frankland '05 Rieslings, with great line and length. Screwcap. 13.5° alc. **RATING** 95 **DRINK** 2015 $ 23
Poison Hill Vineyard Riesling 2005 Flowery bouquet; passionfruit and tropical flavours; the most elegant of the '05 Rieslings, but no shrinking violet. Screwcap. 13° alc. **RATING** 94 **DRINK** 2013 $ 23
Isolation Ridge Vineyard Shiraz 2003 Elegant medium-bodied, counter-cultural style; dark fruits and excellent texture and structure from the fine tannins running through its length; perfect acidity. Screwcap. 14° alc. **RATING** 94 **DRINK** 2013 $ 27

ŸŸŸŸ⁷ **Cooladerra Vineyard Riesling 2005** Apple blossom and mineral aromas; a powerful, long palate with spice, apple and lime; fractionally heavy finish. Screwcap. 13° alc. **RATING** 93 **DRINK** 2010 $ 23
Rocky Gully Shiraz Viognier 2004 Aromatic spice and black cherry; medium-bodied, attractive juicy wine with anise/spice flavours; fine tannins. Screwcap. **RATING** 91 **DRINK** 2010 $ 18

ŸŸŸŸ **Rocky Gully Riesling 2005** Light green-straw; lime and pineapple aromas; a powerful, deep palate, with a core of minerality. Screwcap. **RATING** 89 **DRINK** 2010 $ 16
Olmo's Reward 2002 Expected development; distinctly earthy, savoury, tobacco, bitter chocolate flavours; has more length than generosity. Cabernet Franc/Merlot/Petit Verdot/Cabernet Sauvignon. Screwcap. 13.5° alc. **RATING** 88 **DRINK** 2009 $ 35

Fratin Brothers Vineyard ★★★

Byron Road, Ararat, Vic 3377 **REGION** Grampians
T (03) 5352 3322 **F** (03) 5352 3322 **OPEN** 7 days 11–5
WINEMAKER Michael Fratin **EST.** 1996 **CASES** 500
The Fratin Brothers Vineyard was planted by Dino and Michael Fratin in 1996, 30 years after their father Serge and uncles Dom and Lino established Mount Langi Ghiran Vineyards. Shiraz cuttings were supplied by Mount Langi Ghiran, and 2 ha of shiraz, 1 ha of chardonnay and 0.5 ha of merlot have been planted. The wines are made in open fermentation tanks and basket pressed.

ŸŸŸŸ **Copes Hill Cabernet Sauvignon 2004** Very sweet cassis, blackberry and mulberry fruit on the medium-bodied palate; ripe tannins, subtle oak. Screwcap. 14.5° alc. **RATING** 87 **DRINK** 2011 $ 16

ŸŸŸ⁷ **Shiraz Cabernet Merlot 2003** Firm, earthy, savoury notes around a core of plum and cassis fruit, persistent tannins. Cork. 13.5° alc. **RATING** 86 **DRINK** 2009 $ 22
Copes Hill Shiraz Cabernet 2004 Medium-bodied; clean red and black fruits not quite able to escape the clutches of powerful tannins; time may help. Screwcap. 14° alc. **RATING** 86 **DRINK** 2012 $ 16

ŸŸŸ **Shiraz 2003 RATING** 83 $ 25

Frazer Woods Wines NR

c/- Post Office, Yallingup, WA 6282 **REGION** Margaret River
T (08) 9755 6274 **F** (08) 9755 6295 **OPEN** Not
WINEMAKER Various contract **EST.** 1996 **CASES** 1000
John Frazer has set up a contract sparkling wine business, called the Champagne Shed, although the winemaking is done offsite. He makes the Frazer Woods wines from 2 ha of estate-grown shiraz; the white grapes for the pinot chardonnay sparkling are bought in. The wines are sold through the Margaret River Wine Cellars and the Witchcliffe Liquor Store.

Freeman Vineyards ★★★★☆

RMB 101, Prunevale, NSW 2587 (postal) **REGION** Hilltops
T (02) 6384 4299 **F** (02) 6384 4299 **www**.freemanvineyards.com.au **OPEN** Not
WINEMAKER Dr Brian Freeman **EST.** 2000 **CASES** 250

Dr Brian Freeman has spent much of his long life in research and education, in the latter role as head of Charles Sturt University's viticulture and oenology campus. In 2004 he purchased the 30-year-old vineyard previously known as Demondrille. He has also established a new vineyard next door, and in all has 14 varieties totalling 40.5 ha; these range from staples such as shiraz, cabernet sauvignon, semillon and riesling through to the more exotic, trendy varieties such as tempranillo, and on to corvina and rondinella. It is the latter two grapes which have been used to make the first release. He has had a long academic interest in the effect of partial drying of grapes on the tannins, and (living at Prunevale) was easily able to obtain a prune dehydrator to partially raisin the 2 varieties.

ΥΥΥΥΥ Rondinella Corvina 2003 The first thing to hit are the dead-ringer Italian tannins, then a complex array of cherry and plum fruit. Cork. 14.5° alc. **RATING** 90 **DRINK** 2018 $ 35

Freycinet

15919 Tasman Highway via Bicheno, Tas 7215 **REGION** East Coast Tasmania
T (03) 6257 8574 **F** (03) 6257 8454 **WWW**.freycinetvineyard.com.au **OPEN** 7 days 9.30–4.30
WINEMAKER Claudio Radenti, Lindy Bull, Paula Kloosterman (Assistant) **EST.** 1980 **CASES** 5000
The original 9-ha Freycinet vineyards are beautifully situated on the sloping hillsides of a small valley. The soils are brown dermosol on top of jurassic dolerite, and the combination of aspect, slope, soil and heat summation produce red grapes with unusual depth of colour and ripe flavours. One of Australia's foremost producers of Pinot Noir, with a wholly enviable track record of consistency — rare with such a temperamental variety. The Radenti (sparkling), Riesling and Chardonnay are also wines of the highest quality. Exports to the UK.

ΥΥΥΥΥ Radenti Pinot Noir Chardonnay 1999 Powerful and rich; very complex, sustained citrus, nectarine and white peach fruit, the fruit line flowing and rippling. 12° alc. **RATING** 95 **DRINK** 2010 $ 62
Botrytis 2004 Extremely complex, with a high botrytis impact; lime, honey and malt, the glorious lusciousness off-set by citrussy acidity. Screwcap. 12° alc. **RATING** 95 **DRINK** 2009 $ 40
Riesling 2005 A powerful bouquet, with touches of Alsace; a very concentrated and solid palate shadowing the bouquet; retains balance and elegance, sustained by lingering acidity. Screwcap. 13.5° alc. **RATING** 94 **DRINK** 2013 $ 25
Chardonnay 2004 Fragrant, spicy grapefruit and nectarine is supported by subtle barrel ferment inputs; long, balanced and stylish. Cork. 13.5° alc. **RATING** 94 **DRINK** 2010 $ 30
Pinot Noir 2004 Fresh, bright and lively; unmistakeable Tasmanian acidity and finesse; silky mouthfeel. Cork. **RATING** 94 **DRINK** 2009 $ 62

ΥΥΥΥΥ Louis Pinot Noir 2004 Brilliantly clear; bright, fresh red fruits; good length and balance; impressive second label. Cork. **RATING** 92 **DRINK** 2008 $ 30

ΥΥΥΥ Louis Riesling Schonburger 2005 RATING 86 **DRINK** Now $ 18
Cabernet Sauvignon Merlot 2003 RATING 86 **DRINK** 2008 $ 34

Frog Choir Wines

PO Box 515, Margaret River, WA 6285 **REGION** Margaret River
T (08) 9757 6510 **F** (08) 9757 6501 **WWW**.frogchoir.com **OPEN** Not
WINEMAKER Swings & Roundabouts (Mark Lane) **EST.** 1997 **CASES** 550
Eddie Sawiris and partner Sharon Martin have a micro vineyard of 1.5 ha, equally split between shiraz and cabernet sauvignon. It has immaculate address credentials: adjacent to Leeuwin Estate and Voyager Estate, 6 km from the Margaret River township. The hand-tended vines are grown without the use of insecticides.

ΥΥΥΥ Margaret River Shiraz 2003 Unconvincing colour; light- to medium-bodied, with light, spicy red fruits; minimal tannins, balanced oak. Cork. 13° alc. **RATING** 87 **DRINK** 2009 $ 38

ΥΥΥΥ Margaret River Cabernet Sauvignon 2003 RATING 85 **DRINK** 2008 $ 35

Frog Island ★★★

PO Box 423, Kingston SE, SA 5275 **REGION** Limestone Coast Zone
T (08) 8768 5000 **F** (08) 8768 5008 **WWW**.frogisland.com.au **OPEN** At Ralph Fowler
WINEMAKER Sarah Squire **EST.** 2003 **CASES** 4000
Sarah Squire (née Fowler) has decided to do her own thing, with full support from father Ralph. The quixotic name is taken from a small locality inland from the seaside town of Robe, and the wine is deliberately made in a fresh, fruit-forward style. Exports to Europe and Asia.

ŸŸŸŸ **Shiraz 2004** Light- to medium-bodied; an easy style with light, juicy red fruits; tangy, with little, if any, oak contribution. Screwcap. 12.5° alc. **RATING** 87 **DRINK** 2008 **$** 18

ŸŸŸŸ **Pinot Noir 2004 RATING** 86 **DRINK** Now **$** 18
Sparkling Red NV RATING 84 **DRINK** Now **$** 18

Frog Rock Wines ★★★☆

Edgell Lane, Mudgee, NSW 2850 **REGION** Mudgee
T (02) 6372 2408 **F** (02) 6372 6924 **WWW**.frogrockwines.com **OPEN** 7 days 10–5
WINEMAKER David Lowe, Jane Wilson (Contract) **EST.** 1973 **CASES** 25 000
Frog Rock is the former Tallara Vineyard, established over 30 years ago by leading Sydney chartered accountant Rick Turner. There are now 60 ha of vineyard, with 22 ha each of shiraz and cabernet sauvignon, and much smaller plantings of chardonnay, semillon, merlot, petit verdot and chambourcin. Exports to Ireland, the US, Canada, Singapore and Hong Kong.

ŸŸŸŸŸ **Old Vine Mudgee Semillon 2005** Light straw-green; a delicate, well-balanced, classic mix of mineral, grass and lemon; good length, clean finish. Screwcap. 11.5° alc. **RATING** 91 **DRINK** 2012 **$** 18

ŸŸŸŸ **Old Vine Mudgee Shiraz 2003** Medium-bodied; complex savoury/earthy/brambly aromas and flavours; a good finish lifts the wine. Cork. 13° alc. **RATING** 88 **DRINK** 2010 **$** 25

ŸŸŸŸ **Mudgee Rose 2004** Salmon pink; light red fruits; well-balanced acidity and a little flick of sweetness. Screwcap. 12° alc. **RATING** 86 **DRINK** Now **$** 18
Sticky Frog 2005 RATING 84 **DRINK** Now **$** 30

Frogmore Creek ★★★★☆

208 Denholms Road, Cambridge, Tas 7170 **REGION** Southern Tasmania
T (03) 6248 5844 **F** (03) 6248 5855 **OPEN** At Hood Wines/Wellington
WINEMAKER Andrew Hood **EST.** 1997 **CASES** 2300
Frogmore Creek is a Pacific Rim joint venture, the two owners being Tony Scherer of Tasmania, and Jack Kidwiler of California. They have commenced the establishment of the only organically certified commercial vineyard in Tas, and plan to take the area under vine to 80 ha over the next 4 years. A winery will be constructed; when completed, the development will offer a visitor centre and cellar door sales area; an environmental centre with walking trails and lakeside picnic areas; an organic garden; and a restaurant, accommodation and event facilities. The name is taken from the creek which runs through the property. In late 2003 the Frogmore Creek owners acquired the Wellington wine business of Andrew Hood, and for the foreseeable future will run the 2 operations in tandem, handling all organically grown fruit at the Frogmore Creek winery, and the remainder at the Wellington winery.

ŸŸŸŸŸ **Chardonnay 2005** Considerable intensity and length; stone fruit and citrus mix; controlled but evident oak. **RATING** 93 **DRINK** 2009 **$** 26
Chardonnay 2004 Surprising colour development, already with gold tints; the palate is tighter than the colour would suggest, citrussy, flinty, low alcohol flavours moving the wine towards Chablis in style. Screwcap. 12.9° alc. **RATING** 93 **DRINK** 2011 **$** 26
Riesling 2005 Supple, smooth and ripe; citrus moving almost into stone fruit; fluid line. **RATING** 90 **DRINK** 2010 **$** 24
Cuvee Evermore 2003 Faint blush tones; abundant flavour with a pinot noir emphasis; powerful finish. **RATING** 90 **DRINK** Now **$** 34
Iced Riesling 2005 Very flavoursome and rich, with peachy fruit typical of the vintage. **RATING** 90 **DRINK** 2008 **$** 26

ΥΥΥΥ **Pinot Noir 2004** Light- to medium-bodied; strongly savoury/foresty aromas and flavours; needs more fruit weight. **RATING** 87 **DRINK** Now $ 30

Frogspond   NR

400 Arthurs Seat Road, Red Hill, Vic 3937 **REGION** Mornington Peninsula
T (03) 5989 2941 **F** (03) 9824 7659 **WWW**.frogspond.com.au **OPEN** By appt
WINEMAKER David Lloyd **EST.** 1994 **CASES** 160
The Nelson family has established 2 ha of chardonnay and pinot noir on an ideal north-facing slope. The low yields produce grapes with intense fruit flavours, but only a tiny amount of wine is made.

FUSE   ★★★★☆

PO Box 441, South Melbourne, Vic 3205 **REGION** Clare Valley & Adelaide Hills
T (03) 9696 7018 **F** (03) 9686 4015 **OPEN** Not
WINEMAKER Neil Pike, John Trotter **EST.** 2004 **CASES** 3000
FUSE is a joint venture of the Pikes (Clare Valley), Pike & Joyce (Adelaide Hills) and well-known Melbourne wine distributors Trembath & Taylor. It takes low-cropped grape varieties from *terroir* that best suits them: riesling, cabernet, merlot, shiraz, grenache and mourvedre from the Clare Valley, and semillon, sauvignon blanc, chardonnay and pinot noir from the Adelaide Hills. Distinctive packaging, and a simple price range, makes the proposition easy to understand.

ΥΥΥΥΥ **Clare Valley Riesling 2005** Apple, herb, spice and citrus, but predominant minerally acidity runs through the length of the wine. All gain from here. Screwcap. 12° alc. **RATING** 93 **DRINK** 2012 $ 16
Adelaide Hills Semillon Sauvignon Blanc 2005 Spotless, aromatic, flowery bouquet; passionfruit and gooseberry from the sauvignon blanc; acidity and structure from the semillon. Screwcap. 13° alc. **RATING** 91 **DRINK** 2008 $ 19

ΥΥΥΥ **Adelaide Hills Pinot Noir 2004** Light red-purple; quite sweet red cherry fruit off-set by some briar/forest notes; dry, fractionally stemmy, finish. Screwcap. 14° alc. **RATING** 89 **DRINK** 2010 $ 19

Fyffe Field   NR

1417 Murray Valley Highway, Yarrawonga, Vic 3730 **REGION** Goulburn Valley
T (03) 5748 4282 **F** (03) 5748 4284 **WWW**.fyffefieldwines.com.au **OPEN** 7 days 10–5
WINEMAKER Tisdall Wines (Robin Querre) **EST.** 1993 **CASES** 2500
Fyffe Field has been established by Graeme and Liz Diamond near the Murray River in a mudbrick and leadlight tasting room opposite a historic homestead. They have 2 ha of shiraz, 1 ha each of semillon, verdelho, merlot and cabernet sauvignon, and 0.5 ha each of touriga and petit verdot. A highlight is the collection of ornamental pigs, a display set up long before Babe was born.

Gabriel's Paddocks Vineyard   NR

Deasys Road, Pokolbin, NSW 2320 **REGION** Lower Hunter Valley
T (02) 4998 7650 **F** (02) 4998 7603 **WWW**.gabrielspaddocks.com.au **OPEN** Thurs–Mon 9–5
WINEMAKER Contract **EST.** 1979 **CASES** NA
Formerly Sutherlands Wines, Gabriel's Paddocks is as much about general tourism and small conference accommodation as it is about wine production, and has two separate buildings able to accommodate more than 20 people altogether. The 13.6-ha vineyards are planted to chardonnay, chenin blanc, pinot noir, merlot, shiraz and cabernet sauvignon.

Galafrey   ★★★★

Quangellup Road, Mount Barker, WA 6324 **REGION** Mount Barker
T (08) 9851 2022 **F** (08) 9851 2324 **WWW**.galafreywines.com.au **OPEN** 7 days 10–5
WINEMAKER Vincent Lignac **EST.** 1977 **CASES** 10 000
Relocated to a purpose-built but utilitarian winery after previously inhabiting the exotic surrounds of the old Albany wool store, Galafrey makes wines with plenty of robust, if not rustic, character,

drawing grapes in the main from nearly 13 ha of estate plantings at Mount Barker. Exports to Belgium, Holland, Japan and Singapore.

🍷🍷🍷🍷🍷 **Mount Barker Riesling 2004** Firm and tightly focused; excellent lime and mineral varietal character; good balance, structure and length. Screwcap. **RATING** 92 **DRINK** 2020 $ 15

Mount Barker Semillon Sauvignon Blanc 2004 Clean, crisp and fresh passionfruit and herb aromas; lively lemon, mineral and gooseberry flavours; crunchy acidity. Screwcap. **RATING** 90 **DRINK** 2008 $ 15

🍷🍷🍷🍷 **Frankland River Shiraz 2001** Light- to medium-bodied; spicy, earthy, foresty notes along with touches of cedar and cigar box; almost lemony acidity. Quality cork. **RATING** 88 **DRINK** 2009 $ 22

Mount Barker Sauvignon Blanc 2004 Pale straw-green; faintly sweaty/reduced aromas typical of the variety; gooseberry and citrus fruit; crisp finish. Screwcap. **RATING** 87 **DRINK** Now $ 15

Mount Barker Unoaked Chardonnay 2004 Aromatic, lively, light-bodied wine; fresh and crisp stone fruit; bright flavour and mouthfeel. Screwcap. **RATING** 87 **DRINK** Now $ 15

Mount Barker Shiraz 2002 Very savoury; predominantly red fruits with touches of spice; light- to medium-bodied, low pH style; firm finish. Doubtful cork. **RATING** 87 **DRINK** 2009 $ 22

Mount Barker Cabernet Sauvignon 1999 Attractive bottle-developed style; light- to medium-bodied; earth, olive and blackberry on a long palate. Cork. **RATING** 87 **DRINK** 2008 $ 22

🍷🍷🍷🍷 **Mount Barker Cabernet Merlot 2002** **RATING** 86 **DRINK** Now $ 15

Galah   ★★★

Tregarthen Road, Ashton, SA 5137 **REGION** Adelaide Hills
T (08) 8390 1243 **F** (08) 8390 1243 **OPEN** At Ashton Hills
WINEMAKER Stephen George **EST.** 1986 **CASES** 500
Over the years Stephen George has built up a network of contacts across SA from which he gains some very high-quality small parcels of grapes or wine for the Galah label. These are all sold direct at low prices given the quality. Exports to the UK and the US.

🍷🍷🍷🍷 **Three Sheds Red 2002** Good colour; light- to medium-bodied; supple, lively black fruits, and light, ripe tannins; bargain. Cork. 13.5° alc. **RATING** 87 **DRINK** 2008 $ 12

Gallagher Wines   ★★★★

2770 Dog Trap Road, Murrumbateman, NSW 2582 **REGION** Canberra District
T (02) 6227 0555 **F** (02) 6227 0666 **WWW**.gallagherwines.com.au **OPEN** W'ends & public hols 10–5
WINEMAKER Greg Gallagher **EST.** 1995 **CASES** 2000
Greg Gallagher was senior winemaker at Taltarni for 20 years, working with Dominique Portet. He began planning a change of career at much the same time as did Portet, and started establishing a small vineyard at Murrumbateman in 1995, now planted to 2 ha each of chardonnay and shiraz. He and his family have now moved to the region. Retail distribution in Vic, NSW and the ACT.

🍷🍷🍷🍷🍷 **Canberra District Riesling 2005** Light straw-green; a spotlessly clean bouquet, the palate with good focus and intensity to the mix of lime, lemon and mineral flavours of the palate. Screwcap. 12° alc. **RATING** 91 **DRINK** 2012 $ 17

Canberra District Shiraz 2004 Very powerful; a touch of crushed ant on the bouquet, the long palate, with plum and blackberry, dispelling the slightly questionable bouquet. Screwcap. 14° alc. **RATING** 90 **DRINK** 2014 $ 20

🍷🍷🍷🍷 **Canberra District Sauvignon Blanc 2005** A rich, mouthfilling but not heavy tropical fruit display; slightly soft finish. Screwcap. 13° alc. **RATING** 89 **DRINK** Now $ 17

Canberra District Chardonnay 2004 Light- to medium-bodied; a tightly focused range of nectarine/grapefruit/citrus/melon flavours; clean finish. Screwcap. 12.8° alc. **RATING** 88 **DRINK** 2009 $ 17

Canberra District Merlot 2003 Light- to medium-bodied; fresh red fruits with hints of olive and snow pea; minimal tannin and oak inputs. Screwcap. 14° alc. **RATING** 87 **DRINK** 2009 $ 20

Canberra District Sparkling Shiraz 2003 Strong colour; plenty of flavour, but chops off short on the finish; cellaring may help. 13.5° alc. **RATING** 87 **DRINK** 2010 $ 30

Galli Estate ★★★★☆

1507 Melton Highway, Rockbank, Vic 3335 **REGION** Sunbury
T (03) 9747 1444 **F** (03) 9747 1481 **WWW**.galliestate.com.au **OPEN** 7 days 11–5
WINEMAKER Stephen Phillips **EST.** 1997 **CASES** 12 000
Galli Estate may be a relative newcomer to the scene, but it is a substantial one. The late Lorenzo, and Pam, Galli first planted 34.5 ha of vines at Rockbank, the lion's share to cabernet sauvignon and shiraz, but with 1.5–2.5 ha of semillon, sauvignon blanc, pinot grigio, chardonnay, sangiovese and pinot noir. This was followed by an even larger vineyard at Heathcote, with 106 ha of an even more diverse spread once 55 ha had been allotted for shiraz. A large underground cellar has been constructed; already 50m long, it may be extended in the future. A cellar door sales, restaurant and administration centre were completed in 2002, with former Coldstream Hills winemaker Stephen Phillips in charge of winemaking. Exports to Japan.

ΥΥΥΥΥ **Rockbank Vineyard Chardonnay 2005** Green-straw; spotlessly clean; so perfectly balanced it all seems effortless; citrus, nectarine and white peach with a web of barrel ferment/malolactic/lees contact just visible. Screwcap. 14° alc. **RATING** 94 **DRINK** 2012 $ 22

ΥΥΥΥΥ **Rockbank Vineyard Cabernet Merlot 2003** Medium- to full-bodied; quite rich and luscious cassis/blackcurrant/licorice fruit; nicely balanced oak and tannins; good finish. Cork. 14.3° alc. **RATING** 92 **DRINK** 2015 $ 22

Rockbank Vineyard Sauvignon Blanc Semillon 2005 A faint touch of reduction on the bouquet; a powerful palate with ripe tropical/kiwifruit with a subtext of bright acidity. Screwcap. 13° alc. **RATING** 90 **DRINK** 2008 $ 20

Camelback Vineyard Heathcote Viognier 2005 A clean bouquet; good mouthfeel and weight; a mix of citrus and apricot kernel hides the alcohol. First release. Screwcap. 14.3° alc. **RATING** 90 **DRINK** 2008 $ 24

Rockbank Vineyard Pinot Noir 2004 Spicy/savoury aromas; an elegant, light-bodied wine with a fine, silky palate and good length. Needed a touch more sweet fruit for higher points. Cork. 14° alc. **RATING** 90 **DRINK** 2009 $ 16

Camelback Vineyard Heathcote Shiraz 2003 Good hue; a ripe, sweet melange of black fruits, then persistent, savoury tannins, good oak and even better alcohol. Cork. 14° alc. **RATING** 90 **DRINK** 2013 $ 24

ΥΥΥΥ **Camelback Vineyard Heathcote Tempranillo 2004** Has the power stamp of Heathcote imposed on the variety; certainly has flavour, but tends to varietal anonymity. Cork. 14° alc. **RATING** 89 **DRINK** 2015 $ 24

ΥΥΥΥ **Rockbank Vineyard Shiraz 2003** Alcohol shows through in unusually ripe fruit for this region, affecting both flavour and finish. Cork. 15° alc. **RATING** 86 **DRINK** 2010 $ 22

Gapsted ★★★★

Great Alpine Road, Gapsted, Vic 3737 **REGION** Alpine Valleys
T (03) 5751 1383 **F** (03) 5751 1368 **WWW**.gapstedwines.com.au **OPEN** 7 days 10–5
WINEMAKER Michael Cope-Williams, Shayne Cunningham **EST.** 1997 **CASES** 50 000
Gapsted has emerged from the shadows of the Victorian Alps winery, which started life (and continues) as a large-scale contract winemaking facilities. However, the quality of the wines it made for its own brand (Gapsted) has led to not only the expansion of production under that label, but under a raft of cheaper, subsidiary labels including Tobacco Road, Coldstone, Buckland Gap, Snowy Creek and doubtless others in the pipeline.

ΥΥΥΥΥ **Ballerina Canopy Sauvignon Blanc 2005** Spotlessly clean; very good focus and line; gooseberry, passionfruit, citrus and white peach all intermingle on the long palate. Screwcap. 12.5° alc. **RATING** 93 **DRINK** Now $ 18

Tobacco Road Sauvignon Blanc Semillon 2005 Clean; smooth, flavoursome tropical, lychee aromas and flavours; moderate length, well-made. Screwcap. 13° alc. **RATING** 93 **DRINK** Now $12

Victorian Alps Riesling 2005 Light green-straw; a flowery and fragrant blossom bouquet; very attractive passionfruit and lime; with appealing ripeness. Screwcap. 12.5° alc. **RATING** 91 **DRINK** 2010 $14

ΨΨΨΨ **Ballerina Canopy Chardonnay 2004** Medium-bodied; abundant peach and melon fruit, the oak incidental music to the main theme of generosity. Screwcap. 13.5° alc. **RATING** 89 **DRINK** 2008 $20

Limited Release Sangiovese 2002 Spicy, cherry-accented aromas and flavours; light- to medium-bodied fruit plus fine, powdery, tannins. Screwcap. 13.5° alc. **RATING** 89 **DRINK** 2010 $25

Coldstone Pinot Grigio 2005 Tight grigio varietal character and style; firm pear, citrus and apple with a continuous streak of mineral. Screwcap. 13° alc. **RATING** 88 **DRINK** Now $12

Limited Release Cabernet Franc 2002 Interesting spicy/cedary/tobacco leaf rendition of the variety; slightly dry tannins. Screwcap. 14° alc. **RATING** 88 **DRINK** 2010 $25

Muscato 2005 Intense grapey sweetness balanced by acidity; top stuff in a niche market style. Gewurztraminer/Frontignac. Screwcap. 7.5° alc. **RATING** 87 **DRINK** Now $14

Limited Release Touriga 2002 Thorny savoury mouthfeel; spicy, earthy, brambly flavours, yet, curiously, not much structure. Screwcap. 14° alc. **RATING** 87 **DRINK** 2009 $25

ΨΨΨΫ **Limited Release Petit Manseng 2005** **RATING** 86 **DRINK** 2008 $20

Buckland Gap Traminer Riesling 2004 The tried and true Wyndham TR222 formula, lemon tart with a sweet finish; designed for the local Chinese restaurant. Cork. 12° alc. **RATING** 86 **DRINK** Now $9

Tobacco Road Rose 2005 **RATING** 86 **DRINK** Now $12

Tobacco Road Shiraz 2003 **RATING** 86 **DRINK** 2008 $12

Buckland Gap Cabernet Merlot 2002 **RATING** 86 **DRINK** Now $9

Snowy Creek Reserve Merlot Cabernet Shiraz 2004 Bright red fruits; light- to medium-bodied, attractive, early-drinking style. Screwcap. 13.5° alc. **RATING** 86 **DRINK** 20082008 $6

Tobacco Road Cabernet Sauvignon 2002 **RATING** 86 **DRINK** 2008 $12

Tobacco Road Unwooded Chardonnay 2004 **RATING** 84 **DRINK** Now $12

Buckland Gap Shiraz Cabernet 2003 **RATING** 84 **DRINK** Now $9

Cabernet Merlot 2003 **RATING** 84 **DRINK** Now $14

ΨΨΨ **Buckland Gap Chardonnay 2004** **RATING** 83 $9

Snowy Creek Chenin Blanc Verdelho Chardonnay 2005 **RATING** 83 $6

Snowy Creek Stonefruit 2005 **RATING** 83 $6

Dolcetto Syrah 2005 **RATING** 83 $14

Coldstone Tarrango 2005 **RATING** 83 $12

Garbin Estate ★★★

209 Toodyay Road, Middle Swan, WA 6056 **REGION** Swan Valley
T (08) 9274 1747 **F** (08) 9274 1747 **OPEN** Tues–Sun & public hols 10.30–5.30
WINEMAKER Peter Garbin, Peter Grimwood **EST.** 1956 **CASES** 4500
Peter Garbin, winemaker by weekend and design draftsman by week, decided in 1990 that he would significantly upgrade the bulk fortified winemaking business commenced by his father in 1956. The 11-ha vineyards were replanted, 2 ha of chardonnay was planted at Gingin, the winery was re-equipped, and the first of the new-generation wines was produced in 1994. Exports to Hong Kong; otherwise sold direct from the winery.

ΨΨΨΫ **Verdelho 2005** **RATING** 85 **DRINK** Now $18

Garden Gully NR

1477 Western Highway, Great Western, Vic 3377 **REGION** Grampians
T (03) 5356 2400 **F** (03) 5356 2405 **www**.gardengully.com.au **OPEN** 7 days 11–4
WINEMAKER Contract **EST.** 1987 **CASES** 1000

In mid-2005 a 5-family team purchased Garden Gully. The team is Tom and Sarah Guthrie (owners of Grampians Estate), Robyn and Bruce Dalkin (owners of Westgate Vineyard), Paul Dakis (vineyard manager at Seppelt), Bill and Helen Francis (owners of a small olive grove near Great Western) and Mike and Kate Connellan (local doctor and lawyer). They have reopened the cellar door, selling Garden Gully, Grampians Estate and Westgate Wines, various olive oils and other local produce. The old 5.5-ha vineyard is being rejuvenated.

Garlands   NR

Marmion Street off Mount Barker Hill Road, Mount Barker, WA 6324 **REGION** Mount Barker
T (08) 9851 2737 **F** (08) 9851 1062 **WWW**.garlandswines.com.au **OPEN** 7 days 10.30–4.30; winter
Thurs–Sun 10.30–4.30 or by appt
WINEMAKER Michael Garland **EST.** 1996 **CASES** 5000
Garlands is a partnership between Michael and Julie Garland and their vigneron neighbours, Craig and Caroline Drummond and Patrick and Christine Gresswell. Michael Garland came to grapegrowing and winemaking with a varied background (in biological research, computer sales and retail clothing) and now has a Charles Sturt University degree in oenology. A small but highly functional winery was erected prior to the 2000 vintage; the earlier wines were made elsewhere. The winery has a capacity of 150 tonnes, and will continue contract-making for other small producers in the region as well as making the wine from the 9.25 ha of estate vineyards (planted to shiraz, riesling, cabernet sauvignon, cabernet franc, chardonnay, sauvignon blanc and semillon). Cabernet Franc is the winery specialty, but the quality of all the wines has risen. Exports to the UK, Switzerland, Trinidad, Hong Kong and Singapore.

Gartelmann Hunter Estate   ★★★★

Lovedale Road, Lovedale, NSW 2321 **REGION** Lower Hunter Valley
T (02) 4930 7113 **F** (02) 4930 7114 **WWW**.gartelmann.com.au **OPEN** 7 days 10–5
WINEMAKER Jorg Gartelmann, Monarch Winemaking Services (Jim Chatto) **EST.** 1970 **CASES** 5000
In 1996 Jan and Jorg Gartelmann purchased what was previously the George Hunter Estate — 16 ha of mature vineyards; most established by Sydney restaurateur Oliver Shaul in 1970, the merlot in 1997. They produced a limited amount of wine under the Gartelmann label in 1997, and moved to full production in 1998. Diedrich Shiraz is the flagship, and is consistently good. Exports to UK, Germany and Canada.

▼▼▼▼▽ **Benjamin Semillon 2005** Powerful, with the faintest touch of reduction; lots of grab and power; considerable length. Screwcap. **RATING** 91 **DRINK** 2015 $ 18

▼▼▼▽ **Chardonnay 2004** Solid peachy fruit, but the oak does not sit harmoniously with it; time may help. Screwcap. 13° alc. **RATING** 86 **DRINK** 2008 $ 26

Gawler River Grove   NR

PO Box 280, Virginia, SA 5120 **REGION** Adelaide Plains
T 0438 506 097 **F** (08) 8380 9787 **OPEN** Not
WINEMAKER Steve Black (Contract) **EST.** 2001 **CASES** 200
The vineyards at Gawler River Grove go back to the late 1940s, with 7.7 ha of grenache bush vines. Since then, 5.8 ha of chardonnay and 1.5 ha of shiraz have been added. It was not until 2003 that a small amount of Chardonnay was vinified for the Gawler River Grove label; Grenache followed in 2004.

Gecko Valley   NR

Bailiff Road, via 700 Glenlyon Road, Gladstone, Qld 4680 **REGION** Queensland Coastal
T (07) 4979 0400 **F** (07) 4979 0500 **OPEN** 7 days 10–5
WINEMAKER Bruce Humphery-Smith (Contract) **EST.** 1997 **CASES** 1000
Gecko Valley extends the viticultural map of Qld yet further: it is little more than 50 km off the Tropic of Capricorn in an area better known for beef farming and mineral activities. The 3-ha vineyard (chardonnay, verdelho and shiraz) was established by Tony (an engineer) and Coleen McCray (an accountant). The coastal belt between Gladstone and Rockhampton has a unique climate, with lower rainfall than the more northern and the more southern coastal strips. The climate is hot, but the vineyard is only 1 km from the tempering influence of the sea. It has been planted on free-draining, shallow soil, so excessive vigour is not a problem.

Gehrig Estate

Cnr Murray Valley Highway/Howlong Road, Barnawartha, Vic 3688 **REGION** Rutherglen
T (02) 6026 7296 **F** (02) 6026 7424 **OPEN** Mon–Sat 9–5, Sun 10–5
WINEMAKER Ross Gehrig **EST.** 1858 **CASES** 5000
A historic winery and adjacent house are superb legacies of the 19th century. Progressive modernisation of the winemaking facilities and operations has seen the quality of the white wines improve significantly; the red wines now receive a percentage of new oak. Another recent innovation has been the introduction of the Gourmet Courtyard, which serves lunch on weekends, public holidays and Victorian school holidays.

▼▼▼▼▼ **John Gehrig Durif 2004** Rich black fruits and dark chocolate flavour, with balanced tannins, and improbable pretensions to elegance despite high alcohol. Screwcap. 15.5° alc. **RATING** 94 **DRINK** 2015 **$** 35

Gembrook Hill
★★★★☆

Launching Place Road, Gembrook, Vic 3783 **REGION** Yarra Valley
T (03) 5968 1622 **F** (03) 5968 1699 **WWW**.gembrookhill.com.au **OPEN** By appt
WINEMAKER Timo Mayer **EST.** 1983 **CASES** 2000
The 6-ha Gembrook Hill Vineyard is situated on rich, red volcanic soils 2 km north of Gembrook in the coolest part of the Yarra Valley. The vines are not irrigated, with consequent natural vigour control, and low yields. Harvest usually spans mid-April, 3 weeks later than the traditional northern parts of the valley, and the style is consistently elegant. Exports to the UK and Denmark.

▼▼▼▼▼ **Yarra Valley Chardonnay 2004** Light green-straw; fragrant, flowery, orange blossom aromas; delicious nectarine/melon fruit; exceptional mouthfeel and balance to a wine of breed and finesse. Cork. 13° alc. **RATING** 95 **DRINK** 2011 **$** 30

▼▼▼▼▽ **Mayer Vineyard Yarra Valley Pinot Noir 2004** Light, bright purple-red; light- to medium-bodied cherry, raspberry and plum; quite firm mouthfeel. Cork. 13.2° alc. **RATING** 90 **DRINK** 2011 **$** 23
Yarra Valley Pinot Noir 2004 Light red-purple; light- to medium-bodied, but softer and more expressive fruit than the Mayer; sweet plum and red cherry fruit. Cork. 13° alc. **RATING** 90 **DRINK** 2011 **$** 35

Gemtree Vineyards

PO Box 164, McLaren Vale, SA 5171 **REGION** McLaren Vale
T (08) 8323 8199 **F** (08) 8323 7889 **WWW**.gemtreevineyards.com.au **OPEN** Not
WINEMAKER Mike Brown **EST.** 1998 **CASES** 10 000
The Buttery family, headed by Paul and Jill, and with the active involvement of Melissa as viticulturist, have been grapegrowers in McLaren Vale since 1980, when they purchased their first vineyard. Today the family owns a little over 130 ha of vines. The oldest block, of 25 ha on Tatachilla Road at McLaren Vale, was planted in 1970. Exports to the US, Canada, the UK, The Netherlands, Switzerland and Singapore.

▼▼▼▼▽ **Uncut Shiraz 2004** Delicious blackberry and dark chocolate fruit to both bouquet and palate; soft, ripe tannins; good oak. Screwcap. **RATING** 93 **DRINK** 2014 **$** 20
Obsidian Shiraz 2003 Deep, purple colour; very complex aromas and flavours; slurpy blackberry, licorice, dark chocolate, spice and herb flavours, mouthfilling and long; has eaten the French oak in which it spent 30 months. Cork. **RATING** 93 **DRINK** 2018 **$** 38
Bloodstone McLaren Vale Tempranillo 2004 Considerable depth to colour; strikingly rich and concentrated plum, black fruits and dark chocolate; soft, ripe tannins, and excellent acidity. Screwcap. **RATING** 92 **DRINK** 2015 **$** 25
Cinnabar Cadenzia 2004 Clean, fresh, exuberant red fruits; oozes sweet fruit on the palate; totally seductive. Grenache/Tempranillo/Shiraz. Screwcap. **RATING** 90 **DRINK** 2010 **$** 25

ŶŶŶŶ **Citrine McLaren Vale Chardonnay 2005** Elegant wine with the focus on light melon, peach and citrus fruit; good length, the oak a background echo. Screwcap. **RATING** 89 **DRINK** Now $ 16

Tatty Road 2004 Very good colour; potent, powerful in-your-face style; sombre, dark, black fruits. Cabernet Sauvignon/Petit Verdot/Cabernet Franc/Merlot. Screwcap. 14° alc. **RATING** 89 **DRINK** 2014 $ 18

Gentle Annie

455 Nalinga Road, Dookie, Vic 3646 **REGION** Central Victoria Zone
T (03) 5828 6333 **F** (03) 9602 1349 **WWW**.gentle-annie.com **OPEN** By appt
WINEMAKER David Hodgson, Tony Lacy **EST.** 1997 **CASES** 8000
Gentle Annie was established by Melbourne businessman Tony Cotter; wife Anne and five daughters assist with sales and marketing. The name Gentle Annie refers to an early settler renowned for her beauty and gentle temperament. The vineyard is a substantial one, with 4 ha of verdelho, 31 ha of shiraz and 23 ha of cabernet sauvignon planted on old volcanic ferrosol soils, similar to the red Cambrian loam at Heathcote. The winemaking team is headed by David Hodgson, who also heads up the Oenology faculty at Dookie College. Gentle Annie has hitherto sold the major part of its grape production. The increasing production of Gentle Annie wines has a substantial export component, likely to grow in the future.

ŶŶŶŶŶ **Shiraz 2003** Good colour; an amazing array of flavours coat the mouth, ranging through blackberry, plum, prune, licorice, spice and chocolate. Cork. **RATING** 90 **DRINK** 2013 $ 20

Shiraz Cabernet 2003 Medium- to full-bodied; a rich, ripe blackberry/blackcurrant mix; ripe tannins run through the back-palate; good oak. Cork. **RATING** 90 **DRINK** 2013 $ 20

ŶŶŶŶ **Cabernet Sauvignon 2003** Solid blackcurrant/blackberry/earthy fruit on the medium- to full-bodied palate, potent tannins as yet a little uncomfortable. Cork. **RATING** 89 **DRINK** 2012 $ 20

ŶŶŶŶ **Verdelho 2004** Bright green-yellow; a quite complex bouquet; full-bodied, ripe, tropical fruit salad flavours. Screwcap. 14.5° alc. **RATING** 86 **DRINK** Now $ 14

Geoff Hardy/Pertaringa ★★★★☆

Cnr Hunt Road/Rifle Range Road, McLaren Vale, SA 5171 **REGION** Adelaide Hills
T (08) 8323 8125 **F** (08) 8323 7766 **WWW**.k1.com.au **OPEN** Mon–Fri 10–5, w'ends & public hols 11–5
WINEMAKER Geoff Hardy, Ben Riggs **EST.** 1980 **CASES** 18 000
The Pertaringa wines are made from part of the grapes grown by leading viticulturists Geoff Hardy and Ian Leask. The Pertaringa vineyard of 31 ha was acquired in 1980 and rejuvenated. The ultra-cool Kuitpo vineyard in the Adelaide Hills was begun in 1987 and now supplies leading makers such as Southcorp and Petaluma. Geoff Hardy wines come from 20 ha of vines, with a large percentage of the grape production being sold to other makers. The new premium K1 range is impressive in both quality and value. Exports to Germany, Denmark, Canada and Hong Kong.

ŶŶŶŶŶ **Pertaringa Over The Top McLaren Vale Shiraz 2004** Dense purple-red; immediately proclaims its regional origin with lashings of blackberry fruit coated with chocolate; richly textured, and carries the alcohol well. 15° alc. **RATING** 94 **DRINK** 2014 $ 39

ŶŶŶŶŶ **Pertaringa Undercover McLaren Vale Shiraz 2004** Spotlessly clean, but sombre black fruit and dark chocolate aromas; a round, supple and generous palate; good tannin and acid balance. Screwcap. **RATING** 93 **DRINK** 2014 $ 20

Geoff Hardy K1 Adelaide Hills Shiraz 2004 Good colour; pristine, cool-grown varietal fruit expression; exemplary texture and structure; easily carries the alcohol. Procork. 14.5° alc. **RATING** 93 **DRINK** 2014 $ 28

Geoff Hardy K1 Adelaide Hills Merlot 2003 A mix of olive and dark berries provide clear varietal fruit characters; very good weight, texture and structure, mimicking the Shiraz. Procork. 14° alc. **RATING** 93 **DRINK** 2012 $ 28

Pertaringa Rifle & Hunt Cabernet Sauvignon 2004 Strong purple-red; powerful, focused, bright black fruits; fine persistent tannins, good acidity. Procork. **RATING** 93 **DRINK** 2014 $ 30

Geoff Hardy Tzimmukin Adelaide Hills Cabernet Shiraz 2004 Rich, hyper-concentrated spice, chocolate, licorice and black fruits combination; lingering tannins. Egyptian rather than Italian inspiration. Cork. 15° alc. **RATING** 93 **DRINK** 2015 $75

Pertaringa Understudy Cabernet Sauvignon 2004 Slightly less bright colour than the Rifle & Hunt; an interesting wine; sharper again, brisk acidity; vibrant red and black fruits. Procork. **RATING** 91 **DRINK** 2015 $18

Geoff Hardy K1 Adelaide Hills Sauvignon Blanc 2005 Powerful wine, intense but not heavy; a mix of mineral, gooseberry and redcurrant; good balance. Screwcap. 13° alc. **RATING** 90 **DRINK** Now $18

Geoff Hardy K1 Adelaide Hills Chardonnay 2004 A firm, restrained style; melon, stone fruit and a hint of mineral; good structure and balance. Screwcap. 14° alc. **RATING** 90 **DRINK** 2009 $28

Geoff Hardy K1 Adelaide Hills Rose 2005 Vivid red-purple; much more fruit substance and flavour than most, but without phenolics or sweetness; broad food match. Screwcap. 13° alc. **RATING** 90 **DRINK** Now $18

Pertaringa Over The Top McLaren Vale Shiraz 2003 An unusual mix of mocha, milk and dark chocolate is the driving force. While obviously regional, more black fruits needed. Cork. 15° alc. **RATING** 90 **DRINK** 2011 $35

ŸŸŸŸ **Geoff Hardy K1 Adelaide Hills Cabernet Sauvignon 2004** Firm blackcurrant juicy fruit drives the wine which lacks the great texture of the Shiraz and Merlot. Procork. 13.5° alc. **RATING** 89 **DRINK** 2013 $28

Pertaringa The Full Fronti NV Rich, complex, multi-spice, toffee and Christmas cake; good balance; an average age of 20 years. **RATING** 89 **DRINK** Now $24

Pertaringa Scarecrow Sauvignon Blanc 2005 Clean, fresh and precise but delicate aromas and flavours; touches of citrus and gooseberry. Screwcap. 13.5° alc. **RATING** 88 **DRINK** Now $15

Geoff Hardy K1 Adelaide Hills Pinot Noir 2004 Very savoury, foresty, earthy style; despite the alcohol, doesn't show dead fruit, but still is more dry red than pinot. Screwcap. 14.5° alc. **RATING** 88 **DRINK** 2010 $28

Pertaringa Two Gentlemen's McLaren Vale Grenache 2004 Light- to medium-bodied; juicy berry red fruits; undemanding, quaffing style. Screwcap. 14.5° alc. **RATING** 88 **DRINK** Now $20

Geoff Merrill Wines ★★★★★

291 Pimpala Road, Woodcroft, SA 5162 **REGION** McLaren Vale
T (08) 8381 6877 **F** (08) 8322 2244 **WWW**.geoffmerrillwines.com **OPEN** Mon–Fri 10–5, w'ends 12–5
WINEMAKER Geoff Merrill, Scott Heidrich **EST.** 1980 **CASES** 80 000
If Geoff Merrill ever loses his impish sense of humour or his zest for life, high and not-so-high, we shall all be the poorer. The product range consists of 3 tiers: premium (varietal); reserve, being the older (and best) wines, reflecting the desire for elegance and subtlety of this otherwise exuberant winemaker; and at the top, Henley Shiraz. Mount Hurtle wines are sold exclusively through Vintage Cellars/Liquorland. National retail distribution; exports to all major markets.

ŸŸŸŸŸ **Reserve Cabernet Sauvignon 2002** Cedary earthy to blackcurrant fruit; has great length and persistence; fine tannins. Trophy winner Sydney Wine Show '06. **RATING** 95 **DRINK** 2015

Reserve McLaren Vale Shiraz 1999 Savoury, spicy black fruit aromas and flavours with a touch of regional dark chocolate; light- to medium-bodied, with fine tannins and a lingering finish. Cork. 14.5° alc. **RATING** 94 **DRINK** 2009 $40

ŸŸŸŸŶ **McLaren Vale Shiraz 2002** Good colour; classic McLaren Vale black fruits and dark chocolate mix; attractive spicy oak; savoury, fine tannins. Cork. **RATING** 93 **DRINK** 2012 $22.50

McLaren Vale Grenache Rose 2005 Elegant, supple, perfectly balanced palate; fractionally more fruit than the Sangiovese; splashes of spice on the dry finish. Screwcap. **RATING** 92 **DRINK** Now $18.50

Shiraz Grenache Mourvedre 2002 Very nice wine; excellent fusion of fruit, oak and tannins; juicy, pleasantly jammy, grenache coralled by spicy shiraz and firm mourvedre. Screwcap. **RATING** 92 **DRINK** 2010 $18.50

Reserve Cabernet Sauvignon 2000 Elegant, medium-bodied blackcurrant fruit, with touches of chocolate, mocha and vanilla; the tannins are now a near-invisible support. Cork. 13.5° alc. **RATING** 92 **DRINK** 2010 $ 35

Liquid Asset McLaren Vale Sangiovese Rose 2005 Fresh, lively and spicy red fruits; a long, crisp and near-dry finish. Screwcap. **RATING** 91 **DRINK** Now $ 18.50

Reserve McLaren Vale Shiraz 2000 A medium-bodied, harmonious and seamless blend of black fruits, dark chocolate, mocha/vanilla and tannins; basically to roll now, like a Rioja. Brilliant outcome for such a vintage. Cork. 14° alc. **RATING** 91 **DRINK** 2010 $ 45

Reserve McLaren Vale Chardonnay 2002 A power-packed wine revelling in the cool vintage; layered melon, honey and citrus; emphatic finish. Cork. 14° alc. **RATING** 90 **DRINK** 2009 $ 25

Pimpala Vineyard Cabernet Merlot 2001 Medium-bodied; spicy/savoury/cedary nuances to the gentle black fruits and regional chocolate; mocha, oak and fine tannins. Cork. 13.5° alc. **RATING** 90 **DRINK** 2010 $ 30

McLaren Vale Coonawarra Cabernet Sauvignon 2002 Elegant, light- to medium-bodied wine with cedar, blackcurrant, spice and earth; nicely ripened, fine tannins. Cork. **RATING** 90 **DRINK** 2009 $ 22.50

♥♥♥♥ **Henley Shiraz 1999** Disappointing colour; soft cedar and vanilla with supple but equally soft fruit. A pleasant wine which needs more character and presence to justify the price. Cork. 14° alc. **RATING** 89 **DRINK** 2009 $ 150

McLaren Vale Merlot 2002 Elegant, light-bodied style; spice, tobacco, olive, earth and demure red fruits; fine tannins. Cork. **RATING** 89 **DRINK** Now $ 22.50

Mount Hurtle Grenache Rose 2005 Fragrant, flowery rose petal and strawberry aromas and flavours; lots of flavour, with a hint of sweetness. Ridiculously cheap. Screwcap. 14.5° alc. **RATING** 88 **DRINK** Now $ 8

McLaren Vale Chardonnay 2004 Generously proportioned and flavoured; could not be accused of delicacy or finesse. Screwcap. 13.5° alc. **RATING** 87 **DRINK** 2008 $ 18

Liquid Asset McLaren Vale/Coonawarra Chardonnay 2003 Powerful, ripe, high-toned tropical fruit; slightly hot finish; needs food. Screwcap. **RATING** 87 **DRINK** Now $ 11.95

Geoff Weaver ★★★★☆

2 Gilpin Lane, Mitcham, SA 5062 (postal) **REGION** Adelaide Hills
T (08) 8272 2105 **F** (08) 8271 0177 **WWW**.geoffweaver.com.au **OPEN** Not
WINEMAKER Geoff Weaver **EST.** 1982 **CASES** 5000
This is the full-time business of former Hardys chief winemaker Geoff Weaver. He draws upon a little over 11 ha of vineyard established between 1982 and 1988, and invariably produces immaculate Riesling and Sauvignon Blanc, and one of the longest-lived Chardonnays to be found in Australia, with intense grapefruit and melon flavour. The beauty of the labels ranks supreme with Pipers Brook. Exports to the UK and the US.

♥♥♥♥♥ **Lenswood Riesling 2005** Fragrant, sweet lemon blossom aromas; a very delicate palate, again with persistent blossom characters; drink now or much later. Screwcap. 13.5° alc. **RATING** 93 **DRINK** 2015 $ 23

Ghost Rock Vineyard ★★★

PO Box 311, Devonport, Tas 7310 **REGION** Northern Tasmania
T (03) 6423 1246 **OPEN** Due to open November 2006
WINEMAKER Tamar Ridge **EST.** 2001 **CASES** 450
Cate and Colin Arnold purchased the former Patrick Creek Vineyard (planted in 1989) in August 2001. They run a printing and design business in Devonport, and were looking for a suitable site to establish a vineyard, when the opportunity to buy Patrick Creek came up. The 1-ha vineyard is half chardonnay and a quarter each of pinot noir and sauvignon blanc, planted on a northeasterly aspect on a sheltered slope. In 2004 the vineyard was increased with an additional 3 ha of vines.

♥♥♥♥ **Sauvignon Blanc 2005** Clean and pleasant; not particularly intense, but what is there is nice enough. Screwcap. 13.5° alc. **RATING** 87 **DRINK** Now $ 24

♥♥♥♥ **Pinot Noir 2004** **RATING** 86 **DRINK** 2008 $ 27

Giaconda

NR

McClay Road, Beechworth, Vic 3747 **REGION** Beechworth
T(03) 5727 0246 **F**(03) 5727 0246 **WWW**.giaconda.com.au **OPEN** By appt
WINEMAKER Rick Kinzbrunner **EST.** 1985 **CASES** 2000
These wines have a super-cult status and, given the tiny production, are extremely difficult to find;
they are sold chiefly through restaurants and by mail order. All have a cosmopolitan edge befitting
Rick Kinzbrunner's international winemaking experience. The Chardonnay and Pinot Noir are made
in contrasting styles: the Chardonnay tight and reserved, the Pinot Noir more variable, but usually
opulent and ripe. No tasting samples, no rating. Exports to the UK and the US.

Giant Steps

★★★★★

10–12 Briarty Road, Gruyere, Vic 3770 **REGION** Yarra Valley
T(03) 5962 6111 **F**(03) 5962 6199 **WWW**.giant-steps.com.au **OPEN** By appt
WINEMAKER Phil Sexton, Allison Sexton **EST.** 1998 **CASES** 15 000
Phil Sexton made his first fortune as a pioneer micro-brewer, and invested a substantial part of that
fortune in establishing Devil's Lair. Late in 1996 he sold Devil's Lair to Southcorp, which had
purchased Coldstream Hills earlier that year. Two years later he and Allison Sexton purchased a
hillside property less than 1 km from Coldstream Hills, and sharing the same geological structure
and aspect. The name Giant Steps comes in part from their love of jazz and John Coltrane's album of
that name, and in part from the rise and fall of the property across a series of ridges ranging from
120m to 360m. The 34-ha vineyard is predominantly planted to pinot noir and chardonnay, but with
significant quantities of cabernet sauvignon and merlot, plus small plantings of cabernet franc and
petit verdot. Exports to the US.

ŸŸŸŸŸ **Sexton Bernard Clones Yarra Valley Chardonnay 2004** A very complex bouquet, with
the appropriate touch of Burgundian funk; tightly focused nectarine and some citrus fruit;
extreme length, demands time. Clones 95 and 96. Screwcap. 13.9° alc. **RATING** 95
DRINK 2014 $ 36
Giant Steps Yarra Valley Chardonnay 2004 A complex and powerful mix of melon,
grapefruit and barrel ferment French oak inputs; long finish; controlled alcohol a plus.
Screwcap. 12.9° alc. **RATING** 94 **DRINK** 2010 $ 25
Sexton Dijon Clones Yarra Valley Pinot Noir 2004 Scented, aromatic, spicy red fruits
bouquet; the palate is focused and long, less fearsome than the '03, and particularly
impressive given the big berries and bunches of the vintage. Clones 114 and 115. Screwcap.
13.5° alc. **RATING** 94 **DRINK** 2010 $ 40
Sexton Jones Block McLaren Vale Shiraz 2004 Very good colour; McLaren Vale with a
dose of elegance; finely balanced plum, black cherry and blackberry fruit; fine tannins,
good oak. If you can't beat them, join them. Screwcap. 14.5° alc. **RATING** 94 **DRINK** 2014
$ 45
Sexton Harry's Monster 2004 Rich and (by Yarra Valley standards) opulent; the skilful
blend of cabernet sauvignon, merlot, petit verdot and cabernet franc provides an array of
black fruits without the slightest hint of green; good tannins and oak, not at all monstrous.
Screwcap. 13.9° alc. **RATING** 94 **DRINK** 2015 $ 40

ŸŸŸŸŸ **Sexton Tarraford Yarra Valley Chardonnay 2004** Spotlessly clean, elegant and fresh;
flavours of melon, stone fruit and grapefruit are backed by harmonious oak. Screwcap.
13.4° alc. **RATING** 93 **DRINK** 2011 $ 23
Innocent Bystander Yarra Valley Shiraz Viognier 2004 Light- to medium-bodied;
vibrantly fresh black cherry and blackberry fruit; a nice touch of lift ex the Viognier.
Screwcap. 14.4° alc. **RATING** 93 **DRINK** 2010 $ 19.95
Giant Steps Yarra Valley Merlot 2004 Good purple-red; classic merlot varietal character,
with a mix of small red fruits; good balance and structure. Sadly, the last Merlot to be
made by Giant Steps. (Fickle market demands.) Screwcap. 13.9° alc. **RATING** 92
DRINK 2014 $ 23
Giant Steps First Steps Chardonnay 2004 Unexpectedly complex, showing obvious oak
on the bouquet; melon, nectarine and fig fruit drive the very long palate. Screwcap.
RATING 90 **DRINK** 2009 $ 15.95

Giant Steps Yarra Valley Merlot 2003 Strongly varietal redcurrant and black olive aromas follow through on a powerfully built palate. Screwcap. 14° alc. **RATING** 90 **DRINK** 2013 $ 25

 Innocent Bystander Yarra Valley Sangiovese Merlot 2004 Interesting wine; medium-bodied, fine structure; gently savoury fruit and tannins. Screwcap. 14.2° alc. **RATING** 89 **DRINK** 2009 $ 19.95

Innocent Bystander Yarra Valley Pinot Gris 2005 Perfumed spice and pear aromas; solid, ripe, pear and musk fruit flavour. Screwcap. 13.9° alc. **RATING** 88 **DRINK** Now $ 19.95

Giant Steps Yarra Valley Pinot Noir 2004 Bright red-purple; clean aromas of plum and black cherry; the tannins are somewhat dry and aggressive, demanding time and/or food. Screwcap. 13.5° alc. **RATING** 88 **DRINK** 2010 $ 25

Innocent Bystander Yarra Valley Rose 2005 Clean and fresh; nicely balanced red fruits; long, crisp, dry finish. Screwcap. 13.6° alc. **RATING** 87 **DRINK** Now $ 16.95

Gibraltar Rock ★★★★★

Woodlands Road, Porongurup, WA 6324 **REGION** Porongurup
T (08) 9481 2856 **F** (08) 9481 2857 **WWW**.gibraltarrockwines.com.au **OPEN** Wed–Sun 10–5
WINEMAKER Forest Hill Vineyard (Shane McKerrow) **EST.** 1979 **CASES** 600
A once-tiny Riesling specialist in the wilds of the Porongurups, forced to change its name from Narang because Lindemans felt it could be confused with its (now defunct) Nyrang Shiraz brand; truly a strange world. This beautifully sited vineyard and its long-lived Riesling were acquired by Perth orthopaedic surgeon Dr Peter Honey in 2001. The vineyard now has 23 ha of riesling, chardonnay, merlot, pinot noir, sauvignon blanc and shiraz. Most of the grapes are sold to Houghton under a long-term contract, but Dr Honey intends to slowly increase production from the older vines under the Gibraltar Rock label.

TTTTT **Porongurup Chardonnay 2005** All the best features of the region's chardonnay; a lilting song of blossom, passionfruit, nectarine and grapefruit, the oak merely a refrain. Cork. 13.8° alc. **RATING** 95 **DRINK** 2013 $ 26

Semillon Sauvignon Blanc 2004 Delicious wine, still fresh and lively; finely balanced passionfruit and green apple fruit; a long, harmonious finish. Screwcap. **RATING** 94 **DRINK** 2008 $ 20

TTTTT **Porongurup Riesling 2005** Pale straw-green; intriguing spicy edges to the aromas; ultra-fine, tight, minerally palate, with little fruit yet escaping, but will do so. Screwcap. 12° alc. **RATING** 91 **DRINK** 2013 $ 20

TTTT **Porongurup Pinot Noir 2005** Strong red-purple; big, solid, dark plum, spice and briar; tending tadpole in structure. Polar opposite to the '04. Screwcap. 14.1° alc. **RATING** 89 **DRINK** 2010 $ 28

Porongurup Shiraz 2004 Fragrant, light-bodied red fruits and spice; balanced tannins and extract, though needs more fruit depth. Screwcap. **RATING** 87 **DRINK** 2008 $ 25

Gibson Barossavale ★★★★★

Willows Road, Light Pass, SA 5355 **REGION** Barossa Valley
T (08) 8562 3193 **F** (08) 8562 4490 **WWW**.barossavale.com **OPEN** 7 days 11–5
WINEMAKER Rob Gibson **EST.** 1996 **CASES** 3500
Rob Gibson spent much of his working life as a senior viticulturist for Penfolds. While at Penfolds he was involved in research tracing the characters that particular parcels of grapes give to a wine, which left him with a passion for identifying and protecting what is left of the original vineyard plantings in wine regions around Australia. This led to the acquisition of an additional 8 ha of old shiraz, mourvedre and grenache, plus some of the oldest chardonnay vines in the Barossa (recent arrivals in comparison with shiraz, but planted in 1982). Exports to the UK and Hong Kong.

 2003 Barossa Valley Shiraz Exceptional focus and structure; seamlessly woven tannins and quality oak through abundant black fruits, medium-bodied, just where it should be. Cork. **RATING** 94 **DRINK** 2018 $ 36

ŶŶŶŶ♀ **2003 Old Vine McLaren Vale Grenache** Bright, clear red-purple; medium-bodied; an interesting structure, with fine tannins running throughout giving the wine a savoury caste utterly unlike Barossa Valley grenache; long finish. Cork. **RATING** 92 **DRINK** 2013 $ 48
2003 Barossa Valley Merlot Vibrant colour; a powerful, though not aggressive, wine; doubtful whether Barossa Valley is the right place, but the wine has plenty of black fruits and controlled tannins. Cork. **RATING** 90 **DRINK** 2012 $ 21

ŶŶŶŶ **2005 Loose End Adelaide Hills SBS** A clean bouquet; soft, gentle tropical fruit on the mid-palate before a twitch of lemony acidity enlivens the finish. Sauvignon Blanc/Semillon. Screwcap. **RATING** 89 **DRINK** 2007 $ 14
2004 Loose End Barossa Valley Shiraz Viognier Pleasant, light- to medium-bodied wine; viognier hasn't woven the magic it so often does; easy-going red fruits. Screwcap. **RATING** 88 **DRINK** 2009 $ 18

Gidgee Estate Wines   NR

441 Weeroona Drive, Wamboin, NSW 2620 **REGION** Canberra District
T (02) 6236 9506 **F** (02) 6236 9070 **OPEN** W'ends 12–4
WINEMAKER Kay Brett, Andrew McEwin (Contract) **EST.** 1996 **CASES** 500
Brett and Cheryl Lane purchased the 1-ha vineyard in 1996; it had been planted to riesling, chardonnay, cabernet sauvignon, cabernet franc and merlot over a 10-year period prior to its acquisition, but had been allowed to run down and needed to be rehabilitated.

Gilberts   ★★★★

RMB 438 Albany Highway, Kendenup via Mount Barker, WA 6323 **REGION** Mount Barker
T (08) 9851 4028 **F** (08) 9851 4021 **OPEN** 7 days 10–5
WINEMAKER Plantagenet **EST.** 1980 **CASES** 3500
A part-time occupation for sheep and beef farmers Jim and Beverly Gilbert, but a very successful one. The now mature vineyard, coupled with contract winemaking at Plantagenet, has produced small quantities of high-quality Riesling and Chardonnay. The wines sell out quickly each year. A restaurant and function area opened in 2003, and further plantings are planned. Exports to the US, the UK, Singapore and The Netherlands.

ŶŶŶŶ♀ **Reserve Mount Barker Shiraz 2003** Very good hue; an elegant, medium-bodied wine; spiced plum and blackberry fruit, fine oak and tannins; considerable finesse. Cork. 13° alc. **RATING** 93 **DRINK** 2013 $ 25

ŶŶŶŶ **Three Devils Shiraz 2004** Light- to medium-bodied; clear plum and blackberry fruit; fine, persistent tannins. Screwcap. 15° alc. **RATING** 89 **DRINK** 2010 $ 17
Mount Barker Shiraz Cabernet 2003 In the elegant, medium-bodied winery style, with gentle black fruits and fine tannins. Cork. 14° alc. **RATING** 89 **DRINK** 2012 $ 18

ŶŶŶ♀ **Three Devils Rose 2005** Full pink-purple; soft cherry fruit; I'm not convinced the alcohol is appropriate to this style. Screwcap. 15° alc. **RATING** 86 **DRINK** Now $ 16

Gilead Estate   NR

1868 Wanneroo Road, Neerabup, WA 6031 (postal) **REGION** Swan District
T (08) 9407 5076 **F** (08) 9407 5187 **OPEN** Not
WINEMAKER Gerry Gauntlett **EST.** 1990 **CASES** 400
A retirement — but nonetheless serious — venture for Judy and Gerry Gauntlett, who planted 1.2 ha on the Tuart sands of Wanneroo in 1990. The name comes from the Balm of Gilead produced from trees on the hills northeast of Galilee in Biblical times, and was said to have had healing and purifying qualities. The tiny production is mainly sold by mail order, with occasional tasting days.

Gilgai Winery

NR

Tingha Road, Gilgai, NSW 2360 **REGION** Northern Slopes Zone
T (02) 6723 1204 **OPEN** 7 days 10–5
WINEMAKER Keith Whish **EST.** 1968 **CASES** 550
Inverell medical practitioner Dr Keith Whish has been quietly producing wines from his 6-ha vineyard for almost 40 years. All the production is sold through the cellar door.

Gilligan

★★★★

PO Box 235, Willunga, SA 5172 **REGION** McLaren Vale
T (08) 8323 8379 **F** (08) 8323 8379 **OPEN** Not
WINEMAKER Mark Day, Leigh Gilligan **EST.** 2001 **CASES** 850
Leigh Gilligan is a 20-year marketing veteran, mostly with McLaren Vale wineries (including Wirra Wirra). The Gilligan family have 6 ha of shiraz and 2 ha of grenache on their Old Rifle Range Vineyard, selling the lion's share to Southcorp. In 2001 they persuaded next-door neighbour Drew Noon to make a barrel of Shiraz, which they drank and gave away. Realising they needed more than one barrel, and with no space at Noon's, they moved to Maxwell Wines for 2002 and 2003, with help from Maxwell Wines winemaker Mark Day. They have now migrated to Mark's new Koltz Winery at Blewitt Springs. The longer-term plan is to take all the fruit when the Southcorp contract terminates; they have also planted more grenache, and small parcels of mourvedre, marsanne and roussanne on another property they have acquired in the heart of McLaren Vale. Exports to the US, Canada, Thailand, Germany and Denmark.

TTTT **McLaren Vale Shiraz Grenache Mourvedre 2004** Light- to medium-bodied; smooth, sweet and supple fruit, the grenache component in particular making its presence felt. Easy going style. Stained Diam. 14.5° alc. **RATING** 89 **DRINK** 2009 $ 21

Gin Gin Wines

NR

Gin Gin Historical Village, Mulgrave Street, Gin Gin, Qld 4671 **REGION** Queensland Coastal
T (07) 4157 3099 **F** (07) 4157 3088 **OPEN** 7 days 10–5
WINEMAKER Lyla McLaren **EST.** 2002 **CASES** NA
The 2.5-ha vineyard of Lyla and John McLaren may not be large, but it is planted to a Joseph's Coat of varieties: sauvignon blanc, gewurztraminer, semillon, chardonnay, colombard, verdelho, pinot noir, merlot, grenache, cabernet sauvignon, malbec, shiraz, petit verdot, sangiovese and tempranillo. Similarly, the cellar door offers wine tourists everything they could wish for.

Gisborne Peak

★★★★

69 Short Road, Gisborne South, Vic 3437 **REGION** Macedon Ranges
T (03) 5428 2228 **F** (03) 5428 4816 **WWW**.gisbornepeakwines.com.au **OPEN** 7 days 11–5
WINEMAKER Hanging Rock (John Ellis) **EST.** 1978 **CASES** 1500
Bob Nixon began the development of Gisborne Peak way back in 1978, planting his dream vineyard row-by-row. Bob is married to Barbara Nixon, founder of Victoria Winery Tours, who has been in and out of cellar doors around Australia with greater frequency than any other living person. So it is that the tasting room has wide shaded verandahs, plenty of windows and sweeping views. The 4.5-ha vineyard is planted to chardonnay, pinot noir, semillon and riesling. Exports to the US.

TTTT **Mawarra Vineyard Foundation Block Pinot Noir 2004** Strong purple-red; intensely focused and tightly wound dark cherry and plum fruit, plus pronounced acidity; needs time to open up. Screwcap. **RATING** 92 **DRINK** 2011 $ 28
Mawarra Vineyard Chardonnay 2004 Light- to medium-bodied; supple and smooth stone fruit, ripe citrus and gentle oak; has flourished over the last 2 years. **RATING** 90 **DRINK** 2010 $ 25

TTTT **Mawarra Vineyard Semillon 2005** Good balance and clear varietal character; grass and lemon flavours, with lingering, but not aggressive acidity. Screwcap. **RATING** 89 **DRINK** 2011 $ 18

Mawarra Vineyard Pinot Rose 2005 Bright pink; appealing strawberry and cherry flavours, the hint of sweetness as much from the fruit as residual sugar. Screwcap. 13.6° alc. **RATING** 89 **DRINK** Now $19

Mawarra Vineyard Top Block Pinot Noir 2004 Bright red-purple; bright, fresh and lively strawberry/cherry red fruits; light- to medium-bodied; good length. Screwcap. 12.2° alc. **RATING** 89 **DRINK** 2008 $22

Mawarra Vineyard Unwooded Chardonnay 2005 Clean and crisp citrus, stone fruit and mineral; has considerable structure and length. Screwcap. **RATING** 88 **DRINK** 2009 $16

ŸŸŸŸ **Mawarra Vineyard Duet Chardonnay Semillon 2004** Acidity is very pronounced, in part a reflection of the low alcohol; fresh seafood/oysters match. Screwcap. 12° alc. **RATING** 86 **DRINK** 2008 $15

Glaetzer Wines ★★★★★

34 Barossa Valley Way, Tanunda, SA 5352 (postal) **REGION** Barossa Valley
T (08) 8563 0288 **F** (08) 8563 0218 **WWW**.glaetzer.com **OPEN** Not
WINEMAKER Colin Glaetzer, Ben Glaetzer **EST.** 1996 **CASES** 5000
Colin and son Ben Glaetzer are almost as well known in South Australian wine circles as Wolf Blass winemaker John Glaetzer, Colin's twin brother. Glaetzer Wines purchases its grapes from third and fourth-generation Barossa Valley growers and makes an array of traditional Barossa styles. The winery has a very large contract winemaking business for 140 clients and an annual crush of 10 000 tonnes of 26 grape varieties. The Shiraz comes predominantly from vines that are 80+ years old. Exports to all major markets.

ŸŸŸŸŸ **Barossa Valley Shiraz 2004** Deep but bright purple-red; a luscious array of succulent, perfectly ripened, black fruits; excellent balance and length; nuanced tannins and oak. From 80-year-old vines in the Ebenezer region. Cork. 14.5° alc. **RATING** 96 **DRINK** 2019 $50

Amon-Ra Unfiltered Shiraz 2004 Glorious purple-red; proclaims its old vine origins from the word go, and carries its alcohol. A rich, sumptuous cascade of blackberry, plum, chocolate and quality oak. 15° alc. **RATING** 95 **DRINK** 2024 $90

Bishop Barossa Valley Shiraz 2004 Again, luscious and rich, with cascades of black fruits; perhaps not with quite the same finesse as the Barossa Valley Shiraz; good tannin and oak. Cork. 14.5° alc. **RATING** 95 **DRINK** 2017 $30

Godolphin 2004 Delicious wine; supple and luxuriant blackcurrant, cassis and quality oak all intermingle, the oak perfectly controlled, the tannins fine and long. Barossa Valley Shiraz/Cabernet Sauvignon. Cork. 15° alc. **RATING** 95 **DRINK** 2015 $49

ŸŸŸŸŸ **Wallace Barossa Valley Shiraz Grenache 2004** A well-structured blend without the weakness of some; blackberry, plum, cherry and spice all intermingle on the medium-bodied palate; fine, ripe tannins; has absorbed all the French and American oak in which it was matured. Screwcap. 14.5° alc. **RATING** 93 **DRINK** 2012 $20

Glastonbury Estate Wines NR

Shop 4, 104 Memorial Drive, Eumundi, Qld 4562 **REGION** Queensland Coastal
T (07) 5442 8557 **F** (07) 5442 8745 **WWW**.glastonburyvineyard.com.au **OPEN** Tues 12–5, Wed 9–8, Thurs 12–8, Fri 12–5, Sat 9–8, Sun 12–5
WINEMAKER Peter Scudamore-Smith MW **EST.** 2001 **CASES** 4000
Glastonbury Estate is situated in the hills of Glastonbury, high up in the Sunshine Coast hinterland, 50 mins from Noosa. It is the vision of managing director Steve Davoren, who (in typical Qld tradition) has established a combined wine and tourism venture. Chardonnay, merlot and cabernet sauvignon have been established on terraces cut into the hillsides, with further plantings underway.

Gledswood Homestead & Winery   NR

900 Camden Valley Way, Catherine Fields, NSW 2171 **REGION** Sydney Basin
T (02) 9606 5111 **WWW**.gledswood.com.au **OPEN** 7 days 10–5
WINEMAKER Contract **EST.** 2000 **CASES** NA
The Gledswood Homestead & Winery complex is one of the most historically important properties in Australia, with the collection of buildings dating back to 1810, and the homestead to around 1820. The owners live in the homestead, but the homestead and all its ancillary buildings are devoted to a wide range of tourist activities, supported by the restaurant, which is open 7 days.

Glen Creek Wines   NR

Glen Creek Road, Barjarg, Vic 3722 **REGION** Upper Goulburn
T (03) 5776 4271 **F** (03) 9873 5088 **WWW**.glencreekwines.com.au **OPEN** By appt
WINEMAKER Geoff Alford, MasterWineMakers **EST.** 2001 **CASES** NA
Geoff Alford commenced the establishment of the vineyard in Mt Strathbogie at Barjarg, around 30 km northwest of Mansfield, with the planting of 500 chardonnay vines in 1995. The estate has since grown to 6 ha, with the addition of pinot gris, merlot, cabernet sauvignon and nebbiolo; other local vineyards contribute shiraz, pinot noir and additional cabernet sauvignon. There is a complementary planting of olives. Part of the wine is made onsite, part offsite by MasterWineMakers.

Glen Eldon Wines   NR

Cnr Koch's Road/Nitschke Road, Krondorf, SA 5235 **REGION** Eden and Barossa Valleys
T (08) 8568 2996 **F** (08) 8568 1833 **WWW**.gleneldonwines.com.au **OPEN** Mon–Fri 8.30–5, w'ends 11–5
WINEMAKER Richard Sheedy **EST.** 1997 **CASES** 4000
The Sheedy family — brothers Richard and Andrew, and wives Mary and Sue — have established their base at the Glen Eldon property (which was given its name over 100 years ago); today it is the home of Richard and Mary. The riesling is planted here; the shiraz and cabernet sauvignon come from their vineyards in the Barossa Valley. Exports to the UK, the US and Canada.

Glen Erin Vineyard Retreat   ★★☆

Rochford Road, Lancefield, Vic 3435 **REGION** Macedon Ranges
T (03) 5429 1041 **F** (03) 5429 2053 **WWW**.glenerinretreat.com.au **OPEN** W'ends, public hols 10–6
WINEMAKER Hanging Rock Winery **EST.** 1993 **CASES** 400
Brian Scales acquired the former Lancefield Winery and renamed it Glen Erin. Wines are contract-made from Macedon and other grapes and sold only through the cellar door and restaurant; conferences and events are the major business activity, supported by 24 accommodation rooms.

▼▼▼ **Mystic Park Chardonnay Pinot NV** **RATING** 83 $ 35

Glen Isla Estate   NR

107 Glen Isla Road, Bickley, WA 6076 (postal) **REGION** Perth Hills
T (08) 9293 5293 **F** (08) 9293 5293 **WWW**.glenislaestate.com.au **OPEN** By appt
WINEMAKER John Griffiths (Contract) **EST.** 1998 **CASES** 350
Jim Winterhalder has established 0.84 ha each of merlot and pinot noir, and 2.38 ha of shiraz, on slopes which straddle Piesse Brook, facing variously west, east and north.

Glenalbyn   NR

84 Halls Road, Kingower, Vic 3517 **REGION** Bendigo
T (03) 5438 8255 **F** (03) 5438 8255 **OPEN** 10.30–4.30 most days
WINEMAKER Lee (Leila) Gillespie **EST.** 1997 **CASES** 500
When Leila Gillespie's great-grandfather applied for his land title in 1856, he had already established a vineyard on the property (in 1853). A survey plan of 1857 shows the cultivation paddocks, one marked the Grape Paddock, and a few of the original grape vines have survived in the garden which abuts the National Trust and Heritage homestead. In 1986 Leila and John Gillespie decided on a

modest diversification of their sheep, wool and cereal crop farm, and began the establishment of 4 ha of vineyards. Since 1997 Leila Gillespie has made the wine (she is self-taught), starting with Cabernet Sauvignon, then adding Pinot Noir and Sauvignon Blanc. In 2003 she commemorated 150 years of family ownership of the property; ironically, the 2003 drought meant that no grapes were picked.

GlenAyr   ★★★☆

Back Tea Tree Road, Richmond, Tas 7025 **REGION** Southern Tasmania
T (03) 6260 2388 **F** (03) 6260 2691 **OPEN** Mon–Fri 8–5
WINEMAKER Andrew Hood **EST.** 1975 **CASES** 500
The substantial and now fully mature Tolpuddle Vineyard, managed by Warren Schasser, who is completing a Bachelor of Applied Science (viticulture) at Charles Sturt University, provides the grapes which go to make the GlenAyr wines. The major part of the grape production continues to be sold to Domaine Chandon and Hardys, with most going to make premium still table wine, and a lesser amount to premium sparkling.

▼▼▼▼♀ **Tolpuddle Vineyards Chardonnay 2004** Ripe nectarine fruit, with a hint of honey; long
      fruit carry; balanced sweetness and acidity. **RATING** 92 **DRINK** 2009

▼▼▼♀ **Tolpuddle Vineyards Pinot Noir 2004 RATING** 86 **DRINK** 2008

Glenburnie Vineyard   NR

Black Range Road, Tumbarumba, NSW 2653 **REGION** Tumbarumba
T (02) 6948 2570 **F** (02) 6948 2570 **OPEN** 7 days 10–5
WINEMAKER Cofield Wines **EST.** 1992 **CASES** 800
Robert Parkes has established 12 ha of vineyard planted to riesling, sauvignon blanc, chardonnay and pinot noir. The production is marketed under the Black Range Wines. The cellar door offers barbecue facilities, and accommodation is also available.

Glendonbrook   NR

Lot 2 Park Street, East Gresford, NSW 2311 **REGION** Upper Hunter Valley
T (02) 4938 9666 **F** (02) 4938 9766 **WWW**.glendonbrook.com **OPEN** Mon–Fri 9–5, w'ends & public hols 10.30–4.30
WINEMAKER Geoff Broadfield **EST.** 2000 **CASES** 25 000
Sydney businessman Tom Smith and wife Terese purchased the Bingleburra homestead at East Gresford in the mid-1990s. The 600-ha property raises beef cattle, but in 1997 the decision was taken to plant 12.5 ha of vines (8.3 ha shiraz, 4.2 ha verdelho). This in turn led to the construction (in 2001) of a $2 million, 300-tonne capacity winery, lifting their total investment in the wine industry to $3 million. The estate production is supplemented by contract-grown grapes, and the winery has sufficient capacity to offer contract winemaking facilities for others. It marks a major return to the Gresford area, where Dr Henry Lindeman established his Cawarra vineyards in the mid-1800s.

Glenfinlass   NR

Elysian Farm, Parkes Road, Wellington, NSW 2820 **REGION** Western Plains Zone
T (02) 6845 2011 **F** (02) 6845 3329 **OPEN** Sat 9–5, or by appt
WINEMAKER Brian Holmes **EST.** 1971 **CASES** 500
The weekend and holiday hobby of Wellington solicitor Brian Holmes, who has wisely decided to leave it at that. I have not tasted the wines for many years, but the last wines I did taste were competently made. Wines are in short supply owing to drought (1998), frost (1999) and flooding (2000), promptly followed by 3 more years of drought.

Glengariff Estate Winery   NR

3234 Mount Mee Road, Dayboro Valley, Qld 4521 **REGION** Queensland Coastal
T (07) 3425 1299 **F** (07) 3425 2255 **WWW**.glengariff.com.au **OPEN** By appt
WINEMAKER Contract **EST.** 1999 **CASES** 350
The word 'historic' is as much overused as the word 'passionate', but this is a historic property with a quite remarkable story. The twice-married Honorah Mullins, first to a Mr Doyle and later to a

Mr Mullins, moved with her husband from County Cork, Ireland, to Australia in 1875. In 1876 they established the family dairy farm, now Glengariff Estate. At the age of 90, Honorah Mullins was still milking a herd of 40 cows, and when 111 she continued to take her morning walk with one of her sons, Dennis Doyle. When she died on 1 May 1926, one day before her 115th birthday, she had lived through the reign of six English monarchs, from George III to George V. Tracey Wrightson, the great-great-granddaughter of Honorah Mullins, together with husband Andrew and children, now own and run the 100-ha Glengariff Estate. It operates as a tourist attraction, with a restaurant and wedding function venue and (since 1999) as a grapegrower and wine producer.

Glenguin ★★★★★

Milbrodale Road, Broke, NSW 2330 **REGION** Lower Hunter Valley
T (02) 6579 1009 **F** (02) 6579 1009 **OPEN** At Boutique Wine Centre, Broke Road, Pokolbin
WINEMAKER Robin Tedder MW **EST.** 1993 **CASES** 5000
Glenguin's vineyard has been established along the banks of the Wollombi Brook by Robin and Rita Tedder; Robin is a grandson of Air Chief Marshal Tedder, made Baron of Glenguin by King George VI in recognition of his wartime deeds. There are now two distinct ranges: the Glenguin wines come solely from the 19 ha of estate plantings at Wollombi, and the Maestro label matching grape varieties and site climates in regions as diverse as Orange and the Adelaide Hills. Exports to the UK, Germany and NZ.

ȲȲȲȲȲ **Aristea Shiraz 2003** Powerful, distinguished shiraz from a very good Hunter Valley vintage; medium- to full-bodied, with perfectly balanced blackberry fruit, tannins and oak. Undoubted 20-year development; 250 cases made; high-quality cork. 13.5° alc. **RATING** 94 **DRINK** 2023 $ 70
Stoneybroke Shiraz Tannat 2003 Excellent colour; rich, ripe, not jammy, black fruits; juicy and supple; good length, balanced oak. The tannat contribution is incidental. Screwcap. 14° alc. **RATING** 94 **DRINK** 2015 $ 20

ȲȲȲȲȲ **Schoolhouse Block Shiraz 2003** Substantial wine; an abundance of savoury/earthy black fruits; good texture from ripe tannins; sensible oak. Cork. 13.5° alc. **RATING** 93 **DRINK** 2015 $ 30
Maestro Sangiovese 2003 Intense red cherry flavours boosted by savoury, fine tannins and racy acidity. Still very youthful and needs to settle down a little. From Orange. Screwcap. 14.5° alc. **RATING** 90 **DRINK** 2010 $ 23

ȲȲȲȲ **The Old Broke Block Semillon 2005** Spotlessly clean; plenty of lemon/lemon tart flavour, but a slightly congested finish. Screwcap. 12° alc. **RATING** 89 **DRINK** 2010 $ 19
River Terrace Chardonnay 2004 Medium green-yellow; big, rich, concentrated yellow peach and fig fruit; reflects the very low yield. Screwcap. 14° alc. **RATING** 88 **DRINK** 2009 $ 20

ȲȲȲ **Christina Semillon 1999** Brassy orange; the cork has sabotaged what would otherwise be a very good wine. Cork. 10.5° alc. **RATING** 86 **DRINK** Now $ 25
Maestro Pinot Grigio 2005 **RATING** 86 **DRINK** Now $ 23

Glenhoya Estate ★★★

Uralla Road, Armidale, NSW 2350 **REGION** Northern Slopes Zone
T (02) 6771 1874 **F** (02) 6771 1874 **OPEN** Future opening
WINEMAKER Hunter Wine Services (John Hordern) **EST.** 1997 **CASES** 300
David and Margaret Graf planted an experimental plot of 320 shiraz and riesling vines in the back garden of their 0.7-ha house property in 1997 and 1998. The first wine was produced in 2000, and in November 2001 the Grafs successfully applied for an off-license, the first in the region. In the meantime they have planted a further 1.4 ha on a 4-ha property directly across the road. In 2004 they sold a half-share in the 4-ha property; it is now called Martin's Gully, and the wines produced from this block will be separately labelled, but sold through a future cellar door at Glenhoya Estate.

ȲȲȲȲ **Ironstone Riesling 2003** Gentle tropical fruit aromas and flavours; some CO_2 still showing; crisp acidity on the finish does tighten up the wine. Screwcap. **RATING** 87 **DRINK** 2010 $ 21.50

ȲȲȲ **Armidale Shiraz 2003** **RATING** 83 $ 21.50

🍂 Glenmaggie Wines ★★★

McLachlans Road, Maffra, Vic 3860 **REGION** Gippsland
T (03) 5145 1131 **F** (03) 5145 1131 **OPEN** Sun & public hols 10–5, or by appt
WINEMAKER Tony Dawkins, Fleur Dawkins **EST.** 1998 **CASES** 1500
The origins of Glenmaggie go back to 1983, when trial plantings of shiraz and cabernet were
sufficiently encouraging to prompt the extension of the vineyard to 3 ha (0.5 ha each of chardonnay,
semillon, sauvignon blanc, pinot noir, shiraz and cabernet sauvignon). It is the venture of Fleur and
Tony Dawkins, with occasional assistance from their young son Jack (who at the age of 8 has
graduated to supervision and grape quality assessment, other vineyard tasks being too menial). The
family's background includes nursing, dance, youth work, building and, more recently, dairy
farming, parenthood and, of course, winemaking.

🍷🍷🍷🍷 **Gippsland Cabernet Sauvignon 2004** Plenty of ripe blackcurrant fruit; controlled oak
and tannins; just an element of rusticity. **RATING** 89 **DRINK** 2011 $ 24

🍷🍷🍷🍷 **Bazz Gippsland Shiraz 2004** Fresh and bright plum, raspberry and blackberry fruit;
needs a little more concentration. Twin top. 13.5° alc. **RATING** 86 **DRINK** 2009 $ 22
Gippsland Pinot Noir 2004 RATING 84 **DRINK** Now $ 25

🍂 Glenmore ★★★★

PO Box 201, Yallingup, WA 6282 **REGION** Margaret River
T (08) 9755 2330 **F** (08) 9755 2331 **OPEN** Not
WINEMAKER Ian Bell **EST.** 1990 **CASES** NFP
Ian Bell started his career as a cellar and vineyard hand at Moss Wood; he was encouraged to study
viticulture at the then Roseworthy College in 1987, and returned in 1989 to work for Moss Wood. Between
1990 and 1999 he established 3.6 ha of cabernet sauvignon and 1.2 ha of merlot, petit verdot and malbec
on the Glenmore property, which has been in the family's ownership since 1895. Between 1997 and 2001
all of the Glenmore Vineyard grapes were sold to Moss Wood, and made under the Glenmore Vineyard
Cabernet Sauvignon label. Since then, Ian Bell has developed the Glenmore label in its own right, but
continues to sell grapes to Moss Wood, the wine now being called Amy's Vineyard, named after Ian's
grandmother Amy Beers who still owns and runs beef cattle at the age of 84. A complicated story, it must
said, made more complicated by the Pin Pin Cabernet coming from a separate vineyard.

🍷🍷🍷🍷🍷 **Margaret River Cabernet Sauvignon 2001** Medium- to full-bodied; focused
blackcurrant and earth aromas and flavours; good tannin structure; integrated oak.
Screwcap. **RATING** 92 **DRINK** 2016 $ 45

🍷🍷🍷🍷 **Pinpin Margaret River Cabernet Sauvignon 2002** Light- to medium-bodied; clean,
fresh, gentle cassis and blackcurrant; minimal tannin and oak influence; easy access style.
Cork. **RATING** 87 **DRINK** 2009

Gloucester Ridge Vineyard ★★★☆

Lot 7489 Burma Road, Pemberton, WA 6260 **REGION** Pemberton
T (08) 9776 1035 **F** (08) 9776 1390 **www**.gloucester-ridge.com.au **OPEN** 7 days 10–5
WINEMAKER West Cape Howe Wines (Gavin Berry) **EST.** 1985 **CASES** 6000
Gloucester Ridge is the only vineyard located within the Pemberton town boundary. It is owned and
operated by Don and Sue Hancock. The wines are distributed in 3 ranges: at the bottom the Back
Block range, the Mid range, and the Premium Estate range. The varieties covered are Riesling (in
dessert style), Sauvignon Blanc, Semillon, Chardonnay, Merlot and Cabernet Sauvignon.

🍷🍷🍷🍷 **Sauvignon Blanc 2005** A clean bouquet with herb, grass and mineral flavours; backs off
ever so slightly on the finish, but well-made nonetheless. Screwcap. 12.7° alc. **RATING** 89
DRINK Now $ 16
Pemberton White 2004 Generous fruit with peach, melon and a touch of lemony acidity
from the Sauvignon Blanc; complex wine which works well. Chardonnay/Sauvignon
Blanc. Screwcap. 12.8° alc. **RATING** 89 **DRINK** 2008 $ 14
Unwooded Chardonnay 2005 Clean; has some zest and zip to the grapefruit/stone fruit
flavours; above average for unwooded Chardonnay. Screwcap. 13.3° alc. **RATING** 88
DRINK Now $ 16

Cabernet Sauvignon 2001 Light- to medium-bodied; aging nicely, retaining sweet cassis fruit; good balance and length. Cork. 12.7° alc. **RATING** 88 **DRINK** 2009 $ 25

ΨΨΨΫ **Seduction Rose NV** Abundant black cherry fruit sustains the sweetness demanded by cellar door customers. Cork. **RATING** 86 **DRINK** Now $ 14
Merlot 2003 RATING 85 **DRINK** 2008 $ 20
Chimere Methode Champenoise 2004 RATING 85 **DRINK** Now $ 30
Pemberton Red 2001 RATING 84 **DRINK** 2009 $ 14

Gnadenfrei Estate ★★★★☆

Seppeltsfield Road, Marananga via Nuriootpa, SA 5355 **REGION** Barossa Valley
T (08) 8562 2522 **F** (08) 8562 3470 **OPEN** Tues–Sun 11–5.30
WINEMAKER Malcolm Seppelt **EST.** 1979 **CASES** 750
A strictly cellar door operation, which relies on a variety of sources for its wines but has a core of 2 ha of estate shiraz and 1 ha of grenache. The red wines are from the old estate dry-grown vines, and are not filtered.

ΨΨΨΨΫ **St Michael's Barossa Shiraz 2004** Deep purple-red; intense prune, plum, blackberry aromas; a full-bodied, rich and plush texture. At the end of the day, loses a little more on the alcohol roundabout than it gains on the swings. Cork. 15.8° alc. **RATING** 92 **DRINK** 2015 $ 45

ΨΨΨΨ **Barossa Grenache 2004** Light- to medium-bodied; typical jammy, juicy Barossa style, flavoursome, but again the alcohol is a distraction. Cork. 15.6° alc. **RATING** 88 **DRINK** 2009 $ 25

Gold Dust Wines NR

Southpark, Tallwood Road, Millthorpe, NSW 2798 **REGION** Orange
T (02) 6366 5168 **F** (02) 6361 9165 **OPEN** By appt
WINEMAKER Contract **EST.** 1993 **CASES** 700
John and Jacqui Corrie have established 3 ha each of riesling and chardonnay, electing to sell two-thirds of the production, and have the remainder contract-made. Most of the wine is sold by mail order.

Golden Ball NR

1175 Beechworth–Wangaratta Road, Beechworth, Vic 3747 **REGION** Beechworth
T (03) 5727 0284 **OPEN** By appt
WINEMAKER James McLaurin **EST.** 1996 **CASES** 625
The Golden Ball vineyard is established on one of the original land grants in the Beechworth region. The 2.4-ha vineyard was planted by James and Janine McLaurin in 1996, the major parts being cabernet sauvignon, shiraz and merlot, with lesser plantings of grenache and malbec. All the wines are vinified separately and aged in one-third new French oak, the remainder 2–3 years old. The low yields result in intensely flavoured wines which are to be found in a Who's Who of Melbourne's best restaurants and a handful of local and Melbourne retailers, including Randall's at Albert Park.

Golden Grape Estate NR

Oakey Creek Road, Pokolbin, NSW 2321 **REGION** Lower Hunter Valley
T (02) 4998 7588 **F** (02) 4998 7730 **OPEN** 7 days 10–5
WINEMAKER Neil McGuigan (Consultant) **EST.** 1985 **CASES** NFP
German-owned and unashamedly directed at the tourist, with a restaurant, barbecue and picnic areas, a wine museum and a separate tasting room for bus tours. The substantial range of wines are of diverse origins and style. The operation now has over 42 ha of Hunter Valley plantings.

Golden Grove Estate

NR

Sundown Road, Ballandean, Qld 4382 **REGION** Granite Belt
T (07) 4684 1291 **F** (07) 4684 1247 **OPEN** 7 days 9–5
WINEMAKER Sam Costanzo **EST.** 1993 **CASES** 10 000
Golden Grove Estate was established by Mario and Sebastiana Costanzo in 1946, producing stone fruits and table grapes for the fresh fruit market. The first wine grapes (shiraz) were planted in 1972, but it was not until 1985, when ownership passed to son Sam Costanzo and wife Grace, that the use of the property started to change. In 1993 chardonnay and merlot joined the shiraz, followed by cabernet sauvignon, sauvignon blanc and semillon. Wine quality has steadily improved; national (though limited) retail distribution.

Golden Gully Wines

NR

5900 Midwestern Highway, Mandurama, NSW 2792 **REGION** Orange
T (02) 6367 5148 **F** (02) 6367 4148 **OPEN** W'ends 10–4, or by appt
WINEMAKER Contract **EST.** 1994 **CASES** 1300
Kevin and Julie Bate have progressively established over 5 ha of vineyard (2 ha cabernet sauvignon, 1.6 shiraz, 0.5 merlot and 0.5 each of semillon and sauvignon blanc). The first commercial crop came in 2001, but tiny makes in 1999 (Cabernet Shiraz) and 2000 (Cabernet Sauvignon) both won bronze medals at the Bathurst Cool Climate Wine Show.

Golders Vineyard

★★★★

Bridport Road, Pipers Brook, Tas 7254 **REGION** Northern Tasmania
T (03) 6395 4142 **F** (03) 6395 4142 **WWW**.geocities.com/goldersvineyard **OPEN** By appt
WINEMAKER Richard Crabtree **EST.** 1991 **CASES** 400
The initial plantings of 1.5 ha of pinot noir have been supplemented by 1 ha of chardonnay. The quality of the Pinot Noir has been good from the first vintage in 1995.

▼▼▼▼▼ **Pinot Noir 2004** Plenty of spicy, savoury black fruits; good length and balance; overall elegance. **RATING** 94 **DRINK** 2010 $17

▼▼▼▽ **Chardonnay 2005 RATING** 84 **DRINK** Now $15

Golding Wines

★★★★☆

Western Branch Road, Lobethal, SA 5241 **REGION** Adelaide Hills
T (08) 8389 5120 **F** (08) 8389 5290 **WWW**.goldingwines.com.au **OPEN** By appt
WINEMAKER Justin McNamee **EST.** 2002 **CASES** 1500
The Golding family has lived in the Lobethal area of the Adelaide Hills for several generations, and is one of the larger vignerons, owning and operating 3 separate vineyards with around 40 ha planted to pinot noir, chardonnay, sauvignon blanc, cabernet franc and merlot. They also run a commercial vine propagation business. Over the years, their grapes have gone to some of SA's leading wineries, for good measure being incorporated in some of the icon brands. In 2002 a decision was taken to establish the Golding Wines brand, the owners being Darren and Lucy Golding, together with Darren's parents, Connie and Greg.

▼▼▼▼▼ **Lenswood Pinot Noir 2002** Good colour; very complex aromas of warm spice, briar and berry; a very long, savoury/spicy palate, but with enough plum fruit at its core. Striking packaging. Cork. 13.3° alc. **RATING** 94 **DRINK** 2009 $35

▼▼▼▼▽ **Lenswood Chardonnay 2004** Bright green-yellow; attractive wine, with melon and nectarine fruit the driver, citrussy acidity following on the finish, oak the unseen conductor. Cork. 12.4° alc. **RATING** 92 **DRINK** 2009 $25

▼▼▼▼ **Lenswood Sauvignon Blanc 2005** Spotlessly clean; a restrained style, mainly mineral, chalk and slate, but with some flecks of gooseberry and herb. Screwcap. 13.5° alc. **RATING** 89 **DRINK** Now $18

Gomersal Wines   NR

Lyndoch Road, Gomersal, SA 5352 **REGION** Barossa Valley
T (08) 8563 3611 **F** (08) 8563 3776 **OPEN** 7 days 10–5
WINEMAKER Contract **EST.** 2000 **CASES** 2000
In 1887 Friedrich W Fromm planted the Wonganella Vineyards; following that with a winery on the
edge of the Gomersal Creek in 1891 which remained in operation for 90 years, finally closing in 1983.
In 2000 a group of friends 'with strong credentials in both the making and consumption end of the
wine industry' bought the winery and re-established the vineyard, planting 17 ha of shiraz, 2.25 ha of
mourvedre and 1 ha of grenache via terraced bush vines. The Riesling comes from purchased grapes,
the Grenache Rose, Grenache Shiraz Mataro and Shiraz from the replanted vineyard.

Goona Warra Vineyard   ★★★★

Sunbury Road, Sunbury, Vic 3429 **REGION** Sunbury
T (03) 9740 7766 **F** (03) 9744 7648 **WWW**.goonawarra.com.au **OPEN** 7 days 10–5
WINEMAKER John Barnier, Mark Matthews **EST.** 1863 **CASES** 3000
A historic stone winery, established under this name by a 19th-century Victorian premier. A brief
interlude as part of The Wine Investment Fund in 2001 is over, the Barniers having bought back the
farm. Excellent tasting facilities, an outstanding venue for weddings and receptions, and lunch on
Sunday. Exports to the UK.

▼▼▼▼♀ **2004 Goona Warra Vineyard Sunbury Merlot Cabernet Franc** Ominously developed
colour; spicy, savoury, earthy aromas and flavours, but with rather more character than the
colour suggests; a long, almost lemony, finish; strangely appealing. Screwcap. **RATING** 90
DRINK 2010 $ 25

▼▼▼▼ **2003 Goona Warra Vineyard Sunbury Shiraz** Spicy, peppery, leathery notes to the core
of light- to medium-bodied black fruits; balanced tannins and oak. Screwcap. **RATING** 89
DRINK 2012 $ 29.50

Goorambath   NR

103 Hooper Road, Goorambat, Vic 3725 **REGION** Glenrowan
T (03) 5764 1380 **F** (03) 5764 1320 **WWW**.goorambath.com.au **OPEN** 1st weeknd of month or by appt
WINEMAKER Dookie College (David Hodgson) **EST.** 1997 **CASES** 850
Lyn and Geoff Bath have had a long association with the Victorian wine industry. Since 1982 Geoff
Bath has been senior lecturer in viticulture with the University of Melbourne at Dookie campus; he
and wife Lyn also owned (in conjunction with two other couples) a vineyard at Whitlands for 18
years. In July 2000 they sold their interest in that vineyard to focus on their small vineyard at
Goorambat, hence the clever name. Planting had begun in 1998 with 1 ha of shiraz, subsequently
joined by 1 ha of verdelho, 0.5 ha of orange muscat and 0.2 ha of tannat.

Gordon Sunter Wines   NR

PO Box 12, Tanunda, SA 5352 **REGION** Barossa Valley
T (08) 8563 2349 **OPEN** Not
WINEMAKER Stuart Blackwell **EST.** 1982 **CASES** NA
Gordon Sunter Wines has lived a shadowy existence for over 20 years, as the part-time private label
of St Hallett winemaker Stuart Blackwell. The deliberately low profile is not hard to understand.

🐌 Gotham   ★★★

PO Box 343, Mona Vale, NSW 1660 **REGION** Langhorne Creek
T 0412 124 811 **F** (02) 9973 3586 **OPEN** Not
WINEMAKER Kalleske **EST.** 2004 **CASES** 3500
Bruce Clugston, with a long involvement in the wine industry, has created a virtual winery (or label,
whichever you prefer) sourcing Langhorne Creek shiraz and having the wine made in the Barossa
Valley by Troy Kalleske. The initial vintage of 2004 had an alcohol of 15.5°, a level which many will
find intimidating.

▼▼▼♀ **Langhorne Creek Shiraz 2004** **RATING** 85 **DRINK** 2008 $ 19.95

Goulburn Terrace
★★★☆

340 High Street, Nagambie, Vic 3608 **REGION** Goulburn Valley
T (03) 5794 2828 **F** (03) 5794 1854 **WWW**.goulburnterrace.com.au **OPEN** Sat 10–5, Sun &
most public hols 11–5
WINEMAKER Dr Mike Boudry, Greta Moon **EST.** 1993 **CASES** 1000
Dr Mike Boudry and Greta Moon have established their 7-ha vineyard on the west bank of the
Goulburn River, 8 km south of Lake Nagambie. Planting began in 1993; chardonnay on the alluvial
soils (10 000 years old, adjacent to the river), and cabernet sauvignon on a gravelly rise based on 400
million-year-old Devonian rocks. The wines are made in small volumes, with open fermentation and
hand plunging of the reds; all are basket pressed. The wines are sold by mail order, and at the cellar
door in High Street, Nagambie.

▼▼▼▼ **Wattlevale Shiraz 2001** Holding medium-red hue; plenty of substance and depth; plum,
spice and blackberry; long, savoury finish. Cork. 14.5° alc. **RATING** 89 **DRINK** 2011 $ 28

Goulburn Valley Estate Wines
NR

340 Trotter Road, Mooroopna North, Vic 3629 **REGION** Goulburn Valley
T (03) 5829 0278 **F** (03) 5829 0014 **OPEN** By appt
WINEMAKER Rocky Scarpari **EST.** 2001 **CASES** NA
Rocky Scarpari heads Goulburn Valley Estate Wines, the wine being made under the direction of the
vastly experienced Lee Clarnette. Goulburn Valley Estate has a nominal 1.2 ha of vines; the major
part of its substantial production comes from growers in the Mooroopna area. The wines are sold
under the Goulburn Shed brand. Exports to Hong Kong and Malaysia.

Goundrey
★★★★

Muirs Highway, Mount Barker, WA 6324 **REGION** Mount Barker
T (08) 9892 1777 **F** (08) 9851 1997 **WWW**.goundreywines.com.au **OPEN** 7 days 10–4.30
WINEMAKER David Martin, Michael Perkins, Stephen Craig **EST.** 1976 **CASES** 375 000
Jack Bendat acquired Goundrey when it was on its knees; through significant expenditure on land,
vineyards and winery capacity, it became the House that Jack Built. In late 2002 it was acquired by
Vincor, Canada's largest wine producer, for a price widely said to be more than $30 million, a sum
which would have provided Bendat with a very satisfactory return on his investment. Exports to all
major markets.

▼▼▼▼▽ **Reserve Riesling 2004** Pale, bright straw-green; crisp mineral, slate, spice and
passionfruit aromas; delicate, fresh and well-balanced palate. Screwcap. **RATING** 91
DRINK 2014 $ 20.99
WA Shiraz 2003 Bright, clear hue; a light- to medium-bodied mix of red and black fruits;
good fruit-driven, early drinking, red. Cork. 13.5° alc. **RATING** 90 **DRINK** 2009 $ 15
Reserve Shiraz 2002 Light- to medium-bodied; has some elegance; vibrant cherry,
raspberry and blood plum red fruits; fine tannins, minimal oak. Cork. **RATING** 90
DRINK 2012 $ 32

▼▼▼▼ **Homestead Unwooded Chardonnay 2005** Strong yellow-green; a full-bodied, rich,
yellow peach retro style; gives the impression of skin contact. Gold medal '05 Gisborne
International Chardonnay Challenge NZ and Sydney International Wine Competition.
Screwcap. **RATING** 89 **DRINK** 2008 $ 15
Reserve Cabernet Sauvignon 2003 Direct blackcurrant and cassis, with hints of spicy
earth; medium-bodied palate, closing with fine tannins. Cork. **RATING** 89 **DRINK** 2013 $ 32
Homestead Sauvignon Blanc Semillon 2005 Clean, fresh and firm; a mix of mineral,
grass, apple and citrus, a slightly congested finish the only downside. Screwcap. **RATING** 88
DRINK Now $ 15
Reserve Chardonnay 2003 Surprisingly developed colour; solid, peachy wine; plenty of
depth though not much finesse. Screwcap. **RATING** 87 **DRINK** Now $ 33

▼▼▼▽ **WA Cabernet Merlot 2003** **RATING** 86 **DRINK** 2008 $ 15
Offspring Cabernet Sauvignon 2003 **RATING** 86 **DRINK** 2009 $ 19.99
Offspring Chardonnay 2003 **RATING** 85 **DRINK** Now $ 19.99

Shiraz Cabernet Sauvignon 2003 RATING 85 DRINK Now $ 15
Homestead Cabernet Merlot 2003 RATING 85 DRINK Now $ 15

Governor Robe Selection ★★★☆

Waterhouse Range Vineyards, Lot 11, Old Naracoorte Road, Robe, SA 5276 REGION Limestone Coast Zone
T (08) 8768 2083 F (08) 8768 2190 WWW.waterhouserange.com.au OPEN At The Attic House, Victoria St, Robe
WINEMAKER Cape Jaffa Wines (Nigel Westblade) EST. 1995 CASES 1500
Brothers Bill and Mick Quinlan-Watson, supported by a group of investors, began the development of Waterhouse Range Vineyards Pty Ltd in 1995, planting 15 ha of vines that year, with further plantings over the following few years lifting the total area under vine to just under 60 ha. The majority of the grapes are sold; what is retained is contract-made at Cape Jaffa winery. The unusual name comes from the third Governor of South Australia, Frederick Holt Robe, who in 1845 selected the site for a port and personally put in the first survey peg at Robe.

ꜟꜟꜟꜟ **Chardonnay 2004** Very similar grapefruit, melon and stone fruit to the '05; an abundance of flavour, good length. Screwcap. 13.5° alc. RATING 89 DRINK 2008 $ 15
Chardonnay 2005 Plenty of typical grapefruit and stone fruit flavours of the region; good length and acidity. Quality unwooded style. Screwcap. RATING 87 DRINK 2008 $ 15
The Governor Merlot 2004 Medium-bodied; red fruits and a touch of olive; not much texture, but has fair length. Cork. RATING 87 DRINK 2008 $ 18

Governor's Choice Winery NR

Berghofer Road, Westbrook via Toowoomba, Qld 4350 REGION Queensland Zone
T (07) 4630 6101 F (07) 4630 6701 WWW.governorschoice.com.au OPEN 7 days 9–5
WINEMAKER James Yates EST. 1999 CASES 1500
This is a part winery, part premium guest house venture 18 km from Toowoomba. The estate plantings (3 ha) produce chardonnay, shiraz, verdelho, cabernet sauvignon and malbec, made onsite and sold through the cellar door or to those using the accommodation.

Gowrie Mountain Estate NR

2 Warrego Highway, Kingsthorpe, Qld 4400 REGION Darling Downs
T (07) 4630 0566 F (07) 4630 0366 OPEN 7 days 10–5
WINEMAKER Peter Howland Wines, Preston Peak EST. 1998 CASES 6000
Situated northeast of Toowoomba in the heart of the Darling Downs, this is a substantial entrant, having established 32 ha of mainstream varieties, and the new breed in the form of tempranillo (4 ha) and gamay (2 ha). Part of the production goes to Peter Howland in the Hunter Valley, who makes the red wines, and part to Preston Peak, where the white wines and Tempranillo are made. All the Newberry family members, headed by father Ron, are involved in the venture.

Grace Devlin Wines NR

53 Siddles Road, Redesdale, Vic 3444 REGION Heathcote
T (03) 5425 3101 OPEN By appt
WINEMAKER Brian Paterson, Lee Paterson EST. 1998 CASES 200
Brian and Lee Paterson have 2 ha of cabernet sauvignon and 0.5 ha of merlot at Redesdale. It is one of the most southerly vineyards in the Heathcote region, and most of the vines are over 12 years old. The name comes from the middle names of Brian Paterson's grandmother, mother and daughters. The small production is available from a number of local outlets.

🐌 Gracebrook Vineyards ★★★☆

1446 Wangaratta Whitfield Road, King Valley, Vic 3678 REGION King Valley
T (03) 5729 3562 F (03) 5729 8015 OPEN 7 days 10–5, closed Christmas Day
WINEMAKER David Maples EST. 1989 CASES 2500

David and Rhonda Maples began the establishment of their 37.5-ha vineyard in 1989. The vineyard is planted to merlot, shiraz, riesling, cabernet sauvignon, sangiovese, chardonnay, dolcetto and alborino. Their cellar door is housed in stables built in the 1880s, with panoramic views of the King Valley, and they cater for functions/weddings for up to 100 people.

▼▼▼▼ **King Valley Riesling 2005** A clean, fresh and lively mix of mineral, slate and green apple; pulls up a fraction short. Screwcap. **RATING** 89 **DRINK** 2010 $ 14
The Stables King Valley Chardonnay 2002 Significantly more weight than the '04; melon, stone fruit and citrus; good length, still youthful. Cork. 13.5° alc. **RATING** 88 **DRINK** 2009 $ 18
The Stables Cabernet Sauvignon 2003 Medium-bodied; vibrant cassis and berry fruit with a touch of mint; good finish and aftertaste. 14° alc. **RATING** 88 **DRINK** 2009 $ 16
King Valley Shiraz 2001 Deeper in colour than the '02; a mix of black fruits, spice and savoury/dark chocolate nuances; physiologically ripe. Cork. 14.5° alc. **RATING** 87 **DRINK** 2009 $ 20
King Valley Sangiovese 2003 Light-bodied, but does have authentic cherry and rose petal varietal character, and the tannins are not bitter; hanging in there. Cork. 14° alc. **RATING** 87 **DRINK** Now $ 18

▼▼▼▽ **King Valley Riesling 2004** **RATING** 86 **DRINK** 2008 $ 14
King Valley Shiraz 2000 **RATING** 86 **DRINK** 2008 $ 25
The Stables King Valley Merlot 2003 Medium-bodied; earthy/olive/savoury varietal characters; fine, persistent tannins with some oak contribution. Cork. 13.5° alc. **RATING** 86 **DRINK** 2008 $ 14
The Stables King Valley Chardonnay 2004 **RATING** 84 **DRINK** 2008 $ 14
King Valley Shiraz 2002 **RATING** 84 **DRINK** 2008 $ 16

▼▼▼ **The Stables King Valley Sangiovese Rose 2004** **RATING** 83 $ 10

Gracedale Hills Estate ★★★★

770 Healesville–Kooweerup Road, Healesville, Vic 3777 **REGION** Yarra Valley
T (03) 5967 3403 **F** (03) 5967 3581 **www**.gracedalehills.com.au **OPEN** Not
WINEMAKER Gary Mills **EST.** 1996 **CASES** 450
Dr Richard Gutch has established 1.2 ha of chardonnay and 2 ha of shiraz at a time when most would be retiring from active business, but it represents the culmination of a lifelong love of fine wine, and Richard has no hard feelings towards me — it was I who encouraged him, in the mid-1990s, to plant vines on the north-facing slopes of his property. Here, too, the grapes have been sold to others, but he is now retaining sufficient to make around 450 cases a year.

▼▼▼▼▼ **Hill Paddock Yarra Valley Shiraz 2004** Fine, balanced medium-bodied display of spicy, black cherry, plum and blackberry fruit, showing the Yarra Valley style to best advantage; good acidity. Cork. 13.5° alc. **RATING** 94 **DRINK** 2015 $ 35

▼▼▼▼ **Hill Paddock Yarra Valley Chardonnay 2004** Light straw-green; tightly wound, reserved style; melon, fig and wild ferment characters interwoven; light oak inputs. Screwcap. 12.5° alc. **RATING** 89 **DRINK** 2012 $ 35

▼▼▼▽ **Yarra Valley Rose 2005** **RATING** 84 **DRINK** Now $ 15

Graham Cohen Wines ★★☆

PO Box 195, Bannockburn, Vic 3331 **REGION** Geelong
T (03) 5281 7438 **F** (03) 5281 7387 **OPEN** Not
WINEMAKER Simon Black **EST.** 1985 **CASES** 200
Graham and Jan Cohen have established 1 ha of pinot noir, which produces a sole wine called Captains Birchwood. The unusual name was chosen by the Cohens' 4 sons, each one in turn House Captain of Birchwood House at their school.

▼▼▼▽ **Captains Birchwood Pinot Noir 2004** **RATING** 85 **DRINK** Now $ 23

Gralaine Vineyard ★★★★

65 Feehan's Road, Mount Duneed, Vic 3216 (postal) **REGION** Geelong
T 0429 009 973 **F** (03) 9886 7377 **OPEN** At Hanging Rock Winery
WINEMAKER Hanging Rock Winery **EST.** 1983 **CASES** NA
Graeme and Elaine Carroll have gradually established 4 ha of low-yielding merlot (with a few cabernet sauvignon vines). There are no cellar door sales, but the wine can be tasted at Hanging Rock Winery.

ŸŸŸŸŸ **Cabernet Sauvignon 2002** Supple, smooth and gently ripe fruit with good oak, tannin and extract. Gold medal 2005 Geelong Wine Show. **RATING** 94 **DRINK** 2008

ŸŸŸŸ **Merlot 2002** **RATING** 85 **DRINK** 2008

Gralyn Estate

Caves Road, Wilyabrup, WA 6280 **REGION** Margaret River
T (08) 9755 6245 **F** (08) 9755 6136 **WWW.**gralyn.com.au **OPEN** 7 days 10.30–4.30
WINEMAKER Graham Hutton, Merilyn Hutton, Dr Bradley Hutton **EST.** 1975 **CASES** 3000
The move from primarily fortified wine to table wine production has been completed, and has brought considerable success. The red wines are made in a distinctively different style from most of those from the Margaret River region, with an opulence which is reminiscent of some of the bigger wines from McLaren Vale. The age of the vines (30+ years) and the site are also significant factors. Exports to the US.

ŸŸŸŸŸ **Margaret River Cabernet Sauvignon 2004** Very distinguished cabernet sauvignon; full-bodied, rich, layered cassis/blackcurrant; fine, supple tannins running throughout; quality oak plays a role, too. Cork. **RATING** 95 **DRINK** 2024 **$** 90
Margaret River Chardonnay 2004 A lovely wine; fine but intense nectarine and citrus fruit; oak integration and balance spot on; will develop over many years. Screwcap. 13.8° alc. **RATING** 94 **DRINK** 2015 **$** 35
Single Barrel Reserve Margaret River Shiraz Cabernet 2001 Medium- to full-bodied; abundant mouthfilling black fruits and mocha vanilla oak in similar plenitude; ripe, soft tannins. The single barrel, by some alchemy, is aged in American and French oak barriques. Cork. 14.9° alc. **RATING** 94 **DRINK** 2015 **$** 90

ŸŸŸŸ **Margaret River Cabernet Shiraz 2004** Good colour; a rich, ripe array of black fruits, licorice and spice; ripe tannins and abundant oak; just a little over the top. Cork. **RATING** 93 **DRINK** 2024 **$** 90
Old Vine Margaret River Shiraz 2004 Some development in colour; a complex wine, opening with blackberry and plum, then cedar, spice and earth; fine-grained, savoury tannins. Cork. **RATING** 92 **DRINK** 2015 **$** 60

Grampians Estate

Mafeking Road, Willaura, Vic 3379 **REGION** Grampians
T (03) 5354 6245 **F** (03) 5354 6257 **WWW.**grampiansestate.com.au **OPEN** By appt
WINEMAKER Clayfield Wines **EST.** 1989 **CASES** 1000
Over a decade ago local farmers and graziers Sarah and Tom Guthrie decided to diversify their activities, while continuing to run their fat lamb and wool production. So they planted 2 ha of shiraz and 1.2 ha of chardonnay, and opened the Thermopylae Host Farm business, which offers 2 farm-stay buildings, a 5-bedroom shearer's cottage and a 5-room miner's cottage. The wines are sold to those who stay on the farm, which is able to offer an unusually wide range of activities. The whole property, including the vineyard, was devastated by the 2006 Australia Day bushfires, but the Guthries are determined to rebuild their business.

ŸŸŸŸŸ **Streeton Reserve Shiraz 2003** Great colour; a full-bodied, ultra-powerful wine with deep texture and structure, masses of black fruits and tannins; predictably, a prodigious trophy winner in the highest level of competition. Cork. 14.6° alc. **RATING** 95 **DRINK** 2018 **$** 55
Mafeking Shiraz 2003 Medium-bodied; very good balance and integration of ripe, but not overripe, red and black fruits, fine tannins and good oak. Much readier than the Streeton Reserve. Cork. 14.3° alc. **RATING** 94 **DRINK** 2013 **$** 26

Grancari Estate Wines ★★★

50 Northumberland Road, Onkaparinga Hills, SA 5163 **REGION** McLaren Vale
T (08) 8382 4465 **F** (08) 8382 4465 **OPEN** By appt
WINEMAKER Rino Ozzella, Greta Ozzella, James Hastwell (Consultant) **EST.** 1999 **CASES** 3000
In 1983 Rino and Greta Ozzella purchased a small vineyard in McLaren Vale which had been planted in the early 1940s to a little under 3 ha of grenache; the grapes were sold to other winemakers. Later, they planted a further 2.5 ha of shiraz on a westerly slope facing the sea, and decided to establish their own brand. At the same time they began the conversion to organic production, which has now been certified (in conversion).

TTTT **McLaren Vale Shiraz 2003** **RATING** 84 **DRINK** Now $ 34

Grandview Vineyard ★★★

59 Devlyns Road, Birchs Bay, Tas 7162 **REGION** Southern Tasmania
T (03) 6267 4099 **F** (03) 6267 4779 **WWW**.grandview.au.com **OPEN** 7 days 10–5
WINEMAKER Hood Wines (Andrew Hood) **EST.** 1996 **CASES** 350
Ryan Hartshorn has acquired the vineyard formerly burdened by the impossible name 2 Bud Spur. It is a pocket-handkerchief mix of varieties: 0.35 ha gewurztraminer, 0.7 ha chardonnay, 0.6 ha pinot noir, 0.3 ha sauvignon blanc and 0.05 ha gamay which are now organic.

TTT **Gewurztraminer 2005** **RATING** 83 $ 25

Granite Hills ★★★★☆

1481 Burke and Wills Track, Baynton, Kyneton, Vic 3444 **REGION** Macedon Ranges
T (03) 5423 7264 **F** (03) 5423 7288 **WWW**.granitehills.com.au **OPEN** Mon–Sat 10–6, Sun 12–6
WINEMAKER Llew Knight, Ian Gunter **EST.** 1970 **CASES** 8000
Granite Hills is one of the enduring classics, pioneering the successful growing of riesling and shiraz in an uncompromisingly cool climate. It is based on 11 ha of riesling, chardonnay, shiraz, cabernet sauvignon, merlot and pinot noir (the last used in its sparkling wine). After a quiet period in the 1990s, it has been reinvigorated, with its original two icons once again to the fore. The Rieslings age superbly, and the Shiraz is at the forefront of the cool-climate school in Australia. Exports to the US and the UK.

TTTTT **2005 Granite Hills Macedon Ranges Riesling** Highly fragrant and floral lime/acacia blossom; a vibrant palate; superb fruit line flows through to the perfectly balanced finish; simply outstanding. Screwcap. **RATING** 96 **DRINK** 2020 $ 22

TTTTY **2002 Granite Hills Macedon Ranges Shiraz** Medium red-purple; as befits this label, tightly woven and constructed spicy/peppery/blackberry fruits; fine tannins and good length. Cork. **RATING** 91 **DRINK** 2012 $ 32
2004 Granite Hills Heathcote Merlot In terms of texture, weight and structure, more to do with Macedon Ranges than Heathcote, explained by the fact the vineyard is only 12 km north of Granite Hills, just over the border; spicy, herby, plummy fruit belies the alcohol, though not the varietal character. Altogether interesting. Screwcap. **RATING** 90 **DRINK** 2010 $ 25

TTTT **Knight Macedon Ranges Pinot Noir 2003** Light, fresh, strawberry, cherry and spice; light-bodied but lively palate. Screwcap. 13.5° alc. **RATING** 88 **DRINK** Now $ 24

Granite Range Estate ★★★

183 Wilson Road, Wangandary, Vic 3678 **REGION** Glenrowan
T (03) 5725 3292 **F** (03) 5725 3292 **WWW**.graniterangeestate.com.au **OPEN** Tues–Sun 10–5
WINEMAKER Peter Long **EST.** 1998 **CASES** 2000
This is the retirement venture of Peter and Maureen Long, who acquired a bare-paddock 16-ha property in 1997, with the Warby Ranges behind and a panoramic view of the Australian Alps, complete with 9 snow caps, visible in winter. The following year they established 2.3 ha each of shiraz and merlot, and a grape purchase contract with Baileys of Glenrowan. Until 2003 all but a tiny proportion of the grapes went to Baileys, but since then production has been split between sales to

other producers, and wine under the Granite Range Estate label. The modern building complex comprises the Longs' house, cellar door, barrel store and self-contained accommodation.

ΤΤΤΤ **Merlot 2004** Good colour, body, balance and extract; blackcurrant, earth and black olive flavours; nice wine. Cork. **RATING** 88 **DRINK** 2010 $ 20

ΤΤΤ Υ **Glenrowan Shiraz 2004** **RATING** 84 **DRINK** 2008 $ 20

Granite Ridge Wines ★★★☆

Sundown Road, Ballandean, Qld 4382 **REGION** Granite Belt
T (07) 4684 1263 **F** (07) 4684 1250 **WWW**.graniteridgewines.com.au **OPEN** 7 days 9–5
WINEMAKER Dennis Ferguson, Juliane Ferguson **EST.** 1995 **CASES** 1500
Formerly known as Denlana Ferguson Estate Wines, Granite Ridge had considerable success in the mid-1990s. Its Goldies Unwooded Chardonnay was the first Qld wine to be chosen as the official Parliamentary Wine of the Queensland Government. Most of the production comes from its 5-ha vineyard, which is planted to pinot gris, chardonnay, verdelho, merlot, shiraz, petit verdot, tempranillo and cabernet sauvignon.

ΤΤΤΤ **Granite Grange Cabernet Sauvignon 2002** Deep colour; a powerful, medium- to full-bodied palate with abundant black fruits, the tannins in balance (unlike the Merlot); good length. Cork. 12° alc. **RATING** 89 **DRINK** 2012 $ 18
Traminer 2005 Gentle lychee/rose petal on a light-bodied and soft, but mercifully dry, palate. Screwcap. 12° alc. **RATING** 87 **DRINK** Now $ 18
Cabernet Sauvignon Rose 2005 Clean, fresh and well-made; cassis/berry fruit with residual sugar balanced by acidity. Screwcap. 11° alc. **RATING** 87 **DRINK** Now $ 13

ΤΤΤΥ **Fergies Hill Merlot 2003** **RATING** 85 **DRINK** Now $ 22

Grant Burge ★★★★★

Jacobs Creek, Barossa Valley, SA 5352 **REGION** Barossa Valley
T (08) 8563 3700 **F** (08) 8563 2807 **WWW**.grantburgewines.com.au **OPEN** 7 days 10–5
WINEMAKER Grant Burge **EST.** 1988 **CASES** 320 000
As one might expect, this very experienced industry veteran makes consistently good, full-flavoured and smooth wines chosen from the pick of the crop of his extensive vineyard holdings, which total an impressive 440 ha; the immaculately restored/rebuilt stone cellar door sales buildings are another attraction. The provocatively named The Holy Trinity (Grenache/Shiraz/Mourvedre) joins Shadrach and Meshach at the top of the range. In 1999 Grant Burge repurchased the farm from Mildara Blass by acquiring the Krondorf winery (not the brand) in which he made his first fortune. He has renamed it Barossa Vines (it is in Krondorf Road, Tanunda) and, taking advantage of the great views it offers, has opened a cellar door offering casual food, featuring local produce wherever possible. A third cellar door (Illaparra) is open at Murray Street, Tanunda. Exports to the UK, Europe, the US, Canada and Asia.

ΤΤΤΤΤ **Miamba Shiraz 2004** Medium- to full-bodied; lots of charry oak surrounding black cherry and blackberry fruit. Imposing style. Gold medal National Wine Show '05.
RATING 94 **DRINK** 2015 $ 20
The Holy Trinity Grenache Shiraz Mourvedre 2002 Bright, clear red; fragrant and fresh; elegant, spicy red fruits; fine tannins. Cork. 14.5° alc. **RATING** 94 **DRINK** 2010 $ 36.40

ΤΤΤΤΥ **Abednigo 2002** Light- to medium-bodied; juicy red fruits, clean and still very fresh and vibrant, though doesn't have the structure for long-term aging. Cork. 14° alc. **RATING** 93
DRINK 2010 $ 59.60
Summers Eden Valley Adelaide Hills Chardonnay 2004 Complex, slightly funky aromas; tangy, intense grapefruit and melon flavours; brisk acidity, controlled oak. Strange choice of closure. Cork. **RATING** 90 **DRINK** 2009 $ 19.90
Adelaide Hills Viognier 2004 Clear-cut varietal character on both bouquet and palate; a mix of apricot pastille, musk and honeysuckle; avoids phenolics, ditto oak. Screwcap.
RATING 90 **DRINK** 2008 $ 19.90
Nebuchadnezzar Shiraz Cabernet 2003 A medium-bodied mix of sweet, juicy blackberry and blackcurrant fruit; nicely balanced oak and tannins. Cork. 13.5° alc.
RATING 90 **DRINK** 2010 $ 36.40

TTTT **Miamba Shiraz 2003** Generous, traditional, medium-bodied Barossa Shiraz; blackberry, plum and some spice; good oak and tannin management. Cork. **RATING** 89 **DRINK** 2010 $19.90

Filsell Barossa Valley Shiraz 2003 Traditional blackberry, plum, earth, spice and vanilla; good mouthfeel and length; impressive given the vintage. Cork. **RATING** 89 **DRINK** 2012 $29.90

Barossa Valley Grenache Rose 2005 Light fuchsia-purple; well-balanced strawberry/raspberry fruit; not too sweet. Screwcap. 14° alc. **RATING** 87 **DRINK** Now $16

Balthasar Barossa Valley Shiraz Viognier 2003 Light- to medium-bodied; quite fragrant red fruits and spice bouquet; clean, fresh direct fruit flavours; simple structure. Cork. **RATING** 87 **DRINK** 2008 $36.50

Grassy Point Wines

Coatsworth Farm, 145 Coatsworth Road, Portarlington, Vic 3223 **REGION** Geelong
T 0409 429 608 **WWW**.grassypointwines.com.au **OPEN** By appt
WINEMAKER Mermerus (Dr Paul Champion), Provenance (Scott Ireland) **EST.** 1997 **CASES** 600
Partners David Smith and Robert Bennett and Kerry Jones purchased this 32-ha undeveloped grazing property in 1997. Coatsworth Farm now has 8 ha of vines (chardonnay, sauvignon blanc, pinot noir, shiraz, merlot, malbec and cabernet franc), South Devon beef cattle and Perendale/White Suffolk-cross lambs. The first crops were sold to Mermerus, but the whites have since been made by Dr Paul Champion, the reds by Scott Ireland.

TTTTT **Bellarine Peninsula Chardonnay 2004** Complex smokey/charry barrel ferment inputs sustained by the depth and power of the fruit; good length and finish. **RATING** 94 **DRINK** 2009 $18

TTTT **Bellarine Peninsula Shiraz 2004** Very good colour; powerful, dense blackberry fruit, just a little over-extracted. **RATING** 89 **DRINK** 2012 $20

Bellarine Peninsula Pinot Noir 2004 Youthful purple-red; succulent, luscious plum fruit, but finishes short. **RATING** 87 **DRINK** Now $16

TTTY **Bellarine Peninsula Cabernet Franc 2004** **RATING** 86 **DRINK** 2008 $14

TTT **Bellarine Peninsula Cabernets 2004** **RATING** 83 $14

Bellarine Peninsula Sauvignon Blanc 2005 **RATING** 82 $16

Great Lakes Wines   NR

115 Herivals Road, Wootton, NSW 2423 **REGION** Northern Rivers Zone
T (02) 4997 7255 **F** (02) 4997 7450 **OPEN** 7 days 10–5
WINEMAKER Steve Attkins, David Hook (Consultant) **EST.** 1990 **CASES** NA
Great Lakes Wines is situated south of the Hastings River region but well north of Newcastle. Robyn Piper and Steve Attkins have 4 ha of semillon, chardonnay, verdelho, cabernet sauvignon, shiraz and chambourcin planted, and make the wine onsite with David Hook overseeing proceedings. The cellar door offers light meals and barbecue/picnic facilities.

Green Valley Vineyard

3137 Sebbes Road, Forest Grove, WA 6286 **REGION** Margaret River
T (08) 9757 7510 **F** (08) 9757 7510 **WWW**.greenvalleyvineyard.com.au **OPEN** 7 days 10–5
WINEMAKER Moss Wood **EST.** 1980 **CASES** 3000
Owners Ed and Eleanore Green began developing Green Valley Vineyard in 1980; though still a part-time operation, production has grown steadily from the 7.7 ha of vines, and the Cabernet Sauvignon has been a consistent medal winner. Exports to the US and Singapore.

TTTTY **Margaret River Chardonnay 2003** A complex bouquet, possibly just feral, or a touch reductive; a complex, multi-layered palate, with good length and drive; controlled oak. Screwcap. 14.2° alc. **RATING** 90 **DRINK** 2009 $28

ΨΨΨΨ **Margaret River Cabernet Sauvignon 2003** Significantly more structure and depth than the Shiraz; solid blackcurrant fruit and supporting tannins. Cork. 14° alc. **RATING** 89 **DRINK** 2011 $39

ΨΨΨΫ **Margaret River Riesling 2005 RATING** 86 **DRINK** Now $20
Gelignite Block Shiraz 2003 RATING 85 **DRINK** 2008 $25

🍇 Greenbrier Park Vineyard   ★★★☆

Old South Road, Mittagong, NSW 2575 **REGION** Southern Highlands
T (02) 4862 2028 **F** (02) 4862 2028 **OPEN** Fri–Sun & public hols 10–4
WINEMAKER Eddy Rossi **EST.** 1999 **CASES** 700
Industry veteran Robert Constable, former director of Hungerford Hill, has established Greenbrier Park Vineyard at an altitude of 740m on north-facing basalt soils, with cool winds and low frost risk. The original plantings of 0.35 ha of cabernet sauvignon, 0.48 ha of sauvignon blanc and 0.21 ha of pinot noir have been extended with the planting of 0.35 ha of pinot noir in 2005.

ΨΨΨΨΫ **Mittagong Sauvignon Blanc 2004** Well-made; the screwcap has kept the wine together, with a mix of kiwifruit, gooseberry and tropical flavours. Good line and length. Screwcap. 12° alc. **RATING** 92 **DRINK** Now $30

ΨΨΨΫ **Estate Grown Mittagong Cabernet Merlot 2004 RATING** 86 **DRINK** Now $24

Greenock Creek Wines   NR

Radford Road, Seppeltsfield, SA 5360 **REGION** Barossa Valley
T (08) 8562 8103 **F** (08) 8562 8259 **OPEN** Wed–Mon 11–5 when wine available
WINEMAKER Michael Waugh **EST.** 1978 **CASES** 2500
Michael and Annabelle Waugh are disciples of Rocky O'Callaghan of Rockford Wines, and have deliberately accumulated a series of old dryland, low-yielding Barossa vineyards, aiming to produce wines of unusual depth of flavour and character. They have succeeded handsomely in this aim, achieving icon status and stratospheric prices in the US, making the opinions of Australian scribes irrelevant. They also offer superior accommodation in 'Miriam's', the ancient but beautifully restored 2-bedroom cottage (Michael Waugh is also a skilled stonemason).

Gregory's Wines   NR

1 Lizard Park Drive, Kilkerran, SA 5573 **REGION** The Peninsulas Zone
T (08) 8834 1258 **F** (08) 8834 1287 **OPEN** 7 days 10–4.30
WINEMAKER Ashton Hills **EST.** 1997 **CASES** 500
Rod and Toni Gregory have established 11 ha of vineyard near Maitland, on the western side of the York Peninsula. The plantings are of chardonnay, viognier, shiraz and cabernet sauvignon, and are chiefly sold through the cellar door and by mail order. The site has facilities to cater for concerts or festivals, and tours by arrangement.

Grevillea Estate   NR

Buckajo Road, Bega, NSW 2550 **REGION** South Coast Zone
T (02) 6492 3006 **F** (02) 6492 5330 **WWW**.grevilleawines.com **OPEN** Sept–May Mon–Fri 9–5, w'ends 10–5; June–Aug 7 days 10–4
WINEMAKER Nicola Collins **EST.** 1980 **CASES** 2000
A tourist-oriented winery which successfully sells all its production through the cellar door and local restaurants. The consistency and quality of the wines has improved out of sight; a further label redesign has also lifted the appeal.

Grey Sands

Cnr Kerrisons Road/Frankford Highway, Glengarry, Tas 7275 **REGION** Northern Tasmania
T(03) 6396 1167 **F**(03) 6396 1153 **WWW**.greysands.com.au **OPEN** Last Sunday of each month 10–5,
or by appt
WINEMAKER Bob Richter **EST.** 1989 **CASES** 800
Bob and Rita Richter began the establishment of Grey Sands in 1988, slowly increasing the plantings
over the ensuing 10 years to the present total of 2.5 ha. The ultra-high density of 8900 vines per ha
reflects the experience gained by the Richters during a 3-year stay in England, during which time
they visited many vineyards across Europe, and Bob Richter's graduate diploma in wine from
Roseworthy College.

ȲȲȲȲ **Pinot Gris 2005** A clean bouquet; well-balanced and constructed; however, as is usual
with the variety, struggles for personality, the pear and musk not as convincing as the
lemony acidity on the finish. Screwcap. 13.8° alc. **RATING** 88 **DRINK** 2009 $ 26
Late Release Pinot Gris 2003 A late release of the wine first sold in early 2004. Does
show the variety can stand up to cellaring with surprisingly little change, particularly with
the screwcap. Clean mineral and citrus. **RATING** 88 **DRINK** Now $ 26
Merlot 2003 A somewhat schizophrenic movement from sweet cassis aromas on the
bouquet and fore-palate to ultra-savoury tannins and flavours on the finish. Difficult to
predict how the elements will resolve themselves. Cork. 13.2° alc. **RATING** 88 **DRINK** 2010
$ 30

Griffin Wines

PO Box 221, Clarendon, SA 5157 **REGION** Adelaide Hills
T(08) 8377 1300 **F**(08) 8377 3015 **WWW**.griffinwines.com **OPEN** Not
WINEMAKER Phil Christiansen, Shaw & Smith, Kangarilla Road **EST.** 1997 **CASES** 1500
The Griffin family (Trevor, Tim, Mark and Val) planted 31.2 ha of pinot noir, chardonnay, sauvignon
blanc, merlot and shiraz in 1997, having owned the property for over 30 years. It is situated 3 km
from Kuitpo Hall; its 350m elevation gives sweeping views south down the valley below. Part of the
grape production is sold; a small amount is made offsite, and sold through the website.

ȲȲȲȲȲ **No. 1 Adelaide Hills Shiraz 2002** Dense colour; rich, ripe, focused, intense blackberry,
spice and licorice; fine, lingering tannins; subtle oak. High-quality cork. **RATING** 94
DRINK 2015 $ 25

ȲȲȲȲȲ **No. 3 Adelaide Hills Pinot Noir 2003** Fragrant, complex and spicy aromas and flavours;
cherry, strawberry and a twist of lemon peel; good length and balance. High-quality cork.
RATING 91 **DRINK** 2008 $ 22
No. 2 Adelaide Hills Sauvignon Blanc 2005 Spotlessly clean and fresh; gentle
passionfruit and gooseberry, with skein of sweetness throughout; very approachable.
Screwcap. 13° alc. **RATING** 90 **DRINK** Now $ 20
No. 4 Adelaide Hills Merlot 2003 Clearly articulated varietal character; ripe berry fruit
laced through with hints of black olive, spice and earth; extract and oak well handled.
High-quality cork. **RATING** 90 **DRINK** 2013 $ 22

ȲȲȲȲ **No. 3 Adelaide Hills Pinot Noir 2004** Good colour; sweet varietal cherry and plum fruit
on the medium-bodied palate; just a little too ripe. Screwcap. 14.5° alc. **RATING** 89
DRINK 2010 $ 25
No. 5 Adelaide Hills Unwooded Chardonnay 2005 Citrussy nectarine aromas and
flavours; crunchy acidity lengthens the palate and finish. Screwcap. 13° alc. **RATING** 88
DRINK 2008 $ 15
No. 1 Adelaide Hills Shiraz 2003 A spicy/cedary/savoury style which largely belies its
alcohol until the sweet fruit builds on the back-palate. Cork. 15° alc. **RATING** 88
DRINK 2009 $ 25

ȲȲȲȲ **No. 2 Adelaide Hills Sauvignon Blanc 2004** **RATING** 85 **DRINK** Now $ 18
No. 6 Adelaide Hills Chardonnay 2004 **RATING** 85 **DRINK** Now $ 15

Grosset ★★★★★

King Street, Auburn, SA 5451 **REGION** Clare Valley
T (08) 8849 2175 **F** (08) 8849 2292 **WWW**.grosset.com.au **OPEN** Wed–Sun 10–5 from 1st week of
September for approx 6 weeks
WINEMAKER Jeffrey Grosset **EST**. 1981 **CASES** 10 000
Jeffrey Grosset served part of his apprenticeship at the vast Lindeman Karadoc winery, moving from
the largest to one of the smallest when he established Grosset Wines in its old stone winery. He crafts
the wines with the utmost care from grapes grown to the most exacting standards; all need a certain
amount of time in bottle to achieve their ultimate potential, not the least the Rieslings and Gaia,
which are among Australia's best examples of their kind. He is also a passionate advocate of the use of
screwcaps on all wines. Exports to all major markets mean a continuous shortage of the wines.

ΥΥΥΥΥ **Semillon Sauvignon Blanc 2005** Intense herb, spice, and asparagus aromas; a
beautifully flavoured and structured palate, building fruit intensity all the way through to
the long finish. Clare Semillon/Adelaide Hills Sauvignon Blanc. Screwcap. 13° alc.
RATING 96 **DRINK** 2009 $ 30
Piccadilly Chardonnay 2004 Brilliant green-yellow; fine, elegant and intense; long and
very pure nectarine and grapefruit; immaculate oak handling. Screwcap. 13.5° alc.
RATING 96 **DRINK** 2014 $ 49.50
Pinot Noir 2004 Very good colour; spotlessly clean dark plum and black cherry aromas; a
classy wine, more concentrated than many, though by no means big; excellent use of oak.
Screwcap. 14° alc. **RATING** 95 **DRINK** 2011 $ 59.50

ΥΥΥΥΥ **Gaia 2003** Bright colour; spice, berry and earth aromas and flavours; fruit-driven style;
fine tannins; 75% Cabernet Sauvignon/15% Cabernet Franc/10% Merlot. Screwcap.
14° alc. **RATING** 93 **DRINK** 2013 $ 53

Grove Estate Wines ★★★★★

Murringo Road, Young, NSW 2594 **REGION** Hilltops
T (02) 6382 6999 **F** (02) 6382 4527 **WWW**.groveestate.com.au **OPEN** W'ends 10–5, or by appt
WINEMAKER Clonakilla (Tim Kirk), Madrez Wine Services (Chris Derrez) **EST**. 1989 **CASES** 3000
A partnership of Brian Mullany, John Kirkwood and Mark Flanders has established a 30-ha vineyard
planted to semillon, chardonnay, merlot, shiraz, cabernet sauvignon and zinfandel. Some of the
grapes are sold (principally to Southcorp), but an increasing amount of very good and interesting
wine is contract-made for the Grove Estate label. Exports to the UK.

ΥΥΥΥΥ **Hilltops Semillon 2005** A powerful and aromatic bouquet; excellent restraint and focus
on a long and crisp palate; very good balance. Screwcap. **RATING** 94 **DRINK** 2012 $ 17
Cellar Block Shiraz 2004 Deep colour; powerful dark fruits and spice; integrated oak;
good tannins and length. Quality cork. Gold medal National Wine Show '05. Cork.
RATING 94 **DRINK** 2013 $ 30

ΥΥΥΥ **Hilltops Sangiovese 2004** Good colour; blackberry and black cherry fruit with heaps of
spice and powdery tannins; nice touch of oak sweetness. Cork. 14.5° alc. **RATING** 89
DRINK 2010 $ 19
Hilltops Semillon Frontignac NV Racy, spicy, tangy; a sweet mid-palate and bone-dry
finish. Summer spritzer. Muscat de Beaumes-de-Venise-style. Cork. 18.5° alc. **RATING** 87
DRINK Now $ 18

ΥΥΥΥ **Basazi Barbera Zinfandel Sangiovese 2004** **RATING** 85 **DRINK** 2008 $ 17

Grove Hill NR

120 Old Norton Summit Road, Norton Summit, SA 5136 **REGION** Adelaide Hills
T (08) 8390 1437 **F** (08) 8390 1437 **OPEN** Sunday 11–5, or by appt
WINEMAKER Neville Falkenberg (Contract) **EST**. 1978 **CASES** 500
Grove Hill is a heritage property established in 1846; the original homestead and outbuildings have
been held by the same family since that time. Very tight, slow-developing wines.

Growlers Gully

NR

354 Shaws Road, Merton, Vic 3715 **REGION** Upper Goulburn
T (03) 5778 9615 **F** (03) 5778 9615 **OPEN** W'ends & public hols 10–5, or by appt
WINEMAKER MasterWineMakers **EST.** 1997 **CASES** 380
Les and Wendy Oates began the establishment of the Growlers Gully vineyard in 1997, extending it in 1998 to a total of 4 ha of shiraz and 1 ha of cabernet sauvignon. It sits at an elevation of 375m on fertile brown clay loam soil. A rammed-earth cellar door sales outlet offers light meals and barbecue facilities.

Guichen Bay Vineyards

★★★

PO Box 582, Newport, NSW 2106 **REGION** Mount Benson
T (02) 9997 6677 **F** (02) 9997 6177 **WWW**.guichenbay.com.au **OPEN** At Mount Benson Tourist & Wine Information Centre
WINEMAKER Cape Jaffa Wines (Derek Hooper), Ralph Fowler Wines (Sarah Squires) **EST.** 2003
CASES 800
Guichen Bay Vineyards is one of 3 adjacent vineyards known collectively as the Mount Benson Community Vineyards. Between 1997 and 2001, 120 ha of vines were planted to chardonnay, sauvignon blanc, shiraz, merlot and cabernet sauvignon. While the major part of the production is sold under long-term contracts, the 3 owners have obtained a producer's licence, and a small quantity of grapes is held back and made by local winemakers under the Guichen Bay Vineyards label.

ŸŸŸŸ **Force Ten Mount Benson Shiraz 2004** Light- to medium-bodied; clean, fresh blackberry, plum and cherry; subtle oak. Screwcap. 13.3° alc. **RATING** 88 **DRINK** 2009 $18

ŸŸŸŸ **Force Ten Mount Benson Cabernet Sauvignon 2004** **RATING** 85 **DRINK** Now $18

 # Gypsy Creek Winery

NR

43 School Road, Labertouche, Vic 3816 (postal) **REGION** Gippsland
T (03) 5628 7679 **F** (03) 5628 7679 **OPEN** Not
WINEMAKER Jeff Wright **EST.** 1997 **CASES** 800
Sam Dardha arrived in Australia 35 years ago with wine in his veins from growing up in the Macedonia/Northern Greece/Albania sector of Europe. He and wife Mary purchased the property in 1995, planting 1 ha each of chardonnay and cabernet sauvignon and 0.5 ha each of shiraz and pinot noir in 1997. Up to and including 2003, all the grapes were sold, the first commercial vintage following in 2004.

Haan Wines

★★★★★

Siegersdorf Road, Tanunda, SA 5352 **REGION** Barossa Valley
T (08) 8562 4590 **F** (08) 8562 4590 **WWW**.haanwines.com.au **OPEN** Not
WINEMAKER Mark Jamieson (Contract) **EST.** 1993 **CASES** 4500
Hans and Fransien Haan established their business in 1993 when they acquired a 19-ha vineyard near Tanunda (since extended to 36.7 ha). The primary focus is on Merlot, in particular the luxury Merlot Prestige, supported by Semillon, Viognier and Shiraz. Exports to all major markets.

ŸŸŸŸŸ **Viognier Prestige 2005** Honeysuckle and apricot aromas proclaim the variety; a perfectly poised and balanced palate brings touches of honey and lemon butter; no alcohol heat; 125 dozen made. Screwcap. 14.5° alc. **RATING** 95 **DRINK** Now $35

Wilhelmus 2003 Colour showing some development; cedar, earth and mocha surround the core of sweet and black fruits; pleasurable mouthfeel and balance; silky tannins. Cork. 14.5° alc. **RATING** 95 **DRINK** 2016 $50

Merlot Prestige 2003 As usual, shows clear varietal character, with a mix of black olive, plum and tobacco on the bouquet and the medium-bodied palate. The French oak is just a little over the top. Cork. 14.5° alc. **RATING** 94 **DRINK** 2015 $45

ŸŸŸŸ **Hanenhof Semillon 2005** A big, solid wine; a mix of the old and new approach to Semillon in the Barossa Valley, but lower alcohol would have been better still. Screwcap. 13° alc. **RATING** 87 **DRINK** 2008 $19

Hackersley

Ferguson Road, Dardanup, WA 6236 **REGION** Geographe
T (08) 9384 6247 **F** (08) 9383 3364 **WWW**.hackersley.com.au **OPEN** Thurs–Sun 10–4
WINEMAKER Tony Davis (Contract) **EST.** 1998 **CASES** 1200
Hackersley is a partnership between the Ovens, Stacey and Hewitt families, friends since their
university days, and with (so they say) the misguided belief that growing and making their own wine
would be cheaper than buying it. They found what they describe as a 'little piece of paradise in the
Ferguson Valley just south of Dardanup', and in 1998 they planted a little under 8 ha, extended since
then to 11.5 ha of the mainstream varieties; interestingly, they turned their back on chardonnay. Most
of the crop is sold to Houghton, but a small quantity is made for release under the Hackersley label.

ŸŸŸŸŸ **Merlot 2004** Good depth to colour; substantial texture and structure but right in the slot;
lovely black fruits with touches of olive and spice. Cork. **RATING** 95 **DRINK** 2012 $ 24

ŸŸŸŸŸ **Ferguson Valley Cabernet Sauvignon 2004** Earthy blackcurrant varietal aromas; a fluid,
medium-bodied palate of cassis and blackcurrant; fine, ripe tannins, good length. Cork.
RATING 93 **DRINK** 2012 $ 24
Victor Shiraz Cabernet 2004 Attractive medium-bodied wine with plum, blackberry
and chocolate; excellent mouthfeel and good oak; 60% Shiraz/35% Cabernet
Sauvignon/5% Merlot. 14.5° alc. **RATING** 92 **DRINK** 2014 $ 28

ŸŸŸŸ **Semillon 2005** A crisp, grassy, mineral, herbal mix; finely delineated mouthfeel; poor
cork a real concern. Drink asap. Cork. **RATING** 89 **DRINK** Now $ 22
Ferguson Valley Shiraz 2004 A light- to medium-bodied mix of red and black cherry,
mint, leaf, spice and oak proclaiming its cool-grown provenance. Cork. **RATING** 89
DRINK 2010 $ 24
Ferguson Valley Sauvignon Blanc 2005 Clean, correct, crispy minerally bouquet and
palate; not a lot of effusive fruit, though. Cork. **RATING** 88 **DRINK** Now $ 18

Hahndorf Hill Winery

Lot 10 Pains Road, Hahndorf, SA 5245 **REGION** Adelaide Hills
T (08) 8388 7512 **F** (08) 8388 7618 **WWW**.hahndorfhillwinery.com.au **OPEN** 7 days 10–5
WINEMAKER Geoff Weaver (Consultant) **EST.** 2002 **CASES** 3500
Larry Jacobs and Marc Dobson, both originally from South Africa, purchased Hahndorf Hill Winery
in January 2002. Jacobs gave up a career in intensive care medicine in 1988 when he purchased an
abandoned property in Stellenbosch, and proceeded to establish one of Capetown's best-known
sauvignon blanc producers, Mulderbosch. When Mulderbosch was purchased at the end of 1996, the
pair migrated to Australia and eventually found their way to Hahndorf Hill. A new winery was
upgraded to deal with the ultra-strict effluent disposal requirements of the Adelaide Hills. Rare
German varieties trollinger and lemberger were planted by the prior owners.

ŸŸŸŸŸ **Adelaide Hills Shiraz 2003** Fine, spicy, savoury nuances to plum and blackberry fruit;
has excellent length, texture and balance; lovely finish and aftertaste; 380 cases made.
Cork. 14° alc. **RATING** 94 **DRINK** 2015 $ 26

ŸŸŸŸŸ **Adelaide Hills Chardonnay 2003** Elegant, light-bodied wine; melon, apple, with touches
of fig and cream; perfectly judged barrel ferment and malolactic inputs; delicate fruit
developing impressively. Cork. 13.5° alc. **RATING** 93 **DRINK** 2011 $ 23
Adelaide Hills White Mischief 2005 An aromatic, tangy wine with sauvignon blanc
doing most of the talking; good length and balance; an unwooded blend of Sauvignon
Blanc/Pinot Gris/Chardonnay. Screwcap. 13.5° alc. **RATING** 90 **DRINK** Now $ 17.50

ŸŸŸŸ **Adelaide Hills Sauvignon Blanc 2005** Very pale straw-green; clean, fresh and crisp; the
fruit is just a little too delicate. Screwcap. 13° alc. **RATING** 88 **DRINK** 2009 $ 18.50
Adelaide Hills Trollinger & Lemberger Rose 2005 Bright fuchsia; fresh small berry
fruits; has resisted the temptation to sweeten the finish, although it does shorten slightly.
Screwcap. 13.5° alc. **RATING** 87 **DRINK** Now $ 17

Haig   NR

Square Mile Road, Mount Gambier, SA 5290 **REGION** Mount Gambier
T (08) 8725 5414 **F** (08) 8725 5414 **OPEN** 7 days 11–5
WINEMAKER Bochara Wines **EST.** 1982 **CASES** 1000
The 4 ha of estate vineyards are planted on the rich volcanic soils near the slopes of the famous Blue
Lake of Mt Gambier.

Hainault   NR

255 Walnut Road, Bickley, WA 6076 **REGION** Perth Hills
T (08) 9293 8339 **www**.hainault.com.au **OPEN** W'ends & public hols 11–5, or by appt
WINEMAKER Tony Davis (Contract) **EST.** 1980 **CASES** 2200
Lyn and Michael Sykes became the owners of Hainault in 2002, after previous owner Bill Mackey
and wife Vicki headed off elsewhere. The 11 ha of close-planted vines are hand-pruned and hand-
picked, and the pinot noir is very sensibly used to make a sparkling wine, rather than a table wine.

Halifax Wines   ★★★★

Lot 501 Binney Road, McLaren Vale, Willunga, SA 5172 **REGION** McLaren Vale
T (08) 8557 1000 **F** (08) 8367 0333 **www**.halifaxwines.com.au **OPEN** By appt
WINEMAKER Peter Butcher **EST.** 2000 **CASES** 700
Halifax is owned and operated by Elizabeth Tasker (background in advertising and marketing) and
Peter Butcher (20+ years in the wine industry, in marketing, sales, distribution, education and
winemaking). A passionate proponent of wine's 'sense of place', Peter has worked with some of
Australia's most well-known winemakers — Jeffrey Grosset, Peter Leske, Mike Farmilo and Peter
Gago — and has also been influenced by visits to France and Italy. Currently produces a single-
vineyard Shiraz from 4 ha of estate plantings, supplemented by small quantities of grenache (50-
year-old vines) and cabernet sauvignon (40-year-old vines) added to the roster in 2006. Exports to
the US and Hong Kong.

▼▼▼▼▽ **McLaren Vale Shiraz 2002** Medium-bodied; elegant, spicy overtones to both bouquet
and palate; attractive plum and licorice flavours; good handling of oak and tannins. Cork.
RATING 92 **DRINK** 2012 $ 35

▼▼▼▼ **McLaren Vale Shiraz 2004** Medium-bodied; earthy/savoury nuances to both bouquet
and palate along with blackberry and plum fruit. Screwcap. 14.5° alc. **RATING** 89
DRINK Now $ 32
McLaren Vale Shiraz 2003 Ripe plum, blackberry and chocolate mix; some spicy
tannins; medium-bodied. Screwcap. 14.5° alc. **RATING** 88 **DRINK** 2013 $ 32

Halina Brook Estate   NR

Bindoon Moora Road, Bindoon WA 6502 **REGION** Perth Hills
T (08) 9576 2030 **OPEN** By appt
WINEMAKER Rob Marshall (Contract) **EST.** 1999 **CASES** NA
The Halina Brook Estate cellar door is in an old shearing shed with panoramic views of the Bindoon
area. A little over 16 ha of verdelho, shiraz, chenin blanc and grenache is planted.

Hamelin Bay   ★★★★★

McDonald Road, Karridale, WA 6288 **REGION** Margaret River
T (08) 9758 6779 **F** (08) 9758 6779 **www**.hbwines.com.au **OPEN** 7 days 10–5
WINEMAKER Julian Scott **EST.** 1992 **CASES** 15 000
The 25-ha Hamelin Bay vineyard was established by the Drake-Brockman family. The initial releases
were contract-made, but a winery with cellar door sales facility was opened in 2000; this has enabled
an increase in production. Exports to all major markets.

▼▼▼▼▼ **Five Ashes Vineyard Semillon Sauvignon Blanc 2005** A potent and powerful wine, the
semillon driving the considerable length and line. Overall, great mouthfeel. Screwcap.
12° alc. **RATING** 94 **DRINK** 2009 $ 19

Five Ashes Vineyard Chardonnay 2004 Controlled funky barrel ferment inputs drive the bouquet; delicately sweet stone fruit and melon in the mouth; very good acidity to close. Screwcap. 13.5° alc. RATING 94 DRINK 2012 $ 26

Sauvignon Blanc 2005 Very fine, reserved bouquet; great line and length to palate, with lemony acidity; fresh as a daisy. RATING 94 DRINK Now $ 19

ΨΨΨΨ **Five Ashes Vineyard Reserve Chardonnay 2004** More obvious toasty/nutty oak, and a supple, round, peachy palate. In very different style to the varietal, though of similar appeal (for me). Screwcap. 13.5° alc. RATING 93 DRINK 2011 $ 43

Five Ashes Vineyard Shiraz 2003 Good colour; medium-bodied, with spicy/peppery edges to fresh blackberry and plum fruit; well-controlled tannin and oak. Cork. 13.5° alc. RATING 93 DRINK 2013 $ 29

Five Ashes Vineyard Reserve Shiraz 2003 Slightly more advanced colour; interesting parallels to the Reserve Chardonnay; the oak component is more obvious, and it would appear to have spent a longer time in oak gaining complexity, but with fractional loss of freshness. Cork. 13.5° alc. RATING 92 DRINK 2013 $ 43

Five Ashes Vineyard Cabernet Sauvignon 2002 Developed colour; fragrant blackcurrant, earth, spice and chocolate; excellent medium-bodied mouthfeel, with a silky texture and fine tannins. Cork. 14° alc. RATING 92 DRINK 2012 $ 29

ΨΨΨΨ **Five Ashes Vineyard Sauvignon Blanc 2005** Potent, faintly sweaty varietal bouquet; a solid palate with plenty of depth and richness. A small percentage is barrel-fermented. Screwcap. 13° alc. RATING 89 DRINK Now $ 19

ΨΨΨΨ **Rampant White 2005** RATING 86 DRINK Now $ 17
Rampant Red 2003 RATING 86 DRINK 2008 $ 17

Hamilton's Ewell Vineyards ★★★

Siegersdorf Vineyard, Barossa Valley Way, Nuriootpa, SA 5355 REGION Barossa Valley
T (08) 8231 0088 F (08) 8231 0355 WWW.hamiltonewell.com.au OPEN 7 days 10–5
WINEMAKER Robert Hamilton EST. 1837 CASES 11 000
Mark Hamilton, an Adelaide lawyer by profession, is a sixth-generation direct descendant of Richard Hamilton, who arrived in SA in 1838 (a year after the State was proclaimed) and made his first wine in 1841. Hamilton's Ewell Vineyards remained in the family until 1979, when it was acquired by Mildara Blass, much to Mark Hamilton's dismay. Since 1991 he has set about building another Hamilton wine business by a series of astute vineyard acquisitions, and by buying back the name Hamilton's Ewell from Mildara. Most of the grapes are sold, but there is scope to increase production. Exports to the UK, the US and other major markets.

ΨΨΨΨ **Sturt River Chardonnay 2005** RATING 86 DRINK Now $ 14
Ewell Moselle 2004 RATING 84 DRINK Now $ 14

Hamiltons Bluff NR

Longs Corner Road, Canowindra, NSW 2804 REGION Cowra
T (02) 6344 2079 F (02) 6344 2165 WWW.hamiltonsbluff.com.au OPEN By appt
WINEMAKER Alasdair Sutherland (Contract) EST. 1995 CASES 2000
Hamiltons Bluff is owned and operated by the Andrews family, which planted 45 ha of vines in 1995, with the first crop in 1998. Cellar door sales opened in early 1999, heralding a new stage of development for the Cowra region. Chardonnay, Shiraz, Sangiovese and sparkling wines are made. Exports to the US.

Hanging Rock Winery ★★★★★

88 Jim Road, Newham, Vic 3442 REGION Macedon Ranges
T (03) 5427 0542 F (03) 5427 0310 WWW.hangingrock.com.au OPEN 7 days 10–5
WINEMAKER John Ellis EST. 1982 CASES 40 000
The Macedon area has proved very marginal in spots, and the Hanging Rock vineyards, with their lovely vista towards the Rock, are no exception. John Ellis has thus elected to source additional

grapes from various parts of Vic to produce an interesting and diverse range of varietals at different price points. The low-priced Rock series, with its bold packaging, has replaced the Picnic wines. Exports to the UK and other major markets.

ŸŸŸŸŸ **Macedon Cuvee NV** XI. An elegant wine; long, lively and citrussy, with a crisp clean finish, and perfect dosage; 80% 2000, remainder reserves back to 1987; 51 months on lees. **RATING** 96 **DRINK** 2009 $ 45

Macedon Cuvee (Late Disgorged) NV Six. Excellent fine mousse attests to its very long lees contact, as does its immaculate balance despite its low dosage of only 2 grams per litre of sugar. The complex bready/biscuity characters of the palate are reminiscent of Bollinger, and very good acidity stretches out the long, lingering finish. **RATING** 96 **DRINK** 2008 $ 100

Heathcote Shiraz 2003 Glorious colour; big, rich, condensed fruit and ample tannins; floods the mouth with flavour. **RATING** 95 **DRINK** 2013 $ 55

The Jim Jim Sauvignon Blanc 2005 Attractive gooseberry and citrus aromas and flavours; great drive on a vibrant finish and aftertaste. Screwcap. **RATING** 94 **DRINK** Now $ 27

Kilfara Pinot Noir 2004 Bright purple-red; an interesting wine, with lively, bright plum and spice fruit; particularly good line and mouthfeel, very well-made. Surprise package. Screwcap. 13.5° alc. **RATING** 94 **DRINK** 2011 $ 18

Cambrian Rise Heathcote Shiraz 2003 Great colour; a powerful, rich and focused array of lush black fruits in full-on regional style; does not go over the top. Diam. 14.5° alc. **RATING** 94 **DRINK** 2023 $ 27

ŸŸŸŸŸ **Rowbottoms Heathcote Shiraz 2003** Great colour; powerful black fruits with a savoury edge; very interesting how slightly lower alcohol manifests itself in flavour and mouthfeel, more to '02 than '03 in style. Diam. 14° alc. **RATING** 93 **DRINK** 2018 $ 33

Macedon Brut Rose NV Pale pink; a totally seductive rose style; strawberry fruit and perfect acidity/dosage. Estate-grown pinot noir. 12.5° alc. **RATING** 92 **DRINK** 2010 $ 27

Strathbogie Ranges Chardonnay 2004 Light green-straw; nectarine and citrus fruit seamlessly woven through new French oak; while only light- to medium-bodied, has good length and acidity. Screwcap. 13.5° alc. **RATING** 90 **DRINK** 2010 $ 18

Amaroo Farm Big Rivers Shiraz 2003 Very good colour; remarkable concentration and density of fruit given the region and vintage; lots of plummy fruit flavour, soft tannins and balanced American oak. Cork. 14.5° alc. **RATING** 90 **DRINK** 2013 $ 27

ŸŸŸŸ **Tarzali Strathbogie Ranges Riesling 2003** Herb, mineral and spice aromas; bright, crisp and minerally with just a twitch of lime; dry style. Screwcap. 12° alc. **RATING** 89 **DRINK** 2013 $ 25

Amaroo Farm Shiraz Mourvedre 2003 Bright hue, particularly for its age; light- to medium-bodied, with fresh, lively red fruits and some tannin support from the mourvedre. Diam. 12.5° alc. **RATING** 89 **DRINK** 2008 $ 27

Yin Barum Merlot Cabernet Franc 2003 A quite elegant, medium-bodied wine; fruit-driven by redcurrant and raspberry flavours; light tannins. Cork. 14.5° alc. **RATING** 89 **DRINK** 2010 $ 27

The Jim Jim Gewurztraminer 2005 Clean, crisp and fresh; well-made; still to flesh out and develop varietal fruit character, which it will do with time. Screwcap. **RATING** 87 **DRINK** 2008 $ 25

ŸŸŸŸ **The Jim Jim Pinot Gris 2005** **RATING** 86 **DRINK** Now $ 25

Hanging Tree Wines NR

Lot 2 O'Connors Road, Pokolbin, NSW 2325 **REGION** Lower Hunter Valley
T (02) 4998 6601 **F** (02) 4998 6602 **www**.hangingtreewines.com.au **OPEN** By appt
WINEMAKER Andrew Thomas (Contract) **EST.** 2003 **CASES** 1250
Hanging Tree Wines is the former Van De Scheur Estate. A little under 3 ha of semillon, chardonnay, shiraz and cabernet sauvignon provide the grapes for the wines.

Hankin Estate NR

2 Johnsons Lane, Northwood via Seymour, Vic 3660 **REGION** Goulburn Valley
T (03) 5792 2396 **F** (03) 9353 2927 **OPEN** W'ends & public hols 10–5
WINEMAKER Dr Max Hankin **EST.** 1975 **CASES** 1700

Hankin Estate is now the principal occupation of Dr Max Hankin, who has retired from full-time medical practice. He has had to contend with phylloxera, which decimated the original plantings, but has successfully replanted most of the vineyard.

Hanson-Tarrahill Vineyard ★★★★

49 Cleveland Avenue, Lower Plenty, Vic 3093 (postal) **REGION** Yarra Valley
T (03) 9439 7425 **F** (03) 9439 4217 **OPEN** Not
WINEMAKER Dr Ian Hanson **EST.** 1983 **CASES** 1300

Dental surgeon Ian Hanson planted his first vines in the late 1960s, close to the junction of the Yarra and Plenty Rivers; in 1983 those plantings were extended (with 3000 vines), and in 1988 the Tarrahill property at Yarra Glen was established with a further 4 ha. Hanson is the name which appears most prominently on the labels; Tarrahill Vineyard is in much smaller type. Exports to the UK.

🍷🍷🍷🍷½ **Reserve Yarra Valley Pinot Noir 2002** Developed colour; vibrantly fresh sappy red fruits; long palate; good finish. Cork. 14° alc. **RATING** 92 **DRINK** 2009 **$** 22

LP 2004 Much sweeter, cassis-accented fruit than usual for this blend; pleasing mouthfeel, line and flow. Cabernet Franc (70%)/Cabernet Sauvignon (30%). Cork. 13° alc. **RATING** 90 **DRINK** 2012 **$** 22

🍷🍷🍷🍷 **Yarra Valley Cabernet Sauvignon 2004** Bright red-purple; fresh, medium-bodied cassis and blackcurrant fruit; the tannins just a little assertive, and needed some fining. Time may help. Procork. 13° alc. **RATING** 89 **DRINK** 2013 **$** 22

Yarra Valley Cabernet Sauvignon Cabernet Franc 2002 Very cedary, savoury, earthy traditional Hanson style, accentuated by the very cool '02 vintage. Cork. 13.5° alc. **RATING** 87 **DRINK** 2010 **$** 22

Happs ★★★★★

571 Commonage Road, Dunsborough, WA 6281 **REGION** Margaret River
T (08) 9755 3300 **F** (08) 9755 3846 **www**.happs.com.au **OPEN** 7 days 10–5
WINEMAKER Erl Happ, Mark Warren **EST.** 1978 **CASES** 16 000

Former schoolteacher turned potter and winemaker Erl Happ is an iconoclast and compulsive experimenter. Many of the styles he makes are unusual, and the future is likely to be even more so: the Karridale vineyard planted in 1994 has no less than 28 different varieties established. Merlot has been a winery specialty for a decade. Exports to the US.

🍷🍷🍷🍷🍷 **Three Hills Charles Andreas 2003** Superb colour; a very different blend to the '04; medium- to full-bodied, intense and long palate, the softness of malbec sustained by the other components without losing suppleness; lovely tannin and oak support. Malbec/Merlot/Cabernet Franc/Cabernet Sauvignon. **RATING** 95 **DRINK** 2015 **$** 36

Three Hills Shiraz 2004 Medium- to full-bodied; rich, textured blackberry, licorice and bitter chocolate; fine-grained tannins and good oak; excellent mouthfeel and balance. Cork. 14.1° alc. **RATING** 94 **DRINK** 2014 **$** 55

Three Hills Merlot 2004 Good colour; medium-bodied, supple and smooth; raspberry and cassis fruit with touches of savoury spice; a marvellously elegant merlot. Cork. 14° alc. **RATING** 94 **DRINK** 2011 **$** 35

Three Hills Charles Andreas 2004 Full-bodied; very powerful and concentrated, and, for the moment, forbidding; a rich well of black fruits and tannins, the latter balanced but yet to soften and integrate; good oak; 500 cases made. Cabernet Sauvignon/Merlot/Malbec/Cabernet Franc/Petit Verdot. Cork. **RATING** 94 **DRINK** 2020 **$** 36

ŢŢŢŢŢ **Three Hills Grenache Shiraz Mataro 2004** Good colour; a full-bodied, concentrated wine, radically different from SA blends; has a strong tannin backbone to support the plum and raspberry red fruits; 290 cases made. Cork. 15° alc. **RATING** 93 **DRINK** 2014 **$** 25

Margaret River Cabernet Merlot 2002 An attractive mix of blackberry and cassis; good structure, texture and balance; refined oak and tannins. Cork. **RATING** 92 **DRINK** 2012 **$** 20

Margaret River Sauvignon Blanc 2004 Medium-bodied; complex texture courtesy of the touch of barrel ferment; well-balanced, if light, gooseberry fruit; alternative style. Cork. 13.5° alc. **RATING** 90 **DRINK** Now **$** 15

Margaret River Semillon Sauvignon Blanc 2005 Fresh and crisp grassy/minerally aromas and flavours; bright, clean, dry finish and aftertaste. Cork. 13° alc. **RATING** 90 **DRINK** Now **$** 16

Three Hills Eva Marie Semillon Sauvignon Blanc 2004 A potent, powerful wine with multiple winemaker inputs via barrel fermentation of cloudy juice, lees contact and stirring. Certainly succeeds in altering the normal profile; 104 cases made. Cork. 13.5° alc. **RATING** 90 **DRINK** Now **$** 25

Margaret River Chardonnay 2004 Fragrant and elegant, light- to medium-bodied, fruit-driven style; nectarine, melon and citrus supported by subtle French oak; long finish. Cork. **RATING** 90 **DRINK** 2009 **$** 20

Three Hills Sangiovese 2004 Light- to medium-bodied; spicy cherry and plum fruit; persistent but fine tannins; good length. Cork. 14.5° alc. **RATING** 90 **DRINK** 2009 **$** 28

ŢŢŢŢ **Three Hills Viognier 2004** Another powerful wine, the alcohol more or less immediately apparent, but so is the ginger, apricot kernel and lychee varietal fruit. Cork. 14.5° alc. **RATING** 89 **DRINK** 2008 **$** 35

Margaret River Shiraz 2002 Savoury, earthy edges to medium-bodied black fruits and a touch of bitter chocolate; good tannin structure. Cork. 13.5° alc. **RATING** 89 **DRINK** 2012 **$** 25

Harbord Wines ★★★☆

PO Box 41, Stockwell, SA 5355 **REGION** Barossa Valley
T (08) 8562 2598 **F** (08) 8562 2598 **www**.harbordwines.com.au **OPEN** Not
WINEMAKER Roger Harbord **EST.** 2003 **CASES** 3000
Roger Harbord is a well-known and respected Barossa winemaker, with over 20 years' experience, the last 10 as chief winemaker for Cellarmaster Wines, Normans and Ewinexchange. He has set up his own virtual winery as a complementary activity; the grapes are contract-grown, and he leases winery space and equipment to make and mature the wines. Exports to the UK, the US and other major markets.

ŢŢŢŢ **Mt Crawford Pinot Noir 2004** Strong red-purple; abundant black plum studded with splashes of spice; medium- to full-bodied, with slightly ragged tannins; may improve. Screwcap. 13° alc. **RATING** 89 **DRINK** 2009 **$** 30

The Tendril Barossa Valley Shiraz 2003 Sweet black fruits, chocolate and mocha; ripe tannins; seems higher in alcohol than is the case. 14.5° alc. **RATING** 89 **DRINK** 2013 **$** 35

Harcourt Valley Vineyards ★★★★☆

3339 Calder Highway, Harcourt, Vic 3453 **REGION** Bendigo
T (03) 5474 2223 **F** (03) 5474 2223 **www**.harcourtvalley.com.au **OPEN** 7 days 11–5, (11–6 during daylight savings)
WINEMAKER Barbara Broughton, Adam Marks (Consultant) **EST.** 1976 **CASES** 2000
Established by Ray and Barbara Broughton, the vineyard was handed over to John and Barbara Livingstone in 1998. Barbara's Shiraz was created by Barbara Broughton, but with the arrival of the new 'Barbara' it lives on as the flagship of the vineyard. The Livingstones planted a further 2 ha of shiraz on north-facing slopes with the aid of 2 sons, who, says Barbara, 'have since bolted, vowing never to have anything to do with vineyards, but having developed fine palates'. John Livingstone died in mid-2004, but Barbara continues her role of viticulturist; winemaking is now in the hands of Barbara Broughton and sons Kye and Quinn under the direction of Adam Marks of Bress.

ŶŶŶŶŶ **Chardonnay 2005** A medium-bodied, well-made and harmonious wine; gentle and seamless peach, melon and French oak run through the palate, relatively low alcohol giving freshness. Screwcap. 12.8° alc. **RATING** 91 **DRINK** 2010 $ 20

Riesling 2005 Clean, and full of flavour; the touch of sweetness is neatly balanced by minerally acidity, leaving a dry aftertaste. Headed in the direction of the Mosel. Surprise packet. Screwcap. 11.5° alc. **RATING** 90 **DRINK** 2010 $ 16

Barbara's Shiraz 2003 Medium-bodied; strongly spicy, savoury overtones to the fruit; nonetheless, has good mouthfeel and length. Screwcap. 13.3° alc. **RATING** 90 **DRINK** 2018 $ 25

ŶŶŶŶ **Cabernet Sauvignon 2003** Light- to medium-bodied; sweet, slightly jammy/confection flavours, but as with the Shiraz, texture and structure are redeeming features. Diam. 13.5° alc. **RATING** 89 **DRINK** 2010 $ 25

ŶŶŶŶ **Malbec 2004 RATING** 85 **DRINK** Now $ 20

Hardys   ★★★★☆

Reynell Road, Reynella, SA 5161 **REGION** McLaren Vale
T (08) 8392 2222 **F** (08) 8392 2202 **WWW**.hardys.com.au **OPEN** Mon–Fri 10–4.30, Sat 10–4, Sun 11–4, closed public hols
WINEMAKER Peter Dawson, Paul Lapsley, Ed Carr, Tom Newton **EST.** 1853 **CASES** 16 000
The 1992 merger of Thomas Hardy and the Berri Renmano group may well have had some of the elements of a forced marriage when it took place, but the merged group prospered mightily over the next 10 years. So successful was it that a further marriage followed in early 2003, with Constellation Wines of the US the groom, and BRL Hardy the bride, creating the largest wine group in the world. The Hardys wine brands are many and various, from the lowest price point to the highest, and covering all the major varietals. They also make outstanding Vintage Port and fine, wood-aged Brandy.

ŶŶŶŶŶ **Eileen Hardy Chardonnay 2003** Still light straw-green; amazingly delicate and fresh, the ultimate iron fist in a velvet glove; perfect balance and integration of fruit, barrel ferment, lees contact and malolactic inputs without threatening the fruit. Yarra Valley/Tas/Adelaide Hills. Cork. 13.3° alc. **RATING** 96 **DRINK** 2013 $ 38

Eileen Hardy Shiraz 2002 Retains hue and depth; complex texture and structure; a tapestry of black fruits, chocolate and fine French oak. Cork. 13.9° alc. **RATING** 95 **DRINK** 2020 $ 42

Tintara Shiraz 2000 Strong colour; spice, blackberry, licorice and dark chocolate; excellent mouthfeel, texture and structure; ripe, savoury tannins, balanced and integrated oak. Cork. 14° alc. **RATING** 95 **DRINK** 2015 $ 42

Oomoo McLaren Vale Shiraz 2004 Very rich, luscious red and black fruits, tinged with chocolate. Ripe, well-balanced tannins; dash of oak. Gold medal Sydney Wine Show '06. Cork. **RATING** 94 **DRINK** 2015 $ 12.95

Starvedog Lane Shiraz Viognier 2004 Powerful blackberry fruit lifted by the viognier and by notes of both spice and dark chocolate; ripe tannins, quality oak. **RATING** 94 **DRINK** 2015

Reynell Basket Pressed McLaren Vale Shiraz 2003 Complex, strongly regional wine; black fruits, dark chocolate and high-quality oak handling; uncompromised fruit and varietal character, and mercifully moderate alcohol. Cork. 14.5° alc. **RATING** 94 **DRINK** 2018 $ 40

Reynell McLaren Vale Grenache 2004 Juicy, slippery black (not red, as is more usual) fruits; good structure and gossamer tannins; likely inclusion of 10% or so shiraz. Gold medal National Wine Show '05. Cork. 14.3° alc. **RATING** 94 **DRINK** 2011 $ 32

Starvedog Lane Cabernet Merlot 2004 Totally delicious cassis and blackcurrant fruit, seamless oak and tannins. Gold medal Sydney Wine Show '06. **RATING** 94 **DRINK** 2014

ŶŶŶŶŶ **Starvedog Lane Cabernet Sauvignon 2000** Attractive medium-bodied wine; ripe blackcurrant, plum and sweet oak merge with fine tannins. Cork. 14° alc. **RATING** 93 **DRINK** 2010 $ 27

Sir James Vintage 2002 Bright, fresh, crisp and lively; a mix of citrus, spice and strawberry with creamy malolactic and gentle yeast autolysis characters woven through. **RATING** 92 **DRINK** Now $ 23

TTTT **Padthaway Unwooded Chardonnay 2004** Spotlessly clean; a light mix of stone fruit and grapefruit; has length, and the vivacity so often lacking in unwooded chardonnays. Screwcap. RATING 89 DRINK Now $17

Four Emus Shiraz 2004 A remarkable wine at the price, with quite generous fruit to a light- to medium-bodied frame; soft mouthfeel. Skilled micro-oxygenation at work, one suspects. Screwcap. RATING 89 DRINK Now $9.95

Nottage Hill Cabernet Sauvignon 2004 Clear-cut, ripe varietal blackcurrant/cassis fruit; soft tannins, and nice oak infusion. Another impressive wine at the price from Hardys. Twin top. 13.8° alc. RATING 89 DRINK 2010 $8

Padthaway Cabernet Sauvignon 2001 Clean blackcurrant fruit aromas; a powerful palate, with strong tannins nipping on the finish; needs time to sort itself out. Cork. RATING 88 DRINK 2011 $20

Siegersdorf Riesling 2005 Mineral, citrus and herb aromas; has good length and balance, but a little unfocused. Screwcap. RATING 87 DRINK 2008 $9.75

Sir James Sparkling Pinot Noir Shiraz NV Fragrant spicy (oaky?) aromas; juicy red berry/cherry/strawberry flavours; an interesting blend, pinot the driver. RATING 87 DRINK Now $15

TTTY **Oomoo McLaren Vale Unwooded Chardonnay 2005** RATING 86 DRINK Now $12.95
Nottage Hill Chardonnay 2004 RATING 86 DRINK Now $8.20
Four Emus Rose 2005 RATING 86 DRINK Now $9.95
Nottage Hill Shiraz 2003 RATING 86 DRINK Now $8.20
No Preservatives Added Cabernet Sauvignon 2003 RATING 86 DRINK Now $15.50
Four Emus Chardonnay 2005 RATING 85 DRINK Now $9.95
No Preservatives Added Shiraz 2004 RATING 85 DRINK Now $15.50
Four Emus Cabernet Sauvignon 2004 RATING 84 DRINK Now $9.95

TTT **No Preservatives Added Chardonnay 2004** RATING 83 $15.50
Voyage Gordo Riesling Traminer 2005 RATING 83 $5
Voyage Colombard Semillon Sauvignon Blanc 2005 RATING 83 $5
Regional Reserve Rose 2004 RATING 83 $6.99

Hare's Chase   ★★★★☆

PO Box 46, Melrose Park, SA 5039 REGION Barossa Valley
T (08) 8277 3506 F (08) 8277 3543 WWW.hareschase.com.au OPEN Not
WINEMAKER Peter Taylor EST. 1998 CASES 2500
Hare's Chase is the creation of two families who own a 100-year-old vineyard in the Marananga Valley subregion of the Barossa Valley. The simple, functional winery sits at the top of a rocky hill in the centre of the vineyard, which has some of the best red soil available for dry-grown viticulture. The winemaking arm of the partnership is provided by Peter Taylor, a senior red winemaker with Penfolds for over 20 years, and now Southcorp chief winemaker. Exports to the UK, the US and Switzerland.

TTTTY **Barossa Red Blend 2004** Good colour; medium- to full-bodied, with considerable depth and, unsurprisingly, flavour complexity, though with black cherry and plum shiraz the major player. Shiraz (70%)/Merlot/Cabernet Franc/Tempranillo/Cabernet Sauvignon. Screwcap. 14° alc. RATING 93 DRINK 2014 $14

Harewood Estate   ★★★★★

Scotsdale Road, Denmark, WA 6333 REGION Denmark
T (08) 9840 9078 F (08) 9840 9053 WWW.harewoodestate.com.au OPEN 7 days 10–4
WINEMAKER James Kellie EST. 1988 CASES 4000
In July 2003 James Kellie, who for many years was a winemaker with Howard Park, and was responsible for the contract making of Harewood Wines since 1998, purchased the estate with his father and sister as partners. Events moved quickly thereafter: a 300-tonne winery was constructed, offering both contract winemaking services for the Great Southern region, and the ability to expand the Harewood range to include subregional wines that showcase the region.

ΥΥΥΥΥ **Denmark Sauvignon Blanc Semillon 2005** Utterly compelling line, length and intensity to the mix of grass, herb and snow peas, with tropical nuances in the background; 2 gold medals. Screwcap. 13° alc. **RATING** 95 **DRINK** 2009 $19

Frankland Mount Barker Shiraz 2004 Bright purple-red; perfectly ripened blackberry, spice, licorice and plum fruit on both bouquet and palate; supple mid-palate, then fine, lingering tannins and oak in support roles; 2 trophies. Screwcap. 14.5° alc. **RATING** 95 **DRINK** 2019 $30

Porongurup Riesling 2005 An immaculately clean and precise rendition of riesling; lovely lime and lemon juice flavours; great balance, line and length. Trophy winner. Screwcap. 12° alc. **RATING** 94 **DRINK** 2013 $19

Denmark Chardonnay 2004 Vibrantly fresh and crisp; grapefruit and nectarine, with oak in the background; lingering acidity and a fresh, airy aftertaste. Screwcap. 13.5° alc. **RATING** 94 **DRINK** 2012 $25

ΥΥΥΥΫ **Great Southern Shiraz Cabernet 2004** Ripe, sweet red and black fruits; silky mouthfeel, with a dusting of fine, dark chocolate. Screwcap. **RATING** 93 **DRINK** 2014 $19.50

Mount Barker Cabernet Merlot 2004 Strong colour; controlled, incisive cabernet so typical of Mount Barker; blackcurrant, cassis, cedar and earth run through a long and balanced palate. Screwcap. 14.5° alc. **RATING** 93 **DRINK** 2015 $30

Denmark Pinot Noir 2004 Complex winemaking techniques bear fruit; plum plus spicy, bramble, forest floor notes; good length, and impressive for the region. Screwcap. 14.5° alc. **RATING** 90 **DRINK** 2009 $25

ΥΥΥΥ **Great Southern Classic White 2005** Light- to medium-bodied; clean, fresh gentle fruit salad flavour and soft acidity; no pretensions; unwooded Sauvignon Blanc/Semillon/Chardonnay. Screwcap. 13° alc. **RATING** 88 **DRINK** Now $16

🦆 Harlow Park Estate   NR

72 Baldry's Road, Flinders, Vic 3929 **REGION** Mornington Peninsula
T (03) 5989 0598 **F** (03) 5989 0598 **OPEN** By appt
WINEMAKER Contract **EST.** 1995 **CASES** NFP
Owners John and Kelly Ballis have 26 ha of chardonnay, pinot grigio, pinot noir and merlot, Pinot Noir being the icon wine.

Harmans Ridge Estate   NR

Cnr Bussell Highway/Harmans Mill Road, Wilyabrup, WA 6284 **REGION** Margaret River
T (08) 9755 7409 **F** (08) 9755 7400 **WWW**.harmansridge.com.au **OPEN** 7 days 10.30–5
WINEMAKER Paul Green **EST.** 1999 **CASES** 35 000
Harmans Ridge Estate, with a crush capacity of 1600 tonnes, is primarily a contract maker for larger producers in the Margaret River region which do not have their own winery/winemaker. It does, however, have 2 ha of shiraz, and does make wines under the Harmans Ridge Estate label from grapes grown in Margaret River. Exports to the US and Asia.

Harrington Glen Estate

88 Townsend Road, Glen Aplin, Qld 4381 **REGION** Granite Belt
T (07) 4683 4388 **F** (07) 4683 4388 **OPEN** 7 days 10–4, Sat & public hols 10–5
WINEMAKER Jim Barnes **EST.** 2003 **CASES** 1200
The Ireland family planted 2.8 ha of cabernet sauvignon, shiraz, merlot and verdelho vines in 1997. Red grapes not required for cellar door production are sold to local wine producers, and some white grapes are purchased from other Granite Belt grape producers.

ΥΥΥΥ **Vineyard 88 Reserve Shiraz 2003** A complex wine with some Hunter Valley-like characters to the mix of spicy, leathery, savoury, earthy aromas and flavours. Screwcap. 14.1° alc. **RATING** 89 **DRINK** 2008 $25

Vineyard 88 Reserve Shiraz 2004 Earthy, leathery edges to the sweet bouquet, the medium-bodied palate a replay of the bouquet; just a touch of dead fruit character. Screwcap. 13.7° alc. **RATING** 88 **DRINK** 2009 $ 25

Vineyard 88 Shiraz 2003 Similar to the '03 Reserve, with slightly brighter plum and blackberry fruit, and less oak. Value. Screwcap. 14.1° alc. **RATING** 88 **DRINK** 2009 $ 16

ŸŸŸŸ **Vineyard 88 Cabernet Sauvignon 2003** Light- to medium-bodied; savoury, earthy, chocolatey nuances; good tannin management. Screwcap. 13.1° alc. **RATING** 86 **DRINK** 2008 $ 16

Vineyard 88 Cabernet Shiraz 2003 Chocolate, earth and vanilla, with some spice; typical Harrington Glen tannins, quite ripe, though not bulky. Screwcap. 13.5° alc. **RATING** 86 **DRINK** 2009 $ 16

The Three Graces Rosella Rose 2005 **RATING** 85 **DRINK** Now $ 16

Harris Estate

NR

Paracombe Road, Paracombe, SA 5132 **REGION** Adelaide Hills
T (08) 8380 5353 **F** (08) 8380 5353 **OPEN** By appt
WINEMAKER Trevor Harris **EST.** 1994 **CASES** 1000
Trevor and Sue Harris have established 2.5 ha of chardonnay, shiraz and cabernet sauvignon at Paracombe. The wines are distributed by The Wine Group, Vic, and Jonathan Tolley, SA, and sold by mail order.

🐌 Harris River Estate

★★☆

Lot 1293 Harris River Road, Collie, WA 6225 **REGION** Geographe
T (08) 9734 1555 **F** (08) 9734 1555 **www.**harrisriverestate.com.au **OPEN** W'ends 11–4
WINEMAKER Luis Simian Snr, Siobhan Lynch **EST.** 2001 **CASES** 15 000
In 2000 Karl and Lois Hillier (and their 6 children) purchased the Harris River property to run cattle and have a farm life for the family. When it was subsequently suggested the soils were ideal for vineyards, the family quickly diversified into grapegrowing, and even more quickly formed a company owned by family and friends to fast-track the planting of 27 ha of viognier, verdelho, chardonnay (4 ha each), shiraz (3 ha), and merlot and cabernet sauvignon (6 ha each). At the same time a 200-tonne winery, incorporated in a 3-storey winery/cellar door/restaurant/function centre swung into action with the 2002 vintage.

ŸŸŸŸ **Chardonnay 2004** **RATING** 85 **DRINK** Now $ 15

ŸŸŸ **Cabernet Sauvignon 2004** **RATING** 80 $ 15

Hartley Estate

★★★

260 Chittering Valley Road, Lower Chittering, WA 6084 **REGION** Perth Hills
T (08) 9481 4288 **F** (08) 9481 4291 **OPEN** By appt
WINEMAKER Steve Hagan (Contract) **EST.** 1999 **CASES** 1700
While driving through the Chittering Valley one Sunday with his daughter Angela, and reminiscing about the times he had spent there with his father Hartley, Bernie Stephens saw a For Sale sign on the property, and later that day the contract for sale was signed. Planting of 17 ha of vines began, with Cabernet Sauvignon and Shiraz released in 2003. They form part of the Generations Series, recognising the involvement of three generations of the family. The major part of the crop goes to Western Range Wines; the remainder is under the Hartley Estate label.

ŸŸŸŸ **Cabernet Merlot 2004** Light- to medium-bodied; well-balanced black olive and supple berry fruit; fine tannins, good value. Screwcap. 13.5° alc. **RATING** 88 **DRINK** 2012 $ 14

ŸŸŸŸ **Classic White 2005** **RATING** 85 **DRINK** Now $ 14

Hartz Barn Wines

1 Truro Road, Moculta, SA 5353 **REGION** Eden Valley
T (08) 8563 9002 **F** (08) 8563 9002 **WWW**.hartzbarnwines.com.au **OPEN** By appt
WINEMAKER David Barnett **EST.** 1997 **CASES** 2300
Hartz Barn Wines was formed in 1997 by Penny Hart (operations director), David Barnett (winemaker/director), Katrina Barnett (marketing director) and Matthew Barnett (viticulture/cellar director), which may suggest that the operation is rather larger than it in fact is. The business name and label have an unexpectedly complex background, too, involving elements from all the partners. The grapes come from the 11.5-ha Dennistone Vineyard, which is planted to merlot, shiraz, riesling, cabernet sauvignon, chardonnay and lagrein. Exports to NZ.

ㅜㅜㅜㅜㅜ **Carriages Barossa Cabernet Sauvignon 2003** Good colour; plenty of depth to nicely ripened, expressive, cabernet sauvignon; defies common wisdom about the variety (unsuited to the Barossa Valley) and vintage (difficult). Cork. 14.4° alc. **RATING** 92 **DRINK** 2013 $ 25

ㅜㅜㅜㅜ **General Store Barossa Shiraz 2003** Medium-bodied, gentle, blackberry and plum fruit; soft tannins, controlled oak. Cork. 14.4° alc. **RATING** 89 **DRINK** 2011 $ 25
General Store Eden Valley Riesling 2005 Light straw-green; a clean bouquet, with generous regional lime varietal character but falters on the finish. Screwcap. 12.5° alc. **RATING** 87 **DRINK** 2009 $ 19

ㅜㅜㅜㅜ **The Milliner Chardonnay 2005** **RATING** 86 **DRINK** Now $ 19

ㅜㅜㅜ **Hartz of Gold Autumn Riesling 2005** **RATING** 79 $ 19

Hartzview Wine Centre NR

70 Dillons Road, Gardners Bay, Tas 7112 **REGION** Southern Tasmania
T (03) 6295 1623 **F** (03) 6295 1723 **WWW**.hartzview.com.au **OPEN** 7 days 9–5
WINEMAKER Andrew Hood (Contract), Robert Patterson **EST.** 1988 **CASES** 2000
A combined wine centre, offering wines from a number of local Huon Valley wineries; also offers accommodation for 6 people in a separate, self-contained house. Hartzview table wines (produced from 3 ha of estate plantings) are preferred to the self-produced Pig & Whistle Hill fruit wines.

Harvey River Bridge Estate NR

Third Street, Harvey, WA 6220 **REGION** Geographe
T (08) 9729 2199 **F** (08) 9729 2298 **WWW**.harveyfresh.com.au **OPEN** 7 days 10–4
WINEMAKER Greg Jones **EST.** 2000 **CASES** 35 000
This is a highly focused business which is a division of parent company Harvey Fresh (1994) Ltd, a producer of fruit juice and dairy products exported to more than 12 countries. It has 10 contract growers throughout the Geographe region, with the wines being made in a company-owned winery and juice factory. Exports to the US, Japan, Malaysia, Singapore, Germany and Ireland.

Hastwell & Lightfoot

Foggos Road, McLaren Vale, SA 5171 (postal) **REGION** McLaren Vale
T (08) 8323 8692 **F** (08) 8323 8098 **WWW**.hastwellandlightfoot.com.au **OPEN** By appt
WINEMAKER Goe DiFabio (Contract) **EST.** 1990 **CASES** 2500
Hastwell & Lightfoot is an offshoot of a rather larger grapegrowing business, with the majority of the grapes from the 16 ha of vineyard being sold to others; the vineyard was planted in 1988 and the first grapes produced in 1990. Varieties planted are shiraz, cabernet sauvignon, chardonnay, cabernet franc, viognier, tempranillo and barbera. Incidentally, the labels are once seen, never forgotten. Exports to the UK, the US, Singapore and NZ.

ㅜㅜㅜㅜㅜ **McLaren Vale Shiraz 2003** Deep purple-red, very good for the vintage; medium- to full-bodied blackberry, plum and chocolate with velvety texture, off-set by some savoury tannins; vanilla oak. Cork. 14.5° alc. **RATING** 91 **DRINK** 2015 $ 21

▼▼▼▼ **McLaren Vale Tempranillo 2004** Medium-bodied; black cherry with a touch of bitter chocolate; persistent, fine tannins; lingering fruit length. Cork. 13.5° alc. **RATING** 89 **DRINK** 2012 $ 21

McLaren Vale Cabernet 2003 Unconvincing colour; sweet blackcurrant, spice and dark chocolate regional mix; gentle oak, soft tannins. Cork. 14° alc. **RATING** 88 **DRINK** 2010 $ 21

McLaren Vale Viognier 2005 Crystallised peach and apricot fruit flavours; some acidity to balance. Screwcap. 14° alc. **RATING** 87 **DRINK** 2008 $ 21

Hawkers Gate   NR

Lot 31 Foggo Road, McLaren Flat, SA 5171 **REGION** McLaren Vale
T 0403 809 990 **F** (08) 8323 9981 **www.**hawkersgate.com.au **OPEN** By appt
WINEMAKER James Hastwell **EST.** 2000 **CASES** 500
James Hastwell (son of Mark and Wendy Hastwell of Hastwell & Lightfoot) decided he would become a winemaker when he was 9 years old, and duly obtained his wine science degree from the Adelaide University, working each vintage during his degree course at Haselgrove Wines and later Kay Bros. It is a long way from Hawkers Gate, which takes its name from the gate at the border of Australia's dog fence between SA and NSW, 250 km north of Broken Hill. A small winery in Foggo Road was completed in 2003. A few rows of saperavi have been planted. Exports to the US.

Hawley Vineyard   NR

Hawley Beach, Hawley, Tas 7307 **REGION** Northern Tasmania
T (03) 6428 6221 **F** (03) 6428 6844 **www.**view.com.au/hawley **OPEN** 7 days
WINEMAKER Winemaking Tasmania (Julian Alcorso) **EST.** 1988 **CASES** 1000
Hawley Vineyard overlooks Hawley Beach and thence northeast to Bass Strait. It is established on a historic 200-ha farming property, with Hawley House offering dining and accommodation in a grand style. There are no other vineyards in this unique winegrowing region, and few hoteliers-cum-viticulturists as flamboyant as owner Simon Houghton.

Hay River Wines   NR

'The Springs', RMB 570, Mount Barker, WA 6324 (postal) **REGION** Mount Barker
T (08) 9857 6012 **F** (08) 9857 6112 **OPEN** Not
WINEMAKER Michael Kerrigan **EST.** 1974 **CASES** 200
Hay River first appeared in my Wines and Wineries of Western Australia, published in 1982. The then very remote vineyard was planted in 1974, and I visited the tractor shed-cum-winery with diesel engine-generated power, watching Jane Paul make the 1981 vintage (which turned out very well). These days the grapes from the 6 ha of cabernet sauvignon and 5 ha of chardonnay are sold to Howard Park, but a small amount of wine is made for release under the Hay River label.

Hay Shed Hill Wines   ★★★★

Harmans Mill Road, Wilyabrup, WA 6280 **REGION** Margaret River
T (08) 9755 6046 **F** (08) 9755 6083 **www.**hayshedhill.com.au **OPEN** 7 days 10.30–5
WINEMAKER Nigel Kinsman **EST.** 1987 **CASES** 35 000
When erected in 1987, the winery was a landmark in the Margaret River region, and over the ensuing years the 'sold out' sign was often displayed. Quality wobbled in the lead-up to its ill-fated acquisition by Barrington Estate in 2000, but in November 2002 it joined Alexandra Bridge and Chestnut Grove as part of Mike Calneggia's Australian Wine Holdings Limited group.

▼▼▼▼▽ **Margaret River Sauvignon Blanc 2005** Quiet, clean bouquet; opens up on the complex palate, with sweet citrus, passionfruit and grass; 6% barrel-fermented. Screwcap.
RATING 93 **DRINK** Now $ 21.45

Margaret River Sauvignon Blanc Semillon 2005 High-toned wild herb and grass aromas; very good length, focus and intensity, particularly on the lingering finish and aftertaste. Screwcap. **RATING** 92 **DRINK** 2009 $ 21.45

▼▼▼▼ **The X Trials Margaret River Tempranillo 2003** Light- to medium-bodied; plum, black fruits and all-spice; ripe, soft tannins; interesting wine. Screwcap. **RATING** 87 **DRINK** 2008 $ 45 ᵀᵀᵀ⵾ **Pitchfork Pink 2005** Vivid red-purple; sweet small berry/red cherry fruits; balanced acidity. Screwcap. 13.2° alc. **RATING** 86 **DRINK** Now $16

ᵀᵀᵀ **Pitchfork Unwooded Chardonnay 2004** **RATING** 83 $16.45

🍇 Haywards of Locksley ★★★☆

RMB 6365, Locksley, Vic 3665 (postal) **REGION** Strathbogie Ranges
T 0432 914 747 **OPEN** Not
WINEMAKER David Hayward, Jane Sandilands **EST.** NA **CASES** 500
David Hayward and Jane Sandilands have established a patchwork quilt vineyard of shiraz, riesling, viognier, cabernet franc, petit verdot and cabernet sauvignon, totalling 2.2 ha. By 2006 they had been practising organic growing for 5 years, and biodynamic for 1 year. The Shiraz is estate-grown, the Merlot organically grown at Strath Creek and purchased by Haywards. The Vintage Port comes from Goulburn Valley fruit.

ᵀᵀᵀᵀ **Shiraz 2004** Medium-bodied; a quite powerful structure around spicy black fruits; good tannins on a long finish. Good value. **RATING** 90 **DRINK** 2011 $15
Merlot 2004 Lively, fresh fruit with some cassis; light- to medium-bodied, and entirely fruit-driven. Cork. 13.6° alc. **RATING** 87 **DRINK** 2008 $15

ᵀᵀᵀ⵾ **Vintage Port 2000** **RATING** 86 **DRINK** Now $15

Hazyblur Wines ★★★★

Lot 5, Angle Vale Road, Virginia, SA 5120 **REGION** Adelaide Plains
T (08) 8380 9307 **F** (08) 8380 8743 **OPEN** By appt
WINEMAKER Ross Trimboli **EST.** 1998 **CASES** 2000
Robyne and Ross Trimboli hit the jackpot with their 2000 vintage red wines, sourced from various regions in SA, including one described by Robert Parker as 'Barotta, the most northerly region in South Australia' (it is in fact Baroota, and is not the most northerly), with Parker points ranging between 91 and 95. One of the wines was a Late Harvest Shiraz, tipping the scales at 17° alcohol, and contract-grown at Kangaroo Island. It is here that the Trimbolis have established their own 4.7-ha vineyard, planted principally to cabernet sauvignon and shiraz (first vintage 2004). Needless to say, almost all the wine is exported to the US (lesser amounts to Canada), the importer being the one and only Dan Phillips, aka The Grateful Palate.

ᵀᵀᵀᵀ⵾ **Kangaroo Island Cabernet Sauvignon 2004** Outstanding purple-red colour; a medium-bodied wine with cool-grown cassis cabernet fruit, and just a whisper of herb and grass; long and pure. Cork. 14.5° alc. **RATING** 92 **DRINK** 2015 $25
Kangaroo Island Shiraz 2004 Attractive medium-bodied wine; ripe blackberry fruit and an undoubted touch of gum leaf (as per the label); not at all overblown, with good balance and mouthfeel. Stained cork ominous. Cork. 14.5° alc. **RATING** 91 **DRINK** 2010 $25

ᵀᵀᵀᵀ **McLaren Vale Shiraz 2004** Powerful black fruits, earth, blackberry and bitter chocolate; sustained tannins need to soften. Similarly stained cork. 14.5° alc. **RATING** 89 **DRINK** 2011 $29

🍇 Heafod Glen Winery ★★★

8691 West Swan Road, Henley Brook, WA 6055 **REGION** Swan Valley
T (08) 9296 3444 **F** (08) 9296 3555 **WWW**.heafodglenwine.com.au **OPEN** Wed–Sun 10–5
WINEMAKER Neil Head **EST.** 1999 **CASES** NFP
A combined vineyard and restaurant business, each sustaining the other. The estate plantings are shiraz (2.5 ha), cabernet sauvignon (1 ha), viognier (0.75 ha) and chenin blanc, chardonnay and verdelho (0.25 ha each). The wines are made by vineyard owner Neil Head. Chesters restaurant, created by Paul Smith (famed for establishing Dear Friends restaurant in Perth), is run by Duncan Head and sister Anna, and is situated in a former stable which has been restored with all of the tables, cabinet works and feature walls crafted from the original timber. The homestead on the property is much older again, having been built in the 1880s.

ᵀᵀᵀᵀ **Cabernet Sauvignon 2003** **RATING** 86 **DRINK** Now $25

Healesville Wine Co

189–191a Maroondah Highway, Healesville, Vic 3777 **REGION** Yarra Valley
T (03) 5962 1800 **F** (03) 5962 1833 **WWW**.healesvillewine.com.au **OPEN** 7 days 11–6
WINEMAKER Paul Evans (Contract) **EST.** 2002 **CASES** 700

This is the venture of John Reith and Roger Hocking, who have a small vineyard, planted with chardonnay in 1997, off Don Road, Healesville, plus pinot noir and chardonnay from the Kiah Yallambee Vineyard in Old Don Road. Small amounts of shiraz, cabernet sauvignon, cabernet franc and merlot are obtained from Yarra Valley vineyards managed or controlled by the Healesville Wine Co.

▼▼▼▼ **Yarra Valley Shiraz 2003** Very developed hue; medium-bodied, with spice, licorice, chocolate and earth all coming before the black fruits; ripe tannins. Nice wine. Diam. 14° alc. **RATING** 89 **DRINK** 2011 $ 32
Yarra Valley Pinot Noir 2003 Light, ripe, earthy, spicy style; the oak not entirely convincing. Cork. 14.2° alc. **RATING** 87 **DRINK** 2009 $ 25

▼▼▼▽ **Yarra Valley Chardonnay 2003** Soft, broad yellow peach fruit; a honeyed but soft palate; a poor cork may have caused some oxidation. Cork. 13.7° alc. **RATING** 86 **DRINK** Now $ 20
Yarra Valley Cabernets 2003 Light-bodied; spicy/cedary/minty/leafy aromas and flavours; not over-extracted, the balance good. Diam. 13° alc. **RATING** 86 **DRINK** 2010 $ 23

Heartland Vineyard

PO Box 78, Greta, NSW 2334 **REGION** Lower Hunter Valley
T (02) 4938 6272 **F** (02) 4938 6004 **WWW**.heartlandvineyard.com.au **OPEN** Not
WINEMAKER David Hook **EST.** 1998 **CASES** 1500

Duncan and Libby Thomson, cardiac surgeon and cardiac scrub nurse respectively, say Heartland Vineyard is the result of a sea-change that got a little out of hand. 'After looking one weekend at some property in the Hunter Valley to escape the Sydney rat-race, we stumbled upon the beautiful 90 acres that has become our vineyard.' They have built a rammed-earth house on the property, and the vineyard is now a little over 5 ha, with an exotic mix of shiraz, semillon, merlot, barbera, verdelho and viognier.

▼▼▼▼▽ **Shiraz Viognier 2004** Very good colour; supple, round and mouthfilling even at this (wholly desirable) low alcohol; dark plum and black cherry, the 16% viognier way above that normally used, yet not derailing the wine as it did in '03. I can't help but feel a little less would be better. Screwcap. 12.4° alc. **RATING** 93 **DRINK** 2014 $ 10

▼▼▼▼ **Sticky Monster 2005** Quite intense and long; citrus, mandarin and lemon fruit; good acidity. The Germanic level of alcohol means the wine is not the least bit monstrous. Screwcap. 11° alc. **RATING** 89 **DRINK** 2008 $ 10
Merlot 2004 Light- to medium-bodied; fresh, earthy, savoury, olive aromas and flavours; the natural tendency of the region to maximise earthy characters accentuates the savoury notes; well-made, though. Screwcap. 12.4° alc. **RATING** 88 **DRINK** 2010 $ 10

Heartland Wines

Level 1, 205 Greenhill Road, Eastwood, SA 5063 **REGION** Limestone Coast Zone
T (08) 8357 9344 **F** (08) 8357 9388 **WWW**.heartlandwines.com.au **OPEN** Not
WINEMAKER Ben Glaetzer **EST.** 2001 **CASES** 20 000

This is a joint venture of 4 industry veterans: winemakers Ben Glaetzer and Scott Collett, viticulturist Geoff Hardy and wine industry management specialist Grant Tilbrook. It draws upon grapes grown in the Limestone Coast, Barossa Valley and McLaren Vale, predominantly from vineyards owned by the partners. Its sights are firmly set on exports and it has already had impressive results. The wines are principally contract-made at Barossa Vintners and represent excellent value for money. Exports to all major markets.

▼▼▼▼▽ **Director's Cut Shiraz 2004** Good hue; rich, supple, sweet blackberry, raspberry, plum and spice fruit; soft, ripe tannins; good oak. Langhorne Creek/Limestone Coast. Cork. 14.5° alc. **RATING** 93 **DRINK** 2015 $ 30

Langhorne Creek Limestone Coast Shiraz 2004 Dense colour; a very attractive mix of black fruits, dark chocolate and spice; good tannin and oak management. Cork. **RATING** 91 **DRINK** 2010 $ 16.99

Langhorne Creek Limestone Coast Cabernet Sauvignon 2004 A rich, ripe profusion of flavours from cassis to capsicum, and just about everything in between; good tannins; will repay cellaring. Cork. **RATING** 90 **DRINK** 2012 $ 18

Langhorne Creek Dolcetto Lagrein 2004 Rich, lusciously sweet and ripe red cherry and a wrapping of chocolate — cherry ripe indeed. Soft tannins and minimal oak. Screwcap. **RATING** 90 **DRINK** 2009 $ 20

Limestone Coast Petit Verdot 2004 Very good colour as always; richly robed black cherry, plum and mint; soft, ripe tannins. Cork. **RATING** 90 **DRINK** 2010 $ 18

ΥΥΥΥ **Langhorne Creek Viognier Pinot Gris 2005** Surging aromas a little off-putting at first; intense pear, citrus and apricot flavours; good length though highly idiosyncratic. Screwcap. **RATING** 89 **DRINK** Now $ 20

ΥΥΥΥ **Stickleback White 2005 RATING** 86 **DRINK** Now $ 12
Stickleback Red 2004 RATING 86 **DRINK** Now $ 12

Heath Wines

NR

21–23 Fourth Street, Bowden, SA 5007 (postal) **REGION** Warehouse
T (08) 8346 8488 **F** (08) 8346 4088 **WWW**.heathwines.com.au **OPEN** Not
WINEMAKER Contract **EST.** 2002 **CASES** NA
Since Alan Heath founded the eponymously named winery in 2002, it has built up exports to 8 countries, with a major presence in North America and the Asia Pacific. There are 3 labels: Lizard Flat Cabernet Sauvignon Merlot Sangiovese; Southern Roo Cabernet Sauvignon Shiraz and Chardonnay Viognier; and 4 Southern Sisters wines — Cabernet Sauvignon, Sauvignon Blanc, Riesling and Chardonnay.

Heathcote Estate

★★★★★

1 Garden Street, South Yarra, Vic 3141 (postal) **REGION** Heathcote
T (03) 9251 5375 **F** (03) 9639 1540 **WWW**.heathcoteestate.com **OPEN** Not
WINEMAKER Tod Dexter, Larry McKenna (Consultant) **EST.** 1988 **CASES** 9000
Heathcote Estate is a thoroughly professional venture, a partnership between Louis Bialkower, founder of Yarra Ridge Winery, and Robert G. Kirby, owner of Yabby Lake Vineyards, Director of Escarpment Vineyards (NZ) and Chairman of Village Roadshow Ltd. They purchased a prime piece of Heathcote red Cambrian soil on Drummonds Lane in 1999, and have an experienced and skilled winemaking team in the form of Tod Dexter (ex-Stonier) and Larry McKenna (of NZ) as consultant, who are also responsible for the Yabby Lake wines. They have planted 30 ha of vines, 85% shiraz and 15% grenache, the latter an interesting variant on viognier. A single wine is to be produced, and one suspects that the percentage of grenache will vary from year to year. The wines are matured exclusively in French oak (50% new).

ΥΥΥΥΥ **Shiraz 2003** Elegant and restrained within the context of the region and the drought vintage; plum, blackberry and prune fruit woven through with fine-grained, ripe tannins, and perfectly judged French oak. Quality cork. **RATING** 94 **DRINK** 2013 $ 46

🐌 Heathcote II

★★★★☆

290 Cornella-Toolleen Road, Toolleen, Vic 3551 **REGION** Heathcote
T (03) 5433 6292 **F** (03) 5433 6293 **WWW**.heathcote2.com **OPEN** W'ends 10–5
WINEMAKER Peder Rosdal **EST.** 1995 **CASES** 500
This is the venture of Danish-born, French-trained, Flying Winemaker (California, Spain and Chablis) Peder Rosdal and Lionel Flutto. The establishment of the vineyard dates back to 1995, new plantings in 2004 lifted the total to a little over 5 ha, shiraz with the lion's share of 2.2 ha, then cabernet sauvignon (1.3 ha) with around 0.5 ha each of cabernet franc, merlot and tempranillo. The vines are dry-grown on the famed red Cambrian soil, and since 2004 the wines made onsite. Open fermentation, hand-plunging, basket press and (since 2004) French oak maturation are the techniques used.

🍷🍷🍷🍷🍷 **Shiraz 2004** Typical deep Heathcote colour; abundant blackberry, dark chocolate, licorice and spice fruit; powerfully built with excellent tannin structure; has absorbed the oak. Cork. 15° alc. **RATING** 95 **DRINK** 2017 $ 32

🍷🍷🍷🍷🍷 **Shiraz 2003** Good colour; has a certain elegance notwithstanding the alcohol; quite firm black fruits and spice, but not quite the velvety fruit of the '04. Cork. 15° alc. **RATING** 92 **DRINK** 2015 $ 32

Heathcote Winery ★★★★☆

183–185 High Street, Heathcote, Vic 3523 **REGION** Heathcote
T (03) 5433 2595 **F** (03) 5433 3081 **www**.heathcotewinery.com.au **OPEN** 7 days 10–5
WINEMAKER Jonathan Mepham **EST.** 1978 **CASES** 12 000
The Heathcote Winery is back in business with a vengeance. The wines are being produced predominantly from the 26 ha estate vineyard, and some from local and other growers under long-term contracts; the tasting room facilities have been restored and upgraded. The 2006 vintage was the 10th since owner Stephen Wilkins acquired the pre-existing winery and vineyard, and the 5th for winemaker Jono Mepham. Exports to the UK.

🍷🍷🍷🍷🍷 **Curagee Shiraz 2004** Vibrant, spicy black fruits with a typical lift of even a little (2% in this instance) viognier; very good length and structure. Screwcap. 14.5° alc. **RATING** 94 **DRINK** 2015 $ 40

🍷🍷🍷🍷🍷 **Craven's Place Shiraz 2004** Deep colour; dense blackberry, plum and licorice fruit; good control of tannins and oak. Screwcap. **RATING** 91 **DRINK** 2014 $ 16
Mail Coach Shiraz 2004 Similar lifted fruit to the Curagee, but with some raspberry and overall less intensity; nonetheless, attractive mouthfeel and flavour. Has a splash of viognier. Screwcap. 14.5° alc. **RATING** 91 **DRINK** 2011 $ 24

🍷🍷🍷🍷 **Slaughterhouse Paddock Shiraz 2004** Stacked full of flavour but (excessively) heated by alcohol. A distinctly unappetising name, it must be said. Screwcap. 15.5° alc. **RATING** 88 **DRINK** 2010 $ 32
Mail Coach Viognier 2005 A solid wine, barrel-fermented and spending 6 months in apparently older oak; plenty of impact, heating up on the finish. Screwcap. 15° alc. **RATING** 87 **DRINK** 2008 $ 20

Heathvale NR

Saw Pit Gully Road, via Keyneton, SA 5353 **REGION** Eden Valley
T (08) 8564 8248 **F** (08) 8564 8248 **www**.heathvalewines.com.au **OPEN** By appt
WINEMAKER Ben Radford **EST.** 1987 **CASES** 1250
The origins of Heathvale go back to 1865, when William Heath purchased the property, building the Heathvale home and establishing the fruit orchard and 8 ha of vineyard. The property is now 65 ha and has 10 ha of vineyard in production, with future plantings planned. The wine was made in the cellar of the house which still stands on the property (the house is now occupied by owners Trevor and Faye March). The vineyards were re-established in 1987, and consist of shiraz, cabernet sauvignon, chardonnay and riesling, with a 1000-vine sagrantino trial planted in 2004. Exports to the UK and the US.

Heggies Vineyard ★★★★☆

Heggies Range Road, Eden Valley, SA 5235 **REGION** Eden Valley
T (08) 8565 3203 **F** (08) 8565 3380 **www**.heggiesvineyard.com **OPEN** At Yalumba
WINEMAKER Peter Gambetta **EST.** 1973 **CASES** 13 000
Heggies was the second of the high-altitude (570m) vineyards established by S. Smith & Sons (Yalumba). Plantings on the 120-ha former grazing property began in 1973, and 62 ha is now under vine. Plantings of both chardonnay and viognier were increased in 2002. Exports to all major markets.

🍷🍷🍷🍷🍷 **Museum Reserve Eden Valley Riesling 2001** Glowing green-yellow; a beautiful wine, just entering the prime of what will be a very long life; essence of lime juice without any hint of heaviness; now or 10 years' time, take your pick. Screwcap. **RATING** 96 **DRINK** 2015 $ 27

ŢŢŢŢŶ **Eden Valley Viognier 2004** Complex, rich and mouthfilling apricot, dried fruits and spice; firm but dry finish, the 14.5° alcohol inevitable. Screwcap. 14.5° alc. **RATING** 90 **DRINK** Now $ 27.95

ŢŢŢŢ **Eden Valley Chardonnay 2004** Light- to medium-bodied; citrus, stone fruit and melon; balanced and integrated oak. Why the cork closure? Cork. **RATING** 89 **DRINK** 2008 $ 24.95

Helen's Hill Estate ★★★★☆

16 Ingram Road, Lilydale, Vic 3140 **REGION** Yarra Valley
T (03) 9739 1573 **F** (03) 9739 0350 **WWW**.helenshill.com.au **OPEN** Thurs–Mon 10–5
WINEMAKER Scott McCarthy **EST.** 1984 **CASES** 3000
Helen's Hill Estate is named after the previous owner of the property, Helen Fraser. Allan Nalder, Roma and Lewis Nalder and Andrew and Robyn McIntosh, with backgrounds in banking and finance, grazing and medicine respectively, are the partners in the venture. A small planting of pinot noir and chardonnay dating from the mid-1980s is retained for the Helen's Hill Estate wines; the grapes from the newer plantings are sold to Domaine Chandon and Coldstream Hills. The plantings now cover chardonnay, pinot noir, shiraz, merlot and cabernet sauvignon. A very elegant and relatively large restaurant, with a private function room, looks out over the Yarra Valley.

ŢŢŢŢŶ **Yarra Valley Chardonnay 2003** Light straw-green; finely structured, light- to medium-bodied; melon, nectarine and citrus nuances; a breath of barrel ferment oak on a long finish. Screwcap. 13.8° alc. **RATING** 93 **DRINK** 2012 $ 21

V Cabernet Blend 2004 An elegant, medium-bodied array of red and black fruits; fine, supple mouthfeel; good tannin and oak support. Cabernet Sauvignon/Merlot/Cabernet Franc/Malbec/Petit Verdot. Cork. 12.5° alc. **RATING** 93 **DRINK** 2015 $ 28

Yarra Valley Unfiltered Pinot Noir 2004 Extremely powerful and concentrated, particularly in the context of the vintage; black fruits and substantial tannins. Screwcap. 14.1° alc. **RATING** 90 **DRINK** 2011 $ 25

Helm ★★★☆

Butt's Road, Murrumbateman, NSW 2582 **REGION** Canberra District
T (02) 6227 5953 **F** (02) 6227 0207 **WWW**.helmwines.com.au **OPEN** Thurs–Mon 10–5
WINEMAKER Ken Helm **EST.** 1973 **CASES** 3000
Ken Helm is well known as one of the more stormy petrels of the wine industry and is an energetic promoter of his wines and of the Canberra district generally. His wines have been consistent bronze medal winners, with silvers and golds dotted here and there.

ŢŢŢŢŶ **Canberra District Premium Riesling 2005** Aromatic mineral, herb and lime, with no reduction; lively and fresh; excellent balance and length; 11.2° alcohol works brilliantly. Screwcap. **RATING** 93 **DRINK** 2015 $ 33

ŢŢŢŶ **Canberra District Pinot Noir 2005** Bright colour; a firm wine with dark plum; the finish and aftertaste fractionally green/stemmy. Screwcap. 13° alc. **RATING** 86 **DRINK** 2010 $ 28

Canberra District Cabernet Sauvignon 2003 **RATING** 86 **DRINK** 2009 $ 30
Canberra District Classic Dry Riesling 2005 **RATING** 85 **DRINK** 2009 $ 25

Henderson Hardie NR

PO Box 554, Wangaratta, Vic 3676 **REGION** King Valley
T (03) 5722 1850 **F** (03) 5721 5577 **OPEN** Not
WINEMAKER Howard Anderson (Contract) **EST.** 2000 **CASES** NA
Gayle and Jim Hardie have established 12 ha of gewurztraminer, chardonnay, pinot gris, pinot noir and pinot meunier in their Whitlands vineyard. Jim Hardie has had a long and high-profile career in viticulture and in viticultural research, and the choice of the varieties planted in this high altitude vineyard reflects that knowledge. Winemaker Howard Anderson, too, has many years under his belt as a winemaker in various parts of Vic.

Henke
NR

175 Henke Lane, Yarck, Vic 3719 **REGION** Upper Goulburn
T (03) 5797 6277 **F** (03) 5797 6277 **OPEN** By appt
WINEMAKER Tim Miller, Caroline Miller **EST.** 1974 **CASES** 250
Produces tiny quantities of estate-grown deep-coloured, full-flavoured, minty red wines known only to a chosen few. The 1.5 ha of shiraz and 0.5 ha of cabernet sauvignon are low-yielding, hence the power and longevity of the wines. A range of vintages up to 5 years of age are usually available at the cellar door.

Henkell Wines
NR

Melba Highway, Dixons Creek, Vic 3775 **REGION** Yarra Valley
T (03) 9417 4144 **WWW**.henkellvineyards.com.au **OPEN** Thurs & Sun 11–5, Fri–Sat 11–9
WINEMAKER Contract **EST.** 1988 **CASES** 500
Hans Henkell started with a 57-variety Heinz mix in the vineyard, but has now rationalised it to a total of 25 ha of sauvignon blanc, chardonnay, pinot noir, shiraz and cabernet sauvignon. Most of the grapes are sold, with small amounts contract-made each year. Dinner concerts are held regularly throughout the summer months, bookings essential.

Henley Park Wines
NR

6 Swan Street, Henley Brook, WA 6055 **REGION** Swan Valley
T (08) 9296 4328 **F** (08) 9296 1313 **WWW**.henleywine.com **OPEN** Tues–Sun 10–5
WINEMAKER Claus Petersen, Lisbet Petersen **EST.** 1935 **CASES** 5000
Henley Park, like so many Swan Valley wineries, was founded by a Yugoslav family, but it is now jointly owned by Danish and Malaysian interests, a multicultural mix if ever there was one. Majority owner (with wife Lisbet) and winemaker Claus Petersen arrived in 1986. Exports to Denmark and Japan.

Henry's Drive

Hodgsons Road, Padthaway, SA 5271 **REGION** Padthaway
T (08) 8765 5251 **F** (08) 8765 5180 **WWW**.henrysdrive.com **OPEN** 7 days 10–4
WINEMAKER Kim Johnston, Chris Ringland (Consultant) **EST.** 1998 **CASES** 100 000
The Longbottom families have been farming in Padthaway since the 1940s, with a diverse operation ranging from sheep and cattle to growing onions. In 1992 they decided to plant a few vines, and now have almost 300 ha of vineyard consisting mainly of shiraz and cabernet sauvignon, plus some chardonnay, merlot, verdelho and sauvignon blanc. Henry's Drive is owned and operated by Brian and Kay Longbottom. Exports to all major markets.

ΨΨΨΨΨ **Parson's Flat Padthaway Shiraz Cabernet 2004** Medium- to full-bodied; blackberry, earth and dark chocolate fruit on a solid structure of tannins and oak. Should be long-lived. Cork. **RATING** 91 **DRINK** 2014 **$** 35

Pillar Box Red 2004 Strong colour; medium- to full-bodied; luscious black fruits with a dusting of dark chocolate and earth; good control of extract. Screwcap. 15° alc. **RATING** 90 **DRINK** 2014 **$** 12

ΨΨΨΨ **Dead Letter Office Shiraz 2004** Dense red-purple; medium- to full-bodied, with rich, ripe blackberry, dark chocolate and plum; the alcohol does deliver a kick on the finish; patience (and prayer) may help. Screwcap. 16° alc. **RATING** 89 **DRINK** 2014 **$** 20

ΨΨΨ **Padthaway Cabernet Sauvignon 2004** **RATING** 82 **$** 30

Henschke

Henschke Road, Keyneton, SA 5353 **REGION** Eden Valley
T (08) 8564 8223 **F** (08) 8564 8294 **WWW**.henschke.com.au **OPEN** Mon–Fri 9–4.30, Sat 9–12, public hols 10–3
WINEMAKER Stephen Henschke **EST.** 1868 **CASES** 50 000
Regarded as the best medium-sized red wine producer in Australia, and has gone from strength to strength over the past three decades under the guidance of winemaker Stephen and viticulturist Prue Henschke. The red wines fully capitalise on the very old, low-yielding, high-quality vines and are

superbly made with sensitive but positive use of new small oak: Hill of Grace is second only to Penfolds Grange as Australia's red wine icon. Exports to all major markets.

ŸŸŸŸŸ **Mount Edelstone 2002** Clean blackberry, plum and a touch of prune on the bouquet; the palate utterly belies the alcohol, with a cascade of black fruits and spices; very good oak and tannin management. Screwcap. 15° alc. **RATING** 96 **DRINK** 2022 $ 68

Hill Of Grace 2001 Dusty, earthy, black fruits and mocha aromas; springs into life on the palate, with wonderfully long and persistent red and black fruits; gentle tannins and oak. Quality cork. 14° alc. **RATING** 96 **DRINK** 2021 $ 385

Cyril Henschke Eden Valley Cabernet 2002 Excellent colour; a lovely wine, another in the stable to bounce back; classic cabernet fruit, with long, fine, cedary/savoury tannins; perfect balance. Screwcap. **RATING** 96 **DRINK** 2022 $ 112

Julius Eden Valley Riesling 2005 Light green-straw; spotlessly clean; finer and more directly focused than Green's Hill, with lime, lemon and green apple; great length and finish. Screwcap. 13° alc. **RATING** 95 **DRINK** 2015 $ 27

Mount Edelstone 2003 Good colour; has structure and focus with red and blackberry fruit (no dead fruit); good spice and length, exemplary oak and tannins. A raucous return to top form. Screwcap. **RATING** 95 **DRINK** 2018 $ 92

Tappa Pass Shiraz 2002 Highly charged and fragrant blackberry, licorice and prune aromas; lots of dark chocolate joins in on the palate, with very good French oak in support. A particularly auspicious debut. Screwcap. **RATING** 95 **DRINK** 2022 $ 46

Keyneton Estate Euphonium 2002 An elegant mix of a full range of red and black fruits; medium-bodied, with delicious silky mouthfeel; 70% Shiraz/20% Cabernet Sauvignon/10% Merlot. The Euphonium in question, incidentally, is B Flat. Screwcap. 14.5° alc. **RATING** 95 **DRINK** 2015 $ 32

Green's Hill Lenswood Riesling 2005 Bright green-yellow; spotlessly clean, powerful and somewhat introspective on the bouquet; citrus, passionfruit and mineral all power-up on the finish. Screwcap. **RATING** 94 **DRINK** 2015 $ 30

Green's Hill Lenswood Riesling 2004 Very rich, opulent, lime juice aromas; backs off slightly on the palate, no bad thing; still flooded with flavour and immediate appeal. Screwcap. 13° alc. **RATING** 94 **DRINK** 2014 $ 25

Louis Eden Valley Semillon 2004 Has excellent tangy intensity of fruit in a lemon/citrus/spice spectrum; no hint of phenolics or heat; perfect acidity. Vines up to 50 years old. Screwcap. 13° alc. **RATING** 94 **DRINK** 2011 $ 19.50

Eleanor's Cottage Eden Valley Sauvignon Blanc Semillon 2005 Light straw-green; spotlessly clean, with remarkable drive and intensity on the palate; long and piercing finish. Screwcap. **RATING** 94 **DRINK** 2009 $ 23

Giles Lenswood Pinot Noir 2004 Spotlessly clean; fragrant, spicy, red and black fruit aromas; an elegant, cherry-accented palate; has poise and length. Screwcap. 14.5° alc. **RATING** 94 **DRINK** 2012 $ 46

Johann's Garden Barossa Grenache Mourvedre Shiraz 2004 Bright red-purple; vibrant and fragrant; light- to medium-bodied, but an intense and long spray of red fruits; shows just what can be done with this blend. Screwcap. 15.5° alc. **RATING** 94 **DRINK** 2012 $ 36

ŸŸŸŸŸ **Coralinga Adelaide Hills Sauvignon Blanc 2005** Light straw-green; the bouquet is faintly reductive, but the wine is redeemed by the strength of the palate; long, lingering and focused, finishing with tangy/citrussy acidity. Screwcap. 13.5° alc. **RATING** 93 **DRINK** 2008 $ 24

Lenswood Croft Chardonnay 2004 Gentle nectarine, white peach and French oak all coalesce on the medium-bodied palate; nice touch of minerality on the finish. Screwcap. 14° alc. **RATING** 93 **DRINK** 2010 $ 38

Abbott's Prayer Lenswood Merlot 2002 Clearly delineated varietal character, with a mix of red berries, olive, leaf, spice and herb; good mouthfeel and length. Screwcap. 14° alc. **RATING** 92 **DRINK** 2012 $ 70

Peggy's Hill Eden Valley Riesling 2005 Bright straw-green; a clean bouquet, then a palate with abundant citrus/lime/apple flavours, the Achilles heel lack of focus and structure. Screwcap. 12.5° alc. **RATING** 90 **DRINK** 2010 $ 20

Joseph Hill Eden Valley Gewurztraminer 2005 A bright, clean bouquet with faint spice and rose petal aromas; a tight, reserved palate; fully priced. Screwcap. **RATING** 90 **DRINK** 2011 $ 34

YYYY **Littlehampton Innes Vineyard Adelaide Hills Pinot Gris 2005** Classic spice, pear and a hint of musk; good balance and length, the alcohol no problem. Screwcap. 14.5° alc. **RATING** 89 **DRINK** 2008 $ 31

Tilly's Vineyard 2005 Fresh, clean grassy/spicy/citrussy; light on its feet, as it should be. Best yet under this label. Screwcap. 13° alc. **RATING** 89 **DRINK** Now $ 18

Henry's Seven 2004 Good hue; aromatic; light- to medium-bodied juicy/jammy/confit red fruits; minimal tannin and oak influence. Screwcap. 15° alc. **RATING** 89 **DRINK** 2010 $ 31

Louis Eden Valley Semillon 2005 Abundant flavour and richness; overwhelming case for picking much earlier; alcohol puts lead bags on the saddle. Screwcap. 13° alc. **RATING** 88 **DRINK** 2010 $ 28

🐦 Hentley Farm Wines ★★★★☆

PO Box 246, Tanunda, SA 5352 **REGION** Barossa Valley
T (08) 8562 8427 **F** (08) 8562 8427 **WWW**.hentleyfarm.com.au **OPEN** Not
WINEMAKER Reid Bosward (Contract) **EST.** 1999 **CASES** 2000
Keith and Alison Hentschke purchased the Hentley Farm in 1997, then an old vineyard and mixed farming property. Keith had thoroughly impressive credentials at the time of the purchase, having studied agricultural science at Roseworthy College from 1987 to 1989, then studying wine marketing, and obtaining an MBA. During the 1990s he had a senior production role with Orlando, before moving on to manage one of Australia's largest vineyard management companies, and from 2002–2006 with Nepenthe. Under the direction of their vineyard manager Kevin North, but with significant input from Keith, just under 15 ha of shiraz, 5 ha of grenache, 2 ha of cabernet sauvignon, 0.8 ha of zinfandel and 0.1 ha of viognier are now in production. The vineyard is situated among rolling hills on the banks of Greenock Creek, with red clay loam soils overlaying shattered limestone, lightly rocked slopes and little top soil. It hardly needs to be said the emphasis is on quality.

YYYYY **The Beauty Shiraz 2004** Powerful, medium- to full-bodied with a different fruit register to the varietal, thanks in part to the touch of viognier; lovely licorice, dark plum and blackberry fruit. Cork. 14.5° alc. **RATING** 94 **DRINK** 2019 $ 45

YYYYY **Shiraz 2004** Medium- to full red-purple; medium-bodied, and quite elegant, with gently savoury/earthy edges to the spicy/black fruits. Screwcap. 14.5° alc. **RATING** 93 **DRINK** 2019 $ 32

The Beast Shiraz 2003 Dense colour, good hue; a massive wine in every dimension; fruit, tannins, oak and alcohol. Needs prolonged domestication, but worth the training. Cork. 15.5° alc. **RATING** 93 **DRINK** 2023 $ 75

Shiraz 2003 Leathery, spicy overtones to blackberry fruit; spicy, ripe tannins; hints of mocha and chocolate. Screwcap. **RATING** 90 **DRINK** 2013 $ 32

YYYY **Grenache Shiraz Zinfandel 2004** Bright red; quite perfumed, with predominantly juicy berry fruits, and some fine, spicy tannins. Screwcap. 14.5° alc. **RATING** 89 **DRINK** 2010 $ 28

Henty Brook Estate NR

Box 49, Dardanup, WA 6236 **REGION** Geographe
T (08) 9728 1459 **F** (08) 9728 1459 **OPEN** W'ends 10–4, Mon–Fri by appt
WINEMAKER James Pennington (Contract) **EST.** 1994 **CASES** 400
Shiraz and sauvignon blanc (1 ha each) and semillon (0.5 ha) were planted in the spring of 1994. It has a very low profile.

🐦 Henty Estate ★★★★

657 Hensley Park Road, Hamilton, Vic 3300 (postal) **REGION** Henty
T (03) 5572 4446 **F** (03) 5572 4446 **WWW**.henty-estate.com.au **OPEN** Not
WINEMAKER Peter Dixon **EST.** 1991 **CASES** 600
Peter and Glenys Dixon have hastened slowly with Henty Estate. In 1991 they began the planting of 4.5 ha of shiraz, 1 ha each of cabernet sauvignon and chardonnay, and 0.5 ha of riesling. In their

words, 'we avoided the temptation to make wine until the vineyard was mature', establishing the winery in 2003. Encouraged by neighbours John Thomson and Tamara Irish, they have limited the yield to 3 to 4 tonnes per ha on the VSP-trained, essentially dry-grown, vineyard.

ŶŶŶŶ♀ **Riesling 2005** Fragrant and floral, with some lime blossom; ripe fruit, with masses of flavour, the alcohol just intruding. Cork. **RATING** 90 **DRINK** 2008 $ 20

Riesling 2004 A subdued bouquet, then a finely structured palate, with lime, apple and pear shot through with minerally acidity; fresh finish and aftertaste. Cork. 13.5° alc. **RATING** 90 **DRINK** 2012

Cabernet Sauvignon 2004 Light- to medium-bodied; a finely articulated cool-grown cabernet with cassis, raspberry and blackberry fruit; fine, ripe tannins; minimal oak. **RATING** 90 **DRINK** 2012 $ 24

ŶŶŶŶ **Shiraz Cabernet 2003** Medium-bodied; tangy, spicy red and black fruits; well-integrated vanilla oak and fine tannins. Cork. 13.5° alc. **RATING** 89 **DRINK** 2010 $ 22

Cabernet Sauvignon 2003 Medium-bodied; cool-grown cassis blackcurrant fruit, with some spicy/leafy aspects and light tannins; very well-made. Cork. 13.5° alc. **RATING** 89 **DRINK** 2009 $ 24

Heritage Estate ★★★

Granite Belt Drive, Cottonvale, Qld 4375 **REGION** Granite Belt
T (07) 4685 2197 **F** (07) 4685 2112 **WWW**.heritagewines.com.au **OPEN** 7 days 9–5
WINEMAKER John Handy **EST.** 1992 **CASES** 7000
Bryce and Paddy Kassulke operate a very successful winery, with many awards in recent years. It also showcases its wines through its cellar door at Mt Tamborine (cnr Bartle Road/The Shelf Road, telephone (07) 5545 3144) in an old church converted into a tasting and sales area, which has views over the Gold Coast hinterland, and includes a restaurant, barbecue area and art gallery. The estate plantings, established in 1993, are chardonnay (2.5 ha), merlot (1 ha), shiraz (0.4 ha) and cabernet sauvignon (0.1 ha). The quality of the wines has been consistently good, in the top 10 of the now innumerable Qld wineries.

ŶŶŶŶ **Vintage Brut 2000** Good wine; a well-balanced touch of sweetness presents no problems; generous stone fruit from a 100% chardonnay base spending 3 years on yeast lees. 13.3° alc. **RATING** 88 **DRINK** Now $ 25

ŶŶŶŶ♀ **Cabernet Franc 2004 RATING** 86 **DRINK** 2008
Riley's Durif 2004 RATING 86 **DRINK** 2009
Cabernet Shiraz 2004 RATING 85 **DRINK** 2008
Unwooded Chardonnay 2005 RATING 84 **DRINK** Now $ 15

Heritage Farm Wines NR

RMB 1005 Murray Valley Highway, Cobram, Vic 3655 **REGION** Goulburn Valley
T (03) 5872 2376 **F** (03) 5872 2376 **OPEN** 7 days 9–5
WINEMAKER Roy Armfield **EST.** 1987 **CASES** 3000
Heritage Farm claims to be the only vineyard and orchard in Australia still using horsepower, with Clydesdales used for most of the general farm work. The winery and cellar door area also boasts a large range of restored horse-drawn farm machinery and a bottle collection. All the wines are sold by mailing list and through the cellar door.

Heritage Wines ★★★★☆

106a Seppeltsfield Road, Marananga, SA 5355 **REGION** Barossa Valley
T (08) 8562 2880 **F** (08) 8562 2692 **WWW**.heritagewinery.com.au **OPEN** Mon–Fri 10–5, w'ends & public hols 11–5
WINEMAKER Stephen Hoff **EST.** 1984 **CASES** 5000
A little-known winery which deserves a far wider audience, for Stephen Hoff is apt to produce some startlingly good wines. At various times the Riesling (from old Clare Valley vines), Cabernet Sauvignon and Shiraz (now the flag-bearer) have all excelled. Exports to the UK, US, Malaysia and Netherlands.

ŸŸŸŸŸ **Barossa Shiraz 2004** Excellent colour; controlled alcohol brings the best out of a very good vintage; medium-bodied blackberry and plum, with hints of spice and chocolate; very good texture and structure. Cork. 14.5° alc. **RATING** 94 **DRINK** 2013 $ 25

ŸŸŸŸŸ **Barossa Cabernet Sauvignon 2004** Attractive blackcurrant fruit and (again) dark chocolate; firm, earthy varietal tannins; controlled oak. Cork. 14.5° alc. **RATING** 92 **DRINK** 2014 $ 25

ŸŸŸŸ **Barossa Semillon 2005** Good structure and depth to the grassy/lemony fruit; not phenolic. Screwcap. 12.2° alc. **RATING** 89 **DRINK** 2009 $ 15

Hermes Morrison Wines   NR

253 Swan Ponds Road, Woodstock, NSW 2793 **REGION** Central Ranges Zone
T (02) 6345 0153 **F** (02) 6345 0153 **OPEN** 7 days 10–5 summer, winter w'ends & public hols
WINEMAKER Jill Lindsay (Contract) **EST.** 1990 **CASES** 180
The Morrison family established a Hermes Poll Dorset Stud in 1972, which has now been joined by Hermes Morrison Wines. The cellar door has been built by the side of a large lake fed by cold, clear water welling up from subterranean caves, and a 10-minute walk takes you to the summit of Mt Palatine, one of the highest peaks in the shire, and with a spectacular view of the Canobolas Mountains 80 km away.

Heron Lake Estate   NR

Lot 27, Rendezvous Road, Vasse, WA 6280 **REGION** Margaret River
T (08) 9336 5711 **F** (08) 9433 1297 **WWW**.heronlake.com.au **OPEN** 7 days 10–4
WINEMAKER Frank Kittler **EST.** 1984 **CASES** 1200
Di and Rob Goodwin (plus children Hannah and Callum) purchased the Heron Lake Vineyard from its founders, Mike and Faith Sparrow, in 2001, by which time the vineyard was 20 years old. There is a little over 6 ha of vines, chardonnay accounting for 2.6 ha, the remainder verdelho, semillon, sauvignon blanc, cabernet and merlot. Both Rob and Di are involved in postgraduate viticulture studies at various West Australian campuses. Di is actively involved in the management of the vineyard while Rob continues his involvement in a US sales training consultancy.

Herons Rise Vineyard   NR

Saddle Road, Kettering, Tas 7155 **REGION** Southern Tasmania
T (03) 6267 4339 **F** (03) 6267 4245 **WWW**.heronsrise.com.au **OPEN** By appt
WINEMAKER Andrew Hood **EST.** 1984 **CASES** 250
Sue and Gerry White run a small stone country guest house in the D'Entrecasteaux Channel area and basically sell the wines produced from the surrounding hectare of vineyard to those staying at the 2 self-contained cottages.

Hesperos Wines   ★★★★

PO Box 882, Margaret River, WA 6285 **REGION** Margaret River
T (08) 9757 6565 **F** (08) 9757 6565 **WWW**.hesperoswines.com.au **OPEN** Long w'ends and public hols by appt
WINEMAKER Jurg Muggli **EST.** 1993 **CASES** 2000
Founded by Swiss-born chef Jurg Muggli and partners, Hesperos has planted 6.2 ha of mixed varieties on phylloxera and drought-resistent root stocks. The vines are close-planted, and the vineyard is run with minimal irrigation, the aim being to grow smaller berries with an increased ratio of grape skins to juice, increasing the flavour in the process. Muggli owned a restaurant in Switzerland in his early 20s, and this has left him with a chef's eye for quality ingredients, and says, 'my background reminds me how we were able to improve our recipes every day, sometimes depending on the mood of the hour. As a winemaker we are cooking once a year in big pots for thousands of people.' Exports to Japan, Switzerland and Germany.

ŸŸŸŸ **Margaret River Sauvignon Blanc 2005** Clean, fresh, bright and lively; a neat mix of herbaceous and tropical elements. Screwcap. 13° alc. **RATING** 90 **DRINK** Now $ 18.50

ΥΥΥΥ **Margaret River Syrah 2002** Light- to medium-bodied; strongly spicy, savoury flavours; quite austere. Cork. 14° alc. **RATING** 87 **DRINK** 2008 $ 25

Hewitson ★★★★★

The Old Dairy Cold Stores, 66 London Road, Mile End, SA 5031 **REGION** Southeast Australia
T (08) 8443 6466 **F** (08) 8443 6866 **WWW**.hewitson.com.au **OPEN** By appt
WINEMAKER Dean Hewitson **EST.** 1996 **CASES** 22 000
Dean Hewitson was a winemaker at Petaluma for 10 years, and during that time managed to do 3 vintages in France and one in Oregon as well as undertaking his Masters at UC Davis, California. It is hardly surprising that the wines are immaculately made from a technical viewpoint. However, he has also managed to source 30-year-old riesling from the Eden Valley and 70-year-old shiraz from McLaren Vale, and makes a Barossa Valley Mourvedre from 152-year-old vines at Rowland Flat and a Barossa Valley Shiraz and Grenache from 60-year-old vines at Tanunda. The vineyards are now under long-term contracts to Dean Hewitson. Exports to the UK, the US and other major markets.

ΥΥΥΥΥ **Private Cellar McLaren Vale Shiraz Mourvedre 2003** Deeply coloured; blackberry and dark chocolate aromas and flavours so typical of McLaren Vale; fruit, oak and tannins in complete harmony and balance in a full-bodied frame. Screwcap. 14.5° alc. **RATING** 96 **DRINK** 2018 $ 60
Ned & Henry's Shiraz 2004 Potent black fruits, herbs and spices all intermingle on the bouquet, following through on the medium- to full-bodied, tightly focused palate. Screwcap. **RATING** 95 **DRINK** 2019 $ 26
The Mad Hatter McLaren Vale Shiraz 2003 Spice, chocolate, blackberry and mocha aromas and flavours; full tannins. Carries its alcohol with ridiculous ease. Screwcap. 15° alc. **RATING** 95 **DRINK** 2018 $ 50
Old Garden Barossa Valley Mourvedre 2004 Medium red-purple; sweet red and black fruits akin to grenache, the structure quite different; in fact, the tannins are very well-handled and refined, running through a long finish. Fault-free. Precious wine inheritance from vines planted in 1854. Screwcap. 14.5° alc. **RATING** 94 **DRINK** 2015 $ 49

ΥΥΥΥΥ **Eden Valley Riesling 2005** Floral lime blossom aromas; lime juice fruit built around a core of minerally acidity; very pure. Screwcap. 12° alc. **RATING** 93 **DRINK** 2015 $ 22
Lulu Adelaide Hills Sauvignon Blanc 2005 Light straw-green; spotlessly clean and correct; whispers of gooseberry/tropical fruit, then a crisp, dry finish. Screwcap. 12.5° alc. **RATING** 90 **DRINK** Now $ 23
Miss Harry Dry Grown and Ancient 2004 Fresh, clean, vibrant; light- to medium-bodied red and black fruits with splashes of spice; oak and tannins irrelevant. Screwcap. **RATING** 90 **DRINK** 2008 $ 22

ΥΥΥΥ **Mermaids Lite Dry White 2005** Pear and clove aromas; bone-dry palate, crisp and flinty, finishing with nice acidity; 100% muscadelle. Screwcap. 9.5° alc. **RATING** 87 **DRINK** Now $ 16.50

Heytesbury Ridge ★★★☆

1170 Cooriemungle Road, Timboon, Vic 3268 **REGION** Geelong
T (03) 5598 7394 **F** (03) 5598 7396 **WWW**.heytesburyridge.com.au **OPEN** 7 days 11–5 Nov–Apr, or by appt
WINEMAKER David Newton **EST.** 1998 **CASES** 1200
David and Dot Newton say that after milking cows for 18 years, they decided to investigate the possibility of planting a northeast-facing block of land which they also owned. Their self-diagnosed mid-life crisis also stemmed from a lifelong interest in wine as consumers. They planted 2 ha of chardonnay and pinot noir in December 1998, and another 2 ha of pinot gris, pinot noir and sauvignon blanc the following year. Having done a short winemaking course at Melbourne University (Dookie campus), the Newtons completed a small winery in 2003.

ΥΥΥΥ **Sauvignon Blanc 2005** Intense herb, grass and asparagus aromas, moving more into tropical fruit on the palate; does show its alcohol. Screwcap. 13.7° alc. **RATING** 89 **DRINK** Now $ 18

Chardonnay 2005 Light- to medium-bodied; slightly muted melon fruit; this and the nutty notes suggest malolactic fermentation slightly blurring the fruit profile; subtle oak. Screwcap. 14.5° alc. RATING 88 DRINK 2009 $ 20

Pinot Noir 2004 Dark purple-red; black fruits, herb, spice and mint; has length, but the early picking seems to have given some sweet and sour characters. Screwcap. 12.5° alc. RATING 87 DRINK 2009 $ 22

▼▼▼▽ **Pinot Grigio 2005** RATING 86 DRINK Now $ 18
Rose 2005 RATING 85 DRINK Now $ 15

Hickinbotham of Dromana ★★★★

Nepean Highway (near Wallaces Road), Dromana, Vic 3936 REGION Mornington Peninsula
T (03) 5981 0355 F (03) 5987 0692 www.hickinbotham.biz OPEN 7 days 11–5
WINEMAKER Andrew Hickinbotham EST. 1981 CASES 3000
After a peripatetic period and a hiatus in winemaking, Hickinbotham established a permanent vineyard and winery base at Dromana. It now makes only Mornington Peninsula wines, drawing in part on 6.5 ha of estate vineyards, and in part on contract-grown fruit. The wines are principally sold through the cellar door and by mail order.

▼▼▼▼▽ **David Hickinbotham Sauvignon Blanc 2005** Light straw-green; a spotless, lively and crisp bouquet; tangy, gooseberry, citrus with a strong spine of acidity to give focus. Historic label. Screwcap. 13.5° alc. RATING 91 DRINK Now $ 18

Alan Robb Pinot Noir 2004 Light but good hue; light, fractionally funky strawberry fruit; good balance and length, finishes well; light-bodied but appealing. Screwcap. 13.5° alc. RATING 90 DRINK 2008 $ 18

▼▼▼▼ **Chardonnay with Aligote 2004** Substantial colour development; rich creamy/buttery/peachy style, shortening somewhat on the finish, and the impression of higher alcohol than is in fact present. Cork. 14° alc. RATING 87 DRINK Now $ 25

Hidden Creek NR

Eukey Road, Ballandean, Qld 4382 REGION Granite Belt
T (07) 4684 1383 F (07) 4684 1355 www.hiddencreek.com.au OPEN Mon–Fri 11–3, w'ends 10–4
WINEMAKER Jim Barnes EST. 1997 CASES 1000
A beautifully located vineyard and winery on a 1000m high ridge overlooking the Ballandean township and the Severn River Valley, separated from Girraween National Park by Doctors Creek. The granite boulder-strewn hills mean that the 70-ha property will only provide a little over 6 ha of vineyard, in turn divided into six different blocks. The business has been leased to district veteran Jim Barnes (formerly of Mountview Wines) who is contract winemaker for 10 clients, as well as making the Hidden Creek wines.

Hidden River Estate NR

Mullineaux Road, Pemberton, WA 6260 REGION Pemberton
T (08) 9776 1437 F (08) 9776 0189 www.hiddenriver.com.au OPEN 7 days 9–4
WINEMAKER Brenden Smith, Phil Goldring EST. 1994 CASES 2000
Phil and Sandy Goldring spent 10 years operating farm chalets in the Pemberton area before selling the business and retiring to become grapegrowers, with the intention of selling the grapes to others. However, they found old habits hard to kick, so opened a cellar door and café/restaurant. It is a successful business with a very strong marketing push; a renovated 1901 Kalgoorlie tram (the streetcar named Desire) has been installed to provide more seating for the award-winning restaurant. I hope the Goldrings did not pay much for the tram.

High Valley Wines NR

137 Cassilis Road, Mudgee, NSW 2850 **REGION** Mudgee
T (02) 6372 1011 **F** (02) 6372 1033 **WWW**.highvalley.com.au **OPEN** 7 days 10–5
WINEMAKER Ian MacRae, David Lowe (Contract) **EST.** 1995 **CASES** 2000
The Francis family, headed by Ro and Grosvenor Francis, have operated a sheep, wheat and cattle property at Dunedoo for several generations. When they handed over the property to their sons in 1995, Ro and Grosvenor subdivided and retained a 40-ha block on which they have since established 11 ha of shiraz, 6 ha of cabernet sauvignon and 5 ha of chardonnay. In 1998 they decided to retain a portion of the grapes and develop the High Valley Wines label.

Highbank NR

Riddoch Highway, Coonawarra, SA 5263 **REGION** Coonawarra
T (08) 8736 3311 **F** (08) 8736 3122 **WWW**.highbank.com.au **OPEN** By appt
WINEMAKER Dennis Vice, Trevor Mast (Contract) **EST.** 1986 **CASES** 1000
Mt Gambier lecturer in viticulture Dennis Vice makes a tiny quantity of smooth, melon-accented Chardonnay and stylish, good-quality Coonawarra Cabernet Blend; they are sold through local restaurants and the cellar door, with limited Melbourne distribution. Intermittent exports to various countries.

Higher Plane Wines

Location 1077, Wintarru Rise via Warner Glen Road, Forrest Grove, WA 6286 (postal)
REGION Margaret River
T (08) 9336 7855 **F** (08) 9336 7866 **WWW**.higherplanewines.com.au **OPEN** Not
WINEMAKER Keith Mugford (Contract) **EST.** 1997 **CASES** 6000
Plastic and hand surgeon Dr Craig Smith, and wife Cathie, left nothing to chance in planning and establishing Higher Plane. As a prelude, Cathie obtained a Master of Business in wine marketing from Edith Cowan University, and Craig began the wine marketing course at the Adelaide University. An exhaustive search for the right property ended in 1997, and 7.13 ha of vines were planted, followed by a further 6.58 ha in late 2004, covering all the classic varieties. Its eastern and northern boundaries adjoin Devil's Lair, and the two have similar gravelly, loamy, sandy soil.

ŶŶŶŶŶ **Bellibone Margaret River Chardonnay 2004** A very attractive wine; nectarine, melon and a touch of citrus on the bouquet; very well delineated palate with fused oak and fruit. Screwcap. **RATING** 93 **DRINK** 2009 $ 23
Bellibone Margaret River Cabernet Merlot 2003 A spotlessly clean and fresh mix of cassis, raspberry and blackcurrant; strongly fruit-driven; good length. **RATING** 91 **DRINK** 2013 $ 25
Bellibone Margaret River Sauvignon Blanc 2005 A touch of varietal sweatiness on the bouquet, but with apple, nettle, gooseberry and grass running through a long, bright palate. Screwcap. **RATING** 90 **DRINK** Now $ 22

ŶŶŶŶ **Bellibone Margaret River Semillon Sauvignon Blanc 2005** A similar hint of varietal (sauvignon blanc) sweatiness on the bouquet; stone, grass and nettle flavours; slightly short finish. Cork. **RATING** 88 **DRINK** 2008 $ 20

Highland Heritage Estate NR

Mitchell Highway, Orange, NSW 2800 **REGION** Orange
T (02) 6361 3612 **F** (02) 6361 3613 **WWW**.highlandheritageestate.com.au
OPEN Mon–Fri 9–3, w'ends 9–5
WINEMAKER Hunter Wine Services (John Hordern), Rex D'Aquino **EST.** 1984 **CASES** 3500
The estate plantings have increased from 4 ha to over 15 ha, with 1995 and 1997 plantings now in full production. The tasting facility is unusual: a converted railway carriage overlooking the vineyard. Exports to all major markets.

Highway Wines

NR

612 Great Northern Highway, Herne Hill, WA 6056 **REGION** Swan Valley
T (08) 9296 4354 **OPEN** Mon–Sat 8.30–6
WINEMAKER Tony Bakranich **EST.** 1954 **CASES** 4000
A survivor of another era, when literally dozens of such wineries plied their business in the Swan
Valley. It still enjoys a strong local trade, selling much of its wine in fill-your-own containers and
2-litre flagons, with lesser quantities sold by the bottle.

Hill Smith Estate

★★★★★

Flaxmans Valley Road, Eden Valley, SA 5235 **REGION** Eden Valley
T (08) 8561 3200 **F** (08) 8561 3393 **www**.hillsmithestate.com **OPEN** At Yalumba
WINEMAKER Louisa Rose **EST.** 1979 **CASES** 5000
Part of the Yalumba stable, drawing upon estate plantings, including 15 ha of sauvignon blanc. Over
the years has produced some excellent wines, but the style (and perhaps quality) does seem to vary
significantly with vintage. Exports to all major markets.

♀♀♀♀♀ **Sauvignon Blanc 2005** Spotlessly clean; intense herb, capsicum and gooseberry aromas
and flavours; vibrant and very long; very good finish. Screwcap. **RATING** 94 **DRINK** Now $ 18

Hillbillé

★★★★

Blackwood Valley Estate, Balingup Road, Nannup, WA 6275 **REGION** Blackwood Valley
T (08) 9481 0888 **F** (08) 9486 1899 **www**.hillbille.com **OPEN** W'ends & hols 10–4
WINEMAKER Woodlands Wines (Stuart Watson) **EST.** 1998 **CASES** 3000
Gary Bettridge began the establishment of 19 ha of shiraz, cabernet sauvignon, merlot, chardonnay
and semillon in 1998. The vineyard is situated in the Blackwood Valley between Balingup and
Nannup, which the RAC describes as 'the most scenic drive in the southwest of Western Australia'. A
significant part of the grape production is sold to Goundrey, Vasse Felix, Plantagenet and Evans &
Tate, but since the 2003 vintage, part has been vinified for the Hillbillé label.

♀♀♀♀♀ **Reserve Merlot 2004** Distinctly brighter hue than the varietal; generously flavoured,
supple redcurrant and raspberry fruit; controlled tannins and oak. Cork. 14.5° alc.
RATING 92 **DRINK** 2011 $ 25
Merlot Shiraz 2004 Medium-bodied; a mix of red cherry, plum and cassis fruit; soft
tannins, supple finish. Cork. 14.2° alc. **RATING** 90 **DRINK** 2011 $ 15

♀♀♀♀ **Merlot 2004** Light- to medium-bodied; good texture, gossamer tannins running
throughout; notes of blackcurrant, olive and vanilla oak. Cork. 14.3° alc. **RATING** 88
DRINK 2009 $ 15

♀♀♀♀ **Rose 2005** Light-bodied; well-balanced dry finish to small red fruit flavours. Screwcap.
13.5° alc. **RATING** 86 **DRINK** Now $ 15

Hillbrook

NR

639 Doust Road, Gearys Gap via Bungendore, NSW 2621 **REGION** Canberra District
T (02) 6236 9455 **F** (02) 6236 9455 **OPEN** W'ends & public hols 10–5
WINEMAKER Contract **EST.** 1994 **CASES** 2000
Adolf and Levina Zanzert began the establishment of 8.5 ha of vines at Gearys Gap in 1994. The
wines have retail distribution in the ACT, Bungendore and Cooma, and are also available through the
cellar door and via a mailing list.

Hillbrook Wines

NR

Cnr Hillbrook Road/Wheatley Coast Road, Quinninup, WA 6258 **REGION** Pemberton
T (08) 9776 7202 **F** (08) 9776 7202 **OPEN** By appt
WINEMAKER Castle Rock Estate **EST.** 1996 **CASES** 350
Brian Ede and partner Anne Walsh have established 1 ha of sauvignon blanc and 3 ha of merlot, and
have the wines made for them by Robert Diletti at Castle Rock Estate. They are sold through the
cellar door and via a mailing list, and — increasingly — by word of mouth.

Hillcrest Vineyard

31 Phillip Road, Woori Yallock, Vic 3139 **REGION** Yarra Valley
T (03) 5964 6689 **F** (03) 5961 5547 **www.**hillcrestvineyard.com.au **OPEN** By appt
WINEMAKER Phillip Jones (Contract) **EST.** 1971 **CASES** 400
The small, effectively dry-grown, vineyard was established by Graeme and Joy Sweet, who ultimately sold it to David and Tanya Bryant. The pinot noir, chardonnay, semillon and cabernet sauvignon grown on the property have always been of the highest quality, and, when Coldstream Hills was in its infancy, was a particularly important resource for it. The Bryants have developed the Hillcrest label with the benefit of skilled contract winemaking, and have released several vintages of outstanding wines.

ᵀᵀᵀᵀᵀ **Premium Yarra Valley Pinot Noir 2004** Supple, smooth, silky texture and structure; a perfectly weighted light- to medium-bodied wine, the fruit dominant, the oak harmonious. Remarkably low alcohol. Cork. 12.6° alc. **RATING** 94 **DRINK** 2010 $48

ᵀᵀᵀᵀᵀ **Yarra Valley Chardonnay 2004** Developed colour; rich, mouthfilling, soft stone fruit/peach/melon; integrated oak; at its best now. Cork. 12.8° alc. **RATING** 90 **DRINK** 2008 $37

ᵀᵀᵀᵀ **Yarra Valley Pinot Noir 2004** Similar to the Premium, though less oak influence, the fruit also seeming a bit lighter, although the alcohol is the same. Cork. 12.6° alc. **RATING** 89 **DRINK** 2008 $33
Yarra Valley Cabernet Sauvignon 2004 Light- to medium-bodied; savoury/earthy/minty overtones to the fruit centre all suggest the 34-year-old vines struggled to fully ripen the grapes. Cork. 12.8° alc. **RATING** 89 **DRINK** 2010 $37

Hills of Plenty

370 Yan Yean Road, Yarrambat, Vic 3091 **REGION** Yarra Valley
T (03) 9436 2264 **F** (03) 9436 2264 **www.**hillsofplenty.com.au **OPEN** Last Sun of each month 11–6, or by appt
WINEMAKER Karen Coulston **EST.** 1998 **CASES** 400
Hills of Plenty is just outside the Melbourne metropolitan area, north of Greensborough. There is a tiny 0.2-ha vineyard of riesling, chardonnay and cabernet sauvignon around the winery, but most of the fruit is purchased from other regions, notably Geelong, Gippsland and Swan Hill. The limited production means that the cellar door only opens once a month, but these are festive occasions, with live music, and picnics welcome.

ᵀᵀᵀᵀ **Sweet Enough Riesling Verdelho Sauvignon Blanc 2005** Despite the ominous name and curious blend, it is in fact fresh, lively and crisp, its sweet fruit notes balanced by acidity. Screwcap. 12° alc. **RATING** 87 **DRINK** Now $16

ᵀᵀᵀᵀ **Cabernet Sauvignon 2003 RATING** 84 **DRINK** 2008 $25

Hills View Vineyards

NR

42 Crittenden Road, Findon, SA 5023 **REGION** McLaren Vale
T (08) 8445 7337 **F** (08) 8445 7367 **www.**hillsview.com.au **OPEN** Not
WINEMAKER Brett Howard **EST.** 1998 **CASES** 30 000
District veteran Brett Howard, with 20 years' winemaking experience, is now the winemaker for Hills View Vineyards, producing its range of wines: the Blewitt Springs range and Howard label, a Fleurieu Semillon and a Coonawarra Shiraz which are released only in the best vintages. Exports to the UK, the US and Germany.

Hillside Estate Wines

NR

Marrowbone Road, Pokolbin, NSW 2320 **REGION** Lower Hunter Valley
T (02) 4991 4370 **F** (02) 4991 4371 **OPEN** By appt
WINEMAKER Trevor Drayton (Contract) **EST.** 1995 **CASES** NA
Rena and former noted journalist Ed Barnum have a substantial vineyard of 46 ha, planted to chardonnay, verdelho, traminer, shiraz and cabernet sauvignon; this is substantially more than a quiet retirement hobby. Most of the grapes are sold, the Hillside Estate wines being made by district veteran Trevor Drayton.

Hillwood Vineyard

NR

55 Innocent Street, Kings Meadows, Tas 7249 (postal) **REGION** Northern Tasmania
T 0418 500 672 **OPEN** Not
WINEMAKER Geoff Carr **EST.** NA **CASES** NA
Geoff Carr, owner, viticulturist and winemaker, has established his vineyard on the east bank of the
Tamar River, looking out over the river. He supplements his estate-grown grapes by purchasing some
chardonnay and pinot gris from local growers.

Hirsch Hill Estate

★★★★☆

PO Box 13238, Melbourne, Vic 8010 **REGION** Yarra Valley
T 0425 777 307 **WWW**.hirschhill.com **OPEN** Not
WINEMAKER MasterWineMakers (Martin Williams) **EST.** 1998 **CASES** 3250
The Hirsch family has planted a 13-ha vineyard to pinot noir (predominantly), cabernet sauvignon,
chardonnay, shiraz, merlot and cabernet franc. The vineyard is part of a larger racehorse stud,
situated in a mini-valley at the northern end of the Yarra Valley.

ŸŸŸŸŸ **Yarra Valley Cabernet Sauvignon 2004** Luscious blackcurrant and cassis fruit suggests
greater ripeness/alcohol than the disclosed level of 12.5°; a delicious wine, with good
tannin and extract. Quality cork. 12.5° alc. **RATING** 94 **DRINK** 2012 $ 20

ŸŸŸŸŸ **Yarra Valley Shiraz 2004** Attractive wine; abundant black cherry and blackberry fruit;
mocha/vanilla French oak a little assertive, but should settle down. Quality cork. 13.1° alc.
RATING 90 **DRINK** 2012 $ 20

ŸŸŸŸ **Yarra Valley Pinot Noir 2004** Strong colour; considerable depth to black plum and spice
fruit; just a little extractive. Cork. 13.5° alc. **RATING** 89 **DRINK** 2008 $ 20
Yarra Valley Merlot 2004 Spicy, savoury edges to sweet berry fruit at the core of the
palate; elegant wine which doesn't show green characters despite its relatively low alcohol.
Cork. 12.5° alc. **RATING** 89 **DRINK** 2009 $ 20

ŸŸŸŸ **Yarra Valley Pinot Noir 2003** **RATING** 85 **DRINK** Now $ 20

Hochkirch Wines

★★★☆

Hamilton Highway, Tarrington, Vic 3301 **REGION** Henty
T (03) 5573 5200 **F** (03) 5573 5200 **OPEN** 11–5 by appt
WINEMAKER John Nagorcka **EST.** 1997 **CASES** 2000
Jennifer and John Nagorcka have developed Hochkirch in response to the very cool climate: growing
season temperatures are similar to those in Burgundy. A high-density planting pattern was
implemented, with a low fruiting wire taking advantage of soil warmth in the growing season, and
the focus was placed on pinot noir (4.5 ha), with lesser quantities of riesling, cabernet sauvignon,
semillon and shiraz. The vines are not irrigated, and no synthetic fungicides, pesticides or fertilisers
are used; the Nagorckas have moved to certified biodynamic viticulture.

ŸŸŸŸ **Riesling 2005** Clean, firm mineral structure support spiced apple and some lime. Cork.
12.5° alc. **RATING** 89 **DRINK** 2008 $ 20
Cuvee Blanc Semillon Chardonnay 2005 Cut grass, herbs, spice and lemony acidity; no
oak works well; good length. Not sparkling. Cork. 12.5° alc. **RATING** 88 **DRINK** 2009 $ 17

ŸŸŸŸ **Maximus Pinot Noir 2004** **RATING** 86 **DRINK** 2008 $ 32
Shiraz 2004 **RATING** 84 **DRINK** Now $ 25

Hoddles Creek Estate

★★★★☆

505 Gembrook Road, Hoddles Creek, Vic 3139 **REGION** Yarra Valley
T (03) 5967 4692 **F** (03) 5967 4692 **WWW**.hoddlescreekestate.com.au **OPEN** By appt
WINEMAKER Franco D'Anna **EST.** 1997 **CASES** 10 000
In 1997, the D'Anna family decided to establish a vineyard on the property which had been in the
family since 1960. There are now 2 vineyard blocks totalling 18.5 ha, split by Gembrook Road and
Hoddles Creek, which are hand-pruned and hand-harvested. A 300-tonne, split-level winery was

completed in 2003. Son Franco D'Anna is the viticulturist and winemaker, having started to work in the family liquor store at 13, graduating to chief wine buyer by the time he was 21, then completing a Bachelor of Commerce degree at Melbourne University before studying viticulture at Charles Sturt University. A vintage at Coldstream Hills, then consulting help from Peter Dredge of Red Edge and Mario Marson (ex Mount Mary) has put an old head on young shoulders. Together with his uncle Bruno and one other worker, he is solely responsible for the vineyard and winery.

ŸŸŸŸŸ **Yarra Valley Pinot Noir 2004** Clean, fresh, light- to medium-bodied; attractive plum and red fruits, silky smooth and supple. Screwcap. **RATING** 91 **DRINK** 2010 $ 16.99

Hoffmann's ★★★★☆

Ingoldby Road, McLaren Flat, SA 5171 **REGION** McLaren Vale
T (08) 8383 0232 **F** (08) 8383 0232 **WWW**.hoffmannswine.com.au **OPEN** 7 days 11–5
WINEMAKER Nick Holmes, Hamish McGuire (Consultant) **EST.** 1996 **CASES** 2500
Peter and Anthea Hoffmann have been growing grapes at their property in Ingoldby Road since 1978, and Peter Hoffmann has worked at various wineries in McLaren Vale since 1979. Both he and Anthea have undertaken courses at the Regency TAFE Institute in Adelaide, and (in Peter's words), 'in 1996 we decided that we knew a little about winemaking and opened a small cellar door'. Exports to the UK, the US and other major markets.

ŸŸŸŸŸ **McLaren Vale Shiraz 2004** Big, rich, ripe archetypal McLaren Vale Shiraz oozing blackberry, chocolate and licorice; balanced tannins and oak. Cork. 14.5° alc. **RATING** 91 **DRINK** 2012 $ 21
McLaren Vale Shiraz Cabernet 2004 A strong chocolate coating to an array of black fruits and ripe tannins. A seriously poor cork. 14.5° alc. **RATING** 90 **DRINK** 2012 $ 21
McLaren Vale Cabernet Sauvignon 2004 Good colour; medium-bodied; bright, sweet cassis/blackcurrant fruit, with supple tannins and a juicy finish. Screwcap. 14.5° alc. **RATING** 90 **DRINK** 2011 $ 21

ŸŸŸŸ **McLaren Vale Merlot 2004** **RATING** 86 **DRINK** Now $ 18

Holley Hill ★★☆

140 Ronalds Road, Willung, Vic 3847 **REGION** Gippsland
T (03) 5198 2205 **F** (03) 5198 2205 **OPEN** Thurs–Sun & public hols 10–6
WINEMAKER David Packham **EST.** 1998 **CASES** 350
David Packham has used his background as a Master of Applied Science, formerly a research scientist with the CSIRO, and more recently with the Bureau of Meteorology, to plan the establishment of Holley Hill. He served his apprenticeship at another winery for 2 years before acquiring the then 2-year-old Holley Hill vineyard, planted to approximately 0.5 ha each of chardonnay, sauvignon blanc and pinot noir. A large hay shed on the property was converted to a winery and cellar door.

ŸŸŸŸ **Sauvignon Blanc 2005** Faint oxidative pinking; a long intense palate with driving acidity, the fruit slightly diminished. Cork. 14.5° alc. **RATING** 86 **DRINK** Now $ 16

ŸŸŸ **Johnsonville Pinot Rose 2005** **RATING** 83 $ 15

Hollick ★★★★☆

Riddoch Highway, Coonawarra, SA 5263 **REGION** Coonawarra
T (08) 8737 2318 **F** (08) 8737 2952 **WWW**.hollick.com **OPEN** 7 days 9–5
WINEMAKER Ian Hollick, David Norman **EST.** 1983 **CASES** 40 000
A family business owned by Ian and Wendy Hollick, and winner of many trophies (including the most famous of all, the Jimmy Watson), its wines are well crafted and competitively priced. A $1 million cellar door and restaurant complex opened in 2002. The original cellar door was a heritage-listed cottage built in 1860, and was restored by Ian and Wendy in 1983. The Hollicks have progressively expanded their vineyard holdings: the first is the 12-ha Neilson's Block vineyard, one of the original John Riddoch selections, but used as a dairy farm between 1910 and 1975 when the Hollicks planted cabernet sauvignon and merlot. The second is the 80-plus ha Wilgha vineyard, purchased in 1987 with already established dry-grown cabernet sauvignon and shiraz; total area under vine is 45 ha. The last is the Red Ridge vineyard in Wrattonbully, where 24 ha have been planted including trial plantings of tempranillo and sangiovese. Exports to Europe and Asia.

ŢŢŢŢŢ Wilgha Shiraz 2003 Deep colour; very attractive fruit with a sweet kernel, then ripples of spice and licorice around the edge. **RATING** 93 **DRINK** 2013 $ 45

The Nectar 2005 Aromatic lime and lemon blossom bouquet; very good balance and acidity, midway between spatlese and auslese; long, lingering palate. Cork. 13° alc. **RATING** 93 **DRINK** 2008 $ 24

Sauvignon Blanc Semillon 2005 Clean, lively, fresh flavours ranging through passionfruit to cut grass; minerally acidity on a bright finish. Best yet. Coonawarra/Mount Benson. Screwcap. 12.5° alc. **RATING** 92 **DRINK** Now $ 17

Reserve Chardonnay 2004 Elegant, light-bodied; melon and stone fruit with integrated oak/lees/malolactic inputs; good finish, developing slowly. Cork. 14° alc. **RATING** 91 **DRINK** 2010 $ 22

Wrattonbully Shiraz 2003 Has some of the McLaren Vale chocolate along with blackberry, mocha and vanilla; good balance, ripe tannins. Cork. 14° alc. **RATING** 90 **DRINK** 2013 $ 25

ŢŢŢŢ Hollaia 2004 Fragrant red fruits and flower blooms; light-bodied, but has good fruit intensity; minimal tannins, a nice touch of oak. The Hollick version of the distinguished Italian super-Tuscan Solaia. Sangiovese/Cabernet Sauvignon. Screwcap. 12.5° alc. **RATING** 89 **DRINK** 2010 $ 20

Shiraz Cabernet Sauvignon 2003 Earthy, cedary, savoury aromas; medium-bodied, with some red fruits, but not enough to balance the savoury elements. Cork. 13.5° alc. **RATING** 87 **DRINK** 2009 $ 19

Wrattonbully Tempranillo 2004 Medium-bodied; characteristic black and red cherry fruit; perhaps a touch heavily cropped; supple tannins. Screwcap. 12.5° alc. **RATING** 87 **DRINK** 2008 $ 20

ŢŢŢŢ Coonawarra Cabernet Sauvignon Merlot 2003 RATING 86 **DRINK** 2009 $ 24
Coonawarra Cabernet Sauvignon 2003 RATING 86 **DRINK** 2009 $ 29

Holm Oak

NR

RSD 256 Rowella, West Tamar, Tas 7270 **REGION** Northern Tasmania
T (03) 6394 7577 **F** (03) 6394 7350 **OPEN** 7 days 10–5
WINEMAKER Nick Butler, Winemaking Tasmania (Julian Alcorso) **EST.** 1983 **CASES** 3000
The Butler family produces tremendously rich and strongly flavoured red wines from their vineyard on the banks of the Tamar River. Holm Oak takes its name from its grove of oak trees, planted around the turn of the 20th century, and originally intended for the making of tennis racquets.

Home Hill

★★★★

38 Nairn Street, Ranelagh, Tas 7109 **REGION** Southern Tasmania
T (03) 6264 1200 **F** (03) 6264 1069 **www.**homehillwines.com.au **OPEN** 7 days 10–5
WINEMAKER Peter Dunbaven **EST.** 1994 **CASES** 3000
Terry and Rosemary Bennett planted their first 0.5 ha of vines in 1994 on gentle slopes in the beautiful Huon Valley. The plantings were quickly extended to 3 ha, with another ha planted in 1999. The varieties planted are pinot noir, chardonnay and sylvaner, and the quality of the chardonnay and pinot noir in particular is exemplary.

ŢŢŢŢŢ Kelly's Reserve Pinot Noir 2004 Deep colour; very powerful and strong black fruits; seems late-picked; within a whisker of top points. **RATING** 90 **DRINK** 2010 $ 35

Kelly's Reserve Sticky 2005 Fragrant and elegant; tangy lime juice on a pure palate. Screwcap. 11.5° alc. **RATING** 90 **DRINK** 2011 $ 19

ŢŢŢŢ Unoaked Chardonnay 2005 RATING 86 **DRINK** Now $ 19
Pinot Noir 2004 In typical Home Hill style, extremely powerful and tannic; past history suggests it may come around with time in bottle. **RATING** 86 **DRINK** 2012 $ 26
Sylvaner 2005 RATING 85 **DRINK** Now $ 19
Early Release Pinot Noir 2004 RATING 85 **DRINK** Now $ 26
Kelly Cuvee 2003 RATING 85 **DRINK** Now $ 28

Honeytree Estate

16 Gillards Road, Pokolbin, NSW 2321 **REGION** Lower Hunter Valley
T (02) 4998 7693 **F** (02) 4998 7693 **WWW**.honeytreewines.com **OPEN** Wed–Fri 11–4, w'ends 10–5
WINEMAKER Monarch Winemaking Services (Jim Chatto) **EST.** 1970 **CASES** 1800
The Honeytree Estate vineyard was first planted in 1970, and for a period of time wines were produced. It then disappeared, but the vineyard has since been revived by Dutch-born Henk Strengers and family. Its 10 ha of vines are of shiraz, cabernet sauvignon, semillon and a little clairette, known in the Hunter Valley as blanquette, and a variety which has been in existence there for well over a century. Jancis Robinson comments that the wine 'tends to be very high in alcohol, a little low in acid and to oxidise dangerously fast', but in a sign of the times, the first Honeytree Clairette sold out so quickly (in 4 weeks) that 2.2 ha of vineyard has been grafted over to additional clairette. Exports to The Netherlands.

ΥΥΥΥ **Hunter Valley Clairette 2005** Well-made; an essentially neutral variety, given interest here by counterbalancing acidity with a touch of residual sugar. Screwcap. 13.5° alc. **RATING** 88 **DRINK** Now **$** 20

ΥΥΥΥ **Veronica Semillon 2005** **RATING** 86 **DRINK** 2010 **$** 15

Hope Estate

Cobcroft Road, Broke, NSW 2330 **REGION** Lower Hunter Valley
T (02) 6579 1161 **F** (02) 6579 1373 **WWW**.hopeestate.com.au **OPEN** By appt
WINEMAKER James Campkin **EST.** 1996 **CASES** 40 000
Pharmacist Michael Hope has come a long way since acquiring his first vineyard in the Hunter Valley in 1994. His Hunter Valley empire now encompasses three substantial vineyards and the former Saxonvale Winery, acquired in 1996, renamed Hope Estate, and refurbished at a cost of over $1 million. That, however, proved to be only the first step, for Hope has acquired most of the assets of the former public-listed Vincorp, including its Donnybrook Vineyard in WA, and the Virgin Hills brand, which includes its original 14-ha vineyard, another nearby 32-ha vineyard at Glenhope and a lease of the historic winery. Exports to the UK, the US and other major markets.

ΥΥΥΥΥ **Hunter Valley Chardonnay 2005** A complex wine; the peach/nectarine/melon fruit shows, but stands up to the full bag of winemaking inputs used across 10 different vineyard/fermentation lots. Cork. 13° alc. **RATING** 91 **DRINK** 2009 **$** 18
Hunter Valley Shiraz 2003 Good depth of colour; plenty of fruit weight as expected from the vintage; medium-bodied, supple, blackberry fruit and fine-grained tannins. Cork. 13° alc. **RATING** 90 **DRINK** 2013 **$** 20
Hunter Valley Merlot 2003 Medium-bodied, with a similar supple mouthfeel to that of the Shiraz; red fruits with near-subliminal regional earthy notes; well-controlled oak and extract. Cork. 13° alc. **RATING** 90 **DRINK** 2011 **$** 20

ΥΥΥΥ **Verdelho 2005** A lighter, crisper, more brisk style than usual, with a tangy, citrussy overlay to the tropical fruit; has attitude. Cork. 12.5° alc. **RATING** 88 **DRINK** 2010 **$** 15

Hoppers Hill Vineyard

NR

108 Googodery Road, Cumnock, NSW 2867 **REGION** Central Ranges Zone
T (02) 6367 7270 **OPEN** By appt
WINEMAKER Robert Gilmour **EST.** 1985 **CASES** 450
The Gilmours planted their vineyard in 1979, using organic growing methods; they use no preservatives or filtration in the winery, which was established in 1985. Not surprisingly, the wines cannot be judged or assessed against normal standards, but may have appeal in a niche market.

Hopwood

687 Murray Valley Highway, Echuca, Vic 3564 **REGION** Goulburn Valley
T (03) 5480 7090 **F** (03) 5480 7096 **WWW**.hopwood.com.au **OPEN** Mon–Fri 9–5
WINEMAKER Don Buchanan, Rowan Steward **EST.** 2000 **CASES** 32 000
Previously known first as Echuca Estate Wines, and then by its corporate owner, New Glory Pty Ltd. Since taking the reins, industry veteran Don Buchanan has focused on retrellising and training the

38-ha vineyard planted to verdelho, viognier, shiraz, cabernet sauvignon, durif, sangiovese and petit verdot. The wines are released in 2 price levels: Charlotte's Farm the entry point, and the Hopwood Single Vineyard premium range.

▼▼▼▼ **SMPV Single Vineyard 2004** Good colour; medium-bodied; savoury black fruits with typical grainy tannins of mourvedre and petit verdot; good overall extract. Shiraz/Mourvedre/Petit Verdot. Cork. 13° alc. **RATING** 89 **DRINK** 2010 $ 19
CPVM Single Vineyard 2004 Light- to medium-bodied; savoury blackcurrant, earth and olive; fine tannins and gentle vanilla oak. Cabernet Sauvignon/Petit Verdot/Mourvedre. Cork. **RATING** 88 **DRINK** 2009 $ 19
Charlotte's Farm Sangiovese 2004 Light-bodied, but does have some rose petal and cherry stone varietal character. Cork. 13.5° alc. **RATING** 87 **DRINK** Now $ 13

▼▼▼▽ **Charlotte's Farm Cabernet Sauvignon 2004** **RATING** 86 **DRINK** Now $ 13
Charlotte's Farm Verdelho 2004 **RATING** 85 **DRINK** Now $ 13
Charlotte's Farm Shiraz 2004 **RATING** 84 **DRINK** Now $ 13

▼▼▼ **Charlotte's Farm Chardonnay 2005** **RATING** 83 $ 13

Horndale   ★★★☆

Fraser Avenue, Happy Valley, SA 5159 **REGION** McLaren Vale
T (08) 8387 0033 **F** (08) 8387 0033 **OPEN** Mon–Sat 9–5, Sun & public hols 10–5.30
WINEMAKER Phil Albrecht **EST.** 1896 **CASES** NFP
Established in 1896 and has remained continuously in production in one way or another since that time, though with a number of changes of ownership and direction. My father used to buy Horndale Brandy 60 years ago, but it no longer appears on the extensive price list. The wines are only available from the cellar door and by mail order.

▼▼▼▼▽ **Old Horndale Shiraz 2004** Light- to medium-bodied; well-constructed and balanced blackberry and plum fruit; supple tannins, balanced oak. Gold medal Australian Small Winemakers Show '05. Outstanding value. Langhorne Creek. Cork. 14° alc. **RATING** 92 **DRINK** 2013 $ 15

▼▼▼▼ **Old Horndale Shiraz Grenache 2004** Good colour; more structure than often encountered with this blend; a mix of blackberry and juicy red fruits; minimal oak influence. Screwcap. 14.8° alc. **RATING** 89 **DRINK** 2010 $ 13
Old Horndale Cabernet Merlot Shiraz 2004 Good colour; light- to medium-bodied; attractive sweet berry fruits and no green characters; soft, ripe tannins. Cork. 13.4° alc. **RATING** 88 **DRINK** 2012 $ 13
Old Horndale Cabernet Sauvignon 2004 Bright colour; light- to medium-bodied, clean, fresh and lively cassis berry fruit; minimal tannins and oak. Cork. 13.5° alc. **RATING** 87 **DRINK** 2010 $ 13

Horseshoe Vineyard   NR

Horseshoe Road, Horseshoe Valley via Denman, NSW 2328 **REGION** Upper Hunter Valley
T (02) 6547 3528 **OPEN** W'ends 9–5
WINEMAKER John Hordern **EST.** 1986 **CASES** NFP
Fell by the wayside after its wonderful start in 1986, with rich, full-flavoured, barrel-fermented Semillons and Chardonnays. These days John Hordern's main occupation seems to be as a highly successful contract winemaker (Hunter Wine Services), particularly for Penmara.

Horvat Estate   NR

2444 Burke Street, Landsborough, Vic 3384 **REGION** Pyrenees
T (03) 5356 9296 **F** (03) 5356 9264 **OPEN** 7 days 10–5
WINEMAKER Andrew Horvat, Gabriel Horvat **EST.** 1995 **CASES** 1500
The Horvat family (including Janet, Andrew and Gabriel) began developing their 5-ha vineyard of shiraz in 1995, supplementing production with contract-grown grapes. The wines are made using traditional methods and ideas, deriving in part from the family's Croatian background.

Houghton

Dale Road, Middle Swan, WA 6056 **REGION** Swan Valley
T (08) 9274 9450 **F** (08) 9274 5372 **WWW**.houghton-wines.com.au **OPEN** 7 days 10–5
WINEMAKER Robert Bowen **EST.** 1836 **CASES** 280 000
The 5-star rating was once partially justified by Houghton White Burgundy, one of Australia's largest-selling white wines: it was almost entirely consumed within days of purchase, but was superlative with 7 or so years' bottle age. The Jack Mann red, Gladstones Shiraz, Houghton Reserve Shiraz, the Margaret River reds and Frankland Riesling are all of the highest quality, and simply serve to reinforce the rating. To borrow a saying of the late Jack Mann, 'There are no bad wines here.'

ŸŸŸŸŸ Museum Release Chardonnay 1998 Marvellously elegant and fine (13.5°alcohol); grapefruit, melon and stone fruit aromas and flavours; oak in support role; long, lingering finish. Multiple golds. Frankland River. High-quality cork. 13.5° alc. **RATING** 95 **DRINK** Now $25
Crofters Cabernet Merlot 2003 A lively and fresh array of red and black fruits; finely balanced and integrated oak and tannins. Top gold medal National Wine Show '05. Cork. 13.8° alc. **RATING** 95 **DRINK** 2013 $25
Frankland River Riesling 2002 Lively, crisp and juicy; also toast and mineral notes; excellent life, length and drive. Gold medal National Wine Show '05. Screwcap. 12° alc. **RATING** 94 **DRINK** 2012 $23

ŸŸŸŸŸ Crofters Sauvignon Blanc Semillon 2004 Has developed impressively in bottle; a serious wine, the semillon providing spine and framework; herb, mineral and tropical mix; has both depth and length. **RATING** 93 **DRINK** Now $18
Museum Release White Burgundy 1994 Brilliant green-yellow; great balance, structure and mouthfeel; citrus and mineral, with hints of toast and spice. Unlike some others in this museum release series, the cork has not destroyed the wine. Cork. **RATING** 93 **DRINK** Now $25
Museum Release Riesling 1996 Fully mature, but still crisp and lively; a core of honey, lime and toast; brisk acidity to the finish. Soft, saturated cork. **RATING** 92 **DRINK** Now $25
Museum Release White Burgundy 1995 Light- to medium-bodied; lively and complex toast, lime, lemon and honey; brisk acidity. Crumbly cork. **RATING** 91 **DRINK** Now $25

ŸŸŸŸ Semillon Sauvignon Blanc 2005 Light-bodied; attractive passionfruit, herb and gooseberry aromas and flavours; outstanding value. Twin top. **RATING** 89 **DRINK** Now $10.50
Shiraz 2003 As ever, great value, punching well above its weight; appealing blackberry fruit; fine tannins, minimal oak; good length. Twin top. **RATING** 89 **DRINK** 2010 $10
White Burgundy 2005 An article of faith that it will develop real character with bottle development; faintly reductive aromas; tropical fruit and good acidity. Twin top. **RATING** 88 **DRINK** 2009 $10.50
Cabernet Shiraz Merlot 2004 Good purple-red; a medium-bodied mix of red and black fruits, positive oak and soft tannins; remarkable at the price. Twin top. 13.5° alc. **RATING** 88 **DRINK** 2009 $10.50

ŸŸŸŸ Pemberton Sauvignon Blanc 2005 RATING 86 **DRINK** Now
Chardonnay Verdelho 2005 RATING 84 **DRINK** Now $10.50

ŸŸŸ Chenin Blanc 2005 RATING 83 $10.50

House of Certain Views ★★★★

1238 Milbrodale Road, Broke, NSW 2330 **REGION** Lower Hunter Valley
T (02) 6579 1317 **F** (02) 6579 1267 **WWW**.margan.com.au **OPEN** 7 days 10–5
WINEMAKER Andrew Margan **EST.** 2001 **CASES** 1000
A stand-alone business owned by Andrew and Lisa Margan, with a fascinating portfolio of wines based on exclusive or fairly new winegrowing regions on the western side of the Great Dividing Range. The selection of the vineyard sites (via contract growers) involves a careful correlation of latitude, altitude, soil type and variety — the French catch it all in the single word 'terroir'. The packaging of the wines, incidentally, is brilliant.

ᵀᵀᵀᵀ♀ **Orange Shiraz 2002** Uncertain colour; very interesting spicy/tangy aromas and flavours; long, lingering spicy black fruits; shows the cool climate to advantage. Cork. 15° alc. **RATING** 92 **DRINK** 2012 $ 30

ᵀᵀᵀᵀ **Orange Viognier 2005** Powerful; good varietal character with apricot/tropical fruit; a subliminal touch of oak. Cork. 14° alc. **RATING** 89 **DRINK** 2008 $ 25

Howard Park (Denmark)   ★★★★★

Scotsdale Road, Denmark, WA 6333 **REGION** Great Southern
T (08) 9848 2345 **F** (08) 9848 2064 **WWW**.howardparkwines.com.au **OPEN** 7 days 10–4
WINEMAKER Michael Kerrigan, Andy Browning, Matt Burton **EST.** 1986 **CASES** NFP
All the Howard Park wines are made here at the new, large winery. However, there are three groups of wines: those sourced from either Great Southern or Margaret River; the icon Howard Park Riesling and Cabernet Sauvignon Merlot; and the multi-regional MadFish range. Thus the Leston wines come from Margaret River, the Scotsdale from Great Southern. All are very impressive. Exports to all major markets.

ᵀᵀᵀᵀᵀ **Riesling 2005** Intense, almost pungent, deep lime/citrus aromas; flooded with lime juice on the palate, yet not at all heavy. Outstanding wine. Screwcap. 12.5° alc. **RATING** 96 **DRINK** 2015 $ 25
Chardonnay 2004 Very fragrant and pure citrus, apple, grapefruit, stone fruit and grapefruit aromas and flavours; great line and balance; fruit has easily swallowed the oak. Screwcap. 13.5° alc. **RATING** 96 **DRINK** 2014 $ 35
Scotsdale Great Southern Shiraz 2003 Excellent colour; fragrant spicy, peppery black fruits; long, intense palate; great balance and style; flavour with finesse. Screwcap. **RATING** 96 **DRINK** 2018 $ 35
Scotsdale Great Southern Cabernet Sauvignon 2003 Elegant, intense and very long; classic cool-grown style; cedar, cassis and blackcurrant; has swallowed the oak. Screwcap. **RATING** 95 **DRINK** 2018 $ 35

ᵀᵀᵀᵀ♀ **Sauvignon Blanc 2005** Light straw-green; a spotlessly clean bouquet; mineral, talc, gooseberry and green apple flavours run through to the long, clean finish. Screwcap. 12.5° alc. **RATING** 93 **DRINK** Now $ 25

Howard Park (Margaret River)   ★★★★★

Miamup Road, Cowaramup, WA 6284 **REGION** Margaret River
T (08) 9756 5200 **F** (08) 9756 5222 **WWW**.howardparkwines.com.au **OPEN** 7 days 10–5
WINEMAKER Michael Kerrigan, Andy Browning, Matt Burton **EST.** 1986 **CASES** NFP
In the wake of its acquisition by the Burch family, and the construction of a large state-of-the-art winery at Denmark, a capacious cellar door (incorporating Feng Shui principles) has opened in the Margaret River, where there are also significant estate plantings. The Margaret River flagships are the Leston Shiraz and Leston Cabernet Sauvignon, but the Margaret River vineyards routinely contribute to all the wines in the range, from MadFish at the bottom, to the icon Cabernet Sauvignon Merlot at the top. Exports to all major markets.

ᵀᵀᵀᵀᵀ **Leston Margaret River Cabernet Sauvignon 2003** Outstanding colour; spotlessly clean; floods the mouth with blackcurrant fruit plus wisps of mocha and chocolate; radically different style to Scotsdale. Screwcap. **RATING** 96 **DRINK** 2018 $ 35
MadFish Chardonnay 2004 Bright, light straw-green; a fragrant and stylish fruit-driven style notwithstanding the barrel ferment and maturation in oak; long and crisp, very much in Chablis style. Screwcap. 13.5° alc. **RATING** 95 **DRINK** 2010 $ 22
Leston Margaret River Shiraz 2003 Supple, smooth and sweet red fruits; fine-grained spicy tannins; as elegant as ever; controlled French oak. Screwcap. **RATING** 94 **DRINK** 2015 $ 35

ᵀᵀᵀᵀ♀ **MadFish Sauvignon Blanc Semillon 2005** Spotlessly clean; a lively, bright and fresh mix of light tropical fruit and balanced acidity. Screwcap. 12.5° alc. **RATING** 92 **DRINK** Now $ 18
MadFish Riesling 2005 Very refined style; delicate, yet intense and long palate; delicious lemony acidity to close. Screwcap. **RATING** 91 **DRINK** 2015 $ 16

MadFish Premium Red 2003 Medium-bodied; perfectly ripened blackcurrant and cassis fruit; fresh mouthfeel and finish; minimal oak; fine, ripe tannins. Top value. Cabernet Sauvignon/Merlot/Cabernet Franc, Margaret River/Great Southern. Screwcap. **RATING** 90 **DRINK** 2010 $19.99

ŦŦŦŦ **MadFish Premium White 2005** Fresh, lively stone fruit and citrus, though a ghost of reduction stalks in the background; clean, crisp finish. Screwcap. 13° alc. **RATING** 88 **DRINK** Now $20

ŦŦŦŦ **MadFish Carnelian 2004 RATING** 86 **DRINK** 2012 $24

Howards Lane Vineyard ★★★☆

Howards Lane, Welby, Mittagong, NSW 2575 **REGION** Southern Highlands
T (02) 4872 1971 **WWW**.howardslane.com.au **OPEN** 7 days 10–5
WINEMAKER Michelle Crockett (Contract) **EST.** 1991 **CASES** 600
Tony and Mary Betteridge have developed the plantings over a 10-year period, establishing the Corrie Vineyard first, and recently the McCourt Vineyard. Older vintages of Chardonnay are available.

ŦŦŦŦ **Southern Highlands Chardonnay 2005** Light-bodied; seemingly entirely driven by stone fruit and quince aromas and flavours; good acidity. Screwcap. 12.9° alc. **RATING** 89 **DRINK** 2009 $18
Southern Highlands Unwooded Chardonnay 2005 Light-bodied; clean nectarine, peach and citrus; balanced acidity, and just enough length. Screwcap. 12.9° alc. **RATING** 87 **DRINK** 2008 $18
Southern Highlands Light Red 2005 Bright, light purple-red; apparently unoaked and from unspecified varieties; midway between rose and red wine; the dry finish does shorten slightly. This is indeed a light red. Screwcap. 11.7° alc. **RATING** 87 **DRINK** 2008 $18

ŦŦŦŦ **Southern Highlands Cabernet Sauvignon 2004 RATING** 84 **DRINK** 2008 $22

HPR Wines NR

260 Old Moorooduc Road, Tuerong, Vic 3933 (postal) **REGION** Mornington Peninsula
T (03) 5974 2097 **F** (03) 5974 3099 **OPEN** Not
WINEMAKER Hugh Robinson **EST.** 1988 **CASES** 250
Hugh Robinson is a Mornington Peninsula veteran, and has no less than 22 ha of sauvignon blanc, semillon, chardonnay, pinot gris, pinot noir, merlot and shiraz. The major part of the production is sold as grapes to other makers, with the remainder made by Hugh Robinson onsite.

Hudson's Peak Wines NR

92 Hillsborough Road, Hillsborough, NSW 2320 **REGION** Lower Hunter Valley
T 0409 660 883 **F** (02) 4930 0759 **OPEN** 7 days 10–5
WINEMAKER John Cassegrain (Contract) **EST.** 1998 **CASES** NFP
Hudson's Peak Wines come from a historic property, first gazetted in 1829, and taken up by Beresford Hudson, who gave his name both to a nearby mountain top and (now) this substantial wine venture. The 53-ha property includes 18 ha of vines, almost half to shiraz, the remainder to semillon, chardonnay, verdelho and merlot. Part of the production is sold as grapes, and part is contract-made.

Hugh Hamilton ★★★★★

McMurtrie Road, McLaren Vale, SA 5171 **REGION** McLaren Vale
T (08) 8323 8689 **F** (08) 8323 9488 **WWW**.hughhamiltonwines.com.au **OPEN** Mon–Fri 10–5.30, w'ends & public hols 11–5.30
WINEMAKER Hugh Hamilton **EST.** 1991 **CASES** 19 000
Hugh Hamilton is the most recent member of the famous Hamilton winemaking family to enter the business with a label of his own. Production comes from 18.2 ha of estate plantings, supplemented by contract-grown material. Recent plantings go beyond the mainstream to sangiovese, tempranillo, petit verdot and saperavi. Exports to the US, Canada, the UK, Denmark and Malaysia.

ΨΨΨΨΨ Jekyll & Hyde Shiraz Viognier 2004 Intense, high-toned spice, cherry and apricot aromas; very powerful and long palate, with tangy black cherry, spice and dark chocolate; 7% viognier co-fermented; 5% may have been better. Cork. 14° alc. **RATING** 94 **DRINK** 2015 $ 28.50

The Villain Cabernet Sauvignon 2004 Strong purple-red; archetypal McLaren Vale cabernet, flooded with juicy cassis/blackcurrant fruit swathed in dark chocolate; good tannins and oak. Screwcap. 14.5° alc. **RATING** 94 **DRINK** 2019 $ 24.50

ΨΨΨΨ The Rascal Shiraz 2004 Good colour; medium-bodied black and red cherry, chocolate and spice; fine tannins; restrained style. **RATING** 92 **DRINK** 2014 $ 24

The Mongrel 2005 Fresh, bright cherry fruit ex sangiovese the dominant player; lively and long finish; good balance. Sangiovese (85%)/Merlot/Tempranillo. Cork. 14° alc. **RATING** 90 **DRINK** 2011 $ 19

The Scoundrel Tempranillo 2003 Clean and fragrant; attractive spice component; very good mouthfeel; sweet fruit and supple tannins. Diam. **RATING** 90 **DRINK** 2010 $ 24.50

ΨΨΨΨ The Scallywag Unwooded Chardonnay 2005 RATING 86 **DRINK** Now $ 17.50
The Loose Cannon Viognier 2005 RATING 86 **DRINK** Now $ 19.50
The Trickster Verdelho 2005 RATING 84 **DRINK** Now $ 18.50

Hugo ★★★

Elliott Road, McLaren Flat, SA 5171 **REGION** McLaren Vale
T (08) 8383 0098 **F** (08) 8383 0446 **WWW**.hugowines.com.au **OPEN** Mon–Fri 9.30–5, Sat 12–5, Sun 10.30–5
WINEMAKER John Hugo **EST.** 1982 **CASES** 12 000
A winery which came from relative obscurity to prominence in the late 1980s with some lovely ripe, sweet reds which, while strongly American oak-influenced, were quite outstanding. Has picked up the pace again after a dull period in the mid-1990s. There are 32 ha of estate plantings, with part of the grape production sold to others. Exports to all major markets.

ΨΨΨΨ McLaren Vale Cabernet Sauvignon 2003 Tight, savoury; I'm not sure the screwcap has done this wine any favours — or, perhaps, vice versa. Screwcap. 14.5° alc. **RATING** 86 **DRINK** 2009 $ 19

McLaren Vale Shiraz 2003 RATING 85 **DRINK** 2008 $ 19

Humbug Reach Vineyard ★★★★★

72 Nobelias Drive, Legana, Tas 7277 **REGION** Northern Tasmania
T (03) 6330 2875 **F** (03) 6330 2739 **WWW**.humbugreach.com.au **OPEN** Not
WINEMAKER Winemaking Tasmania (Julian Alcorso) **EST.** 1988 **CASES** 450
The Humbug Reach Vineyard was established in the late 1980s on the banks of the Tamar River, with plantings of pinot noir; riesling and chardonnay followed thereafter. Owned by Paul and Sally McShane since 1999, who proudly tend the 5000 or so vines on the property.

ΨΨΨΨΨ Riesling 2005 Fine, intense and with outstanding structure and length; tightly focused lime juice flavours; elegant minerality to close. **RATING** 94 **DRINK** 2012 $ 22

Chardonnay 2005 Delicious wine; fragrant, gently sweet, stone fruit aromas and flavours; a long, lingering finish sustained by Tasmanian acidity. Screwcap. 13° alc. **RATING** 94 **DRINK** 2012 $ 20

Hundred Tree Hill NR

1 Sally's Lane, Redbank, Vic 3478 **REGION** Pyrenees
T (03) 5467 7255 **F** (03) 5467 7248 **WWW**.sallyspaddock.com.au **OPEN** Mon–Sat 9–5, Sun 10–5
WINEMAKER Huw Robb, Scott Hutton, Sasha Robb **EST.** 1973 **CASES** 6000
The next generation of the Robb family (Emily, Huw and Sasha) have established their own vineyard, with 6 ha each of shiraz, cabernet sauvignon and cabernet franc, plus 2 ha of pinot noir. Hundred Tree Hill was so named to commemorate the 100 trees which went into the building of the Hundred Tree Homestead. Exports to the US, Canada, Germany and Philippines.

Hungerford Hill

1 Broke Road, Pokolbin, NSW 2321 **REGION** Lower Hunter Valley
T 1800 187 666 **F** (02) 4998 7375 **WWW**.hungerfordhill.com.au **OPEN** 7 days 10–5
WINEMAKER Phillip John **EST.** 1967 **CASES** 20 000
Hungerford Hill, sold by Southcorp to the Kirby family in 2002, has emerged with its home base at the impressive winery on the corner of Allandale and Broke Roads, previously known as One Broke Road. The development of the One Broke Road complex proved wildly uneconomic, and the rationalisation process has resulted in Hungerford Hill being the sole owner. Terroir Restaurant and Wine Bar are run by award-winning chef Darren Ho. Exports to all major markets.

ŸŸŸŸŸ **Hunter Valley Semillon 2005** Glowing yellow-green; unusual complexity and depth; maybe a touch of barrel ferment, maybe not. Screwcap. **RATING** 92 **DRINK** 2013 $ 23
Chardonnay 2005 Fragrant nectarine and grapefruit define an elegant, fruit-driven style; very good line and length; perfect acidity against a hint of sweetness. Screwcap. **RATING** 91 **DRINK** 2009 $ 17.99
FishCage Sauvignon Blanc Semillon 2005 Light straw-green; extremely lively, tangy, lemony flavours through to a long, dry finish. Exceptional value. Screwcap. 12° alc. **RATING** 90 **DRINK** 2008 $ 14
Pinot Noir 2004 Powerful pinot dark plum fruit with a core of minerally acidity; will develop slowly but surely. Like the Chardonnay, excellent value. Screwcap. **RATING** 90 **DRINK** 2010 $ 17.99

ŸŸŸŸ **FishCage Shiraz Viognier 2004** Strong colour; rich blackberry, spice and apricot (ex Viognier) aromas and flavours; fleshy and mouthfilling; soft tannins; excellent value. Riverland/Adelaide Hills Shiraz/Swan Hill Viognier. Screwcap. **RATING** 89 **DRINK** 2008 $ 13.99
FishCage Chardonnay Viognier 2004 A surprisingly fresh and vibrant array of ripe citrus aromas and flavours; subliminal oak; great value; 85% Tumbarumba Chardonnay/15% Swan Hill Viognier. Screwcap. **RATING** 88 **DRINK** Now $ 13.99

ŸŸŸŸ **FishCage Cabernet Merlot 2004 RATING** 85 **DRINK** Now $ 14

Hunt's Foxhaven Estate   NR

Canal Rocks Road, Yallingup, WA 6282 **REGION** Margaret River
T (08) 9755 2232 **F** (08) 9255 2249 **WWW**.netserv.net.au/foxhaven **OPEN** W'ends & hols 11–5, or by appt
WINEMAKER David Hunt **EST.** 1978 **CASES** 1000
This long-established (by the standards of Margaret River) vineyard is on land which David Hunt lived as a child from 1946. It was then a dairy farm run by his father Jack. Together with wife Libby, he began planting in 1978 with riesling, followed later by cabernet sauvignon, semillon, sauvignon blanc and merlot.

Hunter Park   NR

PO Box 815, Muswellbrook, NSW 2333 **REGION** Upper Hunter Valley
T (02) 6541 4000 **F** (02) 6543 2456 **OPEN** Not
WINEMAKER Contract **EST.** 1977 **CASES** NA
The origins of Hunter Park go back more than 25 years; the business is based on 80 ha of sauvignon blanc, chardonnay, merlot, cabernet sauvignon and cabernet franc managed by Andrew Dibley. The wines are not widely distributed in Australia (although they are available by mail order) but exports have been established to the UK, Germany and the US.

Hunting Lodge Estate   NR

703 Mt Kilcoy Road, Mount Kilcoy, Qld 4515 **REGION** South Burnett
T (07) 5498 1243 **F** (07) 5498 1025 **WWW**.huntinglodgeestate.com.au **OPEN** 7 days 10–5
WINEMAKER Daryl Higgins **EST.** 1999 **CASES** 9000
Daryl and Vicki Higgins opened Hunting Lodge Estate on their 140-ha cattle property in 1999, originally with a cellar door and B&B. A winery was opened in 2002, and there is now a kaleidoscopic array of table and fortified wines available, mostly with African game park associations. For good measure, there is a personal museum of hunting trophies.

Huntington Estate

NR

Cassilis Road, Mudgee, NSW 2850 **REGION** Mudgee
T (02) 6373 3825 **F** (02) 6373 3730 **WWW**.huntingtonestate.com.au **OPEN** Mon–Fri 9–5, Sat 10–5,
Sun 10–3
WINEMAKER Tim Stevens **EST.** 1969 **CASES** 20 000
In late 2005 the Stevens (of Abercorn) acquired Huntington from the founders Bob and Wendy
Roberts. There is no reason to suppose the quality will change, and the Roberts family intend to
remain involved, with the renowned Huntington Music Festival a major annual event. The red wines
of Huntington Estate are outstanding and sell for relatively low prices.

Huntleigh Vineyards

NR

38 Tunnecliffes Lane, Heathcote, Vic 3523 **REGION** Heathcote
T (03) 5433 2795 **F** (03) 5433 2795 **WWW**.heathcotewinegrowers.com.au **OPEN** 7 days 10–5.30
WINEMAKER Leigh Hunt **EST.** 1975 **CASES** 500
The wines are made at the winery by former stockbroker Leigh Hunt from 5 ha of estate-grown
grapes; the last-tasted Cabernet Sauvignon was of exemplary quality.

Hurley Vineyard

★★★★★

101 Balnarring Road, Balnarring, Vic 3926 **REGION** Mornington Peninsula
T (03) 5931 3000 **F** (03) 5931 3200 **WWW**.hurleyvineyard.com.au **OPEN** By appt
WINEMAKER Kevin Bell **EST.** 1998 **CASES** 600
It's never as easy as it seems. Though Kevin Bell is now a Victorian Supreme Court judge, and his wife
Tricia Byrnes has a busy legal life as a family law specialist in a small Melbourne law firm, they have
done most of the hard work in establishing Hurley Vineyard themselves, with family and friends.
Most conspicuously, Kevin Bell has completed the Applied Science (Wine Science) degree at Charles
Sturt University, and has drawn on Nat White for consultancy advice, and occasionally from Phillip
Jones of Bass Phillip, and Domaine Fourrier and Gevrey Chambertin.

 Homage Mornington Peninsula Pinot Noir 2003 Even greater richness and depth than
the varietal, the even higher alcohol (15.1°) making its statement. Very long, warm finish;
black fruits and spice throughout; 75 cases made. Diam. 15.1° alc. **RATING** 95 **DRINK** 2013
$ 36
Lodestone Pinot Noir 2004 Much riper, richer fruit more towards black fruits and plums,
the texture more to velvet than silk. A choice between finesse and complexity, but not
quality. Diam. 14.3° alc. **RATING** 94 **DRINK** 2012 $ 38
Garamond Pinot Noir 2004 Slightly fresher, brighter hue than Lodestone; a silky mix of
red fruits and spice; long, lingering finish and very fine tannins. Diam. 13.6° alc.
RATING 94 **DRINK** 2010 $ 42
Mornington Peninsula Pinot Noir 2003 Powerful, concentrated black fruits/plum;
intense and long; super-powerful style with high alcohol evident. MV6, 114 and 115 clones;
320 cases made. Diam. **RATING** 94 **DRINK** 2011 $ 36

Hutton Vale Vineyard

★★★★★

Stone Jar Road, Angaston, SA 5353 **REGION** Eden Valley
T (08) 8564 8270 **F** (08) 8564 8385 **WWW**.huttonvale.com **OPEN** By appt
WINEMAKER Torbreck Vintners, Rockford **EST.** 1960 **CASES** 500
John Howard Angas (who arrived in SA in 1843, aged 19, charged with the responsibility of looking
after the affairs of his father, George Fife Angas) named part of the family estate Hutton Vale. It is
here that John Angas, John Howard's great-great-grandson, and wife Jan tend a little over 26 ha of
vines and produce (or, at least, Jan does) a range of jams, chutneys and preserves. Almost all the
grapes are sold, but a tiny quantity has been made by the Who's Who of the Barossa Valley, notably
David Powell of Torbreck and Chris Ringland of Rockford.

 Eden Valley Shiraz 2002 Harks back to the '00 vintage with a similar complex array of
aromas; medium- to full-bodied, with intense black fruits, spice, bitter chocolate and
leather. Cork. 14.4° alc. **RATING** 94 **DRINK** 2022 $ 59

Eden Valley Shiraz 2001 Powerful, ripe blackberry, plum and spice aromas; layers of flavour on the palate in the blackberry/dark chocolate spectrum. Cork. 14.4° alc. **RATING** 94 **DRINK** 2015 $59

Eden Valley Shiraz 2000 Complex black fruits, dark chocolate, leather, spice and earth; excellent mouthfeel, structure, weight and length; controlled oak, alcohol and extract. Cork. 14° alc. **RATING** 94 **DRINK** 2020 $59

ŶŶŶŶŶ **Eden Valley Grenache Mataro 2002** Strongly spicy/earthy; medium-bodied, the structure coming from the Mataro (Mourvedre) tannins; slightly more intensity than the '01. Cork. 14.5° alc. **RATING** 92 **DRINK** 2010 $29

Eden Valley Grenache Mataro 2001 Light- to medium-bodied; spice, earth, chocolate and vanilla with a nice core of ripe fruit; fine, ripe tannins. Cork. 14.5° alc. **RATING** 90 **DRINK** 2009 $29

ŶŶŶŶ **Eden Valley Riesling 2004** Generous, slightly broad style; plenty of citrus/lime flavour and length. Cork. 14° alc. **RATING** 89 **DRINK** 2008 $19

Ibis Wines

NR

239 Kearneys Drive, Orange, NSW 2800 **REGION** Orange
T (02) 6362 3257 **F** (02) 6362 5779 **WWW**.ibiswines.com.au **OPEN** W'ends & public hols 11–5, or by appt
WINEMAKER Phil Stevenson **EST.** 1988 **CASES** 500
Ibis Wines is located just north of Orange (near the botanic gardens) on what was once a family orchard. Planting of the vineyard commenced in 1988, and a new winery was completed on the property in 1998. The grapes are sourced from the home vineyards (at an altitude of 800m), the Habitat Vineyard (at 1100m on Mt Canobolas) (pinot noir and merlot) and the Kanjara Vineyard (shiraz).

Idlewild

★★★★

70 Milbrodale Road, Broke, NSW 2330 **REGION** Lower Hunter Valley
T (02) 6574 5188 **F** (03) 6574 5199 **WWW**.wildbrokewines.com.au **OPEN** At Broke Estate
WINEMAKER Matthew Ryan **EST.** 1999 **CASES** 1000
Idlewild is a spin-off from Broke Estate/Ryan Family Wines; it is a partnership between Matthew Ryan (who continues as viticulturist for Ryan Family Wines on Broke Estate and Minimbah Vineyards) and wife Tina Ryan (who continues to run Wild Rhino PR Marketing & Events in Sydney). It shares the 25 ha of vineyards with Broke Estate/Ryan Family Wines, although the product range is different.

ŶŶŶŶŶ **Wild Yeast Chardonnay 2003** Light green-straw; a complex wine with a rich creamy/nutty overlay to fig and melon fruit; integrated oak; 80 dozen made. Cork. 14.5° alc. **RATING** 91 **DRINK** 2009 $45

Semillon 2003 Still water-white, amazing; the palate is as tight and minerally as the colour suggests. Is this a true Peter Pan wine, or will it develop? I simply don't know. Cork. 11.5° alc. **RATING** 90 **DRINK** 2015 $45

Three Vineyard Chardonnay 2003 Bright straw-green; medium-bodied, smooth peach, fig and melon; subtle oak; aging convincingly; 100 dozen made. Cork. 14° alc. **RATING** 90 **DRINK** 2009 $45

Ilnam Estate

NR

750 Carool Road, Carool, NSW 2486 **REGION** Northern Rivers Zone
T (07) 5590 7703 **F** (07) 5590 7922 **WWW**.ilnam.com.au **OPEN** Mon–Fri 11–4, w'ends 10–5
WINEMAKER Mark Quinn, Lachlan Quinn **EST.** 1998 **CASES** 2500
This is the first vineyard and winery to be established in the Tweed Valley, 30 mins from the Gold Coast. There are 2 ha each of chardonnay, cabernet sauvignon and shiraz, plus a small planting of chambourcin. In addition, Ilnam Estate has a number of growers in the Stanthorpe area who supply grapes. Ione, Lachlan, Nathan, Andrew and Mark Quinn are all involved in the family business.

Immerse

NR

1548 Melba Highway, Yarra Glen, Vic 3775 **REGION** Yarra Valley
T (03) 5965 2444 **F** (03) 5965 2460 **www**.immerseyourself.com.au **OPEN** Thurs–Mon 11–5
WINEMAKER Contract **EST.** 1989 **CASES** 700
Steve and Helen Miles purchased the restaurant, accommodation and function complex previous
known as Lovey's. A spa-based health farm has 8 rooms, with a full range of services. I have to say
that the name chosen both for the facility and for the wines is as far left of centre as it is possible to go.
As previously, a substantial portion of the grapes produced is sold to other makers in the Yarra Valley,
the 6.9-ha vineyards having been rehabilitated.

Inchiquin Wines

NR

PO Box 865, Clare, SA 5453 **REGION** Clare Valley
T (08) 8843 4210 **OPEN** Not
WINEMAKER Stephen McInerney **EST.** 1998 **CASES** 1000
Stephen McInerney learnt his trade on the winery floor in various parts of the world: he started in
1985 at Jim Barry Wines, and spent a number of years there before moving to Pikes. He also worked
as a Flying Winemaker in France, Oregon, Spain and Argentina. He is now assistant winemaker at
the large new Kirribilly Winery in the Clare Valley. He established Inchiquin Wines with his partner
Kate Strachan; she too has great industry credentials, primarily as the viticulturist for Taylor's
(previously Southcorp), which has the largest vineyards in the Clare Valley. The wines are made by
Stephen McInerney at Pikes. Exports to Ireland.

Indigo Ridge

Icely Road, Orange, NSW 2800 **REGION** Orange
T (02) 6362 1851 **F** (02) 6362 1851 **www**.indigowines.com.au **OPEN** First & second weekend of the
month, public hols & w'ends 12–5, or by appt
WINEMAKER Contract **EST.** 1994 **CASES** 800
Paul Bridge and Trish McPherson describe themselves as the owners, labourers and viticulturists at
Indigo Ridge; they planted and tend every vine on the 4-ha vineyard. The plantings are of cabernet
sauvignon, sauvignon blanc, merlot and a few riesling vines.

ΥΥΥΥΥ **Sauvignon Blanc 2005** Spotlessly clean; a lively, vibrant palate enhanced by relatively low
alcohol; passionfruit, gooseberry and a touch of citrussy acidity. Screwcap. 11.7° alc.
RATING 93 **DRINK** Now $ 20

ΥΥΥΥ **Cabernet Sauvignon 2003** Light- to medium-bodied, earthy, savoury style; some dark
berry fruit and acceptable tannins, sweetened by a touch of French oak. Screwcap.
13.1° alc. **RATING** 87 **DRINK** 2010 $ 25

Inghams Skilly Ridge Wines

Gillentown Road, Sevenhill via Clare, SA 5453 **REGION** Clare Valley
T (08) 8843 4330 **F** (08) 8843 4330 **OPEN** W'ends 10–5
WINEMAKER Clark Ingham, O'Leary Walker **EST.** 1994 **CASES** 3000
Clark Ingham has established a substantial 24-ha vineyard of shiraz, cabernet sauvignon,
chardonnay, riesling, merlot and tempranillo. Part of the production is made by contract winemaker
David O'Leary (with input from Clark Ingham); the remaining grape production is sold.

ΥΥΥΥΥ **Clare Valley Riesling 2005** Spotlessly clean; citrus, apple, spice and mineral notes;
classic Clare, with a long, lingering finish. Screwcap. 13° alc. **RATING** 94 **DRINK** 2015 $ 18

ΥΥΥΥ **Clare Valley Shiraz 2001** Medium red-purple; medium-bodied, quite rich and developing
nicely; 18 months in American oak has worked well. Cork. 14° alc. **RATING** 90 **DRINK** 2011
$ 20

Clare Valley Tempranillo 2004 Fresh, lively cherry, plum and berry fruit mix; super-fine
tannins, considerable length. Screwcap. 13° alc. **RATING** 90 **DRINK** 2010 $ 20

ΥΥΥΥ **Clare Valley Merlot 2002** A substantial wine, the cool vintage helping to focus the varietal fruit; strong herb and spice overtones to dark plum fruit. Another of the many faces of Janus. Cork. 14.5° alc. **RATING** 89 **DRINK** 2012 $ 20

Clare Valley Cabernet Sauvignon 2001 Earthy, slightly stemmy characters, part bottle-developed, part from the variety; medium-bodied, and there is blackcurrant fruit at home base. Cork. 13.5° alc. **RATING** 88 **DRINK** 2011 $ 20

ΥΥΥΥ **Para River Barossa Valley Shiraz 2004** **RATING** 86 **DRINK** 2010 $ 20

Ingoldby ★★★★★

Ingoldby Road, McLaren Flat, SA 5171 **REGION** McLaren Vale
T (08) 8383 0005 **F** (08) 8383 0790 **WWW**.ingoldby.com.au **OPEN** 7 days 10–4
WINEMAKER Matt O'Leary **EST.** 1983 **CASES** 170 000
A sister operation to Andrew Garrett, also within the FWE group, with many of the wines now not having a sole McLaren Vale source but instead being drawn from regions across southeastern Australia. Over the past few years, Ingoldby has produced some excellent wines which provide great value for money.

ΥΥΥΥΥ **Golden Vine Reserve McLaren Vale Shiraz 2002** An intense and highly focused mix of blackberry and savoury fruits; 20 months in oak, yet without oak dominating; fine tannins; very long carry and finish. High-quality cork. **RATING** 95 **DRINK** 2020 $ 45

Chardonnay 2005 A complex wine on both bouquet and palate; balanced nectarine fruit and oak; very good finish. Top gold medal National Wine Show '05; surprise performance. **RATING** 94 **DRINK** 2010

ΥΥΥΥΥ **Chardonnay 2004** Quite fragrant; elegant but intense grapefruit and nectarine; minimal oak; very good length. Screwcap. **RATING** 90 **DRINK** Now $ 16.99

ΥΥΥΥ **Cabernet Sauvignon 2003** Light- to medium-bodied; juicy, minty, leafy blackcurrant flavours; light tannins. Cork. **RATING** 87 **DRINK** 2008 $ 16.99

ΥΥΥΥ **McLaren Vale Rose 2005** **RATING** 86 **DRINK** Now $ 17.99

Injidup Point NR

Caves Road, Wilyabrup, WA 6280 **REGION** Margaret River
T 0408 955 770 **F** (08) 9386 8352 **OPEN** By appt
WINEMAKER Belinda Gould, Michael Standish **EST.** 1993 **CASES** 1000
The development of the substantial Injidup Point vineyard began in 1993; there are now 16 ha planted to cabernet sauvignon, shiraz, cabernet franc, merlot, sauvignon blanc, pinot noir and semillon. Most of the grapes are sold to other makers, with a small amount of wine reserved for mail order sale and other local distribution. An extensive native garden surrounds the property, which has views to the adjacent Leeuwin Naturaliste National Park.

Inneslake Vineyards ★★★

The Ruins Way, Inneslake, Port Macquarie, NSW 2444 **REGION** Hastings River
T (02) 6581 1332 **F** (02) 6581 1954 **WWW**.inneslake.com.au **OPEN** 7 days 10–5
WINEMAKER Nick Charley, Cassegrain **EST.** 1988 **CASES** 1500
The property upon which the Inneslake vineyard is established has been in the Charley family's ownership since the turn of the 20th century, but had been planted to vines by a Major Innes in the 1840s. After carrying on logging and fruit growing at various times, the Charley family planted vines in 1988 with the encouragement of John Cassegrain. Around 4.5 ha of vines have been established.

ΥΥΥΥ **Charley Brothers Chardonnay 2004** Entirely fruit-driven by delicate nectarine and peach flavours; some length. Screwcap. 13.5° alc. **RATING** 87 **DRINK** 2008 $ 16

ΥΥΥΥ **Charley Brothers Lindsay Edition Semillon 2003** Well-made; light-bodied, and not a lot of mid-palate fruit, but is crisp. Twin top. 12° alc. **RATING** 86 **DRINK** 2008 $ 15

Charley Brothers Summer Red 2004 **RATING** 85 **DRINK** Now $ 14

Charley Brothers Summer White 2004 **RATING** 84 **DRINK** Now $ 14

Innisfail Vineyards   NR

Cross Street, Batesford, Vic 3221 **REGION** Geelong
T (03) 5276 1258 **F** (03) 5276 1258 **OPEN** By appt
WINEMAKER Nick Farr **EST.** 1980 **CASES** 2000
This 6-ha estate-based producer released its first wines way back in 1988, but has had a very low profile, notwithstanding the quality of its early wines. Nick Farr, son of Gary Farr, is now the winemaker and the profile has increased, as has the quality of the wines.

International Vintners Australia   NR

11 Biralee Road, Regency Park, SA 5010 (postal) **REGION** Yarra Valley
T (08) 8440 6300 **F** (08) 8244 5553 **OPEN** Not
WINEMAKER Mark Jamieson **EST.** 1995 **CASES** 100 000
International Vintners arose from the ashes in 2001 when it provided the capital necessary to sustain the former Andrew Garrett business. The brands have extensive distribution in Australia and overseas.

Iron Gate Estate   NR

Oakey Creek Road, Pokolbin, NSW 2320 **REGION** Lower Hunter Valley
T (02) 4998 6570 **F** (02) 4998 6571 **WWW**.iron-gate-estate.com.au **OPEN** 7 days 10–4
WINEMAKER Craig Perry, Roger Lilliott **EST.** 2001 **CASES** 5000
Iron Gate Estate would not be out of place in the Napa Valley, which favours bold architectural statements made without regard to cost. No expense has been spared in equipping the winery, or on the lavish cellar door facilities. The wines are made from 8 ha of estate plantings of semillon, verdelho, chardonnay, cabernet sauvignon and shiraz, and include such exotic offerings as a sweet shiraz and a chardonnay made in the style of a fino sherry.

Iron Pot Bay Wines   ★★★

766 Deviot Road, Deviot, Tas 7275 **REGION** Northern Tasmania
T (03) 6394 7320 **F** (03) 6394 7346 **WWW**.ironpotbay.com.au **OPEN** Thurs–Sun 11–5 Sept–May, June–Aug by appt
WINEMAKER Andrew Pirie **EST.** 1988 **CASES** 2100
Iron Pot Bay is now part of the syndicate which established Rosevears Estate, with its large, state-of-the-art winery on the banks of the Tamar. The vineyard takes its name from a bay on the Tamar River (now called West Bay) and is strongly maritime-influenced, producing delicate but intensely flavoured unwooded white wines. It has 4.58 ha of vines, over half being chardonnay, the remainder semillon, sauvignon blanc, pinot gris, gewurztraminer and riesling.

ΥΥΥΥ   **Pinot Grigio 2004** A big, fruity style, almost tropical; has benefitted greatly from time in bottle. **RATING** 89 **DRINK** Now $ 22

ΥΥΥΥ   **Vividus Riesling 2005** **RATING** 85 **DRINK** 2008

Ironbark Ridge Vineyard   NR

Middle Road Mail Service 825, Purga, Qld 4306 **REGION** Queensland Coastal
T (07) 5464 6787 **F** (07) 5464 6858 **WWW**.ironbarkridge.com **OPEN** Tues–Sun & public hols 10–5
WINEMAKER Contract **EST.** 1984 **CASES** 250
Ironbark Ridge Vineyard is situated southwest of Ipswich, approximately 40 mins from Brisbane. It has 2.5 ha of vineyard planted to many different varieties, and the tasting room is a restored miners cottage built in the early 1900s.

Ironwood Estate ★★★★☆

RMB 1288, Porongurup, WA 6234 **REGION** Porongurup
T (08) 9853 1126 **F** (08) 9853 1172 **OPEN** By appt
WINEMAKER Dianne Miller, Bill Crappsley (Consultant) **EST.** 1996 **CASES** 2000
Ironwood Estate was established in 1996; the first wines were made from purchased grapes. In the same year, chardonnay, shiraz and cabernet sauvignon were planted on a northern slope of the Porongurup Range. The twin peaks of the Porongurups, seen on the label, rise above the vineyard. The first estate-grown grapes were vinified at the Porongurup Winery, co-owned with Jingalla, Chatsfield and Montgomery's Hill.

ŸŸŸŸŸ **Great Southern Riesling 2005** Intense varietal flavour and profile; green apple blossom and some citrus; tight minerality. Screwcap. 12.5° alc. **RATING** 92 **DRINK** 2012 $15
Reserve Porongurup Chardonnay 2004 Light-bodied; attractive nectarine fruit with a twist of citrus; subtle French barrel ferment oak; good balance and length. Cork. 13.4° alc. **RATING** 92 **DRINK** 2012 $18
Porongurup Merlot 2004 Bright, clear, red-purple; light- to medium-bodied, fresh, fruit-driven; attractive small red berries with touches of spice and savoury tannins; minimal oak influence. Cork. 13.9° alc. **RATING** 90 **DRINK** 2010 $20

ŸŸŸŸ **Rocky Porongurup Rose 2005** Lots of red fruit flavour, verging on light dry red, some sweetness adding to the flavour and impact. Screwcap. 12° alc. **RATING** 87 **DRINK** Now $14

Irvine ★★★★★

PO Box 308, Angaston, SA 5353 **REGION** Eden Valley
T (08) 8564 1046 **F** (08) 8564 1314 **WWW**.irvinewines.com.au **OPEN** At Eden Valley Hotel
WINEMAKER James Irvine, Joanne Irvine **EST.** 1980 **CASES** 7000
Industry veteran Jim Irvine, who has successfully guided the destiny of so many South Australian wineries, quietly introduced his own label in 1991. The vineyard from which the wines are sourced was planted in 1983 and now comprises a patchwork quilt of 10 ha of vines. The flagship is the rich Grand Merlot. Exports to all major markets.

ŸŸŸŸŸ **James Irvine Grand Merlot 2002** Complex, rich and textured; admirable dark fruits, fine, ripe tannins, and the French oak, while obvious, is beautifully integrated. Cork. 14.5° alc. **RATING** 95 **DRINK** 2015 $100
The Baroness 2002 Medium-bodied, with that silky texture which Irvine gets through barrel fermentation; an array of sweet spices, plus fine, ripe tannins on a long palate. Merlot/Cabernet Franc/Cabernet Sauvignon. Cork. 14.5° alc. **RATING** 94 **DRINK** 2012 $45

ŸŸŸŸŸ **Merlot 2002** Holding red-purple hue well; spicy, cedary, savoury aromas; attractive, sweet red and black fruits; silky, fine tannins and controlled oak. Screwcap. 14° alc. **RATING** 91 **DRINK** 2012 $25
Merlot Cabernet 2002 Complex, with typical Irvine supple texture and mouthfeel; black fruits interwoven with mocha oak. Screwcap. 14.5° alc. **RATING** 90 **DRINK** 2014 $25

ŸŸŸŸ **Merlot Cabernet Franc 2002** A distinctly different fruit impact from the cabernet franc, giving a slightly stemmy and sharper edge, though still medium-bodied, with savoury varietal fruits to the fore. Screwcap. 14.5° alc. **RATING** 89 **DRINK** 2011 $22
Reserve Eden Valley Zinfandel 2002 A harmonious combination of vanillan oak and spicy cherry fruit in a medium-bodied framework. Cork. 14.5° alc. **RATING** 89 **DRINK** 2008 $35
Non Vintage Meslier Brut NV Not particularly complex; tangy, lemony, citrussy flavours; good length and perfect dosage. The rarest grape of Champagne, France. 11° alc. **RATING** 88 **DRINK** 2009 $20

ŸŸŸŸ **Springhill Unwooded Chardonnay 2005** Ample stone fruit flavour; inevitably, not complex, but has fruit presence. Screwcap. 13° alc. **RATING** 86 **DRINK** Now $15
Barossa Pinot Gris 2005 Soft peach and pear fruit; has flavour, the dry finish needing a touch more acidity. Screwcap. 14.5° alc. **RATING** 86 **DRINK** Now $22
Barossa Merlot Brut MV NV RATING 86 **DRINK** 2010 $25
Springhill Merlot 2004 RATING 85 **DRINK** 2008 $15

Island Brook Estate

Bussell Highway, Metricup, WA 6280 **REGION** Margaret River
T (08) 9755 7501 **F** (08) 9755 7008 **www**.islandbrook.com.au **OPEN** 7 days 10–5
WINEMAKER Flying Fish Cove **EST.** 1985 **CASES** 2000
Island Brook Estate is a small boutique winery situated in the middle of the Margaret River. Owners Peter and Linda Jenkins have begun the process of seeking certification as organic grapegrowers. Luxurious accommodation set among 45 acres of forest is available.

ΥΥΥΥΥ **Reserve Margaret River Cabernet Sauvignon 2003** Very good colour; a complex, full-bodied, layered array of blackcurrant and cassis fruit, with much more tannin structure than the '04. A blend of the 2 might make the best wine; 3 gold medals in smaller wine shows. Screwcap. 14° alc. **RATING** 92 **DRINK** 2014 $ 38
Reserve Margaret River Cabernet Sauvignon 2004 Light- to medium-bodied; attractive, fresh redcurrant/blackcurrant mix with fine tannins and oak. Good balance, but still tightly wound; fractionally surprising gold medal '05 Margaret River Wine Show. Screwcap. 14.5° alc. **RATING** 91 **DRINK** 2014 $ 34

Ivanhoe Wines

Marrowbone Road, Pokolbin, NSW 2320 **REGION** Lower Hunter Valley
T (02) 4998 7325 **F** (02) 4998 7848 **www**.ivanhoewines.com.au **OPEN** 7 days 10–5
WINEMAKER Stephen Drayton, Tracy Drayton **EST.** 1995 **CASES** 7000
Stephen Drayton is the son of the late Reg Drayton and, with wife Tracy, is the third branch of the family to be actively involved in winemaking in the Hunter Valley. The property on which the vineyard is situated has been called Ivanhoe for over 140 years, and 25 ha of 30-year-old vines provide high-quality fruit for the label. The plans are to build a replica of the old homestead (burnt down, along with much of the winery, in the 1968 bushfires) to operate as a sales area.

ΥΥΥΥ **TLD Semillon 2005** Nicely balanced; plenty of flavour and depth; ripe semillon fruit; slight catch on the finish. **RATING** 88 **DRINK** 2010 $ 19.50
Estate Verdelho 2005 Big wine; quite powerful, ripe fruit salad flavours, and some length. **RATING** 87 **DRINK** 2009 $ 18.50

🦡 Izway Wines

31 George Street, North Adelaide, SA 5006 (postal) **REGION** Barossa Valley
T 0423 040 385 **OPEN** Not
WINEMAKER Craig Isbel, Brian Conway **EST.** 2002 **CASES** 298
Izway Wines is the venture of business partners Craig Isbel and Brian Conway, both of whom have significant Australian and international wine industry experience. It is a virtual winery, purchasing small quantities of grenache from 80-year-old vines in Greenock, mourvedre from 30-year-old vines in Gomersal, and shiraz from 5-year-old vines in Ebenezer.

ΥΥΥΥΥ **Bruce Barossa Valley Shiraz Viognier 2003** Potent, powerful blackberry, dark chocolate and spice; full-bodied, the Viognier subliminal; good oak and length. Cork. 15.3° alc.
RATING 93 **DRINK** 2015 $ 35
Mates Barossa Valley Grenache Mataro Shiraz 2005 Bright red-purple; light- to medium-bodied, vibrantly fresh red berry fruits; good balance with minimal tannin and oak influences. Screwcap. 14.5° alc. **RATING** 90 **DRINK** 2010 $ 20

ΥΥΥΥ **Mates Barossa Valley Grenache Mataro Shiraz 2004** Light- to medium-bodied; fresh, easy red fruits; ready to roll. Screwcap. 14.5° alc. **RATING** 87 **DRINK** Now $ 20

Jackson's Hill Vineyard

NR

Mount View Road, Mount View, NSW 2321 **REGION** Lower Hunter Valley
T 1300 720 098 **F** 1300 130 220 **www**.jacksonshill.com.au **OPEN** By appt
WINEMAKER Christian Gaffey **EST.** 1983 **CASES** 1500
One of the low-profile operations on the spectacularly scenic Mount View Road, making small quantities of estate-grown (3 ha) wine sold exclusively through the cellar door and Australian Wine Selectors.

Jadran

NR

445 Reservoir Road, Orange Grove, WA 6109 **REGION** Perth Hills
T (08) 9459 1110 **OPEN** Mon–Sat 10–8, Sun 11–5
WINEMAKER Steve Radojkovich **EST.** 1967 **CASES** NFP
A quite substantial operation which basically services local clientele, occasionally producing wines of quite surprising quality from a variety of fruit sources.

JAG Wines

72 William Street, Norwood, SA 5067 (postal) **REGION** Warehouse
T (08) 8364 4497 **F** (08) 8364 4497 **www**.jagwines.com **OPEN** By appt
WINEMAKER Grant Anthony White **EST.** 2001 **CASES** 500
The name is doubtless derived from that of owners Julie and Grant White, but might cause raised eyebrows in clothing circles. The project developed from their lifelong love of wine; it started with a hobby vineyard (along with friends) in the Adelaide Hills, then more formal wine studies, then highly successful amateur winemaking. The Whites obtained their producers' licence (and trademark) in 2001, purchasing grapes from the major South Australian regions, bringing them to their suburban house to be fermented and pressed, and then storing the wine offsite in French and American oak until ready for sale.

ΨΨΨΨ **Shiraz 2003** Colour moving to brick-red; a strong mocha vanilla coating to red and black fruits, not surprising given the 27 months maturation in American oak; soft tannins. Langhorne Creek/Clare Valley/McLaren Vale. Screwcap. 14.5° alc. **RATING** 89 **DRINK** 2013 $ 20
Cabernet Sauvignon 2003 Colour change towards brick; similar malty style to the Shiraz, the fruit well and truly coated with oak; mocha and chocolate, rather than fruit, flavours will appeal to some. Screwcap. 14.6° alc. **RATING** 87 **DRINK** 2012 $ 20

James Estate

951 Bylong Valley Way, Baerami via Denman, NSW 2333 **REGION** Upper Hunter Valley
T (02) 6547 5168 **F** (02) 6547 5164 **www**.jamesestatewines.com.au **OPEN** 7 days 10–4.30
WINEMAKER Peter Orr **EST.** 1971 **CASES** 30 000
In 1997 the Cecchini family sold the assets of Serenella (but not the name) to David James, resulting in the change of name to James Estate. It is a large property, planted to 11 different white and red varieties, and with substantial production. In 2005 the business became even more complicated, when Tish Cecchini (winemaker at James Estate prior to its sale) sold the Serenella brand and assets to James Estate (for further details, see James Estate Pokolbin entry). Exports to the UK and the US.

ΨΨΨΨ **Semillon 2005** An attractive, aromatic bouquet; lively lemon, herb and grass flavours; length and delicacy reflects the vintage. Good value. Screwcap. 11.5° alc. **RATING** 92 **DRINK** 2012 $ 14

ΨΨΨΨ **Verdelho 2005** **RATING** 85 **DRINK** Now $ 14
Sundara Semillon Chardonnay 2005 **RATING** 84 **DRINK** Now $ 7

ΨΨΨ **Chardonnay 2004** **RATING** 83 $ 14

James Estate (Pokolbin)

NR

Lot 300 Hermitage Road, Pokolbin, NSW 2325 **REGION** Lower Hunter Valley
T (02) 4998 7992 **F** (02) 4998 7993 **www**.serenella.com.au **OPEN** 7 days 9.30–5
WINEMAKER Letitia 'Tish' Cecchini **EST.** 2005 **CASES** 5000
In 1998 the Cecchini family, having sold their Upper Hunter winery, acquired the 43-ha block on which this business is established. They built a new winery, a restaurant (Arlecchino Trattoria) and a cellar door sales and function area, planting 2.5 ha of sangiovese. In 2005 all of the assets of this venture were sold to James Estate, but Tish Cecchini leased back the winery to enable her to carry on contract winemaking services for others, and to produce the Serenella brand wines for James Estate.

James Haselgrove   ★★★★

PO Box 271, McLaren Vale, SA 5171 **REGION** McLaren Vale
T (08) 8332 0618 **F** (08) 8332 0638 **WWW**.haselgrovevignerons.com **OPEN** Not
WINEMAKER James Haselgrove **EST.** 1981 **CASES** 1000
The Haselgrove/James Haselgrove/Nick Haselgrove brands have been buffeted by numerous storms.
The outcome is that James Haselgrove is now a virtual winery, selling the limited quantities of wine
via phone, mail order and the website. Exports to all major markets.

ＹＹＹＹＹ **HRS Reserve Adelaide Hills Viognier 2005** Aromatic; complex, rich apricot and peach;
50% barrel ferment in older oak gives great texture without compromising the fruit
flavour. Screwcap. 13° alc. **RATING** 91 **DRINK** 2010 $ 25

ＹＹＹＹ **Fleurieu Shiraz 2004** Strong purple-red; light- to medium-bodied, strongly spicy, cool-
grown characters to the bright red fruits. Screwcap. 14° alc. **RATING** 89 **DRINK** 2010 $ 16
HRS Reserve Coonawarra Cabernet Sauvignon 2004 Light- to medium-bodied; very
earthy/dusty/savoury style which needs more blackcurrant fruit, admittedly difficult in
Coonawarra in '04. Screwcap. 13.5° alc. **RATING** 89 **DRINK** 2012 $ 25
MVS Grenache Shiraz Viognier 2005 Bright, juicy red berry fruits; the two components
(grenache and shiraz viognier) each contributing positively; fruit, not sugar, sweetness,
best young. Screwcap. 14° alc. **RATING** 89 **DRINK** 2008 $ 15
Fleurieu Sauvignon Blanc 2005 A faint touch of sweat which (for me) disfigures
sauvignon blanc; however, the light-bodied palate is crisp with touches of passionfruit and
vibrant acidity. Screwcap. 11.5° alc. **RATING** 88 **DRINK** Now $ 15

ＹＹＹＹ **Sovereign Series Cabernet Merlot 2003** **RATING** 84 **DRINK** Now $ 10

ＹＹＹ **Sovereign Series Shiraz 2003** **RATING** 83 $ 10

Jamiesons Run   ★★★★★

Penola-Naracoorte Road, Coonawarra, SA 5263 **REGION** Coonawarra
T (08) 8736 3380 **F** (08) 8736 3307 **WWW**.jamiesonsrun.com.au **OPEN** Mon–Fri 9–4.30, w'ends 10–4
WINEMAKER Andrew Hales **EST.** 1955 **CASES** 160 000
Once the prized possession of Mildara, which spawned a child called Jamiesons Run to fill the need
for a cost-effective second label. Now the name Mildara is very nearly part of ancient wine history,
and the child has usurped the parent. Worldwide distribution.

ＹＹＹＹＹ **Winemakers Reserve Cabernet Sauvignon Shiraz Malbec 2001** A lovely wine, with
gently ripe earth, blackcurrant and blackberry fruit; well-integrated oak and tannins; soft,
mouthfilling and languorous. Cork. 13.5° alc. **RATING** 96 **DRINK** 2016 $ 50
Rothwell Coonawarra Cabernet Sauvignon 2003 Excellent colour; firm, medium-
bodied, high-quality cassis/blackcurrant fruit; fine tannins and cedary oak. Gold medal
National Wine Show '05. Cork. **RATING** 95 **DRINK** 2018
Chardonnay 2005 Impressive stone fruit flavours with a mix of fleshy and more mineral
notes; overall, far more elegance than one might expect from a wine at this price. Trophy
winner Sydney Wine Show '06. **RATING** 94 **DRINK** 2010 $ 14.99
Mildara Coonawarra Shiraz 2003 Voluminous black cherry, plum and blackberry fruit,
with just a hint of spice; medium-bodied, good balance and length. The old Mildara label
returns with a stylish design polish. Screwcap. 14° alc. **RATING** 94 **DRINK** 2013 $ 30
Winemakers Reserve Cabernet Sauvignon Shiraz Malbec 2002 Deep colour; lush but
not jammy black fruits; plump, ripe tannins, good oak and excellent overall balance.
RATING 94 **DRINK** 2017

ＹＹＹＹＹ **Mildara Coonawarra Cabernet Sauvignon 2003** Fragrant and elegant cassis, raspberry
and blackcurrant; medium-bodied, fine tannins and good acidity. Screwcap. 13.5° alc.
RATING 93 **DRINK** 2015 $ 30
Country Select Shiraz 2003 A complex blend of ripe licorice, blackberry and notes of
mocha oak; plenty of tannins. Quality cork. **RATING** 92 **DRINK** 2015 $ 21.99
Mildara Coonawarra Cabernet Sauvignon 2004 Very good colour; medium- to full-
bodied; black fruits and cassis on entry, then uncompromising tannins which are, however,
ripe, and will settle back down within a few years. Screwcap. 14.5° alc. **RATING** 92 **DRINK** 2015

Mildara Blass Galway Pipe 20 Year Old Premium Tawny Port NV Supple, round and generously flavoured; a Christmas cake spice and ginger mix, then a lingering, gently dry finish. Cork. 17.5° alc. **RATING** 92 **DRINK** Now

Robertson's Well Coonawarra Shiraz 2004 Strong purple-red; medium-bodied, with abundant blackberry and mulberry fruit; carefully controlled extract and oak; obvious discipline in the vineyard in a big-yielding vintage. Cork. 14.5° alc. **RATING** 91 **DRINK** 2014

Robertson's Well Cabernet Sauvignon 2004 Good balance, texture and length; black fruits with hints of earth and dark chocolate; positive oak. Tannins still to soften. **RATING** 90 **DRINK** 2014

Country Select Cabernet Sauvignon 2003 Slightly developed colour; a medium-bodied mix of ripe blackberry/mulberry fruit and cedar/mocha oak; soft, ripe tannins; ready now. Cork. **RATING** 90 **DRINK** 2008 $ 21.99

Robertson's Well Cabernet Sauvignon 2003 Bright purple-red; firm, blackcurrant fruit; long, clear-cut, low pH style, with a certain austerity; long finish. Polar opposite to Country Select Cabernet. Cork. **RATING** 90 **DRINK** 2013 $ 21.99

Winemakers Reserve Cabernet Sauvignon 2003 A powerful, slightly austere, rendition of cabernet sauvignon in a blackcurrant, earthy spectrum; needs years to drop its tannin defenses. Cork. **RATING** 90 **DRINK** 2018

Rothwell Coonawarra Cabernet Sauvignon 2002 Very good colour; full-bodied, powerhouse dark fruits; just a little too extractive. **RATING** 90 **DRINK** 2012

ŶŶŶŶ **Limestone Coast Sauvignon Blanc 2005** Bright light straw-green; crisp, lively, mineral herb, spice and passionfruit mix; the line does, however, falter towards the finish. Screwcap. 12° alc. **RATING** 89 **DRINK** Now

Coonawarra Shiraz 2003 Medium-bodied and fruit-driven; plum and blackberry fruit supported by some tannin structure. Cork. **RATING** 89 **DRINK** 2009 $ 21.99

Mildara Coonawarra Cabernet Shiraz 2003 Good hue; largely driven by cabernet sauvignon, with earthy, savoury, medium-bodied black fruits, and fine, persistent tannins. Screwcap. 14° alc. **RATING** 89 **DRINK** 2013

Mildara Coonawarra Cabernet Merlot 2003 Good hue; very savoury earthy/olive/spice aromas and flavours; uncompromising varietal character. Screwcap. 14° alc. **RATING** 88 **DRINK** 2009 $ 30

ŶŶŶ♀ **Coonawarra Cabernet Sauvignon 2003** **RATING** 86 **DRINK** 2008 $ 21.99
Country Select Coonawarra Chardonnay 2005 **RATING** 85 **DRINK** Now

🐛 Jamsheed ★★★★

157 Faraday Street, Carlton, Vic 3053 (postal) **REGION** Yarra Valley
T 0409 540 414 **F** (03) 5967 3581 **OPEN** Not
WINEMAKER Gary Mills **EST.** 2003 **CASES** 200

Jamsheed is the venture of Gary Mills, proprietor of Simpatico Wine Services, a boutique contract winemaking company established at the new Hill Paddock Winery in Healesville. The wines are sourced from a 30-year-old, low-yielding vineyard, and are made using indigenous/wild yeasts and minimal handling techniques. For the short-term future the business will focus on old vine sites in the Yarra Valley, but plans are to include a Grampians and Heathcote Shiraz along with a Strathbogie Gewurztraminer. The name, incidentally, is that of a Persian king recorded in the Annals of Gilgamesh.

ŶŶŶŶ♀ **Yarra Valley Shiraz 2003** Good colour; spice and pepper nuances to ripe black cherry and blackberry fruit; a well-balanced and structured medium-bodied wine. Cork. 14° alc. **RATING** 91 **DRINK** 2013 $ 35

ŶŶŶŶ **Yarra Valley Gewurztraminer 2003** Brilliant green-yellow; rich, harmonious mouthfeel with good length; diminished varietal character, but a nice wine nonetheless. Screwcap. 13° alc. **RATING** 89 **DRINK** Now $ 25

Jane Brook Estate   ★★★★

229 Toodyay Road, Middle Swan, WA 6056 **REGION** Swan Valley
T (08) 9274 1432 **F** (08) 9274 1211 **WWW**.janebrook.com.au **OPEN** Mon–Fri 10–5, w'ends & public hols 12–5
WINEMAKER Julie Smith **EST.** 1972 **CASES** 20 000
Beverley and David Atkinson have worked tirelessly to build up the Jane Brook Estate wine business over the past 30-plus years. The most important changes during that time have been the establishment of a Margaret River vineyard, and sourcing grapes from other southern wine regions in WA; winemaker Julie Smith has also played a major role in lifting wine quality since her appointment as chief winemaker in 2000. Retail distribution in Perth, Sydney, Canberra and Melbourne; exports to the UK, the US and Asia.

▼▼▼▼▽ **Sauvignon Blanc 2005** Lively; plenty of punch to the strongly varietal citrus and gooseberry fruit; excellent length. Pemberton/Margaret River. Screwcap. 12.3° alc.
RATING 91 **DRINK** Now **$** 19.50
Semillon Sauvignon Blanc 2005 Some CO_2 evident; clean, gentle, tropical/passionfruit flavours; cleansing acidity on the finish. Screwcap. 12.5° alc. **RATING** 90 **DRINK** 2008 **$** 19.50
Mountjoy Cabernet Merlot 2002 Holding hue well; medium-bodied, with good structure and balance; cassis, raspberry and blackcurrant fruit plus fine, ripe tannins; good oak. Very impressive for the Swan Valley. Cork. 13.7° alc. **RATING** 90 **DRINK** 2009 **$** 24.50

▼▼▼▼ **Plain Jane Rose 2005** Attractive, clean cherry fruit; perfect balance and mouthfeel; not sweet. Good value. Screwcap. 12° alc. **RATING** 88 **DRINK** Now **$** 13.50
Plain Jane Shiraz 2005 Bright, light red-purple; light- to medium-bodied blackberry and plum; some sweetness along the way; good mouthfeel. Cork. 14.4° alc. **RATING** 87
DRINK 2009 **$** 13
Atkinson Family Reserve Shiraz 2002 Light- to medium-bodied; earthy/savoury/foresty notes throughout, and limited red fruit flavours; minimal tannins. Cork. 13.9° alc.
RATING 87 **DRINK** 2008 **$** 35.50

Jansz Tasmania   NR

1216b Pipers Brook Road, Pipers Brook, Tas 7254 **REGION** Northern Tasmania
T (03) 6382 7066 **F** (03) 6382 7088 **WWW**.jansztas.com **OPEN** 7 days 10–5
WINEMAKER Natalie Fryar **EST.** 1985 **CASES** 15 000
Jansz is part of the S Smith & Son/Yalumba group, and was one of the early sparkling wine labels in Tas, stemming from a short-lived relationship between Heemskerk and Louis Roederer. Its 15 ha of chardonnay, 12 ha of pinot noir and 3 ha of pinot meunier correspond almost exactly to the blend composition of the Jansz wines. It is the only Tasmanian winery entirely devoted to the production of sparkling wine, which is of high quality.

Jarrah Ridge Winery   NR

651 Great Northern Highway, Herne Hill, WA 6056 **REGION** Perth Hills
T 1800 800 047 **F** (08) 9409 8010 **WWW**.jarrahridge.com.au **OPEN** By appt
WINEMAKER Rob Marshall (Contract) **EST.** 1998 **CASES** 8000
Syd and Julie Pond have established a 13.5-ha vineyard with shiraz the most important, the remainder chenin blanc, chardonnay, cabernet sauvignon, verdelho, viognier and merlot. Children Michael and Lisa are also involved in the business. Most of the wines have a degree of sweetness which will doubtless appeal to cellar door and restaurant customers.

Jarretts of Orange   ★★★★

Annangrove Park, Cargo Road, Orange, NSW 2800 **REGION** Orange
T (02) 6364 3118 **F** (02) 6364 3048 **OPEN** By appt
WINEMAKER Chris Derrez **EST.** 1995 **CASES** 2000
Justin and Pip Jarrett have established a very substantial vineyard (140 ha), planted to chardonnay, cabernet sauvignon, shiraz, sauvignon blanc, merlot, pinot noir, riesling, marsanne, cabernet franc and verdelho. As well as managing the vineyard, they provide management and development

services to growers of another 120 ha in the region. Most of the grapes are sold, with a limited amount produced for local distribution and by mail order. The wines are modestly priced.

▼▼▼▼▽ **Chardonnay 2004** Typical Orange regional style; an elegant mix of stone fruit, citrus and mineral, finishing with crisp acidity. Cork. 13° alc. **RATING** 90 **DRINK** 2010 $ 14

Shiraz 2003 Light- to medium-bodied; the components have married well, with supple and elegant red fruits doing the driving; good balance and length. Cork. 13.6° alc. **RATING** 90 **DRINK** 2010 $ 16

▼▼▼▼ **Finger & Thumb Shiraz 2004** A light- to medium-bodied mix of bright, fresh, zesty cherry and raspberry fruits; subtle oak; good length. Screwcap. 14.6° alc. **RATING** 89 **DRINK** 2011 $ 30

Row 72 Sauvignon Blanc 2005 A clean bouquet; the quite powerful palate is driven in part by the alcohol, with ripe, tropical fruit; flavour at the expense of finesse. Screwcap. 13.9° alc. **RATING** 87 **DRINK** Now $ 13

Finger & Thumb 303 Blend NV A somewhat rustic style, but has plenty of depth to the black fruits; solid, earthy tannins. Cork. 14.4° alc. **RATING** 87 **DRINK** 2011 $ 35

Jarvis Estate   ★★★★

Lot 13, Wirring Road, Margaret River, WA 6285 **REGION** Margaret River
T (08) 9758 7526 **F** (08) 9758 8017 **WWW**.jarvisestate.com.au **OPEN** By appt
WINEMAKER Naturaliste Vintners (Bruce Dukes) **EST.** 1995 **CASES** 3000
Matt and Jackie Jarvis carefully researched the Margaret River region, and in particular the Bramley locality, before purchasing their property, where they now live. It is planted to cabernet sauvignon, shiraz, merlot, chardonnay and cabernet franc (8.4 ha). Exports to Taiwan, Greece and Ireland.

▼▼▼▼▽ **Shiraz 2004** Bright red-purple; abundant blackberry, plum, black cherry and spice; good mouthfeel and tannins; more weight than many Margaret River shirazes. Twin top. 14° alc. **RATING** 92 **DRINK** 2014 $ 24

Shiraz 2003 Medium red-purple; lifted spice and black cherry aromas; medium-bodied, fruit-driven; cherry, plum and blackberry. Twin top. 14° alc. **RATING** 90 **DRINK** 2013 $ 24

▼▼▼▼ **Chardonnay 2005** Gentle peach, nectarine and melon fruit; neither oak nor malolactic intrude onto the fruit line. Twin top. 13.5° alc. **RATING** 89 **DRINK** 2010 $ 22

Chardonnay 2004 A very reserved style, similar to the '05; barrel ferment and malolactic inputs all restrained and balanced; developing slowly but surely, although the wet cork is a worry. Cork. 13.5° alc. **RATING** 89 **DRINK** 2008 $ 22

Cabernet Sauvignon 2003 Medium red-purple; a role reversal with the Merlot; quite elegant, medium-bodied cassis and blackcurrant fruit, fine tannins and subtle oak. Cork. 13.5° alc. **RATING** 89 **DRINK** 2014 $ 24

Cabernet Franc 2004 Bright red; brisk, fresh raspberry, mulberry and redcurrant; Margaret River has a good clone of this difficult variety. Cork. 14° alc. **RATING** 89 **DRINK** 2013 $ 28

Cabernet Franc 2003 Slight development in colour; a medium-bodied wine with very similar fruit characters and structure to the '04; fine tannins. Cork. 14° alc. **RATING** 89 **DRINK** 2012 $ 28

Merlot 2004 Full red-purple; uncompromisingly varietal fruit, perhaps too much so, as olive and herb characters crowd in around the fruit core. Cork. 15° alc. **RATING** 88 **DRINK** 2014 $ 24

Verdelho 2005 Nice mid-weight fruit salad flavours; a twist of acidity gives freshness and length. Screwcap. 13° alc. **RATING** 87 **DRINK** 2008 $ 18

Jasper Hill   ★★★★★

Drummonds Lane, Heathcote, Vic 3523 **REGION** Heathcote
T (03) 5433 2528 **F** (03) 5433 3143 **OPEN** By appt
WINEMAKER Ron Laughton, Emily Laughton **EST.** 1975 **CASES** 3500
The red wines of Jasper Hill are highly regarded and much sought after, invariably selling out at the cellar door and through the mailing list within a short time of release. These are wonderful wines in

admittedly Leviathan mould, reflecting the very low yields and the care and attention given to them by Ron Laughton. The oak is not overdone, and the fruit flavours show Heathcote at its best. There has been comment (and some criticism) in recent years about the alcohol level of the wines. Laughton responds by saying he picks the grapes when he judges them to be at optimum ripeness, and is in no way chasing high alcohol, whether to suit the US market or otherwise.

▼▼▼▼▼ **Georgia's Paddock Shiraz 2004** Outstanding colour; a fragrant burst of sweet fruits and spices leaps from the glass; much more elegant than many prior vintages; black fruits and very fine tannins to close. Cork. 15° alc. **RATING** 96 **DRINK** 2024 $ 66

Emily's Paddock Shiraz Cabernet Franc 2004 Less dense colour than Georgia's Paddock; overall, far more savoury and less luscious; bitter chocolate, spice and blackberry power the long finish to redeem the wine. Cork. 15° alc. **RATING** 94 **DRINK** 2019 $ 88

Cornella Vineyard Grenache 2004 Vivid purple-red; fragrant raspberry and cherry bouquet; excellent flavour and structure; an exciting modern style of grenache. Cork. 14.5° alc. **RATING** 94 **DRINK** 2012 $ 48

▼▼▼▼ **Georgia's Paddock Riesling 2005** Quite floral and rich; a powerful mix of lime and tropical fruit; faintly silky finish. Cork. 12° alc. **RATING** 89 **DRINK** 2008 $ 32

Georgia's Paddock Nebbiolo 2004 Light, bright colour; fresh, brisk and firm red cherry fruit; from an opposite universe to the Shiraz; I know it's a pinot correlative, but ... Cork. 13° alc. **RATING** 89 **DRINK** 2014 $ 55

Jasper Valley

NR

RMB 880 Croziers Road, Berry, NSW 2535 **REGION** Shoalhaven Coast
T (02) 4464 1596 **F** (02) 4464 1595 **WWW**.jaspervalleywines.com.au **OPEN** 7 days 9.30–5.30
WINEMAKER Contract **EST.** 1976 **CASES** 1500
A strongly tourist-oriented winery with most of its wine purchased as cleanskins from other makers, but with 2 ha of estate shiraz planted in 1976 by former owner Sidney Mitchell the oldest vines in the region. Features around 1 ha of lawns, barbecue facilities, and sweeping views.

Jeanneret Wines

 ★★★★☆

Jeanneret Road, Sevenhill, SA 5453 **REGION** Clare Valley
T (08) 8843 4308 **F** (08) 8843 4251 **OPEN** Mon–Fri 11–5, w'ends & public hols 10–5
WINEMAKER Ben Jeanneret **EST.** 1992 **CASES** 10 000
Jeanneret's fully self-contained winery has a most attractive outdoor tasting area and equally attractive picnic facilities, on the edge of a small lake surrounded by bushland. While the business did not open until October 1994, its first wine was in fact made in 1992 (Shiraz) and it had already established a loyal following. National distribution; exports to the UK, Canada, Malaysia and Japan.

▼▼▼▼▽ **Clare Valley Shiraz 2004** Full-bodied; dense blackberry and licorice fruit; ripe tannins and controlled oak. Screwcap. 15° alc. **RATING** 93 **DRINK** 2019 $ 22

Clare Valley Riesling 2005 Spice and apple aromas; the palate moves smartly into full-on tropical fruit flavours; good length and finish; drink soonish. Screwcap. 11.8° alc. **RATING** 92 **DRINK** 2011 $ 18

Clare Valley Adelaide Hills Semillon Sauvignon Blanc 2005 A complex structure, driven by semillon 20% oak-fermented with partial wild fermentation; nice balance and weight, with a spine of grassy/minerally/citrussy acidity. Screwcap. 12.5° alc. **RATING** 92 **DRINK** 2009 $ 18

Clare Valley Grenache Shiraz 2004 Bright red-purple; medium-bodied, fresh and vibrant red and black fruits, the blend working very well. Carries the alcohol easily. Screwcap. 15° alc. **RATING** 90 **DRINK** 2012 $ 18

Clare Valley Cabernets 2003 Powerful, rich black fruits range through blackcurrant, blackberry, mulberry and dark plum; the tannins are ripe, the oak balanced. Cabernet Sauvignon/Merlot/Cabernet Franc/Malbec. Screwcap. 14.5° alc. **RATING** 90 **DRINK** 2015 $ 22

Jeir Creek

NR

Gooda Creek Road, Murrumbateman, NSW 2582 **REGION** Canberra District
T (02) 6227 5999 **F** (02) 6227 5900 **WWW**.jeircreekwines.com.au **OPEN** Thurs–Mon & hols 10–5
WINEMAKER Rob Howell **EST.** 1984 **CASES** 4500
Rob Howell came to part-time winemaking through a love of drinking fine wine, and is intent on improving both the quality and the consistency of his wines. It is now a substantial (and still growing) business, with the vineyard plantings increased to 11 ha by the establishment of more cabernet sauvignon, shiraz, merlot and viognier.

Jenke Vineyards

Barossa Valley Way, Rowland Flat, SA 5352 **REGION** Barossa Valley
T (08) 8524 4154 **F** (08) 8524 5044 **OPEN** 7 days 11–5
WINEMAKER Kym Jenke **EST.** 1989 **CASES** 8000
The Jenkes have been vignerons in the Barossa since 1854 and have over 45 ha of vineyards; a small part of the production is now made and marketed through a charming restored stone cottage cellar door. Distribution in Vic and NSW; exports to Singapore, Switzerland and NZ.

ΨΨΨΨ **Reserve Barossa Cabernet Sauvignon 2002** Medium- to full-bodied; sweet, supple, ripe blackcurrant/cassis and a dash of chocolate; velvety tannins, good oak. Screwcap. 15° alc. **RATING** 93 **DRINK** 2015 $ 35
Barossa Shiraz 2004 Aromas of black fruits, mocha, spice and earth; medium-bodied, with quite sweet but not jammy fruit; controlled extract, good finish. Screwcap. 14.5° alc. **RATING** 91 **DRINK** 2015 $ 28

ΨΨΨΨ **Barossa Cabernet Sauvignon 2004** Unusual flavours, seemingly very ripe; substantial tannins and extract; not typical for '04. Screwcap. 14.5° alc. **RATING** 87 **DRINK** 2012 $ 20

ΨΨΨΨ **Barossa Cabernet Franc Rose 2005** **RATING** 85 **DRINK** Now $ 13

🐚 Jeremiah One

PO Box 718, Surry Hills, NSW 2010 **REGION** Warehouse
T (02) 9699 2124 **F** (02) 9699 3354 **WWW**.jeremiahone.com **OPEN** Not
WINEMAKER Jonathon Hyams, Pikes, Chain of Ponds **EST.** 2004 **CASES** 2000
Jeremiah One is a name borne of owner Jonathon Hyams' 20 years' experience in the wine industry. He has set up a virtual winery business, precisely sourcing contract-grown grapes and winemakers to match, spanning Clare Valley Riesling; Adelaide Hills Sauvignon Blanc, Pinot Grigio and Chardonnay; Lenswood Pinot Noir; and Adelaide Hills/Clare Valley Merlot.

ΨΨΨΨΨ **Clare Valley Riesling 2005** Spotlessly clean; elegant and finely boned; apple and lemon flavours; dry finish. Screwcap. 12.5° alc. **RATING** 94 **DRINK** 2012 $ 18.99

ΨΨΨΨ **Barossa Valley Shiraz 2004** Medium-bodied and elegant; blackberry fruit supported by controlled oak, extract and tannins. Screwcap. 14.5° alc. **RATING** 92 **DRINK** 2015 $ 18.99
Adelaide Hills Sauvignon Blanc 2005 Attractive passionfruit and gooseberry bouquet; gentle fruit on the palate needs a little more drive. Screwcap. 13° alc. **RATING** 90 **DRINK** Now $ 18.99
Adelaide Hills Pinot Grigio 2004 Fragrant, flowery bouquet; quite delicate and fresh in the mouth, with touches of pear and musk; nice acidity. Screwcap. 13.5° alc. **RATING** 90 **DRINK** Now $ 18.99

ΨΨΨΨ **Adelaide Hills Clare Valley Merlot 2004** Blackcurrant, olive and earth; medium-bodied; fine but persistent tannins. Screwcap. 14.5° alc. **RATING** 89 **DRINK** 2010 $ 18.99

ΨΨΨΨ **Adelaide Hills Pinot Noir 2004** **RATING** 86 **DRINK** Now $ 18.99

Jerusalem Hollow ★★★★

6b Glyde Street, East Fremantle, WA 6158 (postal) **REGION** Margaret River
T (08) 9339 6879 **F** (08) 9339 5192 **WWW**.jerusalemhollowwines.com.au **OPEN** Not
WINEMAKER Harold Osborne, Frank Kittler (Contract) **EST.** 2000 **CASES** 500
Perth eye surgeon Bill Ward, wife (and former nurse) Louise and family began planting their 5.8 ha vineyard in 2000. Bill, a long term admirer of Champagne, was inspired by an article by Max Allen in the *Weekend Australian Magazine* in which Californian sparkling winemaker Harold Osborne (maker of Pelorus for Cloudy Bay in NZ) expressed the view that Margaret River was a good region for sparkling wine. This remains the main thrust of the business, with a side bet on Cabernet Sauvignon and a small amount of Roussanne Chardonnay to follow in due course. The name, incidentally, is a local one, but it so happens that Bill worked at the St John's eye hospital in Jerusalem as a surgical fellow in the late 1980s to early '90s.

▼▼▼▼▽ **Methode Champenoise 2003** Very flavoursome and complex in the fashion that Harold Osborne has always favoured; peach, honey, cream and nuts with 2 years on lees. 13.5° alc. **RATING** 90 **DRINK** Now $ 21

▼▼▼▼ **Cabernet Sauvignon 2004** Clean and fresh; light-bodied, but despite that lightness is balanced and not green. Young vine influences, one suspects. Cork. 13° alc. **RATING** 87 **DRINK** 2008 $ 18

Jester Hill Wines NR

292 Mount Stirling Road, Glen Aplin, Qld 4381 **REGION** Granite Belt
T (07) 4683 4380 **F** (02) 6622 3190 **WWW**.jesterhillwines.com.au **OPEN** 7 days 9–5
WINEMAKER John Ashwell, James Janda **EST.** 1993 **CASES** 860
A family-run vineyard situated in the pretty valley of Glen Aplin in the Granite Belt. The owners, John and Genevieve Ashwell, aim to concentrate on small quantities of premium-quality wines reflecting the full-bodied style of the region. Believing that good wine is made in the vineyard, John and Genevieve spent the first 7 years establishing healthy, strong vines on well-drained soil.

Jim Barry Wines ★★★★☆

Craig's Hill Road, Clare, SA 5453 **REGION** Clare Valley
T (08) 8842 2261 **F** (08) 8842 3752 **OPEN** Mon–Fri 9–5, w'ends, hols 9–4
WINEMAKER Mark Barry **EST.** 1959 **CASES** 80 000
The patriarch of this highly successful wine business, Jim Barry, died in October 2004, but the business continues under the active management of various of his many children. There is a full range of wine styles across most varietals, but with special emphasis on Riesling, Shiraz and Cabernet Sauvignon. The ultra-premium release is The Armagh Shiraz, with the McCrae Wood red wines not far behind. Jim Barry Wines is able to draw upon 247 ha of mature Clare Valley vineyards, plus a small holding in Coonawarra. Worldwide distribution.

▼▼▼▼▼ **The Armagh 2002** Dense purple-red; absolutely stuffed with blackberry, prune, dark chocolate and plum fruit intermingling with mocha/vanilla oak; gets away with the preposterous alcohol; very long finish. Cork. 15.5° alc. **RATING** 96 **DRINK** 2018 $ 205

▼▼▼▼▽ **McRae Wood Shiraz 2002** Chock-full of black fruits and mocha/vanilla oak; does show the alcohol. Cork. 15.5° alc. **RATING** 93 **DRINK** 2017 $ 39.95
Watervale Riesling 2005 Clean, lemon/lime aromas and similar, generous citrus flavours; good balance and line. Screwcap. 13° alc. **RATING** 92 **DRINK** 2013 $ 13
Silly Mid On Sauvignon Blanc Semillon 2005 Lively, fresh and crisp; delicious passionfruit and lemon flavours; beguiling finish. Clare Valley/Adelaide Hills. Screwcap. 12.5° alc. **RATING** 92 **DRINK** Now $ 18
The Lodge Hill Clare Valley Shiraz 2004 Good hue; an aromatic spice, cherry and blackberry bouquet; medium-bodied; lively, juicy red and black fruits; attractive style. Cork. 14.5° alc. **RATING** 92 **DRINK** 2014 $ 18

ɯɯɯɯ **The Family Vineyards Shiraz Cabernet Sauvignon 2002** For the price, has plenty of complexity; dark chocolate, black plum and vanilla aromas and flavours; good structure. Screwcap. **RATING** 89 **DRINK** 2010 $14.95

The Cover Drive Coonawarra Cabernet Sauvignon 2004 Medium-bodied; gentle blackcurrant, earth and mulberry fruit; fine, ripe tannins, controlled oak. Cork. 15° alc. **RATING** 89 **DRINK** 2012 $18

Jimbour Wines ★★★★

86 Jimbour Station Road, Jimbour, Qld 4406 **REGION** Queensland Zone
T (07) 3878 8909 **F** (07) 3878 8920 **WWW**.jimbourwines.com.au **OPEN** 7 days 10–4.30
WINEMAKER Peter Scudamore-Smith MW **EST**. 2000 **CASES** 30 000
Jimbour Station was one of the first properties opened in the Darling Downs, the heritage-listed homestead built in 1876. The property has been owned by the Russell family since 1923, which has diversified by establishing a 22-ha vineyard and opening a cellar door on the property. Increasing production is an indication of its intention to become one of Qld's major wine producers. Peter Scudamore-Smith MW is winemaker, but also provides marketing and financial advice to one of the State's most successful wine businesses.

ɯɯɯɯ̦ **Jimbour Station Darling Downs Shiraz 2003** Blackberry and black cherry aromas are swathed in vanilla oak, followed by a massively charged and concentrated palate with some prune, and dense, ripe tannins. Procork. **RATING** 90 **DRINK** 2013 $15.99

ɯɯɯɯ **Jimbour Station Chardonnay 2005** Bright colour; plenty of presence with ripe melon and peach fruit; good texture, and just a breath of French oak. Screwcap. 14° alc. **RATING** 89 **DRINK** 2008 $16

Jimbour Station Rose 2005 Cherry strawberry fruit; above-average concentration; dry finish. Screwcap. 14° alc. **RATING** 88 **DRINK** Now $16

Jimbour Station Shiraz Grenache Petit Verdot 2004 Light, bright, clear red; clean and fresh cherry and raspberry fruit aromas and flavours drive the light- to medium-bodied palate. There is an appropriately delicate touch of oak on a wine with good balance and length. Sophisticated winemaking manages to marry 3 different varieties from 3 different regions. **RATING** 88 **DRINK** 2010 $15.99

Jimbour Station Ludwig Leichhardt Reserve Merlot 2004 Medium-bodied; clear varietal expression with olive/earth surrounds to the blackcurrant/cassis fruit. Cork. 13.5° alc. **RATING** 88 **DRINK** 2014 $28

Jimbour Station Cabernet Sauvignon 2003 Clear varietal character in a somewhat austere mode; blackcurrant and earth plus savoury tannins; has absorbed the oak. Screwcap. 14.5° alc. **RATING** 88 **DRINK** 2010 $16

Jimbour Station Verdelho 2005 Some citrussy edges lift and sharpen the focus of the light-bodied fruit salad flavours; good example of the variety. Screwcap. 13° alc. **RATING** 87 **DRINK** Now $16

Jimbour Station Viognier 2005 Light green-straw; peach, apricot, spice and a flick of ginger; has depth, the alcohol and phenolics under control. Screwcap. 14° alc. **RATING** 87 **DRINK** 2008 $16

Ludwig Leichhardt Reserve Pinot Noir Chardonnay 2002 Blush pink; spicy, strawberry aromas and flavours; quite complex, with the base wine barrique-aged for 7 months; 71% Pinot Noir/29% Chardonnay. 11.5° alc. **RATING** 87 **DRINK** 2008 $28

ɯɯɯ̦ **Jimbour Station Ludwig Leichhardt Reserve Chardonnay 2004** Very developed yellow colour; rich, ripe, sweet yellow peach fruit; for immediate consumption. Cork. 14° alc. **RATING** 86 **DRINK** Now $28

Old Monty Tawny Port NV **RATING** 85 **DRINK** Now $18

Jindalee Estate ★★★★

265 Ballan Road, Moorabool, North Geelong, Vic 3221 **REGION** Geelong
T (03) 5276 1280 **F** (03) 5276 1537 **www**.jindaleewines.com.au **OPEN** 7 days 10–5
WINEMAKER Andrew Byers, Chris Sargeant **EST.** 1997 **CASES** 500 000
Jindalee is part of the Littore Group, which currently has 550 ha of premium wine grapes in wine production and under development in the Riverland. Corporate offices are now at the former Idyll Vineyard, acquired by Jindalee in late 1997. Here 14 ha of estate vineyards have been retrellised and upgraded, and produce the Fettlers Rest range. The Jindalee Estate Chardonnay can offer spectacular value. Exports to the UK, Sweden, the US and Canada.

▼▼▼▼♀ **Fettlers Rest Gewurztraminer 2005** Clear-cut, if delicate, spice, musk and rose petal varietal aromas; the main strength of the wine lies in its line, length and balance. Screwcap. 13° alc. **RATING** 90 **DRINK** 2009 $ 15

▼▼▼▼ **Premium Selection Chardonnay 2004** A broader, richer palate than the varietal; more depth and structure, and more oak evident. Cork. 13.5° alc. **RATING** 89 **DRINK** 2008 $ 10
Chardonnay 2004 Surprising focus and length; lively, tangy nectarine and citrus fruit, and a touch of French oak. **RATING** 89 **DRINK** Now $ 20
Shiraz 2004 A clean bouquet; a pleasant, light- to medium-bodied mix of black and red fruits; easy access style, with slightly surprising length. Screwcap. 13.5° alc. **RATING** 87 **DRINK** Now $ 7

▼▼▼♀ **Premium Selection Shiraz 2005** **RATING** 85 **DRINK** Now $ 10
Cabernet Sauvignon 2004 **RATING** 85 **DRINK** Now $ 7
Sauvignon Blanc 2005 **RATING** 84 **DRINK** Now $ 9
Premium Selection Pinot Noir 2004 **RATING** 84 **DRINK** Now $ 10
Merlot 2004 **RATING** 84 **DRINK** Now $ 7
Premium Selection Cuvee NV **RATING** 84 **DRINK** Now $ 10

Jingalla ★★★☆

RMB 1316 Bolganup Dam Road, Porongurup, WA 6324 **REGION** Porongurup
T (08) 9853 1023 **F** (08) 9853 1023 **www**.jingallawines.com.au **OPEN** 7 days 10.30–5
WINEMAKER Diane Miller, Bill Crappsley (Consultant) **EST.** 1979 **CASES** 5000
Jingalla is a family business, owned and run by Geoff and Nita Clarke and Barry and Shelley Coad, the latter the ever-energetic wine marketer of the business. The 8 ha of hillside vineyards are low-yielding, with the white wines succeeding best, but they also produce some lovely red wines. A partner in the new Porongurup Winery, which means it no longer has to rely on contract winemaking. Exports to the UK, Taiwan and Singapore.

▼▼▼▼ **Shiraz 2004** Light- to medium-bodied; fresh red cherry and plum fruit; fine, ripe tannins; easy style. Cork. 14.5° alc. **RATING** 89 **DRINK** 2010 $ 25
Porongurup Cabernet Sauvignon 2004 Medium purple-red; juicy cassis, blackcurrant and mulberry; the tannins are evident, as is the relatively low pH; needs a few years. Cork. 13° alc. **RATING** 88 **DRINK** 2014 $ 20

▼▼▼♀ **Porongurup Merlot 2004** **RATING** 85 **DRINK** 2008 $ 25

Jinglers Creek Vineyard NR

288 Relbia Road, Relbia, Tas 7258 (postal) **REGION** Northern Tasmania
T (03) 6344 3966 **F** (03) 6344 3966 **www**.jinglerscreekvineyard.com.au **OPEN** Thurs–Sun 11–5
WINEMAKER Graham Wiltshire, Tamar Ridge **EST.** 1998 **CASES** 1300
Irving Fong came to grapegrowing later in life, undertaking the viticulture course at Launceston TAFE when 67 years old (where he also met his second wife). They have 1.8 ha of pinot noir, with small plantings of pinot gris and chardonnay.

Jinks Creek Winery ★★★★★

Tonimbuk Road, Tonimbuk, Vic 3815 **REGION** Gippsland
T (03) 5629 8502 **F** (03) 5629 8551 **WWW**.jinkscreekwinery.com.au **OPEN** By appt
WINEMAKER Andrew Clarke **EST.** 1981 **CASES** 1000

Jinks Creek Winery is situated between Gembrook and Bunyip, bordering the evocatively named Bunyip State Park. While the winery was not built until 1992, planting of the 3.64-ha vineyard started back in 1981 and all the wines are estate-grown. The 'sold out' sign goes up each year. Exports to the US and Singapore.

ŢŢŢŢŢ **West Gippsland Chardonnay 2004** Bright green-straw; light- to medium-bodied, with tangy nectarine and citrus fruit, the palate lengthened by delightful lemony acidity. **RATING** 94 **DRINK** 2010 **$** 25

Heathcote Shiraz 2004 Best colour of the two shirazes; potent, powerful black fruit aromas; abundant flavour at the ripe end of the spectrum; good French oak, and considerable length. Cork. 14.2° alc. **RATING** 94 **DRINK** 2019 **$** 30

ŢŢŢŢŢ **East Gippsland Shiraz 2004** Developed hue; attractive licorice/spice/pepper/leather aromas; the spicy, medium-bodied palate finishes with fine, ripe tannins. Cork. 14° alc. **RATING** 91 **DRINK** 2014 **$** 28

West Gippsland Sauvignon Blanc 2005 Light straw-green; floral apple, spice and gooseberry aromas; a clean and lively palate, the fruit flavours tied with a bow of acidity. Cork. 13.5° alc. **RATING** 90 **DRINK** Now **$** 20

ŢŢŢŢ **West Gippsland Pinot Noir 2004** Medium- to full-bodied, rich and ripe; the palate has soft fruit and good flavour, though doesn't drive through to the finish. Cork. 13.9° alc. **RATING** 89 **DRINK** 2009 **$** 28

ŢŢŢŢ **Yarra Valley Cabernet Franc 2003 RATING** 86 **DRINK** 2008 **$** 17
West Gippsland Sauvignon Blanc 2004 RATING 84 **DRINK** Now **$** 20

ŢŢŢ **Rose 2005 RATING** 83

Jinnunger Vineyard NR

588 Nanarup Road, Lower Kalgan, Albany, WA 6330 **REGION** Albany
T (08) 9846 4374 **F** (08) 9846 4474 **WWW**.jinnunger.com.au **OPEN** By appt
WINEMAKER Robert Diletti (Contract) **EST.** 1996 **CASES** 800

Jinnunger Vineyard is owned by research scientist Colin Sanderson. There is 1 ha each of chardonnay and pinot noir, and while he expects to increase the plantings, it will always be a small, hand-tended vineyard. It is ideally situated, on a north-facing slope of Mt Mason close to the Southern Ocean, 18 km east of Albany. The name comes from the local Aboriginal (Nyungah) language, and means 'good views' (the property looks out over the Porongurup and Stirling Ranges).

Joadja Vineyards NR

Joadja Road, Berrima, NSW 2577 **REGION** Southern Highlands
T (02) 4878 5236 **F** (02) 4878 5236 **WWW**.joadja.com **OPEN** 7 days 10–5
WINEMAKER Kim Moginie **EST.** 1983 **CASES** 2000

The strikingly labelled Joadja Vineyards wines, first made in 1990, are principally drawn from 7 ha of estate vineyards situated in the cool hills adjacent to Berrima. Mature vines and greater experience of this emerging region have solved early difficulties in securing full ripeness.

John Duval Wines ★★★★★

9 Park Street, Tanunda, SA 5352 (postal) **REGION** Barossa Valley
T (08) 8563 2591 **F** (08) 8563 0372 **WWW**.johnduvalwines.com **OPEN** Not
WINEMAKER John Duval **EST.** 2003 **CASES** 3500

John Duval is an internationally recognised winemaker, having been the custodian of Penfolds Grange for almost 30 years as part of his role as chief red winemaker at Penfolds. He remains involved with Penfolds as a consultant, but these days is concentrating on establishing his own brand, and providing consultancy services to other clients in various parts of the world. On the principle of if not broken, don't fix, he is basing his business on Shiraz and Shiraz blends from old-vine vineyards in the Barossa Valley. The brand name Plexus, incidentally, denotes a network in an animal body that combines elements into a coherent structure. Exports to the UK, the US, NZ, Hong Kong and Switzerland.

ㅜㅜㅜㅜㅜ **Entity Barossa Valley Shiraz 2004** Deep colour; full-bodied, but supple and smooth; concentrated blackberry and plum with seamless oak and fine tannins; great length. Cork. 14.5° alc. **RATING** 95 **DRINK** 2014 $ 40

Plexus Barossa Valley Shiraz Grenache Mourvedre 2004 Far more structure and substance than the majority of Barossa Valley blends of these varieties; abundant spicy black fruits; excellent tannins and oak. Cork. 14.5° alc. **RATING** 95 **DRINK** 2012 $ 35

John Gehrig Wines ★★★★

Oxley-Milawa Road, Oxley, Vic 3678 **REGION** King Valley
T(03) 5727 3395 **F**(03) 5727 3699 **WWW**.johngehrigwines.com.au **OPEN** 7 days 9–5
WINEMAKER Ross Gehrig **EST.** 1976 **CASES** 5600
Ross Gehrig has taken over from parents John and Elizabeth, but finds getting them to slow down a hard task. As a sign of the times, all of the wines are now screwcapped.

ㅜㅜㅜㅜㅜ **Durif 2004** Classic durif style; dense, rich black fruits and bitter chocolate; built-in tannins; takes no prisoners. Screwcap. 13.6° alc. **RATING** 92 **DRINK** 2019 $ 30

Muscat NV Quality raisined muscat varietal character; Christmas pudding richness; some age. Screwcap. 18° alc. **RATING** 90 **DRINK** Now $ 18

ㅜㅜㅜㅜ **Pinot Noir 2004** A lot of work has gone into making the wine; good colour, structure and texture; midway between dry red and cherry plum pinot varietal character. Screwcap. 13.8° alc. **RATING** 89 **DRINK** 2008 $ 25

ㅜㅜㅜㅜ **Chenin Blanc 2004** Spotlessly clean; light-bodied, gentle fruit salad flavours; mercifully dry finish. Screwcap. 12.4° alc. **RATING** 86 **DRINK** Now $ 15

ㅜㅜㅜ **Gamay 2002 RATING** 81 $ 18

John Kosovich Wines ★★★★★

Cnr Memorial Avenue/Great Northern Highway, Baskerville, WA 6056 **REGION** Swan Valley
T(08) 9296 4356 **F**(08) 9296 4356 **WWW**.johnkosovichwines.com.au **OPEN** 7 days 10–5.30
WINEMAKER John Kosovich **EST.** 1922 **CASES** 4000
The name change from Westfield to John Kosovich Wines does not signify any change in either philosophy or direction for this much-admired producer of a surprisingly elegant and complex Chardonnay; the other wines are more variable, but from time to time there have been attractive Verdelho and excellent Cabernet Sauvignon. Since 1998, wines partly or wholly from the family's planting at Pemberton have been made, the Swan/Pemberton blends released under the Bronze Wing label. Exports to Singapore.

ㅜㅜㅜㅜㅜ **Liqueur Muscat NV** Mahogany colour with an olive rim; powerful and intense, with very good rancio; long and lingering; fine balance. **RATING** 95 **DRINK** Now $ 55

Liqueur Shiraz NV Tawny-olive colour; extremely powerful rancio, likewise age. Great length. More than 20 years old. Cork. 19° alc. **RATING** 95 **DRINK** Now $ 75

ㅜㅜㅜㅜ **Chardonnay 2005 RATING** 86 **DRINK** Now $ 26

Shiraz 2004 RATING 86 **DRINK** 2008 $ 21

John Wade Wines NR

PO Box 23, Denmark, WA 6633 **REGION** Denmark
T(08) 9848 2462 **F**(08) 9848 2087 **OPEN** By appt
WINEMAKER John Wade, Stephanie Wade, Alex Wade **EST.** 2000 **CASES** 1500
John Wade is arguably the most experienced winemaker in WA, with over 20 years' experience following his role as chief winemaker at Wynns Coonawarra Estate. He is best known for his

involvement with Plantagenet and then Howard Park. Having sold his interest in Howard Park, he has become a consultant winemaker to a substantial number of producers; his own label is a relatively small part of his total wine business. The wines are chiefly sold through premium retail outlets and restaurants.

John's Blend ★★★★★

18 Neil Avenue, Nuriootpa, SA 5355 (postal) **REGION** Langhorne Creek
T (08) 8562 1820 **F** (08) 8562 4050 **WWW**.johnsblend.com.au **OPEN** Not
WINEMAKER John Glaetzer **EST.** 1974 **CASES** 3000
John Glaetzer was Wolf Blass' right-hand man almost from the word go, the power behind the throne of the 3 Jimmy Watson trophies awarded to Wolf Blass Wines in 1974, '75 and '76, and a small matter of 11 Montgomery trophies for the Best Red Wine at the Adelaide Wine Show. This has always been a personal venture on the side, as it were, by John and wife Margarete Glaetzer, officially sanctioned of course, but really needing little marketing effort.

ŸŸŸŸŸ **Margarete's Shiraz 2002** Complex wine; rich black fruits, dark, bitter chocolate, vanilla oak and tannins all interwoven. Has length and finesse; best since 1998; 76% Langhorne Creek, 24% McLaren Vale. **RATING** 94 **DRINK** 2015 $ 50
Individual Selection Langhorne Creek Cabernet Sauvignon 2002 Super-saturated with American oak (40 months in new barrels) in traditional Blass/Glaetzer style; amazingly, the fruit does stand up thanks to a very long finish. Nonetheless, less oak might have been better. **RATING** 94 **DRINK** 2017 $ 50

Johnston Oakbank ★★★★

18 Oakwood Road, Oakbank, SA 5243 **REGION** Adelaide Hills
T (08) 8388 4263 **F** (08) 8388 4278 **WWW**.johnston-oakbank.com.au **OPEN** Mon–Fri 8–5
WINEMAKER David O'Leary (Contract), Geoff Johnston **EST.** 1843 **CASES** 4000
The origins of this business, owned by the Johnston Group, date back to 1839, making it the oldest known family-owned business in SA. The vineyard at Oakbank is substantial, with 12.5 ha chardonnay, 12 ha pinot noir, 9 ha sauvignon blanc, 87.5 ha shiraz, 5 ha merlot and 3 ha cabernet sauvignon.

ŸŸŸŸŸ **Adelaide Hills Sauvignon Blanc 2005** Well-constructed and balanced; plenty of mid-palate fruit without heaviness; grass, herb through to tropical; finishes with bright acidity. Good length. Screwcap. 13.3° alc. **RATING** 93 **DRINK** Now $ 18

ŸŸŸŸ **Adelaide Hills Merlot 2002** Light- to medium-bodied; strongly varietal olive, earth, savoury notes; the tannins are fine and has good length; it simply lacks generosity. Screwcap. 14° alc. **RATING** 88 **DRINK** 2009 $ 20

ŸŸŸŸ **Adelaide Hills Pinot Noir 2003** Savoury, spicy, foresty style; good mouthfeel, but the fruit is fading away. Screwcap. 13.8° alc. **RATING** 86 **DRINK** Now $ 20

Jones Winery & Vineyard ★★★★☆

Jones Road, Rutherglen, Vic 3685 **REGION** Rutherglen
T (02) 6032 8496 **F** (02) 6032 8495 **WWW**.joneswinery.com **OPEN** Fri–Sun & public hols 10–5
WINEMAKER Mandy Jones **EST.** 1864 **CASES** 2000
Late in 1998 the winery was purchased from Les Jones by Leanne Schoen and Mandy and Arthur Jones (nieces and nephew of Les). The cellar door sales area is in a building from the 1860s, still with the original bark ceiling and walls made of handmade bricks fired onsite.

ŸŸŸŸŸ **LJ Shiraz 2003** Very good colour; powerful, ripe blackberry and plum fruit; substantial tannin structure to support the wine for many years. Gold medal Victorian Wines Show '05. Cork. 14.8° alc. **RATING** 94 **DRINK** 2018 $ 40

ŸŸŸŸŸ **The Winemaker Marsanne 2004** Pale straw-green; distinct varietal character as in the Northern Rhone; a mix of mineral, talc. and honeysuckle, with a delicate, long palate. Cork. 13.9° alc. **RATING** 91 **DRINK** 2009 $ 18

ŸŸŸŸ **The Winemaker Shiraz 2004** Aromas of spice and hay; medium-bodied black fruits; a gentle hand with extract. Cork. 14.6° alc. **RATING** 89 **DRINK** 2010 $ 18

Journeys End Vineyards ★★★★

248 Flinders Street, Adelaide, SA 5000 (postal) **REGION** Southeast Australia
T 0431 709 305 **www**.journeysendvineyards.com.au **OPEN** Not
WINEMAKER Ben Riggs (Contract) **EST.** 2001 **CASES** 5000
A particularly interesting business in the virtual winery category which, while focused on McLaren Vale shiraz, also has contracts for other varieties in the Adelaide Hills and Langhorne Creek. The shiraz comes in four levels, and, for good measure, uses five different clones of shiraz to amplify the complexity which comes from having grapegrowers in many different parts of McLaren Vale. Exports to the US, the UK, Canada and Singapore.

▼▼▼▼♀ **Arrival McLaren Vale Shiraz 2003** A medium- to full-bodied, savoury, spicy wine with the customary dollop of dark chocolate. Fine-grained tannins, controlled oak. Cork. 15° alc. **RATING** 91 **DRINK** 2013 $45
Ascent McLaren Vale Shiraz 2003 Medium- to full-bodied; interestingly, seems to have sweet fruit and more chocolate than the Arrival (good) and more apparent alcohol (not so good). Cork. 15° alc. **RATING** 91 **DRINK** 2013 $30

▼▼▼▼ **Three Brothers Reunion Shiraz 2004** Light- to medium-bodied; clean and fresh red and black fruits; light tannins. Cork. **RATING** 88 **DRINK** 2009 $15
Three Brothers Reunion Sauvignon Blanc Semillon 2005 Good balance and line; mineral, grass and herb aromas and flavours; semillon tightens the structure. Screwcap. 13.5° alc. **RATING** 87 **DRINK** Now $13

▼▼▼♀ **The Return Watervale Riesling 2005 RATING** 86 **DRINK** 2009 $23
Building Bridges Fleurieu Peninsula Sauvignon Blanc 2005 RATING 86 **DRINK** Now $16

Judds Warby Range Estate ★★☆

Jones Road, Taminick via Glenrowan, Vic 3675 **REGION** Glenrowan
T (03) 5765 2314 **www**.warbyrange-estate.com.au **OPEN** Thurs–Mon 10–5, or by appt
WINEMAKER Ralph Judd **EST.** 1989 **CASES** 500
Ralph and Margaret Judd began the development of their vineyard in 1989 as contract growers for Southcorp. They have gradually expanded the plantings to 4 ha of shiraz and 0.5 ha of durif; they also have 100 vines each of zinfandel, ruby cabernet, cabernet sauvignon, petit verdot, nebbiolo, tempranillo and sangiovese for evaluation. Until 1995, all the grapes were fermented and then sent by tanker to Southcorp, but in 1996 the Judds made their first barrel of wine. They have now opened a small cellar door sales area. The wines are monumental in flavour and depth, in best Glenrowan tradition, and will richly repay extended cellaring. They missed the boat in 2004.

▼▼▼ **Shiraz 2004 RATING** 83 $15

▼▼♀ **Durif 2004 RATING** 79 $15

Juniper Estate ★★★★

Harmans Road South, Cowaramup, WA 6284 **REGION** Margaret River
T (08) 9755 9000 **F** (08) 9755 9100 **www**.juniperestate.com.au **OPEN** 7 days 10–5
WINEMAKER Mark Messenger **EST.** 1973 **CASES** 14 000
This is the reincarnation of Wrights, which was sold by founders Henry and Maureen Wright in 1998. The 10-ha vineyard has been retrellised, and the last 1.5 ha of plantable land has seen the key plantings of shiraz and cabernet sauvignon increase a little. A major building program was completed in 2000, giving Juniper Estate a 250-tonne capacity winery, barrel hall and cellar door facility. Juniper Crossing wines use a mix of estate-grown and purchased grapes from other Margaret River vineyards. The Juniper Estate releases are made only from the 28-year-old estate plantings. Immaculate packaging and background material. Exports to the US, the UK, Denmark, Germany, Hong Kong and Japan.

▼▼▼▼♀ **Juniper Crossing Semillon Sauvignon Blanc 2005** Lively, moderately intense herb, grass and citrus mix; nicely tight and focused. Screwcap. 13° alc. **RATING** 90 **DRINK** Now $16
Juniper Crossing Chardonnay 2004 Attractive, fragrant nectarine and citrus aromas moving more to melon and citrus on the palate; brisk acidity and an airbrush of French oak. Screwcap. **RATING** 90 **DRINK** 2010 $19

ΥΥΥΥ **Margaret River Cabernet Sauvignon 2003** Light- to medium-bodied; bright, fresh, lively dark fruits; just a trifle angular. Cork. 14° alc. **RATING** 89 **DRINK** 2012 $ 32
Margaret River Shiraz 2002 Light- to medium red-purple; very savoury style, with earthy/briary characters; the tannins are in balance, but the wine is somewhat lean overall. Cork. 14.5° alc. **RATING** 88 **DRINK** 2010 $ 30
Cane Cut Riesling 2004 Clean, fresh and lively, inevitably slightly simple; sweet lime juice flavour, the balance good. Cork. 10.5° alc. **RATING** 88 **DRINK** 2009 $ 24

Jupiter Creek Winery

NR

10 Queen Street, Thebarton, SA 5031 (postal) **REGION** Adelaide Hills
T (08) 8354 3744 **F** (08) 8354 3822 **OPEN** Not
WINEMAKER Paul Lindner (Contract) **EST.** 1999 **CASES** NA
Jupiter Creek has 8.9 ha of vineyard at Echunga, under the control of viticulturist Michael Clarken. The varieties planted are sauvignon blanc, grenache, cabernet sauvignon, merlot and shiraz.

Just Red Wines

★★★☆

2370 Eukey Road, Ballandean, Qld 4382 **REGION** Granite Belt
T (07) 4684 1322 **www**.justred.com.au **OPEN** W'ends & public hols 10–5, or by appt
WINEMAKER Michael Hassall **EST.** 1998 **CASES** 2000
Tony, Julia and Michael Hassall have planted 1.8 ha of shiraz and 1.2 ha of merlot at an altitude of just under 900m in the Granite Belt. They run the vineyard minimising the use of chemicals wherever possible, but do not hesitate to protect the grapes if weather conditions threaten an outbreak of mildew or botrytis. The names of the first wines to be released are bittersweet, though more of the former than the latter. The Hassalls' daughter Nikki was very much involved in the creation of the vineyard, and was driving back from university to be there for the first day of picking. By the ultimate cruel finger of fate, the car crashed and she was killed. The Hassalls went on to pick the grapes 'with our hearts broken'; hopefully the quality of the wines will provide some solace.

ΥΥΥΥΥ **Nikki's Vineyard Granite Belt Syrah 2004** Good purple-red hue; well-made; nicely balanced, supple cherry and plum fruit and a touch of vanilla oak; ripe tannins. Fine tribute. Cork. 13° alc. **RATING** 90 **DRINK** 2012 $ 20

ΥΥΥΥ **Nikki's First Pick Granite Belt Shiraz Merlot 2003** Medium red; a complex mix of sweet shiraz and distinctly savoury merlot influences; the Syrah seems to work better. Cork. 13° alc. **RATING** 88 **DRINK** 2011 $ 30

ΥΥΥΥ **Granite Belt Merlot 2004** Light- to medium-bodied; gently sweet, juicy red berry fruit and a touch of mint; no attempt to over-extract. Cork. 13° alc. **RATING** 86 **DRINK** 2009 $ 17

Jylland Vineyard

★★★

77 Ashby Road, Gingin, WA 6503 **REGION** Perth Hills
T (08) 9575 1442 **OPEN** Tues–Sun 10–5
WINEMAKER Bella Ridge Wines (Alon Arbel) **EST.** 1999 **CASES** 2000
Jylland is the Danish spelling for Jutland (the Jutland Peninsula divides the North Sea from the Baltic Sea and is home to mainland Denmark and the northern part of Germany). Co-owner Edel Grocke (with Terry Grocke) brought her Viking heritage with her to Australia, with a particular liking for sunshine, fine food and fresh, fruity wine. They have established a total of 4 ha of vines, the lion's share to chardonnay (1.5 ha); the remainder spread across chenin blanc, verdelho, carnelian, shiraz and cabernet sauvignon.

ΥΥΥΥ **Shiraz Cabernet 2004** Light- to medium-bodied; savoury edges to gently sweet red and black fruits, backed by fine tannins on the finish. Great value. Screwcap. 13.5° alc.
RATING 88 **DRINK** 2009 $ 12

ΥΥΥΥ **Verdelho 2005** **RATING** 84 $ 13

ΥΥΥ **Chardonnay 2005** **RATING** 83 $ 13

Kabminye Wines ★★★★

Krondorf Road, Tanunda, SA 5352 **REGION** Barossa Valley
T(08) 8563 0889 **F**(08) 8563 3828 **www**.kabminye.com **OPEN** 7 days 11–5
WINEMAKER Contract **EST.** 2001 **CASES** 3000
Rick and Ingrid Glastonbury have established a combined café (serving traditional Barossa Valley lunches), art gallery and cellar door, with a surrounding 1.5 ha of vineyard. Architect Rick Glastonbury has been a home winemaker for 30 years, but almost all the wines under the Kabminye label are contract-made from purchased grapes.

ΨΨΨΨΨ **2003 Kabminye Barossa Valley Cabernet Shiraz** Light- to medium-bodied; a savoury, spicy, earthy mix of mulberry, blackberry and blackcurrant fruit; some oak inputs; fine tannins and supple overall mouthfeel. Screwcap. **RATING** 90 **DRINK** 2013 $ 22.50

ΨΨΨΨ **2005 Kabminye Ilona Rose** Bright red-purple; juicy cherry/raspberry/cassis flavours; a long, virtually dry, finish. Cabernet Sauvignon/Grenache/Shiraz. Screwcap. **RATING** 89 **DRINK** Now $ 17.50

Kaesler Wines ★★★★★

Barossa Valley Way, Nuriootpa, SA 5355 **REGION** Barossa Valley
T(08) 8562 4488 **F**(08) 8562 4499 **www**.kaesler.com.au **OPEN** Mon–Sat 10–5, Sunday & public hols 11.30–4
WINEMAKER Reid Bosward **EST.** 1990 **CASES** 12 000
The Kaesler name dates back to 1845, when the first members of the family settled in the Barossa Valley. The Kaesler vineyards date back to 1893, but the Kaesler ownership ended in 1968. After several changes, the present (much-expanded) Kaesler Wines was acquired by a Swiss banking family in conjunction with former Flying Winemaker Reid Bosward and wife Bindy. Bosward's experience shows through in the wines, which now come from 24 ha of estate vineyards which, as well as the 1893 shiraz, grenache and mourvedre, have grenache and mourvedre planted in the 1930s. Exports to US, Canada, Switzerland, Denmark, Sweden, Japan, Hong Kong and NZ.

ΨΨΨΨΨ **Old Bastard Shiraz 2004** Great colour, deep and clear; extreme concentration, focus and power; a super-charged V8 engine idling and waiting to go, with all the fruit one could wish for. Try cellaring for 10 years minimum. Cork. 15° alc. **RATING** 95 **DRINK** 2024 $ 160
Old Vine Shiraz 2004 Smooth, supple, velvety black fruits; against the majestic power of Old Bastard seems positively elegant; long, balanced palate. Cork. 15° alc. **RATING** 94 **DRINK** 2019 $ 60
WOMS Shiraz Cabernet 2004 Concentrated, intense blackberry blackcurrant fruit, tannins and oak all seamlessly interwoven. Parker powerhouse. Cork. 15.5° alc. **RATING** 94 **DRINK** 2020 $ 70

ΨΨΨΨΨ **Stonehorse Shiraz 2004** Strong colour; a powerful array of black fruits and supporting oak and tannins; oak hidden until the last moment, when its snout appears. Cork. 15.5° alc. **RATING** 91 **DRINK** 2015 $ 30

ΨΨΨΨ **Avignon Grenache Shiraz Mourvedre 2005** Complex, spiced plums and black cherries; typical supple and smooth texture, but the alcohol is very obvious. Cork. 15.5° alc. **RATING** 89 **DRINK** 2010 $ 30

ΨΨΨΨ **Cabernet Sauvignon 2004** Just too ripe, however flavoursome, entering into the valley of the dead fruit. Cork. 16° alc. **RATING** 86 **DRINK** 2010 $ 25

Kalari Wines NR

120 Carro Park Road, Cowra, NSW 2794 **REGION** Cowra
T(02) 6342 1465 **F**(02) 6342 1465 **www**.kalariwines.com.au **OPEN** Fri–Mon & public hols 10–5
WINEMAKER Jill Lindsay (Contract) **EST.** 1995 **CASES** 1000
Kalari Vineyards is yet another of the newer brands to appear in the Cowra region. It has 14 ha of vines, with a Verdelho, Chardonnay and Shiraz in the initial release.

Kalleske

★★★★☆

Vinegrove Road, Greenock, SA 5360 **REGION** Barossa Valley
T 0409 339 599 **F** (08) 8562 8118 **WWW**.kalleske.com **OPEN** Not
WINEMAKER Troy Kalleske **EST.** 1999 **CASES** 5000

The Kalleske family has been growing and selling grapes on a mixed farming property at Greenock for over 100 years. Fifth-generation John and Lorraine Kalleske embarked on a trial vintage for a fraction of the grapes in 1999. It was an immediate success, and led to the construction of a small winery with son Troy Kalleske as winemaker. The vineyards, with an average age of 50 years, see no chemical fertilisers or pesticides; some blocks are certified fully organic. The density of the flavour of the Shiraz and Grenache is awesome.

TTTTT **Greenock Shiraz 2004** Deep, dense colour; saturated blackberry, plum and black cherry fruit; ripe tannins and lots of complementary oak. Needs patience. Cork. 15° alc.
RATING 94 **DRINK** 2019 $ 39

TTTTT **Clarry's Barossa Valley Red 2004** Clear, bright red-purple; an attractive array of black and red fruits with ripples of spice and chocolate; much more structure than most, and no jammy characters; oak incidental; 80% Grenache; 20% Shiraz. Screwcap. 14.5° alc.
RATING 93 **DRINK** 2010 $ 20

Johann Georg Old Vine Barossa Valley Shiraz 2003 Dense red-purple; rich black fruits, licorice and prune, with spicy elements; at 15.5° alcohol it just seems a little too ripe. Cork. 15.5° alc. **RATING** 91 **DRINK** 2013 $ 100

Old Vine Barossa Valley Grenache 2003 Typical Barossa Grenache; sweet, jammy, confit fruit, but with nice spicy notes to finish, plus the finest tannins possible; controlled oak. Vines planted 1935. Quality cork. **RATING** 90 **DRINK** 2010 $ 45

TTTT **Clarry's Barossa Valley White 2005** Disciplined winemaking; no oak or skin contact; fresh, firm, minerally fruit with a touch of herb; dry finish; 70% Semillon, 30% Chenin Blanc. Screwcap. **RATING** 87 **DRINK** 2010 $ 16

Kamberra

★★★★★

Cnr Northbourne Avenue/Flemington Road, Lyneham, ACT 2602 **REGION** Canberra District
T (02) 6262 2333 **F** (02) 6262 2300 **WWW**.kamberra.com.au **OPEN** 7 days 10–5
WINEMAKER Alex McKay **EST.** 2000 **CASES** 18 000

Kamberra is part of the Hardys group, established in 2000 with the planting of 40 ha of vines and a winery in the Australian Capital Territory, only a few hundred metres from the showground facilities where the national wine show is held every year. Riesling and Shiraz are fully estate-grown, and most of the wines have a Kamberra component.

TTTTT **Shiraz Viognier 2004** Good colour; nicely balanced blackberry, spice and lift (from the viognier) on the bouquet; the medium-bodied palate follows on in the same spectrum, with fine tannins and good oak. Cork. 13.3° alc. **RATING** 94 **DRINK** 2013 $ 30

Tumbarumba Pinot Noir Chardonnay Pinot Meunier 2000 Very fine and very intense; a long, lingering, citrussy palate, with a seemingly bone-dry finish, although it does have some dosage. 13° alc. **RATING** 94 **DRINK** 2010 $ 30

TTTTT **Meeting Place Chardonnay 2004** An intense, cool-climate, fruit-driven style; a tangy fusion of grapefruit, stone fruit and melon. Screwcap. 13° alc. **RATING** 93 **DRINK** 2010 $ 16

Tumbarumba Chardonnay 2004 A classy wine, with leanings towards Chablis; despite its relatively low alcohol, has absorbed the barrel ferment and maturation in French oak; light nectarine and cashew mix, minerally finish. Screwcap. 12.1° alc. **RATING** 93 **DRINK** 2011 $ 30

Meeting Place Riesling 2004 A clean and generous mix of ripe lime and tropical fruit lingering through to the finish and aftertaste. Screwcap. 12° alc. **RATING** 91 **DRINK** 2010 $ 16

TTTT **Meeting Place Viognier 2004** Complex spice, dried apricot and oak aromas; lightens off somewhat on the palate; perhaps no bad thing. Screwcap. 13.5° alc. **RATING** 89 **DRINK** Now $ 16

Meeting Place Sparkling 2002 Lean, lemony/citrussy aromas and flavours, led by the chardonnay component; a tangy, relatively dry finish. Chardonnay/Pinot Noir/Pinot Meunier. **RATING** 88 **DRINK** Now $ 15

Kancoona Valley Wines

NR

123 Morgan's Creek Road, Kancoona South, Vic 3691 **REGION** Alpine Valleys
T (02) 6028 9419 **F** (02) 6028 9051 **WWW**.kancoonavalleywines.com.au **OPEN** By appt
WINEMAKER Joseph Birti **EST.** 1989 **CASES** 1000
Joseph and Lena Birti began planting their vineyard, situated in a natural amphitheatre 12 km from the Kiewa River, halfway between Myrtleford and Mt Beauty, in 1989. Thermal breezes rising from the Kiewa River valley help protect the vines from fungal disease, and the Birtis do not use any pesticides. From the word go have offered preservative-free alternatives.

Kangarilla Road Vineyard

★★★★

Kangarilla Road, McLaren Vale, SA 5171 **REGION** McLaren Vale
T (08) 8383 0533 **F** (08) 8383 0044 **WWW**.kangarillaroad.com.au **OPEN** Mon–Fri 9–5, w'ends 11–5
WINEMAKER Kevin O'Brien **EST.** 1975 **CASES** 40 000
Kangarilla Road was formerly known as Stevens Cambrai. Long-time industry identity Kevin O'Brien and wife Helen purchased the property in 1997, and have now fully established the strikingly labelled Kangarilla Road brand in place of Cambrai, steadily increasing production. Exports to all major markets.

ŸŸŸŸŸ **McLaren Vale Shiraz Viognier 2004** Dense purple-red; luscious, rich, round and mouthfilling blackberry fruit; oak in the background, alcohol in the foreground. Cork. 15° alc. **RATING** 93 **DRINK** 2015 $ 29

ŸŸŸŸ **McLaren Vale Viognier 2005** Plenty of varietal fruit in a peach, apricot, honeysuckle, lychee spectrum; as ever, viognier is reluctant to concede texture, like high gloss paint, notwithstanding sophisticated winemaking techniques. Screwcap. 14° alc. **RATING** 89 **DRINK** 2008 $ 18
McLaren Vale Zinfandel 2004 Medium red-purple; plum, prune, spice, raisin and chocolate fruit; slightly jagged mouthfeel. Cork. 15.5° alc. **RATING** 88 **DRINK** 2010 $ 29

Kangaroo Island Vines

★★★☆

c/- 413 Payneham Road, Felixstow, SA 5070 **REGION** Kangaroo Island
T (08) 8365 3411 **F** (08) 8336 2462 **OPEN** Not
WINEMAKER Caj Amadio **EST.** 1990 **CASES** 600
Kangaroo Island is another venture of Caj and Genny Amadio, with the wines being sold through the Chain of Ponds cellar door. The Amadios have been the focal point of the development of vineyards on Kangaroo Island, producing the wines from their own tiny planting of 450 vines on quarter of an acre, and from grapes from other vignerons on the island.

ŸŸŸŸ **Florance Cabernet Sauvignon Cabernet Franc Merlot 2001** Good colour; quite fragrant berry, mint, leaf and spice; fruit-driven mulberry and blueberry flavours, slightly savoury tannins. Cork. **RATING** 88 **DRINK** 2009 $ 24.65

Kangderaar Vineyard

★★★

Wehla-Kingower Road, Rheola, Vic 3517 **REGION** Bendigo
T (03) 5438 8292 **F** (03) 5438 8292 **OPEN** Mon–Sat 9–5, Sun 10–5
WINEMAKER James Nealy **EST.** 1980 **CASES** 800
The 4.5-ha vineyard is near the Melville Caves, said to have been the hideout of the bushranger Captain Melville in the 1850s, and surrounded by the Kooyoora State Park. It is owned by James and Christine Nealy.

ŸŸŸŸ **Chardonnay 2005** Big, rich, ripe and generous yellow peach/tropical fruit does all the talking. Screwcap. 13.2° alc. **RATING** 87 **DRINK** 2008 $ 13

ŸŸŸŸ **Cabernet Sauvignon 2004 RATING** 85 **DRINK** 2010 $ 18
Riesling Traminer 2005 RATING 84 **DRINK** Now $ 13
Cabernet Sauvignon 2003 RATING 84 **DRINK** 2009 $ 18

ŸŸŸ **Carmine 2005 RATING** 83 $ 15

Kara Kara Vineyard ★★★★★

99 Edelsten Road, St Arnaud, Vic 3478 (10 km sth St Arnaud) **REGION** Pyrenees
T (03) 5496 3294 **F** (03) 5496 3294 **WWW**.pyrenees.org.au/karakara **OPEN** Mon–Fri 10.30–6, w'ends 9–6
WINEMAKER Steve Zsigmond, Hanging Rock Winery **EST.** 1977 **CASES** 1200
Hungarian-born Steve Zsigmond comes from a long line of vignerons and sees Kara Kara as the eventual retirement occupation for himself and wife Marlene. He is a graduate of the Adelaide University (Roseworthy) wine marketing course, and worked for Yalumba and Negociants as a sales manager in Adelaide and Perth. He looks after sales and marketing from the Melbourne premises of Kara Kara, and the wine is made at Hanging Rock, with consistent results. Draws upon 9 ha of estate plantings.

ŸŸŸŸŸ **Pyrenees Shiraz 2004** Dense, impenetrable colour; extremely concentrated and luscious blackberry, plum and dark chocolate, but not overly tannic or extracted. Best by far from Kara Kara. Cork. 14° alc. **RATING** 94 **DRINK** 2019 $ 24
Pyrenees Cabernet Sauvignon 2004 Similar dense colour; layers of cassis, blackcurrant and mulberry fruit; juicy and not green. A pigeon pair with the Shiraz. Cork. 13° alc. **RATING** 94 **DRINK** 2016 $ 24

ŸŸŸŸ **Pyrenees Sauvignon Blanc 2005** Crisp, minerally style; subdued varietal fruit, but attractive squeaky acidity and length. Screwcap. 13.4° alc. **RATING** 88 **DRINK** Now $ 16

Karatta Wine NR

43/22 Liberman Close, Adelaide, SA 5000 (postal) **REGION** Mount Benson
T (08) 8215 0250 **F** (08) 8215 0450 **OPEN** Not
WINEMAKER Contract **EST.** 1994 **CASES** 1400
This is the former Anthony Dale vineyard, planted to 12 ha of shiraz, cabernet sauvignon, pinot noir, malbec, and more recently sauvignon blanc and chardonnay. It is owned by Karatta Wine Company in association with the Tenison Vineyard. The wines are sold through regional outlets, and by mail order, but with further developments planned.

Karee Estate NR

PO Box 38, Goornong, Vic 3557 **REGION** Bendigo
T (03) 5432 2268 **F** (03) 5432 2274 **OPEN** By appt
WINEMAKER Greg Dedman (Contract) **EST.** 2002 **CASES** NA
The earlier wines were made by Mal Stewart (Wild Dog), but since 2004 they have been made in collaboration with the Bendigo Institute of TAFE winery, now run by Greg Dedman.

Karina Vineyard ★★★★

35 Harrisons Road, Dromana, Vic 3936 **REGION** Mornington Peninsula
T (03) 5981 0137 **F** (03) 5981 0137 **OPEN** W'ends 11–5, 7 days in January
WINEMAKER Gerard Terpstra **EST.** 1984 **CASES** 2000
A typical Mornington Peninsula vineyard, situated in the Dromana/Red Hill area on rising, north-facing slopes, just 3 km from the shores of Port Phillip Bay, immaculately tended and with picturesque garden surrounds. Fragrant Riesling and cashew-accented Chardonnay are usually its best wines. Retail distribution in Vic; exports to Japan.

ŸŸŸŸŸ **Chardonnay 2005** Stylish and intense grapefruit and melon with well-integrated oak; excellent overall balance. Screwcap. 13° alc. **RATING** 93 **DRINK** 2010 $ 21
Terroir Cabernet Merlot 2004 Strong purple-red; fresh, lively, red fruits; light- to medium-bodied, but no green characters. Screwcap. 14° alc. **RATING** 90 **DRINK** 2008 $ 21

Karl Seppelt

NR

Ross Dewells Road, Springton, SA 5235 **REGION** Eden Valley
T (08) 8568 2378 **F** (08) 8568 2799 **OPEN** 7 days 10–5
WINEMAKER Karl Seppelt **EST.** 1981 **CASES** 5000
It is strange that Karl Seppelt, once marketing and sales director of Seppelt (before it was acquired by SA Brewing) should have struggled to gain recognition for his own brand. It has excellent vineyards, the wines made offsite under the direction of Karl. Exports to Canada and Germany.

Karriview

NR

Cnr Scotsdale Road/Roberts Road, Denmark, WA 6333 **REGION** Denmark
T (08) 9840 9381 **F** (08) 9855 1549 **WWW**.karriviewwines.com.au **OPEN** Fri–Sun 11–4, school & public hols 7 days 11–4
WINEMAKER Elizabeth Smith **EST.** 1986 **CASES** 550
A small (1.5 ha each) of immaculately tended pinot noir and chardonnay on ultra-close spacing produce tiny quantities of 2 wines of at times remarkable intensity, quality and style. Available only from the winery, but worth the effort. Typically, back vintages are available; with age, the Pinot Noir acquires strong foresty characters which are quite Burgundian.

Kassebaum Wines

★★★★☆

Nitschke Road, Marananga, SA 5355 **REGION** Barossa Valley
T (08) 8562 2731 **F** (08) 8562 4751 **OPEN** By appt
WINEMAKER Rod Chapman (Contract) **EST.** 2003 **CASES** 260
David and Dianne Kassebaum are third-generation grapegrowers. David has been involved in the wine industry for 20 years, working first with Penfolds in bottling, microbiology and maturation laboratories, and most recently in the Vinpac International laboratory. They have 5.4 ha of shiraz and 1.5 ha of semillon, most of which is sold to Southcorp with a top-quality grade. Yields vary from 1 to 1.5 tonnes per acre. The small amount of shiraz retained for the Kassebaum Magdalena label is matured in new French and American oak for 12 months. Exports to the US.

TTTTT **Magdalena Barossa Valley Shiraz 2004** Deep, intense purple-red; flooded with essence of black fruits, plums and prunes, yet not at all extractive or alcoholic; needs time to develop light and shade. High-quality cork. **RATING** 93 **DRINK** 2019 **$** 35

Katnook Estate

Riddoch Highway, Coonawarra, SA 5263 **REGION** Coonawarra
T (08) 8737 2394 **F** (08) 8737 2397 **WWW**.katnookestate.com.au **OPEN** Mon–Sat 10–5, Sun 11–4
WINEMAKER Wayne Stehbens, Tony Milanowski **EST.** 1979 **CASES** 125 000
Still one of the largest contract grapegrowers and suppliers in Coonawarra, selling more than half its grape production to others. The historic stone woolshed in which the second vintage in Coonawarra (1896) was made, and which has served Katnook since 1980, is being restored. The 1997 launch of the flagship Odyssey and the 2000 follow-up of Prodigy Shiraz point the way to a higher profile for the winemaking side of the venture. Freixenet, the Spanish Cava producer, owns 60% of the business. Exports to the UK, the US and other major markets.

TTTTT **Prodigy Shiraz 2002** A fragrant, elegant mix of black cherry, blackberry, spice and mocha oak; super-fine tannins, long finish. Quality cork. 14° alc. **RATING** 96 **DRINK** 2017 **$** 100
Odyssey Cabernet Sauvignon 2001 A very complex, round and mouthfilling wine; amazing combination of 38 months in predominantly new French and American oak, and low alcohol; cedar, vanilla, mocha and earth, black fruits still there, likewise fine tannins. Cork. 13.5° alc. **RATING** 96 **DRINK** 2016 **$** 100
Coonawarra Chardonnay 2003 Bright, light green-yellow; developing nicely; sweet white peach and nectarine fruit complexed by gently creamy malolactic inputs and sure oak handling. Screwcap. **RATING** 94 **DRINK** 2010 **$** 32
Coonawarra Shiraz 2003 Spice, cedar and polished leather aromas and flavours surround the core of black fruit; a super-elegant style; very good length and mouthfeel. Cork. **RATING** 94 **DRINK** 2015 **$** 45

ΥΥΥΥΥ **Coonawarra Cabernet Sauvignon 2002** Powerful, concentrated and focused black fruits and earth plus touches of bitter chocolate; tannins imposing, but balanced by fruit and oak. Cork. **RATING** 92 **DRINK** 2017 $ 45

Founder's Block Chardonnay 2003 Elegant, delicate, light-bodied grapefruit and nectarine; subtle, spicy oak. Screwcap. **RATING** 90 **DRINK** Now $ 19.99

Coonawarra Merlot 2002 Strong, cedary oak drives both the bouquet and palate; good texture and mouthfeel, with olive-tinged varietal fruit still discernible. Simply too long (2 years) in oak. A pity. Cork. **RATING** 90 **DRINK** 2010 $ 45

Founder's Block Cabernet Sauvignon 2003 Elegant, medium-bodied cedary blackcurrant flavours; fine, ripe, rounded tannins; ready now. Screwcap. **RATING** 90 **DRINK** 2008 $ 19.99

ΥΥΥΥ **Founder's Block Coonawarra Sauvignon Blanc 2005** Herb, mineral, apple and spice; pleasantly crisp and lively; good length, but understated. Screwcap. **RATING** 89 **DRINK** Now $ 19.99

Founder's Block Chardonnay 2004 Light- to medium-bodied; smooth and supple, with restrained stone fruit and grapefruit flavours; minimal oak impact. Screwcap. 13° alc. **RATING** 89 **DRINK** 2009 $ 20

Riddoch Chardonnay 2003 Well-made; good balance and integration of oak with peach and melon fruit; light- to medium-bodied; good length, good value. Screwcap. **RATING** 89 **DRINK** 2008 $ 17

Riddoch Cabernet Sauvignon 2002 Shows considerable development; savoury, spicy, earthy, briary flavours; the finish and aftertaste are the strong points. Quality cork. **RATING** 88 **DRINK** 2009 $ 20

Riesling 2005 Slightly subdued bouquet; tight, crisp, citrussy/minerally palate; pleasantly dry finish. **RATING** 87 **DRINK** 2010 $ 19

Founder's Block Shiraz 2003 Light-bodied; black fruits, spice and a wisp of vanilla oak; fine tannins. Screwcap. **RATING** 87 **DRINK** 2008 $ 19.99

Founder's Block Merlot 2003 Light-bodied; earthy, spicy, savoury, olive aromas and flavours are varietal, but very light. Screwcap. **RATING** 87 **DRINK** Now $ 19.99

Kay Bros Amery ★★★★

Kay Road, McLaren Vale, SA 5171 **REGION** McLaren Vale
T (08) 8323 8211 **F** (08) 8323 9199 **WWW**.kaybrothersamerywines.com **OPEN** Mon–Fri 9–5, w'ends & public hols 12–5
WINEMAKER Colin Kay **EST.** 1890 **CASES** 14 000
A traditional winery with a rich history and nearly 20 ha of priceless old vines; while the white wines have been variable, the red wines and fortified wines can be very good. Of particular interest is Block 6 Shiraz, made from 100-year-old vines; both vines and wine are going from strength to strength. Exports to the UK, the US and other major markets.

ΥΥΥΥΥ **Block 6 Shiraz 2003** Clean, soft, rounded wine; spice, plums, blackberry and mocha; fine tannins, good balance and length; has consumed the oak. Ultimate retro label; from 1.6 ha of 111-year-old vines. Screwcap. 15.5° alc. **RATING** 93 **DRINK** 2018 $ 50

Hillside Shiraz 2003 Good colour; soft, round and rich; gentle plum, mocha and vanilla; everything moulded by 2 years in oak. Shares the ultimate retro-style label with Block 6. Screwcap. 15° alc. **RATING** 92 **DRINK** 2015 $ 40

ΥΥΥΥ **McLaren Vale Shiraz 2003** Fruit-forward style; medium-bodied cherry, plum and mulberry, plus a wisp of chocolate. What you see is what you get. Screwcap. 14.5° alc. **RATING** 89 **DRINK** 2011 $ 25

ΥΥΥΥ **Merlot 2003** **RATING** 85 **DRINK** 2008 $ 25

Keith Tulloch Wine

★★★★☆

Hunter Ridge Winery, Hermitage Road, Pokolbin, NSW 2320 **REGION** Lower Hunter Valley
T (02) 4998 7500 **F** (02) 4998 7211 **www**.keithtullochwine.com.au **OPEN** Thurs–Fri 10–4, Sat 10–5, or by appt
WINEMAKER Keith Tulloch **EST.** 1997 **CASES** 6500

Keith Tulloch is, of course, a member of the Tulloch family which has played such a lead role in the Hunter Valley for over a century. Formerly a winemaker at Lindemans and then Rothbury Estate, he has developed his own label since 1997. I cannot remember being more impressed with an initial release of wines than those under the Keith Tulloch label. The only problem is the small scale of their production. There is the same almost obsessive attention to detail, the same almost ascetic intellectual approach, the same refusal to accept anything but the best. Exports to all major markets.

🍷🍷🍷🍷🍷 **Botrytis Semillon 2004** Full gold; ultra-rich; cordon-cut, but also strong botrytis influence; cumquat, honey and crème brulee off-set by lingering acidity; remarkable wine; 350 dozen made. Screwcap. **RATING** 94 **DRINK** 2009 $ 28

🍷🍷🍷🍷🍷 **Kester Shiraz 2002** Medium-bodied; strongly regional earthy/leathery overtones to the fruit; has considerable length thanks to fine, ripe, lingering tannins; considerable style; 650 dozen made. Stained cork. **RATING** 91 **DRINK** 2012 $ 42.50

Semillon 2005 Quite intense mineral and lime flavours; good length and intensity. Will build from here. Screwcap. **RATING** 90 **DRINK** 2015 $ 26

Chardonnay 2004 Complex barrel ferment inputs to both bouquet and palate; rich, ripe peach and nectarine fruit; gently sweet overall impression, before finishing dry; 250 dozen made. Screwcap. **RATING** 90 **DRINK** 2008 $ 26

Kells Creek Vineyards

NR

Kells Creek Road, Mittagong, NSW 2575 **REGION** Southern Highlands
T (02) 4878 5096 **F** (02) 4878 5097 **www**.kellscreekvineyards.com.au **OPEN** By appt
WINEMAKER Eric Priebee **EST.** 2001 **CASES** 800

Kells Creek is one of the newer businesses in the rapidly expanding Southern Highlands region. Established by Eric Priebee and wife Gaby Barfield, it draws principally on other vineyards around Mittagong, Moss Vale and Aylmerton. Kells Creek itself has 1 ha of riesling planted, and operates an energetic marketing program under the direction of industry veteran Douglas Hamilton. In 2003 a joint venture was set up with Littledale Estates of the Hunter Valley: Kells Creek will make the wines for both partners, and the wines will be marketed under the Littledale Estates Brand. Exports to Canada.

Kelly's Creek

★★★☆

RSD 226a Lower Whitehills Road, Relbia, Tas 7258 **REGION** Northern Tasmania
T (03) 6234 9696 **F** (03) 6231 6222 **OPEN** Not
WINEMAKER Hood Wines (Andrew Hood) **EST.** 1992 **CASES** 650

Kelly's Creek draws on 1 ha of riesling and 0.2 ha each of chardonnay, pinot noir and cabernet sauvignon. Its majority owner is Darryl Johnson, who runs the vineyard with help from Guy Wagner, who describes himself as 'merely a marketing minion'. Small quantities of Riesling are made for Kelly's Creek; all vintages have had success at the Tasmanian Wines Show.

🍷🍷🍷🍷 **Sweet Fruity Riesling 2005** Easy style; sweet lime juice, pineapple and passionfruit; a touch more acidity need for top points. **RATING** 89 **DRINK** 2010

Kellybrook

★★★★☆

Fulford Road, Wonga Park, Vic 3115 **REGION** Yarra Valley
T (03) 9722 1304 **F** (03) 9722 2092 **www**.kellybrookwinery.com.au **OPEN** Mon 11–5, Tues–Sat 9–6, Sun 11–6
WINEMAKER Philip Kelly, Darren Kelly **EST.** 1960 **CASES** 4000

The 8.5-ha vineyard is at Wonga Park, one of the gateways to the Yarra Valley, and has a picnic area and a full-scale restaurant. As well as table wine, a very competent producer of both cider and apple brandy (in Calvados style). When it received its winery licence in 1960, it became the first winery in the Yarra Valley to open its doors in the 20th century, a distinction often ignored or forgotten (by this author as well as others). Exports to the UK and Denmark.

ŸŸŸŸŸ **Yarra Valley Chardonnay 2004** Impressive wine; focused and intense melon and grapefruit, with cashew nuances and subtle oak. Screwcap. **RATING** 93 **DRINK** 2014 $ 24
Yarra Valley Cabernet Merlot 2004 Quite concentrated blackcurrant fruit with touches of cedar, earth and leaf; excellent length. Cork. **RATING** 92 **DRINK** 2014 $ 27
Yarra Valley Pinot Noir 2003 Unfolds progressively on the palate, with attractive spice, plum and black cherry flavours; fine, ripe tannins; ready now. Cork. 14° alc. **RATING** 91 **DRINK** 2008 $ 27

ŸŸŸŸ **Yarra Valley Riesling 2005** A spotlessly clean bouquet; gentle passionfruit and apple mix; trails away slightly on the finish in typical Yarra riesling fashion. Screwcap. 12° alc. **RATING** 88 **DRINK** 2009 $ 20

Kelman Vineyards ★★★★

Cnr Oakey Creek Road/Mount View Road, Pokolbin, NSW 2320 **REGION** Lower Hunter Valley
T (02) 4991 5456 **F** (02) 4991 7555 **WWW**.kelmanvineyards.com.au **OPEN** 7 days 10–4.30
WINEMAKER Stephen Hagan (Contract), David Lowe (Consultant) **EST.** 1999 **CASES** 3000
Kelman Vineyards is a California-type development on the outskirts of Cessnock. A 40-ha property has been subdivided into 80 residential development lots, but with 8 ha of vines wending between the lots, which are under common ownership. Part of the chardonnay has already been grafted across to shiraz before coming into full production, and the vineyard has the potential to produce 8000 cases a year. In the meantime, each owner will receive 12 cases a year of the wines produced by the vineyard.

ŸŸŸŸŸ **Chairman's Reserve Hunter Valley Semillon 2005** Spotlessly clean; a tight, reserved, steely wine with squeaky acidity; not a hair out of place, but needs 5+ years. Screwcap. 11.3° alc. **RATING** 92 **DRINK** 2015 $ 22

ŸŸŸŸ **Chairman's Reserve Hunter Valley Chardonnay 2005** Light straw-green; very restrained style; melon, with some mineral and spice; subtle oak. Needs time, but I'm not sure where it's headed. Cork. 13.7° alc. **RATING** 89 **DRINK** 2010 $ 41
Pond Block Hunter Valley Chardonnay 2004 Good yellow-green; attractive yellow peach fruit, balanced oak and acidity. Screwcap. 13° alc. **RATING** 88 **DRINK** 2009 $ 22
Catherine's Blush Hunter Valley Rose 2005 Bright, pale fuchsia; clearly off-dry, but has good balance and length to its array of small red fruits. Screwcap. 13.1° alc. **RATING** 87 **DRINK** Now $ 19

ŸŸŸŸ **Orchard Block Semillon 2005** **RATING** 84 **DRINK** 2009 $ 19.50

Kelso NR

Princes Highway, Narrawong, Vic 3285 **REGION** Henty
T (03) 5529 2334 **OPEN** By appt
WINEMAKER Contract **EST.** NA **CASES** NA
Howard and Glenda Simmonds have established their vineyard 11 km east of Portland, and produce Riesling and Cabernet Sauvignon.

Kelvedon ★★★☆

PO Box 126, Swansea, Tas 7190 **REGION** Southern Tasmania
T (03) 6257 8283 **F** (03) 6257 8179 **OPEN** Not
WINEMAKER Winemaking Tasmania (Julian Alcorso) **EST.** 1998 **CASES** 260
Jack and Gill Cotton began the development of Kelvedon by planting 1 ha of pinot noir in 1998. The plantings were extended in 2000/01 by an additional 5 ha, half to pinot noir and half to chardonnay; all the production from this is under contract to the Hardy Wine Company. The Pinot Noirs can be of outstanding quality.

ŸŸŸŸ **Pinot Noir 2004** Attractive plum and raspberry fruit; good length; fair balance. **RATING** 87 **DRINK** 2008 $ 25

Kenilworth Bluff Wines

NR

Lot 13 Bluff Road, Kenilworth, Qld 4574 **REGION** Queensland Coastal
T (07) 5472 3723 **F** (07) 5522 8620 **OPEN** W'ends & public hols 10–4
WINEMAKER Marburg Custom Crush **EST.** 1993 **CASES** 800
Brian and Colleen Marsh modestly describe themselves as 'little more than hobbyists', but also admit
that 'our wines show tremendous promise'. They began planting the vineyards in 1993 in a hidden
valley at the foot of Kenilworth Bluff, and now have 4 ha of shiraz, cabernet sauvignon, merlot,
semillon and chardonnay. Presently the wines are made offsite, but one day the Marshes hope it will
be feasible to establish their own winery.

Kennedys Keilor Valley

NR

Lot 3 Overnewton Road, Keilor, Vic 3036 **REGION** Sunbury
T (03) 9311 6246 **F** (03) 9331 6246 **OPEN** By appt
WINEMAKER Peter Dredge **EST.** 1994 **CASES** 300
A small Chardonnay specialist, producing its only wine from 1.8 ha of estate vineyards; half is sold as
grapes, half contract-made and sold by mailing list and word of mouth.

Kersbrook Hill

★★★★

Lot 101 Bagshaw Road, Kersbrook, SA 5231 **REGION** Adelaide Hills
T 0419 570 005 **OPEN** By appt
WINEMAKER Jeanneret Wines **EST.** 1998 **CASES** 1450
Paul Clark purchased what is now the Kersbrook Hill property, then grazing land, in 1997, planting
0.4 ha of shiraz on a reality check basis. Encouraged by the results, 2 years later the plantings were
lifted to 3 ha of shiraz and 1 ha of riesling. Mark Whisson is consultant viticulturist (Whisson has
been growing grapes in the Adelaide Hills for 20 years) and Ben Jeanneret chosen as winemaker
because of his experience with riesling.

** TTTTT** **Adelaide Hills Riesling 2005** Well-balanced lime, citrus and passionfruit; delicate
mouthfeel without sacrificing flavour. Screwcap. 12° alc. **RATING** 90 **DRINK** 2012 $ 22

TTTT **Adelaide Hills Shiraz 2004** An elegant wine; the sweet red and black fruits belie the
relatively low alcohol, perhaps with a whisper of sweetness on the finish. Minimal oak.
Screwcap. 13° alc. **RATING** 89 **DRINK** 2011 $ 25

Kevin Sobels Wines

★★★

Cnr Broke Road/Halls Road, Pokolbin, NSW 2321 **REGION** Lower Hunter Valley
T (02) 4998 7766 **F** (02) 4998 7475 **WWW**.sobelswines.com.au **OPEN** 7 days (no fixed hours)
WINEMAKER Kevin Sobels **EST.** 1992 **CASES** 9000
Veteran winemaker Kevin Sobels draws upon 8 ha of vineyards (originally planted by the Ross Jones
family) to produce wines sold almost entirely through the cellar door and by mail order. In 2005
additional grapes (sauvignon blanc) were sourced from Orange. The Sobels family has a rich
winemaking history in the Barossa and Clare Valleys dating back 150 years.

TTTT **Orange Sauvignon Blanc 2005** Well-made; clean, crisp bouquet; understated palate but
does have varietal fruit and length. Cork. 11.7° alc. **RATING** 88 **DRINK** Now $ 18
Hunter Valley Semillon 2004 Flavoursome, soft, quick-developing style; grass and
preserved lemon flavours; clean finish. Twin top. 12° alc. **RATING** 87 **DRINK** 2008 $ 16
Hunter Valley Shiraz 2003 Light- to medium-bodied; a clean, regional expression with a
mix of black and red fruits plus touches of earth and spice; not over-extracted. Cork.
13.4° alc. **RATING** 87 **DRINK** 2009 $ 22

TTTT **Hunter Valley Chardonnay 2004** **RATING** 85 **DRINK** 2008 $ 16
Hunter Valley Verdelho 2005 **RATING** 85 **DRINK** 2008 $ 18
Hunter Valley Cabernet Merlot 2003 **RATING** 85 **DRINK** 2009 $ 20
Hunter Valley White Port NV **RATING** 85 **DRINK** Now $ 25
Hunter Valley Red Port NV **RATING** 85 **DRINK** Now $ 25
Hunter Valley Merlot 2004 **RATING** 84 **DRINK** Now $ 20

TTT **Hunter Valley Gewurztraminer NV** **RATING** 83 $ 15

Kies Family Wines ★★★★

Barossa Valley Way, Lyndoch, SA 5381 **REGION** Barossa Valley
T (08) 8524 4110 **F** (08) 8524 4544 **WWW**.kieswines.com.au **OPEN** 7 days 9.30–4.30
WINEMAKER Wine Wise Consultancy **EST.** 1969 **CASES** 4000
The Kies family has been resident in the Barossa Valley since 1857, with the present generation of winemakers being the fifth, their children the sixth. Until 1969 the family sold almost all the grapes to others, but in that year they launched their own brand, Karrawirra. The co-existence of Killawarra forced a name change in 1983 to Redgum Vineyard; this business was subsequently sold. Later still, Kies Family Wines opened for business, drawing upon vineyards (up to 100 years old) which had remained in the family throughout the changes, offering a wide range of wines through the 1880 cellar door. Exports to the UK, Canada, Singapore, Hong Kong, China and Japan.

ＴＴＴＴＴ **Dedication Shiraz 2001** Good colour; very concentrated, powerful and dense wine with lots of black fruits and licorice balanced by lashings of oak; the tannins still prominent, the wine needing years yet. Cork. 14.5° alc. **RATING** 93 **DRINK** 2020 $ 39
Monkey Nut Tree Merlot 2004 Strong, clear, bright purple-red; a rich array of red and black fruits drives the wine, tannins and oak mere background presence; has good length and balance. Cork. **RATING** 93 **DRINK** 2014 $ 25

ＴＴＴＴ **White Barossa 2005** An extremely interesting and unconventional wine; lime and lemon juice fruit, with impressive tension between sweetness and acidity. Most unlikely anyone will cellar the wine, but it will repay the few who do — which is not to say don't drink it now. Screwcap. 10.5° alc. **RATING** 89 **DRINK** 2012 $ 15
Hill Block Riesling 2005 A solid, flavoursome, four-square Barossa riesling; power rather than finesse to the citrus and herb flavours. Screwcap. 12° alc. **RATING** 87 **DRINK** 2009 $ 15
Semillon Sauvignon Blanc 2005 Light straw-green; abundant life and freshness; tangy, herbaceous semillon with gooseberry/kiwifruit sauvignon blanc; bright, clean finish; major surprise. Low alcohol a huge plus. Screwcap. 11.5° alc. **RATING** 87 **DRINK** 2009 $ 15
Sparkling Heysen Gold 2005 A spumante style made from frontignac, and with very similar flavours to the still version; has resisted the temptation to sweeten it up unduly. Strange how it sells for the same price. 12° alc. **RATING** 87 **DRINK** 2008 $ 15
Heysen Gold Frontignac 2005 Delicate grapey fruit in true varietal style; not overly sweet, and has very good acidity on a long finish. Spring day stuff. Screwcap. 11.5° alc. **RATING** 87 **DRINK** 2008 $ 15

ＴＴＴＹ **Spring Cabernet 2005** Brilliant colour; a clever halfway house between rose and light dry red; sweet plum fruit with deliberate sweetness on the finish. Screwcap. 13° alc. **RATING** 86 **DRINK** Now $ 15
Deer Stalker Merlot 2005 Cunningly made with obvious, but not cloying, sweetness; the Kies say it can be chilled — good in summer. Screwcap. 14° alc. **RATING** 86 **DRINK** 2009 $ 15

Kilgour Estate ★★★

85 McAdams Lane, Bellarine, Vic 3223 **REGION** Geelong
T (03) 5251 2223 **F** (03) 5251 2223 **WWW**.kilgourestate.com.au **OPEN** Tues–Sun 10.30–6, 7 days in Jan
WINEMAKER Alister Timms **EST.** 1989 **CASES** 3500
Kilgour Estate is a family-owned venture, with just over 10 ha of vines. The beautifully situated cellar door has a restaurant and barbecue facilities.

ＴＴＴＴ **Pinot Gris Reserve 2004** Fresh and clean with hints of grass and mineral; quite crunchy acidity; seemingly lower alcohol style. Cork. 12.5° alc. **RATING** 87 **DRINK** Now $ 25

ＴＴＴＹ **Pinot Noir 2004 RATING** 86 **DRINK** 2008 $ 25
Oaked Chardonnay 2004 RATING 85 **DRINK** 2008
Shiraz 2004 RATING 85 **DRINK** 2009 $ 20

Kilikanoon ★★★★★

Penna Lane, Penwortham, SA 5453 **REGION** Clare Valley
T (08) 8843 4377 **F** (08) 8843 4246 **www**.kilikanoon.com.au **OPEN** Thurs–Sun & public hols 11–5, or by appt
WINEMAKER Kevin Mitchell **EST.** 1997 **CASES** 35 000
Kilikanoon has over 300 ha of vineyards, predominantly in the Clare Valley, but spreading to all regions around Adelaide and the Barossa Valley. It had the once-in-a-lifetime experience of winning 5 of the 6 trophies awarded at the 2002 Clare Valley Wine Show, spanning Riesling, Shiraz and Cabernet, and including Best Wine of Show. Hardly surprising, then, that production has risen sharply. Exports to the UK, the US and other major markets.

▼▼▼▼▼ **Green's Vineyard Barossa Valley Shiraz 2002** Dense colour; powerful, savoury, dense black fruits and bitter chocolate on both bouquet and palate; massively intense and long, but retains balance. Cork. 15° alc. **RATING** 96 **DRINK** 2020 $75

Mort's Block Reserve Riesling 2005 A relatively reserved bouquet; powerful, tightly focused apple and pear on entry to the mouth, lime coming through on a very long finish; excellent structure. Screwcap. 12° alc. **RATING** 95 **DRINK** 2015 $30

Reserve Barossa Valley Shiraz 2003 Dense red-purple; full-bodied, and similarly massively concentrated, but has more light and shade, not all-consuming power; still has layer-upon-layer of flavour. A tiny parcel from Green's Vineyard. Cork. 15° alc. **RATING** 95 **DRINK** 2020 $120

Mort's Block Riesling 2005 Fine, intense lime juice and green apple aromas and flavours; super-long and lingering palate. Screwcap. 12° alc. **RATING** 94 **DRINK** 2015 $22

Killerman's Run Shiraz 2004 Deep red-purple; medium- to full-bodied, a luscious, round, mouthfilling array of black fruits; controlled tannin and oak, and alcohol doesn't intrude. Fruit bomb, but a good one. Screwcap. 15° alc. **RATING** 94 **DRINK** 2019 $19

Oracle Clare Valley Shiraz 2003 Deeper colour than the Covenant; powerful, rich, concentrated blackberry, earthy fruit; impressive structure and texture, with ripe tannins and assured oak. Estate-grown. Cork. 15° alc. **RATING** 94 **DRINK** 2015 $59

Green's Vineyard Barossa Valley Shiraz 2003 Dense purple-red; full-bodied, massively concentrated, thick and almost viscous; black fruits, prunes, dark chocolate and oak; ultra-Parkeresque. Cork. 15° alc. **RATING** 94 **DRINK** 2018 $80

▼▼▼▼▽ **Parable McLaren Vale Shiraz 2004** Dense, impenetrable colour; archetypal McLaren Vale fruit profile with dark chocolate aromas and flavours leading the black fruits; full-bodied, and does carry the alcohol and oak. Cork. 15° alc. **RATING** 93 **DRINK** 2015 $44

Reserve Barossa Valley Shiraz 2002 Super-saturated, dense, saignee-style; everything magnified from colour to flavour, texture and structure; most is not necessarily best. Cork. 15° alc. **RATING** 93 **DRINK** 2020 $105

McLaren Vale Shiraz 2003 Regional chocolate screams from the rooftops investing the wine with character and personality; not overblown, and carries the alcohol. Single vineyard. Cork. **RATING** 92 **DRINK** 2013 $40

Secret Places Barossa Valley Shiraz 2003 Medium- to full-bodied; an interesting array of flavours with lots of chocolate, spice and mocha; plenty of black fruits; good outcome for the vintage. Cork. 15° alc. **RATING** 92 **DRINK** 2015 $44

Killerman's Run Shiraz 2003 Strong colour; medium- to full-bodied black chocolate, spice, dark plum and blackberry fruit; good tannin and oak support. Screwcap. **RATING** 91 **DRINK** 2009 $20

Block's Road Cabernet Sauvignon 2003 Medium- to full-bodied; substantial blackcurrant/blackberry fruit; plenty of depth and structure; good oak. Cork. 14.5° alc. **RATING** 91 **DRINK** 2015 $29

Covenant Clare Valley Shiraz 2003 Abundant spicy dark fruit flavours in a restrained, medium-bodied, framework; positive French and American oak. Cork. 15° alc. **RATING** 90 **DRINK** 2013 $40

ΨΨΨΨ **Baroota Reserve Southern Flinders Shiraz 2003** Ripe, rich, succulent, sweet black fruits, chocolate and spice; ripe tannins. Alcohol heat on the finish detracts, a pity. Procork. 15° alc. **RATING** 89 **DRINK** 2013 $ 29

Prodigal Grenache 2003 Typical perfumed, sweet fruit which seems to be yearning for a bit of gutsy shiraz to stiffen it up. Others may like the softness for what it is. Cork. 15° alc. **RATING** 89 **DRINK** 2008 $ 27

The Medley 2003 Strong colour; a soft, sweet, velvety medley of juicy black fruits, spice and gentle tannins. Grenache/Shiraz/Mourvedre. Cork. 15° alc. **RATING** 89 **DRINK** 2010 $ 25

Killerman's Run Cabernet Sauvignon 2003 A well-made, medium-bodied mix of dark chocolate, ripe blackcurrant and mulberry fruit; ripe tannins, soft oak. Screwcap. **RATING** 89 **DRINK** 2008 $ 18

Second Fiddle Clare Valley Grenache Rose 2005 Vivid fuchsia-purple; good balance, the focus on strawberry/cherry fruit; has length without sweetness. Screwcap. 13.5° alc. **RATING** 88 **DRINK** Now $ 20

Killara Park Estate

Kylie Lane, Seville East, Vic 3139 **REGION** Yarra Valley
T (03) 9790 1255 **F** (03) 9790 1633 **WWW**.killarapark.com.au **OPEN** W'ends & public hols 11–5
WINEMAKER Michael Kyberd **EST.** 1997 **CASES** 5500
The striking label design hints at the involvement of the Palazzo family (the owners) in winemaking in Lombardia (Italy) since the 16th century. It also tells you that this is a highly-focused, modern, wine-producing company. With just over 60 ha of vineyards established since 1997, Killara Park is one of the larger grape suppliers in the Yarra Valley, capable of producing fruit of high quality from its steeply sloping vineyards. Around 90% of the grapes are sold to companies such as Coldstream Hills and McWilliam's, but 10% is now being vinified for the label. Exports to the UK.

ΨΨΨΨ **Yarra Valley Sauvignon Blanc 2005** A clean but relatively closed bouquet; powers up on the palate with a ripe tropical and gooseberry mix. Screwcap. 13.5° alc. **RATING** 89 **DRINK** Now $ 22

Killerby

Caves Road, Wilyabrup, WA 6280 **REGION** Margaret River
T 1800 655 722 **F** 1800 679 578 **WWW**.killerby.com.au **OPEN** Not
WINEMAKER Simon Keall **EST.** 1973 **CASES** 15 000
Has moved from Geographe to Margaret River following the acquisition of a vineyard with 25-year-old chardonnay vines on Caves Road. It has kept its substantial mature vineyards in Geographe, where the wines are still made. Exports to the US and Denmark.

ΨΨΨΨ **Sauvignon Blanc 2005** Spotlessly clean; fresh, crisp mineral characters set against a more textured barrel ferment component; works very well here, with good mouthfeel and length. Screwcap. 13° alc. **RATING** 93 **DRINK** 2008 $ 19

Cabernet Sauvignon 2003 Leafy, scented, briar and cigar box aromas; light- to medium-bodied, with well-defined blackcurrant/cassis flavours; good length. Screwcap. 13.9° alc. **RATING** 90 **DRINK** 2013 $ 24

ΨΨΨΨ **Semillon 2004** A complex wine, the textural gain on the roundabouts, diminished varietal character on the swings. Partially French oak barrel-fermented and aged for 6 months, part stainless steel; every possibility it will cellar well. Screwcap. 12.8° alc. **RATING** 89 **DRINK** 2010 $ 19

Shiraz 2002 Medium-bodied; savoury, slightly leafy/spicy notes around a core of balanced plum and cherry fruit core; fine tannins. Screwcap. **RATING** 89 **DRINK** 2010 $ 24

🍷 Killibinbin Wines ★★★★

PO Box 108, Crafers, SA 5152 **REGION** McLaren Vale
T (08) 8339 8664 **F** (08) 8339 8664 **WWW**.killibinbin.com.au **OPEN** Not
WINEMAKER Rolf Binder, Kym Teusner, Phil Christiansen, Justin Lane **EST.** 1998 **CASES** 4000
Business partners Liz Blanks and Wayne Anderson embarked on their virtual winery (with, they say, 'no money, no winemaker, no vineyard and no winery') with the inaugural 1997 Langhorne Creek Shiraz. Robert Parker promptly gave it 92 points, which meant that all of the production, and all of the subsequent growth, went to the US.

TTTTT **Langhorne Creek Shiraz 2003** A fragrant mix of black fruits, spice, earth and chocolate; the medium-bodied palate is elegant, with good balance and length; fine tannins; high-quality cork. **RATING** 90 **DRINK** 2010 **$** 25
Langhorne Creek Blend 2003 A similar light- to medium-bodied, elegant, fruit-driven style to the shiraz; lots of regional bitter dark chocolate, plus fine tannins and good length; 60% Shiraz/40% Cabernet Sauvignon. Screwcap. **RATING** 90 **DRINK** 2011 **$** 20

TTTT **Langhorne Creek Cabernet Sauvignon 2003** Blackcurrant, earth and bitter chocolate aromas; a potent, powerful wine, still edgy and slightly raw; needs time. Cork. **RATING** 87 **DRINK** 2009 **$** 21

Kiltynane Estate ★★★☆

Cnr School Lane/Yarra Glen-Healesville Road, Tarrawarra, Vic 3775 **REGION** Yarra Valley
T 0418 339 555 **F** (03) 5962 1897 **WWW**.kiltynane.com.au **OPEN** By appt
WINEMAKER Kate Kirkhope **EST.** 2000 **CASES** 300
Kate Kirkhope has owned and run Kiltynane Estate since 1994. Having completed a local viticulture course in 1997, she began the development of the 3.8-ha vineyard, planted to seven clones of pinot noir, in 2000. Her son's education at a Rudolf Steiner School had given her an interest in biodynamics, and biodynamic practices are followed wherever possible. The vines are not irrigated, and no pesticides are used. The winemaking has been carried out with help from Frederic Blanck, of the highly regarded Alsace winery Paul Blanck et Fils, who has been a regular visitor to Australia and the Yarra Valley over the years.

TTTT **Preliminaire Blanc de Noir 2005** Palest blush; delicate strawberry, spice and mineral mix; dry finish; for the adventurous. Free-run pinot noir barrel-fermented with wild yeast. 13.5° alc. **RATING** 87 **DRINK** 2009 **$** 40

Kimbarra Wines ★★★★☆

422 Barkly Street, Ararat, Vic 3377 **REGION** Grampians
T (03) 5352 2238 **F** (03) 5342 1950 **WWW**.kimbarrawines.com.au **OPEN** Mon–Fri 9–4.30
WINEMAKER Peter Leeke, Ian MacKenzie **EST.** 1990 **CASES** 800
Peter and David Leeke have established 21 ha of riesling, shiraz and cabernet sauvignon, varieties which have proved best suited to the Grampians region. The particularly well-made wines deserve a wider audience.

TTTTT **Great Western Riesling 2005** Fine, delicate but intense citrus, passionfruit and apple; good length, high quality. Great value. Screwcap. 13.3° alc. **RATING** 93 **DRINK** 2015 **$** 14
Great Western Shiraz 2003 Medium- to full-bodied; intense blackberry fruit, with some spicy/savoury elements; fine, ripe tannins; outstanding for the drought vintage. Cork. 13.6° alc. **RATING** 93 **DRINK** 2015 **$** 22

TTTT **Great Western Cabernet Sauvignon 2003** Bright, not especially deep, colour; light- to medium-bodied, with attractive cassis and red berry fruit. Out of the clouds, as it were. Golds at regional wine shows. Cork. 12.3° alc. **RATING** 89 **DRINK** 2010 **$** 22
Great Western Late Picked Riesling 2004 Sweet juicy lemon and lime fruit; crisp acidity; halfway house style, patience will unquestionably be rewarded. Screwcap. 12.4° alc. **RATING** 88 **DRINK** 2014 **$** 12

Kimber Wines ★★★

Chalk Hill Road, McLaren Vale, SA 5171 **REGION** McLaren Vale
T (08) 8323 9773 **F** (08) 8323 9773 **WWW**.kimberwines.com **OPEN** 7 days Dec–Apr 9–6, or by appt
WINEMAKER Reg Wilkinson **EST.** 1996 **CASES** 350
Kimber Wines is primarily a grapegrower, selling its production from 2.5 ha each of chardonnay and cabernet sauvignon, and 1.2 ha of petit verdot to larger producers. A very small amount of its grapes are vinified under the Kimber Wines label; they tend to sell out within a few months of release through the cellar door (hence the restricted opening hours). An added attraction is pick-your-own fruit (peaches, apricots and plums) during the summer months.

ᵀᵀᵀᵞ **McLaren Vale Unwooded Chardonnay 2005** Plenty of ripe melon and ripe peach fruit on both bouquet and palate; honest wine. Screwcap. 14° alc. **RATING** 86 **DRINK** Now $ 14

King River Estate NR

3556 Wangaratta–Whitfield Road, Wangaratta, Vic 3678 **REGION** King Valley
T (03) 5729 3689 **F** (03) 5729 3688 **WWW**.kingriverestate.com.au **OPEN** W'ends, or by appt
WINEMAKER Trevor Knaggs **EST.** 1996 **CASES** 6000
Trevor Knaggs, with the assistance of his father Collin (sic), began the establishment of King River Estate in 1990, making the first wines in 1996. The initial plantings were of 3.3 ha each of chardonnay and cabernet sauvignon, followed by 8 ha of merlot and 3 ha of shiraz. More recent plantings have extended the varietal range with verdelho, viognier, barbera and sangiovese, lifting the total plantings to a substantial 24 ha.

Kings Creek Winery ★★★★☆

237 Myers Road, Bittern, Vic 3918 **REGION** Mornington Peninsula
T (03) 5983 1802 **F** (03) 5983 1807 **OPEN** W'ends 11–5
WINEMAKER Sandro Mosele (Contract) **EST.** 1980 **CASES** 750
In the wake of the implosion of the original Kings Creek winery, Graham and Dorothy Turner purchased the name Kings Creek, and acquired the original home vineyard block, taking the decision to radically change the trellis system from lyre to vertical spur. The vines have taken time to recover (as is normal in such circumstances), and winemaker Sandro Mosele forecast at the time that it would take until 2006 for the vines to regain balance and produce their best fruit.

ᵀᵀᵀᵀᵞ **Mornington Peninsula Chardonnay 2004** Complex creamy/nutty malolactic/barrel ferment inputs to stone fruit and melon; good balance and length. Diam. 14° alc.
RATING 93 **DRINK** 2012 $ 25
Mornington Peninsula Pinot Noir 2004 Very good colour; medium-bodied, with excellent texture and structure to the soft, spicy plum and cherry fruit; good finish. Cork. 13.5° alc. **RATING** 93 **DRINK** 2011 $ 20

ᵀᵀᵀᵀ **Mornington Peninsula Rose 2004** A fresh mix of mineral and strawberry; good length and nice, dry finish. Great value. Diam. 14° alc. **RATING** 87 **DRINK** Now $ 12

Kings of Kangaroo Ground NR

15 Graham Road, Kangaroo Ground, Vic 3097 **REGION** Yarra Valley
T (03) 9712 0666 **F** (03) 9712 0566 **WWW**.kkg.com.au **OPEN** Mon–Sat 10–6, Sun 12–6
WINEMAKER Ken King, Geoff Anson, Neil Johannesen **EST.** 1990 **CASES** 600
Ken King's involvement in wine began back in 1984 as an amateur member of the Eltham and District Winemakers Guild. Around that time, the Guild was asked to manage a tiny (0.13 ha) experimental vineyard planted on the rich volcanic soil of Kangaroo Ground. In 1988 Ken King purchased a little under 3 ha of similar land, which he describes as 'chocolate cake', and established 1 ha of chardonnay and 0.6 ha of pinot noir in 1990. Until 2000, the grapes were sold to Diamond Valley, but each year King retained sufficient grapes to produce a barrel or two of Pinot Noir, and began experimenting with multi-vintage blends of pinot with up to 5 years of continuous ageing in French barriques.

Kingsley Grove

49 Stuart Valley Drive, Kingaroy, Qld 4610 (postal) **REGION** South Burnett
T (07) 4162 2229 **F** (07) 4162 2201 **www**.kingsleygrove.com **OPEN** 7 days 10–5
WINEMAKER Michael Berry, Patricia Berry, Simon Berry **EST.** 1998 **CASES** 4000
Michael and Patricia Berry have established a substantial vineyard of 8.8 ha near Kingaroy. It is
planted to verdelho, chardonnay, semillon, shiraz, merlot, sangiovese, chambourcin and cabernet
sauvignon, and the wines are made in a winery built in 2001 and extended in 2003, Michael Berry
having undertaken viticulture studies at Melbourne University.

TTTT **Jimmy's Block Chardonnay 2005** Clean stone fruit and peach aromas; the palate doesn't
deliver the promise of the bouquet, clean, but lacking intensity. Nonetheless, well-made.
Cork. 12.4° alc. **RATING** 86 **DRINK** Now $16
Sweet Berry Red 2005 Very sweet cellar door special, well-named; serve on the rocks.
Cork. 11.5° alc. **RATING** 86 **DRINK** Now $15
Zipp Methode Champenoise NV **RATING** 85 **DRINK** Now $17

TTT **Verde 2005** **RATING** 83 $18
Brian's Bin Sangiovese 2004 **RATING** 83 $15

Kingston Estate

Sturt Highway, Kingston-on-Murray, SA 5331 **REGION** Southeast Australia
T (08) 8130 4500 **F** (08) 8130 4511 **www**.kingstonestatewines.com **OPEN** By appt
WINEMAKER Bill Moularadellis **EST.** 1979 **CASES** 2.5 million
Kingston Estate, under the direction of Bill Moularadellis, has its production roots in the Riverland
region, but it has also set up long-term purchase contracts with growers in the Clare Valley, the
Adelaide Hills, Coonawarra, Langhorne Creek and Mount Benson. It has also spread its net to take in
a wide range of varietals, mainstream and exotic, under a number of different brands at various price
points. Exports to Europe.

TTTTT **Echelon Shiraz 2002** Smooth, supple and intense; an elegant ripple of black fruits and
fine tannins washes across the palate. **RATING** 94 **DRINK** 2015 $22

TTTT **Echelon Cabernet Sauvignon 2002** Firm, medium-bodied, blackberry, earth and bitter
chocolate; fine, lingering tannins. Cork. 15.5° alc. **RATING** 90 **DRINK** 2012 $24

TTTT **Empiric Selection Viognier 2004** Moderately complex; spicy barrel ferment oak inputs
controlled; varietal apricot and dried fruit flavours carry the alcohol of 14.8° well. Cork.
14.8° alc. **RATING** 89 **DRINK** Now $18.99
Empiric Selection Viognier 2004 Bright green-yellow; fresh, floral aromas and flavours
of citrus and apricot; lively acidity balances the alcohol. Screwcap. **RATING** 89 **DRINK** Now
$18.99
Echelon Petit Verdot 2002 Holding hue well; savoury/sombre/earthy black fruits, the
tannins slowly loosening their grip. Cork. 14.5° alc. **RATING** 89 **DRINK** 2010 $21
Empiric Selection Arneis 2004 Very distinct almond aromas; a delicate, crisp palate with
hints of almond and pear. Interesting wine. Screwcap. **RATING** 88 **DRINK** Now $18.99
Merlot 2003 Light- to medium-bodied; blackcurrant and a touch of black olive; good
oak/tannins. Value. Cork. 14° alc. **RATING** 88 **DRINK** 2009 $12
Petit Verdot 2004 The usual good colour, but unusual fruit sweetness; medium-bodied
black plum, blueberry and blackberry; soft tannins. Cork. 14.5° alc. **RATING** 88 **DRINK** 2009
$12
Ambleside Adelaide Hills Shiraz Viognier 2004 Bright red-purple; light- to medium-
bodied and highly aromatic; the viognier is too overt, or the shiraz too light. Screwcap.
RATING 87 **DRINK** 2008 $22
Empiric Selection Petit Verdot 2003 Fragrant, high-toned fruit aromas; flavoursome, but
with slightly sharp edges still needing to soften. Screwcap. **RATING** 87 **DRINK** 2008 $18.99
Empiric Selection Durif 2003 Massively rich dark fruits; tannins still threaten the
balance; barbecue special. Cork. **RATING** 87 **DRINK** 2009 $18.99

♟♟♟♟ **Sarantos Soft Press Merlot 2003** RATING 86 DRINK 2008 $ 14
Outback Chase Merlot 2003 Pleasant, nicely weighted wine, with soft, savoury tannins. Convincing value. Screwcap. 13.5° alc. RATING 86 DRINK Now $ 9
Empiric Selection Barbera 2004 RATING 86 DRINK Now $ 18.99
Empiric Tempranillo 2004 RATING 84 DRINK Now $ 18.99

Kingtree Wines   NR

Kingtree Road, Wellington Mills via Dardanup, WA 6326 REGION Geographe
T (08) 9728 3050 F (08) 9728 3113 OPEN 7 days 12–5.30
WINEMAKER Contract EST. 1991 CASES 1000
Kingtree Wines, with 2.5 ha of estate plantings, is part of the Kingtree Lodge development, a four and a half-star luxury retreat in dense Jarrah forest.

Kinloch Wines

Kainui, Wairere Road, Booroolite, Vic 3723 REGION Upper Goulburn
T (03) 5777 3447 F (03) 5777 3449 WWW.kinlochwines.com.au OPEN W'ends & public hols 10–5 or by appt
WINEMAKER Al Fencaros (Contract) EST. 1996 CASES 2500
In 1996 Susan and Malcolm Kinloch began the development of their vineyard, at an altitude of 400m on the northern slopes of the Great Dividing Range, 15 mins from Mansfield. One of the unusual varieties in the portfolio is Pinot Meunier. The grapes are hand-picked and taken to the Yarra Valley for contract making.

♟♟♟♟ **Mansfield Pinot Noir 2004** Strawberry, spice and a hint of menthol; well-made, the oak largely irrelevant. Cork. 12.8° alc. RATING 89 DRINK 2008 $ 21
Mansfield Unwooded Chardonnay 2005 Interesting cool-grown citrussy overtones reminiscent more of sauvignon blanc than chardonnay; long, tangy finish, and good acidity. Suits the style well. Screwcap. 13.5° alc. RATING 88 DRINK Now $ 17

♟♟♟♟ **Mansfield Pinot Meunier 2004** RATING 84 DRINK Now $ 20

♟♟♟ **Mansfield Merlot 2004** RATING 83 $ 24

Kinvarra Estate   NR

RMB 5141, New Norfolk, Tas 7140 REGION Southern Tasmania
T (03) 6286 1333 F (03) 6286 2026 OPEN Not
WINEMAKER Andrew Hood EST. 1990 CASES 90
Kinvarra is the part-time occupation of David and Sue Bevan, with their wonderful 1827 homestead depicted on the label. There is only 1 ha of vines, half riesling and half pinot noir, and most of the crop is sold to Hood Wines/Wellington.

Kirkham Estate   NR

3 Argyle Street, Camden, NSW 2570 REGION Sydney Basin
T (02) 4655 7722 F (02) 4655 7722 OPEN 7 days 11–5
WINEMAKER Stan Aliprandi EST. 1993 CASES 3000
Kirkham Estate is one of a handful of wine producers near Camden, a far cry from the 18 producers of the mid-19th century, but still indicative of the growth of vineyards and winemakers everywhere. It is the venture of Leif Karlsson and Stan Aliprandi, the latter a former Riverina winemaker. It draws upon 9 ha of vineyards, planted to chardonnay, semillon, verdelho, petit verdot, shiraz, merlot, pinot noir and cabernet sauvignon, supplemented, it would seem, by grapes (and wines) purchased elsewhere.

Kirrihill Wines

Wendouree Road, Clare, SA 5453 **REGION** Clare Valley
T (08) 8842 4087 **F** (08) 8842 4089 **WWW**.kirrihillwines.com.au **OPEN** 7 days 10–4
WINEMAKER David Mavor **EST.** 1998 **CASES** 10 000
A large development, with a 7000-tonne, $10 million, winery designed for modular expansion to 20 000 tonnes, and currently storing 3 million litres of wine. It is associated with the Kirribilly Wine Group, which has developed and now manages 1300 ha of vineyards in the Clare Valley, the Adelaide Hills and Langhorne Creek. Small parcels of its managed vineyards' grapes are taken for the Kirrihill Estates wine range, with a Cabernet Sauvignon from Clare and Langhorne Creek, plus a Sauvignon Blanc from the Adelaide Hills completing the range. The quality of the wines is thus no surprise. Exports to the UK, the US and other major markets.

ＹＹＹＹＹ **Adelaide Hills Sauvignon Blanc 2005** Pure and perfect in every way; tropical/passionfruit/gooseberry flavours, with beautiful line and length; the ultimate Sauvignon Blanc. Top gold medal Sydney Wine Show '06. **RATING** 95 **DRINK** Now $16
Reserve Clare Valley Shiraz 2002 Medium- to full-bodied; powerful, blackberry, bitter chocolate and licorice; a long, intense palate and ripe tannins. Cork. 15.5° alc. **RATING** 94 **DRINK** 2015
Clare Valley Shiraz Mourvedre Grenache 2004 Delicious wine, the components perfectly balanced and integrated on a flowing, medium-bodied palate, finishing with the finest imaginable tannins. Standout example. Screwcap. 14° alc. **RATING** 94 **DRINK** 2014

ＹＹＹＹＹ **Clare Valley Riesling 2005** A clean but muted bouquet; a long, precise palate, with citrus, green apple and acidity interwoven; a slatey, dry finish. Screwcap. 12° alc. **RATING** 92 **DRINK** 2015 $17
Clare Valley Cabernet Sauvignon 2002 Cedary/leafy/spicy/tangy edges to blackcurrant and blackberry fruit; lively mouthfeel. Screwcap. 14.3° alc. **RATING** 91 **DRINK** 2012 $21.95
Adelaide Hills Chardonnay 2004 Developed straw-green; surprisingly ripe fruit flavours have largely absorbed the barrel ferment French oak; total malolactic gives textural richness, but does shorten the finish slightly. Screwcap. 12.5° alc. **RATING** 90 **DRINK** 2009 $17
Clare Valley Shiraz 2003 Attractive mid-weight wine; blackberry and plum, smooth tannins and integrated oak. Screwcap. 14° alc. **RATING** 90 **DRINK** 2013 $23.95
Companions Cabernet Merlot 2004 Good colour; solid blackcurrant fruit with notes of chocolate, and good tannin support; a complex blend which includes malbec. Clare Valley/Langhorne Creek. Screwcap. 14.5° alc. **RATING** 90 **DRINK** 2014
Companions Cabernet Merlot 2002 Excellent wine at the price; complex structure; blackcurrant/blackberry/cassis mix; good tannins and length. Clare Valley/Padthaway/Adelaide Hills. Screwcap. **RATING** 90 **DRINK** 2012 $12.99

ＹＹＹＹ **Companions Semillon Sauvignon Blanc 2005** Bright green-yellow; abundant flavour, texture and depth; ripe, but not overripe, fruit flavours, lightened by good acidity. Clare Semillon/Adelaide Hills Sauvignon Blanc. Screwcap. 13° alc. **RATING** 89 **DRINK** 2008 $13
Companions Semillon Sauvignon Blanc 2004 Bright green-yellow; an abundant mix of juicy, lemony, gooseberry, tropical flavours; rich, sweet and soft; ready to roll; great value. Clare Valley Semillon/Adelaide Hills Sauvignon Blanc. Screwcap. **RATING** 89 **DRINK** Now $12.99
Langhorne Creek Shiraz 2002 Light- to medium-bodied; clean red fruit; understated style, but has length. Screwcap. **RATING** 88 **DRINK** 2011 $21.99
Companions Shiraz 2004 Light- to medium-bodied; a pleasant array of predominantly sweet red and black fruits; fine tannins. Langhorne Creek/Clare Valley. Screwcap. 14.5° alc. **RATING** 88 **DRINK** 2011 $13
Companions Chardonnay 2003 Gently sweet and ripe peachy fruit; a touch of toasty oak; plenty of all up flavour. Screwcap. **RATING** 87 **DRINK** Now $12.99

ＹＹＹＹ **Companions Chardonnay 2004** **RATING** 85 **DRINK** Now $13
Companions Shiraz 2002 **RATING** 85 **DRINK** 2008 $12.99

Kirwan's Bridge Wines   NR

Lobb's Lane/Kirwan's Bridge Road, Nagambie, Vic 3608 **REGION** Nagambie Lakes
T (03) 5794 1777 **F** (03) 5794 1993 **OPEN** 7 days 10–5
WINEMAKER Anna Hubbard **EST.** 1997 **CASES** 1500
A major development, with over 35 ha planted: a major emphasis on the Rhône varietals (7.9 ha marsanne, 2.7 ha viognier, 1.3 ha of roussanne; and 11.2 ha shiraz, 2.7 ha mourvedre and 2.5 ha grenache). A side bet on 4.8 ha cabernet sauvignon, 2.4 ha merlot and 1.3 ha riesling rounds off the planting. The cellar door complex includes a restaurant (open for lunch and dinner Thurs–Sun), conference facility and art gallery.

Kithbrook Estate

RMB 4480, Strathbogie, Vic 3666 (postal) **REGION** Strathbogie Ranges
T (03) 5790 8627 **F** (03) 5790 8630 **OPEN** Not
WINEMAKER Contract **EST.** 1994 **CASES** NA
Kithbrook Estate (formerly Gemleigh Meadows) has 2 vineyards on Broughtons Road, Strathbogie: the first and larger is at an altitude of 480–500m, the second is higher up the hillside at the 560–580m contour lines. By far the most important part of the business is grapegrowing for others, coming from 30 ha of sauvignon blanc, 27 ha of merlot, 15 ha of pinot noir and 14 ha of chardonnay, plus a dash of shiraz. Some of the wines have scored well at the Strathbogie Ranges Wine Show.

ᵀᵀᵀᵀᵀ **Shiraz 2003** Dense, full-bodied, ripe blackberry fruit; ripe tannins. Despite all this, has excellent balance. Trophy 2005 Strathbogie Wine Show. **RATING** 94 **DRINK** 2013 $ 11

ᵀᵀᵀᵀ **Chardonnay 2004 RATING** 84 **DRINK** Now $ 11

Kladis Estate   NR

Princes Highway, Wandanian, NSW 2540 **REGION** Shoalhaven Coast
T (02) 4443 5606 **F** (02) 4443 6485 **WWW.**kladisestatewines.com.au **OPEN** W'ends & public hols 10–5
WINEMAKER Briar Ridge (Steve Dodd) **EST.** 1996 **CASES** 10 000
Jim and Nikki Kladis have developed 11 ha of shiraz, cabernet sauvignon, grenache, verdelho, merlot and muscadelle at their Shoalhaven property, and 4 ha of gewurztraminer and cabernet sauvignon in the Hunter Valley. Additional grapes are also sourced from the Adelaide Hills. The inspiration has been the medium-bodied red wines Jim Kladis grew up with on the Greek island of Zante. The winery has recently had a $1.5 million upgrade to include a conference centre, restaurant and cellar door. Exports to China and Hong Kong.

Knappstein Wines

2 Pioneer Avenue, Clare, SA 5453 **REGION** Clare Valley
T (08) 8842 2600 **F** (08) 8842 3831 **WWW.**knappsteinwines.com.au **OPEN** Mon–Fri 9–5, Sat 11–5, Sun & public hols 11–4
WINEMAKER Paul Smith **EST.** 1976 **CASES** 30 000
Very much part of Lion Nathan's stable, with Paul Smith having taken over from Andrew Hardy, who has returned to Petaluma headquarters. The 115 ha of mature estate vineyards in prime locations supply grapes both for the Knappstein brand and for wider Petaluma use. Exports to the UK, Canada, Japan and NZ.

ᵀᵀᵀᵀᵀ **Single Vineyard Clare Valley Fortified Shiraz 2001** Powerful and concentrated; has classic dry, spicy, savoury mouthfeel in true Vintage Port style. Ironic, given the de facto ban on the use of that term on the label. Cork. 18.5° alc. **RATING** 94 **DRINK** 2015 $ 22

ᵀᵀᵀᵀ **Hand Picked Riesling 2005** Ripe, complex and mouthfilling; ripe apple through to tropical fruit, with balancing acidity. Screwcap. **RATING** 93 **DRINK** 2010 $ 19.99
Clare Valley Semillon Sauvignon Blanc 2005 Bright, lively tangy/lemony aromas and flavours, with touches of apple and stone fruit; particularly good finish; outstanding for the region. Screwcap. 13° alc. **RATING** 93 **DRINK** 2008 $ 18
Ackland Vineyard Watervale Riesling 2005 A clean but reserved bouquet; lime, lemon and ripe apple flavours with a streak of minerality adding length. Screwcap. 13.5° alc. **RATING** 91 **DRINK** 2013 $ 26

ΥΥΥΥ **Enterprise Cabernet Sauvignon 2003** Savoury, leafy, earthy with a touch of barnyard; slightly dry tannins. Screwcap. 14.5° alc. **RATING** 88 **DRINK** 2009 $ 35

ΥΥΥΥ **Clare Valley Shiraz 2003** **RATING** 86 **DRINK** Now $ 19.99
Clare Valley Cabernet Merlot 2003 **RATING** 86 **DRINK** 2009 $ 22
Clare Valley Chardonnay 2005 **RATING** 85 **DRINK** Now $ 18

Knights Vines
NR

655 Henry Lawson Drive, Mudgee, NSW 2850 **REGION** Mudgee
T (02) 6373 3954 **F** (02) 6373 3750 **WWW**.eurundereewines.com.au **OPEN** Wed–Fri & Sun 10–4, Sat 10–5
WINEMAKER Peter Knights **EST.** 1985 **CASES** 1500
Sometimes called Knights Vines, although the wines are marketed under the Eurunderee Flats label. There are 5 ha of vineyards producing white wines of variable quality, and rather better dry red table wines. Exports to Hong Kong.

Knots Wines

A8 Shurans Lane, Heathcote, Vic 3552 **REGION** Heathcote
T (03) 5441 5429 **F** (03) 5441 5429 **WWW**.bendigowine.org.au/knots **OPEN** Select w'ends, or by appt
WINEMAKER Lindsay Ross **EST.** 1997 **CASES** 1000
This is the venture of former Balgownie winemaker Lindsay Ross and wife Noeline, and is part of a broader business known as Winedrops, which acts as a wine production and distribution network for the Bendigo wine industry. The Knots wines are sourced from long-established Heathcote and Bendigo vineyards, providing 0.5 ha each of semillon and chardonnay, and 4 ha each of shiraz and cabernets. The viticultural accent is on low-cropping vineyards with concentrated flavours, the winemaking emphasis on flavour, finesse and varietal expression.

ΥΥΥΥΥ **The Bridge Shurans Lane Shiraz 2003** Full-bodied and strongly structured; opulent black fruits on the bouquet and on entry to the palate, then persistent, fine, ripe tannins run through from the mid-palate to the finish. Outstanding for the vintage. Cork. 14.5° alc. **RATING** 95 **DRINK** 2018 $ 45

ΥΥΥΥ **Sheepshank Shiraz 2003** Good colour; medium-bodied; in every way a lighter version of The Bridge, but with similar dynamics other than a fractionally dry finish. Cork. 14.5° alc. **RATING** 90 **DRINK** 2012 $ 25

ΥΥΥΥ **Lashing Rose 2005** **RATING** 86 **DRINK** Now $ 20

Knowland Estate
NR

Mount Vincent Road, Running Stream, NSW 2850 **REGION** Mudgee
T (02) 6358 8420 **F** (02) 6358 8423 **OPEN** By appt
WINEMAKER Peter Knowland **EST.** 1990 **CASES** 250
The former Mount Vincent Winery, at an altitude of 1080m, which sells much of its grape production from the 4 ha of vineyards to other makers.

Koltz

5 Adams Road, Blewitt Springs, SA 5171 (postal) **REGION** McLaren Vale
T (08) 8383 0023 **F** (08) 8383 0023 **OPEN** Not
WINEMAKER Mark Day **EST.** 1994 **CASES** 2000
Mark Day and Anna Koltunow released their first wine in 1995, using grapes from the Bottin Vineyard in McLaren Vale. Mark Day had worked as winemaker at Maxwell Wines and Wirra Wirra in McLaren Vale, and has been a Flying Winemaker for six consecutive vintages in Europe. Day and Koltunow decided to specialise in Shiraz and Shiraz blends from the McLaren Vale region, but added Sangiovese and Mourvedre to the mix in 2002. The wines are exported to England and the US and can be ordered by mail.

ΥΥΥΥ **McLaren Vale Mourvedre Shiraz Grenache 2003** A rich mix of dark chocolate, plum and prune; mouthfilling, round and plush; fruit-driven. Cork. **RATING** 90 **DRINK** 2013 $ 27

𝕐𝕐𝕐𝕐 **DogDay McLaren Vale Shiraz Viognier 2003** Typical high-toned style driven by the Viognier influence; juicy red berry fruit and lively mouthfeel. Screwcap. **RATING** 88 **DRINK** 2009 $24

𝕐𝕐𝕐𝕐 **McLaren Vale Shiraz 2003** **RATING** 85 **DRINK** Now $27

Kominos Wines ★★★★

27145 New England Highway, Severnlea, Qld 4352 **REGION** Granite Belt
T (07) 4683 4311 **F** (07) 4683 4291 **WWW**.kominoswines.com **OPEN** 7 days 9–5
WINEMAKER Tony Comino **EST.** 1976 **CASES** 4000
Tony Comino is a dedicated viticulturist and winemaker and, with wife Mary, has taken over ownership of the winery from his parents on its 21st vintage. Comino is proud of the estate-grown, made and bottled heritage of the winery and is content to keep a relatively low profile in Australia. Exports to the US and Taiwan and elsewhere in Asia.

𝕐𝕐𝕐𝕐𝕐 **Reserve Granite Belt Merlot 2005** Youthful purple colour of very good depth; a vibrant young wine; good balance, depth and structure, finishing with appropriately fine savoury tannins. Diam. 13.5° alc. **RATING** 90 **DRINK** 2012 $25
Reserve Granite Belt Cabernet Sauvignon 2005 Very powerful and youthful to the point of rebellious; plush blackcurrant fruit then firm, earthy, slightly stringent tannins. All it needs is time for these components to come together. Cork. 13.5° alc. **RATING** 90 **DRINK** 2015 $25

𝕐𝕐𝕐𝕐 **Granite Belt Sauvignon Blanc 2004** Solid wine, now in a lock-down phase on the bouquet and palate, with gooseberry/herb/tropical nuances fighting for their liberty. Diam. 12.5° alc. **RATING** 88 **DRINK** Now $15
Granite Belt Semillon Sauvignon Blanc 2004 Zesty, tangy citrus and mineral characters throughout; long, bone-dry finish. Twin top. 12.3° alc. **RATING** 88 **DRINK** 2008 $15

Kongwak Hills Winery ★★★

1030 Korumburra–Wonthaggi Road, Kongwak, Vic 3951 **REGION** Gippsland
T (03) 5657 3267 **F** (03) 5657 3267 **OPEN** W'ends & public hols 10–5
WINEMAKER Peter Kimmer **EST.** 1989 **CASES** 500
Peter and Jenny Kimmer started the development of their vineyard in 1989 and now have 0.5 ha each of cabernet sauvignon, shiraz and pinot noir, together with lesser quantities of malbec, merlot and riesling. Most of the wines are sold at the cellar door.

𝕐𝕐𝕐𝕐 **Kimmer Cabernet Malbec 2004** **RATING** 85 **DRINK** Now $18
Kimmer Pinot Noir 2004 **RATING** 84 **DRINK** Now $18
Kimmer Shiraz 2004 **RATING** 84 **DRINK** Now $18

Koonara ★★★

Skinner Road, Coonawarra, SA 5263 **REGION** Coonawarra
T (08) 8736 3267 **F** (08) 8736 3020 **WWW**.koonara.com **OPEN** By appt
WINEMAKER Dru Reschke, Peter Douglas (Consultant) **EST.** 1988 **CASES** NA
Koonara is a sister, or, more appropriately, brother company to Reschke Wines. The latter is run by Burke Reschke, Koonara by his brother Dru. Both are sons of Trevor Reschke, who planted the first vines on the Koonara property in 1988. The initial planting was of cabernet sauvignon, followed by shiraz in 1993 and additional cabernet sauvignon in 1998. Peter Douglas, formerly Wynn's chief winemaker before moving overseas for some years, has returned to the district and is consultant winemaker.

𝕐𝕐𝕐𝕐 **Sofiel's Gift 2005** **RATING** 86 **DRINK** 2009 $17
Ezra's Gift Shiraz 2003 **RATING** 86 **DRINK** 2008 $24
Cupra's Gift Cabernet Sauvignon 2003 **RATING** 86 **DRINK** 2008 $19.95

Kooroomba Vineyards

NR

168 FM Bells Road, Mount Alford via Boonah, Qld 4310 **REGION** Queensland Zone
T (07) 5463 0022 **F** (07) 5463 0441 **OPEN** Wed–Sun & public hols 10–5
WINEMAKER Ballandean Estate **EST.** 1998 **CASES** 3000
Kooroomba Vineyards is little more than 1 hour's drive from the Brisbane CBD, and offers cellar door wine tasting and sales, a vineyard restaurant and a lavender farm. The 7.5-ha vineyard is planted to verdelho, marsanne, merlot, shiraz and cabernet sauvignon and chardonnay.

Kooyong

★★★★★

PO Box 153, Red Hill South, Vic 3937 **REGION** Mornington Peninsula
T (03) 5989 7355 **F** (03) 5989 7677 **WWW**.kooyong.com **OPEN** At Port Phillip Estate
WINEMAKER Sandro Mosele **EST.** 1996 **CASES** 5000
Kooyong, owned by Giorgio and Dianne Gjergja, released its first wines in 2001. The 34-ha vineyard is planted to pinot noir and chardonnay. Winemaker Sandro Mosele is a graduate of Charles Sturt University, having previously gained a science degree, and has a deservedly high reputation. He also provides contract winemaking services for others. Exports to the UK, the US and Singapore.

ŢŢŢŢŢ **Single Vineyard Meres Pinot Noir 2003** Lightly coloured; a lovely, lively, juicy, fragrant wine, all about the delicacy of Pinot Noir; ultimate silky mouthfeel, and great length. Diam. 13° alc. **RATING** 96 **DRINK** 2009 **$** 55
Clonale Mornington Peninsula Chardonnay 2005 Very elegant and fresh; while not the least heavy, the fruit has absorbed the oak; long, citrus, grapefruit and nectarine flavours; 10 clones. Diam. 13.5° alc. **RATING** 95 **DRINK** 2011 **$** 25
Estate Pinot Noir 2004 Great hue, still vibrant purple-red; a clean, fragrant red cherry and plum bouquet; light-bodied, but with abundant flavour and silky texture. Quite an achievement. Diam. 13.5° alc. **RATING** 95 **DRINK** 2011 **$** 45
Clonale Mornington Peninsula Chardonnay 2004 Very elegant, very intense and focused; tightly wound palate with a mix of citrus and stone fruit; malolactic and oak a wispy backdrop; extremely long, lingering finish; 10 clones of chardonnay. Diam. **RATING** 94 **DRINK** 2012 **$** 25
Estate Chardonnay 2004 An attractive mix of melon, white peach and fig; well-balanced oak, good line and length. Diam. 13° alc. **RATING** 94 **DRINK** 2010 **$** 39
Massale Mornington Peninsula Pinot Noir 2004 Very good colour; rich, opulent, ripe plum aromas and mid-palate fruit; tightens up nicely on the finish; very good length. Multi-clone. Diam. **RATING** 94 **DRINK** 2010 **$** 26

Kopparossa Wines

★★★★

PO Box 26, Coonawarra, SA 5263 **REGION** Wrattonbully
T (08) 8736 3268 **F** (08) 8736 3363 **OPEN** Not
WINEMAKER Gavin Hogg, Mike Press **EST.** 1996 **CASES** 5000
Kopparossa has undergone several transformations since its establishment in 1996, but the partnership of Gavin Hogg and Mike Press, with more than 60 years' winemaking and grapegrowing experience between them, has continued throughout. The business is now based on 2 estate vineyards, one in the Adelaide Hills, the other in Coonawarra, plus contract-grown grapes from Wrattonbully. The Adelaide Hills property, developed by the Press family and known as Kenton Valley, has 24 ha of pinot noir, merlot, shiraz, cabernet sauvignon and chardonnay planted in 1998 and 1999. The Coonawarra vineyard is called Stentiford, and is, quite literally, Gavin and Julie Hogg's back yard. It was planted in 1992 and '93 with cabernet sauvignon, merlot and chardonnay.

ŢŢŢŢŢ **Limestone Coast Cabernet Sauvignon 2002** Quite powerful dark fruits; not extractive, but a lot of oak; good length. **RATING** 90 **DRINK** 2010

Kotai Estate

NR

South Western Highway, Harvey, WA 6220 **REGION** Geographe
T (08) 9729 1755 **F** (08) 9729 1755 **OPEN** Wed–Sun 10–5
WINEMAKER Peter Stanlake **EST.** 2001 **CASES** 2000
Carol and Peter Jackson have planted 4.2 ha of chenin blanc, semillon, chardonnay, cabernet sauvignon and merlot, using contract-winemaking services. Sales are by mail order and through the cellar door.

Kouark Vineyard

★★★★

300 Thompson Road, Drouin South, Vic 3818 **REGION** Gippsland
T (03) 5627 6337 **F** (03) 5627 6337 **WWW**.gourmetgippsland.com **OPEN** W'ends 12–5
WINEMAKER Phil Gray **EST.** 1997 **CASES** 1000
Dairy farmers Phil and Jane Gray decided to diversify with the establishment of a 4-ha vineyard on part of their farm. They have planted 1.3 ha each of chardonnay and pinot noir, and 0.7 ha each of shiraz and cabernet sauvignon (and a few vines of pinot gris and viognier) on a northeasterly slope, bordered on the east by a 2.4-ha lake. As well as their general farming background, they have undertaken various Charles Sturt University grape and wine production courses, and similar short courses from other education facilities. A simple but appropriately equipped winery has been established, and the wines are sold through local stores and cafés. The name is believed to be the word for kookaburra in the language of the local Kurnai people.

ΨΨΨΨ **Gippsland Chardonnay 2004** A complex wine, with ripe stone fruit balanced by good acidity and positive, but controlled, oak. **RATING** 91 **DRINK** 2011 $15

ΨΨΨΨ **Gippsland Pinot Noir 2003** Powerful/foresty/savoury/spicy fruit flavours, the tannins still solid; should flourish with food. Cork. 13.3° alc. **RATING** 89 **DRINK** 2008 $25
Drouin South Pinot Gris 2005 Pear, spice and baked apple provide plenty of flavour and impact. Diam. 13.2° alc. **RATING** 88 **DRINK** 2009 $22
Gippsland Shiraz 2003 Very good hue; elegant, fresh medium-bodied wine, the acidity on the high side, but certainly makes the wine crisp. **RATING** 88 **DRINK** 2011 $22

ΨΨΨΨ **Rose 2004** **RATING** 85 **DRINK** Now $15

Kraanwood

★★★☆

8 Woodies Place, Richmond, Tas 7025 **REGION** Southern Tasmania
T (03) 6260 2540 **OPEN** Not
WINEMAKER Frank van der Kraan **EST.** 1994 **CASES** 150
Frank van der Kraan and wife Barbara established their 0.5-ha vineyard Kraanwood in 1994 and 1995, with approximately equal plantings of pinot noir, chardonnay and cabernet sauvignon. Frank also manages the 1-ha Pembroke Vineyard, and procures from it small quantities of schonburger, chardonnay, riesling and sauvignon blanc.

ΨΨΨΨ **Sparkling Pinot Noir 2004** Fresh and crisp with delicate strawberry undertones; lingering finish. **RATING** 90 **DRINK** Now $25

ΨΨΨΨ **Semillon 2005** Attractive, crisp herb, stone and lemon; good length and balance; not green. Cork. 12.7° alc. **RATING** 89 **DRINK** 2009 $25

ΨΨΨ **Schonburger 2005** **RATING** 83 $20

Krinklewood

★★★★☆

712 Wollombi Road, Broke, NSW 2330 **REGION** Lower Hunter Valley
T (02) 6579 1322 **F** (02) 9968 3435 **WWW**.krinklewood.com **OPEN** W'ends, long w'ends & by appt
WINEMAKER Monarch Winemaking Services (Jim Chatto) **EST.** 1981 **CASES** 4000
Rod and Suzanne Windrim first ventured to the Hunter Valley in 1981, establishing Krinklewood Cottage at Pokolbin and a 1-ha vineyard. In 1996 they sold that property and moved to the Broke/Fordwich region, where they have planted 20.5 ha with Dr Richard Smart as their viticultural consultant. Exports to Canada.

TTTTT **Hunter Valley Semillon 2005** Bright green-yellow; good intensity, line and length, with floral aromas and controlled ripeness. Screwcap. **RATING** 94 **DRINK** 2015 $17.99

TTTT **Hunter Valley Verdelho 2005** Plenty of ripe varietal fruit flavour; not too sweet. Screwcap. **RATING** 88 **DRINK** 2008 $18

Kurabana ★★★★

580 Hendy Main Road, Mt Moriac, Vic 3240 **REGION** Geelong
T 0438 661 273 **F** (03) 5266 1116 **www**.kurabana.com **OPEN** Not
WINEMAKER Ray Nadeson, Lee Evans **EST.** 1987 **CASES** 2000
The development of the quite extensive Kurabana Vineyard, west of Geelong in the foothills of Mt Moriac, began in 1987. Pinot noir (7.5 ha) is the largest portion, followed by (in descending order) shiraz, chardonnay, sauvignon blanc and pinot gris. While some of the grapes are sold, there are also limited purchases from the Geelong area.

TTTTY **Reserve Geelong Pinot Noir 2004** Very good colour; deserves the Reserve tag with significantly more concentration and weight than the varietal version; abundant, dark plum and black cherry fruit; silky tannins, good oak. Cork. **RATING** 93 **DRINK** 2010 $40
Geelong Pinot Noir 2004 Stylish, medium-bodied wine; a mix of forest, plum and spice through a long palate. **RATING** 92 **DRINK** 2009 $23

TTTY **Traditional Method Pinot Noir 2003** **RATING** 86 **DRINK** Now $26
Geelong Rose 2004 **RATING** 85 **DRINK** Now $18

Kurrajong Downs ★★★★

Casino Road, via Tenterfield, NSW 2372 **REGION** Northern Slopes Zone
T (02) 6736 4590 **F** (02) 6736 1983 **www**.kurrajongdownswines.com **OPEN** Thurs–Mon 9–4
WINEMAKER Ravens Croft Wines (Mark Ravenscroft), Symphony Hill (Mike Hayes) **EST.** 2000
CASES 2400
Jonus Rhodes arrived at Tenterfield in 1858, lured by the gold he mined for the next 40 years, until his death in 1898. He was evidently successful, for the family now runs a 2800-ha cattle grazing property on which Lynton and Sue Rhodes have planted a 5-ha vineyard at an altitude of 850m. Development of the vineyard started in the spring of 1996, and continued the following year.

TTTTT **Louisa Mary Semillon 2005** Spotlessly clean; an attractive wine, with some of the aromatic qualities of riesling; lemony/tangy flavour, with presence and length. Screwcap. 12.5° alc. **RATING** 94 **DRINK** 2013 $16

TTTTY **Louisa Mary Semillon 2004** Bright, light straw-green; a well-made wine, more classic, perhaps, but without the intensity and fruit characters of the '05. Screwcap. 11° alc. **RATING** 90 **DRINK** 2011 $14

TTTT **Timbarra Gold Chardonnay 2005** Attractive melon and grapefruit; a touch of barrel ferment interwoven with the fruit; powerful finish. Screwcap. 13° alc. **RATING** 89 **DRINK** 2008 $16

TTTY **Rose 2004** **RATING** 86 **DRINK** Now $14
All Nations Pinot Noir 2004 Has distinct strawberry and stem varietal character, but is light to the point of rose; at least it is not dead fruit. Screwcap. 13° alc. **RATING** 86 **DRINK** Now $17
The Forge Cabernet Merlot 2004 Light-bodied; pretty, small red fruit flavours; a summer red to be drunk while fresh. Screwcap. 12.5° alc. **RATING** 86 **DRINK** Now $15
Old Racecourse Sweet White 2005 Off-dry cellar door style; a nice twist of lemon helps prevent cloying; simple, though. Screwcap. 13.5° alc. **RATING** 86 **DRINK** Now $14
Darcy's Hill Merlot 2004 **RATING** 85 **DRINK** Now $16

Kurtz Family Vineyards

NR

PO Box 460, Nuriootpa, SA 5355 **REGION** Barossa Valley
T 0418 810 982 **F** (08) 8564 8278 **OPEN** Not
WINEMAKER John Zilm (Contract) **EST.** 1996 **CASES** NA
The Kurtz family has 20 ha of vineyard at Light Pass, planted to semillon, chardonnay, grenache, cabernet sauvignon, merlot, shiraz, cabernet franc, mourvedre and petit verdot. Exports to the US and Hong Kong.

Kyeema Estate

NR

43 Shumack Street, Weetangera, ACT 2614 (postal) **REGION** Canberra District
T (02) 6254 7557 (AH) **F** (02) 6254 7536 **OPEN** Not
WINEMAKER Andrew McEwin **EST.** 1986 **CASES** 1200
Part-time winemaker, part-time wine critic (with *Winewise* magazine) Andrew McEwin produces wines full of flavour and character; every wine released under the Kyeema Estate label has won a show award of some description.

Kyneton Ridge Estate

NR

90 Blackhill School Road, Kyneton, Vic 3444 **REGION** Macedon Ranges
T (03) 5422 7377 **F** (03) 5422 3747 **WWW.**kynetonridge.com.au **OPEN** W'ends & public hols 10–5, or by appt
WINEMAKER John Boucher **EST.** 1997 **CASES** 500
Kyneton Ridge Estate has been established by a family team of winemakers with winemaking roots going back 4 generations in the case of John and Ann Boucher. Together with Pauline Russell they found what they believe is a perfect pinot noir site near Kyneton, and planted 2.5 ha of pinot noir in 1997; 1.5 ha of chardonnay and 0.5 ha of shiraz were added in 2002.

Kyotmunga Estate

NR

287 Chittering Valley Road, Lower Chittering, WA 6084 **REGION** Perth Hills
T (08) 9571 8001 **WWW.**kyotmunga.com.au **OPEN** W'ends 11–5 April-Dec
WINEMAKER Trevor Wallis **EST.** 2000 **CASES** 500
Lynette Chester and Trevor Wallis have planted 3 ha of shiraz, chenin blanc, taminga, grenache and barbera as well as an olive grove. The wines are made onsite, and both they and the estate-made extra virgin olive oil are available for tasting. The cellar door verandah overlooks the estate vineyard and Hartley Estate on the opposite slope, and then on to the Swan Valley National Park.

La Cantina King Valley

5 Honey's Lane, King Valley, Vic 3678 **REGION** King Valley
T (03) 5729 3615 **F** (03) 5729 3613 **WWW.**lacantinakingvalley.com.au **OPEN** 7 days 10–5 (10–6 during daylight savings)
WINEMAKER Gino Corsini **EST.** 1996 **CASES** 1500
Gino and Peter Corsini have 22 ha of riesling, chardonnay, shiraz, merlot and cabernet sauvignon, selling most but making a small amount in a winery 'made of Glenrowan granite stone in traditional Tuscan style'. The wines are made without the use of sulphur dioxide.

▼▼▼ **Cabernet Shiraz Merlot 2003** RATING 83 $ 14

La Curio

11 Sextant Avenue, Seaford, SA 5169 (postal) **REGION** McLaren Vale
T (08) 8327 1442 **F** (08) 8327 1442 **WWW.**lacuriowines.com **OPEN** Not
WINEMAKER Adam Hooper, Elena Golakova **EST.** 2003 **CASES** 500
La Curio has been established by Adam Hooper and partner Elena Golakova, who purchased small parcels of grapes from 5 vineyards in McLaren Vale with an average age of 40 years, the oldest 80 years. They make the wines at Redheads Studio, a boutique winery in McLaren Vale which has been

established to cater for a number of small producers. The manacles depicted on the striking label are those of Harry Houdini, and the brand proposition is very cleverly worked through. Winemaking techniques, too, are avant-garde, and highly successful. Exports to the UK and the US.

ỴỴỴỴỿ **Reserve McLaren Vale Shiraz 2004** Medium- to full-bodied, and carries the alcohol quite well; plum, chocolate, spice and mocha flavours; good length, ripe tannins. Cork. 15° alc. **RATING** 92 **DRINK** 2014 $ 30

Reserve Bush Vine McLaren Vale Grenache 2004 Good purple-red; good varietal expression via juicy/jammy red berry fruits girdled by persistent tannins. Cork. 15° alc. **RATING** 91 **DRINK** 2010 $ 26

The Nubile McLaren Vale Grenache Shiraz 2004 The 30% Shiraz component makes a major difference; juicy, rich black fruits carry the tannins; good oak. Cork. 15° alc. **RATING** 91 **DRINK** 2014 $ 21

La Pleiade ★★★★★

c/- Jasper Hill, Drummonds Lane, Heathcote, Vic 3523 **REGION** Heathcote
T (03) 5433 2528 **F** (03) 5433 3143 **OPEN** By appt
WINEMAKER Ron Laughton, Michel Chapoutier **EST.** 1998 **CASES** NFP
This is the joint venture of Michel and Corinne Chapoutier and Ron and Elva Laughton. In the spring of 1998 a new vineyard using Australian shiraz clones and imported French clones was planted. The vineyard is run biodynamically, and the winemaking is deliberately designed to place maximum emphasis on the fruit quality.

ỴỴỴỴỴ **Heathcote Shiraz 2003** Exceptional red-purple colour; a very powerful and complex wine with blackberry, licorice and pepper fruit; firm tannins tremble on the brink, but time will see these soften well before the fruit starts to fade. Cork. 15° alc. **RATING** 94 **DRINK** 2023 $ 65

Laanecoorie ★★★★

4834 Bendigo/Maryborough Road, Betley, Vic 3472 **REGION** Bendigo
T (03) 5468 7260 **F** (03) 5468 7388 **OPEN** W'ends 10–4, or by appt
WINEMAKER Graeme Jukes, John Ellis (Contract) **EST.** 1982 **CASES** 1000
John McQuilten's 7.5-ha vineyard produces grapes of high quality, and competent contract-winemaking has done the rest.

ỴỴỴỴỴ **McQuilten's Reserve Shiraz 2004** Dense red-purple; crammed to the gills with blackberry, prune, bitter chocolate, spice, tannins, alcohol and oak; vinous black hole in space; give it a minimum of 10 years. Cork. 15° alc. **RATING** 94 **DRINK** 2024 $ 39.50

ỴỴỴỿ **Cabernet Sauvignon Cabernet Franc Merlot 2003** Quite sweet blackcurrant fruit, but very grippy tannins need to soften before the fruit disappears. Cork. 12.8° alc. **RATING** 86 **DRINK** 2010 $ 23

Labyrinth ★★★★★

PO Box 7372, Shepparton, Vic 3632 **REGION** Yarra Valley
T (03) 5831 2793 **F** (03) 5831 2982 **www.**labyrinthwine.com **OPEN** Not
WINEMAKER Rick Hill **EST.** 2000 **CASES** 1100
Rick Hill is running a unique wine business, the name Labyrinth being well chosen. While it is a Pinot Noir-only specialist, one is produced in the southern hemisphere (from the Yarra Valley) and one from the northern hemisphere (Santa Barbara, California) each year. The wines come from individual vineyards: the Bien Nacido Vineyard has a deserved reputation as one of the best sources of pinot noir in California. Rick Hill uses leased space in California and at Goulburn Valley Estate to make the wines, and also has active consultancy work in California.

ỴỴỴỴỴ **Bien Nacido Vineyard Santa Maria Valley Pinot Noir 2001** Youthful, fine and elegant; lovely red fruits; very fine tannins give great length and feel. The Californian sister wine vividly demonstrating the quality of the fruit. Cork. 14.5° alc. **RATING** 96 **DRINK** 2010 $ 60

Viggers Vineyard Yarra Valley Pinot Noir 2003 Complex, rich, foresty/savoury overtones to plum fruit; strong structure; radical style difference to the Valley Farm. Cork. 14.1° alc. **RATING** 94 **DRINK** 2009 $ 40

ỴỴỴỴỴ **Valley Farm Vineyard Yarra Valley Pinot Noir 2003** Very crisp, firm and fresh cherry and strawberry fruit, with just a hint of mint. Cork. 12.5° alc. **RATING** 90 **DRINK** Now $ 36.50

Ladbroke Grove ★★★★

Riddoch Highway, Coonawarra, SA 5263 **REGION** Coonawarra
T (08) 8737 3777 **F** (08) 8737 3777 **www**.ladbrokegrove.com.au **OPEN** Wed–Sun 10–5 or by appt
WINEMAKER Contract **EST.** 1982 **CASES** 5000
Established in 1982, Ladbroke Grove is a relatively old Coonawarra brand. However, while the vineyards remained, winemaking and marketing lapsed until the business was purchased by John Cox and Marie Valenzuela, who have quietly gone about the re-establishment and rejuvenation of the label and were rewarded by a string of wine show results. It has extensive grape sources, including the Killian vineyard (10 ha), planted in 1990 to cabernet sauvignon, merlot and chardonnay. It also leases a little over 1 ha of dry-grown shiraz planted in 1965 in the centre of the Coonawarra township. In the spring of 2002 it planted another 11 ha at the northern end of Coonawarra to cabernet sauvignon, shiraz, viognier, riesling and merlot.

ỴỴỴỴỴ **Riesling 2005** High-toned bouquet; intense and powerful apple and citrus flavours, a hint of sweetness balanced by lemony acidity. Screwcap. **RATING** 94 **DRINK** 2014

ỴỴỴỴ **Township Block Shiraz 2003** **RATING** 85 **DRINK** 2008
Shiraz Viognier 2004 **RATING** 84 **DRINK** Now

ỴỴỴ **Chardonnay 2005** **RATING** 82

Lake Barrington Estate ★★★★★

1133–1136 West Kentish Road, West Kentish, Tas 7306 **REGION** Northern Tasmania
T (03) 6491 1249 **F** (03) 6334 2892 **OPEN** Wed–Sun 10–5 (Nov–Apr)
WINEMAKER Steve Lubiana (Sparkling), Andrew Hood (Table) **EST.** 1986 **CASES** 500
Lake Barrington Estate is owned by the vivacious and energetic Maree Taylor; it is adjacent to Lake Barrington, 30 km south of Devonport, on the northern coast of Tasmania. There are picnic facilities at the 3-ha vineyard, and, needless to say, the scenery is very beautiful.

ỴỴỴỴỴ **Chardonnay 2002** Has developed superbly over the past 3 years; gently complex malolactic and barrel ferment inputs; excellent length and balance; marries finesse with flavour. **RATING** 95 **DRINK** Now

Lake Breeze Wines ★★★★☆

Step Road, Langhorne Creek, SA 5255 **REGION** Langhorne Creek
T (08) 8537 3017 **F** (08) 8537 3267 **www**.lakebreeze.com.au **OPEN** 7 days 10–5
WINEMAKER Greg Follett **EST.** 1987 **CASES** 12 000
The Folletts have been farmers at Langhorne Creek since 1880, grapegrowers since the 1930s. Since 1987, increasing amounts of their grapes have been made into wine. The quality of the releases has been exemplary, with the red wines particularly appealing. Lake Breeze also owns and makes the False Cape wines from Kangaroo Island; there are 12 ha of vines. Exports to the UK, the US and other major markets.

ỴỴỴỴỴ **Langhorne Creek Cabernet Sauvignon 2003** Deep colour and good hue; abundant blackcurrant fruit supported by fine but positive tannins and oak; a lovely wine. Cork. **RATING** 94 **DRINK** 2015 $ 20

ỴỴỴỴ **False Cape The Captain Cabernet Sauvignon 2003** A powerful, concentrated and strongly structured palate; blackcurrant, blackberry and bitter chocolate; oak an incidental by-play, the tannins persistent but balanced. Cork. 13.8° alc. **RATING** 92 **DRINK** 2015 $ 28
Bernoota Shiraz Cabernet 2003 A powerful dark fruit and chocolate bouquet, the palate following suit; lots of depth and structure. Cork. 14.5° alc. **RATING** 91 **DRINK** 2013 $ 18

False Cape Silver Mermaid Sauvignon Blanc 2005 Light straw-green; light-bodied, attractive passionfruit, grapefruit and gooseberry mix; a clean, long finish. Screwcap. 12.5° alc. **RATING** 90 **DRINK** Now $18

TTTT **Langhorne Creek Chardonnay 2005** Spotlessly clean; an elegant, light- to medium-bodied palate with stone fruit, grapefruit, and a touch of barrel ferment adding to the texture. Screwcap. 13° alc. **RATING** 89 **DRINK** 2008 $17

Langhorne Creek White Frontignac 2005 Fresh orange blossom aromas and vibrant, grapey flavours; great on the rocks at the height of summer. Screwcap. 12° alc. **RATING** 88 **DRINK** Now $15

Langhorne Creek Grenache 2004 Light-bodied, relatively simple sweet red fruits; easy drinking summer red. Screwcap. 14.8° alc. **RATING** 87 **DRINK** 2008 $17

Lake Charlotte Wines   NR

4750 Ballup Road, Wooroloo, WA 6558 **REGION** Perth Hills
T (08) 9573 1219 **F** (08) 9573 1616 **OPEN** W'ends & public hols 10–5
WINEMAKER Jim Elson (Contract) **EST.** 2001 **CASES** NA
There is no doubt the Perth Hills is a very pretty wine region, its twisting roads and multiple sub-valleys reminding me in some ways of the Clare Valley. It also has the great advantage of being an easy drive from Perth. Peter and Edwina Carter have set up their cellar door in an idyllic setting on the edge of Lake Charlotte, with a typical wide and open verandah under a low-sloping roof. They have 2.5 ha of verdelho, cabernet sauvignon, shiraz and merlot, and their wines are contract-made by long-term Perth Hills winemaker Jim Elson.

Lake Cooper Estate   ★★★★

1608 Midland Highway, Corop, Vic 3559 **REGION** Heathcote
T (03) 9397 7781 **F** (03) 9397 8502 **www**.lakecooperestate.com.au **OPEN** W'ends & public hols 11–5
WINEMAKER Peter Kelliher, Donald Risstrom **EST.** 1998 **CASES** 1240
Lake Cooper Estate is another substantial venture in the burgeoning Heathcote region, set on the side of Mt Camel Range, with panoramic views of Lake Cooper, Greens Lake and the Corop township. Planting began in 1998 with 12 ha of shiraz, and has since been extended to 18 ha of shiraz, 10 ha of cabernet sauvignon and small plantings of merlot and chardonnay; additional small blocks of more exotic varieties will follow. Owners Gerry and Geraldine McHarg completed the winery in 2003 (the wine was made elsewhere by Peter Kelliher before then) and a new cellar door in 2005.

TTTTY **Reserve Heathcote Shiraz 2004** Very good colour; a complex wine, with more savoury/spice/licorice components, but also greater fruit intensity and length; oak a little more evident. Strange choice of cork closure. Cork. 14.4° alc. **RATING** 93 **DRINK** 2017 $25

Heathcote Shiraz 2004 Medium- to full-bodied; black and red fruits, licorice and savoury tannins, plus a nice touch of mocha/vanilla oak. Screwcap. 14.5° alc. **RATING** 90 **DRINK** 2014 $20

TTTT **Heathcote Cabernet Sauvignon 2004** Slightly hazy colour; solid cassis/blackcurrant fruit and a whisper of mint; appropriate tannins and oak. Screwcap. 13.6° alc. **RATING** 89 **DRINK** 2011 $20

Heathcote Chardonnay 2005 Very reserved style; fruit, oak and minerality all present, but tightly wound; long finish. Screwcap. 14.5° alc. **RATING** 88 **DRINK** 2009 $15

Lake George Winery   NR

Federal Highway, Collector, NSW 2581 **REGION** Canberra District
T (02) 4848 0039 **F** (02) 4848 0039 **www**.lakegeorgewinery.com.au **OPEN** By appt
WINEMAKER Sam Karelas **EST.** 1971 **CASES** 1000
Dr Edgar Riek was an inquisitive, iconoclastic winemaker who was not content with his role as Godfather and founder of the Canberra District, and so was forever experimenting and innovating. His fortified wines, vintaged in northeast Victoria but matured at Lake George, were very good. After a few teething problems, wine quality and consistency has improved.

Lake Moodemere Vineyards ★★★

McDonalds Road, Rutherglen, Vic 3685 **REGION** Rutherglen
T (02) 6032 9449 **F** (02) 6032 9449 **WWW**.moodemerewines.com.au **OPEN** W'ends & public hols
10–5, Mon, Thurs, Fri 10–3.30
WINEMAKER Michael Chambers **EST.** 1995 **CASES** 2500
Michael, Belinda, Peter and Helen Chambers are members of the famous Chambers family of
Rutherglen. They have 22 ha of vineyards (tended by Peter), with the Italian grape variety biancone a
vineyard specialty, made in a light-bodied late-harvest style. The cellar door sits high above Lake
Moodemere, and gourmet hampers can be arranged with 24 hours' notice.

 Late Harvest Biancone 2004 Gentle, sweet lemon/lime/orange flavours balanced by
appropriate acidity; cellar door special. Cork. **RATING** 87 **DRINK** Now $15

Rutherglen Shiraz 2003 Good colour; full-bodied red and black fruit flavours but
unbalanced by over-acidification. Cork. 14.1° alc. **RATING** 86 **DRINK** 2010 $18

Lake's Folly ★★★★☆

Broke Road, Pokolbin, NSW 2320 **REGION** Lower Hunter Valley
T (02) 4998 7507 **F** (02) 4998 7322 **WWW**.lakesfolly.com.au **OPEN** 7 days 10–4 while wine is available
WINEMAKER Rodney Kempe **EST.** 1963 **CASES** 4500
The first of the weekend wineries to produce wines for commercial sale, long revered for its Cabernet
Sauvignon and thereafter its Chardonnay. Very properly, *terroir* and climate produce a distinct
regional influence and thereby a distinctive wine style. Some find this attractive, others are less
tolerant. The winery continues to enjoy an incredibly loyal clientele, with much of each year's wine
selling out quickly by mail order. Lake's Folly no longer has any connection with the Lake family,
having been acquired some years ago by Perth businessman Peter Fogarty. Mr Fogarty's family
company previously established the Millbrook Winery in the Perth Hills, so is no stranger to the joys
and agonies of running a small winery.

 Hunter Valley Chardonnay 2004 A beautifully made and crafted wine; subtle barrel
ferment inputs; the stone fruit and melon with a touch of cream; excellent finish. Cork.
13.5° alc. **RATING** 96 **DRINK** 2014 $50

Hunter Valley Cabernets 2004 Light- to medium-bodied; clean and elegant; lots of
finesse, simply needing a touch more flesh; Cabernet Sauvignon 69%/Petit Verdot
Merlot/Shiraz. Cork. **RATING** 90 **DRINK** 2010 $50

Lambert Vineyards ★★★★

810 Norton Road, Wamboin, NSW 2620 **REGION** Canberra District
T (02) 6238 3866 **F** (02) 6238 3855 **WWW**.lambertvineyards.com.au **OPEN** Thurs–Sun 10–5, or by
appt
WINEMAKER Steve Lambert, Ruth Lambert **EST.** 1998 **CASES** 6000
Ruth and Steve Lambert have established 8 ha of riesling, chardonnay, pinot gris, pinot noir,
cabernet sauvignon, merlot and shiraz. Steve Lambert makes the wines onsite. The café is open
Thurs–Sat evening, Fri–Sun for lunch.

Canberra District Late Harvest Riesling 2004 Amazing citrus blossom and citrus rind
aromas; fresh and lively mouthfeel, the flavours an echo of the bouquet; a highly
commendable style. Screwcap. 13° alc. **RATING** 93 **DRINK** 2014 $18
Canberra District Riesling 2005 Generously flavoured and proportioned; a mix of lime
and passionfruit; juicy finish. Screwcap. 13.1° alc. **RATING** 90 **DRINK** 2013 $18

Canberra District Chardonnay 2003 Full green-yellow; ripe yellow peach fruit and
strong French oak inputs; full-bodied style, drink soon. Screwcap. 14.6° alc. **RATING** 89
DRINK 2008 $20
Reserve Canberra District Shiraz 2003 Unconvincing colour; light- to medium-bodied;
spicy/earthy/savoury/mocha flavours surround the fruit; 22 months in oak was 6 months
too long. Screwcap. 14.4° alc. **RATING** 88 **DRINK** 2010 $30

Canberra District Merlot 2003 Bright red-purple; savoury olive and blackcurrant fruit with assertive tannins; here the 22 months in oak is fully justified, likewise more fining of those tannins. Screwcap. 14.7° alc. **RATING** 88 **DRINK** 2012 $ 22

♥♥♥♡ **Reserve Canberra District Pinot Noir 2004** **RATING** 84 **DRINK** 2008 $ 30

Lamont's
★★★☆

85 Bisdee Road, Millendon, WA 6056 **REGION** Swan Valley
T (08) 9296 4485 **F** (08) 9296 1663 **www**.lamonts.com.au **OPEN** 7 days 10–5
WINEMAKER Digby Leddin, Rachael Robinson **EST.** 1978 **CASES** 7000
Corin Lamont is the daughter of the late Jack Mann, and oversees the making of wines in a style which would have pleased her father. Lamont's also boasts a superb restaurant run by granddaughter Kate Lamont, plus a gallery for the sale and promotion of local arts. The wines are going from strength to strength, utilising both estate grown and contract-grown (from southern regions) grapes. There are 2 cellar doors, the second (open 7 days) in the Margaret River at Gunyulgup Valley Drive, Yallingup.

♥♥♥♥ **Frankland River Riesling 2005** Attractive lime, spice and herb fruit; rich palate with just a hint of phenolics; some CO_2 also. Screwcap. 12.5° alc. **RATING** 89 **DRINK** 2009 $ 25
Margaret River Semillon Sauvignon Blanc 2005 Firm, minerally and crisp; clean and fair length. Screwcap. 13.5° alc. **RATING** 87 **DRINK** 2008 $ 20
Family Reserve 2002 Medium-bodied; solid dark fruits, a splash of oak and firm tannins; has flavour. Cork. 14.3° alc. **RATING** 87 **DRINK** 2009 $ 40

♥♥♥♡ **Verdelho 2005** **RATING** 84 **DRINK** Now $ 16

Lancaster
NR

5228 West Swan Road, West Swan, WA 6055 **REGION** Swan District
T (08) 9250 6461 **F** (08) 9250 7881 **www**.lancasterwines.com.au **OPEN** 7 days 10–5
WINEMAKER Rob Marshall, John Griffiths **EST.** 1960 **CASES** NFP
Carl and Jackie Lancaster own a 10-ha vineyard, with the oldest plantings dating back to 1960, others far more recent. Today the plantings are of chardonnay, chenin blanc, viognier, grenache, shiraz and cabernet sauvignon, supplemented by verdelho and merlot from other growers.

Lancefield Winery
NR

Scrubby Camp Road, Emu Flat, Lancefield, Vic 3435 **REGION** Macedon Ranges
T (03) 5433 5292 **F** (03) 5433 5114 **www**.wineandmusic.net **OPEN** By appt
WINEMAKER Rod Schmidt **EST.** 1985 **CASES** 1000
Lancefield Winery was established by Andrew Pattison, with plantings of 1 ha each of chardonnay and shiraz, and 0.5 ha each of gewurztraminer, pinot noir and cabernets/merlot. With Rod Schmidt in charge, it is in the course of developing its own labels, the other brands having moved across to Pattison's Burke & Wills winery.

Landsborough Valley Estate
★★★★★

850 Landsborough–Elmhurst Road, Landsborough, Vic 3385 **REGION** Pyrenees
T (03) 5356 9390 **F** (03) 5356 9130 **OPEN** Mon–Fri 10–4, w'ends by appt
WINEMAKER Wal Henning **EST.** 1996 **CASES** 6000
LVE (for short) originated in 1963, when civil engineering contractor Wal Henning was engaged to undertake work at Chateau Remy (now Blue Pyrenees). He was so impressed with the potential of the region for viticulture that he began an aerial search for sites with close friend Geoff Oliver. Their first choice was not available; they chose a site which is now Taltarni, developing 40 ha. Taltarni was then sold, and the pair (with Geoff's brother Max) moved on to establish Warrenmang Vineyard. When it, too, was sold the pair was left without a vineyard, but in 1996 they were finally able to purchase the property they had identified 33 years previously, which is now partly given over to LVE and part to the giant Glen Kara vineyard. They have established 20 ha on LVE, the lion's share to shiraz, with lesser amounts of cabernet sauvignon, pinot noir, chardonnay and riesling.

ΤΤΤΤΤ **Geoff Oliver Classic Shiraz 2004** Strong purple-red; masses of dark fruits, blackberry, spice and licorice; tannins in strong support. Gold medal Sydney Wine Show '06. Cork. RATING 94 DRINK 2019 $40

Geoff Oliver Cabernet 2004 Medium- to full-bodied; lots of juicy cassis fruit on entry, then quite persistent tannins still to soften and integrate. Has potential, but will never challenge the marvellous Geoff Oliver Shiraz from the same vintage, which is still gaining complexity and power. Screwcap. 13° alc. RATING 94 DRINK 2019 $26

ΤΤΤΤΤ **Pyrenees Ranges Cabernet Merlot 2003** Good colour; a big, powerful wine, with abundant blackcurrant/blackberry fruit; ample but soft tannins. Screwcap. 14.2° alc. RATING 90 DRINK 2015 $18

ΤΤΤΤ **Pyrenees Ranges Shiraz 2004** Medium-bodied; unexpected spicy/savoury/herbal/dark chocolate flavours at odds with the alcohol; there should be more ripe fruit flavours. Screwcap. 13.9° alc. RATING 89 DRINK 2010 $22

Landscape Wines ★★★★

383 Prossers Road, Richmond, Tas 7025 REGION Southern Tasmania
T (03) 6260 4216 F (03) 6260 4016 WWW.landscapewines.com.au OPEN By appt
WINEMAKER Andrew Hood, Jeremy Direen (Contract) EST. 1998 CASES 120
Knowles and Elizabeth Kerry run the Wondoomarook mixed farming and irrigation property in the heart of the Coal River Valley. In 1998/99 they decided to undertake a small scale diversification, planting 0.5 ha each of riesling and pinot noir. The labels, depicting Antarctic scenes by Jenni Mitchell, hark back to the Kerrys' original occupation in Antarctic scientific research.

ΤΤΤΤΤ **Riesling 2004** Tangy, intense, lime/citrus flavours provide a very different fruit register to the '05; excellent balance, length and finish. Screwcap. 12.1° alc. RATING 91 DRINK 2012 $18

ΤΤΤΤ **Pinot Noir 2005** Light, bright colour; light-bodied, very fresh, and entirely driven by the cherry/strawberry fruit; ideal summer lunch wine. Screwcap. 13.3° alc. RATING 88 DRINK Now $20

Riesling 2005 Bordering on full-bodied; fleshy, tropical ripe fruit with a pleasant twist of citrus to calm things down. RATING 87 DRINK 2008 $20

ΤΤΤΤ **Pinot Noir 2003** RATING 86 DRINK Now $20

Lane's End Vineyard ★★★☆

885 Mount William Road, Lancefield, Vic 3435 (postal) REGION Macedon Ranges
T (03) 5429 1760 F (03) 5429 1760 OPEN Not
WINEMAKER Howard Matthews, Ken Murchison EST. 1985 CASES 450
Pharmacist Howard Matthews (and family) purchased the former Woodend Winery in 2000, with 1.8 ha of chardonnay and pinot noir (and a small amount of cabernet franc) dating back to the mid-1980s. Subsequently, the cabernet franc has been grafted over to pinot noir (with a mix of 4 clones), the chardonnay now totally 1 ha. For the first 2–3 years, the grapes were sold, but by 2003 Howard Matthews was ready to make the first wines. For the 2 preceding vintages he had worked with next-door neighbour Ken Murchison of Portree Wines, gaining winemaking experience; with the exception of the Unoaked Chardonnay, made by David Cowburn, the wines are made there.

ΤΤΤΤ **Macedon Ranges Pinot Noir 2004** Deep, youthful purple-red; super-rich and ripe, with most of the impression coming on entry into the mouth. Radically different from the '03. Patience will be rewarded. Screwcap. RATING 89 DRINK 2012 $29

Langanook Wines ★★★★

91 McKittericks Road, Sutton Grange, Vic 3448 REGION Bendigo
T (03) 5474 8250 F (03) 5474 8250 WWW.bendigowine.org.au/langanook OPEN W'ends & public hols 11 5, or by appt
WINEMAKER Matt Hunter EST. 1985 CASES 1500
The Langanook vineyard was established back in 1985 (the first wines came much later), at an altitude of 450m on the granite slopes of Mt Alexander. The climate is much cooler than in other

parts of Bendigo, with a heat summation on a par with the Yarra Valley. The 20-tonne winery allows minimal handling of the wines. Exports to Belgium and Canada.

▼▼▼▼▼ **Syrah 2004** Strong, deep colour; powerful blackberry and plum fruit throughout, together with a twist of chocolate, but not extractive; impressive length and balance, fine, ripe tannins and controlled oak; 15% Heathcote. Cork. 14.5° alc. **RATING** 94 **DRINK** 2014 $ 28

▼▼▼▼ **Cabernet Sauvignon Merlot Cabernet Franc 2004** A light- to medium-bodied, elegant wine, with attractive cassis/redcurrant fruit, fine tannins and gentle oak. Screwcap. 14° alc. **RATING** 89 **DRINK** 2010 $ 28
Chardonnay Viognier 2004 Big, powerful, ripe wine; yellow peach, fig and a touch of apricot; hearty food style. 14° alc. **RATING** 87 **DRINK** Now $ 19

▼▼▼▽ **Rose 2005** **RATING** 86 **DRINK** Now $ 15

Langleyvale Vineyard   NR

43 Blackhill School Road, Kyneton, Vic 3444 **REGION** Macedon Ranges
T 0417 359 106 **F** (03) 9576 2966 **OPEN** From November 2004
WINEMAKER Richard Beniac **EST.** 2000 **CASES** 250
Richard Beniac purchased his property at Macedon after completing a part-time university viticulture course; he also conducted soil tests and collected weather data before deciding to take on the challenge of cool climate viticulture. The first plantings were 2.6 ha of merlot, followed by 0.6 ha each of shiraz and cabernet franc. Merlot was the first wine produced in 2004; it will be followed in 2006/07 by Shiraz and Cabernet Franc.

Langmeil Winery   ★★★★★

Cnr Para Road/Langmeil Road, Tanunda, SA 5352 **REGION** Barossa Valley
T (08) 8563 2595 **F** (08) 8563 3622 **WWW**.langmeilwinery.com.au **OPEN** 7 days 11–4.30
WINEMAKER Paul Lindner **EST.** 1996 **CASES** 15 000
Vines were first planted at Langmeil in the 1840s, and the first winery on the site, known as Paradale Wines, opened in 1932. In 1996, cousins Carl and Richard Lindner plus brother-in-law Chris Bitter formed a partnership to acquire and refurbish the winery and its 5-ha vineyard (planted to shiraz, and including 2 ha planted in 1846). Another vineyard was acquired in 1998, taking total plantings to 14.5 ha and including cabernet sauvignon and grenache. Exports to the UK, the US and other major markets.

▼▼▼▼▼ **The Freedom Shiraz 2003** Floods every corner of the mouth; rich, dramatic red and black fruits; very good structure, line and mouthfeel. **RATING** 96 **DRINK** 2018 $ 100
Valley Floor Shiraz 2004 Strong, deep purple-red; a rich and succulent array of red and black fruits, ripe tannins and positive oak. Blend of various vineyard sites. Cork. 14.5° alc.
RATING 94 **DRINK** 2014 $ 25

▼▼▼▼▽ **Jackaman's Cabernet Sauvignon 2003** A powerful, substantial medium- to full-bodied wine; blackcurrant, cassis and earth fruit amalgam supported by cabernet tannins. Cork. 14° alc. **RATING** 91 **DRINK** 2013 $ 45
The Blacksmith Barossa Cabernet Sauvignon 2003 Rich, sweet blackcurrant fruit, not dead; supple tannins; success for the vintage. Cork. 14.5° alc. **RATING** 91 **DRINK** 2015 $ 20
Eden Valley Riesling 2005 Clean; abundant aroma and flavour in a relatively soft, tropical/lime spectrum; lacks the diamond-cut precision of the very best. Old, dry-grown vines. Screwcap. 12.5° alc. **RATING** 90 **DRINK** 2010 $ 20

▼▼▼▼ **Three Gardens Barossa Shiraz Grenache Mourvedre 2004** Light- to medium-bodied; sweet juicy, jammy, berry fruit in typical Barossa style; strongly influenced by grenache; ready to roll. Screwcap. 14.5° alc. **RATING** 89 **DRINK** 2010 $ 20
The Fifth Wave Grenache 2003 Typical Barossa Grenache; friendly, medium-bodied and sweet, somewhat jammy fruit, without the structure found in McLaren Vale Grenache. Cork. 15° alc. **RATING** 89 **DRINK** 2008 $ 30

▼▼▼▽ **Barossa Valley Viognier 2005** **RATING** 86 **DRINK** 2008 $ 20

🍇 Lankeys Creek Wines ★★★☆

River Road, Walwa, Vic 3709 **REGION** North East Victoria Zone
T (02) 6037 1577 **WWW**.lankeyscreekwines.com.au **OPEN** By appt
WINEMAKER Steve Thompson **EST.** 2002 **CASES** NA
Lankeys Creek is the former Upper Murray Estate crushing 70 tonnes a year, making wine both for its own label and for other growers within the Tumbarumba region, from which most of the Lankeys Creek grapes come. The white wines are made in Flexitank plastic bags which winemaker Steve Thompson believes prevent oxidation and enhance flavour components, particularly with small batches.

🍷🍷🍷🍷🍷 **Shiraz 2003** A complex juxtaposition of cool spice, leaf and earth with potent black fruits and powerful tannins; lingering finish. Intriguing wine. Twin top. 15° alc. **RATING** 90 **DRINK** 2013 $18

🍷🍷🍷🍷 **Sauvignon Blanc 2005** Clean, firm, predominantly grass and mineral; slightly austere, but well-made. Screwcap. **RATING** 88 **DRINK** Now $15
Unwooded Chardonnay 2004 Light green-gold; light- to medium-bodied, and has developed well; grapefruit and melon flavour; good length and balance. Screwcap. 12.5° alc. **RATING** 88 **DRINK** 2008 $18
Classic White 2004 Fine, citrussy fruit; good length and finesse; sauvignon blanc presumably the driver. Screwcap. 12.7° alc. **RATING** 87 **DRINK** Now $15

🍷🍷🍷🍷 **Pinot Noir 2004** **RATING** 86 **DRINK** 2008 $18
Cabernet Sauvignon 2002 **RATING** 86 **DRINK** 2008 $18
Sauvignon Blanc 2004 **RATING** 85 **DRINK** Now $15
Unwooded Chardonnay 2005 **RATING** 85 **DRINK** 2008 $18

🍇 LanzThomson Wines ★★★☆

Lot 1 Rosedale Scenic Road, Lyndoch, SA 5351 **REGION** Barossa Valley
T (08) 8524 9227 **F** (08) 8524 9227 **WWW**.lanzthomson.com **OPEN** By appt
WINEMAKER Wine Wise Consultancy **EST.** 1998 **CASES** 830
The friendship of the Lanz and Thomson families stretches back for 30 years, although it was the 2 (future) wives who first became friends through Rotary International in the 1970s. In their words 'Brian and Thomas came on the scene over the next few years, sharing stories and bottles of wine'. One thing led to another, and in 1998 they began the establishment of the 15-ha Outlook Vineyard and the 16.5-ha Moolanda Vineyard, each planted predominantly to shiraz, each with around 2 ha of mourvedre and viognier, splitting only with grenache (1.44 ha) on Outlook and cabernet (3.25 ha) on Moolanda. The lion's share of the grapes is sold.

🍷🍷🍷🍷 **Shattered Rock Barossa Valley Shiraz 2004** An interesting rendition of the '04 vintage; offers both red and black fruits with savoury nuances, belying its alcohol. Indifferent oak is the Achilles heel. Cork. 14.5° alc. **RATING** 88 **DRINK** 2010 $20

Lark Hill ★★★★★

521 Bungendore Road, Bungendore, NSW 2621 **REGION** Canberra District
T (02) 6238 1393 **F** (02) 6238 1393 **WWW**.larkhillwine.com.au **OPEN** Wed–Mon 10–5
WINEMAKER Dr David Carpenter, Sue Carpenter **EST.** 1978 **CASES** 4000
The 7-ha Lark Hill vineyard is situated at an altitude of 860m, level with the observation deck on Black Mountain Tower, and offers splendid views of the Lake George escarpment. The Carpenters have made wines of real quality, style and elegance from the start, but have defied all the odds (and conventional thinking) with the quality of their Pinot Noirs.

🍷🍷🍷🍷🍷 **Chardonnay 2004** Tight, long and intense stone fruit and citrus; lingering finish, lemony acidity; subtle oak. Screwcap. **RATING** 94 **DRINK** 2010 $28
Shiraz 2004 The usual good colour and lifted bouquet; a supple, medium-bodied palate with plummy fruit, and ripe, soft, tannins. Screwcap. 13.8° alc. **RATING** 94 **DRINK** 2014 $32

🍷🍷🍷🍷 **Riesling 2005** Light straw-green; clean and fresh passionfruit and apple in a tropical spectrum; substance without heaviness. Screwcap. 12° alc. **RATING** 91 **DRINK** 2012 $22

Lashmar

NR

c/- 24 Lindsay Terrace, Belair, SA 5052 **REGION** Kangaroo Island
T (08) 8278 3669 **F** (08) 8278 3998 **www**.lashmarwines.com **OPEN** Not
WINEMAKER Colin Cooter **EST.** 1996 **CASES** 1000
Colin and Bronwyn Cooter (who are also part of the Lengs & Cooter business) are the driving force behind Antechamber Bay Wines. The wines are in fact labelled and branded Lashmar; the Kangaroo Island Cabernet Sauvignon comes from vines planted in 1991 on the Lashmar family property, which is on the extreme eastern end of Kangaroo Island overlooking Antechamber Bay. The first commercial wines were made in 1999 and released in October 2000. The Three Valleys and Sisters wines (from other regions) give the business added volume. Exports to the US, Canada, Singapore and Japan.

Latara

NR

Cnr McDonalds Road/Deaseys Road, Pokolbin, NSW 2320 **REGION** Lower Hunter Valley
T (02) 4998 7320 **OPEN** Sat 9–5, Sun 9–4
WINEMAKER Brokenwood **EST.** 1979 **CASES** 250
The bulk of the grapes produced on the 6-ha Latara vineyard, which was planted in 1979, are sold to Brokenwood. As one would expect, the wines are very competently made, and are of show medal standard.

🐦 Laughing Jack

★★★★★

Cnr Parbs Road/Boundry Road, Greenock, SA 5360 **REGION** Barossa Valley
T 0427 396 928 **F** (08) 8562 8607 **www**.laughingjackwines.com **OPEN** By appt
WINEMAKER Mick Schroeter, Shawn Kalleske **EST.** 1999 **CASES** 1200
The Kalleske family has many branches in the Barossa Valley. Laughing Jack is owned by Shawn, Nathan and Helen, Ian and Carol Kalleske, and Mick and Linda Schroeter. They have just under 35 ha of vines, the lion's share to shiraz (22 ha), with lesser amounts of semillon, chardonnay, riesling and grenache. Vine age varies considerably, with old dry-grown shiraz the jewel in the crown. A small part of the shiraz production is taken for the Laughing Jack Shiraz. As any Australian knows, the kookaburra (a native member of the kingfisher family) is known as the laughing jackass, and there is a resident flock of kookaburras in the stands of blue and red gum eucalypts surrounding the vineyards.

🍷🍷🍷🍷🍷 **Shiraz 2002** Retaining hue well; medium- to full-bodied; highly focused black fruits, with touches of licorice and chocolate; exceptional length, and balanced tannins and oak. Cork. 14.5° alc. **RATING** 96 **DRINK** 2015 **$** 34
Shiraz 2004 Deep, dense purple-red; full-bodied; extremely rich, concentrated and dense blackberry, plum, licorice and bitter chocolate fruit; good oak and tannins; controlled alcohol. Cork. 14.6° alc. **RATING** 95 **DRINK** 2014

🍷🍷🍷🍷🍷 **Shiraz 2003** A complex mix of confit black fruits, plum and quality oak; the tannins expressive but balanced; excellent outcome for the '03 vintage. Cork. 14.5° alc. **RATING** 93 **DRINK** 2013

Laurance of Margaret River

★★★☆

Lot 549 Caves Road, Wilyabrup, WA 6290 **REGION** Margaret River
T (08) 9755 6199 **F** (08) 9755 6276 **www**.laurancewines.com **OPEN** 7 days 11–5
WINEMAKER Naturaliste Vintners (Bruce Dukes) **EST.** 2001 **CASES** 4000
Dianne Laurance is the driving force of this family business, with husband Peter and son Brendon (plus wife Kerrianne) also involved. Brendon is vineyard manager, living on the property with his wife and family. The 40-ha property had 21 ha planted when it was purchased, and since its acquisition it has been turned into a showplace, with a rose garden to put that of Voyager Estate to shame. While the wine is made offsite by Bruce Dukes, a substantial wine storage facility has been built, and a new cellar door opened in 2005. But it is the tenpin bowling-shaped bottles which will gain the most attention — and doubtless secondary use as lamp stands. Exports to Singapore and Japan.

ȲȲȲȲ **Aussie Jeans Rock White 2005** Fully ripe tropical fruit; pineapple and banana; generous and fleshy. Provocative label. Semillon/Sauvignon Blanc. Screwcap. 13.3° alc. **RATING** 89 **DRINK** Now $ 20

White 2005 Chiefly driven by the Sauvignon Blanc and Semillon components; lively and quite intense lemon and citrus fruit; just a hint of stone fruit from the third component, Chardonnay. Cork. 13.5° alc. **RATING** 89 **DRINK** 2008 $ 27

Red 2003 Light- to medium-bodied; fresh red and black fruits; a pretty wine, with some fruit sweetness, but needing more structure for higher points. Cork. 13.5° alc. **RATING** 89 **DRINK** 2009 $ 30

Rose 2005 An extra $9 for the bowling pin bottle? Strawberries and, paradoxically, a fully dry style. Cork. 13° alc. **RATING** 88 **DRINK** Now $ 26

Aussie Jeans Rock Pink 2005 Well-made; small red fruits with some mineral notes; citrussy acidity, fresh finish. Screwcap. 13.3° alc. **RATING** 87 **DRINK** Now $ 17

ȲȲȲȲ **Aussie Jeans Rock Red 2004** **RATING** 86 **DRINK** 2008 $ 22

Laurel Bank ★★★★

130 Black Snake Lane, Granton, Tas 7030 **REGION** Southern Tasmania
T (03) 6263 5977 **F** (03) 6263 3117 **OPEN** By appt
WINEMAKER Winemaking Tasmania (Julian Alcorso) **EST.** 1987 **CASES** 850
Laurel (hence Laurel Bank) and Kerry Carland began planting their 3-ha vineyard in 1986. They delayed the first release of their wines for some years and (by virtue of the number of entries they were able to make) won the trophy for Most Successful Exhibitor at the 1995 Royal Hobart Wine Show. Things have settled down since; wine quality is solid and reliable.

ȲȲȲȲȲ **Dessert Riesling 2005** A quiet bouquet, but lovely intense palate, more late harvest than botrytis influence, perhaps. Acidity does poke out just a little. **RATING** 94 **DRINK** 2008 $ 18

ȲȲȲȲ **Sauvignon Blanc 2005** **RATING** 86 **DRINK** Now $ 18
Pinot Noir 2004 **RATING** 86 **DRINK** Now $ 24

🐚 Laurellyn Wines NR

'Laurellyn', Bolivia via Tenterfield, NSW 2372 **REGION** Northern Slopes Zone
T (02) 6737 3657 **F** (02) 6737 3657 **www**.laurellynwines.tenterfield.biz **OPEN** By appt only
WINEMAKER Blair Duncan, Shaun Cassidy, Scott Wright (Contract) **EST.** 1997 **CASES** NFP
Richard and Penny Clementson began the planting of their vineyard in 1997 with the intention of selling all but a small portion of the grapes, and have not deviated from that game plan. They have a little less than 1 ha each of sauvignon blanc, verdelho, pinot gris and shiraz, and slightly over 0.5 ha of chardonnay. The varietal mix has changed a little since 1994 with grafting of some of the shiraz to sauvignon blanc and chardonnay, which have proved well suited to the vineyard. The Laurellyn range includes Sauvignon Blanc Semillon, Sauvignon Blanc, Pinot Gris and Shiraz.

Lauren Brook NR

Eedle Terrace, Bridgetown, WA 6255 **REGION** Blackwood Valley
T (08) 9761 2676 **F** (08) 9761 1879 **www**.laurenbrook.com.au **OPEN** Fri–Wed 11–4.30
WINEMAKER Stephen Bullied **EST.** 1993 **CASES** 500
Lauren Brook is on the banks of the beautiful Blackwood River; an 80-year-old barn on the property has been renovated to contain a micro-winery and a small gallery. There is 1 ha of estate chardonnay, supplemented by grapes purchased locally.

Lawrence Victor Estate ★★★

Arthur Street, Penola, SA 5277 **REGION** Coonawarra
T (08) 8737 3572 **F** (08) 8739 7344 **www**.lawrencevictorestate.com.au **OPEN** Not
WINEMAKER Contract **EST.** 1994 **CASES** 1500
Lawrence Victor Estate is part of a large South Australian company principally engaged in harvesting and transport of plantation softwood. The company was established by Lawrence Victor Dohnt in 1932, and the estate has been named in his honour by the third generation of the family.

Though a small part of the group's activities, the plantings (principally contracted to Southcorp) are substantial, with 11 ha of shiraz and 20 ha of cabernet sauvignon established between 1994 and 1999. An additional 12 ha of cabernet sauvignon and 6 ha of pinot noir were planted in 2000.

ŦŦŦŦ **Cabernet Sauvignon 2002** Good varietal character; plenty of focus and length, though needs a tad more weight and structure. **RATING** 89 **DRINK** 2012 $ 18

ŦŦŦŦ **Shiraz 2003 RATING** 85 **DRINK** 2009 $ 15

Lawson Hill Estate   NR

Henry Lawson Drive, Eurunderee, Mudgee, NSW 2850 **REGION** Mudgee
T (02) 6373 3953 **F** (02) 6373 3948 **OPEN** Sat 10–5, Sun 10–1, public hols 10–3, or by appt
WINEMAKER Meerea Park **EST.** 1985 **CASES** 2500
The 5.6-ha Lawson Hill Estate vineyard was purchased from its founders by a group of business associates and friends in 2001. The cellar door takes advantage of the sweeping views out over the vineyards and to the west. A full varietal range is made by noted Hunter winemaker Rhys Eather.

Lazy River Estate   NR

29R Old Dubbo Road, Dubbo, NSW 2830 **REGION** Western Plains Zone
T (02) 6882 2111 **F** (02) 6882 2111 **WWW**.lazyriverestate.com.au **OPEN** By appt
WINEMAKER Briar Ridge **EST.** 1997 **CASES** 1400
The Scott family have planted 3 ha each of chardonnay and semillon, 1 ha of merlot, and 1.5 ha each of petit verdot and cabernet sauvignon. The property is a little under 3 km from the end of the main street of Dubbo.

Le 'Mins Winery   NR

40 Lemins Road, Waurn Ponds, Vic 3216 (postal) **REGION** Geelong
T (03) 5241 8168 **OPEN** Not
WINEMAKER Steve Jones **EST.** 1994 **CASES** 80
Steve Jones presides over 0.5 ha of pinot noir planted in 1998 to the MV6 clone, and 0.25 ha of the same variety planted 4 years earlier to Burgundy clone 114. The tiny production is made for Le 'Mins at Prince Albert Vineyard, and the wine is basically sold by word of mouth.

Leabrook Estate   ★★★★☆

24 Tusmore Avenue, Leabrook, SA 5068 (postal) **REGION** Adelaide Hills
T (08) 8331 7150 **F** (08) 8364 1520 **WWW**.leabrookestate.com **OPEN** By appt
WINEMAKER Colin Best **EST.** 1998 **CASES** 4500
With a background as an engineer, and having dabbled in home winemaking for 30 years, Colin Best took the plunge and moved into commercial scale winemaking in 1998. His wines are now to be found in a Who's Who of restaurants, and in some of the best independent wine retailers on the east coast. Best says 'I consider that my success is primarily due to the quality of my grapes, since they have been planted on a 1.2 x 1.2m spacing and very low yields.' I won't argue with that; he has also done a fine job in converting the grapes into wine. Exports to the UK, Singapore and Japan.

ŦŦŦŦŦ **Adelaide Hills Chardonnay 2004** Complex barrel ferment inputs into stone fruit and citrus fruit; a creamy mid-palate, then a fresh finish with balanced acidity. Screwcap. 13.5° alc. **RATING** 94 **DRINK** 2012 $ 27

ŦŦŦŦ **Three Region Shiraz 2004** Good colour; fragrant fruit aromas; a medium-bodied, synergistic blend with a nice mix of red fruits and subtle savoury notes. Adelaide Hills/Langhorne Creek/Adelaide Plains. Screwcap. 14.3° alc. **RATING** 92 **DRINK** 2014 $ 30

Reserve Adelaide Hills Pinot Noir 2002 The cool vintage and time in bottle has accentuated the foresty, stemmy notes, but there is also spicy fruit there through the long finish. Cork. 14.3° alc. **RATING** 91 **DRINK** 2009 $ 30
Adelaide Hills Sauvignon Blanc 2005 Stuffed full of sweet tropical fruit, unusual for Adelaide Hills and for the variety; points for flavour rather than finesse. Screwcap. 12.9° alc. **RATING** 90 **DRINK** Now $ 20

ŸŸŸŸ **Adelaide Hills Cabernet Franc 2004** Medium red; cedar, tobacco, leaf, spice, earth and berry all come through on the medium-bodied palate; distinctly savoury, yet neither green nor bitter. Screwcap. 14° alc. **RATING** 89 **DRINK** 2010 $ 24

Three Region Cabernet Sauvignon 2004 A medium-bodied mix of savoury and sweet fruit flavours; pleasant enough, though less synergy than with the Shiraz. Adelaide Hills/Langhorne Creek/Adelaide Plains. Screwcap. 14.5° alc. **RATING** 88 **DRINK** 2009 $ 30

Adelaide Hills Pinot Gris 2005 Pear, spice, musk; a powerful finish, seemingly with heat, although the alcohol is low. Screwcap. 13.2° alc. **RATING** 87 **DRINK** Now $ 25

ŸŸŸŸ **Adelaide Hills Merlot 2004** **RATING** 85 **DRINK** 2008 $ 24

Leasingham ★★★★★

7 Dominic Street, Clare, SA 5453 **REGION** Clare Valley
T (08) 8842 2555 **F** (08) 8842 3293 **WWW**.leasingham-wines.com.au **OPEN** Mon–Fri 8.30–5.30, w'ends 10–4
WINEMAKER Simon Osicka **EST.** 1893 **CASES** 70 000

Successive big-company ownerships and various peregrinations in labelling and branding have not resulted in any permanent loss of identity or quality. With a core of high-quality, aged vineyards to draw on, Leasingham is in fact going from strength to strength under Hardys' direction. The stentorian red wines take no prisoners, compacting densely rich fruit and layer upon layer of oak into every long-lived bottle; the Bin 7 Riesling often excels.

ŸŸŸŸŸ **Bin 7 Riesling 2005** A touch of spritz still to dissipate; lovely lime juice and passionfruit flavours, fine and intense; outstanding length. Screwcap. **RATING** 95 **DRINK** 2015 $ 18

Classic Clare Riesling 2005 Well-named; ultra classic Clare Valley style; has refined restraint, yet is extremely intense and long. Screwcap. 12.9° alc. **RATING** 95 **DRINK** 2015 $ 30

Classic Clare Cabernet Sauvignon 2002 Strong colour; has the full gamut of black fruits on the bouquet; a concentrated but not the least heavy palate, with excellent handling of 18 months in French oak. Cork. 14° alc. **RATING** 95 **DRINK** 2015 $ 47

ŸŸŸŸŸ **Bin 61 Clare Valley Shiraz 2002** Deep colour; attractive blackberry, dark chocolate and mocha aromas and flavours; good structure; fine, ripe tannins. Cork. **RATING** 93 **DRINK** 2012 $ 22

Bastion Shiraz Cabernet 2004 Rich, chunky, powerful blackcurrant fruit and substantial, ripe tannins. Gold medal National Wine Show '05. Ridiculously good value. Cork. 13.6° alc. **RATING** 93 **DRINK** 2019 $ 12

Bin 56 Clare Valley Cabernet Malbec 2001 A rich mix of blackcurrant, dark chocolate, earth and savoury tannins. Impressive overall structure. Cork. 14° alc. **RATING** 92 **DRINK** 2015 $ 22

Bastion Clare Valley Riesling 2004 Pale straw-green; spotlessly clean; lively lemon tingle fruit through the length of the palate; outstanding value. Screwcap. **RATING** 90 **DRINK** 2009 $ 13

Bin 61 Clare Valley Shiraz 2003 Strong colour; concentrated, ripe, confit black fruits then an unexpected dip on the back-palate; tannins good, however. Cork. 14° alc. **RATING** 90 **DRINK** 2013 $ 22

ŸŸŸŸ **Bastion Clare Valley Riesling 2005** Clean; generously flavoured, with a ripe, tropical/limefruit mix. Excellent value. Screwcap. 13° alc. **RATING** 89 **DRINK** 2008 $ 13

Classic Clare Sparkling Shiraz 1996 Development obvious in colour; a very complex wine; as always, oak aging of the base wine shows through, spoiling it for some. Needs to be matched with food. **RATING** 89 **DRINK** 2014 $ 47

Bastion Shiraz Cabernet 2002 Archetypal, if slightly rustic, Clare Valley style; a mix of blackberry, blackcurrant, earth and leather; soft tannins, good balance. Great value. Quality cork. **RATING** 88 **DRINK** 2010 $ 13

Leconfield ★★★☆

Riddoch Highway, Coonawarra, SA 5263 **REGION** Coonawarra
T (08) 8737 2326 **F** (08) 8737 2385 **www.**leconfieldwines.com **OPEN** Mon–Fri 9–5, w'ends & public hols 10–4.30
WINEMAKER Paul Gordon, Tim Bailey (Assistant) **EST.** 1974 **CASES** 15 000
A distinguished estate with a proud history. Long renowned for its Cabernet Sauvignon, its repertoire has steadily grown with the emphasis on single-variety wines. The style overall is fruit-rather than oak-driven. Exports to the UK, the US and other major markets.

TTTT **Coonawarra Cabernet Sauvignon 2003** Light- to medium-bodied; fresh cassis, blackcurrant and earth mix; gentle oak and extract. Screwcap. 13.5° alc. **RATING** 88 **DRINK** 2010 $ 29.95

TTT **Old Vines Coonawarra Riesling 2005** **RATING** 83 $ 20

LedaSwan ★★★

179 Memorial Avenue, Baskerville, WA 6065 **REGION** Swan Valley
T (08) 9296 0216 **www.**ledaswan.com.au **OPEN** 7 days 11–4.30
WINEMAKER Duncan Harris **EST.** 1998 **CASES** 250
LedaSwan claims to be the smallest winery in the Swan Valley. It uses organically grown grapes, partly coming from its own vineyard, and partly from contract-grown grapes; the intention is to move to 100% estate-grown in the future, from the 2 ha of estate vineyards. Duncan Harris moved from the coast to Baskerville in 1998, and retired from engineering in 2001 to become a full-time vintner and has won several awards. Tours of the underground cellar are offered, and there is an extensive range of back vintages on offer.

TTTT **Shiraz 2002** Light- to medium-bodied; spicy, savoury, earthy aromas and flavours; good length is the strong suit. Cork. 13° alc. **RATING** 87 **DRINK** 2009 $ 20

TTTY **Fleur de Madeline NV** **RATING** 85 **DRINK** Now $ 23

TTT **Chenin Blanc 2004** **RATING** 83 $ 18

Leeuwin Estate ★★★★★

Stevens Road, Margaret River, WA 6285 **REGION** Margaret River
T (08) 9759 0000 **F** (08) 9759 0001 **www.**leeuwinestate.com.au **OPEN** 7 days 10–4.30, Saturday evening dinner
WINEMAKER Paul Atwood **EST.** 1974 **CASES** 60 000
Leeuwin Estate's Chardonnay is, in my opinion, Australia's finest example, based on the wines of the last 20-odd vintages, and it is this wine alone which demands a 5-star rating for the winery. The Cabernet Sauvignon can be an excellent wine with great style and character in warmer vintages, and Shiraz has made an auspicious debut. Almost inevitably, the other wines in the portfolio are not in the same Olympian class, although the Prelude Chardonnay and Siblings Sauvignon Blanc are impressive at their lower price level. Exports to all major markets.

TTTTT **Art Series Chardonnay 2002** Shows yet again why this is the best Chardonnay in Australia; flawless and seamless balance and integration of all of the chardonnay-making techniques without imperilling the elegant stone fruit and melon running through an endless palate. Cork. 14.5° alc. **RATING** 97 **DRINK** 2015 $ 80

Prelude Vineyards Chardonnay 2004 Beautifully fragrant and spotlessly clean; fine grapefruit, melon and nectarine, with seamless oak. The best second label in the world? Screwcap. 14.5° alc. **RATING** 95 **DRINK** 2012 $ 30

Art Series Chardonnay 2003 Richer, deeper and fuller than most Art Series at this stage of its development; ripe stone fruit and melon fruit. Two bottles tasted; the second slightly tighter and racier than the other. Will develop more quickly than most. Cork. 14° alc. **RATING** 94 **DRINK** 2010 $ 91

Art Series Cabernet Sauvignon 2001 Strong colour; powerful, focused and concentrated blackcurrant and blackberry fruit, with lingering tannins to underwrite a long life. One of the very best ever under this label. Cork. 14° alc. **RATING** 94 **DRINK** 2016 $ 54

ŸŸŸŸŸ **Art Series Shiraz 2003** Bright red-purple; an elegant, medium-bodied array of cherry, plum and blackberry fruits; fine tannins and supporting oak. Screwcap. 13.5° alc. **RATING** 93 **DRINK** 2015 $ 34

Art Series Sauvignon Blanc 2005 Light straw-green; clean, precise, crisp mineral, gooseberry and citrus run through a fine and balanced palate. Screwcap. 12° alc. **RATING** 92 **DRINK** Now $ 32

Siblings Sauvignon Blanc Semillon 2005 Spotlessly clean; vibrantly fresh apple, gooseberry and lemon; lively finish. Screwcap. 12° alc. **RATING** 92 **DRINK** Now $ 22

Siblings Shiraz 2002 Very good colour; has considerable substance and texture; supple black fruits, excellent tannins and quality oak; long finish. Cork. 14.5° alc. **RATING** 92 **DRINK** 2015 $ 22

Art Series Riesling 2004 Clean and fragrant; a delicate mix of apple, lime and mineral with good length. As good as they come from the region. Screwcap. 12° alc. **RATING** 90 **DRINK** 2011 $ 23

ŸŸŸŸ **Prelude Vineyards Cabernet Merlot 2002** Unconvincing colour; light- to medium-bodied, with strongly savoury/earthy flavours, needing more flesh. Cork. 14° alc. **RATING** 87 **DRINK** 2008 $ 30

Leland Estate

NR

PO Lenswood, SA 5240 **REGION** Adelaide Hills
T (08) 8389 6928 **WWW**.lelandestate.com.au **OPEN** Not
WINEMAKER Robb Cootes **EST.** 1986 **CASES** 1000
Former Yalumba senior winemaker Robb Cootes, with a Master of Science degree, opted out of mainstream life when he established Leland Estate, living in a split-level, 1-roomed house built from timber salvaged from trees killed in the Ash Wednesday bushfires. The Sauvignon Blanc is usually good. Exports to the US, Canada and Japan.

Lengs & Cooter

24 Lindsay Terrace, Belair, SA 5042 **REGION** Southeast Australia
T (08) 8278 3998 **F** (08) 8278 3998 **WWW**.lengscooter.com.au **OPEN** Not
WINEMAKER Contract **EST.** 1993 **CASES** 8000
Karel Lengs and Colin Cooter began making wine as a hobby in the early 1980s. Each had (and has) a full-time occupation outside the wine industry, and it was all strictly for fun. One thing has led to another, and although they still possess neither vineyards nor what might truly be described as a winery, the wines graduated to big-boy status, winning gold medals at national wine shows and receiving critical acclaim from writers across Australia. Exports to the UK, Canada, Singapore and Malaysia.

ŸŸŸŸŸ **The Victor Shiraz 2004** Elegant, intensely spicy, peppery black fruits; fluid line and flow; fine tannins, good length. Screwcap. 14.5° alc. **RATING** 94 **DRINK** 2019 $ 18

ŸŸŸŸŸ **Watervale Riesling 2005** Generous, rich lime/citrus aromas and flavours; good balance, long finish; now or later. Screwcap. 12° alc. **RATING** 92 **DRINK** 2012 $ 17

Lenton Brae Wines

Wilyabrup Valley, Margaret River, WA 6285 **REGION** Margaret River
T (08) 9755 6255 **F** (08) 9755 6268 **WWW**.lentonbrae.com **OPEN** 7 days 10–6
WINEMAKER Edward Tomlinson **EST.** 1983 **CASES** NFP
Former architect and town planner Bruce Tomlinson built a strikingly beautiful winery which is now in the hands of winemaker son Edward, who makes elegant wines in classic Margaret River style. Exports to the UK, the US and Canada.

ŸŸŸŸŸ **Margaret River Sauvignon Blanc 2005** Strongly accented gooseberry and passionfruit aromas, verging on slightly sweaty; a powerful palate, full of varietal fruit. Multi gold medal winner. Screwcap. 12.5° alc. **RATING** 94 **DRINK** Now $ 20

Margaret River Chardonnay 2004 Light- to medium-bodied, elegant wine; perfect integration and balance of oak with nectarine/melon fruit; has lovely line and length. Screwcap. 14° alc. **RATING** 94 **DRINK** 2012 $ 36

🍷🍷🍷🍷♆ **Semillon Sauvignon Blanc 2005** Pale straw-green; spotlessly clean passionfruit, gooseberry and citrus aromas; in typically refined and elegant style; good length and balance. Screwcap. **RATING** 91 **DRINK** 2008 $ 19

Margaret River Cabernet Sauvignon 2002 Restrained style; light- to medium-bodied with a mix of blackcurrant, olive and cedary/savoury nuances. Gold medal Qantas West Australia Wine Show. Cork. 13.6° alc. **RATING** 91 **DRINK** 2012 $ 34

Margaret River Cabernet Merlot 2003 A medium-bodied, unforced style; blackcurrant and cassis fruit is supported by restrained oak and light, fine tannins. Screwcap. 13.5° alc. **RATING** 90 **DRINK** 2011 $ 22

Leo Buring

Tanunda Road, Nuriootpa, SA 5355 **REGION** Barossa Valley
T (08) 8560 9408 **F** (08) 8563 2804 **www**.leoburing.com.au **OPEN** Not
WINEMAKER Matthew Pick **EST.** 1931 **CASES** NFP
Australia's foremost producer of Rieslings over a 35-year period, with a rich legacy left by former winemaker John Vickery. After veering away from its core business with other varietal wines, has now been refocused as a specialist Riesling producer.

🍷🍷🍷🍷🍷 **Leonay DW117 Eden Valley Riesling 2005** Spice, mineral, lime and apple aromas; a wine of great finesse which caresses the mouth, with special, almost sweet, lime juice the mark of the region. Screwcap. 13° alc. **RATING** 96 **DRINK** 2020 $ 32.99

Eden Valley Riesling 2005 Fragrant lime blossom and spice; vibrant, fresh and intense lime and lemon fruit; crisp finish; overall finesse and delicacy. Screwcap. **RATING** 95 **DRINK** 2015 $ 17.99

Maturation Reserve Eden Valley Riesling 1999 Bright green-gold; much finer and tighter than the '97, though shares the lime, lemon and toast; bright acidity; very good length and line. Cork. **RATING** 95 **DRINK** 2009 $ 27.50

Maturation Reserve Eden Valley Riesling 1997 Developed green-gold; marvelously intense and complex lime essence and toast aromas; rich, mouthfilling and complete. Cork. **RATING** 95 **DRINK** Now $ 27.50

Maturation Reserve Clare Valley Riesling 1999 Fine toast and mineral aromas lead into an extremely fresh and crisp palate. Flavours of lime and herbs run through to a brisk finish, with excellent acidity. Cork. **RATING** 94 **DRINK** 2009 $ 27.50

🍷🍷🍷🍷♆ **Mount Barker Riesling 2005** Lime, spice, blossom and herb aromas; a lemon sherbet palate (lots of CO_2); for the long haul, and destined for higher points. Screwcap. 12.5° alc. **RATING** 91 **DRINK** 2015 $ 27.99

Clare Valley Riesling 2005 Quite rich tropical/pineapple aromas; abundant, fairly soft, fruit; ready now, though will hold. Screwcap. **RATING** 90 **DRINK** 2010 $ 17.99

Lerida Estate

The Vineyards, Old Federal Highway, Lake George, NSW 2581 **REGION** Canberra District
T (02) 4848 0231 **F** (02) 4848 0232 **www**.leridaestate.com **OPEN** 7 days 10–5, or by appt
WINEMAKER Malcolm Burdett, Sylvain Pabion **EST.** 1999 **CASES** 3000
Lerida Estate continues the planting of vineyards along the escarpment sloping down to Lake George. It is immediately to the south of the Lake George vineyard established by Edgar Riek 30 years ago. Inspired by Edgar Riek's success with pinot noir, Lerida founder Jim Lumbers planted 3.75 ha of pinot noir together with lesser amounts of pinot gris, chardonnay, shiraz, merlot, viognier and cabernet franc (7.4 ha total). The Glenn Murcutt-designed winery, barrel room and cellar door complex (available for weddings and other functions) has spectacular views over Lake George.

🍷🍷🍷🍷 **Lake George Chardonnay 2004** Quite developed colour; flavoursome melon, citrus and peach fruit; acidity balanced by a hint of sweetness. Screwcap. 13.5° alc. **RATING** 89 **DRINK** Now $ 24

Lake George Pinot Gris 2005 Light, crisp and lively; faint musk and pear aromas; nice low alcohol style. Screwcap. 12.8° alc. **RATING** 88 **DRINK** Now $ 26

ƟƟƟƟ **Lake George Shiraz Viognier 2004** Light colour; pleasant, light-bodied palate; well-balanced red fruits; not forced. Screwcap. 13.9° alc. **RATING** 86 **DRINK** Now $18

ƟƟƟ **Lake George Rose 2005 RATING** 83 $14

Lethbridge Wines ★★★★

74 Burrows Road, Lethbridge, Vic 3222 **REGION** Geelong
T (03) 5281 7279 **F** (03) 5281 7221 **WWW**.lethbridgewines.com **OPEN** Thurs–Sun & public hols 10.30–5, or by appt
WINEMAKER Ray Nadeson, Maree Collis **EST.** 1996 **CASES** 2500
Lethbridge was founded by three scientists: Ray Nadeson, Maree Collis and Adrian Thomas. In Ray Nadeson's words, 'Our belief is that the best wines express the unique character of special places'. As well as understanding the importance of *terroir*, the partners have built a unique straw-bale winery, designed for its ability to recreate the controlled environment of cellars and caves in Europe. Winemaking is no less ecological: hand-picking, indigenous yeast fermentations, small open fermenters, pigeage (foot-stamping) and minimal handling of the wine throughout the maturation process are all part and parcel of the highly successful Lethbridge approach.

ƟƟƟƟƟ **Menage a Noir 2004** Light- to medium-bodied; savoury, foresty, earthy style; good texture and length. **RATING** 91 **DRINK** 2009 $18
Shiraz 2004 Medium-bodied; smooth and supple, with excellent balance and flavour. **RATING** 90 **DRINK** 2010 $28

ƟƟƟƟ **Pinot Noir 2004** Medium-bodied; savoury, spicy style with nice weight and good balance. **RATING** 89 **DRINK** 2008 $28
Merlot 2004 A mix of confit dark fruit and more savoury/earthy varietal notes; the oak is still integrating. **RATING** 89 **DRINK** 2008 $35

ƟƟƟƟ **Allegra Chardonnay 2004 RATING** 86 **DRINK** 2008 $38
Indra Shiraz 2003 RATING 85 **DRINK** Now $38

Leura Park Estate ★★★★

1400 Portarlington Road, Curlewis, Vic 3222 **REGION** Geelong
T (03) 5253 3180 **F** (03) 5251 1262 **OPEN** W'ends 11–5
WINEMAKER De Bortoli (Steve Webber) **EST.** 1995 **CASES** 600
Stephen and Lisa Cross gained fame as restaurateurs in the 1990s, first at Touché and then at the outstanding Saltwater at Noosa Heads. They have established a very substantial vineyard, with 8 ha of chardonnay, over 3 ha each of pinot gris, pinot noir and sauvignon blanc, and 1 ha of shiraz. Most of the production is sold to De Bortoli, where the wines for the Leura Park label are made.

ƟƟƟƟƟ **25 d'Gris Pinot Gris 2005** Lively, fresh, zesty and zingy; good length and balance; minerally finish. **RATING** 93 **DRINK** Now $30
Shiraz 2005 Delicious; red and black fruits, warm spices, licorice, and soft, lingering tannins; good oak integration. Screwcap. 14.2° alc. **RATING** 93 **DRINK** 2013 $20

ƟƟƟƟ **Chardonnay 2003 RATING** 86 **DRINK** Now $23

Leven Valley Vineyard NR

321 Raymond Road, Gunns Plains, Tas 7315 **REGION** Northern Tasmania
T (03) 6429 1186 **F** (03) 6429 1369 **WWW**.levenvalleyvineyard.com.au **OPEN** Wed–Mon 10–5, Tues by appt
WINEMAKER Richard Richardson (Contract) **EST.** 1997 **CASES** 700
John and Wendy Weatherly have acquired the former Moonrakers Vineyard from Stephen and Diana Usher, and have changed the name, but otherwise left well alone. The vineyard consists of 0.5 ha each of chardonnay and pinot noir on a north-facing slope above the picturesque valley of Gunns Plains. The deep loam over limestone soil holds much promise.

Liebich Wein

Steingarten Road, Rowland Flat, SA 5352 **REGION** Barossa Valley
T (08) 8524 4543 **F** (08) 8524 4543 **WWW**.liebichwein.com.au **OPEN** Wed–Mon 11–5
WINEMAKER Ron Liebich **EST.** 1992 **CASES** 2500
Liebich Wein is Barossa Deutsch for 'Love I wine'. The Liebich family have been grapegrowers and
winemakers at Rowland Flat since 1919, with CW 'Darkie' Liebich one of the great local characters.
His nephew Ron began making wine in 1969, but it was not until 1992 that he and wife Janet began
selling wine under the Liebich Wein label. Exports to the US, the UK and Germany.

▼▼▼▼▼ **Leveret Barossa Valley Shiraz 2004** Dark but bright purple-red; a complex array of
aromas and flavours, carrying the alcohol with ease, seemingly only medium-bodied;
spice, blackberry, licorice, plum and dark chocolate; fine, savoury tannins. Screwcap.
15° alc. **RATING** 94 **DRINK** 2019 $ 23

🦔 Lightfoot & Sons

Myrtle Point Vineyard, 717 Calulu Road, Bairnsdale, Vic 3875 (postal) **REGION** Gippsland
T (03) 5156 9205 **OPEN** Not
WINEMAKER Dr Robert Brownlee **EST.** 1995 **CASES** 300
Brian and Helen Lightfoot have established just under 30 ha of pinot noir, shiraz, chardonnay,
cabernet sauvignon and merlot, the lion's share to pinot noir and shiraz. The soil bears a striking
resemblance to that of Coonawarra, with terra rossa over limestone on the edge of an escarpment.
The vines are irrigated courtesy of a licence allowing the Lightfoots to pump water from the Mitchell
River, and most of the grapes are sold (as originally planned) to other Gippsland winemakers. In
recent years, limited quantities of wine have been contract-made for them by Dr Robert Brownlee at
Azimuth Estate in Traralgon.

▼▼▼▼▼ **Myrtle Point Vineyard Shiraz 2004** High-quality wine; potent black fruits, with
powerful line and length; controlled oak and tannins. Trophy Best Red Wine of Show,
Gippsland Wine Show '06. **RATING** 94 **DRINK** 2014 $ 22

▼▼▼▼ **Myrtle Point Vineyard Pinot Noir 2004** Light colour; just a hint of development; on the
far side of ripeness, but hasn't lost all varietal character. Slightly earlier picking might have
been better. Cork. 14.3° alc. **RATING** 88 **DRINK** 2009 $ 22
Myrtle Point Vineyard Cabernet Sauvignon Merlot Shiraz 2004 Medium-bodied;
pleasant red and black fruits; slightly milky/soft tannins. **RATING** 87 **DRINK** 2009 $ 20

▼▼▼ **Myrtle Point Vineyard Chardonnay 2004** **RATING** 81 $ 22

Lighthouse Peak   NR

Tumbarumba–Khancohan Road, Bringenbrong, NSW 3707 **REGION** Tumbarumba
T 0500 524 444 **F** 0500 524 445 **OPEN** Not
WINEMAKER Kerry Potocky-Pacay **EST.** 1996 **CASES** NA
Ian Tayles has established a 2-ha vineyard on this historic road. It is planted to sauvignon blanc,
chardonnay, verdelho, pinot noir, cabernet sauvignon and merlot, and the wines are sold by mail
order.

Lilac Hill Estate   ★★★

55 Benara Road, Caversham, WA 6055 **REGION** Swan Valley
T (08) 9378 9945 **F** (08) 9378 9946 **WWW**.lilachillestate.com.au **OPEN** Tues–Sun 10.30–5.00
WINEMAKER Stephen Murfit **EST.** 1998 **CASES** 15 000
Lilac Hill Estate is part of the renaissance which is sweeping the Swan Valley. Just when it seemed it
would die a lingering death, supported only by Houghton, Sandalford and the remnants of the once
Yugoslav-dominated cellar door trade, wine tourism has changed the entire scene. Thus Lilac Hill
Estate, drawing in part upon 4 ha of estate vineyards, has already built a substantial business;
considerable contract winemaking fleshes out the business even further.

▼▼▼▽ **Cape White 2005** **RATING** 85 **DRINK** Now $ 13

Lillian ★★★★☆

Box 174, Pemberton, WA 6260 **REGION** Pemberton
T (08) 9776 0193 **F** (08) 9776 0193 **OPEN** Not
WINEMAKER John Brocksopp **EST.** 1993 **CASES** 400
Long-serving (and continuing consultant) viticulturist to Leeuwin Estate John Brocksopp established 3-ha of the Rhône trio of marsanne, roussanne and viognier and the south of France trio of shiraz, mourvedre and graciano (first vintage in 1998). The varietal mix may seem à la mode, but it in fact comes from John's early experience working for Seppelt at Barooga in NSW, and his formative years in the Barossa Valley. Exports to the UK.

ŸŸŸŸŸ Pemberton Marsanne 2004 A spotless bouquet; considerable fruit weight and intensity without compromising delicacy; honeysuckle, with touches of spice and musk; good finish and balance. Could develop into something quite special. Screwcap. 13.5° alc. **RATING** 92 **DRINK** 2009 $19

Lillico Wines ★★★

297 Copelands Road, Warragul, Vic 3820 **REGION** Gippsland
T (03) 5623 4231 **F** (03) 5623 4231 **WWW.**lillicowines.com.au **OPEN** Thurs–Sun & public hols 11–5, or by appt
WINEMAKER Various contract **EST.** 1998 **CASES** 450
Cattle farmer Robert and senior nurse Marie Young impulsively planted 1.7 ha of cabernet sauvignon on their property in 1998. Two years later they added 1.3 ha of pinot noir, and in the meantime Marie had completed a diploma of horticulture, specialising in viticulture, at Dookie College. The first commercial vintage of cabernet was sold, and encouraged by the quality of the wine made from their grapes, Marie and Rob decided to produce some of their own wine. She promptly enrolled in the diploma of wine technology course, and now makes the wines. The vineyard is run on a no-pesticide and non-residual chemical regime, and the vines are not irrigated. And just to make sure Marie isn't bored, she provides local food platters as an adjunct to the picnic area and barbecue facilities they have also established.

ŸŸŸŸ Gippsland Cabernet Sauvignon 2003 Firm, earthy, savoury, foresty, austere medium-bodied style; some black fruits; tannins help prolong the palate. Screwcap. 13.5° alc. **RATING** 87 **DRINK** 2010 $20

Lilliput Wines ★★★

Withers Road, Springhurst, Vic 3602 **REGION** Rutherglen
T (03) 5726 5055 **F** (03) 5726 5056 **WWW.**lilliputwines.com.au **OPEN** Fri–Sun, public hols or by appt
WINEMAKER Angelica Hellema **EST.** 2001 **CASES** 2000
Angelica and Pieter Hellema have painstakingly developed an 8-ha vineyard planted to cabernet sauvignon, merlot, shiraz, viognier and petit verdot, using only organic principles. Correspondingly, in the winery, only a small quantity of SO_2 is added. Open fermenters and a basket press are used. The name 'Lilliput Wines' dates back to the original crown land allotments (which were extremely small) and the presence of a large family headed by James Gullifer (9 of 16 children survived). In the 1870s there was a Lilliput Winery on the other side of the nearby creek.

ŸŸŸŸ Gullifer's Syrah 2003 A medium-bodied wine which opens with red and black fruits before savoury, earthy tannins take over on the finish. Cork. 15° alc. **RATING** 87 **DRINK** 2009 $16

ŸŸŸ Gullifer's Late Harvest Syrah 2005 **RATING** 83 $16
Gullifer's Merlot 2003 **RATING** 81 $16

Lillydale Estate ★★★★★

45 Davross Court, Seville, Vic 3139 **REGION** Yarra Valley
T (03) 5964 2016 **F** (03) 5964 3009 **WWW.**mcwilliams.com.au **OPEN** 7 days 11–5
WINEMAKER Jim Brayne, Max McWilliam **EST.** 1975 **CASES** NFP
Acquired by McWilliam's Wines in 1994; Max McWilliam is in charge of the business. With a number of other major developments, notably Coonawarra and Barwang, on its plate, McWilliam's has adopted a softly, softly approach to Lillydale Estate.

ΥΥΥΥΥ **Yarra Valley Chardonnay 2004** Delicately fragrant citrus blossom bouquet; stylish and elegant palate with all the hallmark Yarra Valley length; oak barely obvious. Will age superbly. Screwcap. **RATING** 95 **DRINK** 2012 $ 22

Yarra Valley Shiraz 2003 Bright purple-red; red and black cherry and spice aromas and flavours; a fine, medium-bodied palate, revelling in the low alcohol. Screwcap. 12.5° alc. **RATING** 94 **DRINK** 2013 $ 30

ΥΥΥΥΥ **Yarra Valley Gewurztraminer 2004** Very tight, crisp and crunchy, with vibrant acidity, and good length. So far so good, but you do have to go searching to find the varietal character in the faint rose petal and spice. Screwcap. 10.5° alc. **RATING** 92 **DRINK** 2013 $ 19

ΥΥΥΥ **Yarra Valley Sauvignon Blanc 2005** Pale straw-green; spotlessly clean, light-bodied; mineral and herb, not much density to the fruit; clean finish. Screwcap. 12.5° alc. **RATING** 87 **DRINK** Now $ 19

Yarra Valley Pinot Noir 2004 Light, fresh, strawberry and cherry fruit with touches of spice; good varietal character, but lacks concentration. Screwcap. **RATING** 87 **DRINK** Now $ 30

Lillypilly Estate ★★★☆

Lillypilly Road, Leeton, NSW 2705 **REGION** Riverina
T (02) 6953 4069 **F** (02) 6953 4980 **WWW**.lillypilly.com **OPEN** Mon–Sat 10–5.30, Sun by appt
WINEMAKER Robert Fiumara **EST.** 1982 **CASES** 10 000
Botrytised white wines are by far the best from Lillypilly, with the Noble Muscat of Alexandria unique to the winery; these wines have both style and intensity of flavour and can age well. However, table wine quality is always steady. Exports to the UK, the US and Canada.

ΥΥΥΥ **Lexia 2005** Amazingly perfumed grape essence on the bouquet; lots of flavour in the mouth, but needs more acidity to provide better balance. Screwcap. 10° alc. **RATING** 87 **DRINK** Now $ 14

ΥΥΥΥ **Chardonnay 2005** Plenty of gentle yellow peach fruit and mouthfeel; drink asap. Screwcap. 14.5° alc. **RATING** 86 **DRINK** Now $ 14

Tramillon® 2005 A consistent style over the decades; traminer spice and lychee drives the off-dry finish. Gewurztraminer/Semillon. Screwcap. 12.5° alc. **RATING** 86 **DRINK** Now $ 13

Red Velvet 2005 **RATING** 84 **DRINK** Now $ 13

ΥΥΥ **Gypsy Rose 2004** **RATING** 83 $ 14

Lilyvale Wines ★★★

Riverton Road, via Texas, Qld 4385 **REGION** Darling Downs
T 0405 132 507 **F** (07) 3391 3903 **WWW**.lilyvalewines.com **OPEN** By appt 10–4
WINEMAKER Hunter Wine Services (John Hordern), Peter Scudamore-Smith MW (Contract) **EST.** 1997 **CASES** 4000
Yet another new but substantial winery in Qld. It has established 5 ha each of shiraz and chardonnay, 3 ha of cabernet sauvignon, around 2.5 ha each of semillon and verdelho, and 1.5 ha of merlot. The vineyard is situated near the Dumaresq River on the border between Qld and NSW. The wines are made under the direction of Peter Scudamore-Smith MW, who has also been responsible for a marketing alliance with Jimbour wines. Exports to the US, Canada, Singapore and Japan.

ΥΥΥΥ **Texas Gold Late Harvest Semillon 2004** Golden yellow; rich, honeyed peach fruit; good acidity, nice example. Cork. 12.5° alc. **RATING** 87 **DRINK** 2008 $ 16

ΥΥΥΥ **Texas Chardonnay 2004** Developed yellow; soft yellow peach fruit and slightly chunky oak. Screwcap. 13.5° alc. **RATING** 86 **DRINK** Now $ 20

Watson's Crossing Chardonnay Semillon 2004 Semillon has helped to keep the structure and flavour fresh; mixed stone fruit and more mineral/herb. Screwcap. 13.5° alc. **RATING** 86 **DRINK** Now $ 15

Texas Shiraz 2003 Well-made, but the fruit has its limitations; savoury/leafy/minty/earthy nuances. Screwcap. 13.5° alc. **RATING** 86 **DRINK** 2008 $ 20

ΥΥΥ **Watson's Crossing Cabernet Merlot 2003** **RATING** 83 $ 15

Limb Vineyards

NR

PO Box 145, Greenock, SA 5360 **REGION** Barossa Valley
T 0419 846 549 **F** (08) 8347 7484 **OPEN** Not
WINEMAKER Contract **EST.** 1997 **CASES** NA
Julie Limb manages the business, based on 15 ha of cabernet sauvignon, shiraz and mourvedre. The wines are contract-made, the principal market being the US; they are available by mail order within Australia.

Limbic

★★★★☆

295 Morrison Road, Pakenham Upper, Vic 3810 **REGION** Port Phillip Zone
T (03) 5942 7723 **F** (03) 5942 7723 **OPEN** By appt
WINEMAKER Michael Pullar **EST.** 1997 **CASES** 600
Jennifer and Michael Pullar have established a vineyard on the hills between Yarra Valley and Gippsland, overlooking the Mornington Peninsula and Westernport Bay (thus entitled only to the Port Phillip Zone appellation). They have planted 3.1 ha of pinot noir, 1.8 ha of chardonnay and 1.3 ha of sauvignon blanc, increasingly using organic and thereafter biodynamic practices. Trial vintages under the Limbic label commenced in 2001, followed by the first commercial releases in 2003. A winery and cellar door have been constructed, and the 2005 vintage was made onsite. 'Limbic' is the word for a network of neural pathways in the brain that link smell, taste and emotion.

♥♥♥♥♥ **Sauvignon Blanc 2005** Elegant and fragrant (a ghost of reduction); a long and lively palate with passionfruit and gooseberry leading to a clean, vibrant finish. Screwcap. 12.8° alc. **RATING** 94 **DRINK** 2008 $24

♥♥♥♥♡ **Chardonnay 2004** In winery style, fresh and elegant; light- to medium-bodied grapefruit and nectarine; subtle oak, good length and persistence. Diam. 13.5° alc. **RATING** 92 **DRINK** 2010 $36

♥♥♥♥ **Pinot Noir 2004** Very light colour and concomitantly light-bodied; spice, forest and a touch of red fruits; a product of the big berry, big bunch vintage. Diam. 13.5° alc. **RATING** 87 **DRINK** 2008 $36

Lindemans (Coonawarra/Padthaway)

★★★★☆

Memorial Drive, Coonawarra, SA 5263 **REGION** Coonawarra
T (08) 8737 2613 **F** (08) 8737 2959 **WWW**.lindemans.com.au **OPEN** Not
WINEMAKER Brett Sharpe **EST.** 1908 **CASES** NFP
Lindemans' Limestone Coast vineyards are of increasing significance because of the move towards regional identity in the all-important export markets, which has led to the emergence of a range of regional/varietal labels. Exports to all major markets.

♥♥♥♥♡ **Limestone Ridge 2001** Medium- to full red-purple; a rich and substantial palate with blackberry, blackcurrant and mulberry; the tannins, oak and fruit seamlessly interwoven. Cork. 13.5° alc. **RATING** 93 **DRINK** 2015 $50
Pyrus 2000 Holding hue well; elegant cedary, savoury, cigar box aromas; very different fruit register and texture; fine, savoury tannins and good oak. Has developed well over the past 2 years. **RATING** 92 **DRINK** 2012 $50
Rouge Homme Cabernet Merlot 2004 Attractive cassis and blackcurrant on a supple, smooth, medium-bodied palate; fine, ripe tannins. **RATING** 90 **DRINK** 2010 $16
St George 2001 Blackcurrant, chocolate and earth; positive, cedary French oak adds a touch of sweetness; fine tannins. Cork. **RATING** 90 **DRINK** 2013 $42

♥♥♥♥ **Rouge Homme Chardonnay 2005** A touch of funky/leesy character on the bouquet works quite well; elegant and long; nectarine, grapefruit and citrus; subtle oak, good value. Screwcap. **RATING** 89 **DRINK** Now $13.99
Rouge Homme Cabernet Sauvignon 2004 A well-structured and balanced medium-bodied palate; regional earthy notes to blackcurrant fruit; gentle, ripe tannins. Quality cork. **RATING** 89 **DRINK** 2010 $13.99
Reserve Padthaway Shiraz 2004 Juicy damson plum, blackberry and raspberry flavours; medium-bodied, with a flick of vanilla oak. Synthetic. **RATING** 88 **DRINK** Now $12.99

Lindemans (Hunter Valley)

★★★☆

McDonalds Road, Pokolbin, NSW 2320 **REGION** Lower Hunter Valley
T (02) 4998 7684 **F** (02) 4998 7324 **WWW**.lindemans.com.au **OPEN** 7 days 10–5
WINEMAKER Wayne Falkenberg, Greg Clayfield **EST.** 1843 **CASES** NFP
One way or another, I have intersected with the Hunter Valley in general and Lindemans in particular for almost 50 years. The wines are no longer made in the Lower Hunter, and the once mighty Semillon is a mere shadow of its former self. However, the refurbished historic Ben Ean winery (while no longer making wine) is a must-see for the wine tourist.

▼▼▼▼ **Hunter Valley Semillon 2004** Bin 0455. Clean, fresh and lively; herb, grass and hints of melon; well-balanced and plenty of flavour; early developing notwithstanding. From hand-picked, 80-year-old vines. Screwcap. **RATING** 89 **DRINK** 2010 $ 19.95
Hunter River Shiraz 2004 Bin 0403. Firm, clean and fresh; blackberry and red cherry mix; somewhat singular, but should develop more complexity with age. Minimal oak influence. Screwcap. **RATING** 88 **DRINK** 2012 $ 19.95
Hunter Valley Chardonnay 2005 Bin 0581. Pleasant, light- to medium-bodied white peach and fig fruit; minimal oak backdrop. Screwcap. 13° alc. **RATING** 87 **DRINK** 2008 $ 20

▼▼▼▽ **Reserve Verdelho 2005 RATING** 86 **DRINK** 2008 $ 15.50

Lindemans (Karadoc)

★★★

Edey Road, Karadoc via Red Cliffs, Vic 3496 **REGION** Murray Darling
T (03) 5051 3333 **F** (03) 5051 3390 **WWW**.lindemans.com.au **OPEN** 7 days 10–4.30
WINEMAKER Wayne Falkenberg **EST.** 1974 **CASES** 8 million
Now the production centre for all the Lindemans and Leo Buring wines, with the exception of special lines made in Coonawarra. The very large winery allows all-important economies of scale, and is the major processing centre for Southcorp's beverage wine sector (casks, flagons and low-priced bottles). Its achievement in making several million cases of Bin 65 Chardonnay a year is extraordinary given the quality and consistency of the wines. Exports to all major markets.

▼▼▼▼ **Bin 55 Shiraz Cabernet 2004** A clean and fresh array of red and black fruits; fine tannins, minimal oak; drink soon. Synthetic. **RATING** 87 **DRINK** Now $ 8.99
Reserve South Australia Cabernet Sauvignon 2003 Entirely fruit-driven; soft, juicy, ripe blackcurrant and mulberry fruits; ready right now. Synthetic. **RATING** 87 **DRINK** Now $ 12.99

▼▼▼▽ **Reserve South Australia Chardonnay 2004 RATING** 86 **DRINK** Now $ 12.99
Bin 95 Sauvignon Blanc 2005 RATING 85 **DRINK** Now $ 8.99
Bin 65 Chardonnay 2005 RATING 84 **DRINK** Now $ 8.99
Bin 50 Shiraz 2005 RATING 84 **DRINK** Now $ 8.99

▼▼▼ **Bin 35 Rose 2005 RATING** 83 $ 8.99

Lindenderry at Red Hill

NR

142 Arthurs Seat Road, Red Hill, Vic 3937 **REGION** Mornington Peninsula
T (03) 5989 2933 **F** (03) 5989 2936 **WWW**.lindenderry.com.au **OPEN** 7 days 11–5
WINEMAKER Paringa Estate **EST.** 1999 **CASES** 1500
Lindenderry at Red Hill is a sister operation to Lancemore Hill in the Macedon Ranges and Lindenwarrah at Milawa. It has a 5-star country house hotel, conference facilities, a function area, day spa and à la carte restaurant on 16 ha of park-like gardens, but also has a little over 3 ha of vineyards, planted equally to pinot noir and chardonnay 10 years ago. The wines are made by the famed Lindsay McCall, using similar techniques to those he uses for his estate wines.

Lindenton Wines ★★★★

102 High Street, Heathcote, Vic 3523 **REGION** Heathcote
T (03) 5433 3246 **F** (03) 5433 3246 **OPEN** 7 days 10–4 by appt
WINEMAKER Adrian Munari, Greg Dedman (Contract) **EST.** 2003 **CASES** 2000
Jim Harrison established Lindenton Wines as a semi-retirement occupation. His business plan is based on the purchase of grapes from smaller growers in the region who do not have access to winemaking facilities or outlets for their fruit. Right from the word go there has been an extensive range of wines available, running through Verdelho, Chardonnay, Viognier, Marsanne, Merlot, Shiraz, Shiraz Viognier and a top-of-the-tree Melange. Harrison's longer range plan is to make the wines himself.

ŢŢŢŢŢ **Heathcote Merlot 2004** Good purple-red hue; fully ripened, but not over-ripe, luscious black fruits; good tannins and oak. Not particularly varietal, but a very nice wine. Screwcap. 13.8° alc. **RATING** 91 **DRINK** 2014 $18
Valley View Shiraz 2004 Curiously, better colour than the Ridge Estate; medium- to full-bodied, with attractive licorice, blackberry and dark chocolate; good tannin support. Screwcap. 14° alc. **RATING** 90 **DRINK** 2012 $20

ŢŢŢŢ **Ridge Estate Shiraz 2004** Medium-bodied blackberry and plum with a viognier lift; back-palate sweetness seems to show too much viognier (though only 5%). Screwcap. 14.4° alc. **RATING** 89 **DRINK** 2010 $24
Heathcote Chardonnay 2005 Clean, light and fresh; gentle melon and nectarine fruit, with lemony acidity. Screwcap. 13.4° alc. **RATING** 88 **DRINK** 2008 $16.50
Heathcote Melange 2003 Medium-bodied; sweet, slightly confit fruits, with notes of spice and mocha; soft tannins. Screwcap. 14.2° alc. **RATING** 88 **DRINK** 2010 $25
Heathcote Viognier 2004 Rich, ripe apricot and peach aroma and flavour; the alcohol sweetness is not over the top. Screwcap. 14.3° alc. **RATING** 87 **DRINK** Now $22

ŢŢŢŢ **Reserve Heathcote Shiraz 2003** **RATING** 86 **DRINK** 2008 $22
Heathcote Marsanne 2004 **RATING** 85 **DRINK** Now $18
Heathcote Shiraz 2003 **RATING** 85 **DRINK** 2008 $18

ŢŢŢ **Heathcote Verdelho 2005** **RATING** 83 $16.50

Lindrum NR

c/- Level 29, Chifley Tower, 2 Chifley Square, Sydney, NSW 2000 (postal) **REGION** Riverina
T (02) 9375 2185 **F** (02) 9375 2121 **WWW**.lindrum.com **OPEN** Not
WINEMAKER Beelgara Estate **EST.** 2001 **CASES** 650 000
The Lindrum story is a fascinating one; few Australians will not have heard of Walter Lindrum, who reigned as World Professional Billiards and Snooker Champion for over 30 years. What few would know is that his great-grandfather, Frederick Wilhelm von Lindrum, was a renowned vigneron in Norwood, SA, and also became Australia's first professional billiards champion, beating the English champion, John Roberts, in 1869. Lindrum has migrated from Langhorne Creek to the Riverina, where 40 local growers supply 10 000 tonnes of grapes a year, which is made at Beelgara Estate.

Linfield Road Wines ★★★★

PO Box 6, Williamstown, SA 5351 **REGION** Barossa Valley
T (08) 8524 6140 **F** (08) 8524 6427 **WWW**.annandalevineyards.com.au **OPEN** Not
WINEMAKER Rod Chapman (Contract), Steve Wilson, Deb Wilson **EST.** 2002 **CASES** 2000
The Wilson family has been growing grapes at their estate vineyard for over 100 years; Steve and Deb Wilson are the fourth generation of Wilson vignerons. The vineyard is in one of the coolest parts of the Barossa Valley, in an elevated position near the Adelaide Hills boundary. The estate's 19 ha are planted to riesling, cabernet sauvignon, semillon, shiraz, merlot, grenache and chardonnay. In 2002 the Wilsons decided to vinify part of the production. Within 12 months of the release of the first wines under the Linfield Road label, the wines had accumulated three trophies and five gold medals.

ŢŢŢŢŢ **Barossa Valley Cabernet Shiraz 2004** Good red-purple; substantial weight and texture; a mix of blackcurrant, blackberry and ripe tannins; good oak. Cork. 13.5° alc. **RATING** 90 **DRINK** 2014 $22

ŸŸŸŸ **Barossa Valley Shiraz 2004** Light- to medium-bodied; leather, spice and red and black fruits; pleasant, but lacks the concentration of most of the '04s. Cork. 14.5° alc. **RATING** 88 **DRINK** 2010 $ 25

Barossa Valley Cabernet Sauvignon 2004 Medium red; light- to medium-bodied, savoury, earthy blackcurrant and a touch of cassis; balanced tannins. Cork. 13.5° alc. **RATING** 88 **DRINK** 2012 $ 19

Barossa Valley Chardonnay 2004 Clean bouquet; a fruit-driven nectarine and citrus palate; does shorten slightly on the finish, but suffers neither from phenolics or excess alcohol. Screwcap. 12.5° alc. **RATING** 87 **DRINK** 2008 $ 12

Lirralirra Estate

15 Paynes Road, Chirnside Park, Vic 3116 **REGION** Yarra Valley
T (03) 9735 0224 **F** (03) 9735 0224 **OPEN** W'ends & hols 10–6
WINEMAKER Alan Smith **EST.** 1981 **CASES** 400
Alan Smith started Lirralirra with the intention of specialising in a Sauternes-style blend of botrytised semillon and sauvignon blanc. It seemed a good idea — in a sense it still does on paper — but it simply didn't work. He has changed direction to a more conventional mix with dignity and humour.

ŸŸŸŸŸ **Reserve Pinot Noir 2004** Good purple-red; exceptional intensity and drive for the vintage; complex plum and spice fruit; great balance. Screwcap. **RATING** 94 **DRINK** 2011 $ 30

ŸŸŸŸ♀ **Cabernets 2002** Retains good hue and depth; more power and concentration from the low-yielding, cool vintage. Is not green; will be long-lived. Screwcap. 13° alc. **RATING** 92 **DRINK** 2015 $ 25

Cabernets 2004 Light- to medium-bodied; gently sweet, cassis and berry fruit; balanced tannins and judicious oak; nice, unforced style. Screwcap. 13.5° alc. **RATING** 91 **DRINK** 2014 $ 22.50

Cabernets 2003 Light- to medium-bodied; while the origin of the grapes is entirely different from the '04, similar handling techniques in the winery have resulted in a wine of similar style, and slightly more fruit weight. Screwcap. **RATING** 91 **DRINK** 2013 $ 25

Shiraz 2004 Purple-red; light- to medium-bodied; bright, fresh spicy cherry and blood plum fruit; fine tannins. Screwcap. **RATING** 90 **DRINK** 2013 $ 23

Little Brampton Wines

PO Box 61, Clare, SA 5453 **REGION** Clare Valley
T (08) 8843 4201 **F** (08) 8843 4244 **WWW**.littlebramptonwines.com.au **OPEN** By appt
WINEMAKER Contract **EST.** 2001 **CASES** 800
Little Brampton Wines is a boutique, family-owned business operated by Alan and Pamela Schwarz. They purchased their 24-ha property in the heart of the Clare Valley in the early 1990s; Alan graduated from Roseworthy in 1981. The property has produced grapes since the 1860s, but the vineyard had been removed during the Vine Pull Scheme of the 1980s. The Schwarzes have replanted 10 ha to riesling, shiraz and cabernet sauvignon on northwest slopes at 520m; a small proportion of the production is vinified for the Little Brampton label.

ŸŸŸŸŸ **Riesling 2005** Light straw-green; a clean bouquet; attractive lime/grapefruit/lemon aromas and flavours; good line and, particularly, length. Screwcap. 12.9° alc. **RATING** 94 **DRINK** 2015 $ 18

Little Bridge

PO Box 499, Bungendore, NSW 2621 **REGION** Canberra District
T (02) 6251 5242 **F** (02) 6251 4379 **WWW**.littlebridgewines.com.au **OPEN** Not
WINEMAKER Canberra Winemakers (Greg Gallagher, Rob Howell) **EST.** 1996 **CASES** 1000
Little Bridge is a partnership between long-term friends John Leyshon, Rowland Clark, John Jeffrey and Steve Dowton. The partnership was formed in 1996, and 2 ha of chardonnay, pinot noir, riesling and merlot were planted in 1997 on Rowland Clark's property at Butmaroo, near Bungendore, at an

altitude of 860m. In 2004 a further 2.5 ha of shiraz, cabernet sauvignon, sangiovese, grenache and gamay were planted on John Leyshon's property near Yass (560m). Canberra Winemakers make the white wines, and the reds are by the partners at Bungendore.

 TTTTY **Chardonnay 2004** Clean bouquet; ripe melon fruit with attractive creamy/nutty notes, good line, low alcohol a pleasure. Well-made. Screwcap. 12° alc. **RATING** 91 **DRINK** 2008 $15

Riesling 2005 Firm structure, persistent palate; a mix of citrus/grapefruit, apple and mineral; dry finish. Screwcap. 12.5° alc. **RATING** 90 **DRINK** 2008 $18

TTTT **Merlot 2004** Light- to medium-bodied; a fresh mix of red fruits, black olive and spice; minimal tannins and oak, but has good balance and mouthfeel. Screwcap. 13.5° alc. **RATING** 89 **DRINK** 2009 $20

Cabernet Sauvignon 2004 Hue good though not deep; a lot in common with the Merlot, with a mix of sweet and more leafy/earthy characters. Screwcap. 14.5° alc. **RATING** 88 **DRINK** 2009 $20

Little River Estate
NR

c/- 147 Rankins Road, Kensington, Vic 3031 (postal) **REGION** Upper Goulburn
T 0418 381 722 **OPEN** Not
WINEMAKER Philip Challen, Oscar Rosa, Nick Arena **EST.** 1986 **CASES** 250
Philip (a chef and hotelier) and Christine Challen began the establishment of their vineyard in 1986 with the planting of 0.5 ha of cabernet sauvignon. Several years later, 2 ha of chardonnay (and a few vines of pinot noir) followed. Vineyard practice and soil management are based on organic principles; there are low yields, notwithstanding the age of the vines.

Little River Wines
NR

Cnr West Swan Road/Forest Road, Henley Brook, WA 6055 **REGION** Swan Valley
T (08) 9296 4462 **F** (08) 9296 1022 **WWW**.littleriverwinery.com **OPEN** 7 days 10–5
WINEMAKER Bruno de Tastes **EST.** 1934 **CASES** 3000
The former Glenalwyn has as its winemaker the eponymously named Count Bruno de Tastes; the wines come from 4 ha of estate vineyards. Exports to Hong Kong and Malaysia.

Little Valley
NR

RMB 6047, One Chain Road, Merricks North, Vic 3926 **REGION** Mornington Peninsula
T (03) 5989 7564 **F** (03) 5989 7564 **OPEN** By appt
WINEMAKER Moorooduc Estate **EST.** 1998 **CASES** 600
Wesley College teacher Sue Taylor and part-time Anglican minister husband Brian have planted 0.8 ha each of chardonnay and pinot noir on their Little Valley property, and built their house there. Ian MacRae is consultant viticulturist, and Rick McIntyre makes the wines. The Mornington Peninsula is a beautiful place, and the Little Valley property itself a prime example of that beauty, providing a return which cannot be measured in dollars and cents.

Littles
 ★★★★☆

Cnr Palmers Lane/McDonalds Road, Pokolbin, NSW 2321 **REGION** Lower Hunter Valley
T (02) 4998 7626 **F** (02) 4998 7867 **WWW**.littleswinery.com.au **OPEN** Fri–Mon 10–4.30
WINEMAKER Scott Stephens (Contract) **EST.** 1984 **CASES** 6000
Littles is managed by the Kindred family, the ownership involving a number of investors. The winery has mature vineyards planted to shiraz (3.3 ha), semillon (3.1 ha), chardonnay (2.4 ha), pinot noir (1.5 ha), cabernet sauvignon (1.3 ha) and marsanne (1 ha).

TTTTT **Semillon Sauvignon Blanc 2005** Spotlessly clean; a synergistic blend of the delicacy of Hunter Valley Semillon and the fragrant gooseberry, tropical fruit of Orange Sauvignon Blanc. Excellent outcome. Screwcap. 12.5° alc. **RATING** 94 **DRINK** 2008 $16

▼▼▼▼♀ **Hunter Valley Chardonnay 2005** An elegant, fine wine with good focus and intensity to the melon and stone fruit flavours; subtle oak throughout. Screwcap. 13.5° alc. **RATING** 92 **DRINK** 2010 $ 18

Hunter Valley Semillon 2005 A crisp, clean bouquet; elegant and lively lemony fruit, then a clean, lingering finish. Screwcap. 11.5° alc. **RATING** 91 **DRINK** 2012 $ 16

▼▼▼▼ **Hunter Valley Reserve Shiraz 2000** Regional earthy characters starting to emerge; spicy edges to plum cake fruit flavours; fully mature, but will hold. Cork. 13° alc. **RATING** 89 **DRINK** 2010 $ 22

Hunter Valley Unwooded Chardonnay 2005 Straightforward but attractively lively stone fruit and citrus flavours; good length. Screwcap. 13° alc. **RATING** 88 **DRINK** 2008 $ 16

Hunter Valley Shiraz 2002 Light- to medium-bodied; red and black fruits, some primary sweetness still remaining; balanced extract. Cork. 12.5° alc. **RATING** 87 **DRINK** 2008 $ 15

Llangibby Estate   NR

Old Mount Barker Road, Echunga, SA 5153 **REGION** Adelaide Hills
T (08) 8338 5529 **F** (08) 8338 7118 **www**.llangibbyestate.com **OPEN** By appt
WINEMAKER Chris Addams Williams, John Williamson, James Hastwell **EST.** 1998 **CASES** 1000
Chris Addams Williams and John Williamson have established a substantial vineyard cresting a ridge close to Echunga, at a height of 360m. The varietal choice is eclectic, the lion's share to a little over 5 ha each of shiraz and cabernet sauvignon, then 1.95 ha of tempranillo, 1.4 ha of sauvignon blanc, and a tiny planting of pinot noir. Until 2002 this was used to provide a Pinot Hermitage blend, but from that year both a varietal Tempranillo and Pinot Noir have joined the product range alongside Sauvignon Blanc and Shiraz Cabernet. Exports to the UK.

Loch Luna   NR

Morgan Road, Overland Corner, SA 5345 **REGION** Riverland
T (08) 8588 7210 **F** (08) 8588 7210 **www**.riverland.net.au/~lochluna **OPEN** By appt most days 1–5
WINEMAKER Grant Semmens (Contract) **EST.** 1999 **CASES** NA
Raymond Neindorf and Louise Spangler run a small eco-business taking full advantage of the national heritage-listed wetlands reserves; Loch Luna Eco-Stay is part of the world network of biosphere reserves. A cottage for 2–3 people is 300m from the homestead/cellar door. The wines come from 10 ha of vineyards, and are made in limited quantities.

Loch-Lea Vineyard   NR

PO Box 1144, Legana, Tas 7277 **REGION** Northern Tasmania
T (03) 6330 1444 **F** (03) 6330 2190 **www**.loch-lea.com.au **OPEN** Not
WINEMAKER Dr Richard Richardson (Consultant) **EST.** 1984 **CASES** 200
The Loch-Lea Vineyard is owned by John and Luba Richards, and is one of the oldest in the Tamar Valley. The original plantings extended to 2.7 ha of pinot noir, chardonnay and cabernet sauvignon, the wines being sold through an onsite restaurant. The restaurant is no more, nor are the chardonnay and cabernet sauvignon; the pinot noir block of 1000 vines, now over 20 years old, produces the sole wine.

Lochmoore   ★★★★

PO Box 430, Trafalgar, Vic 3824 **REGION** Gippsland
T 0402 216 622 **OPEN** Not
WINEMAKER Lyre Bird Hill, Narkoojee **EST.** 1997 **CASES** 300
The 2 ha of chardonnay, pinot noir, pinot gris and shiraz at Lochmoore are tended by one of the most highly qualified viticulturists one is ever likely to meet. Sue Hasthorpe grew up in Trafalgar, but went on to obtain a Bachelor of Science (Hons) and Doctor of Philosophy in Physiology at the University of Melbourne; thereafter working and travelling as a medical research scientist in Australia, the UK, the US and Europe, and after returning to Australia studied viticulture via the University of Melbourne Dookie College campus (distance education). If this were not enough, she is now doing a Masters of Agribusiness at the University of Melbourne.

♆♆♆♆♀ Chardonnay 2004 Sophisticated, understated wine; nectarine and melon fruit, barrel ferment, malolactic and lees all seamlessly woven together; good length. Submitted unlabelled with a Narkoojee cork. **RATING** 92 **DRINK** 2011 $ 18

♆♆♆♆ Gippsland Pinot Noir 2004 Fragrant; a light- to medium-bodied mix of cherry and more stemmy/minty characters, perhaps some whole bunches, and certainly very low alcohol. Cork. 12.1° alc. **RATING** 88 **DRINK** 2009 $ 20

Logan Wines ★★★★

Castelreagh Highway, Apple Tree Flat, Mudgee, NSW 2850 **REGION** Mudgee
T (02) 6373 1333 **F** (02) 6373 1390 **WWW**.loganwines.com.au **OPEN** 7 days 10–5
WINEMAKER Peter Logan **EST.** 1997 **CASES** 35 000
Logan Wines is a family operation, founded by businessman Mal Logan and assisted by 3 of his children: Peter, who is an oenology graduate from the Adelaide University, Greg (advertising) and Kylie (office administrator). Retail distribution in all states; exports to the UK, the US, Canada, Germany, Sweden, NZ, Singapore and Hong Kong.

♆♆♆♆♀ Orange Sauvignon Blanc 2005 Gooseberry, apple and herb aromas; a long palate, the intensity growing on the minerally/lemony finish and aftertaste. Screwcap. **RATING** 90 **DRINK** Now $ 20
M Cuvee 2000 Fresh, lively and crisp; flavours of strawberry, citrus, apple and stone fruit; good length, nice dry finish; classy wine. 11° alc. **RATING** 90 **DRINK** 2008 $ 35

♆♆♆♆ Weemala Merlot 2002 Holding hue well; likewise has retained attractive raspberry and redcurrant fruit on the light- to medium-bodied palate; fine, ripe tannins. Central Ranges. Screwcap. 14° alc. **RATING** 89 **DRINK** 2008 $ 14.95
Apple Tree Flat Semillon Sauvignon Blanc 2005 Light-bodied, largely driven by Mudgee semillon; lemon and citrus fruit; good length, and a clean, crisp finish. Screwcap. 12° alc. **RATING** 88 **DRINK** 2009 $ 10
Weemala Pinot Gris 2005 Unusual floral and honeysuckle mix of aromas; abundant, rich fruit flavour; solid finish. Screwcap. 14° alc. **RATING** 88 **DRINK** Now $ 15.50
Weemala Pinot Noir 2004 Clear red-purple; cherry and plum fruit with fine, savoury tannins; verges on dry red. Screwcap. **RATING** 87 **DRINK** 2009 $ 16

♆♆♆♀ Orange Chardonnay 2004 RATING 86 **DRINK** Now $ 23
Hannah Rose 2005 RATING 86 **DRINK** Now $ 17
Weemala Pinot Noir 2003 RATING 86 **DRINK** Now $ 15.50
Weemala Shiraz Viognier 2003 RATING 86 **DRINK** 2008 $ 15.50
Apple Tree Flat Shiraz 2002 RATING 86 **DRINK** 2008 $ 10
Weemala Gewurztraminer 2005 RATING 85 **DRINK** Now $ 15.50
Apple Tree Flat Chardonnay 2005 RATING 85 **DRINK** 2008 $ 10

London Lodge Estate NR

Muswellbrook Road, Gungal, NSW 2333 **REGION** Upper Hunter Valley
T (02) 6547 6122 **F** (02) 6547 6122 **OPEN** 7 days 10–9
WINEMAKER Gary Reed (Contract) **EST.** 1988 **CASES** NA
The 16-ha vineyard of Stephen and Joanne Horner is planted to chardonnay, pinot noir, shiraz and cabernet sauvignon, and sold through a cellar door (and restaurant) with a full array of tourist attractions, including arts and crafts.

Lone Crow Wines NR

RSM 343, Busselton, WA 6280 (postal) **REGION** Geographe
T (08) 9753 3023 **F** (08) 9753 3032 **OPEN** Not
WINEMAKER Mark Messenger (Contract) **EST.** 1996 **CASES** 600
The Kennedy (David and Michelle) and Espinos (Kim and Jodie) families progressively established 14 ha of sauvignon blanc, semillon, shiraz, merlot and cabernet sauvignon between 1996 and 1999 in the foothills of the Whicher Ranges, 15 km inland from Busselton. Most of the grapes are sold, principally to Evans & Tate; limited quantities are made under the Lone Crow label.

Long Gully Estate NR

Long Gully Road, Healesville, Vic 3777 **REGION** Yarra Valley
T (03) 9510 5798 **F** (03) 9510 9859 **WWW**.longgullyestate.com **OPEN** 7 days 11–5
WINEMAKER Luke Houlihan **EST.** 1982 **CASES** 16 000
One of the larger Yarra Valley producers to have successfully established a number of export markets, doubtless due to a core of mature vineyards; it is able to offer a range of wines with 2–3 years' bottle age. Recent vineyard extensions underline Long Gully's commercial success. Exports to the UK, Switzerland and Singapore.

Long Point Vineyard NR

6 Cooinda Place, Lake Cathie, NSW 2445 **REGION** Hastings River
T (02) 6585 4598 **F** (02) 6584 8915 **OPEN** Thurs–Sun & public hols 10–6, or by appt
WINEMAKER Graeme Davies **EST.** 1995 **CASES** 600
In turning their dream into reality, Graeme Davies (an educational psychologist) and wife Helen (a chartered accountant) took no chances. After becoming interested in wine as consumers through wine appreciation courses, the Davies moved from Brisbane so that 36-year-old Graeme could begin his study for a postgraduate diploma in wine from Roseworthy. Late in 1993 they purchased a 5-ha property near Lake Cathie, progressively establishing 2 ha of chardonnay, shiraz, chambourcin, cabernet sauvignon and frontignac. As well as having a full-time job at Cassegrain and establishing the vineyard, Graeme built the house, which was designed by Helen and has a pyramid-shaped roof and an underground cellar.

Longview Vineyard ★★★★☆

Pound Road, Macclesfield, SA 5153 **REGION** Adelaide Hills
T (08) 8388 9694 **F** (08) 8388 9693 **WWW**.longviewvineyard.com.au **OPEN** Sun–Fri 11–5
WINEMAKER Shaw & Smith, Kangarilla Road, O'Leary Walker **EST.** 1995 **CASES** 15 000
In a strange twist of fate, Longview Vineyard came to be through the success of Two Dogs, the lemon-flavoured alcoholic drink created by Duncan MacGillivray and sold in 1995 to the Pernod Ricard Group (also the owners of Orlando). Over 60 ha have been planted: shiraz and cabernet sauvignon account for a little over half, and there are significant plantings of chardonnay and merlot, and smaller plantings of viognier, semillon, riesling, sauvignon blanc, zinfandel and nebbiolo. The majority of the production is sold to Southcorp, but $1.2 million has been invested in a cellar door and function area, barrel rooms and an administration centre for the Group's activities. All the buildings have a spectacular view over the Coorong and Lake Alexandrina. Exports to the UK, the US and Canada.

🍷🍷🍷🍷🍷 **Iron Knob Riesling 2005** Excellent, vibrant tangy citrus and herb palate; long, clean finish; a touch of French oak adds more to texture than flavour. Screwcap. 12.3° alc.
RATING 94 **DRINK** 2013 **$** 17

🍷🍷🍷🍷 **Iron Knob Riesling 2005** Very pale straw-green; a clean and powerful bouquet and palate, with zesty herb, lemon and mineral notes; good length. Screwcap. 13° alc.
RATING 93 **DRINK** 2012 **$** 17

Red Bucket Semillon Sauvignon Blanc 2005 Considerable length and intensity; asparagus, grass, herb, spice and mineral with some sweeter fruit substrate. Screwcap. 13° alc. **RATING** 92 **DRINK** 2011 **$** 15

Yakka Shiraz Viognier 2004 Very good colour; powerful licorice, blackberry, spice and apricot mix in emblematic Shiraz Viognier style. Cork. 14.5° alc. **RATING** 92 **DRINK** 2011 **$** 24

Blue Cow Chardonnay 2005 Oak has added as much to texture as to flavour; similar flavour and length to the unwooded, with a strong cool-grown grapefruit component. Screwcap. 13.5° alc. **RATING** 91 **DRINK** 2010 **$** 17

Beau Sea Viognier 2005 Sophisticated winemaking; apricot with touches of honey and spice; oak adds to the texture, rather than the flavour; just a twitch of alcohol heat. Screwcap. 14° alc. **RATING** 91 **DRINK** Now **$** 22

Whippet Sauvignon Blanc 2005 Light- to medium-bodied; grass, herb and gooseberry, then a firm finish. Screwcap. 13° alc. **RATING** 90 **DRINK** 2008 **$** 17

ΥΥΥΥ **Devil's Elbow Cabernet Sauvignon 2004** Blackcurrant, earth and spice; medium- to full-bodied, with firm texture and structure; needs time for the grip to loosen. Cork. 14.5° alc. **RATING** 89 **DRINK** 2014 $ 26

Blue Cow Unwooded Chardonnay 2005 Very pale straw-green; has surprising mid- to back-palate flavour and length, the flavours in a stone fruit/grapefruit spectrum. **RATING** 88 **DRINK** Now $ 17

Red Bucket Cabernet Shiraz 2004 A medium-bodied, fresh red and black fruit mix; gently earthy/savoury tannins, good aftertaste. Screwcap. 14.5° alc. **RATING** 88 **DRINK** 2010 $ 15

ΥΥΥΥ **The Mob Zinfandel 2004 RATING** 86 **DRINK** 2008 $ 32

Black Crow Nebbiolo 2004 RATING 85 **DRINK** 2008 $ 26

Lost Lake
NR

Lot 3 Vasse Highway, Pemberton, WA 6260 **REGION** Pemberton
T (08) 9776 1251 **F** (08) 9776 1919 **www**.lostlake.com.au **OPEN** Wed–Sun 10–4
WINEMAKER Justin Hearn, Melanie Bowater **EST.** 1990 **CASES** 5000
Previously known as Eastbrook Estate, its origins go back to 1990, to the acquisition of an 80-ha farming property which was subdivided into three portions: 16 ha, now known as Picardy, were acquired by Dr Bill Pannell, 18 ha became the base for Lost Lake, and the remainder was sold. The initial plantings in 1990 were of pinot noir and chardonnay, followed by shiraz, sauvignon blanc, merlot and cabernet sauvignon between 1996 and 1998 — 9 ha are now planted. A jarrah and cedar winery with a crush capacity of 300 tonnes was built in 1995, together with a large restaurant. In 1999 the business was acquired by Perth investors. Exports to the UK.

Lost Valley Winery
★★★★

PO Box 4123, Wishart, Vic 3189 **REGION** Upper Goulburn
T (03) 9592 3531 **F** (03) 9551 7470 **www**.lostvalleywinery.com **OPEN** Not
WINEMAKER Alex White (Contract) **EST.** 1995 **CASES** 5000
Dr Robert Ippaso planted the Lost Valley vineyard at an elevation of 450m on the slopes of Mt Tallarook, with 13 ha of merlot, shiraz, cortese and sauvignon blanc. This cortese is the only planting in Australia. It pays homage to Dr Ippaso's birthplace: Savoie, in the Franco-Italian Alps, where cortese flourishes. Exports to the UK and Canada.

ΥΥΥΥΥ **Upper Goulburn Cortese 2005** Quite fragrant; apple, pear and spice on both bouquet and palate; substantial weight and mouthfeel; best yet. Screwcap. 14° alc. **RATING** 90 **DRINK** 2008 $ 30

Thousand Hills Central Victoria Shiraz 2004 Light- to medium-bodied; bright, fresh, spicy, cool-grown black and red cherries; sustained acidity and subtle oak. Cork. 13.5° alc. **RATING** 90 **DRINK** 2010 $ 34

ΥΥΥΥ **Hazy Mountain Central Victoria Merlot 2004** Good red-purple; plenty of substance and weight; opens on the palate with primary red fruits, then a slight twist of leaf and black olive to close, tannins on the aftertaste. Cork. 14° alc. **RATING** 89 **DRINK** 2011 $ 34

Upper Goulburn Sauvignon Blanc 2005 Very pale straw-green; crisp, clean and well-made; mineral and a hint of passionfruit; simply lacks varietal fruit depth. Screwcap. 13° alc. **RATING** 87 **DRINK** Now $ 26

Louee
NR

Cox's Creek Road, Rylstone, NSW 2849 **REGION** Mudgee
T (02) 8923 5373 **F** (02) 8923 5362 **www**.louee.com.au **OPEN** Mon–Sat 10–4, Sun & public hols 11–2
WINEMAKER David Lowe, Jane Wilson (Contract) **EST.** 1998 **CASES** 4000
Jointly owned by Rod James and Tony Maxwell, Louee is a substantial operation. Its home vineyard at Rylstone has over 28 ha of plantings, led by shiraz, cabernet sauvignon, petit verdot and merlot, with chardonnay, cabernet franc, verdelho and viognier making up the balance. The second vineyard is on Nullo Mountain, bordered by the Wollemi National Park, at an altitude of 1100m, high by any standards. Here 4 ha of cool-climate varieties (riesling, sauvignon blanc, pinot noir, pinot gris and nebbiolo) have been planted.

Louis-Laval Wines   NR

160 Cobcroft Road, Broke, NSW 2330 **REGION** Lower Hunter Valley
T (02) 6579 1105 **F** (02) 6579 1105 **WWW**.louislaval.com **OPEN** By appt
WINEMAKER Roy Meyer **EST.** 1987 **CASES** 1200
It is ironic that the winery name should have associations with Alfa Laval, the giant Swiss food and wine machinery firm. Roy Meyer runs an organic vineyard (using only sulphur and copper sprays) and is proud of the fact that the winery has no refrigeration and no stainless steel. The wines produced from the 2.5-ha vineyard are fermented in open barrels or cement tanks, and maturation is handled entirely in oak.

Lovegrove Vineyard & Winery   NR

1420 Heidelberg–Kinglake Road, Cottles Bridge, Vic 3099 **REGION** Yarra Valley
T (03) 9718 1569 **F** (03) 9718 1028 **WWW**.lovegrovewinery.com.au **OPEN** W'ends & public hols 11–6, Mon–Fri by appt
WINEMAKER Stephen Bennett **EST.** 1983 **CASES** 1000
Lovegrove is a long-established winery in the Diamond Valley subregion, and while production is limited, it offers the visitor much to enjoy, with picturesque gardens overlooking the Kinglake Ranges; light lunches; barbecue and picnic tables; and live music on the second Sunday of the month. Intermittent art exhibitions are staged, and the winery caters for private functions. The wines are produced from 3.8 ha of estate plantings and a range of vintages is available.

Lowe Family Wines

Tinja Lane, Mudgee, NSW 2850 **REGION** Mudgee
T (02) 6372 0800 **F** (02) 6372 0811 **WWW**.lowewine.com.au **OPEN** Fri–Mon 10–5, or by appt
WINEMAKER David Lowe, Jane Wilson **EST.** 1987 **CASES** 6000
Former Rothbury winemaker David Lowe and Jane Wilson have consolidated their operations in Mudgee, moving back from their cellar door in the Hunter Valley. They have started a new Mudgee business, Mudgee Growers, at the historic Fairview winery (see separate entry). Exports to the UK, Germany and Canada.

Tinja Orange Sauvignon Blanc 2005 Bright green-straw; lively, zingy blossom aromas with vibrant gooseberry and passionfruit flavour; great length. Screwcap. 13.5° alc. **RATING** 94 **DRINK** Now $18

Mudgee Zinfandel 2004 Light, bright red-purple; fresh, spicy varietal flavour, with good balance and length, sweet tannins; similar to zinfandel from the cooler parts of California; impressive. Cork. 13.5° alc. **RATING** 90 **DRINK** 2010 $35

Tinja Mudgee Sangiovese Barbera Merlot 2004 Typical light colour; the juxtaposition of sweet cherry/berry fruit and dry tannins doesn't really work right now; time may or may not help. Screwcap. 13.5° alc. **RATING** 86 **DRINK** 2009 $18

Lucas Estate

329 Donges Road, Severnlea, Qld 4352 **REGION** Granite Belt
T (07) 4683 6365 **F** (07) 4683 6356 **WWW**.lucasestate.com.au **OPEN** 7 days 10–5
WINEMAKER Colin Sellers, Jim Barnes **EST.** 1999 **CASES** 1000
Louise Samuel and husband Colin Sellers purchased Lucas Estate in 2003. The wines are made from the 2.5-ha estate vineyard (at an altitude of 825m) which is planted to chardonnay, verdelho, cabernet sauvignon, shiraz, merlot and muscat, and also from purchased grapes. The contemporary cellar door houses an art gallery featuring Louise's work.

The Gordon Shiraz 2004 Good colour; excellent balance and structure; blackberry and plum fruit; soft but persistent tannins, and good oak. Very impressive. Cork. 14.5° alc. **RATING** 93 **DRINK** 2014 $30

ΥΥΥΥ   **The Joyce Mary Verdelho 2005** Clean, medium-bodied and well-made; the typical fruit salad of variety, with a slightly flinty, and attractive, finish. Screwcap. 13.5° alc. **RATING** 87 **DRINK** 2008 $ 19

ΥΥΥΫ   **Classic Dry Rose 2005** Fresh, lively and delicate rose petal/cherry fruit; does in fact have some sweetness, though balanced. Screwcap. 12° alc. **RATING** 86 **DRINK** Now $ 17

Lucy's Run   ★★☆

1274 Wine Country Drive, Rothbury, NSW 2335 **REGION** Lower Hunter Valley
T (02) 4938 3594 **F** (02) 4938 3592 **www**.lucysrun.com **OPEN** 7 days 10–5
WINEMAKER David Hook (Contract) **EST.** 1998 **CASES** 1000
The Lucy's Run business has a variety of offerings of wine, cold-pressed extra virgin olive oil and self-catered farm accommodation. The wines are made from 4.2 ha of verdelho, merlot and shiraz. The feisty label design is the work of local artist Paula Rengger, who doubles up as the chef at the nearby Shakey Tables Restaurant, itself the deserving winner of numerous awards.

ΥΥΥ   **Verdelho 2005 RATING** 81 $ 15

Luke Lambert Wines   ★★★★☆

24 Oliver Street, Yarra Glen, Vic 3775 (postal) **REGION** Yarra Valley
T 0438 124 164 **www**.lukelambertwines.com.au **OPEN** Not
WINEMAKER Luke Lambert **EST.** 2003 **CASES** 400
Luke Lambert graduated from Charles Sturt University's wine science course in 2002, aged 23, cramming in winemaking experience at Mount Pleasant, Coldstream Hills, Mount Prior, Poet's Corner, Palliser Estate in Martinborough, and Badia di Morrona in Chianti. With this background he has established a virtual winery, purchasing grapes from quality-conscious growers in the Yarra Valley and Heathcote. After several trial vintages, the first wines were released from the 2005 vintage. In August 2006 he and his partner moved to Piedmont, Italy for an extended stay, with intermittent trips back to the Yarra Valley for the winemaking, sales and continuation of the Luke Lambert wines.

ΥΥΥΥΥ   **Yarra Valley Syrah 2005** Brilliant colour; lovely, vibrant aromas and flavours; blackberry, spice and that touch of viognier lift; super-fine tannins; serious and impressive elegance; 3% viognier, 35% whole bunch shiraz. Cork. 13.7° alc. **RATING** 94 **DRINK** 2015 $ 28

ΥΥΥΥ   **Heathcote Nebbiolo 2005** Typical light colour; fragrant red fruits/cherry/leaf aromas; the savoury tannins demand food, in true Italian fashion. Cork. 13.1° alc. **RATING** 88 **DRINK** 2010 $ 28

Lyre Bird Hill   ★★★★

370 Inverloch Road, Koonwarra, Vic 3954 **REGION** Gippsland
T (03) 5664 3204 **F** (03) 5664 3206 **www**.lyrebirdhill.com.au **OPEN** Wed–Mon 10–5
WINEMAKER Owen Schmidt **EST.** 1986 **CASES** 2000
Former Melbourne professionals Owen and Robyn Schmidt make small quantities of estate-grown wine (the vineyard is 2.4 ha). Various weather-related viticulture problems have seen the Schmidts supplement their estate-grown intake with grapes from contract growers in Gippsland and the Yarra Valley, and also provide contract winemaking services for others.

ΥΥΥΥΥ   **Gewurztraminer 2004** Intensely varietal bouquet of spice, lychee, rose petal and yet more spice; the palate follows on, what it lacks in delicacy, it more than makes up in flavour. No region specified. Screwcap. 12.8° alc. **RATING** 94 **DRINK** 2009 $ 15

ΥΥΥΥΫ   **Gippsland Pinot Noir 2002** Deeper colour than the '03; quite powerful spiced plum and savoury sauce flavours; good structure and length. Cork. 13.6° alc. **RATING** 91 **DRINK** 2010 $ 25

ΥΥΥΥ   **Gippsland Pinot Noir 2003** Light bodied, spicy, savoury fruit; has good length, and the tannins are balanced. No information as to where and when its gold medal was awarded. Cork. 13.3° alc. **RATING** 89 **DRINK** 2008 $ 35

Golden Nectar Botrytis Sauvignon Blanc 2004 Extremely complex, with a high level of botrytis infection; some slightly raw edges, but overall wonderfully luscious. **RATING** 89 **DRINK** 2008 $25

Oaked and Unfiltered Gippsland Chardonnay 2003 Medium- to full yellow with a touch of green; has plenty of structure, but fairly austere fruit suggesting ambient/solids fermentation. Cork. 13.2° alc. **RATING** 87 **DRINK** 2008 $20

Phantasy Pinot Noir Chardonnay 2001 Full-on salmon-pink; spiced bread and strawberry flavours, with a dry finish; has character. 12.4° alc. **RATING** 87 **DRINK** 2008 $25

 Gippsland Riesling 2005 **RATING** 86 **DRINK** 2010 $15

Sauvignon Blanc 2005 **RATING** 86 **DRINK** Now $18

Cabernet Sauvignon 2001 Savoury, cedary, earthy; fine tannins; remarkable given the very low alcohol and time in barrel and bottle. Cork. 11.4° alc. **RATING** 86 **DRINK** Now $18

South Gippsland Shiraz Rose 2005 **RATING** 85 **DRINK** Now $15

South Gippsland Shiraz 2001 **RATING** 84 **DRINK** 2010 $20

Lyrebird Ridge Organic Winery ★★☆

270 Budgong Road, Budgong via Nowra and Kangaroo Valley, NSW 2541 **REGION** Shoalhaven Coast
T (02) 4446 0648 **F** (02) 4446 0648 **WWW**.lyrebirdridge.com **OPEN** Fri–Sun & public hols 10–5
WINEMAKER Larry Moreau **EST.** 1993 **CASES** 110
This is the ultimate organic winery, with no sprays whatsoever being used in the vineyard, and no chemicals — and in particular, no sulphur dioxide — added to the wines. No oak is used, nor are the wines filtered. Chambourcin is, and always will be, the most important grape, its hybrid heritage making it resistant to most of the moulds that require spraying. The absence of SO_2 in the wine means early consumption is essential.

▼▼▼ **Chambourcin 2005** **RATING** 83 $20

M. Chapoutier Australia ★★★★☆

PO Box 437, Robe, SA 5276 **REGION** Mount Benson
T (03) 5433 2411 **F** (03) 5433 2400 **WWW**.chapoutier.com **OPEN** Not
WINEMAKER Benjamin Darnault, Anthony Terlato **EST.** 1998 **CASES** 10 000
M. Chapoutier Australia is the offshoot of the famous Rhône Valley producer. It has established 3 vineyards in Australia: Domaine Tournon at Mount Benson (17 ha shiraz, 10 ha cabernet sauvignon, 4 ha marsanne, 3 ha viognier), Domaine Terlato Chapoutier in the Pyrenees (30 ha shiraz, 2 ha viognier) and a third at Heathcote (10 ha shiraz). It seems likely that increasing emphasis will be placed on the two Victorian vineyards. The business is in the course of re-establishing its operations in Heathcote. The Domaine Terlato and Chapoutier wines are made by Anthony Terlato, a Napa Valley winemaker. Exports to Europe, Asia, the US, NZ, Hong Kong, Japan, Singapore and Indonesia.

▼▼▼▼▼ **Domaine Terlato & Chapoutier Lieu dit Malakoff Pyrenees Shiraz 2004** Much better colour than the Central Victorian Shiraz; radically different, bright plum, cherry and blackberry fruit; good tannin support and a nice touch of oak. Cork. 15° alc. **RATING** 94 **DRINK** 2014 $30

▼▼▼▼ **Domaine Tournon Mt Benson Shiraz 2003** Spicy, savoury, earthy, foresty aromas; medium-bodied, with more blackberry fruit evident, and lingering tannins. Cork. 14° alc. **RATING** 90 **DRINK** 2010 $25

▼▼▼▼ **Domaine Terlato & Chapoutier Central Victorian Shiraz Viognier 2004** Developed colour; elegant, light-bodied, spicy red fruits; very atypical for Central Victoria and viognier; possibly cool-fermented. Cork. 13.5° alc. **RATING** 89 **DRINK** 2010 $15

Mabrook Estate NR

258 Inlet Road, Bulga, NSW 2330 **REGION** Lower Hunter Valley
T (02) 9971 9994 **F** (02) 9971 9924 **WWW**.mabrookestate.com **OPEN** W'ends 10–4
WINEMAKER Larissa Kalt, Tony Kalt **EST.** 1996 **CASES** 800
The Swiss-born Kalt family began the establishment of Mabrook Estate in 1996, planting 3 ha of semillon, 2 ha of shiraz and 1 ha of verdelho. Parents Mona and Tony Kalt decided to use organic

growing methods from the word go, and the vineyard is now certified organic by NASAA (National Association for Sustainable Agriculture Australia). Daughter Larissa, having obtained an Honours degree in Medical Science at the University of Sydney, decided to pursue winemaking by working as a 'lab rat' and cellar hand at a local winery, and visited Switzerland and Italy to observe small-scale family winemaking in those countries. The red wines are all very light in structure and extract, which may be intentional.

Macaw Creek Wines ★★★★☆

Macaw Creek Road, Riverton, SA 5412 **REGION** Mount Lofty Ranges Zone
T (08) 8847 2237 **F** (08) 8847 2237 **WWW.**macawcreekwines.com.au **OPEN** Sun & public hols 11–4
WINEMAKER Rodney Hooper **EST.** 1992 **CASES** 5000
The property on which Macaw Creek Wines is established has been owned by the Hooper family since the 1850s, but development of the estate vineyards did not begin until 1995 (30 ha have since been planted). The Macaw Creek brand was established in 1992 with wines made from grapes from other regions, including the Preservative-Free Yoolang Cabernet Shiraz. Rodney Hooper is a highly qualified and skilled winemaker with experience in many parts of Australia and in Germany, France and the US. Exports to the US, Canada and Malaysia.

ŸŸŸŸŸ **Yoolang Preservative Free Shiraz 2004** Medium-bodied; rich black fruits, dark chocolate and a touch of spice; good tannin, structure and length; best preservative-free red available, particularly protected by screwcap. Screwcap. **RATING** 91 **DRINK** 2008 $ 17
Riesling 2004 Glowing yellow-green; generous, full-bodied, tropical and lime flavours; incipient toast, well-balanced; ready now. Screwcap. 13° alc. **RATING** 90 **DRINK** 2008 $ 15
Semillon Viognier 2004 Bright, glowing green-yellow; soft, gently rich, tropical fruit with a streak of lemony acidity running through; 87% Semillon. Screwcap. 13.5° alc. **RATING** 90 **DRINK** 2010 $ 14
Semillon Viognier 2003 Bright, vivid green-straw; developing slowly but surely; remarkably generous semillon, and similar tropical fruit to the '04; slightly more finesse and length; 96% Semillon; technically invalid labelling. Screwcap. 13.5° alc. **RATING** 90 **DRINK** 2010 $ 14
Yoolang Preservative Free Shiraz 2003 Very good colour; medium-bodied, ripe blackberry fruits; holding on to its freshness without trouble, except that the first bottle tasted was rampantly corked. Cork. 14.5° alc. **RATING** 90 **DRINK** Now $ 17
Shiraz 2002 Medium red-purple; quite youthful, sweet black fruits; fine tannins, well-balanced and integrated oak. Quality cork. **RATING** 90 **DRINK** 2012 $ 15

ŸŸŸŸ **3 Valley Shiraz Cabernet 2003** Medium-bodied; slightly jammy/confit notes to the fruit; soft, ripe tannins. Screwcap. **RATING** 87 **DRINK** 2009 $ 6
Grenache Shiraz 2003 Light- to medium-bodied; not especially complex, but touches of spice add to the flavour and texture. Easy access style, as is the '04. Cork. 14.5° alc. **RATING** 87 **DRINK** Now $ 14

ŸŸŸŸ **Grenache Shiraz 2004** **RATING** 86 **DRINK** 2008 $ 14

McCrae Mist Wines

21 Bass Street, McCrae, Vic 3938 (postal) **REGION** Mornington Peninsula
T 0416 008 630 **F** (03) 5986 6973 **OPEN** Not
WINEMAKER Brien Cole **EST.** 2003 **CASES** 1250
The McCrae Mist vineyard was acquired by Dr Stephen Smith after the Kings Creek business was broken up in 2003. He thus inherited 15.5 ha of pinot grigio, pinot noir, shiraz and sangiovese, adding another 4 ha of chardonnay in 2005.

ŸŸŸŸŸ **Mornington Peninsula Pinot Noir 2004** Medium red-purple; plenty of depth and structure to the mix of plum, forest and spice fruit; firm mouthfeel, long finish. Screwcap. 13.2° alc. **RATING** 93 **DRINK** 2011 $ 16
Reserve Mornington Peninsula Pinot Noir 2004 Slight less bright hue; similar fruit flavours, the main difference appearing to be more oak in this wine; swings and roundabouts. Screwcap. 13.2° alc. **RATING** 93 **DRINK** 2012 $ 29

ΥΥΥΥ **Mornington Peninsula Pinot Grigio 2004** Baked apple, brioche, and a hint of strawberry; the low alcohol gives the wine balance and vitality. **RATING** 89 **DRINK** 2008 $ 15

Mornington Peninsula Shiraz 2004 Light- to medium-bodied; spicy peppery aromas and notes of mint and leaf to the red fruits. Screwcap. 13.2° alc. **RATING** 89 **DRINK** 2010 $ 15

macforbes ★★★★

c/- Sticks, Glenview Road, Yarra Glen, Vic 3775 **REGION** Yarra Valley
T (03) 9818 8099 **F** (03) 9818 8299 **WWW**.macforbes.com **OPEN** Not
WINEMAKER Mac Forbes **EST.** 2004 **CASES** 3000
Mac Forbes cut his vinus teeth at Mount Mary, where he was winemaker for several years before heading overseas in 2002. For the first 2 years he was based in London working for Southcorp in a marketing liaison role, before heading to Portugal and Austria to gain further winemaking experience. He returned to the Yarra Valley prior to the 2005 vintage, purchasing grapes for the 2-tier portfolio: first, the Victorian range (employing unusual varieties or unusual winemaking techniques) and, second, the Yarra Valley range of multiple *terroir*-based offerings of Chardonnay and Pinot Noir.

ΥΥΥΥΥ **Strathbogie Ranges Riesling 2005** Interesting style, with a firm, quite complex structure holding lime juice and sweetness approaching Kabinett (Mosel); will evolve well. Screwcap. 11° alc. **RATING** 90 **DRINK** 2009 $ 22

King Valley Barbera 2004 Deep colour; considerable power and intensity, yet quite supple; poached spiced plums; good acidity and length. Screwcap. 13.5° alc. **RATING** 90 **DRINK** 2012 $ 27

ΥΥΥΥ **Yarra Valley Arneis 2005** Crisp, intense lemon/lemongrass; pronounced acidity, long finish. Screwcap. 13.5° alc. **RATING** 88 **DRINK** 2010 $ 18

Yarra Valley Pinot Rose 2005 Bright colour, with no browning; nicely balanced hints of strawberry followed by a dry finish and perfect acidity. Well above average. Screwcap. 13.5° alc. **RATING** 88 **DRINK** Now $ 18

McGee Wines NR

1710 Wattlevale Road, Nagambie, Vic 3608 **REGION** Nagambie Lakes
T (03) 5794 1530 **F** (03) 5794 1530 **OPEN** By appt
WINEMAKER Don Lewis (Contract) **EST.** 1995 **CASES** 750
Andrew McGee and partner Kerry Smith (the latter the viticulturist) have established 12 ha of vines on the banks of the Goulburn River, the majority planted to shiraz, with lesser quantities of grenache, viognier and mourvedre. Currently, 95% of the production is sold to Mitchelton, where the McGee wines are presently made, but the plan is for the partners to make the wine themselves, and to increase production.

McGlashan's Wallington Estate ★★★★☆

225 Swan Bay Road, Wallington, Vic 3221 **REGION** Geelong
T (03) 5250 5760 **F** (03) 5250 5760 **OPEN** By appt
WINEMAKER Robin Brockett (Contract) **EST.** 1996 **CASES** 1500
Russell and Jan McGlashan began the establishment of their 10-ha vineyard in 1996. Chardonnay and pinot noir make up the bulk of the plantings, with the remainder shiraz, and the wines are made by Robin Brockett. Local restaurants around Geelong and the Bellarine Peninsula take much of the wine, but cellar door sales are available by appointment.

ΥΥΥΥΥ **Bellarine Peninsula Pinot Noir 2004** Complex spicy, savoury, plummy fruit; excellent length and persistence; long and lingering. Screwcap. **RATING** 94 **DRINK** 2010 $ 25

ΥΥΥΥ **Bellarine Peninsula Chardonnay 2004** A fairly lean and spare style; mineral, cashew and light citrussy fruit; some length. Towards Chablis. Screwcap. **RATING** 89 **DRINK** 2009 $ 25

McGuigan Wines ★★★★☆

Cnr Broke Road/McDonald Road, Pokolbin, NSW 2321 REGION Lower Hunter Valley
T (02) 4998 7700 F (02) 4998 7401 WWW.mcguiganwines.com.au OPEN 7 days 9.30–5
WINEMAKER Peter Hall EST. 1992 CASES 1.2 million
A public-listed company which was the ultimate logical expression of Brian McGuigan's marketing drive and vision, on a par with that of Wolf Blass in his heyday. Has been particularly active in export markets, notably the US and more recently China. The overall size of the company has been measurably increased by the acquisition of Simeon Wines; Yaldara and Miranda are now also part of the business, which hit turbulent financial waters in 2006, and saw the retirement of Brian McGuigan from his position as CEO. As the tasting notes show, it has nonetheless continued to produce some excellent wines. Exports to all major markets.

ŸŸŸŸŸ **Bin 9000 Semillon 2005** Very good wine; racy, stylish and refined fruit bolstered and lengthened by the lemony acidity so typical of the vintage. Screwcap. RATING 94 DRINK 2009 $12.50
Genus 4 Adelaide Hills Sauvignon Blanc 2005 Spotlessly clean; a lively, fresh and crisp mix of citrus, tropical and mineral flavours, finishing with lemony acidity. Diam. 12.2° alc. RATING 94 DRINK Now $22

ŸŸŸŸŸ **Bin 2000 Limestone Coast Shiraz 2004** Bright, purple-red; a rich, almost velvety texture; ripe (but not dead) plum and black fruit flavours. Twin top. 13.5° alc. RATING 92 DRINK 2010 $14
Genus 4 Old Vine Hunter Valley Chardonnay 2005 Elegant, light- to medium-bodied wine; stone fruit and melon with well-balanced oak, and citrussy acidity to close. Diam. 13.2° alc. RATING 91 DRINK 2009 $22

ŸŸŸŸ **Personal Reserve Hunter Valley Shiraz 2003** Very good colour; a fresh, bright, light- to medium-bodied, early-picked style; good extract and oak. Cork. 13° alc. RATING 89 DRINK 2012 $49
Personal Reserve Hunter Valley Chardonnay 2004 Bright green-yellow; a very complex wine, but utterly dominated by toasty oak; a pity. Diam. 13° alc. RATING 87 DRINK 2009 $35

ŸŸŸŸ **Genus 4 Old Vine Hunter Valley Chardonnay 2003** RATING 86 DRINK Now $25
Swan Hill Pinot Grigio 2005 RATING 85 DRINK Now $15

ŸŸŸ **Bin 6000 Verdelho 2005** RATING 83 $12.50

McHenry Hohnen Vintners ★★★★☆

PO Box 1480, Margaret River, WA 6285 REGION Margaret River
T (08) 9758 7777 F (08) 9758 7777 WWW.mchv.com.au OPEN Not
WINEMAKER David Hohnen, Freya Hohnen EST. 2004 CASES 6500
McHenry Hohnen is a substantial business owned by the McHenry and Hohnen families, sourcing grapes from 4 vineyards owned by various members of the two families. In all, 120 ha of vines have been established on the McHenry's, Calgardup Brook, Rocky Road and McLeod Creek properties. A significant part of the grape production is sold to others (including Cape Mentelle) but McHenry Hohnen have 18 varieties to choose from in fashioning their wines. The 3 family members with direct executive responsibilities are leading Perth retailer Murray McHenry, Cape Mentelle founder and former longterm winemaker David Hohnen, and Freya Hohnen, who shares the winemaking duties with father David.

ŸŸŸŸŸ **Calgardup Brook Chardonnay 2004** Complex wild yeast barrel ferment characters; a creamy opening to the palate, then fruit takes over and drives through to a long finish. Screwcap. 14.5° alc. RATING 95 DRINK 2014 $31

ŸŸŸŸŸ **Three Amigos Marsanne Chardonnay Viognier 2004** A rich, ripe bouquet, then a palate flooded with soft fruit; tightens up just enough on the finish. Screwcap. 15° alc. RATING 91 DRINK 2009 $24

ŸŸŸŸ **Tiger Country Tempranillo Petit Verdot Cabernet Sauvignon 2004** Clean bouquet; savoury black fruits; a fandango dance indeed. Cork. 14° alc. RATING 89 DRINK 2010 $26
Three Amigos Shiraz Grenache Mataro 2004 Light- to medium-bodied; fresh, bright red fruits and supple tannins; easy come, easy go. Screwcap. 14.5° alc. RATING 88 DRINK 2008 $24

McIvor Creek

NR

Costerfield Road, Heathcote, Vic 3523 **REGION** Heathcote
T (03) 5433 4000 **F** (03) 5433 3456 **OPEN** 7 days 10–5.30
WINEMAKER Peter Turley **EST.** 1973 **CASES** 1000
The beautifully situated McIvor Creek winery is well worth a visit and does offer wines in diverse styles; the red wines are the most regional. Peter Turley has 5 ha of cabernet sauvignon and 2.5 ha of cabernet franc and merlot, and supplements this with grapes from other growers.

McIvor Estate

NR

80 Tooborac–Baynton Road, Tooborac, Vic 3522 **REGION** Heathcote
T (03) 5433 5266 **F** (03) 5433 5358 **WWW.**mcivorestate.com.au **OPEN** W'ends & public hols 10–5, or by appt
WINEMAKER Adrian Munari (Contract) **EST.** 1997 **CASES** 2000
McIvor Estate is situated at the base of the Tooborac Hills, at the southern end of the Heathcote wine region, 5 km southwest of Tooborac. Gary and Cynthia Harbor have planted 5.5 ha of marsanne, roussanne, shiraz, cabernet sauvignon, merlot, nebbiolo and sangiovese.

McKellar Ridge Wines

NR

2 Eureka Avenue, Murrumbateman, NSW 2582 **REGION** Canberra District
T (02) 6258 1556 **F** (02) 6258 9770 **WWW.**mckellarridgewines.com.au **OPEN** By appt
WINEMAKER Dr Brian Johnston **EST.** 2000 **CASES** 300
Dr Brian Johnston and his wife Janet are the partners in McKellar Ridge Wines. He is studying wine science at Charles Sturt University, and in the interim is making the wines at Jeir Creek under the guidance of Rob Howell, Bryan Martin and Greg Gallagher.

McLaren Vale III Associates

130 Main Road, McLaren Vale, SA 5171 **REGION** McLaren Vale
T 1800 501 513 **F** (08) 8323 7422 **WWW.**associates.com.au **OPEN** Mon–Fri 9–5, tasting by appt
WINEMAKER Brian Light **EST.** 1999 **CASES** 14 000
The three associates in question all have a decade or more of wine industry experience; Mary Greer is managing partner, Reginald Wymond chairing partner, and Christopher Fox partner. The partnership owns 34 ha of vines spanning 2 vineyards, one owned by Mary and John Greer, the other by Reg and Sue Wymond. An impressive portfolio of affordable quality wines has been the outcome, precisely as the partners wished. Exports to the US, Canada, Germany and China.

Squid Ink Shiraz 2004 Good colour; elegant, medium-bodied; bright blackberry and dark chocolate fruit, sweet spices, and good oak and tannin handling. If only all McLaren Vale shiraz could be like this. Cork. 14.5° alc. **RATING** 94 **DRINK** 2012 $ 40

Renaissance Merlot Cabernet Petit Verdot 2004 Cedary, savoury, briary aromas, the palate unexpectedly smooth and supple; delicious cassis and blackcurrant fruit, with markedly soft, fine tannins. Cork. 14° alc. **RATING** 93 **DRINK** 2014 $ 23
Sabbatical Sauvignon Blanc 2005 Clean, crisp stone/mineral/herb aromas; attractive tropical/green apple flavours. Screwcap. 13.5° alc. **RATING** 90 **DRINK** Now $ 18
Three Score & 10 Grenache 2003 Strongly varietal and equally regional; more substance than most Barossa examples, but still with spicy/juicy fruit flavours and soft tannins; controlled alcohol; 70-year-old vines. Cork. 14.5° alc. **RATING** 90 **DRINK** 2009 $ 25
The Elder Merlot 2004 Attractive, medium-bodied, mix of savoury olive, earth, black fruits; fine tannins, good oak; as always, a hint of chocolate in the background. Cork. 14° alc. **RATING** 90 **DRINK** 2011 $ 23

The Splinter Chardonnay 2005 **RATING** 86 **DRINK** 2008 $ 18

McLean's Farm Wines

NR

PO Box 403, Tanunda, SA 5352 **REGION** Barossa Valley
T (08) 8564 3340 **F** (08) 8564 3340 **OPEN** At barr-Vinum cellars & restaurant, Angaston, tel (08)
8564 3688
WINEMAKER Bob McLean **EST.** 2001 **CASES** 5000
At various times known as the Jolly Green Giant and Sir Lunchalot, Bob McLean has gone perilously
close to being a marketing legend in his own lifetime, moving from Orlando to Petaluma and then
(for longer and more importantly) St Hallett. He is now free to do his own thing, starting with what
he terms as 'The Virtual Winery' in partnership with long-term friends Dean and Rod Schubert (the
latter a notable Australian artist). Around the corner lies barr-eden, a very real vineyard and winery
in the course of establishment on top of Mengler's Hill at an altitude of 520m.

McLeish Estate

Lot 3 De Beyers Road, Pokolbin, NSW 2320 **REGION** Lower Hunter Valley
T (02) 4998 7754 **F** (02) 4998 7754 **WWW**.mcleishhunterwines.com.au **OPEN** 7 days 10–5, or by appt
WINEMAKER Andrew Thomas **EST.** 1985 **CASES** 3500
Bob and Maryanne McLeish started planting their vineyard in 1985, and now have 10 ha. They have
also opened their cellar door, having accumulated a number of gold medals for their wines.

ŸŸŸŸŸ **Hunter Valley Semillon 2005** Gentle grass, lime and citrus mix; silky mouthfeel; very
good balance, line and length. Cork. **RATING** 95 **DRINK** 2015 $18
Hunter Valley Chardonnay 2005 Melon and nectarine fruit seamlessly interwoven with
French oak and creamy/nutty lees contributions. Screwcap. 14° alc. **RATING** 94
DRINK 2009 $15

ŸŸŸŸŸ **Hunter Valley Semillon Sauvignon Blanc 2005** Bright, clean and fresh; semillon
provides structure and length, the sauvignon blanc some passionfruit nuances; light-
bodied, works well. Screwcap. 11.6° alc. **RATING** 92 **DRINK** 2008 $15
Jessica's Botrytis Semillon 2005 Intensely sweet peachy fruit balanced by crisp acidity
on a long finish. Cork. 10° alc. **RATING** 92 **DRINK** 2008 $25
Hunter Valley Shiraz 2004 Clear, bright colour and a spotlessly clean bouquet; light- to
medium-bodied blackberry, plum and cherry; fresh finish, balanced acidity. Cork.
12.5° alc. **RATING** 90 **DRINK** 2010 $20

ŸŸŸŸ **Hunter Valley Verdelho 2005** Well-made as is typical; gentle fruit salad with nice citrus
components coming through on the finish. Price comparison with Chardonnay is
stupefying. Diam. 12° alc. **RATING** 88 **DRINK** 2009 $16

McPherson Wines

★★★☆

PO Box 529, Artarmon, NSW 1570 **REGION** Nagambie Lakes
T (02) 9436 1644 **F** (02) 9436 3144 **WWW**.mcphersonwines.com **OPEN** Not
WINEMAKER Andrew McPherson, Geoff Thompson **EST.** 1993 **CASES** 350 000
McPherson Wines is not well known in Australia but is, by any standards, a substantial business. Its
wines are almost entirely produced for the export market, with sales in Australia through Safeway
and First Estate. The wines are made at various locations from contract-grown grapes and represent
very good value. For the record, McPherson Wines is a joint venture between Andrew McPherson
and Alister Purbrick (Tahbilk), both of whom have had a lifetime of experience in the industry.
Exports to all major markets.

ŸŸŸŸŸ **Reserve Goulburn Valley Chardonnay 2002** A surprise 3 years on from its birth; has
elegance and freshness, the cool vintage at work; citrus and stone fruit, nice oak. Estate-
grown. Cork. **RATING** 90 **DRINK** 2008 $18.99

ŸŸŸŸ **Murray Darling Chardonnay 2005** Nice wine; aromatic mix of ripe stone fruit and a hint
of citrus; quite long, fruit-driven palate. Twin top. 13° alc. **RATING** 88 **DRINK** 2008 $8.99
Reserve Goulburn Valley Shiraz 2003 Good colour, clean bouquet; plum and blackberry
fruit mark the entry to the palate, then slightly unexpected tannins on the back-palate and
finish. Estate-grown. Cork. 14.5° alc. **RATING** 88 **DRINK** 2010 $19

Basilisk Shiraz Mourvedre 2004 Vivid colour; light- to medium-bodied, bright, fresh black cherry fruit; no sign of tough mourvedre tannins. Cork. 14.5° alc. **RATING** 88 **DRINK** 2009 $ 15

Murray Darling Shiraz Cabernet 2004 Clean, fresh, bright bouquet; light- to medium-bodied, fruit-driven black cherry and blackberry palate; clean finish, minimal oak. Twin top. **RATING** 88 **DRINK** Now $ 8.99

Murray Darling Semillon Sauvignon Blanc 2005 Spicy herb and grass aromas; good balance to the palate with similar flavours; outstanding value, the slightly short finish notwithstanding. Screwcap. 11.5° alc. **RATING** 87 **DRINK** Now $ 8.99

Murray Darling Verdelho 2005 Mainstream style; tropical fruit salad with a twist of citrus. Screwcap. **RATING** 87 **DRINK** Now $ 8.99

Basilisk Marsanne Viognier 2004 Has flavour impact from honeysuckle into tropical fruit, then minerally/citrussy acidity. Cork. 13° alc. **RATING** 86 **DRINK** Now $ 15

Murray Darling Shiraz 2004 **RATING** 85 **DRINK** Now $ 8.99

Murray Darling Merlot 2004 **RATING** 84 **DRINK** Now $ 8.99

Macquariedale Estate

170 Sweetwater Road, Rothbury, NSW 2335 **REGION** Lower Hunter Valley
T (02) 6574 7012 **F** (02) 6574 7013 **WWW**.macquariedale.com.au **OPEN** Fri–Mon, school & public hols 10–5
WINEMAKER Ross McDonald **EST.** 1993 **CASES** 4000
Macquariedale is an acorn to oak story, beginning with a small hobby vineyard in Branxton many years ago, and now extending to 3 certified organic (in conversion) vineyards around the Lower Hunter with a total 15 ha of semillon, chardonnay, pinot noir, shiraz, merlot, mataro and cabernet sauvignon. This has led to Ross McDonald (and his family) leaving a busy Sydney life to be full-time grapegrower and winemaker. Exports to the US, Canada and Japan.

Thomas Shiraz 2003 Light- to medium-bodied; smooth, supple rounded red and black fruits; gentle, ripe tannins, and a nice savoury twist to the finish. Cork. 13.5° alc. **RATING** 90 **DRINK** 2012 $ 20

Hunter Valley Chardonnay 2005 Pleasant, light-bodied yellow peach and melon flavours; the one-third barrel-fermented not obvious in flavour terms, but does add to structure. Screwcap. 13.5° alc. **RATING** 87 **DRINK** 2008 $ 16

Hunter Valley Cabernet Sauvignon 2004 **RATING** 85 **DRINK** 2009 $ 22

McVitty Grove

Wombeyan Caves Road, Mittagong, NSW 2575 **REGION** Southern Highlands
T (02) 4878 5044 **F** (02) 4878 5524 **WWW**.mcvittygrove.com.au **OPEN** Mon–Fri 8–5, w'ends 10–5
WINEMAKER High Range Vintners (Nick Spencer) **EST.** 1998 **CASES** 2000
Notwithstanding his 20-year career in finance, Mark Phillips also had 6 years of tertiary qualifications in horticulture when he and wife Jane began the search for a Southern Highlands site suited to premium grapegrowing and olive cultivation. In 1998 they bought 42 ha of farm land on the Wombeyan Caves Road, just out of Mittagong. They have now established 5.5 ha of pinot noir and pinot gris on deep, fertile soils at the front of the property. In addition, a 1.5-ha olive grove has been planted, which provides the backdrop for the cellar door and café.

Black Label Southern Highlands Pinot Gris 2005 Sweet pear, spice and baked apple aromas and flavours; good acidity and length. Screwcap. 13.1° alc. **RATING** 90 **DRINK** 2008 $ 24

Silver Label Southern Highlands Pinot Gris 2005 Although the alcohol is the same as the Black Label, a less intense version. Screwcap. 13.1° alc. **RATING** 86 **DRINK** Now $ 18

McWilliam's ★★★★★

Jack McWilliam Road, Hanwood, NSW 2680 **REGION** Riverina
T (02) 6963 0001 **F** (02) 6963 0002 **WWW**.mcwilliams.com.au **OPEN** Mon–Sat 9–5
WINEMAKER Jim Brayne, Martin Cooper, Russell Cody **EST.** 1916 **CASES** NFP
The best wines to emanate from the Hanwood winery are from other regions, notably the Barwang
Vineyard at Hilltops (see separate entry) in NSW, Coonawarra (Brand's of Coonawarra) and Eden
Valley. As McWilliam's viticultural resources have expanded, they have been able to produce regional
blends from across southeastern Australia under the Hanwood label; in the last few years, these have
been startlingly good. Exports to many countries via a major distribution joint venture with Gallo.

🍷🍷🍷🍷🍷 **Limited Release Show Reserve Muscat NV** Exceptionally concentrated and aged;
viscous, mouth-coating and powerful, but not stale. A huge string of trophies and gold
medals. Cork. 18° alc. **RATING** 96 **DRINK** Now $ 68
Regional Collection Eden Valley Riesling 2004 Glowing yellow-green; intense
lime/lemon/toast/kerosene aromas; impressive intensity and length; has grown
exponentially in bottle; zesty finish. **RATING** 95 **DRINK** 2013 $ 18.50
Limited Release Riverina Botrytis Semillon 2004 Bright, youthful colour; a well-
balanced wine with preserved lemon, cumquat and peach; well-handled oak, and good
acidity. Cork. 12.5° alc. **RATING** 94 **DRINK** 2008 $ 30

🍷🍷🍷🍷🍸 **Hanwood Estate Sauvignon Blanc 2005** Spotlessly clean, smart wine; intense flavours of
grass, gooseberry and stone fruit; excellent length courtesy of crunchy acidity. Screwcap.
12° alc. **RATING** 90 **DRINK** Now $ 12
Hanwood Estate Chardonnay 2004 Very classy wine at the price; excellent varietal stone
fruit and melon on a smooth, long palate. Still fresh. Twin top. **RATING** 90 **DRINK** Now $ 12

🍷🍷🍷🍷 **Inheritance Semillon Sauvignon Blanc 2005** Clean bouquet; very lively and fresh
lemony/grassy/gooseberry palate; crisp, lemony acidity on the finish. Screwcap. **RATING** 89
DRINK Now $ 9
Hanwood Estate Cabernet Sauvignon 2004 McWilliam's has it down to a fine art; clear
blackcurrant and cassis in a light- to medium-bodied frame; a nice touch of oak, too. Twin
top. 13.5° alc. **RATING** 89 **DRINK** 2008 $ 12
Regional Collection Margaret River Cabernet Merlot 2003 Fragrant cassis and
raspberry; light- to medium-bodied; red fruits, light tannins, nice oak. Cork. **RATING** 88
DRINK 2008 $ 18
Hanwood Special Reserve Tawny Port NV Very sweet raisins and cake style; aimed at a
particular market niche. Cork. 19° alc. **RATING** 88 **DRINK** Now $ 25
Hanwood Estate Semillon Sauvignon Blanc 2005 Clean, correct lemon and
passionfruit aromas and flavours; not particularly intense, but well-balanced. Screwcap.
11.5° alc. **RATING** 87 **DRINK** Now $ 12
Hanwood Estate Semillon Chardonnay 2004 Light- to medium-bodied; good balance,
driven by lemony semillon; chardonnay adds a touch to the mid-palate; good value.
Screwcap. 12° alc. **RATING** 87 **DRINK** Now $ 12
Regional Collection Barossa Shiraz 2004 Light- to medium-bodied; slight confection
notes to juicy berry fruit. Cork. **RATING** 87 **DRINK** 2008 $ 18
Hanwood Estate Shiraz 2004 Light- to medium-bodied; bright, cherry-accented fruit;
good balance and length; incidental oak. Screwcap. 13.5° alc. **RATING** 87 **DRINK** 2008 $ 12
Hanwood Estate Sparkling Shiraz NV Fresh, attractive cherry fruit; simple structure and
texture, but has good balance and length. Value Cork. 13.5° alc. **RATING** 87 **DRINK** 2008 $ 12

🍷🍷🍷🍸 **JJ Chardonnay 2004** Light- to medium-bodied; pleasant stone fruit flavours and an
airbrush of oak; best in the JJ range. Screwcap. 13° alc. **RATING** 86 **DRINK** Now $ 10
Hanwood Estate Merlot 2004 Lively, fresh and bright; ready to roll right now; from
various southeast Australian vineyards. Twin top. 13.5° alc. **RATING** 86 **DRINK** 2009 $ 12
Inheritance Riesling 2005 **RATING** 85 **DRINK** Now $ 9
Hanwood Estate Verdelho 2005 **RATING** 85 **DRINK** Now $ 12
JJ Shiraz 2004 **RATING** 85 **DRINK** Now $ 10
Inheritance Shiraz Cabernet 2004 **RATING** 84 **DRINK** Now $ 9
JJ Merlot 2005 **RATING** 84 $ 10
JJ Cabernet Sauvignon 2004 **RATING** 84 **DRINK** Now $ 10

▼▼▼   Inheritance White Shiraz 2004 RATING 83 $ 9
Hanwood Estate Pinot Noir Chardonnay Brut NV RATING 83 $ 12

McWilliam's Mount Pleasant ★★★★★

Marrowbone Road, Pokolbin, NSW 2320 REGION Lower Hunter Valley
T (02) 4998 7505 F (02) 4998 7761 www.mcwilliams.com.au OPEN 7 days 10–5
WINEMAKER Phillip Ryan, Andrew Leembruggen EST. 1921 CASES NFP
McWilliam's Elizabeth and the glorious Lovedale Semillon are generally commercially available with
4–5 years of bottle age and are undervalued treasures with a consistently superb show record. The
individual vineyard wines, together with the Maurice O'Shea memorial wines, add to the lustre of
this proud name. Exports to many countries, the most important being the UK, the US, Germany
and NZ.

▼▼▼▼▼   Museum Release Elizabeth Semillon 1998 Bright green-yellow; a great mix of youth
and maturity; perfect line and length; citrus/lemon-driven; little toast developing so far.
Multiple trophies. Cork. RATING 96 DRINK 2008 $ 35
Lovedale Semillon 2000 Glowing yellow-green; a complex bouquet, showing the first
signs of toast; intense, lingering grass, citrus and toast flavours; crisp, minerally acidity.
Smart new packaging; numbered bottles. Cork. 11.5° alc. RATING 95 DRINK 2015 $ 50
Elizabeth Semillon 2000 Has come into its own; offers great finesse and delicacy
combined with honey, lime and a touch of toast; typical length and acidity. Four gold
medals. Wet cork a worry, though. Cork. RATING 94 DRINK 2010 $ 18
Maurice O'Shea 2003 Good colour; bright, fresh plum and blackberry fruit; much more
structure than usual; firm, though ripe, tannins make this for the long haul, and probably
higher points down the track. Cork. RATING 94 DRINK 2023 $ 60
Old Paddock & Old Hill Shiraz 2001 The regional influences are obvious, as they should
be; sweet red berry fruit interwoven with mocha/vanilla oak; fine, ripe tannins. Cork.
13.5° alc. RATING 94 DRINK 2011 $ 36.50

▼▼▼▼▽   Old Paddock & Old Hill Shiraz 2002 Bright, clear red-purple; fine, elegant light- to
medium-bodied wine; quite fragrant, with spicy/earthy regional overtones to the core of
black fruits; fine, ripe tannins; good line and length. Cork. RATING 92 DRINK 2017 $ 35
Rosehill Shiraz 2001 Distinctly different fruit register from the Old Paddock & Old Hill,
though still strongly regional; medium-bodied, more savoury/dark chocolate notes, the
tannins a little more solid. Very good outcome for a difficult red vintage. Cork. RATING 91
DRINK 2015 $ 35

▼▼▼▽   Hunter Valley Verdelho 2004 RATING 86 DRINK Now $ 15
Sparkling Pinot Noir 2002 RATING 86 DRINK Now $ 21.50

🐾 Mad Dog Wines ★★★★☆

7a Murray Street, Tanunda, SA 5352 (postal) REGION Barossa Valley
T (08) 8563 1551 F (08) 8563 0754 www.maddogwines.com OPEN Not
WINEMAKER Barossa Vintners EST. 1999 CASES 500
Geoff (aka Mad Dog) Munzberg is a third generation grapegrower who has joined with Jeremy and
Heidi Holmes, Aaron and Kirsty Brasher and son Matthew to create Mad Dog Wines. The principal
wine, Shiraz, comes from 5 ha of vines with an average age of 35 years. The major portion of the
grapes are sold, the best kept for the Mad Dog label. As from 2006, the acquisition of a neighbouring
vineyard will result in the inclusion of some 100-year-old vine fruit, and the range will be slightly
extended with small quantities of Moscato and a few bottles of Sangiovese.

▼▼▼▼▽   Barossa Valley Shiraz 2004 Good colour; a complex array of leather, spice, licorice and
blackberry aromas and flavours; while powerful, is nimble on its feet. Cork. RATING 93
DRINK 2014 $ 37

Madew Wines

NR

Westering, Federal Highway, Lake George, NSW 2581 **REGION** Canberra District
T (02) 4848 0026 **F** (02) 4848 0164 **WWW**.madewwines.com.au **OPEN** Wed–Sun & public hols 10–5
WINEMAKER David Madew **EST.** 1984 **CASES** 5000
Madew Wines bowed to the urban pressure of Queanbeyan and purchased the Westering Vineyard from Captain GP Hood some years ago. Plantings there have now increased to 9.5 ha, with 1 ha each of shiraz and pinot gris coming into bearing. Madew's award-winning restaurant, grapefoodwine, is open Fri–Sat for lunch and dinner, Sun for breakfast and lunch, and also hosts monthly music concerts.

Madigan Vineyard

NR

504 Wilderness Road, Rothbury, NSW 2320 **REGION** Lower Hunter Valley
T (02) 4998 7815 **F** (02) 4998 7116 **WWW**.madiganvineyard.com.au **OPEN** W'ends 10–5
WINEMAKER Rhys Eather (Contract) **EST.** 1996 **CASES** 1200
Bob and Ann Rich have 3.5 ha of shiraz, chardonnay and verdelho at Rothbury, with the infinitely experienced Keith Holder as viticulturist. Virtually all the wine is sold by mailing list and through the cellar door.

Maglieri of McLaren Vale

Douglas Gully Road, McLaren Flat, SA 5171 **REGION** McLaren Vale
T (08) 8383 0177 **F** (08) 8383 0735 **WWW**.maglieri.com.au **OPEN** Mon–Sat 9–4, Sun 12–4
WINEMAKER Charles Hargrave **EST.** 1972 **CASES** 14 000
Was one of the better-kept secrets among the wine cognoscenti, but not among the many customers who drink thousands of cases of white and red Lambrusco every year, an example of niche marketing at its profitable best. It was a formula which proved irresistible to Beringer Blass, which acquired Maglieri in 1999. Its dry red wines are invariably generously proportioned and full of character, the Shiraz particularly so.

ᵀᵀᵀᵀ **Shiraz 2003** A sweet mix of red and black fruits, dark chocolate and vanilla oak; medium-bodied; good flow and mouthfeel. Cork. **RATING** 90 **DRINK** 2011 $ 19
Cabernet Sauvignon 2003 A mix of blackcurrant, earth, cedar and dark chocolate in a medium-bodied frame; ripe tannins; particularly impressive for the vintage. Quality cork. **RATING** 90 **DRINK** 2010 $ 19

ᵀᵀᵀᵀ **Merlot 2004** Fresh, lively redcurrant and raspberry fruit; minimal oak influence; fine tannins, clean finish. Cork. **RATING** 89 **DRINK** 2010 $ 19

ᵀᵀᵀᵀ **Chardonnay 2004 RATING** 86 **DRINK** Now $ 19

Magpie Estate

PO Box 126, Tanunda, SA 5352 **REGION** Barossa Valley
T (08) 8562 3300 **F** (08) 8562 1177 **OPEN** Not
WINEMAKER Rolf Binder, Noel Young **EST.** 1993 **CASES** 6000
This is a partnership between Rolf Binder and Cambridge (England) wine merchant Noel Young. It came about in 1993 when there was limited demand for or understanding of Southern Rhône-style blends based on Shiraz, Grenache and Mourvedre. Initially a small, export-only brand, the quality of the wines was such that it has grown substantially over the years, although the intention is to limit production. The majority of the wines are very reasonably priced (The Schnell! Shiraz Grenache, The Black Sock Mourvedre, The Fakir Grenache, the Callbag Grenache Mourvedre, The Sack Shiraz and The Wit and the Shanker Cabernet); the two super-premiums (The Gomersal Grenache and The Election Shiraz) are more expensive. The labelling is strongly reminiscent of Torbreck and other subsequent ventures, but the quality of the wine needs no assistance. Exports to the UK, the US and other major markets.

ΤΤΤΤΥ **Wit & Shanker Barossa Valley Cabernet Sauvignon 2003** Ripe blackcurrant fruit with whisks of licorice, tar and dark chocolate; good mouthfeel, controlled extract. Cork. 14° alc. **RATING** 91 **DRINK** 2012

The Black Sock Barossa Valley 2003 Good hue; dark fruits, bitter chocolate and earth; impressive control of tannins and balanced oak. Cork. 14° alc. **RATING** 90 **DRINK** 2013

ΤΤΤΤ **The Sack Barossa Valley Shiraz 2003** A complex medium-bodied mix of spice, earth and vanilla over black fruits; light, supple tannins. Cork. 14.5° alc. **RATING** 89 **DRINK** 2010

Main Ridge Estate   ★★★★☆

80 William Road, Red Hill, Vic 3937 **REGION** Mornington Peninsula
T(03) 5989 2686 **F**(03) 5931 0000 **WWW**.mre.com.au **OPEN** Mon–Fri 12–4, w'ends 12–5
WINEMAKER Nat White **EST.** 1975 **CASES** 1300
Nat White gives meticulous attention to every aspect of his viticulture and winemaking, doing annual battle with one of the coolest sites on the Peninsula. The same attention to detail extends to the winery and the winemaking. Despite such minuscule production, exports to the UK and Singapore.

ΤΤΤΤΤ **Mornington Peninsula Chardonnay 2004** Elegant wine; controlled complexity from the rich stone fruit and fig mid-palate and positive barrel ferment components; powerful finish and length. Screwcap. 14° alc. **RATING** 94 **DRINK** 2012 $45

ΤΤΤΤΥ **Half Acre Mornington Peninsula Pinot Noir 2004** Light but good purple-red; light- to medium-bodied, with a spicy, savoury overlay to the red fruits of the palate; controlled oak. May well gain body as it ages. Screwcap. 14° alc. **RATING** 91 **DRINK** 2011 $48

Maiolo Wines   NR

Bussell Highway, Carbunup River, WA 6282 **REGION** Margaret River
T(08) 9755 1060 **F**(08) 9755 1060 **WWW**.maiolowines.com.au **OPEN** 7 days 10–5
WINEMAKER Charles Maiolo **EST.** 1999 **CASES** 4000
Charles Maiolo has established a 28-ha vineyard planted to semillon, sauvignon blanc, chardonnay, pinot noir, shiraz, merlot and cabernet sauvignon. He has a wine science degree from Charles Sturt University, and presides over a winery with a capacity of 250–300 tonnes. The red wines, in particular, show great promise, with Shiraz and Cabernet Sauvignon to the fore. Exports to Canada and Singapore.

Majella   ★★★★☆

Lynn Road, Coonawarra, SA 5263 **REGION** Coonawarra
T(08) 8736 3055 **F**(08) 8736 3057 **WWW**.majellawines.com.au **OPEN** 7 days 10–4.30
WINEMAKER Bruce Gregory **EST.** 1969 **CASES** 14 000
Majella is one of the more important contract grapegrowers in Coonawarra, with 61 ha of vineyard, principally shiraz and cabernet sauvignon, and with a little riesling and merlot. Common gossip has it that part finds its way into the Wynns John Riddoch Cabernet Sauvignon and Michael Shiraz, or their equivalent within the Southcorp Group. The Malleea is one of Coonawarra's best wines. Production under the Majella label has increased substantially over the past few years. Exports to the UK, the US and other major markets.

ΤΤΤΤΤ **Coonawarra Cabernet Sauvignon 2003** Spotlessly clean; a fine, long, supple palate driven by fresh, cassis-accented fruit; fine, ripe tannins. Screwcap. **RATING** 94 **DRINK** 2015 $30

ΤΤΤΤΥ **The Musician Coonawarra Cabernet Shiraz 2004** Excellent deep colour; flooded with luscious blackcurrant, cassis and blackberry fruit; fine, ripe tannins; oak incidental; outstanding value; 70% Cabernet Sauvignon/30% Shiraz. Screwcap. **RATING** 92 **DRINK** 2014 $18

Coonawarra Shiraz 2003 Vibrant cherry and blackberry fruit; linear mouthfeel with fine tannins and controlled oak. Screwcap. **RATING** 90 **DRINK** 2013 $30

ΤΤΤΥ **Riesling 2005** Pleasantly crisp; light apple, pear and citrus aromas and flavours; needs time. **RATING** 86 **DRINK** 2009 $16

🐦 Majors Lane Wines ★★★★

64 Majors Lane, Lovedale, NSW 2320 **REGION** Lower Hunter Valley
T (02) 4930 7328 **F** (02) 4930 7023 **WWW**.majorslane.com **OPEN** Fri–Mon 9.30–5
WINEMAKER Alasdair Sutherland (white wines), David Hook (red wines) **EST.** 1987 **CASES** NFP
Sydney lawyers Ivan and Susan Judd, specialising in contract and industrial law, purchased the Majors Lane vineyard in 2001. Fourteen years earlier Alan and Rosemary MacMillan had planted 3 ha each of semillon, chardonnay and shiraz, plus 1 ha of chambourcin, adding 700 olive trees a decade later. Susan Judd has retired from legal practice to run the cellar door and help in the restaurant, with husband Ivan commuting to and from Sydney.

🍷🍷🍷🍷🍷 **Shiraz 2003** Attractive, fragrant red and blackberry fruits; medium-bodied; good tannins and mouthfeel, likewise oak. Cork. **RATING** 90 **DRINK** 2012 $ 21

🍷🍷🍷🍷 **Semillon 2003** An aromatic mix of gooseberry, tropical and lemon/citrus aromas; a light palate, less intense than the bouquet promises, and more to grassy in style. Screwcap. **RATING** 88 **DRINK** 2009 $ 17

🍷🍷🍷🍷 **Chardonnay 2003** **RATING** 85 **DRINK** Now $ 21

Malcolm Creek Vineyard ★★★★

Bonython Road, Kersbrook, SA 5231 **REGION** Adelaide Hills
T (08) 8389 3235 **F** (08) 8389 3235 **OPEN** W'ends & public hols 11–5, or by appt
WINEMAKER Reg Tolley **EST.** 1982 **CASES** 700
Malcolm Creek is the retirement venture of Reg Tolley, and he keeps a low profile. However, the wines are invariably well-made and develop gracefully; they are worth seeking out, and are usually available with some extra bottle age at a very modest price. Exports to the UK.

🍷🍷🍷🍷🍷 **Adelaide Hills Chardonnay 2005** Abundant flavour in fruit-driven style; nectarine and peach balanced by firm acidity and minimal oak. Screwcap. 13° alc. **RATING** 90 **DRINK** 2008 $ 19

🍷🍷🍷🍷 **Adelaide Hills Cabernet Sauvignon 2003** Light- to medium-bodied; leafy, savoury, earthy wine with a touch of chocolate, but not enough sweet fruit. Cork. 14° alc. **RATING** 86 **DRINK** 2009 $ 22

Mandalay Estate NR

Mandalay Road, Mumballup, WA 6010 **REGION** Geographe
T (08) 9372 2006 **F** (08) 9384 5962 **WWW**.mandalayestate.com.au **OPEN** 7 days 10–5
WINEMAKER Contract **EST.** 1997 **CASES** 400
Terry and Bernice O'Connell have established 6 ha of chardonnay, shiraz, cabernet sauvignon and zinfandel on their 40-ha property, previously owned by Bunnings Tree Farms and abounding with tree stumps. The tasting room has been established in an old plant shed on the property.

Mandurang Valley Wines NR

77 Fadersons Lane, Mandurang, Vic 3551 **REGION** Bendigo
T (03) 5439 5367 **F** (03) 5439 3850 **WWW**.mandurangvalleywines.com.au **OPEN** Fri–Tues 11–5
WINEMAKER Wes Vine, Steve Vine **EST.** 1994 **CASES** 2300
Wes and Pamela Vine planted their first vineyard at Mandurang in 1976 and started making wine as a hobby. Commercial production began in 1993, and an additional vineyard was established in 1997. Wes Vine (a former school principal) has been full-time winemaker since 1999, with son Steve becoming more involved each vintage. The cellar door café (managed by Pamela) has expansive lawns and gardens.

Mann NR

105 Memorial Avenue, Baskerville, WA 6056 **REGION** Swan Valley
T (08) 9296 4348 **F** (08) 9296 4348 **OPEN** W'ends 10–5 & by appt from 1 Aug until sold out
WINEMAKER Dorham Mann **EST.** 1988 **CASES** 600
Industry veteran Dorham Mann has established a one-wine label for what must be Australia's most unusual wine: a dry, only faintly pink, sparkling wine made exclusively from cabernet sauvignon and cygne blanc grown on the 2.5-ha estate surrounding the cellar door. Dorham Mann explains, 'Our family has made and enjoyed the style for more than 30 years, although just in a private capacity until recently.'

Mansfield Wines

204 Eurunderee Lane, Mudgee, NSW 2850 **REGION** Mudgee
T (02) 6373 3871 **F** (02) 6373 3708 **OPEN** Thurs–Tues & public hols 10–5, or by appt
WINEMAKER Bob Heslop **EST.** 1975 **CASES** 2000
Mansfield Wines has moved with the times, moving the emphasis from fortified wines to table wines (though still offering some fortifieds) and expanding the product range to take in new generation reds such as Touriga and Zinfandel.

ΥΥΥΥ **Touriga 2004** Good colour; medium-bodied with black cherry, mulberry and spice flavours, but the main distinction comes from the super-fine, spicy, ripe tannins. Diam. 14° alc. **RATING** 89 **DRINK** 2010 $ 18
Zinfandel 2004 Light red; light- to medium-bodied spicy red fruits in a morello cherry spectrum; nice acidity on the finish. Diam. 14° alc. **RATING** 88 **DRINK** 2009 $ 18

Mantons Creek Vineyard

240 Tucks Road, Main Ridge, Vic 3928 **REGION** Mornington Peninsula
T (03) 5989 6264 **F** (03) 5989 6348 **WWW**.mantonscreekvineyard.com.au **OPEN** 7 days 11–5
WINEMAKER Alex White (Contract) **EST.** 1990 **CASES** 3500
The 19-ha property was originally an orchard, herb farm and horse stud. After the vineyard was established, the grapes were sold to other wineries in the region until 1998, when the first Mantons Creek wines were made from the 10-ha vineyard planted in 1994. A purpose-built cellar door, restaurant and 4-bedroom accommodation unit was opened in 1998; the property was purchased by Dr Michael Ablett, a retired cardiologist, and his wife Judy in March 2001. Exports to Hong Kong and Japan.

ΥΥΥΥΥ **Chardonnay 2003** Attractive wine, developing well; quite intense nectarine and melon fruit; nutty notes from positive oak. Screwcap. 14.6° alc. **RATING** 92 **DRINK** 2008 $ 26

ΥΥΥΥ **Mornington Peninsula Tempranillo 2004** Intriguing aromas and flavours of spice, date and plum; does heat up significantly on the finish and aftertaste. Screwcap. 15.6° alc. **RATING** 87 **DRINK** 2009 $ 37.50

ΥΥΥΥ **Pinot Meunier 2003** **RATING** 85 **DRINK** Now $ 30
Rosado 2004 **RATING** 84 **DRINK** Now $ 25

Margan Family

1238 Milbrodale Road, Broke, NSW 2330 **REGION** Lower Hunter Valley
T (02) 6579 1317 **F** (02) 6579 1267 **WWW**.margan.com.au **OPEN** 7 days 10–5
WINEMAKER Andrew Margan **EST.** 1997 **CASES** 30 000
Andrew Margan followed in his father's footsteps by entering the wine industry 20 years ago and has covered a great deal of territory since, working as a Flying Winemaker in Europe, then for Tyrrell's, first as a winemaker then as marketing manager. His wife Lisa, too, has had many years of experience in restaurants and marketing. They now have over 80 ha of fully yielding vines at their Ceres Hill homestead property at Broke, and lease the nearby Vere Vineyard. Wine quality (and packaging) is consistently good. Exports to the UK, the US and other major markets.

ΥΥΥΥΥ **Hunter Valley Botrytis Semillon 2005** Glowing yellow-green; rich, complex, fruit-driven cumquat, mandarin, yellow peach and lemon; very good acidity. Margan has the style down pat. Screwcap. 10.5° alc. **RATING** 93 **DRINK** 2010 $ 30
Hunter Valley Chardonnay 2005 Nectarine, melon and peach with complex barrel ferment/wild yeast/lees inputs; powerful wine. Screwcap. 13° alc. **RATING** 90 **DRINK** 2011 $ 20

ΥΥΥΥ **Hunter Valley Merlot 2004** Colour not entirely bright; black cherry and plum fruit with spice and savoury/tobacco varietal tannins. Screwcap. 13.5° alc. **RATING** 89 **DRINK** 2012 $ 20
Hunter Valley Shiraz 2004 Nicely balanced medium-bodied wine; blackberry and plum; minimal oak, fine tannins. Cork. 13.5° alc. **RATING** 88 **DRINK** 2009 $ 20
Hunter Valley Barbera 2004 Light- to medium-bodied; juicy red berry fruits, but slightly hollow structure. Screwcap. 14° alc. **RATING** 87 **DRINK** 2008 $ 30

ΥΥΥΥΥ **Hunter Valley Shiraz Saignee 2005** **RATING** 86 **DRINK** Now $ 17
Ceres Hill Limited Release Barbera 2003 **RATING** 86 **DRINK** Now $ 20
Verdelho 2005 **RATING** 85 **DRINK** Now $ 18
Hunter Valley Cabernet Sauvignon 2003 **RATING** 85 **DRINK** 2013 $ 20

ΥΥΥ **Semillon 2005** **RATING** 83 $ 18

ΥΥΥ **Beltree Semillon 2005** **RATING** 79 $ 20

Marienberg   NR

2 Chalk Hill Road, McLaren Vale, SA 5171 **REGION** McLaren Vale
T (08) 8323 9666 **F** (08) 8323 9600 **OPEN** 7 days 10–5
WINEMAKER Peter Orr **EST.** 1966 **CASES** 25 000
A long-established business (founded by Australia's first female owner/vigneron, Ursula Pridham) acquired by James Estate in 2003. Exports to the UK and the US.

Marinda Park Vineyard   ★★★★

238 Myers Road, Balnarring, Vic 3926 **REGION** Mornington Peninsula
T (03) 5989 7613 **F** (03) 5989 7607 **WWW**.marindapark.com **OPEN** Thurs–Mon 11–5, 7 days in January
WINEMAKER Sandro Mosele (Contract) **EST.** 1999 **CASES** 2500
Mark and Belinda Rodman have established 18.7 ha of chardonnay, sauvignon blanc, pinot noir and merlot on their vineyard on the outskirts of Balnarring. They operate the business in conjunction with American partners Norm and Fanny Winton, who are involved in the sale and distribution of the wines in the US and Singapore.

ΥΥΥΥΥ **Mornington Peninsula Sauvignon Blanc 2005** A faintly blurred bouquet; good focus/intensity to the mix of tropical, herb and mineral flavours on the palate. Cork. 13.5° alc. **RATING** 90 **DRINK** Now $ 21

ΥΥΥΥ **Mornington Peninsula Pinot Noir 2004** Ripe plum, with some suggestion of desiccation/dead fruit characters; overall, fairly firm in the mouth. Cork. 13.5° alc. **RATING** 88 **DRINK** 2009 $ 28

ΥΥΥΥ **Mornington Peninsula Rose 2005** Pale pink; strawberry and lemon juice flavours; just a little too brisk and acidic. Cork. 13.5° alc. **RATING** 86 **DRINK** Now $ 19

Mariners Rest   NR

Jamakarri Farm, Roberts Road, Denmark, WA 6333 **REGION** Denmark
T (08) 9840 9324 **F** (08) 9840 9321 **OPEN** 7 days 11–5
WINEMAKER Brenden Smith **EST.** 1996 **CASES** 750
Mariners Rest is the reincarnation of the now defunct Golden Rise winery. A new 2.5-ha vineyard was planted in the spring of 1997, and a slightly odd selection of replacement wines are being marketed.

Maritime Estate

Tucks Road, Red Hill, Vic 3937 **REGION** Mornington Peninsula
T (03) 9848 2926 **F** (03) 9848 2926 **OPEN** W'ends & public hols 11–5, 7 days Dec 27–Jan 26
WINEMAKER Clare Halloran (Contract) **EST.** 1988 **CASES** 1500
John and Linda Ruljancich and Kevin Ruljancich have enjoyed great success since their first vintage in 1994, no doubt due in part to skilled winemaking but also to the situation of their vineyard, looking across the hills and valleys of the Red Hill subregion.

ŢŢŢŢŢ **Mornington Peninsula Chardonnay 2003** Fragrant melon and stone fruit; very fine and elegant, driven by its fruit, the oak purely in support; long finish. Screwcap. **RATING** 95 **DRINK** 2010 $ 26

ŢŢŢŢŢ **Mornington Peninsula Chardonnay 2004** Intense, cool-grown grapefruit, nectarine and melon flavours, with a very long finish; has swallowed all the oak. Screwcap. **RATING** 93 **DRINK** 2012 $ 30
Mornington Peninsula Pinot Noir 2004 Good colour; a quite powerful wine with sombre, spicy fruit; good length, and a pleasantly savoury finish. Screwcap. **RATING** 91 **DRINK** 2011 $ 42

ŢŢŢŢ **Mornington Peninsula Pinot Gris 2005** Clear-cut varietal character achieved without excess alcohol or sweetness; musk, apricot and a touch of ginger spice. A pinot gris with attitude. Screwcap. 13.8° alc. **RATING** 89 **DRINK** 2008 $ 24
Mornington Peninsula Pinot Gris 2004 Water-white; aromatic musk, spice and pear; only 13.8° alcohol, but in a Vendage Tardive Alsace style. Screwcap. 13.8° alc. **RATING** 89 **DRINK** Now $ 22

ŢŢŢŢ **Mornington Peninsula Pinot Noir 2003** AJR. Very light, and needs more flesh, though what is there is pleasant enough. Cork. **RATING** 86 **DRINK** 2008 $ 28

Marius Wines

NR

PO Box 545, Willunga, SA 5172 **REGION** McLaren Vale
T 0402 344 340 **F** (08) 8407 5717 **WWW**.mariuswines.com.au **OPEN** Not
WINEMAKER Mark Day **EST.** 1994 **CASES** 500
Roger Pike says he has loved wine for over 30 years; that for 15 years he has had the desire to add a little bit to the world of wine; and that over a decade ago he decided to do something about it, ripping the front paddock and planting 1.6 ha of shiraz in 1994. He sold the grapes from the 1997–99 vintages, but when the 1998 vintage became a single-vineyard wine (made by the purchaser of the grapes) selling in the US at $40, the temptation to have his own wine became irresistible. Exports to the US.

Markwood Estate

NR

Morris Lane, Markwood, Vic 3678 **REGION** King Valley
T (03) 5727 0361 **F** (03) 5727 0361 **OPEN** 7 days 9–5
WINEMAKER Rick Morris **EST.** 1971 **CASES** 200
A member of the famous Morris family, Rick Morris shuns publicity and relies virtually exclusively on cellar door sales for what is a small output. Of a range of table and fortified wines tasted some years ago, the Old Tawny Port (a cross between Port and Muscat, showing more of the character of the latter than the former) and a White Port (seemingly made from muscadelle) were the best.

🐀 Marlargo Wines

PO Box 371, Glenside, SA 5065 **REGION** Warehouse
T 0438 987 255 **F** (08) 8379 0596 **WWW**.marlargowines.com **OPEN** Not
WINEMAKER Various contract **EST.** 2003 **CASES** 5000
This is the ultimate virtual winery, with virtual homes in Bendigo, Yarra Glen, McLaren Vale, Gumeracha and Clare Valley. Each of the garishly-labelled wines is contract-made by a different winemaker at a different winery, and the range is being extended further. The partners in the venture are Simon Austerberry, a sixth generation farmer in the Pyrenees, and Mark Gibbs, a financial

adviser from Melbourne. The name comes from those of the partners' wives, Margot and Lara. I'm far from convinced by the labels and purple prose (the Latina Cabernet says 'be seduced ... sultry, seductive, sensual' and assures us the wine is matured in 'charismatic oak'); if the wines were at $15 a bottle, that is one thing, but it's another thing again at $33 a bottle — and 5000 cases of production heading north.

ΨΨΨΨ   **Latina Cabernet 2004** By far the best of the Marlargo wines; good, brisk blackcurrant and cassis fruit. Cork. 14.5° alc. **RATING** 88 **DRINK** 2011 $ 33

ΨΨΨΨ   **Soul Searcher Shiraz 2004** Light- to medium-bodied, particularly for the region (McLaren Vale) and vintage; ripe, red fruits with minimal oak tannins; well-made, but seemingly over-cropped vines. Screwcap. 14° alc. **RATING** 86 **DRINK** Now $ 33
Latina Cabernet 2005 Light- to medium-bodied mint/wintergreen notes from early picking; on the plus side, has fresh acidity. Yarra Valley. Screwcap. 12.5° alc. **RATING** 86 **DRINK** 2009 $ 33
Simple Pleasures Sauvignon Blanc 2005 **RATING** 84 **DRINK** Now $ 33
Gypsy Spirit Chardonnay 2005 **RATING** 84 **DRINK** 2008 $ 33

ΨΨΨ   **Temptation Rose 2005** **RATING** 83 $ 33

Maroochy Springs

NR

Musavale Road, Erwah Vale near Eumundi, Qld 4562 **REGION** Queensland Coastal
T (07) 5442 8777 **F** (07) 5442 8745 **WWW**.sunshinecoastwine.com.au **OPEN** 7 days 12–6
WINEMAKER Kevin Watson (Contract) **EST.** 2001 **CASES** NA
Jack and Margaret Connolly have established their winery in the beautiful Erwah Valley at the foothills of the Blackall Range, 30 mins' drive from Noosa and only 6 km west of Eumundi. They have the usual range of general tourist facilities and attractions.

Marquis Phillips

NR

2 Riviera Court, Pasadena, SA 5042 (postal) **REGION** Fleurieu/Limestone Coast Zone
T (08) 8357 4560 **F** (08) 8357 4234 **OPEN** Not
WINEMAKER Sparky Marquis, Sarah Marquis, Kim Johnston **EST.** 1998 **CASES** NA
Marquis Phillips is the export-oriented brand created by the high-profile Sparky and Sarah Marquis winemaking duo. The very large production is directed to the Canadian, German, Singapore and the US markets, but is nominally available by mail order.

Marri Wood Park

Cnr Caves Road/Whittle Road, Yallingup, WA 6282 **REGION** Margaret River
T 0438 525 580 **F** (08) 9386 5087 **WWW**.marriwdpk.com **OPEN** W'ends & public hols 10.30–5.30
WINEMAKER Bob Cartwright, Brian Fletcher (Contract) **EST.** 1993 **CASES** 1800
With plantings commencing back in 1993, Marri Wood Park has 6.5 ha of vineyards: 2 ha of chenin blanc and 1.5 ha each of semillon, sauvignon blanc and cabernet sauvignon. Part of the grapes are sold to other makers, the wine for Marri Wood Park being made by Mark Messenger. The budget-priced Guinea Run range takes its name from the guinea fowl which are permanent vineyard residents, busily eating the grasshoppers, weevils and bugs which cluster around the base of the vines, thus reducing the need for pesticides. The premium Marri Wood Park range takes its name from the giant Marri gum tree depicted on the label.

ΨΨΨΨΨ   **Margaret River Sauvignon Blanc 2005** Fresh, clean, crisp and lively; an attractive mix of grass, gooseberry and tropical fruit, finishing with lemony acidity. Screwcap. 13° alc. **RATING** 92 **DRINK** Now $ 15
Margaret River Semillon Sauvignon Blanc 2005 Light straw-green; a spotlessly clean bouquet, then a well-constituted and constructed palate, with mineral and grass from the semillon, tropical fruit from the sauvignon blanc. Screwcap. 13.5° alc. **RATING** 91 **DRINK** 2008 $ 15

ΨΨΨΨ   **Margaret River Cabernet Sauvignon 2005** Vivid purple-red; virtually entirely fruit-driven by cassis/blackcurrant fruit; possibly used micro-oxygenation; either way, good outcome. Screwcap. 14° alc. **RATING** 89 **DRINK** 2010 $ 16

ỸỸỸỸ Guinea Run Chenin Blanc 2005 RATING 86 DRINK Now $14
Guinea Run Classic White 2005 RATING 85 DRINK Now $14
Guinea Run Cabernet Merlot 2005 RATING 85 DRINK 2008 $16

Marribrook ★★★★

Albany Highway, Kendenup, WA 6323 REGION Mount Barker
T (08) 9851 4651 OPEN W'ends, school & public hols 10.30–4.30
WINEMAKER Harewood Estate (James Kellie) EST. 1990 CASES 2000
The Brooks family purchased the former Marron View 5.6-ha vineyard from Kim Hart in 1994 and
renamed the venture Marribrook Wines; they have also purchased an additional property on the
Albany Highway north of Mount Barker and immediately south of Gilberts. Exports to the UK and
Singapore.

ỸỸỸỸỸ **Botanica Frankland River Chardonnay 2005** Peach, nectarine, fig and melon fruit; good
texture and structure, likely from lees contact, as no oak is used. Several gold medals.
Screwcap. 14° alc. RATING 91 DRINK 2009 $18

ỸỸỸỸ **Frankland River Marsanne 2005** Wild flowers, nuts and honeysuckle; excellent acidity to
sustain the undoubted development potential the wine has. Screwcap. 13.5° alc. RATING 89
DRINK 2015 $15
Members Reserve Frankland River Malbec 2004 Typical slightly jammy confection
fruit, and typical struggle for structure. Such a difficult variety to manage; Great Southern
does it best. Screwcap. 14° alc. RATING 87 DRINK 2009 $28

Marschall Groom Cellars ★★★★☆

28 Langmeil Road, Tanunda, SA 5352 (postal) REGION Barossa Valley
T (08) 8563 1101 F (08) 8563 1102 WWW.groomwines.com OPEN Not
WINEMAKER Daryl Groom EST. 1997 CASES 2000
This is a family venture involving Daryl Groom, former Penfolds but now long-term Geyser Peak
winemaker in California, Jeannette Marschall and David Marschall. It is an export-focused business,
the principal market being the US.

ỸỸỸỸỸ **Barossa Valley Shiraz 2004** Blackberry, spice and leather aromas; a wonderfully silky
smooth and supple palate leaning more to red than black fruits; good oak. Cork. 13.8° alc.
RATING 94 DRINK 2015 $48

ỸỸỸỸỸ **Adelaide Hills Sauvignon Blanc 2005** Spotlessly clean; attractive, gentle apple,
passionfruit and gooseberry; a soft fruity, rather than minerally, finish. Screwcap. 12.9° alc.
RATING 90 DRINK Now $24

Marsh Estate ★★★★

Deasy's Road, Pokolbin, NSW 2321 REGION Lower Hunter Valley
T (02) 4998 7587 F (02) 4998 7884 OPEN Mon–Fri 10–4.30, w'ends 10–5
WINEMAKER Andrew Marsh EST. 1971 CASES 6000
Through sheer consistency, value for money and unrelenting hard work, the Marsh family (who
purchased the former Quentin Estate in 1978) has built up a sufficiently loyal cellar door and mailing
list clientele to allow all the considerable production to be sold direct. Wine style is always direct,
with oak playing a minimal role, and prolonged cellaring paying handsome dividends.

ỸỸỸỸỸ **Hunter River Pokolbin Semillon 2000** Glowing deep gold; rich honey and lightly
browned toast and nuts; balancing acidity. Cork. 12° alc. RATING 91 DRINK 2008 $35
Vat R Hunter River Pokolbin Shiraz 2004 Strong red-purple; well above-average depth
and richness to the blackberry, earth and chocolate fruit plus some vanilla/mocha oak.
Should cellar well. Cork. 12.5° alc. RATING 91 DRINK 2010 $25
Holly's Block Hunter Valley Semillon 2005 Green-gold, already showing some
development; rich, full-bodied style with incipient honey; soft mid-palate, then a tweak of
acidity to close. Cork. 11° alc. RATING 90 DRINK 2012 $27.50

ỸỸỸỸ **Hunter Valley Cremant Brut 2000** RATING 86 DRINK Now $25

Martins Hill Wines
NR

Sydney Road, Mudgee, NSW 2850 **REGION** Mudgee
T (02) 6373 1248 **F** (02) 6373 1248 **OPEN** Not
WINEMAKER Pieter Van Gent (Contract) **EST.** 1985 **CASES** 600
Janette Kenworthy and Michael Sweeny are committed organic grapegrowers and are members of
the Organic Vignerons Association. It is a tiny operation at the moment, with 0.5 ha each of
sauvignon blanc and pinot noir, 1 ha of cabernet sauvignon and 1.5 ha of shiraz in production.
Organic vineyard tours and talks can be arranged by appointment.

Mary Byrnes Wine
NR

Rees Road, Ballandean, Qld 4382 **REGION** Granite Belt
T (07) 4684 1111 **F** (07) 4684 1312 **OPEN** 7 days 10–5 Easter–Oct
WINEMAKER Mary Byrnes **EST.** 1991 **CASES** 3500
Mary Byrnes, who has a wine science degree, acquired her property in 1991, and has since planted 4
ha of shiraz, and 1 ha each of marsanne, viognier, roussanne and mourvedre, and 0.5 ha each of
grenache and black hamburg muscat. She has deliberately grown the vines without irrigation,
thereby limiting yield and (in her words) ensuring a distinctive regional quality and flavour. Exports
to the UK and NZ.

Marybrook Vineyards
NR

Vasse–Yallingup Road, Marybrook, WA 6280 **REGION** Margaret River
T (08) 9755 1143 **F** (08) 9755 1112 **OPEN** Fri–Mon 10–5, 7 days 10–5 school hols
WINEMAKER Aub House **EST.** 1986 **CASES** 2000
Marybrook Vineyards is owned by Aub and Jan House. They have 8 ha of vineyards in production,
with back vintages often available.

mas serrat
NR

PO Box 478, Yarra Glen, Vic 3775 **REGION** Yarra Valley
T (03) 9730 1439 **F** (03) 9730 1579 **WWW**.serrat.com.au **OPEN** Not
WINEMAKER Tom Carson **EST.** 2001 **CASES** 300
mas serrat is the family business of Tom Carson (celebrated winemaker at Yering Station) and
partner Nadege Sune. They have close-planted (at 8800 vines per ha) 1 ha of pinot noir, 0.7 ha of
shiraz, and lesser amounts of chardonnay, viognier and grenache. The intention is to make pinot noir,
chardonnay and, likely, a blend of shiraz, viognier and grenache.

Maslin Old Dunsborough Wines
NR

90 Naturaliste Terrace, Dunsborough, WA 6281 **REGION** Margaret River
T (08) 9755 3578 **F** (08) 9755 3578 **OPEN** W'ends, or by appt
WINEMAKER Robert Maslin **EST.** 1999 **CASES** NA
Yet another entrant in the Margaret River region, established by Robert and Leonie Maslin. They
have planted semillon, sauvignon blanc, chenin blanc, pinot noir, merlot and cabernet sauvignon and
make the wines onsite. The cellar door offers barbecue facilities.

Mason Wines
★★★

27850 New England Highway, Glen Aplin, Qld 4381 **REGION** Granite Belt
T (07) 4684 1341 **F** (07) 4684 1342 **WWW**.masonwines.com.au **OPEN** 7 days 11–4
WINEMAKER Jim Barnes **EST.** 1998 **CASES** NA
Robert and Kim Mason set strict criteria when searching for land suited to viticulture: a long history
of commercial stone fruit production with well-drained, deep soil. The first property was purchased
in 1997, the fruit trees being removed in 1998, the vines planted thereafter. A second orchard was
purchased in 2000, situated on the corner of Booth Lane and New England Highway, and it is here
that the cellar door was constructed. They have planted 25 ha of chardonnay, verdelho, sauvignon
blanc, viognier, semillon, cabernet sauvignon, shiraz, merlot and petit verdot. The wines are released

under 2 labels: Rees Road for the top-of-the-range wines, and Booth Lane for slightly cheaper offerings, although the choice of names does not necessarily reflect the vineyard origin.

ŸŸŸŸ **Rees Road Merlot 2003** RATING 86 DRINK Now $ 15
Rees Road Chardonnay 2003 RATING 84 DRINK Now $ 15
Rees Road Shiraz 2003 RATING 84 DRINK Now $ 15

ŸŸŸ **Rees Road Unwooded Chardonnay 2004** RATING 83 $ 15
Rees Road Cabernet Merlot 2003 RATING 82 $ 11

Massena Vineyards ★★★★☆

PO Box 54, Tanunda, SA 5352 REGION Barossa Valley
T (08) 8564 3037 F (08) 8564 3037 WWW.massena.com.au OPEN By appt
WINEMAKER Dan Standish, Jaysen Collins EST. 2000 CASES 3000
Massena Vineyards draws upon 4 ha of grenache, shiraz, mourvedre, durif and tinta amarella at Nuriootpa. It is an export-oriented business, selling to the US, Denmark and the UK. The wines can, however, be purchased by mail order, which, given both the quality and innovative nature of the wines, seems more than ordinarily worthwhile.

ŸŸŸŸŸ **Barossa Valley Barbera Dolcetto 2004** Very good colour; bright purple; a lovely medium-bodied wine, with an array of sweet berry fruits which are in no way jammy; gossamer tannins; ready now. Cork. 15° alc. RATING 94 DRINK 2012 $ 20

ŸŸŸŸŸ **The Moonlight Run Grenache Shiraz Mataro Cinsaut 2003** Lusciously sweet and ripe; an interesting blend moving close to the Southern Rhône with Cinsaut; the varieties react synergistically, each playing a role. Cork. 15° alc. RATING 93 DRINK 2013 $ 23
The Eleventh Hour Shiraz 2003 Rich, ripe, plum, prune, blackberry and earth aromas and flavours; tannins and oak well-balanced. Cork. 15° alc. RATING 92 DRINK 2015 $ 30

Massoni ★★★☆

PO Box 13261, Law Courts Post Office, Melbourne, Vic 8010 REGION Pyrenees/Mornington Peninsula
T 1300 131 175 F 1300 131 185 WWW.massoniwines.com OPEN Not
WINEMAKER Michael Unwin (Contract) EST. 1984 CASES 20 000
Massoni, under the joint ownership of the Pellegrino and Ursini families, has regained control of its destiny after a proposed public share issue was terminated. The main grape source for Massoni is the very large GlenKara vineyard in the Pyrenees, with a yield well in excess of 1000 tonnes in 2005.

ŸŸŸŸ **Pyrenees Sangiovese 2004** Good colour; light- to medium-bodied fresh, spicy cherry; not forced or over-extracted; excellent food wine, particularly Italian. Screwcap. 13.5° alc. RATING 89 DRINK 2009 $ 17.50
Mornington Peninsula Sauvignon Blanc 2005 A slight touch of reduction on the bouquet; a powerful palate with tropical passionfruit flavours and slight heat from the alcohol. Screwcap. 14° alc. RATING 87 DRINK Now $ 18.50

Matilda's Estate

RMB 654 Hamilton Road, Denmark, WA 6333 REGION Denmark
T (08) 9848 1951 F (08) 9848 1957 WWW.matildasestate.com OPEN Tues–Sun 10–5, 7 days during school hols
WINEMAKER Gavin Berry, Dave Cleary EST. 1990 CASES 4500
In May 2003 the founders of Matilda's Meadow (as it was then known), Don Turnbull and Pamela Meldrum, sold the business to former citizen of the world Steve Hall. It is a thriving business based on 10 ha of estate plantings of chardonnay, semillon, sauvignon blanc, pinot noir, cabernet sauvignon, cabernet franc, merlot and shiraz. Beginning with the 2003 vintage, all the grapes are used for the two ranges of Matilda's Estate wines.

ŸŸŸŸŸ **Sauvignon Blanc 2005** Potent varietal aromas of gooseberry and green apple; the intense palate flows on seamlessly, with bracing acidity on the long finish. RATING 94 DRINK Now

ŢŢŢŢŶ **Fossil Series Pinot Noir 2004** Clearly articulated pinot noir varietal character throughout; light- to medium-bodied, in the savoury/spicy/foresty spectrum; good length. Screwcap. 13.5° alc. **RATING** 90 **DRINK** 2008 $ 23

Mawson Ridge

NR

24–28 Main Road, Hahndorf, SA 5066 **REGION** Adelaide Hills
T (08) 8338 0828 **F** (08) 8338 0828 **WWW**.mawsonridge.com **OPEN** Summer Tues–Sat 11–5, winter Wed–Sat 11–5, Sun 12–5
WINEMAKER Michael Scarpantoni **EST.** 1998 **CASES** 400
You might be forgiven for thinking the winery name carries the cool-climate association a little bit too far. In fact, Sir Douglas Mawson, also a conservationist and forester, arrived in the Lenswood region in the early 1930s, harvesting the native stringybarks and replanting the cleared land with pine trees. A hut that Mawson built on the property still stands today on Mawson Road, which the vineyard fronts. Here Raymond and Madeline Marin have established 5.5 ha of vines, having added 2 ha of pinot gris in 2002.

Maximilian's Vineyard

Main Road, Verdun, SA 5245 **REGION** Adelaide Hills
T (08) 8388 7777 **F** (08) 8388 1371 **WWW**.maximilians.com.au **OPEN** Wed–Sun and public hols Mon from 11
WINEMAKER Grant Burge Wines **EST.** 1994 **CASES** 2500
Maximilian and Louise Hruska opened Maximilian's Restaurant in 1976 in a homestead built in 1851, and planted 2 ha of chardonnay and 6 ha of cabernet sauvignon in 1994, surrounding the restaurant. The Cabernet Sauvignon is made by Grant Burge, the Chardonnay at Scarpantoni Estate under the direction of the Hruskas' eldest son, Paul. Since graduating from Roseworthy, Paul Hruska has completed vintages in Burgundy, Bordeaux, Spain, Margaret River and the Clare Valley; he was winemaker/vineyard manager at The Islander on Kangaroo Island.

ŢŢŢŢ **Madhills Shiraz Cabernet 2004** A perfumed, almost essency bouquet; some seemingly crystallised fruit notes to the plum, spice and licorice fruit, suggesting some Amarone treatment, which is not in fact the case. Screwcap. 14° alc. **RATING** 89 **DRINK** 2010 $ 20
Madhills Sauvignon Blanc 2005 Has a generous dose of the sweaty/reduced aromas common in Sauvignon Blanc, and which I am very sensitive to; a lovely wine hides behind the reduction. Others will give the wine a much higher rating. Screwcap. 13° alc. **RATING** 87 **DRINK** Now $ 21

ŢŢŢŶ **Cabernet Sauvignon 2002** **RATING** 85 **DRINK** 2008 $ 20

Maxwell Wines

★★★★

Olivers Road, McLaren Vale, SA 5171 **REGION** McLaren Vale
T (08) 8323 8200 **F** (08) 8323 8900 **WWW**.maxwellwines.com.au **OPEN** 7 days 10–5
WINEMAKER Mark Maxwell, Elena Golakova **EST.** 1979 **CASES** 12 000
Maxwell Wines has come a long way since opening for business in 1979 using an amazing array of Heath Robinson equipment in cramped surroundings. A state-of-the-art and much larger winery was built in 1997. The brand has produced some excellent white and red wines in recent years. Exports to all major markets.

ŢŢŢŢŶ **Four Roads McLaren Vale Shiraz Grenache Viognier 2004** Excellent colour, the benison of viognier; fragrant, juicy raspberry, plum and blackberry fruit; lively mouthfeel, good tannins; the strange blend works well. Screwcap. 14.5° alc. **RATING** 93 **DRINK** 2012 $ 21

ŢŢŢŢ **Ellen Street McLaren Vale Shiraz 2003** Slightly dull colour; ripe prune, plum and chocolate fruit; persistent tannins run through from start to finish. Off the normal pace for Ellen Street. Cork. 14.5° alc. **RATING** 89 **DRINK** 2011 $ 33
Lime Cave Cabernet Sauvignon 2003 A medium-bodied mix of soft blackcurrant/mulberry fruit, chocolate and mocha; ripe tannins; fully priced. Twin top. 14.5° alc. **RATING** 89 **DRINK** 2012 $ 32

ŢŢŢŶ **Verdelho 2005** **RATING** 84 **DRINK** Now $ 17
Where's Molly McLaren Vale Rose 2005 **RATING** 84 **DRINK** Now $ 15

🐝 Mayer ★★★★

66 Miller Road, Healesville, Vic 3777 **REGION** Yarra Valley
T (03) 5967 3779 **OPEN** By appt
WINEMAKER Timo Mayer **EST.** 1999 **CASES** 700
Timo Mayer, also winemaker at Gembrook Hill Vineyard, teamed with partner Rhonda Ferguson to establish Mayer Vineyard on the slopes of Mount Toolebewoong, 8 km south of Healesville. The steepness of those slopes is presumably self-apparent from the name given to the wines. There is just under 2.5 ha of vineyard, the lion's share to pinot noir, and smaller amounts of shiraz and chardonnay — all high-density plantings. Mayer's winemaking credo is minimal interference and handling, and no filtration.

🍷🍷🍷🍷🍷 **Bloody Hill Yarra Valley Chardonnay 2004** Elegant, light- to medium-bodied, with restrained winemaking inputs to melon and citrus fruit; good length and balance. Cork. 13.5° alc. **RATING** 90 **DRINK** 2009 $ 25
Big Betty Yarra Valley Shiraz 2004 Despite the name, light- to medium-bodied; spicy blackberry fruit with a firm spine of acidity, but not overmuch flesh around the waist. Cork. 14° alc. **RATING** 90 **DRINK** 2009 $ 25

🍷🍷🍷🍷 **Bloody Hill Yarra Valley Pinot Noir 2004** Light red-purple; firm, fresh cherry fruit; trails away somewhat on the finish. Cork. 13.5° alc. **RATING** 88 **DRINK** 2009 $ 25
Bloody Hill Yarra Valley Rose 2005 Salmon pink; spicy strawberry aromas; a light but balanced palate; dry finish. Cork. 13.5° alc. **RATING** 87 **DRINK** Now $ 18

🐝 Mayfield Vineyard ★★★★

Icely Road, Orange, NSW 2800 **REGION** Orange
T (02) 6365 9295 **F** (02) 6365 9294 **WWW**.mayfieldvineyard.com **OPEN** Fri–Sun 10–5, or by appt
WINEMAKER Jon Reynolds (Contract) **EST.** 1998 **CASES** 3000
The property — including the house in which owners Richard and Kathy Thomas now live, and its surrounding aboretum — has a rich history as a leading Suffolk sheep stud, founded upon the vast fortune accumulated by the Crawford family via its biscuit business in the UK (by 1897 producing 13 million biscuits per day). The Thomases planted the 40-ha vineyard in 1998, with merlot (15.3 ha) leading the way, followed (in descending order) by cabernet sauvignon, sauvignon blanc, chardonnay, pinot noir, riesling and sangiovese. The first wines, marketed under the Icely Road brand, were released in 2005.

🍷🍷🍷🍷🍷 **Icely Road Orange Merlot 2004** Bright purple-red; a spotlessly clean bouquet; medium-bodied, with small red fruit flavours, and spicy, savoury, fine tannins; sustained finish. Screwcap. 14° alc. **RATING** 93 **DRINK** 2012 $ 20
Icely Road Orange Chardonnay 2005 Vibrant, tangy, citrussy fruit; good length and intensity; partial barrel ferment and lees contact have disappeared into the fruit-driven components. Screwcap. 13° alc. **RATING** 92 **DRINK** 2010 $ 18

🍷🍷🍷🍷 **Icely Road Orange Riesling 2005** Clean, relatively firm, dry style with some blossom aromas; slate, herb and mineral, with a light twist of lemon on the palate; good acidity. Screwcap. 12.5° alc. **RATING** 89 **DRINK** 2011 $ 18
Pinot Noir Chardonnay NV Pale pink; bright, crisp and fresh strawberry and citrus flavours; excellent balance of dosage and acidity. 12.5° alc. **RATING** 88 **DRINK** 2009 $ 26

Maygars Hill Winery ★★★★

53 Longwood–Mansfield Road, Longwood, Vic 3665 **REGION** Strathbogie Ranges
T (03) 5798 5417 **F** (03) 5798 5457 **WWW**.strathbogieboutiquewines.com **OPEN** By appt
WINEMAKER Plunkett Wines (Sam Plunkett) **EST.** 1997 **CASES** 1200
The 8-ha property was purchased by Jenny Houghton in 1994. The plan, now a reality, was to establish B&B accommodation, and to plant a small vineyard, which now comprises 1.6 ha of shiraz and 0.8 ha of cabernet sauvignon. The name comes from Lieutenant Colonel Maygar, who fought with outstanding bravery in the Boer War in South Africa in 1901, where he won the Victoria Cross. In World War I he rose to command of the 8th Light Horse Regiment, winning yet further medals for bravery. He died on 1 November 1917.

ΥΥΥΥΫ **Reserve Shiraz 2004** Abundant depth and concentration to ample blackberry fruits and soft, round tannins. Cork. 14.5° alc. **RATING** 92 **DRINK** 2012 $ 32

Cabernet Sauvignon 2004 Very ripe; lots of oak and alcohol; blackcurrant and spice; polarises opinions. Screwcap. 14° alc. **RATING** 92 **DRINK** 2014 $ 28

ΥΥΥΥ **Shiraz 2003** Pleasant maturing wine; blackberry, anise and spice; fruit-driven, ripe tannins. Screwcap. **RATING** 89 **DRINK** 2011 $ 28

ΥΥΥΫ **Shiraz 2004** **RATING** 86 **DRINK** 2009 $ 28

Reserve Cabernet Sauvignon 2004 **RATING** 86 **DRINK** 2009 $ 32

Meadowbank Estate ★★★★

699 Richmond Road, Cambridge, Tas 7170 **REGION** Southern Tasmania
T (03) 6248 4484 **F** (03) 6248 4485 **WWW**.meadowbankwines.com.au **OPEN** 7 days 10–5
WINEMAKER Hood Wines (Andrew Hood) **EST**. 1974 **CASES** 10 000
An important part of the Ellis family business on what was once (but is no more) a large grazing property on the banks of the Derwent. Increased plantings are under contract to Hardys, and a splendid winery has been built to handle the increased production. The winery has expansive entertainment and function facilities, capable of handling up to 1000 people, and offering an arts and music program throughout the year, plus a large restaurant (open 7 days). Exports to Hong Kong and Denmark.

ΥΥΥΥΫ **Henry James Pinot Noir 2004** A fragrant mix of berry, spice and a touch of herb on the bouquet; savoury notes behind the red fruits of the long palate. Screwcap. 13.1° alc.
RATING 93 **DRINK** 2010 $ 41

Grace Elizabeth Chardonnay 2004 Very attractive nectarine fruit, with oak playing a balanced supporting role. **RATING** 90 **DRINK** 2010 $ 33

Mardi 2003 Blush pink; plenty of depth to the small red fruit flavours balanced by pleasing acidity. **RATING** 90 **DRINK** Now $ 39

ΥΥΥΥ **Sauvignon Blanc 2005** A potent bouquet, fractionally reductive/sweaty, but with strong varietal character; the palate has good length and gooseberry fruit; others may be more generous with their points. Screwcap. 12.7° alc. **RATING** 89 **DRINK** Now $ 27

Chardonnay 2005 Light- to medium-bodied; some stone fruit and a touch of sweetness, though overall balance is good. **RATING** 89 **DRINK** 2008 $ 25

Cabernet 2004 Strong oak push to help off-set some green fruit/tannins; enough length to satisfy. **RATING** 87 **DRINK** 2008 $ 32

ΥΥΥΫ **Riesling 2005** **RATING** 86 **DRINK** 2008 $ 25

⬚ Medhurst ★★★★

24–26 Medhurst Road, Gruyere, Vic 3770 **REGION** Yarra Valley
T (03) 9821 4846 **F** (03) 9592 5435 **WWW**.medhurstwines.com.au **OPEN** Not
WINEMAKER Dominique Portet **EST**. 2000 **CASES** 1500
The wheel has come full circle for Ross and Robyn Wilson; in the course of a very distinguished corporate career, Ross Wilson was CEO of Southcorp during the time it brought the Penfolds, Lindemans and Wynns businesses under the Southcorp banner. For her part, Robyn spent her childhood in the Yarra Valley, her parents living less than a kilometre away as the crow flies from Medhurst. Immaculately sited and tended vineyard blocks, most on steep, north-facing slopes, promise much for the future, given planting did not commence until 2000. In all there are 13 ha planted to sauvignon blanc, chardonnay, pinot noir, cabernet sauvignon and shiraz, all run on a low-yield basis.

ΥΥΥΥΫ **Shiraz 2004** Aromatic, spicy, peppery nuances to rich black cherry and blackberry fruit; a very distinguished wine from young vines. Cork. 14.5° alc. **RATING** 93 **DRINK** 2014 $ 24

Pinot Noir 2004 Good colour; fresh, clean and pure plum and black cherry fruit, integrated oak, and good mouthfeel and finish. Cork. 13.5° alc. **RATING** 92 **DRINK** 2011 $ 30

Chardonnay 2004 Clean and fresh; light- to medium-bodied, but a quite complex mix of stone fruit and melon with French oak; creeps up on you, with its very long palate and finish. Screwcap. 14° alc. **RATING** 91 **DRINK** 2010 $ 17

ŢŢŢŢ **Rose 2005** Fragrant raspberry and strawberry aromas; a delicate, light but balanced palate; very well-made. Screwcap. 14° alc. **RATING** 88 **DRINK** Now $ 16

ŢŢŢŢ **Cabernet Sauvignon 2003** **RATING** 86 **DRINK** 2009 $ 22

Meerea Park ★★★★★

Lot 3 Palmers Lane, Pokolbin, NSW 2320 **REGION** Lower Hunter Valley
T (02) 4998 7474 **F** (02) 4998 7974 **WWW**.meereapark.com.au **OPEN** At The Boutique Wine Centre, Broke Road, Pokolbin
WINEMAKER Rhys Eather **EST.** 1991 **CASES** 10 000
All the wines are produced from grapes purchased from growers, primarily in the Pokolbin, Broke-Fordwich and Upper Hunter regions, but also from as far afield as Orange and Young. It is the brainchild of Rhys Eather, a great-grandson of Alexander Munro, a leading vigneron in the mid-19th century; he makes the wine at the former Little's Winery on Palmers Lane in Pokolbin. Exports to the UK, The Netherlands, Germany, Canada and Singapore.

ŢŢŢŢŢ **Epoch Semillon 2005** Bright green-yellow; very intense and focused citrus and grass flavours; terrific drive and length; a great Hunter Semillon vintage example once again. Screwcap. 10.5° alc. **RATING** 94 **DRINK** 2013 $ 19
Hell Hole Hunter Valley Shiraz 2003 Slightly more advanced colour (than the Alexander Munro); quite focused and intense black fruits; good structure and length. Screwcap. 14.5° alc. **RATING** 94 **DRINK** 2015 $ 55

ŢŢŢŢŢ **Alexander Munro Semillon 2001** A complex wine, with some deliberately funky characters on the bouquet; still retains grip and length to the ripe citrus and grass flavours. Cork. 10.5° alc. **RATING** 93 **DRINK** 2011 $ 35
Alexander Munro Shiraz 2003 Concentrated, medium- to full-bodied; abundant blackberry, mocha and chocolate fruit; nice earthy tannins; good oak. Screwcap. 14° alc. **RATING** 93 **DRINK** 2015 $ 40

ŢŢŢŢ **Hunter Valley Shiraz Viognier 2004** Light- to medium-bodied; distinctly tangy, though not dense, aromas and flavours; tannins and oak (none new) well controlled; 6% Viognier. Screwcap. 14° alc. **RATING** 89 **DRINK** 2010 $ 19

ŢŢŢŢ **Alexander Munro Semillon 2005** **RATING** 86 **DRINK** 2010 $ 35

Melaleuca Grove ★★★★

8 Melaleuca Court, Rowville, Vic 3178 (postal) **REGION** Upper Goulburn
T (03) 9752 7928 **F** (03) 9752 7928 **WWW**.melaleucawines.com.au **OPEN** Not
WINEMAKER Jeff Wright **EST.** 1999 **CASES** 1000
Jeff and Anne Wright are both Honours graduates in biochemistry who have succumbed to the lure of winemaking after lengthy careers elsewhere; in the case of Jeff, 20 years in research and hospital science. He commenced his winemaking apprenticeship in 1997 at Green Vineyards, backed up by vintage work in 1999 and 2000 at Bianchet and Yarra Valley Hills, both in the Yarra Valley. At the same time he began the external Bachelor of Applied Science (Wine Science) course at Charles Sturt University, while still working in biochemistry in the public hospital system. They purchase grapes from various cool-climate regions, including Yea and the Yarra Valley. Exports to Canada.

ŢŢŢŢ **Yea Valley Merlot 2003** Developed colour; however, good varietal flavour, texture and structure to the medium-bodied palate; olive and earth plus red fruits; fine, savoury tannins. Now at its optimum. Screwcap. 14° alc. **RATING** 91 **DRINK** 2008 $ 19

ŢŢŢŢ **Yarra Valley Marsanne 2004** Interesting wine; while light-bodied, has distinct chalk, honeysuckle and citrus varietal character; 12 months aging in old barriques has contributed texture; balanced, dry finish. Cork. 14° alc. **RATING** 88 **DRINK** 2010 $ 19

ŢŢŢŢ **Yarra Valley Chardonnay 2004** **RATING** 84 **DRINK** Now $ 19

Melange Wines   NR

Farm 1291, Harward Road, Griffith, NSW 2680 **REGION** Riverina
T (02) 6962 7783 **F** (02) 6962 7783 **OPEN** 7 days 10–5
WINEMAKER Angelo D'Aquino **EST.** 2000 **CASES** NA
Melange Wines is a relative newcomer in the Riverina region, although Angelo D'Aquino comes from a family with considerable viticultural experience. There are 25 ha of sauvignon blanc, semillon, chardonnay, verdelho, trebbiano, muscat gordo blanco, shiraz and durif planted. The cellar door offers light meals and winery tours plus tutored tastings.

Mengler View Wines   NR

Magnolia Road, Tanunda, SA 5352 **REGION** Barossa Valley
T (08) 8563 2217 **F** (08) 8563 2408 **WWW**.faith.sa.edu.au **OPEN** By appt
WINEMAKER Bob Mitchell **EST.** 1995 **CASES** 1600
This is the project of the Faith Lutheran School, which began making small batches of wine in 1992 as part of the Year 10 agricultural studies program. Stuart Blackwell of St Hallett monitored the program for many years, during which time the crush has grown from 0.5 tonne to over 20 tonnes. The wines have been exhibited with success in the Barossa Valley Wine Show, and Faith became the first school in Australia to construct a purpose-built winery: the Faith Wine Education Centre opened in 2002. The executive manager in charge is Bob Mitchell, agricultural co-ordinator and winery manager.

Merli   NR

19 One Chain Road, Merricks North, Vic 3926 **REGION** Mornington Peninsula
T (03) 5989 7435 **F** (03) 9380 2555 **OPEN** By appt
WINEMAKER Ennio Merli, David Merli **EST.** 2000 **CASES** NA
Ennio, David and Jonathan Merli have established 4 ha of chardonnay, pinot noir, shiraz, cabernet sauvignon and merlot at Merricks North. The relatively small production is made onsite, and sold by mail order and through the cellar door when open.

Mermerus Vineyard   ★★★☆

60 Soho Road, Drysdale, Vic 3222 **REGION** Geelong
T (03) 5253 2718 **F** (03) 5226 1683 **OPEN** First Sun of each month 11–4; every Sun in Jan
WINEMAKER Paul Champion **EST.** 2000 **CASES** 600
Commencing in 1996, Paul Champion has established 1.5 ha of pinot noir, 1 ha of chardonnay and 0.2 ha of riesling at Mermerus, and also acts as contract winemaker for small growers in the region.

ŸŸŸŸ **Shiraz 2004** Very rich and ripe, with blackberry jam fruit and soft tannins. Diam. 15° alc.
RATING 89 **DRINK** 2012 $ 18
Pope's Eye Rose 2005 Medium salmon; small red fruit flavours; good balance; nice dry finish. Screwcap. 13.5° alc. **RATING** 88 **DRINK** Now $ 14
Riesling 2005 Solidly built and structured; some passionfruit and lime; durable style with a good future. Screwcap. 13° alc. **RATING** 87 **DRINK** 2011 $ 15

ŸŸŸŸ **Chardonnay 2004 RATING** 84 **DRINK** 2008 $ 18

Merops Wines   NR

243 Caves Road, Margaret River, WA 6285 **REGION** Margaret River
T (08) 9757 2691 **F** (08) 9757 3193 **WWW**.meropswines.com.au **OPEN** By appt
WINEMAKER Swings & Roundabouts (Mark Lane) **EST.** 2000 **CASES** 1320
Jim and Yvonne Ross have been involved in horticulture for over 25 years, in production, retail nurseries and viticulture. They established a nursery and irrigation business in the Margaret River township in 1985 on a 3-ha property before establishing a rootstock nursery. In 2000 they removed the nursery and planted 6.3 ha of cabernet sauvignon, cabernet franc, merlot and shiraz on the laterite gravel over clay soils. They use the practices developed by Professor William Albrecht in the US 50 years ago, providing mineral balance and thus eliminating the need for insecticides and toxic sprays.

Merrebee Estate

NR

Lot 3339 St Werburghs Road, Mount Barker, WA 6234 **REGION** Mount Barker
T (08) 9851 2424 **F** (08) 9851 2425 **www**.merrebee.ozware.com **OPEN** By appt
WINEMAKER Contract **EST.** 1986 **CASES** 500
Planting of the Merrebee Estate vineyards commenced in 1986 and have now reached a little over 3.6
ha of riesling, chardonnay and shiraz. It is situated on a gentle hillside 15 km west of Mount Barker
near the historic St Werburgh's Chapel. Exports to the UK, the US and Canada.

Merricks Creek Wines

44 Merricks Road, Merricks, Vic 3916 **REGION** Mornington Peninsula
T (03) 5989 8868 **F** (03) 5989 9070 **www**.pinot.com.au **OPEN** By appt
WINEMAKER Nick Farr, Peter Parker **EST.** 1998 **CASES** 750
Peter and Georgina Parker retained Gary Farr (of Bannockburn) as viticultural consultant before
they began establishing their 2-ha pinot noir vineyard. They say, 'He has been an extraordinarily
helpful and stern taskmaster from day one. He advised on clonal selection, trellis design and planting
density, and visits the vineyard regularly to monitor canopy management.' (Son Nick Farr completes
the circle as contract winemaker.) The vineyard is planted to a sophisticated and rare collection of
new pinot noir clones, and is planted at ultra-high density of 500 mm spacing on 1-m high trellising.

ΥΥΥΥΥ **Nick Farr Pinot Noir 2004** Deeper colour; supple, round and silky/velvety, with the best
mouthfeel of the 3; sweet black cherry and spice; long finish. Cork. 13.5° alc. **RATING** 95
DRINK 2011 **$** 55
Close Planted Pinot Noir 2004 Brilliantly clear red-purple; light- to medium-bodied;
smooth supple predominantly red fruits in a cherry/strawberry/raspberry spectrum; fine-
grained tannins. Cork. 13.5° alc. **RATING** 94 **DRINK** 2011 **$** 43

ΥΥΥΥΫ **Pinot Noir 2004** Brilliantly clear colour; medium-bodied, more powerful, and,
unexpectedly, tannins tremble on the brink. A mix of plum and red fruits; time and prayer
called for. Cork. 13.5° alc. **RATING** 92 **DRINK** 2013 **$** 34

Merricks Estate

★★★★☆

Thompsons Lane, Merricks, Vic 3916 **REGION** Mornington Peninsula
T (03) 5989 8416 **F** (03) 9613 4242 **OPEN** First weekend of each month, each weekend in Jan &
public holiday w'ends 12–5
WINEMAKER Paul Evans **EST.** 1977 **CASES** 2000
Melbourne solicitor George Kefford, with wife Jacquie, runs Merricks Estate as a weekend and
holiday enterprise. Right from the outset it has produced distinctive, spicy, cool-climate Shiraz which
has accumulated an impressive array of show trophies and gold medals.

ΥΥΥΥΫ **Shiraz 2003** Elegant, light- to medium-bodied spicy, cool-grown style as one expects from
Merricks; good balance. Diam. 14° alc. **RATING** 91 **DRINK** 2013 **$** 25
Chardonnay 2003 Generous stone fruit, fig and melon, the oak integrated and balanced;
at the big end of town flavour-wise. Screwcap. 14.5° alc. **RATING** 90 **DRINK** 2010 **$** 25

Merum

Hillbrook Road, Quinninup, WA 6258 **REGION** Pemberton
T (08) 9776 6011 **F** (08) 9776 6022 **www**.merum.com.au **OPEN** By appt
WINEMAKER Jan McIntosh (Contract) **EST.** 1996 **CASES** 1500
Merum is owned and managed by viticulturist Mike Melsom and partner Julie Roberts. The 10-ha
vineyard, planted in 1996, consists of semillon, shiraz and chardonnay. Its wines, led by the Semillon
and Shiraz, have been outstanding since the word go. Exports to the UK and Hong Kong.

ΥΥΥΥΥ **Semillon 2005** Bright, lively and intense; has great structure, with a spine of mineral
running through the lemongrass flavour; crisp finish. Screwcap. 13° alc. **RATING** 94
DRINK 2012 **$** 28
Chardonnay 2005 Elegant, fine and restrained; taut structure, with excellent length and
mouthfeel to the melon and stone fruit, then a top class finish. Screwcap. 14° alc.
RATING 94 **DRINK** 2011 **$** 28

♥♥♥♥♡ Semillon Sauvignon Blanc 2005 A delicate flinty/lemony/citrus/apple mix; good length; balanced acidity. Screwcap. **RATING** 90 **DRINK** 2009 **$** 19

Shiraz 2004 Light- to medium-bodied; spicy, peppery, cool-grown overtones to black cherry and dark plum fruit; fine tannins, controlled oak. Screwcap. 13.3° alc. **RATING** 90 **DRINK** 2012 **$** 28

Metcalfe Valley

283 Metcalfe–Malmsbury Road, Metcalfe, Vic 3448 **REGION** Macedon Ranges
T (03) 5423 2035 **F** (03) 5423 2035 **OPEN** By appt
WINEMAKER Kilchurn Wines (David Cowburn) **EST.** 1994 **CASES** 1000
Ian Pattison, who has a PhD in metallurgy, and a Diploma in horticultural science and viticulture from Melbourne University/Dookie College, purchased Metcalfe Valley from the Frederiksens in 2003. He has 7.3 ha of shiraz and sauvignon blanc, and production is increasing.

♥♥♥♥♡ Shiraz 2004 Plenty of smooth and supple black fruits on the palate before slightly grainy tannins come on the finish. Diam. **RATING** 90 **DRINK** 2010 **$** 25

Metier Wines ★★★★★

Tarraford Vineyard, 440 Healesville Road, Yarra Glen, Vic 3775 (postal) **REGION** Yarra Valley
T 0419 678 918 **F** (03) 5962 2194 **WWW.**metierwines.com.au **OPEN** Not
WINEMAKER Martin Williams MW **EST.** 1995 **CASES** 2000
Metier is the French word for craft, trade or profession; the business is that of Yarra Valley-based Martin Williams MW, who has notched up an array of degrees and had winemaking stints in France, California and Australia which are, not to put too fine a word on it, extraordinary. The focus of Metier is individual vineyard wines, initially based on grapes from the Tarraford and Schoolhouse Vineyards, both in the Yarra Valley. Exports to the UK, the US and Hong Kong.

♥♥♥♥♥ Schoolhouse Vineyard Yarra Valley Chardonnay 2003 Subtly complex aroma and texture; melon, cashew, fig and cream all interwoven. Screwcap. **RATING** 94 **DRINK** 2013 **$** 32

Tarraford Vineyard Yarra Valley Pinot Noir 2002 Light colour, but intense flavour; a finely spun web of tannin support rather than threaten the spicy, savoury fruit; very long finish. Screwcap. **RATING** 94 **DRINK** 2010 **$** 32

♥♥♥♥♡ Manytrees Vineyard Shiraz Viognier 2002 Highly scented and aromatic; a complex array of flavours ranging through spice, sous bois, blackberry and a touch of earth; controlled tannins. Screwcap. **RATING** 93 **DRINK** 2012 **$** 32

♥♥♥♥ Milkwood Yarra Valley Pinot Noir 2003 Light, bright colour; light-bodied, clear-cut varietal fruit; plum, cherry, spice and forest floor; ready. Screwcap. 14° alc. **RATING** 89 **DRINK** Now **$** 19

Milkwood Central Victorian Shiraz 2003 Light- to medium-bodied; bright red and black fruits; far from typical of Central Victoria; possibly young vines. Screwcap. 13.5° alc. **RATING** 88 **DRINK** 2008 **$** 19

Meure's Wines NR

16 Fleurtys Lane, Birchs Bay, Tas 7162 **REGION** Southern Tasmania
T (03) 6267 4483 **F** (03) 6267 4483 **OPEN** Not
WINEMAKER Dirk Meure **EST.** 1991 **CASES** 300
Dirk Meure has established 1 ha of vineyard on the shores of D'Entrecasteaux Channel, overlooking Bruny Island. The Huon Valley is the southernmost wine region in Australia, and it was here that Dirk Meure's parents settled on their arrival from The Netherlands in 1950. He says he has been heavily influenced by his mentors, Steve and Monique Lubiana. The philosophy is to produce low yields from balanced vines and to interfere as little as possible in the winemaking and maturation process.

🐦 Mia Creek   ★★★★☆

365 Wickhams Lane, Glenhope East, Vic 3522 **REGION** Heathcote
T (03) 5433 5324 **OPEN** By appt
WINEMAKER David McKenzie **EST.** 2001 **CASES** 50
David and Dianne McKenzie have planted 2 ha of shiraz and 1 ha of merlot on a mix of granitic soil
and rock, 16 km southwest of Heathcote at an elevation of 340m. The dry-grown vines are, and
always will be, low-yielding, and it is not expected that production will exceed 150 cases. The windy
site means that sprays are seldom required, but the growth of the merlot has been savaged by local
wildlife.

▼▼▼▼▽ **Heathcote Shiraz 2003** Medium- to full-bodied; blackberry, plum, licorice and dark
chocolate with touches of vanilla all come together well. Auspicious debut. Cork. 13.5° alc.
RATING 91 **DRINK** 2013 $ 26

Miceli   ★★★★☆

60 Main Creek Road, Arthurs Seat, Vic 3936 **REGION** Mornington Peninsula
T (03) 5989 2755 **F** (03) 5989 2755 **OPEN** First weekend each month 12–5, public hols, & also every
weekend & by appt in Jan
WINEMAKER Anthony Miceli **EST.** 1991 **CASES** 3000
This may be a part-time labour of love for general practitioner Dr Anthony Miceli, but that hasn't
prevented him taking the whole venture very seriously. He acquired the property in 1989 specifically
to establish a vineyard, planting 1.8 ha in November 1991, followed by a further ha of pinot gris in
1997. Between 1991 and 1997 Dr Miceli did the Wine Science course at Charles Sturt University; he
now manages both vineyard and winery.

▼▼▼▼▼ **Olivia's Chardonnay 2004** Bright green-straw; intense, focused line and purity;
grapefruit and nectarine, oak purely incidental; will be long-lived. Screwcap. **RATING** 94
DRINK 2014 $ 26

▼▼▼▼▽ **Lucy's Choice Pinot Noir 2003** Good hue; light- to medium-bodied, clear-cut varietal
plum and cherry fruit; linear, rather than complex. Screwcap. **RATING** 90 **DRINK** 2010 $ 26

▼▼▼▼ **Iolanda Pinot Grigio 2004** A solid, full-flavoured wine; pear, spice and musk fruit; firm,
mineral finish. Screwcap. 13.5° alc. **RATING** 88 **DRINK** Now $ 20
Pinot Noir 2004 Very light colour, the hue ok; almost pinot rose in style;
cherry/strawberry, crisp finish. Screwcap. 13° alc. **RATING** 88 **DRINK** Now $ 20

▼▼▼▽ **Pinot Rose 2004 RATING** 86 **DRINK** Now $ 20

Michael Unwin Wines   ★★★★★

2 Racecourse Road, Beaufort, Vic 3373 **REGION** Grampians
T (03) 5349 2021 **F** (03) 5349 2032 **www**.michaelunwinwines.com.au **OPEN** 7 days 11–5
WINEMAKER Michael Unwin **EST.** 2000 **CASES** 2000
Established at Ararat, Vic by winemaker Michael Unwin and wife and business partner Catherine
Clark. His track record as a winemaker spans 26 years, and includes extended winemaking
experience in France, NZ and Australia; he has found time to obtain a postgraduate degree in
oenology and viticulture at Lincoln University, Canterbury, NZ. He also does contract winemaking
and consulting; the winemaking takes place in a converted textile factory. The grapes come in part
from the estate plantings of 2 ha shiraz, and 1 ha each of cabernet sauvignon, sangiovese, barbera,
durif, riesling and chardonnay, plus contracts with 5 or 6 local growers.

▼▼▼▼▼ **Acrobat Chardonnay 2003** Complex barrel ferment and lees aromas; the fruit charges
through on the palate, with a bright, zesty finish; aging well. Screwcap. 13° alc. **RATING** 94
DRINK 2013 $ 25
Acrobat Shiraz 2002 Very good colour, still purple; intense, focused black cherry,
blackberry and spice fruit; fine, ripe tannins, oak in support. Not filtered. Screwcap.
13° alc. **RATING** 94 **DRINK** 2015 $ 25

ΨΨΨΨ **Acrobat Cabernet Sauvignon 2002** A powerful, savoury blackcurrant, earth and spice palate, finishing with lingering tannins. Screwcap. 13° alc. **RATING** 90 **DRINK** 2013 $ 25
Acrobat Durif 2004 Densely coloured; rich black fruits so typical of the variety; alcohol and extract under control. Screwcap. 14° alc. **RATING** 90 **DRINK** 2014 $ 25

ΨΨΨΨ **Acrobat Barbera 2004** Cheerful red fruits; rather more to offer than the sister Sangiovese; nicely balanced. Screwcap. **RATING** 87 **DRINK** 2008 $ 19

ΨΨΨΨ **Acrobat Sangiovese 2004** **RATING** 86 **DRINK** Now $ 19

Michelini Wines ★★★☆

Great Alpine Road, Myrtleford, Vic 3737 **REGION** Alpine Valleys
T (03) 5751 1990 **F** (03) 5751 1410 **WWW**.micheliniwines.com.au **OPEN** 7 days 10–5
WINEMAKER Greg O'Keefe **EST.** 1982 **CASES** 8000
The Michelini family are among the best-known grapegrowers in the Buckland Valley of Northeast Victoria. Having migrated from Italy in 1949, the Michelinis originally grew tobacco, diversifying into vineyards in 1982. They now have a little over 42 ha of vineyard on terra rossa soil at an altitude of 300m, mostly with frontage to the Buckland River. The major part of the production is sold (to Orlando and others), but since 1996 an onsite winery has permitted the Michelinis to vinify part of their production. The winery has the capacity to handle 1000 tonnes of fruit, which eliminates the problem of moving grapes out of a declared phylloxera area.

ΨΨΨΨ **Sangiovese 2004** Fragrant spice, rose petal, tea leaf and berry fruit; light-bodied, but well-balanced. Cork. **RATING** 89 **DRINK** 2009 $ 18.50
Unwooded Chardonnay 2005 Fragrant blossom aromas; stone fruit and a hint of fig; good mouthfeel and balance. Above average. Screwcap. 13.5° alc. **RATING** 88 **DRINK** Now $ 15
Pinot Grigio 2004 Spotlessly clean; well-made, the limitations lying with the variety; flecks of stone fruit, spice and apricot. Screwcap. **RATING** 87 **DRINK** Now $ 17.50
Merlot 2004 Faintly hazy colour; ultra savoury/earthy/green olive varietal fruit; fine tannins. Cork. **RATING** 87 **DRINK** 2008 $ 18.50
Barbera 2005 Light, fresh, zippy early drinking style, halfway to rose. Serve slightly chilled. Cork. 13° alc. **RATING** 87 **DRINK** Now $ 18

Middlebrook Estate NR

RSD 43, Sand Road, McLaren Vale, SA 5171 **REGION** McLaren Vale
T (08) 8383 0600 **F** (08) 8383 0557 **WWW**.middlebrookestate.com.au **OPEN** Mon–Fri 10.30–4, w'ends 11.30–4.30
WINEMAKER Joseph Cogno, Michael Petrucci **EST.** 1947 **CASES** 65 000
After a brief period of ownership by industry veteran Bill Clappis (who renovated and reopened the winery), ownership has now passed to the Cogno family, which has been winemaking at Cobbity, near Camden, NSW, since 1964. Through Middlebrook the family has become one of the largest producers of Lambrusco in Australia; it is available Australia-wide through Liquorland stores. Many other wines (18 in all) are produced under the Cogno Brothers label; the Middlebrook cask hall has been given over to production of the Medlow chocolate range. The top wines are still sold under the Middlebrook label.

Middlesex 31 NR

PO Box 367, Manjimup, WA 6258 **REGION** Manjimup
T (08) 9771 2499 **F** (08) 9771 2499 **OPEN** Not
WINEMAKER Brenden Smith, Dave Cleary, Mark Aitken **EST.** 1990 **CASES** 1000
Dr John Rosser (a local GP who runs the Manjimup Medical Centre) and Rosemary Davies have planted 6.5 ha of vines, predominantly to shiraz, chardonnay and verdelho, but with a little patch of pinot noir.

Middleton Wines   NR

Flagstaff Hill Road, Middleton, SA 5213 **REGION** Currency Creek
T (08) 8555 4136 **F** (08) 8555 4108 **OPEN** Fri–Sun 11–5
WINEMAKER Robert Alexandre **EST.** 1979 **CASES** 6000
The Bland family has acquired Middleton Wines and has changed the entire focus of the business. Previously, all the production from the 12 ha of estate plantings was sold either as grapes or as bulk wine; now much is made at the onsite winery.

Midhill Vineyard   ★★★★

PO Box 30, Romsey, Vic 3434 **REGION** Macedon Ranges
T (03) 5429 5565 **OPEN** Not
WINEMAKER Contract **EST.** 1993 **CASES** 200
The Richards family has been breeding Angus cattle for the past 35 years, and diversified into grapegrowing in 1993. The vineyard has been planted on a northeast-facing slope on red volcanic clay loam which is free-draining and moderately fertile. There are 2 ha of chardonnay and 0.5 ha each of pinot noir and gewurztraminer in production. Sparkling Vintage Blanc de Blancs and lightly wooded Chardonnay are made from this planting; the other wine is Gewurztraminer.

TTTT **Macedon Blanc de Blancs 2001** Foaming mousse; attractive, youthful citrus/stone fruit flavours, yet also complex and long. 12° alc. **RATING** 91 **DRINK** Now $ 28

Milford Vineyard   NR

1431 Tasman Highway, Cambridge, Tas 7170 **REGION** Southern Tasmania
T (03) 6248 5029 **F** (03) 6248 5076 **OPEN** Not
WINEMAKER Hood Wines (Andrew Hood) **EST.** 1984 **CASES** 200
Given the tiny production, Milford is understandably not open to the public; the excellent Pinot Noir is quickly sold by word of mouth. The 150-ha grazing property (the oldest Southdown sheep stud in Australia) has been in Charlie Lewis's family since 1830. Only 15 mins from Hobart, and with an absolute water frontage to the tidal estuary of the Coal River, it is a striking site. The vineyard is on a patch of 1.5m-deep sand over a clay base with lots of lime impregnation.

Milhinch Wines   NR

PO Box 655, Greenock, SA 5360 **REGION** Barossa Valley
T (08) 8563 4003 **F** (08) 8563 4003 **WWW**.seizetheday.net.au **OPEN** Not
WINEMAKER Contract **EST.** 2003 **CASES** 600
Peter Milhinch and Sharyn Rogers have established 2 ha each of shiraz and cabernet sauvignon, the first vintage made in 2005 by big name Barossa Valley boutique winemakers.

Milimani Estate   NR

92 The Forest Road, Bungendore, NSW 2621 **REGION** Canberra District
T (02) 6238 1421 **F** (02) 6238 1424 **OPEN** W'ends & public hols 11–4
WINEMAKER Kyeema Estate **EST.** 1989 **CASES** 200
The Preston family (Mary, David and Rosemary) have established a 3.25-ha vineyard at Bungendore planted to sauvignon blanc, chardonnay, pinot noir and cabernet franc.

Millbrook Estate   NR

Lot 18/19 Mt View Road, Millfield, NSW 2325 **REGION** Lower Hunter Valley
T (02) 4998 1155 **F** (02) 4998 1155 **WWW**.millbrookestate.com.au **OPEN** 7 days 10–5
WINEMAKER John Lyons **EST.** 1996 **CASES** 1000
The 2.6 ha of Millbrook Estate vineyards produces between 400 cases (in a dry year) and 800 cases (in a good year). Interestingly, the vineyard is on a geological fault line, and is in fact an uplifted ancient creek bed.

Millbrook Winery ★★★★★

Old Chestnut Lane, Jarrahdale, WA 6124 **REGION** Perth Hills
T (08) 9525 5796 **F** (08) 9525 5672 **WWW**.millbrookwinery.com.au **OPEN** 7 days 10–5
WINEMAKER Tony Davis, Damian Hutton **EST.** 1996 **CASES** 20 000
The strikingly situated Millbrook Winery, opened in December 2001, is owned by the highly
successful Perth-based entrepreneur Peter Fogarty and wife Lee. They also own Lake's Folly in the
Hunter Valley, and Deep Woods Estate in Margaret River, and have made a major commitment to
the quality end of Australian wine. Millbrook draws on 7.5 ha of vineyards in the Perth Hills, planted
to sauvignon blanc, semillon, chardonnay, viognier, cabernet sauvignon, merlot, shiraz and petit
verdot. It also purchases grapes from the Perth Hills and Geographe regions. The wines (Millbrook
and Barking Owl) are of consistently high quality. Exports to the UK, the US and other major
markets.

🍷🍷🍷🍷🍷 **Chardonnay 2004** A super-elegant wine with refined intensity; melon, stone fruit and
citrus; sensitive barrel ferment and lees inputs; very good length; 2 well-deserved trophies
2005 Qantas West Australian Wine Show. Screwcap. 14° alc. **RATING** 95 **DRINK** 2012 $ 25
Limited Release Viognier 2005 Has distinctly more mouthfeel than the other two
'05 releases, partly from the alcohol (which doesn't spoil the finish) and partly from
controlled barrel fermentation inputs. Screwcap. 15° alc. **RATING** 94 **DRINK** 2010 $ 35
Shiraz Viognier 2003 Elegant, scented bouquet; that unmistakable Viognier lift to red
and black fruits; quite silky tannins. 15° alc. **RATING** 94 **DRINK** 2013 $ 22

🍷🍷🍷🍷🍷 **Sauvignon Blanc 2005** Clean, fresh bouquet; an intense fruit profile of passionfruit,
gooseberry and touches of herb/grass. Screwcap. 13.5° alc. **RATING** 92 **DRINK** Now $ 20
Estate Viognier 2005 Aromatic, flowery, orange blossom bouquet, then a relatively tight
palate, with a core of mineral through to stone fruit and apricot flavours. Screwcap. 14° alc.
RATING 92 **DRINK** 2009 $ 35
Semillon Sauvignon Blanc 2005 Firm, lively grass/herb/mineral aromas and flavours;
the texture and structure augmented by partial barrel ferment. Screwcap. 13° alc.
RATING 91 **DRINK** 2010 $ 22
Barking Owl Semillon Sauvignon Blanc 2005 A harmonious blend of many different
components; gooseberry, passionfruit and citrussy acidity; good length. Screwcap.
13.5° alc. **RATING** 91 **DRINK** 2009 $ 17
Viognier 2005 Has lots of personality, with a wide range of flavours ranging through
apricot, spice and clear-cut ginger; doesn't cloy on the finish. Screwcap. 14.5° alc.
RATING 91 **DRINK** 2009 $ 22
Estate Merlot 2004 Good hue; medium-bodied, attractive red berry fruit flavours and
fine tannins; delicious. Screwcap. 14° alc. **RATING** 91 **DRINK** 2010 $ 15
Shiraz 2004 A light- to medium-bodied array of spicy red fruits; fine-grained, ripe
tannins run throughout; controlled oak. Great Southern/Margaret River. Screwcap.
14° alc. **RATING** 90 **DRINK** 2014 $ 25
Cabernet Merlot 2003 Light- to medium-bodied, with lively cassis and mint — indeed
choc mint — flavours; finely structured, subtle oak. Fully priced. Cork. 14.5° alc. **RATING** 90
DRINK 2013 $ 32

🍷🍷🍷🍷 **Barking Owl Chardonnay 2004** Nicely balanced and structured; ripe peach and banana
fruit; subtle oak, slightly sweet. Screwcap. 14° alc. **RATING** 89 **DRINK** 2008 $ 17
Barking Owl Cabernet Sauvignon Merlot Malbec 2004 Rich, sweet dark fruits; some
chocolate and plenty of flavour. Screwcap. 14.5° alc. **RATING** 89 **DRINK** 2012 $ 18
Barking Owl Shiraz Viognier 2003 Rich, very ripe plum, prune and blackberry fruits,
then that tangy note ex viognier (5%). Cork. 15° alc. **RATING** 88 **DRINK** 2010 $ 18

🦉 Miller's Dixons Creek Estate ★★★★

1620 Melba Highway, Dixons Creek, Vic 3775 **REGION** Yarra Valley
T (03) 5965 2553 **F** (03) 5965 2320 **WWW**.graememillerwines.com.au **OPEN** 7 days 10–5
WINEMAKER Graeme Miller **EST.** 1988 **CASES** 6500
Graeme Miller is a Yarra Valley legend in his own lifetime, having established Chateau Yarrinya (now
De Bortoli) in 1971, and as a virtual unknown winning the Jimmy Watson Trophy in the 1978

Melbourne Show with the 1977 Chateau Yarrinya Cabernet Sauvignon. He sold Chateau Yarrinya in 1979, and, together with wife Bernadette, began establishing a new vineyard which has steadily grown to 30 ha with (in descending order of area) chardonnay, cabernet sauvignon, pinot noir, shiraz, sauvignon blanc, petit verdot, pinot gris and merlot. A significant part of the production is sold, but the opening of the winery in 2004, and a cellar door thereafter, has seen production increase.

ΥΥΥΥΥ **Yarra Valley Sauvignon Blanc 2005** Flush with passionfruit and gooseberry flavours running through the length of the palate; well-balanced finish. Screwcap. 13.5° alc. **RATING** 90 **DRINK** Now $ 16

Yarra Valley Shiraz 2004 A light- to medium-bodied, elegant array of black and red fruits, splashes of spice, controlled oak, and fine tannins. Cork. 12.7° alc. **RATING** 90 **DRINK** 2012 $ 20

ΥΥΥΥ **Yarra Valley Chardonnay 2005** Rich, ripe, peachy stone fruit is covered in an overcoat of oak; a pity. Screwcap. 13.8° alc. **RATING** 86 **DRINK** 2008 $ 22

ΥΥΥ **Yarra Valley Rose 2005 RATING** 83 $ 14

Millers Samphire   NR

Watts Gully Road, Robertson Road, Kersbrook, SA 5231 **REGION** Adelaide Hills
T (08) 8389 3183 **F** (03) 8389 3183 **OPEN** 7 days 9–5 by appt
WINEMAKER Tom Miller **EST.** 1982 **CASES** 80
Next after Scarp Valley, one of the smallest wineries in Australia offering wine for sale; pottery also helps. Tom Miller has one of the more interesting and diverse CVs, with an early interest in matters alcoholic leading to the premature but happy death of a laboratory rat at Adelaide University and his enforced switch from biochemistry to mechanical engineering. The Riesling is a high-flavoured wine with crushed herb and lime aromas and flavours.

Millfield   NR

Lot 341, Mount View Road, Millfield, NSW 2325 **REGION** Lower Hunter Valley
T (02) 4998 1571 **F** (02) 4998 0172 **WWW.**millfieldwines.com **OPEN** W'ends 10–4
WINEMAKER David Lowe **EST.** 1997 **CASES** 500
Situated on the picturesque Mount View Road, Millfield made its market debut in 2000. The neatly labelled and packaged wines have won gold medals and trophies right from the first vintage in 1998, and praise from wine writers and critics in Australia and the UK. The wines are sold through the cellar door and by mailing list, and through a limited number of fine wine retail and top-quality restaurants. Exports to the UK.

Millinup Estate   NR

RMB 1280 Porongurup Road, Porongurup, WA 6324 **REGION** Porongurup
T (08) 9853 1105 **F** (08) 9853 1105 **OPEN** W'ends 10–5, or by appt
WINEMAKER Mike Garland (Red), Diane Miller (White) **EST.** 1989 **CASES** 250
The Millinup Estate vineyard was planted in 1978, when it was called Point Creek. Owners Peter and Lesley Thorn purchased it in 1989, renaming it and having the limited production (from 0.5 ha of riesling, supplemented by purchased red grapes) vinified at Garlands and the Porongurup Winery.

Milvine Estate Wines

108 Warren Road, Heathcote, Vic 3523 **REGION** Heathcote
T (03) 5433 2772 **F** (03) 5433 2769 **OPEN** W'ends & public hols 11–5
WINEMAKER Heathcote Winery (Jonathan Mepham) **EST.** 2002 **CASES** 300
Jo and Graeme Millard planted 2 ha of clonally selected shiraz in 1995, picking their first grapes in 1998; in that and the ensuing 4 vintages the grapes were sold to Heathcote Winery, but in 2003 part of the production was vinified by Heathcote Winery for the Millards under the Milvine label. Production will increase in the years ahead, and the Millards have a carefully thought-out business plan to market the wine.

ŶŶŶŶŶ **Heathcote Shiraz 2004** Good colour; notwithstanding the alcohol, medium-bodied and not hot; an array of black and red fruits and spices; fine tannins. Diam. 15° alc. **RATING** 91 **DRINK** 2014 $ 29

Minko Wines

13 High Street, Willunga, SA 5172 **REGION** Southern Fleurieu
T (08) 8556 4987 **F** (08) 8556 2688 **WWW**.minkowines.com **OPEN** 7 days 10–5
WINEMAKER Hawkers Gate (James Hastwell), Mark Day (Consultant) **EST.** 1997 **CASES** 1600
Mike Boerema, Inger Kellett, and children Nick and Margo (the winery name uses letters from each of the family names) established their vineyard on the slopes of Mt Compass at an altitude of 300m. Minko practises sustainable eco-agriculture, and is a member of the Compass Creek Care group; the Nangkita and Tookayerta creeks flow through the property, providing wetlands and associated native vegetation.

ŶŶŶŶ **Pinot Noir 2004** Light- to medium-bodied; cherry and plum fruit with enough varietal character to satisfy; has length and balance. Screwcap. 14° alc. **RATING** 89 **DRINK** 2008 $ 20
Cabernet Merlot 2004 Very good colour; abundant dark berry fruits with touches of savoury olive, and a slight hint of green on the finish. Screwcap. 14.5° alc. **RATING** 88 **DRINK** 2009 $ 24

ŶŶŶŶ **Sparkling Merlot 2004 RATING** 85 **DRINK** Now $ 18
Unwooded Chardonnay 2005 RATING 84 **DRINK** Now $ 15

ŶŶŶ **Pinot Noir Chardonnay 2005 RATING** 83 $ 16

Minot Vineyard ★★★★

Lot 4 Harrington Road, Margaret River, WA 6285 **REGION** Margaret River
T (08) 9757 3579 **F** (08) 9757 2361 **OPEN** By appt
WINEMAKER Harmans Estate (Paul Green) **EST.** 1986 **CASES** 2500
Minot, which takes its name from a small chateau in the Loire Valley in France, is the husband and wife venture of the Miles family, and produces just 2 wines from the 4.2-ha plantings of semillon, sauvignon blanc and cabernet sauvignon.

ŶŶŶŶŶ **Margaret River Semillon Sauvignon Blanc 2005** Spotlessly clean and fresh; delicate, but by no means dilute; a gentle infusion of passionfruit and gooseberry into the crisp, minerally semillon. Screwcap. 12.4° alc. **RATING** 92 **DRINK** 2008

ŶŶŶŶ **Margaret River Cabernet Sauvignon 2003** Light- to medium-bodied; vibrant, direct, blackcurrant and cassis fruit; not complex, the early picking giving some Peter Pan qualities; rigid acidity. Cork. 12.8° alc. **RATING** 89 **DRINK** 2010 $ 27

Mintaro Wines

Leasingham Road, Mintaro, SA 5415 **REGION** Clare Valley
T (08) 8843 9150 **F** (08) 8843 9050 **WWW**.mintarowines.com.au **OPEN** 7 days 10–4.30
WINEMAKER Peter Houldsworth **EST.** 1984 **CASES** 4000
Has produced some very good Riesling over the years, developing well in bottle. The red wines, too, have improved significantly. The labelling is nothing if not interesting, from the depiction of a fish drinking like a fish, not to mention the statuesque belles femmes. Exports to Singapore.

ŶŶŶŶŶ **Clare Valley Shiraz 2003** Altogether more savoury than the Belles Femmes, though still with ample fruit, and likewise not showing its alcohol. Screwcap. 15° alc. **RATING** 94 **DRINK** 2018 $ 25

ŶŶŶŶ **Clare Valley Riesling 2005** A distinct slatey/stoney edge to the familiar lime/citrus fruit coming from the Polish Hill side of the Clare Valley; quite generous mid-palate, good finish. Screwcap. 13° alc. **RATING** 92 **DRINK** 2015 $ 20
Belles Femmes et Grand Vin Shiraz 2003 Very good colour and hue; firm, fresh, vibrant red and black fruits giving no clue about the alcohol, which the wine carries with aplomb; fine tannins, good oak. Screwcap. 15° alc. **RATING** 92 **DRINK** 2015 $ 28

Minto Wines

NR

'Minto', Faraday via Castlemaine, Vic 3450 **REGION** Bendigo
T (03) 5473 3278 **OPEN** By appt
WINEMAKER Alan Elliot **EST.** 1998 **CASES** 130
Alan and Heather Elliot have established a substantial business, anchored around 8 ha of chardonnay, pinot noir, shiraz and cabernet sauvignon, supplemented by contract-grown grapes. The cellar door (when open) is housed in the former Faraday school.

Miramar

NR

Henry Lawson Drive, Mudgee, NSW 2850 **REGION** Mudgee
T (02) 6373 3874 **F** (02) 6373 3854 **WWW**.miramarwines.com.au **OPEN** 7 days 9–5
WINEMAKER Ian MacRae **EST.** 1977 **CASES** 6000
Industry veteran Ian MacRae has demonstrated his skill with every type of wine over the decades, ranging from Rose to Chardonnay to full-bodied reds. All have shone under the Miramar label at one time or another, although the Ides of March are pointing more to the red than the white wines these days. The majority of the production from the 35 ha of estate vineyard is sold to others, the best being retained for Miramar's own use.

Miranda Wines

★★☆

57 Jondaryan Avenue, Griffith, NSW 2680 **REGION** Riverina
T (02) 6960 3000 **F** (02) 6962 6944 **WWW**.mirandawines.com.au **OPEN** 7 days 9–5
WINEMAKER Sam F Miranda, Garry Wall, Hope Golding, Luis E Simian **EST.** 1939 **CASES** 2.5 million
In 2003 Miranda Wines was purchased by the McGuigan/Simeon group; it has kept the brand portfolio largely intact, perhaps investing more in the most successful brands and markets.

ΨΨΨΨ **Mirrool Creek Merlot 2004** RATING 85 DRINK Now $ 9
Mirrool Creek Cabernet Shiraz 2003 RATING 85 DRINK 2008 $ 9
Somerton Brut Reserve Premium Cuvee NV RATING 84 DRINK Now $ 8

ΨΨΨ **Mirrool Creek Semillon Sauvignon Blanc 2004** RATING 83 $ 9
Somerton Semillon Chardonnay 2004 RATING 83 $ 8
Somerton Shiraz Cabernet Merlot 2003 RATING 83 $ 8

Mistletoe Wines

★★★★★

771 Hermitage Road, Pokolbin, NSW 2320 **REGION** Lower Hunter Valley
T (02) 4998 7770 **F** (02) 4998 7792 **WWW**.mistletoe.com.au **OPEN** 7 days 10–6
WINEMAKER Nick Paterson **EST.** 1989 **CASES** 4500
Mistletoe Wines, owned by Ken and Gwen Sloan, can trace its history back to 1909, when a substantial vineyard was planted on what was then called Mistletoe Farm. The Mistletoe Farm brand made a brief appearance in the late 1970s but disappeared until being revived under the Mistletoe Wines label by the Sloans. The wines are made onsite by Nick Paterson, who has long experience in the Hunter Valley, including the family-owned Chateau Pâto. Exports to Japan.

ΨΨΨΨΨ **Semillon 2005** Classic Hunter from a classic vintage; a spotlessly clean wine, with lemon, herb, spice, grass and mineral all intermingling; perfect acidity. Screwcap. 10° alc.
RATING 94 DRINK 2015 $ 20
Reserve Hunter Valley Chardonnay 2005 A slightly more intense version than the varietal, with newer French oak adding a little more texture and structure; very good wine, with length and persistence. Screwcap. 13.5° alc. RATING 94 DRINK 2011 $ 25
Reserve Hunter Valley Shiraz 2004 Much richer fruit, though still in the same flavour register of blackberry, plum and spice; velvety mouthfeel and positive French oak. Screwcap. 13° alc. RATING 94 DRINK 2015 $ 26

ΨΨΨΨ **Hunter Valley Chardonnay 2005** A clean bouquet; unexpected power and precision to the melon, stone fruit and citrus flavours; barrel ferment in older French oak merely a medium; very nice wine. Screwcap. 13.5° alc. RATING 93 DRINK 2010 $ 20

Barrel Fermented Rose 2005 Pale purple-red; among the best roses going around; elegant, long, with considerable fruit, then a delicate, dry finish. Screwcap. 13° alc. **RATING** 91 **DRINK** Now $ 20

▼▼▼▼ **Hunter Valley Shiraz 2004** Clean, light- to medium-bodied plum and spice fruit; a whisper of oak and soft tannins. Screwcap. 13° alc. **RATING** 89 **DRINK** 2010 $ 20
Petite Muscat 2005 Pure grape juice fortified in traditional mistelle style; neatly balanced juicy, grapey fruit with the cut of fortifying spirit. Screwcap. 15.5° alc. **RATING** 88 **DRINK** Now $ 17.50
The Rose 2005 Quite deep but bright colour; a halfway house between light-bodied dry red and rose; works well; for red drinkers. Screwcap. 13° alc. **RATING** 87 **DRINK** Now $ 18

Mitchell   ★★★★★

Hughes Park Road, Sevenhill via Clare, SA 5453 **REGION** Clare Valley
T (08) 8843 4258 **F** (08) 8843 4340 **WWW**.mitchellwines.com **OPEN** 7 days 10–4
WINEMAKER Andrew Mitchell **EST.** 1975 **CASES** 30 000
One of the stalwarts of the Clare Valley, producing long-lived Rieslings and Cabernet Sauvignons in classic regional style. The range now includes very creditable Semillon, Grenache and Shiraz. A lovely old stone apple shed provides the cellar door and upper section of the compact winery. Exports to the US.

▼▼▼▼▼ **Watervale Riesling 2005** Aromatic and floral; classically structured fruit, with dry, spicy minerality; classic style. Screwcap. **RATING** 94 **DRINK** 2015 $ 19
McNicol Shiraz 1998 Restrained, elegant, medium-bodied wine; red plum, raspberry, blackberry and spice flavours; good use of oak; very good line and length. Cork. 14.5° alc. **RATING** 94 **DRINK** 2010 $ 40

▼▼▼▼▽ **Peppertree Vineyard Sparkling Shiraz NV** A very good sparkling Shiraz which achieves full flavour without phenolics or high dosage; spicy black fruits; clean, long finish. Disgorged November 2004 after 2 years on lees. **RATING** 93 **DRINK** 2010 $ 30
Peppertree Vineyard Shiraz 2004 Light- to medium-bodied; soft, cushiony texture to the plum, blackberry and earth fruit; fine tannins, good oak handling. Screwcap. 14.5° alc. **RATING** 92 **DRINK** 2015 $ 25

▼▼▼▼ **Semillon 2004** A complex bouquet and entry promises a little more than the back-palate and finish deliver; I'm not sure why, but still a good wine. Screwcap. 12.5° alc. **RATING** 89 **DRINK** 2010 $ 19

Mitchelton   ★★★★★

Mitchellstown via Nagambie, Vic 3608 **REGION** Nagambie Lakes
T (03) 5736 2222 **F** (03) 5736 2266 **WWW**.mitchelton.com.au **OPEN** 7 days 10–5
WINEMAKER Toby Barlow **EST.** 1969 **CASES** 200 000
Acquired by Petaluma in 1994 (both now part of Lion Nathan), having already put the runs on the board in no uncertain fashion with gifted winemaker Don Lewis (who retired in 2004). Boasts an array of wines across a broad spectrum of style and price, each carefully aimed at a market niche. Exports to all major markets.

▼▼▼▼▼ **Print Shiraz 2003** Cascades of opulent and rich spicy blood plum fruit; fine tannins on a long finish; is not the least bit heavy. Screwcap. **RATING** 94 **DRINK** 2013 $ 21
Parish Shiraz Viognier 2003 A rich, seductive mouthfilling array of black fruits, spices and controlled viognier lift; soft, fine tannins; good oak and length. Screwcap. 14° alc. **RATING** 94 **DRINK** 2015 $ 29
Print Shiraz 2002 Deep red-purple; a powerful wine, the black fruits with considerable texture and structure, supported by savoury tannins. Cork. 14.5° alc. **RATING** 94 **DRINK** 2017 $ 49

▼▼▼▼▽ **Airstrip Marsanne Roussanne Viognier 2003** Glowing yellow-green; rich texture and structure; honey, nuts and honeysuckle, finishing dry. Cork. **RATING** 90 **DRINK** 2008 $ 25
Preece Cabernet Sauvignon 2004 Good colour; light- to medium-bodied, firm, clear-cut varietal fruit, still in a primary phase. Screwcap. 14.5° alc. **RATING** 90 **DRINK** 2012 $ 15

Blackwood Park Botrytis Riesling 2005 Cumquat, lemon, lime and mandarin aromas and flavours; not especially luscious, but good balance and line. Cork. 12.5° alc. **RATING** 90 **DRINK** Now $ 17

ŸŸŸŸ **Blackwood Park Riesling 2005** Crisp, clean and fresh; despite the alcohol, not particularly rich; a ripe but light citrus/lime palate. Screwcap. 13.5° alc. **RATING** 89 **DRINK** 2009 $ 16

Preece Shiraz 2004 Medium-bodied; good texture, balance and mouthfeel to gentle black fruits and nuances of chocolate, mocha and vanilla; over-delivers at the price. Screwcap. 14.5° alc. **RATING** 89 **DRINK** 2010 $ 15

Crescent Shiraz Mourvedre Grenache 2002 Strong colour; full-bodied; richer, stronger and deeper than the '03, albeit flavours in a similar savoury/dark berry spectrum and abundant tannins. Cork. **RATING** 89 **DRINK** 2009 $ 25

Preece Merlot 2004 Light- to medium-bodied; supple, smooth redcurrant/blackcurrant fruit and fine tannins. Trophy at '05 Adelaide Wine Show for Best Merlot simply underlines the shortcomings in Australian Merlot. Goulburn Valley/King Valley. Screwcap. 14.5° alc. **RATING** 89 **DRINK** 2010 $ 15

Preece Sauvignon Blanc 2005 A positive varietal fruit bouquet swells into gently tropical flavours on the mid-palate, sliding away slightly on the finish. Screwcap. 13.5° alc. **RATING** 88 **DRINK** Now $ 15

Preece Chardonnay 2005 Light-bodied; melon/nectarine/peach fruit with touches of cashew and toasty oak. Screwcap. 14° alc. **RATING** 88 **DRINK** 2009 $ 15

Central Victorian Viognier 2004 Well-made, medium-bodied nicely balanced white wine; the only thing lacking is enough varietal character. Screwcap. 14.5° alc. **RATING** 87 **DRINK** 2008 $ 20

Crescent Shiraz Mourvedre Grenache 2003 Medium-bodied; the contribution of each component is obvious, not the least the mourvedre tannins; overall black fruit flavours. Screwcap. **RATING** 87 **DRINK** 2008 $ 25

Mitolo Wines   ★★★★★

PO Box 520, Virginia, SA 5120 **REGION** McLaren Vale
T (08) 8282 9012 **F** (08) 8282 9062 **WWW**.mitolowines.com.au **OPEN** Not
WINEMAKER Ben Glaetzer **EST.** 1999 **CASES** 20 000
Frank Mitolo began making wine in 1995 as a hobby, and soon progressed to undertaking formal studies in winemaking. His interest grew year by year, but it was not until 2000 that he took the plunge into the commercial end of the business, retaining Ben Glaetzer to make the wines for him. Since that time, a remarkably good series of wines have been released. Imitation being the sincerest form of flattery, part of the complicated story behind each label name is pure Torbreck, but Mitolo then adds a Latin proverb or saying to the name. Exports to the UK, the US and other major markets.

ŸŸŸŸŸ **Savitar McLaren Vale Shiraz 2004** Deep, dense colour; clean, dark fruit aromas and archetypal McLaren Vale blackberry and dark chocolate fruit; achieves density without sacrificing mouthfeel. Cork. 15° alc. **RATING** 96 **DRINK** 2015 $ 72

G.A.M. McLaren Vale Shiraz 2004 Deep colour, excellent hue; concentrated and rich red and black fruits, and plenty of dusty tannins. Screwcap. 15° alc. **RATING** 94 **DRINK** 2016 $ 55

Reiver Barossa Shiraz 2004 The medium-bodied weight denies the alcohol, though not so much ripe confit fruit flavours ranging from cherry to blackberry; good length and bright finish. Screwcap. 15° alc. **RATING** 94 **DRINK** 2019 $ 55

Serpico McLaren Vale Cabernet Sauvignon 2004 Potent, powerful blackcurrant, dark chocolate and cassis aromas; very dense and rich mouthfeel, with masses of dusty tannins; some suggestion of juice run-off. Screwcap. 15° alc. **RATING** 94 **DRINK** 2015 $ 72

ŸŸŸŸŸ **Jester McLaren Vale Shiraz 2004** Fragrant spicy berry and leaf aromas, with a whisper of reduction; red cherry, raspberry and plum fruit; fine, ripe tannins; good oak. Screwcap. 14.5° alc. **RATING** 92 **DRINK** 2012 $ 27

Jester McLaren Vale Cabernet Sauvignon 2004 Lifted cassis, berry, olive and leaf aromas; good structure and length; subtle oak. Cork. 14.5° alc. **RATING** 92 **DRINK** 2012 $ 27

ɥɥɥɥ **Jester Rose 2005** Vivid red-purple; a rose with considerable attitude; plum, confit and spice, the alcohol just a touch edgy. Screwcap. 14.5° alc. **RATING** 89 **DRINK** Now $ 21

Molly Morgan Vineyard ★★★☆

Talga Road, Lovedale, NSW 2321 **REGION** Lower Hunter Valley
T(02) 9807 4555 **F**(02) 9807 4544 **WWW**.mollymorgan.com **OPEN** By appt
WINEMAKER John Baruzzi (Consultant) **EST.** 1963 **CASES** 5000
Molly Morgan has been acquired by Andrew and Hady Simon, who established the Camperdown Cellars Group in 1971, which became the largest retailer in Australia, before moving on to other pursuits. They have been recently joined by Grant Breen, their former general manager at Camperdown Cellars. The property has 6.5 ha of 42-year-old unirrigated semillon, which goes to make the Old Vines Semillon, 1 ha for Joe's Block Semillon, 2.4 ha of chardonnay and 3.2 ha of shiraz. Exports to the US, Canada, Ireland, China and Japan.

ɥɥɥɥ **Back Patch Chardonnay 2004** Developed but bright green-yellow; generous melon and stone fruit flavours utterly belie the low alcohol until the tight, fine finish. Interesting wine. Screwcap. 11.5° alc. **RATING** 89 **DRINK** 2008 $ 24
Botrytis Semillon 2003 Rich, luscious peachy fruit off-set by balancing acidity. Cork. 11.7° alc. **RATING** 89 **DRINK** 2008 $ 22
Shiraz 2004 Light- to medium-bodied; clean and fresh red and black fruits; fine tannins, and an airbrush of oak. Cork. 12.6° alc. **RATING** 88 **DRINK** 2011 $ 25
Partner's Reserve Shiraz 2003 Medium red-purple; clean, light-bodied, regional savoury/earthy nuances; more expected of the vintage. Cork. 13.2° alc. **RATING** 88 **DRINK** 2012 $ 38
Red Mistress Sparkling Shiraz NV Gentle cherry/earthy fruit; light- to medium-bodied and no phenolics; pleasantly dry finish. **RATING** 87 **DRINK** Now $ 23

ɥɥɥɥ **Fair Lady Sparkling White NV RATING** 86 **DRINK** Now $ 20

Monahan Estate ★★★

319 Wilderness Road, Rothbury, NSW 2320 **REGION** Lower Hunter Valley
T(02) 4930 9070 **F**(02) 4930 7679 **WWW**.monahanestate.com.au **OPEN** Wed–Sun 10–5
WINEMAKER Monarch Winemaking Services **EST.** 1997 **CASES** 2000
Monahan Estate is bordered by Black Creek in the Lovedale district, an area noted for its high-quality semillon; the old bridge adjoining the property is displayed on the wine label; the wines themselves have been consistent silver and bronze medal winners at the Hunter Valley Wine Show.

ɥɥɥɥ **Old Bridge Hunter Valley Semillon 2005** Relatively late picking is reflected in the alcohol, and has taken the edge off the normal '05 vintage fruit; a pleasant wine, nonetheless. Screwcap. 12.3° alc. **RATING** 87 **DRINK** 2009 $ 15
Old Bridge Hunter Valley Rose 2005 Vivid light purple-red; light, crisp and fresh cherry-accented fruit; a pleasingly dry finish. Screwcap. 13.2° alc. **RATING** 87 **DRINK** Now $ 14

ɥɥɥɥ **Old Bridge Hunter Valley Chardonnay 2005 RATING** 86 **DRINK** Now $ 14

Monbulk Winery NR

Macclesfield Road, Monbulk, Vic 3793 **REGION** Yarra Valley
T(03) 9756 6965 **F**(03) 9756 6965 **OPEN** W'ends & public hols 12–5, or by appt
WINEMAKER Paul Jabornik **EST.** 1984 **CASES** 500
Originally concentrated on kiwifruit wines but now extending to table wines; the very cool Monbulk subregion should be capable of producing wines of distinctive style, but the table wines are not of the same standard as the kiwifruit wines, which are quite delicious.

Mongrel Creek Vineyard

NR

Lot 72, Hayes Road, Yallingup Siding, WA 6281 **REGION** Margaret River
T 0417 991 065 **F** (08) 9755 5708 **OPEN** W'ends, school & public hols 10–5
WINEMAKER Michael Kerrigan, Matt Burton **EST.** 1996 **CASES** 700
Larry and Shirley Schoppe both have full-time occupations, Larry as vineyard supervisor at Howard Park's Leston Vineyard, Shirley as a full-time nurse. Thus the 2.8-ha vineyard, planted to shiraz, semillon, sauvignon blanc in 1996, is still a weekend and holiday business. Given the viticultural and winemaking expertise of those involved, it is hardly surprising that the wines have been consistent show medal winners.

Monichino Wines

1820 Berrys Road, Katunga, Vic 3640 **REGION** Goulburn Valley
T (03) 5864 6452 **F** (03) 5864 6538 **WWW**.monichino.com.au **OPEN** Mon–Sat 9–5, Sun 10–5
WINEMAKER Carlo Monichino, Terry Monichino **EST.** 1962 **CASES** 20 000
This winery was an early pacesetter for the region, with clean, fresh wines in which the fruit character was (and is) carefully preserved; also showed a deft touch with its Botrytis Semillon. It has moved with the times, introducing an interesting range of varietal wines while preserving its traditional base.

White Muscat (500ml) NV Well-made and balanced; good rancio has developed to lift the biscuit and Christmas cake flavours; the base wine is from 1980, the youngest from 1993. Will sell once it's tasted, difficult otherwise. Cork. 18° alc. **RATING** 91 **DRINK** 2008 **$** 60

Montalto Vineyards

33 Shoreham Road, Red Hill South, Vic 3937 **REGION** Mornington Peninsula
T (03) 5989 8412 **F** (03) 5989 8417 **WWW**.montalto.com.au **OPEN** 7 days 11–5
WINEMAKER Robin Brockett **EST.** 1998 **CASES** 3500
John Mitchell and family established Montalto Vineyards in 1998, but the core of the vineyard goes back to 1986. There are 5.6 ha pinot noir, 3 ha chardonnay, 1 ha pinot gris, and 0.5 ha each of semillon, riesling and pinot meunier. Intensive vineyard work opens up the canopy, with yields ranging between 1.5 and 2.5 tonnes per acre. Wines are released under 2 labels, the flagship Montalto and Pennon, the latter effectively a lower-priced, second label. The high-quality restaurant also features guest chefs and cooking classes.

Chardonnay 2004 A seamless fusion of stone fruit, melon, citrus and spicy French oak; flawless balance and length; 13.1° alcohol to be applauded. Quality cork. **RATING** 95 **DRINK** 2011 **$** 32

Pinot Noir 2004 Fragrant cherry and Satsuma plum aromas and flavours; light- to medium-bodied, but with intense fruit; subtle oak, good length. Cork. **RATING** 93 **DRINK** 2010 **$** 37
Mornington Peninsula Riesling 2005 Lime, apple and passionfruit aromas and flavours; above-average length and persistence of flavour (for the Peninsula). Screwcap. 12.5° alc. **RATING** 91 **DRINK** 2010 **$** 23
Pennon Hill Chardonnay 2005 Elegant, fragrant stone fruit/grapefruit aromas; a smooth and supple palate, not as intense as expected. Good nonetheless. Screwcap. 13° alc. **RATING** 90 **DRINK** 2009 **$** 21
Pennon Hill Pinot Noir 2004 Light- to medium-bodied; a smooth and supple mix of plum and cherry fruits; light but well-balanced finish. Screwcap. 13.2° alc. **RATING** 90 **DRINK** 2009 **$** 24

Pennon Hill Rose 2005 Delicate spicy strawberry aromas and flavours; good balance and length; nice dry style. Screwcap. 13° alc. **RATING** 88 **DRINK** Now **$** 18

Montara ★★★★

76 Chalambar Road, Ararat, Vic 3377 **REGION** Grampians
T(03) 5352 3868 **F**(03) 5352 4968 **WWW**.montara.com.au **OPEN** Mon–Sat 10–5, Sun 12–4
WINEMAKER Mike McRae **EST.** 1970 **CASES** NFP
Achieved considerable attention for its Pinot Noirs during the 1980s, but other regions (and other makers) have come along since. It continues to produce wines of distinctive style, and smart label designs help. Exports to the UK, Switzerland, Canada and Hong Kong.

ΨΨΨΨϘ **Chardonnay 2004** Clean, tight, focused and long; fruit-driven palate with a mix of grapefruit, melon and stone fruit; good finish. Screwcap. 14° alc. **RATING** 91 **DRINK** 2010 $ 21

Sauvignon Blanc 2005 A clean bouquet; generous, ripe, tropical fruit on the mid-palate, rounded off by good minerally acidity. Screwcap. 14° alc. **RATING** 90 **DRINK** Now $ 17

ΨΨΨΨ **Shiraz 2004** Developed colour; interesting spicy/peppery/savoury/brambly characters to the medium-bodied blackberry fruit; a little too much perhaps. Screwcap. 14.5° alc. **RATING** 89 **DRINK** 2012 $ 27

Riesling 2005 Green apple and light citrus aromas; soft, ripe fruit on the palate, with a touch of residual sugar. Typical winery style. Screwcap. 13.5° alc. **RATING** 88 **DRINK** 2009 $ 17

Pinot Noir 2003 Does have the varietal character missing in some vintages; sweet, slightly cooked cherry fruit, then a pleasantly sappy finish to give balance. Screwcap. 13.5° alc. **RATING** 87 **DRINK** 2008 $ 25

ΨΨΨϘ **Merlot 2004** **RATING** 86 **DRINK** 2008 $ 25

Montgomery's Hill ★★★★☆

South Coast Highway, Upper Kalgan, Albany, WA 6330 **REGION** Albany
T(08) 9844 3715 **F**(08) 9844 3819 **WWW**.montgomeryshill.com **OPEN** 7 days 11–5
WINEMAKER Dianne Miller, Bill Crappsley (Consultant) **EST.** 1996 **CASES** 6000
Montgomery's Hill is 16 km northeast of Albany on a north-facing slope on the banks of the Kalgan River. The vineyard site was previously used as an apple orchard; it is a diversification for the third generation of the Montgomery family, which owns the property. Chardonnay, cabernet sauvignon and cabernet franc were planted in 1996, followed by sauvignon blanc, shiraz and merlot in 1997.

ΨΨΨΨΨ **Albany Shiraz 2004** Good hue; complex spice, licorice, pepper, black cherry and blackberry all seamlessly interwoven with oak; fine, ripe tannins. Screwcap. 14.5° alc. **RATING** 94 **DRINK** 2015 $ 18

ΨΨΨΨϘ **Albany Sauvignon Blanc 2005** Aromatic nettle, grass and spicy aromas; intense and focused palate, powerful and long; minerally acidity. Screwcap. **RATING** 92 **DRINK** Now $ 15.50

Albany Chardonnay 2004 Light- to medium-bodied; subtle oak/lees infusion; melon, fig and cream flavours; good texture. Screwcap. 14° alc. **RATING** 90 **DRINK** 2010 $ 18

Albany Cabernet Franc 2004 Brilliant fresh colour; light- to medium-bodied; bright, lively red fruits; simply doesn't show the alcohol; nonetheless, chill in summer. Screwcap. 14.5° alc. **RATING** 90 **DRINK** 2010 $ 15

ΨΨΨΨ **Albany Cabernet Sauvignon 2004** Some development in both colour and flavour; savoury, earthy aspects to blackcurrant fruit; the tannins are fine and not green, the oak is good. Given the screwcap, the colour is inexplicable. Screwcap. 14° alc. **RATING** 89 **DRINK** 2012 $ 18

Albany Cabernet Sauvignon Cabernet Franc 2004 Bright red-purple; bright, breezy red fruits; crisp acidity. Not easy to understand what is going on here. Screwcap. 14° alc. **RATING** 89 **DRINK** 2011 $ 15

Montvalley   NR

150 Mitchells Road, Mount View, NSW 2325 (postal) **REGION** Lower Hunter Valley
T (02) 4991 1936 **F** (02) 4991 7994 **www**.montvalley.com.au **OPEN** Not
WINEMAKER Monarch Winemaking Services (Jim Chatto) **EST.** 2002 **CASES** 1500
Having looked at dozens of properties over the previous decade, and having detailed soil analyses done before finalising the deal, John and Deirdre Colvin purchased their 80-ha property in 1998. They chose the name Montvalley in part because it reflects the beautiful valley in the Brokenback Ranges of which the property forms part, and in part because the name Colvin originates from France, 'col' meaning valley and 'vin' meaning vines. Between 1998 and 2001 they have planted a total of 5.7 ha of vines, the lion's share to shiraz, with lesser amounts of chardonnay and semillon.

Monument Vineyard   NR

Cnr Escort Way/Manildra Road, Cudal, NSW 2864 **REGION** Central Ranges Zone
T (02) 9686 4605 **F** (02) 9686 4605 **www**.monumentvineyard.com.au **OPEN** At Underwood Lane Wines, tel (02) 6365 2221
WINEMAKER Alison Eisermann **EST.** 1998 **CASES** 1500
In the early 1990s five mature-age students at Charles Sturt University, successful in their own professions, decided to form a partnership to develop a substantial vineyard and winery on a scale that they could not individually afford, but could do so collectively. After a lengthy search, a large property at Cudal was identified, with ideal terra rossa basalt-derived soil over a limestone base. The property has 110 ha under vine, planted in 1998 and 1999.

Moojelup Farm   ★★★★

Thompson Road, Cookernup, WA 6220 **REGION** Geographe
T (08) 9733 5166 **F** (08) 9733 5490 **www**.moojelup.com.au **OPEN** By appt
WINEMAKER Peter Stanlake **EST.** 1997 **CASES** 275
Moojelup Farm is a historic 40-ha property dating back to the 1870s. The family of present owners, Stephanie and Simon Holthouse, have owned the property for more than half its history. In 1997 they began the planting of 3.2 ha of semillon, cabernet sauvignon and shiraz; most of the grapes are sold to Millbrook Wines in the Perth Hills, with small amounts made for them.

▼▼▼▼▽ **Thompsons Block Semillon 2004** Good wine; excellent texture and structure; grassy semillon fruit supported but not swamped by French oak; good length; barrel-fermented. Quality cork. **RATING** 91 **DRINK** 2009 $ 15

▼▼▼▼ **Thompsons Block Cabernet Sauvignon 2003** Light- to medium-bodied; blackcurrant, spice and black olive flavours; subtle oak; fine tannins. Quality cork. **RATING** 89 **DRINK** 2010 $ 18
Thompsons Block Shiraz 2003 Faintly reduced bouquet; comes alive on the palate, with fine tannins to support blackberry fruit; good length. Screwcap. **RATING** 88 **DRINK** 2009 $ 18

Moombaki Wines   ★★★★★

RMB 1277 Parker Road, Kentdale via Denmark, WA 6333 **REGION** Denmark
T (08) 9840 8006 **F** (08) 9840 8006 **www**.moombaki.com **OPEN** Thurs–Mon 11–5, Wed–Mon summer & school hols, or by appt
WINEMAKER Harewood Estate (James Kellie) **EST.** 1997 **CASES** 1000
David Britten and Melissa Boughey (with three young sons in tow) established 2 ha of vines on a north-facing gravel hillside with a picturesque Kent River frontage. Not content with establishing the vineyard, they put in significant mixed tree plantings to increase wildlife habitats and fenced off wetlands and river from stock grazing and degradation. It is against this background that they chose Moombaki as their vineyard name: a local Aboriginal word meaning 'where the river meets the sky'. Exports to the UK and Switzerland.

▼▼▼▼▼ **Chardonnay 2004** Spotlessly clean; an attractive style marrying elegance and positive varietal melon and nectarine fruit; oak a pure support role; good length and feel. Screwcap. **RATING** 94 **DRINK** 2012 $ 28

Great Southern Shiraz 2004 Elegant, intense, cool-grown style; spice and pepper run through the length of the medium-bodied palate in association with black fruits and fine, ripe tannins; long finish. Screwcap. 14.5° alc. **RATING** 94 **DRINK** 2015 $ 25
Great Southern Cabernet Sauvignon Cabernet Franc Malbec 2004 Bright purple-red; medium-bodied; lively cassis/raspberry/blackcurrant mix; supple and long, with fine-grained tannins. Screwcap. 14° alc. **RATING** 94 **DRINK** 2015 $ 25

Moonbark Estate Vineyard   NR

Lot 11, Moonambel–Natte Yallock Road, Moonambel, Vic 3478 (postal) **REGION** Pyrenees
T 0439 952 263 **F** (03) 9870 6116 **OPEN** Not
WINEMAKER Contract **EST.** 1998 **CASES** 300
Rod Chivers and his family have been slowly establishing their vineyard over the past 7 years, with 0.5 ha of shiraz in bearing. A further ha or so of cabernet sauvignon and merlot are being progressively planted. The wines are sold through local restaurants and retailers.

Moondah Brook

c/- Houghton, Dale Road, Middle Swan, WA 6056 **REGION** Swan Valley
T (08) 9274 5172 **F** (08) 9274 5372 **WWW.**moondahbrook.com.au **OPEN** Not
WINEMAKER Ross Pamment **EST.** 1968 **CASES** 80 000
Part of the Hardy wine group which has its own special character, as it draws part of its fruit from the large Gingin vineyard, 70 km north of the Swan Valley, and part from the Margaret River and Great Southern. From time to time it has excelled even its own reputation for reliability with some quite lovely wines, in particular honeyed, aged Chenin Blanc, generous Shiraz and finely structured Cabernet Sauvignon.

ŸŸŸŸŸ **Cabernet Sauvignon 2002** Clean, elegant, fruit-forward; medium-bodied; excellent varietal definition with cassis and blackcurrant; soft, supple tannins; controlled oak. Cork. **RATING** 92 **DRINK** 2009 $ 14.50

ŸŸŸŸ **Shiraz 2002** Red and black fruit aromas; medium-bodied, with nicely balanced fruit and tannins; good length. Cork. **RATING** 88 **DRINK** 2009 $ 14.50
Cabernet Rose 2005 Vibrant pale pink; carefully pitched at the lunchtime brasserie market; highly floral, slightly sweet; nicely made. Screwcap. **RATING** 87 **DRINK** Now $ 12

ŸŸŸŸ **Classic Dry White 2005** Light-bodied; eager to please tropical passionfruit balanced by a touch of tangy acidity. Screwcap. 13.5° alc. **RATING** 86 **DRINK** Now $ 13
Chenin Blanc 2005 RATING 85 **DRINK** Now $ 12
Verdelho 2005 RATING 85 **DRINK** Now $ 12
Merlot 2003 RATING 85 **DRINK** Now $ 14.50

Moondarra   ★★★

Browns Road, Moondarra, Vic 3825 (postal) **REGION** Gippsland
T (03) 9598 3049 **F** (03) 9598 0677 **OPEN** Not
WINEMAKER Neil Prentice **EST.** 1991 **CASES** NA
In 1991 Neil Prentice and family established their Moondarra Vineyard in Gippsland, planted to 1.5 ha of 11 low-yielding clones of pinot noir, to which they have recently added a 0.25 ha each of nebbiolo and piccolit. The vines are not irrigated, and vineyard management is predicated on the minimum use of any sprays; the aim is to eventually move to Biodynamic farming methods. The winemaking techniques are strongly influenced by the practices of controversial Burgundy consultant Guy Accad, with 10 days pre-fermentation maceration and whole bunches added prior to fermentation. Exports to the US, Japan and Singapore.

ŸŸŸŸ **Holly's Garden Pinot Gris 2004 RATING** 86 **DRINK** Now $ 22

Moorebank Vineyard

NR

Palmers Lane, Pokolbin, NSW 2320 **REGION** Lower Hunter Valley
T (02) 4998 7610 **F** (02) 4998 7367 **WWW**.moorebankvineyard.com.au **OPEN** Fri–Mon 10–5, or by appt
WINEMAKER Iain Riggs (Contract) **EST.** 1977 **CASES** 2000
Ian Burgess and Debra Moore own a mature 6-ha vineyard planted to chardonnay, semillon, gewurztraminer and merlot, with a small cellar door operation offering immaculately packaged wines in avant-garde style.

Moores Hill Estate

3343 West Tamar Highway, Sidmouth, Tas 7270 **REGION** Northern Tasmania
T (03) 6394 7649 **F** (03) 6394 7649 **WWW**.mooreshill.com.au **OPEN** Oct–June Wed–Sun 10–5,
Mon–Tues by appt for group bookings
WINEMAKER Tamar Ridge (Michael Fogarty) **EST.** 1997 **CASES** 3000
Rod and Karen Thorpe, along with their partner Bob Harkness and wife Chris, established Moores Hill Estate in 1997 on the cattle and sheep property of the Thorpes, on the gentle slopes of the West Tamar Valley. The vineyard has 4.9 ha of riesling, chardonnay, pinot noir, merlot and cabernet sauvignon. The vineyard represents a full circle for the Thorpes, who bought the farm nearly 30 years ago and ripped out a small vineyard. The Wine Centre (built in 2002 mainly from timber found on the property) overlooks the vineyard.

ᵠᵠᵠᵠᵠ **Chardonnay 2004** Tangy, lively grapefruit and melon, excellent length and balance.
RATING 94 **DRINK** 2012 $ 18

ᵠᵠᵠᵠᵠ **Riesling 2005** Ultra-ripe passionfruit, almost peachy fruit typical of the vintage. Despite the flavour, retains elegance in a light- to medium-bodied frame. **RATING** 93 **DRINK** 2010 $ 19
Chardonnay 2005 Delicious stone fruit and passionfruit; again minimal oak. **RATING** 92 **DRINK** 2008 $ 19
Pinot Noir 2004 Light- to medium red-purple; pleasant plum and black cherry fruit in a light- to medium-bodied frame; elegance rather than power. **RATING** 90 **DRINK** 2009 $ 24

ᵠᵠᵠᵠ **Cabernet Sauvignon Merlot 2004** Generously flavoured mix of blackberry, raspberry, mint and leaf, the tannins not green. **RATING** 89 **DRINK** 2009 $ 20

Moorilla Estate

★★★★

655 Main Road, Berriedale, Tas 7011 **REGION** Southern Tasmania
T (03) 6277 9900 **F** (03) 6249 4093 **WWW**.moorilla.com.au **OPEN** 7 days 10–5
WINEMAKER Alan Ferry **EST.** 1958 **CASES** 16 000
Moorilla Estate is an icon in the Tasmanian wine industry and is thriving. Wine quality continues to be unimpeachable, and the opening of the museum in the marvellous Alcorso house designed by Sir Roy Grounds adds even more attraction for visitors to the estate, which is a mere 15–20 mins from Hobart. Five-star self-contained chalets are available, with a restaurant open for lunch 7 days. Exports to the US, Hong Kong and Denmark.

ᵠᵠᵠᵠᵠ **Black Label Pinot Noir 2005** Strong colour; plenty of depth and power to the black plum and spice flavours; long palate, sustained acidity. Screwcap. 14° alc. **RATING** 90 **DRINK** 2009 $ 24

ᵠᵠᵠᵠ **Riesling 2005** Crisp array of citrus, passionfruit and apple blossom; good length and balance. **RATING** 88 **DRINK** 2010 $ 19
Black Label Riesling 2005 Fleshy, sweet, ripe fruit with acidity just failing to balance the sweetness. Screwcap. 12° alc. **RATING** 87 **DRINK** 2009 $ 19

ᵠᵠᵠᵠ **Gewurztraminer 2005** **RATING** 86 **DRINK** Now $ 27
Sauvignon Blanc 2005 **RATING** 86 **DRINK** Now $ 23
White Label Pinot Noir 2004 **RATING** 86 **DRINK** 2012 $ 38
Pinot Gris 2005 **RATING** 84 **DRINK** Now $ 23

Moorooduc Estate ★★★★★

501 Derril Road, Moorooduc, Vic 3936 **REGION** Mornington Peninsula
T (03) 5971 8506 **F** (03) 5971 8550 **WWW**.moorooduc-estate.com.au **OPEN** W'ends 11–5, 7 days in January
WINEMAKER Dr Richard McIntyre **EST.** 1983 **CASES** 2500
Richard McIntyre has taken Moorooduc Estate to new heights as he has completely mastered the difficult art of gaining maximum results from wild yeast fermentations. While the Chardonnays remain the jewels in the crown, the Pinot Noirs and other wines are also impressive.

ΨΨΨΨΨ **The Moorooduc Chardonnay 2004** The differences may be subtle, but they absolutely exist. More texture and complexity, stopping short of full-on French funk; woven, layered palate. Screwcap. 14° alc. **RATING** 95 **DRINK** 2014 $58
The Moorooduc Pinot Noir 2004 Significantly greater complexity than the varietal but, most of all, plum and black cherry fruit; impressive wine. Screwcap. 14.5° alc. **RATING** 95 **DRINK** 2013 $58
Devil Bend Creek Chardonnay 2004 Light, glowing yellow-green; supremely elegant, largely fruit-driven notwithstanding the winemaker inputs (including wild yeast) to the citrus and nectarine fruit; lovely finish. Screwcap. 14° alc. **RATING** 94 **DRINK** 2011 $25
Chardonnay 2004 Bright green-straw; very tight, fine and minerally, more restrained than the Devil Bend Creek, and closer to The Moorooduc. A question of style, not quality. Screwcap. 14° alc. **RATING** 94 **DRINK** 2012 $30

ΨΨΨΨΨ **Pinot Noir 2004** A very different bouquet and palate; more powerful, stemmy/foresty notes run through the long palate, the fruit coming through on a peacock's tail finish. Screwcap. 14° alc. **RATING** 93 **DRINK** 2010 $35
Shiraz 2004 Light- to medium-bodied; sweet cherry, plum and blackberry; gentle spice; silky mouthfeel and controlled oak. Screwcap. 14° alc. **RATING** 92 **DRINK** 2014 $30
Devil Bend Creek Pinot Noir 2004 Light- to medium-bodied; spicy, foresty aromas surround red fruits; good length, although the fruit is off-set by slightly assertive tannins. Screwcap. 14° alc. **RATING** 91 **DRINK** 2010 $25

ΨΨΨΨ **Pinot Gris 2005** Good varietal character; medium-bodied pear, apple, musk and spice; not too hot. Screwcap. 14° alc. **RATING** 89 **DRINK** 2008 $30
Cabernet 2004 Savoury, spicy, earthy fruit, sweetened significantly by quality oak. Less effort and cost than with the other varieties, but good for the onsite restaurant. Screwcap. 14° alc. **RATING** 89 **DRINK** 2012 $30

Moothi Estate ★★★

85 Rocky Waterhole Road, Mudgee, NSW 2850 (postal) **REGION** Mudgee
T (02) 9868 6014 **F** (02) 9868 6017 **WWW**.countyview.net **OPEN** Not
WINEMAKER 21C Wine Company (Drew Tuckwell) **EST.** 1995 **CASES** 1000
Phil and Susan Moore purchased a property on the northwest-facing slopes of Mt Frome, at an elevation of 550m, in 1995. The site has reddish-brown clay with limestone, quartz and ironstone gibber soil, well suited to the chardonnay, shiraz, merlot and cabernet sauvignon established on the property, amounting to 24 ha in all. The names for the wines are derived from the Koori name for Mudgee, which is Moothi; 'Moothi Mud' is said to be local slang for Mudgee's full-bodied reds.

ΨΨΨΨΨ **Moothi Mud Merlot 2003** Very distinctive earth, olive, blackcurrant savoury varietal mix; fine tannins; good balance and length. Cork. **RATING** 90 **DRINK** 2010 $15

ΨΨΨΨ **Moothi Mud Shiraz 2003** Medium-bodied; ripe blackberry, plum and prune fruit; well-integrated oak; balanced tannins. Screwcap. **RATING** 88 **DRINK** 2009 $22.50

ΨΨΨΨ **Very Special Selection Shiraz 2004** Light-bodied, savoury/earthy edges; has length, but lacks fruit intensity; as for all of the reds, the problems lie in the vineyard. Screwcap. 13.4° alc. **RATING** 86 **DRINK** 2010 $22
Moothi Waters Very Special Selection Chardonnay 2005 **RATING** 85 **DRINK** 2008 $14
Moothi Dreams Winemakers Reserve Shiraz Cabernet 2004 **RATING** 85 **DRINK** 2009 $25
Very Special Selection Merlot 2004 **RATING** 85 **DRINK** 2009 $22
Very Special Selection Cabernet Sauvignon 2004 **RATING** 84 **DRINK** 2008 $22

Morambro Creek Wines

NR

Riddoch Highway, Padthaway, SA 5271 (postal) **REGION** Padthaway
T (08) 8765 6043 **F** (08) 8765 6011 **OPEN** Not
WINEMAKER Nicola Honeysett **EST.** 1994 **CASES** 6000
The Bryson family has been involved in agriculture for more than a century, moving to Padthaway in 1955 as farmers and graziers. In the early 1990s they began the establishment of 125 ha of vines, planted principally to chardonnay, shiraz and cabernet sauvignon; further plantings are planned. The wines have been consistent winners of bronze and silver medals at Australian wine shows since their release.

Moranghurk Vineyard

1516 Sturt Street, Ballarat, Vic 3350 (postal) **REGION** Geelong
T (03) 5331 2105 **F** (03) 5332 9244 **OPEN** Not
WINEMAKER Dan Buckle (Contract) **EST.** 1996 **CASES** 340
Ross and Liz Wilkie have established a tiny vineyard on the historic Moranghurk property, which was first settled in 1840. They have planted 0.6 ha of clonally selected pinot noir and 0.5 ha of chardonnay on volcanic soil overlying shale and clay. The vineyard is mulched, and is in the course of being converted to organic, with yields of less than 5 tonnes per ha.

TTTTY **Moorabool Valley Pinot Noir 2004** Light- to medium red-purple; lively, fresh plum and black cherry fruit on an elegant palate with good line and length; balanced acidity. Screwcap. 12.5° alc. **RATING** 92 **DRINK** 2008 $ 20

TTTT **Moorabool Valley Chardonnay 2004** Complex barrel ferment inputs work well with the stone fruit and melon flavours; good length. Screwcap. 13.5° alc. **RATING** 89 **DRINK** 2013 $ 22.50

Morgan Simpson

PO Box 39, Kensington Park, SA 5068 **REGION** McLaren Vale
T 0417 843 118 **F** (08) 8364 3645 **WWW**.morgansimpson.com.au **OPEN** Not
WINEMAKER Richard Simpson **EST.** 1998 **CASES** 1800
Morgan Simpson was founded by South Australian businessman George Morgan (since retired) and winemaker Richard Simpson, who is a wine science graduate of Charles Sturt University. The grapes are sourced from the Clos Robert Vineyard (where the wine is made) established by Robert Allen Simpson in 1972. The aim was — and is — to provide drinkable wines at a reasonable price. It succeeds admirably. Exports to the US and NZ.

TTTTY **McLaren Vale Shiraz 2004** Good colour; medium- to full-bodied; voluptuous, sweet blackberry and chocolate fruit; strict tannin control, oak largely incidental. Exceptional value. Cork. 15.2° alc. **RATING** 93 **DRINK** 2015 $ 18

Morgan Vineyards

30 Davross Court, Seville, Vic 3139 **REGION** Yarra Valley
T (03) 5964 4807 **WWW**.morganvineyards.com.au **OPEN** Mon–Fri 11–4, w'ends & public hols 11–5
WINEMAKER Roger Morgan **EST.** 1987 **CASES** 1000
Roger Morgan purchased the Kara Gola vineyard (Aboriginal for 'distant views') in 1987. The original 1971 plantings (cabernet sauvignon and pinot noir) were extended in 1989 (pinot noir), 1991 (cabernet sauvignon and merlot) and 1994 (chardonnay) and now total 4.8 ha. Roger completed a wine science degree at Charles Sturt University in 1997 and Morgan Wines began, and wife Ally retired from teaching in 2004 to become the marketing and events manager. Heathcote Shiraz was recently added to the product range, and they continue to strive to make elegant and distinctive wines.

TTTTY **Yarra Valley Pinot Noir 2004** Excellent colour; ripe, lush plummy fruit; has both depth and length; balanced oak and tannins. Huge improvement. Cork. 14.5° alc. **RATING** 90 **DRINK** 2011 $ 28

ΥΥΥΥ **Yarra Valley Chardonnay 2005** Straw-yellow; an opulent, fleshy style with multiple winemaker fingerprints; ripe fig and stone fruit flavours; atypical. Cork. 14.2° alc. **RATING** 88 **DRINK** 2009 $24

ΥΥΥΥ **Yarra Valley Cabernet Sauvignon 2004** Good colour; light- to medium-bodied; savoury blackcurrant fruit with slight tinges of green, and a question mark on the oak. Cork. 14.2° alc. **RATING** 86 **DRINK** 2011 $25
Yarra Valley Merlot 2004 **RATING** 85 **DRINK** 2012 $24

MorganField ★★★★

104 Ashworths Road, Lancefield, Vic 3435 **REGION** Macedon Ranges
T (03) 5429 1157 **WWW**.morganfield.com.au **OPEN** W'ends & public hols 10–5
WINEMAKER John Ellis (Contract) **EST.** 2003 **CASES** 800
The vineyard (then known as Ashworths Hill) was first planted in 1980 to pinot noir, shiraz, pinot meunier and cabernet sauvignon. When purchased by Mark and Gina Morgan, additional pinot noir and chardonnay plantings increased the area under vine to 4 ha. The wines are deliberately made in a light-bodied, easy-access fashion.

ΥΥΥΥΥ **Macedon Ranges Unwooded Chardonnay 2005** Clean and fresh; intense grapefruit and nectarine supported by lemony acidity on a long finish; well above average. Screwcap. 13.9° alc. **RATING** 90 **DRINK** 2010
Macedon Ranges Cabernet Sauvignon 2004 Bright red-purple; medium-bodied, and while it shows the very cool climate, has achieved more than acceptable ripeness; blackcurrant, tangy fruit, savoury tannins. Surprise packet. Cork. 13.8° alc. **RATING** 90 **DRINK** 2012

Morialta Vineyard ★★★★

195 Norton Summit Road, Norton Summit, SA 5136 **REGION** Adelaide Hills
T (08) 8390 1061 **F** (08) 8390 1585 **WWW**.visitadelaidehills.com.au/morialta **OPEN** By appt
WINEMAKER Jeffrey Grosset **EST.** 1989 **CASES** 500
Morialta Vineyard was planted in 1989 on a site first planted to vines in the 1860s by John Baker, who named his property Morialta Farm. The Bunya pine depicted on the label is one of the few surviving trees from that era, and indeed one of the few surviving trees of that genus. The 20-ha property has 11 ha under vine, planted to chardonnay, pinot noir, cabernet sauvignon, sauvignon blanc, shiraz and merlot. Most of the grapes are sold to Southcorp. Given the age of the vineyard and winemaking by Jeffrey Grosset, it is not surprising that the wines have done well in the Adelaide Hills Wine Show.

ΥΥΥΥΥ **Sauvignon Blanc 2005** A clean, expressive bouquet, with attractive tropical/passionfruit/gooseberry flavours; nicely weighted and balanced. Screwcap. 13.5° alc. **RATING** 92 **DRINK** Now $18

ΥΥΥΥ **Pinot Noir 2003** Light colour, the hue holding; light-bodied, with spicy small red fruits, and touches of forest floor; has length, though not bulk, despite the alcohol. Very different from the '02. Screwcap. 14.9° alc. **RATING** 89 **DRINK** 2009 $18

Morning Star Estate NR

1 Sunnyside Road, Mount Eliza, Vic 3930 **REGION** Mornington Peninsula
T (03) 9787 7760 **F** (03) 9787 7160 **WWW**.morningstarestate.com.au **OPEN** 7 days 10–4
WINEMAKER Sandro Mosele (Contract) **EST.** 1992 **CASES** 4000
In 1992 Judy Barrett purchased this historic property, the house built in 1867, and (with her family) spent the next 10 years repairing years of neglect and planting 10 ha each of pinot gris, chardonnay and pinot noir. Most of the grapes are sold, but the wines made are sold through the Estate's accommodation, conference and function centre, and cellar door.

Morning Sun Vineyard

NR

337 Main Creek Road, Main Ridge, Vic 3928 **REGION** Mornington Peninsula
T (03) 5989 6571 **F** (03) 5989 6572 **WWW**.morningsunvineyard.com.au **OPEN** By appt
WINEMAKER Judy Gifford (Contract) **EST.** 1995 **CASES** NA
Mario Toniolo has managed the development of 6 ha of vineyard at the Main Ridge area of Red Hill.
The varieties planted are semillon, chardonnay, pinot gris, pinot noir and barbera. Meals are
available by arrangement.

Morningside Vineyard

★★★☆

711 Middle Tea Tree Road, Tea Tree, Tas 7017 **REGION** Southern Tasmania
T (03) 6268 1748 **F** (03) 6268 1748 **OPEN** By appt
WINEMAKER Peter Bosworth **EST.** 1980 **CASES** 600
The name Morningside was given to the old property on which the vineyard stands because it gets
the morning sun first; the property on the other side of the valley was known as Eveningside.
Consistent with the observation of the early settlers, the Morningside grapes achieve full maturity
with good colour and varietal flavour. Production will increase as the 2.9-ha vineyard matures,
and as recent additions of clonally selected pinot noir (including 8104, 115 and 777) come into
bearing.

ΤΤΤΤΥ **Chardonnay 2004** A complex wine, with rich, ripe fruit, the overall feeling of sweetness
just a little obvious. **RATING** 90 **DRINK** 2010 $ 23

ΤΤΤΤ **Riesling 2005** Pleasantly abundant and fleshy ripe fruit, needing a touch more
acidity/grip. **RATING** 87 **DRINK** 2008 $ 20

ΤΤΤΥ **Pinot Noir 2004 RATING** 84 **DRINK** Now $ 34

Morris

★★★★★

Mia Mia Road, Rutherglen, Vic 3685 **REGION** Rutherglen
T (02) 6026 7303 **F** (02) 6026 7445 **WWW**.morriswines.com **OPEN** Mon–Sat 9–5, Sun 10–5
WINEMAKER David Morris **EST.** 1859 **CASES** 100 000
One of the greatest of the fortified winemakers, ranking with Chambers Rosewood. If you wish to test
that view, try the Old Premium Rare Muscat and Old Premium Rare Tokay, which are absolute
bargains given their age and quality and which give rise to the winery rating. The Durif table wine is
a winery specialty, the others dependable, the white wines all being made by owner Orlando.

ΤΤΤΤΤ **Old Premium Rare Rutherglen Tokay NV** Deep, aged olive-brown; super-intense, with a
resplendent array of spices, cake and tea leaf surrounded by smoky rancio which cuts the
richness and provide a lingering, intense but pleasingly dry aftertaste. **RATING** 97
DRINK Now $ 62
Old Premium Liqueur Rare Muscat NV Deep mahogany brown with an olive rim; the
ultra-rich bouquet has a complex mix of plum pudding, spice, toffee and coffee; the almost
explosive flavour of the palate is intensely raisiny/dried raisin, then a cleansing finish
investing the wine with enormous length. **RATING** 97 **DRINK** Now $ 62
Old Premium Rare Rutherglen Muscat NV Deep olive brown; dense spice, plum pudding
and raisin aromas; utterly exceptional intensity and length; altogether in another
dimension; while based upon some very old wine, is as fresh as a daisy. **RATING** 97
DRINK Now $ 62
Grand Rutherglen Tokay NV Very rich, very complex tea leaf, spice and Christmas cake
aromas, some honey and butterscotch lurking; floods the mouth, intense and long, with a
pronounced rancio cut, yet not sharp nor volatile. **RATING** 95 **DRINK** Now $ 30
Grand Rutherglen Muscat NV Full olive brown, green rim. A powerful and intense
bouquet, rancio, spice and raisin; while less unctuous than some of its peers, the palate has
outstanding texture, intensity and length. **RATING** 94 **DRINK** Now $ 30

ΤΤΤΤΥ **Classic Rutherglen Liqueur Tokay NV** Olive-brown; a very complex, classic mix of tea
leaf, honey, butterscotch and some fish oil flavours are supported by excellent texture and
balance. **RATING** 93 **DRINK** Now $ 15

Rutherglen Shiraz 2002 Big, rich, ripe voluptuous blackberry and plum; abundant, round tannins. In heroic style. Cork. **RATING** 92 **DRINK** 2015 $14.99

Classic Rutherglen Liqueur Muscat NV A multiplicity of flavours, centred around raisin muscat fruit, but with a spicy jab of rancio to liven up the finish. **RATING** 92 **DRINK** Now $15

Old Premium Tawny Port NV Obvious age, true tawny colour; richly robed and textured into a Liqueur Tawny style; biscuity aftertaste. **RATING** 90 **DRINK** Now

Morrisons Riverview Winery   NR

Lot 2, Merool Lane, Moama, NSW 2731 **REGION** Perricoota
T (03) 5480 0126 **F** (03) 5480 7144 **WWW**.riverviewestate.com.au **OPEN** 7 days 10–5
WINEMAKER John Ellis **EST.** 1996 **CASES** 2500
Alistair and Leslie Morrison purchased this historic piece of land in 1995. Plantings began in 1996 with shiraz and cabernet sauvignon, followed in 1997 by sauvignon blanc, frontignac and grenache in 1998, totalling 6 ha.

Mortimers of Orange   NR

'Chestnut Garth', 786 Burrendong Way, Orange, NSW 2800 **REGION** Orange
T (02) 6365 8689 **F** (02) 6365 8689 **OPEN** 7 days 10–4
WINEMAKER Simon Gilbert, Monarch Winemaking Services (Jim Chatto) **EST.** 1996 **CASES** 2250
Peter and Julie Mortimer began the establishment of their vineyard (named after a quiet street in the Humberside village of Burton Pidsea in the UK) in 1996. They now have just over 4 ha of chardonnay, shiraz, cabernet sauvignon, merlot and pinot noir.

Mosquito Hill Wines

18 Trinity Street, College Park, SA 5069 (postal) **REGION** Southern Fleurieu
T 0411 661 149 **F** (08) 8222 5896 **OPEN** Not
WINEMAKER Glyn Jamieson, Nepenthe **EST.** 2004 **CASES** 2000
Glyn and Elizabeth Jamieson have planted 2.6 ha of chardonnay and 1.8 ha of pinot noir on the slopes of Mt Jagged, and have the wines made under the joint direction of Peter Leske (Nepenthe) and Glyn Jamieson. The prices (from $6.50 to $10) are enticing, to say the least.

▼▼▼   **Pinot Noir 2004 RATING** 83 $10

Moss Brothers

Caves Road, Wilyabrup, WA 6280 **REGION** Margaret River
T (08) 9755 6270 **F** (08) 9755 6298 **WWW**.mossbrothers.com.au **OPEN** 7 days 10–5
WINEMAKER David Moss, Rebecca Tanner **EST.** 1984 **CASES** 30 000
Established by long-term viticulturist Jeff Moss and his family, notably sons Peter and David and Roseworthy graduate daughter Jane. A 100-tonne rammed-earth winery was constructed in 1992 and draws upon both estate-grown and purchased grapes. Exports to the UK, the US and other major markets.

▼▼▼▼▽   **Margaret River Semillon 2005** Clean aromas of grass and herbs; a firm, well-constructed and long palate; alcohol well within the bounds of Margaret River style. Screwcap. 13.5° alc. **RATING** 91 **DRINK** 2012 $20

Jane Moss Semillon Sauvignon Blanc 2005 Firm herb, spice, grass and mineral aromas and flavours; has length; just a ghost of reduction. Screwcap. **RATING** 90 **DRINK** 2008 $19.90

▼▼▼▼   **Moses Rock Margaret River Shiraz 2003** Medium-bodied; lively, spicy cool-grown edges to the black fruits without diminishing a nice touch of fruit sweetness. Very good value. Cork. 15° alc. **RATING** 89 **DRINK** 2012 $16

Cabernet Sauvignon Merlot 2002 Quite attractive cedary/spicy/savoury notes; gentle, ripe tannins; good mouthfeel. Cork. 14.5° alc. **RATING** 89 **DRINK** 2010 $29

Sauvignon Blanc 2005 Faint sweaty reduction; ripe, tropical gooseberry fruit, with some more minerally notes; somewhat hard finish. Screwcap. 13.5° alc. **RATING** 87 **DRINK** Now $20

Moses Rock Shiraz Cabernet Sauvignon 2002 Faintly reductive; still very tight and youthful; firm, fresh red and black berry fruits. Cork. RATING 87 DRINK 2008 $16

Jane Moss Cabernet Merlot 2003 Unconvincing colour; light- to medium-bodied berry, leaf and mint aromas and flavours; gentle tannins and a touch of oak. Screwcap. 14.5° alc. RATING 87 DRINK 2009 $20

ȳȳȳỵ̄ **Margaret River Verdelho 2004** RATING 86 DRINK 2008 $19.90
Moses Rock Shiraz Cabernet Sauvignon 2003 RATING 85 DRINK Now $16

Moss Wood ★★★★★

Metricup Road, Wilyabrup, WA 6284 REGION Margaret River
T (08) 9755 6266 F (08) 9755 6303 WWW.mosswood.com.au OPEN By appt
WINEMAKER Keith Mugford EST. 1969 CASES 18 000
Widely regarded as one of the best wineries in the region, capable of producing glorious Semillon in both oaked and unoaked forms, unctuous Chardonnay and elegant, gently herbaceous, superfine Cabernet Sauvignon which lives for many years. In 2000 Moss Wood acquired the Ribbon Vale Estate, which is now merged within its own business; the Ribbon Vale wines are now treated as vineyard-designated within the Moss Wood umbrella. Exports to all major markets.

ȳȳȳȳȳ **Margaret River Chardonnay 2004** Very complex, strong, funky barrel ferment aromas; ultra rich and complex mouthfeel; manages alcohol well. Screwcap. RATING 94 DRINK 2013 $60

Amy's Margaret River Cabernet Sauvignon 2004 Good hue; classic cassis and blackcurrant varietal fruit in a medium-bodied frame; excellent tannins and good oak. Best Amy's yet; value. Screwcap. 14° alc. RATING 94 DRINK 2019 $30

ȳȳȳỵ̄ **Ribbon Vale Vineyard Semillon Sauvignon Blanc 2005** Fresh, crisp and firm, carrying its alcohol with ease; lemon/lemon grass/herb/mineral/passionfruit; long finish. Screwcap. 14° alc. RATING 93 DRINK 2008 $26

Margaret River Semillon 2005 Light straw-green; powerful as always, with ripe citrus, apple and mineral; supple mouthfeel, deriving in part from the alcohol. Screwcap. 14.5° alc. RATING 92 DRINK 2015 $33

Ribbon Vale Vineyard Cabernet Sauvignon Merlot 2003 Fragrant small red fruits, leaf and mint aromas leading into a palate which changes gear dramatically, with tannins running right through; needs time to come together. Cork. 14.5° alc. RATING 91 DRINK 2013 $40

ȳȳȳȳ **Margaret River Pinot Noir 2003** Bright colour; a pleasant, medium-bodied red wine, with nice texture and structure; well-made; as ever, minimal varietal character. Screwcap. 13.5° alc. RATING 87 DRINK 2009 $52.50

Motton Terraces NR

119 Purtons Road, North Motton, Tas 7315 REGION Northern Tasmania
T (03) 6425 2317 WWW.cradlecoastwines.info/ OPEN W'ends 10–5, or by appt
WINEMAKER Flemming Aaberg EST. 1990 CASES 120
Another of the micro-vineyards which seem to be a Tasmanian specialty; Flemming and Jenny Aaberg planted slightly less than 0.5 ha of chardonnay and riesling in 1990, and are only now increasing that to 1 ha with more riesling and some sauvignon blanc. The exercise in miniature is emphasised by the permanent canopy netting to ward off possums and birds.

Mount Anakie Wines NR

130 Staughton Vale Road, Anakie, Vic 3221 REGION Geelong
T (03) 5284 1256 F (03) 5284 1405 OPEN 7 days 11–5
WINEMAKER Otto Zambelli EST. 1968 CASES 6000
Also known as Zambelli Estate; once produced some excellent wines (under its various ownerships and winemakers), all distinguished by their depth and intensity of flavour. The level of activity seems relatively low.

Mount Appallan Vineyards   NR

239 Mitchell Road, Biggenden, Qld 4621 **REGION** Queensland Coastal
T (07) 4127 1390 **F** (07) 4127 1090 **www**.mtappallan.com.au **OPEN** By appt
WINEMAKER Andrew Hickinbotham **EST.** 1998 **CASES** 400
The Goodchild family settled on the Draycot property in 1912, successive generations carrying on first wool growing and thereafter dairying. The 160-ha farm is 75 km west of Maryborough, in what is known locally as the Wide Bay–Burnett area, where the rich volcanic soils and semi-maritime mild climate is not very different from that of South Burnett. The family has established 7.6 ha of vineyards planted to verdelho, shiraz, merlot, cabernet sauvignon, petit verdot and viognier, with a small amount each of grenache and mourvedre. Third-generation Syd Goodchild returned as a mature-age student to study viticulture at Adelaide University (adding a fourth academic degree), and fourth-generation Bernie Wixon manages the property, including the dairy side.

Mount Avoca Winery   NR

Moates Lane, Avoca, Vic 3467 **REGION** Pyrenees
T (03) 5465 3282 **F** (03) 5465 3544 **www**.mountavoca.com **OPEN** Mon–Fri 9–5, w'ends 10–5
WINEMAKER Matthew Barry **EST.** 1970 **CASES** 15 000
A substantial winery which has long been one of the stalwarts of the Pyrenees region, and is steadily growing, with 23.7 ha of vineyards. There has been a significant refinement in the style and flavour of the red wines over the past few years. I suspect a lot of worthwhile work has gone into barrel selection and maintenance. Reverted to family ownership in July 2003 after a short period as part of the ill-fated Barrington Estates group. Exports to Asia.

Mount Beckworth   NR

RMB 915 Learmonth Road, Tourello via Ballarat, Vic 3363 **REGION** Ballarat
T (03) 5343 4207 **F** (03) 5343 4207 **www**.ballarat.com/clunes/beckworth.htm **OPEN** W'ends 10–6 & by appt
WINEMAKER Paul Lesock **EST.** 1984 **CASES** 1000
The 4-ha Mount Beckworth vineyard was planted between 1984 and 1985, but it was not until 1995 that the full range of wines under the Mount Beckworth label appeared. Until that time much of the production was sold to Seppelt Great Western for sparkling wine use. It is owned and managed by Paul Lesock, who studied viticulture at Charles Sturt University, and his wife Jane. The wines reflect the very cool climate except in warm years.

Mt Billy   ★★★★☆

18 Victoria Street, Victor Harbor, SA 5211 (postal) **REGION** Southern Fleurieu
T 0416 227 100 **F** (08) 8552 8333 **www**.mtbillywines.com.au **OPEN** Not
WINEMAKER Paulett (white), Tobreck (red) **EST.** 1999 **CASES** 2000
Having been an avid wine collector and consumer since 1973, John Edwards (a dentist) and wife Pauline purchased a 3.75-ha property on the hills behind Victor Harbor, planting 1.2 ha each of chardonnay and pinot meunier. The original intention was to sell the grapes, but low yields quickly persuaded Edwards that making and selling a bottle-fermented sparkling wine was the way to go. Since 1999 grenache and Mataro and shiraz have been purchased from the Barossa Valley, and David Powell of Torbreck agreed to make the red wine. Riesling has since joined the portfolio. Exports to the UK and the US.

♥♥♥♥♥ Antiquity Barossa Valley Shiraz 2003 Rich blackberry, licorice aromas and flavours; sweet but not dead fruit; good oak and extract; 80–109-year-old shiraz vines, open-fermented, basket-pressed, French oak. Screwcap. 14.5° alc. **RATING** 94 **DRINK** 2018 $42

♥♥♥♥♡ Harmony Barossa Valley Shiraz Mataro Grenache 2003 Complex aromas of plum, spice and blackberry; medium-bodied; supple and sweet fruit; fine tannins; 7-year-old shiraz/70-year-old mataro (mourvedre)/80-year-old grenache, all dry-grown. Screwcap. 14° alc. **RATING** 91 **DRINK** 2013 $22
Valleys Riesling 2005 Minerally, spicy bouquet; initially reserved fruit on the palate comes charging through on the finish and lingering aftertaste; roughly equal quantities from Eden/Clare Valleys, whole bunch-pressed and co-fermented. Screwcap. 12.3° alc. **RATING** 90 **DRINK** Now $20

Mount Broke Wines ★★☆

130 Adams Peak Road, Broke, NSW 2330 **REGION** Lower Hunter Valley
T (02) 6579 1314 **F** (02) 6579 1314 **www**.mtbrokewines.com.au **OPEN** W'ends 11–4
WINEMAKER Monarch Winemaking Services **EST.** 1997 **CASES** 700
Phil and Jo McNamara began planting 9.6-ha vineyard to shiraz, merlot, verdelho, barbera, semillon, chardonnay and cabernet sauvignon in 1997 on the west side of Wollombi Brook.

ŸŸŸŸ **River Bank Shiraz 2004** Bright colour; fresh, breezy red fruits; not complex or overworked; ripe tannins. Screwcap. 13.5° alc. **RATING** 86 **DRINK** 2010 $25
Sticky Fingers (375 ml) 2005 **RATING** 84 **DRINK** Now $18

ŸŸŸ **River Bank Verdelho 2005** **RATING** 83 $13.70

Mount Buffalo Vineyard NR

6300 Great Alpine Road, Eurobin, Vic 3739 **REGION** Alpine Valleys
T (03) 5756 2523 **F** (03) 5756 2523 **OPEN** 7 days 9–5
WINEMAKER Cyril Ciavarella **EST.** 1998 **CASES** 600
Colin and Lorraine Leita have a substantial horticultural property (Bright Berry Farms) in the foothills of Mt Buffalo. They have diversified into viticulture with 1 ha each of viognier, shiraz and cabernet sauvignon, and 4 ha of merlot. The Great Alpine Road provides a steady stream of visitors to the cellar door.

Mount Buninyong Winery NR

Platts Road, Scotsburn, Vic 3352 **REGION** Ballarat
T (03) 5341 8360 **F** (03) 5341 2442 **www**.mountbuninyong.com **OPEN** 7 days
WINEMAKER Peter Armstrong **EST.** 1993 **CASES** NA
Mount Buninyong Winery is the venture of Peter and Jan Armstrong, assisted by son and daughter-in-law Malcolm and Sandra Armstrong. It is situated just south of Ballarat, with 4 ha of riesling, chardonnay, pinot noir and cabernet sauvignon near Scotsburn. A range of table, fortified, sparkling and organic wines are made under the Mount Buninyong, Ballarat Wines and Ballarat Regional Wines labels.

Mount Burrumboot Estate ★★★★☆

3332 Heathcote–Rochester Road, Colbinabbin, Vic 3559 **REGION** Heathcote
T (03) 5432 9238 **F** (03) 5432 9238 **www**.burrumboot.com **OPEN** W'ends & public hols 11–5, or by appt
WINEMAKER Cathy Branson **EST.** 1999 **CASES** 1500
To quote, 'Mount Burrumboot Estate was born in 1999, when Andrew and Cathy Branson planted vines on the Home Block of the Branson family farm, Donore, on the slopes of Mt Burrumboot, on the Mt Camel Range, above Colbinabbin. Originally the vineyard was just another diversification of an already diverse farming enterprise. However, the wine bug soon bit Andrew and Cathy, and so a winery was established. The first wine was made in 2001 by contract — however, 2002 vintage saw the first wine made by Cathy in the machinery shed, surrounded by headers and tractors. Very primitive, and the appearance of the new 50-tonne winery in August 2002 was greeted with great enthusiasm!' And then you taste the wines. Amazing.

ŸŸŸŸŸ **Heathcote Shiraz 2004** Clear purple-red; excellently controlled winemaking; a spotless bouquet with fragrant wafts of dark fruits; a supple palate with similar blackberry fruit; overall, no more than medium-bodied. Cork. 14° alc. **RATING** 93 **DRINK** 2012 $30
Heathcote Merlot 2004 Very good colour; flooded with sweet red and black fruits, and no green or savoury edges at all; fine tannins are appropriate to the medium-bodied weight. Cork. 14° alc. **RATING** 91 **DRINK** 2012 $30
Mad Uncle Jack's Petit Verdot 2004 Rich, complex and concentrated sweet black fruits; the tannins, however, are far less imposing than expected. Has interesting development potential. Cork. 14° alc. **RATING** 90 **DRINK** 2015 $30

ŸŸŸŸ **Heathcote Sangiovese 2004** Exceptionally strong colour for the variety; rich, jammy, black cherry fruit, the ripeness greater than the alcohol would suggest. Cork. 14° alc. **RATING** 89 **DRINK** 2008 $35

🐏 Mount Camel Ridge Estate ★★★★☆

473 Heathcote Rochester Road, Heathcote, Vic 3523 **REGION** Heathcote
T (03) 5433 2343 **OPEN** By appt
WINEMAKER Ian Langford, Gwenda Langford **EST.** 1999 **CASES** 350
Commencing in 1999, Ian and Gwenda Langford have planted 18 ha of vines, the majority to shiraz (8.5 ha), cabernet sauvignon (3.8 ha) and merlot (3 ha), with a little over 0.5 ha each of petit verdot, viognier and mourvedre. The land has been developed using organic principles, using previously composted chicken manure every 3 years, the manual application of seaweed fertilizer and mulching of the prunings. The vineyard is dry-grown, and no copper, lime or sulphur fungicide has been used. The Langfords say, 'As a result, worms have reappeared, and there is now an extensive frog population, ladybirds and other invertebrates and a range of beautiful spiders.' The very attractive red wines are made in open half-tonne vats, basket-pressed and matured in French oak.

 ▼▼▼▼▽ **Heathcote Shiraz 2004** Youthful purple-red; medium-bodied; fresh maraschino cherry and plum fruit, with a subliminal lift of viognier; very fine tannins, and perfectly integrated oak. Cork. 13.7° alc. **RATING** 92 **DRINK** 2011 $ 26
 Heathcote Cabernet Sauvignon 2004 Bright purple-red; medium-bodied, with juicy cassis and redcurrant flavours, riper than the modest alcohol might suggest. Sensitive extract and oak. Cork. 12.5° alc. **RATING** 90 **DRINK** 2010 $ 26

Mount Cathedral Vineyards NR

125 Knafl Road, Taggerty, Vic 3714 **REGION** Upper Goulburn
T 0409 354 069 **F** (03) 9354 0994 **WWW**.mtcathedralvineyards.com **OPEN** By appt
WINEMAKER Oscar Rosa, Nick Arena **EST.** 1995 **CASES** 1200
The Rosa and Arena families established Mount Cathedral Vineyards in 1995, the vines being planted at an elevation of 300m on the north face of Mt Cathedral. The first plantings were of 1.2 ha of merlot and 0.8 ha of chardonnay, followed by 2.5 ha of cabernet sauvignon and 0.5 ha of cabernet franc in 1996. Oscar Rosa, chief winemaker, has completed two TAFE courses in viticulture and winemaking, and completed a Bachelor of Wine Science course at Charles Sturt University in 2002. He gained practical experience working at Yering Station during 1998 and 1999.

Mount Charlie Winery ★★★☆

228 Mount Charlie Road, Riddells Creek, Vic 3431 **REGION** Macedon Ranges
T (03) 5428 6946 **F** (03) 5428 6946 **WWW**.mountcharlie.com.au **OPEN** Most w'ends 11–3 or by appt
WINEMAKER Trefor Morgan **EST.** 1991 **CASES** 900
Mount Charlie's wines are sold principally by mail order and through selected restaurants. A futures program encourages mailing list sales with a discount of over 25% on the release price. Owner/winemaker Trefor Morgan is perhaps better known as a Professor of Physiology at Melbourne University. He also acts as a contract maker for others in the region.

 ▼▼▼▼▽ **Chardonnay 2004** Nicely balanced nectarine fruit and subtle oak; stylish and focused. **RATING** 90 **DRINK** 2009 $ 20

 ▼▼▼▽ **Malbec 2004** A fresh, light red wine; might well be better to follow the Bloodwood example (Big Men In Tights) and have a compelling rose style. Persuading malbec to make a serious red wine in such a cool climate is a huge ask. Screwcap. 12.3° alc. **RATING** 86 **DRINK** Now $ 22
 Sauvignon Blanc 2005 RATING 85 $ 16

Mount Coghill Vineyard NR

Clunes–Learmonth Road, Coghills Creek, Vic 3364 **REGION** Ballarat
T (03) 5343 4329 **F** (03) 5343 4329 **WWW**.mtcoghillwinery.com **OPEN** W'ends 10–5
WINEMAKER Norman Latta **EST.** 1993 **CASES** 420
Ian (an award-winning photographer) and Margaret Pym began planting their tiny vineyard in 1995 with 1280 pinot noir rootlings, and added 450 chardonnay rootlings the next year. Since 2001 the wine has been made and released under the Mount Coghill Vineyard label.

Mount Delancey Winery NR

60 De Lancey Road, Wandin North, Vic 3139 **REGION** Yarra Valley
T (03) 5964 4964 **OPEN** W'ends 10–5.30, or by appt
WINEMAKER Jordan Metlikovec **EST.** 1985 **CASES** 200
Jordan Metlikovec makes a tiny quantity of wine and fruit wine from a mixed planting of 1 ha which includes chardonnay, pinot noir and cabernet sauvignon. He also purchases approximately 2 tonnes of grapes from other small Yarra Valley vineyards and berry growers.

Mount Duneed NR

Feehan's Road, Mount Duneed, Vic 3216 **REGION** Geelong
T (03) 5264 1281 **F** (03) 5264 1281 **OPEN** Public hols & w'ends 11–5, or by appt
WINEMAKER Ken Campbell, John Darling **EST.** 1970 **CASES** 1000
Rather idiosyncratic wines are the order of the day. Some can develop surprisingly well in bottle; the Botrytis Noble Rot Semillon has, from time to time, been of very high quality. A significant part of the production from the 7.5 ha of vineyards is sold to others.

Mount Eyre Vineyards

173 Gillards Road, Pokolbin, NSW 2321 **REGION** Lower Hunter Valley
T 0438 683 973 **F** (02) 6842 4513 **WWW**.mounteyre.com **OPEN** By appt
WINEMAKER CP Lin **EST.** 1970 **CASES** 5000
Mount Eyre draws on 2 vineyards, the first a 24-ha estate at Broke, planted to semillon, chardonnay, shiraz, chambourcin, cabernet franc and cabernet sauvignon, and the second, Holman Estate, in Gillards Road, Pokolbin, with 4 ha of shiraz and 1.8 ha of merlot. CP Lin, the winemaker, must surely be the only blind Chinese maker in the world. For good measure, having completed the Hunter vintage he crosses to Mountford Winery, near Christchurch, NZ, to work with pinot noir each year. Most amazingly of all, he has translated the *Oxford Companion to Wine* into braille. Exports to Canada, Thailand, Cambodia, Singapore and Finland.

ŸŸŸŸŸ **Heirloom Semillon 2005** Glowing yellow-green; a powerful, rich wine tightened up by lemony acidity; takes flavour to the edge without going over the top. Cork. 11.5° alc.
RATING 92 **DRINK** 2012 $ 30

ŸŸŸŸ **Heirloom Chardonnay 2004** Made in a particular low-profile fruit style; winemaking inputs adding structure and complexity to a web of cashew, cream and fig. Cork. 13.5° alc.
RATING 89 **DRINK** 2008 $ 45
Three Ponds Shiraz 2004 Light- to medium-bodied; a mix of red fruits with touches of earth and leather; gentle acidity. Cork. 13° alc. **RATING** 87 **DRINK** 2009 $ 35

ŸŸŸŸ **Holman Shiraz 2004 RATING** 86 **DRINK** 2008 $ 40
Rose 2005 RATING 85 **DRINK** Now $ 20
Neptune Sparkling Semillon 2005 RATING 84 **DRINK** Now $ 20

ŸŸŸ **Chardonnay 2005 RATING** 83 $ 14

Mount Gisborne Wines

83 Waterson Road, Gisborne, Vic 3437 **REGION** Macedon Ranges
T (03) 5428 2834 **F** (03) 5428 2834 **OPEN** W'ends 10–5
WINEMAKER Stuart Anderson **EST.** 1986 **CASES** 1500
Mount Gisborne Wines is very much a weekend and holiday occupation for proprietor David Ell, who makes the wines from the 7-ha vineyard under the watchful and skilled eye of industry veteran Stuart Anderson, now living in semi-retirement high in the Macedon Hills. The wines are estate-grown from plantings between 1986 and 1990.

ŸŸŸŸ **Macedon Ranges Chardonnay 2004** Minerally, chalky, Chablis style; fruit-driven, though the fruit is itself in a restrained, citrus mode. Cork. 13° alc. **RATING** 89 **DRINK** 2008
$ 23

Mount Horrocks ★★★★☆

The Old Railway Station, Curling Street, Auburn, SA 5451 **REGION** Clare Valley
T (08) 8849 2243 **F** (08) 8849 2265 **WWW**.mounthorrocks.com **OPEN** W'ends & public hols 10–5
WINEMAKER Stephanie Toole **EST.** 1982 **CASES** 4500
Mount Horrocks has well and truly established its own identity in recent years, aided by positive marketing and, equally importantly, wine quality which has resulted in both show success and critical acclaim. Exports to all major markets.

 Cordon Cut Riesling 2005 Lime and honey aromas and flavours; no botrytis complexity, the virtue lying instead in the impeccable balance of the wine. Screwcap. 11.5° alc. **RATING** 93 **DRINK** 2010 $ 32
Semillon 2004 Complex French oak barrel ferment inputs to both bouquet and palate, but well-integrated and balanced; sweet citrussy fruit; good length. Top class wooded Semillon style; 400 cases made. Screwcap. **RATING** 92 **DRINK** 2009 $ 27
Chardonnay 2004 Glowing yellow-green; a chronic over-performer for the Clare Valley; immaculate barrel ferment and oak handling; melon, peach and fig; very good length; 160 cases made. Screwcap. **RATING** 92 **DRINK** 2009 $ 25

Mount Ida ★★★★☆

Northern Highway, Heathcote, Vic 3253 **REGION** Heathcote
T (03) 8626 3340 **OPEN** Not
WINEMAKER Matt Steel **EST.** 1978 **CASES** 2000
Established by the famous artist Leonard French and Dr James Munro but purchased by Tisdall after the 1987 bushfires and by Beringer Blass when it acquired Tisdall. Up to the time of the fires, wonderfully smooth, rich red wines with almost voluptuous sweet, minty fruit were the hallmark. After a brief period during which the name was used as a simple brand (with various wines released), has returned to a single estate-grown wine.

Heathcote Shiraz 2003 Big, heavy hitting style, saved by redeeming acidity; one face of modern Heathcote style. Screwcap. 14.5° alc. **RATING** 90 **DRINK** 2015 $ 45

Mt Jagged Wines ★★★★☆

Main Victor Harbor Road, Mt Jagged, SA 5211 **REGION** Southern Fleurieu
T (08) 8554 9532 **F** (08) 8340 7633 **WWW**.mtjaggedwines.com.au **OPEN** Oct–May 7 days 10–5, June–Sep by appt
WINEMAKER Stephen Pannell, Tom White **EST.** 1989 **CASES** 8500
Jerry White immigrated to Australia in 1970, and after a successful business career, purchased 100 ha at Mt Jagged in 1988. The land is on the main road to Victor Harbor, which he believed would generate ample cellar door sales demand. Being the first to plant in the region, he planted 28 ha, thus producing sufficient grapes to supply large companies, and duly entered into a contract with Penfolds, with semillon, chardonnay, merlot, cabernet sauvignon and shiraz all being sold. The first Mt Jagged wine appeared in 1996, more and more fruit has since been diverted to the Mt Jagged label. The cool, maritime environment was described by John Gladstones as 'what appears to be the best climate in mainland SA for making table wines'. The white wines are exemplary; the red wines, however, seem to struggle for ripeness. Exports to the US and Canada.

 Fleurieu Peninsula Semillon Sauvignon Blanc 2005 A flavoursome wine, with an abundance of fruit characters ranging through gooseberry, green apple and citrus; excellent texture, and extreme length. Screwcap. 12.5° alc. **RATING** 94 **DRINK** 2009 $ 14
Single Vineyard Southern Fleurieu Peninsula Semillon 2003 Has plenty going for it; tight citrussy/grassy palate; good acidity and long finish. Due for release July '08. Nominal points. Screwcap. 11° alc. **RATING** 90 **DRINK** 2013 $ 25
Single Vineyard Southern Fleurieu Peninsula Chardonnay 2005 Light- to medium-bodied; complexity apparently through lees and malolactic fermentation, with little or no oak contribution; whatever, nice wine. Screwcap. 13° alc. **RATING** 89 **DRINK** 2010 $ 14

ΤΤΤ♀ **Southern Fleurieu Merlot Cabernet Sauvignon 1998** RATING 86 DRINK Now $ 60
Single Vineyard Southern Fleurieu Peninsula Shiraz Viognier 2003 RATING 84
DRINK 2008 $ 25

Mount Langi Ghiran Vineyards ★★★★★

Warrak Road, Buangor, Vic 3375 REGION Grampians
T (03) 5354 3207 F (03) 5354 3277 WWW.langi.com.au OPEN Mon–Fri 9–5, w'ends 12–5
WINEMAKER Trevor Mast, Dan Buckle EST. 1969 CASES 45 000
A maker of outstanding cool-climate peppery Shiraz, crammed with flavour and vinosity, and very good Cabernet Sauvignon. The Shiraz points the way for cool-climate examples of the variety. The business was acquired by the Rathbone family group in November 2002, and hence has been integrated with the Yering Station product range, a synergistic mix with no overlap. Trevor Mast continues to run the Mount Langi Ghiran operation. Exports to all major markets.

ΤΤΤΤΤ **Langi Shiraz 2003** Fractionally deeper colour than Cliff Edge; full-bodied, potent, powerful and dense wine; blackberry, spice, bitter chocolate and licorice; very good tannins and oak; long finish. Cork. RATING 95 DRINK 2023 $ 55
Cliff Edge Shiraz 2004 Highly aromatic plum, spice and blackberry fruit; has excellent length and good tannins. RATING 94 DRINK 2014 $ 25
Nowhere Creek Shiraz 2004 Excellent colour; rich, deep, opulent spicy fruit; very good oak; polished tannins. RATING 94 DRINK 2016 $ 30

ΤΤΤΤ♀ **Cliff Edge Shiraz 2003** Good colour; medium- to full-bodied; attractive, complex array of black fruits and spices; good oak and tannins. Cork. RATING 93 DRINK 2015 $ 25
Riesling 2005 Pale straw-green; clean and fresh, with attractive tropical/passionfruit/lime aromas and flavours; good acidity. Grampians/Henty. Screwcap. 13° alc. RATING 91 DRINK 2010 $ 20
Langi Cabernet Merlot 2000 Interesting wine; savoury/earthy/cedary nuances now developing around the blackcurrant fruit; has length and persistence. 14.5° alc. RATING 90 DRINK 2010 $ 38

ΤΤΤΤ **Pinot Gris 2005** Crisp and firm, more grigio than gris in style; has touches of flowers and spice; just gets over the line. Screwcap. RATING 87 DRINK Now $ 22
Billi Billi Creek Shiraz 2003 Light- to medium-bodied; gently sweet red and black fruits; some spice; fine, ripe tannins; ready to roll now. Screwcap. 14.5° alc. RATING 87 DRINK 2009 $ 16

Mt Lofty Ranges Vineyard

Harris Road, Lenswood, SA 5240 REGION Adelaide Hills
T (08) 8389 8339 F (08) 8389 8349 OPEN W'ends 11–5, or by appt
WINEMAKER Nepenthe (Peter Leske) EST. 1992 CASES 700
Mt Lofty Ranges Vineyard is owned by Alan Herath and Jan Reed, who have been involved from the outset in planting, training and nurturing the 5.2-ha vineyard. Both had professional careers but are now full-time vignerons. Skilled winemaking by Peter Leske has already brought rewards and recognition to the vineyard.

ΤΤΤΤΤ **Five Vines Lenswood Riesling 2005** Fragrant herb, spice, apple and lime aromas and flavours; lovely line and length; perfect acidity. Screwcap. 13° alc. RATING 94 DRINK 2015 $ 16

ΤΤΤΤ♀ **Lenswood Chardonnay 2004** Clean, fine, elegant bouquet; nectarine, grapefruit and white peach; subtle oak, long finish. Screwcap. 13.5° alc. RATING 93 DRINK 2011 $ 16
Old Pump Shed Lenswood Pinot Noir 2004 Very good hue; a firm, fresh, tight wine which will flower with bottle age; the points are for the wine now, not how it will be given time to strut its stuff. Screwcap. 14° alc. RATING 91 DRINK 2013 $ 24
Lenswood Sauvignon Blanc 2005 A faintly blurred bouquet; abundant gooseberry/kiwifruit and spice flavours; good balance and length. Screwcap. 12.5° alc. RATING 90 DRINK Now $ 18

Mount Macedon Winery ★★★

433 Bawden Road, Mount Macedon, Vic 3441 **REGION** Macedon Ranges
T (03) 5427 2735 **F** (03) 5427 1071 **WWW**.mountmacedonwinery.com.au **OPEN** 7 days 10–6 (10–5 in winter)
WINEMAKER Kilchurn Wines (David Cowburn) **EST.** 1989 **CASES** 1200
The property on which Mount Macedon Winery is situated was purchased by David and Ronda Collins in August 2003. The 32-ha property, at an altitude of 680m, has 8 ha of gewurztraminer, chardonnay, pinot noir and pinot meunier.

▼▼▼▼ **Oak Aged Chardonnay 2004** Bold, buttery oaky style; yellow peach fruit; soft finish.
RATING 87 **DRINK** Now $ 25

▼▼▼▽ **Vintage Brut Cuvee 2000 RATING** 86 **DRINK** Now $ 35

Mount Majura Vineyard ★★★★

RMB 314 Majura Road, Majura, ACT 2609 (postal) **REGION** Canberra District
T (02) 6262 3070 **F** (02) 6262 4288 **WWW**.mountmajura.com.au **OPEN** Thurs–Mon 10–5
WINEMAKER Dr Frank van de Loo **EST.** 1988 **CASES** 2000
The first vines were planted in 1988 by Dinny Killen on a site on her family property which had been especially recommended by Dr Edgar Riek; its attractions were red soil of volcanic origin over limestone, with reasonably steep east and northeast slopes providing an element of frost protection. The 1-ha vineyard was planted to pinot noir, chardonnay and merlot in equal quantities. The syndicate which purchased the property in 1999 has extended the plantings. Just prior to the 2006 vintage a new winery, office, warehouse and cellar door opened, the cellar door overlooking the barrel cellar.

▼▼▼▼▽ **Canberra Pinot Gris 2005** Potent, aromatic ripe pear and spiced apple aromas; the powerful palate has lots of character and flavour. Screwcap. 13.1° alc. **RATING** 91
DRINK Now $ 16
Canberra Riesling 2005 Rich, fleshy, tropical spice aromas; abundant mid-palate, with just enough acidity; forward style. Screwcap. 11.6° alc. **RATING** 90 **DRINK** Now $ 16

▼▼▼▼ **Tempranillo 2004** Clean; light- to medium-bodied, but with good structure; ripe red fruits, vanilla and mocha; soft tannins. Screwcap. **RATING** 88 **DRINK** 2009 $ 25
Canberra Rose 2005 Light, fresh, strawberry-accented; relatively dry finish. Screwcap.
12° alc. **RATING** 87 **DRINK** Now $ 16

▼▼▼▽ **Canberra Shiraz 2003 RATING** 86 **DRINK** 2008 $ 25

Mount Markey NR

1346 Cassilis Road, Cassilis, Vic 3896 **REGION** Gippsland
T (03) 5159 4264 **F** (03) 5159 4599 **WWW**.omeoregion.com.au/winery **OPEN** Wed–Mon 10–5
WINEMAKER Howard Reddish **EST.** 1991 **CASES** 650
Howard and Christine Reddish have established 2 vineyards, one of 2 ha surrounding the winery, the other of 3 ha on the slopes of Mt Markey, at an altitude of nearly 500m. The winery is built on the site of the Cassilis Wine Palace, which served the local goldmining families for almost 70 years until the gold ran out in the 1940s.

Mount Mary ★★★★★

Coldstream West Road, Lilydale, Vic 3140 **REGION** Yarra Valley
T (03) 9739 1761 **F** (03) 9739 0137 **OPEN** Not
WINEMAKER Dr John Middleton **EST.** 1971 **CASES** 3000
Superbly refined, elegant and intense Cabernets and usually outstanding and long-lived Pinot Noirs fully justify Mount Mary's exalted reputation. The Triolet blend is very good; more recent vintages of Chardonnay are even better. Limited quantities of the wines are sold through the wholesale/retail distribution system in Vic, NSW, Qld and SA.

▼▼▼▼▼ Chardonnay 2004 Very good green-yellow; ultimate elegance and refinement; a seamless marriage of nectarine and melon fruit with perfect oak balance and integration; long, clean finish. Cork. 13.5° alc. **RATING** 96 **DRINK** 2012 $ 43

Triolet 2004 Glowing yellow-green; restrained but intensely focused, the individual components so interwoven they cannot be picked apart; great balance and length. Sauvignon Blanc/Semillon/Muscadelle. Cork. 12.5° alc. **RATING** 94 **DRINK** 2011 $ 43

Quintet 2003 Good colour; considerable depth and power to the array of cassis, blackcurrant and blackberry fruit; very good texture and structure; abundant fine tannins and controlled oak. Cork. 13° alc. **RATING** 94 **DRINK** 2020 $ 85

▼▼▼▼▽ Pinot Noir 2003 Light but bright hue; a light-bodied, elegant wine, the light plum and spice fruit as yet very restrained. History shows it will develop given time. Cork. 13° alc. **RATING** 92 **DRINK** 2010 $ 85

Mount Moliagul ★★★★

Clay Gully Lane, Moliagul, Vic 3472 **REGION** Bendigo
T (03) 9809 2113 **WWW**.mountmoliagulwines.com.au **OPEN** By appt, call 0427 221 641
WINEMAKER Terry Flora **EST.** 1991 **CASES** 400
Terry and Bozenka Flora began their tiny vineyard in 1991, gradually planting 0.5 ha each of shiraz and cabernet sauvignon, and 0.2 ha of chardonnay. Terry Flora has completed two winemaking courses, one with Winery Supplies and the other at Dookie College, and has learnt his craft very well.

▼▼▼▼▼ 2004 Mount Moliagul Shiraz Strong red-purple; rich, plush blackberry and plum fruit; supple texture, with ultra-fine, ripe tannins; good oak. Diam. **RATING** 94 **DRINK** 2019 $ 25

▼▼▼▽ NV Mount Moliagul Non Vintage Unwooded Chardonnay Diam. **RATING** 84 **DRINK** Now $ 15

🐌 Mount Ophir Estate ★★★★

Stillards Lane, Rutherglen, Vic 3685 **REGION** Rutherglen
T (02) 6032 8920 **WWW**.mount-ophir.com **OPEN** W'ends 11–5, or by appt
WINEMAKER Andersons Winery (Howard Anderson) **EST.** 1891 **CASES** 270
When it was built in 1891 by English wine merchant Peter Burgoyne, Mount Ophir Estate was said to be the largest state-of-the-art winemaking facility in the world, and its brick buildings are as impressive today as they were 115 years ago. While the buildings have survived well, the 300 ha vineyard had shrunk to a poorly-tended 4 ha of shiraz when Ruth Hennessy acquired the property and began the refurbishment of the vineyards, discontinuing the use of chemical sprays, and having the Shiraz made with minimal preservatives to organic winemaking standards. The National Trust and Heritage Victoria listed buildings provide B&B in the main homestead, with 2 self-contained farmhouses also available.

▼▼▼▼▽ Organic Rutherglen Shiraz 2005 Deep, dense colour; powerful savoury blackberry fruit with good tannins and length; well-made, and no hint of staleness from lack of SO_2. Cork. 14.4° alc. **RATING** 90 **DRINK** 2014 $ 40

▼▼▼▼ Organic Rutherglen Shiraz 2004 Deep, dense red-purple; extremely concentrated, a chewy array of black fruits and licorice, the tannins controlled. Cork. 14.4° alc. **RATING** 89 **DRINK** 2015 $ 50

Mount Panorama Winery NR

117 Mountain Straight, Mount Panorama, Bathurst, NSW 2795 **REGION** Central Ranges Zone
T (02) 6331 5368 **OPEN** 7 days 10.30–5
WINEMAKER Desmond McMahon **EST.** 1991 **CASES** 600
For all the obvious reasons, Mount Panorama Winery makes full use of its setting: on Mountain Straight after 'Hell Corner' on the famous motor racing circuit. All the winemaking is done onsite, from picking and using the hand-operated basket press through to bottling, labelling, etc.

Mount Pierrepoint Estate ★★★

271 Pierrepoint Road, Tarrington, Vic 3301 (postal) **REGION** Henty
T (03) 5572 5558 **F** (03) 5572 5558 **WWW**.mountpierrepoint.com **OPEN** Not
WINEMAKER Jennifer Lacey **EST.** 1997 **CASES** 300
Mount Pierrepoint Estate has been established by Andrew and Jennifer Lacey on the foothills of
Mount Pierrepoint between Hamilton and Tarrington. The initial planting of pinot noir in 1998 was
followed by plantings of pinot gris in 1999, chardonnay in 2003 and further plantings of pinot gris in
2005. This family-owned and operated business produced its first Chardonnay in 2006; the pinot
gris is sold.

♥♥♥♥ **Pinot Noir 2004** Strawberry, cherry, leaf and mint aromas and flavours, finishing with
brisk acidity. Young vines and early picking have made their mark. Stained and creased
cork. 13.5° alc. **RATING** 87 **DRINK** 2008 **$** 30

Mount Prior Vineyard

1194 Gooramadda Road, Rutherglen, Vic 3685 **REGION** Rutherglen
T (02) 6026 5591 **F** (02) 6026 5590 **WWW**.rutherglenvic.com **OPEN** 7 days 9–5
WINEMAKER Brian Devitt **EST.** 1860 **CASES** 5000
A full-scale tourist facility, with yet more in the pipeline. Full accommodation packages at the
historic Mount Prior House; a restaurant operating weekends under the direction of Trish Hennessy
(for groups of 6 or more), with four consecutive *Age Good Food Guide* awards to its credit; picnic and
barbecue facilities; and a California-style gift shop. The wines are basically sold through the cellar
door and an active mailing list. The 112 ha of vineyards were expanded in 1998 by a further 5 ha of
durif, a mark both of the success of Mount Prior and of interest in Durif.

♥♥♥♥ **Black Label Durif 2003** An immense wine, with black fruits and lashings of bitter
chocolate and licorice; the flavours come from total fruit extract rather than simply
tannins; don't approach without due precaution and protection for at least 5 years. Cork.
14° alc. **RATING** 89 **DRINK** 2023 **$** 29
Reserve Museum Release Port NV While the colour doesn't show it, much more complex
than the Director's Selection, albeit non-classical; Christmas cake and the kitchen sink.
RATING 89 **DRINK** Now **$** 25
Shiraz 2004 Medium-bodied; lively blackberry, chocolate and mocha mix; fine, ripe
tannins, plenty of flavour. Cork. 14° alc. **RATING** 88 **DRINK** 2012 **$** 23
Cabernet Merlot 2003 Earthy, spicy blackberry, chocolate and mocha run through the
bouquet and palate; medium-bodied, well-balanced. Cork. 14.5° alc. **RATING** 88
DRINK 2011 **$** 19
Noble Gold 1997 Golden bronze; soft, honeyed candied orange fruit flavours; good
acidity. Cork. 11.5° alc. **RATING** 88 **DRINK** Now **$** 19
Directors Selection Tokay NV Golden brown; youthful tea leaf, biscuit and toffee flavours
which are strongly varietal. **RATING** 88 **DRINK** Now **$** 18
Director's Selection Muscat NV Raisined and rich; more substance, and seemingly a
little more age than the Tokay. **RATING** 88 **DRINK** Now **$** 17
Domain Chardonnay Durif Rose NV Bright pink; nicely balanced red fruits and a dry,
citrussy finish; a weird blend, but well-made. **RATING** 87 **DRINK** Now **$** 18

♥♥♥♡ **Durif 2004 RATING** 86 **DRINK** 2025 **$** 29
Sparkling Shiraz Durif NV RATING 86 **DRINK** 2010 **$** 27
Directors Selection Port NV RATING 86 **DRINK** Now **$** 16
Brut Cuvee NV RATING 85 **DRINK** Now **$** 24

Mt Samaria Vineyard

3231 Midland Highway, Lima South, Vic 3673 **REGION** Upper Goulburn
T (03) 5768 2550 **WWW**.m-s-v.com.au **OPEN** By appt
WINEMAKER Roger Cowan, Delatite, Auldstone Cellars **EST.** 1992 **CASES** 700
The 3-ha Mt Samaria Vineyard, with shiraz (1.7 ha) and tempranillo (0.8 ha) having the lion's share,
accompanied by a little cabernet and pinot gris, is owned and operated by Judy and Roger Cowan.

Plantings took place over an 8-year period, and in the early days the grapes were sold to Delatite; the Cowans ventured into wine production in 1999.

ΨΨΨΨ **Black Label Shiraz 2004** Much better hue than the Yellow Label; light- to medium-bodied, but with far more red and black fruit flavours; supple tannins, nice oak. Screwcap. 14° alc. **RATING** 91 **DRINK** 2013 $ 16

Tempranillo 2005 Strong colour; a full-flavoured, rich wine especially on the mid-palate, with lots of blackberry, prune and plum; does tail away somewhat on the finish. **RATING** 90 **DRINK** 2015 $ 21

ΨΨΨΨ **Cabernet Shiraz 2004** Early-picked style; intense berry fruits but also fairly sharp acidity; minimal oak/tannins. Cork. 13° alc. **RATING** 87 **DRINK** 2009 $ 18

ΨΨΨ **Yellow Label Shiraz 2004** Light spice, leaf, berry and mint aromas; light-bodied palate with gentle spicy fruit. Screwcap. 13° alc. **RATING** 86 **DRINK** 2009 $ 16

Mt Surmon Wines

Scarlattis Cellar Door Gallery, Basham Road, Stanley Flat, SA 5453 **REGION** Clare Valley
T (08) 8842 1250 **F** (08) 8842 4064 **WWW**.mtsurmon.com.au **OPEN** 7 days 10–5
WINEMAKER Various contract **EST.** 1995 **CASES** 1000
The Surmon family has established just under 20 ha of vineyard, half to shiraz, the remainder to cabernet sauvignon, nebbiolo, chardonnay, pinot gris and viognier. Most of the grapes are sold to other wineries (some on a swap basis for riesling and merlot), but small quantities are contract-made and sold through Scarlattis Gallery and Function Centre (the cellar door) and a few local hotels. The first wines were made in 1999 (Cabernet Merlot and Shiraz); white wines were added later.

ΨΨΨΨ **Clare Valley Shiraz 2004** Deep, dense purple-red; rich, powerful blackberry, earthy, leather, spice and licorice not extractive, the relatively low alcohol a major plus. Terrific value. Screwcap. 13° alc. **RATING** 93 **DRINK** 2019 $ 20

ΨΨΨΨ **Clare Valley Cabernet Sauvignon 2004** Good colour reflects the low pH, low baume and early picking; firm cassis fruit with touches of leaf and mint; a strange decision to pick so early. Screwcap. 12° alc. **RATING** 87 **DRINK** Now $ 20

ΨΨΨ **Nebbiolo 2004** **RATING** 79 $ 20

🐚 Mount Toolleen

103 High Street, Glen Iris, Vic 3146 (postal) **REGION** Barossa Valley/Heathcote
T (03) 9885 1367 **F** (03) 9885 1367 **WWW**.mttoolleen.com.au **OPEN** Not
WINEMAKER James Irvine, Dominic Morris, Krystina Morris (Contract) **EST.** 2000 **CASES** 2000
Mount Toolleen is owned by a group of Melbourne investors by a somewhat complicated joint venture scheme which gives Mount Toolleen permanent access to 4.6 ha of shiraz grown in the Ebenezer district of the Barossa Valley, and 6.9 ha of shiraz from a Heathcote vineyard, the latter still coming into production; in the meantime, grapes are purchased from the Heathcote region. The venture operates under the overall guidance of Peter Scudamore-Smith MW, and achieved early prominence when the 2002 Ebenezer Vineyard Shiraz won the George Mackey Trophy for Best Wine Exported from Australia in the 2004-05 year.

ΨΨΨΨΨ **Ebenezer Vineyard Barossa Valley Shiraz 2002** Dense, deep colour; medium- to full-bodied, flooded with black fruits and dark chocolate; perfect tannins and oak management; easily carries the alcohol. Cork. 15° alc. **RATING** 96 **DRINK** 2017

Premium Reserve Barossa Valley Shiraz 2003 Concentrated, rich blackberry, dark plum and chocolate; shrugs off the limitations of the vintage; plump tannins and good oak. Cork. 14.5° alc. **RATING** 94 **DRINK** 2015 $ 42

Kavel Barossa Valley Shiraz 2002 Medium-bodied; an intense wine which carries the alcohol effortlessly; spice, blackberry and chocolate; fine, long tannins and good oak. Procork. 15° alc. **RATING** 94 **DRINK** 2017 $ 32

Mount Torrens Vineyards ★★★★★

PO Box 1679, Mount Torrens, SA 5244 **REGION** Adelaide Hills
T (08) 8389 4229 **F** (08) 8389 4528 **WWW**.solstice.com.au **OPEN** Not
WINEMAKER Torbreck (David Powell) **EST.** 1996 **CASES** 500
Mount Torrens Vineyards has 2.5 ha of shiraz and viognier, and the distinguished team of Mark Whisson as viticulturist and David Powell as contract winemaker. The wines are available by mail order, but are chiefly exported to England and the US.

 Solstice Shiraz Cabernet 2003 The power of the cabernet takes the wine into yet another dimension, with cassis and blackcurrant joining the fray; retains grace, and has lovely length and finish. Cork. 14° alc. **RATING** 95 **DRINK** 2015 **$** 35
Solstice Shiraz Viognier 2003 Medium- to full-bodied; an epitome of the synergy between shiraz and viognier; a round and velvety complex mix of red and black fruits, and that viognier lift. Cork. 14° alc. **RATING** 94 **DRINK** 2013 **$** 35
Solstice Shiraz 2003 Medium-bodied; an utterly different aromatic profile to that of the Shiraz Viognier; spicier, earthier, with more licorice and blackberry; fine, long palate. Cork. 14° alc. **RATING** 94 **DRINK** 2015 **$** 35
Solstice Shiraz 2002 Deep colour; a complex, rich, mouthfilling array of black fruits, spice and licorice; very good texture and structure; quality French oak. Cork. 14.5° alc. **RATING** 94 **DRINK** 2017 **$** 38

Solstice Viognier 2003 Bright straw-green; very interesting wine which has absorbed 18 months' barrel maturation, and in so doing cuts the edge off what can be a confronting variety; remarkably fresh. Screwcap. 13.5° alc. **RATING** 91 **DRINK** 2008 **$** 28

Mount Trio Vineyard ★★★★

Cnr Castle Rock Road/Porongurup Road, Porongurup WA 6324 **REGION** Porongurup
T (08) 9853 1136 **F** (08) 9853 1120 **OPEN** By appt
WINEMAKER Gavin Berry **EST.** 1989 **CASES** 5000
Mount Trio was established by Gavin Berry and Gill Graham shortly after they moved to the Mt Barker district in late 1988. They have slowly built up the Mount Trio business, based in part on estate plantings of 2 ha of pinot noir and 0.5 ha of chardonnay and in part on purchased grapes. An additional 6 ha was planted in the spring of 1999. Exports to the UK.

Retro Red Shiraz Cabernet 2002 Plush, ripe, red and black fruits; a soft, cosy mouthfeel and good length. Good value. Screwcap. 15° alc. **RATING** 91 **DRINK** 2009 **$** 15
Great Southern Sauvignon Blanc 2005 Ripe, rich, fully charged passionfruit, tropical and gooseberry mix, yet not phenolic. Very good value. Screwcap. 13° alc. **RATING** 90 **DRINK** Now **$** 15
Great Southern Chardonnay 2005 Light green-straw; a subdued bouquet, then a lively palate; crisp nectarine and grapefruit supported by a whisk of oak; good line and length. Screwcap. 13° alc. **RATING** 90 **DRINK** 2009 **$** 17

Great Southern Riesling 2005 Slightly funky/reductive bouquet, a pity, because there is lots of lime juice flavour and length. Others might be less sensitive to the bouquet, and rate the wine much higher. Screwcap. 12° alc. **RATING** 87 **DRINK** 2008 **$** 17

Mount View Estate ★★★★

Mount View Road, Mount View, NSW 2325 **REGION** Lower Hunter Valley
T (02) 4990 3307 **F** (02) 4991 1289 **OPEN** 7 days 10–5
WINEMAKER Andrew Thomas (Consultant) **EST.** 1971 **CASES** 3500
The Tulloch family has neither owned nor had any interest in Mount View Estate since 2000. Winemaking has passed to the capable hands of former Tyrrell's winemaker Andrew Thomas. The 35-year-old vines are paying big dividends.

 Reserve Hunter Valley Chardonnay 2005 Excellent wine; lots of nectarine, white peach and melon fruit; the French barrel ferment oak evident but well-integrated and balanced; good acidity. Screwcap. 14° alc. **RATING** 94 **DRINK** 2010 **$** 19

ΥΥΥΥ **Reserve Semillon 2005** Full fruit expression; citrus, lime and grass; good balance and length. **RATING** 91 **DRINK** 2015 $16

ΥΥΥΥ **Reserve Verdelho 2005** **RATING** 86 **DRINK** 2008 $15
Reserve Limestone Creek Verdelho 2005 **RATING** 86 **DRINK** 2008 $19
Reserve Hunter Valley Pinot Noir 2004 Medium- to full red; a well-made, light- to medium-bodied dry red; with enough age will move to what used to be called Australian Burgundy. Screwcap. 13.2° alc. **RATING** 86 **DRINK** 2015 $25
Reserve Hunter Valley Cabernet Sauvignon 2004 **RATING** 86 **DRINK** 2008 $22

Mt Vincent Estate ★★★★★

8 Main Road, Mount Vincent, NSW 2323 **REGION** Lower Hunter Valley
T (02) 4938 0078 **F** (02) 4938 0048 **WWW**.mvewines.com.au **OPEN** By appt
WINEMAKER Monarch Winemaking Services (Jim Chatto) **EST.** 1999 **CASES** 3000
If you drive from Sydney to the Hunter Valley by the most conventional and quickest route, Mt Vincent Estate is the first vineyard you will come to, at the foot of Mt Vincent in the Mulbring Valley. The 50-ha property includes a 2-ha lake stocked with fish and yabbies, a 5-bedroom accommodation retreat, and a sign which normally says closed. The range of wines extends from Orange to the Hunter Valley to Tas, the common factor contract winemaking of the highest order.

ΥΥΥΥΥ **Morisset Limited Release Hunter Valley Semillon 2005** Pale straw-green; very intense and clearly delineated semillon varietal fruit; long and probing lemon flavours; very well-made. Screwcap. 11.5° alc. **RATING** 94 **DRINK** 2015 $23
Morisset Museum Release Hunter Valley Semillon 1998 Bright green-yellow; developing precisely as it should with lemon, honey and some toast. Minerally acidity provides structure and length. Cork. 10.3° alc. **RATING** 94 **DRINK** 2009 $23

ΥΥΥΥ **Canberra District Riesling 2005** Pale straw-green; fine, elegant, delicate passionfruit, lime and green apple; long, tangy finish. Screwcap. **RATING** 93 **DRINK** 2012
Tamar Valley Pinot Noir 2004 Bright, clear red-purple; ripe, sweet plum and black cherry fruit on a silky smooth palate; good texture and mouthfeel. Screwcap. **RATING** 92 **DRINK** 2010
Awaba Hunter Valley Shiraz 2000 Classic Hunter Valley shiraz, with earthy/leathery overtones to cedary black fruits and fine tannins; good structure and balance; will go on from here. Cork. 13.5° alc. **RATING** 91 **DRINK** 2013 $23
Orange Merlot 2003 Medium-bodied; good varietal fruit definition with cassis, raspberry and blackcurrant flavours; entirely fruit-driven, and still remarkably fresh and youthful. Screwcap. **RATING** 90 **DRINK** 2010
Orange Cabernet Sauvignon 2003 A medium-bodied mix of blackcurrant, cassis and fairly obvious oak, attractive hints of dark chocolate in the background; ripe tannins. Cork. **RATING** 90 **DRINK** 2012

ΥΥΥΥ **Orange Sangiovese 2003** Light- to medium-bodied; spicy, savoury red cherry fruit; good varietal structure and mouthfeel; not forced. Screwcap. **RATING** 89 **DRINK** 2011
Cockle Creek Hunter Valley Chardonnay 2002 Gently soft nectarine and melon with integrated barrel ferment oak inputs; at its peak. Cork. 13.5° alc. **RATING** 88 **DRINK** Now $23

Mount William Winery ★★★★☆

Mount William Road, Tantaraboo, Vic 3764 **REGION** Macedon Ranges
T (03) 5429 1595 **F** (03) 5429 1998 **WWW**.mtwilliamwinery.com.au **OPEN** 7 days 11–5
WINEMAKER Kilchurn Wines (David Cowburn) **EST.** 1987 **CASES** 3500
Adrienne and Murray Cousins established 7.5 ha of vineyards, planted to pinot noir, cabernet franc, merlot and chardonnay, between 1987 and 1999. The wines are made under contract and are sold through a stone cellar door, and through a number of fine wine retailers around Melbourne.

ΥΥΥΥ **Chardonnay 2004** Light green-yellow; silky, lively and tightly focused; peach, nectarine and citrus glide across the tongue; barrel ferment French oak merely a ghost. Screwcap. 13.2° alc. **RATING** 93 **DRINK** 2012 $23

Blanc de Blanc 2001 Fine mousse; extremely fine, minerally, long, intense palate with a skein of citrus and mandarin; very low dosage; 3 years on yeast lees. 12.5° alc. **RATING** 92 **DRINK** 2010 $30

Chardonnay 2003 Obvious creamy/mealy malolactic inputs into a long palate which retains good acidity. **RATING** 91 **DRINK** 2009 $23

Louise Clare NV Light- to medium red; a complex base wine made from pinot noir, shiraz and cabernet sauvignon, not a conventional recipe, but works very well; pleasingly dry finish. **RATING** 91 **DRINK** 2010 $30

Mountadam

High Eden Road, Eden Valley, SA 5235 **REGION** Eden Valley
T (08) 8564 1900 **F** (08) 8564 1999 **OPEN** 7 days 11–4
WINEMAKER Con Moshos **EST.** 1972 **CASES** 25 000
Founded by the late David Wynn for the benefit of winemaker son Adam. Mountadam was (somewhat surprisingly) purchased by Cape Mentelle (doubtless under the direction of Moet Hennessy Wine Estates) in 2000. Rather less surprising has been its sale in September 2005 to Adelaide businessman David Brown, who has extensive interests in the Padthaway region. Con Moshos (long-serving senior winemaker at Petaluma) should lift the quality appreciably in the years ahead.

ꌈꌈꌈꌈ Eden Valley Riesling 2004 Gentle lime and toast aromas and flavours; slow developing, but not particularly intense. Screwcap. 12.5° alc. **RATING** 89 **DRINK** 2010 $24

Barossa Unoaked Chardonnay 2004 Well-made; attractive, ripe stone fruit and melon; good balance and acidity. Screwcap. **RATING** 87 **DRINK** Now $18

Barossa Shiraz 2003 Ripe blackberry and plum fruit; medium-bodied; relatively ripe tannins and minimal oak. Twin top. **RATING** 87 **DRINK** 2008 $18

ꌈꌈꌈꌈ Barossa Cabernet Merlot 2003 **RATING** 86 **DRINK** 2008 $18

Mountford   NR

Bamess Road, West Pemberton, WA 6260 **REGION** Pemberton
T (08) 9776 1345 **F** (08) 9776 1345 **WWW**.mountfordwines.com.au **OPEN** Mon–Fri 10–4, w'ends 10–5
WINEMAKER Andrew Mountford, Saxon Mountford **EST.** 1987 **CASES** 3000
English-born and trained Andrew Mountford and wife Sue migrated to Australia in 1983, and were one of the early movers to select Pemberton for their vineyard. The cool climate and spectacular forested countryside were important considerations in the move. Their strikingly packaged wines are produced from 6 ha of permanently netted, dry-grown vineyards.

Mountilford   NR

Mount Vincent Road, Ilford, NSW 2850 **REGION** Mudgee
T (02) 6358 8544 **F** (02) 6358 8544 **OPEN** 7 days 10–4
WINEMAKER Contract **EST.** 1985 **CASES** 1800
A surprisingly large cellar door operation which has grown significantly over the past few years, utilising 7 ha of estate vineyards. Roughly half the production is sold to other winemakers. I have not, however, had the opportunity to taste the wines.

Mountview Wines   NR

Mount Stirling Road, Glen Aplin, Qld 4381 **REGION** Granite Belt
T (07) 4683 4316 **F** (07) 4683 4111 **WWW**.mountviewwines.com.au **OPEN** Fri–Sun 9.30–4.30, 7 days during school & public hols
WINEMAKER Jim Barnes **EST.** 1990 **CASES** 1250
Mountview Wines has changed hands and is now owned by Pauline Stewart. In the 2006 *Wine Companion* Mountview was inadvertently credited with the wines of Mount View Estate (Hunter Valley). No wines were received for this issue from Mountview Wines.

Mr Riggs Wine Company ★★★★★

Ingleburne, Willunga Road, McLaren Vale, SA 5171 **REGION** McLaren Vale
T (08) 8556 4460 **F** (08) 8556 4462 **WWW**.mrriggs.com.au **OPEN** 7 days 10–5
WINEMAKER Ben Riggs **EST.** 2001 **CASES** 15 000
After 14 years as winemaker at Wirra Wirra, and another 6 at various Australian wineries as well as numerous northern hemisphere vintages, Ben Riggs established his own business. His major activity is as consultant winemaker to Penny's Hill, Pertaringa, Coriole, Geoff Hardy and others, offering a 'grape to plate' service, plus keeping his hand in consulting for Cazal Viel in the south of France. He also makes wine for his Mr Riggs label, initially buying select parcels of grapes from old vines in McLaren Vale, also using grapes from his own vineyard at Piebald Gully, where he has planted shiraz, viognier and petit verdot. Exports to all major markets.

▼▼▼▼▼ **McLaren Vale Shiraz 2004** Clean, rich fruit aromas; lush red and black fruits with a juicy twist giving lively mouthfeel and a delicious finish; amazingly light on its 15° alcohol feet. Procork. 15° alc. **RATING** 96 **DRINK** 2014 **$** 40
Adelaide Viognier 2005 Spotlessly clean; a nicely balanced palate with flavours of honeysuckle, honey, apricot and citrus. Screwcap. 13.5° alc. **RATING** 94 **DRINK** 2008 **$** 24.99
Shiraz Viognier 2004 Immaculately balanced and constructed; supple blackberry and dark chocolate fruit; fine, ripe tannins; good oak. Screwcap. **RATING** 94 **DRINK** 2015 **$** 25

▼▼▼▼♈ **Watervale Riesling 2005** Bright, intense citrus and lime fruit; excellent focus, line and balance; lingering minerally finish. Screwcap. **RATING** 93 **DRINK** 2015 **$** 22
The Gaffer McLaren Vale Shiraz 2004 Rich, generous red and black plum, blackberry, chocolate and vanilla melange; good tannins. Screwcap. 15° alc. **RATING** 92 **DRINK** 2014 **$** 22
Adelaide Hills Riesling 2005 Clean, abundant flavour, with distinct residual sugar sweetness; I am not sure it gels with the alcohol, but time may prove otherwise. Screwcap. 12° alc. **RATING** 90 **DRINK** 2012 **$** 22

Mudgee Growers ★★★

Henry Lawson Drive, Mudgee, NSW 2580 **REGION** Mudgee
T (02) 6372 2855 **F** (02) 6372 2811 **WWW**.mudgeegrowers.com.au **OPEN** 7 days 10–5
WINEMAKER David Lowe, Jane Wilson **EST.** 2004 **CASES** 1200
After closing their operation in the Hunter Valley, David Lowe and Jane Wilson have set up a new business in Mudgee, using grapes from various vineyards in the region. The cellar door is in the heritage winery at Fairview (formerly known as Platt's), which has been returned to working order, once more housing tanks, oak casks and barrels.

▼▼▼▼ **Cabernet Sauvignon 2004** Medium-bodied earthy, chocolatey, blackberry fruit; minimal oak, ripe tannins. Flavoursome. Screwcap. 13.8° alc. **RATING** 89 **DRINK** 2010 **$** 22
Nullo Mountain Riesling 2005 A clean bouquet with nice citrus aromas; the palate has flavour but is loose and wanders. Screwcap. 13.6° alc. **RATING** 87 **DRINK** 2009

▼▼▼♈ **Rose 2005** Bright colour; nicely balanced red fruits and acidity; clean and crisp, even if simple. Screwcap. 13.5° alc. **RATING** 86 **DRINK** Now

Mudgee Wines NR

Henry Lawson Drive, Mudgee, NSW 2850 **REGION** Mudgee
T (02) 6372 2258 **WWW**.mudgeewines.com.au **OPEN** Thurs–Mon 10–5, hols 7 days
WINEMAKER David Conway **EST.** 1963 **CASES** 20 000
Following the acquisition of Mudgee Wines by the Conway family, the organic winemaking practices of the former owner Jennifer Meek have been discontinued; conventional viticultural and winemaking practices have now been adopted.

Mulcra Estate Wines

NR

PO Box 182, Irymple, Vic 3498 **REGION** Murray Darling
T (03) 5022 8991 **F** (03) 5022 8991 **WWW**.mulcraestate.com.au **OPEN** At The Enjoywine Café,
8th St, Mildura
WINEMAKER Glen Olsen **EST.** 2002 **CASES** 1000
Samuel and Anna Andriske were part of a wave of Germans who left their homeland in the 1840s to escape poverty, wars and religious differences. The majority settled in the Barossa Valley, but one group was brought to Geelong by its then Mayor. Grapegrowing was part of a mixed farming business for the Andriskes, but in the wake of phylloxera the third generation (Charles Andriske) moved to Mildura. His sons established Mulcra Estate in 1933, selling grapes to Mildura and also producing table grapes. Finally, the fifth generation, Marlene Andriske and son Mark, have made the move from grapegrowing to winemaking, with 3 ha of chardonnay, supplemented by grapes purchased from a local grower.

Mulligan Wongara Vineyard

NR

603 Grenfell Road, Cowra, NSW 2794 **REGION** Cowra
T (02) 6342 9334 **F** (02) 6342 9334 **OPEN** Sat, public hols (Sundays if a public holiday weekend) 10–4
WINEMAKER Nick Millichip (Consultant) **EST.** 1993 **CASES** 2000
Andrew and Emma Mulligan began the establishment of their 16-ha vineyard in 1993; chardonnay (14 ha), shiraz (2.5 ha), cabernet (3.5 ha) and sangiovese (1 ha) have been planted. A significant proportion of the grapes is sold to others.

Mulyan

NR

North Logan Road, Cowra, NSW 2794 **REGION** Cowra
T (02) 6342 1336 **F** (02) 6341 1015 **OPEN** W'ends & public hols 10–5, or by appt
WINEMAKER 21C Wine Company (Drew Tuckwell) **EST.** 1994 **CASES** 2000
Mulyan is a 1350-ha grazing property purchased by the Fagan family in 1886 from Dr William Redfern, a leading 19th century figure in Australian history. The current-generation owners, Peter and Jenni Fagan, began planting in 1994, and intend the vineyard area to be 100 ha in all. Presently there are 29 ha of shiraz and 14.5 ha of chardonnay, and 4.6 ha each of merlot and viognier. The label features a statue of the Roman God Mercury which has stood in the Mulyan homestead garden since being brought back from Italy in 1912 by Peter Fagan's grandmother.

Munari Wines

★★★★★

Ladys Creek Vineyard, 1129 Northern Highway, Heathcote, Vic 3523 **REGION** Heathcote
T (03) 5433 3366 **F** (03) 5433 3905 **WWW**.munariwines.com **OPEN** 7 days 11–5
WINEMAKER Adrian Munari, Deborah Munari **EST.** 1993 **CASES** 2500
Adrian and Deborah Munari made a singularly impressive entry into the winemaking scene, with both their initial vintages winning an impressive array of show medals, and have carried on in similar vein since then. With a little under 8 ha of estate vines, production is limited, but the wines are well worth seeking out. Exports to Singapore, Malaysia, Indonesia and France.

 Lady's Pass Heathcote Shiraz 2004 Deep colour; full-bodied, almost exotically rich and sweet (sweetness in the best sense) in a black fruit spectrum, together with splashes of anise and licorice. Great structure and length. Cork. 14° alc. **RATING** 96 **DRINK** 2018 **$** 45

The Beauregard Shiraz 2004 A typically good colour; succulent, smooth, rich, ripe plum and dark chocolate smoothie; overall, medium-bodied, with very good balance to ultra-fine tannins and oak. Cork. **RATING** 95 **DRINK** 2015 **$** 30

Schoolhouse Red 2004 Deep, dense purple-red; layer-upon-layer of fruit with the typical viognier fragrant lift; medium- to full-bodied, with very good structure and length; the (relatively) low alcohol provides lovely spice. Shiraz/Viognier. Cork. 13° alc. **RATING** 95 **DRINK** 2016 **$** 30

The Ridge Shiraz 2004 Clear, clean dark fruit aromas; the palate is more powerful than expected, with sweet blackberry and plum fruit, and appropriate supporting tannins. Cork. 14° alc. **RATING** 94 **DRINK** 2014 **$** 25

🍷🍷🍷🍷 **India Red Cabernet Sauvignon 2004** Deep colour; a powerful full-bodied wine with blackcurrant fruit, and firm tannins running through the length of the palate. Good oak. Cork. 13.5° alc. **RATING** 92 **DRINK** 2019 $ 35

Heathcote Merlot 2004 Deep colour; big, deep, rich and luscious; an attractive medium- to full-bodied wine, though not particularly varietal. Cork. 14° alc. **RATING** 90 **DRINK** 2014 $ 30

🍷🍷🍷🍷 **Shiraz Viognier Rose 2005** Bright, pale fuchsia; clean, fresh and fruity strawberry cherry flavours; good balance. Screwcap. 14° alc. **RATING** 88 **DRINK** Now $ 20

Fortified Vintage Shiraz 2005 Abundant flavour, made, however, in traditional Australian style with a distinctly sweet back-palate and finish. Slightly less sweetness would make an even better wine. Cork. **RATING** 88 **DRINK** 2015 $ 25

Mundoonen ★★★★

1457 Yass River Road, Yass, NSW 2582 **REGION** Canberra District
T (02) 6227 1353 **F** (02) 6227 1453 **WWW**.mundoonen.com.au **OPEN** Sun & public hols or by appt
WINEMAKER Terry O'Donnell **EST.** 2003 **CASES** 700
Jenny and Terry O'Donnell released their first wines in August 2003. The winery is situated beside the Yass River, behind one of the oldest settlers' cottages in the Yass River Valley, dating back to 1858. Estate plantings of shiraz and viognier are supplemented by contract-grown riesling, sauvignon blanc and cabernet sauvignon. The barrel shed has been created by refurbishing and insulating a 140-year-old building on the property.

🍷🍷🍷🍷 **Canberra District Riesling 2002** Glowing yellow-green; a spectacular, if unusual, array of aromas and flavours, moving more to a tropical mandarin mix; dry finish. Good example of development under screwcap; gold medal Hyatt Riesling Challenge '05. Screwcap. 12.5° alc. **RATING** 90 **DRINK** 2008 $ 27

Mundrakoona Estate NR

Sir Charles Moses Lane, Old Hume Highway, Mittagong, NSW 2575 **REGION** Southern Highlands
T (02) 4872 1311 **F** (02) 4872 1322 **WWW**.mundrakoona.com.au **OPEN** Mon–Fri 10–5, w'ends & public hols 9–6
WINEMAKER Anton Balog **EST.** 1997 **CASES** 8500
During 1998 and 1999 Anton Balog progressively planted 3.2 ha of pinot noir, sauvignon blanc and tempranillo at an altitude of 680m. He is using wild yeast ferments, hand-plunging and other 'natural' winemaking techniques, with the aim of producing Burgundian-style Pinot and Chardonnay and Bordeaux-style Sauvignon Blanc and Cabernet Sauvignon. For the foreseeable future, estate production will be supplemented by grapes grown in local vineyards.

Murchison Wines ★★★★

105 Old Weir Road, Murchison, Vic 3610 **REGION** Goulburn Valley
T (03) 5826 2294 **F** (03) 5826 2510 **WWW**.murchisonwines.com.au **OPEN** Fri–Mon & public hols 10–5, or by appt
WINEMAKER Guido Vazzoler **EST.** 1975 **CASES** 4000
Sandra (ex kindergarten teacher turned cheesemaker) and Guido Vazzoler (ex Brown Brothers) acquired the long-established Longleat Estate vineyard in 2003, renaming it Murchison Wines, having lived on the property (as tenants) for some years. The wines are estate-grown.

🍷🍷🍷🍷 **Longleat Estate Cabernet Sauvignon 2004** Good hue; bright, crisp, blackcurrant fruit, with fine tannins and controlled oak. Screwcap. 13° alc. **RATING** 91 **DRINK** 2014 $ 18

Longleat Estate Semillon 2005 A spotlessly clean bouquet; a well-balanced palate with lemon and apple fruit, and just a hint of residual sugar to add length. Screwcap. 12.2° alc. **RATING** 90 **DRINK** 2010 $ 13

Longleat Estate Shiraz 2004 Fresh cherry and blackberry mix to a light- to medium- bodied palate, with good balance and length; minimal oak/tannin impact. Screwcap. 14.3° alc. **RATING** 90 **DRINK** 2012 $ 18

TTTT **Longleat Estate Riesling 2005** Clean, lively minerally; just a touch austere, but has good length. Screwcap. 12.7° alc. **RATING** 89 **DRINK** 2011 $ 15

TTTY **Longleat Estate Rose 2005** **RATING** 86 **DRINK** Now $ 15

Murdoch Hill

Mappinga Road, Woodside, SA 5244 **REGION** Adelaide Hills
T (08) 8389 7081 **F** (08) 8389 7991 **WWW**.murdochhill.com.au **OPEN** By appt
WINEMAKER Brian Light (Contract) **EST.** 1998 **CASES** 2600
A little over 21 ha of vines have been established on the undulating, gum-studded countryside of the Downer family's Erinka property, 4 km east of Oakbank. In descending order of importance, the varieties established are sauvignon blanc, shiraz, cabernet sauvignon and chardonnay.

TTTTY **Adelaide Hills Sauvignon Blanc 2005** Bright, fresh, zesty lemony/grassy aromas and flavours, with a streak of minerally acidity; good line and length. Screwcap. 13° alc. **RATING** 90 **DRINK** Now $ 18

Murdock ★★★★★

Riddoch Highway, Coonawarra, SA 5263 **REGION** Coonawarra
T (08) 8737 3700 **F** (08) 8737 2107 **WWW**.murdockwines.com **OPEN** By appt
WINEMAKER Balnaves **EST.** 1998 **CASES** 4000
The Murdock family has established 10.4 ha of cabernet sauvignon, 2 ha of shiraz, 1 ha of merlot, and 0.5 ha each of chardonnay and riesling, and produces small quantities of an outstanding Cabernet Sauvignon, contract-made by Peter Bissell. A second vineyard has been added in the Barossa Valley, with 5.8 ha of shiraz and 2.1 ha each of semillon and cabernet sauvignon. The labels, incidentally, are ultra-minimalist, no flood of propaganda here. Also plans to open a cellar door/café in the Barossa Valley. Exports to the US and Asia.

TTTTT **Barossa Shiraz 2004** Bright purple-red; a top-flight evocation of Barossa shiraz from a very good vintage; medium-bodied, supple blackberry and plum fruit; perfectly balanced and integrated oak. Cork. 14.5° alc. **RATING** 95 **DRINK** 2024 $ 42
The Merger 2004 Deep, clear purple-red; medium- to full-bodied, but has great finesse despite its power; a panoply of blackberry, plum, blackcurrant and cassis, with mocha oak and tannins seamlessly interwoven. Coonawarra Cabernet Sauvignon (60%)/Barossa Shiraz. Screwcap. 13.5° alc. **RATING** 95 **DRINK** 2020 $ 20
Coonawarra Merlot 2004 Powerful, dense plum and blackcurrant fruit; persistent, but ripe and slippery, tannins; rigorous yield control has paid big dividends. Screwcap. 14° alc. **RATING** 94 **DRINK** 2015 $ 28

TTTTY **Coonawarra Merlot 2003** Clear red; light- to medium-bodied, with distinctly earthy, savoury, olive varietal fruit on bouquet and palate; a fraction lean overall. Screwcap. 14° alc. **RATING** 93 **DRINK** 2011 $ 38
Coonawarra Chardonnay 2005 Elegant sculpted style; nectarine and grapefruit, with gentle barrel ferment/malolactic/lees inputs; long finish, and will build with age. Screwcap. 13.7° alc. **RATING** 92 **DRINK** 2011 $ 24
Dos Diablos 2005 A clean and aromatic bouquet; medium-bodied, lively, gently spicy/juicy fruits; minimal oak and tannin inputs, but has a more sustained finish than the varietal Grenache. Grenache (65%)/Tempranillo. 14.7° alc. **RATING** 91 **DRINK** 2010 $ 24

TTTT **Riesling 2005** Fresh, elegant, delicate style; has length and focus; good finish. **RATING** 89 **DRINK** 2010 $ 16
Barossa Grenache 2005 Vivid purple-red; strongly varietal sweet, juicy berry, fruit; flavoursome, but lacks structure; drink-me-quick style. Screwcap. 15.1° alc. **RATING** 89 **DRINK** 2008 $ 18
Barossa Rose 2005 Crisp, dry, spice and herbs; uncompromisingly dry palate; food style. Screwcap. **RATING** 87 **DRINK** Now $ 18

Murdup Wines

NR

Southern Ports Highway, Mount Benson, SA 5275 **REGION** Mount Benson
T (08) 8768 6190 **F** (08) 8768 6190 **WWW**.murdupwines.com.au **OPEN** 7 days 10–4
WINEMAKER Steve Grimley **EST.** 1996 **CASES** 1500
Andy and Melinda Murdock purchased Murdup in 1996, retaining the name of the property which
was first settled as a grazing property in the 1860s. They have planted 10.5 ha of vineyard, the lion's
share going to cabernet sauvignon and shiraz, with smaller patches of chardonnay and sauvignon
blanc.

Murray Darling Collection

NR

PO Box 84, Euston, NSW 2737 **REGION** Murray Darling
T (03) 5026 1932 **F** (03) 5026 3228 **WWW**.murraydarlingcollection.com **OPEN** Not
WINEMAKER Sandro Mosele (Contract) **EST.** 1989 **CASES** 3000
This is the project of Bruce and Jenny Chalmers, who run the largest vine nursery propagation
business in Australia, and Stefano di Pieri. As well as supplying rootlings to vignerons all over
Australia, the Chalmers have established substantial plantings of a range of varietals, running from
mainstream to rare. By using fine, misty, water sprays in the vineyard, Chalmers is able to radically
reduce the canopy temperatures in summer, thus achieving unexpected results with varieties which
theoretically require a far cooler climate. The grapes are taken to the Mornington Peninsula, where
the wines are made by Sandro Mosele.

Murray Estate

NR

Tocumwal–Barooga Road, Yarrawonga, Vic 3730 **REGION** Murray Darling
T (03) 5745 8345 **F** (03) 5745 8346 **WWW**.murrayestatewines.com.au **OPEN** W'ends 11–5
WINEMAKER John Weinert **EST.** 1997 **CASES** NA
John and Sue Weinert were involved from the ground up in planting their 2.6-ha vineyard to riesling,
chenin blanc, merlot, shiraz and cabernet sauvignon. The name was chosen because Murray is John
Weinert's mother's family name, but it so happens the winery overlooks the Murray River.

Murray Street Vineyard

★★★★☆

Lot 723, Murray Street, Greenock, SA 5360 **REGION** Barossa Valley
T (08) 8562 8373 **F** (08) 8562 8414 **OPEN** 7 days 10–4.30
WINEMAKER Andrew Seppelt **EST.** 2003 **CASES** 2000
Andrew and Vanessa Seppelt have moved with a degree of caution in setting up Murray Street
Vineyard, possibly because of inherited wisdom. Andrew Seppelt is a direct descendant of Benno and
Sophia Seppelt, who built Seppeltsfield and set the family company bearing their name on its path to
fame. They have 46 ha of vineyards, one block at Gomersal, the other at Greenock, with the lion's
share going to shiraz, followed by grenache, mourvedre, viognier, marsanne, semillon and zinfandel.
Most of the grapes are sold, with a small (but hopefully increasing) amount retained for the Murray
Street Vineyard brand. The Benno Shiraz Mataro is one icon tribute on the masculine side; the
Sophia Shiraz Grenache the feminine icon. Unusually good point of sale/propaganda material.
Exports to the UK, the US, Canada and Denmark.

ΨΨΨΨΨ **Sophia Barossa Valley Shiraz 2003** Good purple-red; firm blackberry fruit, chocolate
and licorice; the tannins just a fraction dry, but will soften and integrate with a few more
years. Cork. 14.7° alc. **RATING** 94 **DRINK** 2015 $ 45

ΨΨΨΨΨ **Grenache Mourvedre Shiraz 2003** A complex array of spicy, earthy, briary black fruits,
rising to a peak of sweet fruit on the finish; very nice wine. Screwcap. **RATING** 90
DRINK 2009 $ 22
Barossa Valley Shiraz VP (500 ml) 2004 Made in the modern style, quite dry, and with
good fortifying spirit; licorice/blackberry fruit; will show its class given sufficient time.
Cork. 18° alc. **RATING** 90 **DRINK** 2020 $ 38

ΨΨΨΨ **Barossa Valley Shiraz 2003** Medium-bodied; a savoury mix of blackberry, plum, earth
and spice; minimal oak; fine tannins. Screwcap. **RATING** 89 **DRINK** 2008 $ 22

Grenache 2004 Powerful varietal expression; spice, game, black fruits and ripe tannins; juicy, warm finish. Screwcap. **RATING** 89 **DRINK** Now $ 19

Benno Barossa Valley Mataro Shiraz 2003 Radically different from the '02; has the tannins which mourvedre (mataro) is meant to have; they will soften, but so will the fruit; the judgment may prove to be harsh in the fullness of time. Cork. 15° alc. **RATING** 89 **DRINK** 2013 $ 45

Barossa Valley Adelaide Hills Cabernets 2004 Medium red-purple; a mix of blackcurrant, earth, leaf, cedar and mint; slightly sharp acidity. Cabernet Sauvignon/Cabernet Franc. Screwcap. 14.6° alc. **RATING** 88 **DRINK** 2014 $ 35

ŸŸŸŸ **Barossa Valley Viognier Marsanne 2005** **RATING** 86 **DRINK** 2008 $ 25
Barossa Valley Rose 2005 **RATING** 86 **DRINK** Now $ 17

Murrin Bridge Wines ★★★☆

PO Box 16, Lake Cargelligo, NSW 2672 **REGION** Riverina
T (02) 6898 2264 **F** (02) 6898 2263 **www**.murrinbridgewines.com.au **OPEN** Not
WINEMAKER Dom Piromalli (Contract) **EST.** 1999 **CASES** 3500
The Murrin Bridge Vineyard arose out of a program between the Aboriginal and Torres Strait Islander Commission (ATSIC) undertaken in 1999 by 5 members of the Murrin Bridge Aboriginal community, who had received training for a diploma in viticulture from the TAFE college at Griffith. Plantings began with 2 ha of shiraz in 1999, followed by a further 8 ha in 2000, and another extension in 2002 with shiraz, semillon and chardonnay. Very attractive wine bottle stands are handmade from local hardwoods gathered from the paddocks and banks of the Lachlan River.

ŸŸŸŸ **Shiraz 2004** Similar attractive balance to that of the Chardonnay; plum and cherry fruit; quite elegant. Screwcap. 13° alc. **RATING** 89 **DRINK** 2009 $ 15
Chardonnay 2005 Clean bouquet; nicely weighted white peach and melon fruit; good mouthfeel. Screwcap. 13.5° alc. **RATING** 88 **DRINK** Now $ 15

Murrindindi ★★★★

Cummins Lane, Murrindindi, Vic 3717 **REGION** Upper Goulburn
T (03) 5797 8448 **F** (03) 5797 8448 **OPEN** At Marmalades Café, Yea
WINEMAKER Alan Cuthbertson **EST.** 1979 **CASES** 1500
Situated in an unequivocally cool climate, which means that special care has to be taken with the viticulture to produce ripe fruit flavours. In more recent vintages, Murrindindi has succeeded handsomely in so doing.

ŸŸŸŸŸ **Don't Tell Dad Cabernet Sauvignon 2004** A very complex, rich and powerful wine with fruit ranging from mint and cassis through to black fruits; soft tannins and lots of oak. Screwcap. 13.8° alc. **RATING** 91 **DRINK** 2015 $ 19

Murrumbateman Winery NR

Barton Highway, Murrumbateman, NSW 2582 **REGION** Canberra District
T (02) 6227 5584 **F** (02) 6227 5987 **www**.murrumbatemanwines.com.au **OPEN** Thurs–Mon & public hols 10–5
WINEMAKER Mark Farrell **EST.** 1972 **CASES** 1500
Murrumbateman Winery is now owned by its winemaker Mark Farrell, drawing upon 4.5 ha of estate-grown sauvignon blanc, shiraz and cabernet sauvignon. It also incorporates an à la carte restaurant and function room, together with picnic and barbecue areas.

🍷 Mylkappa Wines ★★★★

Mylkappa Road, Birdwood, SA 5234 **REGION** Adelaide Hills
T (08) 8568 5325 **F** (08) 8568 5496 **www**.mylkappawines.com.au **OPEN** W'ends & public hols 10–5
WINEMAKER Contract **EST.** 1998 **CASES** 850
Having left the Adelaide Hills in 1988 with their three children, Patricia and Geoff Porter returned 10 years later to purchase an old dairy farm at Birdwood. Since that time the entire family has worked

tirelessly to progressively establish a large vineyard planted to chardonnay (12.3 ha), sauvignon blanc (8.4 ha), shiraz (3.9 ha), two clones of pinot noir (4 ha), merlot (1.9 ha) and pinot gris (1.8 ha). Almost all of the grape production is sold to other Adelaide Hills winemakers, with small quantities of Sauvignon Blanc, Chardonnay, Pinot Noir, Cabernet Merlot and Cabernet Sauvignon contract-made.

ΨΨΨΨ **Adelaide Hills Chardonnay 2004** Attractive nectarine, melon and citrus fruit aromas; good depth and weight, with creamy/nutty malolactic and barrel ferment influences. Screwcap. **RATING** 93 **DRINK** 2009 $ 20

ΨΨΨΨ **Adelaide Hills Pinot Noir 2004** Light confit cherry and strawberry fruit; clean, gentle palate; not extractive. Screwcap. **RATING** 88 **DRINK** Now $ 21
Adelaide Hills Cabernet Sauvignon 2003 Some slightly raw edges to the youthful blackcurrant and cassis fruit; fractionally green tannins; needs to soften. Cork. **RATING** 87 **DRINK** 2010 $ 18

Myrtaceae   ★★★★

53 Main Creek Road, Main Ridge, Vic 3928 **REGION** Mornington Peninsula
T (03) 5989 2045 **F** (03) 5989 2845 **OPEN** First weekend of each month & public hols
WINEMAKER Julie Trueman **EST.** 1985 **CASES** 250
The development of the Myrtaceae vineyard began in 1985 with the planting of 0.7 ha of cabernet sauvignon, cabernet franc and merlot intended for a Bordeaux-style red blend. It became evident that these late-ripening varieties were not well suited to the site, so between then and 2000 the vineyard was converted to 0.5 ha each of pinot noir and chardonnay. John Trueman (viticulturist) and Julie Trueman (winemaker) are the proprietors. Part of the property is devoted to the Land for Wildlife Scheme.

ΨΨΨΨ **Mornington Peninsula Pinot Noir 2004** Light colour, the hue quite good; an attractive wine with nicely balanced sweet berry fruits and more foresty/spicy/savoury notes; good length. Screwcap. 13.5° alc. **RATING** 91 **DRINK** 2010 $ 27
Mornington Peninsula Chardonnay 2004 Fulsome stone fruit, melon and citrus, long and tangy, the oak subtle. Screwcap. 13.5° alc. **RATING** 90 **DRINK** 2009 $ 25

Naked Range Wines   ★★★☆

125 Rifle Range Road, Smiths Gully, Vic 3760 **REGION** Yarra Valley
T (03) 9710 1575 **F** (03) 9710 1655 **WWW**.nakedrangewines.com **OPEN** By appt
WINEMAKER Kate Goodman, Simon Wightwick (Contract) **EST.** 1996 **CASES** 2500
Mike Jansz began the establishment of the Jansz Estate vineyard at Smiths Gully, in the Diamond Valley area of the Yarra Valley, in 1996. He has established 6.2 ha of vineyard, one-third sauvignon blanc, a small patch of pinot noir and the remainder cabernet sauvignon (predominant), merlot and chardonnay. The wines are made at the Punt Road winery, and marketed under the striking Naked Range label, with a second label for overseas markets using grapes from other Victorian regions. Exports to Indonesia.

ΨΨΨΨ **Yarra Valley Cabernet Sauvignon 2004** Medium-bodied; good blackcurrant varietal fruit; ripe tannins and quality oak; good mouthfeel and weight. Continues a line of superior cabernets from Naked Range. Cork. 13.5° alc. **RATING** 92 **DRINK** 2014 $ 25

ΨΨΨΨ **Yarra Valley Chardonnay 2005** Light-bodied; light smoky barrel ferment aromas, then sweet nectarine and melon fruit. Screwcap. 13.5° alc. **RATING** 87 **DRINK** 2010 $ 20

ΨΨΨΨ **Yarra Valley Merlot 2004** Light-bodied; small red fruits with spice and olive varietal notes; minimal oak and tannins. Cork. 13.5° alc. **RATING** 86 **DRINK** 2008 $ 25

Nandroya Estate   NR

262 Sandfly Road, Margate, Tas 7054 **REGION** Southern Tasmania
T (03) 6267 2377 **OPEN** By appt
WINEMAKER Hood Wines (Andrew Hood) **EST.** 1995 **CASES** 400
John Rees and family have established 0.75 ha each of sauvignon blanc and pinot noir. The Reeses regard it as a holiday and retirement project and modestly wonder whether they deserve inclusion in this work. They certainly do, for wineries of this size are an indispensable part of the Tasmanian fabric.

🐑 Nangwarry Station ★★★★

PO Box 1, Nangwarry, SA 5277 **REGION** Mount Gambier
T (08) 8739 7274 **F** (08) 8739 7009 **WWW.**nangwarrystation.com.au **OPEN** Not
WINEMAKER Peter Douglas **EST.** 1999 **CASES** 2000
Nangwarry Station was purchased by Ian McLachlan in 1964, variously a high profile President of
the National Farmers Federation and Federal Minister of Defence. The property is now managed by
Ian's son Dugald and wife Sophie, ardent supporters of the family's philosophy of long term
sustainability. One example is the wetlands and conservation areas which have created natural
habitats for over 100 species of birds. In what is a large business, the establishment of 9 ha of
vineyard (4 ha of cabernet sauvignon, 3 ha of pinot noir and 1 ha each of chardonnay and sauvignon
blanc) is a small diversification, but it has been a very successful one. The immensely experienced
(and equally likable) Peter Douglas, for many years a winemaker in Coonawarra, has produced some
lovely wines which hold much promise for the future as the vines mature.

YYYYY **Mount Gambier Sauvignon Blanc 2005** Light straw-green; light-bodied, lively, clear-cut
varietal character; a vibrant, though light, crisp finish; very well-made. Screwcap.
12.5° alc. **RATING** 90 **DRINK** Now $ 16

YYYY **Mount Gambier Pinot Noir 2004** Somewhat inauspicious colour; however, positive varietal
character in a slightly stemmy/foresty mode; has good texture, structure and length; adds to
the promise of the region for pinot. Cork. 13.5° alc. **RATING** 89 **DRINK** 2009 $ 18

🐑 Nardone Baker Wines ★★★

PO Box 386, McLaren Vale, SA 5171 **REGION** McLaren Vale
T (08) 8445 8100 **F** (08) 8445 8200 **WWW.**nardonebaker.com **OPEN** Not
WINEMAKER Brian Light (Contract) **EST.** 1999 **CASES** 23 000
Italian-born Joe Nardone and English-born John Baker were brought together by the marriage of
Joe's daughter and John's son. Both were already in the wine industry, John studying at Roseworthy
Agricultural College and establishing a vineyard. The second generation of Frank Nardone and
Patrick Baker, the latter having also studied at Roseworthy, now run what is a significant virtual
winery, sourcing grapes from all over SA, with contract winemaking by Brian Light at the Boar's
Rock winemaking facility. There are 5 ranges, headed by The Wara Manta Reserve, followed by the
Nardone Baker, Blaxland's Legacy, Treeview Selection and Wara Manta (non-reserve). Exports to
various markets including the US and the UK.

YYYY **Chardonnay 2005** Quite fragrant grapefruit and melon aromas; light, fresh palate with a
crisp finish. Good unoaked wine. Cork. 13.5° alc. **RATING** 87 **DRINK** Now $ 13.95
Shiraz 2004 Light- to medium-bodied; ripe plummy fruit with just a hint of sweetness;
cleverly made. Cork. 14° alc. **RATING** 87 **DRINK** Now $ 13.95

YYYY **Cabernet Merlot 2004** **RATING** 85 **DRINK** 2008 $ 13.95

Narkoojee ★★★★★

170 Francis Road, Glengarry, Vic 3854 **REGION** Gippsland
T (03) 5192 4257 **F** (03) 5192 4257 **WWW.**narkoojee.com **OPEN** 7 days 10.30–4.30
WINEMAKER Harry Friend, Axel Friend **EST.** 1981 **CASES** 3000
Narkoojee Vineyard is within easy reach of the old goldmining town of Walhalla and looks out over
the Strzelecki Ranges. The wines are produced from a little over 10 ha of estate vineyards, with
chardonnay accounting for half the total. Harry Friend was an amateur winemaker of note before
turning to commercial winemaking with Narkoojee; his skills show through with all the wines, none
more so than the Chardonnay. Small amounts are exported.

YYYYY **Trafalgar Gippsland Chardonnay 2004** Glowing green-yellow; fine, intense; beautiful
grapefruit and nectarine mix, perfect oak. Just a lovely wine. Cork. 13.5° alc. **RATING** 95
DRINK 2014 $ 18
Reserve Gippsland Chardonnay 2004 A super-elegant and fine style; melon, white
peach and grapefruit; finely integrated and balance oak. The only white wine in a group of
50 wines tasted mid Dec '05 with a cork, perhaps due to the designer bottle. Cork. 14° alc.
RATING 94 **DRINK** 2010 $ 32

Myrtle Point Gippsland Shiraz 2004 Medium purple-red; attractive medium-bodied wine offering raspberry, black cherry and blackberry fruits supported by fine tannins and well-judged oak. Cork. 14° alc. RATING 94 DRINK 2015 $ 20

Gippsland Cabernet Sauvignon 2003 Strong red-purple; perfectly ripened blackcurrant fruit; a silky texture and structure; fine, ripe tannins and exemplary oak. Cork. 14° alc. RATING 94 DRINK 2015 $ 28

ϔϔϔϔϓ **Lily Grace Gippsland Chardonnay 2004** Medium-bodied; peach, nectarine and grapefruit; good structure and balance; oak evident, but suitably restrained. From younger estate-grown material. Cork. 13.5° alc. RATING 92 DRINK 2012 $ 23

Gippsland Pinot Noir 2004 Medium red-purple, no browning; lush, sweet, plum and dark cherry fruit; round and supple texture; much going for it. Cork. 13.5° alc. RATING 92 DRINK 2011 $ 19

ϔϔϔϔ **The Athelstan Gippsland Merlot 2003** Light- to medium-bodied; distinctly varietal cedary/savoury/earthy spicy characters, the tannins fine. Just a little too much of the varietal Worcestershire sauce. Cork. 14° alc. RATING 89 DRINK 2013 $ 35

ϔϔϔϓ **Yorkie's Gully Gippsland Rose 2004** Clean, dry, bright fruits, but acidity too prominent. RATING 86 DRINK Now $ 15

ϔϔϔ **Sparkling Cabernet 2002** RATING 82 $ 25

Nashdale Wines   NR

Borenore Lane, Nashdale, NSW 2800 REGION Orange
T (02) 6365 2463 F (02) 6361 4495 OPEN W'ends 2–6
WINEMAKER Mark Davidson (Contract) EST. 1990 CASES 1000
Orange solicitor Edward Fardell began establishing the 10-ha Nashdale Vineyard in 1990. At an elevation of 1000m, it offers panoramic views of Mt Canobolas and the Lidster Valley; a restaurant/café is open on weekends.

Nassau Estate   NR

Fish Fossil Drive, Canowindra, NSW 2804 REGION Cowra
T (02) 9267 4785 F (02) 9267 3844 OPEN Not
WINEMAKER Andrew Margan (Contract) EST. 1996 CASES 1500
The Curran family established its 110-ha vineyard adjacent to the Belubula River at Canowindra in 1996. The vineyard was named in honour of forebear Joseph Barbeler, who had been involved in a similar endeavour 140 years earlier in the Duchy of Nassau on the river Rhine near Frankfurt. A significant proportion of the grapes is contracted for sale to one of Australia's largest wineries; selected amounts are retained and contract-made for the Nassau Estate label.

Nazaaray   NR

266 Meakins Road, Flinders, Vic 3929 REGION Mornington Peninsula
T (03) 9585 1138 F (03) 9585 1140 WWW.nazaaray.com.au OPEN 1st weekend of each month, or by appt
WINEMAKER Paramdeep Ghumman EST. 1996 CASES 600
Paramdeep Ghumman is, as far as I am aware, the only Indian-born winery proprietor and winemaker in Australia. He and his wife migrated from India over 20 years ago, and purchased the Nazaaray vineyard property in 1991. An initial trial planting of 400 vines in 1996 was gradually expanded to the present level of 1.6 ha of pinot noir, 0.4 ha of pinot gris and 0.15 ha of chardonnay. Notwithstanding the micro size of the estate, all the wines are made and bottled onsite.

Neagles Rock Vineyards   ★★★★★

Lot 1 & 2 Main North Road, Clare, SA 5453 REGION Clare Valley
T (08) 8843 4020 F (08) 8843 4021 WWW.neaglesrock.com OPEN 7 days 10–5
WINEMAKER Steve Wiblin, John Trotter (Consultant) EST. 1997 CASES 10 000
Owner-partners Jane Willson and Steve Wiblin have taken the plunge in a major way, simultaneously raising a young family, resuscitating 2 old vineyards, and — for good measure —

stripping a dilapidated house to the barest of bones and turning it into a first-rate, airy restaurant-cum-cellar door. They bring decades of industry experience, gained at all levels of the wine industry, to Neagles Rock, and built upon this by the 2003 acquisition of the outstanding and mature vineyards of Duncan Estate, adding another level of quality to their wines, which now draw on a total of 24 ha. Exports to the UK, The Netherlands and Malaysia.

ΥΥΥΥΥ **Clare Valley Riesling 2005** Lime, herb, lemon and apple aromas and flavours; very good mouthfeel and balance; delicate but long finish. Screwcap. **RATING** 94 **DRINK** 2015 $ 18
Frisky Filly Reserve Clare Valley Riesling 2005 Tight, reserved, but spotless bouquet; a similarly tightly focused palate, with nigh on perfect acid balance; not unlike a young Hunter semillon; simply needs time. Screwcap. 12.5° alc. **RATING** 94 **DRINK** 2015 $ 30
Clare Valley Shiraz 2004 Medium- to full-bodied; blackberry, plum, licorice and dark chocolate; supple fine-grained tannins; good oak. Cork. 15° alc. **RATING** 94 **DRINK** 2014 $ 22
Clare Valley Sangiovese 2004 Good colour for the variety; medium-bodied, fresh spicy, cherry and strawberry aromas and flavours; strongly varietal and easily carries the alcohol thanks to the acidity. Outstanding example of an often disappointing variety in Australia. Screwcap. 15° alc. **RATING** 94 **DRINK** 2010 $ 22

ΥΥΥΥΥ **Clare Valley Cabernet Sauvignon 2004** Powerful wine; lots of blackcurrant/blackberry/chocolate fruit; balanced, ripe tannins, good oak. Cork. 15° alc. **RATING** 93 **DRINK** 2017 $ 22
Clare Valley Sangiovese 2003 Clean, spicy, cedary aromas; attractive cherry and spice palate; medium-bodied, with balanced and integrated tannins; good example of the variety. Attractive savoury note throughout; carries alcohol. Screwcap. 15° alc. **RATING** 90 **DRINK** 2010 $ 22

ΥΥΥΥ **Clare Valley Semillon Sauvignon Blanc 2005** Clean; light- to medium-bodied; grass, citrus, herb and mineral mix; a clean, lively finish. Screwcap. 13.5° alc. **RATING** 89 **DRINK** 2008 $ 18

ΥΥΥΥ **Sweet Dorothy Cabernet Rose 2005** **RATING** 86 **DRINK** Now $ 18

Neighbours Vineyards

NR

75 Fullarton Road, Kent Town, SA 5067 (postal) **REGION** McLaren Vale
T (08) 8331 8656 **F** (08) 8331 8443 **OPEN** Not
WINEMAKER Chester Osborn **EST.** 1995 **CASES** 500
Esteemed (and dare I say now senior) journalist Bob Mayne planted 1.6 ha of shiraz in McLaren Vale in 1995, without any clear objective in mind; he was certainly not venturing into winemaking. However, one thing leads to another, and in 1998 he formed Neighbours Vineyards Pty Ltd, its 14 shareholders all being McLaren Vale grapegrowers.

Nelson Touch

NR

Hamilton Road, Denmark, WA 6333 **REGION** Denmark
T (08) 9385 3552 **F** (08) 9286 2060 **OPEN** Not
WINEMAKER Michael Staniforth (Contract) **EST.** 1990 **CASES** 2000
Barbara and Brett Nelson began the development of their vineyard back in 1990, and until 1999 sold all the grapes to other wineries, including Howard Park. While Howard Park continues to receive some grapes, the lion's share of the plantings of the 1.5 ha each of sauvignon blanc, pinot noir and cabernet sauvignon, plus 0.5 ha of merlot, is now used for the Nelson Touch label. The name comes from the saying that Admiral Nelson had the 'Nelson touch' when he defeated the French, because everything he did turned to naval gold.

Nelwood Wines

NR

PO Box 237, Paringa, SA 5340 **REGION** Riverland
T (08) 8595 8042 **F** (08) 8595 8182 **WWW**.nelwood.com **OPEN** Not
WINEMAKER Boar's Rock (Mike Farmilo) **EST.** 2002 **CASES** 9000
The wines (released under the Red Mud label) come from 45-ha plantings of shiraz, chardonnay, petit verdot and cabernet sauvignon near Nelwood, 32 km east of Renmark near the SA border. The grapegrowers who are shareholders in the company have been growing grapes for up to 3 generations in the Riverland.

Nepenthe Vineyards ★★★★☆

Jones Road, Balhannah, SA 5242 **REGION** Adelaide Hills
T (08) 8398 8888 **F** (08) 8388 1100 **WWW**.nepenthe.com.au **OPEN** 7 days 10–4
WINEMAKER Peter Leske, Michael Paxton **EST.** 1994 **CASES** 80 000
The Tweddell family has established a little over 160 ha of close-planted vineyards at Lenswood since 1994, with an exotic array of varieties. In late 1996 it obtained the second licence to build a winery in the Adelaide Hills (Petaluma was the only prior successful applicant, back in 1978). Nepenthe quickly established its reputation as a substantial producer of high-quality wines. Exports to all major markets.

♟♟♟♟♟ **Ithaca Adelaide Hills Chardonnay 2003** Elegant and fragrant; a beautifully precise and seamless palate of citrus, stone fruit and oak; long, clean finish. Screwcap. 14° alc.
RATING 94 **DRINK** 2011 $ 38

♟♟♟♟♟ **Adelaide Hills Riesling 2005** Aromatic, flowery and fragrant, the faintest hint of reduction [is] acceptable; a lovely, lively palate with crisp citrus and passionfruit flavours. Screwcap. 13.5° alc. **RATING** 93 **DRINK** 2015 $ 20
Adelaide Hills Sauvignon Blanc 2005 Very pale; strongly mineral-accented aroma; powerful mineral, grass, herb and asparagus flavours; long finish. Screwcap. 13° alc.
RATING 92 **DRINK** 2009 $ 20
The Good Doctor Pinot Noir 2003 Light-bodied; spicy/savoury/foresty notes, but with a core of sweet plum fruit; silky tannins, good finish. Screwcap. **RATING** 90 **DRINK** 2008 $ 38

♟♟♟♟ **Tryst Semillon Sauvignon Blanc 2005** Very pale straw-green; clean, fresh, crisp; ripe apple and kiwifruit; well-balanced. Screwcap. 12.5° alc. **RATING** 89 **DRINK** 2008 $ 14.99
Charleston Pinot Noir 2004 Quite fragrant black fruit aromas; a powerful palate, threatened, though not overwhelmed, by tannins. Screwcap. 14° alc. **RATING** 89
DRINK 2010 $ 22
Adelaide Hills Unoaked Chardonnay 2005 Quite flowery; grapefruit, passionfruit and nectarine aromas and flavours, the fluid palate with length. Screwcap. 14° alc. **RATING** 88
DRINK Now $ 17
Adelaide Hills Zinfandel 2003 Not without some of the contrasting characters of the Tempranillo; spice, herb and berry, fine tannins; good structure. Cork. 15° alc. **RATING** 88
DRINK 2009 $ 35
Adelaide Hills Pinot Gris 2005 Spotlessly clean; one of those painting-with-white-paint styles, correct but unexciting. Screwcap. 14° alc. **RATING** 87 **DRINK** 2008 $ 22
The Fugue 2002 Aromatic and spicy, with touches of pickle on a light- to medium-bodied palate; the tannins in minor support. A 4-variety Bordeaux blend. Cork. 14° alc. **RATING** 87
DRINK 2008 $ 30
Limited Release Tempranillo 2004 A spicy, tangy, zesty mix of sweet and almost lemony notes, yet not sweet and sour. Difficult to categorise. Screwcap. 14° alc. **RATING** 87
DRINK 2009 $ 28

♟♟♟♡ **Tryst Cabernet Tempranillo Zinfandel 2004** **RATING** 86 **DRINK** Now $ 12.80

New England Estate NR

Delungra, NSW 2403 **REGION** Northern Slopes Zone
T (02) 6724 8508 **F** (02) 6724 8507 **OPEN** 7 days 10–5
WINEMAKER John Cassegrain (Contract) **EST.** 1997 **CASES** NA
New England Estate is 33 km west of Inverell; Ross Thomas has established a very substantial vineyard of 36 ha planted to chardonnay, cabernet sauvignon, merlot and shiraz. The cellar door has barbecue and picnic facilities; there is also a museum and accommodation available.

New Era Vineyard

NR

PO Box 239, Woodside, SA 5244 **REGION** Adelaide Hills
T (08) 8389 7562 **F** (08) 8389 7562 **OPEN** Not
WINEMAKER Paracombe **EST.** 1988 **CASES** NA
Patricia Wark's 12.5-ha vineyard, planted to chardonnay, cabernet sauvignon, merlot and shiraz, is under long-term contract to Wolf Blass, providing grapes for the Wolf Blass Adelaide Hills Cabernet Merlot. A tiny proportion of cabernet sauvignon is retained and contract-made.

New Mediterranean Winery

NR

Lot 2 McMillans Road, Boort, Vic 3537 **REGION** Central Victoria Zone
T (03) 5455 2274 **F** (03) 5455 2615 **WWW**.akrasiwine.com.au **OPEN** By appt
WINEMAKER George Tallis **EST.** 1997 **CASES** 500
It is unlikely that you will come across Boort by accident. It falls roughly between the Calder and Loddon highways as they wend their way north towards the Murray River and the NSW border; Kerang, 51 km to the north, is the nearest landmark of any significance. George Tallis commenced home winemaking in the early 1990s, initially simply for his benefit and that of his immediate family. Success led to relatively small commercial winemaking under the Akrasi brand, strongly influenced by Tallis' Greek ancestry. Indeed, the word 'Akrasi' comes from the Greek name of George Tallis' home town. Taking away the letter A you are left with 'krasi' which in Greek means wine.

Nicholson River

★★★☆

Liddells Road, Nicholson, Vic 3882 **REGION** Gippsland
T (03) 5156 8241 **F** (03) 5156 8433 **WWW**.nicholsonriverwinery.com.au **OPEN** 7 days 10–4
WINEMAKER Ken Eckersley **EST.** 1978 **CASES** 3000
The fierce commitment to quality in the face of the temperamental Gippsland climate and frustratingly small production has been handsomely repaid by some massive Chardonnays and quixotic red wines (from 9 ha of estate plantings). Ken Eckersley refers to his Chardonnays not as white wines but as gold wines, and lists them accordingly in his newsletter. Exports to the UK, the US and Thailand.

ㅜㅜㅜㅜ **Botrytis Chardonnay 2001** Rich, complex peachy fruit; holding on very well; great colour. Cork. 14.2° alc. **RATING** 90 **DRINK** 2008 $ 16

ㅜㅜㅜㅜ **Shiraz 2003** Dense colour; chunky, full-bodied style with excellent shiraz varietal fruit, just a little over-extracted. Cork. 13° alc. **RATING** 88 **DRINK** 2012 $ 30

ㅜㅜㅜㅜ **Chardonnay 2004 RATING** 86 **DRINK** Now
Riesling 2004 RATING 84 **DRINK** Now

Nightingale Wines

★★★

1239 Milbrodale Road, Broke, NSW 2330 **REGION** Lower Hunter Valley
T (02) 6579 1499 **F** (02) 6579 1477 **WWW**.nightingalewines.com.au **OPEN** 7 days 10–4
WINEMAKER Nigel Robinson, Paul Nightingale **EST.** 1997 **CASES** 18 000
Paul and Gail Nightingale have wasted no time since establishing their business in 1997. They have planted 3 ha each of verdelho and merlot, 2 ha of shiraz, 1.5 ha each of chardonnay and cabernet sauvignon and 1 ha of chambourcin. Exports to NZ.

ㅜㅜㅜㅜ **Verdelho 2005 RATING** 86 **DRINK** Now $ 19

Nillahcootie Estate

★★★☆

RMB 1637, Lima South, Vic 3673 **REGION** Upper Goulburn
T (03) 5768 2685 **F** (03) 5768 2678 **WWW**.nillahcootieestate.com.au **OPEN** Thurs 2–5, Fri & Sat 12–11, Sun 12–5
WINEMAKER Plunkett Wines (Sam Plunkett), Kilchurn Wines (David Cowburn) **EST.** 1988 **CASES** 1000
Karen Davy and Michael White decided to diversify their primary business of beef cattle production on their 280-ha property in 1988. Between then and 2001 they planted a little over 8 ha of grapes,

initially content to sell the production to other local wineries, but in 2001 they retained a small proportion of the grapes for winemaking, increasing it the following year to its current level. In 2001 they also purchased a 20-ha property overlooking Lake Nillahcootie, on which they have built a strikingly designed restaurant and cellar door.

♥♥♥♥ **Shiraz 2003** Savoury bramble and briar aromas; more black fruit flavours come through on the palate, which finishes with ripe tannins. Cork. 14° alc. **RATING** 89 **DRINK** 2013 $ 22

Sparkling Shiraz 2003 Big, bold style with masses of flavour; dark fruits and controlled dosage; will improve in bottle. 13.5° alc. **RATING** 87 **DRINK** 2010 $ 29

♥♥♥♀ **Unwooded Chardonnay 2005** **RATING** 86 **DRINK** Now $ 20

Nirvana Estate   NR

339 Sandy Creek Road, Kilcoy, Qld 4515 **REGION** Queensland Coastal
T (07) 5498 1055 **F** (07) 5498 1099 **OPEN** Tues–Sun & public hols 10–5
WINEMAKER Contract **EST.** 1996 **CASES** NA
Julie Doolan has 5.3 ha planted to sauvignon blanc, semillon, chardonnay, cabernet sauvignon, merlot and shiraz, contract-made. The cellar door offers light meals, and can cater for concerts.

No Regrets Vineyard   ★★★★

40 Dillons Hill Road, Glaziers Bay, Tas 7109 **REGION** Southern Tasmania
T (03) 6295 1509 **F** (03) 6295 1509 **OPEN** By appt, also at Salamanca Market, Hobart, most Saturdays
WINEMAKER Hood Wines (Andrew Hood, Alain Rousseau) **EST.** 2000 **CASES** 400
Having sold Elsewhere Vineyard, Eric and Jette Phillips have planted another vineyard almost next door, called No Regrets. This is their 'retirement' vineyard, where they will be producing only one wine from 1 ha of pinot noir.

♥♥♥♥ **Pinot Noir 2004** Medium-bodied; gently spicy, savoury; has a nice core of sweet fruit, then good length and persistence. Possibly some volatile acidity. **RATING** 89 **DRINK** 2009 $ 22

🐌 Noland Bay   NR

1/61 Cameron Street, Launceston, Tas 7250 (postal) **REGION** Northern Tasmania
T 0408 127 725 **F** (03) 6223 1802 **OPEN** Not
WINEMAKER Andrew Hood, Guy Wagner (Contract) **EST.** 1984 **CASES** 1100
David Wise began establishing his 6.8 ha vineyard (2 ha each of pinot noir, riesling and cabernet sauvignon, and 0.8 ha of chardonnay) in 1984. The vines are planted on deep red basalt soils, and have been dry-grown since the word go. Rejuvenation of the trellis, and the battle against disease has succeeded, and it is intended to increase plantings to 15 ha over the next 3 years. A cellar door is planned for 2007.

Noon Winery   NR

Rifle Range Road, McLaren Vale, SA 5171 **REGION** McLaren Vale
T (08) 8323 8290 **F** (08) 8323 8290 **OPEN** W'ends 10–5 in November (while stock is available)
WINEMAKER Drew Noon **EST.** 1976 **CASES** 2500
Drew Noon returned to McLaren Vale and purchased Noon's from his parents (though father David still keeps an eye on things), having spent many years as a consultant oenologist and viticulturist in Vic, and thereafter as winemaker at Cassegrain. Some spectacular and unusual wines have followed, such as the 17.9° alcohol Solaire Grenache, styled like an Italian Amarone. Low prices mean each year's release sells out in 4–5 weeks, during which time the cellar door is open; all wines are subject to quantity limits. Exports to all major markets.

Noosa Valley Winery   NR

855 Noosa–Eumundi Road, Doonan, Qld 4562 **REGION** Queensland Coastal
T (07) 5449 1675 **F** (07) 5449 1679 **OPEN** Wed–Sat 11–5
WINEMAKER Robinsons Family Vineyards **EST.** 1999 **CASES** NA
Irish-born George and Sue Mullins came to Australia over 30 years ago, but it was not until 1999 that
they purchased the property and opened a B&B business. The potential for wine became obvious,
and 550 chambourcin vines were planted in 2000 at the front of the 5-ha property, giving rise to the
first vintage in 2003. The cellar door also acts as a satellite cellar door for Robinsons Family
Vineyards.

Norfolk Rise Vineyard   ★★★★☆

Limestone Coast Road, Mount Benson, SA 5265 **REGION** Mount Benson
T (08) 8768 5080 **F** (08) 8768 5083 **WWW**.norfolkrise.com.au **OPEN** Mon–Fri 9–5
WINEMAKER Steve Grimley **EST.** 2000 **CASES** 85 000
This is by far the largest and most important development in the Mount Benson region. It is
ultimately owned by a privately held Belgian company, G & C Kreglinger, established in 1797.
Kreglinger Australia was established in 1893 as an agribusiness export company specialising in sheep
skins. In early 2002 it acquired Pipers Brook Vineyard; it will maintain the separate brands of the
two ventures. The Mount Benson development commenced in 2000, with a 160-ha vineyard and a
2000-tonne winery, primarily aimed at the export market.

▼▼▼▼▼ **Sauvignon Blanc 2005** Light straw-green; a spotless bouquet; delicious passionfruit,
gooseberry and more herbaceous notes; good mouthfeel and length. Screwcap. 13° alc.
RATING 93 **DRINK** Now
Pinot Grigio 2005 Pale straw; quite vibrant green apple, pear and citrus flavours; crisp,
dry, lingering finish. Screwcap. 13° alc. **RATING** 93 **DRINK** Now
Cabernet Sauvignon 2004 Bright colour; particularly elegant, silky mouthfeel; sweet, but
not jammy, cassis/blackcurrant fruit; fine tannins, integrated oak. Screwcap. 14° alc.
RATING 93 **DRINK** 2017
Shiraz 2004 Excellent hue; light- to medium-bodied; an elegant, supple wine with
spicy/peppery black cherry and blackberry fruit; slightly dusty tannins. Screwcap.
13.5° alc. **RATING** 91 **DRINK** 2015

Normanby Wines   ★★★

Rose-Lea Vineyard, 178 Dunns Avenue, Harrisville, Qld 4307 **REGION** Queensland Zone
T (07) 5467 1214 **F** (07) 5467 1023 **WWW**.normanbywines.com.au **OPEN** 7 days Winter 10–5, Summer
10–7
WINEMAKER Rumbalara (Mike Cragg), Symphony Hill (Mike Hayes) **EST.** 1999 **CASES** 700
Normanby Wines, about 50 km due south of Ipswich, fills in more of the Qld viticultural jigsaw
puzzle. The vineyard has just under 3 ha planted to verdelho, shiraz, merlot, viognier, chambourcin,
durif and grenache.

▼▼▼▼ **Verdelho 2005** Well-enough made; has recognisable varietal character, with pear, peach,
fruit salad flavours. Estate-grown. Cork. 14.4° alc. **RATING** 86 **DRINK** Now $ 20
Durif 2004 Has to be the lightest durif made in Australia or anywhere else; a quasi-rose,
with fresh, lively, citrussy flavours, and no (conventional) varietal character, which some
might argue to be a thoroughly good thing. Screwcap. 11.5° alc. **RATING** 86 **DRINK** Now
$ 20
Shiraz 2003 RATING 85 **DRINK** 2008 $ 25
Chambourcin 2003 RATING 84 **DRINK** Now $ 18

▼▼▼ **Sweet Caresse 2003 RATING** 83 $ 15

Normans

NR

Grant's Gully Road, Clarendon, SA 5157 **REGION** Adelaide Hills
T (08) 8383 5555 **F** (08) 8383 5551 **WWW**.xanadunormans.com.au **OPEN** Mon–Sat 9–4
WINEMAKER Natasha Mooney, Hugh Thomson **EST.** 1853 **CASES** 50 000
After 3 years of ownership by Xanadu, Normans and Next Generation Wines were sold in early 2005, taking Xanadu back to its base, and leaving the future of the Normans and Next Generation brands in temporary limbo.

Norse Wines

NR

24 Damascus Road, Gin Gin, Qld 4671 **REGION** Queensland Coastal
T (07) 4157 3636 **F** (07) 4157 3637 **OPEN** 7 days 10–5
WINEMAKER Thomas Janstrom, Peter Janstrom **EST.** 1998 **CASES** NA
Peter and Dianna Janstrom have established their 2-ha vineyard 37 km west of Bundaberg. Here they have chardonnay, verdelho, shiraz, cabernet sauvignon and touriga nationale, producing both table and fortified wines.

Norton Estate

★★★★★

758 Plush Hannan Road, Lower Norton, Vic 3400 **REGION** Western Victoria Zone
T (03) 5384 8235 **F** (03) 8384 8235 **OPEN** 7 days 10–5
WINEMAKER Hamish Seabrook (Contract) **EST.** 1997 **CASES** 1250
Donald Spence worked for the Victorian Department of Forests for 36 years before retiring. In 1996 he and his family purchased a farm at Lower Norton, and, instead of farming wool, meat and wheat, trusted their instincts and planted vines on the lateritic buckshot soil. The vineyard is 6 km northwest of the Grampians GI, and will have to be content with the Western Victoria Zone until a sufficient number of others follow suit and plant on the around 1000 ha of suitable soil in the area.

TTTTT **Shiraz 2004** Great colour; rich, ripe blackberry, licorice, spice and pepper aromas and flavours; despite this abundance, controlled alcohol helps create finesse and elegance. Cork. 13.8° alc. **RATING** 95 **DRINK** 2016 $ 22
Limited Release Cabernet Sauvignon 2003 Good colour notwithstanding 30 months in oak; full-bodied, in complete contrast to the varietal release; powerful, brooding black fruits, with touches of chocolate and mocha; potent tannins which are, however, largely in balance. Cork. **RATING** 94 **DRINK** 2018 $ 22

TTTTY **Sauvignon Blanc 2005** Spotlessly clean; clear-cut varietal fruit midway between grass and tropical; harmonious mouthfeel and balance; very well-made. Screwcap. 12.5° alc. **RATING** 93 **DRINK** Now $ 16
Shiraz 2003 Deep colour; a potent, powerful mix of spice, pepper, blackberry, licorice and prune; drought year tannins twitch the finish. Cork. 14° alc. **RATING** 93 **DRINK** 2013 $ 22

TTTT **Cabernet Sauvignon 2003** Medium-bodied; slightly cooked/jammy cassis and blackcurrant fruit; controlled extract and oak. Cork. 13° alc. **RATING** 89 **DRINK** 2010 $ 22

Nowra Hill Vineyard

NR

222 BTU Road, Nowra Hill, NSW 2540 **REGION** Shoalhaven Coast
T (02) 4447 8362 **F** (02) 4447 8362 **OPEN** W'ends & public hols 10–4
WINEMAKER Bevan Wilson, Bruce McLeod **EST.** 1998 **CASES** 450
Bruce and Judy McLeod progressively established a micro-vineyard of chambourcin, verdelho, malbec, chardonnay and cabernet sauvignon between 1998 and 2004. It is situated on a north-facing slope, with sweeping views of the Cambewarra Mountains, and all the wine is sold through the adjacent cellar door, by mail order and through a handful of local outlets. The quaintly named BTU Road, incidentally, runs off the Princes Highway south of Nowra, and leads to the HMAS Albatross Base. In September 2005 the business was purchased by Mark and Nikki Reminis.

Nugan Estate

60 Banna Avenue, Griffith, NSW 2680 **REGION** Riverina
T (02) 6962 1822 **F** (02) 6962 6392 **OPEN** Mon–Fri 9–5
WINEMAKER Darren Owers **EST.** 1999 **CASES** 400 000
Nugan Estate arrived on the scene like a whirlwind. It is an offshoot of the Nugan group, a family company established over 60 years ago in Griffith as a broad-based agricultural business. It is headed by Michelle Nugan, *inter alia* the recipient of an Export Hero Award in 2000. In the mid-1990s the company began developing vineyards, and is now a veritable giant, with 310 ha at Darlington Point, 52 ha at Hanwood and 120 ha at Hillston (all in NSW), 100 ha in the King Valley, and 10 ha in McLaren Vale. In addition, it has contracts in place to buy 1000 tonnes of grapes per year from Coonawarra. It sells part of the production as grapes, part as bulk wine and part under the Cookoothama and Nugan Estate labels. Exports to the US, Canada, Ireland, Norway, Denmark, Sweden and NZ.

ＹＹＹＹＹ **Frasca's Lane Vineyard Chardonnay 2004** Bright green-yellow; attractive melon and yellow peach fruit; plenty of richness and substance, and a positive French oak backdrop. Screwcap. 13.8° alc. **RATING** 90 **DRINK** 2008 $ 20
Frasca's Lane Vineyard Chardonnay 2003 Attractive stone fruit aromas and flavours; medium-bodied; good balance and length; developing well. Screwcap. **RATING** 90 **DRINK** 2008 $ 20
Alfredo Frasca's Lane Vineyard Sangiovese Merlot 2003 Spicy, savoury black olive and blackcurrant aromas and flavours; a classy, medium-bodied wine with good structure and balance. Cork. **RATING** 90 **DRINK** 2010 $ 24

ＹＹＹＹ **Frasca's Lane Vineyard Pinot Grigio 2005** Very much in grigio style; an appealing mix of mineral, citrus and green apple fruit. Good length. Screwcap. 13.5° alc. **RATING** 89 **DRINK** Now $ 20
Alcira Vineyard Coonawarra Cabernet Sauvignon 2002 Fresh, clean, lively, sweet red and black fruits; medium-bodied; oak and tannins balanced and integrated; nice wine. Cork. **RATING** 89 **DRINK** 2012 $ 24.95
Cookoothama Darlington Point Botrytis Semillon 2004 Rich, almost syrupy peachy fruit partially off-set by acidity. Cork. **RATING** 89 **DRINK** 2008 $ 22.95
Cookoothama King Valley Sauvignon Blanc Semillon 2005 Well-made; nicely balanced tropical Sauvignon Blanc and off-setting Semillon, the small portion barrel-fermented providing texture and length. Screwcap. 13° alc. **RATING** 88 **DRINK** Now $ 15
Talinga Park Sauvignon Blanc 2005 **RATING** 87 **DRINK** Now $ 9.95

ＹＹＹＹ **Cookoothama Darlington Point Shiraz 2003** **RATING** 86 **DRINK** 2008 $ 16.95
Cookoothama King Valley Riesling 2005 **RATING** 85 **DRINK** Now $ 16
Talinga Park Chardonnay 2004 **RATING** 85 **DRINK** Now $ 9.95
Talinga Park Cabernet Merlot 2004 **RATING** 84 **DRINK** Now $ 9.95

Nuggetty Vineyard NR

280 Maldon–Shelbourne Road, Nuggetty, Vic 3463 **REGION** Bendigo
T (03) 5475 1347 **F** (03) 5475 1647 **WWW**.nuggettyvineyard.com.au **OPEN** W'ends & public hols 10–4, or by appt
WINEMAKER Greg Dedman, Jackie Dedman **EST.** 1993 **CASES** 2000
The family-owned vineyard was established in 1993 by Greg and Jackie Dedman. Greg is a Charles Sturt University graduate, while Jackie (having spent 18 months at Bowen Estate in 1997/8) has simultaneously undertaken the wine marketing degree at Charles Sturt University and the winemaking degree at the Adelaide University. They share the vineyard and winery tasks (including contract winemaking for others); these include 6.5 ha of estate plantings (semillon, shiraz and cabernet sauvignon).

Nursery Ridge Estate

NR

Calder Highway, Red Cliffs, Vic 3496 **REGION** Murray Darling
T (03) 5024 3311 **F** (03) 5024 3114 **OPEN** By appt
WINEMAKER Bob Shields **EST.** 1999 **CASES** 5000
The estate takes its name from the fact that it is situated on the site of the original vine nursery at Red Cliffs. It is a family-owned and operated affair, with shiraz, cabernet sauvignon, chardonnay, petit verdot and viognier. A cellar door and winery on the Calder Highway opened in 2001. The well priced wines are usually well-made, with greater richness and depth of fruit flavour than most other wines from the region. Production has risen substantially, and, if all goes well, will continue to do so.

Nyora Vineyard & Winery

★★☆

Cnr Peacock & Williams Roads, The Gurdies, Vic 3984 **REGION** Gippsland
T (03) 5997 6205 **OPEN** Wed–Mon 10–6
WINEMAKER Klaus Griese, Denise Griese **EST.** 1995 **CASES** 600
Klaus and Denise Griese have established a Joseph's Coat of varieties since 1995; in descending order shiraz, chardonnay, cabernet sauvignon, sauvignon blanc, colombard, semillon, pinot noir, pinot gris, merlot, riesling and verdelho totalling a little under 5 ha in all. The vineyard is planted on a northeast slope near the top of the ridge overlooking the Bass River Valley, and a 3-storey winery (the bottom floor underground) has been built. All of the wines are, to a lesser or greater degree, sweet, and aimed at the cellar door.

▼▼▼▼ **Pinot Noir 2005 RATING** 84 $ 20

▼▼▼ **Late Picked Semi Sweet Pinot Noir 2005 RATING** 83 $ 20

O'Donohoe's Find

★★★★☆

PO Box 460, Berri, SA 5343 **REGION** Riverland
T 0414 765 813 **F** (08) 8583 2228 **WWW**.tomsdrop.com.au **OPEN** Not
WINEMAKER Michael O'Donohoe **EST.** 2002 **CASES** 600
Michael O'Donohoe pays tribute to his Irish grandfather, Thomas O'Donohoe, and 6 great-uncles, who arrived from Ireland in 1881 to join their father in the search for gold, ending up distilling salty bore water into fresh water. A century later Michael O'Donohoe runs a small vineyard in the Riverland which was certified organic in 1990, receives very little water, and crops at around 2 tonnes per acre. The wines (released under the Tom's Drop label) are made using a tiny crusher, a small hand-operated basket press, and open fermenters. They deserve to be taken seriously.

▼▼▼▼▼ **Tom's Drop Shiraz 2005** Medium-bodied; very attractive blackberry, plum, spice and anise; fine, feathery tannins run throughout a lovely wine. Screwcap. 14° alc. **RATING** 93 **DRINK** 2015 $ 25

O'Leary Walker Wines

★★★★★

Main Road, Leasingham, SA 5452 (PO Box 49, Watervale, SA 5452) **REGION** Clare Valley
T (08) 8843 0022 **F** (08) 8843 0156 **WWW**.olearywalkerwines.com **OPEN** Mon–Fri 10–7, w'ends by appt
WINEMAKER David O'Leary, Nick Walker **EST.** 2001 **CASES** 15 000
David O'Leary and Nick Walker together have more than 30 years' experience as winemakers working for some of the biggest Australian wine groups. They then took the plunge, and backed themselves to establish their own winery and brand. Their main vineyard is at Watervale in the Clare Valley, with over 36 ha of riesling, shiraz, cabernet sauvignon, merlot and semillon. In the Adelaide Hills they have established 14 ha of chardonnay, cabernet sauvignon, pinot noir, shiraz, sauvignon blanc and merlot. Exports to the US, Canada, the UK, Indonesia and Singapore.

▼▼▼▼▼ **Polish Hill River Riesling 2005** Wonderfully fragrant floral, lime blossom aromas; great balance and mouthfeel; lingering finish. Screwcap. **RATING** 95 **DRINK** 2017 $ 20
Watervale Riesling 2005 Curiously, more minerally and tight than the Polish Hill River at first blush; crisp, fresh lime and lemon fruit then comes through. Screwcap. **RATING** 94 **DRINK** 2015 $ 20

Adelaide Hills Sauvignon Blanc 2005 Spotlessly clean; vibrant, zesty, grassy palate; lovely finish and aftertaste; very long. Screwcap. **RATING** 94 **DRINK** Now $ 20
Clare Valley McLaren Vale Shiraz 2004 Very good colour; medium-bodied plum, blackberry and chocolate fruits; considerable synergy between the 2 regions; supple mouthfeel, yet you sense the firm structure holding the parts together. Screwcap. 14.5° alc. **RATING** 94 **DRINK** 2017 $ 22

♈♈♈♈♈ **Adelaide Hills Pinot Noir 2005** Strong colour; a powerful, complex bouquet; black cherry, plum and a touch of game (good); long palate, deserves time; very different from the '04. Screwcap. 14° alc. **RATING** 91 **DRINK** 2012 $ 22
Clare Valley Cabernet Sauvignon 2004 Good colour; the faintest whiff of reduction, but really irrelevant; vibrant blackcurrant and cassis fruit supported by fine, ripe tannins. Screwcap. **RATING** 91 **DRINK** 2014 $ 22

O'Regan Creek Vineyard and Winery   NR

969 Pialba–Burrum Heads Road, Hervey Bay, Qld 4655 (postal) **REGION** Queensland Coastal
T (07) 4128 7636 **OPEN** Not
WINEMAKER John Fuerst, Cathy Fuerst **EST.** 1998 **CASES** NA
John and Cathy Fuerst have established their vineyard right on the Qld Coast, planting cabernet sauvignon, shiraz, chambourcin (doubtless suited to the climate) and zinfandel.

O'Shea & Murphy Rosebery Hill Vineyard   NR

Rosebery Hill, Pastoria Road, Pipers Creek, Vic 3444 **REGION** Macedon Ranges
T (03) 5423 5253 **F** (03) 5424 5253 **WWW**.osheamurphy.com **OPEN** By appt
WINEMAKER Barry Murphy, John O'Shea **EST.** 1984 **CASES** 3000
Planting of the 8-ha vineyard began in 1984 on a north-facing slope of red basalt soil which runs at the 550m elevation line; it is believed the hill was the site of a volcanic eruption 7 million years ago. The vines were established without the aid of irrigation (and remain unirrigated), and produced the first small crop in 1990. No grapes were produced between 1993 and 1995 owing to mildew: Murphy and O'Shea say, 'We tried to produce fruit with no sprays at all, and learned the hard way.' Part of the production is sold to others, all of whom attest to the quality of the fruit.

Oak Dale Wines   NR

40 Titford Road, Tresco, Vic 3583 **REGION** Swan Hill
T (03) 5037 2911 **F** (03) 5037 2911 **OPEN** By appt
WINEMAKER Robert Zagar (Contract) **EST.** 2000 **CASES** NA
Glen and Anne Cook have established 6.3 ha of mourvedre, muscat and sultana, the latter two especially suited to fortified wines, and the mourvedre dual purpose. The relatively small amount of wine made is sold locally, by mail order and through the cellar door when open.

Oak Valley Estate   NR

3055 Deakin Avenue, Sturt Highway, Mildura South, Vic 3502 **REGION** Murray Darling
T (03) 5021 2379 **F** (03) 5022 7283 **WWW**.oakvalleyestate.com.au **OPEN** 7 days 10–5
WINEMAKER Ferdinando DeBlasio **EST.** 2000 **CASES** 800
Ferdinando DeBlasio left Italy bound for Australia when he was 13 years old, with both grandfather and father having made wine for home consumption every year. In 1963 he purchased a 20-ha paddock on Oak Avenue (near Mildura Airport) with 4 ha of established vines. With the help of wife Joanne the plantings were slowly expanded, and completed by 1972. In 1980 a 4-ha property on Deakin Avenue was purchased, and by 1999 a little under 3 ha of shiraz had been planted, the onsite winery built the following year.

Oakover Estate ★★★

14 Yukich Close, Middle Swan, WA 6056 **REGION** Swan Valley
T (08) 9274 0777 **F** (08) 9274 0788 **WWW**.oakoverwines.com.au **OPEN** 7 days 11–4
WINEMAKER Rob Marshall **EST.** 1990 **CASES** 10 000
Owned by the Yukich family, and part of the Dalmatian Coast/Croatian cultural group in the Swan Valley, whose roots go back to the early 1900s. However, Oakover Estate is very much part of the new wave in the area, with a very large vineyard holding of 64 ha, planted predominantly to chardonnay, shiraz, chenin blanc and verdelho. Part of the production is sold to others, with increasing amounts made under the Oakover label, selling (among the other usual ways) at the large café/restaurant and function centre in the heart of the vineyard.

▼▼▼▼ **Chenin Blanc 2005** Clean, light fruit salad/apple fruit; good length, balanced acidity. Screwcap. 11.4° alc. **RATING** 87 **DRINK** 2008 $ 14

▼▼▼♀ **Verdelho 2005 RATING** 85 **DRINK** Now $ 16
Classic White 2005 RATING 85 **DRINK** Now $ 14
Shiraz 2004 RATING 85 **DRINK** 2009 $ 18
Petit Verdot 2005 RATING 85 **DRINK** 2010 $ 26
Viognier 2005 RATING 84 **DRINK** Now $ 18

Oakridge ★★★★★

864 Maroondah Highway, Coldstream, Vic 3770 **REGION** Yarra Valley
T (03) 9739 1920 **F** (03) 9739 1923 **WWW**.oakridgeestate.com.au **OPEN** 7 days 10–5
WINEMAKER David Bicknell **EST.** 1978 **CASES** NFP
The 1997 capital raising by Oakridge Vineyards Limited led to the opening of a new winery in 1998 on a prominent Maroondah Highway site. In 2001 the then struggling company was acquired by Evans & Tate. The appointment of David Bicknell (formerly for many years at De Bortoli) has revitalised the winemaking, taking it to the highest level notwithstanding the financial turmoil which, as at mid-2006, still surrounded the winery. The 864 range of wines is sold through cellar door and key restaurants nationally. Exports to the US, Canada, Switzerland and Philippines.

▼▼▼▼▼ **864 Chardonnay 2004** Light green-straw; complex barrel ferment aromas; the tight, intense palate brings nectarine, grapefruit and melon first, then a touch of oak, and then an echo of the bouquet; great length and equally great finesse. Single, Upper Yarra, vineyard. Screwcap. 13.5° alc. **RATING** 95 **DRINK** 2014 $ 50
Yarra Valley Shiraz 2004 Outstanding colour; medium-bodied; black cherry, blackberry and fine tannins; supple and smooth; is there a touch of viognier? Screwcap. **RATING** 94 **DRINK** 2015 $ 25
Yarra Valley Cabernet Sauvignon 2004 Medium-bodied; a delicious surge of sweet cassis berry fruits; fine, ripe tannins; good oak. Lovely wine. Screwcap. **RATING** 94 **DRINK** 2015 $ 30
864 Yarra Valley Riesling 2005 Intense lime juice flavours, with no modification of the varietal character; excellent balance to a wine of auslese sweetness. An extraordinary wine, the entire press placed in a refrigerated container, with the grapes (and press) held at minus 10°C, yielding 120 litres per tonne as opposed to 'normal' 750 litres. Screwcap. 9° alc. **RATING** 94 **DRINK** 2015 $ 50

▼▼▼▼♀ **Yarra Valley Chardonnay 2004** Fresh citrus, grapefruit, nectarine, with a skein of mineral woven throughout the long palate, which has absorbed the barrel ferment and French oak. Screwcap. 13.5° alc. **RATING** 93 **DRINK** 2012 $ 25
Yarra Valley Merlot 2004 Bright purple-red; medium-bodied; strongly varietal spice, black olive and blackcurrant fruit; fine tannins, appropriate oak and good length. Screwcap. **RATING** 92 **DRINK** 2015 $ 30
864 Yarra Valley Shiraz 2003 Elegant, light- to medium-bodied style; bright cherry and blackberry fruit has absorbed 14 months of French oak maturation; fine tannins, long finish. Screwcap. 13.5° alc. **RATING** 91 **DRINK** 2013 $ 50
Yarra Valley Sauvignon Blanc 2005 Spotlessly clean; light gooseberry, passionfruit and tropical fruit neatly balanced by acidity. Screwcap. 12° alc. **RATING** 90 **DRINK** Now $ 18

Yarra Valley Pinot Gris 2005 An elegant version of the variety, the lower alcohol providing more citrus notes; lively mouthfeel. Screwcap. 13.5° alc. **RATING** 90 **DRINK** 2009 $ 25

Yarra Valley Cabernet Merlot 2004 Vivid purple-red; rich, juicy blackcurrant fruit on entry, then tannins provide structure on the finish; great value. Screwcap. **RATING** 90 **DRINK** 2014 $ 18

Yarra Valley Chardonnay Pinot Noir 2001 Good mousse; fine, tangy lemon and nectarine fruit; clean finish; 3 years on lees. 12.5° alc. **RATING** 90 **DRINK** Now $ 30

♥♥♥♥ **Yarra Valley Pinot Noir 2004** Clean plum and black cherry fruit; very firm texture, needing time to soften somewhat. Screwcap. 13° alc. **RATING** 89 **DRINK** 2010 $ 24.99

864 Yarra Valley Cabernet Merlot 2003 Good colour; some reduction on the bouquet tends to suppress the fruit, amplifying savoury/earthy/leafy characters. This may be a harsh judgment not shared by others. Screwcap. 13° alc. **RATING** 87 **DRINK** 2011 $ 50

Oakvale ★★★☆

Broke Road, Pokolbin, NSW 2320 **REGION** Lower Hunter Valley
T (02) 4998 7088 **F** (02) 4998 7077 **WWW**.oakvalewines.com.au **OPEN** 7 days 10–5
WINEMAKER Cameron Webster **EST.** 1893 **CASES** 17 000
All the literature and promotional material emphasises the fact that Oakvale has been family-owned since 1893. What it does not mention is that three quite unrelated families have been the owners: first, and for much of the time, the Elliott family; then former Sydney solicitor Barry Shields; and, since 1999, Richard and Mary Owens, who also own the separately run Milbrovale winery at Broke. Be that as it may, the original slab hut homestead of the Elliott family which is now a museum, and the atmospheric Oakvale winery, are in the 'must visit' category. Exports to the UK, the US, Japan and Singapore.

♥♥♥♥ **Block 37 Verdelho 2005** Lively, fresh, citrus-tinged; has good length and life. Cork. **RATING** 88 **DRINK** 2009 $ 19.50

🐌 Oakway Estate ★★★☆

PO Box 205, Donnybrook, WA 6239 **REGION** Geographe
T (08) 9731 7141 **F** (08) 9731 7190 **WWW**.oakwayestate.com.au **OPEN** Not
WINEMAKER Frank Kittler (Contract) **EST.** 1998 **CASES** 1250
Ria and Wayne Hammond run a combined blue gum tree plantation, beef cattle and vineyard property. It has a history of apple and stone fruit orchards, which suggested to the Hammonds that it would be suitable for grapes, and hence they planted a little under 2 ha of chardonnay, merlot, cabernet sauvignon and shiraz in 1998. The wines have won a number of bronze medals in local wine shows.

♥♥♥♥ **Blue Gum Ridge Shiraz 2004** Lively, fresh plum and cherry fruit; gentle tannins, subtle oak. Screwcap. 13.5° alc. **RATING** 89 **DRINK** 2010 $ 14

Blue Gum Ridge Semillon Sauvignon Blanc 2005 An attractive mix of herbaceous/mineral notes from the semillon, and gently tropical from the sauvignon blanc; light- to medium-bodied, and does shorten somewhat. Screwcap. 12.2° alc. **RATING** 88 **DRINK** Now $ 14

Blue Gum Ridge Chardonnay 2005 Fragrant and lively unwooded style; light-bodied nectarine and grapefruit; good balance and length. Screwcap. 13.5° alc. **RATING** 88 **DRINK** 2008 $ 14

Blue Gum Ridge Merlot 2004 Light purple-red; very tangy/savoury/briary style; a light-bodied palate, but balanced; minimal oak. Screwcap. 13.5° alc. **RATING** 88 **DRINK** 2010 $ 16

Blue Gum Ridge Cabernet Shiraz 2004 More blackcurrant and blackberry fruit density and richness than the Cabernet Merlot; balanced tannins and oak. Screwcap. 13.5° alc. **RATING** 88 **DRINK** 2010 $ 14

♥♥♥♡ **Blue Gum Ridge Cabernet Merlot 2004** **RATING** 86 **DRINK** 2008 $ 14

Observatory Hill Vineyard ★★★★☆

107 Centauri Drive, Mt Rumney, Tas 7170 **REGION** Southern Tasmania
T (03) 6248 5380 **OPEN** By appt
WINEMAKER Andrew Hood, Alain Rousseau **EST.** 1991 **CASES** 500
Glenn and Chris Richardson's Observatory Hill Vineyard has been developing since 1991 when Glenn and his late father-in-law Jim Ramsey planted the first of the 8500 vines that now make up the estate. Together with the adjoining property owned by Chris' brother Wayne Ramsey and his wife Stephanie, the vineyard now covers 3 ha with new plantings having been made each year. The name 'Observatory Hill' comes from the State's oldest observatory that is perched on the hill above the vineyard.

▼▼▼▼▽ **Pinot Noir 2005** Easily the best wine in the relatively small '05 pinot class at the Tasmanian Wine Show 2006; supple, smooth, plum and cherry fruit; fine tannins. Screwcap. 14.8° alc. **RATING** 93 **DRINK** 2011 $ 28
Sauvignon Blanc 2005 Faintly reduced bouquet; a powerful, focused palate with green apple, asparagus and minerally acidity providing good length. Screwcap. 12.1° alc. **RATING** 91 **DRINK** Now $ 22
Riesling 2005 Opens quietly with spice, lime and mineral notes, which intensify through to the back-palate and finish; good acidity. Screwcap. 12.1° alc. **RATING** 90 **DRINK** 2012 $ 22

▼▼▼▼ **Cabernet Sauvignon 2004** Bright, light purple-red; predictably doesn't have nearly enough depth to convince, though the flavours are pretty. Screwcap. 12.5° alc. **RATING** 87 **DRINK** 2009 $ 25

Occam's Razor ★★★★☆

c/- Jasper Hill, Drummonds Lane, Heathcote, Vic 3523 **REGION** Heathcote
T (03) 5433 2528 **F** (03) 5433 3143 **OPEN** By appt
WINEMAKER Emily Laughton **EST.** 2001 **CASES** 350
Emily Laughton has decided to follow in her parents' footsteps after first seeing the world and having a range of casual jobs. Having grown up at Jasper Hill, winemaking was far from strange, but she decided to find her own way, buying the grapes from a small vineyard owned by Jasper Hill employee Andrew Conforti and his wife Melissa. She then made the wine 'with guidance and inspiration from my father, and with assistance from winemaker Mario Marson'. The name comes from William of Ockham (also spelt Occam) (1285–1349), a theologian and philosopher responsible for many sayings, including that appearing on the back label of the wine: 'what can be done with fewer is done in vain with more'. Exports to the US, Canada and Singapore.

▼▼▼▼▽ **Heathcote Shiraz 2004** Fragrant spicy fruit aromas; medium- to full-bodied blackberry, earth, licorice, leather and bitter chocolate; savoury tannins, controlled oak. Cork. 15° alc. **RATING** 92 **DRINK** 2019 $ 37

Ocean Eight Vineyard & Winery NR

271 Tucks Road, Shoreham, Vic 3916 **REGION** Mornington Peninsula
T (03) 5989 6471 **F** (03) 5989 6630 **WWW**.oceaneight.com **OPEN** By appt
WINEMAKER Michael Aylward **EST.** 2003 **CASES** 500
Chris, Gail and Michael Aylward were involved in the establishment of Kooyong vineyard and winery, and after selling Kooyong in 2003, retained their 5-ha pinot gris vineyard at Shoreham. After careful investigation, they purchased another property, where they have now planted 10 ha of pinot noir and 5 ha of chardonnay, both of which are yet to come into production. A small winery has been set up, and the focus will always be on quality.

Oddfellows Wines NR

PO Box 88, Langhorne Creek, SA 5255 **REGION** Langhorne Creek
T (08) 8537 3326 **F** (08) 8537 3319 **WWW**.oddfellowswines.com.au **OPEN** At Bremer Place 7 days 11–5
WINEMAKER Greg Follett **EST.** 1997 **CASES** 1500
Oddfellows is the name taken by a group of 5 individuals who decided to put their expertise, energy and investments into making premium wine. Greg Follett leads the winemaking side, David Knight the viticultural side, the others the financial and marketing side. Exports to the US and Asia.

Old Caves Winery

NR

New England Highway, Stanthorpe, Qld 4380 **REGION** Granite Belt
T (07) 4681 1494 **F** (07) 4681 2722 **OPEN** Mon–Sat 9–5, Sun 10–4
WINEMAKER David Zanatta **EST.** 1980 **CASES** 2400
Old Caves is a family business run by David Zanatta, his wife Shirley and their sons, Tony, Jeremy and Nathan, drawing on 5 ha of estate vineyards.

Old Kent River

Turpin Road, Rocky Gully, WA 6397 **REGION** Frankland River
T (08) 9855 1589 **F** (08) 9855 1660 **WWW**.valleyofthegiants.com.au/oldkentriver **OPEN** At Kent River, South Coast Highway
WINEMAKER Alkoomi (Contract), Michael Staniford **EST.** 1985 **CASES** 3000
Mark and Debbie Noack have done it tough all their lives but have earned respect from their neighbours and from the other producers to whom they sell more than half the production from the 16.5-ha vineyard on their sheep property. The quality of their wines has gone from strength to strength. Exports to Canada, the UK, The Netherlands, Hong Kong and Japan.

ΥΥΥΥΥ **Burls Reserve Pinot Noir 2004** Lively and vibrant; clear-cut varietal character; length and balance to the red cherry and plum fruit; silky, supple tannins, a peacock's tail finish. Best yet; sets the bar for WA. Cork. 14° alc. **RATING** 95 **DRINK** 2010 $ 50
Frankland River Chardonnay 2004 An intense, lively wine; barrel ferment French oak interwoven with nectarine and citrus fruit; appealing texture and structure, developing surely. Screwcap. 13.5° alc. **RATING** 94 **DRINK** 2012 $ 20

ΥΥΥΥΫ **Reserve Frankland River Pinot Noir 1997** Fully developed colour; potent, powerful savoury, foresty flavours with great length; I'm far from convinced about the price. Cork. 14.9° alc. **RATING** 93 **DRINK** Now $ 150
Frankland River Shiraz 2004 Purple-red; medium-bodied, with a silky texture to the array of plum, blackberry and spice fruits; controlled extract and oak. Cork. 14° alc. **RATING** 92 **DRINK** 2010 $ 22
Frankland River Sauvignon Blanc 2005 Light straw-green; a clean bouquet; opens up with lively tropical/passionfruit, then a more flinty/grassy/green apple finish. Screwcap. 13° alc. **RATING** 90 **DRINK** Now $ 18
Diamontina 2003 Pale straw-pink; bready/yeasty autolysis; quite sweet fruit, good acidity to balance. 12.5° alc. **RATING** 90 **DRINK** 2010 $ 30

ΥΥΥΥ **Backtrack Frankland River Chardonnay 2005** Light, fresh, crisp citrus and stone fruit; lively acidity. Unoaked. Screwcap. 13° alc. **RATING** 87 **DRINK** 2008 $ 15

Old Loddon Wines

NR

5 Serpentine Road, Bridgewater, Vic 3516 **REGION** Bendigo
T (03) 5437 3197 **F** (03) 5438 3502 **OPEN** W'ends 12–5, Mon–Fri by appt
WINEMAKER Passing Clouds **EST.** 1995 **CASES** 5000
A boutique winery overlooking the scenic Loddon River in Bridgewater, owned and managed by Jill Burdett. The 6-ha vineyard is planted to cabernet franc, merlot, cabernet sauvignon and shiraz. The first vintage was in 1995, and the winery produces full-bodied wines.

Oliverhill

NR

Seaview Road, McLaren Vale, SA 5171 **REGION** McLaren Vale
T (08) 8323 8922 **OPEN** By appt
WINEMAKER Stuart Miller **EST.** 1973 **CASES** 4000
Stuart and Linda Miller purchased the property in a thoroughly run-down state in 1993, and gradually restored the vineyard and winery. Exports to the US, Canada, Denmark, Malaysia and Hong Kong.

Olivers Taranga Vineyards ★★★★☆

Olivers Road, McLaren Vale, SA 5171 **REGION** McLaren Vale
T (08) 8323 8498 **F** (08) 8323 7498 **WWW**.oliverstaranga.com **OPEN** By appt
WINEMAKER Corrina Rayment **EST.** 1841 **CASES** 3500
1839 was the year in which William and Elizabeth Oliver arrived from Scotland to settle at McLaren Vale. Six generations later, members of the family are still living on the Whitehill and Taranga farms, 2 km north of McLaren Vale. The Taranga property has 12 varieties planted on 92 ha; historically, grapes from the property have been sold to up to 5 different wineries, but since 1994 some of the old vine shiraz has been made under the Olivers Taranga label. From the 2000 vintage, the wine has been made by Corrina Rayment (the Oliver family's first winemaker and a sixth-generation family member). Exports to the UK, the US and other major markets.

▼▼▼▼▼ **HJ Reserve Shiraz 2002** Very good colour; a restrained elegance and finesse which belies the alcohol; plum, spice and blackberry run through a long, sustained palate. Cork. 14.5° alc. **RATING** 94 **DRINK** 2013 $ 42

▼▼▼▼▽ **HJ Reserve Shiraz 2003** Good colour; a powerful but supple array of black fruits, dark chocolate and mocha; firm but fine tannins; good oak. Vines planted 1948. Cork. 14.5° alc. **RATING** 93 **DRINK** 2015 $ 42
Corrina's McLaren Vale Cabernet Shiraz 2003 A substantial wine, bringing all of the elements of the varietal mix and regional influence together; supple, ripe fruit and good oak. Cork. 14.5° alc. **RATING** 92 **DRINK** 2013 $ 28
McLaren Vale Shiraz 2003 An attractive melange of plum, blackberry, mocha and chocolate on a medium-bodied palate with good supporting tannins and oak. Cork. 14.5° alc. **RATING** 91 **DRINK** 2012 $ 28

Olsen NR

RMB 252 Osmington Road, Osmington, WA 6285 **REGION** Margaret River
T (08) 9757 4536 **F** (08) 9757 4114 **WWW**.olsen.com.au **OPEN** By appt
WINEMAKER Bernard Abbott **EST.** 1986 **CASES** 2500
Steve and AnnMarie Olsen have planted 3.25 ha of cabernet sauvignon, and 2 ha each of semillon and chardonnay, which they tend with the help of their 4 children. It was the desire to raise their children in a healthy, country environment that prompted the move to establish the vineyard, coupled with a longstanding dream to make their own wine. Not to be confused with Olsen Wines in Melbourne.

Olsen Wines NR

131 Koornang Road, Carnegie, Vic 3163 **REGION** Port Phillip Zone
T (03) 9563 5068 **F** (03) 9563 5038 **WWW**.vin888.com **OPEN** Mon–Thurs 10.30–8, Fri–Sat 10.30–9
WINEMAKER Glenn Olsen **EST.** 1991 **CASES** NFP
Glenn Olsen, a science and engineering graduate of the University of Melbourne, has been involved in the wine industry since 1975, initially importing wines and spirits from Europe, then moving into retailing. In 1991, he started Olsen Wines, claiming to be Melbourne's first inner suburban winery. Several others may dispute this claim, but that is perhaps neither here nor there. Most of the wines come either from grapes grown on the Murray River in Northeast Victoria, or from the Yarra Valley. Not to be confused with Olsen in the Margaret River.

Olssens of Watervale ★★★★☆

Sollys Hill Road, Watervale, SA 5452 **REGION** Clare Valley
T (08) 8843 0065 **F** (08) 8843 0065 **OPEN** Thurs–Sun & public hols 11–5, or by appt
WINEMAKER Contract **EST.** 1994 **CASES** 4000
Kevin and Helen Olssen first visited the Clare Valley in December 1986. Within 2 weeks they and their family decided to sell their Adelaide home and purchased a property in a small, isolated valley 3 km north of the township of Watervale. As a result of the acquisition of the Bass Hill Vineyard, estate plantings have risen to more than 32 ha, including unusual varieties such as carmenere and primitivo di Gioia. The Bass Hill project is a joint venture between parents Kevin and Helen and children David and Jane Olssen.

ŸŸŸŸŸ Clare Valley Riesling 2005 Fragrant lime blossom and passionfruit aromas; intense, lively and long; touch of CO_2; delicious wine. Screwcap. 12.5° alc. **RATING** 95 **DRINK** 2015 $20

ŸŸŸŸŸ Clare Valley Shiraz 2003 Medium- to full-bodied; powerful, rich and concentrated black fruits; well-handled spicy French oak. Screwcap. 15° alc. **RATING** 93 **DRINK** 2013 $25

ŸŸŸŸ Bass Hill Vineyard Mataro 2004 Medium red-purple; supple black and red fruits on the medium-bodied palate; plum and a touch of prune; no excess tannins. Screwcap. 14.5° alc. **RATING** 89 **DRINK** 2010 $35
Clare Valley Merlot 2004 Slightly dull colour; a light- to medium-bodied mix of ripe berry and varietal savoury characters. Screwcap. 14° alc. **RATING** 87 **DRINK** 2009 $25

ŸŸŸŸ Clare Valley Sparkling Riesling 2005 RATING 85 **DRINK** Now $20

Orange Country Wines   NR

Underwood Road, Borenore, NSW 2800 **REGION** Orange
T (02) 6365 2221 **F** (02) 6365 2227 **OPEN** 7 days 10–5
WINEMAKER Don MacLennan, David MacLennan **EST.** 1999 **CASES** NA
Don and David MacLennan have planted sauvignon blanc, semillon, chardonnay, pinot noir, cabernet sauvignon and shiraz, and are making the wines in a winery constructed with sawdust blocks and ironbark posts.

Orange Mountain Wines

Cnr Forbes Road/Radnedge Lane, Orange, NSW 2800 **REGION** Orange
T (02) 6365 2626 **WWW**.orangemountain.com.au **OPEN** W'ends & public hols 9–5
WINEMAKER Terry Dolle **EST.** 1997 **CASES** 2500
Terry Dolle has a total of 6 ha of vineyards, part at Manildra (established 1997) and the remainder at Orange (in 2001). The Manildra climate is distinctly warmer than that of Orange, and the plantings reflect the climatic difference, with pinot noir and sauvignon blanc at Orange, shiraz, cabernet sauvignon, merlot and viognier at Manildra.

ŸŸŸŸŸ Manildra Shiraz Viognier 2004 Typical deep, bright colour; medium-bodied; pleasing blackberry and black cherry fruit with hints of apricot and spice; good tannins, appropriate oak management. Screwcap. 14.5° alc. **RATING** 92 **DRINK** 2014 $25
Manildra Viognier 2005 Interesting orange/apricot blossom aromas; abundant pear and apricot varietal fruit on the palate, good acidity helping to avoid the phenolics. Screwcap. 14° alc. **RATING** 90 **DRINK** Now $22

ŸŸŸŸ Chardonnay 2003 Complex aromas with vanilla (American) oak making its mark; the peach and grapefruit palate has substantial depth and power. Screwcap. 13.5° alc. **RATING** 89 **DRINK** 2008 $18
Mountain Mud Cabernet Merlot 2004 Light- to medium-bodied; an unusual array of aromas and flavours including chopped mint, spice, berry and leaf. Central Ranges. Screwcap. 14.8° alc. **RATING** 89 **DRINK** 2011 $35
Cabernet Sauvignon 2004 Medium-bodied; quite attractive, fresh cassis/blackcurrant varietal fruit; well-balanced. Screwcap. 14.9° alc. **RATING** 89 **DRINK** 2012 $18

Orani Vineyard   NR

Arthur Highway, Sorrel, Tas 7172 **REGION** Southern Tasmania
T (03) 6225 0330 **F** (03) 6225 0330 **OPEN** W'ends & public hols 9.30–6.30
WINEMAKER Winemaking Tasmania (Julian Alcorso) **EST.** 1986 **CASES** NA
The first commercial release from Orani was of a 1992 Pinot Noir, with Chardonnay and Riesling following in the years thereafter; since that time Orani has continued to do well with its Pinot Noir. Owned by Tony and Angela McDermott, the latter the President of the Royal Hobart Wine Show. The wines are released with some years' bottle age.

Oranje Tractor Wine/Lincoln & Gomm Wines   NR

198 Link Road, Albany, WA 6330 **REGION** Albany
T (08) 9842 5175 **F** (08) 9842 5175 **WWW**.oranjetractor.com **OPEN** Sunday, or by appt
WINEMAKER Rob Diletti (Contract) **EST.** 1998 **CASES** 1000
The name tells part of the story of the vineyard owned by Murray Gomm and Pamela Lincoln. Murray Gomm was born next door, but moved to Perth to work in physical education and health promotion. Here he met nutritionist Pamela Lincoln, who completed the wine science degree at Charles Sturt University in 2000, before being awarded a Churchill Fellowship to study organic grape and wine production in the US and Europe. When the partners established their 3-ha vineyard, they went down the organic path, with the aid of a 1964 vintage Fiat tractor, which is orange.

Organic Vignerons Australia   ★★★☆

Section 395 Derrick Road, Loxton North, SA 5333 **REGION** Riverland
T (08) 8541 3616 **F** (08) 8541 3616 **WWW**.ova.com.au **OPEN** Mon–Fri 9.30–4.30
WINEMAKER David Bruer **EST.** 2002 **CASES** 3700
Organic Vignerons Australia is a very interesting winemaking business. It consists of the owners of 5 certified organic South Australian properties: Claire and Kevin Hansen at Padthaway, Bruce and Sue Armstrong at Waikerie, Brett and Melissa Munchenberg at Loxton, Terry Markou at Adelaide Plains and David and Barbara Bruer at Langhorne Creek. The wines are made by David Bruer at Temple Bruer, which is itself a certified organic producer. Exports to Japan.

TTTT **Shiraz Cabernet Sauvignon 2003** Holding colour; medium-bodied, spicy/earthy/cedary characters around a core of fresh, bright fruit; moderate tannins. Screwcap. 14.1° alc.
RATING 89 **DRINK** 2013 $ 18
Bin 621 Mataro Shiraz Grenache 2003 Medium-bodied; the parts come together well, marrying red and black fruits, licorice and earth; supple tannins. Screwcap. 14° alc.
RATING 89 **DRINK** 2013 $ 18

Orlando   ★★★★★

Jacob's Creek Visitor Centre, Barossa Valley Way, Rowland Flat, SA 5352 **REGION** Barossa Valley
T (08) 8521 3000 **F** (08) 8521 3003 **WWW**.jacobscreek.com **OPEN** 7 days 10–5
WINEMAKER Philip Laffer, Bernard Hicken **EST.** 1847 **CASES** NFP
Jacob's Creek is one of the largest-selling brands in the world and is almost exclusively responsible for driving the fortunes of this French-owned (Pernod Ricard) company. A colossus in the export game, chiefly to the UK and Europe, but also to the US and Asia. Wine quality across the full spectrum from Jacob's Creek upwards has been exemplary, driven by the production skills of Philip Laffer. The global success of the basic Jacob's Creek range has had the perverse effect of prejudicing many critics and wine writers who fail (so it seems) to objectively look behind the label and taste what is in fact in the glass. Prejudice, real or imagined, does not enter into the question with the outstanding Lawson's Padthaway Shiraz, Jacaranda Ridge Cabernet Sauvignon, Steingarten Riesling and the Jacob's Creek Limited Release range.

TTTTT **Steingarten Riesling 2005** Delicacy personified; lively apple and lime juice flavours; lovely line and balance. Gold medals National Wine Show '05, Sydney '06. **RATING** 95
DRINK 2012 $ 30
Jacob's Creek Johann Shiraz Cabernet 2001 Very well-made and balanced, especially for the vintage; full-bodied blackberry, dark chocolate and mocha, with quite spicy tannins on the finish. Formidable gold medal and trophy record. Cork. 14° alc. **RATING** 94 **DRINK** 2016 $ 75

TTTTY **Jacob's Creek Reserve Riesling 2005** Light straw-green; elegant mouthfeel and balance to the crisp lime juice fruit; fresh finish and aftertaste. Screwcap. **RATING** 93 **DRINK** 2012 $ 16
Lawson's Padthaway Shiraz 2000 Holding its hue well; an elegant, medium-bodied wine with fine red and black fruits, subtle oak and fine tannins. **RATING** 93 **DRINK** 2010 $ 59.99

Jacob's Creek Reserve Chardonnay 2004 Very well-made; relatively low alcohol tightens the texture and structure of the melon and nectarine fruit, with subtle malolactic and barrel ferment influences. Cork. 12.5° alc. **RATING** 92 **DRINK** 2009 $16

Jacob's Creek Reeves Point Chardonnay 2003 An elegant wine, intense yet understated, and developing slowly but surely; cool-grown grapefruit and passionfruit flavours; subtle oak. Cork. 13° alc. **RATING** 92 **DRINK** 2010 $30

Jacob's Creek Reserve Sauvignon Blanc 2005 Clean, crisp and minerally; correct varietal flavours, but very light. Screwcap. **RATING** 91 **DRINK** 2010 $15.99

Jacob's Creek Reserve Shiraz 2003 Harmonious integration and balance of oak, tannins and an array of black fruit flavours; medium-bodied and supple. Cork. 14.5° alc. **RATING** 91 **DRINK** 2013 $16

St Hugo Coonawarra Cabernet Sauvignon 2003 Medium- to full-bodied; attractive blackcurrant, earth, chocolate and mocha flavours; persistent, but ripe, tannins. Cork. **RATING** 91 **DRINK** 2013 $40

Jacob's Creek Chardonnay 2005 Aromatic stone fruit and grapefruit hinting at some Limestone Coast inclusion; an elegant palate, long and balanced; lingering, dry finish. Remarkable at the price and volume. Quality cork. **RATING** 90 **DRINK** Now $9.99

St Hilary Padthaway Chardonnay 2004 Very elegant, tight and refined; a long palate with citrus, nectarine and grapefruit; will evolve very well. **RATING** 90 **DRINK** Now $17.99

♥♥♥♥ **Gramp's Botrytis Semillon 2004** Quite complex; at the mid-range of lusciousness; apricot, citrus and lemonade flavours. Cork. 11° alc. **RATING** 89 **DRINK** 2008 $16

Jacob's Creek Reserve Cabernet Sauvignon 2003 Good colour; abundant blackcurrant fruit, but the tannins are distinctly assertive. Time will help. Cork. **RATING** 88 **DRINK** 2015 $16

Trilogy 2003 Soft, ripe red and black fruits on entry, then quite firm tannins take over towards the finish. Cabernet Sauvignon/Cabernet Franc/Merlot. Screwcap. 14° alc. **RATING** 88 **DRINK** 2009 $15

Trilogy Semillon Sauvignon Blanc Viognier 2005 Nicely composed and structured; crisp acidity on a relatively long, dry finish; omni-seafood style. Screwcap. 12.5° alc. **RATING** 87 **DRINK** 2008 $15

Jacob's Creek Barossa Valley Shiraz Rose 2005 Has pretensions of style; small red fruit flavours; good balance of acidity and a flick of residual sugar providing length. Screwcap. 12.5° alc. **RATING** 87 **DRINK** Now $9.99

Gramp's Cabernet Merlot 2003 Complex texture and structure; earthy/briary overtones to the spice and tobacco palate; firm tannins. Cork. 14.5° alc. **RATING** 87 **DRINK** 2008 $16

♥♥♥♡ **Jacob's Creek Barossa Valley Sparkling Rose NV** **RATING** 85 **DRINK** Now $11.99

Osborns

NR

166 Foxeys Road, Merricks North, Vic 3926 **REGION** Mornington Peninsula
T (03) 5989 7417 **F** (03) 5989 7510 **WWW**.osborns.com.au **OPEN** W'ends Oct–June & by appt
WINEMAKER Frank Osborn, Richard McIntyre **EST.** 1988 **CASES** 1500
Frank and Pamela Osborn are now Mornington Peninsula veterans, having purchased the vineyard land in Ellerina Road in 1988 and (with help from son Guy) planted the vineyard over the following 4 years. Part of the production from the 5.5 ha of vineyards is sold to others. The wine is fermented at Moorooduc Estate by Richard McIntyre, then matured in barrel at the Osborns barrel store, monitored by Frank Osborn and daughter Lucinda.

Otway Estate

★★★

20 Hoveys Road, Barongarook, Vic 3249 **REGION** Geelong
T (03) 5233 8400 **F** (03) 5233 8343 **WWW**.otwayestate.com.au **OPEN** Mon–Fri 11–4.30, w'ends 10–5
WINEMAKER Ian Deacon **EST.** 1983 **CASES** 3000
The history of Otway Estate dates back to 1983, when the first vines were planted by Stuart and Eileen Walker. The current group of 6 family and friends, including winemaker Ian Deacon, have substantially expanded the scope of the business: there are now 6 ha of vineyard, planted primarily to chardonnay (3 ha) and pinot noir (2 ha) with small patches of riesling, semillon, sauvignon blanc and

cabernet making up the remainder. The wines made from these plantings are sold under the Otway Estate label; wines made from contract-grown grapes in the region are marketed under the Yahoo Creek label. Exports to Canada.

ŶŶŶŶ Semillon Sauvignon Blanc 2005 Vibrant, crisp lemon, lime and herb aromas and flavours; good drive and length; crisp acidity. Screwcap. 13.2° alc. **RATING** 89 **DRINK** Now $ 15
Brut 2002 Spicy strawberry fruit; good length and balance; lively acidity throughout. **RATING** 87 **DRINK** 2009 $ 20

ŶŶŶŶ Pinot Noir 2004 RATING 86 **DRINK** 2008 $ 20

ŶŶŶ Chardonnay 2004 RATING 83 $ 20

Outlook Hill ★★★★

97 School Lane, Tarrawarra, Vic 3777 **REGION** Yarra Valley
T (03) 5962 2890 **F** (03) 5962 2890 **WWW**.outlookhill.com.au **OPEN** Fri–Sun 11–4.45
WINEMAKER Al Fencaros (Contract) **EST.** 2000 **CASES** 1800
After several years overseas, former Melbourne professionals Peter and Lydia Snow returned in 1997 planning to open a wine tourism business in the Hunter Valley. However, they had second thoughts, and in 2000 returned to the Yarra Valley, where they have now established 2 tourist B&B cottages, 5.1 ha of vineyard, a terrace restaurant and adjacent cellar door outlet, backed by a constant temperature wine storage cool room. The wines are made by Al Fencaros at Dixons Creek Winery.

ŶŶŶŶŶ Yarra Valley Pinot Noir 2004 Fragrant cherry and plum fruit; medium-bodied, well-balanced and constructed palate; the sweet fruit avoids jamminess. Cork. 14.5° alc. **RATING** 91 **DRINK** 2010 $ 24
Yarra Valley Chardonnay 2004 Light straw-green; spotlessly clean and fragrant aromas; an elegant, fruit-sweet stone fruit and melon palate; minimal oak impact. Screwcap. 13.5° alc. **RATING** 90 **DRINK** 2011 $ 22

ŶŶŶŶ Yarra Valley Pinot Gris 2005 Attractive though slightly unusual passionfruit elements; no heat on the finish; good balance. Screwcap. 13.5° alc. **RATING** 89 **DRINK** 2009 $ 18

ŶŶŶŶ Yarra Valley Cabernet Merlot 2004 RATING 86 **DRINK** 2008 $ 20

Outram Estate ★★★★

39 Coora Road, Westleigh, NSW 2120 **REGION** Lower Hunter Valley
T 0439 909 818 **F** (02) 9481 7879 **WWW**.outramestate.com **OPEN** By appt
WINEMAKER Peter Howland, Scott Stephens (Contract) **EST.** 1995 **CASES** 1000
Dr Geoff Cutter says his inspiration to start Outram Estate came from Max Lake, a visit to St Emilion/Pomerol in Bordeaux, and my account of the establishment of Coldstream Hills, which he read in one of my books. His aim is to produce quality, not quantity, and with Peter Howland in charge of winemaking, there is no reason why he should not do so. He has 5.5 ha of merlot on rich red volcanic basalt, and 13 ha of verdelho and chardonnay on the sandy grey alluvial soils of Wollombi Creek. Exports to the UK, the US, Fiji and Taiwan.

ŶŶŶŶŶ Jebediah's Block Hunter Valley Merlot 2005 Strong, earthy, savoury varietal aromas and flavours; light- to medium-bodied, with fine tannins; well-made and not forced. Diam. 12.5° alc. **RATING** 90 **DRINK** 2011 $ 27

ŶŶŶŶ St Christopher Canberra Cabernets Merlot 2004 A solid wine, with sombre black fruits and ample structure for the long haul; a curious back label suggesting the cork is a ProCork when it is in fact Diam. Complex Bordeaux blend. Diam. 13.5° alc. **RATING** 89 **DRINK** 2012 $ 40
Limited Release Hunter Valley Verdelho 2003 Attractive, varietal peachy fruit salad flavours; good balance and length; developing nicely. Cork. 13.2° alc. **RATING** 88 **DRINK** 2009 $ 18

Oyster Cove Vineyard

NR

134 Manuka Road, Oyster Cove, Tas 7054 **REGION** Southern Tasmania
T (03) 6267 4512 **F** (03) 6267 4635 **OPEN** By appt
WINEMAKER Andrew Hood **EST.** 1994 **CASES** 100
The striking label of Oyster Cove, with a yacht reflected in mirror-calm water, is wholly appropriate, for Jean and Rod Ledingham have been quietly growing tiny quantities of grapes from the 0.9 ha of chardonnay and pinot noir since 1994.

Padthaway Estate

★★★

Riddoch Highway, Padthaway, SA 5271 **REGION** Padthaway
T (08) 8734 3148 **F** (08) 8734 3188 **www**.padthawayestate.com **OPEN** 7 days 10–4
WINEMAKER Ulrich Grey-Smith **EST.** 1980 **CASES** 6000
For many years, until the opening of Stonehaven, this was the only functioning winery in Padthaway, set in the superb grounds of the Estate in a large and gracious old stone woolshed; the homestead is in the Relais et Chateaux mould, offering luxurious accommodation and fine food. Sparkling wines are the specialty. Padthaway Estate also acts as a tasting centre for other Padthaway-region wines.

▼▼▼▽ **Shiraz 2003 RATING** 86 **DRINK** 2011

Pages Creek

★★★★

624 Middle Teatree Road, Teatree, Tas 7017 **REGION** Southern Tasmania
T (03) 6260 2311 **F** (03) 6331 9884 **www**.pagescreekwine.com.au **OPEN** By appt
WINEMAKER Winemaking Tasmania (Julian Alcorso) **EST.** 1999 **CASES** 1600
In 1999 Peter and Sue Lowrie planted a 4-ha vineyard on their 20-ha Pages Creek property named after the creek that runs through it. They have 1.6 ha of cabernet sauvignon, 1 ha each of pinot noir and chardonnay and 0.4 ha of merlot. The tiny first vintage (2002) was consumed at their wedding; the first full vintage was 2003, and the Pages Creek label was launched in 2004.

▼▼▼▼▽ **Chardonnay 2004** Stone fruit and melon with subliminal sweetness off-set by balancing acidity; gentle oak. Diam. 13.6° alc. **RATING** 90 **DRINK** 2008 **$** 22
Cabernet Merlot 2004 Good hue; bright, vibrant, crisp red berry fruits; light- to medium-bodied, but good length; impressive for Tas. Diam. 13.5° alc. **RATING** 90 **DRINK** 2012 **$** 25

▼▼▼▼ **Pinot Noir 2004** Strong colour; mouthfilling, abundant, ripe confit plum fruit. Diam. 13.2° alc. **RATING** 89 **DRINK** 2009 **$** 22

Palandri Wines

★★★☆

Bussell Highway, Cowaramup, WA 6284 **REGION** Margaret River
T (08) 9755 5711 **F** (08) 9755 5722 **www**.palandri.com.au **OPEN** 7 days 10–5
WINEMAKER Sarah Siddons **EST.** 1999 **CASES** 250 000
A state-of-the-art winery completed in 2000 now has a capacity of 2500 tonnes. The vineyards, which are scheduled to supply Palandri Wines with 50% of its intake, are situated in the Frankland River subregion of the Great Southern. In 1999, 150 ha of vines were planted at Frankland River; the major varieties are shiraz, merlot, cabernet sauvignon, riesling, chardonnay and sauvignon blanc. A further 60 ha were planted in early September 2000; a second block has been purchased south of the Frankland River vineyard, and a further 140 ha are being developed there. Exports to all major markets.

▼▼▼▼▽ **Baldivis Estate Late Harvest Riesling 2004** A zingy mix of lemon rind and clove aromas; fresh, crisp and lively in the mouth, although not as exotic as the bouquet; could well develop if given the chance, although it probably won't (be given the chance). Screwcap. **RATING** 90 **DRINK** 2010 **$** 11.95

▼▼▼▼ **Margaret River Cabernet Merlot 2003** Light- to medium-bodied; nicely balanced and proportioned; sweet red and black fruits; very fine tannins on a long finish. **RATING** 89 **DRINK** 2008 **$** 19.95
Shiraz 2003 Light- to medium-bodied; firm black fruits and some spicy notes; fractionally hard finish, surprising given the fermentation was finished in barrel. Great Southern/Margaret River. Cork. **RATING** 88 **DRINK** 2010 **$** 24.95

ŢŢŢŢ **Great Southern Merlot 2004** RATING 85 DRINK 2009 $17
Baldivis Estate Merlot 2003 RATING 84 DRINK Now $11.95

ŢŢŢ **Baldivis Estate Classic Dry White 2005** RATING 83 $12
Baldivis Estate Classic Dry White 2004 RATING 80 $11.95

Palmara

NR

1314 Richmond Road, Richmond, Tas 7025 **REGION** Southern Tasmania
T (03) 6260 2462 **F** (03) 6260 2462 **WWW**.palmara.com.au **OPEN** Sept–May 7 days 12–6
WINEMAKER Allan Bird **EST.** 1985 **CASES** 300
Allan Bird makes the Palmara wines in tiny quantities (the vineyard is slightly less than 1 ha). The
Pinot Noir has performed consistently well since 1990. The Exotica Siegerrebe blend is unchallenged
as Australia's most exotic and unusual wine, with pungent jujube/lanolin aromas and flavours.

Palmer Wines

★★★★

Caves Road, Dunsborough, WA 6281 **REGION** Margaret River
T (08) 9756 7388 **F** (08) 9756 7399 **OPEN** 7 days 10–5
WINEMAKER Naturaliste Vintners (Bruce Dukes) **EST.** 1977 **CASES** 7000
Stephen and Helen Palmer planted their first ha of vines way back in 1977, but a series of events
(including a cyclone and grasshopper plagues) caused them to lose interest and instead turn to
thoroughbred horses. But with encouragement from Dr Michael Peterkin of Pierro, and after a gap of
almost 10 years, they again turned to viticulture and now have 15 ha planted to the classic varieties.

ŢŢŢŢŢ **Margaret River Sauvignon Blanc 2005** Attractive, if slightly unusual, aromas and
flavours, with a mix of citrus, kiwifruit and stone fruit; good acidity wraps a bow around
the parcel. Screwcap. 13.5° alc. RATING 91 DRINK Now
Margaret River Chardonnay 2004 Complex but restrained melon, fig, stone fruit and oak
melange; has good balance. Screwcap. RATING 90 DRINK 2009

Palmers Wines

NR

Lot 152 Palmers Lane, Pokolbin, NSW 2321 **REGION** Lower Hunter Valley
T (02) 4998 7452 **F** (02) 9949 9884 **OPEN** W'ends 10–5, or by appt
WINEMAKER Contract **EST.** 1986 **CASES** 1100
The name of the vineyard and that of the lane on which it is established came from Henry Palmer,
who arrived in 1862. Three generations of the family continued to work the 40-ha property as a
mixed farming enterprise, but when the last (William) died in the 1970s, the property was to all
intents and purposes abandoned. Purchased in 1986, the new owners set about rebuilding the
original Palmer homestead, which now serves as the cellar door, and establishing 2.6 ha of vineyard
(chardonnay, verdelho, semillon and shiraz). Part of the production is sold.

Pankhurst

★★★★

Old Woodgrove, Woodgrove Road, Hall, NSW 2618 **REGION** Canberra District
T (02) 6230 2592 **F** (02) 6230 2592 **WWW**.pankhurstwines.com.au **OPEN** W'ends, public hols, or by
appt
WINEMAKER Lark Hill (Dr David Carpenter, Sue Carpenter), Brindabella Hills (Dr Roger Harris)
EST. 1986 **CASES** 4000
Agricultural scientist and consultant Allan Pankhurst and wife Christine (with a degree in
pharmaceutical science) have established a 5.7-ha split-canopy vineyard. The first wines produced
showed considerable promise. In recent years Pankhurst has shared success with Lark Hill in the
production of good Pinot Noir. Says Christine Pankhurst, 'the result of good viticulture here and
great winemaking at Lark Hill', and she may well be right.

ŢŢŢŢŢ **Pinot Noir 2004** Deep hue; complex, ripe, plum, spice and forest floor/game aromas; the
palate equally complex and powerful; one for the cellar. Cork. 12.6° alc. RATING 92
DRINK 2013 $35

Dorothy May Cabernet Merlot 2004 Strong colour; medium-bodied; complex flavours ranging from blackcurrant to herb and olive, plus a touch of bitter chocolate along the way. Clear and uncluttered finish. Cork. 13.7° alc. **RATING** 90 **DRINK** 2014 $ 20

ΨΨΨΨ **Chardonnay 2004** Medium-bodied; despite the controlled alcohol, quite sweet tropical peach fruit; oak merely a vehicle for fermentation and maturation. Screwcap. 12.6° alc. **RATING** 87 **DRINK** 2009 $ 20

Panorama

NR

1848 Cygnet Coast Road, Cradoc, Tas 7109 **REGION** Southern Tasmania
T (03) 6266 3409 **F** (03) 6266 3482 **WWW**.panoramavineyard.com.au **OPEN** Wed–Mon 10–5
WINEMAKER Michael Vishacki **EST.** 1974 **CASES** 2250
Michael and Sharon Vishacki purchased Panorama from Steve Ferencz in 1997, and have since spent considerable sums in building a brand new winery and an attractive cellar door sales outlet, and in trebling the vineyard size.

Panton Hill Winery

NR

145 Manuka Road, Panton Hill, Vic 3759 **REGION** Yarra Valley
T (03) 9719 7342 **F** (03) 9719 7362 **WWW**.pantonhillwinery.com.au **OPEN** W'ends & public hols 11–5, or by appt
WINEMAKER Dr Teunis AP Kwak **EST.** 1988 **CASES** 700
Melbourne academic Dr Teunis Kwak has a 4-ha fully mature vineyard, part planted in 1976, the remainder in 1988. The vineyard, established on a fairly steep hillside, is picturesque, and there is a large stone hall available for functions. Part of the production is sold to others.

Paperbark Vines

NR

PO Box 2553, Kent Town, SA 5071 **REGION** Southeast Australia
T (08) 8431 3675 **F** (08) 8431 3674 **OPEN** Not
WINEMAKER Contract **EST.** 2000 **CASES** NA
Paperbark Vines is a virtual winery owned by Mark Cohen of Malesco Imports and Export Pty Ltd. Chardonnay, cabernet sauvignon and shiraz are made under the Paperbark Vines label, and sold only into Malaysia, Singapore, Thailand and the US.

Paracombe Wines

 ★★★★☆

Main Road, Paracombe, SA 5132 (postal) **REGION** Adelaide Hills
T (08) 8380 5058 **F** (08) 8380 5488 **WWW**.paracombewines.com **OPEN** Not
WINEMAKER Paul Drogemuller **EST.** 1983 **CASES** 5700
The Drogemuller family have established 13.3 ha of vineyards at Paracombe, reviving a famous name in South Australian wine history. The wines are ever-stylish and consistent. Exports to the UK, the US and other major markets.

ΨΨΨΨ **Holland Creek Riesling 2005** Fresh, crisp, minerally aromas swing into citrus, lime and apple on the long palate; lively acidity to finish. Screwcap. 12.5° alc. **RATING** 92 **DRINK** 2018 $ 19

Adelaide Hills Shiraz Viognier 2004 Deep, dense colour; very powerful and concentrated, of course, given its huge alcohol; black fruits, prunes, licorice and spice, with a marginally tempering effect from the viognier. Procork. 16.5° alc. **RATING** 92 **DRINK** 2024 $ 23

Adelaide Hills Chardonnay 2004 Elegant citrus, nectarine and melon mix; supportive oak, good acidity. Screwcap. 13° alc. **RATING** 91 **DRINK** 2009 $ 23

Adelaide Hills Cabernet Franc 2004 Strong colour; powerful leaf/tobacco leaf/black fruit aromas; the palate follows on with spices and black fruits. A serious wine. Cork. 15° alc. **RATING** 91 **DRINK** 2015 $ 27

Adelaide Hills Sauvignon Blanc 2005 Light straw-green; clean, gentle tropical/passionfruit flavours; an appealing, early drinking style. Screwcap. 13° alc. **RATING** 90 **DRINK** Now $ 21

Somerville Shiraz 2002 As often, high alcohol determines much of the style, sweetening the flavours into a blackberry/confit/jam and spice spectrum. Cork. 16° alc. **RATING** 90 **DRINK** 2012 $ 69

Paradigm Hill ★★★★☆

26 Merricks Road, Merricks, Vic 3916 **REGION** Mornington Peninsula
T (03) 5989 9000 **F** (03) 9509 5336 **WWW**.paradigmhill.com.au **OPEN** Every weekend Jan; first weekend of month, public hols or by appt
WINEMAKER Dr George Mihaly **EST.** 1999 **CASES** 1000
Dr George Mihaly (with a background in medical research, then thereafter the biotechnology and pharmaceutical industries) and wife Ruth (a former chef and caterer) have realised a 30-year dream of establishing their own vineyard and winery, abandoning their previous careers to do so. George had all the necessary scientific qualifications, and built on those by making the 2001 Merricks Creek wines, moving to home base at Paradigm Hill for the 2002 vintage, all along receiving guidance and advice from Nat White from Main Ridge Estate. The vineyard, under Ruth's control with advice from Shane Strange, is planted to 2.1 ha of pinot noir, 1 ha of shiraz, 0.9 ha of riesling and 0.4 ha of pinot gris. The back labels are a mine of technical information. Exports to the UK.

▼▼▼▼▽ **L'ami Sage Mornington Peninsula Pinot Noir 2004** Light, bright red-purple; fragrant cherry, plum and spice aromas; similar flavours have absorbed the 65% new oak in which it was matured. Formerly called Oracle Pinot Noir. Diam. 14° alc. **RATING** 93 **DRINK** 2011 $ 39

The Oracle Mornington Peninsula Pinot Noir 2003 Deeper colour; distinctly richer, riper style; luscious plum fruit, with silky/velvety texture and mouthfeel, the oak interwoven. Carries its alcohol well. A forced name change after '03 to L'ami Sage. Diam. 14.6° alc. **RATING** 93 **DRINK** 2011 $ 39

Col's Block Mornington Peninsula Shiraz 2004 Light- to medium-bodied; vibrant, fresh red and black cherry with strong spicy notes; seamless oak and tannins. Formerly VH-DOC. Diam. 13° alc. **RATING** 93 **DRINK** 2012 $ 35

Mornington Peninsula Pinot Gris 2005 This is pinot gris with the full works; one-third barrel-fermented, 6 months in new oak, and bone dry. It really ought to be called pinot grigio. Screwcap. 14° alc. **RATING** 90 **DRINK** 2008 $ 35

▼▼▼▼ **Mornington Peninsula Riesling 2005** Very pale straw-green; dry, crisp, minerally, ultra-austere style with light apple and pear fruit. On the evidence of the '04, will forever be Peter Pan. Screwcap. 12.5° alc. **RATING** 87 **DRINK** 2009 $ 24

Paradise Enough ★★☆

Stewarts Road, Kongwak, Vic 3951 **REGION** Gippsland
T (03) 5657 4241 **F** (03) 5657 4229 **OPEN** Sun, public hols 12–5
WINEMAKER John Bell, Sue Armstrong **EST.** 1987 **CASES** 600
Phillip Jones of Bass Phillip persuaded John Bell and Sue Armstrong to establish a small vineyard on a substantial dairy and beef cattle property.

▼▼▼▽ **Pinot Rose 2005** Conter-cultural; salmon-pink; in classic Provence style; genuine food style. **RATING** 86 **DRINK** Now

Chardonnay 2005 **RATING** 84 **DRINK** Now

Paramoor Wines ★★★★☆

439 Three Chain Road, Carlsruhe via Woodend, Vic 3442 **REGION** Macedon Ranges
T (03) 5427 1057 **F** (03) 5427 3927 **WWW**.paramoor.net.au **OPEN** W'ends & public hols 10–5, or by appt
WINEMAKER William Fraser, Keith Brien **EST.** 2003 **CASES** 400
Paramoor Wines is the retirement venture of Will Fraser, formerly Managing Director of Kodak Australasia. To be strictly correct, he is Dr Will Fraser, armed with a PhD in chemistry from the

Adelaide University. Very much later he added a Diploma of wine technology from the University of Melbourne, Dookie Campus, to his degrees. Paramoor's winery is set on 17 ha of beautiful country not far from Hanging Rock, originally a working Clydesdale horse farm, leaving a magnificent heritage-style barn which is now used for cellar door sales and functions. Will has planted 1.3 ha each of pinot noir and pinot gris, and intends to supplement the product range by purchasing varieties more suited to warmer climates than the chilly hills of the Macedon Ranges. He shares the winery with Keith Brien of Silver Wings Winemaking.

ŸŸŸŸŸ **Cabernet Merlot 2004** Medium-bodied cassis and blackcurrant classic varietal character; silky tannins and texture; good oak. Diam. 13.5° alc. **RATING** 92 **DRINK** 2016 $ 22

Shiraz 2004 An elegant, restrained style in the context of the region; spicy, savoury blackberry and plum fruit; integrated oak. Diam. 14° alc. **RATING** 91 **DRINK** 2014 $ 22

Paringa Estate

44 Paringa Road, Red Hill South, Vic 3937 **REGION** Mornington Peninsula
T(03) 5989 2669 **F**(03) 5931 0135 **WWW**.paringaestate.com.au **OPEN** 7 days 11–5
WINEMAKER Lindsay McCall **EST.** 1985 **CASES** 9500
Schoolteacher-turned-winemaker Lindsay McCall has shown an absolutely exceptional gift for winemaking across a range of styles, but with immensely complex Pinot Noir and Shiraz leading the way. The wines have an unmatched level of success in the wine shows and competitions Paringa Estate is able to enter, the limitation being the relatively small size of the production. His skills are no less evident in contract winemaking for others. The restaurant is open 7 days.

ŸŸŸŸŸ **Estate Pinot Noir 2004** Powerful black cherry fruit aromas and flavours backed by perfectly balanced and integrated French oak; fine tannins. Screwcap. 14.9° alc. **RATING** 96 **DRINK** 2010 $ 55

Reserve Special Barrel Selection Pinot Noir 2004 Shows all of the characteristics of Paringa, but with an extra degree of intensity and length; outstanding wine; the third Barrel Selection release. Screwcap. 14.9° alc. **RATING** 96 **DRINK** 2012 $ 80

Reserve Shiraz 2004 Deep colour; medium- to full-bodied; concentrated rich, peppery, spicy fruits more to black than red; seamless oak and tannins; different style to the Estate, but the same quality; both wines picked May 13. Screwcap. 14.4° alc. **RATING** 96 **DRINK** 2024 $ 70

Estate Shiraz 2004 Elegant medium-bodied wine; a seamless balance of spicy cherry and blackberry fruit, oak and tannins; 6 trophies Sydney Wine Show '06 including Best Wine of Show. **RATING** 96 **DRINK** 2015 $ 45

Peninsula Chardonnay 2004 Very complex barrel ferment aromas and flavours, with wild yeast influence; ripe nectarine and citrus, touches of cashew; powerful but not heavy. Screwcap. **RATING** 94 **DRINK** 2009 $ 18

Estate Chardonnay 2004 Glowing green-yellow; a sophisticated wine; nectarine, grapefruit and quality oak up front, then a long, bright finish built around acidity. Screwcap. 14.8° alc. **RATING** 94 **DRINK** 2012 $ 32

Peninsula Pinot Noir 2005 Youthful, bright purple red; vibrant plum and cherry with touches of stem and oak; silky mouthfeel, will develop very well. Screwcap. 14.6° alc. **RATING** 94 **DRINK** 2012 $ 25

Peninsula Shiraz 2004 More developed colour than the Estate Shiraz; fragrant, lively red fruits in a cherry, damson plum and spice spectrum; fine tannins and oak; great mouthfeel and length. Screwcap. 14.4° alc. **RATING** 94 **DRINK** 2019 $ 25

ŸŸŸŸŸ **Estate Riesling 2005** Pale straw-green; tight, reserved bouquet; a fine, elegant and crisp palate, fruit swelling on the lime and mineral finish. Screwcap. 13.4° alc. **RATING** 92 **DRINK** 2013 $ 15

Estate Pinot Gris 2005 Faint pink tinge from the variety; far more flavour than the vast majority; ripe apple, musk and pear; improbably carries its alcohol with aplomb. Screwcap. 15.2° alc. **RATING** 91 **DRINK** 2008 $ 20

Parish Hill Wines   NR

Parish Hill Road, Uraidla, SA 5142 **REGION** Adelaide Hills
T (08) 8390 3927 **F** (08) 8390 0394 **WWW**.parishhillwines.com.au **OPEN** By appt
WINEMAKER Andrew Cottell **EST.** 1998 **CASES** 1000
Andrew Cottell and Joy Carlisle have a tiny 1.6-ha vineyard on a steep, sunny, exposed slope adjacent
to their house, and a micro-winery (which has approval for a total crush of 15 tonnes), but have taken
the venture very seriously. Andrew Cottell studied wine science and viticulture at Charles Sturt
University, where he was introduced to the Italian varieties; this led to the planting of 0.2 ha of arneis
and 0.5 ha of nebbiolo. The other two varieties are new French clones selected by Professor Bernard
at Dijon University. An attempt to use an organic spray program in 2002 failed, and while they adopt
integrated pest management, soft environmental practices and beneficial insects, they have moved to
conventional vineyard management for the time being at least.

Park Wines   NR

RMB 6291, Sanatorium Road, Allan's Flat, Yackandandah, Vic 3691 **REGION** Alpine Valleys
T (02) 6027 1564 **F** (02) 6027 1561 **OPEN** W'ends & public hols 10–5
WINEMAKER Rod Park, Julia Park **EST.** 1995 **CASES** NA
Rod and Julia Park have a 6-ha vineyard of riesling, chardonnay, merlot, cabernet franc and cabernet
sauvignon, set in the beautiful hill country of the Ovens Valley. Part of the vineyard is still coming
into full bearing, and the business is still in its infancy.

Parker Coonawarra Estate   ★★★★☆

Riddoch Highway, Coonawarra, SA 5263 **REGION** Coonawarra
T (08) 8737 3525 **F** (08) 8737 3527 **WWW**.parkercoonawarraestate.com.au **OPEN** 7 days 10–4
WINEMAKER Peter Bissell (Contract) **EST.** 1985 **CASES** 5000
Parker Coonawarra Estate is at the southern end of Coonawarra, on rich terra rossa soil over
limestone. Cabernet Sauvignon is the predominant variety, with minor plantings of merlot and petit
verdot. Acquired by the Rathbone family in May 2004. Exports to the UK, the US and other major
markets.

▼▼▼▼▽ **Terra Rossa Cabernet Sauvignon 2003** Medium- to full-bodied; rich, round and
mouthfilling; luscious blackcurrant fruit; ripe tannins, sure French oak handling. Cork.
RATING 93 **DRINK** 2013 $ 34.95

🐌 Parnassus Vineyard   ★★★

180 Lardners Track, Drouin East, Vic 3818 **REGION** Gippsland
T (03) 5626 8522 **F** (03) 5626 8502 **WWW**.parnassus.com.au **OPEN** By appt
WINEMAKER Mal Stewart **EST.** 1998 **CASES** 600
Gary and Judy Surman bought Parnassus Guest House in 1989, developing a function centre
specialising in weddings and conferences. Wishing to take further advantage of the great views, the
Surmans planted 1 ha each of pinot noir and chardonnay in 1998. In 2005 they purchased Wild Dog
Winery, where their son Luke and Japanese wife Kunie manage the 12 ha vineyard, the cellar door
and assist in the winery. Mal Stewart has the same wide-ranging brief for Parnassus as he has for
Wild Dog.

▼▼▼▼ **Pinot Noir Chardonnay 2004** Crisp and clean, with balanced citrussy fruit flavours; nice
acidity and length. **RATING** 88 **DRINK** Now $ 24
The Delphi Chardonnay 2004 Good green-yellow; rich, ripe, fig and peach fruit, with a
slightly phenolic finish. No shortage of overall flavour. Screwcap. 14° alc. **RATING** 87 **DRINK**
2008 $ 20

▼▼▼▽ **Chardonnay 2004 RATING** 85 **DRINK** 2008 $ 18
Pinot Noir 2003 RATING 85 **DRINK** 2008 $ 25
Summer Pinot Noir 2004 RATING 84 **DRINK** Now $ 18
Pinot Noir 2004 RATING 84 **DRINK** Now $ 25

Parri Estate

Sneyd Road, Mount Compass, SA 5210 **REGION** Southern Fleurieu/McLaren Vale
T (08) 8554 9660 **F** (08) 8554 9694 **WWW.**parriestate.com.au **OPEN** 7 days 11–5
WINEMAKER Linda Domas **EST.** 1998 **CASES** 10 000
Alice, Peter and John Phillips have established a substantial business with a clear marketing plan
and an obvious commitment to quality. The 33-ha vineyard is planted to chardonnay, viognier,
sauvignon blanc, semillon, pinot noir, cabernet sauvignon and shiraz, using modern trellis and
irrigation systems. The protected valley in which the vines are planted has a creek which flows
throughout the year, and which has been rejuvenated by the planting of 3000 trees. In 2004 a 9-ha
property on Ingoldby Road, McLaren Vale was acquired, with a modern warehouse and shiraz,
grenache and cabernet sauvignon up to 60 years old. A new cellar door has also been built on the
property. Exports to the UK, Canada, Germany and Asia.

Southern Fleurieu Sauvignon Blanc 2005 Aromatic, clean and fresh gooseberry and
passionfruit aromas and flavours; vibrantly fresh and long; lovely cleansing acidity.
Screwcap. **RATING** 94 **DRINK** Now $ 18

Southern Fleurieu Shiraz Viognier 2004 Good colour; typically lifted aromas, with an
attractive mix of red and black fruits; supple tannins. Estate-grown. Cork. 13° alc.
RATING 92 **DRINK** 2012 $ 20

Southern Fleurieu Viognier Chardonnay 2005 Viognier dominant, though no
percentage specified; an appealing mix of yellow peach and apricot fruit; long, clean and
bright finish. Screwcap. **RATING** 90 **DRINK** Now $ 18

Southcote Southern Fleurieu Dry White 2005 Lively, fresh, sweet lemon juice/citrus
flavours; a lovely summer drink. Value. Semillon/Chardonnay. Screwcap. 13.5° alc.
RATING 90 **DRINK** Now $ 13

Southern Fleurieu Cabernet Shiraz 2004 Bright, clear colour; a light- to medium-
bodied array of fresh red fruits, with touches of spice; fine tannins, subtle oak. Excellent
value. Twin top. 13° alc. **RATING** 90 **DRINK** 2009 $ 15

McLaren Vale Rose 2005 Bright, pale fuchsia; clean, fresh bouquet of delicate red fruits
and spice; dry palate; good balance and length. Cabernet/Grenache/Shiraz. Screwcap.
RATING 89 **DRINK** Now $ 16

Salmon Brut 2004 Highly fragrant lemon blossom bouquet; fresh, direct, bracing palate,
with crisp acidity. **RATING** 87 **DRINK** 2008 $ 22

Southern Fleurieu Pinot Noir 2004 RATING 86 **DRINK** 2008 $ 25

Passing Clouds

RMB 440 Kurting Road, Kingower, Vic 3517 **REGION** Bendigo
T (03) 5438 8257 **F** (03) 5438 8246 **WWW.**passingclouds.com.au **OPEN** W'ends 12–5, Mon–Fri by
appt
WINEMAKER Graeme Leith, Susie McDonald **EST.** 1974 **CASES** 4000
Graeme Leith and Sue Mackinnon planted the first vines at Passing Clouds in 1974, 60 km northwest
of Bendigo. Graeme Leith is one of the great personalities of the wine industry, with a superb sense of
humour, and makes lovely regional reds with cassis, berry and mint fruit. Sheltered by hills of
ironbark forest, the valley offers an ideal growing climate for premium red wine. The main varieties
planted on the 6-ha vineyard are shiraz, cabernet sauvignon, and pinot noir. Additional varieties are
sourced from local grapegrowers. Exports to the US.

Graeme's Blend 2004 Distinctly better colour/hue than Angel; more powerful and
distinct array of black fruits; ripe tannins, good oak. For release 2007. Screwcap. 14.2° alc.
RATING 93 **DRINK** 2017 $ 25

Yarra Valley Pinot Noir 2004 Bright, light red-purple; shows very early-picked characters
throughout; leaf, mint and fresh red fruits; a foot in the rose camp. Diam. 11.7° alc.
RATING 89 **DRINK** Now $ 23

Reserve Shiraz 2004 Medium-bodied, savoury, spicy plum and blackberry; sweet fruit on
the mid-palate, fine tannins to close. Screwcap. 14.5° alc. **RATING** 89 **DRINK** 2012 $ 35

Pasut Family Wines

NR

Block 445 Calder Highway, Sunnycliffs, Vic 3496 **REGION** Murray Darling
T (03) 5024 2361 **OPEN** By appt
WINEMAKER Stuart Kilmister (Contract) **EST.** 2000 **CASES** NA
Denis and Pauline Pasut have 10 ha of vineyards, with a very interesting range of varietals planted: pinot gris, sangiovese, barbera, fragola, nebbiolo and vermentino, all of which (with the qualified exception of pinot gris) are grapes grown chiefly in Italy. If the varieties planted are exotic, the brands are more so: Pasut, Pinkbits, Fatbelly and Alpino Misto.

Paternoster

NR

17 Paternoster Road, Emerald, Vic 3782 **REGION** Yarra Valley
T (03) 5968 3197 **F** (03) 5968 3197 **WWW**.paternosterwines.com.au **OPEN** W'ends 11–6
WINEMAKER Philip Hession **EST.** 1985 **CASES** 700
The densely planted, non-irrigated vines (at a density of 5000 vines per ha) cascade down a steep hillside at Emerald in one of the coolest parts of the Yarra Valley. Pinot Noir is the specialty of the winery, producing intensely flavoured wines with a strong eucalypt mint overlay.

Paterson's Gundagai Vineyard

★★★★☆

474 Old Hume Highway Road, Tumblong, NSW 2729 **REGION** Gundagai
T (02) 6944 9227 **F** (02) 9410 1466 **OPEN** 7 days 9.30–5
WINEMAKER Celine Rousseau (Contract) **EST.** 1996 **CASES** 700
The Paterson family began developing the 23-ha vineyard in 1996, with 12 ha shiraz, 6 ha cabernet sauvignon and 5 ha chardonnay. It is a powerful team: Robert Paterson (M.Ec. — Sydney, PMD — Harvard) was a Senior Vice-President of Coca Cola and his wife Rhondda was a teacher, before both turned to cattle farming in the early 1980s and grapegrowing in the mid-'90s. Son Stuart Paterson has a PhD in Chemical Engineering from the University of NSW, and has studied viticulture and wine science at Charles Sturt University in Wagga; wife Rainny is an architect. Most of the grapes grown elsewhere in Gundagai are sold to major wine companies for blended wines; Paterson's is one of the few estate-based operations.

▼▼▼▼▽ **Shiraz 2004** Vivid purple-red; rich, luscious, but not jammy, blackberry and dark plum fruit with controlled oak and extract. Plastered with gold medals and trophies from Boutique/Small Winemakers shows. Cork. 14° alc. **RATING** 93 **DRINK** 2014 **$** 18

Patrick T Wines

★★★★☆

Cnr Ravenswood Lane/Riddoch Highway, Coonawarra, SA 5263 **REGION** Coonawarra
T (08) 8737 3687 **F** (08) 8737 3689 **OPEN** 7 days 10–4.30
WINEMAKER Pat Tocaciu **EST.** 1996 **CASES** 1500
Patrick Tocaciu is a district veteran, setting up Patrick T Winemaking Services after prior careers at Heathfield Ridge Winery and Hollick Wines. He and his partners have almost 44 ha of vines at Wrattonbully, and another 2 ha of cabernet sauvignon in Coonawarra. The Wrattonbully plantings cover all the major varieties, while the Coonawarra plantings give rise to the Home Block Cabernet Sauvignon. Also carries out contract winemaking for others.

▼▼▼▼▽ **The Caves Vineyard Riesling 2005** Bright green-yellow; abundant, rich, tropical and citrus mix with squeaky, lemony acidity. Blessed with both a cork and screwcap for some archaic marketing reason, one supposes. Screwcap. 12° alc. **RATING** 91 **DRINK** 2008 **$** 20
The Caves Vineyard Shiraz 2003 Vibrant blackberry, raspberry and cherry fruit; light- to medium-bodied, with minimal tannin and oak impact. Zork. 14° alc. **RATING** 91 **DRINK** 2012 **$** 27
Home Block Vineyard Cabernet Sauvignon 2003 Medium-bodied; and supple, quite sweet, blackcurrant and cassis fruit; fine, ripe tannins; integrated oak. Zork. 13.5° alc. **RATING** 90 **DRINK** 2013 **$** 27

Patrick's Vineyard ★★★

Croziers Road, Cobaw via Mount Macedon, Vic 3441 (postal) REGION Macedon Ranges
T 0419 598 401 F (03) 9521 6266 OPEN Not
WINEMAKER Alan Cooper (Contract) EST. 1996 CASES 480
Noell and John McNamara and Judy Doyle planted 2 ha of pinot noir in 1996 and 1997. The vineyard
stands high on the southern slopes of the Cobaw Ranges with an 1862 settler's cottage still standing
and marking the first land use in the region. At an altitude of 600m, even pinot ripens very late in the
season, typically at the end of April or early May, but in the right years, when the canopy has turned
entirely from green to yellow-gold, the results can be impressive.

Macedon Ranges Pinot Noir 2004 Light colour; elegant, delicate, fragrant aromas; a
very light palate, drink asap. Value in its category. The '02 vintage shows just what the
vineyard can achieve. Diam. 13° alc. RATING 86 DRINK Now $ 17

Patritti Wines NR

13–23 Clacton Road, Dover Gardens, SA 5048 REGION Adelaide Zone
T (08) 8296 8261 F (08) 8296 5088 OPEN Mon–Sat 9–5
WINEMAKER G Patritti, J Mungall EST. 1926 CASES 100 000
A traditional, family-owned business offering wines at modest prices, but with impressive vineyard
holdings of 10 ha of shiraz in Blewitt Springs and 6 ha of grenache at Aldinga North.

Patterson Lakes Estate NR

Riverend Road, Bangholme, Vic 3175 (postal) REGION Port Phillip Zone
T (03) 9773 1034 F (03) 9772 5634 OPEN Not
WINEMAKER Bill Christophersen EST. 1998 CASES 1500
Former property developer James Bate has followed in the footsteps of the late Sid Hamilton (who
established Leconfield in Coonawarra when he was 80) by starting Patterson Lakes Estate not long
before he turned 80. The original planting was of 3 ha of shiraz, with a further 3 ha of shiraz, 0.8 ha
each of viognier and tempranillo, a patch of cabernet franc, petit verdot, and merlot for a Bordeaux
blend, and small amounts of mourvedre, cinsaut and grenache to go with the shiraz. A small winery
was completed in 2004. Sullivan Wine Agencies handles the domestic distribution; exports to the US.

Pattersons NR

St Werburghs Road, Mount Barker, WA 6234 REGION Mount Barker
T (08) 9851 2063 F (08) 9851 2063 OPEN Sat–Wed 10–5, or by appt
WINEMAKER Plantagenet EST. 1982 CASES 500
Schoolteachers Sue and Arthur Patterson have grown chardonnay, shiraz and pinot noir and grazed
cattle as a weekend relaxation for 2 decades. The cellar door is in a beautiful rammed-earth house,
and a number of vintages are on sale at any one time. Good Chardonnay and Shiraz have been
complemented by the occasional very good Pinot Noir.

Paul Bettio Wines

34 Simpsons Lane, Moyhu, Vic 3732 REGION King Valley
T (03) 5727 9308 F (03) 5727 9344 WWW.paulbettiowines.com.au OPEN 7 days 10–5
WINEMAKER Daniel Bettio EST. 1995 CASES 3000
The Bettio family, with Paul and Daniel at the helm, have established 27.5 ha of vines in the King
Valley. The plantings are of sauvignon blanc, chardonnay, merlot and cabernet sauvignon, and the
wines, including a range of back vintages, are chiefly sold through the cellar door and by mail order.

King Valley Sauvignon Blanc Chardonnay 2005 A synergistic blend with lifted aromatic
qualities, good length and good balance. Very good value. Screwcap. RATING 88
DRINK Now $ 9.90
King Valley Cabernet Shiraz Merlot 2005 Medium-bodied; has a little more structure
than some of the other Bettio wines; nice black and red fruit mix; value. Screwcap.
14.5° alc. RATING 88 DRINK Now $ 12

King Valley Chardonnay 2005 Light citrus and nectarine fruit drives both the bouquet and palate. The French oak is at a subliminal level, gentle acidity lengthening the finish. Screwcap. **RATING** 87 **DRINK** Now $ 11.95

King Valley Shiraz 2005 Light- to medium-bodied; spicy, peppery touches to blackberry fruit; minimal extract. Screwcap. 14.5° alc. **RATING** 87 **DRINK** 2009 $ 14

King Valley Merlot 2005 Enticing, bright, clear colour; light-bodied, clean and fresh red fruits with a touch of olive; no distracting oak or tannins. Screwcap. 14.5° alc. **RATING** 87 **DRINK** 2008 $ 14

ҀҀҀ҇ **King Valley Cabernet Sauvignon 2005** **RATING** 86 **DRINK** 2008 $ 14
King Valley Sauvignon Blanc 2005 **RATING** 85 **DRINK** Now $ 14
King Valley Riesling 2005 **RATING** 84 **DRINK** Now $ 14
King Valley Cabernet Merlot 2005 **RATING** 84 **DRINK** Now $ 10

Paul Conti Wines ★★★★

529 Wanneroo Road, Woodvale, WA 6026 **REGION** Greater Perth Zone
T (08) 9409 9160 **F** (08) 9309 1634 **WWW**.paulcontiwines.com.au **OPEN** Mon–Sat 9.30–5.30, Sun by appt
WINEMAKER Paul Conti, Jason Conti **EST.** 1948 **CASES** 8000
Third-generation winemaker Jason Conti has now assumed day-to-day control of winemaking, although father Paul (who succeeded his father in 1968) remains interested and involved in the business. Over the years Paul Conti challenged and redefined industry perceptions and standards; the challenge for Jason Conti was to achieve the same degree of success in a relentlessly and increasingly competitive market environment, and he is doing just that. Exports to the UK, Indonesia, Singapore, Malaysia and Japan.

ҀҀҀҀ҇ **The Tuarts Cabernet Sauvignon 2005** Spotlessly clean bouquet; medium-bodied, perfectly ripened cabernet fruit-driven style, French oak (and a touch of merlot) in the background along with a twist of chocolate; very good mouthfeel, likewise value. Screwcap. 14° alc. **RATING** 93 **DRINK** 2015 $ 19

Medici Ridge Pinot Noir 2004 Good hue and depth; abundant plum and cherry in unambiguous varietal spectrum; supple, fleshy fruit, then a touch of forest floor. By far the best yet. Cork. 13.5° alc. **RATING** 91 **DRINK** 2010 $ 19

ҀҀҀҀ **The Tuarts Chardonnay 2005** Fruit-forward, oak ex partial barrel ferment well into the background; light- to medium-bodied melon and fig fruit flavours. Screwcap. 13.5° alc. **RATING** 88 **DRINK** 2009 $ 19

Mariginiup Shiraz 2003 Strong colour; very ripe plum, prune and blackberry fruit with soft tannins and controlled oak. Cork. 14.5° alc. **RATING** 88 **DRINK** 2010 $ 27

The Tuarts Chenin Blanc 2005 If you like chenin blanc, this is for you. Light- to medium-bodied, with pleasant, ripe fruit salad flavours and balanced acidity. Screwcap. 13.5° alc. **RATING** 87 **DRINK** 2010 $ 15

Late Harvest Muscat 2005 Cleverly made; sweet grapey entry to the mouth, then a twist of lemony acidity and CO_2 spritz. Cork. 10° alc. **RATING** 87 **DRINK** Now $ 15

ҀҀҀ҇ **Grenache Shiraz 2004** **RATING** 84 **DRINK** Now $ 15

Paul Osicka NR

Majors Creek Vineyard at Graytown, Vic 3608 **REGION** Heathcote
T (03) 5794 9235 **F** (03) 5794 9288 **OPEN** Mon–Sat 10–5, Sun 12–5
WINEMAKER Paul Osicka **EST.** 1955 **CASES** NFP
A low-profile producer but reliable, particularly when it comes to its smooth but rich Shiraz. Exports to the UK, Hong Kong and Japan.

Paulett ★★★★★

Polish Hill Road, Polish Hill River, SA 5453 **REGION** Clare Valley
T (08) 8843 4328 **F** (08) 8843 4202 **WWW**.paulettwines.com.au **OPEN** 7 days 10–5
WINEMAKER Neil Paulett **EST.** 1983 **CASES** 12 500
The Paulett story is a saga of Australian perseverance, commencing with the 1982 purchase of a property with 1 ha of vines and a house, promptly destroyed by the terrible Ash Wednesday bushfires of the following year. Son Matthew has joined Neil and Alison Paulett as a partner in the business, responsible for viticulture, and the plantings now total 25 ha on a much-expanded property holding of 147 ha. The winery and cellar door have wonderful views over the Polish Hill River region, the memories of the bushfires long gone. Exports to the UK and NZ.

TTTTT Anotonina Polish Hill River Riesling 2004 Fine spice, apple and mineral aromas; vibrant apple and citrus fruit on the palate; diamond-like clarity and purity. Screwcap.
RATING 94 **DRINK** 2015 $ 38

Paulmara Estate NR

47 Park Avenue, Rosslyn Park, SA 5072 (postal) **REGION** Barossa Valley
T 0417 895 138 **F** (08) 8364 3019 **WWW**.paulmara.com.au **OPEN** Not
WINEMAKER Paul Georgiadis, Neil Pike **EST.** 1999 **CASES** 450
Born to an immigrant Greek family, Paul Georgiadis grew up in Waikerie, where his family owned vineyards and orchards. His parents worked sufficiently hard to send him first to St Peters College in Adelaide and then to do a marketing degree at Adelaide University. He became the whirlwind grower relations manager for Southcorp, and one of the best-known faces in the Barossa Valley. Paul and wife Mara established a 10.9-ha vineyard in 1995, planted to semillon, shiraz, sangiovese, merlot and cabernet sauvignon. Part of the production is sold, and the best shiraz goes to make the Syna Shiraz ('syna' being Greek for together). Exports to the UK and the US.

Paxton ★★★★☆

Wheaton Road, McLaren Vale, SA 5171 **REGION** McLaren Vale
T (08) 8323 8645 **F** (08) 8323 8903 **WWW**.paxtonvineyards.com **OPEN** Thurs–Sun 10–5, pub hols by appt
WINEMAKER Michael Paxton **EST.** 1997 **CASES** 3500
David Paxton is one of Australia's best-known viticulturists and consultants. He founded Paxton Vineyards in McLaren Vale with his family in 1979, and has since been involved in various capacities in the establishment and management of vineyards in various leading regions across the country. Sons Ben (general manager) and former Flying Winemaker Michael (with 14 years' experience in Spain, South America, France and Australia) are responsible for making the wines. There are 4 vineyards in the family holdings: the Thomas Block, the Jones Block, Quandong Farm and Landcross Farm Settlement and Homestead. Here an underground barrel store has been completed and a cellar door opened in the original shearing shed. Exports to Denmark and Canada.

TTTTT McLaren Vale Shiraz 2003 Strong red-purple; a particularly impressive outcome for the vintage; supple, succulent blackberry, bitter chocolate and mocha; sustained finish thanks to fine tannins and quality oak. Cork. 14.5° alc. **RATING** 94 **DRINK** 2013 $ 39

TTTTT AAA McLaren Vale Shiraz Grenache 2004 Fresh, fragrant and delicious fruit-driven style; raspberry, cherry and blackberry; minimal tannin and oak inputs, but excellent length. Screwcap. 14° alc. **RATING** 91 **DRINK** 2009 $ 24

Peacetree Estate ★★★☆

Harmans South Road, Wilyabrup, WA 6280 **REGION** Margaret River
T (08) 9755 5170 **F** (08) 9755 9275 **WWW**.peacetreeestate.com **OPEN** 7 days 10–6
WINEMAKER Paul Green, Severine Maudoux (Contract) **EST.** 1995 **CASES** 1400
Three generations of the Tucker family were involved in the first plantings at Peacetree Estate in 1995; however, it was of olive trees, not vines. One ha each of sauvignon blanc and cabernet sauvignon followed, 0.8 ha viognier coming later. For the first 3 vintages the grapes were sold, and in 2001 the Tuckers decided to take the plunge and have the wine bottled under the Peacetree Estate label.

Margaret River Semillon Sauvignon Blanc 2005 A ripe, rich style running into the tropical/peach spectrum, bolstered by alcohol. Screwcap. 14.3° alc. **RATING** 89 **DRINK** 2008 $ 19

Unoaked Cabernet Sauvignon 2004 Interesting style; certainly puts the focus on blackcurrant/cassis fruit, finishing with soft tannins. The pricing rationale is not obvious. Screwcap. 13.2° alc. **RATING** 89 **DRINK** 2012 $ 26

Margaret River Cabernet Sauvignon 2004 A very substantial wine; rich blackcurrant fruit, good oak and tannin management. Cork. 13.5° alc. **RATING** 89 **DRINK** 2012 $ 26

Lumiere Rouge 2005 Fresh, bright red fruits; more cassis than blackcurrant; nicely balanced. Cabernet rose. Screwcap. 14.5° alc. **RATING** 88 **DRINK** Now $ 22

Margaret River Cabernet Merlot 2004 Good colour; fresh, light- to medium-bodied red and black fruits with a touch of mint; subtle oak, but a little underdone in the winery. Screwcap. 12.9° alc. **RATING** 88 **DRINK** 2010 $ 24

Peacock Hill Vineyard

29 Palmers Lane, Pokolbin, NSW 2320 **REGION** Lower Hunter Valley
T (02) 4998 7661 **F** (02) 4998 7661 **WWW**.peacockhill.com.au **OPEN** Thurs–Mon, public & school hols 10–5, or by appt
WINEMAKER George Tsiros, Bill Sneddon, Rod Russell (Contract) **EST.** 1969 **CASES** 1500

The Peacock Hill Vineyard was first planted in 1969 as part of the Rothbury Estate, originally owned by a separate syndicate but then moving under the direct control and ownership of Rothbury. After several further changes of ownership as Rothbury sold many of its vineyards, George Tsiros and Silvi Laumets acquired the 8-ha property in October 1995. Since that time they have rejuvenated the vineyard.

Top Block Hunter Valley Chardonnay 2002 Has aged very well; nectarine and citrus fruit much tighter; better acidity. **RATING** 90 **DRINK** Now $ 35

Top Block Hunter Valley Chardonnay 2005 Light straw-green; stone fruit, fig and melon; not particularly intense, but clean and well-balanced; minimal oak. Cork. 13.5° alc. **RATING** 89 **DRINK** 2008 $ 26

Top Block Hunter Valley Chardonnay 2004 Peach, stone fruit and melon; very similar style to the '05; soft fruit, easy access. Cork. 13.5° alc. **RATING** 88 **DRINK** Now $ 26

Jaan Hunter Valley Shiraz 2003 Firm, fresh; light- to medium-bodied red and black fruits; crisp finish, low tannin profile. Cork. 13° alc. **RATING** 88 **DRINK** 2011 $ 30

Pearson Vineyards

Main North Road, Penwortham, SA 5453 **REGION** Clare Valley
T (08) 8843 4234 **F** (08) 8843 4141 **OPEN** Mon–Fri 11–5, w'ends 10–5
WINEMAKER Jim Pearson **EST.** 1993 **CASES** 800

Jim Pearson makes the Pearson Vineyard wines at Mintaro Cellars. The 1.5-ha estate vineyards surround the beautiful little stone house which acts as a cellar door — and which appears on the cover of my book, *The Wines, The History, The Vignerons of the Clare Valley.*

Riesling 2005 Pale, bright straw-green; very strong mineral, slate and spice characters lock up the fruit; interesting, and time may reveal all. Screwcap. 12.3° alc. **RATING** 89 **DRINK** 2015 $ 18

Peel Estate

Fletcher Road, Baldivis, WA 6171 **REGION** Peel
T (08) 9524 1221 **F** (08) 9524 1625 **WWW**.peelwine.com.au **OPEN** 7 days 10–5
WINEMAKER Will Nairn **EST.** 1974 **CASES** 6000

The icon wine is the Shiraz, a wine of considerable finesse and with a remarkably consistent track record. Every year Will Nairn holds a Great Shiraz Tasting for 6-year-old Australian Shirazs, and pits Peel Estate (in a blind tasting attended by 100 or so people) against Australia's best. It is never disgraced. The white wines are workmanlike, the wood-matured Chenin Blanc another winery specialty, although not achieving the excellence of the Shiraz. Exports to the UK, the US, Malaysia, Hong Kong and Japan.

ŦŦŦŦ℣ **Cabernet Sauvignon 2001** Some colour development, not 100% bright; a substantial wine; with rich, but not jammy, blackcurrant fruit; nice touch of cigar box; balanced, ripe tannins. Cork. 14.5° alc. **RATING** 93 **DRINK** 2015 $ 30

ŦŦŦŦ **Rose Sec 2005** Light, lively, fresh and — indeed — is virtually dry; citrus and cherry flavours; good example. Screwcap. 13° alc. **RATING** 88 **DRINK** Now $ 14
Merlot Cabernet Franc 2003 Light- to medium-bodied; savoury/minty/leafy/spicy characters all reflect the blend. Estate-grown. Screwcap. 13.5° alc. **RATING** 87 **DRINK** 2008 $ 16

ŦŦŦ℣ **Premium White 2005** The 2 varieties come together quite well, sauvignon blanc giving some vitality to the finish. Chenin Blanc/Sauvignon Blanc. Screwcap. 13.5° alc. **RATING** 86 **DRINK** Now $ 14

ŦŦŦ **Zinfandel 2001 RATING** 83 $ 40

Peerick Vineyard ★★★★☆

Wild Dog Track, Moonambel, Vic 3478 **REGION** Pyrenees
T (03) 5467 2207 **F** (03) 5467 2207 **WWW**.peerick.com.au **OPEN** W'ends & public hols 11–4
WINEMAKER Mount Langhi Ghiran (Dan Buckle) **EST.** 1990 **CASES** 2000
Peerick is the venture of Chris Jessup and wife Meryl. They have mildly trimmed their Joseph's Coat vineyard by increasing the plantings to 5.6 ha and eliminating the malbec and semillon, but still grow cabernet sauvignon, shiraz, cabernet franc, merlot, sauvignon blanc and viognier. Quality has improved as the vines have reached maturity. Exports to NZ.

ŦŦŦŦ℣ **Reserve Pyrenees Shiraz 2002** Medium red-purple; a medium-bodied combination of sweet plum and blackberry fruit, and cedar and vanilla oak; ripe tannins, good length. Cork. 14° alc. **RATING** 93 **DRINK** 2013 $ 28
Pyrenees Viognier 2005 Complex winemaking inputs work well; creamy/nutty nuances around varietal apricot/orange fruit. Partial malolactic fermentation and maturation in new French oak works well; no phenolics. Screwcap. 14.5° alc. **RATING** 92 **DRINK** 2009 $ 25
Pyrenees Shiraz Viognier 2004 Bright purple-red; sweet black plum and blackberry fruit in an elegant, medium-bodied frame; viognier just a little bit over the top (9%). Cork. 14° alc. **RATING** 92 **DRINK** 2009 $ 28

ŦŦŦŦ **Pyrenees Sauvignon Blanc 2005** A complex dusty/chalky/slatey bouquet, and a similarly complex palate, with partial barrel ferment adding to texture and mouthfeel. Screwcap. 14° alc. **RATING** 89 **DRINK** Now $ 17

Pegeric NR

PO Box 227, Woodend, Vic 3442 **REGION** Macedon Ranges
T (03) 9354 4961 **F** (03) 9354 4961 **WWW**.pegeric.com **OPEN** Not
WINEMAKER Chris Cormack, Ian Gunter, Llew Knight (Contract) **EST.** 1987 **CASES** 100
Owner and viticulturist Chris Cormack accumulated an oenological degree and experience in every facet of the wine industry here and overseas before beginning the establishment of the close-planted, non-irrigated, low-yielding Pegeric Vineyard at an altitude of 640m on red volcanic basalt soil. As a separate exercise, he has also made several vintages of a cross-regional blend of Cabernet Shiraz named Tumbetin. He has recently planted a small block of riesling.

🦭 Pelican's Landing Maritime Wines ★★★★☆

PO Box 1143, Stirling, SA 5152 **REGION** Southern Fleurieu
T 0411 552 077 **F** (08) 8370 9208 **WWW**.plmwines.com **OPEN** At Boccabella's, w'ends & public hols 9–5, school hols Thurs–Sun 9–5
WINEMAKER Helen Marzola **EST.** 2001 **CASES** 240
Helen Marzola is the owner and winemaker of Pelican's Landing, the second vineyard to be established on Hindmarsh Island. The 32-ha property was previously a cattle farm; it now has 7.3 ha of cabernet sauvignon, chardonnay and viognier in production, the first vintage in 2004.

ŸŸŸŸ🍷 **Mr Percival Cabernet Sauvignon 2004** The clean bouquet offers cassis, chocolate and French oak aromas in abundance. A strongly structured palate brings together all the elements of the bouquet in impressive fashion, with fine and ripe tannins. Screwcap. **RATING** 93 **DRINK** 2014 $30

Pembroke ★★★☆

191 Richmond Road, Cambridge, Tas 7170 **REGION** Southern Tasmania
T (03) 6248 5139 **F** (03) 6234 5481 **www**.pembrokewines.com **OPEN** By appt
WINEMAKER Hood Wines (Andrew Hood) **EST.** 1980 **CASES** 350
The 2.3-ha Pembroke vineyard was established in 1980 by the McKay and Hawker families and is still owned by them. It is predominantly planted to pinot noir and chardonnay, with tiny quantities of riesling and sauvignon blanc.

ŸŸŸŸ🍷 **North Block Lightly Wooded Chardonnay 2005** Definitive cool-grown chardonnay, with grapefruit, melon, racy acidity and a lively finish; the oak barely surfaces. Screwcap. 14.6° alc. **RATING** 92 **DRINK** 2012 $25

ŸŸŸ **Pinot Noir 2004 RATING** 83 $25

Penbro Estate NR

Cnr Melba Highway/Murrindindi Road, Glenburn, Vic 3717 **REGION** Upper Goulburn
T 0408 548 717 **F** (03) 9215 2346 **www**.penbroestate.com.au **OPEN** At Glenburn Pub
WINEMAKER Scott McCarthy (Contract) **EST.** 1997 **CASES** 3250
Since 1997 the Bertalli family has established 40 ha of premium cool-climate vineyards on their highly regarded Black Angus cattle farm. The vineyards are high up in the rolling hills of the Great Dividing Range, flanked by the Toolangi Forest and the alluvial plains of the Yea River, halfway between Yarra Glen and Yea. Part of the grape production is sold.

Pendarves Estate NR

110 Old North Road, Belford, NSW 2335 **REGION** Lower Hunter Valley
T (02) 9913 1088 **F** (02) 9970 6152 **www**.winedoctor.info **OPEN** By appt
WINEMAKER Monarch Winemaking Services (Greg Silkman) **EST.** 1986 **CASES** 12 000
The perpetual-motion general practitioner and founder of the Australian Medical Friends of Wine, Dr Philip Norrie, is a born communicator and marketer as well as a wine historian of note. He also happens to be a passionate advocate of the virtues of Verdelho, inspired in part by the high regard held for that variety by vignerons around the turn of the century. His ambassadorship for the cause of wine and health, in Australia and overseas, has led to a joint venture to produce and export a large-volume brand, 'The Wine Doctor'. Exports to the UK, Germany and India.

🐚 Pende Valde NR

PO Box 668, Kent Town, SA 5071 **REGION** McLaren Vale
T (08) 8363 8793 **www**.pendevalde.com.au **OPEN** Not
WINEMAKER Various contract **EST.** 1835 **CASES** 2000
Pende Valde is, to put it mildly, an unusual business, its raison d'etre being the female descendants of Mary (nee Holt) and Christopher Rawson Penfold. We are told that 'Mrs Mary became one of Australia's first founding female winemakers and the Pende Valde family matriarch'. The wines come from 12 ha of cabernet sauvignon, 9 ha of shiraz and 1.6 ha of bush-pruned grenache and 4 ha of trellised chardonnay. They have not hitherto been sold (large format bottles donated to charity) but with the opening of the website the wines are generally available.

Penfolds ★★★★★

Tanunda Road, Nuriootpa, SA 5355 **REGION** Barossa Valley
T (08) 8568 9389 **F** (08) 8568 9489 **www**.penfolds.com.au **OPEN** Mon–Fri 10–5, w'ends & public hols 11–5
WINEMAKER Peter Gago **EST.** 1844 **CASES** 1.4 million

Senior among the numerous wine companies or stand-alone brands in Southcorp Wines and undoubtedly one of the top wine companies in the world in terms of quality, product range and exports. The consistency of the quality of the red wines and their value for money is recognised worldwide; the white wines, headed by the ultra-premium Yattarna Chardonnay, are steadily improving in quality. Exports to the UK and the US.

ΤΤΤΤΤ **Yattarna Chardonnay 2003** A wonderful wine; very complex, yet has elegance and finesse; superb fruit and oak balance; flawless winemaking. **RATING** 96 **DRINK** 2012 $ 120

Grange 2001 It is extraordinary how this wine has gained power, weight and complexity since first bottled; now majestic black fruits, licorice and chocolate/mocha notes run through the palate. Great tannins sustain and support the back-palate and finish. Please move to screwcaps; this wine would live forever. Cork. 14.5° alc. **RATING** 96 **DRINK** 2030 $ 300

St Henri Shiraz 2002 Excellent colour; a medium-bodied wine which lives up to the expectations of a great vintage; intense black fruits run through a long, perfectly balanced palate, finishing with fine tannins, oak largely unseen. Cork. 14.5° alc. **RATING** 96 **DRINK** 2020 $ 70

Cellar Reserve Eden Valley Gewurztraminer 2005 A rare beast; crystal-clear spice, musk, lychee and rose petal aromas and flavours, the palate delivering on the bouquet but avoiding phenolics. Ready, set, go. Screwcap. 13.5° alc. **RATING** 95 **DRINK** 2010 $ 30

RWT Shiraz 2003 Great outcome for a lesser vintage; right from the outset, a fusion of black fruits and fine French oak each supporting the other; silky and caressing. Cork. 14.5° alc. **RATING** 95 **DRINK** 2018 $ 150

Great Grandfather Port NV Deep tawny with an olive-green rim; both bouquet and palate are extraordinarily concentrated and rich, very much into the liqueur style of port which is unique to Australia. Shows the brandy spirit which was used in the fortifying process, and which adds yet extra complexity. **RATING** 95 **DRINK** Now

Bin 311 Tumbarumba Chardonnay 2005 Complex, faintly funky, French oak barrel ferment aromas lead into intense nectarine and grapefruit flavours, the oak just emerging again on the finish. High quality cool climate style. Screwcap. 13° alc. **RATING** 94 **DRINK** 2010 $ 35

Reserve Bin Chardonnay 2004 Bin 04A. Obvious funky, wild yeast barrel ferment inputs don't overwhelm the surprisingly delicate and fine fruit. Screwcap. **RATING** 94 **DRINK** 2010 $ 27

ΤΤΤΤ **Old Vine Barossa Valley Bin 138 Grenache Shiraz Mourvedre 2004** Good red-purple; a medium-bodied array of red and black berry fruits, with excellent texture and structure; balanced tannins, and a long finish. Screwcap. 14.5° alc. **RATING** 93 **DRINK** 2014 $ 27

Bin 407 Cabernet Sauvignon 2003 A stylish, medium-bodied wine; gentle cassis and blackcurrant fruit with very fine tannins running through the length of the palate, oak merely a support vehicle. Cork. 14.5° alc. **RATING** 93 **DRINK** 2015 $ 35

Bin 389 Cabernet Shiraz 2003 Good hue; medium-bodied, complex blackcurrant, blackberry, plum, chocolate, spice and vanilla, the whole works; will richly repay cellaring if the cork permits. Very good outcome for a challenging vintage. Cork. 14.5° alc. **RATING** 93 **DRINK** 2018 $ 40

Reserve Bin Eden Valley Riesling 2005 Very youthful, tight and reserved; mineral, talc. and slate; does have considerable length, and needs 5 years plus to come into full flower. Screwcap. **RATING** 90 **DRINK** 2015 $ 25.99

Thomas Hyland Chardonnay 2005 Elegant, light- to medium-bodied, fruit-driven style; very attractive melon and citrus flavours, good balance. Screwcap. 13.5° alc. **RATING** 90 **DRINK** 2009 $ 20

Koonunga Hill Chardonnay 2004 Fragrant citrus, nectarine and white peach fruit-driven, elegant style; good length; will hold. Screwcap. **RATING** 90 **DRINK** 2008 $ 14.99

Kalimna Bin 28 Shiraz 2003 Big, sturdy, archetypal Penfolds red; masses of black fruits and strong but balanced tannins in support; simply needs time. Barossa Valley/Clare Valley/McLaren Vale. Cork. 14.5° alc. **RATING** 90 **DRINK** 2015 $ 26

Koonunga Hill Cabernet Sauvignon 2002 Very traditional Koonunga Hill style, even though 100% cabernet. Solid black fruits with sustained, but not aggressive, tannins add to the length; will age very well; good oak handling. Screwcap. **RATING** 90 **DRINK** 2015 $ 14.99

Cellar Reserve Barossa Valley Sangiovese 2004 Plenty of cherry fruit; good length, balance and structure, with an appealing twist of lemon and earth on the finish. Cork. **RATING** 90 **DRINK** 2010

▼▼▼▼ **Koonunga Hill Semillon Sauvignon Blanc 2005** Fresh and crisp; an attractive mix of zesty lemony flavours around the structural core of Semillon; works well. Screwcap. 12.5° alc. **RATING** 89 **DRINK** Now $14.99

Thomas Hyland Chardonnay 2004 A moderately complex bouquet; nicely balanced, with good length to citrus and melon fruit; subtle oak. Screwcap. 13.5° alc. **RATING** 89 **DRINK** 2008 $20

Cellar Reserve Adelaide Hills Pinot Noir 2004 Strong colour; interesting spicy/bramble/ferny aromas, then powerful, dense and ripe plum fruit; seems late picked. Cork. **RATING** 89 **DRINK** 2008

Rawson's Retreat Shiraz Cabernet 2005 Ample mouthfeel; a ripe, but not overripe, palate of red and black fruits, plus layers of dark chocolate and mocha. Impressive and great value. What a pity the synthetic cork means you must not cellar the wine. Synthetic. 13.5° alc. **RATING** 89 **DRINK** 2008 $11

Thomas Hyland Cabernet Sauvignon 2003 Good colour; a well-balanced and structured medium-bodied palate, with gentle cassis and blackberry fruit; subtle oak. Screwcap. **RATING** 89 **DRINK** 2008 $19.99

Koonunga Hill Shiraz 2003 Smooth and supple, medium-bodied; leather, earth, blackberry and spice aromas and flavours; shortens slightly. Screwcap. **RATING** 88 **DRINK** 2013 $14.99

Bin 128 Coonawarra Shiraz 2003 Medium-bodied; a mix of black fruits and dark chocolate; controlled oak and tannins; nice line. **RATING** 88 **DRINK** 2011 $26

Rawson's Retreat Shiraz Cabernet 2004 Nice easy style; aromatic red and black fruits; fruit-driven, works well; immediate drinking. Synthetic. **RATING** 88 **DRINK** Now $10.99

Koonunga Hill Shiraz Cabernet 2003 Gently ripe black fruits on the medium-bodied palate; some mocha and vanilla. Screwcap. **RATING** 88 **DRINK** 2009 $14.99

Koonunga Hill Cabernet Merlot 2003 Well-balanced, medium-bodied blackcurrant fruit with fine, ripe tannins; minimal oak impact. Screwcap. 14° alc. **RATING** 87 **DRINK** 2009 $14.99

Rawson's Retreat Cabernet Sauvignon 2005 Good purple-red colour; light- to medium-bodied, with clean cassis/blackcurrant varietal fruit; light-framed structure. Screwcap. 13.5° alc. **RATING** 87 **DRINK** Now $11

Rawson's Retreat Cabernet Sauvignon 2004 Pleasing blackcurrant, cassis and blackberry fruit; minimal tannin and oak inputs; good value. Synthetic. **RATING** 87 **DRINK** Now $10.99

▼▼▼▽ **Rawson's Retreat Chardonnay 2005** **RATING** 86 **DRINK** Now $11
Rawson's Retreat Semillon Chardonnay 2005 **RATING** 86 **DRINK** Now $11
Rawson's Retreat Merlot 2005 **RATING** 86 **DRINK** Now $11

Penfolds Magill Estate ★★★★☆

78 Penfold Road, Magill, SA 5072 **REGION** Adelaide Zone
T (08) 8301 5400 **F** (08) 8301 5544 **WWW**.penfolds.com **OPEN** 7 days 10.30–4.30
WINEMAKER Peter Gago **EST.** 1844 **CASES** NFP
The birthplace of Penfolds, established by Dr Christopher Rawson Penfold in 1844, his house still part of the immaculately maintained property. It includes 6 ha of precious shiraz used to make Magill Estate; the original and subsequent winery buildings, most still in operation or in museum condition; the Penfolds corporate headquarters; and the much-acclaimed Magill Restaurant, with panoramic views back to the city, a great wine list and fine dining. All this a 20-minute drive from Adelaide's CBD.

▼▼▼▼▽ **Shiraz 2003** Medium-bodied; a wine as much about texture and structure as flavour; savoury black fruits, touches of spice, and a gentle oak echo. Cork. 14.5° alc. **RATING** 92 **DRINK** 2013 $90

Penley Estate ★★★★★

McLeans Road, Coonawarra, SA 5263 **REGION** Coonawarra
T (08) 8736 3211 **F** (08) 8736 3124 **WWW**.penley.com.au **OPEN** 7 days 10–4
WINEMAKER Kym Tolley **EST.** 1988 **CASES** 30 000
Owner winemaker Kym Tolley describes himself as a fifth-generation winemaker, the family tree involving both the Penfolds and the Tolleys. He worked 17 years in the industry before establishing Penley Estate and has made every post a winner since, producing a succession of rich, complex, full-bodied red wines and stylish Chardonnays. These are made from 91 precious ha of estate plantings. Exports to all major markets.

ᵀᵀᵀᵀᵀ **Hyland Shiraz 2004** Filled with powerful blackberry fruit; superb line and length; perfectly integrated and balanced oak. Trophy Best Commercial Dry Red Sydney Wine Show '06. **RATING** 95 **DRINK** 2014 $ 20
Phoenix Cabernet Sauvignon 2004 Delicious, supple mouthfeel; cassis fruit flavours; good oak and tannin management. **RATING** 94 **DRINK** 2014 $ 20

ᵀᵀᵀᵀᵀ **Merlot 2004** Bright colour; vibrantly fresh mix of red and black fruits; fine, soft tannins; good oak. Quality cork. **RATING** 93 **DRINK** 2011 $ 19.99
Condor Cabernet Shiraz 2004 Dusty/cedary notes to the underlying mix of blackcurrant and blackberry fruit; still coming together, but should do so. Cork. 14.5° alc. **RATING** 92 **DRINK** 2010 $ 20

ᵀᵀᵀᵀ **Chardonnay 2004** Ripe peach and citrus aromas; sweet peachy fruit; full-bodied palate; ready now. Screwcap. **RATING** 88 **DRINK** Now $ 19.99

ᵀᵀᵀᵀ **Over The Moon Rose 2005 RATING** 85 **DRINK** Now $ 15

Penmara ★★★

159 Corunna Road, Stanmore, NSW 2048 (postal) **REGION** Upper Hunter Valley/Orange
T (02) 9569 1703 **F** (02) 9560 7031 **WWW**.penmarawines.com.au **OPEN** Not
WINEMAKER Hunter Wine Services (John Horden) **EST.** 2000 **CASES** 35 000
Penmara was formed with the banner '5 Vineyards: 1 Vision'. In fact a sixth vineyard has already joined the group, the vineyards pooling most of their grapes, with a central processing facility, and marketing focused exclusively on exports. The members are Lilyvale Vineyards, in the Northern Slopes region near Tenterfield; Tangaratta Vineyards at Tamworth; Birnam Wood, Rothbury Ridge and Martindale Vineyards in the Hunter Valley; and Highland Heritage at Orange. In all, these vineyards give Penmara access to 128 ha of shiraz, chardonnay, cabernet sauvignon, semillon, verdelho and merlot, mainly from the Hunter Valley and Orange. Exports to the US, Canada, Singapore and Japan.

ᵀᵀᵀᵀᵀ **Sauvignon Blanc 2005** Light straw-green; a clean bouquet, then delicate passionfruit and gooseberry; the sweet fruit is neatly balanced by crisp acidity. Orange. Screwcap. 13.5° alc. **RATING** 91 **DRINK** Now $ 13

ᵀᵀᵀᵀ **Chardonnay 2005 RATING** 86 **DRINK** Now $ 13

ᵀᵀᵀ **Merlot 2003 RATING** 83 $ 13
Cabernet Sauvignon 2003 RATING 82 $ 13
Shiraz 2003 RATING 80 $ 13

Penna Lane Wines ★★★★☆

Lot 51, Penna Lane, Penwortham via Clare, SA 5453 **REGION** Clare Valley
T (08) 8843 4364 **F** (08) 8843 4349 **WWW**.pennalanewines.com.au **OPEN** Thurs–Sun & public hols 11–5, or by appt
WINEMAKER Paulett Wines **EST.** 1998 **CASES** 3000
Ray and Lynette Klavin, then living in the Riverland, purchased their 14-ha property in the Skilly Hills in 1993. It was covered with rubbish, Salvation Jane, a derelict dairy and a tumbledown piggery, and every weekend they travelled from Waikerie to clean up the property, initially living in a tent and thereafter moving into the dairy, which had more recently been used as a shearing shed. Planting

began in 1996, and in 1997 the family moved to the region, Lynette to take up a teaching position and Ray to work at Knappstein Wines. Ray had enrolled at Roseworthy in 1991, and met Stephen Stafford-Brookes, another mature-age student. Both graduated from Roseworthy in 1993, having already formed a winemaking joint venture for Penna Lane. Exports to the US.

ΥΥΥΥΥ **The Willsmore Shiraz 2002** Dense colour; full-bodied, dense and concentrated but a supple mix of blackberry and dark chocolate; ripe tannins, good oak, good balance. **RATING** 94 **DRINK** 2020 $ 40

ΥΥΥΥΥ **Clare Valley Riesling 2005** Spice, slate and mineral; very lively palate, with bright acidity. Screwcap. 12° alc. **RATING** 91 **DRINK** 2012 $ 19
The Willsmore Shiraz 2003 Smooth, supple blackberry, dark chocolate and mocha run through a medium-bodied palate, the oak integrated, the tannins soft. Screwcap. 14° alc. **RATING** 90 **DRINK** 2013 $ 22
Cabernet Sauvignon 2003 Again medium-bodied; distinctly savoury/earthy edges to the black fruits, but has considerable length; controlled tannins. Screwcap. 14° alc. **RATING** 90 **DRINK** 2012 $ 22

ΥΥΥΥ **Clare Valley Rambling Rose 2005** Deep, bright fuchsia; a rich style, with lots of cherry fruit; carries a touch of sweetness on the finish. Screwcap. 13.5° alc. **RATING** 88 **DRINK** Now $ 18
The Willsmore Shiraz 2003 A savoury, earthy, leaner medium-bodied style; some black fruits, the tannins in check. Cork. 14° alc. **RATING** 87 **DRINK** 2009 $ 40

Penny's Hill   ★★★★

Main Road, McLaren Vale, SA 5171 **REGION** McLaren Vale
T (08) 8556 4460 **F** (08) 8556 4462 **WWW**.pennyshill.com.au **OPEN** 7 days 10–5
WINEMAKER Ben Riggs (Contract) **EST.** 1988 **CASES** 11 500
Penny's Hill is owned by Adelaide advertising agency businessman Tony Parkinson and wife Susie. The vineyard is 43.5 ha and, unusually for McLaren Vale, is close-planted with a thin vertical trellis/thin vertical canopy, the work of consultant viticulturist David Paxton. The innovative red dot packaging was the inspiration of Tony Parkinson, recalling the red dot sold sign on pictures in an art gallery and now giving rise to the Red Dot Art Gallery opening at Penny's Hill. Exports to the UK, the US and other major markets, particularly via the Woop Woop joint venture between Ben Riggs and Penny's Hill.

ΥΥΥΥΥ **McLaren Vale Shiraz 2004** Toasty oak a little assertive on the bouquet, but good palate richness and structure. **RATING** 92 **DRINK** 2014 $ 25
McLaren Vale Shiraz 2003 Medium- to full-bodied; rich blackberry and dark chocolate fruit; ripe tannins; good balance, length and quality French oak. Well above average for the vintage. Quality cork. **RATING** 92 **DRINK** 2013 $ 27
Red Dot Fleurieu Shiraz 2004 Strong colour; strongly regional blackberry and dark chocolate; a clean, medium-bodied, well-balanced palate carries 15° alcohol remarkably well. Zork. 15° alc. **RATING** 90 **DRINK** 2009 $ 19

ΥΥΥΥ **Red Dot Chardonnay Viognier 2005** Apricot and marzipan viognier dominates both the bouquet and palate despite being the junior partner; a complex, multi-region/varietal blend, full of interest. Zork. 13.5° alc. **RATING** 89 **DRINK** Now $ 15
McLaren Vale Cadenzia Grenache 2004 Sweet, rounded, juicy/jammy grenache; some kick on the finish from alcohol. Cork. 15° alc. **RATING** 88 **DRINK** 2009 $ 22
Woop Woop Shiraz 2004 Supple, smooth, medium-bodied; black and red fruits with good balance and length; fruit-driven. Cork. **RATING** 87 **DRINK** 2008 $ 12.99
Woop Woop Cabernet Sauvignon 2004 Strong colour; a big, brawny, barbecue-style red for real men, best left for a year or two. Cork. **RATING** 87 **DRINK** 2008 $ 12.99

ΥΥΥΥ **Woop Woop Chardonnay 2004** **RATING** 85 **DRINK** Now $ 12.99

ΥΥΥ **Woop Woop Verdelho 2005** **RATING** 83 $ 12.99

Pennyfield Wines
NR

Pennyfield Road, Berri, SA 5343 **REGION** Riverland
T (08) 8582 3595 **F** (08) 8582 3205 **WWW**.pennyfieldwines.com.au **OPEN** Not
WINEMAKER David Smallacombe **EST.** 2000 **CASES** 3500
Pennyfield Wines is named in memory of the pioneering family which originally developed the property, part of which is now owned by the Efrosinis family. Pennyfield draws on 17.7 ha of estate vineyards (principally planted to cabernet sauvignon and shiraz) but is also supplied with chardonnay, merlot, petit verdot, touriga and viognier by 4 local growers. Exports to the US, Canada, Denmark, Hong Kong, China and Japan.

Pennyweight Winery
NR

Pennyweight Lane, Beechworth, Vic 3747 **REGION** Beechworth
T (03) 5728 1747 **F** (03) 5728 1704 **WWW**.pennyweight.com.au **OPEN** 7 days 10–5
WINEMAKER Stephen Newton Morris **EST.** 1982 **CASES** 1000
Pennyweight was established by Stephen Morris, great-grandson of GF Morris, founder of Morris Wines. The 4 ha of vines are not irrigated and are organically grown. The business is run by Stephen, together with his wife Elizabeth and assisted by their 3 sons; Elizabeth Morris says, 'It's a perfect world', suggesting that Pennyweight is more than happy with its lot in life.

Peos Estate
★★★★

Graphite Road, Manjimup, WA 6258 **REGION** Manjimup
T (08) 9772 1378 **F** (08) 9772 1372 **WWW**.peosestate.com.au **OPEN** 7 days 10–4
WINEMAKER Shane McKerrow (Contract) **EST.** 1996 **CASES** 3000
The Peos family has farmed the West Manjimup district for 50 years, the third generation of 4 brothers commencing the development of a substantial vineyard in 1996; there is a little over 33 ha of vines, with shiraz (10 ha), merlot (7 ha), chardonnay (6.5 ha), cabernet sauvignon (4 ha) and pinot noir, sauvignon blanc and verdelho (2 ha each). Exports to Denmark.

 Four Acres Shiraz 2004 Allspice, blackberry and plum aromas lead into a rich blackberry, dark chocolate and spice palate, with good length and texture. Totally stained cork a worry. Cork. 14.5° alc. **RATING** 92 **DRINK** 2010 $ 30

♥♥♥♥ **Four Acres Chardonnay 2004** Soft, peachy fruit; a slightly broad but flavoursome palate. 14° alc. **RATING** 87 **DRINK** 2008 $ 28

Pepper Tree Wines
★★★★★

Halls Road, Pokolbin, NSW 2321 **REGION** Lower Hunter Valley
T (02) 4998 7539 **F** (02) 4998 7746 **WWW**.peppertreewines.com.au **OPEN** Mon–Fri 9–5, w'ends 9.30–5
WINEMAKER Chris Cameron, Janelle Zerk **EST.** 1993 **CASES** 50 000
The Pepper Tree winery is part of a complex which also contains The Convent guest house and Roberts Restaurant. In October 2002 it was acquired by a company controlled by Dr John Davis, who owns 50% of Briar Ridge and has substantial vineyard interests throughout NSW and SA, all of which contribute to its top-flight Grand Reserve and Reserve (single region) varietal ranges. Exports to the UK, the US and other major markets.

 Grand Reserve Hunter Valley Semillon 1999 Glowing yellow-green; a lovely wine, now moving towards the peak of maturity, holding the zesty freshness of youth but with a cloak of sweet lime and honey, the toast still to come. Cork. 10.5° alc. **RATING** 95 **DRINK** 2010 $ 39

Hunter Valley Semillon 2005 A quiet but clean bouquet; springs into life on the palate, with every combination of lemon imaginable, and echoes of other fruits, too. Cork. **RATING** 94 **DRINK** 2015 $ 25

Grand Reserve Orange Chardonnay 2005 Well-made and balanced; nectarine fruit and oak seamlessly interwoven on a long, harmonious palate. Cork. 13.5° alc. **RATING** 94 **DRINK** 2012 $ 35

Reserve Orange Shiraz 2004 Medium-bodied; rich, supple, plum, blackberry and licorice fruit; good tannin and oak management; no shortage of flavour or depth. Cork. 14.5° alc. RATING 94 DRINK 2010 $30

ŶŶŶŶŶ **Reserve Wrattonbully Shiraz 2004** An elegant, fluid wine, almost a role reversal with the Reserve Orange Shiraz; light- to medium-bodied red and black fruits; fine tannins and oak. Cork. 14.5° alc. RATING 91 DRINK 2014 $30
Limited Release Hunter Valley Viognier 2005 Big, generous, mouthfilling style; the ripe stone fruit, ginger and spice fruit has eaten the 100% barrel ferment oak. Cork. 13.5° alc. RATING 90 DRINK Now $25
Limited Release Hunter Valley Shiraz 2004 Medium red-purple; light- to medium-bodied, distinctly regional, soft, earthy fruit; has length and grows on retasting. Cork. 13° alc. RATING 90 DRINK Now $26

ŶŶŶŶ **Reserve Semillon 1999** Still very light, delicate and reserved; mineral, dried herbs and touches of spice and lanolin. Re-release. Cork. RATING 89 DRINK 2008 $25
Hunter Valley Verdelho 2005 Much more aroma and flavour than usual; attractive fruit salad and honey balanced by acidity. Cork. RATING 89 DRINK 2008 $22
Grand Reserve Wrattonbully Tannat 2004 Good colour; a powerful wine, fruit at the centre surrounded by a forest of the legendary tannat tannins; blend it or do more micro-oxygenation. Cork. 14.5° alc. RATING 89 DRINK 2014 $46
Hunter Valley Shiraz Viognier 2004 Light red; fresh, breezy, juicy berry style; fruit-driven, early drinking style. Screwcap. 12.5° alc. RATING 88 DRINK 2009 $18
Grand Reserve Wrattonbully Merlot 2004 Very ripe dark berry fruit, slightly anomalous for the vintage, and not particularly varietal, but has abundant flavour. RATING 88 DRINK Now $52
Orange Verduzzo 2005 Light straw-green; an unexpected, highly floral, spicy bouquet; the palate an anticlimax, seeming with some residual sugar; nonetheless, interesting. Cork. 14° alc. RATING 87 DRINK 2009 $25

ŶŶŶŶŶ **Reserve Wrattonbully Chardonnay 2005** Picked too late, the alcohol far too high; a rescue job in the winery was partially successful. Cork. 15.5° alc. RATING 86 DRINK 2009 $20
McLaren Vale Merlot 2001 RATING 85 DRINK Now $18
Reserve Coonawarra Classics 2002 RATING 84 DRINK 2009 $25

ŶŶŶ **Grand Reserve Hunter Valley Semillon 2005** RATING 83 $39
Limited Release Semillon 2005 RATING 83 $25

ŶŶŶ **Limited Release Verdelho 2005** RATING 79 $20

Peppin Ridge ★★★★

Peppin Drive, Bonnie Doon, Vic 3720 REGION Upper Goulburn
T (03) 5778 7430 F (03) 5778 7430 OPEN 7 days 11–5
WINEMAKER Don Adams EST. 1997 CASES 400
Peppin Ridge is planted on the shores of Lake Eildon; the land forms part of a vast station property established in 1850, and now partly under Lake Eildon. The property was acquired by the Peppin family, who developed the Peppin Merino sheep, said to be the cornerstone of the Australian wool industry. The plantings of marsanne, verdelho, shiraz and merlot cover 4 ha, and the wine is made onsite.

ŶŶŶŶŶ **Shiraz 2004** Very good balance, texture and overall mouthfeel; sweet spiced plum fruit; fine-grained, ripe tannins. Cork. RATING 91 DRINK 2014 $20
Merlot 2004 An attractive medium-bodied wine with clear varietal character; small red fruits and hints of spice and olive; good structure and tannins. Cork. RATING 90 DRINK 2010 $18

Perrini Estate

NR

Bower Road, Meadows, SA 5201 **REGION** Adelaide Hills
T (08) 8388 3210 **F** (08) 8388 3210 **OPEN** Wed–Sun & public hols 10–5
WINEMAKER Antonio Perrini **EST.** 1997 **CASES** 3500
Perrini Estate is very much a family affair; Tony and Connie Perrini had spent their working life in the retail food business, and Tony purchased the land in 1988 as a hobby farm and retirement home (or so he told Connie). In 1990 Tony planted his first few grapevines, began to read everything he could about making wine, and thereafter obtained vintage experience at a local winery. Next came highly successful entries into amateur winemaker competitions, and that was that. Together the family established the 6 ha of vineyard and built the winery and cellar door. Exports to Singapore.

Peschar's

NR

179 Wambo Road, Bulga, NSW 2330 **REGION** Lower Hunter Valley
T (02) 4927 1588 **F** (02) 4927 1589 **WWW.**peschar.com.au **OPEN** Not
WINEMAKER Tyrrell's **EST.** 1995 **CASES** 8000
In 1995 John and Mary Peschar purchased the historic Meerea Park property which had been in the ownership of the Eather family, the name of which continues to be used by the Eathers for a quite separate winemaking operation. The property is situated at the foot of the Wollemi National Park which rises steeply behind the vineyard. There are 16 ha of chardonnay, planted on sandy alluvial soils. While the focus is on Chardonnay, the Peschars have sourced 6 ha of vines in the Limestone Coast Zone for the production of Shiraz and Cabernet Merlot.

Petaluma

Spring Gully Road, Piccadilly, SA 5151 **REGION** Adelaide Hills
T (08) 8339 9300 **F** (08) 8339 9301 **WWW.**petaluma.com.au **OPEN** At Bridgewater Mill, Mount Barker Road, Bridgewater
WINEMAKER Con Moshos (former) **EST.** 1976 **CASES** 30 000
The Petaluma empire comprises Knappstein Wines, Mitchelton, Stonier and Smithbrook, since 2001 part of the Lion Nathan group. The range has been expanded beyond the core group of Croser sparkling, Clare Valley Riesling, Piccadilly Chardonnay and Coonawarra (Cabernet Sauvignon/Merlot). Newer arrivals of note include Adelaide Hills Viognier and Adelaide Hills Shiraz. Bridgewater Mill is the second label, which consistently provides wines most makers would love to have as their top label. Exports to the UK, US and Japan.

ŸŸŸŸŸ **Hanlin Hill Clare Valley Riesling 2005** Light, bright and crisp; fine lime and apple flavours, good length; a deliciously airy finish. Screwcap. 13° alc. **RATING** 94 **DRINK** 2013 $ 27

ŸŸŸŸŸ **Bridgewater Mill Viognier 2004** Strong musk, apricot and honeysuckle aromas lead into a powerful palate with integrated and balanced acidity holding the precocious fruit together. Cork. 14.5° alc. **RATING** 93 **DRINK** Now $ 21
Adelaide Hills Viognier 2004 Extremely rich and dense, yet not heavy nor (obviously) alcoholic; sweet apricot, musk and peach, the barely perceptible oak adding to texture rather than flavour. Cork. **RATING** 92 **DRINK** 2008 $ 36
Croser 2003 Fine, minerally notes to the bouquet; intense, long and tight white peach/apple/citrus mix, though not particularly complex as yet. **RATING** 92 **DRINK** 2008 $ 35
Adelaide Hills Shiraz 2003 Spice and blackberry with hints of leaf, mint and apricot; a powerful palate, with distinct tannins; needs time to soften. Cork. **RATING** 91 **DRINK** 2013 $ 42

ŸŸŸŸ **Bridgewater Mill Shiraz Viognier 2003** Aromatic red and black fruits with the telltale apricot lift; a clean, fresh and lively red fruit palate; fine tannins. Screwcap. **RATING** 89 **DRINK** 2010 $ 21

Peter Howland Wines

2/14 Portside Crescent, Wickham, NSW 2293 **REGION** Hunter Valley
T (02) 4920 2622 **F** (02) 4920 2699 **WWW**.peterhowlandwines.com **OPEN** By appt
WINEMAKER Peter Howland **EST.** 2001 **CASES** 4000
Peter Howland graduated from Adelaide University in 1997 with a first-class Honours degree in oenology. He has worked in the Hunter Valley, Margaret River, Hastings Valley, Macedon Ranges and Puglia in Italy. Newcastle may seem a strange place for a winery cellar door, but this is where his insulated and refrigerated barrel shed is located. From 2004 he has fermented his wines at Serenella Estate, where he also acts as contract winemaker. His wines are sourced from both sides of the continent: Great Southern and the Hunter Valley.

ŸŸŸŸŸ **Maxwell Vineyard Chardonnay 2004** A complex wine, with an à la mode hint of feral on the bouquet. An excellent palate, long, intense and perfectly balanced. A tour de force for the Hunter Valley. Screwcap. 13.7° alc. **RATING** 95 **DRINK** 2011 $ 30

Parsons Vineyard Frankland River Shiraz 2004 Deep purple-red; medium- to full-bodied; potent, powerful, intense blackberry fruit and a long, lingering palate; firm tannins give backbone. Cork. 14.5° alc. **RATING** 95 **DRINK** 2016 $ 33

Langley Vineyard Donnybrook Shiraz 2004 Medium-bodied, supple and smooth; a core of sweet plum and blackberry fruit supported by gentle vanillan oak and fine tannins. Cork. 14.5° alc. **RATING** 94 **DRINK** 2014 $ 33

Pine Lodge Vineyard Mount Barker Shiraz 2004 Medium-bodied; black fruits with whispers of dark chocolate; the wine expands through the length of the palate to the finish and aftertaste, almost in the fashion of a high-quality pinot noir. Cork. 14.2° alc. **RATING** 94 **DRINK** 2014 $ 33

ŸŸŸŸŸ **Maxwell Vineyard Chardonnay 2003** A rich and complex wine which does, however, show its alcohol; ripe, full peachy fruit and well-integrated French oak. Cork. 14.5° alc. **RATING** 91 **DRINK** 2009 $ 30

Peter Lehmann

Para Road, Tanunda, SA 5352 **REGION** Barossa Valley
T (08) 8563 2100 **F** (08) 8563 3402 **WWW**.peterlehmannwines.com **OPEN** Mon–Fri 9.30–5, w'ends & public hols 10.30–4.30
WINEMAKER Andrew Wigan, Leonie Lange, Ian Hongell, Kerry Morrison **EST.** 1979 **CASES** 200 000
After one of the more emotional and intense takeover battles in the latter part of 2003, Peter Lehmann fought off the unwanted suit of Allied Domeq, and is now effectively controlled by the Swiss/Californian Hess Group. The takeover has reinforced the core business, and protected the interests of employees, and of Peter Lehmann's beloved Barossa Valley grapegrowers. Exports to the UK, the US and other major markets.

ŸŸŸŸŸ **Reserve Riesling 2001** Bright green-yellow; a flowery lime juice bouquet with the barest hint of toast; brilliantly incisive palate with pure lime juice and lovely, slippery acidity. Screwcap. 12° alc. **RATING** 96 **DRINK** 2016 $ 24

Stonewell Shiraz 2000 Ultra-careful selection of grapes; seductive, velvety mouthfeel, with black fruits, prunes, tannins and oak seamlessly interwoven; developing slowly and surely. Quality cork. **RATING** 95 **DRINK** 2020 $ 80

Barossa Riesling 2005 Scented, lively and long tropical/citrus fruit; very good mouthfeel. Gold medal Sydney Wine Show '06. Screwcap. **RATING** 94 **DRINK** 2009 $ 12

Eden Valley Riesling 2005 Elegant wine; an appealing mix of lemon, lime and mineral aromas and flavours; cleverly balanced. Gold medal National Wine Show '05. Screwcap. **RATING** 94 **DRINK** 2015 $ 15

Reserve Semillon 2002 Highly aromatic and complex; a quite lovely wine, showing how well Peter Lehmann has mastered this variety in the Barossa Valley. Gold medal Sydney Wine Show '06. Screwcap. 12° alc. **RATING** 94 **DRINK** 2012 $ 24

The Futures Shiraz 2003 An elegant, medium-bodied wine which has risen above the limitations of the vintage; attractive plum fruit, good oak handling and fine tannins run through the long palate. Cork. 14.5° alc. **RATING** 94 **DRINK** 2015 $ 30

Eight Songs Shiraz 2001 Red berry, leaf, spice and mocha aromas; an elegant wine, with appealing red fruits, savoury tannins and quality French oak. Cork. 14° alc. **RATING** 94 **DRINK** 2011 $ 40

Light Pass Cabernet Sauvignon 2002 Excellent varietal definition on both bouquet and palate; blackcurrant, blackberry, chocolate and earth; fine but persistent tannins. Cork. 14° alc. **RATING** 94 **DRINK** 2017 $ 28

ＹＹＹＹＹ **The Mentor 2001** Smooth, supple amalgam of blackcurrant and spicy fruit; fine tannins; compelling length. Cabernet Sauvignon/Merlot/Shiraz. Cork. **RATING** 93 **DRINK** 2016 $ 38

Barossa Semillon 2004 Spotlessly clean; stylish palate reflects the low (11.5°) alcohol; a crisp interplay between grass, pea pod, apple, mineral and acidity. Still fresh, and still developing. Screwcap. 11.5° alc. **RATING** 90 **DRINK** 2010 $ 12

Barossa Rose 2005 Vivid red-purple; elegant, fresh and precise red fruits; fearlessly near-dry; delicious finish. Screwcap. **RATING** 90 **DRINK** Now $ 15

ＹＹＹＹ **Adelaide Hills Semillon Sauvignon Blanc 2005** An appealing mix of ripe fruit flavours, ranging from citrus to gooseberry to yellow peach. Screwcap. 12.5° alc. **RATING** 89 **DRINK** Now $ 15

Barossa Shiraz 2003 A pleasing mix of ripe blackberry fruit and a dash of chocolate; gentle tannins/extract. Screwcap. **RATING** 87 **DRINK** 2009 $ 18

ＹＹＹＹ **Chenin Blanc 2005 RATING** 85 **DRINK** Now $ 12
Shiraz Grenache 2004 RATING 85 **DRINK** Now $ 12

ＹＹＹ **GSM Grenache Shiraz Mourvedre 2003 RATING** 83 $ 16

Peterson Champagne House

NR

Cnr Broke Road/Branxton Road, Pokolbin, NSW 2320 **REGION** Lower Hunter Valley
T (02) 4998 7881 **F** (02) 4998 7882 **OPEN** 7 days 9–5
WINEMAKER Contract **EST.** 1994 **CASES** 7000
Prominently and provocatively situated on the corner of Broke and Branxton Roads as one enters the main vineyard and winery district in the Lower Hunter Valley. It is an extension of the Peterson family empire and, no doubt, very deliberately aimed at the tourist. While the dreaded word 'Champagne' has been retained in the business name, the wine labels now simply say Peterson House, which is a big step in the right direction.

Petersons

NR

Mount View Road, Mount View, NSW 2325 **REGION** Lower Hunter Valley
T (02) 4990 1704 **F** (02) 4991 1344 **WWW**.petersonswines.com.au **OPEN** Mon–Sat 9–5, Sun 10–5
WINEMAKER Colin Peterson, Gary Reed **EST.** 1971 **CASES** 15 000
Ian and Shirley Peterson were among the early followers in the footsteps of Max Lake, contributing to the Hunter Valley renaissance which has continued to this day. Grapegrowers since 1971 and winemakers since 1981, the second generation of the family, headed by Colin Peterson, now manages the business. It has been significantly expanded to include 16 ha at Mount View, a 42-ha vineyard in Mudgee (Glenesk), and an 8-ha vineyard near Armidale (Palmerston).

Pettavel

★★★★☆

65 Pettavel Road, Waurn Ponds, Vic 3216 **REGION** Geelong
T (03) 5266 1120 **F** (03) 5266 1140 **WWW**.pettavel.com **OPEN** 7 days 10–5.30
WINEMAKER Peter Flewellyn **EST.** 2000 **CASES** 20 000
This is a major landmark in the Geelong region. Mike and wife Sandi Fitzpatrick sold their large Riverland winery and vineyards, and moved to Geelong, where, in 1990, they began developing vineyards at Sutherlands Creek. Here they have been joined by daughter Robyn (who has overseas management of the business) and son Reece (who coordinates the viticultural resources). A striking and substantial winery/restaurant complex was opened in 2002. Exports to the UK, the US, Sweden and Germany.

ΥΥΥΥΥ **Evening Star Shiraz 2004** Highly flavoured; masses of licorice and spice overtones to small berry red and black fruits; controlled oak and tannins; striking wine. Screwcap. 14° alc. RATING 93 DRINK 2014 $ 18

Platina Viognier 2005 Clearly articulated peach, apricot and pear varietal character; clever winemaking (fermented in 4-year-old barriques and partial malolactic fermentation) adds to the texture and structure, without heat or phenolics. Screwcap. 13.5° alc. RATING 91 DRINK 2008 $ 27

Southern Emigre Shiraz Viognier 2003 Very strong Viognier impact on medium-bodied Shiraz; likewise obvious French oak inputs. Love it or hate it. Cork. 14.5° alc. RATING 91 DRINK 2008 $ 42

Evening Star Late Harvest Riesling 2005 A complex and incredibly luscious and rich palate with spice and cumquat, but really needs a little more acidity to balance that luscious sweetness. Screwcap. 10.5° alc. RATING 91 DRINK Now $ 18

Evening Star Sauvignon Blanc 2005 Attractive light- to medium-bodied wine with herb, passionfruit and gooseberry; good length and balance. Screwcap. 12.5° alc. RATING 90 DRINK Now $ 18

ΥΥΥΥ **Platina Chardonnay 2003** Full, rich and ripe peach and stone fruit; fractionally oily acidity. Screwcap. 13.5° alc. RATING 89 DRINK Now $ 27

Platina Merlot Petit Verdot 2003 Pleasant medium-bodied wine, with good line and length; appropriately ripe fruit flavours though an unusual blend. RATING 89 DRINK 2012 $ 27

Platina Cabernet Sauvignon Cabernet Franc 2002 Holding hue well; cedary/savoury/leafy/minty aromas and flavours surround a core of cassis/red fruits; fine tannins. Cork. 13° alc. RATING 88 DRINK 2008 $ 27

Evening Star Riesling 2005 Flavoursome, tropical fruit in a big, and somewhat cumbersome, wine. Screwcap. 13° alc. RATING 87 DRINK 2008 $ 18

Evening Star Cabernet Merlot 2003 Lively herbaceous style; not over-extracted, though not particularly rich, either. RATING 87 DRINK 2009 $ 18

ΥΥΥΥ **Evening Star Cabernet Merlot 2004** RATING 86 DRINK 2008 $ 18

Platina Cabernet Sauvignon Cabernet Franc 2003 RATING 86 DRINK Now $ 27

Platina Pinot Noir 2003 RATING 85 DRINK Now $ 27

Pewsey Vale   ★★★★★

Browns Road, Eden Valley, SA 5353 (postal) REGION Eden Valley
T (08) 8561 3200 F (08) 8561 3393 WWW.pewseyvale.com OPEN At Yalumba
WINEMAKER Louisa Rose EST. 1847 CASES 18 000
Pewsey Vale was a famous vineyard established in 1847 by Joseph Gilbert, and it was appropriate that when S Smith & Son (Yalumba) began the renaissance of the Adelaide Hills plantings in 1961, they should do so by purchasing Pewsey Vale and establishing 40 ha of riesling and 2 ha each of gewurztraminer and pinot gris. The Riesling has also finally benefited from being the first wine to be bottled with a Stelvin screwcap in 1977. While public reaction forced the abandonment of the initiative for almost 20 years, Yalumba/Pewsey Vale never lost faith in the technical advantages of the closure. A quick taste (or better, a share of a bottle) of 5–7-year-old Contours Riesling will tell you why. Exports to all major markets.

ΥΥΥΥΥ **The Contours Eden Valley Riesling 2001** Classic lime juice riesling fruit supported by a streak of mineral; power and depth with grace. Top gold medal National Wine Show '05. RATING 95 DRINK 2016 $ 26

Pfeiffer   ★★★★

167 Distillery Road, Wahgunyah, Vic 3687 REGION Rutherglen
T (02) 6033 2805 F (02) 6033 3158 WWW.pfeifferwines.com.au OPEN Mon–Sat 9–5, Sun 10–5
WINEMAKER Christopher Pfeiffer, Jen Pfeiffer EST. 1984 CASES 20 000
Ex-Lindeman fortified winemaker Chris Pfeiffer occupies one of the historic wineries (built 1880) which abound in Northeast Victoria and which is worth a visit on this score alone. The fortified wines are good, and the table wines have improved considerably over recent vintages, drawing upon 36 ha

of estate plantings. Exports to the UK, the US, Canada, Malaysia and China (under the Carlyle and Three Chimneys labels).

ŸŸŸŸŸ **Cabernet Sauvignon 2002** Nicely balanced and weighted medium-bodied wine; blackcurrant and black olive; good oak. Cork. 14° alc. **RATING** 91 **DRINK** 2012 $18.50
Old Distillery Classic Rutherglen Tokay NV Pale golden-brown; elegant tea leaf, cake and touches of caramel and toffee; good balance and length; still fresh. **RATING** 90 **DRINK** Now $22

ŸŸŸŸ **Carlyle Riesling 2005** Clean, crisp ripe apple and a touch of citrus; good mouthfeel and length, finishing with a faint hint of sweetness. Screwcap. 12° alc. **RATING** 89 **DRINK** 2009 $16
Gamay 2005 Powerful black plum fruit and a touch of spice; presence without phenolics. Screwcap. 13.5° alc. **RATING** 89 **DRINK** 2010 $15.50
Shiraz 2002 Rich, ripe, confit fruit characters; some spice, fine tannins. Cork. 14° alc. **RATING** 89 **DRINK** 2010 $18.50
Christopher's VP 2004 Spicy berry and chocolate fruit, good spirit; a medium-bodied style, towards ruby but not too sweet. Screwcap. 18° alc. **RATING** 89 **DRINK** 2010 $22
Old Distillery Classic Rutherglen Muscat NV Midway to mahogany in colour; distinctly more complex than the basic muscat; rich, raisiny, with some plum pudding. **RATING** 89 **DRINK** Now $22
Riesling 2005 Herb, slate and mineral aromas with an unusual touch of earth; slightly austere style, has good length. Screwcap. 12.5° alc. **RATING** 88 **DRINK** 2008 $15.90
Merlot 2001 Mature, but very savoury/earthy/briary fruit; demands appropriate food. Cork. 13.5° alc. **RATING** 87 **DRINK** 2008 $31
Rutherglen Muscat NV Young, intensely grapey muscat varietal character; rich and sweet; needs more age to cut the sweetness and gain complexity. However, to be accepted for what it is. Cork. 18° alc. **RATING** 87 **DRINK** Now $22

ŸŸŸŸ **Pinot Noir 2003** A miracle to have as much varietal character as it does; light- to medium-bodied but sweet and ripe; fine tannins. Screwcap. 13.5° alc. **RATING** 86 **DRINK** 2009 $18
Frontignac 2005 **RATING** 85 **DRINK** Now $13
Old Distillery Rutherglen Tawny NV **RATING** 85 **DRINK** Now $16

Pfitzner ★★★★☆

PO Box 1098, North Adelaide, SA 5006 **REGION** Adelaide Hills
T (08) 8390 0188 **F** (08) 8390 0188 **OPEN** Not
WINEMAKER Petaluma **EST.** 1996 **CASES** 1500
The subtitle to the Pfitzner name is Eric's Vineyard. The late Eric Pfitzner purchased and aggregated a number of small, subdivided farmlets to protect the beauty of the Piccadilly Valley from ugly rural development. His three sons inherited the vision, with a little under 6 ha of vineyard planted principally to chardonnay and pinot noir, plus small amounts of sauvignon blanc and merlot. Half the total property has been planted, the remainder preserving the natural eucalypt forest. Roughly half the production is sold in the UK.

ŸŸŸŸŸ **Eric's Vineyard Piccadilly Valley Pinot Noir 2002** Holding hue very well; fresh plum and spice fruit; perfect balance and length; top Adelaide Hills example. Cork. 13.6° alc. **RATING** 94 **DRINK** 2010 $18

ŸŸŸŸŸ **Eric's Vineyard Piccadilly Valley Sauvignon Blanc 2004** Still quite fresh and crisp, with a mix of lemon, gooseberry and passionfruit flavours. Screwcap. 13° alc. **RATING** 90 **DRINK** Now $14

Phaedrus Estate ★★★★☆

220 Mornington–Tyabb Road, Moorooduc, Vic 3933 **REGION** Mornington Peninsula
T (03) 5978 8134 **F** (03) 5978 8134 **WWW**.phaedrus.com.au **OPEN** W'ends & public hols 11–5
WINEMAKER Ewan Campbell, Maitena Zantvoort **EST.** 1997 **CASES** 1500
Ewan Campbell and Maitena Zantvoort established Phaedrus Estate in 1997. At that time both had already had winemaking experience with large wine companies, and were at the point of finishing

their wine science degrees at Adelaide University. They decided they wished to (in their words) 'produce ultra-premium wine with distinctive and unique varietal flavours, which offer serious (and light-hearted) wine drinkers an alternative to mainstream commercial styles'. Campbell and Zantvoort believe that quality wines involve both art and science, and I don't have any argument with that.

ɪɪɪɪ̵ **Reserve Mornington Peninsula Pinot Noir 2004** Bright but lighter colour than the varietal; elegant, fine and focused; has greater length than the varietal; has absorbed 20 months in oak. Screwcap. 13.5° alc. **RATING** 93 **DRINK** 2011 $ 45

Mornington Peninsula Chardonnay 2005 A powerful wine, with lots of flavour and textural complexity to the fruit; malolactic fermentation, solids fermentation and wild yeast all substitute for oak. Screwcap. 13° alc. **RATING** 90 **DRINK** 2012 $ 18

Mornington Peninsula Pinot Noir 2004 Clean, supple and smooth; light- to medium-bodied with sweet, confit black cherry fruit; 4 clones; multiple fermentation techniques. Screwcap. 13.6° alc. **RATING** 90 **DRINK** 2010 $ 20

Mornington Peninsula Shiraz 2004 Clear, bright fruit style; a light- to medium-bodied mix of cherry, raspberry and blackberry fruit; good length and finish. Screwcap. 13.6° alc. **RATING** 90 **DRINK** 2010 $ 20

ɪɪɪ̵ **Mornington Peninsula Pinot Gris 2005** **RATING** 85 **DRINK** Now $ 18

Philip Shaw ★★★★☆

PO Box 2473, Caldwell Lane, Orange, NSW 2800 **REGION** Orange
T(02) 6365 2334 **F**(02) 6365 2449 **WWW**.philipshaw.com.au **OPEN** Not
WINEMAKER Philip Shaw **EST.** 1989 **CASES** NFP
Philip Shaw, former chief winemaker of Rosemount Estate and then Southcorp Wines, first became interested in the Orange region in 1985. In 1988 he purchased the Koomooloo Vineyard, and began the planting of sauvignon blanc, chardonnay, shiraz, merlot, cabernet franc and cabernet sauvignon. As one might expect, the first wines released are of high quality.

ɪɪɪɪɪ **No. 11 Orange Chardonnay 2004** A sophisticated wine in all respects; subtle wild yeast barrel ferment inputs; a gently creamy/nutty palate; melon and stone fruit expands on the finish Screwcap. 13.5° alc. **RATING** 94 **DRINK** 2009 $ 30

ɪɪɪɪ̵ **No. 19 Orange Sauvignon Blanc 2005** Spotlessly clean bouquet; an intense mix on the palate of herb, grass, asparagus, gooseberry and redcurrant; long carry and finish. Screwcap. 12.5° alc. **RATING** 93 **DRINK** Now $ 23

No. 89 Orange Shiraz Viognier 2004 High-toned spice, leather and apricot nuances on the bouquet; medium-bodied palate, with excellent tannin management and good oak. Screwcap. **RATING** 92 **DRINK** 2014 $ 44

No. 17 Orange Merlot Cabernet Sauvignon Cabernet Franc 2004 An attractive, well-made wine; gentle black and redcurrant fruit; fine tannins and integrated oak. Screwcap. **RATING** 92 **DRINK** 2014 $ 25

Phillip Island Vineyard ★★★★★

Berrys Beach Road, Phillip Island, Vic 3922 **REGION** Gippsland
T(03) 5956 8465 **F**(03) 5956 8465 **WWW**.phillipislandwines.com.au **OPEN** 7 days 11–5
WINEMAKER David Lance, James Lance **EST.** 1993 **CASES** 3000
1997 marked the first harvest from the 2.5 ha of the Phillip Island Vineyard, which is totally enclosed in the permanent silon net which acts both as a windbreak and protection against birds. The quality of the wines across the board make it clear that this is definitely not a tourist-trap cellar door; it is a serious producer of quality wine. Exports to South-East Asia.

ɪɪɪɪɪ **Chardonnay 2004** Intense grapefruit, citrus and stone fruit on a crisp and lively palate; well-integrated oak, lively finish and good acidity. Screwcap. 14° alc. **RATING** 94 **DRINK** 2012 $ 28

Chardonnay 2003 Bright, light straw-green; fresh, pure and still very youthful; super-elegant nectarine and grapefruit flavours, supported by lingering, fine acidity; fresh aftertaste. Cork. 14.5° alc. **RATING** 94 **DRINK** 2011 $ 28

Pinot Noir 2004 Fragrant, bordering on exuberant, aromas of spices and plums; light- to medium-bodied, with great mouthfeel; lovely pinot fruit. Cork. 15° alc. **RATING** 94 **DRINK** 2011 $ 50

The Pinnacles Botrytis Riesling 2004 An elegant wine, with lime juice flavours in a Spatlese sweetness spectrum; great balance and lingering finish. Twin top. 11.5° alc. **RATING** 94 **DRINK** 2010 $ 19

ＹＹＹＹＹ **Cabernet Sauvignon 2003** Firm, cool-grown varietal character; a mix of black fruits, earth, cedar and olive; lingering tannins and overall austerity. Cork. 14° alc. **RATING** 92 **DRINK** 2013 $ 28

Sauvignon Blanc 2005 Very light and elegant; crisp and clean; touches of gooseberry, then a cleansing finish. Screwcap. 13° alc. **RATING** 90 **DRINK** Now $ 29.50

ＹＹＹＹ **Merlot 2003** An ultra-fragrant spray of spicy, leafy, minty aromas; elegant, light- to medium-bodied wine which does, however, shorten slightly. Cork. 14° alc. **RATING** 89 **DRINK** 2008 $ 30

Phillips Brook Estate

118 Redmond-Hay River Road, Redmond, WA 6332 **REGION** Albany
T (08) 9845 3124 **F** (08) 9845 3126 **WWW**.phillipsbrook.com.au **OPEN** By appt
WINEMAKER Harewood Estate (James Kellie) **EST.** 1975 **CASES** 800
Bronwen and David Newbury first became viticulturists near the thoroughly unlikely town of Bourke, in western New South Wales. They were involved with Dr Richard Smart in setting up the First Light vineyard, with the aim of making the first wine in the world each calendar year. Whatever marketing appeal the idea may have had, the wine was never going to be great, so in May 2001 they moved back to the Great Southern region. The name comes from the adjoining Phillips Brook Nature Reserve, and the permanent creek on their property. Riesling and cabernet sauvignon (4.5 ha in all) had been planted in 1975, but thoroughly neglected. The Newburys have rehabilitated the old plantings, and have added 7.5 ha of chardonnay, merlot, cabernet franc and sauvignon blanc.

ＹＹＹＹＹ **Great Southern Riesling 2005** Spotlessly clean and tightly focused; sundry citrus flavours seamlessly interwoven with acidity; a particularly long, bone-dry, finish. Screwcap. 12.5° alc. **RATING** 94 **DRINK** 2015 $ 18

ＹＹＹＹＹ **Albany Sauvignon Blanc 2005** Bright green-straw; a clean, relatively restrained bouquet, springing into life on the palate with passionfruit and tropical flavours; a long, well-balanced finish; value. Screwcap. 13° alc. **RATING** 92 **DRINK** 2015 $ 16

ＹＹＹＹ **Albany Cabernet Merlot 2004** Light colour; light-bodied, with more red fruits than the colour suggests; cherry and raspberry, not green. Screwcap. 13.5° alc. **RATING** 89 **DRINK** 2008 $ 20

Nine Redgums Clairet 2004 A throwback to the origin of the word 'Claret', when Bordeaux wines were made from indiscriminate, mixed red and white grapes, giving rise to the term 'Clairet' in the 13th century, a forerunner of today's rose. Screwcap. 12.5° alc. **RATING** 87 **DRINK** Now $ 14

Phillips Estate

NR

Lot 964a Channybearup Road, Pemberton, WA 6230 **REGION** Pemberton
T (08) 9776 0381 **F** (08) 9776 0381 **OPEN** 7 days 10.30–4
WINEMAKER Phillip Wilkinson **EST.** 1996 **CASES** 5000
Phillip Wilkinson has developed 4.5 ha of vines framed by an old-growth Karri forest on one side and a large lake on the other. As well as the expected varieties, he has planted 1 ha of zinfandel; as far as I know, it is the only zinfandel in the Pemberton region. Sophisticated winemaking techniques are used at the fermentation stage, but fining and filtration are either not used at all, or employed to a minimum degree. Exports to the UK.

Pialligo Estate

18 Kallaroo Road, Pialligo, ACT 2609 **REGION** Canberra District
T (02) 6247 6060 **F** (02) 6262 6074 **www.**pialligoestate.com.au **OPEN** Thurs–Sun & public hols 10–5
WINEMAKER Andrew McEwin, Greg Gallagher (Contract) **EST.** 1999 **CASES** 1500
Sally Milner and John Nutt planted their 4-ha vineyard (1.5 ha of merlot, 1 ha of riesling and 0.5 ha each of shiraz, cabernet sauvignon and sangiovese) in 1999. The cellar door sales area and café opened July 2002, with views of Mt Ainslie, Mt Pleasant, Duntroon, the Telstra Tower, Parliament House and the Brindabella Ranges beyond. The property, which has a 1-km frontage to the Molonglo River, also includes an olive grove, yet is only 5 mins' drive from the centre of Canberra.

ŸŸŸŸŸ **Riesling 2005** Floral and fragrant apple blossom aromas; elegant and long; excellent acidity. Delicious. Screwcap. **RATING** 94 **DRINK** 2013 **$** 20

ŸŸŸŸŸ **Merlot 2003** Bright, small red fruits; attractive overall flavour and mouthfeel in the fruit-driven style of the winery. Screwcap. **RATING** 91 **DRINK** 2011 **$** 20
Shiraz 2003 Clean and fresh; direct, fruit-driven; a mix of spicy red and black fruits on the medium-bodied palate; fine tannins. Screwcap. **RATING** 90 **DRINK** 2012 **$** 20
Sangiovese 2004 Clean, fresh red fruits and spice; more precision and length on the palate than many from this variety. Screwcap. **RATING** 90 **DRINK** 2008 **$** 30

ŸŸŸŸ **Chardonnay 2005** Fragrant and fresh, light-bodied, with a strong streak of mineral; austere, but may develop. **RATING** 87 **DRINK** 2010 **$** 20

ŸŸŸŸ **Rose 2005** **RATING** 86 **DRINK** Now **$** 20

Piano Gully NR

Piano Gully Road, Manjimup, WA 6258 **REGION** Manjimup
T (08) 9772 3140 **F** (08) 9316 0336 **www.**pianogully.com.au **OPEN** By appt
WINEMAKER Ashley Lewkowski **EST.** 1987 **CASES** 4000
The 5-ha vineyard was established in 1987 on rich Karri loam, 10 km south of Manjimup, with the first wine made from the 1991 vintage. The name of the road (and the winery) commemorates the shipping of a piano from England by one of the first settlers in the region. The horse and cart carrying the piano on the last leg of the long journey were within sight of their destination when the piano fell from the cart and was destroyed.

Picardy ★★★★★

Cnr Vasse Highway/Eastbrook Road, Pemberton, WA 6260 **REGION** Pemberton
T (08) 9776 0036 **F** (08) 9776 0245 **www.**picardy.com.au **OPEN** By appt
WINEMAKER Bill Pannell, Dan Pannell **EST.** 1993 **CASES** 5000
Picardy is owned by Dr Bill Pannell, wife Sandra and son Daniel; Bill and Sandra were the founders of Moss Wood winery in the Margaret River region (in 1969). Picardy reflects Bill Pannell's view that the Pemberton area has proved to be one of the best regions in Australia for Pinot Noir and Chardonnay, but it is perhaps significant that the wines include a Shiraz, and a Bordeaux-blend of 50% Merlot, 25% Cabernet Franc and 25% Cabernet Sauvignon. Time will tell whether Pemberton has more Burgundy, Rhône or Bordeaux in its veins. Exports to the UK, the US and other major markets.

ŸŸŸŸŸ **Pemberton Chardonnay 2004** Altogether stylish wine; complex but not over the top barrel ferment and malolactic ferment inputs; intense stone fruit and grapefruit flavours; long finish. High-quality cork. **RATING** 95 **DRINK** 2010 **$** 30

Pemberton Merlot Cabernet Sauvignon Cabernet Franc 2003 Very good purple-red; attractive cassis, blackberry and cedar mix; very good balance and mouthfeel; likewise tannins and oak. Cork. 14° alc. **RATING** 94 **DRINK** 2015 **$** 25

ᵞᵞᵞᵞ♀ **Tête de Cuvee Pemberton Pinot Noir 2003** Light red, with some purple remaining; leafy, spicy, savoury aromas; an elegant, supple and fine structure; ultra-restrained. Cork. 14° alc. **RATING** 91 **DRINK** 2008 $ 40

Tête de Cuvee Pemberton Pinot Noir 2002 Light- to medium-bodied; complex spice and forest floor nuances to the fine red and black fruits; long finish. Cork. **RATING** 91 **DRINK** 2008 $ 40

Pemberton Shiraz 2003 Bright colour; fragrant black cherry fruit with a background of spicy, peppery notes; fine, savoury tannins. Dodgy cork. **RATING** 90 **DRINK** 2011 $ 20

ᵞᵞᵞ♀ **Merlimont 2002 RATING** 86 **DRINK** 2010 $ 30

Pemberton Merlot Cabernet Sauvignon Cabernet Franc 2002 RATING 86 **DRINK** 2011 $ 20

Pemberton Pinot Noir 2003 RATING 85 **DRINK** Now

🐖 Piedmont Wines ★★★

3430 Yarra Junction–Noojee Road, Noojee, Vic 3833 **REGION** Gippsland
T (03) 9733 0449 **F** (03) 9733 0449 **WWW**.piedmontwines.com.au **OPEN** W'ends & public hols 10–5
WINEMAKER Ivan Juric **EST.** 1991 **CASES** 1000
Quite where the name Piedmont Wines came from, I do not know, but Ivan and Ljubica Juric started the venture as a hobby, with only 360 vines planted in 1991. Since that time they have expanded twice, the vineyard now comprising 1 ha each of chardonnay, sauvignon blanc and shiraz.

ᵞᵞᵞᵞ **Chardonnay 2004** Light green-straw; fresh, citrussy/tangy fruit and brisk acidity. **RATING** 87 **DRINK** 2009 $ 14

ᵞᵞᵞ♀ **Sauvignon Blanc 2005 RATING** 85 **DRINK** Now $ 14

Pier 10 NR

10 Shoreham Road, Shoreham, Vic 3916 **REGION** Mornington Peninsula
T (03) 5989 8848 **F** (03) 5989 8848 **WWW**.pier10.com.au **OPEN** Wed–Sun 11–5, 7 days Dec–Mar
WINEMAKER Kevin McCarthy (Contract) **EST.** 1996 **CASES** NA
Eric Baker and Sue McKenzie began the development of Pier 10 with the aim of creating first a lifestyle, then perhaps a retirement business. Both helped set up the vineyard while continuing to work in Melbourne before handing over viticultural management of the 3.2 ha to Mark Danaher. The varieties planted are chardonnay, pinot gris and pinot noir, and with ultra-competent winemaking, the sold-out sign goes up regularly.

Pierro ★★★★★

Caves Road, Wilyabrup via Cowaramup, WA 6284 **REGION** Margaret River
T (08) 9755 6220 **F** (08) 9755 6308 **WWW**.pierro.com.au **OPEN** 7 days 10–5
WINEMAKER Dr Michael Peterkin **EST.** 1979 **CASES** 10 000
Dr Michael Peterkin is another of the legion of Margaret River medical practitioners; for good measure, he married into the Cullen family. Pierro is renowned for its stylish white wines, which often exhibit tremendous complexity. The Chardonnay can be monumental in its weight and complexity. Exports to the UK, the US, Japan and Indonesia.

ᵞᵞᵞᵞᵞ **Semillon Sauvignon Blanc LTC 2005** A complex fruit expression reflecting the cepage on both bouquet and palate; ripe lemon, gooseberry and nectarine fruit in a harmonious flow. The little touch of chardonnay works well. Screwcap. 13° alc. **RATING** 94 **DRINK** 2008 $ 25

Margaret River Chardonnay 2004 Complex yet elegant, reflecting multiple winemaker inputs; nectarine, fig, cashew and cream; great balance. Screwcap. 13.5° alc. **RATING** 94 **DRINK** 2012 $ 65

ᵞᵞᵞᵞ **Margaret River Cabernet Sauvignon Merlot LTCf 2003** Bright purple-red hue; firm, almost youthful, fruit profile; has considerable length, but not so much depth. Still evolving, and will improve. (LTCf stands for 'little touch of cabernet franc'.) Cork. 13.5° alc. **RATING** 89 **DRINK** 2013 $ 31

Piesse Brook

NR

226 Aldersyde Road, Bickley, WA 6076 **REGION** Perth Hills
T (08) 9293 3309 **F** (08) 9293 3309 **OPEN** Sat 1–5, Sun & public hols 10–5 & by appt
WINEMAKER Di Bray, Ray Boyanich **EST.** 1974 **CASES** 1000
Surprisingly good red wines made in tiny quantities; they have received consistent accolades over the years. The first Chardonnay was made in 1993; a trophy-winning Shiraz was produced in 1995. Now has 4 ha of chardonnay, shiraz, merlot and cabernet sauvignon under vine. Exports to the UK.

Piggs Peake

★★★★★

697 Hermitage Road, Pokolbin, NSW 2321 **REGION** Lower Hunter Valley
T (02) 6574 7000 **F** (02) 6574 7070 **WWW**.piggspeake.com **OPEN** 7 days 10–5
WINEMAKER Steve Langham, Hugh Jorgen **EST.** 1998 **CASES** 3000
The derivation of the name remains a mystery to me; if it is a local landmark, I have not heard of it. It sources its grapes from a wide variety of places, to make a range of wines which are well outside the straight and narrow. Piggs Peake has secured listings at a number of leading Sydney metropolitan and NSW country restaurants. The arrival of Steve Langham (having previously worked 4 vintages at Allandale) has seen a marked increase in quality.

ΨΨΨΨΨ **Sows Ear Semillon 2005** A top example of the vintage, stacked with lemony fruit, yet without any heaviness; fluid line and length; great finish. Screwcap. 11° alc. **RATING** 95 **DRINK** 2015
House of Bricks Cabernet Merlot 2004 Resplendent with blackcurrant and mulberry fruit; medium- to full-bodied but velvety smooth; fruit rides over the alcohol and American oak. Seriously good blend. Orange Cabernet Sauvignon (70%)/Mudgee Merlot (25%). Screwcap. 15.3° alc. **RATING** 95 **DRINK** 2014

ΨΨΨΨ **Hogshead Chardonnay 2005** Very powerful and rich wine; lusciously ripe yellow peach fruit has absorbed the oak from 7 months in new French hogsheads. Food style. Screwcap. 13.5° alc. **RATING** 91 **DRINK** 2009

Pike & Joyce

★★★★☆

Mawson Road, Lenswood, SA 5240 (postal) **REGION** Adelaide Hills
T (08) 8843 4370 **F** (08) 8843 4353 **WWW**.pikeandjoyce.com.au **OPEN** Not
WINEMAKER Neil Pike, John Trotter **EST.** 1998 **CASES** 4000
This is a partnership between the Pike family (of Clare Valley fame) and the Joyce family, related to Andrew Pike's wife, Cathy. The Joyce family have been orchardists at Lenswood for over 100 years, but also have extensive operations in the Riverland. Together with Andrew Pike (formerly chief viticulturist for the Southcorp group) they have established 1 ha of vines; the lion's share to pinot noir, sauvignon blanc and chardonnay, followed by merlot, pinot gris and semillon. The wines are made at Pikes Clare Valley winery. Exports to the UK, the US and other major markets.

ΨΨΨΨΨ **Adelaide Hills Chardonnay 2004** A complex bouquet and palate; melon, fig, cashew and cream all seamlessly interwoven into a harmonious whole. Screwcap. 13.5° alc. **RATING** 94 **DRINK** 2010 $ 28

ΨΨΨΨ **Adelaide Hills Sauvignon Blanc 2005** Good intensity and length; ripe but not heavy tropical/passionfruit food style. Screwcap. 13.5° alc. **RATING** 92 **DRINK** Now $ 20
Adelaide Hills Pinot Gris 2005 The faintest blush of pink to the colour; attractive spicy notes, also hints of wild strawberry; greater than usual fruit complexity. Screwcap. 13.5° alc. **RATING** 90 **DRINK** Now $ 22
Adelaide Hills Pinot Noir 2004 Medium- to full-bodied; potent, savoury, foresty aromas and flavours; considerable texture and structure. Food style. Screwcap. 13.5° alc. **RATING** 90 **DRINK** 2009 $ 28

Pikes

★★★★☆

Polish Hill River Road, Sevenhill, SA 5453 **REGION** Clare Valley
T (08) 8843 4370 **F** (08) 8843 4353 **WWW**.pikeswines.com.au **OPEN** 7 days 10–4
WINEMAKER Neil Pike, John Trotter **EST.** 1984 **CASES** 35 000
Owned by the Pike brothers: Andrew was for many years the senior viticulturist with Southcorp, Neil was a winemaker at Mitchell. Pikes now has its own winery, with Neil Pike presiding. In most vintages its white wines, led by Riesling, are the most impressive. Exports to the UK, the US and other major markets.

ΨΨΨΨΨ **The Merle Clare Valley Riesling 2005** Relatively subdued aromas, but explodes on the super-intense and long palate; lime and lemon with lingering, but balanced, acidity. Screwcap. 12.5° alc. **RATING** 95 **DRINK** 2015 $ 32

ΨΨΨΨΨ **Clare Valley Riesling 2005** Very restrained in typical Polish Hill River style; a bone-dry finish, and certain to repay cellaring. Screwcap. **RATING** 93 **DRINK** 2014 $ 19
Clare Valley Sauvignon Blanc Semillon 2005 A clean but relatively subdued bouquet; springs into life on the palate with lemon zest fruit and a fresh finish. Bravo. Screwcap. 13° alc. **RATING** 92 **DRINK** Now $ 18
Eastside Clare Valley Shiraz 2003 A complex wine, with some not unpleasant earthy/gamey overtones to plum, blackberry and spice; good oak, fine tannins. Screwcap. **RATING** 90 **DRINK** 2015 $ 22

ΨΨΨΨ **Clare Valley Chardonnay 2004** Glowing yellow-green; rises above its regional station in life; attractive, medium-bodied stone fruit and fig, controlled oak. Screwcap. 14° alc. **RATING** 89 **DRINK** 2008 $ 22
The Dogwalk Cabernet Merlot 2003 A medium-bodied, clean and fresh mix of blackcurrant and cassis; oak and balance good. Screwcap. **RATING** 88 **DRINK** 2009 $ 18
Gill's Farmer Clare Valley Viognier 2004 Moderately rich apricot and honeysuckle fruit; medium-bodied, tailing off slightly, but could develop. Screwcap. **RATING** 87 **DRINK** 2008 $ 24
Edwards Road Clare Valley Merlot 2003 Slightly dull colour; medium-bodied; savoury, earthy red berry fruit; warm vanilla oak doesn't enhance the varietal profile. Screwcap. 14.5° alc. **RATING** 87 **DRINK** 2010 $ 20

ΨΨΨΨ **Eastside Shiraz 2003 RATING** 86 **DRINK** 2008 $ 24
The Dogwalk Cabernet Merlot 2002 RATING 86 **DRINK** Now $ 18
The Hill Block Cabernet Sauvignon 2003 RATING 86 **DRINK** Now $ 24
Luccio White 2004 RATING 85 **DRINK** Now $ 16
Luccio Red 2003 RATING 85 **DRINK** Now $ 16
The Assemblage Shiraz Mourvedre Grenache 2003 RATING 84 **DRINK** Now $ 20

Pinnacle Wines

NR

50 Pinnacle Road, Orange, NSW 2800 **REGION** Orange
T (02) 6365 3316 **OPEN** By appt
WINEMAKER David Lowe, Jane Wilson (Contract) **EST.** 1999 **CASES** 400
Peter Gibson began Pinnacle Wines in 1999, with the planting of 2 ha of pinot gris on the slopes of Mt Canobolas, at an elevation of around 1000m. The vineyard is close to Brangayne of Orange, and Peter Gibson says that Brangayne's success played a considerable part in his decision to plant the vineyard. Just over 1 ha of viognier and 1.6 ha of pinot noir (using the new Burgundy clones 777 115 and 114 in conjunction with MV6), plus a little riesling, have been added.

Pipers Brook Vineyard

★★★★★

1216 Pipers Brook Road, Pipers Brook, Tas 7254 **REGION** Northern Tasmania
T (03) 6382 7527 **F** (03) 6382 7226 **WWW**.pipersbrook.com **OPEN** 7 days 10–5
WINEMAKER Rene Bezemer **EST.** 1974 **CASES** 90 000
The Pipers Brook Tasmanian empire has over 220 ha of vineyard supporting the Pipers Brook and Ninth Island labels, with the major focus, of course, being on Pipers Brook. Fastidious viticulture and

winemaking, immaculate packaging and enterprising marketing create a potent and effective blend. Pipers Brook operates two cellar door outlets, one at headquarters, the other at Strathlyn . In 2001 it became yet another company to fall prey to a takeover, in this instance by Belgian-owned sheepskin business Kreglinger, which has also established a large winery and vineyard at Mount Benson in SA. Exports to all major markets.

ϷϷϷϷϷ **Kreglinger Vintage 1999** Fragrant white peach and citrus aromas; very fine, tight and long palate; still extremely fresh and vibrant; lovely wine. RATING 96 DRINK 2010 $ 46.50

Estate Chardonnay 2003 A complex wine, with toasty hazelnut and cashew nuances from barrel ferment and malolactic, which don't overwhelm the still fresh and delicate fruit. Excellent finish, length and aftertaste. Cork. 13.5° alc. RATING 94 DRINK 2009 $ 33.95

Reserve Chardonnay 2002 Complex barrel ferment inputs, the fruit intensity not quite as high as might be expected, but certainly has elegance and length. Cork. 14.5° alc. RATING 94 DRINK 2009 $ 44.95

Reserve Pinot Noir 2003 Stylish, silky, savoury mouthfeel; spice, stem and red fruits; long and fine; lingering finish. Cork. RATING 94 DRINK 2010 $ 65

ϷϷϷϷϷ **Kreglinger Blanc de Blancs 2000** Pale green-straw; a vibrant, steely, tight no-compromise style; citrus and white peach, with lingering acidity and clean aftertaste. RATING 93 DRINK 2010 $ 65

Ninth Island Sauvignon Blanc 2005 Abundant mouthfeel, with tropical gooseberry and melon fruit well outside the normal spectrum for Tas. Screwcap. 13.7° alc. RATING 91 DRINK Now $ 21.50

Estate Chardonnay 2004 Slightly more grip and texture than many chardonnays of the vintage, even with a slight undercover of sweetness. RATING 91 DRINK 2011 $ 25

Ninth Island Riesling 2004 Crisp, mineral, green apple aromas and flavours; well-balanced acidity on a long finish. Screwcap. RATING 90 DRINK 2012 $ 19.95

Ninth Island Sparkling NV Bright straw-green; crisp, lively, crunchy/punchy with obvious Tasmanian clarity of line and vibrant acidity. Good yeast autolysis characters. RATING 90 DRINK Now $ 26.95

ϷϷϷϷ **Ninth Island Pinot Grigio 2005** Very cleverly made, with a touch of residual sugar balanced by crisp acidity; light pear and musk varietal fruit notes. Screwcap. 13.5° alc. RATING 88 DRINK Now $ 21.50

Ninth Island Riesling 2005 A big, muscular wine, very much the product of the vintage; big in flavour, but not finesse. RATING 87 DRINK 2008 $ 20

Estate Gewurztraminer 2005 Hints of rose petal; fine and crisp; will undoubtedly develop with time in bottle. RATING 87 DRINK 2009 $ 27

Estate Pinot Gris 2005 Blush-pink; has flavour, but achieves this with a certain degree of phenolics. RATING 87 DRINK Now $ 27

ϷϷϷϷ **Estate Riesling 2005** RATING 86 DRINK 2008 $ 23
Ninth Island Cabernet Sauvignon 2004 RATING 84 DRINK 2008 $ 23

Pirie Estate ★★★★☆

17 High Street, Launceston, Tas 7250 (postal) REGION Northern Tasmania
T (03) 6334 7772 F (03) 6334 7773 www.andrewpirie.com OPEN Not
WINEMAKER Andrew Pirie EST. 2004 CASES 8000
After a relatively short break, Andrew Pirie has re-established his winemaking activities in Tas. He has leased the Rosevears winery, where he will oversee the production of wines for the Rosevears group, for his own brands, and for others on a contract basis. His main responsibility, however, is now his role as CEO of Tamer Ridge, where he will also oversee winemaking.

ϷϷϷϷϷ **Pinot Noir 2004** Deeply coloured; spotlessly clean dark berry, plum and spice aromas; a fleshy, long and stylish palate; from clones 114, 115 and MV6. Screwcap. RATING 95 DRINK 2010 $ 35.50

ϷϷϷϷ **Pirie South Riesling 2005** Big, slightly broad, noticeably ripe fruit; abundant flavour. RATING 87 DRINK 2009 $ 22

Piromit Wines

NR

113 Hanwood Avenue, Hanwood, NSW 2680 **REGION** Riverina
T (02) 6963 0200 **F** (02) 6963 0277 **WWW**.piromitwines.com.au **OPEN** Mon–Fri 9–5
WINEMAKER Dom Piromalli, Sam Mittiga **EST.** 1998 **CASES** 50 000
I simply cannot resist quoting directly from the background information kindly supplied to me.
'Piromit Wines is a relatively new boutique winery situated in Hanwood, NSW. The 1000-tonne
capacity winery was built for the 1999 vintage on a 14-acre site which was until recently used as a
drive-in. Previous to this, wines were made on our 100-acre vineyard. The winery site is being
developed into an innovative tourist attraction complete with an Italian restaurant and landscaped
formal gardens.' It is safe to say this extends the concept of a boutique winery into new territory, but
then it is a big country. It is a family business run by Pat Mittiga, Dom Piromalli and Paul Hudson.

Pirramimma

Johnston Road, McLaren Vale, SA 5171 **REGION** McLaren Vale
T (08) 8323 8205 **F** (08) 8323 9224 **WWW**.pirramimma.com.au **OPEN** Mon–Fri 9–5, Sat 11–5, Sun &
public hols 11.30–4
WINEMAKER Geoff Johnston **EST.** 1892 **CASES** 50 000
A long-established, family-owned company with outstanding vineyard resources. It is using those
resources to full effect, with a series of intense old-vine varietals including Semillon, Sauvignon
Blanc, Chardonnay, Shiraz, Grenache, Cabernet Sauvignon and Petit Verdot, all fashioned without
over-embellishment. There are 2 quality tiers, both offering excellent value, the packaging recently
significantly upgraded. Exports to the UK, the US, Canada and Germany.

TTTT **Stock's Hill Shiraz 2003** An attractive medium-bodied mix of black fruits, spice and
regional chocolate; fine, ripe tannins. Smart new packaging; good value. Screwcap.
RATING 90 **DRINK** 2010 $ 16

Old Bush Vine Grenache 2003 Brilliant clear colour; fragrant plum, black cherry and
spice; light- to medium-bodied; good length and finish. Screwcap. **RATING** 90 **DRINK** 2008
$ 18

McLaren Vale Petit Verdot 2003 Over the years, one of the best examples of the variety in
Australia; no more than medium-bodied, cedary and elegant; does fall partial victim to
the '03 vintage, but still a worthy wine. Cork. 14° alc. **RATING** 90 **DRINK** 2012 $ 26

TTTT **Stock's Hill Sauvignon Blanc Semillon 2005** A dry style from start to finish,
mineral/stone/acidity driving the firm, but not phenolic, palate. Screwcap. 12.5° alc.
RATING 87 **DRINK** 2008 $ 13

TTTT **McLaren Vale Late Harvest Riesling (500 ml) 2004 RATING** 86 **DRINK** 2009 $ 17

Pizzini

★★★☆

Lano–Trento Vineyard, 175 King Valley Road, Whitfield, Vic 3768 **REGION** King Valley
T (03) 5729 8278 **F** (03) 5729 8495 **WWW**.pizzini.com.au **OPEN** 7 days 10–5
WINEMAKER Alfred Pizzini, Joel Pizzini **EST.** 1980 **CASES** 14 000
Fred and Katrina Pizzini have been grapegrowers in the King Valley for over 25 years, with over 50 ha
of vineyard. Grapegrowing (rather than winemaking) still continues to be the major focus, but their
move into winemaking has been particularly successful, and I can personally vouch for their Italian
cooking skills. It is not surprising, then, that their wines should span both Italian and traditional
varieties. Exports to Hong Kong and China.

TTTT **King Valley Riesling 2005** Clean, crisp citrus/spice/mineral mix; good balance and
length, well-made. Screwcap. 13° alc. **RATING** 89 **DRINK** 2012 $ 14

King Valley Cabernet Sauvignon 2002 Neatly balanced and constructed; blackcurrant,
licorice and blackberry fruit on the medium-bodied palate; good balance and length. Cork.
13.8° alc. **RATING** 89 **DRINK** 2011 $ 20

Il Barone 2001 Relatively finely-boned and structured; a blend of spicy, cedary, savoury
aromas and flavours; fine, soft tannins. Cabernet Sauvignon/Shiraz/Sangiovese/Nebbiolo.
Cork. 14.2° alc. **RATING** 89 **DRINK** 2011 $ 48

King Valley Sauvignon Blanc 2005 A strongly minerally style, with some green apple and spice; well-made, but not particularly intense. Screwcap. 12.5° alc. **RATING** 88 **DRINK** Now $15

King Valley Sangiovese 2004 Far better colour than most; a massive wine for the variety, with dark cherry fruit largely obscured by extract and tannins. It is conceivable the wine will come out of its shell with enough time in bottle. Cork. 14.2° alc. **RATING** 87 **DRINK** 2009 $24

ȲȲȲȲ King Valley Verduzzo 2005 Gently floral, spicy bouquet; the fruit flavours are akin to those of pinot grigio, likewise the slightly hot finish. Work in progress. Screwcap. 14° alc. **RATING** 86 **DRINK** 2008 $18

Plantagenet

Albany Highway, Mount Barker, WA 6324 **REGION** Mount Barker
T (08) 9851 3111 **F** (08) 9851 1839 **WWW**.plantagenetwines.com **OPEN** 7days 9–5
WINEMAKER Richard Robson **EST.** 1974 **CASES** 130 000
The senior winery in the Mount Barker region, making superb wines across the full spectrum of variety and style: highly aromatic Riesling, tangy citrus-tinged Chardonnay, glorious Rhône-style Shiraz and ultra-stylish Cabernet Sauvignon. Exports to all major markets.

ȲȲȲȲȲ Great Southern Riesling 2005 Classic riesling aroma, flavour and profile; apple, passionfruit and citrus, the very good balancing acidity also contributing to length. 13° alc. **RATING** 94 **DRINK** 2012 $19

ȲȲȲȲȲ Mount Barker Cabernet Sauvignon 2003 Good hue; clearly articulated varietal fruit in a cassis/blackcurrant spectrum; medium-bodied, with good tannin and oak management. Cork. 14° alc. **RATING** 93 **DRINK** 2016 $35

Mount Barker Shiraz 2003 Spicy notes to both bouquet and palate; gentle blackberry, plum and licorice fruit with slightly unexpected tannins to add structure. Cork. 14.5° alc. **RATING** 92 **DRINK** 2015 $40

Omrah Sauvignon Blanc 2005 Crisp, lively and fresh; gentle passionfruit and gooseberry; good length, and delivers the goods at the price. Screwcap. 13° alc. **RATING** 90 **DRINK** Now $17

Omrah Shiraz 2004 Good depth; medium-bodied blackberry, dark chocolate, mocha and spice, finishing with ripe tannins; excellent value. Screwcap. 14.5° alc. **RATING** 90 **DRINK** 2011 $17

ȲȲȲȲ Eros Rose 2005 Positive strawberry and cherry fruit; has length and a well-balanced, dry finish. Screwcap. 13° alc. **RATING** 89 **DRINK** Now $16

Hazard Hill Semillon Sauvignon Blanc 2005 Tropical orange blossom aromas; a solid palate, with plenty of flavour; excellent value. Screwcap. 12.5° alc. **RATING** 88 **DRINK** 2015 $12

Omrah Merlot 2003 Attractive light- to medium-bodied wine; good savoury/olive varietal character; rests well in the mouth. Screwcap. **RATING** 88 **DRINK** Now $17.50

Omrah Shiraz 2003 Light- to medium-bodied; spicy/peppery red and black fruits; fresh finish; entirely fruit-driven. Screwcap. 14° alc. **RATING** 87 **DRINK** 2008 $17.50

ȲȲȲȲ Omrah Cabernet Sauvignon 2003 **RATING** 86 **DRINK** Now $17.50
Omrah Chardonnay 2005 **RATING** 85 **DRINK** Now $17

ȲȲȲ Omrah Pinot Noir 2004 **RATING** 83 $17.50

Platypus Lane Wines

PO Box 1140, Midland, WA 6936 **REGION** Swan District
T (08) 9250 1655 **F** (08) 9274 3045 **WWW**.platypuswines.com.au **OPEN** Not
WINEMAKER Brenden Smith (Contract) **EST.** 1996 **CASES** NA
Platypus Lane, with a small core of 2.5 ha of chardonnay, shiraz and muscat, gained considerable publicity for owner Ian Gibson when its Shiraz won the inaugural John Gladstones Trophy at the Qantas Western Australian Wines Show for the wine showing greatest regional and varietal typicity.

Much of the credit can no doubt go to winemaker Brenden Smith, who handles significant quantities of grapes brought in from other producers as well as from the core vineyards. Exports to the UK and the US.

TTTT **Unwooded Chardonnay 2005** Well-made; a mix of white peach and more tropical fruits; good acidity; good packaging. Screwcap. 13.6° alc. **RATING** 87 **DRINK** Now $ 15

🐚 Plum Hill Vineyard ★★★★

45 Coldstream West Road, Chirnside Park, Vic 3116 **REGION** Yarra Valley
T (03) 9735 0985 **F** (03) 9735 4109 **OPEN** By appt
WINEMAKER Rachel Dutton **EST.** 1998 **CASES** 2500
Ian and June Delbridge had been breeding cattle on their 36-ha property since the early 1970s, before deciding to establish a vineyard in 1998. They planted a little over 7 ha of merlot, pinot noir, cabernet sauvignon and shiraz, in the distinguished neighbourhood of Mount Mary, Bianchet and Yarre Edge. Grapes from the first 2 vintages were sold, but in 2003 the decision was taken to make and bottle the wines under the Plum Hill Vineyard label.

TTTTY **Yarra Valley Shiraz 2004** Strong purple-red; warm licorice, multi-spice aromas; the medium-bodied palate picks up the bouquet with blackberry, pepper and spice, and a lingering core of sweet fruit. Stained Diam cork is unusual. 13.5° alc. **RATING** 91 **DRINK** 2012 $ 20
Yarra Valley Pinot Noir 2004 Medium red; a light- to medium-bodied spicy, savoury plum and black cherry mix; while relatively light, does have good length.

Diam. 13.5° alc. **RATING** 90 **DRINK** 2009 $ 20

TTTT **Yarra Valley Merlot 2004** Very good colour; a powerful wine, with sombre dark fruits and a hint of game; remarkable concentration for '04. Similar stained Diam. 13.5° alc. **RATING** 89 **DRINK** 2015 $ 20
Yarra Valley Cabernet 2004 Youthful purple-red; ample blackcurrant and cassis; a fruit-driven style with minimal oak; not yet complex, but has the potential to become so. Diam. **RATING** 89 **DRINK** 2010 $ 20

Plunkett Wines ★★★★★

Cnr Hume Highway/Lambing Gully Road, Avenel, Vic 3664 **REGION** Strathbogie Ranges
T (03) 5796 2150 **F** (03) 5796 2147 **WWW**.plunkett.com.au **OPEN** 7 days 10–5 (cellar door),
Thurs–Mon 10–5 (restaurant)
WINEMAKER Sam Plunkett, Victor Nash **EST.** 1980 **CASES** 13 000
The Plunkett family first planted grapes way back in 1968, establishing 1.2 ha with 25 experimental varieties. Commercial plantings commenced in 1980, with 100 ha now under vine, and more coming. Though holding a vigneron's licence since 1985, the Plunketts did not begin serious marketing of the wines until 1992. They now produce an array of wines which are pleasant and well priced; the Reserves are in another quality and price league. Exports to the UK, the US and other major markets.

TTTTT **Reserve Strathbogie Ranges Shiraz 2003** The best '03 red in the Sydney Wine Show '06; polished, elegant, fine and long; no dead fruit character; classy oak handling. One of 2 gold medals to Plunkett in Class 57, topping the 7 gold medals in this large class. Cork. **RATING** 95 **DRINK** 2013 $ 38
Reserve Strathbogie Ranges Shiraz 2002 Powerful and concentrated, medium- to full-bodied; abundant luscious black fruits; very good tannins, oak and structure. Significant wine show awards. Cork. 14.5° alc. **RATING** 94 **DRINK** 2012 $ 38

TTTTY **Strathbogie Ranges Riesling 2005** Fragrant lime blossom; nicely balanced residual sugar and acidity; good fruit, line and length. Screwcap. **RATING** 90 **DRINK** 2010 $ 16

TTTT **Strathbogie Ranges Cabernet Merlot 2003** Powerful wine; plenty of black fruits and dark chocolate along with touches of mint and leaf. Cork. **RATING** 89 **DRINK** 2010 $ 19
Strathbogie Ranges Sauvignon Blanc 2005 Clean; a mineral streak to gentle tropical fruit, good length and nice lemony acidity. Screwcap. **RATING** 88 **DRINK** Now $ 16

ΨΨΨΨ **Blackwood Ridge Unwooded Chardonnay 2005** RATING 86 DRINK Now $17
Strathbogie Ranges Chardonnay 2004 RATING 86 DRINK 2008 $20
Blackwood Ridge Shiraz 2003 RATING 85 DRINK Now $17
Blackwood Ridge Traminer Riesling 2004 RATING 84 DRINK Now $17

Poacher's Ridge Vineyard ★★★★

163 Jersey Street, Wembley, WA 6014 (postal) REGION Mount Barker
T (08) 9387 5003 F (08) 9387 5503 WWW.prv.com.au OPEN Not
WINEMAKER Robert Diletti (Contract) EST. 2000 CASES 2000
Alex and Janet Taylor purchased the Poacher's Ridge property in 1999; before then it had been used for cattle grazing. In 2000, 7 ha of vineyard (in descending order: shiraz, cabernet sauvignon, merlot, riesling, marsanne and viognier) were planted. The first small crop came in 2003, a larger one in 2004, together making an auspicious debut. A cellar door and café is expected to be completed in late 2006.

ΨΨΨΨΨ **2004 Poacher's Ridge Vineyard Sophie's Yard Great Southern Shiraz** Bright colour; light- to medium-bodied; juicy red cherry, raspberry and blood plum fruit; fine tannins. Procork. RATING 90 DRINK 2012
2004 Poacher's Ridge Vineyard Louis' Block Great Southern Merlot Strongly varietal olive, herb and spice edges to plum/blackcurrant fruit; fine-boned, long and savoury; has absorbed 18 months of French oak.Procork. RATING 90 DRINK 2014

Poet's Corner ★★★

Craigmoor Road, Mudgee, NSW 2850 REGION Mudgee
T (02) 6372 2208 F (02) 6372 4464 WWW.poetscornerwines.com OPEN Mon–Sat 10–4.30, Sun & public hols 10–4
WINEMAKER Trent Nankivell EST. 1858 CASES 150 000
Poet's Corner is located in one of the oldest wineries in Australia to remain open and in use one way or another since it was founded in 1858. It is now the public face for the Mudgee brands of Orlando Wyndham, which are made at Montrose (which has no cellar door) and which are sent to the Barossa for bottling.

ΨΨΨΨ **Shiraz Cabernet Sauvignon 2004** Quite fragrant; spicy oak and soft fruit aromas, then a light- to medium-bodied, neatly balanced palate. Cork. RATING 87 DRINK Now $9.99
Montrose Barbera 2002 Light, clear red; fresh berry, leaf and spice aromas; light-bodied, with silky red fruits and minimal tannins. Cork. 14° alc. RATING 87 DRINK 2008 $20.99

ΨΨΨΨ **Shiraz 2004** RATING 86 DRINK Now $9.99

🍂 Point Leo Road Vineyard ★★★★☆

214 Point Leo Road, Red Hill South, Vic 3937 REGION Mornington Peninsula
T 0409 882 402 F (03) 9882 0327 WWW.pointleoroad.com.au OPEN By appt
WINEMAKER Phillip Kittle, Kilchurn Wines (David Cowburn) EST. 1996 CASES 350
John Law and family planted 2 ha of pinot noir and 1.6 ha of chardonnay in 1996 as contract growers for several leading Mornington Peninsula wineries. They subsequently planted 1 ha of pinot gris and 0.6 ha of lagrein which came into production in 2006. These have in turn been followed by 1.4 ha of gewurztraminer and sauvignon blanc, lifting total plantings to 6.6 ha, although the latest additions will not come into bearing until 2008. They have decided to have part of the grapes contract-made, and the amounts released under the Point Leo Road label will increase in the years ahead.

ΨΨΨΨΨ **Mornington Peninsula Chardonnay 2004** A clean, fresh and fragrant bouquet; incisive grapefruit and nectarine flavours; a touch of oak on a long finish. Screwcap. 13.5° alc. RATING 92 DRINK 2010 $23
Mornington Peninsula Pinot Noir Chardonnay 2004 Fine mousse; elegant sparkling wine, with delicate, citrussy fruit, and impeccable balance. 12.5° alc. RATING 92 DRINK 2009 $29
Mornington Peninsula Pinot Noir 2004 Attractive light- to medium-bodied wine; spiced plum aromas and flavours; good balance and, in particular, length. Diam. 13.5° alc. RATING 91 DRINK 2008 $27.50

TTTT **Rose 2005** Fresh, light and crisp; strawberry fruit off-set by lemony acidity; delicious summer drink. Screwcap. 13.5° alc. **RATING** 89 **DRINK** Now $ 20

Pokolbin Estate ★★★★

McDonalds Road, Pokolbin, NSW 2321 **REGION** Lower Hunter Valley
T (02) 4998 7524 **F** (02) 4998 7765 **www**.pokolbinestate.com.au **OPEN** 7 days 10–6
WINEMAKER Andrew Thomas (Contract) **EST.** 1980 **CASES** 2500
If you go to the lengths that Pokolbin Estate has done to hide its light under a bushel, you end up with something like 7 vintages of Semillon, 6 of Riesling, 7 of Shiraz, 3 of Tempranillo, 2 each of Nebbiolo and Sangiovese and sundry other wines adding up to more than 30 in total. Between 1998 and 2000 Neil McGuigan and Gary Reid shared the winemaking tasks; since 2001 Andrew Thomas has skilfully made the wines from vineyards over 25 years old.

TTTTY **Hunter Valley Semillon 2005** Powerful, intense and long; a touch of CO_2 spritz needs to settle down, but will do so. Screwcap. **RATING** 90 **DRINK** 2015 $ 25

Polin & Polin Wines NR

Wyameta, Bell's Lane, Denman, NSW 2328 **REGION** Upper Hunter Valley
T (02) 6547 2955 **F** (02) 9969 9665 **www**.polinwines.com.au **OPEN** Not
WINEMAKER Peter Orr (Contract) **EST.** 1997 **CASES** 1200
The 6-ha vineyard was established by Lexie and Michael Polin (and family) in 1997. It is not named for them, as one might expect, but to honour Peter and Thomas Polin, who migrated from Ireland in 1860, operating a general store in Coonamble. Limb of Addy has a distinctly Irish twist to it, but is in fact a hill immediately to the east of the vineyard.

Politini Wines NR

65 Upper King River Road, Cheshunt, Vic 3678 **REGION** King Valley
T (03) 5729 8277 **F** (03) 5729 8373 **www**.politiniwines.com.au **OPEN** 7 days 11–5
WINEMAKER Contract **EST.** 1989 **CASES** 2200
The Politini family have been grapegrowers in the King Valley supplying major local wineries since 1989, selling to Brown Brothers, Miranda and the Victorian Alps Winery. In 2000 they decided to withhold 20 tonnes per year for the Politini Wines label.

Polleters ★★★★☆

Polleters Road, Moonambel, Vic 3478 **REGION** Pyrenees
T (03) 9569 5030 **www**.polleters.com **OPEN** W'ends 10–5
WINEMAKER Mark Summerfield **EST.** 1994 **CASES** 1500
Pauline and Peter Bicknell purchased the 60-ha property on which their vineyard now stands in 1993, at which time it was part of a larger grazing property. The first vines were planted in spring 1994, and there are now 2 ha each of shiraz and cabernet sauvignon, 1.25 ha of cabernet franc and 0.75 ha of merlot. In the first few years the grapes were sold, but since 2001 part of the production has been used to produce the impressively rich and powerful wines. The grapes are hand-picked, fermented in open vats with hand-plunging, and matured for 18 months in American oak.

TTTTT **Moonambel Cabernet Sauvignon 2004** Medium purple-red; rich, luxuriant blackcurrant and cassis floods the mouth; good oak, plump tannins. Screwcap. 14.5° alc. **RATING** 94 **DRINK** 2019 $ 25

TTTTY **Moonambel Shiraz 2004** Deep red-purple; a medium-bodied but complex array of black fruits and savoury/spicy notes; firm, earthy tannins; American oak barely to be seen. Screwcap. 14.3° alc. **RATING** 92 **DRINK** 2015 $ 25
Courtney's Choice 2003 Retains good hue; has abundant flavour, the alcohol ok. Shiraz/Cabernet Sauvignon/Cabernet Franc/Merlot. Screwcap. 14.3° alc. **RATING** 90 **DRINK** 2013 $ 25
Moonambel Merlot 2004 Deep colour; abundant, rich fruit with touches of dark chocolate; a supple wine, saying much more about the region than the variety. Screwcap. 14.5° alc. **RATING** 90 **DRINK** 2014 $ 25

▼▼▼▼ **Moonambel Cabernet Franc 2004** Good colour; quite fragrant spice, tobacco and earth all pointing to varietal character, but lacking enough flesh on the mid-palate. Screwcap. 14° alc. **RATING** 89 **DRINK** 2012 $ 25

🐾 Pollocksford Vineyards ★★★★

Level 3, 68 Myers Street, Geelong, Vic 3221 (postal) **REGION** Geelong
T 0419 888 700 **F** (03) 5229 9869 **OPEN** Not
WINEMAKER Scott Ireland **EST.** 1991 **CASES** 200
Drew Hewson and Craig Scott purchased the Pollocksford property in 1991 and planted a little under 2 ha of pinot noir, shiraz, chenin blanc and cabernet franc between 1992 and 1994. It is on the typical regional chocolate clay-loam from weathered basalt over powdery limestone, with a northerly aspect to the Barwon River, and was the site of a distinguished winery 150 years ago until phylloxera led to the compulsory removal of all vines from the Geelong district.

▼▼▼▼▽ **Geelong Unfiltered Pinot Noir 2003** An attractive mix of spice and plum aromas and flavours; good length and persistence; developing slowly. Screwcap. **RATING** 91 **DRINK** 2008 $ 18
Geelong Shiraz 2001 Has more substance and structure than the 2002; a mix of spice, bitter chocolate and black fruits; medium-bodied, good length. Cork. **RATING** 90 **DRINK** 2008 $ 20

▼▼▼▼ **Geelong Chenin Blanc 2002** Interesting wine; complex, spicy, nutty notes, with good acidity and length. Could easily be mistaken for Chardonnay. Cork. **RATING** 87 **DRINK** Now $ 12

Pondalowie Vineyards ★★★★★

6 Main Street, Bridgewater-on-Loddon, Vic 3516 **REGION** Bendigo
T (03) 5437 3332 **F** (03) 5437 3332 **WWW**.pondalowie.com.au **OPEN** W'ends 12–5, or by appt
WINEMAKER Dominic Morris, Krystina Morris **EST.** 1997 **CASES** 1500
Dominic and Krystina Morris both have strong winemaking backgrounds, gained from working in Australia, Portugal and France. Dominic has worked alternate vintages in Australia and Portugal since 1995, and Krystina has worked there, at St Hallett, and Boar's Rock. They have established 5.5 ha of shiraz, 2 ha each of tempranillo and cabernet sauvignon, and a little viognier and malbec. Incidentally, the illustration on the Pondalowie label is not a piece of barbed wire, but a very abstract representation of the winery kelpie dog. Exports to the UK.

▼▼▼▼▼ **Shiraz Viognier 2004** Dense colour; riper, more dense and more complex aromas and flavours than the Shiraz; bordering viscous, with the apricot nuances of viognier running along with multi-spice and licorice notes. Screwcap. 15° alc. **RATING** 95 **DRINK** 2010 $ 30
Shiraz 2004 Good colour; complex blackberry, spice, mocha and vanilla interplay; fine, rounded tannins and controlled oak. Screwcap. 14.5° alc. **RATING** 94 **DRINK** 2014 $ 25
Vineyard Blend 2004 Vibrant purple-red; an unlikely marriage, but a successful one; supple and smooth medium-bodied black fruits; balanced tannins, good oak. Cabernet/Shiraz/Tempranillo. Screwcap. 14° alc. **RATING** 94 **DRINK** 2012 $ 20

▼▼▼▼▽ **Special Release Sparkling Shiraz 2002** As to be expected, a serious wine; black cherry fruit with no phenolics or oak; a long, clean finish, nigh-on dry. 14° alc. **RATING** 92 **DRINK** 2010 $ 36
Cabernet Malbec 2003 Lots of blackcurrant, mulberry, earthy, spice and dark chocolate; the tannins firm and needing to soften. Screwcap. **RATING** 90 **DRINK** 2013 $ 30
Vintage Port (500 ml) 2003 Authentic Portuguese style; spicy, dry fruit with considerable complexity; just a touch of hot spirit on the finish. **RATING** 90 **DRINK** 2012 $ 25

Poole's Rock/Cockfighter's Ghost ★★★★☆

De Beyers Road, Pokolbin, NSW 2321 **REGION** Lower Hunter Valley
T (02) 4998 7356 **F** (02) 4998 6866 **WWW**.poolesrock.com.au **OPEN** 7 days 9.30–5
WINEMAKER Patrick Auld **EST.** 1988 **CASES** NFP

Sydney merchant banker David Clarke has had a long involvement with the wine industry. The 18-ha Poole's Rock vineyard, planted purely to chardonnay, is his personal venture; it was initially bolstered by the acquisition of the larger, adjoining Simon Whitlam Vineyard. However, the purchase of the 74-ha Glen Elgin Estate, upon which the 2500-tonne former Tulloch winery is situated, takes Poole's Rock (and its associated brands, Cockfighter's Ghost and Firestick) into another dimension. Retail distribution throughout Australia; exports to the UK, the US and other major markets.

ΨΨΨΨΨ **Cockfighter's Ghost Hunter Valley Semillon 2005** An unusually aromatic lemon zest and blossom bouquet; great flavour intensity; very good example of a great semillon vintage. Screwcap. 12.2° alc. RATING 95 DRINK 2012 $18

ΨΨΨΨΨ **Cockfighter's Ghost McLaren Vale Shiraz 2002** A strongly regional coating of dark chocolate around supple, blackberry fruit; medium-bodied; relatively low 14.3° alcohol a relief; great vintage. Cork. RATING 92 DRINK 2012 $25

Cockfighter's Ghost Coonawarra Cabernet Sauvignon 2001 Maturing Cabernet with earthy regional character; elegant palate with good length and attractive, cedary oak. Cork. 13.5° alc. RATING 91 DRINK 2011 $30

Cockfighter's Ghost Tasmanian Pinot Noir 2004 Clean; light- to medium-bodied; plum and spice with controlled oak and extract, good balance and firm structure. Screwcap. 14.1° alc. RATING 90 DRINK 2009 $35

Cockfighter's Ghost McLaren Vale Merlot 2002 Intense, savoury, black fruits with the unmistakable stamp of the vintage, and a nice touch of olive, courtesy of the variety. Cork. 13.9° alc. RATING 90 DRINK 2009 $25

ΨΨΨΨ **Cockfighter's Ghost Clare Valley Riesling 2005** Light green-yellow; relatively full-bodied, with ripe tropical fruits; solid finish. Screwcap. 12.7° alc. RATING 89 DRINK 2010 $23

Cockfighter's Ghost Clare Valley Riesling 2004 Quite developed colour; powerful toast and lime aromas; similar lemony/toasty flavours with balancing acidity; more power than finesse. Screwcap. RATING 89 DRINK 2010 $23

Cockfighter's Ghost Langhorne Creek Cabernet Sauvignon 2002 Soft, cedary, blackberry aromas; an easy, soft palate with ripe tannins. Blue Gold medal Sydney International Wine Competition 2006. Cork. 14.2° alc. RATING 89 DRINK 2010 $25

Cockfighter's Ghost Hunter Valley Chardonnay 2005 Generous ripe flavour ranging from stone fruit to tropical plus a whisper of oak; not particularly long. Screwcap. 13.7° alc. RATING 87 DRINK 2008 $20

Poole's Rock Hunter Valley Shiraz 2001 Light- to medium-bodied; earthy regional aromas and flavours; fine tannins, but an overall lack of concentration. Cork. 12.5° alc. RATING 87 DRINK 2008 $35

ΨΨΨΨ **Firestick Chardonnay 2004** A thoroughly honest wine with obvious varietal character, though not much complexity or finesse; low alcohol both help and hindrance. Screwcap. 12.4° alc. RATING 86 DRINK Now $15

Cockfighter's Ghost Hunter Valley Verdelho 2005 RATING 86 DRINK 2008 $18

Cockfighter's Ghost McLaren Vale Shiraz 2003 RATING 86 DRINK 2008 $25

Cockfighter's Ghost Hunter Valley Unwooded Chardonnay 2005 RATING 85 DRINK Now $18

Pooley Wines ★★★★★

Cooinda Vale Vineyard, Barton Vale Road, Campania, Tas 7026 REGION Southern Tasmania
T (03) 6260 2895 F (03) 6260 2895 WWW.pooleywines.com.au OPEN 7 days 10–5
WINEMAKER Matt Pooley, Andrew Hood (Contract) EST. 1985 CASES 2000
Three generations of the Pooley family have been involved in the development of Pooley Wines, although the winery was previously known as Cooinda Vale. Plantings have now reached 6.4 ha in a region which is substantially warmer and drier than most people realise. In 2003 the family planted 1 ha of pinot noir at Richmond on a heritage property with an 1830s Georgian home (and 28 ha in all) which will be known as the Belmont Vineyard, and will have a cellar door in an old sandstone barn on the property.

ŸŸŸŸŸ **Coal River Riesling 2004** Highly fragrant lime and apple blossom; glorious palate with superb balance and length; some Mosel overtones. Multiple trophies including Best Wine of Show Tasmanian Wine Show '06. **RATING** 96 **DRINK** 2012 $ 20

ŸŸŸŸŸ **Coal River Riesling 2005** Fragrant, flowery bouquet; exceptionally generous and ripe tropical/lime fruit mix; mouthfilling; good balance and length. **RATING** 92 **DRINK** 2010 $ 20

Coal River Chardonnay 2003 Medium-bodied; solid stone fruit and melon supported by gentle oak. **RATING** 90 **DRINK** 2009 $ 22

Coal River Pinot Noir 2005 Good, bright hue; medium-bodied spiced plum fruit, then a relatively firm finish. Will develop. Screwcap. **RATING** 90 **DRINK** 2011 $ 26

ŸŸŸŸ **Family Reserve Merlot 2005** Vibrant colour; sweet redcurrant and raspberry fruit; supple, medium-bodied palate; no problem with ripeness; good finish. Cork. **RATING** 89 **DRINK** 2012 $ 35

ŸŸŸŸ **Coal River Pinot Noir 2004 RATING** 86 **DRINK** 2008 $ 26

Family Reserve Cabernet Shiraz Merlot 2004 RATING 86 **DRINK** 2009 $ 35

Coal River Pinot Gris 2005 RATING 85 **DRINK** Now $ 26

Poplar Bend   NR

465 Main Creek Road, Main Ridge, Vic 3928 **REGION** Mornington Peninsula
T (03) 5989 6046 **F** (03) 5989 6278 **OPEN** W'ends & public hols 10–5, also by appt
WINEMAKER Paul Wallace **EST.** 1988 **CASES** 350
Poplar Bend was the child of Melbourne journalist, author and raconteur Keith Dunstan and wife Marie, who moved into full-scale retirement in 1997, selling Poplar Bend to David Briggs. The changes are few; the label still depicts Chloe in all her glory, which could be calculated to send the worthy inhabitants of the Bureau of Alcohol, Tobacco and Firearms (of the US) into a state of cataleptic shock.

Port Phillip Estate   ★★★★★

261 Red Hill Road, Red Hill, Vic 3937 **REGION** Mornington Peninsula
T (03) 5989 2708 **F** (03) 5989 3017 **WWW**.portphillip.net **OPEN** W'ends & public hols 11–5
WINEMAKER Sandro Mosele **EST.** 1987 **CASES** 4000
Established by leading Melbourne QC Jeffrey Sher, who, after some prevarication, sold the estate to Giorgio and Dianne Gjergja in February 2000. The Gjergjas are rightly more than content with the quality and style of the wines; the main changes are enhanced cellar door facilities and redesigned labels. Exports to the UK.

ŸŸŸŸŸ **Chardonnay 2004** Pale green-straw; super-fine crisp and elegant stone fruit, melon and citrus mix, oak in a pure support role. Diam. 14° alc. **RATING** 95 **DRINK** 2012 $ 30

Pinot Noir 2004 Strong red-purple; medium-bodied; smooth, velvety, sweet plummy fruit; excellent balance and length. Diam. 14° alc. **RATING** 94 **DRINK** 2011 $ 35

Shiraz 2004 Medium- to medium-full-bodied; has good structure, texture and mouthfeel to relatively sweet, spicy blackberry fruit; skilled tannin and oak management. Diam. 14° alc. **RATING** 94 **DRINK** 2014 $ 35

ŸŸŸŸ **Sauvignon Blanc 2005** A rich wine, full of varietal fruit at the passionfruit/tropical end of the spectrum; clean, dry finish. Diam. 13.5° alc. **RATING** 92 **DRINK** Now $ 22

Port Stephens Winery   NR

69 Nelson Bay Road, Bobs Farm, NSW 2316 **REGION** Northern Rivers Zone
T (02) 4982 6411 **F** (02) 4982 6766 **WWW**.portstephenswinery.com **OPEN** 7 days 10–5
WINEMAKER Contract **EST.** 1984 **CASES** 3500
Planting of the quite substantial Port Stephens Winery vineyard began in 1984, and there are now 4 ha of vines in production. The wines are made under contract in the Hunter Valley but sold through the attractive Boutique Wine Centre, which offers over 100 wines from 30 wineries (as far afield as Manjimup in WA).

Portree
NR

72 Powells Track via Mount William Road, Lancefield, Vic 3455 **REGION** Macedon Ranges
T (03) 5429 1422 **F** (03) 5429 2205 **WWW**.portreevineyard.com.au **OPEN** W'ends & public hols 11–5
WINEMAKER Ken Murchison **EST.** 1983 **CASES** 1500
Owner Ken Murchison selected his 5-ha Macedon vineyard after studying viticulture at Charles Sturt
University and being strongly influenced by Dr Andrew Pirie's doctoral thesis. All the wines show
distinct cool-climate characteristics, the Quarry Red having clear similarities to the wines of Chinon
in the Loire Valley. However, Portree has done best with Chardonnay, its principal wine (in terms of
volume). Exports to Hong Kong.

Possums Vineyard

31 Thornber Street, Unley Park, SA 5061 (postal) **REGION** McLaren Vale
T (08) 8272 3406 **F** (08) 8272 3406 **WWW**.possumswines.com.au **OPEN** Not
WINEMAKER Boar's Rock Winery **EST.** 2000 **CASES** 5000
Possums Vineyard is owned by the very distinguished wine scientist and researcher Dr John
Possingham, and Carol Summers. They have 22 ha of shiraz, 17 ha of cabernet sauvignon, 18 ha of
chardonnay, 1 ha of viognier and 0.5 ha of grenache established in 2 vineyards (at Blewitt Springs and
Willunga). They regard themselves as grapegrowers, rather than winemakers, with the bulk of the
grapes sold to Beringer Blass and d'Arenberg. However, with the advent of Boar's Rock Winery, and
the contract-making facilities it offers, they have embarked on making wines under the Possums
Vineyard label. Exports to the US, the UK and other markets.

Willunga Shiraz 2004 Spicy, earthy, leathery, savoury nuances to the light- to medium-
bodied red and black fruits; supple, silky mouthfeel. Intriguingly, no alcohol disclosed on
the front or back label. Screwcap. **RATING** 91 **DRINK** 2015 $ 17

Potters Clay Vineyards
NR

Main Road, Willunga, SA 5172 **REGION** McLaren Vale
T (08) 8556 2799 **F** (08) 8556 2922 **WWW**.pottersclayvineyards.com.au **OPEN** By appt
WINEMAKER John Bruschi **EST.** 1994 **CASES** 900
John and Donna Bruschi are second-generation grapegrowers who assumed full ownership of the
16-ha Potters Clay Vineyard in 1994 with the aim of establishing their own winery and label. In 1999
they completed stage one of a two-stage boutique winery. Stage one is a winery production facility;
stage two (at some future date) is to be cellar door, restaurant and garden/picnic area.

🐎 Prancing Horse Estate

39 Paringa Road, Red Hill South, Vic 3937 **REGION** Mornington Peninsula
T (03) 5989 2602 **F** (03) 9827 1231 **WWW**.prancinghorseestate.com **OPEN** By appt
WINEMAKER Sergio Carlei **EST.** 1990 **CASES** 600
Anthony and Catherine Hancy acquired the Lavender Bay Vineyard in early 2002, renaming it the
Prancing Horse Estate, and embarking on a radical upgrade of the existing plantings of 1 ha each of
chardonnay and pinot noir. They will progressively extend the plantings by 2.5 ha, planted equally to
chardonnay, pinot gris and pinot noir, using selected clones. The Hancys also made a decision to
avoid the use of pesticides, herbicides and fungicides. Having appointed Sergio Carlei as winemaker,
the following year they became joint owners with Sergio in Carlei Wines.

Mornington Peninsula Chardonnay 2004 Medium straw-green; distinctly richer,
sweeter, riper fruit, more to tropical peach than the '03; supple and mouthfilling. Diam.
13.5° alc. **RATING** 94 **DRINK** 2010 $ 40
Mornington Peninsula Pinot Noir 2004 Good colour; fine structure and balance; elegant
but intense black cherry, plum, spice and forest floor. Diam. 13.5° alc. **RATING** 94
DRINK 2011 $ 40

Mornington Peninsula Chardonnay 2003 Fine, elegant light-bodied wine; understated
nectarine and melon fruit plus a whisk of oak. Diam. 13.5° alc. **RATING** 92 **DRINK** 2009
$ 40

Preston Peak

NR

31 Preston Peak Lane, Toowoomba, Qld 4352 **REGION** Darling Downs
T (07) 4630 9499 **F** (07) 4630 9499 **WWW**.prestonpeak.com **OPEN** Wed–Sun 10–5
WINEMAKER Rod MacPherson **EST.** 1994 **CASES** 5000
Dentist owners Ashley Smith and Kym Thumpkin have a substantial tourism business. The large, modern cellar door can accommodate functions of up to 150 people, and is often used for weddings and other events. It is situated less than 10 mins' drive from the Toowoomba city centre, with views of Table Top Mountain, the Lockyer Valley and the Darling Downs.

Pretty Sally Estate

NR

PO Box 549, Kilmore East, Vic 3764 **REGION** Central Victoria Zone
T (03) 5783 3082 **F** (03) 5783 2027 **WWW**.prettysally.com **OPEN** Not
WINEMAKER Hanging Rock **EST.** 1996 **CASES** 1000
The McKay, Davies and Cornew families have joined to create the Pretty Sally business. It is based on estate plantings of 11.7 ha of shiraz, 23.8 ha of cabernet sauvignon and a splash of sauvignon blanc. The wines are chiefly exported to the US, where Pretty Sally has a permanent office.

Preveli Wines

Bessell Road, Rosa Brook, Margaret River, WA 6285 **REGION** Margaret River
T (08) 9757 2374 **F** (08) 9757 2790 **WWW**.preveliwines.com.au **OPEN** At Prevelly General Store
WINEMAKER Andrew Gaman Jnr, Frank Kittler, Mike Lemmes (Contract) **EST.** 1995 **CASES** 8000
Andrew and Greg Home have turned a small business into a substantial one, with 15 ha of vineyards at Rosabrook (supplemented by contracts with local growers), and winemaking spread among a number of contract makers. The wines are of impressive quality. The Prevelly General Store (owned by the Homes) is the main local outlet.

Margaret River Cabernet Sauvignon 2002 Attractive cedar and cigar box edges to strongly varietal blackcurrant fruit; slinky, smooth and supple; lingering finish. Screwcap. **RATING** 93 **DRINK** 2012 $ 31.95

Margaret River Pinot Noir 2003 A surprise packet; has good varietal character and style; foresty/sappy undertones to small dark fruits; excellent length. One of the best Margaret River Pinots to date. Screwcap. **RATING** 92 **DRINK** 2009 $ 16.95

Margaret River Chardonnay 2004 Elegant, fresh and lively; light- to medium-bodied; gentle stone fruit and melon; subtle oak, good length and balance. Screwcap. **RATING** 90 **DRINK** 2010 $ 22.95

Margaret River Shiraz Cabernet 2003 Light- to medium-bodied; strongly savoury/briary/spicy cool-grown style; fine-grained tannins. Screwcap. **RATING** 89 **DRINK** 2010 $ 21.95

Margaret River Semillon Sauvignon Blanc 2004 Clean and fresh; herb, grass and mineral notes from the semillon; has more length than depth. Screwcap. **RATING** 88 **DRINK** 2008 $ 16.95

Margaret River Sauvignon Blanc 2004 Light-bodied, clean, fresh and crisp; lively and well-made, but lacks the fruit intensity for higher points. Screwcap. **RATING** 87 **DRINK** Now $ 16.95

Primo Estate

Old Port Wakefield Road, Virginia, SA 5120 **REGION** Adelaide Plains
T (08) 8380 9442 **F** (08) 8380 9696 **WWW**.primoestate.com.au **OPEN** June–Aug Mon–Sat 10–4, Sept–May Mon–Fri 10–4
WINEMAKER Joseph Grilli **EST.** 1979 **CASES** 25 000
Roseworthy dux Joe Grilli has risen way above the constraints of the hot Adelaide Plains to produce innovative and always excellent wines. The biennial release of the Joseph Sparkling Red (in its tall Italian glass bottle) is eagerly awaited, the wine immediately selling out. Also unusual and highly regarded are the vintage-dated extra virgin olive oils. However, the core lies with the La Biondina (Colombard), the Il Briccone Shiraz Sangiovese and the Joseph Cabernet Merlot. The business has

expanded to take in both McLaren Vale and Clarendon, with 36.3 ha of cabernet sauvignon, colombard, shiraz, merlot, riesling, nebbiolo, sangiovese, riesling, sauvignon blanc and pinot grigio. Exports to all major markets.

TTTTT Joseph Moda Cabernet Merlot 2003 Strong, high-toned cassis blackcurrant fruit aromas; a luscious but not jammy cascade of black fruits, fine tannins and nice oak. Cork. 14.5° alc. **RATING** 95 **DRINK** 2013 $45

Joseph Sparkling Red NV As ever, immaculate balance and length. A spicy mix of dark fruits and nutty characters, the dosage low simply because it is not required. The shiraz base dates back to the 1980s, the reserve dosage to the 1960s and '70s. Disgorged September 2003. **RATING** 94 **DRINK** 2013 $50

TTTTY La Biondina Colombard 2005 As ever, vibrantly fresh and precise grapefruit, stone fruit and mineral flavours; amazing finish and aftertaste. Screwcap. **RATING** 93 **DRINK** Now $14.50

Joseph Pinot Grigio d'Elena 2005 Abundant texture and mouthfeel; an attractive cool-grown twist of citrus over apple and pear; neatly balanced acidity. Screwcap. **RATING** 93 **DRINK** 2008 $23

Joseph Angel Gully Shiraz 2003 Rich and clean blackberry and dark chocolate; good tannin structure and controlled oak. **RATING** 93 **DRINK** 2010 $45

Joseph La Magia 2005 Spicy rose petal aromas; great balance between sweetness and acidity; grows on you with each sip. Screwcap. 10.5° alc. **RATING** 93 **DRINK** 2009 $26

Prince Albert ★★★☆

100 Lemins Road, Waurn Ponds, Vic 3216 **REGION** Geelong
T (03) 5241 8091 **F** (03) 5241 8091 **OPEN** By appt
WINEMAKER Bruce Hyett **EST.** 1975 **CASES** 300
Australia's true Pinot Noir specialist (it has only ever made the one wine), which also made much of the early running with the variety: the wines always show good varietal character and have rebounded after a dull patch in the second half of the 1980s. In 1998 the vineyard and winery was certified organic by OVAA Inc. Apart from the mailing list, the wine is sold through fine wine retailers in Sydney and Melbourne, with a little finding its way to the UK. The impact of the drought resulted in a radically decreased production of the 2002 and 2003 vintages.

TTTY Pinot Noir 2004 **RATING** 86 **DRINK** 2008 $24

Prince of Orange ★★★★

'Cimbria', The Escort Way, Borenore, NSW 2800 **REGION** Orange
T (02) 6365 2396 **F** (02) 6365 2396 **www**.princeoforangewines.com.au **OPEN** Sat & long w'ends 10–5, or by appt
WINEMAKER Monarch Winemaking Services (Jim Chatto) **EST.** 1996 **CASES** 3000
Harald and Coral Brodersen purchased the 40-ha Cimbria property in 1990, and planted 3 ha of sauvignon blanc and 2 ha of cabernet sauvignon in 1996, followed by more recent and smaller plantings of merlot, viognier, shiraz and semillon. The name and label design were inspired by the link between Thomas Livingstone Mitchell, Surveyor-General of NSW, who served in the British Army during the Peninsular Wars against Napoleon alongside Willem, Prince of Orange, who was aide-de-camp to the Duke of Wellington. It was Mitchell who named the town Orange in honour of his friend, who had by then been crowned King Willem II of The Netherlands.

TTTTY Sauvignon Blanc 2005 Pale, bright straw-green; a spotlessly clean bouquet; delicate, well-balanced citrus and passionfruit palate. Screwcap. 12.5° alc. **RATING** 91 **DRINK** 2009 $19.99

TTTT Cabernet Sauvignon 2004 Very savoury, spicy, bordering green, aromas; light- to medium-bodied, with some bright cassis fruit and lingering tannins; just on the cusp of ripeness. Cork. 13.5° alc. **RATING** 87 **DRINK** 2010 $24.99

TTTY Cabernet Rose 2005 Vivid, light purple-red; full-on cellar door sweetness over the top. Cork. 14.5° alc. **RATING** 86 **DRINK** Now $20.99

Principia ★★★★

139 Main Creek Road, Red Hill, Vic 3937 (postal) **REGION** Mornington Peninsula
T (03) 5931 0010 **WWW**.principiawines.com.au **OPEN** Not
WINEMAKER Rebecca Gaffy **EST.** 1995 **CASES** 400

Darren and Rebecca Gaffy spent their honeymoon in SA, and awakened their love of wines. In due course they gravitated to Burgundy, and began the search in Australia for a suitable cool-climate site to grow pinot noir and chardonnay. In 1995 they began to develop their vineyard, with 2.6 ha of pinot noir, and 0.8 ha of chardonnay. Darren continues to work full-time as a toolmaker (and in the vineyard on weekends and holidays); while Rebecca's career as a nurse took second place to the Bachelor of Applied Science (Wine Science) course at Charles Sturt University, graduating in 2002. Along the way she worked at Red Hill Estate, Bass Phillip, Virgin Hills and Tuck's Ridge, and as winemaker at Massoni Homes. They have built a rammed-earth house, where they live with their children. A cellar door is planned.

TTTTY **Pinot Noir 2004** Colour still good; light- to medium-bodied, complexity due in part to a long time in barrel; fragrant plum and spice fruit, with considerable length. Cork. 13° alc.
RATING 91 **DRINK** 2010 $ 32

Printhie Wines ★★★★

Yuranigh Road, Molong, NSW 2866 **REGION** Orange
T (02) 6366 8422 **F** (02) 6366 9328 **WWW**.printhiewines.com.au **OPEN** Mon–Sat 10–4
WINEMAKER Robert Black **EST.** 1996 **CASES** 12 000

Jim and Ruth Swift have planted 32 ha of viognier, cabernet sauvignon, merlot and shiraz, and built the largest winery in the region. As well as making the Printhie wines, full-time winemaker Robert Black oversees contract winemaking for others. Adding further weight, Printhie supplements the estate-grown grapes with grapes purchased from growers in the region. The wines are modestly priced, and will gain weight as the vines age.

TTTTY **Orange Chardonnay 2005** Very elegant and beautifully balanced; light- to medium-bodied; nectarine and grapefruit with ultra-fine oak/lees/malolactic inputs. Great value. Screwcap. 13.8° alc. **RATING** 92 **DRINK** 2010 $ 15

TTTT **Orange Merlot 2005** Good hue; elegant, light- to medium-bodied; predominant cassis/raspberry fruit flavours, with minimal oak and tannins. Screwcap. **RATING** 89 **DRINK** 2011 $ 15

Provenance Wines ★★★☆

870 Steiglitz Road, Sutherlands Creek, Vic 3331 **REGION** Geelong
T (03) 5281 2230 **F** (03) 5281 2205 **WWW**.provenancewines.com.au **OPEN** By appt
WINEMAKER Scott Ireland, Kirilly Gordon **EST.** 1995 **CASES** 3000

A joint venture between Pam and Richard Austin of Austin's Barrabool wines and Scott Ireland has resulted in a new winery being built on land owned by the Austins at Sutherlands Creek, and leased to winemaker Scott Ireland. Here he makes the Provenance wines, Austin's wines and provides contract winemaking services for small companies in the region.

TTTT **Geelong Pinot Gris 2005** Clean bouquet; pear, apple and musk flavours; has good length and balance. Screwcap. **RATING** 88 **DRINK** Now $ 27
Geelong Chardonnay 2004 Big, ripe, lush style with pungent stone fruit and a hint of sweetness, possibly from the alcohol. **RATING** 87 **DRINK** 2008 $ 27

TTTY **Geelong Shiraz 2003** **RATING** 86 **DRINK** 2008 $ 29
Kismet Late Pick Pinot Gris 2005 **RATING** 85 **DRINK** Now $ 16

Providence Vineyards ★★★☆

236 Lalla Road, Lalla, Tas 7267 **REGION** Northern Tasmania
T (03) 6395 1290 **F** (03) 6395 2088 **WWW**.providence-vineyards.com.au **OPEN** 7 days 10–5
WINEMAKER Hood Wines (Andrew Hood) **EST.** 1956 **CASES** 800

Providence incorporates the pioneer vineyard of Frenchman Jean Miguet, now owned by the Bryce family, which purchased it in 1980. The original 1.3-ha vineyard has been expanded to a little over 3 ha, and unsuitable grenache and cabernet (left from the original plantings) have been grafted over to chardonnay, pinot noir and semillon. Miguet called the vineyard 'La Provence', reminding him of the part of France he came from, but after 40 years the French authorities forced a name change. The cellar door offers 70 different Tasmanian wines.

ŸŸŸŸ **Miguet Reserve Chardonnay 2004** Ripe citrus and stone fruit flavours, almost into tropical. A fractionally disappointing vintage for a normally distinguished wine. Screwcap. 13.3° alc. **RATING** 89 **DRINK** 2010 $28

ŸŸŸŸ **Miguet Reserve Pinot Noir 2004 RATING** 86 **DRINK** Now $120
Pinot Noir 2004 RATING 84 **DRINK** Now $26

Puddleduck Vineyard ★★★★☆

992 Richmond Road, Richmond, Tas 7024 **REGION** Southern Tasmania
T (03) 6260 2301 **F** (03) 6260 2301 **WWW**.puddleduckvineyard.com.au **OPEN** 7 days 10–5
WINEMAKER Hood Wines (Andrew Hood) **EST.** 1997 **CASES** 500
Puddleduck Vineyard is owned and run by Darren and Jackie Brown. Darren's career began at Moorilla Estate, mowing lawns (aged 16), eventually ending up as assistant winemaker to Julian Alcorso. With the changing of the guard at Moorilla Darren left to become vineyard manager of both Craigow and 572 Richmond Road in the Coal Valley. Jackie moved to Craigow when its cellar door opened, then worked in the restaurant and cellar door at Coal Valley Vineyard (formerly Treehouse). In the meantime, they had purchased a house with a block of land suitable for viticulture. So far, they have planted 0.6 ha of pinot noir and 0.4 ha of sauvignon blanc; they are sourcing grapes from other vineyards in the region (particularly those managed by Darren) until they have sufficient vineyards of their own.

ŸŸŸŸŸ **Sparkling Bubbleduck 2004** Quite delicious apple, lime and mineral flavours; fine, long and clean finish. **RATING** 94 **DRINK** Now $35

ŸŸŸŸŸ **Chardonnay 2005** A very pretty wine, with nectarine and stone fruit supported by minimal oak; good balance. **RATING** 91 **DRINK** 2008 $26

ŸŸŸŸ **Sauvignon Blanc 2005** A ripe, tropical fruit style, with a rich mix of gooseberry and pineapple. **RATING** 88 **DRINK** Now $22

ŸŸŸŸ **Riesling 2005 RATING** 86 **DRINK** 2008 $24

ŸŸŸ **Pinot Noir 2004 RATING** 83 $28

🐌 Punch ★★★★★

2130 Kinglake Road, St Andrews, Vic 3761 (postal) **REGION** Yarra Valley
T (03) 9710 1155 **F** (03) 9710 1369 **WWW**.punched.com.au **OPEN** Not
WINEMAKER James Lance **EST.** 2004 **CASES** 150
In the wake of Graeme Rathbone taking over the brand (but not the real estate) of Diamond Valley, the Lances' son James and wife Claire leased the vineyard and winery from David and Catherine Lance including the 0.25 ha block of the close-planted pinot noir. The tiny production from this block will be the only release in 2006. In all Punch (as the business will be known) has 2.25 ha of pinot noir (including the close planted), 0.8 ha of chardonnay and 0.4 ha of cabernet sauvignon.

ŸŸŸŸŸ **Close Planted Pinot Noir 2004** Strong red-purple; richly textured and structured spicy plum fruit; controlled oak and extract; simply needs more time to reveal all. Screwcap. **RATING** 94 **DRINK** 2012 $80

Punt Road ★★★★☆

10 St Huberts Road, Coldstream, Vic 3770 **REGION** Yarra Valley
T (03) 9739 0666 **F** (03) 9739 0633 **WWW**.puntroadwines.com.au **OPEN** 7 days 10–5
WINEMAKER Kate Goodman **EST.** 2000 **CASES** 9000
Punt Road was originally known as The Yarra Hill, a name abandoned because of the proliferation of wineries with the word 'Yarra' as part of their name. The winery (opposite St Huberts) produces the

Punt Road wines, as well as undertaking substantial contract winemaking for others. The Punt Road wines are made from the best parcels of fruit grown on 100 ha of vineyards owned by members of the Punt Road syndicate, and represent the tip of the iceberg.

🍷🍷🍷🍷🍷 **MVN Yarra Valley Chardonnay 2004** Lots of winemaker thumbprints on a complex, relatively rich, wine; notes of melon, fig, cream and nuts all there; long, balanced finish. Cork. 13.5° alc. **RATING** 94 **DRINK** 2012 $35

🍷🍷🍷🍷♀ **Yarra Valley Shiraz 2003** Very good colour; elegant, supple light- to medium-bodied plum, blackberry and spice; smooth tannins, not forced. Cork. 13° alc. **RATING** 92 **DRINK** 2011 $25
MVN Yarra Valley Cabernet Sauvignon 2003 Elegant, medium-bodied; gently ripe blackcurrant and cassis fruit; well-integrated oak, balanced tannins. Cork. 13.5° alc. **RATING** 91 **DRINK** 2013 $48
Botrytis Semillon 2004 Luscious yellow peach, cumquat and crystallised fruit flavours balanced by acidity; length and verve. Riverina. Cork. 13° alc. **RATING** 91 **DRINK** 2008 $30
Yarra Valley Chardonnay 2004 Elegant, light-bodied wine with pure melon and stone fruit; good length, minimal oak. Screwcap. 13° alc. **RATING** 90 **DRINK** 2009 $19.99
Yarra Valley Merlot 2004 Interesting wine, the flavours seemingly sweetened by oak; a mix of red and black fruits; good structure, length and mouthfeel. Screwcap. **RATING** 90 **DRINK** 2012 $25
Yarra Valley Cabernet Sauvignon 2003 Powerful bouquet, faintly earthy; blackcurrant, dark chocolate and earth; good extract. Cork. 13° alc. **RATING** 90 **DRINK** 2013 $24.99

🍷🍷🍷🍷 **Yarra Valley Sauvignon Blanc 2005** Fresh, lively and crisp; green pea, passionfruit and citrus flavours; bright finish. Screwcap. 12.5° alc. **RATING** 89 **DRINK** Now $17.99
Yarra Valley Pinot Noir 2004 Light colour; hue ok; a touch of reduction and stemmy, foresty overtones to the fruit; does have length. Screwcap. 13.5° alc. **RATING** 89 **DRINK** 2009 $25
Yarra Valley Pinot Gris 2005 White paint skilfully applied. Screwcap. 13.5° alc. **RATING** 87 **DRINK** 2008 $20

Punters Corner ★★★★★

Cnr Riddoch Highway/Racecourse Road, Coonawarra, SA 5263 **REGION** Coonawarra
T (08) 8737 Now **F** (08) 8737 3138 **WWW**.punterscorner.com.au **OPEN** 7 days 10–5
WINEMAKER Balnaves (Peter Bissell) **EST.** 1988 **CASES** 10 000
Punters Corner started off life in 1975 as James Haselgrove, but in 1992 was acquired by a group of investors who evidently had few delusions about the uncertainties of viticulture and winemaking, even in a district as distinguished as Coonawarra. The arrival of Peter Bissell as winemaker at Balnaves paid immediate (and continuing) dividends. Sophisticated packaging and label design add to the appeal of the wines. Exports to the UK, the US and Asia.

🍷🍷🍷🍷🍷 **Spartacus Reserve Shiraz 2003** Fragrant spicy berry aromas; elegant, medium-bodied spice, black fruit, tannins and integrated, barrel ferment oak. Sophisticated winemaking. Procork. **RATING** 95 **DRINK** 2018 $59.50
Cabernet Sauvignon 2003 A complex amalgam of nicely ripened blackcurrant, cassis and mocha oak; good tannin structure. Procork. 14° alc. **RATING** 94 **DRINK** 2013 $30

🍷🍷🍷🍷♀ **Single Vineyard Coonawarra Chardonnay 2004** Light straw-green; an elegant and harmonious light- to medium-bodied wine with super-sophisticated winemaking using the full bag of tricks without obliterating the fruit. Screwcap. 13° alc. **RATING** 93 **DRINK** 2010 $26
Triple Crown 2003 Good colour; medium-bodied, clean blackcurrant, blackberry, plum and spice; good structure and oak management. Screwcap. **RATING** 91 **DRINK** 2011 $24

🍷🍷🍷🍷 **Coonawarra Shiraz 2003** Fresh, elegant, light- to medium-bodied; spice, black cherry and blackberry fruit; fine tannins; controlled oak. Screwcap. **RATING** 89 **DRINK** 2008 $20

🐦 Purple Hen Wines

★★★★

96 McFees Road, Rhyll, Vic 3923 **REGION** Gippsland
T (03) 5956 9244 **F** (03) 5956 9244 **WWW**.purplehenwines.com.au **OPEN** Fri–Mon 11–5.30
WINEMAKER Marcus Satchell **EST.** 2002 **CASES** 1000
This is the family owned business of Rick Lacey and wife Maira Vitols. They purchased the property, situated on a small peninsula that is part of Phillip Island, in 2001, and planted the first 2 ha of vines in 2002. Subsequent plantings have increased the area to 4.7 ha, half of the total to pinot noir and chardonnay, the other half to more or less equal amounts of cabernet sauvignon, merlot, shiraz, sauvignon blanc and viognier. Rick Lacey had a horticultural background, and his professional life prior to Purple Hen was as an agricultural economist. In 2006 he was a little over halfway through degrees in wine science and viticulture at Charles Sturt University. They profess to being 'a bit taken aback' by the success they have had in the first 2 wine shows they entered, Gippsland and the Cool Climate Wine Show; it is a fair assumption that they can look forward to further success in the future.

ΥΥΥΥΫ **Gippsland Shiraz 2005** Very good purple-red; spotlessly clean bouquet with gently rich blackberry and plum fruit; soft, slurpy mouthfeel and tannins. **RATING** 92 **DRINK** 2015 $24
Gippsland Pinot Noir 2004 Good colour; light- to medium-bodied with varietal plummy fruit, and nice balance and length. **RATING** 90 **DRINK** 2009 $26

ΥΥΥΥ **Gippsland Chardonnay 2005** Barrel ferment and extended lees contact seem to have underlined the minerally/citrussy/Chablis-like characters of the Purple Hen Chardonnays; considerable length and classic austerity. **RATING** 89 **DRINK** 2011 $24
Gippsland Cabernet Sauvignon 2004 Clear, bright red-purple; fresh, cassis berry fruit; lively finish, minimal tannins. Screwcap. 14° alc. **RATING** 88 **DRINK** 2011 $24
Gippsland Unwooded Chardonnay 2005 Crisp, minerally/river pebble notes to the palate, and a citrussy finish. Well-made. Screwcap. 13.5° alc. **RATING** 87 **DRINK** 2008 $18

ΥΥΥ **Gippsland Rose 2005** **RATING** 83 $16

Purple Patch Wines

NR

101 Main Avenue, Merbein, Vic 3505 **REGION** Murray Darling
T (03) 5025 3558 **F** (03) 5025 2253 **OPEN** By appt
WINEMAKER Brian Davey **EST.** 2001 **CASES** NA
The neatly named Purple Patch Wines has been established by Brian Davey with a 2.5 ha planting of cabernet sauvignon, merlot and shiraz. Brian Davey makes the wines with assistance from a contract winemaker. The small production is principally sold by mail order.

Pycnantha Hill Estate

★★★★

Benbournie Road, Clare, SA 5453 (postal) **REGION** Clare Valley
T (08) 8842 2137 **F** (08) 8842 2137 **WWW**.pycnanthahill.com.au **OPEN** Not
WINEMAKER Jim Howarth **EST.** 1997 **CASES** 1000
The Howarth family progressively established 2.4 ha of vineyard from 1987, and made its first commercial vintage in 1997. Acacia pycnantha is the botanic name for the golden wattle which grows wild over the hills of the Howarth farm, and they say it was 'a natural choice to name our vineyards Pycnantha Hill'. I am not too sure that marketing gurus would agree, but there we go.

ΥΥΥΥΫ **Clare Valley Shiraz 2004** Good colour; medium- to full-bodied blackberry, dark plum and dark chocolate fruit carries the alcohol very well; lots of character. Screwcap. 15° alc. **RATING** 92 **DRINK** 2019 $18
Clare Valley Riesling 2005 Light straw-green; delicate lime, passionfruit, apple and spice fruit aromas and flavours; good acidity and length. Screwcap. 12.5° alc. **RATING** 91 **DRINK** 2012 $16

TTTT **Clare Valley Cabernet Merlot 2004** Light- to medium-bodied; a mix of savoury red- and black-berry fruit with notes of mint and leaf; unexpectedly, sweet fruit comes through on the finish. Screwcap. 13.8° alc. **RATING** 88 **DRINK** 2012 $16

Clare Valley Chardonnay 2004 Perfectly good French oak has been given a hard task; sweet peach and stone fruit, balanced acidity. The end result is better than most Clare Valley chardonnays. Screwcap. 13.5° alc. **RATING** 87 **DRINK** Now $18

Howarth's Clare Valley Sangiovese 2004 Lots of confit/morello cherry fruit; slightly disjointed tannins; work in progress. Screwcap. 13° alc. **RATING** 87 **DRINK** 2010 $16

Pyramid Hill Wines NR

194 Martindale Road, Denman, NSW 2328 **REGION** Upper Hunter Valley
T (02) 6547 2755 **F** (02) 6547 2735 **WWW**.pyramidhillwines.com **OPEN** 7 days 10–5
WINEMAKER Monarch Winemaking Services **EST.** 2002 **CASES** 6000
Pyramid Hill is a partnership between the Adler and Hilder families. Richard Hilder is a veteran viticulturist who oversaw the establishment of many of the Rosemount vineyards. Nicholas Adler and Caroline Sherwood made their mark in the international film industry before moving to Pyramid Hill in 1997 with their 4 young children. There are now 72 ha of chardonnay, semillon, verdelho, shiraz, merlot, cabernet sauvignon and ruby cabernet, with a computer-controlled irrigation system backed up by a network of radio-linked weather and soil moisture sensors which constantly relay data detailing the amount of available moisture at different soil depths to a central computer, thus avoiding excess irrigation and preventing stress. Most of the grapes are sold, but a small amount has been vinified under the Pyramid Hill label, with cautious expansion planned. Exports to the UK.

Pyramids Road Wines NR

Pyramids Road, Wyberba, Qld 4382 **REGION** Granite Belt
T (07) 4684 5151 **F** (07) 4684 5151 **WWW**.pyramidsroad.com.au **OPEN** Wed–Sun, school & public hols 10–4.30
WINEMAKER Warren Smith **EST.** 1999 **CASES** 750
Warren Smith and partner Sue moved to the Granite Belt region in 1999. With encouragement and assistance from the team at Ballandean Estate, the first vines were planted in November 1999, the first vintage following in 2002. Current vineyard area is just 2 ha; further plantings are planned but will not exceed 4 ha. All wines are made onsite and the production area can be viewed from the cellar door.

🐂 Pyren Vineyard ★★★★

22 Errard Street North, Ballarat, Vic 3350 (postal) **REGION** Pyrenees
T (03) 5467 2352 **F** (03) 5021 0804 **WWW**.pyrenvineyard.com **OPEN** Not
WINEMAKER Mount Avoca Winery, Pyrenees Ridge **EST.** 1999 **CASES** 5500
Although it is still early days, this is a substantial venture. Martin and Kevyn Joy have planted 25 ha of shiraz, 3 ha each of cabernet sauvignon and viognier, 1 ha of durif and 2 ha comprising cabernet franc, malbec and petit verdot on the slopes of the Warrenmang Valley near Moonambel. The initial releases in 2005 were of Shiraz, a Cabernet blend followed in 2006, and Durif and Viognier will follow in the future as the vines mature. So far, winemaking duties have been shared between Matthew Barry at Mount Avoca and Graham Jukes at Pyrenees Ridge. Yield is restricted to between 1.5 and 2.5 tonnes per acre.

TTTTY **Block E Pyrenees Shiraz 2004** Dense purple-red; rich blackberry, damson plum, licorice and spice; controlled extract, oak and tannin. Made by Graham Jukes. Cork. 14° alc. **RATING** 92 **DRINK** 2015 $18

TTTT **Broken Quartz Pyrenees Shiraz 2004** Spicy black fruit aromas; a quite complex medium-bodied array of gently sweet fruits supported by fine tannins. Twin top. 14° alc. **RATING** 89 **DRINK** 2009 $17

Pyrenees Ridge Vineyard ★★★★★

532 Caralulup Road, Lamplough via Avoca, Vic 3467 **REGION** Pyrenees
T (03) 5465 3710 **WWW**.pyreneesridge.com.au **OPEN** Thurs–Mon & public hols 10–5
WINEMAKER Graeme Jukes **EST.** 1998 **CASES** 2500
Notwithstanding the quite extensive winemaking experience (and formal training) of Graeme Jukes, this started life as a small-scale, winemaking in the raw version of the French garagiste approach. Graeme and his wife, Sally-Ann, now have another 10 ha of shiraz, cabernet sauvignon and chardonnay; the grape intake is supplemented by purchases from other growers in the region. Contract winemaking for others will also be expanded. Exports to the US, Canada, China and Hong Kong.

ᵀᵀᵀᵀᵀ **Reserve Shiraz 2004** A medium- to full-bodied, attractive wine with blackberry, spice, pepper, mocha, and fine, ripe tannins. Great vintage. Cork. 14.5° alc. **RATING** 94 **DRINK** 2018 $ 45
Shiraz 2004 Similar bright colour; slightly lower alcohol and slightly brighter, sweeter black and red fruits, still with spice; nice tannins. Distinguished show record. Cork. 14.2° alc. **RATING** 94 **DRINK** 2015 $ 25

Queen Adelaide NR

Eddy Road, Karadoc, Vic 3496 **REGION** Southeast Australia
T (03) 5051 3333 **F** (03) 5051 3390 **OPEN** Not
WINEMAKER Various **EST.** 1858 **CASES** NFP
The famous brand established by Woodley Wines and some years ago, subsumed into the Seppelt and now FWE Group. It is a pure brand, without any particular home either in terms of winemaking or fruit sources, but is very successful; Queen Adelaide Chardonnay is and has been for some time one of the largest-selling Chardonnays in Australia, in 2006 holding second place behind Jacob's Creek.

Racecourse Lane Wines ★★★☆

PO Box 215, Balgowlah, NSW 2093 **REGION** Lower Hunter Valley
T 0408 242 490 **F** (02) 9949 7185 **WWW**.racecourselane.com.au **OPEN** Not
WINEMAKER David Fatches (Contract) **EST.** 1998 **CASES** 1000
Mike and Helen McGorman purchased their 15-ha property in 1998. They have established 1.8 ha of shiraz and 1.2 ha sangiovese and 1 ha each of semillon and verdelho and 0.2 ha viognier. Consultancy viticultural advice from Brian Hubbard, and winemaking by David Fatches, a long-term Hunter Valley winemaker (who also makes wine in France each year) has paid dividends. Exports to the UK.

ᵀᵀᵀᵀ **Hunter Valley Verdelho 2005** Unusually rich, ripe and flavoursome, seemingly beyond 13° alcohol; abundant tropical/honeyed fruit. Screwcap. **RATING** 89 **DRINK** 2008 $ 19
Hunter Valley Semillon 2005 Bright colour; full-bodied young Semillon; ripe citrus, soft finish. Quick-developing style. Screwcap. 12.5° alc. **RATING** 88 **DRINK** Now $ 19
Hunter Valley Sangiovese 2005 Attractive, fresh, light-bodied wine with cherry, spice and fine tannins. One jump up from outright rose, and best drunk sooner rather than later. Screwcap. 12.5° alc. **RATING** 88 **DRINK** 2009 $ 19
Hunter Valley Shiraz 2003 While again light- to medium-bodied and with the same alcohol, works a little better than the '04, the fruit a little sweeter, the finish a little smoother. Cork. 12.5° alc. **RATING** 87 **DRINK** 2010 $ 22

ᵀᵀᵀ⸮ **Hunter Valley Shiraz 2004** Light- to medium-bodied; driven and shaped by the relatively low alcohol, opening with pleasant red fruits but thinning out on the finish. Cork. 12.5° alc. **RATING** 86 **DRINK** 2010 $ 22

🐦 Radford Dale ★★★★★

RSD 355, Eden Valley, SA 5235 (postal) **REGION** Eden Valley
T (08) 8565 3256 **F** (08) 8565 3244 **OPEN** Not
WINEMAKER Ben Radford **EST.** 2003 **CASES** 1150
I first met Ben Radford when he was working as a head winemaker at the Longridge/Winecorp Group in Stellenbosch, South Africa. A bevy of international journalists grilled Ben, a French winemaker and a South African about the wines they were producing for the group. The other two refused to admit there were any shortcomings in the wines they had made (and there were), while Ben took the opposite tack, criticising his own wines even though they were clearly the best. He and Gillian Radford are now the proud owners of a 4 ha vineyard in the Eden Valley, with 1.2 ha of riesling planted in 1930, 1.1 ha planted in 1970, and 1.7 ha of shiraz planted in 2000. Ben also acts as a contract winemaker for a number of other Barossa Zone businesses.

🍷🍷🍷🍷🍷 **Eden Valley Riesling 2005** Light straw-green; extremely fine and elegant blossom aromas; a long, intense yet delicate, lime and apple palate; perfect acidity and length. Screwcap. 12° alc. **RATING** 95 **DRINK** 2015 **$** 18
Eden Valley Riesling 2003 Near-identical to the 2005 light straw-green, slow-developing; spice, apple and citrus blossom aromas; a glorious palate starting to develop; intense lime, lemon and apple; very long finish. Screwcap. 12.5° alc. **RATING** 95 **DRINK** 2015 **$** 18
Eden Valley Riesling 2004 Bright straw-green; the tightest and most mineral-structured of the 3 wines; shy lime juice starting to poke its nose through; will take longer to fully emerge. Screwcap. 12° alc. **RATING** 94 **DRINK** 2017 **$** 18
Eden Valley Shiraz 2004 A medium-bodied, complex, seamless fusion of plum and blackberry fruit with quality oak and soft, ripe tannins. Classy minimalist packaging. Cork. 14.5° alc. **RATING** 94 **DRINK** 2015 **$** 30

Rahona Valley Vineyard ★★★★☆

PO Box 256, Red Hill South, Vic 3939 **REGION** Mornington Peninsula
T (03) 5989 2924 **F** (03) 5989 2924 **WWW**.rahonavalley.com.au **OPEN** Not
WINEMAKER John Salmons, Rebecca Gaffy (Consultant) **EST.** 1991 **CASES** 200
John and Leonie Salmons have one of the older and more interesting small vineyards in the Mornington Peninsula, on a steep north-facing slope of a small valley in the Red Hill area. The area takes its name from the ancient red basalt soils. In all there are 1.2 ha of pinot noir planted to 5 different clones and a few hundred vines each of pinot meunier and pinot gris.

🍷🍷🍷🍷🍷 **Reserve Mornington Peninsula Pinot Noir 2004** Similar colour to the varietal; despite fractionally lower alcohol, has distinctly more fruit, with a mix of plum and black cherry; good line and length. Cork. 13.9° alc. **RATING** 92 **DRINK** 2011 **$** 27
Mornington Peninsula Pinot Noir 2004 Light- to medium-bodied; spicy, savoury nuances around a red fruit centre; good length and balance. Cork. 14° alc. **RATING** 90 **DRINK** 2010 **$** 20
Mornington Peninsula Pinot Meunier 2004 Light but bright hue; one of the few meuniers to have real merit as a table wine; strawberry/raspberry fruit; fresh mouthfeel. Cork. 13.6° alc. **RATING** 90 **DRINK** 2009 **$** 20

Raleigh Winery NR

Queen Street, Raleigh, NSW 2454 **REGION** Northern Rivers Zone
T (02) 6655 4388 **F** (02) 6655 4265 **WWW**.raleighwines.com **OPEN** Wed–Sun 10–5, 7 days during school hols
WINEMAKER Lavinia Dingle **EST.** 1982 **CASES** 500
Raleigh Winery lays claim to being Australia's most easterly vineyard. The vineyard was begun in 1982 and purchased by Lavinia and Neil Dingle in 1989. The wine is produced in part from 1 ha of vines planted to no less than 6 varieties.

Ralph Fowler Wines ★★★★

Limestone Coast Road, Mount Benson, SA 5275 **REGION** Mount Benson
T (08) 8768 5000 **F** (08) 8768 5008 **www**.ralphfowlerwines.com.au **OPEN** 7 days 10–5
WINEMAKER Sarah Squires **EST.** 1999 **CASES** 4000
Established in February 1999 by the Fowler family, headed by well-known winemaker Ralph Fowler, with wife Deborah and children Sarah (Squires) and James all involved in the 40-ha property. Ralph Fowler began his winemaking career at Tyrrell's, moving to the position of chief winemaker before moving to Hungerford Hill, then the Hamilton/Leconfield group. In 2005 he passed on the operation of the business to Sarah. Exports to Europe and Asia.

ΨΨΨΨ **Mount Benson Viognier 2005** Rich, ripe apricot, pear and honey floods the mouth without apparent alcohol heat; long finish. Screwcap. 14.5° alc. **RATING** 92 **DRINK** 2008 $ 25

ΨΨΨΨ **Mount Benson Merlot 2004** Fragrant spicy, leafy blackberry aroma and flavour; does have good tannin structure on the finish. Cork. 14° alc. **RATING** 88 **DRINK** 2010 $ 25
Limestone Coast Cabernet Sauvignon 2004 Light- to medium-bodied; savoury minty berry with quite good balance and length; minimal oak. Cork. 13.5° alc. **RATING** 88 **DRINK** 2009 $ 25

ΨΨΨΨ **Mount Benson Shiraz 2003** **RATING** 86 **DRINK** 2008 $ 25

Ramsay's Vin Rose ★★★

30 St Helier Road, The Gurdies, Vic 3984 **REGION** Gippsland
T (03) 5997 6531 **F** (03) 5997 6158 **OPEN** 7 days 1–5
WINEMAKER Dianne Ramsay **EST.** 1995 **CASES** 400
The slightly curious name (which looks decidedly strange in conjunction with Riesling and Cabernet Sauvignon) stems from the original intention of Alan and Dianne Ramsay to grow roses on a commercial scale on their property. Frank Cutler, at Western Port Winery, persuaded them to plant wine grapes instead; they established the first 2 ha of riesling and cabernet sauvignon in 1995. They opened their micro-winery in 1999, and have 4 self-contained units set around their 800-bush rose garden.

ΨΨΨΨ **Cabernet Sauvignon Cabernet Franc Merlot 2003** Quite complex; medium-bodied, with soft, ripe tannins, and a welcoming mouthfeel. **RATING** 88 **DRINK** 2009 $ 18

ΨΨΨΨ **Merlot 2004** **RATING** 86 **DRINK** 2009 $ 18

ΨΨΨ **Riesling 2004** **RATING** 83 $ 15

Random Valley Organic Wines NR

PO Box 11, Karridale, WA 6288 **REGION** Margaret River
T (08) 9758 6707 **F** (08) 9758 6707 **www**.randomvalley.com **OPEN** Not
WINEMAKER Saxon Mountford **EST.** 1995 **CASES** 3000
The Little family has established 7 ha of sauvignon blanc, semillon, shiraz and cabernet sauvignon, with a no-holds-barred organic grapegrowing program. No chemical-based fertilisers, pesticides or herbicides are used in the vineyard, building humus and biological activity in the soil. Given that the 7 ha produce 50 tonnes per year, it is evident that the approach has worked well.

Rangemore Estate NR

366 Malling-Boundary Road, Maclagan, Qld 4352 **REGION** Darling Downs
T (07) 4692 1338 **F** (07) 4692 1338 **OPEN** Fri–Sun 10–5
WINEMAKER Ravens Croft Wines **EST.** 1999 **CASES** 600
The 4.5-ha vineyard of Rangemore Estate, planted to verdelho, shiraz, cabernet and merlot, is high in the southern foothills of the Bunya Mountains. The soil is a sandy loam over sandstone, and the low-yielding vines are grown with little or no irrigation. The founding Allen family operate a cellar door and café, with B&B accommodation, offering spectacular views of the Bunya Mountains.

Ravens Croft Wines

★★★★

274 Spring Creek Road, Stanthorpe, Qld 4380 **REGION** Granite Belt
T (07) 4683 3252 **OPEN** Fri–Sun & public hols 10.30–sunset, or by appt
WINEMAKER Mark Ravenscroft **EST.** 2002 **CASES** 500

Mark Ravenscroft was born in South Africa, and studied oenology there. He moved to Australia in the early 1990s, and in 1994 became an Australian citizen. In addition to his winemaking for Robert Channon, he makes wines for 10 other clients with separate labels. Finally, he makes 500 cases of wine under the Ravenscroft label, with limited quantities of grapes purchased from other growers in the Granite Belt to supplement the estate-grown fruit.

ΨΨΨΨΨ **Reserve Cabernet Sauvignon 2002** Excellent colour; a stylish wine, with pristine cabernet blackcurrant fruit, good touches of cedar and earth, and appropriately firm tannins. Cork. **RATING** 94 **DRINK** 2017 **$** 49

ΨΨΨΨ **Cabernet Sauvignon 2004** Good colour; blackcurrant/cassis fruit and tannins still coming together as at February '06, however, they are in balance, even though as yet in compartments. Diam. **RATING** 89 **DRINK** 2014 **$** 26
Petit Verdot 2004 Bright red-purple; fresh, sweet black fruits are off-set by firm but not aggressive tannins. Just a little simple. Incorrectly labelled as Petite Verdot. Screwcap. 14° alc. **RATING** 88 **DRINK** 2010 **$** 24

Ravensworth

★★★★☆

Rosehill Vineyard, PO Box 116, Mawson, ACT 2607 **REGION** Canberra District
T 1300 302 292 **F** (02) 6262 2161 **WWW**.ravensworthwines.com.au **OPEN** Not
WINEMAKER Bryan Martin **EST.** 2000 **CASES** 1400

Winemaker, vineyard manager and partner Bryan Martin (with dual wine science and wine growing degrees from Charles Sturt University) has a background of wine retail, food and beverage in the hospitality industry, and teaches part-time in that field. He is also assistant winemaker to Tim Kirk at Clonakilla, after seven years at Jeir Creek. Judging at wine shows is another arrow to his bow. Ravensworth has 7 ha of vineyards spread over 2 sites; Rosehill planted in 1998 to cabernet sauvignon, merlot and sauvignon blanc, and Martin Block (planted 2000/2001) to shiraz, viognier, marsanne and sangiovese.

ΨΨΨΨΨ **Canberra District Shiraz 2004** Intense, rich plum and blackberry fruit; lovely texture and structure; fine, ripe tannins. Screwcap. 14° alc. **RATING** 94 **DRINK** 2012 **$** 22.50

ΨΨΨΨ **Canberra District Riesling 2005** Considerable spritz needs to settle down; elegant lime and passionfruit flavour; crisp finish. Screwcap. 12° alc. **RATING** 90 **DRINK** 2012 **$** 16.25
The Tinderry Red 2004 Fresh red fruit aromas; a similar entry to the mouth, then twists of herb and tobacco; light- to medium-bodied blend of Cabernet Franc and Merlot. Screwcap. 14° alc. **RATING** 90 **DRINK** 2008 **$** 22.50

ΨΨΨΨ **Canberra District Sangiovese 2005** Medium-bodied, sweet, spicy cherry and mocha; fine tannins, good length; works well. Screwcap. 14° alc. **RATING** 89 **DRINK** 2010 **$** 19
Canberra District Sangiovese 2004 A mix of sour cherry, spice, lemon and herb; typical light- to medium-bodied; very fine tannins. Screwcap. **RATING** 88 **DRINK** Now **$** 16.25
Canberra District Marsanne 2005 Light- to medium yellow-green; quite complex and developed (some oak?); faintly honeyed, the chalky acidity of the variety coming through on the finish. Screwcap. 13.5° alc. **RATING** 87 **DRINK** 2008 **$** 19
Canberra District Marsanne 2004 Unusual lemon rind and lantana mix; light- to medium-bodied, good acidity; where will it go? Screwcap. **RATING** 87 **DRINK** 2008 **$** 16.25

Ray-Monde

NR

250 Dalrymple Road, Sunbury, Vic 3429 **REGION** Sunbury
T (03) 5428 2657 **F** (03) 5428 3390 **OPEN** Sundays, or by appt
WINEMAKER John Lakey **EST.** 1988 **CASES** 700

The Lakey family has established 5 ha of pinot noir on their 230-ha grazing property at an altitude of 400m. Initially the grapes were sold to Domaine Chandon, but in 1994 son John Lakey (who had gained experience at Tarrawarra, Rochford, Virgin Hills and Coonawarra, plus a vintage in Burgundy) began making the wine — and very competently.

Raydon Estate ★★★★

Lake Plains Road, Langhorne Creek, SA 5255 **REGION** Langhorne Creek
T (08) 8537 3158 **F** (08) 8537 3158 **OPEN** At Bremer Place, Langhorne Creek
WINEMAKER Wayne Dutschke (Contract) **EST.** 1999 **CASES** 1200
The establishment date of any winery business can have a wide number of meanings. In this instance it is the date of the first vintage, but Colleen and Joe Borrett planted 8 ha each of shiraz and cabernet sauvignon many years ago, selling the majority of the grapes to Bleasdale and Southcorp. A small parcel of shiraz not under contract gave them the opportunity to move into the winemaking business, now extended with a little cabernet sauvignon. Exports to the UK and the US.

ᵀᵀᵀᵀᵀ **Tails South Cabernet Sauvignon 2002** Good colour depth and hue; powerful and long; abundant blackcurrant and blackberry fruit; lingering, ripe tannins; shows the mark of a top vintage. A much-awarded wine. Cork. 14.6° alc. **RATING** 94 **DRINK** 2012 $ 20

ᵀᵀᵀᵀ **Tails South Shiraz 2003** Firm, medium- to full-bodied; earthy blackberry fruit, and acidity verging on lemony; at odds with the alcohol. Cork. 15° alc. **RATING** 88 **DRINK** 2013 $ 20

🐝 RBJ ★★★★

PO Box 34, Tanunda, SA 5352 **REGION** Barossa Valley
T (08) 8563 0080 **F** (08) 8563 0080 **WWW.**rbjwines.com **OPEN** Not
WINEMAKER Chris Ringland **EST.** 1991 **CASES** 1000
The name comes from the 3 owners of this venture: Ringland, Bruce and Johnstone. They have 1 ha each of old, dry-grown grenache and mourvedre, and have quietly gone about their work over the past 15 years, secure in the knowledge that there would always be demand than supply. Their stated aim 'is to work with this great fruit and make wines that are driven by the vineyard with little influence of oak'. Needless to say, the winemaker is Chris Ringland. Microscopic quantities are released in Sydney through Ultimo Wines, Melbourne through Rathdowne Cellars, Perth through Chateau Gilford and Adelaide East End, Edinburgh and Melbourne Street Cellars.

ᵀᵀᵀᵀᵀ **Theologicum Mataro 2002** Developed colour; good structure; juicy, berry black fruit flavours and tannins in balance. Screwcap. **RATING** 90 **DRINK** 2010 $ 30

Reads NR

Evans Lane, Oxley, Vic 3678 **REGION** King Valley
T (03) 5727 3386 **F** (03) 5727 3386 **OPEN** Mon–Sat 9–5, Sun 10–6
WINEMAKER Kenneth Read **EST.** 1972 **CASES** 1900
Limited tastings have not impressed, but there may be a jewel lurking somewhere, such as the medal-winning though long-gone 1990 Sauvignon Blanc.

🐝 Red Centre Wines NR

Stuart Highway, Ti Tree, NT 0872 **REGION** Northern Territory
T (08) 8956 9828 **F** (08) 8956 9837 **WWW.**redcentrefarm.com **OPEN** 7 days 9–7, tasting by appt
WINEMAKER Geoff Patritti **EST.** 1988 **CASES** 1000
Chateau Hornsby may be no more (previously the only winery in the State), but John and Shirley Crayford have filled the void by establishing Red Centre Wines on the Stuart Highway, 180 km north of Alice Springs. They have established a small planting of shiraz, ruby cabernet, riesling and chardonnay, but specialise in mango wines. The conventional wines are made for them by Geoff Patritti in McLaren Vale.

Red Clay Estate NR

269 Henry Lawson Drive, Mudgee, NSW 2850 **REGION** Mudgee
T (02) 6372 4569 **F** (02) 6372 4596 **OPEN** Jan–Sept 7 days 10–5, Oct–Dec Mon–Fri 10–5, or by appt
WINEMAKER Ken Heslop **EST.** 1997 **CASES** NA
Ken Heslop and Annette Bailey are among the more recent arrivals in Mudgee, with a 2.5-ha vineyard planted to a diverse range of varieties.

Red Earth Estate Vineyard ★★★

18L Camp Road, Dubbo, NSW 2830 **REGION** Western Plains Zone
T (02) 6885 6676 **F** (02) 6882 8297 **WWW**.redearthestate.com.au **OPEN** Thurs–Tues 10–5
WINEMAKER Ken Borchardt **EST.** 2000 **CASES** 2500
Ken and Christine Borchardt look set to be the focal point of winegrowing and making in the future
Macquarie Valley region of the Western Plains Zone. They have planted 1.3 ha each of riesling,
verdelho, frontignac, grenache, shiraz and cabernet sauvignon at the winery, and gamay, tempranillo,
barbera and carmenere at the Macquarie Grove Vineyard at Narromine. The winery has a capacity of
14 000 cases, and the Borchardts are offering contract winemaking facilities in addition to their own
brand.

ŸŸŸŸ **Toccolato 2004** Sweet cellar door style; made using a method similar to Amarone; has
surprisingly good structure, and works well, if this is what you are after. Screwcap.
14.4° alc. **RATING** 87 **DRINK** Now $ 90

ŸŸŸŸ **Shiraz 2005 RATING** 84 **DRINK** Now $ 18.50

Red Edge ★★★★★

Golden Gully Road, Heathcote, Vic 3523 **REGION** Heathcote
T (03) 9337 5695 **F** (03) 9337 7550 **OPEN** By appt
WINEMAKER Peter Dredge, Judy Dredge **EST.** 1971 **CASES** 1000
Red Edge is a relatively new name on the scene, but the vineyard dates back to 1971, and the
renaissance of the Victorian wine industry. In the early 1980s it produced the wonderful wines of
Flynn & Williams and has now been rehabilitated by Peter and Judy Dredge, producing two quite
lovely wines in their inaugural vintage and have continued that form in succeeding vintages. They
now have a little over 15 ha under vine, and Red Edge has become a full-time occupation for Peter
Dredge. Exports to the UK and the US.

ŸŸŸŸŸ **Heathcote Shiraz 2004** A beautifully weighted wine; spice, black cherry, blackberry,
licorice and a dash of chocolate for good measure; ripe tannins and oak. A strange closure
decision. Cork. 14.8° alc. **RATING** 96 **DRINK** 2020 $ 45
Degree Heathcote Shiraz 2004 Spotlessly clean bouquet; an elegant, medium-bodied
wine; spicy black fruits with flavour complexity which is hard to pin down until you find
there is 12% mourvedre and 3% riesling in this most interesting blend. Screwcap.
14.5° alc. **RATING** 94 **DRINK** 2019 $ 25
Heathcote Cabernet Sauvignon 2004 Strong colour; a particularly good example of
high-quality cabernet, bursting with cassis/berry fruit; ripe tannins and positive oak; once
again, challenges conventional thinking with 25% whole-bunch inclusion. Cork. 14.8° alc.
RATING 94 **DRINK** 2020 $ 45

Red Hill Estate ★★★★★

53 Shoreham Road, Red Hill South, Vic 3937 **REGION** Mornington Peninsula
T (03) 5989 2838 **F** (03) 5931 0143 **WWW**.redhillestate.com.au **OPEN** 7 days 11–5
WINEMAKER Michael Kyberd, Luke Curry **EST.** 1989 **CASES** 30 000
Red Hill Estate was established by Sir Peter Derham and family, and has 3 vineyard sites: Range
Road, with a little over 31 ha, Red Hill Estate (the home vineyard) with 10 ha, and The Briars with 2
ha. Taken together, the vineyards make Red Hill Estate one of the larger producers of Mornington
Peninsula wines. The tasting room and ever-busy restaurant have a superb view across the vineyard
to Westernport Bay and Phillip Island. Production continues to surge, and the winery goes from
strength to strength. Exports to the US, Canada, the UK and Sweden.

ŸŸŸŸŸ **Mornington Peninsula Chardonnay 2004** Intense and very stylish; grapefruit and
nectarine are seamlessly interwoven with barrel ferment French oak and malolactic
ferment influences; has finesse and length. Screwcap. 14° alc. **RATING** 96 **DRINK** 2012 $ 22
Mornington Peninsula Pinot Noir 2003 An effortlessly powerful and very attractive
wine; plum and black cherry with seamless oak and tannins through to a long finish. Cork.
12.5° alc. **RATING** 94 **DRINK** 2010 $ 22

♟♟♟♟♡ Bimaris Sauvignon Blanc 2005 Spotlessly clean; lots of aromatic and flavoursome tropical/gooseberry fruit; mouthfilling, but not heavy. Screwcap. 13° alc. **RATING** 91 **DRINK** Now $ 14
Mornington Peninsula Cabernet Sauvignon 2004 Medium-bodied; savoury, spicy edges to black fruits; has good balance and length; controlled oak. A role reversal with the Pinot. Cork. **RATING** 90 **DRINK** 2015 $ 30

♟♟♟♟ Mornington Peninsula Pinot Grigio 2005 Bright, crisp and clean; apple, melon and pear fruit in diminuendo, as is normal for the variety. Screwcap. 13.5° alc. **RATING** 88 **DRINK** Now $ 22
Mornington Peninsula Pinot Noir 2004 Firm, savoury, almost minerally style; seemingly lower alcohol than is in fact the case; cherry, plum and mint fruit with brisk acidity. Screwcap. 13.7° alc. **RATING** 88 **DRINK** 2011 $ 22
Mornington Peninsula Shiraz 2004 Light red-purple; light, fresh, spicy red and black fruits; needs more flesh on the bones. Screwcap. **RATING** 88 **DRINK** 2009 $ 22
Bimaris Chardonnay 2004 Light- to medium-bodied; clean melon, fig and peach fruit; unforced style. Screwcap. 13.5° alc. **RATING** 87 **DRINK** 2008 $ 14

🐝 Red Nectar Wines

Stonewell Road, Marananga, SA **REGION** Barossa Valley
T 0409 547 478 **F** (08) 8563 3624 **WWW**.rednectar.com.au **OPEN** Not
WINEMAKER Troy Kalleske **EST.** 1997 **CASES** 700
Tammy Pfeiffer may be a sixth generation grape grower, but she was only 19 when she purchased the 27-ha property now known as Red Nectar Estate in 1997. At that time there were 2.4 ha plantings of shiraz, the remainder grazing land with a beautiful view towards the Seppeltsfield palm avenue. The existing shiraz had been sourced from 80-year-old vines grown in the Moppa district, and Tammy has since established another 5.3 ha of shiraz and 2 ha of cabernet sauvignon. She carries out much of the work on the vineyards herself, using sustainable vineyard practices wherever possible. The Stonewell area, in which the vineyard is situated, is well-known for its high-quality shiraz fruit. The winemaking is done by her good friend and cousin Troy Kalleske.

♟♟♟♟♟ Barossa Valley Shiraz 2004 Delicious wine; lovely balance and mouthfeel; blackberry, dark plum and some spicy notes; fine, soft tannins; oak integrated and balanced. Most happily, 14° alcohol. Cork. **RATING** 94 **DRINK** 2013 $ 25

♟♟♟♟♡ Barossa Valley Cabernet Sauvignon 2004 Savoury, earthy, cedary, briary tones to blackcurrant fruit; a bright, clean finish bringing fruit back to the fore. Cork. **RATING** 90 **DRINK** 2012 $ 25

Red Rock Winery

NR

Red Rock Reserve Road, Alvie, Vic 3249 **REGION** Western Victoria Zone
T (03) 5234 8382 **F** (03) 5234 8382 **WWW**.redrockwinery.com.au **OPEN** 7 days 10–5
WINEMAKER Rohan Little **EST.** 1981 **CASES** 5000
Red Rock Winery has progressively established 10 ha of sauvignon blanc, semillon, pinot noir and shiraz, and is a part-time occupation for Rohan Little. It takes its name from the now dormant Red Rock Volcano which created the lakes and craters of the Western District when it last erupted, 8000 years ago.

Red Tail Wines

NR

15 Pinnacle Place, Marlee, NSW 2429 **REGION** Northern Rivers Zone
T (02) 6550 5084 **F** (02) 6550 5084 **OPEN** 7 days 11–4
WINEMAKER Cecchini Winemaking **EST.** 1992 **CASES** 800
Warren and Sue Stiff have planted 0.5 ha each of colombard, semillon and verdelho, and 0.25 ha of merlot, at their property northwest of Taree. The vineyard takes its name from the red-tailed black cockatoo which inhabits the area. The wines are reasonably priced.

Redbank Victoria ★★★☆

Whitfield Road, King Valley, Vic 3678 **REGION** King Valley
T (03) 5729 3604 **F** (08) 8561 3411 **WWW**.redbankwines.com **OPEN** Fri–Mon 11–11
WINEMAKER Natalie Fryar **EST.** 2005 **CASES** 75 000
The Redbank brand was for decades the umbrella for Neill and Sally Robb's Sally's Paddock. In 2005 long-term distributor of Redbank, the Yalumba Wine Group, acquired the Redbank brand from the Robbs, leaving them with the winery and Sally's Paddock. Redbank Victoria now draws almost all its grapes from the King Valley, purchasing viognier from the Taylor's vineyard, and pinot gris from the Cavedon Vineyard. In October 2005 Redbank opened a cellar door in conjunction with the Sartori family.

ŸŸŸŸŸ **The Fugitive Cabernet Sauvignon 2002** Spotlessly clean; medium-bodied; clear blackcurrant and earth fruit in strongly varietal mode; good structure and length; minimal oak. Impressive. Cork. **RATING** 90 **DRINK** 2012 $ 21

ŸŸŸŸ **Fighting Flat King Valley Shiraz 2002** Good colour; light- to medium-bodied but quite firm; a mix of blackberry and spice, with fine-grained tannins. Cork. **RATING** 88 **DRINK** 2009 $ 21

ŸŸŸ **Viognier 2005 RATING** 83

Redbox Vineyard & Winery ★★★☆

2 Ness Lane, Kangaroo Ground, Vic 3097 **REGION** Yarra Valley
T (03) 9712 0440 **F** (03) 9712 0422 **WWW**.redboxvineyard.com.au **OPEN** W'ends & public hols 11–6, or by appt
WINEMAKER Phil Kelly (Contract) **EST.** 2004 **CASES** 5000
Colin and Clayton Spencer have moved quickly since establishing their business, with a kaleidoscopic array of wines, partly from the Yarra Valley, and partly from the Perricoota region north of the River Murray. The wines are released under the Redbox, Wildfell Estate and Murray Flyer labels, with all of the red wines (other than Pinot Noir) coming from Perricoota. Their estate plantings in the Yarra comprise 2 ha of cabernet sauvignon, 0.8 ha of chardonnay and 0.4 ha of riesling; they also purchase pinot gris from the Yarra Valley region. It is strange to see a Perricoota Shiraz at a significantly higher price than a Yarra Valley Cabernet.

ŸŸŸŸŸ **Perricoota Shiraz 2004** Plenty of lush blackberry, dark plum, spice and dark chocolate fruit; good tannins and oak. Screwcap. 14.3° alc. **RATING** 90 **DRINK** 2014 $ 24

ŸŸŸŸ **Yarra Valley Riesling 2005** Delicate, flowery aromas; driven by distinct residual sugar, balanced in turn by acidity; outside the square, vaguely Germanic. Screwcap. 12.5° alc. **RATING** 89 **DRINK** 2010 $ 18
Yarra Valley Cabernet Sauvignon 2004 Savoury elements of leaf and mint to the light- to medium-bodied palate; some cassis notes, light tannins. Screwcap. 12.3° alc. **RATING** 87 **DRINK** 2010 $ 18

ŸŸŸ **Perrictoota Barbera 2005 RATING** 84 **DRINK** Now $ 18

Redesdale Estate Wines ★★★★☆

North Redesdale Road, Redesdale, Vic 3444 **REGION** Heathcote
T (03) 5425 3236 **F** (03) 5425 3122 **WWW**.redesdale.com **OPEN** By appt
WINEMAKER Tobias Ansted (Contract) **EST.** 1982 **CASES** 900
Planting of the Redesdale Estate vines began in 1982 on the northeast slopes of a 25-ha grazing property, fronting the Campaspe River on one side. The rocky quartz and granite soil meant the vines had to struggle for existence, and when Peter Williams and wife Suzanne Arnall-Williams purchased the property in 1988 the vineyard was in a state of disrepair. They have rejuvenated the vineyard, planted an olive grove, and, more recently, erected a 2-storey cottage surrounded by a garden which is part of the Victorian Open Garden scheme (and cross-linked to a villa in Tuscany).

🍷🍷🍷🍷🍷 **Heathcote Shiraz 2004** Strong purple-red; medium-bodied, clean and fresh, somewhat lighter than the alcohol would suggest; black fruits and fine tannins. Screwcap. 15° alc. **RATING** 92 **DRINK** 2013 $ 40

Heathcote Cabernet Sauvignon Cabernet Franc 2004 Firm, bracing fruit; blackcurrant, cedar and cigar box, lemony acidity allied with powerful tannins, warning to stay away for 3 or 4 years. Screwcap. 14.5° alc. **RATING** 90 **DRINK** 2014 $ 40

🐟 Redfin ★★★★☆

80 Vancouver Street, Albany, WA 6330 (postal) **REGION** Warehouse
T (08) 8554 2894 **F** (08) 8554 2493 **WWW**.redfinwines.com.au **OPEN** Not
WINEMAKER Plantagenet **EST.** 2002 **CASES** 1500
Given the approach of owners Caroline and Jonathan O'Neill to the creation of Redfin, it comes as no surprise to find that Jonathan has been Plantagenet Wines' marketing manager for 7 years, and in fact continues in that role. Wife Caroline (a pharmacist) also brings some expertise into the technical side of the venture. That said, they have neither vineyards nor winery, using contract growers in the Mount Barker region, and Plantagenet to make the wines. They have set themselves the goals which any new winery venture could well adopt, number one in the list being 'only produce what you can sell to make sure the brand doesn't become compromised'. They also believe that a little bit of fun should be part of the formula. Being true to the region, there are only 2 wines in the portfolio: Shiraz and Riesling.

🍷🍷🍷🍷🍷 **Mount Barker Riesling 2005** Classic regional style, clean and intense mineral, lime and lemon; a fresh, vibrant finish, with squeaky acidity and perfect alcohol. Screwcap. 12° alc. **RATING** 93 **DRINK** 2015 $ 17

Mount Barker Riesling 2004 Similar to the '05, and more punch from the slightly higher alcohol; ripe apple, lime and mineral. Screwcap. 13.5° alc. **RATING** 93 **DRINK** 2015 $ 17

Redgate ★★★★★

Boodjidup Road, Margaret River, WA 6285 **REGION** Margaret River
T (08) 9757 6488 **F** (08) 9757 6308 **WWW**.redgatewines.com.au **OPEN** 7 days 10–5
WINEMAKER Andrew Forsell **EST.** 1977 **CASES** 8000
Founder and owner of Redgate, Bill Ullinger, chose the name not simply because of the nearby eponymous beach, but also because — so it is said — a local farmer (with a prominent red gate at his property) had run an illegal spirit still 100 or so years ago, and its patrons would come to the property and ask whether there was any 'red gate' available. True or not, Ullinger was one of the early movers in the Margaret River, and there is now a little over 21 ha of mature estate plantings (the majority to sauvignon blanc, semillon, cabernet sauvignon, cabernet franc, shiraz and chardonnay). Former Flying Winemaker Andrew Forsell joined the team in 1995, and has helped create both consistency and quality in the wines. Exports to all major markets.

🍷🍷🍷🍷🍷 **Margaret River Sauvignon Blanc Semillon 2005** Spotlessly clean; a lively mix of passionfruit, gooseberry and citrus; bright finish. Screwcap. 12.5° alc. **RATING** 94 **DRINK** Now $ 18.50

Chardonnay 2004 Elegant and intense; perfect balance and integration of oak and nectarine/grapefruit; long palate and finish. Screwcap. 12.5° alc. **RATING** 94 **DRINK** 2010 $ 30

🍷🍷🍷🍷🍷 **OFS Semillon 2005** Clean, fragrant and fresh; lots of citrus and gooseberry flavours almost into Sauvignon Blanc; admirable restraint in not seeking to guild the lily. Screwcap. 12° alc. **RATING** 93 **DRINK** 2011 $ 19

🍷🍷🍷🍷 **Shiraz 2003** Fresh, lively black fruits, licorice, spice and mint; restrained oak, good length. Screwcap. 14.5° alc. **RATING** 89 **DRINK** 2013 $ 22

Margaret River Rose 2005 Vivid fuchsia; gentle red berry/raspberry fruit; plenty of flavour, balanced finish. 14° alc. **RATING** 88 **DRINK** Now $ 16

Bin 588 Cabernet Shiraz Cabernet Franc 2003 Bright and fresh in zesty winery style; fruit forward, and not over-much structure. Screwcap. 13.5° alc. **RATING** 87 **DRINK** 2008 $ 19

ΥΥΥΨ **Cabernet Sauvignon 2003** RATING 86 DRINK 2008 $26
Margaret River Chenin Blanc 2005 RATING 85 DRINK Now $16
Cabernet Franc 2003 RATING 84 DRINK Now $36
Ezabello 2004 RATING 84 DRINK Now $19

Redman ★★★☆

Riddoch Highway, Coonawarra, SA 5263 REGION Coonawarra
T (08) 8736 3331 F (08) 8736 3013 WWW.redman.com.au OPEN Mon–Fri 9–5, w'ends 10–4
WINEMAKER Bruce Redman, Malcolm Redman EST. 1966 CASES 17 000
After a prolonged period of mediocrity, the Redman wines are showing sporadic signs of
improvement, partly through the introduction of modest amounts of new oak, even if principally
American. It would be nice to say the wines now reflect the full potential of the fully mature vineyard,
but there is still some way to go.

ΥΥΥΥΨ **Coonawarra Cabernet Sauvignon Merlot 2001** Retains good colour; ripe blackcurrant
fruit; considerable texture and structure courtesy of more tannins than usual. Time in
front of it. Cork. 14.7° alc. RATING 90 DRINK 2014 $33

ΥΥΥΥ **Premium Blend 2002** Medium-bodied; somewhat austere, but is elegant, and has good
line. RATING 87 DRINK 2009 $33

ΥΥΥΨ **Shiraz 2003** RATING 84 DRINK Now $21

Reedy Creek Vineyard NR

Reedy Creek, via Tenterfield, NSW 2372 REGION Northern Slopes Zone
T (02) 6737 5221 F (02) 6737 5200 WWW.reedycreekwines.com.au OPEN 7 days 9–5
WINEMAKER Contract EST. 1971 CASES 2800
Like so many Italian settlers in the Australian countryside, the De Stefani family has been growing
grapes and making wine for its own consumption for over 30 years at its Reedy Creek property in the
far north of NSW. What is more, like their compatriots in the King Valley, the family's principal
activity until 1993 was growing tobacco, but the continued rationalisation of the tobacco industry
prompted the De Stefanis to turn a hobby into a commercial exercise. The vineyard has now been
expanded to 6.1 ha.

Rees Miller Estate ★★★☆

5355 Goulburn Highway, Yea, Vic 3717 REGION Upper Goulburn
T (03) 5797 2101 F (03) 5797 3276 WWW.reesmiller.com OPEN 7 days 10–6
WINEMAKER David Miller EST. 1996 CASES 3000
Partners Sylke Rees and David Miller purchased the 64-ha property in 1998 with 7 ha of vines
already planted to pinot noir, cabernet sauvignon, merlot and shiraz, all of which came into
production in 2002. The entire property, including the vineyard, is undergoing organic and
biodynamic certification and they deliberately irrigate sparingly, the upshot being yields typically
5 tonnes per ha. Some of the wines are named after the original owners of the property, Daniel
Joseph and Wilhemina Therese Sier. Exports to Canada and Germany.

ΥΥΥΥΨ **Thousand Hills Shiraz 2003** Interesting cool-grown spicy aromas and flavours; mocha
oak; fine, long tannins. Cork. RATING 91 DRINK 2010 $25

ΥΥΥΥ **Sier's Field Upper Goulburn Cabernet Sauvignon 2003** Medium- to full-bodied; ripe,
sweet, slightly jammy blackcurrant fruit, with elements of dark chocolate; ripe tannins.
Cork. 14.5° alc. RATING 87 DRINK 2013 $20

ΥΥΥΨ **Wilhelmina Upper Goulburn Pinot Noir 2003** Good colour; essentially a well-balanced,
medium-bodied dry red, lacking definitive pinot noir varietal character. Cork. 15° alc.
RATING 86 DRINK 2009 $16
Cotton's Pinch Merlot 2003 RATING 85 DRINK 2008 $18

Reg Drayton Wines

NR

Cnr Pokolbin Mountain Road/ McDonalds Road, Pokolbin, NSW 2321 **REGION** Lower Hunter Valley
T (02) 4998 7523 **F** (02) 4998 7523 **WWW**.regdraytonwines.com.au **OPEN** 7 days 10–5
WINEMAKER Tish Cecchini, Robyn Drayton **EST.** 1989 **CASES** 5500
Reg and Pam Drayton were among the victims of the Seaview/Lord Howe Island air crash in October 1984, having established Reg Drayton Wines after selling their interest in the long-established Drayton Family Winery. Their daughter Robyn (a fifth-generation Drayton and billed as the Hunter's first female vigneron) and husband Craig continue the business, which draws chiefly upon the Pokolbin Hills Estate but also takes fruit from the historic Lambkin Estate vineyard.

Reilly's Wines

NR

Cnr Hill Street/Burra Street, Mintaro, SA 5415 **REGION** Clare Valley
T (08) 8359 3550 **F** (08) 8359 3133 **WWW**.reillyswines.com **OPEN** 7 days 10–5
WINEMAKER Justin Ardill **EST.** 1994 **CASES** 15 000
Cardiologist Justin and Julie Ardill are no longer newcomers in the Clare Valley, with 10 or so vintages under their belt. An unusual sideline of Reilly's Cottage is the production of extra virgin olive oil, made from wild olives found in the Mintaro district of the Clare Valley. Justin Ardill also does some contract making for others. In 2005 a second cellar door was opened in Adelaide which will also hold wine classes. Exports to the US, Ireland, Malaysia and Singapore.

Remo & Son's Vineyard

NR

58 Blaxland Ridge Road, Kurrajong, NSW 2758 **REGION** South Coast Zone
T (02) 4576 1539 **F** (02) 4576 0072 **OPEN** W'ends by appt
WINEMAKER Remo Crisante **EST.** 1998 **CASES** NA
Remo and Mark Crisante have pushed the viticultural envelope that little bit further by planting 2 ha of chardonnay, verdelho, merlot, cabernet sauvignon and traminer at Kurrajong, for long a holiday destination for Sydneysiders. The fact that Kurrajong is in the South Coast Zone may come as a surprise, since it is 100 km northwest of Sydney, but the Zone boundaries have always been a matter of convenience, and had to be so drawn as to cover all of the State. A restaurant and accommodation are available, pointing to the conference and function market.

Renewan Murray Gold Wines

NR

Murray Valley Highway, Piangil, Vic 3597 **REGION** Swan Hill
T (03) 5030 5525 **F** (03) 5030 5695 **OPEN** 7 days 9–5
WINEMAKER Hanging Rock **EST.** 1989 **CASES** 220
In 1990 former senior executive at Nylex Corporation in Melbourne, Jim Lewis, and artist wife Marg, retired to what is now Renewan Vineyard, set on the banks of the Murray River. It is a small business, based on 2.5 ha of estate plantings.

Reschke Wines

★★★★☆

Level 1, 183 Melbourne Street, North Adelaide, SA 5006 (postal) **REGION** Coonawarra
T (08) 8239 0500 **F** (08) 8239 0522 **WWW**.reschke.com.au **OPEN** Not
WINEMAKER Peter Douglas (Contract) **EST.** 1998 **CASES** 10 000
It's not often that the first release from a new winery is priced at $100 per bottle, but that was precisely what Reschke Wines achieved with its 1998 Cabernet Sauvignon. The family has been a landholder in the Coonawarra region for 100 years, with a large landholding which is partly terra rossa, part woodland. There are 15.5 ha of merlot, 105 ha of cabernet sauvignon, 0.5 ha of cabernet franc and 2.5 ha of shiraz in production, with a further 26 ha planted in 2001, mostly to shiraz, and with a little petit verdot. Exports to the US, Canada and Singapore.

 Bos Cabernet Sauvignon 2003 Perfectly ripened cassis, blackcurrant and blackberry; good structure, ripe tannins and appropriate oak. High-quality cork. 14° alc. **RATING** 94 **DRINK** 2012 $ 35

ΥΥΥΥΥ **Vitulus Cabernet Sauvignon 2003** Good colour; clear-cut blackcurrant and cassis fruit; medium-bodied, with good texture and structure throughout; controlled oak. Cork. **RATING** 91 **DRINK** 2013 $ 25

ΥΥΥΥ **Coonawarra Sauvignon Blanc 2005** Light-bodied; clean, fresh and firm; mineral and herb through to a dry finish; food style. Unadorned simplicity. Screwcap. 12.4° alc. **RATING** 88 **DRINK** Now $ 18

Rex Vineyard   NR

Beaufort, WA 6315 **REGION** Central Western Australia Zone
T (08) 9384 3210 **F** (08) 9384 3210 **OPEN** Not
WINEMAKER Julie White (Contract) **EST.** 1991 **CASES** 500
Peter and Gillian Rex have established 2 ha of chardonnay, cabernet sauvignon, merlot and shiraz. Approximately half of each year's production is sold as grapes, the remainder is contract-made.

Ribarits Estate Wines   NR

Sturt Highway, Trentham Cliffs, NSW 2738 (postal) **REGION** Murray Darling
T 0409 330 997 **F** (03) 5024 0332 **OPEN** Not
WINEMAKER Contract **EST.** 1998 **CASES** 4000
Adrian Ribarits has developed over 82 ha of chardonnay, merlot, shiraz and cabernet sauvignon, primarily as a contract grapegrower for Simeon Wines. A small part of the grape production is vinified for Ribarits Estate and sold by mail order at yesterday's prices.

Richard Hamilton

Main Road, Willunga, SA 5172 **REGION** McLaren Vale
T (08) 8556 2288 **F** (08) 8556 2868 **WWW**.richardhamiltonwines.com **OPEN** Mon–Fri 10-5, w'ends & public hols 11-5
WINEMAKER Paul Gordon **EST.** 1972 **CASES** 20 000
Richard Hamilton has outstanding estate vineyards, some of great age, all fully mature. The arrival (in 2002) of former Rouge Homme winemaker Paul Gordon has allowed the full potential of those vineyards to be expressed. Exports to all major markets.

ΥΥΥΥΥ **Hamilton Lot 148 Merlot 2004** A particularly attractive, medium-bodied wine with good varietal character from a mix of red fruits, olive and spice; tangy finish. Screwcap. 13.5° alc. **RATING** 92 **DRINK** 2014 $ 18.48

ΥΥΥΥ **Hut Block Cabernet Sauvignon 2003** Savoury/earthy/leafy fruit notes, with a touch of mint; not entirely ripe. Cork. 14° alc. **RATING** 87 **DRINK** 2009 $ 18.45

Richfield Estate

Bonshaw Road, Tenterfield, NSW 2372 **REGION** Northern Slopes Zone
T (02) 6737 5488 **F** (02) 6737 5598 **WWW**.richfieldvineyard.com.au **OPEN** 7 days 10-4
WINEMAKER John Cassegrain **EST.** 1997 **CASES** 15 000
Singapore resident Bernard Forey is the Chairman and majority shareholder of Richfield Estate. The 500-ha property, at an altitude of 720m, was selected after an intensive survey by soil specialists. Just under 30 ha of shiraz, cabernet sauvignon, merlot, semillon, chardonnay and verdelho have been planted, the first vintage being made in 2000. Winemaker John Cassegrain is a shareholder in the venture, and it is expected that the bulk of the sales will come from the export markets of South-East Asia and Japan.

ΥΥΥΥΥ **Reserve Tenterfield Shiraz 2002** Elegant, spicy/cedary/savoury characters to both bouquet and palate attesting to a relatively cool climate; long, fine, supple palate. Cork. 14° alc. **RATING** 91 **DRINK** 2012 $ 25
Reserve Tenterfield Merlot 2002 Spicy/cedary/savoury overtones to blackcurrant and cassis berry fruit; medium-bodied, with good balance and length; grows on retasting. Cork. 13° alc. **RATING** 90 **DRINK** 2010 $ 25

▼▼▼▼ **Tenterfield Chardonnay 2004** Full-bodied, rich peach and melon; oak not obvious; good bottle development but drink asap. Twin top. 13.5° alc. **RATING** 88 **DRINK** Now $ 15
Tenterfield Verdelho Semillon 2004 Clever winemaking; fruit salad and citrus; a tangy interplay between acidity and residual sugar on the finish. Cork. 13° alc. **RATING** 87 **DRINK** Now $ 15

Richmond Estate

NR

99 Gadds Lane, North Richmond, NSW 2754 **REGION** Sydney Basin
T (02) 4573 1048 **OPEN** W'ends 11–6
WINEMAKER Tony Radanovic **EST.** 1967 **CASES** 600
Richmond Estate featured in a number of books I wrote between 1979 and 1984, as then-proprietor Barry Bracken (a Sydney orthopaedic surgeon) was making excellent Shiraz and Cabernet Sauvignon. However, he sold the property in 1984, and it went through several owners before being purchased by Monica and Tony Radanovic in 1987. The Radanovics have restored the vineyard, which had been run-down in the years prior to their purchase, and while only 3 ha are under vine, the vineyard is used by the University of Western Sydney as its field laboratory for undergraduate and wine production courses.

Richmond Grove

Para Road, Tanunda, SA 5352 **REGION** Barossa Valley
T (08) 8563 7303 **F** (08) 8563 7330 **WWW**.richmondgrovewines.com **OPEN** 7 days 10.30–4.30 except Good Friday, Christmas and Boxing Day
WINEMAKER Steve Clarkson, John Vickery **EST.** 1983 **CASES** 150 000
Richmond Grove, owned by Orlando Wyndham, draws its grapes from diverse sources. The Richmond Grove Barossa Valley and Watervale Rieslings made by the team directed by consultant winemaker John Vickery represent excellent value for money (for Riesling) year in, year out. If these were the only wines produced by Richmond Grove, it would have 5-star rating. Exports to the UK.

▼▼▼▼▼ **Watervale Riesling 2005** Highly aromatic; a classic Clare Valley mix of lime juice and firm, minerally acidity. Gold medal Sydney Wine Show '06. Screwcap. **RATING** 94 **DRINK** 2014

▼▼▼▼▽ **Limited Release Watervale Riesling 2004** Bright, light colour; fresh and crisp; still a baby on its way to growing up; delicacy and finesse. Should develop as well as the now beautiful '98 and '99 wines under screwcap. **RATING** 93 **DRINK** 2014 $ 16
Footbridge Riesling 2005 Very firm, rather austere style with flecks of mineral and slate running through the palate. Will age well. Screwcap. 12.5° alc. **RATING** 90 **DRINK** 2011 $ 14
Barossa Shiraz 2002 Retaining hue well; light- to medium-bodied; attractive spicy, red and black fruits; good oak, and the fine tannins and elegance of an excellent vintage. Cork. **RATING** 90 **DRINK** 2010

▼▼▼▼ **French Cask Chardonnay 2005** Lively, fresh citrus and melon fruit, suggesting some Limestone Coast components; restrained oak and good finish. Value. Cork. 13° alc. **RATING** 89 **DRINK** 2008 $ 14
Weather Vane Cabernet Merlot 2004 Good colour; medium- to full-bodied in a powerful, earthy/austere mode; does have a strong fruit backbone. Cork. 14.5° alc. **RATING** 89 **DRINK** 2014 $ 14

▼▼▼▽ **Black Cat Shiraz 2004 RATING** 86 **DRINK** 2009 $ 14

Richmond Park Vineyard

Logie Road, Richmond, Tas 7025 (postal) **REGION** Southern Tasmania
T (03) 6265 2949 **F** (03) 6265 3166 **OPEN** Not
WINEMAKER Hood Wines (Andrew Hood) **EST.** 1989 **CASES** 250
A small vineyard owned by Tony Park, which gives the clue to the clever name. It is 20 mins' drive from Hobart; a particular (and uncommon) attraction for mailing list clients is the availability of 375ml bottles.

ŸŸŸŸŸ **Chardonnay 2005** Gentle apple, stone fruit and melon, with a hint of creamy malolactic inputs; good length and acidity. **RATING** 90 **DRINK** 2008

ŸŸŸŸŸ **Chardonnay 2004** **RATING** 86 **DRINK** 2008
Pinot Noir 2004 **RATING** 85 **DRINK** Now

Rickety Gate ★★★★

RMB 825, Scotsdale Road, Denmark, WA 6333 **REGION** Denmark
T (08) 9840 9504 **F** (08) 9840 9502 **www**.ricketygate.com.au **OPEN** Fri–Mon & hols 11–4
WINEMAKER John Wade **EST.** 2000 **CASES** 2600
The 3-ha vineyard of Rickety Gate is situated on north-facing slopes of the Bennet Ranges, in an area specifically identified by Dr John Gladstones as highly suited to cool-climate viticulture. The property was purchased by Russell and Linda Hubbard at the end of 1999, and 1.8 ha of merlot, 0.8 ha of riesling and 0.5 ha of chardonnay and pinot noir were planted in 2000. John Wade contract-makes the wines at the small onsite winery.

ŸŸŸŸŸ **Riesling 2005** The minerally bouquet has subdued fruit, the wine springing into life on the palate, with a wonderful, ripe apple and lime juice mix; seamless line and length; perfect balance. Screwcap. **RATING** 94 **DRINK** 2012 $ 22

ŸŸŸŸ **Shiraz 2004** Bright colour; super cool-grown spicy, leafy aromas and flavours; sweet fruit, then slightly green notes. Screwcap. **RATING** 89 **DRINK** 2010 $ 19
Merlot 2004 Light red-purple; a light-bodied wine in similar style to the Shiraz; very fresh, tangy, almost citrussy, edges to small red berry fruits. Screwcap. **RATING** 89 **DRINK** 2010 $ 24
Late Harvest Riesling 2005 Barely more than off-dry; crisp and lively, needing 5 years to flower. Screwcap. **RATING** 89 **DRINK** 2013 $ 16
Cabernet Merlot 2004 Light-bodied; bright fruits with a nice touch of cassis; harmonious mouthfeel to an attractive lunch/summer red offering great value. Screwcap. **RATING** 88 **DRINK** 2009 $ 15

Riddells Creek Winery ★★★☆

296 Gap Road, Riddells Creek, Vic 3431 **REGION** Macedon Ranges
T (03) 5428 7222 **F** (03) 5428 7221 **www**.riddellscreekwinery.com.au **OPEN** Wed–Sun 11–5, or by appt
WINEMAKER John Ellis, Trefor Morgan, Peter Evans **EST.** 1998 **CASES** 2300
Partners Peter Evans, Sonia Mailer, Craig Wellington and Susan Wellington commenced planting the 18.5-ha vineyard in 1998; the varieties chosen were riesling, chardonnay, cabernet sauvignon, shiraz and merlot. While it is situated at the extreme southern end of the Macedon Ranges, only 8 km from Sunbury, the partners correctly anticipated that achieving full ripeness with the red varieties might be difficult in cooler vintages. However, winemakers John Ellis and Trefor Morgan, with input from Peter Evans, have done an excellent job with the white wines since the inaugural vintage of 2001.

ŸŸŸŸŸ **The Sarah Ivy Chardonnay 2004** Beautifully balanced and styled wine; long, intense nectarine and citrus; excellent line. **RATING** 94 **DRINK** 2010 $ 18

ŸŸŸŸ **James Henry Shiraz 2004** **RATING** 86 **DRINK** 2008 $ 16
The Leigh Craig Cabernet Sauvignon 2004 **RATING** 84 **DRINK** 2010 $ 16

ŸŸŸ **Amee Alyce Riesling 2005** **RATING** 81 $ 19

Ridgeback Wines NR

New Chum Gully Estate, Howards Road, Panton Hill, Vic 3759 **REGION** Yarra Valley
T (03) 9719 7687 **F** (03) 9719 7667 **www**.ridgebackwines.com.au **OPEN** By appt
WINEMAKER MasterWineMakers **EST.** 2000 **CASES** 1200
Ron and Lynne Collings purchased their Panton Hill property in March 1990, clearing the land and making it ready for the first vine planting in 1992; there are now a little over 4 ha on the hillside

slopes beneath their house. Ron Collings completed the degree in winegrowing at Charles Sturt University in 1997, with the Dean's Award for Academic Excellence. Most of the grapes were sold, but Ron Collings made small batches of wine himself each year, which ultimately led to the decision to establish the Ridgeback label, with contract winemaking, although Collings is never far from the scene at vintage. Exports to the UK.

Ridgeline

PO Box 695, Healesville, Vic 3777 **REGION** Yarra Valley
T 0421 422 154 **F** (03) 5962 2670 **OPEN** By appt
WINEMAKER Mark Haisma **EST.** 2001 **CASES** 800
Mark Haisma has established 2 ha of dry-grown pinot noir, shiraz, cabernet sauvignon and merlot on a small hillside vineyard on Briarty Road; his neighbours include such well-known producers as Yarra Yering and Giant Steps, and 2 substantial vineyards, one owned by Coldstream Hills, the other by Malcolm Fell.

ᵀᵀᵀᵀᵀ **Single Vineyard Yarra Valley Pinot Noir 2004** Firm, savoury, spicy early-picked style; black fruits, spice and a touch of forest; good length. Diam. 12.2° alc. **RATING** 90 **DRINK** 2011 $ 28

ᵀᵀᵀᵀ **Single Vineyard Yarra Valley Shiraz 2003** Some colour development; the flavours are at odds with the alcohol, complex, but with some sweet and sour characters, although fruit sweetness does finally prevail. Cork. 14.7° alc. **RATING** 89 **DRINK** 2013 $ 34
Single Vineyard Yarra Valley Cabernet Merlot 2003 Developed colour; complex savoury/briary edges to black fruits; sustained tannins. Cork. 13.8° alc. **RATING** 89 **DRINK** 2012 $ 28
Single Vineyard Yarra Valley Pinot White 2004 Pale salmon; has intensity and length mainly due to the good natural acidity; touches of spice and herb, dry finish. Diam. 12° alc. **RATING** 87 **DRINK** Now $ 38

Ridgemill Estate

218 Donges Road, Severnlea, Qld 4352 **REGION** Granite Belt
T (07) 3368 4911 **F** (07) 3368 3410 **OPEN** Fri–Sun 10–5
WINEMAKER Jim Barnes **EST.** 1998 **CASES** 800
Martin Cooper and Dianne Maddison acquired what was then known as Emerald Hill Winery in 2004. In 2005 they expanded the existing 2 ha of vineyard (planted to chardonnay, tempranillo, shiraz, merlot and cabernet sauvignon) by adding 0.2 ha each of saperavi, lagrein and viognier, firmly setting a course down the alternative variety road. The 2005 Chardonnay is said to be the only Qld wine to win an international gold medal (at the 2005 International Chardonnay Challenge in Gisborne, NZ).

ᵀᵀᵀᵀᵀ **Reserve Chardonnay 2005** Very reserved fruit, minerally and textured. One of only 5 Australian wines to win gold at the 2005 International Chardonnay Challenge in Gisborne, NZ (460 entries). The 'international' style obviously appealed to the judges. Screwcap. 12.9° alc. **RATING** 90 **DRINK** Now $ 28

ᵀᵀᵀᵀ **Merlot 2005** Vivid hue; fresh, vibrant red fruit flavours; a smart move to bottle and release the wine quickly. Screwcap. 14° alc. **RATING** 88 **DRINK** 2008 $ 24
First Press Rose 2005 Attractive tangy, strawberry, lime mix; good balance and acidity. Screwcap. 12.5° alc. **RATING** 87 **DRINK** Now $ 16

ᵀᵀᵀᵀ **The Spaniard Tempranillo 2005** Deep hue; a faintly reduced bouquet, the palate still locked up; may make it. Screwcap. 12.8° alc. **RATING** 86 **DRINK** 2008 $ 16

Rigel Wines

NR

PO Box 18062, Collins Street East, Melbourne, Vic 8004 **REGION** Mornington Peninsula
T 1300 131 081 **F** 1300 131 281 **WWW**.rigelwines.com.au **OPEN** At the General Store, Merricks
WINEMAKER MasterWineMakers **EST.** 1989 **CASES** 5000
Rigel Wine Company is owned by Dr Damian and Sue Ireland, and Michael and Mary Calman; the Irelands own the Mornington Peninsula vineyard at Shoreham, which provides the grapes for the

super-premium Rigel label. The second property is at Tocumwal and has 80 ha of vines with 6 km of Murray River frontage. Most of these grapes are sold to other makers, but part of the production is vinified for both the local and export markets.

Rimfire Vineyards ★★★

Bismarck Street, Maclagan, Qld 4352 **REGION** Darling Downs
T (07) 4692 1129 **F** (07) 4692 1260 **www**.rimfirewinery.com.au **OPEN** 7 days 10–5
WINEMAKER Louise Connellan **EST.** 1991 **CASES** 6000
The Connellan family (Margaret and Tony and children Michelle, Peter and Louise) began planting the 12-ha, 14-variety Rimfire Vineyards in 1991 as a means of diversification of their large (1500-ha) cattle stud in the foothills of the Bunya Mountains, 45 mins' drive northeast of Toowoomba. They produce a kaleidoscopic array of wines, the majority without any regional claim of origin. The wine (and variety) simply called 1893 is said to be made from a vine brought to the property by a German settler in about 1893; the vineyard ceased production in the early 1900s, but a single vine remained, and DNA testing has established that the vine does not correspond to any vine cultivar currently known in Australia. Rimfire propagated cuttings, and a small quantity is made each year.

▼▼▼▼ **Vin Gris Aleatico 2005** Very pale blush; attractive lemon and passionfruit flavours; cunningly balanced residual sugar and acidity. Screwcap. 13.8° alc. **RATING** 87 **DRINK** Now $ 18

▼▼▼▽ **Verdelho 2005** Clean tangy citrussy flavours more to sauvignon blanc than verdelho, which is, perhaps, no bad thing. Well-made. Screwcap. 13.5° alc. **RATING** 86 **DRINK** Now $ 18
1893 2005 RATING 85 **DRINK** Now $ 18
Touriga Nacional 2004 RATING 85 **DRINK** 2009 $ 21

Riseborough Estate NR

Lot 21, Petersen Rise, off Mooliabeenee Road, Gingin, WA 6503 **REGION** Swan District
T (08) 9575 1211 **F** (08) 9575 1211 **OPEN** Wed–Sun 10–4
WINEMAKER Flying Fish Cove, Oakover Wines **EST.** 1998 **CASES** 5000
Don Riseborough and Susan Lamp began developing their 8.7-ha vineyard, a stone's throw from Moondah Brook, in 1998. They have planted shiraz, cabernet sauvignon, merlot, cabernet franc and grenache; the grapes take the slightly unusual trip south to Margaret River where the red wines are made by Flying Fish Cove. A small selection of non-estate white wines (Chenin Blanc, Chardonnay and Verdelho, all with a small amount of residual sweetness) are made by Rob Marshall in the Swan Valley.

Rivendell ★★★★

Lot 328 Wildwood Road, Yallingup, WA 6282 **REGION** Margaret River
T (08) 9755 2090 **F** (08) 9755 2301 **www**.rivendellwines.com.au **OPEN** 7 days 10.30–5
WINEMAKER James Pennington **EST.** 1987 **CASES** 3000
Rivendell was established in 1987 by a local family and became recognised for its gardens, restaurant, jams, preserves and wines. The property has recently been purchased by private investors who intend to upgrade the property. The new owners wish to lift wine quality and have employed James Pennington to oversee the improvements to the winery and its production.

▼▼▼▼▽ **Margaret River Cabernet Merlot 2003** Strong colour; luscious, ripe blackcurrant and cassis fruit; balanced tannins and oak; good finish. Screwcap. **RATING** 92 **DRINK** 2013 $ 20

▼▼▼▼ **Margaret River Semillon Sauvignon Blanc 2005** Clean bouquet; plenty of flavour in a tropical gooseberry spectrum, the structure provided by the semillon. Screwcap. 12.5° alc.
RATING 89 **DRINK** 2008 $ 15
Pennington Margaret River Cabernet Merlot 2002 Light- to medium-bodied; spicy, earthy, bramble nuances to berry fruit; tannins in balance. Cork. 14° alc. **RATING** 88
DRINK 2009 $ 27
Margaret River Chardonnay 2003 Very big, rich, ripe bottle-developed wine, with yellow peach fruit. Cork. **RATING** 87 **DRINK** Now $ 20

▼▼▼▽ **Margaret River Rose 2005** Pleasant strawberry fruit; a neatly balanced touch of residual sugar and controlled alcohol. Screwcap. 11° alc. **RATING** 86 **DRINK** Now $ 13

River Park ★★☆

River Park Road, Cowra, NSW 2794 **REGION** Cowra
T (02) 6342 3596 **F** (02) 6341 3711 **OPEN** Mon–Fri 9–5, w'ends 10–5
WINEMAKER Hunter Wine Services (John Hordern) **EST.** 1994 **CASES** 780
Bill and Chris Murphy established River Park with 7 ha chardonnay and 5.5 ha cabernet sauvignon on the banks of the Lachlan River, on the outskirts of Cowra, in 1994. Most of the grapes are sold to major wine companies; some is made under contract and has been stocked by Liquorland, Woolworths and Dan Murphy.

ŸŸŸŸ **Cowra Chardonnay 2004** **RATING** 85 **DRINK** Now $ 16
Cowra Cabernet Sauvignon 2003 **RATING** 85 **DRINK** 2008 $ 16

RiverBank Estate ★★★

126 Hamersley Road, Caversham, WA 6055 **REGION** Swan Valley
T (08) 9377 1805 **F** (08) 9377 2168 **WWW.**riverbankestate.com.au **OPEN** 7 days 10–5
WINEMAKER Robert James Bond, Pheobe Thomas **EST.** 1993 **CASES** 6000
Robert Bond, a graduate of Charles Sturt University and a Swan Valley viticulturist for 20 years, established RiverBank Estate in 1993. He draws upon 11 ha of estate plantings and, in his words, 'The wines are unashamedly full bodied, produced from ripe grapes in what is recognised as a hot grapegrowing region'. Wines extending back over several vintages are available at the cellar door. Bond conducts 8-week wine courses affiliated with the Wine Industry Association of WA. Exports to Poland.

ŸŸŸŸ **Verdelho 2005** Apple, pear and fruit salad; good fruit line and length; dry finish. Screwcap. 12.5° alc. **RATING** 87 **DRINK** Now $ 18

ŸŸŸŸ **Cabernet Shiraz Merlot 2002** **RATING** 85 **DRINK** Now $ 18

Riversands Vineyards NR

Whytes Road, St George, Qld 4487 **REGION** Queensland Zone
T (07) 4625 3643 **F** (07) 4625 5043 **WWW.**riversandswines.com **OPEN** Mon–Sat 8–6, Sunday 9–4
WINEMAKER Ballandean Estate (Contract) **EST.** 1990 **CASES** 4000
Riversands is on the banks of the Balonne River in the southwest corner of Queensland. It is a mixed wine grape and table grape business, acquired by present owners Alison and David Blacket in 1996.

RiverStone Wines NR

105 Skye Road, Coldstream, Vic 3770 **REGION** Yarra Valley
T (03) 5962 3947 **F** (03) 5962 6616 **WWW.**riverstonewine.com.au **OPEN** Thurs–Mon 10–6
WINEMAKER Punt Road (Contract) **EST.** 1995 **CASES** NA
Peter and Jenny Inglese began the establishment of 10 ha of sauvignon blanc, chardonnay, pinot noir, shiraz and cabernet sauvignon in 1995. They also built a bluestone homestead and cellar door, incorporating 100-year-old reclaimed timber. The site has 360-degree views of the Yarra Valley and surrounding mountains, and antipasto platters are available for those who wish to stay a little longer and absorb the beauty of the valley.

Robert Channon Wines ★★★★☆

32 Bradley Lane, Stanthorpe, Qld 4380 **REGION** Granite Belt
T (07) 4683 3260 **F** (07) 4683 3109 **WWW.**robertchannonwines.com **OPEN** 7 days 10–5
WINEMAKER Ravens Croft Wines **EST.** 1998 **CASES** 3500
Peggy and Robert Channon have established 8 ha of chardonnay, verdelho, shiraz, merlot and cabernet sauvignon under permanent bird protection netting. The initial cost of installing permanent netting is high, but in the long term it is well worth it: it excludes birds and protects the grapes against hail damage. Also, there is no pressure to pick the grapes before they are fully ripe. The winery has established a particular reputation for its Verdelho.

▼▼▼▼♀ **Verdelho 2005** Clean, floral fruit salad aromas; a very good palate, back to the best Channon standard, with plenty of fruit flavour and length; good acidity. Screwcap. 14° alc. RATING 92 DRINK 2008 $ 24.50
Reserve Chardonnay 2004 Medium green-yellow; attractive, complex barrel ferment aromas; a rich palate, with lots of ripe stone fruit, trailing away slightly on the finish. Cork. RATING 91 DRINK 2008 $ 29
Reserve Cabernet Sauvignon 2004 Good hue, moderate depth; medium-bodied, pure cassis and blackcurrant varietal fruit; balanced tannins and oak. Cork. RATING 90 DRINK 2012 $ 29

▼▼▼▼ **Reserve Merlot 2004** Very light colour and body; what is present is quite attractive, but really needs more weight and concentration. Cork. RATING 87 DRINK 2009 $ 29

▼▼▼♀ **Singing Lake Chardonnay Verdelho 2005** RATING 84 DRINK Now $ 14

Robert Johnson Vineyards ★★★★☆

PO Box 6708 Halifax Street, Adelaide, SA 5000 REGION Eden Valley
T (08) 8227 2800 F (08) 8227 2833 OPEN Not
WINEMAKER Robert Johnson EST. 1997 CASES 2500
The home base for Robert Johnson is a 12-ha vineyard and olive grove purchased in 1996, with 0.4 ha of merlot (previously sold to Irvine Wines for Grand Merlot) and 5 ha of dilapidated olive trees. The olive grove has been rehabilitated, and 2.1 ha of shiraz, 1.2 ha of merlot and a small patch of viognier have been established. Wines made from the estate-grown grapes are released under the Robert Johnson label; these are supplemented by Alan & Veitch wines purchased from the Sam Virgara vineyard in the Adelaide Hills, and named after Robert Johnson's parents.

▼▼▼▼▼ **Eden Valley Shiraz Viognier 2004** Excellent purple-red; that unmistakable aromatic lift and flavour intensity of the blend; silky texture, with underlying warmth to the red and black fruits; finest tannins, good oak. Cork. 14.5° alc. RATING 94 DRINK 2015 $ 36

▼▼▼▼♀ **Eden Valley Merlot 2004** Medium purple-red; very different, and quite unusual aromas and flavours; rich, ripe spiced plum fruit, some licorice, and warm oak inputs. Cork. 14.5° alc. RATING 91 DRINK 2014 $ 40
Alan & Veitch Woodside Merlot 2004 Light, clear purple-red; light- to medium-bodied, but with considerable length to the bright, small red fruits, fine, slippery tannins, and background notes of green olive. Screwcap. 14° alc. RATING 90 DRINK 2012 $ 24

▼▼▼▼ **Alan & Veitch Lobethal Sauvignon Blanc 2005** A spotlessly clean bouquet; ultra-powerful style; intense citrus and gooseberry, the alcohol haunting the finish. Screwcap. 13.5° alc. RATING 89 DRINK Now $ 22
Alan & Veitch Charleston Viognier 2005 Light straw-green; a complex wine both in terms of flavour and structure; musk, pear and apricot; the alcohol does intrude on the finish, not uncommon for the variety. Screwcap. 14° alc. RATING 89 DRINK 2008 $ 24
Eden Valley Riesling 2005 A solidly-built wine, with regional lime flavour; balanced, but not particularly expressive; time may help. Screwcap. 12.5° alc. RATING 88 DRINK 2012 $ 17

Robert Stein Vineyard ★★★

Pipeclay Lane, Mudgee, NSW 2850 REGION Mudgee
T (02) 6373 3991 F (02) 6373 3709 WWW.robertstein.com.au OPEN 7 days 10–4.30
WINEMAKER Robert Stein, Moore Haszard EST. 1976 CASES 8500
The sweeping panorama from the winery is its own reward for cellar door visitors. Right from the outset this has been a substantial operation but has managed to sell the greater part of its production direct from the winery by mail order and cellar door, with retail distribution in Sydney, Vic and SA. Wine quality, once variable, albeit with top wines from time to time, has become much more consistent. Exports to the UK and Germany.

ŸŸŸŸ **Cabernet Sauvignon 2004** Light- to medium-bodied; savoury/earthy/minty/menthol aromas and flavours; needs more ripe fruit; a curious gold medal at the 2005 Mudgee Wine Show. Screwcap. 13.6° alc. **RATING** 89 **DRINK** 2008 $ 20
Semillon Sauvignon Blanc 2005 Faintly smoky aromas; hay, asparagus, grass and mineral, with an authoritative finish and aftertaste driven by semillon. Screwcap. 12.1° alc. **RATING** 88 **DRINK** 2010 $ 14

ŸŸŸŸ **Unwooded Chardonnay 2005** **RATING** 85 **DRINK** Now $ 14
Semillon Riesling 2005 **RATING** 85 **DRINK** Now $ 14
Cabernet Rose 2005 **RATING** 85 **DRINK** Now $ 15

ŸŸŸ **Gewurztraminer 2005** **RATING** 83 $ 14

Roberts Estate ★★☆

Game Street, Merbein, Vic 3505 **REGION** Murray Darling
T (03) 5024 2944 **F** (03) 5024 2877 **WWW**.robertsestatewines.com **OPEN** Not
WINEMAKER John Pezzaniti **EST.** 1998 **CASES** 20 000
A very large winery acting as a processing point for grapes grown up and down the Murray River. Over 10 000 tonnes are crushed each vintage; much of the wine is sold in bulk to others, but a limited amount is vinified under the Roberts Estate label.

ŸŸŸŸ **Semillon Sauvignon Blanc 2005** Strong aroma and flavour in a grass/herb/gooseberry spectrum; good balance. Excellent value. Screwcap. 12.5° alc. **RATING** 87 **DRINK** Now $ 11

ŸŸŸ **Commissioners Block Chardonnay 2004** **RATING** 82 $ 11

🐦 Robertson & de Bilde Wines NR

3/2 Niangala Close, Austlink Corporate Park, Belrose, NSW 2085 (postal) **REGION** Clare Valley
T (02) 9479 7188 **F** (02) 9450 0808 **WWW**.rdbwines.com.au **OPEN** Not
WINEMAKER Simon Gilbert, Leigh Eldredge **EST.** 2004 **CASES** 1000
This is the new venture of Simon Gilbert, established after he ceased to have an executive position with Simon Gilbert Wines in Mudgee. He has joined with Clare Valley vigneron Leigh Eldredge to produce limited quantities of Clare Valley wines. The first release, MAX V, was sourced from 3 growers in the Clare Valley, utilising the 5 grapes of Bordeaux: cabernet sauvignon, cabernet franc, merlot, malbec and petit verdot. The wine was made using various sophisticated winemaking techniques and an amazing mix of new French oak barrels, at Sevenhill Cellars.

Robinsons Family Vineyards ★★★★

Curtin Road, Ballandean, Qld 4382 **REGION** Granite Belt
T (07) 4684 1216 **F** (07) 4684 1216 **WWW**.robinsonswines.com.au **OPEN** Sat–Wed 10–5, Thurs & Fri by appt
WINEMAKER Craig Robinson **EST.** 1969 **CASES** 2000
One of the pioneers of the Granite Belt, with the second generation of the family Robinson now in control. One thing has not changed: the strongly held belief of the Robinsons that the Granite Belt should be regarded as a cool, rather than warm, climate. It is a tricky debate, because some climatic measurements point one way, others the opposite. Embedded in all this are semantic arguments about the meaning of 'cool' and 'warm'. Suffice it to say that shiraz and (conspicuously) cabernet sauvignon are the most suitable red varieties for the region; semillon, verdelho and chardonnay are the best white varieties.

ŸŸŸŸ **Shiraz 2000** Retains very good hue and depth; velvety, rich blackberry and spice fruit; exemplary texture and structure. Cork. 13° alc. **RATING** 92 **DRINK** 2010 $ 30
Cabernet Sauvignon 2002 Good colour; is developing well, with good varietal blackcurrant fruit supported by ripe tannins. Cork. 14.2° alc. **RATING** 91 **DRINK** 2011 $ 26

ŸŸŸŸ **Shiraz Cabernet 2002** **RATING** 86 **DRINK** 2008 $ 26
Pinot Noir 2002 **RATING** 84 **DRINK** Now $ 35

Robinvale

NR

Sea Lake Road, Robinvale, Vic 3549 **REGION** Murray Darling
T (03) 5026 3955 **F** (03) 5026 1123 **WWW**.organicwines.com.au **OPEN** Mon–Fri 9–6, Sun 1–6
WINEMAKER Bill Caracatsanoudis **EST.** 1976 **CASES** 10 000
Robinvale was one of the first Australian wineries to be fully accredited with the Biodynamic Agricultural Association of Australia. Most, but not all, of the wines are produced from organically grown grapes, with some made preservative-free. Production has grown dramatically, no doubt reflecting the interest in organic and biodynamic viticulture and winemaking. Exports to the UK, Japan, Belgium, Canada and the US.

Roche Wines

NR

Broke Road, Pokolbin, NSW 2320 **REGION** Lower Hunter Valley
T (02) 4998 7600 **F** (02) 4998 7706 **WWW**.hvg.com.au **OPEN** 7 days 10–5
WINEMAKER Tempus Two Wines **EST.** 1999 **CASES** 10 000
Roche Wines, with its 45.77 ha of semillon, shiraz and chardonnay (plus a few bits and pieces), is but the tip of the iceberg of the massive investment made by Bill Roche in the Pokolbin subregion. He has transformed the old Hungerford Hill development on the corner of Broke and McDonalds Roads, and built a luxurious resort hotel with extensive gardens and an Irish pub on the old Tallawanta Vineyard, as well as resuscitating the vines on Tallawanta. The wines are all sold through the various outlets in the overall development; excess grapes are sold to other makers.

Rochford Wines

Cnr Maroondah Highway/Hill Road, Coldstream, Vic 3770 **REGION** Yarra Valley
T (03) 5962 2119 **F** (03) 5962 5319 **WWW**.rochfordwines.com **OPEN** 7 days 10–5
WINEMAKER David Creed **EST.** 1988 **CASES** 25 000
Following the acquisition of the former Eyton-on-Yarra by Helmut and Yvonne Konecsny, major changes have occurred. Most obvious is the renaming of the winery and brand, slightly less so the move of the winemaking operations of Rochford to the Yarra Valley. The large restaurant is open 7 days for lunch, extended with light refreshments 10–5, and Rochford is well-known for the numerous concerts it stages in its lakeside amphitheatre.

ΨΨΨΨΨ **Yarra Valley Pinot Noir 2004** Good purple-red hue; attractive, silky red and black cherry fruit; good length bolstered by fine tannins and quality French oak. Screwcap. 14° alc. **RATING** 94 **DRINK** 2013 $ 27
Reserve Macedon Ranges Pinot Noir 2004 Excellent colour; very elegant, fine and focused; seamless French oak, savoury tannins and spiced plum fruit. A decidedly curious choice of cork when the varietal gets Diam. Cork. 13.5° alc. **RATING** 94 **DRINK** 2010 $ 54
Reserve Yarra Valley Shiraz 2003 Fragrant black fruit, spice and herb aromas; a medium-bodied, supple and smooth palate with mocha and spice; 18 months new French oak. **RATING** 94 **DRINK** 2013 $ 44

ΨΨΨΨ **Reserve Yarra Valley Chardonnay 2004** Oak certainly makes an impact on the bouquet and palate, but melon/nectarine fruit handles the 18 months in new French barrels well. Perhaps a touch more acid needed. Diam. 14° alc. **RATING** 93 **DRINK** 2014 $ 38
2003 Latitude Chardonnay Fresh, fine and elegant, developing slowly but surely; lovely nectarine fruit and sotto voce oak. The back label exposes it comes from a single premium Yarra Valley vineyard. Screwcap. 14° alc. **RATING** 93 **DRINK** 2009 $ 18
Yarra Valley Sauvignon Blanc 2005 Water-white; a spotlessly clean bouquet, with lively, fresh apple, citrus and pear fruit; crisp and clean. Screwcap. 14° alc. **RATING** 91 **DRINK** Now $ 23
Yarra Valley Chardonnay 2005 A light- to medium-bodied, elegant wine; gentle melon and stone fruit with well-integrated and balanced French oak; good finish. Screwcap. 13.5° alc. **RATING** 90 **DRINK** 2010 $ 23
Macedon Ranges Chardonnay 2004 Toasty oak and intense lemony/citrussy fruit; long and sinuous. **RATING** 90 **DRINK** 2009 $ 27

Macedon Ranges Pinot Gris 2005 Vibrant colour, aroma and lemony flavour; not especially varietal, but has zip and presence. **RATING** 90 **DRINK** Now $ 27

Macedon Ranges Pinot Noir 2004 Very well-made, medium-bodied wine; complex spicy black fruits/plums, with very fine, ripe tannins. Diam. 14° alc. **RATING** 90 **DRINK** 2011 $ 30

ҮҮҮҮ **Yarra Valley Shiraz 2003** Good hue; a savoury, spicy medium-bodied style, the dark fruits sustained by fine tannins. **RATING** 89 **DRINK** 2011 $ 23

Latitude Pinot Noir 2003 Undoubted cool-grown, southern Victorian origins; savoury/earthy/spicy flavours; some length. **RATING** 88 **DRINK** Now $ 18

Yarra Valley Cabernet Sauvignon 2003 Offers a range of spicy/cedary/leafy aromas and riper, sweet blackcurrant fruit on the palate. Cork. 14° alc. **RATING** 88 **DRINK** 2010 $ 29

ҮҮҮҮ **Yarra Valley Chardonnay 2004 RATING** 86 **DRINK** Now $ 24

Rock House

NR

St Agnes Hill, Calder Highway, Kyneton, Vic 3444 (postal) **REGION** Macedon Ranges
T (03) 5422 2205 **F** (03) 9388 9355 **OPEN** Not
WINEMAKER Malcolm Stewart **EST.** 1990 **CASES** 350
Ray Lacey and partners have established 6 ha of riesling, cabernet sauvignon and merlot. By far the greatest percentage of the production is sold as grapes, with 5 tonnes being used for the Rock House wines.

RockBare

★★★★☆

PO Box 63, Mt Torrens, SA 5244 **REGION** McLaren Vale
T (08) 8389 9584 **F** (08) 8389 9587 **WWW**.rockbare.com.au **OPEN** Not
WINEMAKER Tim Burvill **EST.** 2000 **CASES** 12 000
A native of WA, Tim Burvill moved to SA in 1993 to do the winemaking course at the Adelaide University Roseworthy Campus. Having completed an Honours degree in oenology, he was recruited by Southcorp, and quickly found himself in a senior winemaking position, with responsibility for super-premium whites including Penfolds Yattarna. He makes the RockBare wines under lend-lease arrangements with other wineries. Exports to all major markets.

ҮҮҮҮҮ **McLaren Vale Shiraz 2004** Good purple-red; black fruits, leather, spice and dark chocolate aroma and flavour. Excellent structure and length; controlled oak. Screwcap. 14.5° alc. **RATING** 92 **DRINK** 2019 $ 21

Barossa Babe Shiraz 2003 Very rich, full-bodied, sweet blackberry and dark chocolate fruit; just a little too sweet/confit/jammy, the vintage no doubt a contributing factor. Cork. **RATING** 91 **DRINK** 2013 $ 40

ҮҮҮҮ **McLaren Vale Chardonnay 2005** Impressive unwooded style; abundant fruit and length, but a fractionally congested finish. Screwcap. 13.5° alc. **RATING** 88 **DRINK** Now $ 18

Rockfield Estate

★★★★

Rosa Glen Road, Margaret River, WA 6285 **REGION** Margaret River
T (08) 9757 5006 **F** (08) 9757 5006 **WWW**.rockfield.com.au **OPEN** Wed–Sun & hols 11–5, or by appt
WINEMAKER Andrew Gaman Jr, John Durham (Consultant) **EST.** 1997 **CASES** 8000
Rockfield Estate Vineyard is very much a family affair. Dr Andrew Gaman wears the hats of chief executive officer, assistant winemaker and co-marketing manager; wife Anne Gaman is a Director; Alex Gaman is the viticulturist; Andrew Gaman Jr is winemaker; and Anna Walter (née Gaman) helps Dr Andrew Gaman with the marketing. Chapman Brook meanders through the property, the vines running from its banks up to the wooded slopes above the valley floor. Exports to the US and UK.

ҮҮҮҮҮ **Reserve Margaret River Cabernet Sauvignon 2003** Firm, fresh cassis berry fruit drives the wine; fleeting touches of leaf and mint; needs more time to settle down. Screwcap. 13.5° alc. **RATING** 90 **DRINK** 2013 $ 39

ҮҮҮҮ **Semillon Sauvignon Blanc 2005** Minerally, spicy aromas; predominantly herbaceous flavour, with a hint of tropical; clean finish. Screwcap. **RATING** 89 **DRINK** Now $ 17

Cabernet Merlot 2003 Clean; a quite firm, cool-grown mix of berry, leaf and spice; tannins ripe. Screwcap. **RATING** 89 **DRINK** 2012 $ 24

Semillon 2005 Faintly reduced bouquet; very tight and reserved, needing — and deserving — patience. Screwcap. **RATING** 87 **DRINK** 2010 $ 22

Rockford ★★★★★

Krondorf Road, Tanunda, SA 5352 **REGION** Barossa Valley
T (08) 8563 2720 **F** (08) 8563 3787 **OPEN** 7 days 11–5
WINEMAKER Robert O'Callaghan, Chris Ringland **EST.** 1984 **CASES** NFP
The wines are sold only through Adelaide retailers (and the cellar door) and are unknown to most eastern Australian wine-drinkers, which is a great pity because these are some of the most individual, spectacularly flavoured wines made in the Barossa today, with an emphasis on old, low-yielding dryland vineyards. This SA slur on the palates of Vic and NSW is exacerbated by the fact that the wines are exported to Switzerland, the UK, the US, Canada and NZ; it all goes to show we need proper authority to protect our living treasures.

ΨΨΨΨΨ **Black Shiraz NV** As good as ever; flavour without heaviness or overt sweetness; black fruits and spices; length and balance. Disgorged Sept '05. **RATING** 95 **DRINK** 2015 $ 53
Handpicked Eden Valley Riesling 2003 Light straw-green; tight, fine lime and apple blossom aromas, moving into slate and mineral on the palate; long, fine finish; still very youthful. Cork. 11.5° alc. **RATING** 94 **DRINK** 2011 $ 17
Basket Press Barossa Valley Shiraz 2003 Good colour; ripe, sweet cherry, plum and spice; delicious fruit profile and weight; silky texture, ripe tannins. Cork. 14.8° alc.
RATING 94 **DRINK** 2018 $ 46

Rocklea Vineyard NR

Londons Road, Lovedale, NSW 2325 (postal) **REGION** Lower Hunter Valley
T (02) 9980 7000 **F** (02) 9980 2833 **OPEN** Not
WINEMAKER Bill Sneddon (Contract) **EST.** 1989 **CASES** NA
Allan Brown has 10 ha planted to semillon, chardonnay and shiraz. The wine is available by mail order, and limited amounts are exported.

Rocky Passes Wines ★★★★

1590 Highlands Road, Seymour, Vic 3660 **REGION** Upper Goulburn
T (03) 5796 9366 **F** (03) 5796 9366 **WWW**.goulburnrandr.com.au **OPEN** W'ends 10–5
WINEMAKER Vitto Oles **EST.** 2000 **CASES** 800
Vitto Oles and Candida Westney run this tiny, cool climate vineyard situated at the southern end of the Strathbogie Ranges which in fact falls in the Upper Goulburn region. They have planted 1.6 ha of shiraz and 0.4 ha of viognier, growing the vines with minimal irrigation and preferring organic and biodynamic soil treatments.

ΨΨΨΨΨ **Syrah 2004** Strong colour; abundant blackberry, plum and spice fruit; equally abundant tannins needed a little fining; nonetheless great value and potential. Cork. 14.4° alc.
RATING 90 **DRINK** 2015 $ 15

Rocland Estate ★★★★☆

PO Box 679, Nuriootpa, SA 5355 **REGION** Barossa Valley
T (08) 8562 2142 **F** (08) 8562 2182 **OPEN** Not
WINEMAKER Simon Adams, Sam Scott **EST.** 2000 **CASES** 1000
Rocland Wines is primarily a bulk winemaking facility for contract work, but Frank Rocca does have 6 ha of shiraz which is used to make Rocland Wines, largely destined for export markets, but with retail distribution in Adelaide.

ΨΨΨΨΨ **Lot 147 Barossa Valley Shiraz 2004** Good colour; a medium-bodied, interesting combination of spice, herb, black fruits and bitter chocolate; quality oak, fine tannins; 3% viognier from Adelaide Hills. Screwcap. 14.5° alc. **RATING** 93 **DRINK** 2016 $ 19

Rodericks

NR

90 Goshnicks Road, Murgon, Qld 4605 **REGION** South Burnett
T (07) 4168 4768 **F** (07) 4168 4768 **OPEN** 7 days 10–5
WINEMAKER Colin Roderick, Robert Roderick **EST.** 1996 **CASES** NA
The Roderick family (Wendy, Colin and Robert) have a 22-ha vineyard planted to semillon, chardonnay, colombard, verdelho, cabernet sauvignon, merlot, malbec, shiraz, white muscat, muscat hamburg and tarrango, and make the wine onsite.

Roehr

NR

Roehr Road, Ebenezer near Nuriootpa, SA 5355 **REGION** Barossa Valley
T (08) 8565 6242 **F** (08) 8565 6242 **OPEN** Not
WINEMAKER Contract **EST.** 1995 **CASES** NFP
Karl Wilhelm Roehr arrived in Australia in 1841, and was amongst the earliest settlers at Ebenezer, in the northern end of the Barossa Valley. His great-great grandson Elmor Roehr is the custodian of 20 ha of shiraz, grenache, mataro on a vineyard passed down through the generations. In 1995 he decided to venture into winemaking and produced a Shiraz from 80-year-old vines which typically crop at less than 1.5 tonnes to the acre; he has subsequently expanded the range significantly.

Rogues Gallery

NR

PO Box 10295, Adelaide BC, SA 5000 **REGION** McLaren Vale
T 0413 263 713 **F** (08) 8410 0918 **WWW.**roguesgallery.com.au **OPEN** Not
WINEMAKER Contract **EST.** 1996 **CASES** NA
Stephen Inglis sources the material for the Rogues Gallery wines in various ways, part coming from 4 ha of vineyards in the heart of McLaren Vale, 2.4 ha at Blewitt Springs and 1.7 ha on the Willunga Scarp. Less than 20 tonnes are crushed for the Rogues Gallery label, the remainder headed elsewhere. Exports to the UK, the US and Canada.

🐌 Rogues Lane Vineyard

★★★★☆

370 Lower Plenty Road, Viewbank, Vic 3084 (postal) **REGION** Heathcote
T 0409 202 103 **F** (03) 9457 2811 **WWW.**rogueslane.com.au **OPEN** Not
WINEMAKER John Ellis (Contract) **EST.** 1998 **CASES** 600
Pauline and Eric Dowker have planted 4 ha of shiraz (including a smattering of malbec), the first vintage coming in 1998. 'Dowker' is an ancient word meaning 'herder of ducks and geese', making the location of the vineyard on Wild Duck Creek doubly appropriate.

🍷🍷🍷🍷🍷 **Heathcote Shiraz Malbec 2003** Dense colour; similar to the Shiraz, the juicy malbec subsumed in the ever-so-dense blackberry fruit of the shiraz. The tannins, however, are slightly less robust. Ultimate Parker special. Cork. 16° alc. **RATING** 94 **DRINK** 2023 **$** 45

🍷🍷🍷🍷🍷 **Heathcote Shiraz 2003** Deep colour; crammed full of dark fruits, blackberry and licorice; has absorbed 18 months oak maturation, but has not shed its robust tannins. Ideally, leave for 10 years. Diam. 16° alc. **RATING** 93 **DRINK** 2023 **$** 45

Rojo Wines

★★★☆

34 Breese Street, Brunswick, Vic 3056 **REGION** Port Phillip Zone
T (03) 9386 5688 **F** (03) 9386 5699 **OPEN** W'ends 10–6
WINEMAKER Graeme Rojo **EST.** 1999 **CASES** 600
Rojo Wines is part of Melbourne's urban winery at Brunswick. Core production is cool-climate wines from the Strathbogie Ranges (Sauvignon Blanc, Chardonnay, Shiraz and Merlot). Fruit is also sourced from various regions in Vic. Production is low, allowing maximum time to be spent with each wine through its development.

🍷🍷🍷🍷🍷 **Terip Chardonnay 2005** Very well-made wine; good balance and structure to pleasing nectarine and stone fruit flavours. **RATING** 92 **DRINK** 2010 **$** 18

♥♥♥♥ **Terip Sauvignon Blanc 2004** Pale straw-green; well-made; while not overly varietal is lengthened by good acidity. **RATING** 88 **DRINK** Now $ 18
Terip Chardonnay 2004 Light- to medium-bodied, but quite tightly wound; light nectarine fruit and a hint of sweetness. **RATING** 87 **DRINK** Now $ 18

♥♥♥♡ **Terip Reserve Shiraz 2004 RATING** 86 **DRINK** 2008 $ 18
Cabernet Shiraz Nebbiolo 2002 Light- to medium-bodied; has a definite Italianate touch partly via the tannins, which are, however, fine, not abrasive; has length, food style. Cork. 13.5° alc. **RATING** 86 **DRINK** 2008 $ 14

♥♥♥ **Terip Chardonnay 2001 RATING** 83 $ 16
Terip Merlot 2004 RATING 82 $ 18

Rolf Binder

Cnr Seppeltsfield Road/Stelzer Road, Tanunda, SA 5352 **REGION** Barossa Valley
T (08) 8562 3300 **F** (08) 8562 1177 **WWW**.rolfbinder.com **OPEN** Mon–Fri 10–4.30, Saturdays 11–4
WINEMAKER Rolf Binder, Christa Deans, Kym Teusner **EST.** 1955 **CASES** 25 000
The change of name from Veritas to to Rolf Binder came with the 50th anniversary of the winery, established by Rolf's and sister Christa Deans' parents. The growth in production and sales is due to the quality of the wines rather than the (hitherto) rather laid back approach to marketing.

♥♥♥♥♥ **Heinrich Barossa Valley Shiraz Grenache Mataro 2004** Excellent purple-red; complex aroma, flavour and structure attests to the varietal mix; herb, spice and small berry fruits; fine, ripe tannins. The blend seldom comes better than this. Cork. 14° alc. **RATING** 94
DRINK 2014 $ 25

♥♥♥♥♡ **Christa Rolf Barossa Valley Shiraz Grenache 2004** Good hue; an aromatic, spiced bouquet followed by a medium-bodied, supple and soft palate; juicy berry grenache supported by shiraz structure; works well. Screwcap. 14° alc. **RATING** 91 **DRINK** 2010 $ 20
Highness Barossa Riesling 2002 Full-flavoured, fleshy, lime, lemon and tropical fruit; aging very well. Screwcap. 13° alc. **RATING** 90 **DRINK** 2010
Barossa Valley Cabernet Sauvignon Merlot 2004 Fresh, vibrant cassis and blackcurrant fruit; medium-bodied; silky tannins and an airbrush of oak. Screwcap. 14° alc. **RATING** 90
DRINK 2011
JJ Hahn 1979 Barossa Valley Cabernet Sauvignon 2002 Developed colour moving to brick; soft, cedary, earthy black fruits; warm oak, soft tannins. Cork. 14.5° alc. **RATING** 90
DRINK 2012

♥♥♥♡ **Binder's Bull's Blood Shiraz Mataro Pressings 2003 RATING** 85 **DRINK** 2008 $ 35
Hanisch Barossa Valley Shiraz 2003 RATING 84 **DRINK** Now

Romavilla

NR

Northern Road, Roma, Qld 4455 **REGION** Queensland Zone
T (07) 4622 1822 **F** (07) 4622 1822 **WWW**.romavilla.com **OPEN** Mon–Fri 8–5, Sat 9–12, 2–4
WINEMAKER David Wall, Richard Wall **EST.** 1863 **CASES** 2000
An amazing historic relic, seemingly untouched since its 19th-century heyday, producing conventional table wines but still providing some extraordinary fortifieds, including a truly stylish Madeira made from Riesling and Syrian (the latter variety originating in Persia). David Wall has now been joined by son Richard in the business, which will hopefully ensure continuity for this important part of Australian wine history. The vineyard has been increased with the planting of 0.4 ha of the Italian grape garganega. Exports to Hong Kong and Canada.

Rosabrook Estate

Rosa Brook Road, Margaret River, WA 6285 **REGION** Margaret River
T (08) 9757 2286 **F** (08) 9757 3634 **WWW**.rosabrook.com **OPEN** 7 days 10–4
WINEMAKER Bill Crappsley **EST.** 1980 **CASES** 4000
The 14-ha Rosabrook Estate vineyards were established progressively between 1984 and 1996, with sauvignon blanc, semillon, chardonnay, shiraz, merlot, cabernet sauvignon and petit verdot. The

cellar door is housed in what was Margaret River's first commercial abbatoir, built in the early 1930s, hence the icon red is named Slaughterhouse Block. Exports to the UK, Canada and Vietnam.

ΥΥΥΥΥ **Margaret River Semillon Sauvignon Blanc 2005** Quite fragrant and delicate aromas which intensify on the palate, the barrel ferment portion adding to structure and excellent length. Clever winemaking; two-thirds Semillon, one-third Sauvignon Blanc. Screwcap. 13° alc. **RATING** 94 **DRINK** 2008 $ 18

Margaret River Chardonnay 2004 Elegant, fruit-driven wine; the skilled use of restrained barrel ferment inputs to the passionfruit and stone fruit flavours results in excellent texture, structure and length. 14° alc. **RATING** 94 **DRINK** 2009 $ 23

ΥΥΥΥΥ **Margaret River Shiraz 2003** Bright purple-red hue; spicy, cherry aromas; light- to medium-bodied, typically elegant, with cherry fruit and fine tannins. Screwcap. 13° alc. **RATING** 91 **DRINK** 2010 $ 23

Rosebrook Estate

NR

1092 Maitlandvale Road, Rosebrook, NSW 2320 **REGION** Lower Hunter Valley
T (02) 4930 6961 **F** (02) 4930 6963 **WWW**.rosebrookestatewines.com.au **OPEN** By appt
WINEMAKER Graeme Levick **EST.** 2000 **CASES** 2000
Graeme and Tania Levick run Rosebrook Estate and Hunter River Retreat as parallel operations. They include self-contained cottages, horse-riding, tennis, canoeing, swimming, bushwalking, fishing, riverside picnic area, recreation room and minibus for winery tours and transport to functions or events in the area. Somewhere in the middle of all this they have established 2.5 ha each of chardonnay and verdelho, purchasing shiraz and muscat to complete the product range.

Rosemount Estate (Hunter Valley)

★★★★☆

Rosemount Road, Denman, NSW 2328 **REGION** Upper Hunter Valley
T (02) 6549 6400 **F** (02) 6549 6499 **WWW**.rosemountestates.com **OPEN** 7 days 10–4
WINEMAKER Matthew Koch **EST.** 1969 **CASES** NFP
Rosemount Estate achieved a miraculous balancing act, maintaining wine quality while presiding over an ever-expanding empire and dramatically increasing production. The wines were consistently of excellent value; all had real character and individuality, and more than a few were startlingly good. The outcome was the merger with Southcorp in March 2001; what seemed to be a powerful and synergistic merger turned out to be little short of a disaster. Southcorp lost more than its market capitalisation and more than half of its most effective and talented employees. Now part of FWE. Exports to all major markets.

ΥΥΥΥΥ **Hill of Gold Mudgee Cabernet Sauvignon 2004** Medium- to full-bodied; loaded with cassis blackcurrant fruit; excellent, fine tannins and well-integrated oak. Gold medal Sydney Wine Show '06. **RATING** 94 **DRINK** 2014 $ 19

ΥΥΥΥΥ **Hill of Gold Mudgee Shiraz 2004** Strong colour; well-made, with black fruits, chocolate, spice and earth; appropriate warm oak; good overall mouthfeel. Cork. 13° alc. **RATING** 93 **DRINK** 2014 $ 19

Show Reserve Chardonnay 2005 Brilliant green-yellow; a powerful, well-made wine, with excellent melon/fig/peach fruit and oak balance and integration. Cork. 13.5° alc. **RATING** 91 **DRINK** 2009 $ 23

ΥΥΥΥ **Show Reserve Chardonnay 2004** A complex wine showing long experience with the variety, but also the limitations of the region (and American oak). Cork. 13° alc. **RATING** 89 **DRINK** 2008 $ 22.99

Diamond Label Shiraz 2004 Attractive juicy berry red fruit flavours, but not a great deal of depth or structure. **RATING** 89 **DRINK** 2009 $ 13.50

Diamond Label Semillon Sauvignon Blanc 2005 Nicely balanced and structured; gentle herbaceous/tropical mix. Synthetic. **RATING** 87 **DRINK** Now $ 10.99

ΥΥΥ **Traminer Riesling 2005** Tried and true; actually has surprising varietal character from spice/musk traminer, and — of course — substantial sweetness. Chinese food special. Cork. 11.5° alc. **RATING** 86 **DRINK** Now $ 10.99

Limited Edition Rose 2005 Bright, crisp and clean; small red fruit flavours; nice dry finish. Screwcap. 13.5° alc. **RATING** 86 **DRINK** Now $ 11

Diamond Label Pinot Noir 2005 Rich, with some ripe plum pinot varietal character within a dry red shell. The synthetic cork should encourage immediate consumption. Synthetic. 13.5° alc. **RATING** 86 **DRINK** Now $ 15

Grenache Shiraz 2004 Clean, fresh, harmonious juicy berry fruit; easy drinking. Synthetic. **RATING** 86 **DRINK** Now $ 10.99

Diamond Label Semillon 2005 RATING 85 **DRINK** 2009 $ 14.99

ŸŸŸ **Diamond Label Rose 2005 RATING** 83 $ 10.99

Rosemount Estate (McLaren Vale) ★★★★☆

Chaffeys Road, McLaren Vale, SA 5171 **REGION** McLaren Vale
T (08) 8323 8250 **F** (08) 8323 9308 **WWW**.rosemountestate.com.au **OPEN** Mon–Sat 10–5, Sun & public hols 11–4
WINEMAKER Charles Whish **EST.** 1888 **CASES** NFP
The specialist red wine arm of Rosemount Estate, responsible for its prestigious Balmoral Syrah, Show Reserve Shiraz and GSM, as well as most of the other McLaren Vale-based Rosemount brands. These wines come in large measure from 325 ha of estate plantings.

ŸŸŸŸŸ **Show Reserve Shiraz 2001** Previously tasted in September 2003 when I noted it was still coming together. It has now done so splendidly, with dense, fat and luscious red and black fruits, avoiding the alcohol and extract traps. **RATING** 94 **DRINK** 2015 $ 23

ŸŸŸŸŸ **Show Reserve Shiraz 2002** A positively elegant mix of red and black cherry, chocolate and plum; fine tannins, quality oak. Cork. 14° alc. **RATING** 93 **DRINK** 2010 $ 27.99

ŸŸŸŸ **Show Reserve Coonawarra Cabernet Sauvignon 2002 RATING** 85 **DRINK** 2010 $ 24

Rosenvale Wines ★★★★

Lot 385 Railway Terrace, Nuriootpa, SA 5355 **REGION** Barossa Valley
T 0407 390 788 **F** (08) 8565 7206 **WWW**.rosenvale.com.au **OPEN** By appt
WINEMAKER James Rosenzweig, Mark Jamieson **EST.** 2000 **CASES** 2000
The Rosenzweig family has 80 ha of vineyards, some old and some new, planted to riesling, semillon, pinot noir, grenache, shiraz and cabernet sauvignon. Most of the grapes are sold to other producers, but since 1999 select parcels have been retained and vinified for release under the Rosenvale label. Exports to the UK, the US, Singapore, China and Taiwan.

ŸŸŸŸ **Barossa Valley Shiraz Cabernet 2004** Good hue; medium-bodied; a complex array of fresh red and black fruits, with touches of spice and chocolate; fine, ripe, sweet tannins to close. Cork. **RATING** 92 **DRINK** 2015 $ 25

Barossa Valley Cabernet Sauvignon 2003 Ripe, luscious, sweet blackcurrant and cassis; fine tannins, good French oak support. No dead fruit. Vines planted 1960. Cork. 14° alc. **RATING** 91 **DRINK** 2013 $ 25

ŸŸŸŸ **Barossa Valley Semillon 2005** A highly, and unusually, fragrant bouquet; lemongrass and spice flavours, then a fair burst of heat from the alcohol. A wine in 2 parts; oh for lower alcohol. Vines planted 1940. Screwcap. 13° alc. **RATING** 89 **DRINK** 2010 $ 14

Barossa Valley Shiraz 2003 An abundance of blackberry and plum; while it has plenty of sweet flavour, there are touches of dead fruit character. Twin top. 15° alc. **RATING** 88 **DRINK** 2011 $ 25

ŸŸŸŸ **Barossa Valley Chardonnay 2005 RATING** 84 **DRINK** Now $ 14

ŸŸŸ **Barossa Valley Grenache 2004 RATING** 83 $ 25

Rosevears Estate

1a Waldhorn Drive, Rosevears, Tas 7277 **REGION** Northern Tasmania
T (03) 6330 1800 **F** (03) 6330 1810 **WWW**.rosevearsestate.com.au **OPEN** 7 days 10–4
WINEMAKER Andrew Pirie **EST.** 1999 **CASES** 3000
The multi-million dollar Rosevears Estate winery and restaurant complex was opened by the Tasmanian premier in November 1999. Built on a steep hillside overlooking the Tamar River, it is certain to make a lasting and important contribution to the Tasmanian wine industry. It is owned by a syndicate of investors headed by Dr Mike Beamish, and incorporates both Notley Gorge and Ironpot Bay. Offers spacious, high-quality accommodation units with a splendid view over the Tamar River.

ŸŸŸŸ **Unwooded Chardonnay 2005** **RATING** 86 **DRINK** Now $ 22
Notley Gorge Unwooded Pinot Noir 2005 **RATING** 86 **DRINK** 2008
Pinot Noir 2004 **RATING** 86 **DRINK** 2008 $ 28

Rosily Vineyard

Yelveton Road, Wilyabrup, WA 6284 **REGION** Margaret River
T (08) 9755 6336 **F** (08) 9221 3309 **WWW**.rosily.com.au **OPEN** W'ends 10–5, every day over Christmas
WINEMAKER Mike Lemmes, Dan Pannell (Consultant) **EST.** 1994 **CASES** 6500
The partnership of Mike and Barb Scott and Ken and Dot Allan acquired the Rosily Vineyard site in 1994. Under the direction of consultant Dan Pannell (of *the Pannell family*) 12 ha of vineyard were planted over the next 3 years: first up sauvignon blanc, semillon, chardonnay and cabernet sauvignon, and thereafter merlot, shiraz and a little grenache and cabernet franc. The first crops were sold to other makers in the region, but in 1999 Rosily built a winery with a 120-tonne capacity, and is now moving to fully utilise that capacity.

ŸŸŸŸŸ **Margaret River Sauvignon Blanc 2005** Aromatic, clean and crisp; grass, asparagus, gooseberry and mineral flavours; good line and drive through the long finish. Screwcap. 13.9° alc. **RATING** 94 **DRINK** Now $ 18

ŸŸŸŸŸ **Semillon Sauvignon Blanc 2005** A complex wine with a cleverly handled barrel ferment component; overall good balance. **RATING** 93 **DRINK** 2008 $ 19
Chardonnay 2004 Slightly smoky barrel ferment inputs; delicate stone fruit and citrus flavours; good balance and length; will develop. Screwcap. **RATING** 90 **DRINK** 2010 $ 20

Rosnay Organic Wines

NR

Rivers Road, Canowindra, NSW 2804 **REGION** Cowra
T (02) 6344 3215 **F** (02) 6344 3229 **WWW**.organicfarms.com.au **OPEN** By appt
WINEMAKER Various contract **EST.** 2002 **CASES** 3000
Rosnay Organic Wines is, to put it mildly, an interesting business venture, with the Statham and Gardner families at its centre. There are 36 ha of vineyard on the 140-ha property, part of which has been divided into 12 blocks ranging from 8–10 ha, along with 10 housing blocks, each of 5000m², with all the requisite building approvals and services provided. The viticulture is organic, and the management company provides active growers or absentee investors with a range of specialist organic farming machinery and contract management. Winemaking is split between John Cassegrain of Cassegrain Wines, Kevin Karstrom of Botobolar and Rodney Hooper of Windowrie, each one of whom has expertise in organic grapegrowing and organic winemaking.

Ross Estate Wines

Barossa Valley Way, Lyndoch, SA 5351 **REGION** Barossa Valley
T (08) 8524 4033 **F** (08) 8524 4533 **WWW**.rossestate.com.au **OPEN** Mon–Fri 10–4.30, w'ends 11–4.30
WINEMAKER Rod Chapman, Andrew Hercock **EST.** 1999 **CASES** 18 000
Darius and Pauline Ross laid the foundation for Ross Estate Wines when they purchased 43 ha of vines which included two blocks of 75- and 90-year-old grenache. Also included were blocks of 30-year-old riesling and semillon, and 13-year-old merlot. Chardonnay, sauvignon blanc, cabernet

sauvignon, cabernet franc and shiraz followed. The immensely experienced Rod Chapman, with many vintages under his belt, including 18 years as red winemaker with Southcorp/Penfolds, is in charge of winemaking. Exports to all major markets.

ΨΨΨΨ **2003 Ross Estate Lynedoch Cabernet Sauvignon Cabernet Franc Merlot** Medium- to full-bodied; substantial black and red fruits, dark chocolate, and mocha/vanilla oak; prominent but ripe tannins; all works very well. Cork. **RATING** 91 **DRINK** 2015 $25

Ross Hill Vineyard ★★★★

62 Griffin Road, via Ammerdown, Orange, NSW 2800 **REGION** Orange
T (02) 6360 0175 **F** (02) 6363 1674 **WWW**.rosshillwines.com.au **OPEN** By appt
WINEMAKER David Lowe, Stephen Doyle (Contract) **EST.** 1994 **CASES** 3000
Peter and Terri Robson began planting 12 ha of vines in 1994. Chardonnay, sauvignon blanc, merlot, cabernet sauvignon, shiraz and cabernet franc have been established on north-facing, gentle slopes at an elevation of 800m. No insecticides are used in the vineyard, the grapes are hand-picked and the vines are hand-pruned. Ross Hill also has an olive grove with Italian and Spanish varieties and a free-range organic snail production business. Exports to the UK.

ΨΨΨΨΨ **Jack's Lot Limited Release Cabernet Franc 2004** Very good colour for the variety; a powerful wine, with dark fruits, tobacco, cedar and spice aromas and flavours; still young, will open up more. One of the best cabernet francs going around. Cork. 14.5° alc.
RATING 91 **DRINK** 2015 $28
Isabelle Cabernet Franc Merlot 2004 Bright red-purple; powerful and intense blackcurrant, plum and mint, again with some slight sweet and sour characters, but the fruit line is much better. Cork. 14.5° alc. **RATING** 90 **DRINK** 2012 $24

ΨΨΨΨ **Jessica Cabernet Merlot 2004** Good colour; a curious array of sweet and sour red fruit and pickle flavours, strange given the alcohol; may sort itself out. Cork. 14.2° alc.
RATING 87 **DRINK** 2010 $18

ΨΨΨΨ **Orange Sauvignon Blanc 2005** **RATING** 85 **DRINK** Now $18

Rothbury Ridge NR

Talga Road, Rothbury, NSW 2320 **REGION** Lower Hunter Valley
T (02) 4930 7122 **F** (02) 4930 7198 **OPEN** Mon–Sat 9–5, Sun 10–5
WINEMAKER Peter Jorgensen **EST.** 1998 **CASES** 10 000
Rothbury Ridge has an extraordinarily eclectic choice of varieties planted, with between 1.2 ha and 2.4 ha each of chardonnay, semillon, verdelho, chambourcin, durif, shiraz and cabernet sauvignon. It is owned by a public company (not listed on the Stock Exchange) with an imposing array of directors, and actively markets its wines through a wine club.

Rothvale Vineyard NR

223 Deasy's Road, Pokolbin NSW 2320 **REGION** Lower Hunter Valley
T (02) 4998 7290 **F** (02) 4998 7926 **WWW**.rothvale.com.au **OPEN** 7 days 10–5
WINEMAKER Max Patton, Luke Patton **EST.** 1978 **CASES** 10 000
Owned and operated by the Patton family, headed by Max Patton, who has the fascinating academic qualifications of BVSc, MSc London, BA Hons Canterbury — the scientific part has no doubt been useful for winemaking. The wines have accumulated an impressive array of medals. Exports to China.

Roundstone Winery & Vineyard

54 Willow Bend Drive, Yarra Glen, Vic 3775 **REGION** Yarra Valley
T (03) 9730 1181 **F** (03) 9730 1151 **WWW**.roundstonewine.com.au **OPEN** Wed–Sun & public hols 10–5, or by appt
WINEMAKER John Derwin, Rob Dolan and Kate Goodman (Consultants) **EST.** 1998 **CASES** 4000
John and Lynne Derwin have moved quickly since establishing Roundstone, planting 8 ha of vineyard (half to pinot noir with a mix of the best clones), building a small winery and opening a

cellar door and restaurant on the side of a dam. The Derwins tend the vineyard, enlist the aid of friends to pick the grapes; John makes the wine with advice from Rob Dolan and Kate Goodman; Lynne is the chef and sommelier. Her pride and joy is a shearer's stove which was used at the Yarra Glen Grand Hotel for 100 years before being abandoned, and which is now at the centre of the kitchen. The restaurant has established itself as one of the best winery restaurants in the valley.

ΨΨΨΨΥ **Rubies Pinot Noir 2004** Deeper red-purple than the varietal; distinctly richer and more complex notwithstanding the same alcohol; plums, spices and good tannins. Once again, cork, not screwcap, for the better wine. Why? Cork. 13.2° alc. **RATING** 93 **DRINK** 2012 $ 28
Lightning Hill Cabernets 2003 Good hue; clean, attractive, fresh mulberry, raspberry and blackcurrant fruits; silky, supple mouthfeel; good oak. Cork. 13° alc. **RATING** 93 **DRINK** 2013 $ 25
Pinot Noir 2004 Bright colour; clean, fresh red cherry and plum fruit; sweetness on the mid-palate; nice, fine tannins lengthen the finish. Screwcap. 13.2° alc. **RATING** 91 **DRINK** 2010 $ 20
Charmed Chardonnay 2004 A complex bouquet, with obvious oak, the fruit seeming lighter than the varietal; a curious juxtaposition of closures. Cork. 13° alc. **RATING** 90 **DRINK** 2009 $ 28
Chardonnay 2004 Spotlessly clean, fruit-driven nectarine and melon; smooth and supple, good length and mouthfeel. Screwcap. 13.2° alc. **RATING** 90 **DRINK** 2010 $ 18
Gamay 2005 Vivid purple-red; very bright and lively red fruits, and a bone-dry finish; good mouthfeel and length; top example, good vintage. Screwcap. 13.1° alc. **RATING** 90 **DRINK** Now $ 18

ΨΨΨΨ **Shiraz Viognier 2004** Pleasant, medium-bodied spicy red berry fruit; supple texture; the viognier seems to dilute, rather than intensify. Cork. 13.7° alc. **RATING** 88 **DRINK** 2009 $ 25

ΨΨΨΥ **Merlot 2004** **RATING** 86 **DRINK** 2008 $ 18

Roundtable Wines

PO Box 117, East Brunswick, Vic 3057 **REGION** Warehouse
T (03) 9380 9729 **F** (03) 9380 9609 **WWW**.roundtablewines.com **OPEN** Not
WINEMAKER Nick Bickford **EST.** 2005 **CASES** 12 000
Owner/winemaker Nick Bickford has had, to put it mildly, an interesting career, starting in McLaren Vale, carousing through Roseworthy Agricultural College for a few years, then Flying Winemaking in California and Oregon, briefly settling for vintages at Dromana Estate and Tarrawarra before flying off again to winemaking in Provence, Brazil and Moldova. Oh, and a stint at the legendary McCoppins bottle shop in Melbourne. Somewhere along the way he picked up a strong belief in organic/biodynamic practices, so the grapes for the first 2 wines (grown at Canowindra) come from organic certified, low-yielding vineyards, the wines likewise accredited. Neither spends any time in oak, helping to keep the price user-friendly.

ΨΨΨΥ **Rosso Verde Shiraz 2005** **RATING** 85 **DRINK** Now $ 15
Bianco Verde Unwooded Chardonnay 2005 **RATING** 84 **DRINK** Now $ 15

Rowans Lane Wines ★★★☆

135 Rowans Lane, Allansford, Vic 3277 (postal) **REGION** Henty
T (03) 5565 1586 **F** (03) 5565 1586 **WWW**.rowanslanewines.com.au **OPEN** Not
WINEMAKER Ted Rafferty **EST.** 2003 **CASES** 370
Ted and Judy Rafferty expanded their lifetime interest in wine by establishing an experimental 0.8 ha vineyard at their Rowans Lane property in 1999, making their first Pinot Noir in 2003. This encouraged them to expand their plantings to 3.6 ha at a second site at Dennington, on the banks of the Merri River. To supplement their own production, they have purchased grapes from other leading Henty grapegrowers, each with an impressive track record. The Dennington site is visible from the Princes Highway, and close to Port Fairy; plans for a cellar door facility were with the council in April 2006.

ΨΨΨΨ **Merlot 2004** Attractive small red fruits with spice and olive nuances; good tannins/oak/extract balance. Cork. 13.1° alc. **RATING** 89 **DRINK** 2010 $ 18
Cabernet Merlot 2004 Bright, light- to medium-bodied; fresh cassis, raspberry and blackcurrant fruit; fine tannins and oak. Cork. 13.2° alc. **RATING** 89 **DRINK** 2011 $ 18

Ɣɣɣ⛢ **Pinot Noir 2004** Light, but not jammy, dry red; flavours in a varietal spectrum, simply
very light. Cork. 13.2° alc. **RATING** 86 **DRINK** Now $ 18
Botrytis Chardonnay 2003 Some botrytis evident, especially on the bouquet, with
cumquat and peach aromas, but not especially sweet or luscious; acidity in balance. Cork.
13° alc. **RATING** 86 **DRINK** Now

🍇 Rowanston on the Track ★★★

2710 Burke & Wills Track, Glenhope, Vic 3444 **REGION** Macedon Ranges
T (03) 5425 5492 **F** (03) 5425 5493 **OPEN** Fri–Sun 9–5, or by appt
WINEMAKER John Frederiksen **EST.** 2003 **CASES** 1500
John (a social worker) and Marilyn (a former teacher turned viticulturist) Frederiksen are no strangers to
grapegrowing and winemaking in the Macedon Ranges. They founded Metcalfe Valley Vineyard in 1995,
planting 5.6 ha of shiraz, going on to win gold medals at local wine shows. They sold the vineyard in early
2003, moving to their new property in the same year. It has 3.6 ha of shiraz, 1.8 ha of merlot (planted
between 1998 and 2000), and 2 ha of pinot noir and 1.3 ha of riesling (planted between 2000 and 2002).

ƔƔƔƔ **Cabernet Sauvignon 2003** Firm cassis and blackcurrant fruit; still to build complexity.
RATING 87 **DRINK** 2010 $ 25
Sparkling Shiraz 2004 Rich and full-bodied, with abundant black fruits; fairly high
dosage necessary to cover the phenolics. **RATING** 87 **DRINK** 2010 $ 30

ƔƔƔ⛢ **Shiraz 2003** **RATING** 86 **DRINK** 2010 $ 25

🍇 Rubicon ★★★★

186 Blue Range Road, Rubicon, Vic 3172 **REGION** Upper Goulburn
T (03) 9802 2174 **OPEN** By appt
WINEMAKER Robert Zagar **EST.** 2004 **CASES** 1000
Douglas Gordan and wife Lillian purchased Rubicon in 2004 intending to expand their cattle
enterprise. The property included a 5.4-ha vineyard planted in 1992 to chardonnay, pinot noir and
cabernet sauvignon by the original owners. When the sale of the grapes fell through, Douglas Gordan
decided to have the wines made. Douglas is studying viticulture/wine production at Swinburne
TAFE, and manages the vineyard using minimal intervention techniques with the help of his family.

ƔƔƔƔ⛢ **Upper Goulburn Chardonnay 2005** Interesting wine; an intense, citrussy tang to the
fruit, and a spine of acidity; has consumed the oak; long finish. Whole bunch-pressed and
barrel-fermented. Twin top. 13.5° alc. **RATING** 90 **DRINK** 2012 $ 22
Upper Goulburn Cabernet Sauvignon 2005 Brilliant purple-red; extremely youthful,
fractionally raw, cassis, spice, blackcurrant and raspberry; 12 months in French oak, yet
tasted Feb '06. Given the benefit of the doubt. Cork. 14.2° alc. **RATING** 90 **DRINK** 2015 $ 32

Rumbalara NR

Fletcher Road, Fletcher, Qld 4381 **REGION** Granite Belt
T (07) 4684 1206 **F** (07) 4684 1299 **OPEN** 7 days 9–5
WINEMAKER Wayne Beecham (Contract) **EST.** 1974 **CASES** 1500
Has produced some of the Granite Belt's finest honeyed Semillon and silky, red berry Cabernet
Sauvignon, but quality does vary. The winery incorporates a spacious restaurant, and there are also
barbecue and picnic facilities.

Rumball Sparkling Wines NR

55 Charles Street, Norwood, SA 5067 **REGION** Adelaide Zone
T (08) 8332 2761 **F** (08) 8364 0188 **WWW**.rumball.com.au **OPEN** Mon–Fri 9–5
WINEMAKER Peter Rumball **EST.** 1988 **CASES** 10 000
Peter Rumball has been making and selling sparkling wine for as long as I can remember, but has led
a somewhat peripatetic life, starting in the Clare Valley but now operating one of the larger Methode
Champenoise lines in Australia, in the Adelaide suburb of Norwood. His particular specialty has
always been Sparkling Shiraz, and was so long before it became 'flavour of the month'. Exports to the
UK, US and Japan.

Rusden Wines

NR

Magnolia Road, Tanunda, SA 5352 (postal) **REGION** Barossa Valley
T (08) 8563 2976 **F** (08) 8563 0885 **WWW**.rusdenwines.com.au **OPEN** Not
WINEMAKER Christian Canute **EST.** 1998 **CASES** 2250
The Canute family (Dennis, Christine and Christian) have been long-term grapegrowers with 14 ha of sauvignon blanc, chenin blanc, grenache, cabernet sauvignon, merlot, shiraz, mourvedre and zinfandel. While only part of the production is vinified under the Rusden label, exports have been established to all major markets.

Russet Ridge

NR

Cnr Caves Road/Riddoch Highway, Naracoorte, SA 5271 **REGION** Wrattonbully
T (08) 8762 0114 **F** (08) 8762 0341 **WWW**.orlandowines.com **OPEN** 7 days 11–4.30
WINEMAKER Nigel Logos **EST.** 2000 **CASES** 35 000
This is the former Heathfield Ridge winery, built in 1998 as a contract crush and winemaking facility for multiple clients, but purchased by Orlando in 2000. It is the only winery in the large Wrattonbully region, and also receives Orlando's Coonawarra and Padthaway grapes, and other Limestone Coast fruit.

Rusticana

NR

Lake Plains Road, Langhorne Creek, SA 5255 **REGION** Langhorne Creek
T (08) 8537 3086 **F** (08) 8537 3220 **WWW**.rusticanawines.com.au (coming soon) **OPEN** 7 days 10–5
WINEMAKER Bremerton Wines **EST.** 1998 **CASES** 2400
Brian and Anne Meakins are also owners of Newman's Horseradish, which has been on the SA market for over 80 years. Increasing demand for the horseradish forced them to move from Tea Tree Gully to Langhorne Creek in 1985. It wasn't until 1997 that they succumbed to the urging of neighbours and planted 5 ha each of shiraz and cabernet, adding 1 ha each of durif and zinfandel several years later. In a slightly unusual arrangement, the premium Black Label wines are made at Bremerton, the White Label range at the Langhorne Creek winery.

Rutherglen Estates

★★★★

Cnr Great Northern Road/Murray Valley Highway, Rutherglen, Vic 3685 **REGION** Rutherglen
T (02) 6032 7999 **F** (02) 6032 7998 **OPEN** 7 days 10–4, Tuileries Building, Drummond St, Rutherglen
WINEMAKER Nicole Esdaile **EST.** 2000 **CASES** 45 000
The Rutherglen Estates brand is an offshoot of a far larger contract crush and make business, with a winery capacity of 4000 tonnes (roughly equivalent to 280 000 cases). Rutherglen is in a declared phylloxera region, which means all the grapes grown within that region have to be vinified within it, itself a guarantee of business for ventures such as Rutherglen Estates. It also means that some of the best available material can be allocated for the brand, with an interesting mix of varieties. Exports to the UK, the US, Canada, NZ and Brazil.

ΥΥΥΥΥ **Durif 2003** Deep, dense colour; ripe, rich and dense, but not jammy or pruney. Has good structure, and savoury notes which add to the complexity and appeal. Screwcap.
RATING 93 **DRINK** 2018 $ 19.95

Marsanne 2005 A well-made wine; slate, talc, and lemon with just a touch of well-judged oak; has length and balance, good acidity to close. Screwcap. 14.5° alc. **RATING** 90
DRINK 2012 $ 19

Viognier 2003 Strongly accented apricot varietal bouquet; rich, intense apricot and cumquat palate; good acid balance. If from the Northern Rhone, would cost a fortune. Cork. **RATING** 90 **DRINK** 2010 $ 19.95

Durif 2004 Potent, powerful black fruit aromas; chocolate, licorice and blackberry marry with ripe tannins on the palate. Will evolve. Screwcap. 14.5° alc. **RATING** 90 **DRINK** 2014 $ 20

ΥΥΥΥ **The Alliance Marsanne Viognier 2005** The blend of 70% Marsanne and 30% Viognier works well, the acidity of the marsanne and the broader spectrum of fruit from the viognier combining synergistically. Clean finish and excellent value. Screwcap. 14.5° alc.
RATING 89 **DRINK** 2009 $ 16

Red 2004 Prune and red fruit confit aromas; an expectedly powerful palate, but not over the top; will age indefinitely. Shiraz/Durif. Screwcap. **RATING** 89 **DRINK** 2019 $ 12.95

Viognier 2005 A moderately intense range of fruit flavours, no one dominant; good length, though does show a twitch from the combined effect of alcohol and acidity on the finish. Screwcap. 14.5° alc. **RATING** 88 **DRINK** 2010 $ 21

Shiraz 2003 Blackcurrant, prune and licorice aromas and flavours; supple, medium-bodied palate. Nice wine. Screwcap. **RATING** 88 **DRINK** 2012 $ 17.95

The Reunion 2005 Bright, fresh juicy fruit style; excellent restraint with tannins; lively and good value. Mourvedre (60%)/Shiraz (20%)/Grenache (20%). Screwcap. 14.5° alc. **RATING** 88 **DRINK** Now $ 15

The Reunion 2004 Light purple-red; strongly accented sweet fruit (not sugar); minimal tannins; like a super-charged Rose; brasserie lunch style. Screwcap. **RATING** 87 **DRINK** Now $ 14.95

Sangiovese 2004 Typical pale colour; spice, rose petal and cherry aromas; spicy tannins to close and give length. Screwcap. **RATING** 87 **DRINK** 2008 $ 17.95

ŶŶŶŶ **Nebbiolo 2004** **RATING** 84 **DRINK** Now $ 17.95

ŶŶŶ **Rose 2003** **RATING** 83 $ 14.95

Rymill Coonawarra   ★★★☆

The Riddoch Run Vineyards, Riddoch Highway, Coonawarra, SA 5263 **REGION** Coonawarra
T (08) 8736 5001 **F** (08) 8736 5040 **WWW**.rymill.com.au **OPEN** 7 days 10–5
WINEMAKER John Innes, Sandrine Gimon **EST.** 1974 **CASES** 50 000
The Rymills are descendants of John Riddoch and have long owned some of the finest Coonawarra soil, upon which they have grown grapes since 1970; present plantings are 150 ha. The output from the modern winery is substantial, the quality dependable rather than exciting. Quite why this should be so is an interesting question without an obvious answer. Exports to all major markets.

ŶŶŶŶŶ **Shiraz 2002** A medium-bodied mix of sweet black fruits and more spicy, savoury notes, but by no means sweet and sour; good tannin, structure and oak; nice wine. Cork. 14.5° alc. **RATING** 90 **DRINK** 2012 $ 23

ŶŶŶŶ **Sauvignon Blanc 2005** Clean, fresh, zesty and lively; light-bodied with a touch of passionfruit; shows the low alcohol to advantage. Screwcap. 12° alc. **RATING** 89 **DRINK** Now $ 17

ŶŶŶŶ **Rose 2005** **RATING** 86 **DRINK** Now $ 17

Cabernet Sauvignon 2002 Savoury, herbal, green bean, spicy cabernet from the cool vintage; the limitations lie in the vineyard, not the winery. Cork. **RATING** 86 **DRINK** 2009 $ 28

MC² 2003 Screwcap. **RATING** 86 **DRINK** Now $ 17

S Kidman Wines   ★★★☆

Riddoch Highway, Coonawarra, SA 5263 **REGION** Coonawarra
T (08) 8736 5071 **F** (08) 8736 5070 **WWW**.kidmanwines.com.au **OPEN** 7 days 10–5
WINEMAKER John Innes (Contract) **EST.** 1984 **CASES** 8000
One of the district pioneers, with a 16-ha estate vineyard which is now fully mature. Limited retail distribution in Melbourne and Adelaide; exports through Australian Prestige Wines.

ŶŶŶŶŶ **Coonawarra Cabernet Sauvignon 2001** Medium-bodied; starting to move towards the secondary phase of its development; blackcurrant with notes of earth, leaf and cigar box; fine tannins, good length. Cork. 13.5° alc. **RATING** 90 **DRINK** 2011 $ 20

ŶŶŶŶ **Coonawarra Riesling 2005** Aromatic bouquet; ripe lime juice flavours; just a fraction heavy. **RATING** 87 **DRINK** 2008 $ 14

Coonawarra Sauvignon Blanc 2005 Clean; a very light-bodied mix of tropical and more grassy components. Well-made. Screwcap. 12° alc. **RATING** 87 **DRINK** Now $ 15

Sabella Vineyards   NR

PO Box 229, McLaren Vale, SA 5171 **REGION** McLaren Vale
T 0416 361 369 **F** (08) 8323 8270 **OPEN** Not
WINEMAKER Michael Petrucci **EST.** 1999 **CASES** 450
Giuseppe (Joe) Petrucci was born in the Molise region of Italy, where his family were farmers. His father migrated to Australia in 1960, the rest of the family following him in 1966. In 1976 Joe and wife Rosa (and their children) moved to McLaren Vale where they purchased their first vineyard in McMurtrie Road. Over the years their vineyards have increased from 10 ha to 44 ha, their grapes sold to various leading wineries. In 1999 they decided to keep some grapes back for release under the Sabella label; Sabella derives from a pseudonym given to the Petrucci name 6 generations ago.

Saddlers Creek   NR

Marrowbone Road, Pokolbin, NSW 2320 **REGION** Lower Hunter Valley
T (02) 4991 1770 **F** (02) 4991 2482 **WWW**.saddlerscreekwines.com.au **OPEN** 7 days 9–5
WINEMAKER John Johnstone **EST.** 1989 **CASES** 20 000
Made an impressive entrance to the district with consistently full-flavoured and rich wines, and has continued on in much the same vein, with good wines across the spectrum. Exports to Canada, NZ and Mauritius.

St Aidan   ★★★

754 Ferguson Road, Dardanup, WA 6236 **REGION** Geographe
T (08) 9728 3007 **F** (08) 9728 3006 **WWW**.saintaidan.com **OPEN** Mon–Fri 10–3, w'ends & public hols 10–5
WINEMAKER Mark Messenger (Contract) **EST.** 1996 **CASES** 1500
Phil and Mary Smith purchased their property at Dardanup in 1991, 20 mins' drive from the Bunbury hospitals for which Phil Smith works. They first ventured into Red Globe table grapes, planting 1 ha in 1994–5, followed by 1 ha of mandarins and oranges. With this experience, and with Mary completing a TAFE viticulture course, they extended their horizons by planting 1 ha each of cabernet sauvignon and chardonnay in 1997. A little muscat followed in 2001.

ŸŸŸŸ   **Cabernet Sauvignon 2001** Holding hue well; medium-bodied; good blackcurrant varietal fruit with slightly earthy tones; balanced tannins. Cork. 14° alc. **RATING** 88 **DRINK** 2011 $ 17
         Sister Series Sybil Unwooded Chardonnay 2005 Light-bodied; tangy grapefruit and melon; crisp, clean finish. Screwcap. 13.5° alc. **RATING** 87 **DRINK** 2008 $ 14

ŸŸŸŸ   **Chardonnay 2004** Light- to medium-bodied; gently sweet nectarine fruit, with the faintest whisk of oak. Screwcap. 13.5° alc. **RATING** 86 **DRINK** 2008 $ 20
         Sister Series XS Rose 2004 RATING 86 **DRINK** Now $ 14
         Cabernet Sauvignon 2003 RATING 85 **DRINK** 2009 $ 17

ŸŸŸ   **Sister Series Myra Muscat Chardonnay 2005 RATING** 83 $ 14

St Anne's Vineyards   NR

Cnr Perricoota Road/24 Lane, Moama, NSW 2731 **REGION** Perricoota
T (03) 5480 0099 **F** (03) 5480 0077 **OPEN** 7 days 9–5, also at Garrards Lane, Myrniong
WINEMAKER Richard McLean **EST.** 1972 **CASES** 18 000
St Anne's is by far the most active member of the newly registered Perricoota region. Richard McLean has established 80 ha of estate vineyards, with another 120 ha of grower vineyards to draw upon. Shiraz, cabernet sauvignon, grenache and mourvedre account for over 75% of the plantings, but there is a spread of the usual white wines and few red exotics. The wines are all competently made.

Saint Derycke's Wood Winery   NR

Cnr Greenhills Road/Joadja Road, Berrima, NSW 2576 **REGION** Southern Highlands
T (02) 4878 5439 **F** (02) 4878 5133 **WWW**.saintderyckeswood.com.au **OPEN** W'ends & public hols 10–5, or by appt
WINEMAKER Sean O'Regan **EST.** 1995 **CASES** NA
Sue and John Rappell own the intriguingly-named winery, one of the many newcomers to the Southern Highlands region. He has planted 6.5 ha to riesling, chardonnay, marsanne, pinot noir, cabernet sauvignon, merlot, shiraz and cabernet franc and the wines are made onsite — except, one would imagine, the fortified wines.

St Gregory's   NR

Bringalbert South Road, Bringalbert South via Apsley, Vic 3319 **REGION** Henty
T (03) 5586 5225 **OPEN** By appt
WINEMAKER Gregory Flynn **EST.** 1983 **CASES** NFP
Unique Port-only operation selling its limited production direct to enthusiasts (mainly by mailing list).

St Hallett   ★★★★★

St Hallett Road, Tanunda, SA 5352 **REGION** Barossa Valley
T (08) 8563 7000 **F** (08) 8563 7001 **WWW**.sthallett.com.au **OPEN** 7 days 10–5
WINEMAKER Stuart Blackwell, Di Ferguson, Matt Gant **EST.** 1944 **CASES** 100 000
Nothing succeeds like success. St Hallett merged with Tatachilla to form Banksia Wines, which was then acquired by NZ's thirsty Lion Nathan. St Hallett understandably continues to ride the Shiraz fashion wave, but all its wines are honest and well priced. Exports to the UK, the US, Canada, Hong Kong and Japan.

ΥΥΥΥΥ **Old Block Barossa Valley Shiraz 2002** Very good colour; excellent texture, structure and length, befitting the '02 vintage; plum, blackberry, dark chocolate and a touch of mocha oak; supple, silky and harmonious. Screwcap. **RATING** 96 **DRINK** 2015 $ 75
Eden Valley Riesling 2005 Attractive tropical lime aromas; generous palate, with rich passionfruit and lime juice flavours; very good length and finish. Gold medal Sydney Wine Show '06. Screwcap. **RATING** 94 **DRINK** 2010 $ 19

ΥΥΥΥΥ **Poacher's Blend 2005** Attractive gooseberry and tropical fruit aromas; fills the mouth; brilliantly balanced; seductive. Semillon/Sauvignon Blanc. Screwcap. **RATING** 91
DRINK Now $ 12.50
Faith Barossa Valley Shiraz 2004 Bright colour; attractive juicy berry fruits; good oak and tannin support. Screwcap. 14° alc. **RATING** 90 **DRINK** 2010 $ 19
Barossa GST 2004 Bright colour; fragrant stewed plum, black cherry and spice aromas; a lively palate with juicy berry fruit. Cork. **RATING** 90 **DRINK** 2008 $ 21

St Huberts   ★★★★☆

St Huberts Road, Coldstream, Vic 3770 **REGION** Yarra Valley
T (03) 9739 1118 **F** (03) 9739 1096 **WWW**.sthuberts.com.au **OPEN** Mon–Fri 9–5, w'ends 10.30–5.30
WINEMAKER Shavaughn Wells **EST.** 1966 **CASES** 15 000
A once famous winery (in the context of the Yarra Valley) which is now part of Beringer Blass. The wines are very reliable, and the cellar door — if somewhat humble — is well situated.

ΥΥΥΥΥ **Yarra Valley Sauvignon Blanc 2005** Clean and fresh; attractive passionfruit and gooseberry sustained by lively, lemony acidity and refreshingly low alcohol. Screwcap. 11.5° alc. **RATING** 92 **DRINK** Now $ 23.99
Yarra Valley Cabernet Merlot 2004 Good colour; medium-bodied, luscious cassis and blackcurrant mix; fine, soft but lingering tannins. Cork. 13.5° alc. **RATING** 92 **DRINK** 2014 $ 23.99
Yarra Valley Roussanne 2004 Fresh, lively lemon/mineral/green apple aromas and flavours; may well age with distinction. Screwcap. 12.5° alc. **RATING** 91 **DRINK** 2010 $ 24.99

Yarra Valley Cabernet Merlot 2003 Attractive juicy berry fruit; cassis, raspberry and blackcurrant; lively mouthfeel and finish. Best soon. Cork. 13.5° alc. **RATING** 91 **DRINK** 2009 $ 26.99

Yarra Valley Chardonnay 2004 Super-restrained, light-bodied, elegant wine, partly the function of vintage, towards Petit Chablis in style. Cork. 13.5° alc. **RATING** 90 **DRINK** 2008 $ 24.99

Yarra Valley Cabernet Sauvignon 2003 Well-made; medium-bodied, fresh cassis and blackcurrant fruit; fine tannins, good finish and aftertaste. Cork. 13° alc. **RATING** 90 **DRINK** 2012 $ 26.99

ＹＹＹＹ **Yarra Valley Chardonnay 2005** Light straw-green; light-bodied and gentle melon and stone fruit; the oak a little rough on the finish. Screwcap. 13.5° alc. **RATING** 88 **DRINK** 2008 $ 24.99

Yarra Valley Pinot Noir 2004 Medium red, fractionally opaque; a pleasant wine with fair varietal character — spice, forest and red fruits — but not particularly intense. Screwcap. 13° alc. **RATING** 88 **DRINK** 2009 $ 25.99

St Ignatius Vineyard ★★★

Sunraysia Highway, Avoca, Vic 3467 **REGION** Pyrenees
T (03) 5465 3542 **F** (03) 5465 3542 **WWW**.stignatiusvineyard.com.au **OPEN** 7 days 10–5
WINEMAKER Enrique Diaz **EST.** 1992 **CASES** 2000
Silvia and husband Enrique Diaz began establishing their vineyard, winery and restaurant complex in 1992. They have planted 8 ha of shiraz, chardonnay, cabernet sauvignon, sauvignon blanc, merlot and sangiovese. The vineyard has received 3 primary production awards. Exports to the UK.

ＹＹＹＹ **Hangmans Gully Chardonnay 2005** Light- to medium-bodied; clean, gentle peach fruit with a good streak of mineral, but does finish slightly short. Screwcap. 13° alc. **RATING** 87 **DRINK** 2010 $ 20

ＹＹＹＹ **Hangmans Gully Shiraz 2004** **RATING** 86 **DRINK** 2009 $ 25
Hangmans Gully Cabernet Sauvignon 2004 **RATING** 84 **DRINK** 2008 $ 25

St John's Road ★★★★★

PO Box 286, Rundle Mall, SA 5000 **REGION** Barossa Valley
T (08) 8342 9070 **F** (08) 8342 9007 **WWW**.stjohnsroad.com **OPEN** Not
WINEMAKER Veritas, Turkey Flat **EST.** 2002 **CASES** 3500
Martin Rawlinson (with a background of politics and defence) and wife Vivienne (journalism and music) were running a small B&B (equivalent) in France surrounded by vineyards. One thing led to another, and in 2002 they purchased a small vineyard in the Eden Valley, planted to 30-year-old riesling on lean, rocky soils. The following year they purchased a much larger property at Greenock, established by the Helbig family in the 1880s, but subsequently extended with other varieties. In all, they had 24 ha of riesling, semillon, chardonnay, grenache, cabernet sauvignon and shiraz. Out of the blue Martin was diagnosed with motor neurone disease, dying in March 2005. Says Vivienne, 'I am grateful that Martin had a chance to see and taste the realisation of his dream with the bottling of our 2003 Julia (named after their young daughter) and the other wines of the 2004 vintage'.

ＹＹＹＹＹ **Peace of Eden Riesling 2005** Bright green-yellow; highly fragrant, with strong regional essence of lime juice flavour; balance and alcohol excellent; totally delicious. Eden Valley. Screwcap. 11.5° alc. **RATING** 95 **DRINK** 2015 $ 20

Julia Shiraz 2004 Slightly more purple than Blood & Courage; while also medium-bodied, has excellent intensity, focus and length, albeit in the same flavour spectrum. Controlled alcohol and oak. Screwcap. 14.5° alc. **RATING** 94 **DRINK** 2019 $ 30

ＹＹＹＹＹ **Blood & Courage Shiraz 2004** Medium red-purple; attractive medium-bodied red and black fruits, with some spice and a touch of mocha/vanilla oak. Screwcap. 14.5° alc. **RATING** 93 $ 21

ＹＹＹＹ **The Stockman Old Vine Chardonnay 2005** Medium-bodied; ripe stone fruit and a hint of fig; abundant flavour though fractionally sweet, possibly/probably due to the alcohol. Screwcap. 14.1° alc. **RATING** 88 **DRINK** 2009 $ 18

TTTT First Eleven Semillon 2004 Traditional Barossa style, full-bodied, heavy and somewhat phenolic. The polar opposite of the Eden Valley riesling. Screwcap. 13.5° alc. RATING 86 DRINK Now $18

Julia Shiraz 2003 RATING 86 DRINK 2008 $30

St Leonards Vineyard ★★★☆

St Leonards Road, Wahgunyah, Vic 3687 REGION Rutherglen
T (02) 6033 1004 F (02) 6033 3636 WWW.stleonardswine.com.au OPEN 7 days 10–5
WINEMAKER Dan Crane EST. 1860 CASES 20 000
An old favourite, relaunched in late 1997 with a range of three premium wines cleverly marketed through a singularly attractive cellar door and bistro at the historic winery on the banks of the Murray. All Saints and St Leonards were wholly owned by Peter Brown, tragically killed in a road accident in late 2005. Ownership has passed to Peter Brown's children, Eliza, Angela and Nicholas, and it is the intention to keep the business in the family.

TTTTT Dry Orange Muscat 2005 A quiet bouquet, but opens with a lovely, flowery, gently grapey palate; perfect sugar/acid balance. Screwcap. 11.9° alc. RATING 90 DRINK Now $16.50

TTTT Wahgunyah Shiraz 2004 A very, very unusual wine, the '04 Shiraz re-fermented on the skins of 2005 Vintage Port. The wine is not dense, but sweetness ex the 17° alcohol is evident. For the insatiably curious. Cork. RATING 89 DRINK 2009 $49

TTTT Wahgunyah Chardonnay 2004 RATING 86 DRINK Now $29
Shiraz Viognier 2004 RATING 86 DRINK Now $25
Pinot Noir 2004 RATING 85 DRINK Now $21.50
Wahgunyah Sparkling Shiraz NV RATING 85 DRINK Now $27.50

St Mary's ★★★

V & A Lane, via Coonawarra, SA 5277 REGION Penola
T (08) 8736 6070 F (08) 8736 6045 WWW.stmaryswines.com OPEN 7 days 10–4
WINEMAKER Barry Mulligan EST. 1986 CASES 4000
The Mulligan family has lived in the Penola/Coonawarra region since 1909. In 1937 a 250-ha property 15 km west of Penola, including an 80-ha ridge of terra rossa over limestone, was purchased for grazing. The ridge was cleared, the remainder of the property was untouched and is now a private wildlife sanctuary. In 1986 Barry and Glenys Mulligan planted shiraz and cabernet sauvignon on the ridge, followed by merlot in the early 1990s. Exports to the UK, the US, Canada, Singapore, Belgium and Switzerland.

TTTT House Block Penola Cabernet Sauvignon 2002 Very lean and minty, very much a child of the cool '02 vintage, but does have length. Cork. 14° alc. RATING 87 DRINK 2009 $25

St Matthias ★★★☆

113 Rosevears Drive, Rosevears, Tas 7277 REGION Northern Tasmania
T (03) 6330 1700 F (03) 6330 1975 WWW.moorilla.com.au OPEN 7 days 10–5
WINEMAKER Michael Glover (former) EST. 1983 CASES 16 000
After an uncomfortable period in the wilderness following the sale of the vineyard to Moorilla Estate, and the disposal of the wine made by the previous owners under the St Matthias label, Moorilla has re-introduced the label, and markets a full range of competitively priced wines which are in fact made at Moorilla Estate.

TTTTT Vintage Brut 2003 Straw-pink; a brisk, crisp minerally style with some depth to the back-palate before a long, fresh finish. RATING 90 DRINK Now $24

TTTT Pinot Noir 2004 RATING 86 DRINK 2008 $19

St Michael's Vineyard ★★★☆

503 Pook Road, Toolleen, Vic 3521 **REGION** Heathcote
T (03) 5433 2580 **F** (03) 5433 2612 **OPEN** By appt
WINEMAKER Mick Cann **EST.** 1994 **CASES** 300
Owner/winemaker Mick Cann has established just over 4 ha of vines on the famous deep red Cambrian clay loam on the east face of the Mt Camel Range. Planting began in 1994, continued in 1995, with a further extension in 2000. Shiraz (2.5 ha), merlot (1.25 ha) and petit verdot (0.3 ha) are the main varieties, with a smattering of cabernet sauvignon and semillon. Part of the production is sold to David Anderson of Wild Duck Creek, the remainder made by Mick Cann, using open fermentation, hand-plunging of skins and a basket press, a low-technology but highly effective way of making high-quality red wine.

ᵞᵞᵞᵞᵞ **Personal Reserve Heathcote Shiraz 2004** Good colour; medium-bodied; sweet cherry, plum and blackberry fruit; ripe tannins and good oak. Cork. 14.5° alc. **RATING** 93 **DRINK** 2015 $ 30

ᵞᵞᵞᵞ **Personal Reserve Heathcote Petit Verdot 2004** Vibrant purple-red; very nearly makes the big time, but the pH is too low/the acid too high for more than a brief taste. Cork. 13.3° alc. **RATING** 86 **DRINK** 2010 $ 30
Heathcote Merlot 2003 **RATING** 84 **DRINK** 2008 $ 30

St Petrox NR

352 Luskintyre Road, Luskintyre, NSW 2321 **REGION** Lower Hunter Valley
T (02) 4930 6120 **F** (02) 4930 6070 **OPEN** Not
WINEMAKER Peter Jorgensen **EST.** 2000 **CASES** 3000
Peter Jorgensen has established 4 ha of vines, choosing to plant two varieties ignored by all others in the Hunter Valley: mondeuse and durif. If recognised at all, most people will associate mondeuse with Brown Brothers and northeast Victoria, but it is a rarely propagated yet interesting red varietal.

St Regis ★★★★☆

35 Princes Highway, Waurn Ponds, Vic 3216 **REGION** Geelong
T (03) 5241 8406 **F** (03) 5241 8946 **www**.stregis.com.au **OPEN** 7 days 11–6
WINEMAKER Peter Nicol **EST.** 1997 **CASES** 600
St Regis is a family-run boutique winery focusing on estate-grown Shiraz, Chardonnay and Pinot Noir. Each year the harvest is hand-picked by 40 people (members of the family and friends), with Peter Nicol (assisted by wife Viv) the executive, onsite winemaker. While Peter has a technical background in horticulture, he is a self-taught winemaker, and has taught himself well.

ᵞᵞᵞᵞᵞ **Wild Reserve Pinot Noir 2004** Good colour; a very powerful wine with plum, forest floor and spice; excellent balance, line and length; likewise varietal definition. **RATING** 95 **DRINK** 2010 $ 30

ᵞᵞᵞᵞ **The Reg Shiraz 2004** More structure, mouthfeel and extract than the varietal; similar spicy/peppery black cherry fruit, and more apparent oak. Screwcap. 14.8° alc. **RATING** 93 **DRINK** 2017 $ 30
Geelong Shiraz 2004 Good colour; medium-bodied, supple, black cherry and spice; fine tannins, good length. Screwcap. 14.8° alc. **RATING** 91 **DRINK** 2015 $ 20
Geelong Pinot Noir 2004 Fragrant and bright plummy/spicy fruit; attractive texture and structure. **RATING** 90 **DRINK** 2009 $ 20

ᵞᵞᵞᵞ **Geelong Chardonnay 2005** Notwithstanding the screwcap, very developed yellow-green; rich, full-bodied flavours; both the colour and mouthfeel/weight suggest skin contact pre-fermentation. Screwcap. 14° alc. **RATING** 88 **DRINK** 2008 $ 20

Salem Bridge Wines

NR

Salem Bridge Road, Lower Hermitage, SA 5131 **REGION** Adelaide Hills
T (08) 8380 5240 **F** (08) 8380 5240 **OPEN** Not
WINEMAKER Barry Miller **EST.** 1989 **CASES** 300
Barry Miller acquired the 45-ha Salem Bridge property in 1988. A little under 2 ha of cabernet franc
were planted in 1989, and Cabernet Franc was the only commercial release prior to 1999. However, a
further 14 ha have been planted to cabernet sauvignon, shiraz and merlot, with a Shiraz and
Cabernet Sauvignon release in the pipeline. The core business is contract growing, with only 10% of
the production vinified for Salem Bridge.

Salena Estate

NR

Bookpurnong Road, Loxton, SA 5333 **REGION** Riverland
T (08) 8584 1333 **F** (08) 8584 1388 **WWW**.salenaestate.com.au **OPEN** Mon–Fri 8.30–4.30
WINEMAKER Robert Patynowski **EST.** 1998 **CASES** 480 000
This business, established in 1998, encapsulates the hectic rate of growth across the entire Australian
wine industry. Its 1998 crush was 300 tonnes, and by 2001 it was processing around its present level
7000 tonnes. This was in part produced from over 200 ha of estate vineyards, supplemented by
grapes purchased from other growers. It is the venture of Bob and Sylvia Franchitto, the estate being
named after their daughter Salena. Exports to the US, the UK and other major markets.

Salitage

★★★★☆

Vasse Highway, Pemberton, WA 6260 **REGION** Pemberton
T (08) 9776 1771 **F** (08) 9776 1772 **WWW**.salitage.com.au **OPEN** 7 days 10–4
WINEMAKER Patrick Coutts, Greg Kelly **EST.** 1989 **CASES** 20 000
Salitage is the showpiece of Pemberton. If it had failed to live up to expectations, it is a fair bet the
same fate would have befallen the whole of the Pemberton region. The quality and style of Salitage
did vary substantially, presumably in response to vintage conditions and yields, but since 1999 seems
to have found its way, with a succession of attractive wines. Exports to the UK, the US and other
major markets.

Chardonnay 2004 A lovely wine; stone fruit and citrus drive both the bouquet and palate,
French oak merely a backdrop; long, clean and perfectly balanced finish. Screwcap.
13° alc. **RATING** 95 **DRINK** 2014 $ 33

Pemberton Sauvignon Blanc 2005 Clean, fresh and well-balanced, ranging through
herb/citrus to tropical/passionfruit; light-bodied, but focused. Screwcap. 12.5° alc.
RATING 91 **DRINK** Now $ 20
Treehouse Sauvignon Blanc 2005 Attractive tropical bouquet, and similar fruit on the
palate, bolstered by a touch of sweetness. Screwcap. 12.5° alc. **RATING** 91 **DRINK** Now $ 17
Pemberton Unwooded Chardonnay 2005 Fragrant, cool-grown nectarine and grapefruit
palate with flavour and length; very good example of the style. Screwcap. 13.5° alc.
RATING 90 **DRINK** 2009 $ 19

Rose 2005 Full-on salmon; dry Tavel style; outside the mainstream. Screwcap. **RATING** 87
DRINK Now $ 18
Treehouse Pinot Noir 2004 Light-bodied; typical savoury/foresty style, with a nice twist
of spice on the finish. Screwcap. 13° alc. **RATING** 87 **DRINK** 2008 $ 20
Treehouse Shiraz 2003 Fresh, light-bodied, driven by cherry and raspberry fruit flavours;
minimal tannins and oak. Screwcap. 13° alc. **RATING** 87 **DRINK** 2008 $ 20

Treehouse Chardonnay 2005 **RATING** 86 **DRINK** Now $ 17
Treehouse Chardonnay Verdelho 2005 **RATING** 86 **DRINK** Now $ 17
Treehouse Cabernet Merlot 2003 **RATING** 85 **DRINK** Now $ 20

Sally's Paddock ★★★★☆

Redbank Winery, 1 Sally's Lane, Redbank, Vic 3478 **REGION** Pyrenees
T (03) 5467 7255 **F** (03) 5467 3478 **WWW**.sallyspaddock.com.au **OPEN** Mon–Sat 9–5, Sun 10–5
WINEMAKER Neill Robb **EST.** 1973 **CASES** 8000
The Redbank brand and stocks (Long Paddock, etc) were acquired by the Hill Smith Family
Vineyards (aka Yalumba) several years ago. The winery and surrounding vineyard which produces
Sally's Paddock were retained by Neill and Sally Robb, and continue to produced (and sell) this
single-vineyard, multi-varietal red wine and the new Sally's Hill range.

ᵀᵀᵀᵀᵀ **Sally's Hill Shiraz 2004** Good purple-red; dense, ripe blackberry fruit with nuances of
spice and licorice; good oak tannins; textured, plush finish. Cork. 14° alc. **RATING** 93
DRINK 2015 **$** 20
Sally's Hill Cabernet 2004 Good, deep purple-red; clean, rich blackcurrant fruit; fine,
gently earthy, savoury cabernet tannins; nice oak. Cork. 13.5° alc. **RATING** 93 **DRINK** 2015
$ 20
2004 Sally's Paddock Similar colour to the Cabernet; an elegant wine with cassis,
blackcurrant and spice backed by lingering, fine, savoury tannins; good oak. Cork.
13.5° alc. **RATING** 93 **DRINK** 2015 **$** 47

ᵀᵀᵀᵀ **2003 Sally's Paddock RATING** 86 **DRINK** 2009 **$** 47
Sally's Hill Pinot Noir 2005 RATING 84 **DRINK** 2009 **$** 20

Salomon Estate ★★★★☆

PO Box 829, McLaren Vale, SA 5171 **REGION** Currency Creek
T 0417 470 590 **F** (08) 8323 8668 **OPEN** Not
WINEMAKER Bert Salomon, Boar's Rock (Mike Farmilo) **EST.** 1997 **CASES** 7000
Bert Salomon is an Austrian winemaker with a long-established family winery in the Kremstal
region, not far from Vienna. He became acquainted with Australia during his time with import
company Schlumberger in Vienna; he was the first to import Australian wines (Penfolds) into
Austria in the mid-1980s, and later became head of the Austrian Wine Bureau. He was so taken by
Adelaide that he moved his family there for the first few months each year, sending his young
children to school and setting in place an Australian red winemaking venture. He has now retired
from the Bureau, and is a full-time travelling winemaker, running the family winery in the northern
hemisphere vintage, and overseeing the making of the Salomon Estates wines at Boar's Rock in the
first half of the year. The circle closes as Mike Farmilo, former Penfolds chief red winemaker, now
makes Salomon Estate wines.

ᵀᵀᵀᵀᵀ **Finniss River Shiraz 2003** Good hue; medium-bodied, elegant style with a range of black
spicy fruits and fine, lingering tannins; excellent finish and aftertaste. Cork. 14° alc.
RATING 94 **DRINK** 2014 **$** 35

ᵀᵀᵀᵀ **Norwood Shiraz Cabernet Merlot 2004** Bright purple-red; light- to medium-bodied
cassis/plum/blackcurrant fruit with good texture and structure; a touch of bitter chocolate
to close. Cork. 14° alc. **RATING** 90 **DRINK** 2011 **$** 20
Finniss River Cabernet Merlot 2003 Savoury, spicy nuances; good structure and weight
to the medium-bodied palate; merlot seems to be an important part, some black olive
flavours; fine tannins. Cork. 14° alc. **RATING** 90 **DRINK** 2012 **$** 35

Saltram ★★★★★

Nuriootpa Road, Angaston, SA 5355 **REGION** Barossa Valley
T (08) 8561 0200 **F** (08) 8561 0232 **WWW**.saltramwines.com.au **OPEN** Mon–Fri 9–5, w'ends & public
hols 10–5
WINEMAKER Nigel Dolan **EST.** 1859 **CASES** NFP
There is no doubt that Saltram has taken giant strides towards regaining the reputation it held 30 or
so years ago. Under Nigel Dolan's stewardship, grape sourcing has come back to the Barossa Valley
for the flagship wines, a fact of which he is rightly proud. The red wines, in particular, have enjoyed
great show success over the past few years, with No. 1 Shiraz, Mamre Brook and Metala leading the
charge. Exports to the UK, the US and other major markets.

♥♥♥♥♥ **Pepperjack Barossa Shiraz 2004** A seductive, succulent red wine, the viognier
component working its full magic. The first Shiraz Viognier under the Pepperjack brand.
Gold medal Sydney Wine Show '06. **RATING** 94 **DRINK** 2015
No. 1 Shiraz 2003 Very powerful, dense and concentrated; interesting spice, chocolate
and licorice nuances to the core of blackberry fruit; good oak and tannin management;
great outcome for the vintage. Screwcap. **RATING** 94 **DRINK** 2018
The Eighth Maker Barossa Shiraz 2002 Excellent hue, still purple-red; a prime example
of a great, cool vintage in the Barossa; tight, blackberry fruit; long, lingering tannins. Cork.
RATING 94 **DRINK** 2017

♥♥♥♥♡ **Pepperjack Barossa Shiraz 2004** Good colour; attractive medium-bodied wine;
blackberry, plum and a touch of chocolate; good oak and tannins. Cork. 14° alc. **RATING** 93
DRINK 2015
Mamre Brook Barossa Shiraz 2003 Extremely powerful black fruits and oak, just
avoiding going over the top; long and convincing. Archetypal Barossa Shiraz. Gold medal
National Wine Show '05. Cork. **RATING** 93 **DRINK** 2013 $23
No. 1 Shiraz 2002 A big, rich and dense mix of blackberry, licorice and chocolate
supported by appropriate oak and tannins. Heroic style. Probably needs more time to
show its best. **RATING** 93 **DRINK** 2022 $65
Pepperjack Cabernet Sauvignon 2004 Bright, deep colour; medium- to full-bodied,
with excellent blackcurrant cabernet fruit, particularly so for the Barossa; fruit, oak and
tannins all integrated and balanced. Cork. 14° alc. **RATING** 93 **DRINK** 2015
Metala Langhorne Creek Shiraz Cabernet 2003 Stylish, harmonious, medium-bodied
wine; gentle blackberry and blackcurrant fruit; supple mouthfeel, good oak/extract.
Quality cork. 14.5° alc. **RATING** 92 **DRINK** 2013 $17.99
The Eighth Maker Barossa Shiraz 2001 Starting to develop secondary earthy aromas
and flavours along with a dusting of chocolate and spice; well ripened tannins. Daunting
price. Cork. **RATING** 91 **DRINK** 2011 $180
Mr Pickwick's Limited Release Particular Port NV Lighter, sweeter and perhaps finer
than others in its class; cleansing finish and aftertaste. Cork. 18° alc. **RATING** 91 **DRINK** Now

♥♥♥♥ **Pepperjack Barossa Valley Grenache Rose 2005** Vivid fuchsia-purple; the naturally
sweet fruit of grenache works very well; clean and bright, with a dry finish. Screwcap.
14° alc. **RATING** 89 **DRINK** Now
Pepperjack Barossa Valley Shiraz Grenache Mourvedre 2004 Sweet, ripe (not overripe) black and red fruits; a juicy contribution from the grenache. Cork. 14° alc. **RATING** 89
DRINK 2011
Mamre Brook Barossa Cabernet Sauvignon 2003 Clean, ripe, sweet blackcurrant/cassis
fruit is off-set by earthy/savoury tannins; plenty of structure; rump steak style. Cork.
RATING 89 **DRINK** 2012 $23
Mamre Brook Barossa Valley Chardonnay 2004 Nicely balanced white peach fruit and
oak; flavourful, though not particularly long. Screwcap. 13° alc. **RATING** 88 **DRINK** 2009
$19

♥♥♥♡ **Pepperjack Barossa Valley Viognier 2005** **RATING** 85 **DRINK** Now

Sam Miranda of King Valley ★★★☆

Cnr Snow Road/King Valley Road, Oxley, Vic 3678 **REGION** King Valley
T (03) 5727 3888 **F** (03) 5727 3851 **OPEN** 7 days 10–5
WINEMAKER Sam Miranda **EST.** 2004 **CASES** 12 000
Sam Miranda, grandson of Francesco Miranda, joined the family business in 1991, striking out on his
own in 2004 after Miranda Wines was purchased by McGuigan Simeon. The High Plains Vineyard is
in the Myrrhee district of the Upper King Valley at an altitude of 450m; 13 ha of vines are
supplemented by some purchased grapes. In July 2005 Sam Miranda purchased the Symphonia
Wines business, and intends to keep its identity intact and separate from the Sam Miranda brand.

ΥΥΥΥ **High Plains Merlot 2004** Light- to medium-bodied; fresh, clean red fruits, spice and black olive; fine, ripe tannins; subtle oak. Cork. 13.8° alc. **RATING** 89 **DRINK** 2009 $18.50
High Plains Cabernet Shiraz 2004 Bright colour; an attractive mix of cassis, raspberry and blackcurrant on a medium-bodied palate; long, clean finish. Cork. 13° alc. **RATING** 89 **DRINK** 2010 $18.50
High Plains King Valley Durif 2004 Much more approachable and balanced than many; attractive juicy dark fruits; good balance. Cork. 14.5° alc. **RATING** 89 **DRINK** 2008 $18
High Plains Sauvignon Blanc 2005 Light, clean and fresh, with touches of tropical fruit; a neatly balanced flick of residual sugar against good acidity; easy access style. Screwcap. 12.5° alc. **RATING** 87 **DRINK** Now $16

ΥΥΥΫ **High Plains Traminer Riesling 2005** **RATING** 86 **DRINK** Now $16
High Plains King Valley Rose 2005 **RATING** 86 **DRINK** Now $17
High Plains Late Harvest Verdelho 2005 **RATING** 86 **DRINK** Now $20

Samson Hill Estate

NR

360 Eltham–Yarra Glen Road, Kangaroo Ground, Vic 3097 **REGION** Yarra Valley
T (03) 9712 0715 **F** (03) 9712 0815 **OPEN** 7 days 10–6
WINEMAKER Steven Sampson, Pago Sampson **EST.** 1997 **CASES** 3000
In a region noted for its spectacular scenery, Samson Hill Estate has been established by Steven and Pago Sampson on one of the most spectacular sites of all. At the very top of Kangaroo Ground, it looks to the city of Melbourne (with the buildings clearly visible), thence to Kinglake and the Dandenongs, and then all the way to Mt Macedon. They have planted 3 ha of pinot noir, 2 ha of verdelho and 0.5 ha of shiraz, the verdelho firmly aimed at the cellar door market. The cellar door restaurant offers catering for all functions, one of the few winery restaurants in the Yarra Valley to be open weeknights for dinner.

Samuel's Gorge

 ★★★★☆

Lot 10 Chaffeys Road, McLaren, SA 5171 **REGION** McLaren Vale
T (08) 8323 8651 **F** (08) 8323 8673 **WWW**.gorge.com.au **OPEN** First weekend of spring until sold out, or by appt
WINEMAKER Justin McNamee **EST.** 2003 **CASES** 1250
After a wandering winemaking career in various parts of the world, Justin McNamee became a winemaker at Tatachilla in 1996, where he remained until December 2003, leaving to found Samuel's Gorge. He has established his winery in a barn built in 1853, part of a historic property known as the old Seaview Homestead. The property was owned by Sir Samuel Way, variously Chief Justice of the South Australian Supreme Court and Lieutenant Governor of the State. The grapes come from small contract growers spread across the ever-changing (unofficial) subregions of McLaren Vale, and are basket-pressed and fermented in old open slate fermenters lined with beeswax.

ΥΥΥΥΫ **McLaren Vale Shiraz 2003** Dark colour; flooded with regional dark chocolate woven through soft blackberry and plum fruit; nice oak; just about gets away with the alcohol. Cork. 15.4° alc. **RATING** 92 **DRINK** 2013 $35
McLaren Vale Grenache 2003 Massively rich and ripe confit berry fruit with a splash of chocolate; ripe tannins, of course. Make sure you share the bottle with others. Cork. 15.8° alc. **RATING** 90 **DRINK** 2011 $35
McLaren Vale Tempranillo 2004 Extremely concentrated and powerful; dark fruits in abundance. A little less extract would be better still, though the alcohol is fine. Cork. 13.6° alc. **RATING** 90 **DRINK** 2013 $35

Sand Hills Vineyard

NR

Sandhills Road, Forbes, NSW 2871 **REGION** Western Plains Zone
T (02) 6852 1437 **F** (02) 6852 4401 **OPEN** Mon–Sat 9–5, Sun 12–5
WINEMAKER John Saleh, Jill Lindsay (Contract) **EST.** 1920 **CASES** 400
Having purchased Sand Hills from long-term owner Jacques Genet, the Saleh family has replanted the vineyard to appropriate varieties, with over 6 ha of premium varieties having been established.

Sandalford ★★★★★

3210 West Swan Road, Caversham, WA 6055 **REGION** Margaret River
T (08) 9374 9374 **F** (08) 9274 2154 **WWW**.sandalford.com **OPEN** 7 days 10–5
WINEMAKER Paul Boulden **EST.** 1840 **CASES** 80 000
Some years ago the upgrading of the winery and the appointment of Paul Boulden as chief winemaker resulted in far greater consistency in quality, and the proper utilisation of the excellent vineyard resources of Sandalford in Margaret River and Mount Barker. Things have continued on an even keel since. Exports to the UK, the US and other major markets.

▼▼▼▼▼ **Prendiville Reserve Cabernet Sauvignon 2002** Classic cedar, spice, earth and cassis aromas; a long palate; fine but persistent tannins will help hold the wine for a long future. Cork. 14.5° alc. **RATING** 95 **DRINK** 2020 $ 90
Margaret River Cabernet Sauvignon 2004 Very good colour; elegant, medium-bodied with fine structure and texture; pristine blackcurrant and cassis; controlled tannins and oak, long finish. Screwcap. 14.5° alc. **RATING** 94 **DRINK** 2015 $ 32

▼▼▼▼▽ **Margaret River Semillon Sauvignon Blanc 2005** A crisp, clean and very lively mix of lemon and gooseberry is augmented by slippery acidity on the good finish. Screwcap. 12.5° alc. **RATING** 93 **DRINK** Now $ 22.50
Margaret River Chardonnay 2004 Light- to medium-bodied; quite complex, nutty barrel ferment and maturation inputs to peachy, butterscotch fruit; does pull up a little short. Screwcap. 14° alc. **RATING** 90 **DRINK** 2008 $ 33.95

▼▼▼▼ **Element Chardonnay 2005** Aromatic and scented; nectarine and peach fruit with subtle oak; finishes with lemony acidity. Very good value. Screwcap. 13° alc. **RATING** 89 **DRINK** 2008 $ 12
Element Cabernet Sauvignon 2004 Attractive cassis and blackcurrant flavour to a medium-bodied palate, with more mouthfeel and texture than expected at this price point; good finish and aftertaste. Bargain. Screwcap. 14° alc. **RATING** 89 **DRINK** 2008 $ 12
Margaret River Riesling 2005 Unusual orange peel and spice aromas; flavoursome, but relatively soft; limitations of the region are all too apparent. Screwcap. 12.5° alc. **RATING** 88 **DRINK** 2010 $ 22.50
Margaret River Verdelho 2005 A substantial wine with dimensions not always found in Verdelho; ripe pear fruit. Screwcap. 14° alc. **RATING** 87 **DRINK** Now $ 22.50
Protege Classic Dry White 2005 Clean, fresh and crisp, precisely in style; light mineral, herb and tropical fruit blend. Screwcap. 13° alc. **RATING** 87 **DRINK** Now $ 18.95
Protege Cabernet Merlot 2004 Light-bodied; fresh, light mint, leaf and red berry mix. Screwcap. 14° alc. **RATING** 87 **DRINK** Now $ 18.95

▼▼▼▽ **Element Classic White 2005** **RATING** 86 **DRINK** Now $ 12.50
Element Shiraz Cabernet 2004 **RATING** 86 **DRINK** Now $ 12

▼▼▼ **Element Late Harvest 2005** **RATING** 83 $ 12

Sandalyn Wilderness Estate ★★★

162 Wilderness Road, Rothbury, NSW 2321 **REGION** Lower Hunter Valley
T (02) 4930 7611 **F** (02) 4930 7611 **WWW**.huntervalleyboutiques.com.au **OPEN** 7 days 10–5
WINEMAKER Lindsay Whaling **EST.** 1988 **CASES** 6000
Sandra and Lindsay Whaling preside over the picturesque cellar door building of Sandalyn on the evocatively named Wilderness Road, where you will find a one-hole golf range and views to the Wattagan, Brokenback and Molly Morgan ranges. The estate has 9 ha of vineyards planted to chardonnay, pinot noir, verdelho and semillon. Exports to Ireland.

▼▼▼▼ **Chardonnay 2004** A powerful wine with ripe melon, fig and peach fruit; some alcohol heat, but certainly has presence. Cork. **RATING** 88 **DRINK** 2009 $ 22

▼▼▼▽ **Hunter Valley Verdelho 2002** Hanging in there surprisingly well, all things considered; gentle fruit salad flavour. Cork. 11.5° alc. **RATING** 86 **DRINK** Now $ 18
Semillon Verdelho 2005 Clean, medium- to full-bodied, with some sweetness, the Verdelho talking more loudly than the Semillon. Screwcap. 12° alc. **RATING** 86 **DRINK** 2008 $ 18

ŢŢŢ   **Cuvee Pinot Noir 99/00** RATING 83 $25
         Hunter Valley Shiraz 2001 RATING 83 $22

Sandhurst Ridge   NR

156 Forest Drive, Marong, Vic 3515 **REGION** Bendigo
T(03) 5435 2534 **F**(03) 5435 2548 **WWW**.sandhurstridge.com.au **OPEN** Wed–Mon 11–5, or by appt
WINEMAKER Paul Greblo, George Greblo **EST.** 1990 **CASES** 2500
The Greblo brothers (Paul and George), with combined experience in business, agriculture, science and construction and development began the establishment of Sandhurst Ridge in 1990 with the planting of the first 2 ha of shiraz and cabernet sauvignon. Plantings have now been increased to over 7 ha, principally cabernet and shiraz, but also a little merlot, sauvignon blanc and nebbiolo. The fully equipped winery was completed in 1996 with a cellar capacity of 400 barriques. The winery rating is given for its red wines. Exports to the US, Canada and Hong Kong.

Sandow's End   NR

Sandow Road, Verdun, SA 5245 **REGION** Adelaide Hills
T(08) 8388 7008 **F**(08) 8388 7100 **WWW**.sandowsend.com.au **OPEN** By appt
WINEMAKER Matt Wenk (Contract) **EST.** 2001 **CASES** 1000
Kati and Andrew Wenk purchased the former Pibbin Vineyard in 2001, acquiring 20-year-old vines which, with some refurbishment, are producing grapes of very high quality. Both a varietal and Reserve Pinot Noir are made from the 2.8-ha vineyard. The wines are made by Andrew Wenk's brother Matt, and are being sold through the website, and through restaurants in Adelaide Hills, Mt Hotham and Falls Creek, the link being, according to Kati Wenk, altitude.

Sandstone

Cnr Johnson Road/Caves Road, Wilyabrup, WA 6280 **REGION** Margaret River
T(08) 9755 6271 **F**(08) 9755 6292 **OPEN** 7 days 11–4
WINEMAKER Jan McIntosh **EST.** 1988 **CASES** 4000
There have been a number of changes at Sandstone over recent years, Jan McIntosh is now winemaker and runs the business. It will eventually be estate-based following the planting of 9 ha (semillon and cabernet sauvignon).

ŢŢŢŢ   **Margaret River Cabernet Sauvignon Merlot 2002** Developing colour; blackcurrant, earth and spice plus a touch of sweet vanilla oak. Cork. 13.5° alc. **RATING** 89 **DRINK** 2008 $30
       Margaret River Semillon 2003 Complex bottle-developed toasty aromas; plenty of flavour, though does shorten slightly. Screwcap. 13.3° alc. **RATING** 88 **DRINK** Now $18

Sandy Farm Vineyard   NR

RMB 3734 Sandy Farm Road, Denver via Daylesford, Vic 3641 **REGION** Macedon Ranges
T(03) 5348 7610 **WWW**.sandyfarm.primetap.com **OPEN** W'ends 10–5, or by appt
WINEMAKER Peter Comisel **EST.** 1988 **CASES** 800
Peter Comisel and Dot Hollow have acquired Sandy Farm from founder Peter Covell. There are 1.5 ha of cabernet sauvignon, cabernet franc and merlot and 0.5 ha of pinot noir, with a small, basic winery in which they make preservative-free Cabernet Sauvignon, Merlot and Pinot Noir, attracting a loyal local following.

Sanguine Estate   NR

77 Shurans Lane, Heathcote, Vic 3523 (postal) **REGION** Heathcote
T(03) 9646 6661 **F**(03) 9646 1746 **WWW**.sanguine-estate.com.au **OPEN** Not
WINEMAKER Mark Hunter, Peter Dredge (Contract) **EST.** 1997 **CASES** 450
The Hunter family, with parents Linda and Tony at the head, and their 2 children, Mark and Jodi, with their respective partners Melissa and Brett, began establishing the vineyard in 1997. From a starting base of 4 ha of shiraz planted that year, it has now grown to 20.7 ha of shiraz, and 2 ha of

8 different varieties, including chardonnay, viognier, merlot, tempranillo, zinfandel, petit verdot, cabernet sauvignon, merlot and cabernet franc. Low-yielding vines and the magic of the Heathcote region have produced Shiraz of exceptional intensity, which has received rave reviews in the US, and led to the 'sold out' sign being posted almost immediately upon release. With the ever-expanding vineyard, Mark Hunter has become full-time vigneron, and Jodi Marsh part-time marketer and business developer. For the foreseeable future the wines will continue to be contract-made. Exports to the US.

Saracen Estates   NR

731 Caves Road, Wilyabrup, WA 6280 **REGION** Margaret River
T (08) 9221 4955 **F** (08) 9221 4966 **www**.saracenestates.com.au **OPEN** By appt
WINEMAKER Bill Crappsley **EST.** 1998 **CASES** 40 000
The Cazzolli and Saraceni families have established 40 ha of vines on their 80-ha property, with a striking restaurant and cellar door opened in 2005. The name not only echoes one of the founding families, but also pays tribute to the Saracens, one of the most advanced races in cultural and social terms at the time of the Crusades. Exports to the UK, Singapore, Malaysia, Hong Kong, India and Denmark.

Sarsfield Estate   NR

345 Duncan Road, Sarsfield, Vic 3875 **REGION** Gippsland
T (03) 5156 8962 **F** (03) 5156 8970 **OPEN** By appt
WINEMAKER Dr Suzanne Rutschmann **EST.** 1995 **CASES** 1000
The property is owned by Suzanne Rutschmann, who has a PhD in Chemistry, a Diploma in Horticulture and and a BSc (Wine Science) from Charles Sturt University, and Swiss-born Peter Albrecht, a civil and structural engineer who has also undertaken various courses in agriculture and viticulture. For a part-time occupation, these are exceptionally impressive credentials. Their 2-ha vineyard was planted between 1991 and 1998; the first vintage made at the winery was 1998, the grapes being sold to others in previous years. High-quality packaging is a plus.

Savaterre   NR

PO Box 337, Beechworth, Vic 3747 **REGION** Beechworth
T (03) 5727 0551 **F** (03) 5727 0551 **www**.savaterre.com **OPEN** Not
WINEMAKER Keppell Smith **EST.** 1996 **CASES** NA
Keppell Smith embarked on a career in wine in 1996, studying winemaking at Charles Sturt University and (at a practical level) with Phillip Jones at Bass Phillip. He purchased the 40-ha property on which Savaterre has been established, and has close planted (7500 vines per ha) 1 ha each of chardonnay and pinot noir at an elevation of 440m. Organic principles govern the viticulture, and the winemaking techniques look to the old world rather than the new. Smith's stated aim is to produce outstanding, individualistic wines far removed from the mainstream.

Sawtooth Ridge   NR

Lot 295 Waggon Road, Victor Harbor, SA 5211 **REGION** Southern Fleurieu
T (08) 8552 8450 **F** (08) 8552 8450 **www**.sawtoothridge.com.au **OPEN** 7 days 9–5
WINEMAKER Harry Duerden **EST.** 1996 **CASES** NA
The former Duerden's Wines was purchased by Andrea Sutherland and Frank Falco in 2003, and renamed Sawtooth Ridge. The unique overhead sawtooth trellis (a traditional structure in parts of Italy) remains unchanged, and the panoply of conventional wines, liqueurs (including quandong), syrups, honeys, jelly and vinegar remain available.

Scaffidi Wines   ★★★★

Talunga Cellars, Adelaide–Mannum Road, Gumeracha, SA 5233 **REGION** Adelaide Hills
T (08) 8389 1222 **F** (08) 8389 1233 **www**.talunga.com.au **OPEN** Wed–Sun & public hols 10.30–5
WINEMAKER Vince Scaffidi **EST.** 1994 **CASES** 2000
Owners Vince and Tina Scaffidi have a one-third share of the 62-ha Gumeracha Vineyards, and it is from these vineyards that the wines are sourced, including distinguished Sangiovese. The cellar door and restaurant is named Talunga Cellars. The wines are exceptionally well priced given their quality.

ŢŢŢŢŸ **One Tree Hill Shiraz 2004** Good purple-red; an abundance of luscious, but not jammy, black and red fruits, licorice and spice; medium- to full-bodied, ripe tannins, good oak. Screwcap. **RATING** 93 **DRINK** 2014 $ 10
One Tree Hill Gulf Breeze Cabernet Merlot 2002 Firm blackcurrant, earth and spice flavours; a particularly long and well-structured finish. Screwcap. 14° alc. **RATING** 92 **DRINK** 2017 $ 13.50

ŢŢŢŢ **Shiraz Nebbiolo Sangiovese Grenache 2004** Light- to medium-bodied; fresh, lively, spicy/savoury cherry aromas and flavours; fine tannins; 70% Shiraz. Screwcap. **RATING** 89 **DRINK** 2010 $ 10

ŢŢŢŢŸ **Unwooded Chardonnay 2005** Fairly austere lemony/citrussy/minerally fruit; a summer seafood style. Screwcap. **RATING** 86 **DRINK** Now $ 10
One Tree Hill Gulf Breeze Nebbiolo 2003 **RATING** 85 **DRINK** 2008 $ 25

🐌 Scaramouche Wines NR

PO Box 161, Gulgong, NSW 2852 **REGION** Mudgee
T (02) 6374 1178 **F** (02) 6374 1178 **OPEN** Not
WINEMAKER 21C Wine Company (Drew Tuckwell) **EST.** 1998 **CASES** 150
Brendan Shaw has established 6 ha of cabernet sauvignon, 4 ha of shiraz and 1 ha of merlot on his Peregrine Vineyard. All of the grapes are sold with the exception of 150 cases of Shiraz, which is contract-made and sold only by mail order.

Scarborough ★★★★

179 Gillards Road, Pokolbin, NSW 2320 **REGION** Lower Hunter Valley
T (02) 4998 7563 **F** (02) 4998 7786 **WWW**.scarboroughwine.com.au **OPEN** 7 days 9–5
WINEMAKER Ian Scarborough, Jerome Scarborough **EST.** 1985 **CASES** 15 000
Ian Scarborough honed his white winemaking skills during his years as a consultant, and has brought all those skills to his own label. He makes 3 different styles of Chardonnay: the Blue Label in a light, elegant, Chablis style for the export market and a richer barrel-fermented wine (Yellow Label) primarily directed to the Australian market, the third is the White Label, a cellar door-only wine made in the best vintages. However, the real excitement for the future lies with the portion of the old Lindemans Sunshine Vineyard which he has purchased (after it lay fallow for 30 years) and planted with semillon and (quixotically) pinot noir. The first vintage from the legendary Sunshine Vineyard was made in 2004; in the meantime, Ian has kept his hand in with contract-grown semillon. Exports to the UK and the US.

ŢŢŢŢŸ **White Label Chardonnay 2004** Tighter and more focused than the Blue Label; melon and peach with touches of citrus; fruit-driven, good length. Cellar door sales only. Screwcap. 13° alc. **RATING** 91 **DRINK** 2009 $ 25

ŢŢŢŢ **Semillon 2005** Bright green-straw; a fuller style of semillon, the alcohol determining the outcome; plenty of fruit on entry, but does tail off slightly on the finish. Screwcap. 12° alc. **RATING** 89 **DRINK** 2008 $ 19
Blue Label Chardonnay 2004 Rich, sweet fig and peach fruit; abundant mouthfeel, the oak incidental. Screwcap. 13.5° alc. **RATING** 89 **DRINK** 2008 $ 19

ŢŢŢŸ **Non Vintage Pinot Noir NV** **RATING** 86 **DRINK** 2010 $ 21

Scarp Valley Vineyard NR

6 Robertson Road, Gooseberry Hill, WA 6076 **REGION** Perth Hills
T (08) 9454 5748 **OPEN** By appt
WINEMAKER Contract **EST.** 1978 **CASES** 25
Owner Robert Duncan presides over what has to be one of the smallest producers in Australia, with 0.1 ha (quarter of an acre) of shiraz and 30 cabernet sauvignon vines producing a single cask of wine each year if the birds do not get the grapes first.

Scarpantoni Estate

NR

Scarpantoni Drive, McLaren Flat, SA 5171 **REGION** McLaren Vale
T (08) 8383 0186 **F** (08) 8383 0490 **WWW**.scarpantoni-wines.com.au **OPEN** Mon–Fri 9–5, w'ends &
public hols 11–5
WINEMAKER Michael Scarpantoni, Filippo Scarpantoni **EST.** 1979 **CASES** 30 000
With 20 ha of shiraz, 11 ha of cabernet sauvignon, 3 ha each of chardonnay and sauvignon blanc, 1 ha
each of merlot and gamay, and 0.5 ha of petit verdot, Scarpantoni has come a long way since
Domenico Scarpantoni purchased his first property of 5.6 ha in 1958. At that time he was working for
Thomas Hardy at its Tintara winery; he subsequently became vineyard manager for Seaview Wines,
responsible for the contoured vineyards which were leading edge viticulture in the 1960s. In 1979 his
two sons, Michael and Filippo, built the winery, which has now been extended to enable all the grapes from the estate plantings to be used to make wine under the Scarpantoni label. As the vines
have matured, quality has improved. Exports to the US, the UK and other major markets.

Schild Estate Wines

Cnr Barossa Valley Way/Lyndoch Valley Road, Lyndoch, SA 5351 **REGION** Barossa Valley
T (08) 8524 5560 **F** (08) 8524 4333 **WWW**.schildestate.com.au **OPEN** 7 days 10–5
WINEMAKER Wine Wise Consultancy **EST.** 1998 **CASES** 24 000
Ed Schild is a Barossa Valley grapegrower who first planted a small vineyard at Rowland Flat in 1952,
steadily increasing his vineyard holdings over the next 50 years to their present 140 ha. Currently
12% of the production from these vineyards (now managed by son Michael Schild) is used to produce
Schild Estate Wines, and the plan is to increase this percentage. The flagship wine is made from
155-year-old shiraz vines on the Moorooroo Block. The cellar door is in the old ANZ Bank at
Lyndoch, and provides the sort of ambience which can only be found in the Barossa Valley. Exports to
the UK, the US and Canada.

♥♥♥♥♥ Barossa Shiraz 2004 A medium- to full-bodied mix of blackberry, mocha, dark chocolate
and licorice; ripe tannins; sweetness without dead fruit characters. Diam. 14.5° alc.
RATING 94 **DRINK** 2017 $ 24

♥♥♥♥♡ Barossa Cabernet Sauvignon 2004 Good colour; a fragrant bouquet, then riper
blackcurrant, blackberry, chocolate and mocha flavours; ripe tannins, a touch of cigar box;
quality oak. Diam. 14.5° alc. **RATING** 93 **DRINK** 2017 $ 24

♥♥♥♥ Barossa Merlot 2004 Medium-bodied; sweet red fruits and plums; fine, ripe tannins and
controlled oak. Cork. 14.5° alc. **RATING** 89 **DRINK** 2010 $ 24
Barossa Riesling 2005 Substantial citrus, lime, tropical fruit mix; plenty of honest
flavour. Screwcap. 12° alc. **RATING** 88 **DRINK** 2009 $ 15
Barossa Unwooded Semillon 2005 Definitely a step in the right direction, but it's still a
difficult balancing act. Screwcap. 12.5° alc. **RATING** 88 **DRINK** 2011 $ 15
Moorooroo Limited Release Barossa Valley Shiraz 2001 Medium-bodied; ripe spicy
fruit; despite the moderate alcohol, some cooked characters, the tannins slightly broken;
nowhere near where it should be. Conceivably an oxidised bottle. Cork. 14° alc. **RATING** 88
DRINK 2009 $ 85
Barossa GMS 2005 Fresh, light red fruits; minimal tannins; nice summer red.
Grenache/Mourvedre/Shiraz. Screwcap. 15° alc. **RATING** 87 **DRINK** 2008 $ 19

♥♥♥♡ Barossa Unwooded Chardonnay 2005 RATING 86 **DRINK** 2008 $ 15
Barossa Frontignac 2005 Intensely grapey and fully sweet; irresistible for beginners and
the cellar door; balanced acidity. Screwcap. 11.5° alc. **RATING** 86 **DRINK** Now $ 14

Schindler Northway Downs

★★★

437 Stumpy Gully Road, Balnarring, Vic 3926 **REGION** Mornington Peninsula
T (03) 5983 1945 **F** (03) 9580 4262 **OPEN** First weekend each month
WINEMAKER Tammy Schindler-Hands **EST.** 1996 **CASES** 250
The Schindler family planted the first 2 ha of pinot noir and chardonnay in 1996. A further 4 ha of
pinot noir was planted on an ideal north-facing slope in 1999, and the first vintage followed in 2000.
The cellar door offers Austrian food and live Austrian music on the Sunday.

ŸŸŸŸ **Mornington Peninsula Chardonnay 2004** Very pale straw-green; a complex bouquet with touches of solids/French funk; the palate heads off in an opposite direction with sweet stone fruit flavours. Diam. 13.6° alc. **RATING** 89 **DRINK** 2009 $ 20

ŸŸŸŸ **Hands On Mornington Peninsula Pinot Noir 2004** Light colour; light-bodied, savoury/stemmy overtones to the red fruit flavours; strange, given the substantial alcohol. Cork. 14.9° alc. **RATING** 86 **DRINK** 2008 $ 24

Schubert Estate ★★★★☆

Roennfeldt Road, Marananga, SA 5355 **REGION** Barossa Valley
T (08) 8562 3375 **F** (08) 8562 4338 **WWW**.schubertestate.com.au **OPEN** Not
WINEMAKER Steve Schubert, Cecilia Schubert **EST.** 2000 **CASES** 240
Steve and Cecilia Schubert are primarily grapegrowers, with 13 ha of shiraz and 2 ha of viognier, and almost all the production is sold to Torbreck. They purchased the 25-ha property from a relative in 1986, when it was in such a derelict state that there was no point trying to save the old vines. Moreover, both were working in other areas, so it was some years before they began replanting, at a little under 2 ha per year. In 2000 they decided to keep enough grapes to make a barrique of wine for their own (and friends') consumption. They were sufficiently encouraged by the outcome to obtain the necessary licence and venture into the dizzy heights of 2 hogsheads a year. The wine is made with wild yeast, open fermentation, basket pressing and bottling without filtration. Exports to the US, Denmark and Japan.

ŸŸŸŸŸ **Goose Yard Block Barossa Valley Shiraz 2004** Saturated, dense red-purple; a rich tapestry of textures and flavours; plum, blackberry and spice, with ripe tannins. Cork. 14° alc. **RATING** 95 **DRINK** 2019 $ 55

ŸŸŸŸŸ **The Gosling Barossa Valley Shiraz 2004** Good colour; elegant, medium-bodied wine with appealing blackberry and spice fruit, finishing with fine tannins. Very good value. Screwcap. 14.5° alc. **RATING** 90 **DRINK** 2011 $ 22

Scorpo Wines ★★★★☆

23 Old Bittern–Dromana Road, Merricks North, Vic 3926 **REGION** Mornington Peninsula
T (03) 5989 7697 **F** (03) 9813 3371 **WWW**.scorpowines.com.au **OPEN** By appt
WINEMAKER Paul Scorpo, Sandro Mosele (Contract) **EST.** 1997 **CASES** 2600
Paul Scorpo has a 27-year background as a horticulturist and landscape architect, and has worked in major projects ranging from private gardens to golf courses in Australia, Europe and South-East Asia. His family has a love of food, wine and gardens, all of which led to them buying a derelict apple and cherry orchard on gentle rolling hills halfway between Port Phillip and Westernport Bay. It is part of a ridge system which climbs up to Red Hill, and offers north and northeast-facing slopes on red-brown, clay loam soils. Here they have established 4.5 ha of pinot noir, chardonnay, pinot gris and shiraz. The wines are made by Paul Scorpo and Sandro Mosele at Kooyong.

ŸŸŸŸŸ **Mornington Peninsula Chardonnay 2004** Intense grapefruit and nectarine flavours drive the long palate; oak seamlessly interwoven; very good line, length and aftertaste. Diam. 13.5° alc. **RATING** 95 **DRINK** 2012 $ 36

ŸŸŸŸŸ **Mornington Peninsula Pinot Noir 2004** Good hue; quite complex aromas and flavours in a plum, cherry and spice spectrum, plus a touch of forest. Light- to medium-bodied, good balance. Diam. 14° alc. **RATING** 93 **DRINK** 2011 $ 38
Mornington Peninsula Shiraz 2004 A medium-bodied, fresh, bright and lively assemblage of red fruits, spice and pepper; well-controlled oak and extract. Diam. 14° alc. **RATING** 93 **DRINK** 2010 $ 38

ŸŸŸŸ **Mornington Peninsula Pinot Gris 2005** Moderately distinctive apple and pear varietal fruit, with a flick of sweetness on the finish to add mouthfeel. Diam. 14° alc. **RATING** 88 **DRINK** 2009 $ 32

Scotchmans Hill

190 Scotchmans Road, Drysdale, Vic 3222 **REGION** Geelong
T (03) 5251 3176 **F** (03) 5253 1743 **WWW**.scotchmanshill.com.au **OPEN** 7 days 10.30–5.30
WINEMAKER Robin Brockett **EST.** 1982 **CASES** 70 000
Situated on the Bellarine Peninsula, southeast of Geelong, with a well-equipped winery and first-class vineyards. It is a consistent performer with its Pinot Noir and has a strong following in Melbourne and Sydney for its astutely priced, competently made wines. A doubling in production has seen the establishment of export markets in the UK, Holland, Switzerland, Hong Kong and Singapore. The second label, Swan Bay, has been joined at the other end of the spectrum with top-end individual vineyard wines.

ΨΨΨΨΨ **2004 Scotchmans Hill Geelong Chardonnay** Bright green-yellow; a very stylish and elegant wine; vibrant stone fruit and grapefruit flavours, the oak balanced and integrated; drives through to a long finish. Screwcap. **RATING** 94 **DRINK** 2012 $ 27

ΨΨΨΨΨ **2005 Scotchmans Hill Geelong Sauvignon Blanc** Spotlessly clean; crisp, lively, focused passionfruit/citrus/gooseberry mix; a long, bright finish. Screwcap. **RATING** 92 **DRINK** Now $ 22.50

2004 Scotchmans Hill Geelong Pinot Noir Medium red-purple; firm dark plum fruit aromas and flavours; foresty tannins, complex but austere. Screwcap. **RATING** 91 **DRINK** 2010 $ 29

2004 Scotchmans Hill Swan Bay Shiraz Good colour; light- to medium-bodied, driven by spicy red and black fruits; a lively finish with slippery, fine tannins. Screwcap. **RATING** 90 **DRINK** 2009 $ 17.50

2004 Scotchmans Hill Geelong Cabernet Sauvignon A faint touch of reduction on the bouquet clears up on the palate; medium-bodied, well-balanced cassis and blackcurrant fruit supported by fine, persistent tannins and quality oak. Screwcap. **RATING** 93 **DRINK** 2019 $ 29

ΨΨΨΨ **2004 Scotchmans Hill Geelong Riesling** Plenty of honest flavour, but lacks the focus and precision of wines from inland regions; riesling does not like to be beside the seaside. Screwcap. **RATING** 87 **DRINK** 2010 $ 27

2005 Scotchmans Hill Swan Bay Sauvignon Blanc Semillon A piercing fresh-squeezed lemon juice palate backed by some minerality; seafood on the rocks. Screwcap. **RATING** 89 **DRINK** Now $ 17.50

2005 Scotchmans Hill Swan Bay Chardonnay Light- to medium-bodied, driven by attractive nectarine/white peach/melon fruit; some oak adds to complexity. Screwcap. **RATING** 89 **DRINK** Now $ 17.50

2005 Scotchmans Hill Swan Bay Pinot Grigio A clean but reticent bouquet; tangy lemon rind edges to the more usual pinot gris fruit profile; good balance and finish. Screwcap. **RATING** 88 **DRINK** Now $ 17.50

2005 Scotchmans Hill Swan Bay Rose Full-on salmon colour, Tavel-style; spicy, strawberry flavours, then a pleasantly dry finish; much merit. Screwcap. **RATING** 89 **DRINK** Now $ 17.50

2005 Scotchmans Hill Hill Cabernet Shiraz Fresh, vibrant, juicy red fruits; a lively finish, crisp and crunchy, almost as if it were white rather than red. Value plus. Screwcap. **RATING** 87 **DRINK** 2008 $ 10

Scotts Brook

Scotts Brook Road, Boyup Brook, WA 6244 **REGION** Blackwood Valley
T (08) 9765 3014 **F** (08) 9765 3015 **OPEN** 7 days 10–5
WINEMAKER Vasse River **EST.** 1987 **CASES** 1000
The Scotts Brook winery at Boyup Brook (equidistant between the Margaret River and Great Southern regions) has been developed by local schoolteachers Brian Walker and wife Kerry. There are 15 ha of vineyards, but the majority of the production is sold to other winemakers, with limited quantities being made by contract.

ΨΨΨΨ **Chardonnay 2004** A harmonious blend of stone fruit, melon and citrus, oak a largely invisible net; long finish. Screwcap. 13.3° alc. **RATING** 92 **DRINK** 2011 $ 16

ＴＴＴＴ **Shiraz 2004** Pleasant, light- to medium-bodied wine; predominantly red fruits, with some spices; fine tannins and a hint of vanilla oak. Cork. 13.8° alc. **RATING** 88 **DRINK** 2011 $ 20

Cabernet Sauvignon 2004 Minty, leafy notes to cassis and blackcurrant fruit on a light- to medium-bodied palate; slightly green overall. Cork. 14° alc. **RATING** 87 **DRINK** 2010 $ 20

Scotts Hill Vineyard   NR

280 Lillicur Road, Amherst, Vic 3371 (postal) **REGION** Pyrenees
T (03) 5463 2468 **OPEN** Not
WINEMAKER Lester Scott, Pamela Scott **EST.** 2000 **CASES** NA
Lester and Pamela Scott have established 3 ha of pinot noir, cabernet sauvignon, merlot, shiraz, cabernet franc and petit verdot at Amherst. They make the wine onsite.

Scrubby Creek Wines   NR

566 Crystal Creek Road, Alexandra, Vic 3714 **REGION** Upper Goulburn
T (03) 5772 2191 **F** (03) 5772 1048 **WWW**.scrubbycreek.com **OPEN** 7 days 9–5
WINEMAKER MasterWineMakers **EST.** 1995 **CASES** 400
The Stastra and Napier families are next-door neighbours who have jointly planted 3.5 ha of chardonnay. Exports to the UK and the US.

Sea Winds Vineyard   NR

PO Box 511, Dromana, Vic 3936 **REGION** Mornington Peninsula
T (03) 5989 6204 **F** (03) 5989 6204 **OPEN** Not
WINEMAKER Kevin McCarthy (Contract) **EST.** 1990 **CASES** NA
Douglas Schwebel has established 3 ha of sauvignon blanc, chardonnay and pinot noir; the wines are sold by mail order.

Seaforth Vineyard   ★★★★☆

520 Arthurs Seat Road, Red Hill, Vic 3937 **REGION** Mornington Peninsula
T (03) 5989 2362 **F** (03) 5989 2506 **WWW**.seaforthwines.com.au
OPEN Spring and summer w'ends 11–5
WINEMAKER Contract (Phillip Kittle) **EST.** 1994 **CASES** 1850
Andrew and Venetia Adamson planted their 3.6 ha vineyard to chardonnay (2.2 ha), pinot noir (1 ha) and pinot gris (0.4 ha) in 1994. At 300m, it is one of the highest on the Mornington Peninsula, and is always amongst the last to pick. All of the wines are 100% estate-grown, and all of the standard vineyard operations are carried out personally by Andrew and Venetia Adamson, with only picking bringing in outside contractors. Kevin McCarthy of T'Gallant was the winemaker for the first 10 years, but following the acquisition of T'Gallant by Fosters Wine Estates, Phillip Kittle has been appointed contract winemaker.

ＴＴＴＴＹ **Mornington Peninsula Pinot Noir 2005** Good colour; rich, ripe black fruits with spicy/foresty nuances adding complexity; oak plays a background role. Screwcap. 13.6° alc. **RATING** 93 **DRINK** 2012 $ 28

Mornington Peninsula Pinot Noir 2004 Much lighter colour than the '05, but good hue; a fresh, lively array of red, rather than black, fruits with good length; a very different style to the '05, but appealing. Screwcap. 13.4° alc. **RATING** 93 **DRINK** 2012 $ 28

Mornington Peninsula Chardonnay 2004 A similar elegant, tightly focused style, driven by melon/citrus fruit; excellent bright finish. Screwcap. 13.4° alc. **RATING** 92 **DRINK** 2009 $ 26

Mornington Peninsula Chardonnay 2005 Intense, elegant citrus and nectarine flavours; a clear, clean fruit line throughout, the oak in subtle support. Screwcap. 13.8° alc. **RATING** 91 **DRINK** 2010 $ 26

ＴＴＴＴ **Mornington Peninsula Pinot Gris 2005** Powerful varietal musk and spice, but has some heat to the finish. Screwcap. 13.8° alc. **RATING** 88 **DRINK** 2008 $ 24

Mornington Peninsula Pinot Gris 2004 Although the alcohol is higher than the '05, seems to have less heat; musk and spice flavours sustain the considerable length of the palate. Screwcap. 14.2° alc. **RATING** 88 **DRINK** Now $ 24

Mornington Peninsula Wild Rose 2005 A fresh, virtually dry, strawberry/cherry mix; good alcohol and acid balance. Screwcap. 12.8° alc. **RATING** 87 **DRINK** Now $ 18

Seashell Wines   NR

Ammon Road, Balingup, WA 6253 (postal) **REGION** Blackwood Valley
T (08) 9307 1469 **F** (08) 9307 1469 **WWW**.seashellwines.com.au **OPEN** Not
WINEMAKER Stephen Bullied (Contract) **EST.** 1994 **CASES** 1500
Dr Barry Wilson is a biologist and specialist on Australian marine shells and marine ecology, and a director of the Australian Wildlife Conservancy. He and his family planted the first 4 ha of semillon and shiraz in 1993, subsequently extending the plantings to 6 ha. Part of the proceeds of the sale of the wines is donated to various wildlife conservation activities, particularly the restoration of endangered species.

Secret Garden Wines   NR

251 Henry Lawson Drive, Mudgee, NSW 2850 **REGION** Mudgee
T (02) 6373 3874 **F** (02) 6373 3854 **OPEN** Fri–Sun & public hols 9–5
WINEMAKER Ian MacRae **EST.** 2000 **CASES** NA
Secret Garden Wines is owned by Ian and Carol MacRae, and is a sister operation to their main business, Miramar Wines. Estate plantings consist of 10 ha of shiraz and around 2 ha each of cabernet sauvignon and chardonnay. The wines are made at Miramar, the cellar door is at Secret Garden. The property is only 5 km from Mudgee, and also fronts Craigmoor Road, giving it a prime position in the so-called 'golden triangle'.

Sedona Estate   ★★★★★

182 Shannons Road, Murrindindi, Vic 3717 **REGION** Upper Goulburn
T (03) 9730 2883 **F** (03) 9730 2583 **OPEN** By appt
WINEMAKER Paul Evans **EST.** 1998 **CASES** 1500
The Sedona Estate vineyard was chosen by Paul and Sonja Evans after a long search for what they considered to be the perfect site. Situated on north-facing and gently undulating slopes, with gravelly black soils, it is planted (in descending order) to 4 ha of shiraz, cabernet sauvignon, merlot and sangiovese. Paul Evans (former Oakridge winemaker) also contract-makes wines for a number of other small Yarra Valley producers.

ŦŦŦŦŦ **Yea Valley Cabernet Merlot 2004** Bright purple-red; appealing medium- to full-bodied blackcurrant and cassis fruit runs through a very well-balanced palate; excellent tannin and oak management. Diam. 13° alc. **RATING** 94 **DRINK** 2015 $ 18
Yea Valley Cabernet Sauvignon 2003 Ultra-rich blackcurrant, dark chocolate and mocha aromas and flavours; ripe, soft tannins add to velvety mouthfeel. Diam. 13.5° alc. **RATING** 94 **DRINK** 2013 $ 22

ŦŦŦŦ🙾 **Yea Valley Merlot 2003** Good structure, body and weight; attractive varietal savoury/olive overtones to blackcurrant fruit; the oak and tannins balanced. Diam. 13.5° alc. **RATING** 92 **DRINK** 2010 $ 24

ŦŦŦŦ **Yea Valley Riesling 2005** Solid, firm, ripe citrus fruit; plenty of overall flavour. Cork. 13° alc. **RATING** 88 **DRINK** 2010 $ 22

Seppelt ★★★★★

1 Seppeltsfield Road, Seppeltsfield via Nuriootpa, SA 5355 **REGION** Barossa Valley
T (08) 8568 6217 **F** (08) 8562 8333 **WWW**.seppelt.com.au **OPEN** Mon–Fri 10–5, w'ends &
public hols 11–5
WINEMAKER James Godfrey **EST.** 1851 **CASES** NFP
A multi-million dollar expansion and renovation program has seen the historic Seppeltsfield winery
become the production centre for the Seppelt fortified and SA table wines, adding another
dimension to what was already the most historic and beautiful major winery in Australia. It is now
home to some of the world's great fortified wines, nurtured and protected by the passionate James
Godfrey. Exports to all major markets.

♆♆♆♆♆ **100 Year Old Para Liqueur 1906** Honey, treacle consistency; impenetrable olive-brown
colour; a nuclear explosion of flavour starting with Christmas pudding, molasses and
chocolate, ending miraculously balanced by perfect acidity. One of the great ones.
RATING 98 **DRINK** 2100 $ 1050

Rare Tawny Port DP90 NV By common consent, the greatest Australian tawny, but with
no similarity whatsoever to Para Liqueur. Superb, scintillating length, balance and
harmony; so much finesse with so much flavour. 500 m.l. 20.5° alc. **RATING** 97 **DRINK** Now
$ 59.50

Rare Rutherglen Tokay DP59 NV Deep olive-brown; spice, toffee, caramel and tea leaf
aromas intermingle with pronounced rancio. The super-elegant, intense, and long palate
has a refined and controlled complexity, the flavours peeling off like layers of onion skin.
Significantly more viscous than the Rare Muscat. 500 ml. 17.5° alc. **RATING** 97 **DRINK** Now
$ 59.50

Rare Rutherglen Muscat GR113 NV Deep mahogany-brown; olive rim; a mix of almond,
smoke, spice, rose petal and raisin; a Joseph's coat of flavours; dances in the mouth, the
finish lasting forever. 500 ml. 17.5° alc. **RATING** 96 **DRINK** Now $ 59.50

Oloroso DP38 NV Mid-brown, with a hint of green on the rim; nutty rancio complexity,
with just a touch of sweetness; finely balanced with a constant interplay between nutty,
honeyed sweetness and drier, rancio characters. The finish lingers in the mouth for
minutes, without any hint of alcohol heat. 21° alc. **RATING** 95 **DRINK** Now $ 19.50

1985 Seppelt Para Liqueur Luscious and almost creamy mouthfeel; a density and
complexity well above Bin 124; raisins, nuts, honey and spice all coalesce; this is serious
seduction. Progressive 21-year-old releases. **RATING** 95 **DRINK** Now $ 47.90

Amontillado DP116 NV Glowing golden-bronze; enticing richness with
brandysnap/biscuit aromas; super-intense and long palate, sweet and fruity on the entry,
then bitingly dry on the long finish. Exhilarating stuff. 22° alc. **RATING** 94 **DRINK** Now
$ 19.50

Fino DP117 NV The alcohol is less than many Barossa Valley red wines; finesse and grace
so well-constructed you do not think it is dry until the aftertaste, which is as clear as a
spring day. Serve chilled; do not cellar. 15.5° alc. **RATING** 94 **DRINK** Now $ 19.50

♆♆♆♆♈ **NV Seppelt Para Liqueur Aged Tawny Bin 124** Glowing golden; a seductive mix of nuts,
honey, preserved fruits and more biscuity characters; great balance, the rancio cutting
back any suggestion of cloying sweetness. **RATING** 93 **DRINK** Now $ 18.50

Seppelt (Great Western) ★★★★★

Moyston Road, Great Western, Vic 3377 **REGION** Grampians
T (03) 5361 2222 **F** (03) 5361 2200 **WWW**.seppelt.com.au **OPEN** 7 days 10–5
WINEMAKER Arthur O'Connor **EST.** 1865 **CASES** NFP
Australia's best-known producer of sparkling wine, always immaculate in its given price range but
also producing excellent Great Western-sourced table wines, especially long-lived Shiraz and
Australia's best Sparkling Shirazes. The glitzy labels of the past have rightly been consigned to the
rubbish bin, and the product range has been significantly rationalised. Exports to the UK, the US and
other major markets.

ŸŸŸŸŸ **Drumborg Riesling 2005** Very pale straw-green; a wonderfully delicate, pure, flowery bouquet, followed by an intense, yet feather-light, array of bright and crisp flavours. Screwcap. 13° alc. RATING 97 DRINK 2020 $ 30
Jaluka Drumborg Vineyard Chardonnay 2005 Light straw-green; extremely tangy, citrussy, intense and long; the fruit has devoured the French oak; cellaring special. Screwcap. 13.5° alc. RATING 94 DRINK 2015 $ 25
St Peters Grampians Shiraz 2003 Good colour; a powerful, ripe wine with savoury black fruits plus a twist of licorice and spice; ripe tannins. From 80-year-old plantings around the winery. Screwcap. 13.5° alc. RATING 94 DRINK 2018 $ 61

ŸŸŸŸŸ **Victoria Pinot Noir 2005** Strong purple-red; a powerful, strongly structured and deep-flavoured pinot; should age superbly to develop as yet subtle complexity. Drumborg. Screwcap. 13° alc. RATING 93 DRINK 2012 $ 18
Salinger 2002 Good mousse; a gentle mix of toasty/bready yeast and tangy fruit in a bright citrus, nectarine and white peach spectrum; excellent balance, long and dry. RATING 93 DRINK 2008 $ 25.99
Coborra Drumborg Vineyard Pinot Gris 2005 Tangy lemony, citrussy, floral bouquet; a light year away from warmer-grown pinot gris; long and lingering, with perfect acidity. Ultimate summer seafood wine. Screwcap. 13.5° alc. RATING 92 DRINK 2008 $ 25
Chalambar Grampians Bendigo Shiraz 2004 An elegant, medium-bodied wine, benefitting from the controlled alcohol; red and black fruits, fine, velvety tannins; balanced oak. Screwcap. 13° alc. RATING 92 DRINK 2014 $ 25
Victoria Shiraz 2004 Good colour; medium- to full-bodied, the strength coming from balanced but persistent tannins rather than alcohol; an array of black fruits; cellaring special. Screwcap. 13.5° alc. RATING 92 DRINK 2019 $ 18
Victoria Riesling 2005 Well-balanced; gentle citrus and tropical fruit; good length. Great Western/Drumborg. Screwcap. 13° alc. RATING 90 DRINK 2010 $ 18
Victorian Sauvignon Blanc 2005 Spotlessly clean, crisp and minerally; good length and balance, but not quite enough varietal fruit. Screwcap. 13.5° alc. RATING 90 DRINK Now $ 16.99
Moyston Cabernet Merlot 2003 Medium-bodied; blackcurrant and blackberry fruit mix gaining complexity and structure from oak and tannins; solid wine. Bendigo/Grampians/Pyrenees. Screwcap. RATING 90 DRINK 2013 $ 23.95

ŸŸŸŸ **Victorian Cabernet Merlot 2004** Medium red-purple; blackcurrant fruit almost immediately off-set by earth/olive/forest notes. A consistent style over the years. Screwcap. 13° alc. RATING 89 DRINK 2012 $ 18

ŸŸŸŸ **Victoria Pinot Noir 2004** RATING 86 DRINK Now $ 16.99

Serafino Wines ★★★★☆

McLarens on the Lake, Kangarilla Road, McLaren Vale, SA 5171 REGION McLaren Vale
T (08) 8323 0157 F (08) 8323 0158 OPEN Mon–Fri 10–5, w'ends & public hols 10–4.30
WINEMAKER Scott Rawlinson EST. 2000 CASES 20 000
In wake of the sale of Maglieri Wines to Beringer Blass in 1998, Maglieri founder Steve Maglieri acquired the McLarens on the Lake complex originally established by Andrew Garrett. The accommodation has been upgraded and a larger winery was commissioned prior to the 2002 vintage. The operation draws upon 40 ha each of shiraz and cabernet sauvignon, 7 ha of chardonnay, 2 ha each of merlot, semillon, barbera, nebbiolo and sangiovese, and 1 ha of grenache. Part of the grape production is sold to others, the remainder goes to wines under the Serafino and McLarens on the Lake labels. Exports to the UK, the US, Asia, Italy and NZ.

ŸŸŸŸŸ **McLaren Vale Cabernet Sauvignon 2003** Medium-bodied; savoury/earthy/olive nuances to blackcurrant fruit; fine-grained tannins. Gold medal National Wine Show '05. RATING 94 DRINK 2013 $ 20

ŸŸŸŸ **McLaren Vale Shiraz 2003** Predominantly black fruits and strongly accented regional bitter chocolate; substantial framework, but yet to fill out. RATING 90 DRINK 2013 $ 20

Serventy Organic Wines ★★★

Rocky Road, Forest Grove, WA 6286 **REGION** Margaret River
T (08) 9757 7534 **F** (08) 9757 7272 **WWW**.serventy.com **OPEN** 7 days 10–5
WINEMAKER Frank Kittler **EST.** 1984 **CASES** 1700
In 2003 a small group of wine enthusiasts from Perth acquired the business from the famous
naturalist Serventy family (one of the early movers in organic viticulture and winemaking).
Substantial investments have been made to both vineyard and winery, and the house on the property
has been restored for short-term holiday stays. The quality of the wines has improved significantly,
without losing the original identity. Exports to the UK.

♥♥♥♥ **Purely Organic Shiraz Merlot Cabernet 2003** An array of ripe red fruits reflecting the
alcohol; prune and dark chocolate; fine tannins. Some suggestion of brett. Screwcap.
15° alc. **RATING** 87 **DRINK** 2009 $ 18

♥♥♥♡ **Purely Organic Solstice Rose 2004** Distinctly sweet cellar door style, but well enough
made. Cork. 12.5° alc. **RATING** 86 **DRINK** Now $ 18

Setanta Wines ★★★★★

RSD 43 Williamstown Road, Forreston, SA 5233 (postal) **REGION** Adelaide Hills
T (08) 8380 5516 **F** (08) 8380 5516 **WWW**.setantawines.com.au **OPEN** Not
WINEMAKER Rod Chapman, Rebecca Wilson **EST.** 1997 **CASES** 2500
Setanta is a family-owned operation involving Sheilagh Sullivan, her husband Tony, and brother
Bernard; the latter is the viticulturist, while Tony and Sheilagh manage marketing, administration
and so forth. Of Irish parentage (they are first-generation Australians), they chose Setanta, Ireland's
most famous mythological hero, as the brand name. The beautiful and striking labels tell the
individual stories which give rise to the names of the wines. Exports to Ireland, of course; also to the
UK, the US, Canada, Singapore and Hong Kong.

♥♥♥♥♥ **Black Sanglain Cabernet Sauvignon 2004** Very good purple-red; fragrant cassis
aromas; wonderfully supple, sweetly fruit-driven wine, with cassis, blackcurrant and silky
smooth tannins; subtle oak. Cork. 13.9° alc. **RATING** 95 **DRINK** 2019
Cuchulain Shiraz 2004 Deep purple-red; inviting, scented aromas; medium- to full-
bodied palate with rich, concentrated plum, blackberry and spice; lingering tannins, high-
quality oak, long finish. Trophy Adelaide Hills Wine Show 2005. Cork. 15.5° alc. **RATING** 94
DRINK 2015 $ 26
Cuchulain Shiraz 2002 Fragrant and elegant; bright blackberry, plum, licorice and spice
fruit; medium-bodied; perfect balance between oak and fruit; very fine tannins. High-
quality cork. **RATING** 94 **DRINK** 2012 $ 22
Black Sanglain Cabernet Sauvignon 2002 A complex wine; highly focused blackcurrant
fruit; hints of cassis and earth; fine, lingering tannins; balanced oak. Trophy winner
Adelaide Hills Wine Show 2004. Cork. **RATING** 94 **DRINK** 2015 $ 22

♥♥♥♥♡ **Speckled House Adelaide Hills Riesling 2004** Clean, tight apple blossom, spice and
lime aromas; lemon/lime acidity; good flow and line, still very fresh. Cork. 12.5° alc.
RATING 93 **DRINK** 2010 $ 17
Emer Chardonnay 2004 Light- to medium-bodied; very fine, elegant melon, nectarine
and fig subtly interwoven with oak; good mouthfeel, still developing. Cork. 13.1° alc.
RATING 93 **DRINK** 2010 $ 22

Settlers Ridge Organic Wines NR

54b Bussell Highway, Cowaramup, WA 6284 **REGION** Margaret River
T (08) 9755 5883 **F** (08) 9755 5883 **WWW**.settlersridge.com.au **OPEN** 7 days 10–5
WINEMAKER Wayne Nobbs **EST.** 1994 **CASES** 3500
Wayne and Kaye Nobbs have established what they say is the only vineyard in WA with organic
certification and the only producer in Australia with dual classification from NASAA (National
Association for Sustainable Agriculture Australia) and OVAA (Organic Vignerons Association of
Australia Inc). They have 7.5 ha of vineyard, including shiraz, cabernet sauvignon, merlot,
sangiovese, malbec, chenin blanc and sauvignon blanc. Exports to Germany.

Settlers Rise Montville

249 Western Avenue, Montville, Qld 4560 **REGION** Queensland Coastal
T (07) 5478 5558 **F** (07) 5478 5655 **WWW**.settlersrise.com.au **OPEN** 7 days 10–5
WINEMAKER Peter Scudamore-Smith MW (Contract) **EST.** 1998 **CASES** 3500
Settlers Rise is located in the beautiful highlands of the Blackall Range, 75 min drive north of Brisbane and 20 mins from the Sunshine Coast. A little over 1 ha of chardonnay, verdelho, shiraz and cabernet sauvignon have been planted at an elevation of 450m on the deep basalt soils of the property. First settled in 1887, Montville has gradually become a tourist destination, with a substantial local arts and crafts industry and a flourishing B&B and lodge accommodation.

ⵖⵖⵖⵖⵖ Reserve Shiraz 2002 Light- to medium-bodied, but has style and length in a savoury, spicy mode, with sweet fruit at the core; well-controlled oak inputs. Striking label. Granite Belt/Darling Downs. Cork. 14° alc. **RATING** 90 **DRINK** 2010 $ 27

ⵖⵖⵖⵖ Verdelho 2005 Extremely pale colour; clean fruit salad with a nice drizzle of lemony acidity; avoids sweetness on the finish. Screwcap. 14° alc. **RATING** 87 **DRINK** Now $ 18

ⵖⵖⵖⵖ Blackall Range White 2005 RATING 85 **DRINK** Now $ 17
Lake Baroon Cabernet Merlot 2002 RATING 85 **DRINK** Now $ 20

7 Acres Winery NR

374 Mons Road, Forest Glen, Buderim, Qld 4556 **REGION** Queensland Coastal
T (07) 5445 1198 **F** (07) 5445 1799 **WWW**.sunshinecoastwine.com.au/7acres_winery.htm
OPEN Mon–Fri 10–4, w'ends 10–5
WINEMAKER Tom Weidmann **EST.** 1985 **CASES** 3000
When Swiss-trained winemaker Tom Weidmann bought the former Moonshine Valley Winery, which had originally been established to produce fruit wines, he changed both the name and the focus of the business. The 2005 vintage was Tom Weidmann's 24th, and he seeks to make wines from single-vineyard sources, showing the grower and the place of the vineyard on the label. At the other extreme, there is also a range of ports and liqueurs for the general tourist, and the first sparkling wine from the Sunshine Coast, named Rose of Buderim.

Seven Mile Vineyard NR

84 Coolangatta Road, Shoalhaven Heads, NSW 2535 **REGION** Shoalhaven Coast
T (02) 4448 5466 **F** (02) 9357 3141 **WWW**.sevenmilevineyard.com.au **OPEN** Wed–Sun 10–6 (summer), Thurs–Sun 10–5 (winter)
WINEMAKER Eric Swarbrick **EST.** 1997 **CASES** 1500
The 1.8-ha Seven Mile Vineyard was established by Joan and Eric Swarbrick in 1997, east of the town of Berry, and within the sound of the surf on the Seven Mile Beach. The vineyard overlooks Coomonderry Swamp, one of the largest coastal wetlands in NSW.

Sevenhill Cellars

College Road, Sevenhill, SA 5453 **REGION** Clare Valley
T (08) 8843 4222 **F** (08) 8843 4382 **WWW**.sevenhillcellars.com.au **OPEN** Mon–Fri 9–5, w'ends & public hols 10–5
WINEMAKER Brother John May, Liz Heidenreich **EST.** 1851 **CASES** 35 000
One of the historical treasures of Australia; the oft-photographed stone wine cellars are the oldest in the Clare Valley, and winemaking is still carried out under the direction of the Jesuitical Manresa Society, and in particular Brother John May. Quality is very good, particularly of the powerful Shiraz; all the wines reflect the estate-grown grapes from old vines. Exports to NZ, Switzerland and the UK.

ⵖⵖⵖⵖ Riesling 2005 Massive CO_2 evident in the glass; fine apple and citrus fruit flavours behind the spritz. Needs time. Screwcap. **RATING** 89 **DRINK** 2012 $ 19
Merlot 2002 Good colour; savoury, earthy bouquet; quite pungent leafy, savoury, olive flavours; some length. Stained cork. **RATING** 88 **DRINK** 2009 $ 21

Sevenoaks Wines

NR

304 Doyles Creek Road, Jerrys Plains, NSW 2330 **REGION** Upper Hunter Valley
T (02) 6576 4285 **F** (02) 9586 3685 **WWW**.sevenoakswines.com.au **OPEN** By appt
WINEMAKER Hunter Wine Services (John Hordern) **EST.** 1997 **CASES** 1800
Robert and Deborah Sharp established Sevenoaks Wines in 1997, with the intention of selling the grapes to other winemakers. With only 2 ha of shiraz, 1.5 ha of sangiovese and 0.5 ha of petit verdot, it was inevitable that the wine from their grapes would be blended with many others, so in 2000 the Sharps changed course, retaining John Hordern as winemaker. The vineyard is part of a 68-ha property which abuts the Wollemi National Park at the bottom of the slopes that rises to be Mt Woodlands. Exports to Singapore, Malaysia and China.

Severn Brae Estate

NR

Lot 2 Back Creek Road (Mount Tully Road), Severnlea, Qld 4352 **REGION** Granite Belt
T (07) 4683 5292 **F** (07) 3391 3821 **OPEN** Mon–Fri 12–3, w'ends 10–5, or by appt
WINEMAKER Bruce Humphery-Smith **EST.** 1987 **CASES** 1400
Patrick and Bruce Humphery-Smith have established 5.5 ha of chardonnay with relatively close spacing, and trained on a high 2-tier trellis. Two-thirds of the production is sold, one-third used for the Severn Brae label.

Seville Estate

65 Linwood Road, Seville, Vic 3139 **REGION** Yarra Valley
T (03) 5964 2622 **F** (03) 5964 2633 **WWW**.sevilleestate.com.au **OPEN** 7 days 10–5
WINEMAKER Dylan McMahon **EST.** 1970 **CASES** 4000
In December 2005 Graham and Margaret Van Der Meulen acquired Seville Estate from the Brokenwood-based syndicate which had acquired it (from Brokenwood) several years earlier. Margaret Van Der Meulen is studying for a graduate certificate in viticulture and oenology from the University of Melbourne, and when the course is upgraded to a Masters Degree in 2007, she will continue her studies. She and husband Graham will be fully hands-on in the vineyard and winery, although Dylan McMahon (grandson of original owners Peter and Margaret McMahon) will continue as chief winemaker.

▼▼▼▼ **Rose 2005** Deep colour for rose, the hue good. There is plenty of flavour in a red fruit spectrum followed by a dry but well-balanced finish. Screwcap. 14° alc. **RATING** 89 **DRINK** Now $16
Beechworth Pinot Gris 2005 Quite deep colour; substantial richness, almost into honey; not phenolic, but not particularly varietal. Screwcap. **RATING** 88 **DRINK** Now $19

Seville Hill

8 Paynes Road, Seville, Vic 3139 **REGION** Yarra Valley
T (03) 5964 3284 **F** (03) 5964 2142 **WWW**.sevillehill.com.au **OPEN** 7 days 10–6
WINEMAKER Dom Bucci, John D'Aloisio **EST.** 1991 **CASES** 3000
John and Josie D'Aloisio have had a long-term involvement in the agricultural industry, which ultimately led to the establishment of the Seville Hill vineyard in 1991. There they have 2.4 ha of cabernet sauvignon and 1.3 ha each of merlot, shiraz and chardonnay. John D'Aloisio makes the wines with Dominic Bucci, a long-time Yarra resident and winemaker.

▼▼▼▼▼ **Reserve Yarra Valley Shiraz 2004** Light- to medium-bodied; bright, savoury, spicy red and black fruits; fine tannins, balanced oak. Diam. 14.8° alc. **RATING** 90 **DRINK** 2015 $29

▼▼▼▼ **Yarra Valley Cabernet Shiraz 2003** Lusciously sweet cassis raspberry fruit, sweetness which carries through all the way to the finish. Doubtless a crowd pleaser. Cork. 14.5° alc. **RATING** 87 **DRINK** 2008 $15

▼▼▼ **Yarra Valley Rose 2005 RATING** 83 $15
Yarra Valley Pinot Noir 2004 Light purple-red; focused and intense spiced plum fruit; good oak and tannin balance and support. Diam. 13.5° alc. **RATING** 81 **DRINK** 2014 $30

Sewards

NR

Lot 2, Wildwood Road, Yallingup, WA 6282 **REGION** Margaret River
T 0413 567 693 **F** (08) 6267 8009 **OPEN** Not
WINEMAKER Michael Kelly (Contract) **EST.** 1995 **CASES** 625
The 10-ha vineyard was established by Dr John McCarthy Seward in 1995, and is now run by family members. Most of the grapes are sold to Fermoy Estate, where the wines are contract-made. For the moment, sales are by mail order only, but a cellar door may be opened down the track.

Shadowfax

★★★★★

K Road, Werribee, Vic 3030 **REGION** Geelong
T (03) 9731 4420 **F** (03) 9731 4421 **WWW**.shadowfax.com.au **OPEN** 7 days 11–5
WINEMAKER Matt Harrop **EST.** 2000 **CASES** 15 000
Shadowfax is part of an awesome development at Werribee Park, a mere 20 mins from Melbourne. The truly striking winery, designed by Wood Marsh architects, built in 2000, is adjacent to the extraordinary 60-room private home built in the 1880s by the Chirnside family and known as The Mansion. It was then the centrepiece of a 40 000-ha pastoral empire, and the appropriately magnificent gardens were part of the reason why the property was acquired by Parks Victoria in the early 1970s. The Mansion is now The Mansion Hotel, with 92 rooms and suites, with the emphasis on conference bookings during the week and general tourism on the weekend. Exports to the UK, Japan, NZ and Singapore.

ŸŸŸŸŸ **Geelong Chardonnay 2004** Lovely complex, wild yeast barrel ferment aromas with a touch of funk adding complexity; long grapefruit, citrus and melon flavours; excellent acidity; 150 cases made. Trophy 2005 Geelong Wine Show. **RATING** 96 **DRINK** 2014 **$** 38

One Eye Heathcote Shiraz 2002 Fragrant spice overtones to black fruits; finely structured and perfectly balanced; power without alcohol. Has developed superbly over the last year. Screwcap. **RATING** 96 **DRINK** 2017 **$** 70

Adelaide Hills Sauvignon Blanc 2005 Eloquent varietal expression on both bouquet and palate; rich but not over the top gooseberry/tropical fruit; tightens nicely on the finish. Screwcap. 13° alc. **RATING** 94 **DRINK** Now **$** 20

Pinot Noir 2004 Very good hue; nicely ripened mix of plum and cherry; fine texture and structure; good length and finish. Geelong/Gippsland. Screwcap. 13.5° alc. **RATING** 94 **DRINK** 2011 **$** 30

Pink Cliffs Heathcote Shiraz 2003 Slightly more purple hue than the One Eye; firmer and slightly fresher, with more red fruit components; possibly slightly earlier picked, though the tannins are nonetheless firm. Screwcap. **RATING** 94 **DRINK** 2018 **$** 70

One Eye Heathcote Shiraz 2003 Ripe, rich, full-bodied palate, with sweet blackberry, dark plum and a hint of spice; ripe tannins run through the length of the palate. Screwcap. **RATING** 94 **DRINK** 2013 **$** 70

McLaren Vale Barossa Shiraz 2002 Very different mouthfeel and flavour spectrum to the Heathcote One Eye. Chocolate, blackberry, leather and spice; attractive, ripe tannins; good oak and tannin management. **RATING** 94 **DRINK** 2015 **$** 25

ŸŸŸŸ♀ **Landscape Tallarook Viognier 2004** Fragrant and fresh; gentle peach, apricot and lemon fruit; stylish and subtle. From the Landscape Vineyard at Tallarook. Screwcap. **RATING** 91 **DRINK** 2008 **$** 27

Victorian Rose 2005 Complex, distinctive pinot noir spice and strawberry base; mouthfeel ex old oak fermentation; right up there. Screwcap. 13.5° alc. **RATING** 91 **DRINK** Now **$** 20

Chardonnay 2004 Bright, fresh, crisp tangy style; long finish and aftertaste, all helped by restrained alcohol. Geelong/Beechworth/Cardinia Ranges. Screwcap. **RATING** 90 **DRINK** 2009 **$** 28

Landscape Tallarook Viognier 2005 Subdued bouquet, springing into life on the palate; apricot and peach fruit, but neither phenolic nor heavy; good acidity, food-friendly. Screwcap. 13° alc. **RATING** 90 **DRINK** Now **$** 25

Shiraz 2003 A complex, savoury, spicy mix of cool-grown, lighter components from Geelong and the power of Heathcote. The former wins the day. Screwcap. 14° alc. **RATING** 90 **DRINK** 2013 **$** 29

♥♥♥♥ **Adelaide Hills Pinot Gris 2005** Clean and correct, but simply shows the limitations of the variety; crisp finish. Screwcap. 13.5° alc. **RATING** 88 **DRINK** Now $ 24

Werribee Shiraz 2004 Deep colour; complex, with toasty/charry oak; blackberry fruit and slightly congested tannins. **RATING** 88 **DRINK** 2010 $ 29

Landscape Shiraz Viognier 2003 Fragrant aromatic, spicy, apricot overtones; has plenty of character in the mouth, but viognier dominates. Screwcap. **RATING** 88 **DRINK** 2010 $ 31

Shantell ★★★★

1974 Melba Highway, Dixons Creek, Vic 3775 **REGION** Yarra Valley
T (03) 5965 2155 **F** (03) 5965 2331 **WWW**.shantellvineyard.com.au **OPEN** 7 days 10.30–5
WINEMAKER Shan Shanmugam, Turid Shanmugam **EST.** 1980 **CASES** 2500
The substantial and fully mature Shantell vineyards provide the winery with a high-quality fruit source; part is sold to other Yarra Valley makers, the remainder vinified at Shantell. Chardonnay, Semillon and Cabernet Sauvignon are its benchmark wines, sturdily reliable, sometimes outstanding.

♥♥♥♥♥ **Yarra Valley Chardonnay 2004** Fragrant citrus overtones to the melon and stone fruit flavours; very good acidity and length, the oak merely a vehicle. Twin top. **RATING** 93 **DRINK** 2012 $ 28

Yarra Valley Pinot Noir 2003 Unusually sweet plummy fruit, with some vanilla and 5-spice on the aftertaste; a haunting style. Cork. 13° alc. **RATING** 92 **DRINK** 2009 $ 35

♥♥♥♥ **Yarra Valley Shiraz 2002** **RATING** 86 **DRINK** 2009 $ 28

Yarra Valley Cabernet Sauvignon 2002 **RATING** 86 **DRINK** 2010 $ 28

Sharmans ★★★

Glenbothy, 175 Glenwood Road, Relbia, Tas 7258 **REGION** Northern Tasmania
T (03) 6343 0773 **F** (03) 6343 0773 **OPEN** Thurs–Sun 11–5, closed during winter
WINEMAKER Pirie Consulting (Andrew Pirie) **EST.** 1987 **CASES** 1000
Mike Sharman pioneered one of the more interesting wine regions of Tas, not far south of Launceston but with a distinctly warmer climate than (say) Pipers Brook. Ideal north-facing slopes are home to a vineyard now approaching 4 ha. This additional warmth gives the red wines greater body than most Tasmanian counterparts.

♥♥♥♥ **Cabernet Sauvignon 2004** Light- to medium-bodied; spicy, leafy, cedary aromas and flavours; fair length. **RATING** 87 **DRINK** 2010 $ 18

♥♥♥♥ **Sauvignon Blanc 2005** **RATING** 86 **DRINK** Now $ 19

Pinot Noir 2004 **RATING** 85 **DRINK** 2008 $ 23

Unoaked Chardonnay 2005 **RATING** 84 **DRINK** Now $ 18

Sharpe Wines of Orange ★★★☆

Stagecoach Road, Emu Swamp, Orange, NSW 2800 **REGION** Orange
T (02) 6361 9046 **F** (02) 6361 1645 **WWW**.sharpewinesoforange.com.au **OPEN** W'ends 12–4
WINEMAKER Margot Sharpe, Rob Black **EST.** 1998 **CASES** 1200
When Margot and Tony Sharpe began planting their 3-ha vineyard, predominantly to cabernet sauvignon, with lesser amounts of merlot and cabernet franc, the wheel turned in a somewhat wayward full circle. Sharpe Bros Cordials was established in 1868 by strict Methodists to give the working man something to drink other than the demon alcohol. Says Margot Sharpe, 'I do believe there might be some serious grave turning over the product.' The Rose and Single Barrel Cabernet Sauvignon were made by the Sharpes in a tiny winery established in small stables at the back of their house; the Jack Demmery Cabernet Sauvignon was named in honour of Margot Sharpe's late father, who died just as planting of the vineyard was completed.

YYYY Chardonnay 2004 Clean; appealing nectarine and grapefruit flavours; light-bodied; good balance and length. Screwcap. 13° alc. **RATING** 89 **DRINK** 2009 $18

Reserve Cabernet Sauvignon 2003 A curious role reversal with the Merlot; this more elegant, medium-bodied wine has spicy/cedary/earthy flavours, perhaps partly due to the extra year in bottle. Diam. 13.6° alc. **RATING** 89 **DRINK** 2012 $20

Merlot 2004 Strong red-purple colour; medium- to full-bodied, with no shortage of flavour or extract; much denser than the '03, and less would have been better. Diam. 14.1° alc. **RATING** 87 **DRINK** 2012 $18

Shaw & Smith

★★★★★

Lot 4 Jones Road, Balhannah, SA 5242 **REGION** Adelaide Hills
T (08) 8398 0500 **F** (08) 8398 0600 **WWW**.shawandsmith.com **OPEN** W'ends 11–4
WINEMAKER Martin Shaw, Darryl Catlin **EST**. 1989 **CASES** 35 000
Has progressively moved from a contract grape-grown base to estate production with the development of a 51.5-ha vineyard at Balhannah, followed in 2000 by a state-of-the-art, beautifully designed and executed winery, which ended the long period of tenancy at Petaluma. Exports to the UK, the US, Canada, Hong Kong, Japan and Singapore.

YYYYY M3 Vineyard Chardonnay 2004 A wine of marvellous finesse; elegant but intense melon, citrus, nectarine and pear; malolactic and barrel ferment inputs there without trumpeting their presence. Vibrant. Cork. 13° alc. **RATING** 96 **DRINK** 2012 $35

Riesling 2005 Powerful, intense aromas and flavours; lime, spice and ripe apple; lingering finish. Screwcap. **RATING** 95 **DRINK** 2013 $19

Adelaide Hills Sauvignon Blanc 2005 Ultra-pure and refined wine; intense but elegant palate, with tangy, lemony acidity, and a lingering, dry finish. Screwcap. **RATING** 95 **DRINK** Now $25

Shiraz 2004 Elegantly balanced and crafted; predominantly spicy red fruits, supported by fine, persistent tannins. Quality cork. 14° alc. **RATING** 94 **DRINK** 2014 $35

YYYYY Pinot Noir 2004 Good colour; light- to medium-bodied; supple, smooth, spicy plummy fruit; restrained oak, good length; promising start. High-quality cork. **RATING** 90 **DRINK** 2008 $45

Shaw Vineyard Estate

★★★★

Isabelle Drive, Murrumbateman, NSW 2582 **REGION** Canberra District
T 0412 633 542 **WWW**.shawvineyards.com.au **OPEN** Wed–Sun & public hols 9.30–5
WINEMAKER Bill Calabria, Ken Helm (Contract) **EST**. 1999 **CASES** 1500
Graeme and Michael Shaw have established 32 ha of vineyard, planted to semillon, riesling, shiraz, merlot and cabernet sauvignon. Most of the production is sold to Hardys. A winery, cellar door and restaurant opened in 2005.

YYYYY Canberra Riesling 2005 Straw-green; a clean bouquet; well-structured citrus and a touch of passionfruit; good length and intensity. Screwcap. 12° alc. **RATING** 94 **DRINK** 2013 $22

YYYYY Canberra Semillon 2004 Very similar style and structure to the '05, though with slightly more focus and intensity (and, perhaps, bottle development). Screwcap. 12° alc. **RATING** 90 **DRINK** 2010 $20

YYYY Canberra Semillon 2005 Clean, easy access style; patience not really needed; soft lemony fruit, balanced finish. Screwcap. 12° alc. **RATING** 89 **DRINK** 2010 $20

Canberra Cabernet Merlot 2003 Clean, fresh red fruits, but very light-bodied; on the other hand, the components are balanced. Screwcap. 13.5° alc. **RATING** 87 **DRINK** 2008 $20

Cabernet Sauvignon 2003 Some colour development; medium-bodied; cedary, earthy edges to blackcurrant fruit; gentle tannins and oak. Screwcap. 13.2° alc. **RATING** 87 **DRINK** 2009 $20

Cabernet Sauvignon 2002 Continued colour development; more cedary/leafy, but does have nice line and length. Cork. 13.2° alc. **RATING** 87 **DRINK** 2008 $20

Shawwood Estate   NR

Cnr Craigmoor Road/Henry Lawson Drive, Mudgee, NSW 2850 **REGION** Mudgee
T (02) 6372 0237 **F** (02) 6372 0355 **WWW**.shawwood.com.au **OPEN** W'ends & public hols 10–4
WINEMAKER Craig Bishop **EST.** 1998 **CASES** 3000
Shawwood Estate has been established a mere 2.5 km from Mudgee, on a slight rise on the northern
side overlooking the township. A group of investors, including Charles Tym, Alison Bishop and Craig
Bishop, have planted 3.3 ha each of shiraz and cabernet sauvignon, and 1.7 ha each of chardonnay
and verdelho.

Shays Flat Vineyard

3A Brookville Road, Toorak, Vic 3142 (postal) **REGION** Pyrenees
T 0407 644 184 **F** (03) 9826 6191 **WWW**.shaysflat.com **OPEN** Not
WINEMAKER Michael Unwin Wines **EST.** 1999 **CASES** 500
With advice from leading viticultural consultant Di Davidson, Rob and Isabella Burns have planted
11 ha of shiraz, 3.5 ha of cabernet sauvignon, 3.1 ha of merlot and 0.9 ha of sangiovese on the western
slopes of the Pyrenees Ranges in the Landsborough-Elmhurst Valley. Since the arrival of Glenlofty
Vineyard in 1995, almost 1000 ha of vines have been planted in the valley. The Shays Flat soil has a
thin layer of loam over a red-orange duplex clay heavily dispersed with quartz particles, the quartz
providing favourable water holding and draining properties. Situated at an altitude of 300–330m on
gently rising ridges, the property is situated at the end of the Great Dividing Range, and is slightly
warmer than most of the Pyrenees and Grampians vineyards.

ΥΥΥΥΥ **Pyrenees Shiraz 2003** Very ripe confit plum and blackberry fruit; the wine does show
some drought impact, and the oak is still integrating. Screwcap. 14.5° alc. **RATING** 96
DRINK 2011 $ 20
Pyrenees Shiraz 2002 Retains very good colour; medium-bodied, elegant, long and
supple; black fruits with a caress of French oak. Cork. 14° alc. **RATING** 94 **DRINK** 2015 $ 20

ΥΥΥΥ **Pyrenees Sangiovese 2003** Light cherry, spice and earth; fine tannins, savoury. The
Burns' describe it as a wild child, and I wonder whether it (along with so many other
Sangioveses) would rather be back in Italy. Screwcap. 13.5° alc. **RATING** 87 **DRINK** 2008
$ 18

She-Oak Hill Vineyard   NR

82 Hope Street, South Yarra, Vic 3141 (postal) **REGION** Heathcote
T (03) 9866 7890 **OPEN** Not
WINEMAKER Hanging Rock (John Ellis) **EST.** 1995 **CASES** 600
Gordon, Judith and Julian Leckie selected a vineyard site on the east side of She-Oak Hill, lying
between Jasper Hill Emily's Paddock and Mount Ida, sharing the same Cambrian red soil and an
immaculate address pedigree. They opted for a dry-grown vineyard, but years of drought meant the
establishment phase was prolonged, and it was not until 2001 (6 years after the vines were planted)
that the first commercial crop was obtained. The vines now have a deep root system and are
producing well without any supplementary water. They have 1.4 ha of shiraz and 0.6 ha of
chardonnay, producing around 400–600 cases of Shiraz and 200–300 cases of Chardonnay, with
yearly variation depending on the growing conditions. Lower than usual alcohol levels is a feature of
the wines.

Sheep's Back   NR

PO Box 441, South Melbourne, Vic 3205 **REGION** Barossa Valley
T (03) 9696 7018 **F** (03) 9686 4015 **OPEN** Not
WINEMAKER Dean Hewitson **EST.** 2001 **CASES** 3000
Sheep's Back is a joint venture between Neil Empson (with 30 years' experience as an exporter to
Australia and elsewhere of Italian wines) and Dean Hewitson. They decided to produce a single
estate-grown shiraz after an extensive search found a 6-ha vineyard of 75-year-old vines. Exports to
the US and Canada.

Shelmerdine Vineyards ★★★★★

Merindoc Vineyard, Lancefield Road, Tooborac, Vic 3522 **REGION** Heathcote
T (03) 5433 5188 **F** (03) 5433 5118 **WWW**.shelmerdine.com.au **OPEN** 7 days 10–5
WINEMAKER De Bortoli (Stephen Webber) **EST.** 1989 **CASES** NA
Stephen Shelmerdine has been a major figure in the wine industry for well over 20 years, like his
family before him (who founded Mitchelton Winery), and has been honoured for his many services to
the industry. The venture has 130 ha of vineyards spread over 3 sites: Lusatia Park in the Yarra Valley
and Merindoc Vineyard and Willoughby Bridge in the Heathcote region. Substantial quantities of
the grapes produced are sold to others; a small amount of high-quality wine is contract-made. The
cellar door is at the Merindoc Vineyard.

▼▼▼▼▼ **Heathcote Shiraz 2004** Bright purple; finely balanced and structured blackberry and
plum fruit; fine tannins. Benefits greatly from the controlled alcohol; long finish, subtle
oak. Screwcap. 13.5° alc. **RATING** 95 **DRINK** 2019 $ 30
Heathcote Viognier 2005 Gloriously fragrant apricot, pear and fig aromas and flavours;
carries its alcohol with aplomb; good acidity to close. Screwcap. 14.6° alc. **RATING** 94
DRINK Now $ 25
Heathcote Cabernet Sauvignon 2004 Medium-bodied, with bright cassis, mulberry and
blackcurrant fruit; nicely balanced oak and tannins; good length and aftertaste. Screwcap.
13° alc. **RATING** 94 **DRINK** 2014 $ 30

▼▼▼▼▽ **Yarra Valley Sauvignon Blanc 2005** Spotlessly clean bouquet; a refined but intense mix
of gooseberry, passionfruit and green apple; good acidity. Screwcap. **RATING** 92
DRINK Now $ 20
Yarra Valley Pinot Noir 2004 Fragrant, light spicy fruit; foresty characters on a long,
savoury finish. Screwcap. **RATING** 90 **DRINK** 2010 $ 24

▼▼▼▼ **Yarra Valley Chardonnay 2004** Crisp, crunchy and lively melon and citrus fruit which
does, however, dip on the mid-palate; may fill out with time. Screwcap. 13.5° alc.
RATING 89 **DRINK** 2009 $ 24
Heathcote Merlot 2004 Pleasant light- to medium-bodied wine; raspberry, cherry and
touches of spice; tannins and oak incidental. Screwcap. **RATING** 89 **DRINK** Now $ 24

Shepherd's Hut ★★★☆

PO Box 194, Darlington, WA 6070 **REGION** Porongurup
T (08) 9299 6700 **F** (08) 9299 6703 **WWW**.shepherdshutwines.com **OPEN** Not
WINEMAKER Rob Diletti **EST.** 1996 **CASES** 1600
The shepherd's hut which appears on the wine label was one of four stone huts used in the 1850s to house
shepherds tending large flocks of sheep. When WA pathologist Dr Michael Wishart (and family)
purchased the property in 1996, the hut was in a state of extreme disrepair. It has since been entirely
restored, and still features the honey-coloured Mt Barker stone. A total of 18 ha of riesling, chardonnay,
sauvignon blanc, shiraz and cabernet sauvignon have been established; the daily running of the vineyard
is the responsibility of son Philip, who also runs a large farm of mainly cattle; son William helps with
marketing and sales. Most of the grapes are sold to other makers in the region. Exports to the UK.

▼▼▼▼▽ **Porongurup Riesling 2005** Light straw-green; ripe apple, citrus and passionfruit, a trace
of sweetness on the finish will add to the appeal for many. Screwcap. 13° alc. **RATING** 90
DRINK 2012 $ 18

▼▼▼▼ **Moulin Great Southern Rose 2005** Sweet, aromatic cherry blossom aromas, the quite dry
palate coming as a (pleasant) surprise. Screwcap. 12.8° alc. **RATING** 87 **DRINK** Now $ 15

Shepherd's Moon ★★★★

Barwang Ridge, 1 Barwang Road, via Young, NSW 2594 **REGION** Hilltops
T (02) 6382 6363 **F** (02) 6382 6363 **OPEN** Sat–Mon 10–5 or by appt
WINEMAKER Canberra Winemakers (Greg Gallagher) **EST.** 1979 **CASES** 1500
Rick and Julie Hobba purchased the Hansen Hilltops property in 2002. They have since engaged in an
extensive rehabilitation program in the vineyard, with minimal crops in the meantime. The plantings
are 2 ha cabernet sauvignon, 1.5 ha riesling, and 1 ha each of chardonnay, shiraz and semillon.

ŶŶŶŶŶ **Cabernet Sauvignon 2004** Very good colour; medium-bodied, with stylish restraint, fine texture and balance; the blackcurrant fruit is supported by quality oak, and a long finish. Screwcap. 14° alc. **RATING** 93 **DRINK** 2019 $20

Shiraz 2004 Despite the alcohol, light- to medium-bodied and quite graceful; spicy/cedary/briary overtones to the blackberry fruit; fine tannins. Screwcap. 14.4° alc. **RATING** 90 **DRINK** 2012 $22

ŶŶŶŶ **Chardonnay 2005** Good structure and texture provided by a minerally core to the tight melon and fig fruit. Apparently unoaked. Screwcap. 11.9° alc. **RATING** 89 **DRINK** 2009 $15

Riesling 2005 Light straw-green; a clean, soft, lime/tropical/passionfruit mix of flavours, finishing with a touch of sweetness. Screwcap. 11.5° alc. **RATING** 88 **DRINK** 2009 $15

Sherwood Estate   NR

1187 Gowings Hill Road, Sherwood, NSW 2440 **REGION** Hastings River
T (02) 6581 4900 **WWW**.sherwoodestatewines.com.au **OPEN** Fri–Sun & public hols 11–4, or by appt
WINEMAKER Karen Legget **EST.** 1998 **CASES** 750
John and Helen Ross began planting the Sherwood Estate vineyard in 1998, with 2 ha of chambourcin. Subsequently, verdelho, chardonnay, cabernet franc, semillon and (most recently) sangiovese have been planted, with 10 ha now under vine. The vineyard is in the Macleay Valley, 15 mins west of Kempsey on the NSW North Coast. The property has a total of 43 ha of undulating fertile soils, rich in limestone. The wines are also available from the Sherwood Wine Embassy, Port Macquarie.

Shingleback

1 Main Road, McLaren Vale, SA 5171 **REGION** McLaren Vale
T (08) 8323 7388 **F** (08) 8323 7336 **WWW**.shingleback.com.au **OPEN** 7 days 10–5
WINEMAKER John Davey, Dan Hills **EST.** 1995 **CASES** 100 000
Shingleback has 100 ha of vineyards in McLaren Vale, all of which is vinified for the Shingleback labels. Originally a specialist export business, but now the wines are also available in Australia. Exports to the US, the UK, Canada and Europe.

ŶŶŶŶŶ **The Gate McLaren Vale Shiraz 2002** Redolent with regional dark chocolate surrounding a supple core of black fruits; delicious, almost silky, mouthfeel; long finish. Deserves better than the poor cork it gets. **RATING** 95 **DRINK** 2017 $45

ŶŶŶŶŶ **McLaren Vale Chardonnay 2005** Quite powerful stone fruit/grapefruit aromas and flavours, balanced by a nice touch of oak; good length, ready now. Screwcap. 13.5° alc. **RATING** 90 **DRINK** 2009 $22

Grenache 2004 Soft, but not jammy or vapid, gently spicy raspberry, plum and black cherry fruit; minimal oak interference in a delicious early-drinking example of Grenache. Cork. 14.5° alc. **RATING** 90 **DRINK** 2009 $27

Red Knot McLaren Vale Cabernet Sauvignon 2004 Fresh, clean cassis and blackcurrant; exuberant but not heavy; great early drinking style. Zork. **RATING** 90 **DRINK** Now $15

ŶŶŶŶ **McLaren Vale Cabernet Sauvignon 2003** Medium-bodied; blackcurrant, blackberry and a touch of chocolate; firm tannins, but should soften. Cork. **RATING** 88 **DRINK** 2009 $27

Black Bubbles McLaren Vale Sparkling Shiraz NV Rich black fruits; good balance and dosage; not phenolic or oaky; worth time on cork. 14° alc. **RATING** 88 **DRINK** 2010 $25

Red Knot McLaren Vale Shiraz 2004 Light- to medium-bodied; clean, fresh and well-made; blackberry and spice fruit; just a hint of green tannins. Zork. **RATING** 87 **DRINK** 2008 $15

McLaren Vale Shiraz 2003 Leather, dark chocolate, blackberry and earth aromas and flavours; slight astringency on the finish. Cork. **RATING** 87 **DRINK** 2008 $27

Red Knot Cadenzia 2004 Powerful, potent wine; very ripe, slightly jammy fruit and tannins still to come to terms with each other, Grenache/Shiraz. Zork. 14.5° alc. **RATING** 87 **DRINK** 2009 $14

▼▼▼♡ **White Knot McLaren Vale Chardonnay 2005** Rich, full peachy fruit unassisted by oak, but plenty of mouthfeel. Well enough priced. Zork. 13.5° alc. **RATING** 86 **DRINK** Now $ 14
McLaren Vale Grenache Rose 2005 **RATING** 85 **DRINK** Now $ 17

Shiralee Wines   NR

PO Box 260, Nuriootpa, SA 5355 **REGION** Barossa Valley
T (08) 8564 2799 **F** (08) 8564 2799 **OPEN** Not
WINEMAKER Bob Mitchell **EST.** 2001 **CASES** NA
Shiralee Wines is the venture of Graeme Ruwoldt and Bob Mitchell, with access to 25 ha of chardonnay and shiraz in the Barossa Valley. Only part of the output is vinified for the Shiralee brand; the major market is the US.

Shirvington   NR

PO Box 220, McLaren Vale, SA 5171 **REGION** McLaren Vale
T (08) 8383 0554 **F** (08) 8383 0556 **WWW**.shirvington.com **OPEN** Not
WINEMAKER Kim Johnston **EST.** 1996 **CASES** 2700
The Shirvington family began the development of their McLaren Vale vineyards in 1996 under the direction of viticulturist Peter Bolte, and now have 35 ha under vine, the majority to shiraz and cabernet sauvignon, and with small additional plantings of merlot, cabernet franc and verdelho. A substantial part of the production is sold as grapes, the best reserved for the Shirvington wines. Exports to NZ and the US.

Shottesbrooke

Bagshaws Road, McLaren Flat, SA 5171 **REGION** McLaren Vale
T (08) 8383 0002 **WWW**.shottesbrooke.com.au **OPEN** Mon–Fri 10–4.30, w'ends & public hols 11–5
WINEMAKER Nick Holmes, Hamish Maguire **EST.** 1984 **CASES** 12 000
For many years now the full-time business of former Ryecroft winemaker Nick Holmes (now with stepson Hamish Maguire), drawing primarily on estate-grown grapes at his Myoponga vineyard. He has always stood out for the finesse and elegance of his wines compared with the dam-buster, high-alcohol reds for which McLaren Vale has become famous (or infamous, depending on one's point of view). Now the wheel has started to turn full circle, and finesse and elegance are much more appreciated. Exports to the UK, the US and Europe.

▼▼▼▼♡ **McLaren Vale Shiraz 2004** Blackberry and black plum giving fruit sweetness on the mid-palate; fine, smooth tannins on a long finish; subtle oak. Screwcap. 14.5° alc. **RATING** 91
DRINK 2011 $ 18
McLaren Vale Merlot 2004 In generous, rich, regional style, but is strongly varietal, with juicy blackcurrant and olive flavours through the palate, the sweeter end of the spectrum prevailing. Screwcap. 14° alc. **RATING** 90 **DRINK** 2011 $ 17

▼▼▼▼ **Fleurieu Adelaide Hills Sauvignon Blanc 2005** Very pale straw-green; crisp, lively, delicate apple, pear and passionfruit. Screwcap. 14° alc. **RATING** 89 **DRINK** Now $ 15
McLaren Vale Cabernet Sauvignon 2003 Quite powerful; at the briary/earthy end of the spectrum, but the tannins are seamlessly interwoven to aid structure. Counter-cultural style. Screwcap. 13.5° alc. **RATING** 88 **DRINK** 2010 $ 18
McLaren Vale Chardonnay 2004 Clean, light- to medium-bodied, with relatively subdued melon and fig fruit; neatly balanced oak. Screwcap. 14° alc. **RATING** 87
DRINK 2008 $ 15
Merlette 2005 Bright, light red-purple; attractive rose style, with positive raspberry and red cherry fruit; although slightly sweet, has good balance and length. Screwcap. 14° alc.
RATING 87 **DRINK** Now $ 14
McLaren Vale Cabernet Sauvignon 2004 Herb, olive and leaf aromas suggest some lack of ripeness; the palate, however, has quite sweet fruit. Screwcap. 13.5° alc. **RATING** 87
DRINK 2009 $ 18

Sienna Estate ★★★★☆

Canal Rocks Road, Yallingup, WA 6282 **REGION** Margaret River
T (08) 9755 2028 **F** (08) 9755 2101 **WWW**.siennaestate.com.au **OPEN** W'ends & hols 10–5
WINEMAKER Egidijus Rusilas **EST.** 1978 **CASES** 2000
The 3.7-ha vineyard, planted to semillon, sauvignon blanc, riesling and cabernet sauvignon, was established by David Hunt in 1978. It has now passed into the ownership of the Rusilas family.

ΨΨΨΨΨ **Momentum of Passion Semillon Sauvignon Blanc 2005** Spotlessly clean, fresh and lively; very attractive lemony bouquet, with touches of passionfruit (what else?) on the long, bright palate. Screwcap. 13° alc. **RATING** 94 **DRINK** 2009 $ 17

ΨΨΨΨΨ **Momentum of Freedom Chardonnay 2005** Tangy, vibrant grapefruit and melon; long, clean finish; oak (if any) invisible. Screwcap. 13° alc. **RATING** 93 **DRINK** 2010 $ 17
Momentum of Love Cabernet Sauvignon 2003 Good colour; medium-bodied, smooth cassis, blackcurrant and mulberry fruit; well-knit tannins a plus. Cork. 12.5° alc.
RATING 93 **DRINK** 2013 $ 20
Momentum of Youth Semillon 2005 An intense bouquet, virtually free of the sweaty characters of the Riesling; the palate likewise stacked with flavours of grass, herbs and more tropical notes akin to sauvignon blanc. Screwcap. 13° alc. **RATING** 92 **DRINK** 2011 $ 16

ΨΨΨΨ **Momentum of Life Riesling 2005** **RATING** 85 **DRINK** 2009 $ 16

Silk Hill ★★★☆

324 Motor Road, Deviot, Tas 7275 **REGION** Northern Tasmania
T (03) 6394 7385 **F** (03) 6394 7392 **OPEN** By appt
WINEMAKER Gavin Scott **EST.** 1989 **CASES** 500
Pharmacist Gavin Scott has been a weekend and holiday viticulturist for many years, having established the Glengarry Vineyard, which he sold, and then establishing the 1.5-ha Silk Hill (formerly Silkwood Vineyard) in 1989, planted exclusively to pinot noir. Growing and making Pinot Noir and fishing will keep him occupied when he sells his pharmacy business.

ΨΨΨΨ **Pinot Noir 2004** Good colour; medium-bodied, with plenty of ripe plummy fruit, and quite substantial tannins. For the long haul. **RATING** 89 **DRINK** 2009
The Supply Pinot Noir 2004 Big, rich, ripe, fleshy and luscious black fruits and ripe tannins plus oak. **RATING** 89 **DRINK** 2010

Silkwood Wines NR

Lot 5204 Channybearup Road, Pemberton, WA 6260 **REGION** Pemberton
T (08) 9776 1584 **F** (08) 9776 0019 **WWW**.silkwoodwines.com.au **OPEN** 7 days 11–4
WINEMAKER Contract **EST.** 1998 **CASES** 800
Third-generation farmers Pam and John Allen returned from a short break running small businesses in Adelaide and Perth to purchase Silkwood in 1998. Plantings began with 5 ha of shiraz and sauvignon blanc in 1999, followed by a further 5.5 ha of riesling, pinot noir, merlot and cabernet sauvignon in 2000. The vineyard is patrolled by a large flock of guinea fowl, eliminating most insect pests, and reducing the use of chemicals.

Silver Wings Winemaking ★★★★☆

Paramoor Farm, 439 Three Chain Road, Carlsruhe, Vic 3442 **REGION** Central Victoria Zone
T (03) 5429 2444 **F** (03) 5429 2442 **OPEN** By appt
WINEMAKER Keith Brien **EST.** 2003 **CASES** 1500
This is the new venture of Keith Brien, formerly of Cleveland. After a brief shared occupation with Goona Warra Winery in Sunbury, he has moved Silver Wings to a little winery at Carlsruhe, near Lancefield. Here he offers contract winemaking and export consulting, as well as making the Silver Wings wines from 4 ha of contract-grown grapes (3 ha of mourvedre, 1 ha of shiraz) coming from 50-year-old vines.

Ⓨ Ⓨ Ⓨ Ⓨ Ⓨ **Grand Reserve Macedon Ranges Brut XO 1993** Elegant and fine; still very fresh; subtle complexity; long and lingering. Ten years on lees; liqueured with XO Cognac. **RATING** 94 **DRINK** 2010 $ 50

Ⓨ Ⓨ Ⓨ Ⓨ Ⓨ **Vincenzo OV 2004** Good colour; a supple and smooth medium-bodied palate, with red and black fruits; fine-grained tannins; good length and finish. Old Vine Mourvedre (60%)/Shiraz (40%). Diam. 13.5° alc. **RATING** 93 **DRINK** 2014 $ 27

🐀 Silverwaters Vineyard

PO Box 41, San Remo, Vic 3925 **REGION** Gippsland
T (03) 5678 8230 **F** (03) 5678 5989 **OPEN** Not
WINEMAKER Paul Evans (Contract) **EST.** 1995 **CASES** 1000
Lyn and Lionel Hahn planted 0.5 ha each of chardonnay, pinot gris, pinot noir, shiraz and cabernet sauvignon in 1995. The first commercial vintage followed 5 years later, and the wines have gone from strength to strength, the 2003 Pinot Noir winning the trophy and gold medal for Pinot Noir at the International Cool Climate Wine Show 2005.

Ⓨ Ⓨ Ⓨ Ⓨ Ⓨ **Pinot Noir 2003** Deep colour; complex, ripe dark plum and spice aromas and flavours; good varietal character, good mouthfeel. Cork. 14° alc. **RATING** 91 **DRINK** 2008 $ 20

Silverwood Wines ★★★★☆

Bittern–Dromana Road, Balnarring, Vic 3926 **REGION** Mornington Peninsula
T 0419 890 317 **F** (03) 9888 5303 **WWW**.silverwoodwines.com.au **OPEN** Not
WINEMAKER Paul Dennis, Phillip Kittle **EST.** 1997 **CASES** 350
Paul and Denise Dennis were inspired to establish Silverwood by living in France for a year. They, with members of their family, did much of the establishment work on the vineyard, which is meticulously maintained. Most of the grapes are sold to other Mornington Peninsula wineries, but a small amount of attractive wine is made under the Silverwood label.

Ⓨ Ⓨ Ⓨ Ⓨ Ⓨ **Mornington Peninsula Pinot Noir 2004** Clear but deep purple-red; generous, ripe plum and black cherry; velvety mouthfeel; will grow in bottle. Screwcap. 13.9° alc. **RATING** 93 **DRINK** 2011 $ 31
Mornington Peninsula Chardonnay 2004 Medium green-yellow; powerful, tangy citrus and grapefruit; excellent length and focus; quality French oak. Screwcap. 13.5° alc. **RATING** 92 **DRINK** 2010 $ 24

Ⓨ Ⓨ Ⓨ Ⓨ **Mornington Peninsula Pinot Rose 2005** Light style; crisp and balanced; strawberries and lemony acidity. Screwcap. 14.2° alc. **RATING** 86 **DRINK** Now $ 17

Simon Gilbert Wines ★★★☆

1220 Sydney Road, Mudgee, NSW 2850 **REGION** Mudgee
T (02) 6373 1245 **F** (02) 6373 1350 **WWW**.simongilbertwines.com.au **OPEN** 7 days 9–5
WINEMAKER Andrew Ewart, David Darlow **EST.** 1993 **CASES** 35 000
The arrival of high-profile, ex-Southcorp senior executives David Coombe as Chairman and Paul Pacino as Chief Executive has seen a complete restructuring of this $20 million, 5000-tonne winery. In late 2005 the company merged with Cassegrain, which extends the vineyard resources to include the burgeoning Northern Slopes/New England areas of NSW. There will also be rationalisation of the winemaking business of Cassegrain, albeit with the active and continued involvement of John Cassegrain, who has become a shareholder in Simon Gilbert. The wines, with new products being introduced, continue to be predominantly sourced from the Central Ranges regions of NSW, including Orange, Mudgee and Cowra. Exports to all major markets.

Ⓨ Ⓨ Ⓨ Ⓨ **Card Series Central Ranges Semillon Sauvignon Blanc 2005** The clean aromas and flavours are primarily those of semillon, the sauvignon blanc impact minimal; long, minerally finish. Screwcap. 13° alc. **RATING** 89 **DRINK** 2010 $ 15
Card Series Central Ranges Verdelho 2005 Has more going for it than most, with a nice twist of lemony acidity to give length and freshness. Screwcap. 14° alc. **RATING** 88 **DRINK** Now $ 15

Card Series Central Ranges Riesling 2005 Soft, ripe, flavoursome apple, lime and tropical mix; needs a touch more acidity and drive. Screwcap. 12° alc. **RATING** 87 **DRINK** 2009 $15

Card Series Central Ranges Chardonnay 2005 Fruit-driven nectarine, peach and melon; plenty of flavour and well-enough balanced. Screwcap. 13.5° alc. **RATING** 87 **DRINK** 2008 $15

Card Series Central Ranges Cabernet Rose 2005 Light-bodied; red fruits with neatly counterpoised acidity and residual sugar. Screwcap. 13° alc. **RATING** 87 **DRINK** Now $15

Card Series Central Ranges Sangiovese Barbera 2004 Light, bright red; light- to medium-bodied, clean cherry fruit; persistent, slightly dry tannins; food style. Cork. 14° alc. **RATING** 87 **DRINK** Now $15

ΨΨΨΨ **Card Series Central Ranges Pinot Grigio 2005 RATING** 86 **DRINK** Now $15

Simon Hackett

Budgens Road, McLaren Vale, SA 5171 **REGION** McLaren Vale
T (08) 8323 7712 **F** (08) 8323 7713 **OPEN** Wed–Sun 11–5
WINEMAKER Simon Hackett **EST.** 1981 **CASES** 20 000
In 1998 Simon Hackett acquired the former Taranga winery in McLaren Vale, which has made his winemaking life a great deal easier. He has 8 ha of estate vines, and has contract growers in McLaren Vale and the Barossa Valley, with another 32 ha of vines.

ΨΨΨΨΨ **Old Vine McLaren Vale Grenache 2004** Has the substantial structure of McLaren Vale grenache without losing the juicy fruit which is the varietal marker. Cork. 14° alc. **RATING** 91 **DRINK** 2012 $15

ΨΨΨΨ **McLaren Vale Shiraz 2003** Ripe blackberry and plum fruit flavours; a savoury, chocolatey finish. Stained cork. 14° alc. **RATING** 89 **DRINK** 2010 $18

Brightview Barossa Valley Chardonnay 2005 Sweet peachy fruit balanced by oak; generous mouthfeel; barrel-fermented, lees contact. Screwcap. 13.5° alc. **RATING** 88 **DRINK** Now $15

ΨΨΨΨ **McLaren Vale Cabernet Sauvignon 2003** Those '03 fruit characters surrounded by swathes of regional dark chocolate, which do help the wine, though not necessarily the varietal character. Cork. 14° alc. **RATING** 86 **DRINK** 2009 $18

Sinclair Wines

Graphite Road, Glenoran, WA 6258 **REGION** Manjimup
T (08) 9335 6318 **F** (08) 9433 5489 **WWW**.sinclairwines.com.au **OPEN** By appt
WINEMAKER Brenden Smith (Contract) **EST.** 1994 **CASES** 2800
Sinclair Wines is the child of Darelle Sinclair, a science teacher, wine educator and graduate viticulturist from Charles Sturt University, and John Healy, a lawyer, traditional jazz musician and graduate wine marketing student of Adelaide University, Roseworthy campus. The 5 ha of estate plantings underpin high-quality wines at mouthwatering prices. Exports to the UK, The Netherlands and Japan.

ΨΨΨΨΨ **Giovanni Manjimup Cabernet Sauvignon 2004** Medium-bodied; good blackcurrant and cassis fruit; balanced tannins, good length. Cork. 13° alc. **RATING** 90 **DRINK** 2012 $20

ΨΨΨΨ **Swallow Hill Manjimup Sauvignon Blanc 2005** Pale straw-green; clean, light-bodied, gentle tropical and mineral mix. Screwcap. 12.5° alc. **RATING** 89 **DRINK** Now $16

Jeremy Cabernet Shiraz 2005 Light- to medium-bodied; bright, fresh, juicy berry style; very well put together and great value. Drink while young. Screwcap. 13° alc. **RATING** 89 **DRINK** 2008 $15

Lady Claire Manjimup Chardonnay 2005 Clever, restrained use of 25% barrel fermentation gives both texture and the impression of more nectarine fruit sweetness to the unwooded version. Screwcap. 13° alc. **RATING** 88 **DRINK** 2008 $18

Rose of Glenoran 2005 Light- to medium-bodied; bright, fresh, light cassis fruit; off-dry finish. Surprising Blue Gold medal from the Sydney International Wine Competition '06. Screwcap. 13° alc. **RATING** 87 **DRINK** Now $16

ƳƳƳƳ **Jezebel Manjimup Cabernet Merlot 2002** **RATING** 85 **DRINK** 2008 $18
The Nikstar Manjimup Unwooded Chardonnay 2005 **RATING** 84 **DRINK** Now $15

Sinclair's Gully ★★★★

Colonial Drive, Norton Summit, SA 5136 **REGION** Adelaide Hills
T (08) 8390 1995 **www**.sinclairsgully.com **OPEN** By appt
WINEMAKER Contract **EST.** 1998 **CASES** 600
In 1997 Sue and Sean Delaney purchased their 10.5 ha property at Norton Summit. The property had a significant stand of remnant native vegetation, with a State Conservation Rating, and since acquiring the property much energy has been spent in restoring 8 ha of pristine bushland, home to 130 species of native plants and 66 species of native birds, some recorded as threatened or rare. It has been a DIY venture for the Delaneys (supported by family and friends) with Sue Delaney hand-pruning the 0.4 ha each of chardonnay and sauvignon blanc planted in 1998.

ƳƳƳƳƳ **Adelaide Hills Chardonnay 2005** Elegant wine with a vibrant, fresh and lively citrus/passionfruit/tropical mix; good length. Screwcap. 12.5° alc. **RATING** 92 **DRINK** Now $22.50
Adelaide Hills Chardonnay 2003 Elegant, light- to medium-bodied; quite complex bottle-developed characters emerging around melon, stone fruit and citrus fruit. Screwcap. 13.5° alc. **RATING** 90 **DRINK** 2010 $24.50

ƳƳƳƳ **Adelaide Hills Chardonnay 2004** Very light and crisp citrussy/minerally aromas and flavours; early picked style, needing more flesh. Screwcap. 12.5° alc. **RATING** 87 **DRINK** 2009 $24.50

Sir Paz Estate NR

384 George Street, Fitzroy, Vic 3065 (postal) **REGION** Yarra Valley
T (03) 9417 9337 **F** (03) 9417 3981 **www**.sirpaz.com **OPEN** Not
WINEMAKER Scott McCarthy, John Zapris **EST.** 1997 **CASES** 4600
The Zapris family established Sir Paz Estate in 1997, planting just under 11 ha of shiraz; the first release of 2001 scored an emphatic gold medal at the Victorian Wines Show 2003 as the highest scored entry. Subsequent vintages have not disappointed, and the success led to the planting of an additional 7 ha of merlot (even though the original intention was to simply make one wine).

Sirromet Wines ★★★★☆

850–938 Mount Cotton Road, Mount Cotton, Qld 4165 **REGION** Queensland Coastal
T (07) 3206 2999 **F** (07) 3206 0900 **www**.sirromet.com **OPEN** 7 days 10–5
WINEMAKER Adam Chapman, Craig Stevenson, Velten Tiemann **EST.** 1998 **CASES** 66 500
This was an unambiguously ambitious venture, which has succeeded in its aim of creating Qld's premier winery. The Morris family, founders of Sirromet Wines, which owns Mount Cotton Estate, retained a leading architect to design the striking state-of-the-art winery with an 80 000-case production capacity; the State's foremost viticultural consultant to plant the 4 major vineyards (in the Granite Belt) which total over 100 ha; and the most skilled winemaker practising in Qld, Adam Chapman, to make the wine. It has a 200-seat restaurant, a wine club offering all sorts of benefits to its members, and is firmly aimed at the domestic and international tourist market, taking advantage of its situation, halfway between Brisbane and the Gold Coast. Exports to the UK, the US and The Netherlands.

ƳƳƳƳƳ **Seven Scenes Cabernet Sauvignon 2002** Immaculately crafted; blackcurrant and blackberry fruit plus fine, ripe tannins; very good balance and length. Has developed impressively, gaining elegance and a trio of gold medals along the way. **RATING** 92 **DRINK** 2012 $22

TM Queensland Chardonnay 2003 Stylish wine; a light- to medium-bodied array of nectarine, fig and cashew flavours; well-balanced acidity, good length. Cork. 14° alc. **RATING** 91 **DRINK** 2008 $ 30

Vineyard Selection Pinot Gris 2005 Pale bronze-pink; very attractive, scented, floral musk and spice; even flow and line in the mouth, though backing off a little on varietal intensity. Screwcap. **RATING** 90 **DRINK** Now $ 16

ΥΥΥΥ **Vineyard Selection Viognier Marsanne 2005** Lots of presence; an intriguing mix of apricot, honeysuckle, pear and nutmeg spice; soft in the mouth. Screwcap. **RATING** 88 **DRINK** Now $ 16

Vineyard Selection Semillon 2003 Pleasant wine; some toasty notes starting to develop along with a touch of honey. Screwcap. **RATING** 87 **DRINK** 2008 $ 16

Vineyard Selection Verdelho 2005 Nicely proportioned, with pleasant mouthfeel to the tropical fruit salad flavours; of more than average interest. **RATING** 87 **DRINK** Now $ 16

ΥΥΥΥ **Perfect Day Rose 2005** **RATING** 84 **DRINK** Now $ 12

Sittella Wines ★★★☆

100 Barrett Road, Herne Hill, WA 6056 **REGION** Swan Valley
T (08) 9296 2600 **F** (08) 9296 2600 **WWW**.sittella.com.au **OPEN** Tues–Sun & public hols 11–4
WINEMAKER John Griffiths, Matthew Bowness **EST**. 1998 **CASES** 5000
Perth couple Simon and Maaike Berns acquired a 7-ha block (with 5 ha of vines) at Herne Hill, making the first wine in 1998 and opening a most attractive cellar door facility later in the year. They also own the 10-ha Wildberry Springs Estate vineyard in the Margaret River region.

ΥΥΥΥΥ **Berns Reserve Cabernet Shiraz 2004** Good colour; medium- to full-bodied, supple and round blackcurrant, blackberry and plum fruit; soft, ripe tannins. Cork. 14.2° alc. **RATING** 91 **DRINK** 2012 $ 32

ΥΥΥΥ **Muscat of Alexandria 2005** Floral, spicy, grapey, true to variety; quite delicate, though, of course, sweet. Screwcap. 10° alc. **RATING** 87 **DRINK** Now $ 13

ΥΥΥΥ **Shiraz 2004** **RATING** 86 **DRINK** 2009 $ 17
Silk 2005 **RATING** 85 **DRINK** Now $ 15
Verdelho 2005 **RATING** 84 **DRINK** Now $ 18

Skillogalee ★★★★

Off Hughes Park Road, Sevenhill via Clare, SA 5453 **REGION** Clare Valley
T (08) 8843 4311 **F** (08) 8843 4343 **WWW**.skillogalee.com.au **OPEN** 7 days 10–5
WINEMAKER Dave Palmer, Daniel Palmer **EST**. 1970 **CASES** 10 000
David and Diana Palmer purchased the small hillside stone winery from the George family at the end of the 1980s and have fully capitalised on the exceptional fruit quality of the Skillogalee vineyards. The winery also has a well-patronised lunchtime restaurant. All the wines are generous and full flavoured, particularly the reds. In 2002 the Palmers purchased next-door neighbour Waninga Vineyards, with 30 ha of 30-year-old vines, allowing a substantial increase in production without any change in quality or style. Exports to the UK, Switzerland, the US, Malaysia and Hong Kong.

ΥΥΥΥΥ **Clare Valley Riesling 2005** Ripe tropical/pineapple/citrus mix; a long and very even carry in the mouth; ready to roll. Screwcap. 13° alc. **RATING** 93 **DRINK** 2008 $ 19.50

ΥΥΥΥ **Liqueur Frontignac NV** Some butterscotch and spice notes; medium-bodied, and showing some barrel age. Made from vines since removed. **RATING** 88 **DRINK** Now $ 38.50

Clare Valley Rose 2005 Aromatic red fruits; solid length and flavour, with a touch of sweetness on the finish. Screwcap. 13.5° alc. **RATING** 87 **DRINK** Now $ 17.50

Small Gully Wines

NR

Roenfeldt Road, Greenock, SA 5355 (postal) **REGION** Barossa Valley
T 0411 690 047 **F** (08) 8376 4276 **OPEN** Not
WINEMAKER Stephen Black **EST.** 2000 **CASES** 2000
Stephen Black is producing a carefully positioned range of wines, from Barossa Valley Semillon and Gawler River Shiraz in cleanskin form progressing upwards to the Ringbark Red Shiraz Cabernet and the flagship, Small Gully Shiraz.

☙ Smallfry Wines

★★★☆

13 Murray Street, Angaston, SA 5353 **REGION** Barossa Valley
T (08) 8564 2182 **F** (08) 8564 2182 **WWW**.smallfrywines.com.au **OPEN** Thurs 4.30–8, Fri–Sun & public hols 12–4.30
WINEMAKER Wayne Ahrens, Colin Forbes, Tim Smith **EST.** 2005 **CASES** 450
The engagingly-named Smallfry Wines is the venture of Wayne Ahrens and partner Suzi Hilder. Wayne comes from a fifth-generation Barossa family, Suzi is the daughter of well-known Upper Hunter viticulturist Richard Hilder and wife Del, partners in Pyramid Hill Wines. Both have degrees from Charles Sturt University, and both have extensive experience; Wayne's track record includes 7 vintages as a cellar hand at Orlando Wyndham and other smaller Barossa wineries. They have 5.5 ha of cabernet sauvignon, 2.3 ha of riesling, 1.5 ha of shiraz and a few vines of mataro/mourvedre, and purchase small lots of interesting grapes which become available — hence wines such as Grenache and Bordeaux blends including cabernet franc, merlot and petit verdot.

🍷🍷🍷🍷🍷 **Eden Valley Riesling 2005** Pale, bright straw-green; touches of herb and nettle on the bouquet; balanced palate of lime juice and mineral. Screwcap. 12.5° alc. **RATING** 92 **DRINK** 2012 $ 18

🍷🍷🍷🍷 **Eden Valley Cabernet Shiraz 2004** **RATING** 85 **DRINK** 2008 $ 22
Barossa Shiraz 2004 **RATING** 84 **DRINK** Now $ 28
Barossa Cabernet Franc Merlot 2004 **RATING** 84 **DRINK** Now $ 22

Smidge Wines

NR

62 Austral Terrace, Malvern, SA 5061 (postal) **REGION** Southeast Australia
T (08) 8272 0369 **F** (08) 8272 0369 **WWW**.smidgewines.com **OPEN** Not
WINEMAKER Matt Wenk **EST.** 2004 **CASES** 900
Matt Wenk and Trish Callaghan have many things in common: their joint ownership of Smidge Wines, their marriage, and their real day jobs. Matt has a distinguished record as Flying Winemaker and, in Australia, with Tim Knappstein and then Peter Leske at Nepenthe Wines. These days he is the winemaker for Two Hands Wines (and Sandow's End). Trish holds a senior position in one of the world's largest IT services companies, and in 2003 was a finalist in the Australian Young Business Woman of the Year. The elegantly labelled wines are Le Grenouille (The Frog) Adelaide Hills Merlot, from a small vineyard in Verdun, and The Tardy Langhorne Creek Zinfandel which (and I quote) 'is named The Tardy in honour of Matt's reputation for timekeeping (or lack thereof)'.

Smithbrook

★★★★

Smith Brook Road, Pemberton, WA 6260 **REGION** Pemberton
T (08) 9772 3557 **F** (08) 9772 3579 **WWW**.smithbrook.com.au **OPEN** Mon–Fri 9–4, w'ends by appt
WINEMAKER Michael Symons, Jonathan Farrington **EST.** 1988 **CASES** 15 000
Smithbrook is a major player in the Pemberton region, with over 60 ha of vines in production. Owned by Petaluma/Lion Nathan, but continues its role as a contract grower for other companies, as well as supplying Petaluma's needs and making relatively small amounts of wine under its own label. Perhaps the most significant change has been the removal of Pinot Noir from the current range of products, and the introduction of Merlot. Exports to the UK and Japan.

🍷🍷🍷🍷🍷 **The Yilgarn Blanc 2005** A very complex wine built around barrel ferment and maturation in 100% new French oak; this plus the alcohol creates a radically different style; rich and powerful in the mouth; some echoes of white Bordeaux. Sauvignon Blanc/Semillon. Screwcap. 14° alc. **RATING** 93 **DRINK** 2009 $ 28

Sauvignon Blanc 2005 A clean and aromatic bouquet with classic passionfruit/tropical notes, the powerful palate following suit; the alcohol just a notch hot. Screwcap. 14° alc. **RATING** 92 **DRINK** Now $ 19

ŶŶŶŶ   **Merlot 2003** Not entirely convincing colour; at the savoury/earthy/briary/olivaceous end of the spectrum, with slightly green tannins. Cork. **RATING** 87 **DRINK** 2011 $ 24

ŶŶŶŶ   **Naked Grape Cabernet Merlot 2003** **RATING** 86 **DRINK** 2008 $ 15

SmithLeigh Vineyard   NR

53 Osborne Road, Lane Cove, NSW 2066 (postal) **REGION** Lower Hunter Valley
T 0418 484 565 **F** (02) 9420 2014 **OPEN** Not
WINEMAKER Andrew Margan (Contract) **EST.** 1997 **CASES** 3000
As the name suggests, a partnership between Rod and Ivija Smith and John and Jan Leigh, which purchased part of the long-established Lindeman Cobcroft Road vineyard from Southcorp in 1996. A lot of work in the vineyard, and skilled winemaking, has produced the right outcomes.

Smiths Vineyard   ★★★★★

27 Groom Lane, Beechworth, Vic 3747 **REGION** Beechworth
T 0412 475 328 **WWW**.smithsvineyard.com.au **OPEN** W'ends & public hols 10–5 or by appt
WINEMAKER Jeanette Henderson, Will Flamsteed **EST.** 1978 **CASES** 600
Pete Smith established the first vineyard in Beechworth in 1978, with the encouragement of John Brown Jnr of Brown Brothers. Most of the production of the Smiths' 2.5 ha of chardonnay, cabernet sauvignon and merlot is sold to Shadowfax, the remainder being made and sold under the Smiths Vineyard and Flamsteed labels.

ŶŶŶŶŶ   **Beechworth Chardonnay 2004** An elegant, finely crafted wine; melon and cashew with subtle oak and contrasting splashes of cream and minerality. Totally delicious. Screwcap. 13.1° alc. **RATING** 94 **DRINK** 2012 $ 28

Snobs Creek Wines   ★★★★☆

486 Goulburn Valley Highway, via Alexandra, Vic 3714 **REGION** Upper Goulburn
T (03) 5774 2017 **F** (03) 5774 2017 **WWW**.snobscreekvineyard.com.au **OPEN** W'ends 11–5, closed in winter
WINEMAKER MasterWineMakers **EST.** 1996 **CASES** 3500
The vineyard is situated where Snobs Creek joins the Goulburn River, 5 km below the Lake Eildon wall. Originally planted in 1996, the vineyard has recently been increased to 16 ha. The varieties grown are pinot gris, pinot noir, shiraz, viognier, chardonnay, merlot and dolcetto.

ŶŶŶŶŶ   **Lake Eildon Sauvignon Blanc 2005** A clean, aromatic bouquet with a mix of tropical and grass nuances; the palate is at the gooseberry/tropical end of the spectrum, with positive varietal character. Strathbogie Ranges/Upper Goulburn Valley. Screwcap. 13° alc. **RATING** 91 **DRINK** Now $ 18

  Reserve Upper Goulburn Pinot Noir 2003 Strong colour; a powerful wine but does have enough varietal character to take it away from the Dry Red category; dark plum fruit with good structure and texture. A surprise packet. Cork. 13.4° alc. **RATING** 91 **DRINK** 2010 $ 40

  Reserve Lake Eildon Shiraz 2004 Quite fragrant spicy, bramble aromas; medium-bodied, with attractive, spicy red and black fruits, fine tannins and balanced oak. Screwcap. 13° alc. **RATING** 90 **DRINK** 2012 $ 40

ŶŶŶŶ   **Lightly Wooded Upper Goulburn Chardonnay 2004** **RATING** 85 **DRINK** Now $ 18

Snowy River Winery   NR

Rockwell Road, Berridale, NSW 2628 **REGION** Southern New South Wales Zone
T (02) 6456 5041 **F** (02) 6456 5005 **OPEN** Wed–Sun, 7 days during school hols
WINEMAKER Manfred Plumecke **EST.** 1984 **CASES** 2500
An operation which relies entirely on the substantial tourist trade passing through or near Berridale on the way to the Snowy Mountains. The product range is, to put it mildly, eclectic; all the wines are said to be made onsite, and the grapes for all the white varietals are estate-grown.

Somerbury Estate ★★★★☆

133 Jones Road, Somerville, Vic 3912 (postal) **REGION** Mornington Peninsula
T (03) 5977 7795 **F** (03) 5977 9695 **WWW**.jonesroad.com.au **OPEN** Not
WINEMAKER Sticks (Rob Dolan) **EST.** 1998 **CASES** 5000
It's a long story, but after establishing a very large and very successful herb-producing business in the UK, Rob Frewer and family migrated to Australia in 1997. By another circuitous route they ended up with a property on the Mornington Peninsula, promptly planting pinot noir and chardonnay, then pinot gris, sauvignon blanc and merlot, and have since leased another vineyard at Mt Eliza. Production is set to increase significantly from its already substantial level. Exports to the UK.

ŢŢŢŢŢ **Jones Road Chardonnay 2004** An attractively complex bouquet with barrel ferment and malolactic aromas; very good intensity, depth and length to the grapefruit and nectarine flavours; good oak. Screwcap. **RATING** 94 **DRINK** 2011 $ 23

ŢŢŢŢŢ **Jones Road Pinot Noir 2004** Fresh, bright, cherry, plum and spice; medium-bodied; good texture, line and balance. Screwcap. 14° alc. **RATING** 93 **DRINK** 2011 $ 32
Jones Road Cabernet Merlot 2004 Similar fresh fruit to the pinot; an array of cassis, blackcurrant and raspberry fruit on the supple, medium-bodied palate; ripe tannins to close. Screwcap. 13.6° alc. **RATING** 91 **DRINK** 2014 $ 32

ŢŢŢŢ **Jones Road Sauvignon Blanc 2005** Clean, fresh, crisp bouquet; some mineral joining lemon and gooseberry on the palate; good balance. Screwcap. 13.5° alc. **RATING** 89 **DRINK** Now $ 19

Somerled ★★★★☆

7 Heath Road, Crafers, SA 5152 (postal) **REGION** McLaren Vale
T (08) 8339 2617 **F** (08) 8339 2617 **OPEN** Not
WINEMAKER Robin Moody **EST.** 2001 **CASES** 1000
This is the venture of Robin and Heather Moody, and daughters Emma and Lucinda. The quietly spoken Robin Moody (with a degree in oenology) joined Penfolds in 1969, and remained with Penfolds/Southcorp until 2001. This is a classic negociant business in the strict sense of that term: it produces only full-bodied McLaren Vale Shiraz, selected by Robin from exceptional parcels of young wine, during or soon after fermentation. The wines are blended and matured at Boar's Rock Winery at McLaren Vale. The name, incidentally, comes from the bay gelding which Robin's grandfather raced to victory in the amateur steeplechase at the famous Oakbank Picnic Races in 1908, which in turn took its name from the Scottish king who defeated the Vikings in 1156. So there you are.

ŢŢŢŢŢ **McLaren Vale Shiraz 2002** Holding hue; delicious blackberry fruit, with nuances of chocolate, spice and vanilla; excellent balance and length. Cork. 14.5° alc. **RATING** 94 **DRINK** 2015 $ 27

ŢŢŢŢŢ **McLaren Vale Shiraz 2001** Likewise holding hue well; attractive blackberry, blood plum and lots of dark chocolate; juicy mouthfeel, good oak. Cork. 14° alc. **RATING** 93 **DRINK** 2014 $ 27
McLaren Vale Shiraz 2003 Attractive, medium-bodied, strongly regional wine; blackberry, chocolate and mocha; supple mouthfeel and ripe tannins. Cork. 14.9° alc. **RATING** 91 **DRINK** 2014 $ 27

Somerset Hill Wines NR

891 McLeod Road, Denmark, WA 6333 **REGION** Denmark
T (08) 9840 9388 **F** (08) 9840 9394 **WWW**.somersethillwines.com.au **OPEN** 7 days 11–5 summer, winter 11–4
WINEMAKER Harewood Estate (James Kellie) **EST.** 1995 **CASES** 3000
Graham Upson commenced planting 11 ha of pinot noir, chardonnay, semillon, merlot and sauvignon blanc in 1995, on one of the coolest and latest-ripening sites in WA. The limestone cellar door sales area has sweeping views out over the ocean. Exports to Denmark, Russia and Poland.

Somervaille Estate

NR

Belubula Valley Vineyard, Golden Gully, Mandurama, NSW 2798 (postal) **REGION** Orange
T (02) 6367 5236 **F** (02) 6362 4726 **OPEN** Not
WINEMAKER David Somervaille **EST.** 1986 **CASES** 650
Somervaille Estate is a foundation member of the Central Highlands Grapegrowers Association (now ORVA), centred on Orange; the vineyard is on the Belubula River, near Carcoar. David Somervaille was the chairman of partners of the national law firm Blake Dawson Waldron. Like myself, he is a self-taught winemaker, his early experience with wine coming through his participation in a partnership which operated the Oakdale Vineyard (now Audrey Wilkinson) in the Hunter Valley (which was sold in 1980). Wines are available in small quantities by mail order.

Sorrenberg

★★★☆

Alma Road, Beechworth, Vic 3747 **REGION** Beechworth
T (03) 5728 2278 **WWW**.sorrenberg.com **OPEN** Mon–Fri by appt, most w'ends 1–5 (by appt)
WINEMAKER Barry Morey **EST.** 1986 **CASES** 1200
Barry and Jan Morey keep a low profile, but the wines from their 2.5-ha vineyard at Beechworth have a cult following not far removed from that of Giaconda; chardonnay, sauvignon blanc, cabernet sauvignon and gamay are the principal varieties planted on the north-facing, granitic slopes. Gamay and Chardonnay are two of the winery specialties.

▼▼▼▼ **Beechworth Cabernet Sauvignon Cabernet Franc Merlot 2002** Medium-bodied; savoury earth, bramble and a touch of dark chocolate flavours; fine tannins. Cork. 14° alc. **RATING** 89 **DRINK** 2012 $ 42

Soul Growers

★★★★★

34 Maria Street, Tanunda, SA 5352 (postal) **REGION** Barossa Valley
T 0417 851 317 **OPEN** Not
WINEMAKER James Lindner, Paul Lindner **EST.** 1998 **CASES** 240
James Lindner is a fifth generation Barossan, working in every area of the wine industry since he left school. In 1998 he acquired a small property on the hills of Seppeltsfield, planting 1.6 ha of shiraz, 0.8 ha of grenache, 0.3 ha of mourvedre, and a little cabernet sauvignon and black muscat. The first 3 varieties are separately open-fermented and given 2 years barrel age before the wine is blended and bottled (without filtration or fining).

▼▼▼▼▼ **Barossa Valley Shiraz Grenache Mourvedre 2003** Has risen above the challenges of the vintage; generous, supple mouthfilling juicy, sweet red fruits with touches of mocha and spice; total control of extract and oak. Cork. 15.5° alc. **RATING** 95 **DRINK** 2015 $ 28
Barossa Valley Shiraz Grenache Mourvedre 2002 Holding hue very well; similarly generous, but slightly firmer and more toward black fruits, but retains elegance, balance and mouthfeel on a long finish. Cork. 15.5° alc. **RATING** 95 **DRINK** 2016 $ 28
Barossa Valley Shiraz Grenache Mourvedre 2001 Equally good hue; has more strength in structural terms, but slightly less mid-palate vinosity. Good length. Cork. 14° alc. **RATING** 94 **DRINK** 2013 $ 28

Southern Dreams

NR

10293 Deeside Coast Road, Northcliffe, WA 6262 **REGION** Pemberton
T (08) 9775 1027 **F** (08) 9389 9242 **OPEN** By appt
WINEMAKER John Wade (Contract) **EST.** 1997 **CASES** NA
John Akehurst and family have planted 12 ha of sauvignon blanc, chardonnay, merlot, shiraz and cabernet sauvignon. Giant Karri, Marri and Jarrah trees surround the property, which has the Shannon National Park on one side. The adjacent 10-ha dam is home to a family of black swans, ducks and visiting pelicans.

Southern Highland Wines ★★★

Oldbury Road, Sutton Forest, NSW 2577 **REGION** Southern Highlands
T (02) 4868 2300 **F** (02) 4868 1808 **WWW**.southernhighlandwines.com **OPEN** 7 days 10–5
WINEMAKER Eddy Rossi **EST.** 2003 **CASES** 10 000
The venture is owned by its 5 directors, who together have 50 years of experience in the wine industry and in commerce. John Gilbertson ran Ericsson in NZ and then China between 1983 and 2000. Darren Corradi and Eddy Rossi, respectively in charge of viticulture and winemaking, both had lengthy careers in various Griffith wineries, also the training ground for production director Frank Colloridi. NZ-born Simon Gilbertson graduated from Lincoln University with a degree in agriculture, and after 13 years in corporate life, purchased 3 vineyards in Hawke's Bay, NZ; he is de facto general manager and sales director. There are 41 ha of vines, a veritable fruit salad of pinot gris, riesling, gewurztraminer, sauvignon blanc, chardonnay, viognier, nebbiolo, sangiovese, pinot noir, shiraz and cabernet sauvignon.

ΥΥΥΥ **Altitude 676 Rose 2005** Vibrant, long and tangy; innovative winemaking ferments sauvignon blanc on shiraz skins; the resultant flavour carries the residual sugar sweetness well. Drop dead cellar door style. Screwcap. 12° alc. **RATING** 89 **DRINK** Now $11
Cool Climate Cabernet Sauvignon 2003 Light colour; light-bodied; spicy/savoury/cedary style with minty aspects; needs more extract and ripeness, but well enough made, and has length. Quality cork. **RATING** 87 **DRINK** 2008 $20

ΥΥΥΥ **Cool Climate Shiraz 2003** Light, spicy, peppery, cherry/berry fruit; nice flavour, but not much extract or structure. Quality cork. **RATING** 86 **DRINK** 2008 $20
Cool Climate Chardonnay 2004 **RATING** 84 **DRINK** Now $20

🐌 SpearGully Wines NR

455 Lusatia Park Road, Hoddles Creek, Vic 3139 (postal) **REGION** Yarra Valley
T 0409 258 348 **F** (03) 5967 4496 **OPEN** Not
WINEMAKER Tony Jordan **EST.** 1999 **CASES** 700
SpearGully is the venture of Dr Anthony (Tony) and Michele Jordan, both prominent figures in the Australian wine industry, albeit in different fields. Tony Jordan has had a distinguished career, first as a lecturer and consultant, and thereafter as CEO of Domaine Chandon, broken for several years as the senior technical director for the worldwide operations of Moet Hennessy, before returning to Domaine Chandon and the Yarra Valley. Wife Michele has spent many years in public relations, marketing and sales, based variously in the UK and Australia. They have established 2 ha of chardonnay and 1 ha of shiraz on the hillsides surrounding their home in the Upper Yarra Valley, and the wines have both domestic and international distribution, albeit in small quantities.

🐌 Spence's Vineyard ★★★☆

760 Burnside Road, Murgheboluc, Vic 3221 **REGION** Geelong
T (03) 5264 1181 **F** (03) 5265 1181 **OPEN** By appt
WINEMAKER Scott Ireland, Peter Spence **EST.** 1997 **CASES** 800
Peter and Anne Spence were sufficiently inspired by an extended European holiday, which included living on a family vineyard in Provence, to purchase a small property specifically for the purpose of establishing a vineyard and winery. It remains a part-time occupation; Peter is an engineering manager at the Ford product development located at Geelong, Anne a teacher, but presently full-time mother looking after 2 very young children. They have planted 3.2 ha on a north-facing slope in a valley 7 km south of Bannockburn; the lion's share has gone to 3 clones of shiraz (1.83 ha), the remainder to chardonnay, pinot noir and fast-diminishing cabernet sauvignon (which is being grafted over to viognier for use in the Shiraz).

ΥΥΥΥΥ **Shiraz 2003** Ripe, dense blackberry and plum fruit; has length and persistence.
RATING 92 **DRINK** 2012 $25

ΥΥΥ **Chardonnay 2004** **RATING** 83 $25

⚡ Spinifex ★★★★★

PO Box 511, Nuriootpa, SA 5355 **REGION** Barossa Valley
T (08) 8562 1914 **F** (08) 8562 1409 **OPEN** Not
WINEMAKER Peter Schell **EST.** 2001 **CASES** 1500
Peter Schell and Magali Gely are a husband and wife team from NZ who came to Australia in the early 1990s to study oenology and marketing respectively at Roseworthy Agricultural College (now the Adelaide University). Together they have spent 4 vintages making wine in France, mainly in the south where Magali's family were vignerons for generations near Montpellier. The focus at Spinifex is the red varieties which dominate in the south of France: mataro (more correctly mourvedre), grenache, shiraz and cinsaut. The wine is made in open top fermenters, basket pressed, partial wild (indigenous) fermentations, and relatively long post-ferment maceration. This is at once a very old approach, but nowadays à la mode. The wines are made at Spinifex's winery in Vine Vale, where Peter also makes wines for a number of clients to which he consults.

ΥΥΥΥΥ **Eden Valley Shiraz Viognier 2004** Superb colour; gloriously high-toned aromas and flavours; supple texture to the black cherry, blackberry, licorice and spice fruit; good length; 5% viognier. Cork. 14.5° alc. **RATING** 96 **DRINK** 2024 **$** 44

Esprit 2004 Medium- to full-bodied; velvety richness, but no hint of dead fruit; a seamless array of blackberry/blackcurrant/licorice/spice flavours; excellent structure. Grenache/Shiraz/Mataro/Cinsaut. Cork. 14.8° alc. **RATING** 95 **DRINK** 2020 **$** 28

Indigene 2004 Deep purple-red; unashamedly full-bodied, but the fruit is more than sufficient to fill the frame; luscious black fruits with seamless, built-in tannins from the mataro. Mataro (64%)/Shiraz. Cork. 14.5° alc. **RATING** 95 **DRINK** 2020 **$** 44

Barossa Valley Grenache 2004 Very good colour; a rare Barossa grenache which has great depth and structure, and no confection or dead fruit; you cannot entirely get away from the alcohol, but is carried by the built-in spicy black fruits. Special late harvest. Cork. 15.5° alc. **RATING** 94 **DRINK** 2020 **$** 32

Papillon 2005 Bright purple-red; vivid red fruit flavours in a strawberry/red cherry/raspberry spectrum; the ultimate summer lunch red. Grenache (75%)/Cinsaut. Screwcap. 14° alc. **RATING** 94 **DRINK** 2020 **$** 25

ΥΥΥΥ **Lola 2005** Extremely tight, focused and minerally; way out of the Barossa mainstream white style; long, lingering, bone-dry finish. Marsanne/Ugni Blanc/Grenache Gris. Screwcap. 12.5° alc. **RATING** 92 **DRINK** 2010 **$** 25

Barossa Valley Rose 2005 Vivid fuchsia; bright, small red fruits and spice; a long, bone-dry finish; wild yeast, sur lies. Grenache/Cinsaut. Screwcap. 14° alc. **RATING** 91 **DRINK** Now **$** 23

Splitters Swamp Vineyards NR

Rose Valley, Bolivia via Tenterfield, NSW 2372 **REGION** Northern Slopes Zone
T (02) 6737 3640 **F** (02) 6737 3640 **OPEN** By appt
WINEMAKER Ravens Croft Wines **EST.** 1997 **CASES** 550
Ken Hutchison and Mandy Sharpe have made a cautious entry, planting a 1-ha vineyard equally to shiraz, cabernet sauvignon and merlot. As knowledge of the region grows, and as their experience as vignerons increases, they intend to increase the size of the vineyard and plant additional varieties. In the meantime they are producing Shiraz, Cabernet Merlot and Merlot, which have won several bronze medals.

Spoehr Creek Wines NR

Greenhill Road, Balhannah, SA 5242 **REGION** Adelaide Hills
T (08) 8398 0884 **F** (08) 8398 0885 **OPEN** W'ends 11–5, or by appt
WINEMAKER Stephen Black **EST.** 2001 **CASES** 2000
Philip Reid and Margie Ringwood purchased the former Pibbin vineyard and winery (excluding the brand name and stock) in March 2001. It is one of a handful of onsite wineries in the Adelaide Hills; very few licences have been issued due to the desire to protect the quality of the ground water, which is an important source of Adelaide's water supply. The 6-ha vineyard is planted to merlot, pinot noir, sauvignon blanc and viognier, and the grape intake is supplemented by purchases from Adelaide Hills growers, and from the Riverland and Adelaide Plains for the Rose and Shiraz (at lower price points).

Spring Ridge Wines

880 Darbys Falls Road, Cowra, NSW 2794 **REGION** Cowra
T (02) 6341 3820 **F** (02) 6341 3820 **OPEN** W'ends, public hols or by appt
WINEMAKER 21C Wine Company (Drew Tuckwell) **EST.** 1997 **CASES** NA
Peter and Anne Jeffery have established 12.5 ha of shiraz, chardonnay, semillon, cabernet sauvignon and merlot. They sell the greatest part of the grape production, having only a small amount made under the Spring Ridge Wines label.

TTTT **Cowra Rose 2005** Bright red-purple; fresh, vibrant cherry and strawberry fruit; good balancing acidity. Screwcap. 13.1° alc. **RATING** 88 **DRINK** Now $14
Cowra Chardonnay 2004 Yellow peach, nectarine and fig fruit; controlled oak but uncontrolled alcohol makes the finish slightly soft and sweet. Screwcap. 14.4° alc. **RATING** 87 **DRINK** Now $18
Cowra Shiraz 2003 Good hue; light- to medium-bodied, bright plum and black fruit flavours; fine tannins, minimal oak; well-made. Open-fermented and basket-pressed. Screwcap. 13.1° alc. **RATING** 87 **DRINK** 2009 $18
Cowra Shiraz 2000 Has retained excellent hue; light- to medium-bodied, fresh, red and black fruits; gentle tannins. Drink asap. Cork. 13.5° alc. **RATING** 87 **DRINK** Now $16

TTTT **Cowra Cabernet Sauvignon 2003** **RATING** 86 **DRINK** 2010 $18

Spring Vale Vineyards

★★★★

130 Spring Vale Road, Cranbrook, Tas 7190 **REGION** East Coast Tasmania
T (03) 6257 8208 **F** (03) 6257 8598 **WWW.**springvalewines.com **OPEN** Mon–Fri 10–5, or by appt
WINEMAKER Kristen Cush, David Cush **EST.** 1986 **CASES** 5000
Rodney Lyne progressively established 1.5 ha each of pinot noir and chardonnay and then added 0.5 ha each of gewurztraminer and pinot gris; the latter produced its first crop in 1998. Spring Vale produces first-class wines when the frost stays away. Exports to the UK.

TTTTT **Gewurztraminer 2004** Has more than fulfilled the considerable promise it showed a year ago, the lime juice now with hints of spice and rose petal. The outstanding wine in the Gewurztraminer class at Tasmanian Wine Show '06. **RATING** 94 **DRINK** 2009 $23

TTTT **Pinot Gris 2005** Very fragrant and rich; fruit bomb style, crammed with flavour and some residual sugar. Screwcap. 13.8° alc. **RATING** 87 **DRINK** 2009 $23

TTTT **Salute 2002** **RATING** 86 **DRINK** Now $35
Unwooded Chardonnay 2005 **RATING** 85 **DRINK** 2008 $18

SpringLane

★★★★

PO Box 390, Yarra Glen, Vic 3775 **REGION** Yarra Valley
T (03) 9730 1107 **F** (03) 9739 0135 **OPEN** Not
WINEMAKER Yering Station (Tom Carson) **EST.** 1998 **CASES** 1800
SpringLane is the separately owned wine business of Graeme Rathbone, brother of Doug Rathbone, who is the (corporate) owner of Yering Station. The wines are made at Yering Station from grapes grown on the 14-ha SpringLane vineyard planted to merlot, pinot noir, shiraz, cabernet sauvignon, viognier and cabernet franc. Part of the production is sold to Yering Station, part used for the SpringLane label.

TTTTT **Yarra Valley Shiraz Viognier 2004** Typical brilliant purple-red colour; excellent black and red fruits lifted by a controlled touch of viognier; medium-bodied and fine tannins. Screwcap. **RATING** 94 **DRINK** 2015 $25

TTTT **Yarra Valley Pinot Noir 2004** Firm style, with not inconsiderable tannins to the plummy fruit, and a hint of forest. Screwcap. **RATING** 89 **DRINK** 2010 $24
Yarra Valley Cabernet Merlot 2003 Generous red and black fruits with hints of dark chocolate; the tannins are not entirely convincing, but a nice wine nonetheless. Cork. **RATING** 89 **DRINK** 2013 $22

Springton Cellars

NR

14 Miller Street, Springton, SA 5235 **REGION** Southern Flinders Ranges
T 0429 709 081 **F** (08) 8346 9533 **WWW**.agale.com.au/winery.htm **OPEN** 7 days 10–5
WINEMAKER Chris Thomas, Colin Forbes **EST.** 1999 **CASES** NA
Dr Allen E Gale has a CV of extraordinary length, specialising in allergy. Together with Chris Thomas he has established 1 ha of vines at Wilmington, a very promising new area. The Cabernet Sauvignon and Shiraz are made offsite by Chris Thomas, and are sold at the adjoining Café C Restaurant.

Springviews Wine

NR

Woodlands Road, Porongurup, WA 6324 **REGION** Porongurup
T (08) 9853 2088 **F** (08) 9853 2098 **OPEN** 7 days 10–5
WINEMAKER Harewood Estate (Contract) **EST.** 1994 **CASES** 400
Andy and Alice Colquhoun planted their 5-ha vineyard (chardonnay, cabernet sauvignon and riesling) in 1994. The wine is sold through the cellar door and by mailing list.

Stanley Brothers

NR

Barossa Valley Way, Tanunda, SA 5352 **REGION** Barossa Valley
T (08) 8563 3375 **F** (08) 8563 3758 **WWW**.stanleybrothers.com.au **OPEN** 7 days 9–5
WINEMAKER Lindsay Stanley **EST.** 1994 **CASES** 15 000
Former Anglesey winemaker and industry veteran Lindsay Stanley established his own business in the Barossa Valley when he purchased (and renamed) the former Kroemer Estate in late 1994. As one would expect, the wines are competently made, although usually very light-bodied. The 21 ha of estate plantings have provided virtually all the grapes for the business. Exports to Switzerland, France, Luxembourg, Japan, Hong Kong, Malaysia and the US.

Stanton & Killeen Wines

★★★★★

Jacks Road, Murray Valley Highway, Rutherglen, Vic 3685 **REGION** Rutherglen
T (02) 6032 9457 **WWW**.stantonandkilleenwines.com.au **OPEN** Mon–Sat 9–5, Sun 10–5
WINEMAKER Chris Killeen **EST.** 1875 **CASES** 20 000
Chris Killeen has skilfully expanded the portfolio of Stanton & Killeen but without in any way compromising its reputation as a traditional maker of smooth, rich reds, some of Australia's best Vintage Ports, and attractive, fruity Muscats and Tokays. All in all, deserves far greater recognition. Exports to the UK, the US and NZ.

Rare Rutherglen Muscat NV Deep brown, olive-rimmed; has fantastic flair and style; in the mouth, there is still a core of fresh muscat fruit encased in a complex web of nutty, raisin-accented rancio, spirit the hidden scalpel. **RATING** 96 **DRINK** Now

Rutherglen Vintage Port 2001 Elegant, intense multi-spice fruit; long and penetrating with a relatively dry finish; perfect profile and mouthfeel, spirit a mere accessory after the fact. A blend of 6 varieties, headed by shiraz, and including 4 of the classic Portuguese varieties. Cork. 18.4° alc. **RATING** 95 **DRINK** 2011 $ 27

Rutherglen Durif 2004 Extremely powerful and concentrated; layer-upon-layer of black fruits and warm spices; avoids over-extraction. Cork. **RATING** 94 **DRINK** 2020 $ 30

Grand Rutherglen Muscat NV Full olive-brown; clear-cut rancio aligns with clean spirit and spicy/grapey fruit; excellent balance and structure, the tannins subliminal, but giving another dimension to the flavour; very long, fine finish. **RATING** 94 **DRINK** Now $ 75

Moodemere Shiraz 2004 Good colour; strong blackberry and dark chocolate fruit; fine, ripe tannins provide structure and texture; sustained length. Diam. 14.5° alc. **RATING** 93 **DRINK** 2017 $ 18

Rutherglen Shiraz Durif 2004 As expected, even bigger, richer and stronger than the Shiraz in a style unique to Rutherglen. Cork. **RATING** 92 **DRINK** 2018 $ 18

Classic Rutherglen Tokay NV Light- to medium golden-brown; great clarity and freshness, with honey and tea leaf aromas; lively and vibrant with similar finesse and harmony to the Campbell wines. Finishes with excellent acidity and a clean, crisp aftertaste. **RATING** 92 **DRINK** Now $ 25

Classic Rutherglen Muscat NV Has a great display of grapey varietal fruit, skilfully combining younger and older material. Fine tannins give the wine extra structure and intensity. **RATING** 92 **DRINK** Now $ 25

Stanton Estate

NR

135 North Isis Road, Childers, Qld 4660 **REGION** Queensland Zone
T (07) 4126 1255 **F** (07) 4126 1823 **OPEN** W'ends 10–5, or by appt
WINEMAKER Symphony Hill **EST.** 2000 **CASES** 500
Keith and Joy Stanton have established 2 ha of verdelho, marsanne, cabernet sauvignon and merlot using organic growing methods, and are seeking organic certification, making Stanton Estate one of the leaders of organically grown wine in Qld. The wines are also made to BFA standards, which permit the use of some SO_2, but within strictly controlled limits. The wines sell out rapidly through the cellar door and Woodgate Restaurant.

Star Lane

NR

RMB 1167 Star Lane, Beechworth, Vic 3747 **REGION** Beechworth
T (03) 5728 7268 **OPEN** By appt
WINEMAKER Savaterre **EST.** 1996 **CASES** NA
Liz and Brett Barnes have established 4 ha of shiraz and merlot (planted in 1996) with further plantings of riesling and chardonnay planned. When Liz Barnes completes her winemaking course, she will take responsibility for winemaking from Keppell Smith (of Savaterre), but even then, they will continue to sell 70% of their grape production.

Statford Park

NR

Farmgate at Statford Park, Pearson's Lane, Wildes Meadow, NSW 2577 **REGION** Southern Highlands
T (02) 4885 1101 **F** (02) 4885 1035 **www**.statford.com.au **OPEN** 7 days 10–5
WINEMAKER Contract **EST.** 1997 **CASES** 1000
Statford Park is situated in the triangle bounded by Robertson 5 km east, Burrawang 5 km to the northwest and Wildes Meadow, some 6 km southwest. The Wildes Meadow Creek rises in the northeastern end of the valley, runs east–west through to Lake Fitzroy a few kilometres further west. In 1997/8, 6500 vines were planted, the first wine release following in June 2001. The cellar door has an exotic array of lavender and other products.

Station Creek

NR

Edi Road, Cheshunt, Vic 3678 **REGION** King Valley
T (03) 5729 8265 **F** (03) 5729 8056 **OPEN** 7 days
WINEMAKER Warren Proft (Contract) **EST.** 1999 **CASES** 2000
David and Sharon Steer have established 5 ha of vineyards at Cheshunt, planted to sauvignon blanc, cabernet sauvignon, merlot and shiraz. The cellar door offers light meals, crafts, a gallery and local produce.

Staughton Vale Vineyard

NR

20 Staughton Vale Road, Anakie, Vic 3221 **REGION** Geelong
T (03) 5284 1477 **F** (03) 5284 1229 **OPEN** Fri–Mon & public hols 10–5, or by appt
WINEMAKER Paul Chambers **EST.** 1986 **CASES** 2000
Paul Chambers has 6 ha of closely planted vines, with the accent on the classic Bordeaux mix of cabernet sauvignon, merlot, cabernet franc and petit verdot, although chardonnay and pinot noir are also planted. Weekend lunches are available at the Staughton Cottage Restaurant.

Steels Creek Estate ★★★☆

1 Sewell Road, Steels Creek, Vic 3775 **REGION** Yarra Valley
T (03) 5965 2448 **F** (03) 5965 2448 **WWW**.steelsckestate.com.au **OPEN** W'ends & public hols 10–6, or by appt
WINEMAKER Simon Peirce **EST.** 1981 **CASES** 400
A 1.7-ha vineyard, family-operated since establishment in 1981, is located in the picturesque Steels Creek Valley with views towards to the Kinglake NP. Red wines are made onsite, white wines with the assistance of consultants. Visitors can view the winemaking operations from the cellar door.

▼▼▼▼ **Yarra Valley Shiraz 2003** Cool climate berry, spice, pepper and licorice fruit characters; just a whisper of green on the finish. Cork. 13.5° alc. **RATING** 89 **DRINK** 2012 $ 28
Yarra Valley Cabernet Sauvignon 2003 Good colour; powerful, fractionally hard-edged blackcurrant fruit allied with controlled oak. Cork. 13.5° alc. **RATING** 89 **DRINK** 2013 $ 25
Yarra Valley Colombard 2005 Clear varietal character courtesy of the racy acidity which runs through the palate to the finish. Screwcap. 12.8° alc. **RATING** 87 **DRINK** 2009 $ 18

▼▼▼▽ **Yarra Valley Chardonnay 2004** Medium green-yellow; melon and citrus fruit, but simply doesn't sing. Screwcap. 13° alc. **RATING** 86 **DRINK** 2008 $ 22

Stefani Estate ★★★★☆

389 Heathcote–Rochester Road, Heathcote, Vic 3523 **REGION** Heathcote
T (03) 9570 8750 **F** (03) 9579 1532 **OPEN** By appt
WINEMAKER Mario Marson **EST.** 2002 **CASES** 1100
Stefano Stefani came to Australia in 1985. Business success has allowed Stefano and wife Rina to follow in the footsteps of Stefano's grandfather, who had a vineyard and was an avid wine collector. The first property they acquired was at Long Gully Road in the Yarra Valley, with pinot grigio, cabernet sauvignon, chardonnay and pinot noir. The next acquisition was in Heathcote, where he acquired a property adjoining that of Mario Marson, and both built a winery and established 8.5 ha of vineyard, planted predominantly to shiraz, then cabernet sauvignon and merlot and a mixed block of cabernet franc, malbec and petit verdot. In 2003 a second Yarra Valley property was purchased where Dijon clones of chardonnay and pinot noir have been planted. Mario Marson (ex Mount Mary) oversees the operation of all the vineyards and is also the winemaker. He is also able to use the winery to make his own brand wines, completing the business link.

▼▼▼▼▽ **Heathcote Shiraz 2003** Dense, inky colour; ripe blackberry fruit with touches of bitter chocolate and earth; strong structure; positive French oak. Cork. 14.5° alc. **RATING** 93 **DRINK** 2013 $ 37
Yarra Valley Cabernet Sauvignon 2004 Deep colour; a very powerful and concentrated wine with masses of blackcurrant, cassis and blackberry fruit; better balanced extract and tannins than the Pinot, and — anyway — this is Cabernet Sauvignon. Diam. 13.5° alc. **RATING** 93 **DRINK** 2019 $ 39
Yarra Valley Chardonnay 2004 Sophisticated, complex barrel ferment/malolactic/lees inputs to powerful, underlying fruit. Diam. 13.5° alc. **RATING** 90 **DRINK** 2012 $ 54

▼▼▼▼ **Yarra Valley Pinot Grigio 2004** Clean, fresh spice, musk and apple; good balance and length. Diam. 14° alc. **RATING** 89 **DRINK** Now $ 20
Yarra Valley Pinot Noir 2004 A fraction cloudy; a huge wine, particularly for the vintage; heavy extraction has liberated abundant plum fruit, but even more tannins. In a particular style which will have great appeal to some. Diam. 14° alc. **RATING** 89 **DRINK** 2015 $ 39
Yarra Valley Pinot Noir 2003 Incredibly deep colour; massively rich, full and concentrated; more to dry red in style, but will live forever. Diam. 14.5° alc. **RATING** 89 **DRINK** 2013 $ 35

Stefano Lubiana

60 Rowbottoms Road, Granton, Tas 7030 **REGION** Southern Tasmania
T (03) 6263 7457 **WWW**.slw.com.au **OPEN** Sun–Thurs 11–3 (closed some public hols)
WINEMAKER Steve Lubiana **EST.** 1990 **CASES** 12 000
When Stefano (Steve) Lubiana moved from the Riverland to Tas, he set up a substantial contract sparkling winemaking facility to help cover the costs of the move and the establishment of his new business. Over the years, he has steadily decreased the amount of contract winemaking, now focusing on the estate-grown wines from 18 ha of beautifully located vineyards sloping down to the Derwent River. Exports to Italy, Sweden, Korea, Indonesia and Japan.

▼▼▼▼▼ **Sauvignon Blanc 2004** Spotlessly clean; spice, herb, mineral and gooseberry aromas; excellent mouthfeel, more to tropical fruit; very good length; a subliminal hint of sweetness. Screwcap. **RATING** 94 **DRINK** 2008 $ 24

▼▼▼▼▽ **Sauvignon Blanc 2005** Tangy and lively, quite sweet citrus and passionfruit followed by hints of grass and mineral on the back-palate and a slightly sweet finish. Screwcap.
RATING 90 **DRINK** Now $ 24
Primavera Pinot Noir 2005 Bright colour; a light- to medium-bodied mix of black cherry and plum, touches of forest add complexity. Good length and structure. Screwcap.
13.5° alc. **RATING** 90 **DRINK** 2010 $ 25

▼▼▼▼ **Riesling 2005** Plenty of fleshy tropical fruit, with good length and intensity, although overall bordering too sweet. **RATING** 89 **DRINK** 2009 $ 24
Estate Pinot Noir 2004 Spicy, savoury stemmy edge to sweet plum fruit; good length and balance. **RATING** 89 **DRINK** 2009 $ 42
Pinot Grigio 2005 Medium-bodied; fair balance, with touches of varietal pear and musk.
RATING 87 **DRINK** 2008 $ 24

Steler Estate Wines

NR

26 Belvedere Close, Pakenham Upper, Vic 3810 **REGION** Gippsland
T (03) 9796 5766 **F** (03) 9796 5695 **WWW**.stelerestatewines.com.au **OPEN** By appt
WINEMAKER Tomo Steler **EST.** 1996 **CASES** 460
Croatian-born Tomo Steler had a tough upbringing as an orphan in his native country, but he overcame many obstacles to obtain a degree in forestry before migrating to Australia in 1970. Shortly thereafter he met wife Suzanna, and together they established a successful UV coating and spray-painting business. They planted the first vines in 1996, intending simply to make wine for their own consumption, but further plantings in 1997 have resulted in a little less than a ha of shiraz and merlot.

Stellar Ridge Estate

NR

Clews Road, Cowaramup, WA 6284 **REGION** Margaret River
T (08) 9755 5635 **F** (08) 9755 5636 **WWW**.stellar-ridge.com **OPEN** 7 days 10–5
WINEMAKER Swings & Roundabouts (Mark Lane) **EST.** 1994 **CASES** 2000
Colin and Helene Hellier acquired a 49-ha grazing property at Cowaramup in 1993; it included 2.5 ha of chardonnay and sauvignon blanc planted in 1987. A large dam was constructed in 1994, and the following year 11 ha of new vineyards and 4 ha of olive trees were planted; 1.6 ha of zinfandel followed in 1996, bringing total plantings to 15.1 ha. The majority of the 100 tonne grape production is sold to other local wineries, with 14–15 tonnes being retained for the Stellar Ridge label.

Step Road Winery

Davidson Road, Langhorne Creek, SA 5255 (postal) **REGION** Langhorne Creek
T (08) 8537 3342 **F** (08) 8537 3357 **WWW**.steprd.com **OPEN** Not
WINEMAKER Rob Dundon, Scott McIntosh **EST.** 1998 **CASES** 160 000
Step Road has 92 ha of vineyard in Langhorne Creek, and 40 ha in the Adelaide Hills, supplementing the production from those vineyards with cabernet sauvignon and shiraz purchased from McLaren Vale. It is an autonomous business, but operationally part of the Beresford Wines group. Exports to the UK, the US, Denmark, Hong Kong and NZ.

ettett **Langhorne Creek Shiraz 2003** Densely coloured; a potent mix of blackberry, dark chocolate and plum; while full-bodied, shows excellent control of alcohol and extract. Screwcap. 14° alc. **RATING** 94 **DRINK** 2018 $ 20

etttt **Langhorne Creek Shiraz 2004** Good colour; a rich, opulent and powerful array of black fruits, licorice and a touch of chocolate; fine, persistent tannins. Compelling value. Screwcap. 14° alc. **RATING** 92 **DRINK** 2014 $ 20

etttt **Black Wing Chardonnay 2004** Elegant, fragrant grapefruit and melon fruit-driven style; light- to medium-bodied, but has length; very good value. Screwcap. **RATING** 89 $ 14
Adelaide Hills Sauvignon Blanc 2005 Clean, light and crisp apple and gooseberry aromas and flavours; dry finish. Screwcap. 13.5° alc. **RATING** 88 **DRINK** Now $ 18
Langhorne Creek Cabernet Sauvignon 2003 Clean bouquet; light- to medium-bodied; savoury, bramble edges to blackcurrant fruit; unforced. Screwcap. 14.5° alc. **RATING** 88 **DRINK** 2010 $ 20

etttt **Black Wing Cabernet Sauvignon 2003** **RATING** 85 **DRINK** Now $ 14
Black Wing Langhorne Creek Pinot Noir Chardonnay NV **RATING** 84 **DRINK** Now $ 15

Stephen John Wines ★★★★

Government Road, Watervale, SA 5452 **REGION** Clare Valley
T (08) 8843 0105 **F** (08) 8843 0105 **OPEN** 7 days 11–5
WINEMAKER Stephen John **EST.** 1994 **CASES** 10 000
The John family is one of the best-known in the Barossa Valley, with branches running Australia's best cooperage (AP John & Sons) and providing the chief winemaker of Lindemans (Philip John) and the former chief winemaker of Quelltaler (Stephen John). Stephen and Rita John have now formed their own family business in the Clare Valley, based on a 6-ha vineyard overlooking Watervale, and supplemented by modest intake from a few local growers. The cellar door is a renovated 80-year-old stable full of rustic charm. Exports to the UK, the US, Malaysia and Singapore.

etttt **Estate Reserve Shiraz 2000** Complex and powerful, more in black fruit/blackberry/black plum spectrum; luscious, yet only 13° alcohol. Cork. **RATING** 93 **DRINK** 2017 $ 40

Sterling Heights NR

PO Box 115, Launceston, Tas 7250 **REGION** Northern Tasmania
T (03) 6376 1419 **OPEN** Not
WINEMAKER Moorilla Estate (Contract) **EST.** 1988 **CASES** 400
Geoff and Jenny Wells have sold their 2-ha vineyard at Winkleigh, which was the source for the Sterling Heights wines. They have retained the Sterling Heights brand, and will continue to sell the packaged wine they have in stock. A new planting at St Helens is being contemplated.

Stevens Brook Estate NR

620 High Street, Echuca, Vic 3564 **REGION** Perricoota
T (03) 5480 1916 **F** (03) 5480 2004 **OPEN** 7 days 10–5
WINEMAKER Mal Stewart, Kilchurn Wines (David Cowburn) **EST.** 1996 **CASES** 8000
The Stevens Brook Estate vineyard was established in 1996, with the first commercial production in 1999. Initially the grapes were sold; they are now being used for the Stevens Brook Estate label. The yield is restricted to 3–4 tonnes per acre, roughly half the regional average. The 1500-tonne winery was built in 1999 on a separate 40 ha property on the Echuca side of the Murray River, which will be fully planted. Just to complicate the picture a little further, Bill Stevens has established the cellar door operation in the Port of Echuca district, the philosophy being to take the cellar door to the customer, rather than try to draw the customer to the vineyard.

Sticks ★★★★

Glenview Road, Yarra Glen, Vic 3775 **REGION** Yarra Valley
T (03) 9739 0666 **F** (03) 9739 0633 **www**.sticks.com.au **OPEN** 7 days 10–5
WINEMAKER Rob Dolan **EST.** 2000 **CASES** 25 000
In February 2005 the former Yarra Ridge winery, with a 3000-tonne capacity, and 24 ha of vineyards planted mainly in 1983, was acquired by a partnership headed by Rob 'Sticks' Dolan. He will make all the Sticks wines here, and also provide contract making facilities for wineries throughout the Yarra Valley.

TTTTT **Yarra Valley Sauvignon Blanc 2005** Some of those slightly sweaty/reduced aromas, part of varietal character; delicate grassy, passionfruit, gooseberry, asparagus flavours; crisp finish. Screwcap. **RATING** 90 **DRINK** Now $ 15
Yarra Valley Pinot Noir 2004 Light- to medium-bodied; elegant, savoury style typical of the vintage; spiced plums; good length. Screwcap. **RATING** 90 **DRINK** 2009 $ 18

TTTT **Yarra Valley Merlot 2004** Attractive light- to medium-bodied wine with savoury olive and earth varietal nuances; fine tannins. Screwcap. 13.5° alc. **RATING** 88 **DRINK** Now $ 18

Stirling Wines NR

PO Box 12, Lochinvar, NSW 2321 **REGION** Lower Hunter Valley
T (02) 4930 6189 **F** (02) 4930 6186 **OPEN** Not
WINEMAKER David Hook (Contract) **EST.** 2000 **CASES** 3000
The Stirling Wines vineyard is adjacent to the original Hunter Valley vineyard of WC Wentworth, one of the leading pioneers of NSW, who established Windermere Vineyard in the 1830s. There are 1.5 ha each of semillon and verdelho and 0.25 ha of shiraz planted. Small exports to Hong Kong.

Stone Bridge Estate NR

RMB 189 Holleys Road, Manjimup, WA 6258 **REGION** Manjimup
T (08) 9773 1371 **F** (08) 9773 1309 **OPEN** By appt
WINEMAKER Syd Hooker, Kate Hooker **EST.** 1991 **CASES** 3000
Syd and Sue Hooker purchased the property on which Stone Bridge Estate is established in 1990, and planted the first vines that year. A subsequent planting in 1996 has increased the vineyard size to 8 ha, with shiraz, pinot noir and chardonnay, cabernet sauvignon, merlot, caberent franc, semillon, sauvignon blanc and sangiovese. The pinot noir and chardonnay go to provide the Methode Champenoise, made by daughter Kate, a graduate winemaker and viticulturist from the Lycée Viticole d'Avize in Champagne.

Stone Chimney Creek NR

PO Box 401, Angaston, SA 5353 **REGION** Barossa Valley
T (08) 8565 3339 **F** (08) 8565 3339 **OPEN** Not
WINEMAKER Chris Ringland **EST.** 1989 **CASES** 70
Another tiny production wine produced by ringmaster Chris Ringland, and effectively sold only in the US through The Grateful Palate: 2 ha of old-vine shiraz produce between 60 and 100 cases per year of wine at a breathtaking price. Chris Ringland politely explains that due to the tiny production, he cannot routinely provide bottles for evaluation.

Stone Coast Wines ★★★

18 North Terrace, Adelaide, SA 5000 (postal) **REGION** Wrattonbully
T (08) 8239 4949 **F** (08) 8239 4959 **www**.stonecoastwines.com **OPEN** Not
WINEMAKER Steve Maglieri, Scott Rawlinson **EST.** 1997 **CASES** 2200
The development of the 33 ha of cabernet sauvignon and 11 ha of shiraz (with an addition of 0.5 ha of pinot gris planted in 2004) which constitutes the vineyard was exceptionally difficult. It is situated on a terra rossa ridge top, but had unusually thick limestone slabs running through it, which had caused others to bypass the property. A 95-tonne bulldozer was hired to deep-rip the limestone, but was unequal to the task, and ultimately explosives had to be used to create sufficient inroads to allow planting. Only 15% of the production from the vineyard is used by the immensely experienced Steve Maglieri to make the wines.

ΨΨΨΨ **Adelaide Hills Pinot Gris 2005** Unusual herbal/citrus aromas, possibly deriving from the low alcohol; similar flavours, but also some pear and musk; an interesting picking option. Screwcap. 12.9° alc. **RATING** 87 **DRINK** 2008

ΨΨΨΨ **Limestone Coast Shiraz 2003 RATING** 86 **DRINK** 2010

Stone Ridge

NR

35 Limberlost Road, Glen Aplin, Qld 4381 **REGION** Granite Belt
T (07) 4683 4211 **F** (07) 4683 4211 **www**.stoneridgewine.com **OPEN** 7 days by appt
WINEMAKER Jim Lawrie, Anne Kennedy **EST.** 1981 **CASES** 1100
Jim Lawrie and Anne Kennedy were among the first arrivals at the start of the expansion of the Granite Belt region. They have progressed from a tiny make of Shiraz in a microscopic winery to a very much larger business, with some particularly interesting varietal wines.

Stonebrook Estate

RSM 361, Busselton, WA 6280 **REGION** Margaret River
T (08) 9755 1104 **F** (08) 9755 1001 **www**.stonebrookestate.com **OPEN** By appt
WINEMAKER John Durham (Consultant) **EST.** 1997 **CASES** 900
Perth lawyer Jonathan Meyer decided on a sea change in 1992, moving with his family to their beach house at Dunsborough. From the outset, the intention was to establish a vineyard, and a property was selected in 1996; planting of 7.4 ha of chardonnay, cabernet sauvignon and merlot began in 1997. Most of the production is sold, part made under the Stonebrook Estate label, and a small amount under the second label, Station Gully.

ΨΨΨΨ **The Small Block Chardonnay 2005** Light-bodied; fine, delicate melon fruit notwithstanding the alcohol; subtle French oak is well-integrated and balanced. Screwcap. 14.3° alc. **RATING** 89 **DRINK** 2010 $ 22
Margaret River Cabernet Sauvignon 2004 Light- to medium-bodied; clean, fresh, cassis, mulberry and blackcurrant; the balance is good, the wine simply needing more depth. Screwcap. 13.5° alc. **RATING** 87 **DRINK** 2009 $ 21

ΨΨΨΨ **Margaret River Merlot 2004 RATING** 86 **DRINK** 2008 $ 21

Stonehaven

★★★★★

Riddoch Highway, Padthaway, SA 5271 **REGION** Padthaway
T (08) 8765 6166 **F** (08) 8765 6177 **www**.stonehavenvineyards.com.au **OPEN** 7 days 10–4
WINEMAKER Susanne Bell, Gary Stokes **EST.** 1998 **CASES** 200 000
It is, to say the least, strange that it should have taken 30 years for a substantial winery to be built at Padthaway. However, when Hardys took the decision, it was no half measure: $20 million has been invested in what is the largest greenfields winery built in Australia for more than 20 years. Exports to the US, Canada and the UK.

ΨΨΨΨΨ **Rat & Bull Cabernet Shiraz 2002** Totally delicious; a seamless marriage of the varieties and oak; fluid line and mouthfeel. Screwcap. 13.5° alc. **RATING** 95 **DRINK** 2015 $ 16
Hidden Sea Viognier 2005 Very good Viognier; citrussy overtones to the core of varietal fruit freshen the wine, and cut away the oily heaviness which often marks the variety. Screwcap. 14° alc. **RATING** 94 **DRINK** 2008 $ 17

ΨΨΨΨΨ **Hidden Sea Cabernet Sauvignon 2001** Good colour; elegant cabernet varietal fruit with ripe blackcurrant, cassis and mulberry; harmonious oak, tannins and overall mouthfeel. Bargain. Cork. **RATING** 93 **DRINK** 2010 $ 16
Limited Vineyard Release Cabernet Sauvignon 1999 A powerful wine, chock-full of blackcurrant, blackberry, earth and a touch of chocolate; substantial oak and tannins in typical winery style; still evolving. Cork. 13.5° alc. **RATING** 93 **DRINK** 2015 $ 30
Limited Vineyard Release Padthaway Chardonnay 2002 Has flourished since it was first tasted over 3 years ago; grapefruit and melon flavours run through to a fine, tight finish. Cork. **RATING** 92 **DRINK** 2010 $ 26

Hidden Sea Shiraz 2003 Good colour; medium- to full-bodied, complex wine; lots of dark fruits and spice; good extract and structure. Cork. 14.2° alc. **RATING** 92 **DRINK** 2013 $17

Winemaker's Release Riesling 2005 Has the richness which many of the wines from the region obtained in 2005; sweet tropical fruit to the fore. **RATING** 91 **DRINK** 2008

Hidden Sea Cabernet Sauvignon 2002 Medium-bodied; cassis, black fruits and earth; overall elegance and good balance. Cork. 13.5° alc. **RATING** 91 **DRINK** 2012 $17

Hidden Sea Sangiovese 2004 Very attractive wine; supple cherry/cherry pip/spice; very good balance; major surprise. **RATING** 91 **DRINK** 2008

Limited Release Padthaway Shiraz 2003 Medium- to medium-full-bodied; supple blackberry fruit and soft tannins. Integrated oak. Cork. **RATING** 90 **DRINK** 2010 $30

Hidden Sea Shiraz 2002 Good colour; aromatic, spicy blackberry and mulberry fruit; clean, balanced palate; good length, fine tannins. Cork. **RATING** 90 **DRINK** 2010 $16

Hidden Sea Cabernet Sauvignon 2000 Clean, clear-cut, black olive and earth varietal fruit; fine, ripe tannins, and good length. Cork. **RATING** 90 **DRINK** 2013 $17

▼▼▼▼ **Hidden Sea Chardonnay 2003** A complex wine, bringing together nectarine fruit, crunchy mineral and nutty oak/malolactic influences; does shorten slightly. Cork. **RATING** 89 **DRINK** 2010 $17

Hidden Sea Shiraz 2001 Striking spicy, peppery, licorice overtones to bright red fruits; lingering tannins just a tad dry. Cork. **RATING** 89 **DRINK** 2012 $17

Stepping Stone Merlot 2004 Big wine, medium- to full-bodied; dark berry fruits; depth and length, though not strongly varietal. Cork. 13.9° alc. **RATING** 88 **DRINK** 2009 $12

Limited Vineyard Release Sangiovese 2003 Light- to medium red; spicy savoury, cedary, tobacco overtones to a core of red cherry fruit; ripe tannins; has come on well in bottle. Cork. 14° alc. **RATING** 88 **DRINK** 2009 $19

▼▼▼▽ **Padthaway Viognier 2004** **RATING** 86 **DRINK** Now $17

Limited Vineyard Release Cabernet Sauvignon 2002 **RATING** 86 **DRINK** 2011 $30

Stonehurst Cedar Creek

NR

Wollombi Road, Cedar Creek, NSW 2325 **REGION** Lower Hunter Valley
T (02) 4998 1576 **F** (02) 4998 0008 **WWW**.cedarcreekcottages.com.au **OPEN** 7 days 10–5
WINEMAKER Monarch Winemaking Services **EST.** 1995 **CASES** 3500
Stonehurst (subtitled Cedar Creek) has been established by Daryl and Phillipa Heslop on a historic 220-ha property in the Wollombi Valley, underneath the Pokolbin Range. They have 6.5 ha of vineyards, planted to chambourcin, semillon, chardonnay and shiraz. A substantial part of the business, however, is the 6 self-contained cottages on the property.

Stonemont

★★★★

421 Rochford Road, Rochford, VIC 3442 **REGION** Macedon Ranges
T (03) 5429 1540 **F** (03) 5429 1878 **OPEN** By appt
WINEMAKER Contract **EST.** 1997 **CASES** 500
Ray and Gail Hicks began the establishment of their vineyard in 1993, extending plantings to a total of 1.5 ha each of chardonnay and pinot noir in 1996. The tiny production of Chardonnay, Pinot Noir and Sparkling Macedon is contract-made by various Macedon Ranges winemakers, and the wines are sold by mail order and (by appointment) through the cellar door, which is situated in a heritage stone barn in the vineyard.

▼▼▼▼▽ **Pinot Noir 2003** Far more weight and depth than many '03s from the region; plum and spice; supple fruit and good extract. **RATING** 91 **DRINK** 2008

⚘ Stonewell Vineyards

★★★★☆

Stonewell Road, Tanunda, SA 5352 **REGION** Barossa Valley
T (08) 8563 3624 **F** (08) 8563 3624 **WWW**.stonewell.com.au **OPEN** By appt
WINEMAKER Troy Kalleke **EST.** 1965 **CASES** 360
Owners John and Yvonne Pfeiffer, together with daughters Lisa and Tammy, represent the fifth and sixth generations of this Barossa winegrowing family. John and Yvonne transformed what was an

unviable mixed fruit and farming property, into 50 ha of mainstream varieties. The vineyard has a common boundary with the vineyard which produces Peter Lehmann's renowned Stonewell Shiraz, which may or may not cause confusion with the names. The successful conversion owes much to John, who has been growing grapes since he was 17 years old. The grapes from the vineyard have been sold to local growers for decades, but in 2004 a decision was taken to have specially selected parcels contract-made under the Daughters of the Valley brand, the derivation of the name being self-evident.

▼▼▼▼▼ **Daughters of the Valley Cabernet Sauvignon 2004** Strong red-purple; ripe cassis blackcurrant fruit aromas; a powerful, long and intense palate, with exceptional varietal definition for the Barossa Valley; very good oak and tannins. 13.5° alc. **RATING** 94 **DRINK** 2017

▼▼▼▼▽ **Daughters of the Valley Shiraz 2004** Good colour; round, fleshy mouthfeel yet bright fruit flavours; very good ripeness/alcohol; soft tannins, gentle oak. Unusual elegance. Cork. 13.5° alc. **RATING** 92 **DRINK** 2014

Daughters of the Valley Grenache Rose 2005 A nicely balanced wine; has flavour and length without overt sweetness; tangy, spicy, strawberry flavours; uncommonly good. Screwcap. 15° alc. **RATING** 90 **DRINK** Now

Stoney Rise ★★★★

Hendersons Lane, Gravelly Beach, Tas 7276 **REGION** Northern Tasmania
T (03) 6394 3678 **F** (03) 6394 3684 **OPEN** 7 days 11–5
WINEMAKER Joe Holyman **EST.** 2000 **CASES** 2000

Changes came fast at Stoney Rise in 2004. Surf and sun-loving Joe Holyman has gone back to his native Tas, having purchased one of the State's most distinguished vineyard sites, Rotherhythe. Though small, this Tamar Valley vineyard has produced magnificent Pinot Noir and Cabernet Sauvignon (the latter to be replaced by Chardonnay) in the past. The South Australian wines in the Stoney Rise portfolio (Sauvignon Blanc, Shiraz and Hey Hey Rose) are still produced; 2005 was the first vintage from the Tamar Valley. Exports to the US.

▼▼▼▼▽ **Tamar Valley Chardonnay 2005** Pale, bright green-straw; vibrant fresh aromas and flavour; mineral, grapefruit and melon; subtle French oak. Screwcap. 14° alc. **RATING** 90 **DRINK** 2010 $ 25

▼▼▼▼ **Tamar Valley Pinot Noir 2004** The frequently occurring sweet, confit fruit characters (plums and prunes) of the vintage. Screwcap. 13.5° alc. **RATING** 89 **DRINK** 2009 $ 25

Holyman Pinot Noir 2004 Generous dark plum and berry fruit, soft and round, but still stalked by sweetness. **RATING** 88 **DRINK** 2009 $ 29

Stonier Wines ★★★★★

362 Frankston–Flinders Road, Merricks, Vic 3916 **REGION** Mornington Peninsula
T (03) 5989 8300 **F** (03) 5989 8709 **WWW**.stoniers.com.au **OPEN** 7 days 11–5
WINEMAKER Geraldine McFaul **EST.** 1978 **CASES** 25 000

One of the most senior wineries on the Mornington Peninsula, now part of the Petaluma group, which is in turn owned by Lion Nathan of NZ. Wine quality is assured, as is the elegant, restrained style of the majority of the wines. Exports to all major markets.

▼▼▼▼▼ **Chardonnay 2004** Very elegant, fine ripe apple, spice and stone fruit aromas and flavours; ultra-subtle oak and malolactic inputs; an exercise in restraint. Screwcap. 13.5° alc. **RATING** 95 **DRINK** 2010 $ 23

Reserve Chardonnay 2004 Intense, aromatic, high-toned and complex bouquet; barrel ferment and malolactic inputs to supple nectarine and grapefruit flavours; stylish wine. Screwcap. 14° alc. **RATING** 94 **DRINK** 2011 $ 39

▼▼▼▼▽ **KBS Vineyard Chardonnay 2002** The extra concentration of the '02 vintage very obvious; ripe, white peach and melon; mouthfilling; subtle oak; good fruit weight. Cork. **RATING** 93 **DRINK** 2008 $ 55

Pinot Noir 2004 Distinctive cherry/strawberry fruit aromas; long, firm, clean palate; subtle oak. Screwcap. **RATING** 92 **DRINK** 2010 $ 24

Pinot Noir Chardonnay 2002 Quality sparkling wine; tangy, lively grapefruit/stone fruit mix; fresh acidity on a long finish. **RATING** 92 **DRINK** 2010 $ 29

Reserve Pinot Noir 2004 Very pale but bright colour; firm, bright red fruits in the Stonier style, restrained and tight, asking for 3+ years in bottle. Screwcap. 13.5° alc. **RATING** 91 **DRINK** 2010 $ 45

▼▼▼▼ **Pinot Noir Chardonnay 2003** Fine, elegant and crisp with citrus and strawberry echoes; a clean, bright, dry finish. Spends a minimum of 18 months on lees. 12.5° alc. **RATING** 89 **DRINK** Now $ 45

Windmill Vineyard Pinot Noir 2003 Greater complexity than the KBS Vineyard; spice and forest nuances to an attractive core of cherry, raspberry fruit; long, savoury tannins. **RATING** 87 **DRINK** Now $ 55

KBS Vineyard Pinot Noir 2003 Fragrant and delicate, but really too light on at this price point; fair length and balance, but lacks heart. Cork. **RATING** 87 **DRINK** Now $ 55

Strath Valley Vineyard   NR

Strath Valley Road, Strath Creek, Vic 3658 **REGION** Upper Goulburn
T (03) 5784 9229 **F** (03) 5784 9381 **OPEN** W'ends 10–5, or by appt
WINEMAKER Contract **EST.** 1994 **CASES** 1300
Chris and Robyn Steen have established 12.5 ha of chardonnay, sauvignon blanc, cabernet sauvignon and shiraz. By far the largest part of the production is sold as grapes, with around 1300 cases of Sauvignon Blanc and Shiraz being sold through the cellar door.

Stratherne Vale Estate   NR

Campbell Street, Caballing, WA 6312 **REGION** Central Western Australia Zone
T (08) 9881 2148 **F** (08) 9881 3129 **OPEN** Not
WINEMAKER Contract **EST.** 1980 **CASES** 600
Stratherne Vale Estate stretches the viticultural map of Australia yet further. It is near Narrogin, which is north of the Great Southern region and south of the most generous extension of the Darling Ranges. The closest viticultural area of note is at Wandering, to the northeast.

Strathewen Hills   NR

1090 Strathewen Road, Strathewen, Vic 3099 **REGION** Yarra Valley
T (03) 9714 8464 **F** (03) 9714 8464 **OPEN** By appt
WINEMAKER William Christophersen **EST.** 1991 **CASES** NA
Joan and William (whom I have always called Bill) Christophersen began the slow process of establishing Strathewen Hills in 1991. The vineyard was established with ultra-close spacing, with 3 ha planted predominantly to pinot noir, chardonnay, shiraz, merlot and small amounts of cabernet sauvignon, cabernet franc and a few bits and pieces, but frost caused persistent losses until protective sprinklers were installed. Since then a series of high-quality small volume wines have been made.

Strathkellar   NR

Murray Valley Highway, Cobram, Vic 3644 **REGION** Goulburn Valley
T (03) 5873 5274 **F** (03) 5873 5270 **OPEN** 7 days 10–5
WINEMAKER Tahbilk **EST.** 1990 **CASES** 2000
Dick Parkes planted his 6-ha vineyard to chardonnay, shiraz and chenin blanc in 1990. Prices are modest.

Straws Lane   NR

1282 Mount Macedon Road, Hesket, Vic 3442 **REGION** Macedon Ranges
T (03) 9654 9380 **F** (03) 9663 6300 **OPEN** W'ends & public hols 10–4, or by appt
WINEMAKER Stuart Anderson, John Ellis (Contract) **EST.** 1987 **CASES** 1800
The Straws Lane vineyard was planted in 1987, but the Straws Lane label arrived on the scene with the highly successful 1995 vintage. Adverse weather in 1996 and 1997 meant that little or no wine was

made in those years, but the pace picked up again with later vintages. Stuart Anderson guides the making of the Pinot Noir, Hanging Rock Winery handles the Gewurztraminer and the sparkling wine base. It's good to have co-operative neighbours.

Stringy Brae of Sevenhill ★★★★

Sawmill Road, Sevenhill, SA 5453 **REGION** Clare Valley
T (08) 8843 4313 **WWW**.stringybrae.com.au **OPEN** W'ends & public hols 11–5, Mon–Fri refer to sign
WINEMAKER O'Leary Walker **EST.** 1991 **CASES** 3500
Donald and Sally Willson began planting their vineyard in 1991, having purchased the property in 1983. In 2004 daughter Hannah Rantanen took over day-to-day management from father Donald. Over the years, plantings have increased dramatically to the point where there now a little over 70 ha of cabernet sauvignon, shiraz and riesling, well in excess of the requirement for the Stringy Brae label. Exports to the UK.

ŸŸŸŸŸ **Clare Valley Cabernet Sauvignon 2002** Good colour; firm, blackcurrant, earth, cedar and chocolate; excellent length, ripe tannins. Screwcap. **RATING** 92 **DRINK** 2015 $ 22
Clare Valley Shiraz 2002 Ripe, lush black fruits, earth and chocolate bouquet; medium-to full-bodied; good flavour and mouthfeel. Screwcap. **RATING** 90 **DRINK** 2012 $ 22

ŸŸŸŸ **Clare Valley Riesling 2005** Potent minerally, spicy, earthy aromas; rich, mouthfilling ripe fruit; lacks finesse. Screwcap. **RATING** 89 **DRINK** 2012 $ 18

ŸŸŸŸ **Clare Valley Cabernet Shiraz 2004 RATING** 86 **DRINK** 2008 $ 17

Stringybark ★★★★

2060 Chittering Road, Chittering, WA 6084 **REGION** Perth Hills
T (08) 9571 8069 **F** (08) 9561 6547 **OPEN** Wed–Sat 12–late, Sun 9–8
WINEMAKER Lilac Hill Estate (Steven Murfitt) **EST.** 1985 **CASES** 600
Bruce and Mary Cussen have a vineyard dating back to 1985, but the development of the cellar door and restaurant complex is far more recent. The vineyard consists of 2 ha of verdelho, chardonnay and cabernet sauvignon. Impressive contract winemaking makes its mark.

ŸŸŸŸŸ **Chittering Chardonnay 2005** Lovely texture and mouthfeel; ripe stone fruit, yet retains focus and freshness; subtle oak; seriously good wine. Screwcap. 13.2° alc. **RATING** 95 **DRINK** 2011 $ 22

ŸŸŸŸ **Chittering Cabernet Shiraz 2005** Fresh, bright and youthful; a simple, fruit-driven palate, though French and American oak used; minimal extract and tannins. Cork. 13.2° alc. **RATING** 88 **DRINK** 2009 $ 22

ŸŸŸŸ **Rose 2005 RATING** 86 **DRINK** Now $ 19

Stuart Range ★★★

67 William Street, Kingaroy, Qld 4610 **REGION** South Burnett
T (07) 4162 3711 **F** (07) 4162 4811 **WWW**.stuartrange.com.au **OPEN** 7 days 9–5
WINEMAKER Graham Helmhold **EST.** 1997 **CASES** 5000
Stuart Range has had a turbulent history since 1997, when a newly-equipped winery was established in a large, old butter factory in Kingaroy. Seven growers with 52 ha under vine were involved in the establishment of the business. Prior to the 2005 vintage an administrator was appointed, and ultimately the principal creditor, Graham Helmhold, purchased the business and assumed the role of winemaker. Part of the winery was also leased to Glastonbury.

ŸŸŸŸ **Red Ant Shiraz Cabernet 2002** Attractive, small berry sweet fruit; holding on very well thanks to good acidity. The name and striking label come from the Aboriginal Kingaroori name for red ants. Cork. 12.6° alc. **RATING** 87 **DRINK** 2008 $ 14

ŸŸŸŸ **Goodger Verdelho 2005 RATING** 85 **DRINK** Now $ 16

Stuart Wines ★★★★

93A Killara Road, Gruyere, Vic 3770 (postal) **REGION** Yarra Valley
T(03) 5964 9000 **F**(03) 5964 9313 **OPEN** Not
WINEMAKER Peter Wilson **EST.** 1999 **CASES** 2000
The Indonesian Widjaja family have major palm oil plantations in Java, with downstream refining.
Under the direction of Hendra Widjaja it has decided to diversify into the Australian wine business,
establishing two very significant vineyards, one in the Yarra Valley planted to no less than 12
varieties, and an even larger one in Heathcote, with 7 varieties — shiraz, nebbiolo, tempranillo,
merlot, cabernet sauvignon, viognier and chardonnay. Between them the 2 vineyards cover 128 ha.
Since 2004 all the wines have been made at a new winery at Heathcote. While the major part of the
production will be exported to Asia and the US, there are also direct sales in Australia. Wines are
released under the Cahillton, White Box and Buddha's Wine labels.

ᵀᵀᵀᵀᵀ̣ Buddha's Wine Chardonnay 2004 Ripe melon, stone fruit and fig with citrussy acidity
contributing to the length and balance; controlled oak. Screwcap. 14° alc. **RATING** 91
DRINK 2009 $16
Buddha's Wine Tempranillo 2004 Strong colour; dark fruits, chocolate and spice
flavours; considerable tannin extract, and should develop very well. The variety holds
much promise for this producer. Cork. 14.5° alc. **RATING** 90 **DRINK** 2016 $18
2004 Stuart White Box Heathcote Shiraz Viognier An elegant wine which belies its 15°
alcohol; an aromatic, lifted bouquet, then flavours of black fruits, spice and a distinct
touch of apricot. Controlled oak and extract. Cork. **RATING** 92 **DRINK** 2015

ᵀᵀᵀᵀ White Box Heathcote Shiraz 2004 Greater colour density expected given the
provenance; sweet confit fruit characters dominate the palate running all the way through
to the finish. Cork. 15° alc. **RATING** 89 **DRINK** 2012 $18

ᵀᵀᵀᵀ̣ Buddha's Wine Rose 2004 RATING 84 **DRINK** Now $14

Studley Park Vineyard NR

5 Garden Terrace, Kew, Vic 3101 (postal) **REGION** Port Phillip Zone
T(03) 9254 2777 **F**(03) 9853 4901 **WWW**.studleypark.com **OPEN** Not
WINEMAKER Llew Knight (Contract) **EST.** 1994 **CASES** 250
Geoff Pryor's Studley Park Vineyard is one of Melbourne's best-kept secrets. It is on a bend of the
Yarra River barely 4 km from the Melbourne CBD, on a 0.5-ha block once planted to vines, but for a
century used for market gardening, then replanted with cabernet sauvignon. A spectacular aerial
photograph shows that immediately across the river, and looking directly to the CBD, is the epicentre
of Melbourne's light industrial development, while on the northern and eastern boundaries are
suburban residential blocks.

Stumpy Gully ★★★★★

1247 Stumpy Gully Road, Moorooduc, Vic 3933 **REGION** Mornington Peninsula
T(03) 5978 8429 **F**(03) 5978 8419 **WWW**.stumpygully.com.au **OPEN** W'ends 11–5
WINEMAKER Wendy Zantvoort, Maitena Zantvoort, Ewan Campbell **EST.** 1988 **CASES** 7500
When Frank and Wendy Zantvoort began planting their first vineyard in 1988 there were no
winemakers in the family, now there are 3, plus 2 viticulturists. Mother Wendy was first to obtain her
degree from Charles Sturt University. She was followed by daughter Maitena, who then married
Ewan Campbell, also a winemaker. Father Frank and son Michael look after the vineyards. The
original vineyard has 9 ha of vines, but in establishing the new 20-ha Moorooduc vineyard (first
harvest 2001) the Zantvoorts have deliberately gone against prevailing thinking, planting it solely to
red varieties, predominately cabernet sauvignon, merlot and shiraz. They believe they have one of the
warmest sites on the Peninsula, and that ripening will in fact present no problems. In all they now
have 10 varieties planted, producing a dozen different wines. Exports to Hong Kong.

ᵀᵀᵀᵀᵀ Mornington Peninsula Sauvignon Blanc 2005 Spotlessly clean; most attractive
passionfruit, gooseberry, tropical flavours; a long, well-balanced, harmonious palate.
Screwcap. 13.2° alc. **RATING** 94 **DRINK** Now $18

Mornington Peninsula Chardonnay 2005 A youthful and clean bouquet; light-bodied melon and nectarine fruit, with a gentle touch of French oak. Needs time to develop more complexity. Screwcap. 14.4° alc. **RATING** 94 **DRINK** Now $18

ΥΥΥΥ **Mornington Peninsula Pinot Noir 2004** Despite the alcohol, the bouquet has touches of mint/menthol/forest although there is more red fruit expression on the palate. Screwcap. 14° alc. **RATING** 89 **DRINK** 2010 $25

ΥΥΥΥ **Mornington Peninsula Merlot 2004 RATING** 86 **DRINK** 2009 $25
Red Dog Red 2004 RATING 85 **DRINK** Now $20

Suckfizzle/Stella Bella ★★★★★

PO Box 536, Margaret River, WA 6285 **REGION** Margaret River
T (08) 9757 6377 **F** (08) 9757 6022 **WWW**.stellabella.com.au **OPEN** Not
WINEMAKER Janice McDonald **EST.** 1997 **CASES** 50 000
First things first. The back label explains: 'the name Suckfizzle has been snaffled from the 14th century monk and medico-turned-writer Rabelais and his infamous character the great Lord Suckfizzle.' Suckfizzle was established by two well-known Margaret River winemakers who, in deference to their employers, did not identify themselves on any of the background material or the striking front and back labels of the wines. In the wake of increased financial backing, Janice McDonald has (oenologically) come out. Production has increased dramatically in the wake of deserved market success, with exports to the UK, the US and other major markets.

ΥΥΥΥΥ **Suckfizzle Cabernet Sauvignon 2003** A fragrant bouquet of cassis, raspberry and blackcurrant; excellent balance and structure; perfectly poised tannins to sustain a long life if the already-stained cork holds. 14° alc. **RATING** 96 **DRINK** 2018 $45
Stella Bella Sauvignon Blanc 2005 Fragrant, clean, spice and passionfruit aromas; a lively and crisp palate; excellent finish. Screwcap. 13.5° alc. **RATING** 95 **DRINK** Now $22
Suckfizzle Sauvignon Blanc Semillon 2004 A very complex fusion of fruit and oak on the bouquet; delicious lemon, citrus, apple and gooseberry in the mouth, the oak in restraint; long, clean finish. Cork. 13° alc. **RATING** 95 **DRINK** 2012 $45
Stella Bella Semillon Sauvignon Blanc 2005 Spotlessly clean; aromatic herb, grass, spice and gooseberry fruit runs through a lively, crisp and clean palate; vibrant finish. Screwcap. **RATING** 95 **DRINK** 2008 $21
Stella Bella Chardonnay 2004 Fine fruit focused and driven; very fresh and lively nectarine/grapefruit; subtle barrel ferment inputs. Screwcap. 13° alc. **RATING** 95 **DRINK** 2014 $25
Stella Bella Cabernet Sauvignon Merlot 2003 Vibrant purple-red; immaculately crafted; spotless cassis and blackcurrant aromas and flavours; super-fine, ripe tannins and skilled French oak handling. Cork. 14° alc. **RATING** 95 **DRINK** 2013 $26
Stella Bella Viognier 2004 Bright straw-green; aromatic, flowery citrus blossom/honeysuckle aromas; while full-on varietal character in the mouth, it is not phenolic or overly alcoholic; good acidity. Screwcap. 14° alc. **RATING** 94 **DRINK** Now $25
Stella Bella Sangiovese Cabernet Sauvignon 2004 A powerful wine; spicy, cedary, earthy black cherry and spice aromas; very good structure on the palate, and good length. Interesting take on Tuscany. Screwcap. 14.5° alc. **RATING** 94 **DRINK** 2012 $27

ΥΥΥΥΥ **Stella Bella Tempranillo 2004** Strong red-purple; fragrant, almost flowery aroma and flavours, with hints of nutmeg, spice and cherry pip; abrasive tannins need to soften, however. Screwcap. 14.5° alc. **RATING** 92 **DRINK** 2015 $27
Stella Bella Shiraz 2004 Light- to medium-bodied; bright, fresh and lively red fruits; well-handled oak warms up the palate. Screwcap. **RATING** 91 **DRINK** 2012 $24

ΥΥΥΥ **Skuttlebutt Cabernet Shiraz Merlot 2004** Bright purple-red; vibrant and intense spicy black fruits; positive tannins, firm finish. Screwcap. 14° alc. **RATING** 89 **DRINK** 2010 $16
Skuttlebutt Sauvignon Blanc Semillon Chardonnay 2005 Pale straw-green; a delicate, fresh and gently aromatic bouquet; a fresh and light palate with a touch of passionfruit. What is there is lovely. Screwcap. **RATING** 87 **DRINK** Now $16

Sugarloaf Creek Estate

20 Zwars Road, Broadford, Vic 3658 **REGION** Goulburn Valley
T (03) 5784 1291 **F** (03) 5784 1291 **WWW**.sugarloafcreek.com **OPEN** By appt
WINEMAKER Munari Wines **EST.** 1998 **CASES** 600
The 2-ha vineyard, planted exclusively to shiraz, was established by the Blyth and Hunter families in the 1990s, the first vintage in 2001. While situated in the Goulburn Valley, it is in fact near the boundary of the Upper Goulburn, Goulburn Valley and Macedon Ranges regions, and the climate is significantly cooler than that of the major part of the Goulburn Valley. Adding the skilled winemaking by Adrian Munari, it became immediately apparent that this is a distinguished producer of Shiraz.

Central Victoria Shiraz 2004 Bright, clear purple-red; a silky smooth and long medium-bodied palate with delicious plum, raspberry and a touch of blackberry; fine tannins and controlled oak. Cork. 14.5° alc. **RATING** 94 **DRINK** 2014 $ 25

Sugarloaf Ridge

★★★☆

336 Sugarloaf Road, Carlton River, Tas 7173 **REGION** Southern Tasmania
T (03) 6265 7175 **F** (03) 6266 7275 **WWW**.sugarloafridge.com **OPEN** Fri–Mon 10–5 Oct–May
WINEMAKER Winemaking Tasmania (Julian Alcorso) **EST.** 1999 **CASES** 300
Dr Simon and wife Isobel Stanley are both microbiologists, but with thoroughly unlikely specialties: he in low-temperature microbiology, taking him to the Antarctic, and she in a worldwide environmental geosciences company. Sugarloaf Ridge is an extended family business, with daughter Kristen and husband Julian Colvile partners. Since 1999, multiple clones of pinot noir, sauvignon blanc, pinot gris, viognier and lagrein have been planted, and 1580 native trees, 210 olive trees and 270 cherry trees have also helped transform the property from bare, sheep grazing pasture.

Chardonnay 2004 Some colour develoment; surprisingly rich and mouthfilling (given the modest alcohol) with quite sweet nectarine and peach fruit, the oak barely perceptible. Screwcap. 13° alc. **RATING** 90 **DRINK** 2011 $ 26

Pinot Noir 2004 RATING 86 **DRINK** 2008 $ 32

Summerfield

NR

5967 Stawell–Avoca Road, Moonambel, Vic 3478 **REGION** Pyrenees
T (03) 5467 2264 **F** (03) 5467 2380 **WWW**.summerfieldwines.com **OPEN** 7 days 9–5.30
WINEMAKER Mark Summerfield **EST.** 1979 **CASES** 8000
A specialist red wine producer, the particular forte of which is Shiraz. The red wines are consistently excellent: luscious and full-bodied and fruit-driven, but with a slice of vanillin oak to top them off. Samples were sent for this edition of the *Wine Companion*, but were not received in time. Exports to the US and the UK.

Summerhill Wines

★★★☆

65 Dandenong–Hastings Road, Somerville, Vic 3912 **REGION** Mornington Peninsula
T (08) 9884 5687 **OPEN** By appt
WINEMAKER Robert Zagar **EST.** 1998 **CASES** 1000
Robert Zagar has established 2.6 ha of pinot noir and shiraz, and (with material from elsewhere) makes both table and fortified wines. Exports to Malaysia.

Chardonnay 2003 Surprising style and quality given the Swan region; melon, fig and cashew; good balance and length. Cork. 13.5° alc. **RATING** 88 **DRINK** Now $ 15
Limited Release Reserve Shiraz 2002 Powerful but hay/straw/prune/dead fruit aromas and flavours; taken too far. Cork. 14.8° alc. **RATING** 87 **DRINK** 2009 $ 28
Limited Release Reserve Cabernet Sauvignon 2002 Medium-bodied; a mix of chocolate, earth and black fruits; balanced tannins. Both the colour and the new cork suggest recent bottling. Cork. 14.8° alc. **RATING** 87 **DRINK** 2010 $ 28

TTTT **Sauvignon Blanc Semillon 2003** Quite surprising, clean varietal character; finishes slightly short, but has developed incredibly slowly, showing no collapse. Like other wines, may have spent extra time in tank before being bottled. Screwcap. 13.5° alc. RATING 86 DRINK Now $15

Late Harvest Gold Muscat 1999 Incredibly youthful; grapey flavours balanced by fresh acidity; said to be from 80-year-old vines grown on the Mornington Peninsula. Cork. 11° alc. RATING 86 DRINK Now

Oak Matured Merlot 2003 RATING 85 DRINK Now $15

Late Harvest Gold Muscat 1998 RATING 85 DRINK Now

Limited Release Reserve Shiraz Mourvedre 2002 RATING 84 DRINK Now $28

Limited Release Reserve Vintage Port 2001 RATING 84 DRINK Now $28

Limited Release Reserve Liqueur Muscat 2000 RATING 84 DRINK Now $35

TTT **Oak Matured Cabernet Shiraz 2003** RATING 83 $15

Summit Estate

NR

291 Granite Belt Drive, Thulimbah, Qld 4377 REGION Granite Belt
T (07) 4683 2011 F (07) 4683 2600 WWW.summitestate.com.au OPEN 7 days 9–5
WINEMAKER Paola Cabezas Rhymer EST. 1997 CASES 4500
Summit Estate is the public face of the Stanthorpe Wine Co., owned by a syndicate of 10 professionals who work in Brisbane, and share a love of wine. They operate the Stanthorpe Wine Centre, which offers wine education as well as selling wines from other makers in the region (and, of course, from Summit Estate). The 17-ha vineyard is planted to chardonnay, marsanne, pinot noir, shiraz, merlot, tempranillo, petit verdot and cabernet sauvignon, and they have set up a small, specialised contract winemaking facility.

Sunnyhurst Winery

NR

Lot 16 Doust Street, Bridgetown, WA 6255 REGION Blackwood Valley
T (08) 9761 4525 F (08) 9761 4525 WWW.sunnyhurst.com.au OPEN 7 days 10–6
WINEMAKER Ashley Lewkowski, Mark Staniford EST. 2000 CASES 700
Mark and Lainie Staniford purchased a 108-year-old stone house surrounded by extensive gardens on the outskirts of Bridgetown in 2000. It gave Mark Staniford the opportunity of realizing a lifelong dream of making wine after he opened WA's first specialist wine shop in North Freemantle in 1965. He has established 0.25 ha each of semillon, sauvignon blanc, cabernet sauvignon and merlot, the original intention being to make the equivalents of white and red Bordeaux respectively. However, son-in-law and winemaker Ashley Lewkowski acquired a property planted to 0.5 ha each of shiraz and chardonnay in 1990, which has led to a slightly different path. Both red and white wines are pressed in hand-operated basket presses, the whites barrel-fermented, the reds mainly open-fermented.

Sunset Winery

NR

Main Penneshaw–Kingscote Road, Penneshaw, SA 5222 REGION Kangaroo Island
T (08) 8553 1378 F (08) 8553 1379 WWW.sunset-wines.com.au OPEN 7 days 11–5
WINEMAKER Colin Hopkins EST. 2003 CASES 2200
This boutique winery is owned and run by friends and business partners Colin Hopkins and Athalie and David Martin. Construction of the winery and cellar door, with elevated sea views overlooking Eastern Cove and beyond, was completed in April 2003. It is otherwise surrounded by 14 ha of native bushland, with a profusion of wildlife. Sunset Winery was the first dedicated cellar door on Kangaroo Island, and offers a range of products to accompany the Chardonnay, Cabernet Sauvignon, Shiraz and Sparkling Shiraz produced at the winery.

Surveyor's Hill Winery

215 Brooklands Road, Wallaroo, NSW 2618 **REGION** Canberra District
T (02) 6230 2046 **WWW**.survhill.com.au **OPEN** W'ends & public hols, or by appt
WINEMAKER Brindabella Hills Winery (Dr Roger Harris) **EST.** 1986 **CASES** 500
Surveyor's Hill has just over 6 ha of vineyard, but most of the grapes are sold to Hardys Kamberra, which vinifies the remainder for Surveyor's Hill, which should guarantee the quality of the wines.

▼▼▼▼ **Hills of Hall Shiraz 2003** Good hue; medium-bodied, but quite intense black fruits, spice
and bitter chocolate; balanced tannins, good length. Cork. 12.7° alc. **RATING** 90
DRINK 2013 $18

▼▼▼▼ **Hills of Hall Touriga Nacionale 2004** Aromas of nutmeg, spice, cedar and dried leaves;
small red fruits in a light- to medium-bodied frame; has good balance. Screwcap. 11.5° alc.
RATING 89 **DRINK** 2010 $18
Hills of Hall Semillon 2005 Glowing green-yellow; abundant, if slightly broad flavour; an
approach which works better with semillon than riesling. Screwcap. 12.7° alc. **RATING** 87
DRINK 2009 $15

▼▼▼▼ **Hills of Hall Riesling 2005 RATING** 86 **DRINK** Now $15

Susannah Brook Wines   NR

43 Beryl Avenue, Millendon, WA 6056 **REGION** Swan District
T (08) 9296 4129 **OPEN** By appt
WINEMAKER John Daniel **EST.** 1984 **CASES** NA
Susannah Brook is a small but long-established Swan Valley business, where John Daniel has 2 ha of chenin blanc, chardonnay, verdelho, cabernet sauvignon, merlot, malbec, shiraz and muscat, and makes the range of table and fortified wines onsite.

Sutherland Estate

2010 Melba Highway, Dixons Creek, Vic 3775 **REGION** Yarra Valley
T 0402 052 287 **F** (03) 9762 1122 **OPEN** 7 days 10–5 summer, or Thurs–Sun & public hols
WINEMAKER Alex White (Contract) **EST.** 2000 **CASES** 2000
The Phelan family (father Ron, mother Sheila, daughter Catherine and partner Angus Ridley) established Sutherland Estate in 2000, when they acquired a mature 2-ha vineyard at Dixons Creek. Later that year they planted another 3.2 ha, including a small amount of tempranillo. Catherine and Angus are in the final year of the part-time viticulture and oenology course at Charles Sturt University, in the meantime, Angus is gaining further experience as a winemaker at Coldstream Hills. The DHV range is estate-grown on Daniel's Hill Vineyard.

▼▼▼▼▼ **DHV Chardonnay 2003** An elegant, complex melange of melon, nectarine, fig and
cashew; controlled alcohol a plus. Cork. 13.4° alc. **RATING** 92 **DRINK** 2010 $30
DHV Unwooded Chardonnay 2004 Clean, fresh nectarine and grapefruit, with the length
and intensity typical of the Yarra Valley. Screwcap. **RATING** 90 **DRINK** 2009 $16
DHV Tempranillo 2004 Good purple colour; a firm, fresh and lively array of red fruits, the
cool climate massaging the flavours and the elegant structure. Cork. **RATING** 90
DRINK 2012 $30

Sutherland Smith Wines   NR

Cnr Falkners Road/Murray Valley Highway, Rutherglen, Vic 3685 **REGION** Rutherglen
T (02) 6032 8177 **F** (02) 6032 8177 **OPEN** W'ends, public & Vic school hols and other Fridays 10–5
WINEMAKER George Sutherland-Smith **EST.** 1993 **CASES** 1000
George Sutherland-Smith, for decades managing director and winemaker at All Saints, has opened up his own small business at Rutherglen, making wine in the refurbished Emu Plains winery, originally constructed in the 1850s. He draws upon fruit grown in a leased vineyard at Glenrowan and also from grapes grown in the King Valley.

Sutton Grange Winery

PO Box 181, East Kew, Vic 3102 **REGION** Bendigo
T (03) 5474 8277 **F** (03) 9859 5655 **www**.suttongrangewines.com **OPEN** By appt
WINEMAKER Gilles Lapalus **EST.** 1998 **CASES** 2200
The 400-ha Sutton Grange property is a thoroughbred stud acquired in 1996 by Peter Sidwell, a Melbourne-based businessman with horse racing and breeding among his activities. A lunch visit to the property by long-term friends Alec Epis and Stuart Anderson led to the decision to plant 12 ha of syrah, merlot, cabernet sauvignon, viognier and sangiovese, and to the recruitment of French winemaker Gilles Lapalus, who just happens to be the partner of Stuart Anderson's daughter. The winery, built from WA limestone, was completed in 2001. Exports to the UK and Switzerland.

TTTTT **Estate Syrah 2003** A medium- to full-bodied wine with blackberry, spice and nuances of dark chocolate; persistent, ripe tannins. An impressive first vintage; 19 months in French oak. Cork. 14° alc. **RATING** 93 **DRINK** 2020 **$** 45
Fairbank Syrah 2004 Deep, bright purple-red; medium- to full-bodied; powerful blackberry, black plum, spice and earth flavours, the tannins ripe but substantial. Screwcap. **RATING** 92 **DRINK** 2019 **$** 25

TTTT **Fairbank Viognier 2005** Gentle apricot, peach and ginger fruit; good balance, and no alcohol heat whatsoever. Screwcap. 14° alc. **RATING** 88 **DRINK** Now **$** 25
Fairbank Rose 2005 Pale salmon; dry Tavel style, with spicy notes ex barrel ferment; clean finish; alternative style. Screwcap. **RATING** 87 **DRINK** Now **$** 20
Fairbank Cabernet Sauvignon 2004 Medium-bodied; minty, spicy, leafy, savoury aromas and flavours, with slightly dry, dusty tannins. Disappointing in the overall context. Screwcap. **RATING** 87 **DRINK** 2010 **$** 25

Swallows Welcome NR

Wallis Road, East Witchcliffe, WA 6286 **REGION** Margaret River
T (08) 9757 6312 **F** (08) 9757 6312 **www**.margaretriver.com **OPEN** 7 days by appt
WINEMAKER Tim Negus **EST.** 1994 **CASES** 560
Tim Negus has planted a 2.6-ha vineyard to cabernet sauvignon, merlot and cabernet franc, and makes the wine onsite. The wine is sold by mail order and through the cellar door, which offers barbecue and garden facilities for the visitor.

Swan Valley Wines

261 Haddrill Road, Baskerville, WA 6065 **REGION** Swan Valley
T (08) 9296 1501 **F** (08) 9296 1733 **www**.swanvalleywines.com.au **OPEN** Fri–Sun & public hols 10–5
WINEMAKER Julie White (Consultant) **EST.** 1999 **CASES** 6600
Peter and Paula Hoffman, with sons Paul and Thomas, acquired their 6-ha property in 1989. It had a long history of grapegrowing, and the prior owner had registered the name Swan Valley Wines back in 1983. In 1999 the family built a new winery to handle the grapes from 5.5 ha of chenin blanc, grenache, semillon, malbec, cabernet sauvignon and shiraz. Exports to Japan.

TTTTT **Shiraz 2005** The vibrant colour expected of a young wine; ripe, luscious plum and prune fruit; soft, ripe spicy tannins. Screwcap. 15° alc. **RATING** 90 **DRINK** 2012 **$** 17

TTTT **Chardonnay 2004** Pleasant, light- to medium-bodied melon/fig/peach fruit; good balance and faintly citrussy acidity. Screwcap. 13.6° alc. **RATING** 87 **DRINK** Now **$** 15

TTTT **Chenin Blanc 2005** No doubt perfect for its target market, and actually a good example of the style in a sweet fruit salad spectrum. Screwcap. 11.9° alc. **RATING** 86 **DRINK** Now **$** 14
Semillon 2005 **RATING** 85 **DRINK** 2008 **$** 14
Chardonnay 2005 **RATING** 85 **DRINK** Now **$** 15

Sweet Water Hill Wines   NR

17 Roberts Road, Anderleigh, Qld 4570 **REGION** Queensland Zone
T (07) 5485 7007 **F** (07) 5485 7007 **OPEN** 7 days 10–5
WINEMAKER Tony Totivan **EST.** 1999 **CASES** NA
Tony Totivan has established 5 ha of semillon, chardonnay, cabernet sauvignon, shiraz, muscat hamburg and white muscat, and makes the wine onsite. A range of table and fortified wines are available. The cellar door offers light meals and picnic and barbecue facilities.

Swings & Roundabouts   ★★★★

Caves Road, Wilyabrup, WA 6280 **REGION** Margaret River
T (08) 9756 6640 **F** (08) 9286 1933 **WWW**.swings.com.au **OPEN** 7 days 10–5
WINEMAKER Mark Lane **EST.** 2004 **CASES** NA
The winemaking skills of Mark Lane and the marketing skills of Ian Latchford have come together to create 3 ranges: the super-premium Swings & Roundabouts (Chardonnay, Semillon Sauvignon Blanc, Shiraz and Cabernet Merlot); the varietal Laneway series of The Italian, Tempranillo and Shiraz, targeted at on-premise sales, and with exceptionally striking labels; and the premium Kiss Chasey range.

TTTTT **Margaret River Cabernet Merlot 2004** Good deep colour; clean bouquet; powerful blackcurrant and cassis fruit supported by substantial but ripe tannins; long finish. Screwcap. **RATING** 92 **DRINK** 2016 $19
Laneway Chardonnay 2004 A similar light- to medium-bodied wine in winery style; barrel ferment oak on the bouquet is obvious, with gentle citrus and melon fruit on the palate. Screwcap. 14° alc. **RATING** 90 **DRINK** 2012 $35
Laneway Shiraz Viognier 2004 Aromatic; very pronounced viognier on both bouquet and the medium-bodied palate, with distinct apricot nigh-on distracting; fine mocha/vanilla nuances on the finish. Screwcap. 14° alc. **RATING** 90 **DRINK** 2012 $29

TTTT **Semillon Sauvignon Blanc 2005** Clean and fresh, driven by grassy/minerally semillon; good balance; all-purpose food style. Screwcap. 12.5° alc. **RATING** 89 **DRINK** 2010 $17
Chardonnay 2005 Elegant and light- to medium-bodied; stone fruit, melon and citrus run through to the finish; no oak evident. Screwcap. 14° alc. **RATING** 89 **DRINK** 2011 $19
Laneway The Italian 2004 Light-bodied; a mix of tannins of all shapes and sizes, red fruits trying to escape from their clutches. A blend for the adventurous. Sangiovese/Nebbiolo/Tempranillo. Screwcap. 13.5° alc. **RATING** 87 **DRINK** 2011 $25

TTTT **Viognier 2005** **RATING** 86 **DRINK** Now $19
Margaret River Shiraz 2004 **RATING** 86 **DRINK** 2008 $19
Kiss Chasey Chenin Blanc 2005 **RATING** 85 **DRINK** Now $14
Kiss Chasey Rose 2005 **RATING** 85 **DRINK** Now $14
Kiss Chasey Red 2004 **RATING** 84 **DRINK** Now $16

TTT **Kiss Chasey Chenin Blanc 2004** **RATING** 83 $16

🐦 Swooping Magpie   NR

Lot 14 Commonage Road, Yallingup, WA 6282 **REGION** Margaret River
T 0417 921 003 **F** (08) 9756 6222 **WWW**.swoopingmagpie.com.au **OPEN** By appt
WINEMAKER Mark Standish (Contract) **EST.** 1998 **CASES** 1000
Neil and Leann Tuffield have established their 2-and-a-bit-ha vineyard in the hills behind the coastal town of Yallingup. The name, they say, 'was inspired by family of magpies who consider the property part of their territory'. One ha each of semillon and cabernet franc is supplemented by purchased sauvignon blanc to produce three wines, Semillon Sauvignon Blanc, Semillon and Cabernet Franc. An adjacent sales and pottery studio offers olive oil tastings, sales and, of course, pottery.

Sylvan Springs

NR

RSD 405 Blythmans Road, McLaren Flat, SA 5171 (postal) **REGION** McLaren Vale
T (08) 8383 0500 **F** (08) 8383 0499 **WWW**.sylvansprings.com.au **OPEN** Not
WINEMAKER Brian Light (Consultant) **EST.** 1974 **CASES** 2200
The Pridmore family has been involved in grapegrowing and winemaking in McLaren Vale for
4 generations, spanning over 100 years. The pioneer was Cyril Pridmore, who established The
Wattles Winery in 1896, and purchased Sylvan Park, one of the original homesteads in the area, in
1901. The original family land in the township of McLaren Vale was sold in 1978, but not before
third-generation Digby Pridmore had established new vineyards (in 1974) near Blewitt Springs.
When he retired in 1990, his son David purchased the 45-ha vineyard (planted to 11 different
varieties) and, with sister Sally, began winemaking in 1996. Exports to the US.

Symphonia Wines

RMB 1760, Myrrhee, Vic 3732 (postal) **REGION** King Valley
T (03) 5727 3888 **F** (03) 5727 3851 **OPEN** At Sam Miranda
WINEMAKER Sam Miranda **EST.** 1998 **CASES** 4000
Peter Read and his family were veterans of the King Valley, commencing the development of their
vineyard in 1981 to supply Brown Brothers. As a result of extensive trips to both Western and Eastern
Europe, Peter Read embarked on an ambitious project to trial a series of grape varieties little known
in this country. The process of evaluation and experimentation produced a number of wines with
great interest and no less merit. In July 2005 Rachel Miranda (wife of Sam Miranda) with parents
Peter and Suzanne Evans, purchased the business, and intends to keep its identity intact and
separate from the Sam Miranda brand.

King Valley Pinot Chardonnay 2001 Attractive strawberry and stone fruit flavours;
generous without flabbiness; attractive yeast autolysis; very good balance and length;
4 years on yeast lees. 12° alc. **RATING** 91 **DRINK** Now $ 25

King Valley Petit Manseng 2005 Powerful and intense; fresh lemon zest and preserved
lemon rind flavours supported by racy acidity; good length. Screwcap. 13.8° alc. **RATING** 89
DRINK 2008 $ 24

King Valley Pinot Grigio 2005 Plenty of mouthfeel and palate weight, more to Pinot Gris
in style, with pear and honey flavours. The alcohol seems higher than it in fact is.
Screwcap. 12.5° alc. **RATING** 88 **DRINK** Now $ 24

King Valley Arneis 2005 Very clever winemaking; an aromatic and floral bouquet,
followed by pear and tropical fruit flavours, with a touch of sweetness on the finish.
Screwcap. 13° alc. **RATING** 88 **DRINK** Now $ 24

Las Triadas 2004 A punchy wine with a spice and licorice infusion into black fruits; the
acidity just a little jumpy. Screwcap. 13.9° alc. **RATING** 88 **DRINK** 2010 $ 24

Symphony Hill Wines

2017 Eukey Road, Ballandean, Qld 4382 **REGION** Granite Belt
T (07) 4684 1388 **F** (07) 4684 1399 **WWW**.symphonyhill.com.au **OPEN** 7 days 10–4
WINEMAKER Mike Hayes **EST.** 1999 **CASES** 3000
Ewen and Elissa Macpherson purchased what was then an old table grape and orchard property in
1996. In partnership with Ewen's parents, Bob and Jill Macpherson, they have developed 4 ha of
vineyards, while Ewen has completed his Bachelor of Applied Science in viticulture (in 2003). The
vineyard has been established using state-of-the-art technology; vineyard manager and winemaker
Mike Hayes has a degree in viticulture and is a third-generation viticulturist in the Granite Belt
region. Between he and Ewen Macpherson, a trial block of 50 varieties has been established,
including such rarely encountered varieties as picpoul, tannat and mondeuse.

Release 1 Chardonnay 2005 Bright green-straw; well-made, having impressive texture
and structure; melon, fig and creamy/nutty flavours. Screwcap. 14° alc. **RATING** 91
DRINK 2009 $ 25

Release 1 Viognier 2005 Attractive fruit, with similar vibrancy to that of the Verdelho;
peach, apricot and citrus; neither heat nor phenolics. Screwcap. 13.5° alc. **RATING** 91
DRINK 2008 $ 28

Reserve Sauvignon Blanc 2005 Bright, light green-straw; a lively, crisp palate with good focus and intensity to the green apple, lime and tropical fruit; good balance and line. Screwcap. 13° alc. **RATING** 90 **DRINK** Now $18

Reserve Verdelho 2005 Unusually lively and intense, with strong citrussy overtones to bouquet and palate; excellent length. Screwcap. 14° alc. **RATING** 90 **DRINK** Now $25

 TTTY **Danying Shiraz Cabernet 2004** Light- to medium-bodied; red and black fruits, with minty/leafy overlays. Screwcap. 13.5° alc. **RATING** 86 **DRINK** 2009 $25

White Serenade 2005 RATING 84 **DRINK** Now $16

Syrahmi ★★★★☆

PO Box 438, Heathcote, Vic 3523 **REGION** Heathcote
T 04007 057 471 **OPEN** Not
WINEMAKER Adam Foster **EST.** 2004 **CASES** 110
Adam Foster trained and worked as a chef in Vic and London before moving to the front of house and becoming increasingly interested in wine. He then worked as a cellar hand with a who's who in Australia and France, including Torbreck, Chapoutier, Mitchelton, Domaine Ogier, Heathcote Winery, Jasper Hill and Domaine Pierre Gaillard. He became convinced that the Cambrian soils of Heathcote could produce the best possible shiraz, and since 2004 has purchased grapes (rising from 1.5 tonnes in 2004 to 4 tonnes in 2006) from Heathcote Winery, using the full bag of open ferment techniques, co-fermenting 3.4% viognier with the 2 separate clonal batches of shiraz. The wine spends 14 months in French oak (25% new) and is neither fined nor filtered. The wine, Syrahmi SV², has 2 separately fermented clones, each with 3.4% viognier, which are subsequently blended.

TTTTY **SV² Heathcote Shiraz Viognier 2004** Typical vivid colour; light- to medium-bodied, reflecting the restrained alcohol; lovely bright red fruits; fine tannins. Screwcap. 14° alc. **RATING** 93 **DRINK** 2012 $34

T'Gallant ★★★★☆

1385 Mornington–Flinders Road, Main Ridge, Vic 3928 **REGION** Mornington Peninsula
T (03) 5989 6565 **F** (03) 5989 6577 **www.**tgallant.com.au **OPEN** 7 days 10–5
WINEMAKER Kathleen Quealy, Kevin McCarthy **EST.** 1990 **CASES** 30 000
Husband and wife consultant winemakers Kevin McCarthy and Kathleen Quealy carved out such an important niche market for the T'Gallant label that in April 2003, after protracted negotiations, it was acquired by Beringer Blass. The acquisition of a 15-ha property, and the planting of 10 ha of pinot gris gives the business a firm geographic base, as well as providing increased resources for its signature wine. The yearly parade of new (usually beautiful and striking, it is true) labels designed by Ken Cato do not make my life at all easy. La Baracca Trattoria is open 7 days for lunch and for specially booked evening events. Exports to the UK and the US.

TTTTT **Tribute Pinot Gris 2004** Very, very unusual honeyed bouquet aromas (described as wild honey on the back label!) carry through on the palate, with just a touch of viscosity. Screwcap. 14.5° alc. **RATING** 95 **DRINK** 2009 $27

TTTTY **Lot 2 Chardonnay 2004** Very good mouthfeel, texture and structure; a tangy/creamy/spicy mix, expanding on the finish like a peacock's tail. Screwcap. 14° alc. **RATING** 93 **DRINK** 2012

Viognier 2004 Brilliant green-yellow; a harmonious yet elusive bouquet of flowery fruits; honeysuckle, lime, apricot and peach; good finish. Screwcap. 14° alc. **RATING** 93 **DRINK** 2008 $27

The T'Gallant Chardonnay 2003 Very nice wine; has developed very well; melon and nectarine fruit supported by lingering, citrussy acidity; harmonious mouthfeel. Screwcap. 13.5° alc. **RATING** 92 **DRINK** 2009

Mornington Peninsula Pinot Noir 2003 Light-bodied; pleasant varietal cherry/strawberry fruit definition; nice mouthfeel, not forced in any way. Cork. 13° alc. **RATING** 91 **DRINK** 2008 $28

Pinot Grigio 2005 As always, spotlessly clean; pear, spice and apple; excellent balance, no heat, phenolics or sugar. Screwcap. 13.5° alc. **RATING** 90 **DRINK** 2008

Tribute Mornington Peninsula Pinot Noir 2004 Light-bodied but very seductive strawberry confit with a dusting of spice; sits easy in the mouth, but don't delay. Screwcap. 13° alc. **RATING** 90 **DRINK** Now $ 29

▼▼▼▼ **Imogen Pinot Gris 2005** A super abundance of pear, musk, lychee and spice fruit flavours; no doubting the variety. Screwcap. 14.5° alc. **RATING** 89 **DRINK** Now
Mornington Peninsula Pinot Noir 2004 Very fresh, clean, direct light-bodied wine with good balance and uncomplicated red fruits. Screwcap. 13° alc. **RATING** 89 **DRINK** 2009

▼▼▼▽ **Imogen Pinot Gris 2004** **RATING** 86 **DRINK** Now $ 20

Tahbilk ★★★★★

Goulburn Valley Highway, Tabilk, Vic 3608 **REGION** Nagambie Lakes
T (03) 5794 2555 **F** (03) 5794 2360 **WWW**.tahbilk.com.au **OPEN** Mon–Sat 9–5, Sun 11–5
WINEMAKER Alister Purbrick, Neil Larson, Alan George **EST.** 1860 **CASES** 120 000
A winery steeped in tradition (with National Trust classification), which should be visited at least once by every wine-conscious Australian, and which makes wines — particularly red wines — utterly in keeping with that tradition. The essence of that heritage comes in the form of the tiny quantities of Shiraz made entirely from vines planted in 1860. In 2005 Tahbilk opened its substantial wetlands project, with a series of walks connected (if you wish) by short journeys on a small punt. Exports to the UK and the US.

▼▼▼▼▼ **Riesling 2005** A powerful, slightly old-fashioned style, with overtones of Alsace; has good balance and length, tightened by limey acidity. **RATING** 94 **DRINK** 2010 $ 13
1927 Vines Marsanne 1998 Still as fresh as a daisy; crisp lemon and honeysuckle fruit; outstanding balance and length; 250 cases made from what is some of the oldest marsanne vines in the world. Cork. 13° alc. **RATING** 94 **DRINK** 2018 $ 37
Viognier 2005 Glowing yellow-green; very rich multi-fruit style, drizzled with honey; avoids phenolics on the finish. Screwcap. **RATING** 94 **DRINK** 2008 $ 19
Cabernet Franc 2004 While the wine dips on the mid- to back-palate, it finishes particularly well, with fine, lingering tannins. Altogether superior example of a notoriously difficult variety. Screwcap. 14° alc. **RATING** 94 **DRINK** 2012 $ 13

▼▼▼▼▽ **Marsanne 2005** Fragrant blossom, honeysuckle and passionfruit aromas and flavours; long and vibrant; lovely acidity. Screwcap. **RATING** 93 **DRINK** 2015 $ 14
Cabernet Sauvignon 2002 Good colour; attractive medium-bodied wine with delicious blackcurrant/blackberry fruit; ample tannins, gentle oak. One of the best yet. Cork. **RATING** 93 **DRINK** 2015 $ 21
Shiraz 2002 Strong colour; medium-bodied with latent power to the supple blackberry fruit; fine tannins; should evolve excellently. Cork. **RATING** 90 **DRINK** 2011 $ 21
1860 Vines Shiraz 2000 A typically restrained wine, light- to medium-bodied, with red and black fruits, and a little more oak showing early in its life than preceding vintages. Cork. 13.5° alc. **RATING** 90 **DRINK** 2015 $ 110

▼▼▼▼ **Reserve Cabernet Sauvignon 2000** Medium- to full-bodied; straight blackcurrant/blackberry fruit; slightly stringy tannins. Still coming to terms with itself, and may flourish with 5+ years in bottle. Cork. 13.5° alc. **RATING** 89 **DRINK** 2014 $ 64

Tait Wines NR

Yaldara Drive, Lyndoch, SA 5351 **REGION** Barossa Valley
T (08) 8524 5000 **WWW**.taitwines.com.au **OPEN** W'ends & public hols 11–5, or by appt
WINEMAKER Bruno Tait **EST.** 1994 **CASES** 2000
The Tait family has been involved in the wine industry in the Barossa for over 100 years, making not wine but barrels. Their more recent venture into winemaking was immediately successful. Exports to the US, Germany, Malaysia and Singapore.

Talijancich

★★★☆

26 Hyem Road, Herne Hill, WA 6056 **REGION** Swan Valley
T (08) 9296 4289 **F** (08) 9296 1762 **OPEN** Sun–Fri 11–5
WINEMAKER James Talijancich **EST.** 1932 **CASES** 10 000
A former fortified wine specialist (with old Liqueur Tokay) now making a select range of table wines, with particular emphasis on Verdelho — in August each year there is a tasting of fine 3-year-old Verdelho table wines from both Australia and overseas. James Talijancich is an energetic and effective ambassador for the Swan Valley as a whole. Exports to China, Japan and Hong Kong.

ΨΨΨΨΨ **JJ Reserve Muscat 1961 Solero NV** Dark colour; complex raisin/raisin toast/Christmas cake flavours; a lively, clean finish. The solera system has kept the wine fresh, the 1961 base now only a minor portion. Cork. 18° alc. **RATING** 94 **DRINK** Now

ΨΨΨΨ **Tempranillo 2005** Good purple-red; herb, spice and cedar aromas; plenty of dark fruits on the medium-bodied palate, though not overmuch structure; well-made. Screwcap. **RATING** 88 **DRINK** 2009
Liqueur Verdelho NV Quite pleasant nutty/butter shortbread flavours; the spirit is not sharp and the wine has balance. Cork. 16° alc. **RATING** 87 **DRINK** Now

ΨΨΨΨ **Graciano 2003** **RATING** 85 **DRINK** Now

Taliondal

NR

270 Old North Road, Pokolbin, NSW 2320 **REGION** Lower Hunter Valley
T (02) 9427 6812 **F** (02) 9427 6812 **OPEN** By appt
WINEMAKER Frank Brady **EST.** 1974 **CASES** 240
The Brady Bunch, headed by Frank Brady, acquired Taliondal in 1974 as a family hideaway. Says Frank Brady, 'When in the Hunter, do as the Hunter does', so 1 ha of cabernet sauvignon was planted in 1974, and 1.5 ha of traminer the following year. For many years the family was content to sell the grapes to local vignerons; they now take a small portion of the production and make wine on the property. The Cabernet Sauvignon has been a consistent medal winner at Hunter shows.

Tall Poppy Wines

NR

PO Box 4147, Mildura, Vic 3502 **REGION** Murray Darling
T (03) 5022 7255 **F** (03) 5022 7250 **WWW**.tallpoppywines.com **OPEN** 7 days 8.30–5
WINEMAKER Barossa Vintners **EST.** 1997 **CASES** 20 000
Tall Poppy Wines has lofty ambitions. It owns 4.5 ha each of shiraz and viognier, but is able to draw upon grapes sourced from 170 ha of vineyards owned by its directors, with a volume potential of 300 000–400 000 cases aimed at the export market (the UK, Vietnam, Malaysia, Singapore, NZ and Philippines).

Tallarook

NR

2 Delaney's Road, Warranwood, Vic 3134 (postal) **REGION** Upper Goulburn
T (03) 9876 7022 **F** (03) 9876 7044 **WWW**.tallarook.com **OPEN** Not
WINEMAKER MasterWineMakers **EST.** 1987 **CASES** 1200
Tallarook has been established on a property between Broadford and Seymour at an elevation of 200–300m. Since 1987, 14 ha of vines have been planted, mainly to chardonnay, shiraz and pinot noir. The retaining of MasterWineMakers in 1998 brought a substantial change in emphasis, and the subsequent releases of impressive Chardonnays and other good wines. Subsequently, the second label Terra Felix was sold. Exports to the UK and Europe.

Tallavera Grove Vineyard & Winery

NR

749 Mount View Road, Mount View, NSW 2325 **REGION** Lower Hunter Valley
T (02) 4990 7535 **F** (02) 4990 5232 **WWW**.tallaveragrove.com.au **OPEN** Fri–Mon 10–5
WINEMAKER Chris Cameron **EST.** 2000 **CASES** 1800
Tallavera Grove is one of the many wine interests of John Davis and family. The family is a 50% owner of Briar Ridge, a 12-ha vineyard in Coonawarra, a 100-ha vineyard at Wrattonbully (the Stonefields Vineyard), and a 36-ha vineyard at Orange (Jokers Peak). The Mount View winery will eventually be equipped to handle 200–300 tonnes of fruit.

Tallis Wine

★★★★

PO Box 10, Dookie, Vic 3646 **REGION** Central Victoria Zone
T (03) 5823 5383 **F** (03) 5828 6532 **WWW**.talliswine.com.au **OPEN** Not
WINEMAKER Richard Tallis, Gary Baldwin (Consultant) **EST.** 2000 **CASES** 2000
Richard, Mark and Alice Tallis have a substantial vineyard, with 16 ha of shiraz, 5 ha of cabernet sauvignon, 2 ha of viognier and 1 ha of merlot. While most of the grapes are sold, they have embarked on winemaking with the aid of Gary Baldwin, and have had considerable success. The philosophy of their viticulture and winemaking is to create a low-input and sustainable system; all environmentally harmful sprays are eliminated.

ΨΨΨΨΨ **The Silent Showman Shiraz Viognier 2003** Typically good purple-red; a very concentrated wine, courtesy of the drought perhaps; viognier has fully tamed the tannins as it so often does; plenty of rich blackberry plum fruit, however. Cork. 14.2° alc. **RATING** 91 **DRINK** 2013 $ 25

Dookie Hills Shiraz 2004 Strong, deep purple-red; rich blackberry and plum fruit, with some stylistic similarity to the Shiraz of Heathcote; cooler vintage a plus. Cork. 14.2° alc. **RATING** 90 **DRINK** 2014 $ 19

Dookie Hills Cabernet Sauvignon 2004 Bright purple-red hue; lively, fresh cassis, raspberry and mulberry fruit; good length and line. Cork. 14° alc. **RATING** 90 **DRINK** 2010 $ 19

ΨΨΨΨ **Dookie Hills Sangiovese 2004** Sweet morello cherry fruit; alcohol seems higher than it in fact is; a tweak of acidity on the finish. Cork. 13.6° alc. **RATING** 88 **DRINK** 2010 $ 18

ΨΨΨΨ **Dookie Hills Rose 2005** Enticing deep but bright fuchsia-purple; just a pity the wine is so unashamedly sweet. Screwcap. 12.1° alc. **RATING** 86 **DRINK** Now $ 17

Dookie Hills Viognier 2005 **RATING** 85 **DRINK** Now $ 19

Taltarni

★★★★★

339 Taltarni Road, Moonambel, Vic 3478 **REGION** Pyrenees
T (03) 5459 7918 **F** (03) 5467 2306 **WWW**.taltarni.com.au **OPEN** 7 days 10–5
WINEMAKER Leigh Clarnette, Loic Le Calvez, Louella McPhan **EST.** 1972 **CASES** 70 000
After a hiatus of 2 years or so following the departure of long-serving winemaker and chief executive Dominique Portet, Taltarni gathered momentum and inspiration with a new winemaking team. Major changes in the approach to the vineyards; major upgrading of winery equipment and investment in new oak barrels; a long-term contract for the purchase of grapes from the Heathcote region; and the release of a flagship wine, Cephas, are the visible signs of the repositioning of the business. Exports to all major markets.

ΨΨΨΨΨ **Heathcote Shiraz 2004** Dense colour; clean blackberry aromas, rich but supple and round in the mouth; essentially fruit-driven, but the tannins and oak are there in support. Impressive. Cork. 14° alc. **RATING** 96 **DRINK** 2015 $ 42

Pyrenees Cabernet Sauvignon 2004 Medium-bodied and well-balanced red and black fruits supported by soft, but persistent, tannins. Cork. 14° alc. **RATING** 95 **DRINK** 2014 $ 32

Victoria Tasmania Sauvignon Blanc 2005 Spotlessly clean aromas; a vibrant palate, with long, zesty lemony citrussy flavours plus passionfruit; excellent finish. Screwcap. 13° alc. **RATING** 94 **DRINK** Now $ 19

Three Monks Cabernet Merlot 2003 Strong colour; attractive blackcurrant, cassis and mulberry in an elegant, medium-bodied and well-balanced palate; lovely ripe fruit, soft tannins and positive oak. Cork. **RATING** 94 **DRINK** 2013 $ 21

ŸŸŸŸŸ **Lalla Gully Chardonnay 2003** Light- to medium-bodied; nutty/creamy flavours from the malolactic fermentation have likewise taken the edge off the strong Tasmanian acidity; gentle grapefruit and melon and balanced French oak. Cork. 13° alc. **RATING** 92 **DRINK** 2009 $ 27

Lalla Gully Riesling 2005 Light- to medium-bodied; clean, gentle lime juice, with plenty of mid-palate flavour; good balance and length. **RATING** 91 **DRINK** 2010 $ 22

Brut Tache 2004 Pale blush pink; crisp and lively with touches of spice and strawberry; low dosage, long finish. 13° alc. **RATING** 90 **DRINK** 2010 $ 22

ŸŸŸŸ **Sauvignon Blanc 2005** Herb, grass and green pea aromas; lively, racy acidity; good length. Screwcap. **RATING** 89 **DRINK** Now $ 19

Lalla Gully Sauvignon Blanc 2005 Tangy, citrussy/lemony fruit, with a long and lingering finish. **RATING** 89 **DRINK** Now $ 22

Rose 2005 Bright purple-red; an excellent juxtaposition of small red fruits and crisp acidity on the finish. Screwcap. 13° alc. **RATING** 88 **DRINK** Now $ 20

Three Monks Cabernet Merlot 2004 Strong colour; powerful blackcurrant and earth fruit, the tannins a little cumbersome and needing to settle down. Screwcap. **RATING** 88 **DRINK** 2014 $ 21

Lalla Gully Pinot Noir 2004 Good colour; medium-bodied, soft texture with plummy fruit. **RATING** 87 **DRINK** 2008 $ 28

ŸŸŸŸ **Lalla Gully Pinot Gris 2005** **RATING** 86 **DRINK** 2008 $ 24

Tamar Ridge   ★★★★★

Auburn Road, Kayena, Tas 7270 **REGION** Northern Tasmania
T (03) 6394 1111 F (03) 6394 1126 **WWW**.tamarridgewines.com.au **OPEN** 7 days 10–5
WINEMAKER Andrew Pirie, Matt Lowe **EST.** 1994 **CASES** 50 000
In April 2003 Gunns Limited, a large, publicly listed Tasmanian forestry and agribusiness entity, purchased Tamar Ridge. With the retention of Dr Richard Smart as viticultural advisor, the largest expansion of Tasmanian plantings is now underway, with 137 ha of wines, 72.5 in bearing, in the vicinity of the winery. A further development at Coombend, on the east coast, is also underway. Dr Andrew Pirie became CEO and chief winemaker in September 2005, adding further lustre to the brand. Exports to the UK, the US and other major markets.

ŸŸŸŸŸ **Chardonnay 2004** Classy barrel ferment inputs to a complex wine built around stone fruit flavours; excellent line, length and balance. Top gold medal Tasmanian Wine Show '06. Screwcap. 13° alc. **RATING** 95 **DRINK** 2011 $ 21

Riesling 2004 The initially fearsome acidity to the wine has duly softened and integrated; now has an intense, vibrant and lingering palate with lime juice and steely acidity in balance. **RATING** 94 **DRINK** 2014 $ 19

Sauvignon Blanc 2005 Sweet fruit with tropical edges; passionfruit/tropical fruit giving a coating of fruit sweetness. Screwcap. **RATING** 94 **DRINK** Now $ 20

ŸŸŸŸŸ **Devils Corner Chardonnay 2004** A very aromatic and fragrant citrus blossom bouquet; bright acidity streaks through the vibrant grapefruit flavours of the palate. Little or no oak. **RATING** 92 **DRINK** 2010 $ 17

ŸŸŸŸ **Riesling 2005** Generous, fleshy ripe fruit and good balancing acidity; needs time to show its wares. Screwcap. 13° alc. **RATING** 89 **DRINK** 2012 $ 19

Late Harvest Riesling 2005 Nicely balanced; has length and a mix of lime sherbet and tropical fruit. A touch more acidity needed. Screwcap. 9° alc. **RATING** 89 **DRINK** 2010 $ 22

Pinot Noir 2004 Abundant, ripe, sweet confit/plum fruit and substantial tannins; some sugared fruit characters. Screwcap. 13.5° alc. **RATING** 88 **DRINK** 2009 $ 25

Devils Corner Pinot Noir 2004 Medium-bodied; smooth and supple but slightly sweet fruit off-set by a savoury backdrop. **RATING** 87 **DRINK** 2009 $ 18

ＹＹＹＹ　**Pinot Gris 2005** RATING 86 DRINK 2008 $21
Devils Corner Rose 2005 RATING 86 DRINK Now $14

🐝 Tambo Estate ★★★★

96 Pages Road, Bumberrah, Vic 3902 **REGION** Gippsland
T (03) 5156 4921 **F** (03) 5156 4291 **OPEN** W'ends, public & school hols 10–5, or by appt
WINEMAKER Bill Williams, David Coy **EST.** 1994 **CASES** 650
Bill and Pam Williams returned to Australia in the early 1990s after 7 years overseas, and began the search for a property which met the specific requirements for high-quality table wines established by Dr John Gladstones in his masterwork *Viticulture and Environment*. They chose a property in the foothills of the Victorian Alps on the inland side of the Gippsland Lakes, with predominantly sheltered, north-facing slopes. They planted a little over 5 ha of chardonnay (the lion's share of the plantings with 3.44 ha), sauvignon blanc, pinot noir, cabernet sauvignon and a splash of merlot. Until 1999 the grapes were sold to other producers in the region, and part continues to be sold. They have been rewarded with high-quality Chardonnay and Pinot Noir.

ＹＹＹＹＹ　**Gippsland Lakes Chardonnay 2002** Some faintly funky complexity to the bouquet; excellent intensity and length on the palate; grapefruit and white peach; subtle oak. **RATING** 92 **DRINK** 2008 $18
Gippsland Lakes Pinot Noir 2003 Spicy, foresty edge to the bouquet; excellent length and line, with plum, dark cherry and spice flavours; tight and stylish, still developing; 120 cases made. Cork. **RATING** 91 **DRINK** 2009 $18

ＹＹＹＹ　**Gippsland Lakes Chardonnay 2004** Strongly influenced by what appears to be malolactic fermentation, giving a creamy, nutty overlay to the fruit. **RATING** 86 **DRINK** 2008
Gippsland Lakes Cabernet Sauvignon 2001 RATING 86 DRINK 2008 $18

Tamborine Estate Wines ★★☆

32 Hartley Road, North Tamborine, QLD 4272 **REGION** Queensland Coastal
T (07) 5545 1711 **F** (07) 5545 3522 **WWW**.tamborineestate.com.au **OPEN** 7 days 10–4
WINEMAKER John Cassegrain **EST.** 1990 **CASES** 4000
Tamborine Estate is a joint venture between the well-known John Cassegrain (of Cassegrain Wines at Port Macquarie) and French-born entrepeneur Bernard Forey (owner of the large Richfield Vineyard at Tenterfield in northern NSW). They have acquired the former Mount Tamborine Winery and its 2.5 ha of merlot, cabernet franc and malbec, planted adjacent to the winery. Exports to Switzerland, Singapore and Thailand.

ＹＹＹＹ　**Shiraz Cabernet 2001** Light- to medium-red; has matured very well; light- to medium-bodied, with gently earthy black fruits and fine tannins; 100% Qld fruit. Cork. 14° alc. **RATING** 87 **DRINK** 2008 $22

ＹＹＹＹ　**Hinterland Botrytis Semillon Chardonnay NV** RATING 85 DRINK Now $19
Cuvee NV RATING 84 DRINK Now $17
Sparkling Shiraz NV RATING 84 DRINK Now $19

ＹＹＹ　**Cabernet Franc 2004** RATING 83 $22
Rosso Dolce NV RATING 83 $15
Bianco Dolce NV RATING 83 $15

Tamburlaine NR

358 McDonalds Road, Pokolbin, NSW 2321 **REGION** Lower Hunter Valley
T (02) 4998 7570 **F** (02) 4998 7763 **WWW**.mywinery.com **OPEN** 7 days 9.30–5
WINEMAKER Mark Davidson, Jeremy Gordon **EST.** 1966 **CASES** 50 000
A thriving business which, notwithstanding the fact that it has doubled its already substantial production in recent years, sells over 90% of its wine through the cellar door and by mailing list (with an active tasting club members' cellar program offering wines which are held and matured at Tamburlaine). The maturing of the estate-owned Orange vineyard has led to a dramatic rise in quality across the range. Exports to Europe, the US and Japan.

Taminick Cellars ★★★☆

Booth Road, Taminick via Glenrowan, Vic 3675 **REGION** Glenrowan
T (03) 5766 2282 **F** (03) 5766 2151 **WWW**.taminickcellars.com.au **OPEN** Mon–Sat 9–5, Sun 10–5
WINEMAKER Peter Booth **EST.** 1904 **CASES** 4000
Peter Booth is a member of the fourth generation of the family owners of the winery started when
Esca Booth purchased the property in 1904. He makes massively flavoured and very long-lived red
wines, most sold to long-term customers and through the cellar door.

▼▼▼▼▽ **Premium Shiraz 2003** Distinctly better colour than the varietal; notwithstanding the
even higher alcohol, has more fruit and less overt tannins in the context of the whole
palate; heroic proportions. Cork. 16° alc. **RATING** 92 **DRINK** 2018 $16

▼▼▼▼ **Shiraz 2003** A massive wine, with black fruits, licorice and truck loads of tannins. Cork.
15° alc. **RATING** 88 **DRINK** 2013 $12
Durif 2004 The colour stains the glass; massive total extract; the ultimate truth will take
20 years to discover, but at $14 you can afford it. Cork. 15.5° alc. **RATING** 88 **DRINK** 2024
$14
Cabernet Sauvignon 2002 Strong purple-red; big, chewy, earthy
blackcurrant/blackberry, chocolate and licorice all coming together on a totally
formidable palate. Cork. 14.7° alc. **RATING** 87 **DRINK** 2015 $12

▼▼▼▽ **Chardonnay 2005** A full-flavoured wine with peachy fruit and vanilla oak; a little old-
fashioned, the region not helping. Cork. 13.5° alc. **RATING** 86 **DRINK** Now $10
Liqueur Muscat NV RATING 86 **DRINK** Now $14
Vintage Port 2001 RATING 85 **DRINK** Now $15

Tandou Wines ★★★

Nixon Road, Monash, SA 5342 **REGION** Riverland
T (08) 8583 6500 **F** (08) 8583 6599 **WWW**.tandou.com.au **OPEN** Mon–Fri 10–4
WINEMAKER Stuart Auld, John Lempens **EST.** 2001 **CASES** 30 000
Tandou is a subsidiary of a diversified public company which has 17 000 ha of land 142 km southeast
of Broken Hill and 50 km from Mildura. At its Millewa vineyard, 450 ha of vines have been planted
to chardonnay, verdelho, cabernet sauvignon, merlot, shiraz and sangiovese. A winery with a 21 000-
tonne capacity has been built, and produces a range of wine sold in bulk, as cleanskin bottles and
under the proprietary Broken Earth and Wontanella brands (the latter is a cheaper, second label).

▼▼▼▽ **Broken Earth Merlot 2003** Savoury, within the varietal spectrum, though just a little too
much earthy/savoury/olive flavour. Cork. 13.5° alc. **RATING** 86 **DRINK** 2008 $13

Tangaratta Estate NR

RMB 637 Old Winton Road, Tamworth, NSW 2340 **REGION** Northern Slopes Zone
T (02) 6761 5660 **F** (02) 6766 5383 **OPEN** Sun–Fri 10–5
WINEMAKER Hunter Wine Services (John Hordern) **EST.** 1999 **CASES** 23 000
Another substantial operation in the Northern Slopes Zone, with a 29-ha vineyard planted to
verdelho, cabernet sauvignon, merlot and shiraz. The cellar door has light meals and barbecue
facilities. Exports to the US, Canada, Japan, Malaysia and Singapore.

Tanglewood Downs NR

Bulldog Creek Road, Merricks North, Vic 3926 **REGION** Mornington Peninsula
T (03) 5974 3325 **F** (03) 5974 4170 **OPEN** Sun–Mon 12–5
WINEMAKER Ken Bilham, Wendy Bilham **EST.** 1984 **CASES** 1200
One of the smaller and lower-profile wineries on the Mornington Peninsula, with Ken Bilham quietly
doing his own thing on 2.5 ha of estate plantings. Lunch and dinner are available by arrangement.

Tanglewood Vines

NR

RMB 383, Bridgetown, WA 6255 (postal) **REGION** Blackwood Valley
T (08) 9764 4051 **OPEN** Not
WINEMAKER Contract **EST.** 1999 **CASES** NA
Tanglewood Vines has established 2.4 ha of cabernet sauvignon and 2 ha of merlot, with a planting of viognier in 2002.

Tanjil Wines

1171 Moe Road, Willow Grove, Vic 3825 (postal) **REGION** Gippsland
T (03) 9773 0378 **F** (03) 9773 0378 **WWW**.tanjilwines.com **OPEN** Not
WINEMAKER Robert Hewet, Olga Garot **EST.** 2001 **CASES** 1200
Robert Hewet and Olga Garot planted 4 ha of pinot noir and pinot grigio on a north-facing slope at an altitude of 200m between the Latrobe and Tanjil Valleys. The cool climate allows the vines to grow without irrigation, yields are kept low and the wines are made onsite using traditional methods and minimal intervention.

▼▼▼▼ **Gippsland Pinot Grigio 2005** Spotlessly clean; lively, citrussy edges to bright, fresh fruit; good length. Not particularly varietal, however. Screwcap. 12.6° alc. **RATING** 88 **DRINK** Now $ 16

Tannery Lane Vineyard

NR

174 Tannery Lane, Mandurang, Vic 3551 **REGION** Bendigo
T (03) 5439 3227 **F** (03) 5439 4003 **OPEN** By appt
WINEMAKER Lindsay Ross (Contract) **EST.** 1990 **CASES** 250
In 1990 planting of the present total of 2 ha of shiraz, cabernet sauvignon, cabernet franc, sangiovese, merlot and nebbiolo began. Their sangiovese was one of the first plantings of the variety in the Bendigo region. The micro-production is sold through the cellar door while stocks last, which typically is not for very long. Now owned by the Williams family.

Tantemaggie

NR

Mullineaux Road, Pemberton, WA 6260 **REGION** Pemberton
T (08) 9776 1164 **F** (08) 9776 1810 **OPEN** By appt
WINEMAKER Contract **EST.** 1987 **CASES** 300
Tantemaggie was established by the Pottinger family with the help of a bequest from a deceased aunt named Maggie. It is part of a mixed farming operation, and by far the greatest part of the 28 ha is under long-term contract to Houghton. The bulk of the plantings are cabernet sauvignon, verdelho, chardonnay and sauvignon blanc, the former producing the light-bodied style favoured by the Pottingers.

Tapanappa

★★★★★

PO Box 174, Crafers, SA 5152 **REGION** Wrattonbully
T 0418 818 223 **F** (08) 8370 8374 **WWW**.tapanappawines.com.au **OPEN** Not
WINEMAKER Brian Croser **EST.** 2002 **CASES** 1400
Arguably the most interesting of all new wineries to be announced in Australia over the past few years. Its partners are Brian Croser of Petaluma, Jean-Michel Cazes of Chateau Lynch-Bages in Pauillac and Societe Jacques Bollinger, the parent company of Champagne Bollinger. The core of the business is the Koppamurra vineyard acquired from Koppamurra Wines prior to the 2003 vintage.

▼▼▼▼▼ **Whalebone Vineyard Cabernet Shiraz 2003** Abounds with soft and warm black fruits followed by fine, ripe and gently persistent tannins from the mid-palate through to the finish. Quality French oak rounds the wine off. **RATING** 95 **DRINK** 2018 $ 74

Whalebone Vineyard Cabernet Shiraz 2004 Medium red-purple, not star-bright; a very attractive mix of sweet red and black fruits with seamless quality oak and fine, ripe tannins. Cork. **RATING** 95 **DRINK** 2014 $ 75

Tapestry ★★★★★

Olivers Road, McLaren Vale, SA 5171 **REGION** McLaren Vale
T (08) 8323 9196 **F** (08) 8323 9746 **www**.tapestrywines.com.au **OPEN** 7 days 11–5
WINEMAKER Jon Ketley **EST.** 1971 **CASES** 13 000
After a relatively brief period of ownership by Brian Light, the former Merrivale Winery was acquired in 1997 by the Gerard family, previously owners of Chapel Hill. It has 40 ha of 30-year-old vineyards, 6.5 ha in McLaren Vale and 33.5 ha in Bakers Gully. Less than half the grapes are used for the Tapestry label. Exports to the UK, the US, Canada, Singapore, Hong Kong and NZ.

ŸŸŸŸŸ **The Vincent McLaren Vale Shiraz 2003** Elegant spicy/savoury/chocolatey fruit, with
excellent intensity and length. Utterly atypical for icon McLaren Vale style. Cork. 14° alc.
RATING 94 **DRINK** 2013 **$** 40
Fifteen Barrels McLaren Vale Cabernet Sauvignon 2003 Medium-bodied; fine, supple
velvety/silky texture; perfumed cassis berry fruits which have absorbed all the oak; very
good tannins. Up to 15 barrels are selected; in this vintage only 10 made the grade. Cork.
14° alc. **RATING** 94 **DRINK** 2015 **$** 40

ŸŸŸŸŸ **McLaren Vale Sauvignon Blanc 2005** Apple and passionfruit aromas and flavours; quite
intense, good balance and length. Screwcap. 12.5° alc. **RATING** 93 **DRINK** 2009 **$** 18
McLaren Vale Chardonnay 2004 An aromatic, almost flowery, bouquet; lovely nectarine,
grapefruit and melon flavours; similar balance and length; oak merely a vehicle. Screwcap.
13.5° alc. **RATING** 93 **DRINK** 2009 **$** 18
McLaren Vale Shiraz 2002 A substantial wine, with a big framework and powerful
tannins; just lacks that little bit of mid-palate flesh. **RATING** 92 **DRINK** 2012 **$** 20
McLaren Vale Cabernet Sauvignon 2003 Attractive medium-bodied wine, a not-so-
junior brother of Fifteen Barrels; similar cassis/berry fruit and structure; ripe tannins.
Cork. 14° alc. **RATING** 90 **DRINK** 2013 **$** 20

ŸŸŸŸ **McLaren Vale Shiraz 2003** Medium-bodied; riper and softer than the Shiraz Viognier,
with regional chocolate and soft tannins. Cork. 14.5° alc. **RATING** 89 **DRINK** 2008 **$** 20
McLaren Vale Merlot 2003 Medium-bodied; clear varietal character, more savoury/olive
than usual from McLaren Vale; fractionally grippy tannins. Cork. 14° alc. **RATING** 88
DRINK 2010 **$** 25
Langhorne Creek McLaren Vale Shiraz Viognier 2003 Light- to medium-bodied; has
the lift, but not the concentration or focus for higher points; pleasant red fruits and soft
tannins. Screwcap. 14.5° alc. **RATING** 87 **DRINK** 2008 **$** 20

ŸŸŸŸ **McLaren Vale Riesling 2005** Pleasant enough, but this is the wrong region; soft and
bland. Screwcap. 12.5° alc. **RATING** 86 **DRINK** 2008 **$** 16
McLaren Vale Verdelho 2005 **RATING** 84 **DRINK** Now **$** 18

🐏 Tarcombe Valley Vineyard ★★★☆

1125 Tarcombe Road, Avenel, Vic 3664 (postal) **REGION** Strathbogie Ranges
T (03) 9899 3835 **OPEN** Not
WINEMAKER Elgo Estate (Cameron Atkins) **EST.** 1999 **CASES** 900
The Long Road name was inspired by the circuitous path taken by owners Barbara Cosson and
Martin McKinnon towards establishment of their vineyard. Both immigrants to Australia — one
from Scotland, the other NZ — they quickly came face to face with the Australian outback when, in
1999, they planted 7.5 ha of shiraz, 3 ha of cabernet sauvignon and 1.4 ha of pinot noir. Challenges
included leaking dams, a rare black beetle pest, and the impact of hail and drought. The infertile soils
and constant wind moderate vine growth, keeping yields low and around 3.7–5 tonnes per ha. Elgo
Estate (Cameron Atkins) has been responsible for the wines since 2004, the earlier vintage made by
Sam Plunkett.

ŸŸŸŸŸ **Reserve Shiraz 2004** Very powerful and concentrated; needs some fining, but has loads
of potential. Barrel sample. Cork. **RATING** 90 **DRINK** 2014 **$** 28

▼▼▼▼ **Long Road for a Little Dog Reserve Pinot Noir 2002** Similar firm style to the '04, but with more depth to the fruit in a black plum spectrum; well-made, not over-extracted; surprise for the region. Cork. 13° alc. **RATING** 89 **DRINK** 2010 $ 17

▼▼▼▽ **Long Road for a Little Dog Pinot Noir 2004** Clean, firm, fresh cherry and plum fruit; needs more texture. Screwcap. 14° alc. **RATING** 86 **DRINK** 2009 $ 14

Tarcoola Estate   NR

60 Spiller Road, Lethbridge, Vic 3332 **REGION** Geelong
T (03) 5281 9337 **F** (03) 5281 9311 **OPEN** W'ends 10–5, or by appt
WINEMAKER Keith Wood **EST.** 1970 **CASES** 3250
The 7.2-ha vineyard was planted between 1972 and 1974. When Keith Wood who worked for Seppelt at Great Western, purchased the property in 1990, the winery and the vineyard needed rehabilitation. He decided to gain experience working weekends at other vineyards in 1990 and 1991; during that time he met wife-to-be Annelies, who took over the resurrection of the vineyards. Between 1991 and 1996 the grapes were sold; from 1997 to 1999 wine was made in bulk, but also sold; and it was not until the 2000 vintage that Keith Wood made the wine for sale by Tarcoola Estate (Muller Thurgau, Riesling, Chardonnay, Shiraz, Cabernet Shiraz and Cabernet Sauvignon). Significant wine show success followed, and Tarcoola Estate is already buying grapes from other growers in the region, and making the wine for another local producer.

Tarrangower Estate   NR

17 Baldry Street, Malmsbury, Vic 3446 **REGION** Macedon Ranges
T (03) 5423 2088 **WWW**.macedonranges.com/tarrangowerestate **OPEN** W'ends 10–5, or by appt
WINEMAKER Tom Gyorffy **EST.** 1993 **CASES** 200
Tarrangower Estate is on the northeastern edge of Malmsbury, at the western end of the Macedon Ranges. At an altitude of 470m, it is one of the warmest sites in the region, and is planted to chardonnay, shiraz, cabernet sauvignon and merlot. Tom Gyorffy is a Melbourne lawyer, but as a mature-age student he graduated with an associate degree in applied science (winegrowing) from Charles Sturt University in 1997. His philosophy is to make 'natural wines' and to deliberately oxidise the chardonnay (hyper-oxidation).

Tarrawarra Estate   ★★★★★

Healesville Road, Yarra Glen, Vic 3775 **REGION** Yarra Valley
T (03) 5962 3311 **F** (03) 5962 3887 **WWW**.tarrawarra.com.au **OPEN** 7 days 11–5
WINEMAKER Clare Halloran, Bruce Walker **EST.** 1983 **CASES** 20 000
Clare Halloran has lightened the Tarrawarra style, investing it with more grace and finesse, but without losing complexity or longevity. The opening of the large art gallery (and its attendant café/restaurant) in early 2004 added another dimension to the tourism tapestry of the Yarra Valley. The gallery is open Wed–Sun, but as the Michelin Guide says, it is definitely worth a detour. Tin Cows is the second label, with most of the grapes for the Chardonnay and Pinot Noir estate-grown, merlot is contract-grown. The ratings for the Tin Cows range speak for themselves. Exports to the UK, the US, Switzerland, Belgium, Italy and Singapore.

▼▼▼▼▼ **Yarra Valley Chardonnay 2003** A complex blend of cashew, barrel ferment and melon and nectarine fruit; imposing length, line and drive; retains grace and elegance. Screwcap. 13.5° alc. **RATING** 96 **DRINK** 2010 $ 40

Yarra Valley Chardonnay 2004 Light straw-green; powerful and intense, yet restrained; a complex palate reflecting barrel ferment, lees and apparent malolactic; has got it all together. Screwcap. 13.8° alc. **RATING** 94 **DRINK** 2013 $ 40

▼▼▼▼▽ **Tin Cows Yarra Valley Pinot Noir 2004** Deeply coloured; a powerful, robust wine reminiscent of Tarrawarra in bygone years; abundant plum and blackberry fruit; will develop. Screwcap. **RATING** 93 **DRINK** 2010 $ 20

Yarra Valley Pinot Noir 2003 A substantial but balanced wine; abundant plum/dark fruits, the tannins balanced, oak likewise; will develop further. Screwcap. 13.7° alc. **RATING** 93 **DRINK** 2012 $ 50

Tin Cows Yarra Valley Heathcote Shiraz 2003 Medium-bodied; excellent balance and mouthfeel to sweet black fruits, chocolate and mocha; fine tannins, controlled oak. Uncommon regional blend works well. Screwcap. 14° alc. **RATING** 92 **DRINK** 2010 $20

Tin Cows Yarra Valley Chardonnay 2004 Attractive regional melon and nectarine fruit, with good length and plenty of richness; controlled barrel ferment oak inputs. Screwcap. 13° alc. **RATING** 90 **DRINK** 2010 $20

Tin Cows Yarra Valley Merlot 2003 An attractive medium-bodied mix of red fruits plus touches of olive and earth; good flow and line; fine tannins. Screwcap. 14° alc. **RATING** 90 **DRINK** 2011 $20

▼▼▼▼ **Tin Cows Yarra Valley Sauvignon Blanc 2005** Light-bodied; clean, crisp mineral, grass and gooseberry fruit; fresh finish. Screwcap. 12.8° alc. **RATING** 89 **DRINK** Now $20

▼▼▼▽ **Tin Cows Yarra Valley Rose 2005** **RATING** 86 **DRINK** Now $20

Tarrington Vineyards ★★★★★

Hamilton Highway, Tarrington, Vic 3301 **REGION** Henty
T (03) 5572 4509 **F** (03) 5572 4509 **WWW**.tarrington.net.au **OPEN** By appt
WINEMAKER Tamara Irish, Dianne Nagorcka **EST.** 1993 **CASES** 400
The grape growing and winemaking practices of Burgundy permeate every aspect of Tarrington Vineyards. While its establishment began in 1993, there has been no hurry to bring the vineyard into production. Two varieties only have been planted: pinot noir and chardonnay, with a planting density varying between 3333 and 8170 vines per ha. There are no less than nine clones in the 2 ha of pinot noir, and 4 clones in the 0.5 ha of chardonnay. The approach to making the Pinot Noir is common in Burgundy, while the unoaked Chardonnay is kept in tank on fine lees for 9 months, the traditional method of making Chablis. Everything about the operation speaks of a labour of love, with a high standard of packaging and presentation of all background material. The exemplary wines are to be found on a thoroughly impressive collection of Vic's top restaurant wine lists. Miniscule exports to the UK.

▼▼▼▼▼ **Chardonnay 2004** Very tight, focused and intense; pure nectarine, grapefruit and melon; long, linear finish and aftertaste. Cork. **RATING** 96 **DRINK** 2012 $47

Pinot Noir 2004 Racy, fine, intense spice and plum aromas and flavours; perfect acidity and extreme length. Cork. 13.5° alc. **RATING** 96 **DRINK** 2012 $45

De Ireys Chardonnay 2004 Extremely fine and crisp; long, lingering, intensely lemony acidity; the aftertaste lasts for upwards of a minute. As usual, no oak used. Cork. **RATING** 94 **DRINK** 2019 $95

Artemisia Pinot Noir 2004 Deeply coloured; powerful, rich, ripe black cherry and black plum fruit; a quite fleshy palate, tightening on the finish. Cork. 13.4° alc. **RATING** 94 **DRINK** 2010 $30

De Ireys Syrah 2004 Attractive, lively mix of spice, pepper and slippery red fruits; a long, lingering finish to a distinguished wine. Cork. **RATING** 94 **DRINK** 2016 $95

Tarwin Ridge NR

Wintles Road, Leongatha South, Vic 3953 **REGION** Gippsland
T (03) 5664 3211 **F** (03) 5664 3211 **OPEN** W'ends & hols 10–5
WINEMAKER Brian Anstee **EST.** 1983 **CASES** 700
Brian Anstee makes his wines at Nicholson River, under the gaze of fellow social worker Ken Eckersley. The wines come from 2 ha of estate pinot and 0.5 ha each of cabernet and sauvignon blanc.

Tashinga Estates ★★☆

2a/21 Castray Esplanade, Battery Point, Tas 7004 (postal) **REGION** Southern Tasmania
T (03) 6224 0368 **OPEN** Not
WINEMAKER Winemaking Tasmania (Julian Alcorso) **EST.** 1990 **CASES** NA
Tashinga Estates has a number of investments in the Tasmanian wine industry, having been a partner in Bream Creek Vineyard since 1995 as well as establishing the 3 ha Tashinga Vineyard in 1990, and

the 14 ha Meehans Vineyard in 1999. The bulk of the grapes from both vineyards is sold to Hardys, and this arrangement will continue, however, in some years selected parcels of grapes from both vineyards are contract-made for the Tashinga Estates label. A cellar door is planned.

ΨΨΨ♀ **Botrytis Pinot Gris 2004 RATING** 85 **DRINK** Now $ 16

Tassell Park Wines ★★★★

Treeton Road, Cowaramup, WA 6284 **REGION** Margaret River
T (08) 9755 5440 **F** (08) 9755 5442 **WWW**.tassellparkwines.com **OPEN** 7 days 10.30–5
WINEMAKER Peter Stanlake (Consultant) **EST.** 2001 **CASES** 2500
One of the light brigade of newcomers to the Margaret River region. Ian and Tricia Tassell have 7 ha of sauvignon blanc, chenin blanc, semillon, cabernet sauvignon, merlot, shiraz and petit verdot.

ΨΨΨΨΨ **Margaret River Sauvignon Blanc 2005** Intense, herbaceous slightly smokey bouquet; gun barrel-straight palate, with outstanding length; multiple gold medal and trophy winner. Screwcap. 13.5° alc. **RATING** 94 **DRINK** Now $ 20

ΨΨΨΨ♀ **Margaret River Sauvignon Blanc Semillon 2005** A clean bouquet; tightly focused mineral, herb and gooseberry flavour; clear-cut line and finish. Screwcap. 13° alc. **RATING** 93 **DRINK** 2008 $ 19

ΨΨΨΨ **Margaret River Shiraz 2004** Youthful purple-red; light- to medium-bodied; fresh cherry and plum fruit, controlled extract. Cork. 14.5° alc. **RATING** 89 **DRINK** 2009 $ 22

ΨΨΨ♀ **Margaret River Chenin Blanc 2005 RATING** 85 **DRINK** Now $ 18

Tatachilla ★★★★☆

151 Main Road, McLaren Vale, SA 5171 **REGION** McLaren Vale
T (08) 8323 8656 **WWW**.tatachillawines.com.au **OPEN** Mon–Sat 10–5, Sunday & public hols 11–5
WINEMAKER Fanchon Ferrandi **EST.** 1903 **CASES** 100 000
Tatachilla was reborn in 1995 but has had an at-times tumultuous history going back to 1903. Between 1903 and 1961 the winery was owned by Penfolds. It was closed in that year and reopened in 1965 as the Southern Vales Co-operative. In the late 1980s it was purchased and renamed The Vales but did not flourish; in 1993 it was purchased by local grower Vic Zerella and former Kaiser Stuhl chief executive Keith Smith. After extensive renovations, the winery was officially reopened in 1995 and won a number of tourist awards and accolades. Became part of Banksia Wines in 2001, in turn acquired by Lion Nathan in 2002. Exports to the UK, the US and NZ.

ΨΨΨΨ♀ **McLaren Vale Shiraz 2004** Medium-bodied; silky, supple plum, blackberry and just a hint of dark chocolate; good oak and tannins. Screwcap. **RATING** 92 **DRINK** 2015 $ 23
Keystone McLaren Vale Shiraz Viognier 2003 Rich and round; a very attractive amalgam of dark cherry, blackberry and chocolate, with the Viognier lift not excessive; very good for the vintage. Screwcap. **RATING** 92 **DRINK** 2013 $ 18
McLaren Vale Shiraz 2002 Powerful and focused in best 2002 vintage style; likewise, dark chocolate regional wrapping to the black cherry fruit; long, elegant palate, ripe tannins. Cork. **RATING** 92 **DRINK** 2012 $ 23
McLaren Vale Cabernet Sauvignon 2002 Blackcurrant, blackberry, olive and earth in a medium- to full-bodied palate; good structure and balance; lots to build on. Cork. **RATING** 91 **DRINK** 2012 $ 23
McLaren Vale Merlot 2002 Olive, earth, blackcurrant, spice and bitter chocolate aromas and flavours; has length, intensity and persistence. Cork. **RATING** 90 **DRINK** 2010 $ 23

ΨΨΨΨ **Keystone McLaren Vale Cabernet Sauvignon 2003** Powerful blackcurrant and regional dark chocolate; abundant tannins; needs time. Screwcap. **RATING** 89 **DRINK** 2013 $ 18
McLaren Vale Cabernet Sauvignon 2003 Ever-so-typical regional overlay of chocolate to blackcurrant fruit; a slightly sharp finish. Screwcap. 14.5° alc. **RATING** 89 **DRINK** 2012 $ 23
Growers Semillon Sauvignon Blanc 2005 A clean bouquet; herb, grass, asparagus, snow pea and lemon all to be found; good length, likewise value. Screwcap. 13.5° alc. **RATING** 88 **DRINK** 2008 $ 13

Keystone McLaren Vale Grenache Shiraz 2002 Light- to medium-bodied; savoury, spicy notes; some jam/confit grenache varietal character; fine tannins. Cork. **RATING** 88 **DRINK** Now $ 18

McLaren Vale Merlot 2003 Spicy, savoury, herbal varietal aromas and flavours; light- to medium-bodied, with appropriate tannins and oak. Screwcap. 14.9° alc. **RATING** 88 **DRINK** 2010 $ 23

Keystone McLaren Vale Chardonnay 2005 Starts quietly, but grows progressively through the palate, complexity possibly from lees and/or malolactic; no oak apparent. Screwcap. 14.8° alc. **RATING** 87 **DRINK** 2008 $ 18

Keystone McLaren Vale Cabernet Sangiovese 2003 Tangy, almost lemony, savoury backdrop to the fruit; similar, slightly savoury tannins. Screwcap. **RATING** 87 **DRINK** 2008 $ 18

Partners Cabernet Sauvignon Shiraz 2004 An honest, gutsy wine, skilfully assembled from various parts of southeast Australia; good value. Screwcap. 14.5° alc. **RATING** 87 **DRINK** 2009 $ 13

♟♟♟♟ **Keystone McLaren Vale Chardonnay 2004** **RATING** 84 **DRINK** Now $ 18

Tatehams Wines   NR

Main North Road, Auburn, SA 5451 **REGION** Clare Valley
T (08) 8849 2030 **F** (08) 8849 2260 **OPEN** Wed–Sun 10–5
WINEMAKER Mike Jeandupeux **EST.** 1998 **CASES** 500
Mike and Isabel Jeandupeux left the French-speaking part of Switzerland in 1997 to begin a new life in Australia. They now operate a restaurant and guest house at Auburn, in the southern end of the Clare Valley. The 1863 stone building, which originally operated as a general store and stables, has been completely refurbished, with several buildings offering a variety of upmarket accommodation. The winemaking side of the business is effectively an add-on.

Tatler Wines

477 Lovedale Road, Lovedale, NSW 2321 **REGION** Lower Hunter Valley
T (02) 4930 9139 **F** (02) 4930 9145 **WWW**.tatlerwines.com **OPEN** 7 days 9.30–5.30
WINEMAKER Monarch Winemaking Services (Jim Chatto), Ross Pearson, Alasdair Sutherland, Jenny Bright (Contract) **EST.** 1998 **CASES** 2000
Tatler Wines is a family-owned company headed by Sydney hoteliers Theo and Spiro Isak (Isakidis). The name comes from the Tatler Hotel on George Street, Sydney, which was purchased by James (Dimitri) Isak from the late Archie Brown, whose son Tony is general manager of the wine business. Together with wife Deborah (who he met at the Tatler Hotel many years ago) they now run the vineyard, cellar door, café and accommodation. The 40-ha property has 10 ha of shiraz, semillon and chardonnay.

♟♟♟♟♟ **Nigel's Hunter Valley Semillon 2005** Light straw-green; elegant and poised lemon/lemongrass/herb/mineral; long minerally finish. Screwcap. 10.5° alc. **RATING** 93 **DRINK** 2015 $ 19

Over the Ditch Sauvignon Blanc Semillon 2005 There is no reason why the blend shouldn't work, and it in fact does so very well, retaining the structure of semillon and building the flavour with passionfruit and gooseberry. Hunter Valley Semillon (60%)/Marlborough Sauvignon Blanc. Screwcap. 11.3° alc. **RATING** 93 **DRINK** 2009 $ 22

Tawonga Vineyard   NR

2 Drummond Street, Tawonga, Vic 3697 **REGION** Alpine Valleys
T (03) 5754 4945 **F** (03) 5754 4925 **WWW**.tawongavineyard.com **OPEN** By appt
WINEMAKER John Adams **EST.** 1994 **CASES** 500
Diz and John Adams' vineyard is at the head of the Kiewa Valley, looking out onto the four main mountains of the area: Mt Bogong, Mt Emu, Mt York and Mt Tawonga. It is on a northeast slope with a mixture of deep, red loam/clay and shallow red loam over ancient river stone soils, at an altitude of 1200 ft. Over the years, the Shiraz has won many wine show medals, not surprising given the extensive Flying Winemaker experience of John Adams; he has spent 10 weeks in each of the last 4 years as a consultant senior winemaker in France, overseeing the production of wines for the UK market.

Taylors ★★★★★

Taylors Road, Auburn, SA 5451 **REGION** Clare Valley
T(08) 8849 2008 **F**(08) 8849 2240 **WWW**.taylorswines.com.au **OPEN** Mon–Fri 9–5, Sat & public hols 10–5, Sun 10–4
WINEMAKER Adam Eggins, Helen McCarthy **EST.** 1969 **CASES** 400 000
The family-founded and owned Taylors continues to flourish and expand, its vineyards now total over 500 ha, by far the largest holding in Clare Valley. There have also been substantial changes both in terms of the winemaking team and in terms of the wine style and quality, particularly through the outstanding St Andrews range. Exports (under the Watchfield brand due to trademark reasons) to the UK, the US and other major markets.

❦❦❦❦❦ **Adelaide Hills Sauvignon Blanc 2005** Clean, lively, fresh and zesty; lovely balance, line and length; citrus and a touch of tropical fruit. Gold medal National Wine Show '05. Screwcap. 13° alc. **RATING** 94 **DRINK** 2008 $18
St Andrews Cabernet Sauvignon 2000 Cedary, earthy, spice aromas and flavours; medium-bodied, with very good mouthfeel and balance to a wine of considerable elegance; particularly good tannins. Quality cork. **RATING** 94 **DRINK** 2015 $60

❦❦❦❦ **Clare Valley Estate Sauvignon Blanc 2005** Remarkably pronounced varietal aromas; backs off a little on the apple and gooseberry palate. Screwcap. **RATING** 88 **DRINK** Now

❦❦❦❦ **Promised Land White Cabernet 2005 RATING** 86 **DRINK** Now $14
Promised Land Semillon Sauvignon Blanc 2005 RATING 85 **DRINK** Now $14
Promised Land Shiraz Cabernet 2003 RATING 84 **DRINK** Now
Promised Land Cabernet Merlot 2004 RATING 84 **DRINK** Now

❦❦❦ **Promised Land Unwooded Chardonnay 2005 RATING** 83 **DRINK** Now

Te-Aro Estate ★★★★

Lot 501 Fromm Square Road, Williamstown, SA 5351 **REGION** Barossa Valley
T(08) 8524 6116 **F**(08) 8524 7289 **WWW**.te-aroestate.com **OPEN** By appt
WINEMAKER Rod Chapman, Mark Jamieson **EST.** 1919 **CASES** 800
Te-Aro Estate has been in the Fromm family since 1919, when Carl Hermann Fromm purchased the land and married Elizabeth Minnie Kappler. With the aid of a crowbar, they planted 2 ha of madeira clone semillon and a shiraz block of 1.2 ha, both of which remain in production to this day. Te-Aro is not a Maori name, nor are the Fromms related to the Marlborough (NZ) Fromm family. It is a latin-derived phrase meaning 'to plough'. With a second family-developed property now also owned by Te-Aro Estate, the Fromms' main occupation is grape production for others from the 57 ha of dry-grown estate vines.

❦❦❦❦❦ **Harold's Creek Barossa Valley Shiraz 2002** Deep colour; medium- to full-bodied; perfectly ripened black fruits and fine, ripe tannins; velvety mouthfeel. Stained cork. **RATING** 93 **DRINK** 2010 $20
Harold's Creek Barossa Valley Cabernet Sauvignon 2004 Good colour; clean, firm, bright blackcurrant fruit does all the talking; impressive young wine; good length. Screwcap. **RATING** 92 **DRINK** 2014 $20

❦❦❦❦ **Harold's Creek Barossa Valley Shiraz 2003** Medium-bodied; a smooth and supple mix of blackberry, cherry and vanilla oak; nicely balanced, long finish. Screwcap. **RATING** 89 **DRINK** 2012 $20
Crocket's Block Dry Grown Barossa Valley Grenache 2003 Big, juicy, grapey Barossa style; high alcohol part of the scenery; American oak not over the top. Screwcap. **RATING** 89 **DRINK** 2009 $23
Crocket's Block Dry Grown Barossa Valley Cabernet Sauvignon 2003 Strong, robust black fruits with dashes of earth and chocolate; plenty of tannins; needs patience. Screwcap. **RATING** 89 **DRINK** 2013 $25
1919 Madeira Clone Old Vine Barossa Valley Semillon 2003 Clean, fresh, lemon zest and herb aromas; notes of mineral and talc on the firm, dry finish. Screwcap. **RATING** 88 **DRINK** 2010 $12

Teakles Hill Wines NR

PO Box 251, Woodside, SA 5244 **REGION** Adelaide Hills
T (08) 8389 9375 **F** (08) 8389 9375 **OPEN** Not
WINEMAKER Contract **EST.** 2001 **CASES** 1000
William Borchardt and James Bidstrup have established 4 ha of vineyard, planted to pinot noir, cabernet sauvignon and shiraz. A small amount is made for sale under the Teakles Hill brand.

Temple Bruer

Milang Road, Strathalbyn, SA 5255 **REGION** Langhorne Creek
T (08) 8537 0203 **F** (08) 8537 0131 **WWW**.templebruer.com.au **OPEN** Mon–Fri 9.30–4.30
WINEMAKER David Bruer, Vanessa Altmann **EST.** 1980 **CASES** 10 000
Always known for its eclectic range of wines, Temple Bruer (which also carries on a substantial business as a vine propagation nursery) has seen a sharp lift in wine quality. Clean, modern redesigned labels add to the appeal of a stimulatingly different range of red wines. Part of the production from the 19.2 ha of estate vineyards is sold to others, the remainder made under the Temple Bruer label. The vineyard is now certified organic and organic wines are an increasingly important part of the business. Exports to the US and Japan.

▼▼▼▼▽ **Shiraz Malbec 2002** Retains purple hue; plum, mulberry, herb and spice aromas; strongly structured; nice touch of sweet oak; ripe tannins. Screwcap. **RATING** 93 **DRINK** 2015 $ 17

Templer's Mill NR

The University of Sydney, Leeds Parade, Orange, NSW 2800 **REGION** Orange
T (02) 6360 5570 **F** (02) 6362 7625 **WWW**.orange.usyd.edu.au/ **OPEN** 7 days 11–4
WINEMAKER Reynolds Wines **EST.** 1997 **CASES** 1300
Templer's Mill was one of Australia's first flour mills, providing flour for early goldfields at Ophir near Orange. this historic mill is now a ruin on Narrambla, a property adjacent to the University of Sydney's Orange campus farm, and the birthplace of AB (Banjo) Paterson. The 19.4-ha vineyard is planted to cabernet sauvignon, chardonnay, shiraz, sauvignon blanc and merlot (in descending order of magnitude); part of the production is made under the Temper's Mill label, part sold as grapes, the operation overseen by viticulture lecturer Peter Hedberg.

Tempus Two Wines ★★★☆

Broke Road, Pokolbin, NSW 2321 **REGION** Lower Hunter Valley
T (02) 4993 3999 **F** (02) 4993 3988 **WWW**.tempustwo.com.au **OPEN** 7 days 9–5
WINEMAKER Sarah-Kate Dineen **EST.** 1997 **CASES** 50 000
Tempus Two is the name for what was once Hermitage Road Wines. It is a mix of Latin (Tempus means time) and English; the change was forced on the winery by the EU Wine Agreement and the prohibition of the use of the word 'hermitage' on Australian wine labels. Occupies a controversial new winery on Broke Road (I like it). Exports to the UK.

▼▼▼▼▽ **Mayday Hill Sangiovese 2004** An impressive example of sangiovese; a mix of cherry and spice, supported by persistent, perfectly ripe and fine tannins; good oak. Beechworth. Cork. 14° alc. **RATING** 90 **DRINK** 2010 $ 30

▼▼▼▼ **Hunter Valley Semillon Sauvignon Blanc 2005** Driven by Semillon, but with a positive contribution from the tropical Sauvignon Blanc; good overall flavour, balance and length. Screwcap. 11° alc. **RATING** 89 **DRINK** 2008 $ 14
Vine Vale Barossa Shiraz 2004 Medium-bodied; appealing plum, black cherry and blackberry fruit, with touches of chocolate . Cork. 14.5° alc. **RATING** 89 **DRINK** 2010 $ 30
Wilde Chardonnay 2005 Rich, ripe, seductive, full-bodied peachy fruit; enjoy now style. Screwcap. 14° alc. **RATING** 88 **DRINK** Now $ 19
Melange a Trois 2005 A complex, tropical array of flavours marking a rich entry to the mouth, but does tail off a little on the back-palate. Marsanne/Viognier/Roussanne. Screwcap. **RATING** 88 **DRINK** Now

Ziggy Viognier 2005 Very attractive wine at the price; plenty of apricot and peach varietal character; good mouthfeel, carries alcohol. Cork. 14.5° alc. **RATING** 87 **DRINK** Now $ 10

Cabernet Merlot 2004 Bright purple-red; light- to medium-bodied, juicy cassis and blackcurrant; entirely fruit-driven. Barossa Valley/Langhorne Creek. Screwcap. 14° alc. **RATING** 87 **DRINK** 2010 $ 19

TTTY **Lisa McGuigan Chardonnay 2003** **RATING** 86 **DRINK** Now

King Valley Pinot Gris 2005 Faint musk and pear fruit; has some mouthfeel from a touch of sweetness. Cork. **RATING** 86 **DRINK** Now $ 25

Spring Rock Hunter Valley Verdelho 2005 Generously proportioned, ripe fruit salad flavours and soft acidity. Screwcap. 12.5° alc. **RATING** 86 **DRINK** Now $ 14

Cannon Ball Hill Cabernet Merlot 2004 **RATING** 86 **DRINK** 2010 $ 14

Pinot Noir Chardonnay NV **RATING** 84 **DRINK** Now

TTT **Verdelho 2005** **RATING** 83 $ 12

Ziggy Sangiovese 2004 **RATING** 83 **DRINK** Now $ 10

Ten Minutes by Tractor Wine Co ★★★★★

1333 Mornington-Flinders Road, Main Ridge, Vic 3928 **REGION** Mornington Peninsula
T (03) 5989 6455 **WWW**.tenminutesbytractor.com.au **OPEN** W'ends & hols 11–5, 7 days in Jan
WINEMAKER Richard McIntyre, Alex White (Contract) **EST.** 1999 **CASES** 2500
Ten Minutes by Tractor was sold to Martin Spedding in early 2004, but the same three families (Judd, McCutcheon and Wallis), with their vineyards 10 mins by tractor from each other, continue to supply the fruit, and the contract winemaking continues. There are now three wine ranges: Individual Vineyard at the top; Reserve in the middle; and 10 x Tractor, with its striking label graphics, the base range. There are strong elements of *The Da Vinci Code* in the new labels for the Reserve and Individual Vineyard, but I suppose a $60 bottle of Pinot is not an impulse buy.

TTTTT **Wallis Vineyard Chardonnay 2004** Light straw-green; in very similar style; fine, elegant and long nectarine and grapefruit; a very pure, restrained style. Screwcap. **RATING** 95 **DRINK** 2014 $ 52

McCutcheon Vineyard Chardonnay 2004 Light straw-green; controlled complexity, with stylish barrel ferment inputs to the nectarine and melon fruit; vibrant acidity and length. Screwcap. **RATING** 95 **DRINK** 2014 $ 47

10 x Tractor Chardonnay 2004 Bright straw-green; light-bodied, with excellent balance of fruit, barrel ferment, lees and malolactic inputs to the nectarine and citrus fruit; good length. Screwcap. **RATING** 94 **DRINK** 2012 $ 28

TTTTY **Pinot Noir 2004** Fragrant red fruits; more length and a brighter array of plum, strawberry and cherry than the 10 x Tractor; good oak. Screwcap. **RATING** 92 **DRINK** 2011 $ 52

10 x Tractor Pinot Gris 2005 Vibrant fruit, the unusual citrussy overtones a distinct plus; long palate and finish; 9 months maturation in old French oak a textural vehicle. Screwcap. 14.5° alc. **RATING** 91 **DRINK** 2009 $ 30

10 x Tractor Sauvignon Blanc 2005 Pale straw-green; clean gooseberry passionfruit flavours with minerally acidity woven through from start to finish. Screwcap. 12.5° alc. **RATING** 90 **DRINK** Now $ 23

TTTT **10 x Tractor Pinot Gris 2004** Greater aromatic and flavour impact than the majority, due to the astute use of 10 months maturation in old French oak; some citrus and stone fruit; a chameleon. **RATING** 89 **DRINK** 2008 $ 30

10 x Tractor Pinot Noir 2004 Slightly unusual spicy/herbal/minty aromas; light- to medium-bodied red fruits; spicy finish. Screwcap. **RATING** 89 **DRINK** 2009 $ 34

10 x Tractor Tempranillo 2004 Savoury, minty, leafy and, above all, spicy aromas; light- to medium-bodied; some pretty good French oak helps the wine along; 60 cases made. Cork. 14.6° alc. **RATING** 89 **DRINK** 2008 $ 40

Terrace Vale ★★★★

Deasys Road, Pokolbin, NSW 2321 **REGION** Lower Hunter Valley
T (02) 4998 7517 **F** (02) 4998 7814 **WWW**.terracevale.com.au **OPEN** 7 days 10–4
WINEMAKER Alain Leprince **EST.** 1971 **CASES** 14 000
In April 2001, the Batchelor family (headed by former AMP chief executive Paul Batchelor) acquired Terrace Vale. In late 2004 Terrace Vale (and its various second labels and brands) were merged with Cheviot Bridge/The Long Flat Wine Co, of which Paul Batchelor is now non-executive chairman. Marketing of the brands in Australia and overseas is being undertaken by Cheviot Bridge.

ŦŦŦŦŦ **Old Vine Semillon 2005** Bright green-yellow; bursting with lemon and lime fruit, with a dusting of spice, in best '05 fashion; good balance and length. A capsule over the screwcap even fooled this old dog. 10.8° alc. **RATING** 94 **DRINK** 2013 $ 22

ŦŦŦŦŦ **Old Vine Chardonnay 2003** Bright green-yellow; rich, peachy/buttery regional style, and controlled French oak. Cork. 13.3° alc. **RATING** 90 **DRINK** 2009 $ 22
Old Vine Shiraz 2003 A supple, smooth, medium-bodied palate with a mix of red and black fruits, fine tannins and appropriate oak. Cork. 13.3° alc. **RATING** 90 **DRINK** 2013 $ 22

ŦŦŦŦ **Old Vine Chardonnay 2004** Deep yellow-green; soft peach/stone fruit flavours developing at a rate of knots; plenty of flavour, but drink asap. Cork. **RATING** 87 **DRINK** Now $ 27
Hunter Valley Cabernet Sauvignon 2002 Strong regional overlay to a variety which seldom prospers in the Hunter, old vine or not. Does have charm within the limits of the region. Cork. 12.8° alc. **RATING** 87 **DRINK** 2012

ŦŦŦŦ **Hunter Valley Cabernet Sauvignon 2003** **RATING** 85 **DRINK** 2008 $ 35

Terrel Estate Wines NR

Whitton Stock Route, Yenda, NSW, 2681 **REGION** Riverina
T (02) 6968 1110 **F** (02) 6968 1120 **OPEN** By appt
WINEMAKER Robert Guadagnini **EST.** 1994 **CASES** NA
Gonzalo Terrel Sr heads a very large operation, little known in the domestic market, but with 250 ha of all the major varietals and a few out of left field, such as tempranillo. It is primarily a bulk processing facility, with much of the wine sold in bulk to other winemakers; part is vinified under the Terrel Estate, Morning Mist, Pebblestone and Majestic brands.

Teusner ★★★★☆

29 Jane Place, Tanunda, SA 5352 (postal) **REGION** Barossa Valley
T (08) 8563 0898 **F** (08) 8562 1177 **WWW**.teusner.com.au **OPEN** Not
WINEMAKER Kym Teusner **EST.** 2001 **CASES** 3000
Teusner is a partnership between former Torbreck winemaker Kym Teusner and brother-in-law Michael Page, and is typical of the new wave of winemakers determined to protect very old, low-yielding, dry-grown Barossa vines. The winery approach is based on lees ageing, little racking, no fining or filtration, and no new American oak. The very reasonably priced wines are made either from 100% shiraz or from Southern Rhône blends. Limited exports to the US, Canada and the UK.

ŦŦŦŦ **Joshua Barossa Valley Grenache Mataro Shiraz 2005** Light- to medium-bodied; lovely fresh, lively, juicy fruits; excellent line and length; ready to roll right now. Cork. 14.5° alc. **RATING** 92 **DRINK** 2008 $ 24
Avatar Barossa Valley Grenache Mataro Shiraz 2004 Light- to medium-bodied; fresh, juicy berry fruit; fine, silky tannins; slightly more structure. Cork. 14.5° alc. **RATING** 91 **DRINK** 2008 $ 29

Thalgara Estate

NR

De Beyers Road, Pokolbin, NSW 2321 **REGION** Lower Hunter Valley
T (02) 4998 7717 **F** (02) 4998 7774 **OPEN** 7 days 10–5
WINEMAKER Steve Lamb **EST.** 1985 **CASES** 3000
A low-profile winery which had its moment of glory at the 1997 Hunter Valley Wine Show, when it
won the Doug Seabrook Memorial Trophy for Best Dry Red of Show with its 1995 Show Reserve
Shiraz.

The Blok Estate

Riddoch Highway, Coonawarra, SA 5263 **REGION** Coonawarra
T (08) 8737 2734 **F** (08) 8737 2994 **WWW**.blok.com.au **OPEN** 7 days 10–5
WINEMAKER Kopparossa Wines (Gavin Hogg) **EST.** 1999 **CASES** 2000
The Trotter family (Luke, Rebecca, Gary and Ann) purchased The Blok Estate in October 2005, and
have significantly increased production. The cellar door is in a renovated, old stone home surrounded
by gardens.

Coonawarra Riesling 2005 Fragrant lime and nettle aromas; lively, crisp and intense, yet
delicate, apple and lime; long finish, squeaky acidity. Coonawarra riesling at its best.
Screwcap. 11.5° alc. **RATING** 94 **DRINK** 2012 $ 17

Coonawarra Chardonnay 2005 Elegant and lively unwooded style; restrained melon and
citrus; brisk finish and acidity. Screwcap. 13.5° alc. **RATING** 89 **DRINK** 2011 $ 17
Coonawarra Cabernet Sauvignon 2003 A light- to medium-bodied mix of earth, mint
and sweet berry; fine tannins, controlled oak. Cork. 13° alc. **RATING** 89 **DRINK** 2013 $ 24
Coonawarra Cabernet Merlot 2002 Elegant, light- to medium-bodied
spicy/cedary/earthy/blackcurrant aromas and flavours; fine tannins, good length. Cork.
13.5° alc. **RATING** 88 **DRINK** 2012 $ 24

Limestone Coast Pinot Noir Chardonnay NV Quite pleasant, lively sweet fruits and
balanced finish. Cork. 12.5° alc. **RATING** 86 **DRINK** 2008 $ 24
Coonawarra Shiraz 2002 RATING 84 **DRINK** 2008 $ 24

The Carriages Vineyard

549 Kotta Road, Echuca, Vic 3564 **REGION** Goulburn Valley
T (03) 5483 7767 **F** (03) 5483 7767 **OPEN** By appt
WINEMAKER Plunkett Wines (Sam Plunkett) **EST.** 1996 **CASES** 1000
David and Lyndall Johnson began the development of The Carriages in 1996, planting 2.5 ha of
merlot and 3.5 ha of cabernet sauvignon. The wines are made at Plunkett, where David Johnson was
previously employed. The name and the extremely innovative packaging stems from 4 old railway
carriages which the Johnsons have painstakingly rehabilitated, and now live in. Each bottle is
identified with a cardboard rail ticket which is strikingly similar to the tickets of bygone years.
Vertically bisected, with brown on the left side and yellow on the right side, the ticket manages to
show the brand name, the vintage, the variety, the number of standard drinks, the alcohol and the
bottle number (which is in fact the ticket number, or vice versa). The ticket is fixed to the label with
fine twine, so it can be removed either as a memento or for further orders.

Reserve Echuca Cabernet Sauvignon 2003 Very good colour for an '03; a curate's egg:
bright, fresh fruits, but jumpy acidity and slightly dry tannins on the way through. The
colour and fruit flavour get it over the line. Cork. 14.5° alc. **RATING** 89 **DRINK** 2012 $ 28
Echuca Cabernet Merlot 2004 Good colour; light- to medium-bodied; plenty of
blackcurrant, cassis and blackberry fruit; good balance and length. Cork. 13.3° alc.
RATING 88 **DRINK** 2010 $ 19
Echuca Merlot 2003 Has creditable varietal character; light-bodied; black olive, earth
and cedar; plenty of mouthfeel and structure. Cork. 14.5° alc. **RATING** 87 **DRINK** Now $ 17

The Cups Estate ★★★★

269 Browns Road, Fingal, Vic 3939 **REGION** Mornington Peninsula
T 1300 131 741 **F** (03) 9886 1254 **WWW**.thecupsestate.com **OPEN** 7 days 10–5
WINEMAKER Moorooduc Estate **EST.** 1999 **CASES** 3000
Joe Fisicaro has returned to his roots after a career as a financial executive, establishing The Cups Estate near Rye. The name comes from the rolling dune region of the Peninsula known as 'the cups country'; the soils are light, with relatively low fertility, but drainage is excellent. Wind and frost have been problems, but the 3.6 ha of pinot noir, 1.2 ha merlot, 1 ha shiraz and 0.2 ha pinot grigio are now coming through with interesting wines, also thanks to the skills of winemaker Rick McIntyre.

ΥΥΥΥΥ **Silver Dune Pinot Noir 2004** Much brighter colour and hue; lighter, more aromatic, lively cherry and plum fruit; some spice. Diam. **RATING** 92 **DRINK** 2011 $ 19.95
Raimondo Reserve Pinot Noir 2004 Unexpectedly, very powerful and concentrated briary/foresty/spicy bouquet; the palate seems sweeter overall than the Silver Dune, although the alcohol is the same. Diam. 13.5° alc. **RATING** 92 **DRINK** 2011 $ 28
Mornington Peninsula Shiraz 2004 Complex; strong cool climate characters of spice, mint and lemongrass; tangy, peppery flavours; challenging wine. Diam. **RATING** 90 **DRINK** 2012 $ 24.95

ΥΥΥΥ **Mornington Peninsula Pinot Noir 2004** Medium-bodied; firm, fruit-driven palate; spice, black cherry and plum; long finish. Needs time. Diam. **RATING** 89 **DRINK** 2009 $ 29.95
Mornington Peninsula Pinot Rose 2005 Very similar dry style to the White Pinot, with a touch more strawberry fruit and a little more bite to the finish. Screwcap. 13.5° alc. **RATING** 87 **DRINK** Now $ 17

ΥΥΥΥ **Mornington Peninsula White Pinot 2005** Light lemon and strawberry mix; crisp acidity, dry finish; seafood minimalism. Screwcap. 13.5° alc. **RATING** 86 **DRINK** Now $ 15
Mornington Peninsula Merlot 2004 **RATING** 85 **DRINK** Now $ 22.95

The Deanery Vineyards ★★★☆

PO Box 1172, Balhannah, SA 5242 **REGION** Adelaide Hills
T (08) 8390 1948 **F** (08) 8390 0321 **OPEN** Not
WINEMAKER Duncan Dean (Sangiovese), Phil Christiansen (Shiraz), Petaluma (Sauvignon Blanc)
EST. 1995 **CASES** 500
The Dean family — Pat and Henry, and sons Duncan, Nick and Alan — purchased a 30-ha dairy farm at Balhannah in late 1994, and planted 6.5 ha of chardonnay, sauvignon blanc and semillon in the spring of 1995, subsequently adding 0.67 ha of shiraz. Pinot noir and a tiny block of sangiovese were also planted at a property at Piccadilly. A further 8 ha are now being developed on a third property, adjacent to the original Balhannah holding. Alan Dean, a Charles Sturt University-trained viticulturist and former Petaluma vineyard manager, is in charge of the vineyards, working alongside brother Duncan, and with part-time help from the third generation. The primary aim of the business is contract grapegrowing, the purchasers including Petaluma, Tower Estate and Jeffrey Grosset.

ΥΥΥΥΥ **Quartz Block Sauvignon Blanc 2005** Clean and crisp; powerful varietal fruit, with rich, ripe tropical passionfruit flavours; clean finish; 120 cases made. Screwcap. 13° alc. **RATING** 92 **DRINK** Now $ 18

ΥΥΥΥ **Bull Paddock Shiraz 2003** **RATING** 85 **DRINK** 2008 $ 16

The Duke Vineyard ★★★

38 Paringa Road, Red Hill South, Vic 3937 **REGION** Mornington Peninsula
T (03) 5989 2407 **F** (03) 5989 2407 **OPEN** W'ends, public & summer hols 12–5
WINEMAKER Geoff Duke **EST.** 1989 **CASES** 600
Geoff and Sue Duke run a tiny, low-key winery with a 1.6-ha vineyard equally divided between chardonnay and pinot noir. Its establishment goes back to 1989; 1994 marked the first commercial Chardonnay and 1997 the first Pinot Noir. The wines are made in an onsite micro-winery and back vintages are available; none of the wines are sold until they are 2 years old. A moment of glory at the Sydney Wine Show '06 where its '02 Riesling was awarded a trophy.

TTTT **Early Release Chardonnay 2004** Ripe, rich, peach into tropical fruit; a sturdy full-bodied, mouthfilling style. Cork. 14° alc. **RATING** 88 **DRINK** Now $ 20

Chardonnay 2003 Medium- to full-bodied, in vineyard style; ripe, rich peachy fruit; mouthfilling food wine. Cork. 13.5° alc. **RATING** 88 **DRINK** Now $ 25

The Falls Vineyard ★★★

RMB 2750 Longwood–Gobur Road, Longwood East, Vic 3665 **REGION** Strathbogie Ranges
T (03) 5798 5291 **F** (03) 5798 5437 **WWW**.cameronsbythefalls.com.au **OPEN** W'ends & public hols 10–5, or by appt
WINEMAKER Andrew Cameron **EST.** 1969 **CASES** 1000
The Falls Vineyard was planted by Andrew and Elly Cameron way back in 1969, as a minor diversification for their pastoral company. Two ha of shiraz, originally established on a wide T-trellis, but now converted to vertical spur positioning, provides both the Longwood Shiraz and the Longwood Reserve Shiraz. The exceptionally beautiful property was sold at the end of 2005.

TTTT **Longwood Old Vineyard Reserve Shiraz 2004** Light colour; light- to medium-bodied, with lifted aromas, gentle fruit and vanilla oak. Screwcap. 14° alc. **RATING** 87 **DRINK** 2008 $ 20

TTTT **Nine Mile Shiraz 2004** **RATING** 84 **DRINK** Now $ 18

TTT **Longwood Rose 2005** **RATING** 83 $ 12

The Fleurieu NR

Main Road, McLaren Vale, SA 5171 **REGION** McLaren Vale
T (08) 8323 8999 **F** (08) 8323 9332 **OPEN** 7 days 9–5
WINEMAKER Boar's Rock (Mike Farmilo) **EST.** 1994 **CASES** 3500
A specialist Shiraz producer, with 6.5 ha of estate vineyards and contract winemaking by former long-serving Seaview/Edwards & Chaffey winemaker Mike Farmilo. Exports to the UK, the US, Singapore, Hong Kong, Japan, Philippines and Canada.

The Gap Vineyard

Pomonal Road, Halls Gap, Vic 3381 **REGION** Grampians
T (03) 5356 4252 **F** (03) 5356 4645 **OPEN** Wed–Sun 10–5, 7 days school & public hols
WINEMAKER Trevor Mast, Dan Buckle **EST.** 1969 **CASES** 3000
The Gap is the reincarnation of Boroka, a spectacularly situated vineyard 5 km east of Halls Gap, with the slopes of the Mt William Range forming a backdrop. The vineyard was planted in 1969 but following its acquisition by Mount Langi Ghiran has been rehabilitated (including transplanting the riesling vines); the plantings are 4 ha shiraz, 3 ha each of cabernet sauv ignon and riesling and 1 ha merlot. Exports to Germany.

TTTTY **Cabernet Sauvignon 2003** Medium-bodied; nicely balanced and structured; cedar, earth, blackcurrant and chocolate; fine, ripe tannins. Cork. 14.5° alc. **RATING** 90 **DRINK** 2013 $ 26

TTTT **Riesling 2004** Straw-green; very tight and restrained, with more mineral than fruit until a twist of lime on the finish Screwcap. 12.7° alc. **RATING** 89 **DRINK** 2008 $ 18

Chardonnay 2004 Spotlessly clean, delicate, light-bodied wine; light melon fruit with touches of citrus and oak. Screwcap. 13.7° alc. **RATING** 89 **DRINK** Now $ 16

Late Harvest Riesling 2004 Lime and apple blossom aromas; a subdued minerally palate, the balance okay; will develop. Screwcap. 13° alc. **RATING** 87 **DRINK** 2010 $ 16

TTTTY **Four Sisters Merlot 2003** **RATING** 86 **DRINK** Now

TTT **Four Sisters Shiraz 2003** **RATING** 83

The Garden Vineyard   NR

174 Graydens Road, Moorooduc, Vic 3933 **REGION** Mornington Peninsula
T (03) 5978 8336 **F** (03) 5978 8343 **OPEN** By appt
WINEMAKER Moorooduc Estate **EST.** 1995 **CASES** 800
This captures the delights of the Mornington Peninsula in so many ways. As the name suggests, it is
as much a garden as it is a vineyard; Di and Doug Johnson began establishing a walled garden
10 years ago, at much the same time that they decided to increase the existing 0.5 ha of pinot noir
(planted in 1989) by an additional 1 ha of pinot noir and 0.5 ha of pinot gris.

The Grove Vineyard   NR

Cnr Metricup Road/Carter Road, Wilyabrup, WA 6284 **REGION** Margaret River
T (08) 9755 7458 **F** (08) 9755 7458 **www**.thegrovevineyard.com.au **OPEN** 7 days 9–4
WINEMAKER Steven Hughes **EST.** 1995 **CASES** 1500
Steve and Val Hughes gave their vineyard its name to acknowledge their former residence in a street
called The Grove, which was in turn part of an olive grove near Perth planted by the monks from the
New Norcia monastery north of Perth. They have planted a fruit salad vineyard, the major varieties
being sauvignon blanc (2.65 ha), chardonnay (1.5 ha), cabernet sauvignon (1.88 ha), with lesser but
not insignificant plantings of semillon, pinot noir, shiraz, merlot, verdelho, tempranillo and graciano.
They run a restaurant, provide accommodation, feature coffee roasting sales and tastings, a gourmet
delicatessen, olive oil and, of course, cellar door sales with a wide range of wines reflecting the fruit
salad plantings.

The Gurdies   NR

St Helier Road, The Gurdies, Vic 3984 **REGION** Gippsland
T (03) 5997 6208 **F** (03) 5997 6511 **OPEN** 7 days 10–5, or by appt
WINEMAKER Peter Kozik **EST.** 1991 **CASES** 1500
The only winery in the southwest Gippsland region, established on the slopes of The Gurdies hills
overlooking Westernport Bay and French Island. Plantings of the 3.5-ha vineyard commenced in
1981, but no fruit was harvested until 1991, owing to bird attack. A winery has been completed, and it
is intended to increase the vineyards to 8 ha and ultimately build a restaurant.

The Islander Estate Vineyards   ★★★★★

PO Box 96, Parndana, SA 5220 **REGION** Kangaroo Island
T (08) 8553 9008 **F** (08) 8553 9228 **www**.iev.com.au **OPEN** By appt
WINEMAKER Jacques Lurton **EST.** NA **CASES** 5000
Established by one of the most famous Flying Winemakers in the world, Bordeaux-born, trained and
part-time resident Jacques Lurton, who has established 10 ha of close-planted vineyard. The
principal varieties are sangiovese and cabernet franc; then lesser amounts of semillon, viognier,
grenache, malbec and merlot. The wines are made and bottled at the onsite winery, in true estate
style. The ultimate flagship wine will be an esoteric blend of Sangiovese, Cabernet Franc and Malbec.
Production of this wine will be limited to 2000 cases, with another 2000 cases of the Bark Hut Road
label. Tastings from barrel in late 2004 leave no doubt that some outstandingly different wines will
come from this venture. Exports to France, Denmark, Sweden and Japan.

▼▼▼▼▼ **Old Rowley Bush Vine Grenache 2004** Bright, clear red-purple; light- to medium-
bodied; lovely satiny texture from the fine, ripe spicy tannins; no hint of confection; a very
different style to any other South Australian grenache. Cork. 14.5° alc. **RATING** 94
DRINK 2010 $ 44

The Lane   ★★★★

Ravenswood Lane, Hahndorf, SA 5245 **REGION** Adelaide Hills
T (08) 8388 1250 **F** (08) 8388 7233 **www**.thelane.com.au **OPEN** 7 days 10–4.30
WINEMAKER Robert Mann **EST.** 1993 **CASES** 8000
With their sales and marketing background, John and Helen Edwards opted for a major lifestyle
change when they began establishing the first of the present 28.1 ha of vineyards in 1993. Initially,

part of the production was sold to Hardys, but now some of the wine is made for release under The Lane label (until 2003, Ravenswood Lane). A joint venture with Hardys has been terminated, which has resulted in the Starvedog Lane brand being owned by Hardys, and a revamped Ravenswood Lane label (and a new, cheaper Off The Leash label) carrying the flag for The Lane. John Edwards has applied to build a 500-tonne winery, and plans to open a cellar door and café. Exports to all major markets.

ŸŸŸŸŸ **Adelaide Hills Sauvignon Blanc 2005** Spotlessly clean; lively and intense tropical/herb/gooseberry mix; crisp acidity on the finish. Screwcap. 13.5° alc. **RATING** 92 **DRINK** Now $ 24

Adelaide Hills Pinot Grigio 2005 Water white; good length and, in particular, balance to the finish; smooth pear, spice and musk; good acidity. A pinot gris you can drink. Screwcap. 14° alc. **RATING** 91 **DRINK** 2008 $ 30

Beginning Chardonnay 2004 Elegant, light- to medium-bodied, fresh white peach, grapefruit and melon; any oak component is incidental. Screwcap. **RATING** 90 **DRINK** 2009

ŸŸŸŸ **The Gathering Sauvignon Blanc Semillon 2005** Flinty, minerally, grassy style; has good length; hints of a possible barrel ferment component. Screwcap. 13.5° alc. **RATING** 89 **DRINK** 2008

Adelaide Hills Viognier 2005 Light straw-green; strongly varietal apricot kernel, peach and lychee; a characteristic touch of phenolics on the finish. Screwcap. 14° alc. **RATING** 89 **DRINK** Now $ 30

Off The Leash Max Shiraz Viognier 2005 Plenty of dark berry fruits and some spicy lift ex the viognier; overall, slightly rustic/briary. Screwcap. 13.9° alc. **RATING** 88 **DRINK** 2009 $ 22

Reunion Shiraz 2001 Plenty of dark berry, spicy flavours, but edgy tannins dog the wine. Cork. 13.5° alc. **RATING** 88 **DRINK** 2010

ŸŸŸŸ **Off The Leash Finn No Oak White 2005** **RATING** 85 **DRINK** Now $ 22

The Lily Stirling Range   NR

Lot 3004 Chester Pass Road, Stirling Range via Borden, WA 6338 **REGION** Porongurup
T (08) 9827 9205 **F** (08) 9827 9206 **www**.thelily.com.au **OPEN** Tues–Sun 10–5
WINEMAKER Pleun Hitzert **EST.** 1990 **CASES** NA
An interesting, indeed exotic, tourism complex owned and run by two Dutch families, Hennie and Pleun Hitzert and Ron and Sue Terwijn. It features The Lily Railway Station restaurant, on the reconstructed 1924 Gnowangerup Railway Station, and a windmill. The windmill was completed in August 2003 with the help of a group of millwrights from Schiedam in The Netherlands; a 3-tonne heavy grinding stone now produces flour (available from The Lily and outlets around WA). Less exotic, perhaps, is the 3-ha vineyard planted to chenin blanc, chardonnay, grenache, cabernet sauvignon and cabernet franc.

The Little Wine Company   ★★★

824 Milbrodale Road, Broke, NSW 2330 **REGION** Lower Hunter Valley
T (02) 6579 1111 **F** (02) 6579 1440 **www**.thelittlewinecompany.com.au **OPEN** At the Small Winemakers Centre, Pokolbin
WINEMAKER Ian Little, Suzanne Little **EST.** 2000 **CASES** 13 000
Having sold their previous winery, Ian and Susan Little moved in stages to their new winery at Broke. The Little Wine Company is part-owner of the 20-ha Lochleven Vineyard in Pokolbin, and contracts 3 vineyards in the Broke–Fordwich area. It also has access to the Talga Vineyard in the Gundaroo Valley near Canberra.

ŸŸŸŸ **Olivine Viognier 2005** Well-made; gentle apricot and peach fruit, finishing with clean, lemony acidity. Screwcap. 13° alc. **RATING** 87 **DRINK** Now $ 19

ŸŸŸŸ **Olivine Gewurztraminer 2005** **RATING** 86 **DRINK** 2008 $ 19
Olivine Sangiovese Rose 2005 **RATING** 86 **DRINK** Now $ 19

The Mews

NR

84 Gibson Street, Kings Meadows, Tas 7249 (postal) **REGION** Northern Tasmania
T (03) 6344 2780 **F** (03) 6343 2076 **OPEN** Not
WINEMAKER Graham Wiltshire **EST.** 1984 **CASES** 300
Robin and Anne Holyman have established 0.4 ha of pinot noir and 9.2 ha of chardonnay at Kings
Meadows, only 4 km from the centre of Launceston. Most of the grapes are sold; industry veteran
Graham Wiltshire acts as winemaker for the remainder.

The Minya Winery

NR

Minya Lane, Connewarre, Vic 3227 **REGION** Geelong
T (03) 5264 1397 **F** (03) 5264 1097 **WWW**.theminya.com.au **OPEN** Public hols, or by appt
WINEMAKER Susan Dans **EST.** 1974 **CASES** 1400
Geoff Dans first planted vines in 1974 on his family's dairy farm, followed by further plantings in
1982 and 1988 lifting the total to 4 ha. Grenache is a highly unusual variety for this neck of the woods.
I have not tasted any of the wines, but the concerts staged in summer sound appealing.

The Natural Wine Company

NR

217 Copley Road, Upper Swan, WA 6069 **REGION** Swan Valley
T (08) 9296 1436 **F** (08) 9296 1436 **OPEN** Wed–Sun & public hols 10–5
WINEMAKER Colin Evans **EST.** 1998 **CASES** 1500
Owners Colin and Sandra Evans say the name of the business is intended to emphasise that no
herbicides or systemic pesticides are used in the vineyard, which is on the western slopes of the
Darling Range (weed control is achieved through mulching). Sandra does the vineyard work and
helps with the night shift during vintage, she was also responsible for the koala emerging from the
barrel on the label. The vineyard is within a short walk of Bells Rapids and close to the Walunga
National Park.

The Oaks Vineyard & Winery

★★★☆

31 Melba Highway, Yering, Vic 3770 **REGION** Yarra Valley
T (03) 9739 0070 **F** (03) 9739 0577 **OPEN** W'ends 10.30–5, or by appt
WINEMAKER Karen Coulston (Contract) **EST.** 2000 **CASES** 500
The Oaks has been established in what was originally a Presbyterian manse, the change in use
coming after a long period of neglect, and thus not incurring the wrath of the previous occupants.
Owner Pauline Charlton spent 12 months restoring the Victorian homestead to its former glory prior
to opening. A gallery features photographs by Pauline Charlton's daughter, Mackenzie, and fellow
students of the Photography Studies College. The vineyard is close-planted, and the wine
competently made.

🍷🍷🍷🍷 **For Lyn Yarra Valley Shiraz 2004** Light colour; light- to medium-bodied red and black
fruits, possibly young vine influences; not concentrated, but what is there is pleasant.
Cork. 13.5° alc. **RATING** 87 **DRINK** 2010 $ 25
For Lyn Yarra Valley Cabernet Franc Shiraz 2004 Savoury, briary fruit with persistent,
slightly dry, tannins; one way or another, more sweet fruit is needed. Cork. 13.5° alc.
RATING 87 **DRINK** 2009 $ 22

The Rothbury Estate

Broke Road, Pokolbin, NSW 2321 **REGION** Lower Hunter Valley
T (02) 4998 7363 **F** (02) 4993 3559 **OPEN** 7 days 9.30–4.30
WINEMAKER Mike de Garis **EST.** 1968 **CASES** 82 500
Not long after bringing back Mike de Garis from NZ (de Garis was for many years a senior
winemaker at Tyrrell's before departing to NZ), FWE announced that it was selling the Rothbury
Estate winery, but retaining the brand. It is hard to imagine the slow erosion in the value of the brand
and the quality of the wines will be halted.

ŸŸŸŸ **Pinot Noir Chardonnay NV** RATING 86 DRINK 2009
Brokenback Semillon 2005 RATING 85 DRINK 2009 $28
Black Label Verdelho 2005 RATING 85 DRINK 2008 $21

ŸŸŸ **Hunter Valley Semillon 2005** RATING 82

The Settlement Wine Co   ★★★☆

Cnr Olivers Road/Chalk Hill Road, McLaren Vale, SA 5171 **REGION** McLaren Vale
T (08) 8323 7344 **F** (08) 8323 7355 **WWW**.thesettlementwineco.com.au **OPEN** 7 days 10–5
WINEMAKER Vincenzo Berlingieri **EST**. 1992 **CASES** 3500
Vincenzo Berlingieri, one of the great characters of the wine industry, arrived in Sydney with beard
flowing and arms waving in the 1970s, and gained considerable publicity for his then McLaren Vale
winery. Fortune did not follow marketing success for this research scientist, who had arrived to work
in plant genetics at Melbourne University's Botany Department in 1964, armed with a doctorate in
agricultural science from Perugia University, Italy. However, after various moves he is in business
again with his children — Jason, John and Annika — sourcing most of the grapes from Langhorne
Creek and McLaren Vale.

ŸŸŸŸŸ **Black Pedro Ximinex NV** Obvious age; dark colour; olive rim; extremely luscious raisin fruit;
authentic Pedro Ximinex style. Multiple trophies to its credit. **RATING** 91 **DRINK** Now $30
McLaren Vale Vintage Port 2004 Powerful spice, blackcurrant and dark chocolate; good
fortifying spirit; best of all, has been kept relatively dry. Will age well. 18.5° alc. **RATING** 90
DRINK 2014 $30

ŸŸŸŸ **Verdelho Liqueur NV** Correct pale orange-brown colour and Christmas cake flavours;
gentle biscuity finish. **RATING** 88 **DRINK** Now $25
White Pedro NV Sweet raisin and biscuit mix cleansed by fortifying spirit; some age;
Pedro Ximinez/Palomino. **RATING** 87 **DRINK** Now $30

ŸŸŸŸ **Muscat Liqueur NV** RATING 86 DRINK Now $25

ŸŸŸ **Red Dingo NV** RATING 83 $9

The Silos Estate   NR

Princes Highway, Jaspers Brush, NSW 2535 **REGION** Shoalhaven Coast
T (02) 4448 6082 **F** (02) 4448 6246 **WWW**.thesilos.com **OPEN** 7 days 10–5
WINEMAKER Bevan Wilson **EST**. 1985 **CASES** 1000
Since 1995, Gaynor Sims and Kate Khoury, together with viticulturist Jovica Zecevic, have worked
hard to improve the quality of the wine, both in the 5 ha of estate vineyards and in the winery. The
winery continues to rely on the tourist trade, and the wines do not appear in normal retail outlets.

The Standish Wine Company   ★★★★☆

PO Box 498, Angaston, SA 5353 **REGION** Barossa Valley
T (08) 8564 3634 **F** (08) 8564 3634 **WWW**.standishwineco.com **OPEN** Not
WINEMAKER Dan Standish **EST**. 1999 **CASES** 800
Dan Standish is an extremely experienced winemaker, adding work in the Napa and Sonoma Valleys
in California, La Rioja in Spain and the Rhone Valley in France to his domestic winemaking. In 1999
he was able to negotiate a small parcel of 96-year-old shiraz from his parents' vineyard in the Vine
Vale subregion of the Barossa Valley. This produces 300 cases of The Standish, a wild yeast, open-
fermented and basket-pressed shiraz matured in French oak for 30 months. The Standish, which
uses his Rhone Valley experience led to the creation of The Relic, 93% shiraz and 7% viognier co-
fermented, otherwise made with similar techniques to The Standish.

ŸŸŸŸŸ **The Relic Single Vineyard Shiraz Viognier 2002** Good colour; a luscious, slurpy
testament to the marriage of shiraz and viognier; crammed with sweet fruit, the tannins
and oak under tight control. Cork. 14.5° alc. **RATING** 94 **DRINK** 2015 $85

ŸŸŸŸŸ **The Standish Single Vineyard Shiraz 2001** Holding hue and depth very well; a massive
wine, with layers of black fruits, the tannins still to fully soften and integrate. Leave it
alone for another 5 years. Cork. 14.5° alc. **RATING** 93 **DRINK** 2016 $85

The Vineyards Estate

NR

555 Hermitage Road, Pokolbin, NSW 2320 **REGION** Lower Hunter Valley
T (02) 4998 7822 **F** (02) 6574 7276 **WWW**.thevineyardsestate.com.au **OPEN** 7 days 10–5
WINEMAKER Monarch Winemaking Services (Greg Silkman) **EST.** 1993 **CASES** 500
The major investment and principal business of The Vineyards Estate is the 8-studio-suite guest house sitting among the 5 ha of vines. There is also the high-quality Splash restaurant offering the prospect of all-inclusive gourmet weekends for couples. The estate wines are sold through the restaurant and guest house, with other local wines available in the restaurant.

The Wanderer

 ★★★☆

2850 Launching Place Road, Gembrook, Vic 3783 **REGION** Yarra Valley
T (03) 5968 1622 **F** (03) 5968 1699 **OPEN** By appt
WINEMAKER Andrew Marks **EST.** 2005 **CASES** 800
Andrew Marks is the son of Ian and June Marks, owners of Gembrook Hill, and after graduating from Adelaide University with a degree in oenology he joined Southcorp, working for 6 years with Penfolds in the Barossa Valley and Seppelt at Great Western, as well as undertaking vintages in Coonawarra and France. Since then he has worked in the Hunter Valley, the Great Southern, Sonoma County in the US and Costa Brava in Spain — hence the name of his business. He made the 2005 vintage wines at Gembrook Hill, lending a hand with the Gembrook Hill vintage while doing so.

TTTT **Moscatito 2005** Lovely lemony flavours and good balance; clever, clever, but who will buy it? Technically, it's not even wine, but is said to be 'the breakfast wine for all occasions'. Screwcap. 5.5° alc. **RATING** 88 **DRINK** Now $10

Yarra Valley Rose 2005 Light pink; bright, fresh, crisp, minerally, bone-dry style, with a little strawberry peeping out. Screwcap. 13.3° alc. **RATING** 87 **DRINK** Now $13

TTTY **Yarra Valley Gewurztraminer Chardonnay 2005** A very strange blend; each neutralise the other; necessity the mother of invention? Screwcap. 12.8° alc. **RATING** 86 **DRINK** Now $15

The Warren Vineyard

NR

Conte Road, Pemberton, WA 6260 **REGION** Pemberton
T (08) 9776 1115 **F** (08) 9776 1115 **WWW**.warrenvineyard.com.au **OPEN** 7 days 11–5
WINEMAKER Phillip Wilkinson **EST.** 1985 **CASES** 700
The 1.5-ha vineyard was established in 1985 and is one of the smallest in the Pemberton region. It is owned and run by Anne Wandless and husband Arthur Hawke. An extensive range of back-vintage wines is available at the cellar door.

The Willows Vineyard

★★★★☆

Light Pass Road, Light Pass, Barossa Valley, SA 5355 **REGION** Barossa Valley
T (08) 8562 1080 **F** (08) 8562 3447 **WWW**.thewillowsvineyard.com.au **OPEN** Wed–Mon 10.30–4.30, Tues by appt
WINEMAKER Peter Scholz, Michael Scholz **EST.** 1989 **CASES** 6000
The Scholz family have been grapegrowers for generations and have almost 40 ha of vineyards, selling part and retaining the remainder of the crop. Current generation winemakers Peter and Michael Scholz make smooth, well-balanced and flavoursome wines under their own label, all marketed with bottle age. Exports to the UK, the US and Singapore.

TTTTT **Bonesetter Barossa Valley Shiraz 2002** Outstanding focus, intensity and balance; smooth, supple, velvety black fruits; seamless French oak and fine-grained tannins. Great vintage, great wine. Quality cork. **RATING** 97 **DRINK** 2025 $52

TTTTY **Barossa Valley Cabernet Sauvignon 2002** Firm and quite austere, with earth, mint, bitter chocolate and black fruits; controlled tannins and oak. Stained cork. **RATING** 90 **DRINK** 2012 $25.50

The Wine & Truffle Co

PO Box 1538, Osborne Park, WA 6916 **REGION** Pemberton
T (08) 9228 0328 **WWW**.wineandtruffle.com.au **OPEN** Not
WINEMAKER Mark Aitken **EST.** 1996 **CASES** NA
The name precisely describes this unusual venture. It is owned by a group of investors from various parts of Australia who share the common vision of producing fine wines and black truffles. The winemaking side is under the care of Mark Aitken, who, having graduated as dux of his class in applied science at Curtin University in 2000, joined Chestnut Grove as assistant winemaker in February 2002. He now is contract maker for the Wine & Truffle Company, as well as working for Chestnut Grove. The truffle side of the business is under the care of former CSIRO scientist Dr Nicholas Malajcsuk. He has overseen the planting of 13,000 truffle-inoculated hazelnut and oak trees on the property, which has now produced truffles, some of prodigious size.

ΥΥΥΥΥ **Hazel Hill Estate Reserve Chardonnay 2004** Smooth white and yellow peach, with some citrus; powerful drive, with nutty oak inputs to a substantial wine; good balancing acidity. Screwcap. **RATING** 90 **DRINK** 2009 $ 24.99
Hazel Hill Estate Black Gold Shiraz 2004 Very complex spicy, earthy aromas and a hint of game; intense cool climate style. Cork. **RATING** 90 **DRINK** 2009 $ 18.99

ΥΥΥΥ **Hazel Hill Estate Reserve Riesling 2004** Tight lemon rind and mineral fruit; considerable CO_2 spritz needs to settle down. Screwcap. **RATING** 89 **DRINK** 2013 $ 22.99
Hazel Hill Estate Sauvignon Blanc Semillon 2004 Nicely balanced hints of passionfruit on a delicate palate; good finish. Screwcap. **RATING** 88 **DRINK** Now $ 18.99
Hazel Hill Estate Black Gold Merlot 2004 Surprisingly, has slightly more structure than the Cabernet Merlot; tangy black olive and spice aromas and flavour. Cork. **RATING** 88 **DRINK** 2009 $ 18.99
Hazel Hill Estate Black Gold Cabernet Merlot 2004 Light- to medium-bodied; clean, fresh cassis and blackcurrant fruit; ultra-fine tannins. Cork. **RATING** 87 **DRINK** 2008 $ 18.99

ΥΥΥΥ **Hazel Hill Estate Angel White 2004** **RATING** 85 **DRINK** Now $ 14.99
Hazel Hill Estate Devil's Blend 2004 **RATING** 84 **DRINK** Now $ 14.99

Thistle Hill NR

McDonalds Road, Mudgee, NSW 2850 **REGION** Mudgee
T (02) 6373 3546 **F** (02) 6373 3540 **WWW**.thistlehill.com.au **OPEN** Mon–Sat 9.30–4.30, Sun & public hols 9.30–4
WINEMAKER Lesley Robertson, Robert Paul (Consultant) **EST.** 1976 **CASES** 3000
The Robertson family has put the sudden death of husband and father Dave behind it. The estate-grown wines are made onsite with the help of Robert Paul. Whatever additional assistance is needed is happily provided by the remaining wine community of Mudgee. The vineyard, incidentally, is registered by the National Association for Sustainable Agriculture Australia (NASAA), which means no weedicides, insecticides or synthetic fertilisers — the full organic system.

🐌 Thomas Vineyard Estate

PO Box 490, McLaren Vale, SA 5171 **REGION** McLaren Vale
T (08) 8557 8583 **F** (08) 8557 8583 **WWW**.thomasvineyard.com.au **OPEN** Not
WINEMAKER Trevor Tucker **EST.** 1998 **CASES** 1200
Merv and Dawne Thomas thought long and hard before purchasing the property on which they have established the vineyard. It is 3 km from the coast of the Gulf of St Vincent on the Fleurieu Peninsula, with a clay over limestone soil known locally as 'Bay of Biscay'. They had a dream start to the business when the 2004 Shiraz won the trophy for Best Single Vineyard Wine (red or white) at the 2005 McLaren Vale Wine Show, the Reserve Shiraz also winning a gold medal.

ΥΥΥΥΥ **McLaren Vale Shiraz 2004** Deep colour; inky black fruit, licorice and chocolate aromas and flavours; very concentrated and full-bodied with a multi-layered palate and an abundance of tannins. Demands patience. A nonsensical back label. Cork. 14.5° alc.
RATING 93 **DRINK** 2010 $ 20

Thomas Wines

c/- The Small Winemakers Centre, McDonalds Road, Pokolbin, NSW 2321 **REGION** Lower Hunter
Valley
T (02) 6574 7371 **F** (02) 6574 7371 **WWW**.thomaswines.com.au **OPEN** 7 days 10–5
WINEMAKER Andrew Thomas **EST.** 1997 **CASES** 2000
Andrew Thomas came to the Hunter Valley from McLaren Vale, to join the winemaking team at
Tyrrell's. After 13 years with Tyrrell's, he left to undertake contract work and to continue the
development of his own winery label, a family affair run by himself and his wife, Jo. The Semillon is
sourced from a single vineyard owned by local grower Ken Bray, renowned for its quality. The wines
are available at the Small Winemakers Centre.

ꭗꭗꭗꭗꭗ Braemore Semillon 2005 Extremely potent and powerful; intense lime and citrus fruit;
long, minerally finish. Screwcap. **RATING** 95 **DRINK** 2015 **$** 24
Kiss Hunter Valley Shiraz 2004 Powerful, rich, concentrated blackberry and plum;
supple mouthfeel; excellent tannin and oak management; 350 cases made. Cork. 14° alc.
RATING 94 **DRINK** 2012 **$** 48

Thompson Estate

Harmans Road South, Wilyabrup, WA 6284 **REGION** Margaret River
T (08) 9386 1751 **F** (08) 9386 1708 **WWW**.thompsonestate.com **OPEN** Fri–Sun 11–4
WINEMAKER Various contract **EST.** 1998 **CASES** 4000
Cardiologist Peter Thompson planted the first vines at Thompson Estate in 1994. He was inspired by
his and his family's shareholdings in the Pierro and Fire Gully vineyards, and by visits to many of the
world's premium wine regions. A total of 12 ha has since been established: cabernet sauvignon,
cabernet franc, merlot, chardonnay and pinot noir. The Thompsons have split the winemaking
between specialist winemakers: Cabernet Merlot by Mark Messenger of Juniper Estate (previously of
Cape Mentelle), Pinot Noir by Flying Fish Cove, and Pinot Chardonnay by Harold Osborne of Fraser
Woods.

ꭗꭗꭗꭗꭙ Margaret River Semillon Sauvignon Blanc 2005 Clean, bright, fresh apple, grass, lemon
and gooseberry flavours, the small percentage of barrel ferment adding to the texture; a
clean and powerful finish. Screwcap. 12.6° alc. **RATING** 93 **DRINK** 2009 **$** 22
Margaret River Chardonnay 2004 Light-bodied, fresh melon and citrus flavours; almost
delicate; interestingly, 8 months in French oak does not overwhelm the fruit. Screwcap.
13.5° alc. **RATING** 90 **DRINK** 2010 **$** 35
ꭗꭗꭗꭗ Margaret River Cabernet Merlot 2003 Bright purple-red; light- to medium-bodied, with
strongly earthy/savoury/briary characters, but does have length and balance. Cork.
13.5° alc. **RATING** 88 **DRINK** 2009 **$** 25

Thomson Brook Wines NR

Lot 1, Thomson Road, Donnybrook, WA 6239 **REGION** Geographe
T (08) 9731 0590 **F** (08) 9731 0590 **OPEN** Wed–Sun & public hols
WINEMAKER Terry Foster **EST.** 1993 **CASES** NA
Pam and Terry Foster have established 6 ha of riesling, sauvignon blanc, semillon, chardonnay,
verdelho, pinot noir, shiraz, merlot, cabernet sauvignon and barbera, and make the wine onsite. The
cellar door offers barbecue facilities and local produce.

Thorn-Clarke Wines

Milton Park, Gawler Park Road, Angaston, SA 5353 **REGION** Barossa Valley
T (08) 8564 3036 **F** (08) 8564 3255 **WWW**.thornclarkewines.com **OPEN** Mon–Fri 9–5
WINEMAKER Derek Fitzgerald **EST.** 1997 **CASES** 90 000
Established by David and Cheryl Clarke (née Thorn), and son Sam. Thorn-Clarke is one of the largest
Barossa grapegrowers, with 270 ha across 4 vineyard sites. Shiraz (136 ha), cabernet sauvignon
(49 ha) and merlot (20 ha) are the principal plantings, with lesser amounts of petit verdot, cabernet
franc, nebbiolo, chardonnay, riesling and pinot gris. As with many such growers, most of the grape
production is sold, but the best is retained for the Thorn-Clarke label. Thorn-Clarke received several

important tropies in 2005, underlining the quality and value of the wines. Exports to the US, Europe, Canada and NZ.

ᵀᵀᵀᵀᵀ **Shotfire Ridge Barossa Valley Shiraz 2004** Deep purple-red; a dense, rich and powerful wine which retains true elegance, no doubt due in part to the controlled alcohol. Oak, fruit and tannins coalesce in a wine of great quality, with a number of significant gold medals under its belt. Cork. 14° alc. **RATING** 95 **DRINK** 204 $ 20

Shotfire Ridge Barossa Valley Quartage 2004 Strong purple-red colour; a potent, youthful and concentrated array of a full range of dark fruit/berry characters; oak and tannins a pure support role; 4 trophies 2005 Adelaide Wine Show. Cabernet Sauvignon/Merlot/Malbec/Petit Verdot. Cork. 13.9° alc. **RATING** 94 **DRINK** 2019 $ 24

ᵀᵀᵀᵀᵞ **Sandpiper The Blend 2004** Good hue; medium-bodied, sweet red and black fruits; fine tannins; delicious mouthfeel and overall flavour. Screwcap. 14° alc. **RATING** 93 **DRINK** 2015 $ 13

Sandpiper Barossa Valley Merlot 2004 Good hue; excellent medium-bodied texture and structure; ripe red fruits with touches of spice and olive; controlled oak. Cork. 14.1° alc. **RATING** 93 **DRINK** 2014 $ 16

Sandpiper Barossa Cabernet Sauvignon 2004 Medium red-purple; supple and smooth; cassis, mulberry and blackcurrant fruit; fine, ripe tannins, good mouthfeel. Cork. 14° alc. **RATING** 92 **DRINK** 2014 $ 13

Sandpiper Eden Valley Chardonnay 2005 Bright green-yellow; light- to medium-bodied; fresh melon and nectarine fruit-driven style; just a touch of oak; good length. Curious role reversal with Riesling. Screwcap. 14° alc. **RATING** 90 **DRINK** 2009 $ 13

ᵀᵀᵀᵀ **Sandpiper Barossa Shiraz 2004** Medium red-purple; light- to medium-bodied, but ripe black and red fruits, some spice; fine tannins. Screwcap. 14.5° alc. **RATING** 89 **DRINK** 2014 $ 13

Sandpiper Eden Valley Riesling 2005 Light- to medium-bodied; regional lime and apple aromas and flavours; slight break in line. Screwcap. 13° alc. **RATING** 88 **DRINK** 2009 $ 13

ᵀᵀᵀᵞ **Sandpiper Eden Valley Pinot Gris 2005** **RATING** 86 **DRINK** Now $ 13

Thornborough Estate   NR

PO Box 678, Virginia, SA 5120 **REGION** Adelaide Plains
T (08) 8235 0419 **OPEN** Not
WINEMAKER George Girgolas **EST.** 2000 **CASES** 2000
George Girgolas has been a long-term grapegrower near Virginia in the Adelaide Plains region, with 116 ha of 38-year-old vines, the grapes all previously contract-sold to Yalumba (he was Yalumba's Grower of the Year in 2000). Three years ago he and his family acquired the Thornborough property (5 km from the vineyard) which includes a 2-storey stone house built in 1827, and straddles the Gawler River. The plans are to convert Thornborough into a guest house.

3 Drops   ★★★★

PO Box 1828, Applecross, WA 6953 **REGION** Mount Barker
T (08) 9315 4721 **F** (08) 9315 4724 **WWW**.3drops.com **OPEN** Not
WINEMAKER Robert Diletti (Contract), John Wade (Consultant) **EST.** 1998 **CASES** 4000
The 3 Drops are not the three owners (John Bradbury, Joanne Bradbury and Nicola Wallich), but wine, olive oil and water, all of which come from the property, a substantial vineyard at Mount Barker. The 16 ha are planted to riesling, sauvignon blanc, semillon, chardonnay, cabernet sauvignon, merlot, shiraz and cabernet franc.

ᵀᵀᵀᵀᵞ **Mount Barker Riesling 2005** Fragrant, flowery, lime and apple blossom aromas; delicate, crisp, minerally palate, with brisk acidity and good length. Screwcap. **RATING** 90 **DRINK** 2010 $ 19

Shiraz 2004 Plenty of spiced plum and blackberry fruit flavour; balanced oak and tannins. Screwcap. 14.5° alc. **RATING** 90 **DRINK** 2010 $ 19

▼▼▼▼ **Mount Barker Merlot 2004** Very sweet red and black fruits, the sweetness carrying through to the finish. Screwcap. 14.5° alc. **RATING** 88 **DRINK** 2010 $ 22
Cabernets 2004 Elegant, light-bodied, fresh cassis, berry, leaf and mint; light tannins and oak appropriate to the fruit weight. Screwcap. 14.5° alc. **RATING** 87 **DRINK** 2009 $ 19

▼▼▼▼ **Mount Barker Sauvignon Blanc 2005** **RATING** 86 **DRINK** Now $ 19

Three Willows Vineyard

NR

46 Montana Road, Red Hills, Tas 7304 **REGION** Northern Tasmania
T (03) 6362 2478 **WWW**.threewillowsvineyard.com.au **OPEN** By appt
WINEMAKER Philip Pares **EST.** 2002 **CASES** 50
Philip Pares and Lyn Prove have planted a micro-vineyard, with 1.2 ha of pinot noir, pinot gris, baco noir (a hybrid) and chardonnay. It is 50 km west of Launceston near Deloraine on a gentle north-facing slope at an elevation of 220–250m. The present tiny production will peak at around 250 cases, sold to in-house guests at the B&B accommodation, and by mail and phone order.

Three Wise Men

★★★★★

Woongarra Estate, 95 Hayseys Road, Narre Warren East, Vic 3804 **REGION** Port Phillip Zone
T (03) 9796 8886 **F** (03) 9796 8580 **WWW**.threewisemen.com.au **OPEN** Thurs–Sun 9–5 by appt
WINEMAKER Graeme Leith, Susie McDonald **EST.** 1994 **CASES** 800
The Three Wise Men label was conceived to make a top-quality single vineyard Pinot Noir grown at Woongarra Estate, a well-drained, cool and moist site close to the Yarra Valley. An agreement between the Jones's of Woongarra and Passing Clouds winemaker Graeme Leith means that the wine is made at Passing Clouds at Kingower, near Bendigo. A variety of winemaking techniques are used, varying according to vintage conditions. Each of the partners takes half of the resulting wine and sells it through their respective cellar doors.

▼▼▼▼▼ **Pinot Noir 2004** Spicy, foresty cherry and plum aromas; medium-bodied; very good balance and length, with fine tannins; the aftertaste brings back the sweet fruit. Diam.
RATING 94 **DRINK** 2011 $ 20

Three Wishes Vineyard

★★★★☆

604 Batman Highway, Hillwood, Tas 7252 **REGION** Northern Tasmania
T (03) 6331 2009 **F** (03) 6331 0043 **OPEN** W'ends & public hols 11–5, or by appt
WINEMAKER Bass Fine Wines **EST.** 1998 **CASES** 1000
Peter and Natalie Whish-Wilson began the establishment of their vineyard in 1998 while they were working in Hong Kong, delegating the management tasks to parents Rosemary and Tony Whish-Wilson until 2003. Peter and Natalie then took a year's sabbatical to do the first vintage, with their children aged 6 and 4 also involved in tending the vines. One thing led to another, and the seachange became permanent, Peter completing his winegrowing degree from Charles Sturt University in 1996. The original 2.8 ha of pinot noir, chardonnay and riesling are being extended by the planting of a further ha of pinot noir in the spring of 2006.

▼▼▼▼▼ **Pinot Noir 2004** Generous but not jammy; supple blood plum fruit; good tannins, oak and length. **RATING** 94 **DRINK** 2009 $ 26

▼▼▼▼▼ **Pinot Noir 2005** Very deep purple-red colour; of heroic proportions, with masses of dark plum and spice fruit, reminiscent of some Central Otago pinots. A 10-year pinot. Screwcap. 13.5° alc. **RATING** 92 **DRINK** 2015 $ 30
Chardonnay 2005 Light straw-green; a spotless, super-elegant wine with nectarine and grapefruit; has absorbed 9 months maturation in 50% new French oak. Screwcap. 13° alc. **RATING** 90 **DRINK** 20112011 $ 25

▼▼▼▼ **Riesling 2005** Full of deliciously ripened grapefruit/tropical fruit salad, but doesn't quite drive through to the finish. Screwcap. **RATING** 89 **DRINK** 2009 $ 20

Thumm Estate Wines

NR

87 Kriedeman Road, Upper Coomera, Qld 4209 **REGION** Queensland Coastal
T (07) 5573 6990 **F** (07) 5573 4099 **WWW**.thummestate.com **OPEN** 7 days 9.30–5
WINEMAKER Robert Thumm **EST.** 2000 **CASES** 3000
Robert Thumm, born in 1950 (eldest son of Hermann Thumm, founder of Chateau Yaldara in the
Barossa Valley), gained his degree in oenology from the University of Geisenheim, Germany. In 1999,
when the family business was sold, he and wife Janet decided to move to Qld, establishing the new
winery in a valley below the Tamborine Mountain Tourist Centre. Here they have planted cabernet
sauvignon and petit verdot; they also have 1.5 ha of riesling and 1.2 ha of sauvignon blanc in
production in the Adelaide Hills. The venture, and its associated wine club, is firmly aimed at the
general tourist market; this part of Australia relies heavily on tourism, and offers a great deal to
tourists.

Tibooburra Wines

Stringybark Lane, off Beenak Road, Yellingbo, Vic 3139 (postal) **REGION** Yarra Valley
T 0418 367 319 **F** (03) 5964 8577 **WWW**.tibooburra.com **OPEN** Not
WINEMAKER Paul Evans (Contract) **EST.** 1996 **CASES** 1000
The Kerr family has done much with Tibooburra since they began assembling their 1000-ha
property in 1967. They have established a champion Angus herd, planted a 32.5-ha vineyard in 1996
on elevated northern and northwest slopes, established a truffliere in 2001 to supply Japanese and
northern hemisphere restaurants with black truffles, and launched the Tibooburra Wines label in
2002. Four generations have been, and are now, involved in the business, which is, by any standards,
a substantial one. Most of the grapes are sold under long-term contract to Oakridge and Yering
Station. Plantings (in descending order of magnitude) are pinot noir, chardonnay, shiraz, sauvignon
blanc, merlot and cabernet sauvignon, and the quality of the early releases is all one could possibly
ask for.

ŸŸŸŸŸ **Yarra Valley Chardonnay 2004** Complex barrel ferment characters supported by fine but
quite intense fruit; good length. Cork. 12.5° alc. **RATING** 91 **DRINK** 2012 $ 22
Yarra Valley Shiraz 2004 Medium-bodied; lively, fresh, focused blackberry and plum
fruit with distinct spice; balanced oak, good length. Cork. 13° alc. **RATING** 91 **DRINK** 2014
$ 28
Yarra Valley Sauvignon Blanc 2005 A fresh herb, green pea and apple bouquet; crisp
palate, lingering finish. Screwcap. 13.5° alc. **RATING** 90 **DRINK** Now $ 19

ŸŸŸŸ **Yarra Valley Pinot Noir 2004** Light-bodied and quite tight; savoury/spicy/foresty edges to
plum fruit; good length. Cork. 13° alc. **RATING** 89 **DRINK** Now $ 26

Tidswell Wines

PO Box 94, Kensington Park, SA 5068 **REGION** Limestone Coast Zone
T (08) 8363 5800 **F** (08) 8363 1980 **WWW**.tidswellwines.com.au **OPEN** Not
WINEMAKER Wine Wise Consultancy **EST.** 1997 **CASES** 7000
The Tidswell family has 2 large vineyards in the Limestone Coast Zone near Bool Lagoon; in total
there are 114 ha, the lion's share planted to shiraz and cabernet sauvignon, with smaller plantings of
merlot, chardonnay and sauvignon blanc. Most of the production is sold to Russet Ridge, part
vinified for the Tidswell label. Exports to Canada and Japan.

ŸŸŸŸŸ **Jennifer Cabernet Sauvignon 2002** Fragrant, elegant, cedary/cigar box with silky
cassis/mulberry/blackberry fruit. Cork. 14° alc. **RATING** 93 **DRINK** 2015 $ 30
2002 A rich, soft and supple marriage of blackberry fruit and warm mocha oak in typical
James Irvine fashion. Cork. 14.5° alc. **RATING** 90 **DRINK** 2012 $ 12

ŸŸŸŸ **Caves Road Chardonnay 2004** Light-bodied; minerally, citrussy flavours which have very
good length, if not depth; affinities with Chablis. Screwcap. 13.5° alc. **RATING** 89 **DRINK**
2008 $ 13

Tilba Valley

NR

Lake Corunna Estate, 947 Old Highway, Narooma, NSW 2546 **REGION** South Coast Zone
T (02) 4473 7308 **F** (02) 4473 7484 **WWW**.tilbavalleywines.com **OPEN** Oct–April 7 days 10–5,
May–Sept Wed–Sun 11–4 (closed August)
WINEMAKER Bevan Wilson **EST.** 1978 **CASES** 600
A strongly tourist-oriented operation, serving a ploughman's lunch daily from 12–2. Has 8 ha of
estate vineyards.

Tilbrook

NR

17/1 Adelaide Lobethal Road, Lobethal, SA 5241 **REGION** Adelaide Hills
T (08) 8389 5315 **F** (08) 8389 5318 **OPEN** Fri–Sun 11–5 & public hols, or by appt
WINEMAKER James Tilbrook **EST.** 2001 **CASES** 2000
James and Annabelle Tilbrook have 4.4 ha of multi-clone chardonnay and pinot noir, and 0.4 ha of
sauvignon blanc, planted in 1999 at Lenswood. The winery and cellar door are in the old
Onkaparinga Woollen Mills building in Lobethal; this not only provides an atmospheric home, but
also helps meet the very strict environmental requirements of the Adelaide Hills region in dealing
with winery waste water. English-born James Tilbrook came to Australia in 1986, aged 22; a car
accident led to his return to England. Working for Oddbins for 7 years, and passing the WSET
diploma set his future course. He returned to Australia, met wife-to-be Annabelle, purchased the
vineyard and began planting the vineyard in 1999. Plantings are continuing, and for the moment
most of the chardonnay and pinot noir is sold to Beringer Blass. Exports to the UK.

Tim Adams

★★★★

Warenda Road, Clare, SA 5453 **REGION** Clare Valley
T (08) 8842 2429 **F** (08) 8842 3550 **WWW**.timadamswines.com.au **OPEN** Mon–Fri 10.30–5, w'ends
11–5
WINEMAKER Tim Adams **EST.** 1986 **CASES** 35 000
After almost 20 years slowly and carefully building the business, based on 11 ha of the Clare Valley
classic varieties of riesling, semillon, grenache, shiraz and cabernet sauvignon, Tim and Pat Adams
have decided to more than double their venture. Like their move to a total reliance on screwcaps,
there is nothing unexpected in that. However, the makeup of the new plantings is anything but usual:
they will give Tim Adams more than 10 ha of tempranillo and pinot gris, and about 3.5 ha of viognier,
in each case with a very clear idea about the style of wine to be produced. Exports to the UK, the US,
Canada, Singapore and Sweden.

🍷🍷🍷🍷 **The Aberfeldy Clare Valley Shiraz 2003** Good colour; powerful black fruits; full-bodied,
with solid structure and extract; lots of vanilla oak. Big, traditional style. Screwcap.
14.5° alc. **RATING** 92 **DRINK** 2013 $ 50
Clare Valley Shiraz 2004 Medium-bodied, quite sweet blackberry and plum fruit; fine,
silky tannins; controlled oak and alcohol. Screwcap. 14° alc. **RATING** 91 **DRINK** 2015

🍷🍷🍷🍷 **Clare Valley Semillon 2004** Generous frame; quite ripe tropical fruit; hollows slightly on
the back-palate. Screwcap. 12° alc. **RATING** 89 **DRINK** 2008 $ 22
Clare Valley Cabernet 2003 Light- to medium-bodied; cassis, mulberry and blackberry,
the softening influence of malbec quite obvious. Easy style. Cabernet Sauvignon
(86%)/Malbec/Merlot Screwcap. 14° alc. **RATING** 89 **DRINK** 2013

🍷🍷🍷🍷 **The Fergus 2004 RATING** 86 **DRINK** Now $ 24

Tim Gramp

★★★★

Mintaro/Leasingham Road, Watervale, SA 5452 **REGION** Clare Valley
T (08) 8344 4079 **F** (08) 8342 1379 **WWW**.timgrampwines.com.au **OPEN** W'ends & hols 10–4
WINEMAKER Tim Gramp **EST.** 1990 **CASES** 6000
Tim Gramp has quietly built up a very successful business with a limited product range, and by
keeping overheads to a minimum, provides good wines at modest prices. The operation is supported
by 2 ha of cabernet sauvignon around the cellar door. Exports to the UK, the US, Malaysia and NZ.

ΥΥΥΥΥ **Watervale Riesling 2005** Lime and lemon zest aromas; an intense and very long palate with good mouthfeel. Screwcap. 13° alc. **RATING** 94 **DRINK** 2015 $ 19.50

ΥΥΥΥ **Watervale Cabernet Sauvignon 2003** Medium-bodied; earthy/savoury aromas; an austere palate with a quite dry finish. Screwcap. 14° alc. **RATING** 88 **DRINK** 2012 $ 19.50

Tim Smith Wines

PO Box 446, Tanunda, SA 5352 **REGION** Barossa Valley
T (08) 8563 0939 **F** (08) 8563 0939 **WWW**.timsmithwines.com.au **OPEN** Not
WINEMAKER Tim Smith **EST.** 2001 **CASES** 1000
Tim Smith aspires to make wines in the mould of the great producers of Cote Rotie and Chateauneuf du Pape, but using a New World approach. It is a business in its early stages, with only 3 wines, a Shiraz, Botrytis Semillon and Grenache/Shiraz/Mourvedre. Exports to the UK and the US.

ΥΥΥΥΥ **Barossa Valley Shiraz 2004** A velvety, intense array of dark plum, blackberry, licorice, and a touch of chocolate, flavours; fine tannins, controlled oak on a long finish. Screwcap. 14.5° alc. **RATING** 94 **DRINK** 2019

ΥΥΥΥΥ **Grenache Mataro Shiraz 2004** Atypical Barossa Valley; lusciously sweet cornucopia of juicy berry, confit and jam fruit flavours, but has good structure, and controlled alcohol. Screwcap. 14.5° alc. **RATING** 91 **DRINK** 2012

Timmins Wines

7 Durham Street, Hunters Hill, NSW 2110 (postal) **REGION** Hunter Valley/Orange
T (02) 9816 1422 **F** (02) 9816 1477 **WWW**.timminswines.com.au **OPEN** Not
WINEMAKER John Timmins **EST.** 2001 **CASES** 500
Unusually, this is a micro-wine operation without its own vineyard. Pharmacist John Timmins completed his Bachelor of Applied Science (Wine Science) degree in 2003, and is using his qualifications to make wines in small volumes from grapes grown in the Hunter Valley and Orange regions. Exports to Singapore.

ΥΥΥΥΥ **Chardonnay 2005** A well-balanced, elegant fruit-driven style, the nectarine and melon fruit supported by appealing acidity and subtle barrel ferment inputs. Interesting price. Screwcap. **RATING** 92 **DRINK** 2011 $ 35

ΥΥΥΥ **Hunter Valley Shiraz 2004** **RATING** 84 **DRINK** 2008 $ 20

Tin Shed Wines NR

PO Box 504, Tanunda, SA 5352 **REGION** Eden Valley
T (08) 8563 3669 **F** (08) 8563 3669 **WWW**.tinshedwines.com **OPEN** Not
WINEMAKER Andrew Wardlaw, Peter Clarke **EST.** 1998 **CASES** 3000
Tin Shed proprietors Andrew Wardlaw and Peter Clarke weave all sorts of mystique in producing and marketing the Tin Shed wines. They say, 'our wines are hand-made so we can only produce small volumes; this means we can take more care at each step of the winemaking process ... most bizarre of all we use our nose, palette (sic) and commonsense as opposed to the safe and reliable formula preached by our University's and peers.' The Tin Shed newsletter continues with lots of gee-whizz, hayseed jollity, making one fear the worst, when the reality is that the wines (even the Wild Bunch Riesling, wild-fermented without chemicals) are very good. Exports to the UK, the US, NZ and Japan.

Tinderbox Vineyard

Tinderbox, Tas 7054 **REGION** Southern Tasmania
T (03) 6229 2994 **F** (03) 6229 2994 **OPEN** By appt
WINEMAKER Hood Wines (Andrew Hood) **EST.** 1994 **CASES** 185
Liz McGown is a Hobart nurse who has established her vineyard on the slope beneath her house, overlooking the entrance to the Derwent River and the D'Entrecasteaux Channel, doubling the size from 1 to 2 ha in 2003. The attractive label was designed by Barry Tucker, who was so charmed by Liz McGown's request that he waived his usual (substantial) fee.

ŸŸŸŸŸ **Pinot Noir 2005** Good purple-red; sumptuous, rich, dark cherry and plum fruit, not at all over-extracted; supple tannins, lovely wine. Screwcap. **RATING** 94 **DRINK** 2012 $ 30

ŸŸŸŸ **Pinot Noir 2004** Light red; light-bodied; savoury spicy foresty characters; good length; radically different to the '05. Screwcap. 12.5° alc. **RATING** 89 **DRINK** 2009 $ 30

Tingle-Wood   NR

Glenrowan Road, Denmark, WA 6333 **REGION** Denmark
T (08) 9840 9218 **F** (08) 9840 9218 **WWW**.tinglewoodwines.com.au **OPEN** Thurs–Mon 9–5, 7 days during hols
WINEMAKER Brenden Smith (Contract) **EST.** 1976 **CASES** 1000
An intermittent producer of Riesling of extraordinary quality, although birds and other disasters do intervene and prevent production in some years. The Riesling remains a sentimental favourite of mine. Exports to the UK.

Tinklers Vineyard

Pokolbin Mountains Road, Pokolbin, NSW 2330 **REGION** Lower Hunter Valley
T (02) 4998 7435 **F** (02) 4998 7469 **OPEN** 7 days 10–5
WINEMAKER Usher John Tinkler **EST.** 1997 **CASES** 1000
Three generations of the Tinkler family have been involved with the property since 1942. Originally a beef and dairy farm, vines have been both pulled out and replanted at various stages along the way, and part of the adjoining old Ben Ean Vineyard acquired, the net result being a little over 41 ha of vines. The major part of the production is sold as grapes to McWilliam's, but when Usher John Tinkler returned from Charles Sturt University in 2001, he turned the tractor shed into a winery, and since then the wines have been made onsite. The wines have had significant show success.

ŸŸŸŸŸ **School Block Hunter Valley Semillon 2005** Vibrantly clean, fresh and crisp; ultra-pure mineral, herb and lemon; great length and finish; cries for 5–10 years in the bottle. Screwcap. 11.5° alc. **RATING** 94 **DRINK** 2015 $ 16

ŸŸŸŸŸ **U&I Hunter Valley Shiraz 2003** Good colour; well above-average depth and concentration; blackberry, spice and leather; long palate, good tannins. Cork. 14.7° alc. **RATING** 92 **DRINK** 2018 $ 20

ŸŸŸŸ **Poppy's Vineyard Hunter Valley Chardonnay 2005** Relatively tight and restrained, though there is considerable length and intensity to the palate; a mix of barrel ferment and lees on melon/fig/stone fruit; good length. Screwcap. 13.6° alc. **RATING** 89 **DRINK** 2010 $ 20

ŸŸŸŸ **Pokolbin Mountains Hunter Valley Merlot 2005** Not particularly varietal, but has bright, fresh red fruits; minimal tannins/oak; summer red, serve slightly chilled. Screwcap. 13.8° alc. **RATING** 86 **DRINK** Now $ 18

Lucerne Paddock Hunter Valley Verdelho 2005 RATING 85 **DRINK** Now $ 15

Tinlins   NR

Kangarilla Road, McLaren Flat, SA 5171 **REGION** McLaren Vale
T (08) 8323 8649 **F** (08) 8323 9747 **OPEN** 7 days 9–5
WINEMAKER Warren Randall **EST.** 1977 **CASES** 30 000
A very interesting operation run by former Seppelt sparkling winemaker Warren Randall, drawing upon 100 ha of estate vineyards, and specialising in bulk-wine sales to major Australian wine companies. A small proportion of the production is sold direct through the cellar door at mouthwateringly low prices to customers who provide their own containers and purchase by the litre. McLaren Vale's only bulk-wine specialist.

Tinonee Vineyard
NR

Milbrodale Road, Broke, NSW 2330 **REGION** Lower Hunter Valley
T (02) 6579 1308 **F** (02) 9719 1833 **WWW**.tinoneewines.com.au **OPEN** W'ends & public hols 11–4
WINEMAKER Andrew Margan, Ray Merger (Contract) **EST.** 1997 **CASES** 384
Ian Craig has established 14 ha of vineyards on a mix of red volcanic and river flat soils at Broke. Part are in production, the remainder are coming into bearing; ultimately, production of 5000 cases of wine per year will be possible.

Tintagel Wines
NR

Sebbes Road, Forest Grove, WA 6286 **REGION** Margaret River
T (08) 9386 2420 **F** (08) 9386 2420 **WWW**.tintagelwines.com.au **OPEN** By appt
WINEMAKER Mark Messenger (Contract) **EST.** 1993 **CASES** 1000
The Westphal family began establishing their 8-ha vineyard in 1993, which now has 2 ha each of chardonnay, shiraz and cabernet sauvignon, and 1 ha each of semillon and merlot. It is just south of the township of Margaret River, rubbing shoulders with names such as Leeuwin Estate and Devil's Lair. Part of the crop is sold to other makers. Exports to Malaysia.

Tintilla Wines

725 Hermitage Road, Pokolbin, NSW 2320 **REGION** Lower Hunter Valley
T (02) 6574 7093 **F** (02) 9767 6894 **WWW**.tintilla.com.au **OPEN** 7 days 10.30–6
WINEMAKER James Lusby, Monarch Winemaking Services (Jim Chatto) **EST.** 1993 **CASES** 4000
The Lusby family has established a 25-ha vineyard (including 1 ha of sangiovese) on a northeast-facing slope with red clay and limestone soil. They have also planted an olive grove producing 4 different types of olives, which are cured and sold from the estate.

▼▼▼▼▼ **Reserve Hunter Semillon 2005** A classic example of the variety and the '05 vintage; a clean, crisp opening, then fruit and power progressively unfold through the long, lemony finish and lingering aftertaste. Screwcap. 10.5° alc. **RATING** 94 **DRINK** 2015 **$** 18

▼▼▼▼▽ **Hunter Valley Semillon 2005** Chalky/dusty/minerally aromas with a touch of herb; lovely tight, lemon-tinged palate; very long finish. 10.5° alc. **RATING** 92 **DRINK** 2015 **$** 18
Chardonnay 2005 Clean, lively and aromatic; melon and nectarine fruit with integrated French oak; bright finish, good acidity. Screwcap. 13° alc. **RATING** 92 **DRINK** 2011 **$** 25

▼▼▼▼ **Justine Merlot 2004** Bright colour; light-bodied; fresh red and black fruits; minimal tannins and oak. Screwcap. 13.5° alc. **RATING** 88 **DRINK** 2010 **$** 26
Reserve Hunter Valley Shiraz 2004 Light- to medium-bodied; spicy, earthy, savoury, with a quiet choir of red and black fruits singing in the background; needs the Three Tenors. Screwcap. 13° alc. **RATING** 87 **DRINK** 2014 **$** 26

Tipperary Estate
 ★★☆

167 Tipperary Road, Moffatdale via Murgon, Qld 4605 **REGION** South Burnett
T (07) 4168 4802 **F** (07) 4168 4839 **WWW**.tipperaryestate.com.au **OPEN** 7 days 10–4
WINEMAKER Clovely Estate (Luke Fitzpatrick) **EST.** 2002 **CASES** 600
The 2.5-ha vineyard of Tipperary Estate, planted to shiraz, verdelho and chardonnay, has been established high on the northern slopes overlooking the Barambah Valley. Additional grapes are purchased from other growers in the South Burnett region.

▼▼▼ **Verdelho 2005** **RATING** 83 **$** 15

Tipperary Hill Estate ★★★

Alma–Bowendale Road, Alma via Maryborough, Vic 3465 **REGION** Bendigo
T (03) 5461 3312 **F** (03) 5461 3312 **OPEN** W'ends 10–5, or by appt
WINEMAKER Paul Flowers **EST.** 1986 **CASES** 250
Paul Flowers says production depends 'on the frost, wind and birds', which perhaps explains why this is very much a part-time venture. Situated 7 km west of Maryborough, Tipperary Hill Estate is the only winery operating in the Central Goldfields Shire. Paul built the rough-cut pine winery and the bluestone residential cottage next door with the help of friends.

ΤΤΤΤ **Tulkara Shiraz 2004** Good colour; a powerful if somewhat rustic wine, with black fruit flavours and slightly edgy tannins. Cork. 13.5° alc. **RATING** 87 **DRINK** 2011 $ 16

Cabernets 2004 Similarly powerful and rustic; some good blackcurrant fruit; simply needs more work in the winery and a softer touch. Cork. 13.5° alc. **RATING** 87 **DRINK** 2011 $ 18

Tizzana Winery NR

518 Tizzana Road, Ebenezer, NSW 2756 **REGION** Sydney Basin
T (02) 4579 1150 **F** (02) 4579 1216 **www**.tizzana.com.au **OPEN** W'ends, hols 12–6, or by appt
WINEMAKER Peter Auld **EST.** 1887 **CASES** 500
Tizzana has been a weekend and holiday occupation for Peter Auld for many years now. It operates in one of the great historic wineries built (in 1887) by Australia's true renaissance man, Dr Thomas Fiaschi. The wines may not be great, but the ambience is. Moreover, the cabernet sauvignon and shiraz have been replanted on the same vineyard as that first planted by Fiaschi in 1885. Peter Auld has also developed Tizzana as a wine education centre.

TK Wines ★★★★★

c/- Kilikanoon Wines, Penna Lane, Penwortham, SA 5453 **REGION** Adelaide Hills
T (08) 8843 4377 **F** (08) 8843 4246 **www**.tkwines.com.au **OPEN** Not
WINEMAKER Tim Knappstein **EST.** 1991 **CASES** 10 000
Yet another name change for the wine business of Tim and Annie Knappstein, although on this occasion doing no more than reflecting the difficulty of using the Lenswood Vineyards name, thanks to the Geographic Indication legislation. The label will be used for all the wines, regardless of whether they come entirely from the Lenswood Vineyard, and hence Lenswood GI. Exports to all major markets.

ΤΤΤΤΤ **Adelaide Hills Sauvignon Blanc 2005** Perfectly articulated gooseberry/passionfruit varietal flavour; well above-average intensity, with a crisp apple finish. Screwcap. 12.5° alc. **RATING** 94 **DRINK** 2008 $ 21

Reserve Pinot Noir 2003 Clean, fragrant red fruits; more finesse than usual; light-bodied, but long and precise; good aftertaste. Quality cork. **RATING** 94 **DRINK** 2009 $ 42

ΤΤΤΤΥ **Pinot Noir 2003** Spice, forest and bracken surrounds the core of red fruits; lingering finish. Screwcap. **RATING** 92 **DRINK** 2009 $ 22

ΤΤΤΤ **Shiraz 2003** Light- to medium-bodied; spicy notes to the black fruits at the core; light tannins. Screwcap. **RATING** 88 **DRINK** 2009 $ 22

Tobin Wines NR

34 Ricca Road, Ballandean, Qld 4382 **REGION** Granite Belt
T (07) 4684 1235 **F** (07) 4684 1235 **OPEN** By appt
WINEMAKER Adrian Tobin, David Gianini, Ravens Croft Wines **EST.** 1964 **CASES** 1000
In the early 1900s the Ricca family planted table grapes, planting shiraz and semillon in 1964/5, which are said to be the oldest vinifera vines in the Granite Belt region. The Tobin family (headed by Adrian and Frances Tobin) purchased the vineyard in 2000 and have substantially increased plantings. There are now nearly 10 ha planted to semillon, verdelho, chardonnay, sauvignon blanc, shiraz, merlot, cabernet sauvignon and tempranillo, with some remaining rows of table grapes. However, one thing has not changed — bulk wine made in traditional Italian style and sold in 15-litre drums at enticingly low prices.

Tokar Estate

6 Maddens Lane, Coldstream, Vic 3770 **REGION** Yarra Valley
T (03) 5964 9585 **F** (03) 5964 9587 **WWW**.tokarestate.com.au **OPEN** 7 days 10–5
WINEMAKER Paul Evans **EST.** 1996 **CASES** 5000
Leon Tokar is one of the number of new arrivals on Maddens Lane, having established 12 ha of pinot noir, shiraz, cabernet sauvignon and tempranillo. Part of the grape production is sold to Southcorp, the remainder contract-made.

ŸŸŸŸ **2003** Powerful and rich dark fruits and ripe tannins; the oak is very strong, and may not come back into balance, but there is plenty of fruit there. Diam. 14.5° alc. **RATING** 89 **DRINK** 2015 $60

Tollana

Tanunda Road, Nuriootpa, SA 5355 **REGION** Barossa Valley
T (08) 8568 9389 **F** (08) 8568 9489 **WWW**.australianwines.com.au/tollana **OPEN** Not
WINEMAKER Andrew Baldwin **EST.** 1888 **CASES** NFP
Tollana survived a near-death experience during the turbulent days of the Rosemount management of Southcorp; where it will ultimately fit in the FWE scheme of things remains to be seen, but in the meantime, Tollana is back in business producing Riesling, Viognier, Shiraz, and Cabernet Sauvignon.

ŸŸŸŸŸ **Cabernet Sauvignon Bin TR222 2004** An elegant wine, showing crystal clear varietal fruit courtesy of perfectly ripened cassis and supporting tannins. Value-plus. Screwcap. 13.5° alc. **RATING** 93 **DRINK** 2014 $20
Cabernet Sauvignon Bin TR222 2003 Clean and fragrant; a lovely elegant, medium-bodied palate; gentle cassis flavours with a cedary backdrop; fine, ripe tannins. Screwcap. **RATING** 93 **DRINK** 2013 $21.95
Bin TR16 Shiraz 2004 Medium-bodied blackberry, black cherry and spice fruit; controlled French oak, fine tannins and good length. Adelaide Hills/Clare Valley. Screwcap. 14° alc. **RATING** 90 **DRINK** 2012 $20

ŸŸŸŸ **High Eden Vineyard Riesling 2004** Solid, substantial bouquet and palate; ripe tropical fruit, balanced acidity. Cork. 13° alc. **RATING** 89 **DRINK** 2008 $21.95
Adelaide Hills Viognier 2005 Very well-made; supple, round, apricot and peach fruit; controlled alcohol. Screwcap. 14° alc. **RATING** 89 **DRINK** 2008 $21

Tom's Waterhole Wines

Felton, Longs Corner Road, Canowindra, NSW 2804 **REGION** Cowra
T (02) 6344 1819 **F** (02) 6344 2172 **WWW**.tomswaterhole.com.au **OPEN** W'ends & public hols 10–4, or by appt
WINEMAKER Graham Kerr **EST.** 1997 **CASES** 800
Graham Timms and Graham Kerr started the development of Tom's Waterhole Wines in 1997, progressively establishing 6 ha of shiraz, cabernet sauvignon, semillon and merlot, completing the planting program in 2001. They have decided to bypass the use of irrigation, so the yields will always be low.

ŸŸŸŸŸ **Semillon 2005** Light green-straw; clean bouquet; a very good mix of intense lemon/citrus, and a mineral framework; very impressive, especially the value. Screwcap. 10.5° alc. **RATING** 92 **DRINK** 2010 $12

ŸŸŸŸ **The Waterhole Blend Dry White 2005** Fair flavour; lemon and mineral, the acidity helping the freshness, likewise the low alcohol. Semillon/Chardonnay. Screwcap. 11.5° alc. **RATING** 86 **DRINK** Now $10
Cabernet Sauvignon 2003 RATING 85 **DRINK** 2009 $14
Chardonnay 2005 RATING 84 **DRINK** Now $12
Shiraz 2003 RATING 84 **DRINK** 2008 $14
The Waterhole Blend Cabernet Shiraz Merlot 2005 RATING 84 **DRINK** Now $10

Tomboy Hill

★★★★★

204 Sim Street, Ballarat, Vic 3350 (postal) **REGION** Ballarat
T(03) 5331 3785 **OPEN** Not
WINEMAKER Scott Ireland (Contract) **EST.** 1984 **CASES** 1550
Former schoolteacher Ian Watson seems to be following the same path as Lindsay McCall of Paringa Estate (also a former schoolteacher) in extracting greater quality and style than any other winemaker in his region, in this case Ballarat. Since 1984 Watson has slowly and patiently built up a patchwork quilt of small plantings (most from 0.33 ha to 2 ha), all clustered around the town of Ballarat. In the better years, the single vineyard wines of Chardonnay and/or Pinot Noir are released; Rebellion Chardonnay and Pinot Noir are multi-vineyard blends, but all 100% Ballarat. There are 6 vineyards contributing to the wines up to 2003, with a total area of 7.5 ha.

ÝÝÝÝÝ **The Scotsburn Chardonnay 2004** A gently complex fusion of nutty barrel ferment oak and white peach/grapefruit; long, even palate with line and balance. Screwcap. 13.5° alc. **RATING** 95 **DRINK** 2014 $ 38

Tombstone Estate

NR

5R Basalt Road, Dubbo, NSW 2830 **REGION** Western Plains Zone
T(02) 6882 6624 **F**(02) 6882 6624 **OPEN** Fri–Mon & school hols 10–5, or by appt
WINEMAKER Ian Robertson **EST.** 1997 **CASES** 600
The ominously named Tombstone Estate has been established by Rod and Patty Tilling, who have planted 5 ha of chardonnay, pinot noir, shiraz, cabernet sauvignon, sangiovese, barbera and muscat. The wine is made onsite, and the cellar door offers barbecue and picnic facilities.

Toms Cap Vineyard

★★★

322 Lays Road, Carrajung Lower, Vic 3844 **REGION** Gippsland
T(03) 5194 2215 **F**(03) 5194 2369 **WWW**.tomscap.com.au **OPEN** Fri–Sun & public hols, or by appt
WINEMAKER Owen Schmidt (Contract) **EST.** 1994 **CASES** 570
Graham Morris began the development of the vineyard in 1992 on a 40-ha property surrounded by the forests of the Strezlecki Ranges, the 90-mile beach at Woodside, and the Tarra Bulga National Park, one of the 4 major areas of cool temperature rainforest in Vic. The vineyard has 2.4 ha of cabernet sauvignon, chardonnay, sauvignon blanc and riesling.

ÝÝÝÝ **Sauvignon Blanc 2004** Light straw-green; a clean but reserved bouquet, then classic sauvignon blanc structure, impact and flavours of herb, grass and asparagus on the palate; long, clean finish. **RATING** 89 **DRINK** Now $ 15

ÝÝÝÝ **Chardonnay 2002** Very ripe yellow peach/tropical fruit, the colour suggesting the wine is near its use by date. **RATING** 86 **DRINK** Now $ 16
Cabernet Sauvignon 2002 Light- to medium-bodied; savoury, leafy, earthy notes to a substrate of blackcurrant fruit; just avoids outright bitterness. Cork. 12.1° alc. **RATING** 86 **DRINK** 2010 $ 24
Chardonnay 2004 **RATING** 85 **DRINK** 2008 $ 16

Toolangi Vineyards

★★★★★

PO Box 5046, Glenferrie South, Vic 3122 **REGION** Yarra Valley
T(03) 9822 9488 **F**(03) 9804 3365 **WWW**.toolangi.com **OPEN** Not
WINEMAKER Yering Station, Giaconda, Shadowfax **EST.** 1995 **CASES** 7000
Garry and Julie Hounsell acquired their property in the Dixons Creek subregion of the Yarra Valley, adjoining the bottom edge of the Toolangi State Forest, in 1995. Plantings have taken place progressively since then, with 13 ha now in the ground. The primary accent is on pinot noir, chardonnay and cabernet, accounting for all but 1 ha, which is predominantly shiraz, and a few rows of merlot. As only half the vineyards are in bearing, production is supplemented by chardonnay and pinot noir from the Coldstream subregion, cropped at 2 tonnes per acre. Winemaking is by Tom Carson of Yering Station, Rick Kinzbrunner of Giaconda and Matt Harrop of Shadowfax, as impressive a trio of winemakers as one could wish for. A 24-ha property was acquired in late 2005 on which a cellar door will be built, and further chardonnay planted.

ŦŦŦŦŦ **Reserve Yarra Valley Chardonnay 2004** Ultra-complex and concentrated; remarkable for the '04 vintage, having outstanding richness, texture and structure to the ripe stone fruit flavours; quite Burgundian. Made by Rick Kinzbrunner. Cork. 14° alc. **RATING** 96 **DRINK** 2015 $ 65

Estate Yarra Valley Chardonnay 2004 Fine, intense and elegant; seamless fruit, barrel ferment and malolactic inputs; great length and perfect balance; 680 dozen made by Tom Carson. Cork. 13° alc. **RATING** 95 **DRINK** 2012 $ 35

Yarra Valley Chardonnay 2004 Bright, clear straw-green; excellent varietal definition, then notable structural complexity on the back-palate. Impressive at any price; 850 dozen made by Tom Carson. Screwcap. 13.5° alc. **RATING** 94 **DRINK** 2012 $ 20

ŦŦŦŦŧ **Yarra Valley Pinot Noir 2003** Light- to medium-bodied; fine and long, with spicy, sous bois undertones to cherry and plum fruit; controlled oak and extract; 830 dozen made by Matt Harrop and Tom Carson, blended at Yering Station. Cork. 13.5° alc. **RATING** 93 **DRINK** 2008 $ 35

Reserve Yarra Valley Pinot Noir 2003 Deeper colour; a bigger wine in all respects than the varietal version; intense fruit, but sumo wrestler tannins will intimidate some; 90 cases made by Matt Harrop. Cork. 14° alc. **RATING** 93 **DRINK** 2012 $ 90

Toolleen Vineyard ★★★★

2004 Gibb Road, Toolleen, Vic 3551 (postal) **REGION** Heathcote
T (03) 5433 6397 **F** (03) 5433 6397 **OPEN** Not
WINEMAKER Dominque Portet **EST.** 1996 **CASES** 1500
Owned by Mr KC Huang and family, Toolleen's 14.7 ha of shiraz, cabernet sauvignon, merlot, cabernet franc and durif are planted on the western slope of Mt Camel, 18 km north of Heathcote. The lower Cambrian red soils are now well recognised for their suitability for making full-bodied and strongly structured red wines. Most of the wine (80%) is exported to Taiwan, Malaysia, Singapore, Hong Kong and the US.

ŦŦŦŦŧ **Heathcote Cabernet Sauvignon 2004** Powerful blackcurrant/cassis varietal fruit; still wound up, but balanced and sure to develop well, given time. Cork. 14° alc. **RATING** 92 **DRINK** 2016 $ 45

ŦŦŦŦ **Heathcote Shiraz 2004** Strong colour; a powerful wine, with abundant black fruits and slightly chunky tannins needing to settle down; will improve. Cork. 14.5° alc. **RATING** 89 **DRINK** 2014 $ 45

Toomah Wines NR

'Seven Oaks' 635 Toomuc Valley Road, Pakenham, Vic 3810 **REGION** Port Phillip Zone
T (03) 5942 7583 **F** (03) 5942 7583 **OPEN** W'ends 11–6, or by appt
WINEMAKER Matt Robinson **EST.** 1996 **CASES** 2000
Toomah Wines is owned and managed by Matt and Michelle Robinson; the 6.5 ha of vineyards have been planted on Matt's parents' historically important 226-ha grazing property. Once owned by the Kitchen family (of Lever & Kitchen fame), the property boasted the largest orchard in the southern hemisphere in its 1930s heyday. Matt Robinson has a Bachelor of Agricultural Science from Melbourne University, and is completing his Bachelor of Applied Science (Wine Science) degree (by correspondence) through Charles Sturt University. Various historic buildings on the property are being restored: one serves as the winery, the other as cellar door.

Toorak Estate

Toorak Road, Leeton, NSW 2705 **REGION** Riverina
T (02) 6953 2333 **F** (02) 6953 4454 **WWW**.toorakwines.com.au **OPEN** Mon–Sat 10–5
WINEMAKER Robert Bruno **EST.** 1965 **CASES** 400 000
A traditional, long-established Riverina producer with a strong Italian-based clientele around Australia. Production has been increasing significantly, utilising 150 ha of estate plantings and grapes purchased from other growers.

ŢŢŢŢ **Willandra Estate Leeton Selection Cabernet Merlot 2005** RATING 84 DRINK Now $8

ŢŢŢ **Willandra Estate Leeton Selection Unwooded Chardonnay 2005** RATING 83 $8

Toowoomba Hills Estate   NR

5 Berrys Road, Vale View, Qld 4352 REGION Queensland Zone
T (07) 4696 2459 F (07) 4696 2459 OPEN W'ends & hols 9–6 or by appt
WINEMAKER Matthew Chersini, Irene Wilson EST. 1995 CASES 600
The 2.5-ha vineyard (cabernet sauvignon, shiraz, chardonnay, semillon, cabernet franc and malbec)
was planted in the late 1980s and early 1990s by Matthew Chersini and family. Irene Wilson (then
working in NZ wineries) and Matthew met at Charles Sturt University during their wine science
degree course; they now have 3 children, and together run the vineyard, winery, wine garden and
cellar door on the outskirts of Toowoomba. The winery produces small quantities of Chardonnay,
Semillon, Shiraz, Cabernet Sauvignon, Shiraz Cabernet Malbec, plus sweet and fortified wines.

Top-Paddock Winery   ★★★

Elard Farm, Lot 9 Fleay Road, Harvey, WA 6220 REGION Geographe
T (08) 9729 3240 F (08) 9729 1569 WWW.top-paddock.com OPEN 7 days 12–5
WINEMAKER Peter Stanlake EST. 2003 CASES 700
Richard Warren and Elaine George have planted 3 ha of cabernet sauvignon on a property high in
the Darling Ranges, forming part of Elard Farm. The grapes are hand-picked and basket-pressed,
but are then made into no less than 4 different styles: White Cabernet Sauvignon, Cabernet Rose,
Carbonic Macerated Cabernet Sauvignon and traditional Cabernet Sauvignon, designed, says
Richard Warren, 'to suit all tastes'.

ŢŢŢŢ **Geographe Cabernet Sauvignon 2003** RATING 86 DRINK Now $12
     Geographe Cabernet Rose 2005 RATING 85 DRINK Now $10
     Geographe Cabernet Blanc 2004 RATING 84 DRINK Now $10

Torbreck Vintners   ★★★★★

Roennfeldt Road, Marananga, SA 5352 REGION Barossa Valley
T (08) 8562 4155 F (08) 8562 4195 WWW.torbreck.com OPEN 7 days 10–6
WINEMAKER David Powell EST. 1994 CASES 50 000
Of all the Barossa Valley wineries to grab the headlines in the US, with demand pulling prices up to
undreamt of levels, Torbreck stands supreme. David Powell has not let success go to his head, or
subvert the individuality and sheer quality of his wines, all created around very old, dry-grown, bush-
pruned vineyards. The top trio are led by The RunRig (Shiraz/Viognier), then The Factor (Shiraz)
and The Descendant (Shiraz/Viognier); next The Struie (Shiraz) and The Steading
(Grenache/Shiraz). Notwithstanding the depth and richness of the wines, they have a remarkable
degree of finesse.

ŢŢŢŢŢ **The Descendant 2004** Almost impenetrable purple-red colour; marries elegance
bordering on restraint with intense blackberry fruit and viognier lift; controlled oak,
tannins and alcohol. Shiraz/Viognier. Cork. 14.5° alc. RATING 96 DRINK 2024 $125
The Factor 2003 Immensely powerful and concentrated aromas; a full-bodied, richly
robed array of black fruits, spice, licorice, vanilla and chocolate; persistent, ripe tannins.
Ultra-careful fruit selection has paid big dividends. Quality cork. 14.5° alc. RATING 96
DRINK 2023 $150
The RunRig 2003 Deep colour and hue; highly fragrant, spiced blackberry aromas; the
intensity of flavour hits the mouth like a gale, the inbuilt tannins neither hard nor dry.
Controlled oak. The '04 should be celestial. Cork. 14.5° alc. RATING 96 DRINK 2023 $225
The Struie 2004 Good colour; bursting with layers of juicy, sweet, blackberry, plum,
cherry and dark chocolate fruit flavours; oak and tannins just a backdrop. Barossa/Eden
Valley. Cork. 14.5° alc. RATING 94 DRINK 2019 $48

ŢŢŢŢŢ **The Steading 2003** Relatively light colour; a light- to medium-bodied mix of fresh, juicy
red berry fruit and fine tannins; needed a touch more bulk. Grenache/Shiraz/Mataro.
Quality cork. 14.5° alc. RATING 93 DRINK 2009 $45

ΨΨΨΨ **Woodcutter's Semillon 2004** Bright green-yellow; a spotless bouquet, the fruit flavour somewhat suppressed by the impact of oak. Screwcap. 14.5° alc. **RATING** 87 **DRINK** 2008 $19

Saignee 2005 Well-made, with light, spicy elements to the red fruit flavours; dry finish. Cork. 14.5° alc. **RATING** 87 **DRINK** Now $23

The Juveniles 2004 Disconcertingly light colour; light- to medium-bodied; pleasant, gently sweet fruit; for immediate drinking. Screwcap. **RATING** 87 **DRINK** Now $17.20

Torresan Estate   NR

42 Estate Drive, Flagstaff Hill, SA 5159 **REGION** McLaren Vale
T (08) 8270 2500 **F** (08) 8270 3848 **OPEN** Mon–Fri 8–5
WINEMAKER Michael Torresan, Damien Torresan **EST.** 1958 **CASES** 500
This long-established family-owned (Michael and John Torresan) business has provided contract bottling services for many years. It has, however, moved with the times, its Beehive range bottled under screwcap, and expanding the offering with a tiny amount of Sauvignon Blanc sourced from the Adelaide Hills. The principal release of Beehive Shiraz is a blend of McLaren Vale and Southern Fleurieu grapes.

Torzi Matthews Vintners   NR

Cnr Eden Valley Road/Sugarloaf Hill Road, Mount McKenzie, SA 5353 **REGION** Eden Valley
T (08) 8565 3393 **F** (08) 8565 3393 **www**.edenvalleyshiraz.com.au **OPEN** By appt
WINEMAKER Domenic Torzi **EST.** 1996 **CASES** 1000
Domenic Torzi and Tracey Matthews, former Adelaide Plains residents, searched for a number of years before finding a 4 ha block at Mount McKenzie in the Eden Valley. The block they chose is in a hollow and the soil is meagre, and they were in no way deterred by the knowledge that it would be frost-prone. The result is predictably low yields, concentrated further by drying the grapes on racks and reducing the weight by around 30% (the Appassimento method is used in Italy to produce Amarone-style wines). Two wines are made, both under the Frost Dodger label: Eden Valley Riesling and Eden Valley Shiraz, the Shiraz wild yeast-fermented and neither fined nor filtered.

Totino Wines   NR

982 Port Road, Albert Park, SA 5014 (postal) **REGION** Adelaide Hills
T (08) 8268 8066 **F** (08) 8268 3597 **OPEN** Not
WINEMAKER Scott Rawlinson **EST.** 1992 **CASES** 15 000
Don Totino migrated from Italy in 1968, and at the age of 18 became the youngest barber in Australia. He soon moved on, into general food and importing and distribution. Festival City, as the business is known, has been highly successful, recognised by a recent significant award from the Italian government. In 1998 he purchased a run-down vineyard at Paracombe in the Adelaide Hills, since extending the plantings to 29 ha of chardonnay, pinot grigio, sauvignon blanc, sangiovese, shiraz and cabernet sauvignon. Various members of his family, including daughter Linda, are involved in the business.

Touchwood Wines   NR

PO Box 91, Battery Point, Tas 7004 **REGION** Southern Tasmania
T (03) 6223 3996 **F** (03) 6223 2384 **OPEN** Not
WINEMAKER Moorilla Estate **EST.** 1992 **CASES** 1500
Peter and Tina Sexton planted 5 ha of vineyard in the early 1990s; pinot noir and chardonnay are the principal varieties, with a small amount of cabernet sauvignon and merlot. While on a north-facing hill, with heavy black soil over a calcareous lime base, it has never been an easy site; frost has claimed some vintages, and lack of heat others.

Tower Estate

Cnr Broke Road/Hall Road, Pokolbin, NSW 2320 **REGION** Lower Hunter Valley
T (02) 4998 7989 **F** (02) 4998 7919 **www**.towerestatewines.com.au **OPEN** 7 days 10–5
WINEMAKER Scott Stephens **EST.** 1999 **CASES** 10 000
Tower Estate is a joint venture headed by Len Evans, featuring a luxury conference centre and accommodation. It draws upon varieties and regions which have a particular synergy, coupled with the enormous knowledge of Len Evans and the winemaking skills of Scott Stephens. Exports to the UK, Denmark, Singapore, Canada and Japan.

ΨΨΨΨΨ **Hunter Valley Semillon 2005** Herb, slate and grass aromas; classic Hunter semillon from a classic vintage; fine but intense lemon and mineral flavours; long finish. Pray for the cork. 11.5° alc. **RATING** 95 **DRINK** 2015 $ 26
Adelaide Hills Sauvignon Blanc 2005 Potent, intense, varietal passionfruit, gooseberry and a hint of gun smoke on the bouquet; the palate fully delivers, rich and mouthfilling; as good as they come in the bigger style. Oh for a screwcap. Cork. 13.5° alc. **RATING** 95 **DRINK** Now $ 32
Adelaide Hills Chardonnay 2004 Light straw-green; restrained, yet intense, with great line and length to the nectarine and citrus fruit; French oak a backdrop. Cork. 14.5° alc. **RATING** 94 **DRINK** 2011 $ 28

ΨΨΨΨΨ **Clare Valley Riesling 2005** Bright green-yellow; highly focused and intense; totally typical mineral/lime flavours; good balance. Cork. 13° alc. **RATING** 93 **DRINK** 2010 $ 26
Coonawarra Cabernet Sauvignon 2003 Bell-clear varietal fruit on both bouquet and palate supported by ripe tannins and quality oak; good length. Cork. 13.5° alc. **RATING** 93 **DRINK** 2015 $ 42
Barossa Valley Shiraz 2003 A mix of blackberry, spice, earth and fruit in an overall sweet spectrum; good oak and tannins. Cork. 14.5° alc. **RATING** 91 **DRINK** 2015 $ 42
Tasmania Pinot Noir 2004 A pretty wine with black cherry, spice and plum fruit; very fine tannins. Cork. 13.5° alc. **RATING** 90 **DRINK** 2010 $ 45

Towerhill Estate NR

Albany Highway, Mount Barker, WA 6324 **REGION** Mount Barker
T (08) 9851 1488 **F** (08) 9851 2982 **OPEN** Fri–Sun 10–5 (7 days during school hols)
WINEMAKER Harewood Estate (James Kellie) **EST.** 1993 **CASES** 750
The Williams family, headed by Alan and Diane, began the establishment of Towerhill Estate in 1993, planting 6.5 ha of chardonnay, cabernet sauvignon, riesling and merlot. Initally the grapes were sold to other producers, but since 1999 limited quantities have been made for Towerhill.

Trafford Hill Vineyard NR

Lot 1 Bower Road, Normanville, SA 5204 **REGION** Southern Fleurieu
T (08) 8558 3595 **www**.traffordhillwines.com.au **OPEN** Thurs–Mon & hols 10.30–5
WINEMAKER John Sanderson **EST.** 1996 **CASES** 650
Irene and John Sanderson have established 2 ha of vineyard on the coast of the Fleurieu Peninsula, near to its southern extremity. Irene carries out all the viticulture, and John makes the wine with help from district veteran Allan Dyson.

Train Trak ★★★☆

957 Healesville–Yarra Glen Road, Yarra Glen, Vic 3775 **REGION** Yarra Valley
T (03) 9429 4744 **F** (03) 9427 1510 **www**.traintrak.com.au **OPEN** By appt
WINEMAKER MasterWineMakers **EST.** 1995 **CASES** 10 000
The unusual name comes from the Yarra Glen to Healesville railroad, which was built in 1889 and abandoned in 1980 — part of it passes by the Train Trak vineyard. The 15.95 ha vineyard is planted (in descending order) to pinot noir, cabernet sauvignon, chardonnay and shiraz. A cellar door and restaurant is planned for late 2006.

🍷🍷🍷🍷 **Yarra Valley Chardonnay 2004** Attractive wine; melon, stone fruit and cashew flavour with good length and balance. Screwcap. 14° alc. **RATING** 90 **DRINK** 2010 $ 22

🍷🍷🍷🍷 **Yarra Valley Shiraz 2004** Soft, spicy, savoury fruit; light- to medium-bodied, showing some development; drink sooner rather than later. Cork. 14° alc. **RATING** 89 **DRINK** 2008 $ 27

🍷🍷🍷 **Yarra Valley Pinot Rose 2005** **RATING** 86 **DRINK** Now $ 20

Tranquil Vale

325 Pywells Road, Luskintyre, NSW 2321 **REGION** Lower Hunter Valley
T (02) 4930 6100 **F** (02) 4930 6105 **WWW**.tranquilvalewines.com.au **OPEN** Thurs–Mon 10–4, or by appt
WINEMAKER Phil Griffiths **EST.** 1996 **CASES** 2000
Phil and Lucy Griffiths purchased the property sight unseen from a description in an old copy of the *Weekend Australian* found in the High Commission Office in London. The vineyard they established is on the banks of the Hunter River, opposite Wyndham Estate, on relatively fertile, sandy clay loam. Irrigation has been installed, and what is known as VSP trellising. Competent winemaking has resulted in good wines, some of which have already had show success.

🍷🍷🍷🍷 **Hunter Valley Semillon 2005** Crisp, lively, lemony aromas and flavours; a long palate, and a firm, minerally finish. Screwcap. 11.5° alc. **RATING** 91 **DRINK** 2010 $ 17

🍷🍷🍷 **Hunter Valley Shiraz 2004** Clean enough, but lacks concentration; some red fruits, but seemingly picked too early. Screwcap. 12° alc. **RATING** 86 **DRINK** 2008 $ 19
Shiraz Merlot 2004 **RATING** 85 **DRINK** 2008 $ 18
Pukka Methode Champenoise 2003 **RATING** 85 **DRINK** Now $ 25

Transylvania Winery NR

Monaro Highway, Cooma, NSW 2630 **REGION** Southern New South Wales Zone
T (02) 6452 4374 **F** (02) 6452 6281 **OPEN** 7 days 9–5, restaurant 11–11
WINEMAKER Peter Culici **EST.** 1989 **CASES** NA
Peter Culici operates the vineyard and winery, 14 km north of Cooma, drawing in part on a 2.4-ha vineyard of sauvignon blanc, gewurztraminer, chardonnay, pinot noir, cabernet sauvignon, merlot and muscadelle. Table and fortified wines are sold through the cellar door and restaurant.

Trappers Gully

Lot 6 Boyup Road, Mount Barker, WA 6324 **REGION** Mount Barker
T (08) 9851 2565 **F** (08) 9851 3565 **OPEN** By appt
WINEMAKER Clea Candy, James Kellie (Consultant) **EST.** 1998 **CASES** 1000
The Lester and Candy families began the development of Trappers Gully in 1998, bringing varied backgrounds with them. Clea Candy has the most directly relevant CV, as a qualified viticulturist and practised winemaker, and, according to the official history, 'mother, daughter and wife, and pretty much the instigator of all heated discussions'. The families have progressively planted 1.2 ha each of chenin blanc, sauvignon blanc, cabernet sauvignon and shiraz, and slightly less than 1 ha of cabernet sauvignon.

🍷🍷🍷🍷 **Mount Barker Shiraz 2004** Good colour; medium-bodied; delicious, spicy black fruits glide across the tongue; fine-grained tannins and seamless oak. Screwcap. 13.6° alc.
RATING 93 **DRINK** 2017 $ 19

🍷🍷🍷🍷 **Mount Barker Semillon Sauvignon Blanc 2005** Delicate and crisp herb, nettle, citrus and stone fruit; bright finish. Screwcap. 12.5° alc. **RATING** 89 **DRINK** 2009 $ 17

🍷🍷🍷 **Mount Barker Chenin Blanc 2005** **RATING** 85 **DRINK** Now $ 17

Treen Ridge Estate

NR

Packer Road, Pemberton, WA 6260 **REGION** Pemberton
T (08) 9776 1131 **F** (08) 9776 0442 **WWW**.wn.com.au/treenridgeestat **OPEN** Wed–Fri 11–5, w'ends
10–5
WINEMAKER Andrew Mountford (Contract) **EST.** 1992 **CASES** 600
The 1.7-ha Treen Ridge vineyard and 3-room accommodation is set between the Treen Brook State
Forest and The Warren National Park and is operated by Mollie and Barry Scotman.

Treeton Estate

North Treeton Road, Cowaramup, WA 6284 **REGION** Margaret River
T (08) 9755 5481 **F** (08) 9755 5051 **WWW**.treetonestate.com.au **OPEN** 7 days 10–6
WINEMAKER David McGowan **EST.** 1984 **CASES** 6000
In 1982 David McGowan and wife Corinne purchased the 30-ha property upon which Treeton Estate
is established, planting the 7.1-ha vineyard 2 years later. David has done just about everything in his
life, and in the early years was working in Perth, which led to various setbacks for the vineyard. The
wines are light and fresh, sometimes rather too much so.

▼▼▼▼▽ **Margaret River Shiraz 2004** Good, youthful purple-red hue; attractive spicy blood plum
and blackberry fruit; medium-bodied, and supple tannins. Outstanding bargain. Cork.
14.3° alc. **RATING** 91 **DRINK** 2010 $ 18

▼▼▼▼ **Margaret River Sauvignon Blanc 2005** Clean, fresh and crisp; a direct, unadorned style
with a light citrus/tropical mix. Great value. Twin top. 12.7° alc. **RATING** 88 **DRINK** Now
$ 16

Trentham Estate

Sturt Highway, Trentham Cliffs, NSW 2738 **REGION** Murray Darling
T (03) 5024 8888 **F** (03) 5024 8800 **WWW**.trenthamestate.com.au **OPEN** 7 days 9.30–5
WINEMAKER Anthony Murphy, Shane Kerr **EST.** 1988 **CASES** 60 000
Remarkably consistent tasting notes across all wine styles from all vintages since 1989 attest to the
expertise of ex-Mildara winemaker Tony Murphy, making the Trentham wines from his family
vineyards. All the wines offer great value for money. Exports to the US, the UK, Belgium and NZ.

▼▼▼▼▽ **Viognier 2005** That Tony Murphy touch; fragrant apricot and peach aromas and flavours;
balanced palate, neither phenolic nor alcoholic. Screwcap. **RATING** 91 **DRINK** Now $ 18
Chardonnay 2005 Light straw-green; a complex, rich wine with mouthfilling and ripe
stone fruit and fig; a subtle touch of oak. Screwcap. **RATING** 90 **DRINK** Now $ 14.50
La Famiglia Pinot Gris 2005 Crisp pear aromas; a bright and fresh palate with pear and
citrus; elegant and balanced. Screwcap. **RATING** 90 **DRINK** Now $ 14.50
Cellar Reserve Shiraz 2002 Very good hue; light- to medium-bodied, elegant red fruits
and hints of spice; quite firm and long; 50-year-old vines and a miracle vintage at work.
Screwcap. 13.5° alc. **RATING** 90 **DRINK** 2010 $ 20

▼▼▼▼ **Merlot 2003** Strong red-purple; soft, supple, light- to medium-bodied wine; dark fruits
with a hint of olive, good balance and extract. Good value. Screwcap. 13.5° alc. **RATING** 89
DRINK 2009 $ 14.50
Petit Verdot 2004 Strong colour; typical dark, black fruits to the bouquet; more lush mid-
palate fruit than most; good balance. Screwcap. 13.5° alc. **RATING** 89 **DRINK** 2012 $ 18
Shiraz 2002 Slightly less focused than the Cellar Reserve in hue and body; softer plummy
fruit with touches of mocha and chocolate. Screwcap. 13.5° alc. **RATING** 88 **DRINK** 2008
$ 15
La Famiglia Moscato 2005 Intensely grapey/spicy; expected level of sweetness; broad
appeal as aperitif or dessert wine. Screwcap. 7.5° alc. **RATING** 87 **DRINK** Now $ 12
Pinot Noir 2004 As in prior vintages, flies in the face of accepted wisdom; light-bodied;
crisp, savoury varietal fruit; unforced. Screwcap. 13.5° alc. **RATING** 87 **DRINK** Now $ 12.50
Brut 2004 Nicely made and balanced; sweet strawberry fruit; good dosage. Cork.
10.5° alc. **RATING** 87 **DRINK** Now $ 18

Ruby Sparkling Shiraz 2003 Not especially complex, but is well-balanced and has nice varietal character; isn't too oaky nor too sweet, and will repay cellaring. 13.5° alc. **RATING** 87 **DRINK** 2010 $ 18

▼▼▼▽ **Sauvignon Blanc 2005** **RATING** 86 **DRINK** Now $ 12
Two Thirds Semillon Sauvignon Blanc 2005 **RATING** 86 **DRINK** Now $ 12.50
Viognier 2004 **RATING** 86 **DRINK** Now $ 18
Murphy's Lore Chardonnay 2005 **RATING** 85 **DRINK** Now $ 10
Murphy's Lore Autumn Red 2005 **RATING** 85 **DRINK** Now $ 10
La Famiglia Nebbiolo 2003 **RATING** 85 **DRINK** Now $ 14.50
Murphy's Lore Shiraz Cabernet 2003 **RATING** 84 **DRINK** Now $ 10
Murphy's Lore Spatlese Lexia 2005 **RATING** 84 **DRINK** Now $ 10

Trevelen Farm ★★★★★

Weir Road, Cranbrook, WA 6321 **REGION** Great Southern
T (08) 9826 1052 **F** (08) 9826 1209 **WWW**.trevelenfarmwines.com.au **OPEN** Thurs–Mon 10–4.30, or by appt
WINEMAKER Harewood Estate (James Kellie) **EST.** 1993 **CASES** 3000
John and Katie Sprigg, together with their family, operate a 1300-ha wool, meat and grain-producing farm, run on environmental principles with sustainable agriculture at its heart. As a minor, but highly successful, diversification they established 5 ha of sauvignon blanc, riesling, chardonnay, cabernet sauvignon and merlot in 1993, adding 1.5 ha of shiraz in 2000. The quality of the wines is as consistent as the prices are modest, and visitors to the cellar door have the added attraction of both garden and forest walks, the latter among 130 ha of remnant bush home to many different orchids which flower May–Dec. Exports to the UK, Hong Kong, Malaysia and Japan.

▼▼▼▼▼ **Reserve Shiraz 2004** Very good colour; highly fragrant berry aromas; lovely flavour and mouthfeel to the black cherry/plum/blackberry fruit; fine tannins, quality oak. Screwcap. 14.5° alc. **RATING** 95 **DRINK** 2019 $ 25
Riesling 2005 An attractive touch to the lime and green apple fruit aromas; good focus, line, length, and overall intensity. Screwcap. 13° alc. **RATING** 94 **DRINK** 2015 $ 18
Chardonnay 2004 Light- to medium-bodied; super-elegant, restrained, fruit-driven style with grapefruit and nectarine supported by subtle oak; long finish. Screwcap. 13.5° alc. **RATING** 94 **DRINK** 2011 $ 18

▼▼▼▼ **Sauvignon Blanc 2005** A clean, pleasant wine with gooseberry, passionfruit and grass, but wanders off on its own on the finish. Screwcap. 13.5° alc. **RATING** 89 **DRINK** Now $ 16
Cabernet Merlot 2004 Slightly leafy, gamey aromas; light- to medium-bodied red berry, mint and leaf. No particular reason why this wine should be off the pace of the others. Screwcap. 13.5° alc. **RATING** 87 **DRINK** 2010 $ 18

▼▼▼▽ **Katie's Kiss Soft Sweet Riesling 2005** **RATING** 86 **DRINK** 2009 $ 14

Trevor Jones/Kellermeister ★★★★★

Barossa Valley Highway, Lyndoch, SA 5351 **REGION** Barossa Valley
T (08) 8524 4303 **F** (08) 8524 4880 **WWW**.kellermeister.com.au **OPEN** 7 days 9–6
WINEMAKER Trevor Jones **EST.** 1996 **CASES** 20 000
Trevor Jones is an industry veteran, with vast experience in handling fruit from the Barossa Valley, the Eden Valley and the Adelaide Hills. His business operates on 2 levels: Kellermeister was founded in 1979 with the emphasis on low-cost traditional Barossa wine styles. In 1996 he expanded the scope by introducing the ultra-premium Trevor Jones range, with a strong export focus on the US (lesser amounts elsewhere). Exports to the US, Japan, Switzerland and France.

▼▼▼▼▼ **Trevor Jones Wild Witch Reserve Barossa Valley Shiraz 2002** Very similar to the standard release, except that the intensity is even more pronounced, the length likewise; an inherent elegance despite all the power; oak and tannins just where they should be. Cork. **RATING** 97 **DRINK** 2022 $ 70

Trevor Jones Dry Grown Barossa Shiraz 2002 Intense, elegant, focused and very long in the mouth; vanilla oak, blackberry, spice and dark chocolate flavours; great finish and aftertaste. Cork. **RATING** 95 **DRINK** 2017 $ 38

Trevor Jones Reserve Eden Valley Riesling 2005 Above-average intensity and focus; a classic mix of lime juice and lemon, flooded with flavour. Screwcap. 12.5° alc. **RATING** 94 **DRINK** 2015 $ 35

▼▼▼▼▽ **Trevor Jones Boots Shiraz 2004** A lively, flavoursome wine with sweet black and red fruits, spice and chocolate; pleasant, savoury tannins; good length, ditto value. Screwcap. 14.5° alc. **RATING** 91 **DRINK** 2014 $ 19

▼▼▼▼ **Trevor Jones Grenache Merlot Cabernet Franc 2002** The strange blend does work quite well to add a touch of savoury/olive/herb character to the finish of the predominant (and juicy fruit) grenache. Screwcap. 15° alc. **RATING** 89 **DRINK** 2008 $ 17

Trevor Jones Virgin Chardonnay 2003 Some tropical/canned fruit flavours; malolactic and lees contact, but no oak. Presumably the derivation of the name. Screwcap. 13.5° alc. **RATING** 87 **DRINK** Now $ 18

▼▼▼▽ **Trevor Jones Red Cebo 2005** **RATING** 85 **DRINK** Now $ 14

🐚 Tscharke Wines/Glaymond Wines ★★★☆

PO Box 657, Greenock, SA 5360 **REGION** Barossa Valley
T 0438 628 178 **F** (08) 8562 4920 **www**.glaymondwines.com **OPEN** Not
WINEMAKER Damien Tscharke **EST.** 2001 **CASES** 1500
Damien Tscharke grew up in the Barossa Valley amongst the vineyards at Seppeltsfield and Marananga. In 2001 he began the production of 4 estate-grown wines based on what he calls the classic varieties (following the contemporary trend of having catchy, snappy names) followed by 4 wines under the Tscharke brand using the alternative varieties of tempranillo, graciano, zinfandel, montepulciano and albarino. Like the Glaymond wines (made from traditional varieties), these are estate-grown, albeit in very limited quantities.

▼▼▼▼ **Tscharke Only Son Tempranillo 2004** Unusual aromas of spice and pickled lime leaf; spicy bramble fruit; good texture, balance and length. Damien Tscharke is the 'only son'. Screwcap. 14° alc. **RATING** 89 **DRINK** 2010 $ 22

Tscharke The Curse Zinfandel 2004 Massively ripe and concentrated, though not especially tannic, confit fruit of prune and jam. A tribute to the difficulty of growing zinfandel. Screwcap. 16.1° alc. **RATING** 88 **DRINK** 2011 $ 30

Tscharke The Master Montepulciano 2004 Good colour; elegant red and black fruits on the mid-palate; carries the alcohol, but has dry tannins on the finish. Father Glen persuaded Damien Tsharke to plant the variety. Screwcap. 15° alc. **RATING** 88 **DRINK** 2012 $ 30

Tscharke Girl Talk Albarino 2005 Very pale straw-green; clean, crisp and light lemon/mineral notes; fresh finish. Said to be the first Albarino in Australia. A Spanish variety more correctly spelt 'alvarinho'. A tribute to Damien Tscharke's '4 beautiful sisters'. Screwcap. 13° alc. **RATING** 87 **DRINK** Now $ 18

Tuart Ridge NR

344 Stakehill Road, Baldivis, WA 6171 **REGION** Peel
T (08) 9524 3333 **F** (08) 9524 2168 **www**.tuartridgewines.com **OPEN** W'ends 10–4
WINEMAKER Phil Franzone **EST.** 1996 **CASES** 2000
Phil Franzone has established 5 ha of chardonnay, verdelho, shiraz, cabernet sauvignon, grenache and merlot on the coastal tuart soils. Phil Franzone also acts as contract winemaker for several of the many new ventures springing up in the Peel region.

Tuck's Ridge

37 Shoreham Road, Red Hill South, Vic 3937 **REGION** Mornington Peninsula
T (03) 5989 8660 **F** (03) 5989 8579 **WWW.**tucksridge.com.au **OPEN** 7 days 11–5
WINEMAKER Peninsula Winemakers **EST.** 1988 **CASES** 6000
Tuck's Ridge has changed focus significantly since selling its large Red Hill vineyard. Estate plantings are now an eclectic mix of pinot noir (3 ha), 1 ha each of chardonnay and albarino, and contract grape purchases have been reduced. Quality, not quantity, is the key. Exports to the US.

ŸŸŸŸŸ **Buckle Vineyard Chardonnay 2004** Exceptional nectarine, citrus and melon fruit of great length drives a beautifully poised wine; oak incidental. Cork. 13.5° alc. **RATING** 95 **DRINK** 2012 $ 50
Buckle Vineyard Pinot Noir 2004 Very good texture and structure, the peacock's tail opening on the back-palate; supple, plum and spice fruit with great tannins and natural acidity, oak the backdrop for the orchestra. Cork. 13.5° alc. **RATING** 95 **DRINK** 2011 $ 50

ŸŸŸŸŸ **Sauvignon Blanc 2005** Very pale colour; clean, faintly spicy bouquet; the palate crisp, lively, fresh and long. Screwcap. 13° alc. **RATING** 92 **DRINK** Now $ 23
Merlot 2003 Strongly varietal, bright red fruits with an attractive touch of olive. Only light- to medium-bodied, but has good length and texture. Screwcap. 13° alc. **RATING** 91 **DRINK** 2010 $ 27

ŸŸŸŸ **Mornington Peninsula Chardonnay 2004** Faintly funky complexity to the bouquet; the palate finishes slightly sweet, though not from residual sugar; should settle down with time. Screwcap. **RATING** 89 **DRINK** 2009 $ 27
Pinot Gris 2005 Much more flavour than most, with ripe pear and apple and a mercifully low alcohol level. Screwcap. 13° alc. **RATING** 89 **DRINK** Now $ 27
Mornington Peninsula Pinot Noir 2004 Quite complex, savoury/spicy edges to red and black cherry fruit; quite long finish; lacks the density for higher points. Screwcap. **RATING** 89 **DRINK** 2008 $ 27
Victorian Shiraz 2002 Bright colour; driven by attractive red and black cherry/plum/blackberry fruit; oak and tannins playing second fiddle. Cork. 13.5° alc. **RATING** 88 **DRINK** 2012 $ 22
Cabernet Sauvignon 2004 Good colour; savoury, cool-grown fruit flavours; firm tannins. Screwcap. 13° alc. **RATING** 87 **DRINK** 2009 $ 32

Tulley Wells ★★★

Lot 4, RMB 33 Tulley Road, Lima South, Vic 3673 (postal) **REGION** North East Victoria Zone
T (03) 9723 4353 **F** (03) 9720 1855 **OPEN** Not
WINEMAKER Roz Ritchie **EST.** 1997 **CASES** 375
When Dan and Margaret Mary Zaal purchased the Tulley Wells vineyard in 1998, they came with a background of owning and running restaurants. The vineyard had 0.75 ha of (then) 17-year-old grenache, and in 1999 they extended the plantings with 1 ha of shiraz. In 2002 they planted 350 grenache vines, grown in the traditional bush vine fashion, without any trellising.

ŸŸŸŸ **Lima Valley Shiraz Grenache 2003** Sweet, gently jammy fruit, soft and supple; driven more by the grenache flavours than shiraz, but the structure (such as it is) comes from the shiraz. Quality cork. **RATING** 87 **DRINK** Now $ 21

ŸŸŸŸ **Lima Valley Grenache 2003** **RATING** 86 **DRINK** Now $ 14
Lima Valley Grenache 2001 **RATING** 84 **DRINK** Now $ 17

Tulloch

'Glen Elgin' 638 De Beyers Road, Pokolbin, NSW 2321 **REGION** Lower Hunter Valley
T (02) 4998 7580 **F** (02) 4998 7226 **WWW.**tulloch.com.au **OPEN** 7 days 10–5
WINEMAKER Jay Tulloch, Monarch Winemaking Services (Jim Chatto) **EST.** 1895 **CASES** 30 000
The revival of the near-death Tulloch brand continues apace. Angove's, the national distributors for the brand, have invested in the business, the first time the Angove family has taken a strategic holding in any business other than its own. Inglewood Vineyard (aka Two Rivers) also has a

shareholding in the new venture, and will be the primary source of grapes for the brand. A lavish new cellar door and function facility has opened, and Jay Tulloch is in overall control, with his own label, JYT Wines, also available at the cellar door.

ŶŶŶŶŶ **JYT Julia Hunter Valley Semillon 2005** Light straw-green; a more delicate, yet more intensely fruit-flavoured wine than the '05 varietal; sweet lemon juice, bone-dry finish. **RATING** 95 **DRINK** 2018 $ 28

JYT Julia Hunter Valley Semillon 2004 Light straw-green; mineral, herb and grass; while less seductive, has more authority than the '05, flavour with balance and length; totally impressive. Screwcap. **RATING** 95 **DRINK** 2015 $ 28

Hunter Valley Semillon 2005 Light straw-green; spotlessly clean; fine, bright lemon/slate/herb/mineral flavours; vibrant mouthfeel; perfect fruit ripeness for the long haul. Screwcap. 10.5° alc. **RATING** 94 **DRINK** 2015 $ 15

ŶŶŶŶŶ **Hunter Valley Verdelho 2005** Attractive fruit salad aromas and flavours, with a twist of lemon on the finish; way above average. Screwcap. 13° alc. **RATING** 90 **DRINK** Now $ 14.99

Hector of Glen Elgin Shiraz 2000 Light- to medium-bodied; strongly regional, very earthy style; has elegance and length; potentially compromised by poor quality cork. 13° alc. **RATING** 90 **DRINK** 2010 $ 38

ŶŶŶŶ **Hector of Glen Elgin Shiraz 2004** Light- to medium-bodied; sweet plum and blackberry mixed with more earthy regional notes, and a touch of oak. Screwcap. **RATING** 89 **DRINK** 2010 $ 38

Hector of Glen Elgin Shiraz 2003 Firm, fresh, savoury/earthy regional fruit; may have had a little too rigorous acid adjustment, which on the other hand may serve it well in the long term. Screwcap. **RATING** 89 **DRINK** 2015 $ 38

Hunter Valley Semillon 2004 Very fleshy and full style, suggesting higher alcohol than 11°; best now, rather than later. Screwcap. **RATING** 88 **DRINK** Now $ 14.99

Eileen Mary Tulloch Limited Release Chardonnay 2005 Light- to medium-bodied; gentle peachy fruit, the French oak balanced and integrated. Screwcap. 14° alc. **RATING** 88 **DRINK** Now $ 28

Pokolbin Dry Red 2004 Light- to medium-bodied; slightly simpler but brighter red fruits than the Hector, less time in oak, perhaps; minimal tannins. Shiraz. Screwcap. **RATING** 88 **DRINK** 2009 $ 25

ŶŶŶŶ **Hunter Valley Chardonnay 2005** **RATING** 86 **DRINK** Now $ 14.99

Hunter Valley Cabernet Sauvignon 2004 **RATING** 86 **DRINK** 2011 $ 20

Hunter Valley Shiraz 2003 **RATING** 85 **DRINK** 2008 $ 14.99

Tumbarumba Wine Estates   NR

Glenroy Hills Road, Tumbarumba, NSW 2653 **REGION** Tumbarumba
T (02) 6948 8326 **F** (02) 6948 8326 **OPEN** 7 days
WINEMAKER Monarch Winemaking Services **EST.** 1989 **CASES** 2000
Within sight of the Snowy Mountains, Tumbarumba Wine Estates' Mannus Vineyard was established by a group of Sydney businessmen, all wine enthusiasts, with the aim of producing high-quality cool-climate wines. The vineyard is currently undergoing some refinement, with some cabernet sauvignon being grafted to more suited varieties (sauvignon blanc and chardonnay). The major part of the production from the 21 ha of vineyard (principally chardonnay and sauvignon blanc) is sold to other producers.

Tumbarumba Wine Growers   NR

Sunnyside, Albury Close, Tumbarumba, NSW 2653 **REGION** Tumbarumba
T (02) 6948 3055 **F** (02) 6948 3055 **OPEN** W'ends & public hols, or by appt
WINEMAKER Contract **EST.** 1996 **CASES** 600
Tumbarumba Wine Growers has taken over the former George Martins Winery (established in 1990) to provide an outlet for wines made from Tumbarumba region grapes. It is essentially a co-operative venture, involving local growers and businessmen, and with modest aspirations to growth.

Turkey Flat

Bethany Road, Tanunda, SA 5352 **REGION** Barossa Valley
T (08) 8563 2851 **F** (08) 8563 3610 **WWW**.turkeyflat.com.au **OPEN** 7 days 11–5
WINEMAKER Julie Campbell **EST.** 1990 **CASES** 25 000

The establishment date of Turkey Flat is given as 1990 but it might equally well have been 1870 (or thereabouts), when the Schulz family purchased the Turkey Flat vineyard, or 1847, when the vineyard was first planted to the very shiraz which still grows there today. In addition there are 8 ha of very old grenache and 8 ha of much younger semillon and cabernet sauvignon, together with a total of 7.3 ha of mourvedre, dolcetto and (a recent arrival) marsanne. Exports to the US, Canada, the UK, Germany, Switzerland and NZ.

ŶŶŶŶŶ **Barossa Valley Shiraz 2003** A classic wine, seriously underpriced, coming predominantly from the 1847 estate plantings. Superb structure and mouthfeel, with blackberry fruit, and seamless French oak in the background. Screwcap. **RATING** 96 **DRINK** 2023 $ 45

Barossa Valley Cabernet Sauvignon 2003 High-toned, pure Cabernet varietal character; deliciously ripened and focused blackcurrant and cassis fruit; exceptional vintage for Barossa Cabernet; 20 months in French oak. Cork a worry. 14.5° alc. **RATING** 96 **DRINK** 2015 $ 40

Barossa Valley Shiraz 2004 As complex and elegant as ever, notwithstanding higher than usual alcohol; gently spicy blackberry and blood plum fruit; fine tannins, fine French oak. Cork. 15° alc. **RATING** 95 **DRINK** 2019 $ 40

Barossa Valley Rose 2005 Light, bright fuchsia; spotlessly clean red fruits; achieves length and persistence without reliance on residual sugar. Grenache/Shiraz/Cabernet/Dolcetto. **RATING** 94 **DRINK** Now $ 19

Barossa Valley Cabernet Sauvignon 2004 Very good colour; firm, medium- to full-bodied blackcurrant and cassis; excellent structure and length; controlled French oak. Cork. 15° alc. **RATING** 94 **DRINK** 2015 $ 35

Barossa Valley Sparkling Shiraz NV Intense and flavoursome, yet very elegant; best of all, both phenolics and dosage under control; great balance. Numbered bottle 1276, disgorged January 2004, crown seal. **RATING** 94 $ 45

ŶŶŶŶŶ **Butchers Block Marsanne Viognier 2004** A complex wine; ripe pear and apricot fruit has absorbed the oak; good depth and structure. Screwcap. 14.2° alc. **RATING** 93 **DRINK** 2010 $ 22

The Last Straw Marsanne 2004 A very complex, eclectic style using partially dried grapes; flavour and structure ranging through honey, hay and malt; not overly sweet, cellaring will certainly yield much. Cork. 14.5° alc. **RATING** 92 **DRINK** 2014 $ 35

Butchers Block Marsanne Viognier 2005 Excellent texture and structure; a backbone of minerally acidity carries the alcohol with ease, and also the pear, apricot and green apple flavours. Screwcap. 14.5° alc. **RATING** 92 **DRINK** 2013 $ 22

Butchers Block 2004 Strong red-purple; a mix of juicy berry and more spicy, savoury characters reflecting the blend; has more weight and texture than almost all others with the very old vine mourvedre dominant; 93% Mourvedre/7% Grenache. Screwcap. 14.5° alc. **RATING** 92 **DRINK** 2014 $ 29

Butchers Block 2002 Fresh, elegant, spicy/earthy/red fruit mix; attractively firm texture, the oak incidental. Mourvedre/Shiraz/Grenache. Cork. **RATING** 92 **DRINK** 2012 $ 30

The Last Straw Marsanne 2003 Honeysuckle, spice and dried apricots; a spaetlese level of sweetness; has absorbed all the new French oak in which it was barrel-fermented and matured. Classy if esoteric. Screwcap. **RATING** 92 **DRINK** 2010 $ 40

ŶŶŶŶ **Barossa Valley Grenache 2004** Very much in the lighter Barossa style; sweet, juicy red berry fruits; minimal tannins. Screwcap. **RATING** 89 **DRINK** 2008 $ 23

Barossa Valley Grenache 2003 Some confection notes to the aroma; light- to medium-bodied, with a range of flavours from spice and raspberry through to prune. Screwcap. **RATING** 89 **DRINK** 2008 $ 25

🐾 Turner's Crossing Vineyard ★★★★★

1 Alber Road, Upper Beaconsfield, Vic 3808 **REGION** Bendigo
T (03) 5944 4599 **F** (03) 5944 4599 **WWW**.turnerscrossing.com **OPEN** W'ends
WINEMAKER Sergio Carlei **EST.** 1999 **CASES** 10 000
The name of this outstanding vineyard comes directly from the name given by local farmers crossing the Loddon River in the mid to late 1800s on their way to the nearest town. The 40-ha vineyard was planted in 1999 by former corporate executive and lecturer in the business school at La Trobe University, Paul Jenkins. However, Jenkins' experience as a self-taught viticulturist dates back to 1985, when he established his first vineyard at Prospect Hill, planting all the vines himself. The grapes from both vineyards have gone to a who's who of winemakers in Central Victoria, but an increasing amount is being made under the Turner's Crossing label, not surprising given the exceptional quality of the wines. Phil Bennett and winemaker Sergio Carlei have joined Paul Jenkins as co-owners of the vineyard, in the case of Sergio putting his money where his winemaking mouth is.

TTTTT **Bendigo Shiraz Viognier 2004** Very good colour; abundant, rich, sweet black and red fruits clearly lifted by the viognier component; medium-bodied, with spot-on tannins, alcohol and subdued oak. To be called Shiraz Viognier the wine should contain at least 5% viognier, not the 4% in this instance. Diam. 14° alc. **RATING** 95 **DRINK** 2019 $ 25
The Cut Shiraz 2003 Similar colour; fragrant blackberry, prune and chocolate aromas; very sweet, ripe fruit, just a little too juicy, although the alcohol is under good control. Diam. 14.1° alc. **RATING** 94 **DRINK** 2018 $ 75
Bendigo Cabernet Sauvignon 2003 Once again, excellent colour; medium- to full-bodied, firm blackcurrant/cassis fruit and firm but controlled tannins in support. Simply needs another 5 years. Diam. 14.3° alc. **RATING** 94 **DRINK** 2018 $ 25

Turner's Flat Vineyard NR

PO Box 104, Inglewood, Qld 4387 **REGION** Granite Belt
T (07) 4652 1179 **F** (07) 4652 1179 **OPEN** Not
WINEMAKER Contract **EST.** 1999 **CASES** NA
Bruce and Lynette Babington have established their vineyard at the far western outskirts of the Granite Belt, where they have planted 16 ha of semillon, chardonnay, cabernet sauvignon, shiraz and ruby cabernet. The wines are sold only by mail order.

Turner's Vineyard NR

Mitchell Highway, Orange, NSW 2800 **REGION** Orange
T (02) 6369 1045 **F** (02) 6369 1046 **WWW**.turnersvineyard.com.au **OPEN** 7 days 10–5
WINEMAKER Contract **EST.** 1996 **CASES** 8000
Turner's Vineyard is one of the larger developments in the Orange region, and includes a substantial motel with 30 suites, and 12 luxury 1- and 2-bedroom spa villa units.

Turramurra Estate ★★★★☆

295 Wallaces Road, Dromana Vic 3936 **REGION** Mornington Peninsula
T (03) 5987 1146 **F** (03) 5987 1286 **WWW**.turramurraestate.com.au **OPEN** W'ends 11–5
WINEMAKER David Leslie **EST.** 1989 **CASES** 4500
Dr David Leslie gave up his job as a medical practitioner after completing the Bachelor of Applied Science (Wine Science) at Charles Sturt University, to concentrate on developing the family's 10-ha estate at Dromana; wife Paula is the viticulturist. It has also established what is described as the first purpose-built cooking school in an Australian vineyard. Exports to the UK, the US and Hong Kong. As at April 2006 the Leslies were reluctantly seeking to sell Turramurra Estate as the physical demands of viticulture and winemaking were becoming too great.

TTTTT **2003 Turramurra Estate Shiraz** Bright purple-red; supple and round; classic cool-grown, medium-bodied flavour and structure; dark plum, blackberry and warm fruit spices; lovely texture. Diam. **RATING** 94 **DRINK** 2015 $ 35

ŶŶŶŶỲ **2003 Turramurra Estate Cabernet** Light- to medium-bodied; cassis, leaf and mint aromas and flavours; a particularly pleasing finish, in a ripe, not green, spectrum of red fruits. Diam. **RATING** 90 **DRINK** 2012 $ 30

Twelve Acres   NR

Nagambie–Rushworth Road, Bailieston, Vic 3608 **REGION** Goulburn Valley
T (03) 5794 2020 **F** (03) 5794 2020 **OPEN** Thurs–Mon 10.30–5.30, July weekends only
WINEMAKER Peter Prygodicz, Jana Prygodicz **EST.** 1994 **CASES** 600
The charmingly named Twelve Acres is a red wine specialist, with Peter and Jana Prygodicz making the wines onsite in a tiny winery. The wines could benefit from renewal of the oak in which they are matured; the underlying fruit is good.

Twelve Staves Wine Company   NR

Box 620, McLaren Vale, SA 5171 **REGION** McLaren Vale
T (08) 8178 0900 **F** (08) 8178 0900 **OPEN** Not
WINEMAKER Peter Dennis, Brian Light (Consultant) **EST.** 1997 **CASES** 600
Twelve Staves has a single vineyard block of a little under 5 ha of 70-year-old, bush-pruned grenache vines. The highly experienced team of Peter Dennis and Brian Light (in a consulting role) produce an appealing Grenache in a lighter mode and a monumental Shiraz. Exports to the US, Canada and the UK.

Twin Bays   NR

Lot 1 Martin Road, Yankalilla, SA 5203 **REGION** Southern Fleurieu
T (08) 8267 2844 **F** (08) 8239 0877 **WWW**.twinbays.net **OPEN** W'ends & hols
WINEMAKER Bruno Giorgio **EST.** 1989 **CASES** 2700
Adelaide doctor and specialist Dr Bruno Giorgio, together with wife Ginny, began planting their vineyard back in 1989, but have opted to keep it small (and beautiful). The principal plantings are of cabernet sauvignon, with lesser amounts of shiraz and riesling, taking the total plantings to 2 ha. It was the first vineyard to be established in the Yankalilla district of the Fleurieu Peninsula, and has spectacular views from the vineyard, on the slopes above Normanville, taking in hills, valleys, the coastal plains, and the rugged Rapid Bay and more tranquil Lady Bay.

Twin Oaks   NR

146 Windsor Street, Woodford, Qld 4514 **REGION** Queensland Coastal
T (07) 5496 1368 **F** (07) 5496 1076 **WWW**.twinoaks.com.au **OPEN** 7 days 10–5
WINEMAKER Trevor Phillips **EST.** 1998 **CASES** NA
The Twin Oaks property was purchased by Trevor and Carlin Phillips in 1980, but it was not until 1998 that the first plantings of verdelho, chardonnay and cabernet sauvignon took place. The first vintage followed 2 years later, and the winery and restaurant were opened in 2002.

Two Hands Wines   ★★★★★

Neldner Road, Marananga, SA 5355 **REGION** Various
T (08) 8562 4566 **F** (08) 8562 4744 **WWW**.twohandswines.com **OPEN** Wed–Fri 11–5, w'ends 10–5
WINEMAKER Matthew Wenk **EST.** 2000 **CASES** 20 000
The 'Hands' in question are those of SA businessmen Michael Twelftree and Richard Mintz, Twelftree in particular having extensive experience in marketing Australian wine in the US (for other producers) and now turning that experience to his and Mintz's account. On the principle that if big is good, bigger is better, and biggest is best, the style of the wines has been aimed fairly and squarely at the palate of Robert Parker Jnr and the *Wine Spectator*'s Harvey Steiman. Grapes are sourced from the Barossa Valley, McLaren Vale, Clare Valey, Langhorne Creek and Padthaway, and each of the wines is made in microscopic quantities (down to 50 dozen). Exports to the US, Canada and the UK.

ŶŶŶŶŶ **Bella's Garden Barossa Valley Shiraz 2004** Very strong, deep, purple-red; a full-bodied, luscious array of blackberry, plum and licorice; supple, ripe tannins. Just copes with the alcohol. Cork. 15° alc. **RATING** 95 **DRINK** 2024 $ 55

Bad Impersonator Barossa Valley Shiraz 2004 Achieves elegance through the intensity of the black fruits, spice and seamless French oak; fine tannins; long, fruit-driven finish. Screwcap. 14.5° alc. **RATING** 94 **DRINK** 2019 $45

Lily's Garden McLaren Vale Shiraz 2004 Dense colour; gloriously generous blackberry and dark chocolate fruit; firm structure and tannin backbone. Quality cork. **RATING** 94 **DRINK** 2014 $55

Max's Garden Heathcote Shiraz 2004 Deep, almost opaque, purple-red; intense, finely boned palate; masses of spicy black fruits, and almost delicate tannins. Quality cork. 14° alc. **RATING** 94 **DRINK** 2014 $55

Samantha's Garden Clare Valley Shiraz 2004 A less bright hue than that of Bella's; full-bodied, complex black fruits, earth and chocolate; good length, fine tannins. Cork. 15° alc. **RATING** 94 **DRINK** 2020 $55

ΥΥΥΥΥ **Brave Faces Barossa Valley Shiraz Grenache 2004** Good colour; once again, no reduction evident; a range of blackberry, raspberry, plum and spice flavours; fine, silky tannins; overall elegance and length. Screwcap. 14.5° alc. **RATING** 93 **DRINK** 2012 $32.50

The Wolf Clare Valley Riesling 2005 Clean, mineral, slate and apple aromas; long, intense lemon/lime palate; good balancing acidity. Screwcap. **RATING** 92 **DRINK** 2015 $20

Harry & Edward's Garden Langhorne Creek Shiraz 2004 Aromatic blackberry, confit and polished leather aromas; luscious black fruits and chocolate; lingering finish, and a twist of the 15°alcohol. Quality cork. **RATING** 92 **DRINK** 2015 $55

Sophie's Garden Padthaway Shiraz 2004 Dense colour; ripe plum, prune, blackberry and leather; the alcohol fractionally hollows the palate. Cork. 16° alc. **RATING** 92 **DRINK** 2019 $55

Yesterday's Hero Grenache 2004 Brightly coloured; sweet raspberry, black cherry and blackberry fruit; fine tannins, subtle oak. Screwcap. **RATING** 92 **DRINK** 2011 $35

Angel's Share McLaren Vale Shiraz 2004 Youthful purple-red; clean bouquet, no reduction; generous juicy blackberry, plum and dark chocolate fruit; subtle oak; carries 14.5° alcohol easily. Screwcap. **RATING** 91 **DRINK** 2014 $25

Aphrodite Barossa Valley Cabernet Sauvignon 2003 Medium-bodied, elegant style; clean blackcurrant, cassis and mulberry fruit; finely balanced tannins and oak. Quality cork. **RATING** 91 **DRINK** 2012 $120

ΥΥΥΥ **Brilliant Disguise Barossa Valley Moscato 2005** **RATING** 86 **DRINK** Now $13.50

Two People's Bay Wines   NR

RMB 8700, Nanarup Road, Lower Kalgan, WA 6331 **REGION** Albany
T (08) 9846 4346 **F** (08) 9846 4346 **OPEN** 7 days 12–4, 11–5 in peak season
WINEMAKER Diane Miller (Contract) **EST.** 1998 **CASES** 2700
The Saunders family (Phil and Wendy Saunders, with sons Warren and Mark) began the establishment of their 10-ha vineyard, planted to sauvignon blanc, riesling, semillon, shiraz, cabernet sauvignon, cabernet franc and pinot noir, in 1998, continuing the plantings in 1999. The name comes from the Two People's Bay Nature Reserve, which can be seen from the vineyard to the east; it also has spectacular views to the Porongurups and Stirling Ranges 60 km north.

Two Rivers   ★★★☆

2 Yarrawa Road, Denman, NSW 2328 (postal) **REGION** Upper Hunter Valley
T (02) 6547 2556 **F** (02) 6547 2546 **WWW**.tworiverswines.com.au **OPEN** By appt
WINEMAKER Monarch Winemaking Services (Jim Chatto) **EST.** 1988 **CASES** 15 000
A significant part of the viticultural scene in the Upper Hunter Valley, with almost 170 ha of vineyards established, involving a total investment of around $7 million. Part of the fruit is sold under long-term contracts, and part is made for the expanding winemaking and marketing operations of Two Rivers, the chief brand of Inglewood Vineyards. The emphasis is on Chardonnay and Semillon, and the wines have been medal winners on the wine show circuit. It is also a partner in the Tulloch business, together with the Tulloch and Angove families.

ŸŸŸŸŸ **Lightning Strike Chardonnay 2005** Light green-straw; a lively, fruit-driven style; melon and nectarine fruit, with good acidity and length; oak a whisper in the background. Screwcap. 13.5° alc. **RATING** 90 **DRINK** 2010 $ 13

ŸŸŸŸ **Hidden Hive Verdelho 2005** A solid, ripe wine with plenty of flavour in typical varietal mode. Screwcap. **RATING** 87 **DRINK** Now $ 13

ŸŸŸŸ **Stones Throw Semillon 2005** Somewhat loose flavours and structure, but does have appealing lemon/lemon tart flavours, and finishes with balanced acidity. Screwcap. 11° alc. **RATING** 86 **DRINK** 2009 $ 13

Thunderbolt Shiraz 2003 Medium-bodied; distinct fruit sweetness; gentle vanilla oak; easy access style. Screwcap. 13.5° alc. **RATING** 86 **DRINK** 2011 $ 15

Two Tails Wines

NR

963 Orara Way, Nana Glen, NSW 2450 **REGION** Northern Rivers Zone
T (02) 6654 3633 **F** (02) 6654 3633 **OPEN** 7 days 10–5
WINEMAKER Jeff Maher **EST.** 1998 **CASES** NA
Four members of the Maher family have established Two Tails Wines, with an exotic mix of gewurztraminer, semillon, chardonnay, verdelho, pinot noir, shiraz, chambourcin, ruby cabernet and villard blanc on their 2-ha vineyard. The wines are made onsite; the cellar door offers barbecue/picnic facilities.

🐏 Twofold

★★★★★

142 Beulah Road, Norwood, SA 5067 (postal) **REGION** Clare Valley/Heathcote
T 0418 544 001 **OPEN** Not
WINEMAKER Neil Pike, Sergio Carlei (Contract) **EST.** 2002 **CASES** 800
This is the venture of brothers Nick and Tim Stock, both of whom have had a varied background in the wine industry (primarily at the marketing end, whether as sommeliers or in wholesale) and both of whom have had excellent palates. Their contacts have allowed them to source a single vineyard riesling from Sevenhill in the Clare Valley, and a single vineyard shiraz from Heathcote, both under ongoing arrangements. As one might expect, the quality of the wines is excellent.

ŸŸŸŸŸ **Clare Valley Riesling 2005** Light straw-green; full of regional character and flavour in a lime/citrus/grapefruit spectrum; very good balance and length. Screwcap. 12.5° alc. **RATING** 94 **DRINK** 2015 $ 24

Clare Valley Riesling 2004 Light straw-green; a similar style to the '05, bottle age adding just a little weight and complexity, but the same lime/grapefruit flavours; long and fine. Screwcap. 12° alc. **RATING** 94 **DRINK** 2014 $ 24

Heathcote Shiraz 2002 Similar depth in colour, the hue a little more developed; spicy/savoury/earthy/meaty cool vintage style; excellent intensity, focus and length. Cork. 13.5° alc. **RATING** 94 **DRINK** 2012 $ 38

ŸŸŸŸŸ **Heathcote Shiraz 2003** Good hue, light- to medium-depth; very much the more elegant face of Heathcote; medium-bodied black and red fruits, supple tannins. Diam. 13.5° alc. **RATING** 93 **DRINK** 2015 $ 38

🐏 Tyler Wines

★★★★☆

PO Box 244, Rosedale, Vic 3847 **REGION** Gippsland
T (03) 5199 2788 **F** (03) 5199 2064 **www.**tylerwines.com.au **OPEN** Not
WINEMAKER Ben Tyler **EST.** 2004 **CASES** 1500
This is the business of Ben Tyler and his father Peter, initially established on the family farm at Willung, but moving to a much larger unused facility in Rosedale (also in Gippsland) prior to the 2005 vintage. Ben graduated with a degree in Applied Science (winemaking) from Charles Sturt University; during his time at the university he was offered and accepted the position of trainee winemaker. The following year he was employed as assistant winemaker, before returning to Vic. In 2000 he became the winemaker at Clyde Park, producing a series of excellent wines over the following years. He now works full-time for Tyler Wines, developing the estate label, and also providing contract winemaking services for other clients.

ŦŦŦŦ♀ **Cabernet Sauvignon 2004** Very good colour; medium-bodied; bright, sweet cassis, blackcurrant and chocolate; fine, ripe tannins; good oak. 14.7° alc. **RATING** 92 **DRINK** 2015 $ 18

Chardonnay 2004 Light green-yellow; lively, ripe grapefruit, stone fruit and melon; integrated French oak; some length. Screwcap. 14.5° alc. **RATING** 90 **DRINK** 2009 $ 18

Shiraz 2004 Abundant blackberry, dark plum and spice varietal fruit; warm vanilla oak; soft tannins. 15.5° alc. **RATING** 90 **DRINK** 2014 $ 18

ŦŦŦŦ♀ **Illamahta Pinot Noir 2004** Medium red, some colour development; savoury/spicy/earthy bouquet; light- to medium-bodied; good texture and length; needs a touch more pinot fruit, though certainly not alcohol. Screwcap. 14.5° alc. **RATING** 89 **DRINK** 2010 $ 18

Tyrrell's ★★★★★

Broke Road, Pokolbin, NSW 2321 **REGION** Lower Hunter Valley
T (02) 4993 7000 **F** (02) 4998 7723 **WWW**.tyrrells.com.au **OPEN** Mon–Sat 8–5
WINEMAKER Andrew Spinaze, Mark Richardson **EST.** 1858 **CASES** 500 000
One of the most successful family wineries, a humble operation for the first 110 years of its life which grew out of all recognition over the past 40 years. In 2003 it cleared the decks by selling its Long Flat range of wines for an 8-figure sum, allowing it to focus on its premium, super-premium and ultra-premium wines: Vat 1 Semillon is one of the most dominant wines in the Australian show system, and Vat 47 Chardonnay is one of the pace-setters for this variety. It has an awesome portfolio of single-vineyard Semillons released when 5–6 years old. Exports to the US, Canada and the UK.

ŦŦŦŦŦ **Vat 1 Semillon 1999** Bright green-straw; fine, floral lemon juice aromas, as much akin to Riesling as Semillon; brilliantly fresh, fine, long and lingering mouthfeel. Bottles as good as this one are to die for. Top gold medal Sydney Wine Show '06. Cork. 10.3° alc. **RATING** 97 **DRINK** 2009 $ 40

Vat 1 Semillon 1994 Fantastic, glowing green-yellow; an utterly magical combination of complexity and vibrant freshness; its 12 trophies and 30 gold medals say it all. Cork. 10.8° alc. **RATING** 97 **DRINK** 2010 $ 70

Lost Block Semillon 2005 Fragrant lemon blossom aromas; has great balance and, above all, length; delicacy, but with abundant flavour. A bargain. Screwcap. **RATING** 95 **DRINK** 2015 $ 15

Belford Reserve Semillon 1999 Complex herb, grass, citrus and mineral aromas; a vibrant palate, extremely long finish and lingering aftertaste. Cork. 9.7° alc. **RATING** 95 **DRINK** 2014 $ 35

Vat 1 Semillon 2005 Particularly elegant and fine; long, gently minerally finish intermixed with lemon. Screwcap. **RATING** 94 **DRINK** 2015 $ 25

ŦŦŦŦ♀ **Vat 47 Chardonnay 2004** Has the finesse one expects from Vat 47; citrus, melon and stone fruit, with well-balanced and integrated oak. Screwcap. 12.5° alc. **RATING** 93 **DRINK** 2010 $ 40

Stevens Reserve Semillon 2001 Has considerable length and drive; lemon, herb, spice and talc; bone-dry, flinty finish. Cork. **RATING** 92 **DRINK** 2011 $ 19

Rufus Stone McLaren Vale Shiraz 2003 Clean (no reduction); rich, ripe blackberry/black cherry/dark chocolate fruit, the oak well-integrated; good line and mouthfeel; successful vintage outcome. Screwcap. **RATING** 90 **DRINK** 2013 $ 19.95

ŦŦŦŦ **Stevens Reserve Shiraz 2002** Strongly regional earthy, savoury notes through bouquet and palate; long finish, but lacks mid-palate fruit. Cork. **RATING** 89 **DRINK** 2008 $ 24

Vat 9 Shiraz 2000 Holding hue very well; light- to medium-bodied with earthy regional nuances to the red and black fruits; has good tannins. Cork. 13° alc. **RATING** 89 **DRINK** 2012 $ 45

Old Winery Verdelho 2005 Light- to medium-bodied; clean, fresh fruit salad varietal flavour; good balance. Screwcap. **RATING** 88 **DRINK** 2008 $ 14

Lost Block Merlot 2004 Light- to medium-bodied; a direct, fresh array of small red berry fruits unburdened by more than a touch of tannins or oak. Screwcap. 14° alc. **RATING** 87 **DRINK** Now $ 14.99

ᵀᵀᵀ♀ **Old Winery Chardonnay 2004 RATING** 86 **DRINK** Now $ 13
Old Winery Semillon Sauvignon Blanc 2005 RATING 85 **DRINK** Now $ 13
Rufus Stone McLaren Vale Cabernet Sauvignon Malbec 2003 RATING 85 **DRINK** 2008
$ 19.95

ᵀᵀᵀ **Old Winery Chardonnay Semillon 2005 RATING** 83 $ 10.99

Uleybury Wines ★★★★★

Uley Road, Uleybury, SA 5114 **REGION** Adelaide Zone
T (08) 8280 7335 **F** (08) 8280 7925 **WWW**.uleybury.com **OPEN** 7 days 10–5
WINEMAKER Tony Pipicella **EST.** 1995 **CASES** 10 000
The Pipicella family — headed by Italian-born Tony — has established nearly 45 ha of vineyard near
One Tree Hill in the Mt Lofty Ranges; 10 varieties have been planted, with more planned. Daughter
Natalie Pipicella, who has completed the wine marketing course at the University of SA, was
responsible for overseeing the design of labels, the promotion and advertising, and the creation of the
website. Exports to the UK, Canada, Denmark and Japan.

ᵀᵀᵀᵀᵀ **AP Pipicella Reserve Semillon 2002** Brilliant green-straw; highly aromatic; bursting
with lemony fruit; benchmark style (and price!). Screwcap. 13.8° alc. **RATING** 94
DRINK 2010 $ 35
AP Pipicella Reserve Shiraz 2004 Deep colour; rich dark fruits on both bouquet and
palate; blackberry and chocolate, the tannins well-balanced and composed. Cork. 15° alc.
RATING 94 **DRINK** 2017 $ 35
Block V Shiraz 2004 Good colour; a massive wine in the style of Chapel, though with
more focused fruit; tannins still formidable. Cork. 15° alc. **RATING** 94 **DRINK** 2017 $ 19

ᵀᵀᵀᵀ♀ **Primitivo 2004** Strong colour; deep and rich red and black fruits; not common to find
Zinfandel such as this in Australia, though it is in California. Screwcap. 15.5° alc.
RATING 90 **DRINK** 2012 $ 25

ᵀᵀᵀᵀ **Uley Chapel Shiraz 2004** Exotic spicy bouquet; very rich, ripe — bordering overripe —
flavours of prunes, black fruits and lots of tannins; needs time to sort itself out. Screwcap.
15° alc. **RATING** 89 **DRINK** 2014 $ 19
Merlot Shiraz 2004 Rich, textured, layered, ripe black fruits and a splash of chocolate;
merlot varietal character submerged. Screwcap. 15° alc. **RATING** 89 **DRINK** 2014 $ 19
Petit Verdot 2004 Dense purple-red; a black hole in vinous space, though the tannins are
ripe. Cork. 13.5° alc. **RATING** 88 **DRINK** 2015 $ 19

ᵀᵀᵀ♀ **Sangiovese Rose 2005** Cherry and raspberry fruit with balanced sweetness; a pretty
wine. Screwcap. 11° alc. **RATING** 86 **DRINK** Now $ 13
AP Pipicella Reserve Cabernet Sauvignon 2004 Dense, inky/soupy purple-red; why do
this to cabernet sauvignon, or indeed any wine? Way over the top. Cork. 17° alc. **RATING** 86
DRINK 2019 $ 35

Ulithorne ★★★★☆

PO Box 487, McLaren Vale, SA 5171 **REGION** McLaren Vale
T (08) 8382 5528 **F** (08) 8382 5528 **OPEN** Not
WINEMAKER Brian Light (Contract) **EST.** 1971 **CASES** 800
If ever a wine had an accidental, not to say off-putting, birth, Ulithorne is it. The vineyard was
planted in 1971 to absorb the effluent from the piggery which Frank Harrison (father/father-in-law
of the now-owners) wished to establish. The council was not persuaded, the piggery did not go ahead,
and the vineyard was neglected. In 1997 abstract painter Sam Harrison and marketing consultant
partner Rose Kentish purchased the vineyard, becoming full-time vignerons and resurrecting it from
its near-derelict state. They extended the plantings with 8 ha of cabernet sauvignon, 3 ha of merlot
and an additional 3 ha of shiraz. Exports to the UK, France, The Netherlands, the US and NZ.

ᵀᵀᵀᵀᵀ **McLaren Vale Frux Frugis Shiraz 2004** Deep purple-red; lush, mouthfilling plum,
blackberry and dark chocolate; positive, ripe tannins and controlled oak. Unfiltered. Cork.
14.5° alc. **RATING** 94 **DRINK** 2019 $ 42

ŸŸŸŸŸ **McLaren Vale Frux Frugis Shiraz 2003** Medium- to full-bodied; has a very strong regional bitter chocolate and earth wrapping around the sweet fruit at the core; slips past the alcohol. Cork. 15.3° alc. **RATING** 93 **DRINK** 2013 $ 42

Unavale Vineyard ★★☆

10 Badger Corner Road, Flinders Island, Tas 7255 **REGION** Northern Tasmania
T (03) 6359 3632 **F** (03) 6359 3632 **OPEN** Mon–Wed 10–4, w'ends 10–6, or by appt
WINEMAKER Andrew Hickinbotham (Contract) **EST.** 1999 **CASES** 100
Roger and Bev Watson have pioneered viticulture on Flinders Island, planting 1 ha of pinot noir, and 0.5 ha each of chardonnay, sauvignon blanc, riesling and cabernet sauvignon. The windswept environment has slowed the development of the vines, and will always keep yields low, but production will rise over the next few years.

ŸŸŸŸ **Sauvignon Blanc 2005 RATING** 86 **DRINK** Now

ŸŸŸ **Riesling 2005 RATING** 83 $ 20

Undercliff NR

Yango Creek Road, Wollombi, NSW 2325 **REGION** Lower Hunter Valley
T (02) 4998 3322 **F** (02) 4998 3322 **WWW.**undercliff.com.au **OPEN** 7 days 10–5, or by appt
WINEMAKER David Carrick **EST.** 1990 **CASES** 1600
Peter and Jane Hamshere are the new owners of Undercliff, but it continues to function as both winery cellar door and art gallery. The wines, produced from 2.5 ha of estate vineyards, have won a number of awards in recent years at the Hunter Valley Wine Show and the Hunter Valley Small Winemakers Show.

Upper Reach Vineyard ★★★☆

77 Memorial Avenue, Baskerville, WA 6056 **REGION** Swan Valley
T (08) 9296 0078 **F** (08) 9296 0278 **WWW.**upperreach.com.au **OPEN** Thurs–Mon 11–5
WINEMAKER Derek Pearse **EST.** 1996 **CASES** 3000
This 10-ha property on the banks of the upper reaches of the Swan River was purchased by Laura Rowe and Derek Pearse in 1996. The original vineyard was 4 ha of 12-year-old chardonnay, which has been expanded by 1.5 ha of shiraz, 1 ha of cabernet sauvignon, 0.5 ha each of verdelho and merlot and 0.2 ha graciano. All wines are estate-grown. The fish on the label, incidentally, is black bream, which can be found in the pools of the Swan River during the summer months. Exports to the UK.

ŸŸŸŸŸ **Reserve Chardonnay 2005** Very well-made; whole bunch-pressed and new French oak fermentation; rich stone fruit and seamless oak; a mouthfilling, generous wine. Screwcap. 14° alc. **RATING** 90 **DRINK** 2009 $ 23

ŸŸŸŸ **Verdelho 2005** A quite complex bouquet, with a hint of spice; moderately rich palate, with subliminal sweetness. Screwcap. 13° alc. **RATING** 88 **DRINK** Now $ 16
Shiraz 2004 Medium-bodied; good structure and texture; black fruits, controlled oak. Screwcap. 14° alc. **RATING** 88 **DRINK** 2011 $ 25
Unwooded Chardonnay 2005 Light straw-green; a particularly well-made and balanced wine given its Upper Swan Valley origin; nectarine, peach and a nice touch of acidity. Screwcap. 13° alc. **RATING** 87 **DRINK** Now $ 15
Reserve Chardonnay 2004 Pleasant peachy fruit; well-integrated oak and good mouthfeel. Screwcap. 13.5° alc. **RATING** 87 **DRINK** Now $ 23

ŸŸŸŸ **Cabernet Merlot 2003 RATING** 84 **DRINK** Now $ 18

Vale Wines ★★★☆

2914 Frankston–Flinders Road, Balnarring, Vic 3926 **REGION** Mornington Peninsula
T (03) 5983 1521 **F** (03) 5983 1942 **WWW**.valewines.com.au **OPEN** 7 days 11–5
WINEMAKER John Vale **EST.** 1991 **CASES** 500
After a lifetime in the retail liquor industry, John and Susan Vale took a busman's retirement by purchasing a grazing property at Balnarring in 1991. They planted a little under 0.5 ha of cabernet sauvignon (since grafted over to gewurztraminer), and John Vale undertook what he describes as 'formal winemaking training' before building a 20-tonne winery in 1997. In 2000 they extended the plantings with 1.4 ha of tempranillo, riesling and durif, seeking to move outside the square. In the meantime the wine range has been extended by the purchase of chardonnay and pinot grigio from local growers.

ŸŸŸŸŸ **Riesling 2005** Substantial power and drive, with a mix of lemon, lime and tropical fruit stalling fractionally on the finish. Cork. 12.9° alc. **RATING** 90 **DRINK** 2008 $ 18

ŸŸŸŸ **Chardonnay 2004** Developed green-yellow; ripe, soft yellow peach fruit; early drinking style. Cork. 13.8° alc. **RATING** 87 **DRINK** Now $ 25

ŸŸŸŸ **Tempranillo Dry Rose 2005 RATING** 86 **DRINK** Now $ 18
Pinot Grigio 2004 RATING 85 **DRINK** Now $ 18
Durif 2004 RATING 85 **DRINK** 2008 $ 29

Valley View Vineyard ★★★

21 Boundary Road, Coldstream, Vic 3770 (postal) **REGION** Yarra Valley
T (03) 9739 1692 **F** (03) 9739 0430 **OPEN** Not
WINEMAKER Contract **EST.** 2000 **CASES** 200
Judy and John Thompson purchased their property in 1998, and with the unanimous advice of various contacts in the wine industry they planted 2.2 ha of pinot noir on a north and northwest-facing rocky slope.

ŸŸŸŸ **Yarra Valley Pinot Noir 2004** Very light but clear savoury varietal character; super-fine extract/tannins gives a silky feel, but the wine does need more sweet fruit. Screwcap. 13.5° alc. **RATING** 87 **DRINK** 2008 $ 26

Valley Wines NR

352 Lennard Street, Herne Hill, WA 6056 **REGION** Swan District
T (08) 9296 4416 **F** (08) 9296 4754 **OPEN** Wed–Sun
WINEMAKER Charlie Zannino **EST.** 1973 **CASES** NA
Valley Wines is a long-established, traditional Swan Valley winery owned by Charlie Zannino. Primarily a grapegrower, he has 16 ha of chenin blanc, semillon, chardonnay, grenache, shiraz and pedro ximenez, and makes table and fortified wines from a small portion of the annual production.

Vardon Lane/Kanta ★★★★

22–26 Vardon Lane, Adelaide, SA 5000 (postal) **REGION** Adelaide Hills
T (08) 8232 5300 **F** (08) 8232 2055 **OPEN** Not
WINEMAKER Egon Muller **EST.** 2005 **CASES** NA
This is the ultimate virtual winery, a joint venture between famed Mosel-Saar-Ruwer winemaker (and proprietor) Egon Muller, Michael Andrewartha from Adelaide's East End Cellars, and Armenian-born vigneron and owner of La Corte from Italy's Puglia region, Vahe Keushguerian. A 3-year search for the perfect riesling site ended almost where the journey began, at the Shaw & Smith Adelaide Hills vineyard. Muller arrived on the day of picking to oversee the whole production, carried out at Shaw & Smith with input from Steve Pannell and Shaw & Smith's winemaker, Daryl Catlin. The grapes were crushed and cold-soaked for up to 16 hours, the juice settled without enzyme and kept at 12°C until spontaneous fermentation began. Small wonder that the wine is so different from other Australian Rieslings, and even more different from the gloriously fine wines which Muller makes at home.

ŸŸŸŸŸ **Kanta Riesling 2005** Concentrated, powerful and firm; strong mineral line from start to finish; uncompromisingly dry. Screwcap. 13.5° alc. **RATING** 90 **DRINK** 2012 $ 28

Varrenti Wines

'Glenheather', Blackwood Road, Dunkeld, Vic 3294 **REGION** Grampians
T (03) 5577 2368 **F** (03) 5577 2367 **OPEN** 7 days 12–5
WINEMAKER Ettore Varrenti **EST.** 1999 **CASES** 400
Ettore Varrenti has established 4 ha of pinot noir, shiraz, sangiovese, barbera and cabernet sauvignon at the extreme southern end of the Grampians National Park. It is remote from any other winery, and appears to be on the edge of the Grampians region.

ΥΥΥΥ **Glen Heather Dunkeld Sangiovese 2003** **RATING** 84 **DRINK** Now $ 15

Vasse Felix ★★★★★

Cnr Caves Road/Harmans Road South, Wilyabrup, WA 6284 **REGION** Margaret River
T (08) 9756 5000 **F** (08) 9755 5425 **WWW**.vassefelix.com.au **OPEN** 7 days 10–5
WINEMAKER David Dowden **EST.** 1967 **CASES** 150 000
In 1999 the production of Vasse Felix wines moved to a new 2000-tonne winery; the old winery is now dedicated entirely to the restaurant and tasting rooms. A relatively new 140-ha vineyard at Jindong in the north of the Margaret River region supplies a large part of the increased fruit intake. Exports to all major markets.

ΥΥΥΥΥ **Margaret River Semillon 2005** Very sophisticated and skilled winemaking with barrel fermentation and maturation in (old?) barriques adds more to the texture than to flavour; excellent mouthfeel; gently ripe herb and lemon flavours. Screwcap. 13.5° alc. **RATING** 95 **DRINK** 2010 $ 22.50
Heytesbury Chardonnay 2004 At once elegant and complex; perfectly judged French barrel ferment and lees inputs to the melon and stone fruit of the palate; very long finish. Screwcap. 14° alc. **RATING** 95 **DRINK** 2014 $ 35
Heytesbury 2003 Medium- to full-bodied; very good balance and structure; a complex array of black and red fruits; positive oak and ripe tannins. Cork. 14.5° alc. **RATING** 95 **DRINK** 2023 $ 65

ΥΥΥΥΥ **Margaret River Cabernet Sauvignon 2004** Good red-purple; medium- to full-bodied; rich, quite lush, blackcurrant and chocolate fruit; quality mocha oak and ripe tannins. Cork. 14° alc. **RATING** 93 **DRINK** 2019 $ 30
Cane Cut Semillon 2005 Lovely lemony fruit and lingering, lemony acidity; almost riesling-like. Very different from the '04. Grapes left to shrivel for 6 weeks. Screwcap. 10.5° alc. **RATING** 93 **DRINK** 2012 $ 19

ΥΥΥΥ **Classic Dry White 2005** A nicely balanced mix of ripe citrus, grass and mineral; good length and balance. Semillon/Sauvignon Blanc. Screwcap. **RATING** 88 **DRINK** Now $ 19
Classic Dry Red 2003 Medium-bodied; bright and cheerful red and black fruits, but with enough structure to satisfy. Cork. 14° alc. **RATING** 88 **DRINK** 2009 $ 19

Vasse River Wines

c/- Post Office, Carbunup, WA 6280 **REGION** Margaret River
T (08) 9755 1111 **F** (08) 9755 1011 **WWW**.vasseriver.com.au **OPEN** Not
WINEMAKER Sharna Kowalazuh **EST.** 1993 **CASES** 2500
This is a major and rapidly growing business owned by the Credaro Family; 90 ha of chardonnay, semillon, verdelho, sauvignon blanc, cabernet sauvignon, merlot and shiraz have been planted on the typical gravelly red loam soils of the region. The wines are released under two labels: Vasse River for the premium, and Carbunup Estate for the lower-priced varietals.

ΥΥΥΥΥ **Margaret River Semillon Sauvignon Blanc 2005** Light- to medium-bodied; a complex array of aromas and flavours; gooseberry, passionfruit and tropical, yet avoids heaviness. Screwcap. 12.5° alc. **RATING** 91 **DRINK** Now $ 17
Margaret River Chardonnay 2005 Light straw-green; ripe peach, melon and fig fruit; well-balanced and integrated oak; harmonious mouthfeel. Screwcap. 13.5° alc. **RATING** 90 **DRINK** 2008 $ 18

Margaret River Shiraz 2003 Bright red-purple; light- to medium-bodied, with fresh, predominantly red fruit, flavours; gentle tannins, minimal oak. Screwcap. 14° alc. **RATING** 90 **DRINK** 2011 $ 21

ŸŸŸŸ **Margaret River Verdelho 2004** Quite well-made; a light citrus overlay to equally light tropical fruit salad; typically inoffensive. Screwcap. 13.8° alc. **RATING** 87 **DRINK** Now $ 14

ŸŸŸŸ **Margaret River Cabernet Merlot 2003** **RATING** 86 **DRINK** 2009 $ 25

🍇 Velo Wines ★★★

755 West Tamar Highway, Legana, Tas 7277 **REGION** Northern Tasmania
T 0418 526 858 **F** (03) 6330 2321 **WWW**.velowines.com.au **OPEN** Wed–Sun 10–6
WINEMAKER Micheal Wilson, Winemaking Tasmania (Julian Alcorso) **EST.** 1966 **CASES** 1000
The story behind Velo Wines is a fascinating one, wheels within wheels. The 0.9 ha of cabernet sauvignon and 0.5 ha of pinot noir of the Legana Vineyard were planted in 1966 by Graham Wiltshire, legitimately described as one of the 3 great pioneers of the Tasmanian wine industry. Fifteen years ago Micheal and Mary Wilson returned to Tas after living in Italy and France for a decade. Micheal Wilson was an Olympic cyclist, following which he joined the professional ranks racing in all of the major European events. Imbued with a love of wine and food, they spent '7 long hard years in the restaurant game'. Somehow, Micheal Wilson found time to become a qualified viticulturist, and was vineyard manager for Moorilla Estate based at St Matthias for 7 years. Wife Mary has spent 5 years working in wine wholesaling for leading distributors. In 2001 they purchased the Legana Vineyard planted so long ago, and have painstakingly rehabilitated the 40-year-old vines. They have erected a small winery where Micheal makes the red wines, Julian Alcorso makes the white wines, sourced in part from 0.6 ha of estate riesling and from grapes grown on the East Coast.

ŸŸŸŸ **Riesling 2005** A generous mid-palate, with plenty of soft, tropical fruit. Early developing style. **RATING** 87 **DRINK** 2009 $ 24
Unwooded Chardonnay 2004 Sweet stone fruit flavours; has some depth and length. **RATING** 87 **DRINK** Now $ 20

ŸŸŸŸ **Unwooded Chardonnay 2005** **RATING** 85 **DRINK** Now $ 20
Pinot Noir 2004 **RATING** 84 **DRINK** Now $ 25
Cabernet Sauvignon 2004 **RATING** 84 **DRINK** 2008 $ 25

🍇 Vercoe's Vineyard ★★★★

PO Box 145, Cessnock, NSW 2325 **REGION** Lower Hunter Valley
T 0410 541 663 **F** (02) 6574 7352 **WWW**.vercoesvineyard.com.au **OPEN** Not
WINEMAKER Monarch Winemaking Services (Jim Chatto) **EST.** 2002 **CASES** 700
In the mid-1960s a young John Vercoe toyed with the idea of establishing a wine bar, but it took another 30 years for his interest in wine to translate itself into Vercoe's Vineyard. Together with wife Elizabeth, and adult children, the property on the evocatively-named Sweetwater Ridge was purchased in 1999. After 3 years of soil preparation, 1.8 ha of verdelho was planted in 2002, followed by merlot (1.3 ha) and semillon and chardonnay (0.8 ha each).

ŸŸŸŸŸ **Hunter Valley Verdelho 2005** Very attractive example of the variety; tropical fruit salad is cut by delicious lemony acidity. Better, even, than the bronze medal won at the 2005 Hunter Valley Wine Show. Screwcap. 14° alc. **RATING** 90 **DRINK** 2008 $ 18

Verona Vineyard NR

Small Winemakers Centre, McDonalds Road, Pokolbin, NSW 2321 **REGION** Lower Hunter Valley
T (02) 4998 7668 **F** (02) 4998 7430 **OPEN** 7 days 10–5
WINEMAKER Monarch Winemaking Services **EST.** 1972 **CASES** NA
Verona has had a chequered history, and is still a significant business, acting as a sales point for a number of other Hunter Valley winemakers from its premises, which are directly opposite Brokenwood. The wines come from 22 ha at Muswellbrook and 5 ha surrounding the winery.

Vicarys

NR

Northern Road, Luddenham, NSW 2745 **REGION** Sydney Basin
T (02) 4773 4161 **F** (02) 4773 4411 **WWW**.vicaryswinery.com.au **OPEN** Tues–Fri 9–5, w'ends 10–5
WINEMAKER Chris Niccol **EST.** 1923 **CASES** 3000
Vicarys justifiably claims to be the Sydney region's oldest continuously operating winery, having been established in a large and very attractive stone shearing shed built about 1890. Most of the wines come from other parts of Australia, but the winery does draw upon 1 ha of estate traminer and 3 ha of chardonnay for those wines, and has produced some good wines of all styles over the years.

Vico

NR

Farm 1687 Beelbangera Road, Griffith, NSW 2680 **REGION** Riverina
T (02) 6962 2849 **OPEN** Mon–Fri 9–5
WINEMAKER Ray Vico **EST.** 1973 **CASES** 1200
Ray Vico has been growing grapes for many years with his 9 ha of vines; more recently he has decided to bottle and sell part of the production under the Vico label. On last advice, the prices were positively mouthwatering.

Victor Harbor Winery

NR

Cnr Mont Rosa Road/Adelaide Road, Hindmarsh Valley, SA 5211 **REGION** Southern Fleurieu
T (08) 8554 6504 **F** (08) 8554 6504 **WWW**.victorharborwinery.com.au **OPEN** Wed–Sun & public hols 10–5
WINEMAKER Alan Dyson (Contract) **EST.** 1999 **CASES** 500
Victor Harbor's first winery was established in 1991 by Adrienne and Neville Scott in the picturesque Southern Fleurieu Peninsula Hills behind Victor Harbor. Planting of a 4-ha vineyard to serve the winery commenced in 1992. The first wine from cabernet sauvignon and shiraz was produced in 1996 and the cellar door opened in 1999.

🐾 Victory Point Wines

★★★★☆

121 Rosalie Street, Shenton Park, WA 6008 (postal) **REGION** Margaret River
T (08) 9381 5765 **F** (08) 9388 2449 **WWW**.victorypointwines.com **OPEN** Not
WINEMAKER Keith Mugford, Frank Kittler (Contract) **EST.** 1997 **CASES** 1200
Judith and Gary Berson (the latter a partner in the Perth office of a national law firm) have set their aims high. With viticultural advice from Keith and Clare Mugford of Moss Wood, they have established their 12-ha vineyard without irrigation, emulating those of the Margaret River pioneers (including Moss Wood). The plantings comprise 2 ha chardonnay, the remainder the Bordeaux varieties, with cabernet sauvignon accounting for 6 ha, merlot for 2 ha, cabernet franc 1.5 ha and malbec and petit verdot 0.3 ha each. There will thus be 2 wines each year: a Chardonnay and a Cabernet blend.

▼▼▼▼▼ **Margaret River Chardonnay 2005** Light straw-green; very fine, almost Chablis-like, built for the long haul; melon and stone fruit; subtle oak, good acidity. Screwcap. 13.5° alc.
RATING 94 **DRINK** 2015 $ 33

▼▼▼▼▽ **Margaret River Cabernet Sauvignon 2003** Elegant, medium-bodied style; an attractive mix of blackcurrant, cassis and raspberry, which has absorbed 18 months in French oak. Dry-grown Cabernet Sauvignon/Malbec/Cabernet Franc/Petit Verdot. Screwcap.
RATING 91 **DRINK** 2015 $ 33

Viking Wines

★★★★☆

RSD 108 Seppeltsfield Road, Marananga, SA 5355 **REGION** Barossa Valley
T (08) 8562 3842 **F** (08) 8562 4266 **WWW**.vikingwines.com **OPEN** 7 days 11–5
WINEMAKER Rolf Binder (Contract) **EST.** 1995 **CASES** 1500
Based upon 50-year-old, dry-grown and near-organic vineyards with a yield of only 1–1.5 tonnes per acre, Viking Wines has been 'discovered' by Robert Parker with inevitable consequences for the price of its top Shiraz. There are 5 ha of shiraz and 3 ha of cabernet sauvignon. The Odin's Honour wines

(made by sister company Todd-Viking Wines) also come from old (20–100 years) dry-grown vines around Marananga and Greenoch. Exports to the US, the UK, Singapore and France.

ŶŶŶŶ **Grand Shiraz 2004** Deep colour; immensely powerful and concentrated, awash with black fruits, spice and dark chocolate, which have in turn consumed the oak; 50-year-old dry-grown vines. Cork. 14.5° alc. **RATING** 93 **DRINK** 2019 **$** 35

Grand Shiraz Cabernet 2004 Strong purple-red; powerful, dense blackberry and blackcurrant fruit; substantial tannins make their presence felt from start to finish. Patience will be rewarded. Cork. 14.5° alc. **RATING** 92 **DRINK** 2020 **$** 28

Odin's Honour Reserve Shiraz 2003 Very ripe; the slightly stewed/confit character of many '03 reds, but does have licorice and dark chocolate along with the fruit to even the ship. Cork. 15° alc. **RATING** 91 **DRINK** 2018 **$** 30

Villa Caterina Wines ★★★★☆

4 Wattletree Road, Drumcondra, Geelong, Vic 3215 (postal) **REGION** Geelong
T (03) 5278 2847 **F** (03) 5278 4884 **OPEN** Not
WINEMAKER Ernesto Vellucci **EST.** 2001 **CASES** 300
Ernesto Vellucci was born in Italy where his parents owned a vineyard. He was brought up in the traditional and cultural way of Italian winemaking, a legacy he has not forgotten. On the other hand, he has qualified as an industrial chemist, with years of working with laboratory equipment and techniques. He offers the only wine laboratory services in Geelong with microbiological testing facilities and gas chromotography, directed to the detection of brettanomyces/dekkera yeasts. His small production is made from purchased grapes.

ŶŶŶŶ **Cabernet Sauvignon 2004** Good colour; potent, powerful cassis and black fruits; a little less emphasis would have been even better. Cork. 13.5° alc. **RATING** 92 **DRINK** 2012

Geelong Shiraz 2004 Medium- to full-bodied; while there is plenty of weight and depth to the black fruit flavours, the palate is quite supple. Cork. 15° alc. **RATING** 90 **DRINK** 2012

Villa d'Esta Vineyard NR

2884 Wallambah Road, Dyers Crossing, NSW 2429 **REGION** Northern Rivers Zone
T (02) 6550 2236 **F** (02) 6550 2236 **WWW.**villadesta.com.au **OPEN** 7 days 9–5
WINEMAKER Zoltan Toth **EST.** 1997 **CASES** 1000
Zolton Toth and Maria Brizuela have 5.5 ha of chardonnay, verdelho, chasselas dore, pinot noir, cabernet sauvignon, merlot, shiraz, muscat, hamburg and chambourcin. They make the wines onsite.

Villa Terlato NR

1200 Bass Highway, The Gurdies, Vic 3984 **REGION** Gippsland
T (03) 5997 6381 **OPEN** 7 days
WINEMAKER John Terlato **EST.** 1988 **CASES** NA
John and Francis Terlato have planted 2 ha of riesling, chardonnay, pinot noir and cabernet sauvignon, and make the wine onsite. The cellar door offers barbecue and picnic facilities.

Villa Tinto ★★★☆

Krondorf Road, Tanunda, SA 5352 **REGION** Barossa Valley
T (08) 8563 3044 **F** (08) 8563 0460 **WWW.**villatinto.com.au **OPEN** W'ends & public hols 10–5,
Mon–Fri by appt
WINEMAKER Albert Di Palma **EST.** 1987 **CASES** 700
Albert and Dianne Di Palma began the development of their business in 1987, planting a little under 2 ha of cabernet sauvignon and 0.7 ha of shiraz. They were content to sell their grapes until 1999, but they are now making an increasing amount of wine at their small winery. The wines are also available at the Barossa Small Winemakers Centre at Chateau Tanunda.

ŶŶŶŶ **Albert's Block Barossa Valley Shiraz 2004** An extremely powerful, robust wine with a hint of reduction largely swamped by the tsunami waves of black fruits and savoury tannins; the texture is particularly good. Cork. 14° alc. **RATING** 93 **DRINK** 2014 **$** 33

▼▼▼▼ **Barossa Valley Cabernet Sauvignon 2002** Good colour; savoury, earthy edges to blackcurrant fruit and bitter chocolate, well within expected varietal terms of reference. The balance and tannins are good; the benefit of a cool vintage. Cork. 14° alc. **RATING** 89 **DRINK** 2012 $16
Barossa Valley Cabernet Sauvignon 2003 Black fruits, licorice, prune and dark chocolate; less extractive and tannic than Albert's Block, though still fairly rustic. Cork. 14.5° alc. **RATING** 87 **DRINK** 2013 $16

▼▼▼▼ **Albert's Block Barossa Valley Cabernet Sauvignon 2003** **RATING** 86 **DRINK** 2015 $27
Barossa Valley Cabernet Shiraz 2003 **RATING** 86 **DRINK** 2009 $18

Villacoola Vineyard & Winery NR

Carnarvon Highway, Surat, Qld 4417 **REGION** Queensland Zone
T (07) 4626 5103 **F** (07) 4626 5516 **OPEN** 7 days 10–5
WINEMAKER Contract **EST.** 1992 **CASES** NA
Ron Ritchie has ventured far to the west to establish Villacoola Vineyard & Winery — its nearest neighbour is Romavilla (at Roma), 78 km to the north. The 2.5-ha vineyard is planted to sauvignon blanc, semillon, chardonnay, merlot, shiraz and muscat; the muscats provide the fortified wines for which Romavilla has been famous for 140 years.

Vinden Estate ★★★☆

17 Gillards Road, Pokolbin, NSW 2320 **REGION** Lower Hunter Valley
T (02) 4998 7410 **F** (02) 4998 7421 **WWW**.vindenestate.com.au **OPEN** 7 days 10–5
WINEMAKER Guy Vinden, John Baruzzi (Consultant) **EST.** 1998 **CASES** 3500
Sandra and Guy Vinden have bought their dream home, with landscaped gardens in the foreground, and 9 ha of vineyard, and the Brokenback mountain range in the distance. Much of the winemaking is now done onsite, and increasingly from the estate vineyards. The wines are available through the cellar door and wine club.

▼▼▼▼▼ **Hunter Valley Chardonnay 2004** While light- to medium-bodied, has good length and balance; fresh melon and stone fruit, plus a kiss of oak. Screwcap. 13° alc. **RATING** 90 **DRINK** 2009 $22

▼▼▼▼ **Hunter Valley Alicante Bouschet 2005** Bright, pale fuchsia; neatly balanced strawberry fruit, residual sugar and acidity; astute handling of picking date/alcohol. Rose style, of course. Screwcap. 10.5° alc. **RATING** 88 **DRINK** Now $22.50
Hunter Valley Unwooded Chardonnay 2005 A pleasant, uncomplicated medium-bodied wine with stone fruit and touches of citrus. Screwcap. 12.5° alc. **RATING** 87 **DRINK** 2008 $20

▼▼▼▼ **Reserve Verdelho 2005** **RATING** 86 **DRINK** Now $22

Vinea Marson NR

PO Box 222, Heathcote, Vic 3523 **REGION** Heathcote
T (03) 5433 2768 **F** (03) 5433 2768 **WWW**.vineamarson.com **OPEN** Not
WINEMAKER Mario Marson **EST.** 2000 **CASES** NFP
Owner-winemaker Mario Marson spent many years as the winemaker viticulturist with Dr John Middleton at the celebrated Mount Mary. He purchased the Vinea Marson property in 1999, on the eastern slopes of the Mt Camel Range, and in 2000 planted syrah and viognier, plus Italian varieties, sangiovese, nebbiolo and barbera. Since leaving Mount Mary, he has undertaken vintage work at Isole e Olena in Tuscany, worked as winemaker at Jasper Hill vineyard, and as consultant and winemaker for Stefani Estate.

Vinecrest ★★★

Cnr Barossa Valley Way/Vine Vale Road, Tanunda, SA 5352 **REGION** Barossa Valley
T (08) 8563 0111 **F** (08) 8563 0444 **WWW**.vinecrest.com.au **OPEN** 7 days 11–4.30
WINEMAKER Mos Kaesler **EST.** 1999 **CASES** 5000
The Mader family has a long connection with the Barossa Valley. Ian Mader is a fifth-generation descendant of Gottfried and Maria Mader, who immigrated to the Barossa Valley in the 1840s, and his wife, Suzanne, is the daughter of a former long-serving vineyard manager for Penfolds. In 1969 Ian and Suzanne established their Sandy Ridge Vineyard, and more recently the Turrung Vineyard (together a total of 30 ha), a few mins from Tanunda. Having been grapegrowers for 30 years, in 1999 they established Vinecrest, using a small portion of the production from their vineyards.

ŸŸŸŸ **Barossa Valley Shiraz 2003** Touches of leather and game on the bouquet; light- to medium-bodied palate, with dark fruits and soft tannins. Cork. **RATING** 87 **DRINK** 2008 $24

ŸŸŸ̈Ÿ **Sparkling Shiraz 2002 RATING** 86 **DRINK** 2010 $28
Two Colours White Semillon Sauvignon Blanc 2005 RATING 85 **DRINK** Now $16
One Colour White Semillon 2005 RATING 84 **DRINK** Now $16

Vineyard 28 ★★☆

Lot 1, Bagieau Road, Harvey, WA 6220 **REGION** Geographe
T (08) 9733 5605 **F** (08) 9733 4500 **OPEN** 7 days 10–5
WINEMAKER Contract **EST.** 1998 **CASES** 600
In 1997 Mark and Pippa Cumbers decided to leave Melbourne (where they had worked and become wine lovers) and return to Mark's home state of WA. They chose a 4-ha property on coastal tuart sands, and have planted cabernet sauvignon (0.8 ha) and nebbiolo, sauvignon blanc and chenin blanc (0.4 ha each). Nebbiolo was planted as a point of difference, but has so far proved as difficult to come to terms with here as elsewhere.

ŸŸŸ̈Ÿ **Nebbiolo 2004 RATING** 84 **DRINK** Now $18

Vinifera Wines ★★★☆

194 Henry Lawson Drive, Mudgee, NSW 2850 **REGION** Mudgee
T (02) 6372 2461 **F** (02) 6372 6731 **WWW**.viniferawines.com.au **OPEN** 7 days 10–5.30
WINEMAKER Phillip van Gent, Tony McKendry **EST.** 1997 **CASES** 2500
Having lived in Mudgee for 15 years, Tony McKendry (a regional medical superintendent) and wife Debbie succumbed to the lure; they planted their small (1.5-ha) vineyard in 1995. In Debbie's words, 'Tony, in his spare 2 mins per day, also decided to start Wine Science at Charles Sturt University in 1992.' She continues, 'His trying to live 27 hours per day (plus our four kids!) fell to pieces when he was involved in a severe car smash in 1997. Two months in hospital stopped full-time medical work, and the winery dreams became inevitable.' Financial compensation finally came through and the small winery was built. The vineyard is now 11 ha, including 2 ha of tempranillo and 1 ha of graciano.

ŸŸŸŸŸ̈ **Limited Release Semillon 2005** Has the precision and focus the Riesling lacks; lemon, herb and grass fruit running through to a long, dry, minerally finish. Screwcap. **RATING** 90 **DRINK** 2012 $16

ŸŸŸŸ **Gran Tinto 2004** A light- to medium-bodied spicy, savoury mix of red and black fruits which never veer off their essential juicy berry flavours; fine, ripe tannins. Cabernet Sauvignon/Grenache/Tempranillo Screwcap. **RATING** 89 **DRINK** 2010 $19

ŸŸŸ̈Ÿ **Mudgee Riesling 2005** Glowing light green-straw; nice varietal flavour, but fairly loose structure. Screwcap. **RATING** 86 **DRINK** 2008 $16
Mudgee Cabernet Sauvignon 2004 Quite powerful but distinctly savoury/earthy/rustic style; the tannins linger on the finish, but not entirely to the disadvantage of the wine. Screwcap. **RATING** 86 **DRINK** 2012 $24

ŸŸŸ **Mudgee Rose 2005 RATING** 83 $15

Vino Italia

NR

81 Campersic Road, Middle Swan, WA 6056 **REGION** Swan District
T (08) 9396 4336 **F** (08) 9296 4924 **OPEN** 7 days 10–5
WINEMAKER Eugenio Valenti, Allesandro Calabrese **EST.** 1954 **CASES** NA
Surprising though it may seem to some, the Italian winemaking community in the Swan Valley is significantly smaller than that from Dalmatia. Nonetheless, this business is well named, for Eugenio Valenti and Alessandro Calabrese have 34 ha of chenin blanc, semillon, grenache, shiraz and muscadelle; they make both table and fortified wines.

🐚 Vinrock

★★★★☆

23 George Street, Thebarton, SA 5031 (postal) **REGION** McLaren Vale
T (08) 8234 8288 **F** (08) 8234 8266 **WWW**.vinrock.com **OPEN** Not
WINEMAKER Serafino (Scott Rawlinson) **EST.** 2004 **CASES** 2000
Owners Don Luca, Marco Iannetti and Anthony De Pizzol all have a background in the wine industry, none more than Don Luca, a former board member of Tatachilla, and who planted the 30-ha Luca Vineyard in 1999. The majority of the grapes are sold, but since 2004 limited quantities of wine have been made from the best blocks in the vineyard.

▼▼▼▼▼ **McLaren Vale Shiraz 2004** Very good bouquet; medium-bodied, supple, smooth and velvety blackberry, plum and chocolate fruit; ripe tannins, controlled oak. Cork. 14.5° alc. **RATING** 94 **DRINK** 2017 $ 20

▼▼▼▼▽ **McLaren Vale Grenache 2004** Good varietal fruit and structure; juicy, halfway between red and black fruit, with splashes of spice and chocolate; nice oak. Cork. 14° alc. **RATING** 92 **DRINK** 2010 $ 17

Virgin Block Vineyard

NR

Caves Road, Yallingup, WA 6282 **REGION** Margaret River
T (08) 9755 2394 **F** (08) 9755 2357 **WWW**.virginblock.com **OPEN** 7 days 10–5
WINEMAKER Bruce Dukes, Anne-Coralie Fleury (Contract) **EST.** 1995 **CASES** 3000
Virgin Block has been established on a 30-ha property, 3 km from the Indian Ocean, and is surrounded by large Jarrah and Marri forest trees.

Virgin Hills

NR

Salisbury Road, Lauriston West via Kyneton, Vic 3444 **REGION** Macedon Ranges
T (03) 5422 7444 **F** (03) 5422 7400 **OPEN** By appt
WINEMAKER Josh Steele **EST.** 1968 **CASES** 2500
Virgin Hills has passed through several ownership changes in a short period. It is now owned by Michael Hope, who presides over the Hope Estate in the Hunter Valley. The absence of tastings over recent years has forced the removal of the previous 5-star rating. Exports to the UK and the US.

Voyager Estate

★★★★★

Lot 1 Stevens Road, Margaret River, WA 6285 **REGION** Margaret River
T (08) 9757 6354 **F** (08) 9757 6494 **WWW**.voyagerestate.com.au **OPEN** 7 days 10–5
WINEMAKER Cliff Royle **EST.** 1978 **CASES** 35 000
Voyager Estate has come a long way since it was acquired by Michael Wright (of the mining family) in May 1991. It now has a high-quality 103-ha vineyard which means it can select only the best parcels of fruit for its own label, and supply surplus (but high-quality) wine to others. The Cape Dutch-style tasting room and vast rose garden are a major tourist attraction. Exports to the UK, the US and other major markets.

▼▼▼▼▼ **Margaret River Cabernet Sauvignon Merlot 2002** Spotlessly clean black fruit aromas; outstanding texture and structure, blackcurrant/redcurrant fruit interwoven with fine, ripe tannins and immaculate oak. Cork. 14° alc. **RATING** 96 **DRINK** 2017 $ 39.50

Sauvignon Blanc Semillon 2005 A fresh, lively and zesty mix of passionfruit and lemon, with excellent mouthfeel; lingering finish and aftertaste. Screwcap. 13° alc. **RATING** 95 **DRINK** 2009 $22

Shiraz 2004 Fragrant, spicy black fruits on the bouquet; concentrated and focused sweet blackberry and licorice flavours; good oak and tannins. Cork. **RATING** 95 **DRINK** 2020 $29.50

Margaret River Cabernet Sauvignon Merlot 2003 Strong red-purple; medium- to full-bodied; rich, round, blackcurrant fruit, supple tannins and quality oak all seamlessly interwoven. Cork. 14° alc. **RATING** 95 **DRINK** 2025 $39

Sauvignon Blanc 2005 Fresh, precise passionfruit and kiwifruit aromas, then a lively palate in delicious, early-picked style. Screwcap. 12.8° alc. **RATING** 94 **DRINK** Now $22

Chardonnay 2004 Pale green-straw; very elegant nectarine and apple on a light-bodied palate, which grows in intensity through its length to the finish and aftertaste. Screwcap. 13.2° alc. **RATING** 94 **DRINK** 2012 $38

ΨΨΨΨ **Margaret River Chenin Blanc 2005** Gentle fruit salad; tangy acidity helps the wine, which will grow with time. Screwcap. 13° alc. **RATING** 87 **DRINK** 2008 $20

Wadjekanup River Estate   NR

Flatrocks Road, Broomehill, WA 6318 **REGION** Central Western Australia Zone
T (08) 9825 3080 **F** (08) 9825 3007 **OPEN** By appt
WINEMAKER Alkoomi (Michael Staniford) **EST.** 1995 **CASES** 400
The Witham family (Scott and Sue, Jim and Ann) began the development of Wadjekanup River Estate in 1995 as a minor diversification for a 3000-ha wool, prime lamb, beef and cereal cropping enterprise worked by the family. They began with 1.2 ha of shiraz and sauvignon blanc, since extended to 8 ha, including a 1-ha block of merlot. The aims for the future include a purpose-built cellar for storage and sales, with a possibility of farm-stay accommodation. The present wine range of Sauvignon Blanc and Shiraz will be extended with a varietal Merlot, and perhaps a Semillon.

Wagga Wagga Winery   NR

RMB 427, Oura Road, Wagga Wagga, NSW 2650 **REGION** Riverina
T (02) 6922 1221 **F** (02) 6922 1101 **OPEN** 7 days 11–late
WINEMAKER Peter Fitzpatrick **EST.** 1987 **CASES** 1805
Planting of the 4-ha vineyard, 200m from the Murrumbidgee River and just 15 mins from Wagga Wagga, began in 1987, with further plantings in 1990, 1995, 2000 and 2001. Chardonnay, riesling, shiraz, cabernet sauvignon, cabernet franc and touriga have been established.

🐌 Walden Woods Farm   NR

469 Donald Road, Armidale, NSW 2350 (postal) **REGION** Northern Slopes Zone
T (02) 6772 8966 **OPEN** Not
WINEMAKER Doug Hume, Scott Wright (Contract) **EST.** 2001 **CASES** 130
Doug Hume and Nadine McCrea have established 0.3 ha of close-planted pinot gris, using certified organic growing and management techniques from the outset. The necessarily small production sells out quickly by word of mouth, phone, email and mail orders.

Walla Wines   NR

RMB 201, Walla Walla, NSW 2659 **REGION** Big Rivers Zone
T (02) 6029 2128 **F** (02) 6029 2508 **www**.wallawines.com.au **OPEN** W'ends & public hols 10–5, or by appt
WINEMAKER Paul Robey **EST.** 1998 **CASES** NA
Paul and Chris Robey moved to Walla Walla in 1981 after working in Papua New Guinea, the NT and at Puckapunyal in Vic. Paul is an agriculturist and teacher; Chris is a registered nurse. After making wine as a hobby for some years, they planted the vineyard to semillon, shiraz, taminga and tarrango. Paul has completed a graduate diploma in viticulture at Charles Sturt University, and has also completed short courses in winemaking at the Dookie campus of Melbourne University. The pair do all the vineyard and winemaking operations except bottling.

🐾 Wallaroo Wines ★★★☆

PO Box 272, Hall, ACT, 2618 **REGION** Canberra District
T (02) 6230 2831 **F** (02) 6230 2830 **WWW**.wallaroowines.com.au **OPEN** Not
WINEMAKER Roger Harris (Contract) **EST.** 1996 **CASES** 800

Leading international reporters and journalists Carolyn Jack and Philip Williams purchased the property on which they have subsequently established Wallaroo Wines in 1996, after a 5-year sojourn in Japan led to a desire for space. They retained leading viticultural consultant Di Davidson to evaluate the property and recommend varieties, and she quickly encouraged them to proceed. In 1997 they planted 2 ha of riesling, 4 ha of cabernet sauvignon and 6 ha of shiraz, leading to the first vintage in 2000. Approximately 80% of the production is sold to Hardys Kamberra winery, and is used in Kamberra's Meeting Place gold medal-winning wines. Much of the production has been done by remote control, as they lived in the UK from 2000 to 2005, Philip as the European correspondent for the ABC covering the Iraq war, the Madrid bombing and the Beslan Siege, all making the return to Wallaroo and its elegant house especially rewarding.

♥♥♥♥♡ Canberra District Riesling 2002 Glowing yellow-green; quite powerful and rich; toast, lime, kerosene and spice; much the best of the 4 Rieslings between '02 and '05, suggesting patience with the younger wines. Screwcap. 12.5° alc. **RATING** 90 **DRINK** Now $ 20

♥♥♥♥ Canberra District Cabernet Sauvignon 2004 Elegant, light- to medium-bodied; cassis and blackcurrant fruit; fine, supple tannins. Cork. 14.5° alc. **RATING** 89 **DRINK** 2010 $ 24

Canberra District Shiraz 2004 Slightly dull colour; blackberry and dark plum fruit; gentle tannins and well-integrated oak. Cork. 13° alc. **RATING** 88 **DRINK** 2009 $ 24

Canberra District Cabernet Sauvignon 2003 Powerful savoury, bramble, black fruits; persistent, slightly dry, tannins. Cork. 14° alc. **RATING** 87 **DRINK** 2009 $ 24

Wallington Wines NR

Nyrang Creek Vineyard, Canowindra, NSW 2904 **REGION** Cowra
T (02) 6344 7153 **F** (02) 6344 7105 **WWW**.wallingtonwines.com.au **OPEN** By appt
WINEMAKER Murray Smith (Consultant), Margaret Wallington **EST.** 1992 **CASES** 1500

Margaret and the late Anthony Wallington began their Nyrang Creek Vineyard in 1994. Today there are 15.95 ha of chardonnay, shiraz, cabernet sauvignon, grenache, mourvedre, tempranillo, petit verdot, cabernet franc, viognier and semillon. Most of the production is sold. Exports to the US.

Wandana Estate NR

113 Oakey Creek Road, Hall, NSW 2618 **REGION** Canberra District
T (02) 6230 2140 **F** (02) 6230 2151 **OPEN** By appt
WINEMAKER Various contract **EST.** 1997 **CASES** 300

The small Wandana Estate is managed by Colin Bates; it has 4.25 ha of cabernet sauvignon, merlot and shiraz.

Wandering Brook Estate NR

North Wandering Road, Wandering, WA 6308 **REGION** Peel
T (08) 9884 1084 **F** (08) 9884 1064 **OPEN** W'ends 9.30–6
WINEMAKER Jadran **EST.** 1989 **CASES** 1400

Laurie and Margaret White have planted 10 ha of vines on their 130-year-old family property in a move to diversify. Until 1994 the winery was known as Red Hill Estate. Over half the annual production of grapes is sold.

Wandin Valley Estate ★★★★

Wilderness Road, Lovedale, NSW 2320 **REGION** Lower Hunter Valley
T (02) 4930 7317 **F** (02) 4930 7814 **WWW**.wandinvalley.com.au **OPEN** 7 days 10–5
WINEMAKER Matthew Burton, **EST.** 1973 **CASES** 10 000

After 15 years in the wine and hospitality business, owners Phillipa and James Davern decided to offer the property as a going concern, with vineyard, winery, accommodation, function centre, cricket ground and restaurant in the package, aiming to keep its skilled staff as part of the business, and ensure that all existing contracts are ongoing. Ironically, being offered for sale just as the overall quality has increased. Exports to the UK, the US and other major markets.

ΨΨΨΨΨ **Reserve Hunter Valley Semillon 2005** Pale straw-green, crisp mineral, grass and lemony acidity; lingering finish; classic style; long-term development. Screwcap. **RATING** 92 **DRINK** 2015 $17

Bridie's Reserve Hunter Valley Shiraz 2003 Excellent colour; clean, fresh, vibrant red and black fruits; good acidity and length; will develop complexity and regional character. Cork. **RATING** 90 **DRINK** 2015 $28

ΨΨΨΨ **Pavilion Hunter Valley Rose 2005** Spotlessly clean bouquet of small red fruits; touches of raspberry and cherry on the palate; excellent balancing acidity. Screwcap. **RATING** 89 **DRINK** Now $17

Hunter Valley Verdelho 2005 Typical tropical fruit salad; good expression of region and variety; not sweet. Screwcap. **RATING** 87 **DRINK** Now $17

ΨΨΨΨ **Hunter Valley Orange Cabernet Sauvignon Merlot 2003** **RATING** 86 **DRINK** Now $18

Wandoo Farm   NR

'Glencraig', Duranillin, WA 6393 **REGION** Central Western Australia Zone
T (08) 9863 1066 **F** (08) 9863 1067 **OPEN** By appt
WINEMAKER Camilla Vote **EST.** 1997 **CASES** 1750
Wandoo Farm lies outside any of the existing wine regions, due east of the Blackwood Valley (its nearest regional neighbour). Donald Cochrane owns a 650-ha sheep, cattle and grain farm near Duranillin, with a 23-inch annual rainfall and abundant underground water. His maternal grandfather came to Australia from Kaiser Stuhl in Germany, later settling near Kojonup, where he planted a vineyard and made the community wine. Donald Cochrane has one of his original vines (malbec) growing in the present day Wandoo Farm vineyard. Here there are 7 ha of cabernet sauvignon, shiraz, zinfandel, verdelho, viognier and marsanne.

Wangolina Station   ★★★★☆

Cnr Southern Ports Highway/Limestone Coast Road, Kingston SE, SA 5275 **REGION** Mount Benson
T (08) 8768 6187 **F** (08) 8768 6149 **WWW**.wangolinastation.com.au **OPEN** 7 days 10–5
WINEMAKER Anita Goode **EST.** 2001 **CASES** 3000
Four generations of the Goode family have been graziers at Wangolina Station, renowned for its shorthorn cattle stud. The family now has two connections with the wine industry: it sold the land to Kreglinger for its Norfolk Rise Vineyard and winery, and also sold land to Ralph Fowler. The second connection is even more direct: fifth-generation Anita Goode has become a vigneron, with 3.2 ha of shiraz and 1.6 ha each of cabernet sauvignon, sauvignon blanc and semillon established on the family property.

ΨΨΨΨΨ **Mount Benson Sauvignon Blanc 2005** Clean, fresh, flowery blossom aromas; delicate but perfectly balanced gooseberry and green apple fruit; fine finish. Major surprise. Screwcap. 11.5° alc. **RATING** 94 **DRINK** Now $16

ΨΨΨΨΨ **Mount Benson Semillon 2005** Clear-cut varietal character on both bouquet and palate; the flavour intensity builds through the back-palate and finish; well-made. Screwcap. 11.5° alc. **RATING** 90 **DRINK** 2010 $15

ΨΨΨΨ **Mount Benson Cabernet Shiraz 2003** **RATING** 85 **DRINK** Now $17

Wansbrough Wines   NR

Richards Road, Ferguson, WA 6236 **REGION** Geographe
T (08) 9728 3091 **F** (08) 9728 3091 **OPEN** W'ends 10–5
WINEMAKER Willespie Wines **EST.** 1986 **CASES** 250
Situated east of Dardanup in the picturesque Ferguson Valley, Wansbrough enjoys views of the distant Geographe Bay and the nearer State forest, and has the Bibblemun Track running along the vineyard's northern and eastern borders.

Wantirna Estate

Bushy Park Lane, Wantirna South, Vic 3152 **REGION** Yarra Valley
T (03) 9801 2367 **F** (03) 9887 0225 **OPEN** Not
WINEMAKER Maryann Egan, Reg Egan **EST.** 1963 **CASES** 900
Situated well within the boundaries of the Melbourne metropolitan area, Wantirna Estate is an outpost of the Yarra Valley. It was one of the first established in the rebirth of the valley. Maryann Egan has decided it is time to come in from the cold, and have the wines rated, self-evidently a very sensible decision.

ΥΥΥΥΥ **Isabella Yarra Valley Chardonnay 2004** Fine, elegant; primarily fruit-driven but complex; melon and nectarine fruit with barrel ferment/lees inputs; excellent acidity and length. Cork. 14.5° alc. **RATING** 94 **DRINK** 2015 $ 45
Lily Yarra Valley Pinot Noir 2004 Light but bright hue; light- to medium-bodied; lively red cherry and strawberry fruits; lovely line and balance; you don't need power for pinot to shine. Cork. 14° alc. **RATING** 94 **DRINK** 2010 $ 50
Amelia Yarra Valley Cabernet Merlot 2003 Good colour; medium-bodied, with similar freshness to the Pinot Noir; excellent cassis and blackcurrant married to silky tannins, oak the bridesmaid. An impressive trio. Cork. 12.5° alc. **RATING** 94 **DRINK** 2013 $ 50

Waratah Hills Vineyard ★★★

20 Promentary Road, Fish Creek, Vic 3959 **REGION** Gippsland
T (03) 5683 2441 **F** (03) 9650 0525 **WWW**.waratahhills.com.au **OPEN** Wed–Sun 11–4 (summer 10–5)
WINEMAKER Owen Schmidt **EST.** 1995 **CASES** 450
Peter and Liz Rushen turned to Phillip Jones (of Bass Phillip) for advice when they planned the planting of their vineyard on a northeast slope in a beautiful domed valley formed by the Battery Creek. The outcome was high-density planting with low trellising similar to that of Bass Phillip and, of course, Burgundy. They have 3 ha of pinot noir and 1 ha of chardonnay, together with a sprinkle of merlot. The vines have developed slowly, the first vintage coming in 2004.

ΥΥΥΥ **Pinot Noir 2004** Very ripe, sweet plummy fruit, but has nice brightness. **RATING** 87 **DRINK** 2008 $ 18

ΥΥΥΥ **Chardonnay 2005** **RATING** 84 **DRINK** Now $ 20

Waratah Vineyard NR

11852 Gladstone Road, Mungungo via Monto, Qld 4630 **REGION** Queensland Zone
T (07) 4166 5100 **F** (07) 4166 5200 **WWW**.waratahvineyard.com.au **OPEN** Tues–Sun & public hols 10–5
WINEMAKER Peter Scudamore-Smith MW (Consultant) **EST.** 1998 **CASES** 900
David Bray is one of the doyens of wine journalism in Brisbane, and, indeed, Australia. After decades of writing about wine he and wife Pamela have joined Max Lindsay (Pamela's brother) and partner Lynne Tucker in establishing the Waratah Vineyard at Mungungo, near Monto, at the top of the Burnett Valley. The wines are principally sourced from the 4-ha Waratah Vineyard, with 3.2 ha of vineyard planted to chardonnay, verdelho, semillon, marsanne, viognier, shiraz, merlot and petit verdot, supplemented by grapes grown at Inglewood and Murgon.

Warburn Estate NR

700 Kidman Way, Griffith, NSW 2680 **REGION** Riverina
T (02) 6963 8300 **F** (02) 6962 4628 **WWW**.warburnestate.com.au **OPEN** Mon–Fri 9–5, Sat 10–4
WINEMAKER Sam Trimboli, Moreno Chiappin, Roberto Delgado, Sally Whittaker **EST.** 1969 **CASES** 650 000
One of the large producers of the region, drawing upon 1100 ha of estate plantings. While much of the wine is sold in bulk to other producers, selected parcels of the best of the grapes are made into table wines, with at one time spectacular success. Exports to the US.

Warrabilla

Murray Valley Highway, Rutherglen, Vic 3685 **REGION** Rutherglen
T (02) 6035 7242 **F** (02) 6035 7298 **WWW**.warrabillawines.com.au **OPEN** 7 days 10–5
WINEMAKER Andrew Sutherland Smith **EST.** 1990 **CASES** 10 000
Andrew Sutherland Smith and wife Carol have built a formidable reputation for their wines, headed by the Reserve trio of Durif, Cabernet Sauvignon and Shiraz, quintessential examples of Rutherglen red wine at its best. Their 18.5-ha vineyard has been extended with the planting of some riesling and zinfandel. Andrew spent 15 years with All Saints, McWilliam's, Yellowglen, Fairfield and Chambers before setting up Warrabilla, and his accumulated experience shines through in the wines.

Parola's Limited Release Shiraz 2005 Black fruits and vanilla oak; these wines have few parallels anywhere in the world. You have to look at the alcohol in the context of food in the same way as tannins in Italian red wines. Diam. 16.5° alc. **RATING** 94 **DRINK** 2020 $ 30
Reserve Durif 2005 Needless to say, impenetrable colour; a profusion of black fruits, dark chocolate, licorice, spice are all welded together; the tannins are soft, the oak incidental. Diam. 15.5° alc. **RATING** 94 **DRINK** 2020 $ 22

Parola's Limited Release Cabernet Sauvignon 2005 The slightly lower alcohol, and the new French oak, mean that this wine will always be easier to approach than the Reserve, whether in 5 or 25 years time; potent, supple blackcurrant and cassis fruit with a touch of chocolate. Diam. 16.1° alc. **RATING** 93 **DRINK** 2020 $ 30
Reserve Shiraz 2005 Predictably massive, mouth-flooding, blackberry fruit is the first sensation, alcohol kicking in hard on the finish. Diam. 16° alc. **RATING** 92 **DRINK** 2020 $ 22
Reserve Durif 2004 Completely opaque, with no sign of lightening to the colour; massively luscious and rich, with cascades of black chocolate, spice and licorice; amazingly, the 16.5° alcohol does not burn. A wine for heroes. Cork. **RATING** 91 **DRINK** 2013 $ 22

Reserve Cabernet Sauvignon 2005 Massive cassis and blackcurrant, the alcohol sinking its fangs in right from the start of the palate, and not letting go. Why Warrabilla would suggest only 4–5 years cellaring, I have no idea. Say the Smiths 'We don't like thin, weedy wines, and this is big, old-fashioned cabernet at its best'. Diam. **RATING** 89 **DRINK** 2015 $ 22

Warramate

27 Maddens Lane, Gruyere, Vic 3770 **REGION** Yarra Valley
T (03) 5964 9219 **F** (03) 5964 9219 **WWW**.warramatewines.com.au **OPEN** 7 days 10–6
WINEMAKER David Church **EST.** 1970 **CASES** 1500
A long-established and perfectly situated winery reaping the full benefits of its 36-year-old vines; recent plantings will increase production. All the wines are well-made, the Shiraz providing further proof (if such be needed) of the suitability of the variety to the region.

Black Label Cabernet Sauvignon 2004 Excellent hue; ripe blackcurrant and cassis run through the medium-bodied palate; good tannins and oak. Screwcap. 13.5° alc. **RATING** 93 **DRINK** 2011 $ 19
Shiraz 2003 Clean, bright blackberry and spice; medium-bodied, with good balance, structure, texture and length. Screwcap. 13.5° alc. **RATING** 91 **DRINK** 2013 $ 38

Riesling 2005 Crisp and elegant, with good minerally acidity; the fruit is not particularly expressive (it seldom is in the Yarra Valley) but the wine has a pleasantly dry finish. Screwcap. 12.5° alc. **RATING** 88 **DRINK** 2009 $ 25
Pinot Noir 2004 Bright purple-red; abundant plum and black cherry fruit, then somewhat dry and aggressive tannins join the fight. Patience should be rewarded. Screwcap. 14.5° alc. **RATING** 88 **DRINK** 2010 $ 19
Black Label Shiraz 2004 Very good colour; light- to medium-bodied black cherry, spice, leaf and mint aromas and flavours; controlled extract and oak. A newly introduced second label to the premier white label releases. Screwcap. 13.5° alc. **RATING** 88 **DRINK** 2012 $ 19
Cabernet Merlot 2002 Slightly dull hue; a super-savoury, slightly green, hostage to the ultra-cool vintage. Screwcap. 13.1° alc. **RATING** 87 **DRINK** 2009 $ 30

Warraroong Estate ★★★★☆

247 Wilderness Road, Lovedale, NSW 2321 **REGION** Lower Hunter Valley
T (02) 4930 7594 **F** (02) 4930 7199 **www**.warraroongestate.com **OPEN** Thurs–Mon 10–5
WINEMAKER Andrew Thomas, Adam Rees **EST.** 1978 **CASES** 3000
Warraroong Estate, formerly Fraser Vineyard, adopted its new name after it changed hands in 1997. 'Warraroong' is an Aboriginal word for hillside, reflecting the southwesterly aspect of the property, which looks back towards the Brokenback Range and Watagan Mountains. The label design is from a painting by Aboriginal artist Kia Kiro who, while coming from the NT, is now living and working in the Hunter Valley. The mature vineyard plantings were extended in 2004 with a little over 1 ha of verdelho.

🍷🍷🍷🍷🍷 **Hunter Valley Semillon 2005** Medium- to full yellow-green; smooth, supple and ripe lemon/lemon tart flavours; generous, but not flabby. Multiple trophy winner 2005 Hunter Valley Wine Show. Screwcap. **RATING** 95 **DRINK** 2015 $ 28

🍷🍷🍷🍷♀ **Hunter Valley Chardonnay 2005** Elegant, fresh, light-bodied; melon fruit with creamy lees and French oak; long finish. Screwcap. 13.5° alc. **RATING** 92 **DRINK** 2010 $ 20
Hunter Valley Chardonnay 2003 Elegant melon fruit, with all the characters the '05 will develop given time; moving closer to maturity. **RATING** 90 **DRINK** 2008 $ 20

🍷🍷🍷🍷 **Hunter Valley Chardonnay 2004** A complex bouquet, with obvious barrel ferment inputs; white and yellow peach fruit; soft finish. Screwcap. 13.5° alc. **RATING** 88 **DRINK** 2009 $ 20
Hunter Valley Verdelho 2005 Pleasant light- to medium-bodied style, with a touch of apricot to the fruit salad flavours; correct balance. Screwcap. **RATING** 87 **DRINK** 2008 $ 17

🍷🍷🍷♀ **Hunter Valley Sauvignon Blanc 2005** **RATING** 86 **DRINK** Now $ 14
Hunter Valley Long Lunch White 2005 Very clever, commercial cellar door style; slightly sweet, but well enough balanced. Value. Screwcap. 12.5° alc. **RATING** 86 **DRINK** Now $ 13

Warrego Wines NR

9 Seminary Road, Marburg, Qld 4306 **REGION** Queensland Coastal
T (07) 5464 4400 **F** (07) 5464 4800 **www**.warregowines.com.au **OPEN** 7 days 10–4
WINEMAKER Kevin Watson **EST.** 2000 **CASES** 27 000
Kevin Watson has completed his wine science degree at Charles Sturt University, and the primary purpose of his business is custom winemaking for the many small growers in the region, including all the clients of Peter Scudamore-Smith MW. In 2001, the Marburg Custom Crush company developed a state-of-the-art winery (as the cliché goes), cellar door and restaurant. $500 000 in government funding, local business investment and significant investment from China provided the funds, and the complex opened in April 2002. Since then, the business has expanded further with a public shareholder raising. (In 2004 Warrego crushed over 400 tonnes, 95% of which was contract winemaking for others.) The 3000-case own-brand Warrego wines come from 0.5 ha of estate chambourcin, plus grapes purchased in various regions. Exports to the US and China.

Warrenmang Vineyard & Resort ★★★★☆

Mountain Creek Road, Moonambel, Vic 3478 **REGION** Pyrenees
T (03) 5467 2233 **F** (03) 5467 2309 **www**.bazzani.com.au **OPEN** 7 days 10–5
WINEMAKER Chris Collier **EST.** 1974 **CASES** 11 000
The proposed merger of Warrenmang with other wine interests in 2004 failed to eventuate, through no fault of Luigi and Athalie Bazzani, who resumed full control of the business in February 2005, securing a number of large export orders to the US and Singapore. The Bazzanis emphasise it is business as usual, all thoughts of sale terminated.

🍷🍷🍷🍷🍷 **Black Puma Pyrenees Shiraz 2004** Dense, deep colour; extremely powerful dark fruits, the tannins interwoven, and the balance good, but leave it for 5 years. Cork. 15° alc. **RATING** 94 **DRINK** 2020 $ 80

🍷🍷🍷🍷♀ **Estate Shiraz 2004** Spicy, earthy nuances to the bouquet and palate; medium- to full-bodied blackberry fruit, with good length, finish and aftertaste. Cork. 14.5° alc. **RATING** 93 **DRINK** 2016 $ 60

Bazzani Vinello 2004 Bright purple-red; much more substance and structure than expected, the alcohol perfectly judged; red fruit and savoury notes are neatly counterpoised. Dolcetto/Nebbiolo/Barbera. Cork. 13° alc. **RATING** 91 **DRINK** 2014 $ 20

ŸŸŸŸ **Bazzani Shiraz Cabernet 2004** Red-purple; attractive savoury/spicy tannins run through the medium-bodied palate; good balance. Cork. 13.5° alc. **RATING** 89 **DRINK** 2010 $ 14

Warrina Wines

NR

Back Road, Kootingal, NSW 2352 **REGION** Northern Slopes Zone
T (02) 6760 3985 **F** (02) 6765 5746 **OPEN** W'ends 10–4
WINEMAKER David Nicholls **EST.** 1989 **CASES** 100
David and Susan Nicholls began the establishment of their 2.5-ha vineyard back in 1989, and for some years were content to sell the grapes to other producers and make occasional forays into winemaking. Commercial winemaking commenced in 2001.

Watchbox Wines

Indigo Creek Road, Indigo Valley, Vic 3688 **REGION** Rutherglen
T (02) 6026 9299 **F** (02) 6026 9325 **WWW**.watchbox.org **OPEN** Wed–Fri 10–4, Sat & public hols 10–5, closed Good Friday, Christmas & Boxing Day
WINEMAKER Alan Clark **EST.** 2001 **CASES** NA
Alan and Lisa Clark have established an 11-ha vineyard in the Indigo Valley, planted to sauvignon blanc, chardonnay, cabernet sauvignon, merlot, shiraz, durif and muscat. The wines are made onsite and sold through mail order and through the cellar door and café.

ŸŸŸŸŸ **Indigo Valley Durif 2004** Dense colour; voluminous blackberry, black plum, licorice, prune and spice — so much so, you almost don't notice the extraordinary alcohol. Cork. 16.5° alc. **RATING** 90 **DRINK** 2020 $ 25

ŸŸŸŸ **Indigo Valley Cabernet Sauvignon 2004** Very savoury, leafy minty aromas belying its alcohol; some cassis notes on the palate. Cork. 14° alc. **RATING** 87 **DRINK** 2009 $ 20

Water Wheel

Bridgewater-on-Loddon, Bridgewater, Vic 3516 **REGION** Bendigo
T (03) 5437 3060 **F** (03) 5437 3082 **WWW**.waterwheelwine.com **OPEN** Mon–Fri 9–5, w'ends & public hols 12–4
WINEMAKER Peter Cumming, Bill Trevaskis **EST.** 1972 **CASES** 35 000
Peter Cumming, with more than 2 decades of winemaking under his belt, has quietly built on the reputation of Water Wheel year by year. The winery is owned by the Cumming family, which has farmed in the Bendigo region for 50+ years, with horticulture and viticulture special areas of interest. The wines are of remarkably consistent quality and modest price. Exports to all major markets.

ŸŸŸŸŸ **Bendigo Shiraz 2004** Good colour; supple but complex medium- to medium-full-bodied palate; classic Bendigo/Central Victorian Shiraz, rich in fruit. Doesn't really show its alcohol. Screwcap. 15.5° alc. **RATING** 93 **DRINK** 2014 $ 18

ŸŸŸŸ **Bendigo Chardonnay 2005** Nicely balanced and integrated stone fruit and gentle oak; understated style. Screwcap. 13° alc. **RATING** 89 **DRINK** 2008 $ 15
Memsie Shiraz Cabernet Sauvignon Malbec 2004 Good purple-red hue; medium-bodied, with well above-average depth and complexity at this price point. Blackberry and touches of chocolate and mulberry fruit; ripe tannins. Very consistent. Screwcap.
RATING 89 **DRINK** 2009 $ 12
Bendigo Cabernet Sauvignon 2004 A little more tannin and extract than is normal for Water Wheel; blackberry fruit in uncompromising style; a trophy for Best Cabernet at the Daylesford Wine Show. Screwcap. 14° alc. **RATING** 89 **DRINK** 2013 $ 18
Bendigo Sauvignon Blanc 2005 Some colour; powerful, full-bodied wine; definitely needs food. Screwcap. 14° alc. **RATING** 88 **DRINK** Now $ 15

ŸŸŸŸ **Memsie Sauvignon Blanc Semillon Roussanne 2005** **RATING** 86 **DRINK** Now $ 12
Bendigo Cabernet Sauvignon 2003 **RATING** 86 **DRINK** 2008 $ 18

Watershed Wines ★★★★★

Cnr Bussell Highway/Darch Road, Margaret River, WA 6285 **REGION** Margaret River
T (08) 9758 8633 **F** (08) 9757 3999 **WWW**.watershedwines.com.au **OPEN** 7 days 10–5
WINEMAKER Cathy Spratt **EST.** 1999 **CASES** 76 000
Watershed Wines has been established by a syndicate of investors, and no expense has been spared in
establishing the vineyard and building a striking cellar door sales area, and a 200-seat café and
restaurant. Situated towards the southern end of the Margaret River region, its neighbours include
Voyager Estate and Leeuwin Estate. Exports to all major markets.

ŸŸŸŸŸ **Sauvignon Blanc Semillon 2005** Amazingly youthful; lively, fresh, grassy style in the best
sense. Gold medal National Wine Show '05. **RATING** 95 **DRINK** 2008 $ 18
Awakening Sauvignon Blanc 2005 Light straw-green; the key to the wine is to be found
in the palate rather than the bouquet; partial barrel ferment and lees aging has added to
the texture, introducing a spread from creamy to minerally; just when least expected,
citrussy acidity on the finish. Screwcap. 13° alc. **RATING** 94 **DRINK** 2009 $ 32
Awakening Chardonnay 2005 Tangy, cool-grown fruit with excellent length, structure
and persistence. Gold medal Sydney Wine Show '06. **RATING** 94 **DRINK** 2011 $ 32

ŸŸŸŸŸ **Shiraz 2004** Spicy, savoury black fruit aromas; medium-bodied, complex texture from
fine tannins throughout interwoven with fruit and oak. Cork. 14.5° alc. **RATING** 92
DRINK 2014 $ 27
Awakening Chardonnay 2004 A generous and rich mix of ripe tropical fruit, the creamy
lees characters and barrel ferment French oak just a little overblown. Silver medal in
Germany. Cork. 13.5° alc. **RATING** 91 **DRINK** 2010 $ 32
Cabernet Merlot 2003 Medium-bodied; good structure and mouthfeel from fine tannins
and sweet cassis berry fruit. Cork. 13.5° alc. **RATING** 91 **DRINK** 2013 $ 27

ŸŸŸŸ **Viognier 2005** Well-made; good mouthfeel, length and balance; the problem is that
viognier varietal character has gone awol, leaving no more than an echo. Screwcap.
13.5° alc. **RATING** 88 **DRINK** 2010 $ 27

ŸŸŸŸ **Unoaked Chardonnay 2005** **RATING** 86 **DRINK** 2008 $ 18
Zinfandel 2004 **RATING** 85 **DRINK** 2008 $ 27

Watson Wine Estates ★★★☆

PO Box 6243, Halifax Street, Adelaide, SA 5000 **REGION** Coonawarra
T (08) 8299 9299 **F** (08) 8299 9355 **WWW**.watsonwine.com **OPEN** Not
WINEMAKER Roger Harbord **EST.** 1997 **CASES** NFP
After he sold his highly successful industrial services business to Brambles Group in 1998, Rex
Watson decided to build on the core of a small 10-ha vineyard he had acquired in Coonawarra the
year before. The business rapidly expanded, and today owns, controls and manages almost 400 ha
over 3 vineyards all within the Coonawarra region, and acquires additional grapes for the Limestone
Coast range. The wines are made by industry veteran Roger Harbord at the Russet Ridge winery.
Current releases are under the Gum Bear label, other brands will follow.

ŸŸŸŸ **Gum Bear Coonawarra Sauvignon Blanc 2005** Attractive, ripe passionfruit and
gooseberry aromas and flavours; good balance and length. Screwcap. 12.5° alc. **RATING** 89
DRINK Now $ 16.50
Gum Bear Coonawarra Unwooded Chardonnay 2005 Fresh, direct grapefruit/citrus; a
lively wine. **RATING** 87 **DRINK** Now $ 11
Gum Bear Limestone Coast Cabernet Shiraz Merlot 2004 Light-bodied; a fruit-driven,
fresh, mix of red and black fruits; easy drinking, early access style. Screwcap. 13.5° alc.
RATING 87 **DRINK** 2008 $ 12

ŸŸŸŸ **Gum Bear Coonawarra Cabernet Sauvignon 2003** **RATING** 86 **DRINK** 2008 $ 12

Wattagan Estate Winery

NR

'Wattagan', Oxley Highway, Coonabarabran, NSW 2357 **REGION** Western Plains Zone
T (02) 6842 2456 **F** (02) 6842 2656 **OPEN** 7 days 10–5
WINEMAKER Contract **EST.** 1996 **CASES** NFP
Coonabarabran is known for its sheep grazing, but most emphatically not for viticulture. As far north of Sydney as Port Macquarie, it is 440 km west of that town, with the striking Warrumbungle Range on one side and the national park on the other. The modest production is sold through three outlets in Coonabarabran, and 'exported' to Gunnedah and Boggabri.

Wattle Mist Wines

NR

Taste Mount Barker Wine Café, 26 Langton Road, Mount Barker, WA 6324 **REGION** Mount Barker
T (08) 9851 4314 **F** (08) 9851 2569 **OPEN** 7 days 10.30–5 winter, w'ends 10.30–5 summer
WINEMAKER Mike Garland (Contract) **EST.** 1992 **CASES** 800
Wattle Mist Wines is the retirement vehicle for Ray Burring and Joan Bath. With a desire for a relaxed country lifestyle, Ray and Joan purchased their 100-acre property in Mount Barker in 1992 and have developed the vineyard slowly. The wines are made in an early-drinking style, and are available through the Taste Mount Barker Wine Café (also owned by Ray and Joan), which stocks around 50 local wines and offers light lunches and local produce.

Wattle Ridge Vineyard

★★★☆

Loc 11950 Boyup–Greenbushes Road, Greenbushes, WA 6254 **REGION** Blackwood Valley
T (08) 9764 3594 **F** (08) 9764 3594 **OPEN** 7 days 10–5
WINEMAKER Contract **EST.** 1997 **CASES** 2000
James and Vicky Henderson have established 6.25 ha of vines at their Nelson Vineyard, planted to riesling, verdelho, merlot and cabernet sauvignon. The wines are sold by mail order and through the cellar door, which offers light meals, crafts and local produce.

▼▼▼▼ **Two Tinsmiths Reserve Cabernet Sauvignon 2002** Light- to medium-bodied; cedary bottle-developed aromas and flavours around a core of redcurrant/raspberry fruit; good balance and length. Cork. 14.2° alc. **RATING** 89 **DRINK** 2011 $ 18

Two Tinsmiths Cabernet Sauvignon 2004 Good colour; herb, spice and leaf overtones to small red and black berry fruits; light, but firm, tannins. Screwcap. 14.7° alc. **RATING** 88 **DRINK** 2010 $ 15

▼▼▼▽ **Pink Monet 2005** **RATING** 84 **DRINK** Now $ 18

Wattlebrook Vineyard

NR

Fordwich Road, Broke, NSW 2330 **REGION** Lower Hunter Valley
T (02) 9929 5668 **F** (02) 9929 5668 **WWW**.wattlebrook.com **OPEN** By appt
WINEMAKER Andrew Margan (Contract) **EST.** 1994 **CASES** 1000
Wattlebrook Vineyard was founded by NSW Supreme Court Justice Peter McClellan and family in 1994, with a substantial vineyard lying between the Wollemi National Park and Wollombi Brook. The family planted another major vineyard, in 1998, on Henry Lawson Drive at Mudgee, to shiraz, merlot and cabernet sauvignon. The Wollombi Vineyard is planted to chardonnay, semillon, verdelho, cabernet sauvignon and shiraz. The wines have been consistent medal winners at various local wine shows.

Waverley Estate

NR

Waverley-Honour, Palmers Lane, Pokolbin, NSW 2320 **REGION** Lower Hunter Valley
T (02) 4998 7953 **F** (02) 4998 7952 **WWW**.wineloverslane.com.au **OPEN** 7 days 10–5
WINEMAKER Gary Reed (Contract) **EST.** 1989 **CASES** 4500
Waverley Estate Aged Wines (to give it its full name) is the new name for the Maling Family Estate; as its name suggests, it specialises in offering a range of fully mature wines. Vintages stretching back more than 10 years are available for most of the wines at the cellar door. The wines are chiefly made from the 21.5 ha of estate plantings (shiraz, semillon, chardonnay, cabernet sauvignon).

Wayaree Estate ★★★☆

4391 Main Road, Lunawanna, Bruny Island, Tas 7150 (postal) **REGION** Southern Tasmania
T (03) 6293 1088 **F** (03) 6293 1088 **OPEN** Not
WINEMAKER Winstead Winery **EST.** 1998 **CASES** 100
Richard and Bernice Woolley have established the only vineyard on Bruny Island, the southernmost commercial planting in Australia. They have a total of 2 ha of chardonnay and pinot noir, not all in production. Bernice has a degree in marketing from Curtin University, and she and Richard have operated budget-style holiday accommodation on the property since 1999.

TTTT **Bruny Island Unwooded Chardonnay 2004** Bright green-yellow; lively, crisp, citrus and stone fruit, with typical bracing acidity; good length. Twin top. **RATING** 89 **DRINK** Now $ 20

Bruny Island Pinot Noir 2004 Strong colour; powerful plummy fruit on entry, with spicy notes; shortens/toughens somewhat on the back-palate and finish. **RATING** 88 **DRINK** 2010 $ 25

Waybourne ★★☆

60 Lemins Road, Waurn Ponds, Vic 3221 **REGION** Geelong
T (03) 5241 8477 **F** (03) 5241 8477 **OPEN** By appt
WINEMAKER Kilchurn Wines (David Cowburn) **EST.** 1980 **CASES** 730
Owners Tony and Kay Volpato began planting in 1978, and have continued until recently, shiraz being added to previously established riesling, chardonnay, pinot gris, cabernet, merlot, trebbiano and muscat. The vineyard and winery are located on a ridge, and the Volpatos say 'one glance at the surrounding Barrabool hills explains the choice made by the early Swiss settlers for establishing their vineyards on this land'.

TTT **Pinot Gris 2004** **RATING** 83

Wayne Thomas Wines ★★★★

26 Kangarilla Road, McLaren Vale, SA 5171 **REGION** McLaren Vale
T (08) 8323 9737 **F** (08) 8323 9737 **OPEN** Not
WINEMAKER Wayne Thomas, Tim Geddes **EST.** 1994 **CASES** 5000
Wayne Thomas is a McLaren Vale veteran, having started his winemaking career in 1961, working for Stonyfell, Ryecroft and Saltram before establishing Fern Hill with his late wife Pat in 1975. When they sold Fern Hill in 1994 they started again, launching the Wayne Thomas Wines label, using grapes sourced from 10 growers throughout McLaren Vale. Exports to the UK, the US, Canada and Hong Kong.

TTTTY **McLaren Vale Cabernet Sauvignon 2004** Good colour; as for the '04 Shiraz, excellent depth and flavour; blackcurrant, a touch of chocolate, ripe tannins and convincing oak. Cork. 13.5° alc. **RATING** 92 **DRINK** 2015 $ 28

McLaren Vale Shiraz 2004 Strong colour and hue; medium- to full-bodied; rich, firm and deep blackberry fruit; good length; needs time, but the best from Wayne Thomas for years. Cork. 14.5° alc. **RATING** 91 **DRINK** 2014 $ 28

TTTT **McLaren Vale Petit Verdot 2004** Dense, dark colour; extreme concentration and power, with very savoury/earthy tannins. Needs time or a barbecue rump steak. Cork. 14.5° alc. **RATING** 89 **DRINK** 2015 $ 30

McLaren Vale Shiraz 2003 Solid, medium-bodied wine, with savoury/earthy notes and regional chocolate; controlled oak. Cork. 14.5° alc. **RATING** 88 **DRINK** 2012 $ 28

TTTY **McLaren Vale Cabernet Sauvignon 2003** **RATING** 86 **DRINK** Now $ 28

McLaren Vale Petit Verdot 2003 **RATING** 85 **DRINK** Now $ 30

We're Estate

Cnr Wildberry Road/Johnson Road, Wilyabrup, WA 6280 **REGION** Margaret River
T (08) 9755 6273 **F** (08) 9755 6273 **WWW**.werewines.com.au **OPEN** Wed–Sun & public hols 10.30–5
WINEMAKER Jan Davies (Contract) **EST.** 1998 **CASES** 4000
Owners Diane and Gordon Davies say, 'We are different. We're original, we're bold, we're innovative'. This is all reflected in the design of the unusual back labels, incorporating pictures of the innumerable pairs of braces which real estate agent Gordon Davies wears on his Perth job; in the early move to screwcaps for both white and red wines; and, for that matter, in the underground trickle irrigation system in their Margaret River vineyard which can be controlled from Perth. Exports to the US, Philippines and Singapore.

ŸŸŸŸŸ **Margaret River Semillon Sauvignon Blanc 2005** Clean and fresh bouquet; deliciously brisk, bright and airy mouthfeel; perfect seafood wine. Screwcap. 13.3° alc. **RATING** 94 **DRINK** Now $18
Shiraz 2003 Very attractive supple, medium-bodied wine; red and black fruits with a touch of spice; good balance and length. **RATING** 94 **DRINK** 2013 $20

ŸŸŸŸŸ **Margaret River Sauvignon Blanc 2005** Attractive tropical, gooseberry and passionfruit mix; pleasing mouthfeel, good length. Screwcap. 14.6° alc. **RATING** 92 **DRINK** Now $20
Margaret River Semillon 2005 Well-made; big, generous and complex without being too heavy, thanks to the controlled alcohol; 5 months French oak maturation has done as much for texture as flavour. Screwcap. 12.9° alc. **RATING** 91 **DRINK** 2012 $22

ŸŸŸŸ **Cabernet Sauvignon 2003** Light- to medium-bodied; some blackcurrant fruit with savoury/earthy overtones; lingering tannins. Screwcap. 13.9° alc. **RATING** 87 **DRINK** 2008 $30

Wedgetail Estate

40 Hildebrand Road, Cottles Bridge, Vic 3099 **REGION** Yarra Valley
T (03) 9714 8661 **F** (03) 9714 8676 **WWW**.wedgetailestate.com.au **OPEN** W'ends & public hols 12–5, or by appt, closed from 25 Dec — reopens Australia Day weekend
WINEMAKER Guy Lamothe **EST.** 1994 **CASES** 1500
Canadian-born photographer Guy Lamothe and partner Dena Ashbolt started making wine in the basement of their Carlton home in the 1980s. The idea of their own vineyard started to take hold, and the search for a property began. Then, in their words, 'one Sunday, when we were "just out for a drive", we drove past our current home. The slopes are amazing, true goat terrain, and it is on these steep slopes that in 1994 we planted our first block of pinot noir.' While the vines were growing — they now have 5.5 ha in total — Lamothe enrolled in the wine-growing course at Charles Sturt University, having already gained practical experience working in the Yarra Valley (Tarrawarra), the Mornington Peninsula and Meursault. The net result is truly excellent wine. Exports to the UK, China and Singapore.

ŸŸŸŸŸ **Single Vineyard Pinot Noir 2004** Deeper colour than the Reserve; no reduction whatsoever; riper, more complex and more structure, though no more finesse. A whisker in it. Screwcap. 13.5° alc. **RATING** 94 **DRINK** 2013 $38

ŸŸŸŸŸ **Reserve Pinot Noir 2004** A classic example of how the colour (in this instance light) is no guide to the quality of pinot (in this instance long, intense and stylish). Cherry, plum and fine spice, the oak a pure support role. Diam. **RATING** 93 **DRINK** 2010 $60
Single Vineyard Shiraz 2004 Once again, no reduction; good colour, medium-bodied, smooth, supple spicy black cherry and plum fruit; ripe tannins. Screwcap. 14° alc. **RATING** 92 **DRINK** 2014 $38
Single Vineyard Chardonnay 2004 Rich, ripe melon, stone fruit and fig, the oak sotto voce, if at all; starting to show bottle development, and more flavour than finesse. Cork. 14° alc. **RATING** 90 **DRINK** 2010 $32

ŸŸŸŸ **The North Face Single Vineyard Cabernet Merlot 2003** Medium-bodied; savoury, earthy edges to the black fruits and mint, then quite warm mocha oak and ripe tannins. Cork. 13° alc. **RATING** 89 **DRINK** 2011 $32

Wedgetail Ridge Estate

NR

656 Kingsthorpe-Haden Road, Kingsthorpe, Qld 4400 **REGION** Darling Downs
T(07) 4699 3029 **F**(07) 4699 3371 **OPEN** 7 days 10–4
WINEMAKER Ross Whiteford **EST.** 1999 **CASES** NA
Suzanne Nation has established an 8-ha vineyard 30 km northeast of Toowoomba. It is planted to chardonnay, viognier, merlot, shiraz, cabernet sauvignon and durif, and the wine is made on the premises. Light meals are available at the café, but the primary purpose of the business is as a contract winemaking facility.

Wehl's Mount Benson Vineyards

NR

Wrights Bay Road, Mount Benson, SA 5275 **REGION** Mount Benson
T(08) 8768 6251 **F**(08) 8678 6251 **OPEN** 7 days 10–4
WINEMAKER Contract **EST.** 1989 **CASES** 1800
Peter and Leah Wehl were the first to plant vines in the Mount Benson area, beginning the establishment of their 24-ha vineyard (two-thirds shiraz and one-third cabernet sauvignon) in 1989. While primarily grapegrowers, they have moved into winemaking via contract makers, and plan to increase the range of wines available by grafting 1 ha of merlot and 1.5 ha of sauvignon blanc onto part of the existing plantings.

Wellington

★★★★★

Cnr Richmond Road/Denholms Road, Cambridge, Tas 7170 **REGION** Southern Tasmania
T(03) 6248 5844 **F**(03) 6248 5855 **OPEN** W'ends 10–5
WINEMAKER Andrew Hood, Jeremy Dineen **EST.** 1990 **CASES** 50 000
In 2003 the Wellington winery was acquired by Tony Scherer and Jack Kidwiler of Frogmore Creek. The Wellington winery will continue to operate as previously, making both its own label wines and wines for its other contract customers while a new winery is constructed on the Frogmore Creek property. The latter will be exclusively devoted to organically-grown wines; Andrew Hood will remain in charge of winemaking both at Wellington and at the new Frogmore Creek operation.

▼▼▼▼▼ **Chardonnay 2002** Superb intensity and focus; has the core of fine, minerally acidity which is peculiarly Tasmanian; citrus and stone fruit surrounds; extreme length. Has got better and better over the past 2 years. **RATING** 95 **DRINK** 2012 $ 32
Sauvignon Blanc 2005 Big juicy fruit style crammed with flavour and balancing acidity. Very much a reflection of the vintage. **RATING** 94 **DRINK** Now $ 23

▼▼▼▼▽ **Roaring 40s Chardonnay 2005** Ultra fragrant grapefruit and stone fruit; classic cool-grown wine; very subtle oak. **RATING** 93 **DRINK** 2009 $ 18

▼▼▼▼ **Riesling 2005** Firm and tightly focused mineral and citrus aromas and flavours; has good length. Simply needs time for higher points. **RATING** 89 **DRINK** 2012 $ 19
Chardonnay 2004 Sweet, ripe peachy fruit, but not particularly intense. **RATING** 87 **DRINK** 2009 $ 32
Roaring 40's Sparkling NV Attractive biscuity/brioche aromas; crisp, lively and long; lemony acidity. **RATING** 87 **DRINK** 2008 $ 19

▼▼▼▽ **Gewurztraminer 2005 RATING** 86 **DRINK** Now $ 23
Pinot Noir 2004 RATING 86 **DRINK** Now $ 50

Wellington Vale Wines

★★☆

'Wellington Vale', Deepwater, NSW 2371 (postal) **REGION** Northern Slopes Zone
T(02) 6734 5226 **F**(02) 6734 5226 **OPEN** Not
WINEMAKER Preston Peak (Rod McPherson) **EST.** 1997 **CASES** 230
David and Dierdri Robertson-Cuninghame trace their ancestry (via David) back to the Duke of Wellington, with Cuninghame Senior being the ADC to the Duke, and his son, Arthur Wellesley-Robertson, the godson. Arthur Wellesley migrated to Australia and took up the land upon which Wellington Vale is situated in 1839. Planting began in 1997 with 0.7 ha of semillon, and

continued with 1 ha of pinot noir and 0.3 ha of riesling. The first vintage was in 2000, and the subsequent vintages have won bronze medals at the competitive Australian Small Winemakers Show.

TTTT **Deepwater Red Pinot Noir 2005** RATING 84 DRINK Now $15

Wells Parish Wines   NR

Benerin Estate, Sydney Road, Kandos, NSW 2848 **REGION** Mudgee
T(02) 6379 4168 **F**(02) 6379 4996 **OPEN** By appt
WINEMAKER Philip Van Gent **EST.** 1995 **CASES** 1000
Richard and Rachel Trounson, with help from father Barry Trounson, have established 18 ha of vineyards at Benerin Estate since 1995. Most of the grapes are sold to Southcorp, but small quantities of wine are made for the Wells Parish label. The vineyards are at the eastern extremity of the Mudgee region, near Rylstone, and both the soils and climate are distinctly different from those of the traditional Mudgee area.

Welshmans Reef Vineyard   NR

Maldon–Newstead Road, Welshmans Reef, Vic 3462 **REGION** Bendigo
T(03) 5476 2733 **F**(03) 5476 2537 **WWW**.welshmansreef.com **OPEN** W'ends & public hols 10–5
WINEMAKER Ronald Snep **EST.** 1994 **CASES** 1200
The Snep family (Ronald, Jackson and Alexandra) began developing Welshmans Reef Vineyard in 1986, planting cabernet sauvignon, shiraz and semillon. Chardonnay and merlot were added in the early 1990s, with sauvignon blanc and tempranillo later. For some years the grapes were sold to other wineries, but in the early 1990s the Sneps decided to share winemaking facilities established in the Old Newstead Co-operative Butter Factory with several other small vineyards. When the Butter Factory facility was closed down, the Sneps built a winery and mudbrick tasting room onsite, 6 km north of Newstead.

Welwyn Meadows   NR

PO Box 62, Legana, Tas 7277 **REGION** Northern Tasmania
T(03) 6330 1467 **F**(03) 6330 3005 **WWW**.questhinterland.com **OPEN** Not
WINEMAKER Corey Baker (Contract) **EST.** 1998 **CASES** NA
Judith and Keith Starkey planted 1 ha each of chardonnay and pinot noir in 1998, doing it themselves with the benefit of a TAFE viticulture course, and followed up with a small winery commissioned for the 2005 vintage. A cellar door is planned, meanwhile the wines are available through the website and by mail order.

Wendouree

Wendouree Road, Clare, SA 5453 **REGION** Clare Valley
T(08) 8842 2896 **OPEN** By appt
WINEMAKER Tony Brady **EST.** 1895 **CASES** 2500
The iron fist in a velvet glove best describes these extraordinary wines. They are fashioned with passion and precision from the very old vineyard with its unique *terroir* by Tony and Lita Brady, who rightly see themselves as custodians of a priceless treasure. The 100-year-old stone winery is virtually unchanged from the day it was built; this is in every sense a treasure beyond price. For two reasons, neither Tony Brady nor I see any point in providing tasting notes for the most recently released vintage. First, the wines will have sold out (and there is no room for newcomers on the mailing list for the next release). Second, all I will ever be able to say is wait for 20 years before drinking the wine. I have purchased (as I always do) some of the most recent release wines, but neglected to taste them in time for this edition. Hence, the retention of the 5-star rating.

Wenzel Family Wines ★★★★

'Glenrowan', Step Road, Langhorne Creek, SA 5255 **REGION** Langhorne Creek
T (08) 8537 3035 **F** (08) 8537 3435 **WWW**.langhornewines.com.au **OPEN** By appt
WINEMAKER Greg Follett (Contract) **EST.** 2000 **CASES** 140
The Wenzel family left the Hartz Mountains in Germany in 1846 for Australia, and settled in
Langhorne Creek in 1853. Six generations later Dale and Lisa Wenzel run two vineyards, with a little
over 46 ha of chardonnay, merlot, shiraz, cabernet sauvignon and petit verdot. Over 90% of the
grapes are sold to other makers, with 65 cases of Shiraz and 85 cases of Cabernet produced each year;
'The Old Man's' label is a respectful tribute to Oscar (and Hazel) Wenzel who planted the first vines in
1968.

ϙϙϙϙϙ **The Old Man's Langhorne Creek Cabernet Sauvignon 2003** An attractive mix of cassis,
blackcurrant and spice; fine, ripe tannins; excellent medium-bodied, balanced palate.
RATING 90 **DRINK** 2010 $ 19

ϙϙϙϙ **The Old Man's Langhorne Creek Shiraz 2003** Spicy, cedary, earthy overtones to the core
of black fruits on the medium-bodied palate; the oak balanced, the alcohol restrained.
14° alc. **RATING** 88 **DRINK** 2009 $ 19

West Cape Howe Wines ★★★★★

Lot 42 South Coast Highway, Denmark, WA 6333 **REGION** Denmark
T (08) 9848 2959 **F** (08) 9848 2903 **OPEN** 7 days 10–5
WINEMAKER Gavin Berry, Dave Cleary, Coby Ladwig **EST.** 1997 **CASES** 55 000
After a highly successful 7 years, West Cape Howe founders Brenden and Kylie Smith moved on,
selling the business to a partnership including Gavin Berry (until May 2004, senior winemaker at
Plantagenet) and viticulturist Rob Quenby. As well as existing fruit sources, West Cape Howe now
has the 80-ha Lansdale Vineyard, planted in 1989, as its primary fruit source. The focus now will be
less on contract winemaking, and more on building the very strong West Cape Howe brand. Exports
to the US, Hong Kong, Singapore, Japan, Denmark and The Netherlands.

ϙϙϙϙϙ **Semillon Sauvignon Blanc 2005** Spotless, fine and elegant aromatic mix of gooseberry
and tropical fruit; a nice core of minerality woven through to a harmonious finish.
Screwcap. **RATING** 94 **DRINK** 2008 $ 16
Shiraz Viognier 2004 Attractive wine; lush black fruits with the touch of rounded
sweetness from the viognier; also a touch of chocolate and soft tannins. Cork. **RATING** 94
DRINK 2014 $ 24

ϙϙϙϙϙ **Riesling 2005** Floral apple and passionfruit; a smooth but powerful palate with lime
joining the characters of the bouquet; long finish. Screwcap. **RATING** 92 **DRINK** 2013 $ 19
Sauvignon Blanc 2005 Clean, crisp, correct and lively aromas; bright apple and
gooseberry palate; delicate, fresh finish. Screwcap. **RATING** 92 **DRINK** Now $ 19
Viognier 2005 Intensely fragrant aromas of apricot and gingerbread; a richly textured
palate with a touch of almost inevitable phenolics. Has a back label which tells the truth.
Screwcap. **RATING** 91 **DRINK** Now $ 19

ϙϙϙϙ **Unwooded Chardonnay 2005** As usual, offers more than most unwooded Chardonnays
on the market. Grapefruit and nectarine run through the light-bodied but long palate.
Screwcap. **RATING** 87 **DRINK** Now $ 16
Rose 2005 Strong pink colour; greater depth of flavour than many; red fruits and a twist
of spice and tobacco; 100% Cabernet Franc. Screwcap. **RATING** 87 **DRINK** Now $ 16

ϙϙϙϙ **Cabernet Merlot 2004** **RATING** 86 **DRINK** Now $ 16

Westend Estate Wines ★★★★

1283 Brayne Road, Griffith, NSW 2680 **REGION** Riverina
T (02) 6964 1506 **F** (02) 6969 0800 **WWW**.westendestate.com **OPEN** Mon–Fri 8.30–5, w'ends 10–4
WINEMAKER William Calabria, Bryan Currie **EST.** 1945 **CASES** 100 000
Along with a number of Riverina producers, Westend Estate is making a concerted move to lift both
the quality and the packaging of its wines. Its leading 3 Bridges range, which has an impressive array

of gold medals to its credit since being first released in 1997, is anchored in part on 20 ha of estate vineyards. Bill Calbaria has been involved in the Australian wine industry for more than 40 years, and is understandably proud of the achievements both of Westend and the Riverina wine industry as a whole. Exports to all major markets.

ΨΨΨΨΨ **3 Bridges Reserve Shiraz 2003** Exceptional colour for the vintage and region; medium-bodied blackberry and plum fruit married with mocha/vanilla oak; good tannins. Open-fermented, hand-plunged. **RATING** 92 **DRINK** 2013 $ 29.99

3 Bridges Golden Mist Botrytis Semillon 2004 Intense botrytis; honeyed cumquat and marmalade; citrussy acidity; good length. Cork. **RATING** 92 **DRINK** 2008 $ 20

3 Bridges Shiraz 2003 Traditional ripe shiraz style, with plenty of sweet black fruits welded with vanilla (American) oak. Estate-grown. Cork. 14.5° alc. **RATING** 91 **DRINK** 2008 $ 20

Calabria Private Bin Saint Macaire 2004 Good colour; very unusual spicy chocolate fruit characters, almost floral; not much structure on the finish other than lots of vanilla oak. An extremely rare and (says Jancis Robinson) inferior variety once planted in Bordeaux. Blue Gold medal Sydney International Wine Competition '06. Cork. 14° alc. **RATING** 90 **DRINK** 2012 $ 15

ΨΨΨΨ **3 Bridges Limited Release Merlot 2003** Far riper in taste than the alcohol suggests; cassis and blackcurrant closer to cabernet sauvignon in flavour; however, a nice red wine. Cork. 14° alc. **RATING** 89 **DRINK** 2010 $ 20

3 Bridges Durif 2003 Powerful and concentrated, but does keep the tannins under control; a full range of black fruits and prune. Cork. **RATING** 89 **DRINK** Now $ 25

3 Bridges Reserve Durif 2003 Dense, impenetrable colour; potent, powerful black fruits, leather and licorice; enthusiastic extraction not so necessary. Cork. 14.5° alc. **RATING** 89 **DRINK** 2013 $ 25

Richland Shiraz 2005 Strong purple-red; much more fruit depth and richness than most in this price bracket; possible skilled use of micro-oxygenation. Screwcap. 14.5° alc. **RATING** 88 **DRINK** 2009 $ 11

Richland Sauvignon Blanc 2005 Far more going for it than one might expect; good balance and mouthfeel; gooseberry and tropical fruit. Value. Screwcap. 12.5° alc. **RATING** 87 **DRINK** Now $ 11

Richland Viognier 2005 Light- to medium-bodied; ripe apricot and fruit salad; controlled alcohol and surprising varietal character; good mouthfeel. Screwcap. 14.5° alc. **RATING** 87 **DRINK** Now $ 11

3 Bridges Winemakers Selection Shiraz 2002 Very sweet fruit and lots of American oak; a pleasant wine from a great Riverland vintage, but not a patch on the Reserve. Cork. 14.5° alc. **RATING** 87 **DRINK** 2009 $ 20

ΨΨΨΨ **Richland Merlot 2005** **RATING** 86 **DRINK** 2008 $ 11

Richland Cabernet Sauvignon 2005 **RATING** 86 **DRINK** 2009 $ 11

3 Bridges Show Reserve Cabernet Sauvignon 2003 **RATING** 86 **DRINK** 2010 $ 25

Richland Chardonnay 2005 **RATING** 85 **DRINK** Now $ 11

3 Bridges Chardonnay 2004 **RATING** 85 **DRINK** Now $ 20

3 Bridges Winemakers Selection Cabernet Sauvignon 2002 **RATING** 85 **DRINK** Now $ 20

Western Range Wines ★★★★☆

1995 Chittering Road, Lower Chittering, WA 6084 **REGION** Perth Hills
T (08) 9571 8800 **F** (08) 9571 8844 **www**.westernrangewines.com.au **OPEN** Wed–Sun 10–5
WINEMAKER Ryan Sudano, John Griffiths (Consultant) **EST.** 2001 **CASES** 40 000
Between the mid-1990s and 2001, several prominent West Australians, including Marilyn Corderory, Malcolm McCusker, Terry and Kevin Prindiville and Tony Rechner, have established approximately 125 ha of vines (under separate ownerships) in the Perth Hills, with a kaleidoscopic range of varietals. The next step was to join forces to build a substantial winery. This is a separate venture, but takes the grapes from the individual vineyards and markets the wine under the Western Range brand. In 2004 the releases were rebranded and regrouped at 4 levels: Lot 88, Goyamin Pool, Julimar and Julimar Organic. The label designs are clear and attractive. Exports to the UK, the US and other major markets.

ɣɣɣɣ¥ **Julimar Shiraz Viognier 2004** Light- to medium-bodied; attractive spicy elements throughout blackberry and black cherry fruit, plus the usual viognier lift; fine tannins and overall elegance. Cork. 14° alc. **RATING** 93 **DRINK** 2012 $ 22
Julimar Viognier 2005 A lively array of varietal flavours: peach, musk, lychee, apricot kernel, yet avoids heaviness or cloying characters. Screwcap. 14° alc. **RATING** 90 **DRINK** Now $ 22
Lot 88 Chenin Verdelho 2005 A surprise, with tangy citrussy flavours and acidity stopping the wine from cloying; academic good cellaring capacity. Screwcap. 13.5° alc. **RATING** 90 **DRINK** 2009 $ 13
Goyamin Pool Chardonnay Viognier 2005 Attractive peach, apricot and passionfruit aromas and flavours; both the oak and the alcohol have been very well controlled. Screwcap. 13.5° alc. **RATING** 90 **DRINK** Now $ 16

ɣɣɣɣ **Julimar Tempranillo 2004** Vivid hue, though very light; a light lunch red with nicely balanced cherry and strawberry fruit. Screwcap. 13.5° alc. **RATING** 87 **DRINK** 2009 $ 22

ɣɣɣ¥ **Goyamin Pool Cabernet Malbec 2004** **RATING** 86 **DRINK** 2009 $ 16

Westgate Vineyard

180 Westgate Road, Armstrong, Vic 3377 **REGION** Grampians
T (03) 5356 2394 **F** (03) 5356 2594 **WWW.**westgatevineyard.com.au **OPEN** At Garden Gully
WINEMAKER Bruce Dalkin **EST.** 1997 **CASES** 400
Westgate has been in the Dalkin family ownership since the 1860s, the present owners Bruce and Robyn Dalkin being the sixth generation owners of the property, which today focuses on grape production, a small winery and 4-star accommodation. There are now 14 ha of vineyards, progressively established since 1969, including a key holding of 10 ha of shiraz; most of the grapes are sold to Mount Langi Ghiran and others, but a vigneron's licence was obtained in 1999 and a small amount of high-quality wine is made under the Westgate Vineyard label.

ɣɣɣɣɣ **Endurance Shiraz 2004** A wonderfully elegant and fragrant medium-bodied wine, with very pure blackberry shiraz fruit; fine tannins, long finish. Screwcap. 13.5° alc. **RATING** 95 **DRINK** 2018 $ 48
Shiraz Cabernet 2002 Holding hue well; deliciously fragrant and elegant in typical Westgate style; while no more than medium-bodied, the lovely, fresh blackcurrant and blackberry fruit has immaculate length and tannin support. Cork. 13° alc. **RATING** 94 **DRINK** 2015 $ 20

ɣɣɣɣ¥ **Riesling 2005** Crisp, elegant, floral lime and citrus; good length and acidity. Screwcap. 13° alc. **RATING** 90 **DRINK** 2011 $ 22

Whale Coast Wines   NR

65 Ocean Street, Victor Harbor, SA 5211 **REGION** Southern Fleurieu
T (08) 8552 1444 **F** (08) 8552 2611 **OPEN** By appt
WINEMAKER Cascabel, TK Wines **EST.** 1994 **CASES** 2000
This is the venture of obstetrician and general practitioner David Batt, partner Chris and their 5 children, no longer a hobby, as one of the daughters is completing oenology studies at Adelaide University. Since purchasing the 64-ha farm in 1994, 25 ha of vineyard has been planted, to shiraz, cabernet sauvignon, riesling, sauvignon blanc, viognier, tempranillo, merlot and petit verdot. The house on the Whale Coast Wines vineyard (built in 1852) is being gradually restored. Most of the grapes have been sold to Cascabel who make the red wines. The first white wine, 2004 Crockery Bay Sauvignon Blanc, was made by Tim Knappstein. Exports to the US and the UK.

Wharncliffe ★★★

Summerleas Road, Kingston, Tas 7050 **REGION** Southern Tasmania
T (03) 6229 7147 **F** (03) 6229 2298 **OPEN** W'ends by appt, phone 0438 297 147
WINEMAKER Hood Wines (Andrew Hood) **EST.** 1990 **CASES** 125
With total plantings of 0.75 ha, Wharncliffe could not exist without the type of contract-winemaking service offered by Andrew Hood, which would be a pity, because the vineyard is beautifully situated on the doorstep of Mt Wellington, the Huon Valley and the Channel regions of southern Tasmania.

ŸŸŸŸ **Chardonnay 2005** Nice balance, and some length; nectarine and stone fruit through to a soft finish. **RATING** 87 **DRINK** Now

Whiskey Gully Wines NR

Beverley Road, Severnlea, Qld 4352 **REGION** Granite Belt
T (07) 4683 5100 **F** (07) 4683 5155 **WWW**.whiskeygullywines.com.au **OPEN** 7 days 9–5
WINEMAKER Philippa Hambleton, Rod MacPherson (Contract) **EST.** 1997 **CASES** 500
Close inspection of the winery letterhead discloses that The Media Mill Pty Ltd trades as Whiskey Gully Wines. It is no surprise, then, to find proprietor John Arlidge saying, 'Wine and politics are a heady mix; I have already registered the 2000 Republic Red as a voter in 26 marginal electorates and we are considering nominating it for Liberal Party pre-selection in Bennelong'. Wit to one side, John Arlidge has big plans for Whiskey Gully Wines: to establish 40 ha of vineyards, extending the varietal range with petit verdot, malbec, merlot, semillon and sauvignon blanc. So far, the plans are moving very slowly.

Whispering Brook ★★★★☆

Hill Street, Broke, NSW 2330 **REGION** Lower Hunter Valley
T (02) 9818 4126 **F** (02) 9818 4156 **WWW**.whispering-brook.com **OPEN** By appt
WINEMAKER Nick Patterson, Susan Frazier **EST.** 2000 **CASES** 900
Susan Frazier and Adam Bell say the choice of Whispering Brook was the result of a 5-year search to find the ideal viticultural site (while studying for wine science degrees at Charles Sturt University). Some may wonder whether the Broke subregion of the Hunter Valley needed such persistent effort to locate, but the property does in fact have a combination of terra rossa loam soils on which the reds are planted, and sandy flats for the white wines. The partners have also established an olive grove and accommodation for 6–14 guests in the large house set in the vineyard. Exports to the UK and South-East Asia.

ŸŸŸŸŸ **Limited Release Chardonnay 2005** Very good focus; intense, lingering grapefruit and nectarine; oak in support role; clean, fresh finish. Beautifully made. Cork. 13.7° alc. **RATING** 94 **DRINK** 2010 $ 21

Whispering Hills ★★★★☆

580 Warburton Highway, Seville, Vic 3139 **REGION** Yarra Valley
T (03) 5964 2822 **F** (03) 5964 2064 **WWW**.whisperinghills.com.au **OPEN** 7 days 10–6
WINEMAKER Murray Lyons **EST.** 1985 **CASES** 1200
Whispering Hills is owned and operated by the Lyons family (Murray, Marie and Audrey). Murray (with a degree in viticulture and oenology from Charles Sturt University) concentrates on the vineyard and winemaking, Marie (with a background in sales and marketing) and Audrey take care of the cellar door and distribution of the wines. The 3.5-ha vineyard was established in 1985 (riesling, chardonnay and cabernet sauvignon), with further plantings in 1996, and some grafting in 2003.

ŸŸŸŸŸ **The Reserve Yarra Valley Pinot Noir 2004** Saturated, sweet plummy fruit; well above-average intensity and length for the high-yielding '04 vintage, but not over-extracted. Screwcap. 14° alc. **RATING** 94 **DRINK** 2011 $ 35

ŸŸŸŸ **Audrey Mae Yarra Valley Chardonnay 2004** Delicate stone fruit and citrus aromas; light-bodied nectarine fruit with minimal oak impact. Screwcap. 13° alc. **RATING** 88 **DRINK** 2010 $ 22

Whisson Lake

Lot 2, Gully Road, Carey Gully, SA 5144 **REGION** Adelaide Hills
T (08) 8390 1303 **F** (08) 8390 3822 **WWW**.whissonlake.com **OPEN** By appt
WINEMAKER Mark Whisson **EST.** 1985 **CASES** 400
Mark Whisson (a plant biochemist) is primarily a grapegrower, with 5 ha of close-planted, steep-sloped north-facing vineyard on Mt Carey in the Piccadilly Valley. Over the years small portions of the grape production have been vinified under the Whisson Lake label, initially by Roman Bratasiuk, then Dave Powell of Torbreck, but since 2002 by Mark Whisson. The wine has a consistent style, distinctly savoury, and ages well. His partners in the venture are Bruce Lake (a Perth-based engineer) and Bill Bisset, who has helped broaden the business base to include Pinot Gaz (an early-drinking Pinot), Shiraz from the Adelaide Hills, and Grenache from Blewitt Springs. Tiny quantities are exported to the US and the UK.

TTTT **Grenache 2004** Opens with sweet, juicy red fruits then quickly changes gear into persistent tannins with savoury overtones. Could well be accused of being schizoid. Screwcap. **RATING** 89 **DRINK** 2012 $ 38

Whistle Stop Wines NR

8 Elk Street, Nanango, Qld 4615 **REGION** South Burnett
T (07) 4163 2222 **F** (07) 4163 2288 **WWW**.whistlestop.com.au **OPEN** Wed–Sun 10–5
WINEMAKER Symphony Hill (Mike Hayes) **EST.** 1998 **CASES** 400
Terry and Margaret Walsh are the fourth generation to have carried on farming on the property settled by their ancestor John Walsh in 1861. The location of the cellar door, a renovated 1937 cottage in the town of Nanango, gave rise to the name, as it is next to a railway line which operated between 1911 and 1964. The wines are made from 1.5 ha of cabernet sauvignon, 0.5 ha of recently grafted verdelho and a small amount of viognier, and also from purchased grapes.

Whistler Wines

Seppeltsfield Road, Marananga, SA 5355 **REGION** Barossa Valley
T (08) 8562 4942 **F** (08) 8562 4943 **WWW**.whistlerwines.com **OPEN** 7 days 10.30–5
WINEMAKER Troy Kalleske, Christa Deans (Contract) **EST.** 1999 **CASES** 7000
Whistler Wines had a dream start at the 2000 Barossa Valley Wine Show, when its 2000 Semillon won trophies for Best Dry White and for Most Outstanding Barossa White Table Wine. Add to that the distinguished US importer Weygandt-Metzler, and it is no surprise to find the sold out sign going up on the extremely attractive (modern) galvanised iron cellar door building. The operation is presently based on 5 ha of shiraz, 2 ha each of semillon and merlot and 1 ha of cabernet sauvignon, with an additional 4 ha of grenache, mourvedre and riesling planted in 2001. The hope is to gradually increase production to match existing demand. Exports to the US and Canada.

TTTT **The Reserve Barossa Semillon 2004** Brilliant, glowing green-yellow; a rich, flavoursome style with lemon tart flavours and abundant mouthfeel; quick developing. Screwcap. 12° alc. **RATING** 89 **DRINK** 2008 $ 19
Riesling 2005 A powerful mix of tropical fruit and firm acidity, the dry finish a distinct plus. Screwcap. 12° alc. **RATING** 88 **DRINK** 2009 $ 15
The Rose Barossa Grenache 2004 Quite complex; distinct grenache varietal character; multi-spice and cherry jam fruit; dry finish. Has character. Screwcap. 12.8° alc. **RATING** 87 **DRINK** Now $ 15
Barossa Merlot 2003 Very ripe and sweet, not especially varietal; mocha/vanilla oak a contributor to the overall flavour, though not necessarily the varietal character. Screwcap. 14° alc. **RATING** 87 **DRINK** 2011 $ 23

TTTY **The Black Piper Sparkling Merlot NV** Plenty of flavour, with intriguing touches of chocolate; far better than imagined; I am not normally well disposed to anything other than sparkling shiraz. **RATING** 86 **DRINK** Now $ 28
Barossa Cabernet Merlot 2004 **RATING** 85 **DRINK** 2008 $ 19

Whitehorse Wines

NR

4 Reid Park Road, Mount Clear, Vic 3350 **REGION** Ballarat
T (03) 5330 1719 **F** (03) 5330 1288 **OPEN** W'ends 11–5
WINEMAKER Noel Myers **EST.** 1981 **CASES** 900
The Myers family has moved from grapegrowing to winemaking, using the attractive site on its sloping hillside south of Ballarat. There are 4 ha of vines in production, with pinot noir and chardonnay the principal varieties.

Whitsend Estate

52 Boundary Road, Coldstream, Vic 3770 **REGION** Yarra Valley
T (03) 9739 1917 **F** (03) 9739 0217 **WWW**.whitsend.com.au **OPEN** By appt
WINEMAKER Quercus Oenology (Paul Evans) **EST.** 1998 **CASES** 500
The Baldwin family, headed by Ross and Simone, but with Trish, Tim and Jenny all involved in one way or another, have planted a 13-ha vineyard to pinot noir, shiraz, merlot, viognier and cabernet sauvignon. Most of the production is sold to local wineries; a small amount is retained for the Baldwins. Exports to the US and Canada.

🍷🍷🍷🍷🍷 **Yarra Valley Cabernet Sauvignon 2004** Impressively deep colour; rich, ripe blackcurrant and cassis fruit is the heart of a lovely wine, good tannin and oak management the icing on the cake. Cork. 13.5° alc. **RATING** 94 **DRINK** 2016 $ 23

🍷🍷🍷🍷🍷 **Yarra Valley Merlot 2004** An admirable varietal mix of red fruits, spice and black olive flavours, with fine tannin structure; the finish and aftertaste are good. Diam. 13.5° alc. **RATING** 90 **DRINK** 2011 $ 24

Wignalls Wines

448 Chester Pass Road (Highway 1), Albany, WA 6330 **REGION** Albany
T (08) 9841 2848 **F** (08) 9842 9003 **WWW**.wignallswines.com.au **OPEN** 7 days 11–4
WINEMAKER Rob Wignall **EST.** 1982 **CASES** 6000
A noted producer of Pinot Noir which extended the map for the variety in Australia, the 2004 and 2005 Pinots a welcome return to form. The white wines are elegant, and show the cool climate to good advantage. A winery was constructed in 1998 and uses the production from the 16 ha of estate plantings. Exports to the UK, Japan, Taiwan and Denmark.

🍷🍷🍷🍷🍷 **Albany Pinot Noir 2005** Good colour; rich plum fruit; much more depth than in earlier vintages; good balance, and will develop well. Screwcap. **RATING** 94 **DRINK** 2010 $ 30

🍷🍷🍷🍷🍷 **Albany Pinot Noir 2004** Bright, light red-purple; fragrant and delicate; fresh strawberry and cherry fruit, well-balanced and unforced. Trophy for Best Pinot Noir at 2005 Qantas WA Wine Show. Cork. 13.5° alc. **RATING** 92 **DRINK** 2008 $ 27
Chardonnay 2005 Clean, fresh and lively stone fruit/nectarine/grapefruit supported by subtle oak; good length. Screwcap. 13° alc. **RATING** 90 **DRINK** 2009 $ 25
Shiraz 2004 Fresh, bright, elegant fruit-driven style; raspberry and blackberry flavours, fine tannins. Cork. 14° alc. **RATING** 90 **DRINK** 2010 $ 21

🍷🍷🍷🍷 **Unwooded Chardonnay 2005** Quite intense and rich; a mix of ripe stone fruit and lemony acidity; nice balance and length. Well above average. Screwcap. 14° alc. **RATING** 87 **DRINK** Now $ 16.80

🍷🍷🍷 **Chardonnay 2004 RATING** 86 **DRINK** Now $ 19.50

🐌 Wild Cattle Creek Winery

473 Warburton Highway, Wandin, Vic 3139 **REGION** Yarra Valley
T (03) 5964 4755 **F** (03) 5967 1182 **WWW**.wildcattlecreek.com **OPEN** Wed–Sun 11–5, or by appt
WINEMAKER Jeff Wright **EST.** 1996 **CASES** 800
This is the (much-altered) reincarnation of Langbrook Estate Vineyard, continuing under the ownership of Graeme and Ingrid Smith. It has 10 ha of pinot noir, chardonnay, sauvignon blanc, pinot gris and cabernet sauvignon, and the Sauvignon Blanc, in particular, has had significant show success.

ŸŸŸŸ℩ Yarra Valley Sauvignon Blanc 2005 Clean, gently tropical bouquet; excellent line, intensity and minerally grip to the palate; demands attention. Screwcap. 13.6° alc.
RATING 93 DRINK Now $19
Yarra Valley Sauvignon Blanc 2004 Spotlessly clean bouquet; attractive passionfruit and grapefruit mix, the palate lengthened by a flick of sweetness on the finish. That sweetness did not faze the judges at the '05 Yarra Valley Wine Show, which awarded the wine a gold medal. Screwcap. 12.9° alc. RATING 92 DRINK Now $21
Yarra Valley Rose 2004 A particularly attractive style; vibrant, zesty red fruits with a long finish which is not sweet, the wine still very much alive. Screwcap. 13.3° alc. RATING 90
DRINK Now $18

ŸŸŸŸ Yarra Valley Chardonnay 2004 Light-bodied and direct; clean, fresh, zesty, citrus-tinged nectarine fruit. Screwcap. 13.7° alc. RATING 89 DRINK 2008 $19
Yarra Valley Pinot Noir 2004 Clean and correct; notwithstanding the alcohol, only light- to medium-bodied, with sweet black cherry fruit and minimal oak impact. Cork. 14.3° alc.
RATING 89 DRINK 2009 $22

ŸŸŸ℩ Yarra Valley Cabernet Merlot 2003 RATING 86 DRINK 2008 $23
Yarra Valley Cabernet Merlot 2004 RATING 85 DRINK 2008 $23
Yarra Valley Cabernet Sauvignon 2002 RATING 85 DRINK Now $22

Wild Dog ★★★★

South Road, Warragul, Vic 3820 **REGION** Gippsland
T (03) 5623 1117 **F** (03) 5623 6402 **www**.wilddogwinery.com **OPEN** 7 days 10–5
WINEMAKER Mal Stewart **EST.** 1982 **CASES** 3500
An aptly named winery which produces somewhat rustic wines from the 12 ha of estate vineyards; even the Farringtons say that the 'Shiraz comes with a bite', but they also point out that there is minimal handling, fining and filtration. Following the acquisition of Wild Dog by Gary and Judy Surman, Mal Stewart was appointed winemaker with a far ranging brief to build on the legacy of the previous owners. As the tasting notes indicate, there is much to be confident about.

ŸŸŸŸ℩ Gippsland Riesling 2005 Bright straw-green; clean, tight minerally/savoury flavour; good length and line; lingering, dry finish. Screwcap. 13° alc. RATING 92 DRINK 2015 $19
Shiraz 2004 Good purple-red; clean, aromatic black cherry and spice fruit; medium- to full-bodied, supple black cherry, plum and blackberry; good oak, quality wine. Screwcap. 14° alc. RATING 92 DRINK 2015 $20
Gippsland Pinot Noir 2004 Rich, ripe plum, spice and black cherry fruit; good mouthfeel and length. Screwcap. 13° alc. RATING 91 DRINK 2009 $20
Gippsland Chardonnay 2005 Bright, light straw-green; gentle nectarine and white peach fruit with a hint of sweetness; subtle oak. Screwcap. 13° alc. RATING 90 DRINK 2008 $20

ŸŸŸŸ Gippsland Cabernets 2003 Powerful, rustic, earthy wine; black fruits and persistent tannins. Screwcap. 13° alc. RATING 88 DRINK 2010 $20
Unoaked Chardonnay 2005 Light- to medium-bodied; clean, fresh citrus and nectarine fruit flavours; well-made unoaked style. RATING 87 DRINK Now $20
Gippsland Wild Rose 2005 Some attractive juicy red fruit flavours; balancing acidity. Screwcap. 13° alc. RATING 87 DRINK Now $17
Red Dog NV Plenty of red and black fruit; good structure and length; good value. Screwcap. 13° alc. RATING 87 DRINK 2008 $15

ŸŸŸ℩ Museum Release Gippsland Riesling 1998 Golden yellow, hanging in there rather better than the colour might suggest; still has intact flavour and acidity. Cork. 13° alc.
RATING 86 DRINK Now $22
White Dog NV RATING 86 DRINK Now $15

ŸŸŸ Dancing Dog NV RATING 83 $15

Wild Duck Creek Estate

NR

Spring Flat Road, Heathcote, Vic 3523 **REGION** Heathcote
T (03) 5433 3133 **F** (03) 5433 3133 **OPEN** By appt
WINEMAKER David Anderson **EST.** 1980 **CASES** 4000
The first release of Wild Duck Creek Estate from the 1991 vintage marked the end of 12 years of effort by David and Diana Anderson. They began planting the 4.5-ha vineyard in 1980, made their first tiny quantities of wine in 1986, the first commercial quantities of wine in 1991, and built their winery and cellar door facility in 1993. Exports to the US (where Duck Muck has become a cult wine), the UK and other major markets.

Wild Geese Wines

★★★

PO Box 1157, Balhanna, SA 5242 **REGION** Adelaide Hills
T (08) 8388 4464 **F** (08) 8388 4464 **OPEN** Not
WINEMAKER Patrick O'Sullivan **EST.** 2000 **CASES** 400
Patrick, a graduate of Charles Sturt University, and Amanda O'Sullivan (and 2 business partners) have established a trial planting of 4 clones of merlot, and have found the difference between each of the clones to be substantial. The Wild Geese name, incidentally, comes from the Irish emigres who fled religious and political persecution in the 18th century to settle elsewhere.

▼▼▼▼ **Adelaide Hills Merlot 2003** Strongly varietal, particularly on the savoury acidity to the finish; spicy fruit with green and black olive accents. **RATING** 88 **DRINK** 2009 $ 24

Wild Orchid Wines

★★★★☆

PO Box 165, Boyup Brook, WA 6244 **REGION** Blackwood Valley
T (08) 9767 3058 **F** (08) 9767 3058 **WWW**.wildorchidwines.mysouthwest.com.au **OPEN** Not
WINEMAKER Frank Kittler (Contract), Brad Skraha **EST.** 1997 **CASES** 1000
Orest, Robyn and Brad Skraha have established a little under 16 ha of chardonnay, shiraz, merlot and cabernet sauvignon. Most of the grapes are sold, the remainder made by Brad Skraha. Brad completed his bachelor of science in viticulture and oenology at Curtin University after working at the Chappellet winery in the Napa Valley. His time in California has led to a small export market to Canada; in Australia the wines are available through mail order.

▼▼▼▼▼ **Blackwood Valley Cabernet Merlot 2003** Fragrant, clean and fresh blackcurrant, cassis, mocha and chocolate; fine tannins support the light- to medium-bodied frame; good length. Attractive. Screwcap. **RATING** 91 **DRINK** 2010 $ 19.50
Blackwood Valley Shiraz 2003 A savoury, spicy backdrop to the medium-bodied plum and dark cherry fruit; fine tannins and gentle oak; very nice wine. Screwcap. **RATING** 90 **DRINK** 2010 $ 18

Wild Soul

NR

Horans Gorge Road, Glen Aplin, Qld 4381 **REGION** Granite Belt
T (07) 4683 4201 **F** (07) 4683 4201 **WWW**.wildsoul.netfirms.com **OPEN** W'ends & public hols 10–4
WINEMAKER Andy Boullier **EST.** 1996 **CASES** 350
Andy and Beth Boullier have been on the land their whole lives, in various capacities, before buying their small property at Glen Aplin. They have established a little over 1 ha of vines, more or less equally split between cabernet sauvignon and shiraz, with a little merlot. They use organic principles in growing the fruit, which is a challenge for themselves, compounded by birds, drought, kangaroos and bushfires. Andy Boullier makes the wine onsite.

Wildcroft Estate

NR

98 Stanleys Road, Red Hill South, Vic 3937 **REGION** Mornington Peninsula
T (03) 5989 2646 **F** (03) 9783 9469 **OPEN** 7 days 10–5
WINEMAKER Bass Phillip **EST.** 1988 **CASES** 650
Wildcroft Estate is the brainchild of Devendra Singh, best known as the owner of one of Vic's oldest Indian restaurants. In 1988 he purchased the land upon which 4 ha of pinot noir, chardonnay, shiraz

and cabernet sauvignon have been established, with the management and much of the physical work carried out by Devendra's wife Shashi Singh, who is currently undertaking a viticulture course. The vineyard is one of the few unirrigated vineyards on the Peninsula. The mudbrick cellar door also has a restaurant — Café 98 — allowing Devendra Singh to explore the matching of Indian food with wine. Chef Lindsey Perry serves modern cuisine with Indian and Middle Eastern influences, using local produce wherever possible.

Wildwood
NR

St John's Lane, Wildwood, Bulla, Vic 3428 **REGION** Sunbury
T (03) 9307 1118 **F** (03) 9331 1590 **WWW**.wildwoodvineyards.com.au **OPEN** 7 days 10–5
WINEMAKER Dr Wayne Stott, Clarissa Park **EST.** 1983 **CASES** 800
Wildwood is just 4 km past Melbourne airport, at an altitude of 130m in the Oaklands Valley, which provides unexpected views back to Port Phillip Bay and the Melbourne skyline. Plastic surgeon Dr Wayne Stott has taken what is very much a part-time activity rather more seriously than most by completing the wine science degree at Charles Sturt University.

Wildwood of Yallingup
NR

PO Box 108, Yallingup, WA 6282 **REGION** Margaret River
T (08) 9755 2066 **F** (08) 9755 2301 **WWW**.wildwoodwines.com **OPEN** Not
WINEMAKER James Pennington **EST.** 1984 **CASES** 3000
In the wake of the demise of the Hotham Valley wine group, and its subsequent restructuring and renaming, James Pennington acquired the 5.5-ha Wildwood vineyard, planted in the mid-1980s. The vineyard was established without irrigation and remains dry-grown. All the future releases will be under the Wildwood of Yallingup label or Pennington.

Wilkie Estate
NR

Lot 1, Heaslip Road, Penfield, SA 5121 **REGION** Adelaide Plains
T (08) 8284 7655 **F** (08) 8284 7618 **OPEN** 7 days 10–5
WINEMAKER Trevor Spurr **EST.** 1990 **CASES** NA
Trevor and Bill Spurr have 17.5 ha of organic-certified vineyards planted to verdelho, cabernet sauvignon, merlot and ruby cabernet. They make the wine onsite, and have established exports to the UK and Japan.

Will Taylor Wines

1B Victoria Avenue, Unley Park, SA 5061 **REGION** Southeast Australia
T (08) 8271 6122 **F** (08) 8271 6122 **OPEN** By appt
WINEMAKER Various contract **EST.** 1997 **CASES** 1500
Will Taylor is a partner in the leading Adelaide law firm Finlaysons, and specialises in wine law. He and Suzanne Taylor have established a classic negociant wine business, having wines contract-made to their specifications. Moreover, they choose what they consider the best regions for each variety. Exports to the UK, Hong Kong and Malaysia.

TTTTT **Adelaide Hills Sauvignon Blanc 2005** Straw-green; clean, lively and zesty citrus and passionfruit; a long and lingering palate built on the framework of good acidity. Screwcap. 13° alc. **RATING** 94 **DRINK** 2008 $ 21

TTTTY **Yarra Valley Geelong Pinot Noir 2004** Some colour development; a complex array of flavours, all gentle; spice, plum and cherry; silky tannins; seductive, early-drinking style. Cork. 13.5° alc. **RATING** 93 **DRINK** 2009 $ 37

TTTT **Coonawarra Cabernet Sauvignon 2004** Cedary/earthy/spicy black fruits; ripe tannins, and assistance from French oak. Cork. 14.5° alc. **RATING** 89 **DRINK** 2015 $ 37

Willespie ★★★★☆

Harmans Mill Road, Wilyabrup via Cowaramup, WA 6284 **REGION** Margaret River
T (08) 9755 6248 **F** (08) 9755 6210 **WWW**.willespie.com.au **OPEN** 7 days 10.30–5
WINEMAKER Kevin Squance **EST.** 1976 **CASES** 7000
Willespie has produced many attractive white wines over the years, typically in brisk, herbaceous
Margaret River style, all are fruit, rather than oak, driven. The wines have had such success that the
Squance family (which founded and owns Willespie) has substantially increased winery capacity,
drawing upon an additional 24 ha of estate vineyards now in bearing. Exports to the UK, the US and
other major markets.

ŸŸŸŸŸ **Chardonnay 1999** Persuasive green-yellow; has aged as well as all high-quality Margaret
River chardonnays can do; nectarine, melon and a touch of citrus; good acidity, the oak
long since integrated. What a bargain; looks as if it may have been recorked. Cork.
13.5° alc. **RATING** 94 **DRINK** 2010 $ 22

ŸŸŸŸŸ **Shiraz 2001** Spicy, dusty, herbal aromas; light- to medium-bodied; cherry and spice fruit
continues through the long finish; developing well, a classic vintage. Cork. 13.5° alc.
RATING 91 **DRINK** 2011 $ 25
Sauvignon Blanc 2005 Very pale; a relatively soft, but flavoursome, mix of ripe varietal
flavours from gooseberry, passionfruit through to herbs and grass. Screwcap. 13° alc.
RATING 90 **DRINK** Now $ 18
Semillon Sauvignon Blanc 2005 Remarkably similar to the Sauvignon Blanc, but with
more mineral and grass components, albeit still with soft, mouthfilling fruit. This despite
92.5% Semillon. Screwcap. 13.5° alc. **RATING** 90 **DRINK** 2010 $ 18

ŸŸŸŸ **Verdelho 2005 RATING** 86 **DRINK** 2008 $ 17
Cabernet Sauvignon 1999 RATING 86 **DRINK** 2008 $ 35
Verdelho 2001 RATING 85 **DRINK** Now $ 1750

William Downie ★★★★☆

PO Box 1024, Healesville, Vic 3777 **REGION** Yarra Valley
T 0400 654 512 **F** (03) 5962 6630 **OPEN** Not
WINEMAKER William Downie **EST.** 2003 **CASES** 300
William Downie spends 6 months each year making wine in Burgundy, the other 6 based in the Yarra
Valley with De Bortoli. He uses purchased grapes from older vines to make the wines, avoiding the
use of pumps, filtration and fining. The striking label, designed by artist Reg Mombassa, has helped
obtain listings at The Prince Wine Store and elsewhere.

ŸŸŸŸ **Yarra Valley Pinot Noir 2004** Star-bright, light red-purple; bright, tight, fresh red fruits;
an ascetic Burgundian influence is very obvious; relatively early picked (13° alcohol).
Diam. **RATING** 92 **DRINK** 2011 $ 45

Williams Springs Road NR

76 Dauncey Street, Kingscote, Kangaroo Island, SA 5223 **REGION** Kangaroo Island
T (08) 8553 2053 **F** (08) 8553 3042 **OPEN** By appt
WINEMAKER Contract **EST.** 1995 **CASES** 500
Roger and Kate Williams have established 11 ha of chardonnay, cabernet sauvignon, shiraz and petit
verdot. Most of the grapes are sold to Kangaroo Island Trading Co; a small amount of Chardonnay
and Shiraz are made under the Williams Springs Road label.

Willow Bridge Estate ★★★★★

Gardin Court Drive, Dardanup, WA 6236 **REGION** Geographe
T (08) 9728 0055 **F** (08) 9728 0066 **WWW**.willowbridgeestate.com **OPEN** 7 days 11–5
WINEMAKER David Crawford **EST.** 1997 **CASES** 40 000
The Dewar family has followed a fast track in developing Willow Bridge Estate since acquiring the
spectacular 180-ha hillside property in the Ferguson Valley in 1996: 70 ha of chardonnay, semillon,
sauvignon blanc, shiraz and cabernet sauvignon were planted, with tempranillo added in 2000. The

winery is capable of handling the 1200–1500 tonnes from the estate plantings. Exports to the UK, the US and other major markets.

ŢŢŢŢŢ Family Reserve Pemberton Sauvignon Blanc 2005 Spotlessly clean; delicate, but perfectly poised and balanced, citrus, passionfruit and herb flavours; very good acidity on the bright finish. Screwcap. 13.5° alc. **RATING** 94 **DRINK** Now $ 20
Geographe Sauvignon Blanc Semillon 2005 Clean, fine, vibrant and long; lemon, citrus and passionfruit; good length and acidity. Screwcap. 13.5° alc. **RATING** 94 **DRINK** 2008 $ 14.50
The Black Dog Shiraz 2002 Sumptuous, velvety, rich black and red fruits; fine, ripe tannins; good oak. **RATING** 94 **DRINK** 2017 $ 60

ŢŢŢŢŢ Family Reserve Pemberton Semillon 2005 A complex, rich wine; the strong winemaker inputs (barrel ferment, lees contact and oak maturation) work well, enriching the fruit and giving texture. Needed just a touch more acidity. Cork. 13° alc. **RATING** 93 **DRINK** 2012 $ 20
Rose 2005 Bright pink-purple; fresh cherry and raspberry flavours; unusual length, and excellent balance between sweetness and acidity. Gold medal 2005 Qantas WA Wine Show. Screwcap. 13.5° alc. **RATING** 92 **DRINK** Now $ 14

ŢŢŢŢ Geographe Unwooded Chardonnay 2005 A pretty wine, with sweet nectarine fruit, and fresh acidity. Screwcap. 13.5° alc. **RATING** 88 **DRINK** 2009 $ 14.50
Geographe Cabernet Merlot 2004 Good hue; light- to medium-bodied; lively, sweet red and black fruits; entirely fruit-driven, but so what. Screwcap. 14.5° alc. **RATING** 88 **DRINK** 2009 $ 15
Geographe Shiraz 2004 Light- to medium-bodied; plum, red cherry, raspberry and spice; soft tannins plus mocha/vanilla oak. Screwcap. 14.5° alc. **RATING** 87 **DRINK** 2009 $ 15

ŢŢŢŢ Geographe Chenin Blanc 2005 RATING 86 **DRINK** Now $ 13.50
Family Reserve Pemberton Tempranillo 2004 Light- to medium-bodied; gently spicy, savoury fruit, but not a lot of distinction. A variety which can easily be over-cropped. Cork. 14° alc. **RATING** 86 **DRINK** 2008 $ 17

Willow Creek   ★★★★★

166 Balnarring Road, Merricks North, Vic 3926 **REGION** Mornington Peninsula
T (03) 5989 7448 **F** (03) 5989 7584 **WWW**.willow-creek.com.au **OPEN** 7 days 10–5
WINEMAKER Phil Kerney **EST.** 1989 **CASES** 7000
A significant presence in the Mornington Peninsula area, with 12 ha of vines planted to cabernet sauvignon, chardonnay, pinot noir and sauvignon blanc. The grape intake is supplemented by purchasing small, quality parcels from local growers. Salix restaurant is out of the ordinary, winning a 'Chefs Hat' from the *Age Good Food Guide,* and with a wine list which includes wines from all 31 of Burgundy's Grand Cru vineyards. The wines from Willow Creek aren't bad, either. Exports to the US.

ŢŢŢŢŢ Tulum Chardonnay 2004 A very stylish wine, with bright nectarine/citrus fruit woven through creamy/nutty malolactic and wild yeast influences; French oak in a pure support role. Screwcap. 13.5° alc. **RATING** 94 **DRINK** 2012 $ 35
Pinot Noir 2002 Tangy, foresty, savoury style; length and persistence, with distinct elements of Burgundy, even down to the 2002 vintage. Screwcap. **RATING** 94 **DRINK** 2009 $ 25

ŢŢŢŢŢ Benedictus Pinot Noir 2004 Fresh, lively tangy red fruits with a hint of mint; well-managed oak and a long finish. Cork. 14° alc. **RATING** 90 **DRINK** 2009 $ 50
Tulum Cabernet Sauvignon 2003 Good colour; a clean bouquet, the palate opening with red fruits then a savoury, ever-so-slightly green, finish. The dog preaching. Screwcap. 14° alc. **RATING** 90 **DRINK** 2013 $ 35

ŢŢŢŢ Chardonnay 2005 Light- to medium-bodied, clean and soft with no alcohol heat; creamy/nutty notes from the wild yeast and lees inputs. Very good unoaked style. Screwcap. 13.5° alc. **RATING** 89 **DRINK** 2008 $ 20

Tulum Pinot Noir 2004 A touch of reduction evident on the bouquet; red fruits with quite strong mint/menthol and spice characters. Screwcap. 14° alc. **RATING** 88 **DRINK** Now $ 35
Pinot Saignee 2005 Delicate spicy strawberry fruit, the hints of green not covered up by residual sugar; food style. Screwcap. 13° alc. **RATING** 87 **DRINK** Now $ 20

ƔƔƔƔ **Pinot Noir 2004 RATING** 86 **DRINK** Now $ 25

Willowvale Wines

NR

Black Swamp Road, Tenterfield, NSW 2372 **REGION** Northern Slopes Zone
T (02) 6736 3589 **F** (02) 6736 3753 **WWW**.willowvalewines.com.au **OPEN** 7 days 9–5
WINEMAKER John Morley **EST.** 1994 **CASES** 1200
John and Lyn Morley progressively established 1.8 ha of vineyard of chardonnay, merlot and cabernet sauvignon between 1994 and 2000. The vineyard is at an altitude of 940m, and was the first in the growing Tenterfield region. Advanced vineyard climatic monitoring systems have been installed, and a winery was built in 2000.

Wills Domain

Cnr Brash Road/Abbey Farm Road, Yallingup, WA 6281 **REGION** Margaret River
T (08) 9755 2327 **F** (08) 9755 2327 **WWW**.willsdomain.com.au **OPEN** 7 days 10–5
WINEMAKER Naturaliste Vintners (Bruce Dukes) **EST.** 1992 **CASES** 7500
Another arrival on the Margaret River scene, with a little over 10 ha of semillon, chardonnay, viognier, cabernet sauvignon, merlot, malbec, shiraz, cabernet franc and petit verdot under the control of Darren Haunold, whose ancestor Ulrich commenced winemaking in 1383 in modern day Austria. Between 1992 and 2001 the grapes were sold to local winemakers, but since 2002 have been made into a series of good wines (with its curious map of Australia on the back label). Exports to the UK, the US, Philippines, Singapore and Hong Kong.

ƔƔƔƔƔ **Margaret River Semillon 2004** Bright, light green-yellow; a complex bouquet with a subliminal hint of oak; a rich palate with citrus and herb; good acidity to close. Screwcap. 13.5° alc. **RATING** 91 **DRINK** 2014 $ 21

ƔƔƔƔ **Margaret River Semillon 2005** Unusually aromatic, ripe aromas, almost into stone fruit and citrus; the palate doesn't really work, being too rich. Screwcap. 13.5° alc. **RATING** 89 **DRINK** Now $ 22
Cabernet Sauvignon 2003 Light- to medium-bodied; elegant and bright fruit with good varietal articulation, though not much depth. Cork. 13.5° alc. **RATING** 89 **DRINK** 2008 $ 32
Semillon Sauvignon Blanc 2005 Clean, fresh, crisp and correct; light mineral, green apple and gooseberry fruit. Screwcap. **RATING** 87 **DRINK** Now $ 18
Margaret River Shiraz 2004 Light- to medium-bodied; very spicy, savoury, earthy style; controlled tannins. Cork. 14° alc. **RATING** 87 **DRINK** 2009 $ 23

Willunga Creek Wines

Lot 361 Delabole Road, Willunga, SA 5172 **REGION** McLaren Vale
T (08) 8556 2244 **F** (08) 8556 4660 **WWW**.willungacreekwines.com.au **OPEN** W'ends 10–5, or by appt
WINEMAKER Goe De Fabio, Phil Christiansen **EST.** 2002 **CASES** NA
David and Julie Cheesley purchased the property in the early 1990s, planting 6 ha each of shiraz and cabernet sauvignon in 1994, adding 0.5 ha of merlot in 2000. The vines are planted on terraced sloping hills, the wind exposure helping the Cheesley's organic management of the vineyard. The Willunga name and the Black Duck brand come from the Aboriginal word 'willangga', which means black duck. A new cellar door opens late 2006, replacing the one established in 2002 in a refurbished circa 1850 building in the town of Willunga.

ƔƔƔƔƔ **Black Duck Cabernet Merlot 2004** Good colour; supple cassis, blackcurrant, raspberry fruit on the medium-bodied palate; fine tannins; elegant and unforced. Cork. 13° alc. **RATING** 90 **DRINK** 2012 $ 20

ƔƔƔƔ **Black Duck Shiraz 2004** Medium-bodied; savoury, spicy, chocolatey nuances to the core of black fruits; controlled oak. Cork. 14° alc. **RATING** 89 **DRINK** 2011 $ 20

Black Duck Merlot 2004 A typical McLaren Vale version of the variety; rich, ripe and sweet, with slightly cooked/confit fruit and chocolate sauce; strange characters given the vintage and moderate alcohol. Cork. 14° alc. **RATING** 87 **DRINK** 2010 $ 20

▼▼▼▽ **Black Duck Sauvignon Blanc 2004** Clean, well-made, but fairly soft, broad tropical fruit; drink asap. Screwcap. 13° alc. **RATING** 86 **DRINK** Now $ 13

Black Duck Rose 2005 At the big end of the spectrum, quite full-bodied by rose standards; some sweetness adds emphasis to this. Screwcap. 14° alc. **RATING** 86 **DRINK** 2011 $ 13

Willy Bay   NR

19 Third Avenue, Mount Lawley, WA 6050 (postal) **REGION** Geographe
T (08) 9271 9890 **F** (08) 9271 7771 **www**.willybay.com.au **OPEN** Not
WINEMAKER Peter Stanlake **EST.** 2003 **CASES** 700
Willy Bay Wines is jointly owned and run by the Siciliano and Edwards families, who have established 6.5 ha of shiraz, 2.8 ha of cabernet sauvignon and 1.7 ha of chardonnay, employing Peter Stanlake as winemaker. The wine styles are unusual, not the least the Last Fling Cane Cut Cabernet Sauvignon. One suspects that young vine influences are at work. Samples were sent for this edition, but went astray; the rating is that for 2006.

Wilmot Hills Vineyard   NR

407 Back Road, Wilmot, Tas 7310 **REGION** Northern Tasmania
T (03) 6492 1193 **F** (03) 6492 1193 **www**.wilmothills.tascom.net **OPEN** 7 days 9–7
WINEMAKER John Cole, Ruth Cole **EST.** 1991 **CASES** NA
The beautiful Wilmot Hills Vineyard is on the western side of Lake Barrington, not far from the Cradle Mountain road, with marvellous views to Mt Roland and the adjacent peaks. It is very much a family affair, and produces both wine and cider. John Cole spent 18 years in Melbourne in engineering design and some graphic art, and Ruth worked in the hospitality industry for 10 years and making fruit wines for 20 years. The neat onsite winery was designed and built by the Coles, as was much of the wine- and cider-making equipment.

Wilson Vineyard   ★★★★★

Polish Hill River, Sevenhill via Clare, SA 5453 **REGION** Clare Valley
T (08) 8843 4310 **www**.wilsonvineyard.com.au **OPEN** W'ends 10–4
WINEMAKER Dr John Wilson, Daniel Wilson **EST.** 1974 **CASES** 4000
After working at the shoulder of his father John for many years, Daniel Wilson took responsibility for the winemaking in 2003. The Wilson Vineyard of today is a far cry from that of 10 years ago, taking its place in the upper echelon of the Clare Valley. Exports to the US.

▼▼▼▼▼ **DJW Clare Valley Riesling 2005** Intense, classic lime/lime blossom/mineral aromas; a long, highly focused and intense palate, retaining elegance. Screwcap. **RATING** 96 **DRINK** 2012 $ 19.50

Polish Hill River Riesling 2005 Floral spice and apple; mouthfilling and long; very good balance; powerful, and built for the long haul. Screwcap. **RATING** 95 **DRINK** 2015 $ 22

Hand Plunge Shiraz 2003 Attractive cedary, spicy edges to black cherry/blackberry aromas; an intense, medium- to full-bodied palate with long, graceful tannins. Screwcap. 15° alc. **RATING** 94 **DRINK** 2010 $ 30

Wily Trout

Marakei–Nanima Road, via Hall, NSW 2618 **REGION** Canberra District
T (02) 6230 2487 **F** (02) 6230 2211 **www**.wilytrout.com.au **OPEN** 7 days 10–5
WINEMAKER Dr Roger Harris, Andrew McEwen (Contract) **EST.** 1998 **CASES** 3000
The 21-ha Wily Trout vineyard shares its home with the Poachers Pantry, a renowned gourmet smokehouse. Thus the Smokehouse Café doubles as a tasting room and a cellar door. The quality of the wines is very good, and a testament to the skills of the contract winemakers. The northeast-facing slopes, at an elevation of 720m, provide some air drainage and hence protection against spring frosts.

ȲȲȲȲȲ **Canberra District Pinot Noir 2004** Light- to medium-bodied; spicy/foresty/stemmy overtones but has nice cherry/strawberry fruit at the centre. Screwcap. 13.5° alc. **RATING** 90 **DRINK** 2010 $ 26

ȲȲȲȲ **Canberra District Chardonnay 2005** Clean, light-bodied, rather shy nectarine and melon fruit, despite the low yields. Screwcap. 13° alc. **RATING** 87 **DRINK** 2009 $ 21

ȲȲȲȲȲ **Canberra District Sauvignon Blanc 2005** **RATING** 86 **DRINK** Now $ 25

Wimbaliri Wines
★★★☆

Barton Highway, Murrumbateman, NSW 2582 **REGION** Canberra District
T (02) 6227 5921 **F** (02) 6227 5921 **OPEN** 7 days 10–5
WINEMAKER John Andersen **EST.** 1988 **CASES** 700
John and Margaret Andersen moved to the Canberra district in 1987 and began establishing their vineyard at Murrumbateman in 1988; the property borders highly regarded Canberra producers Doonkuna and Clonakilla. The vineyard is close-planted with a vertical trellis system, with a total of 2.2 ha planted to chardonnay, pinot noir, shiraz, cabernet sauvignon and merlot (plus a few vines of cabernet franc).

ȲȲȲȲ **Chardonnay 2004** Quite rich and firm mouthfeel; nectarine and peach with a minimalist oak backdrop; good length. Cork. 12.6° alc. **RATING** 89 **DRINK** 2009 $ 20
Gravel Block Shiraz 2004 Good colour; blackberry, spice and plum in a firm, low pH style; slightly peaky acidity, possibly adjusted. Cork. 14° alc. **RATING** 89 **DRINK** 2013 $ 24

ȲȲȲȲȲ **Cabernet Sauvignon 2003** **RATING** 86 **DRINK** 2008 $ 22
Pinot Noir 2004 **RATING** 85 **DRINK** Now $ 24
Cabernet Shiraz 2002 **RATING** 84 **DRINK** Now $ 20

Winbirra Vineyard
★★★☆

173 Point Leo Road, Red Hill South, Vic 3937 **REGION** Mornington Peninsula
T (03) 5989 2109 **F** (03) 5989 2109 **WWW**.winbirravineyards.com.au **OPEN** 1st weekend each month & public hols 10.30–5.30, or by appt
WINEMAKER Tuerong Winery **EST.** 1990 **CASES** 700
Winbirra is a small, family-owned and run vineyard which has been producing grapes since 1990, between then and 1997 selling the grapes to local winemakers. Since 1997 the wine has been made and sold under the Winbirra label. There is 1.5 ha of pinot noir (with three clones) at Merricks and 1.5 ha on a second site at Merricks South.

ȲȲȲȲ **Mornington Peninsula Pinot Noir 2004** Complex wine with plum/black cherry fruit off-set by savoury/forest floor/herb notes, and fractionally bitter tannins. Diam. 14° alc. **RATING** 89 **DRINK** 2009 $ 28

Winbourne Wines
NR

Bunnan Road, Scone, NSW 2337 **REGION** Upper Hunter Valley
T 0417 650 834 **F** (02) 6545 1636 **WWW**.winbournewines.com **OPEN** By appt
WINEMAKER Stephen Hagan, De Iuliis, Kevin Sobels Wines **EST.** 1996 **CASES** 1500
A legal contemporary of mine, whom I have known for over 40 years, is one of the faces behind Winbourne Wines. He still practises law at his law firm in Muswellbrook, but has also established a little under 50 ha of vineyards planted to semillon, chardonnay, verdelho, shiraz, merlot and cabernet sauvignon. Most of the production is sold as grapes, a little made into wine. Says David White, 'It could well be wondered why we are doing — have done — this.' I guess it simply proves that old lawyers are not necessarily wise lawyers.

Winburndale

116 Saint Anthony's Creek Road, Bathurst, NSW 2795 **REGION** Central Ranges Zone
T (02) 6337 3134 **F** (02) 6337 3106 **WWW**.winburndalewines.com.au **OPEN** By appt
WINEMAKER Mark Renzaglia, David Lowe (Consultant) **EST.** 1998 **CASES** 2500
Michael Burleigh and family acquired the 200-ha Winburndale property in September 1998: 160 ha is forest, to be kept as a nature reserve; 3 separate vineyards, each with its own site characteristics, have been planted under the direction of viticulturist Mark Renzaglia. The winery paddock has 2.5 ha of shiraz facing due west at an altitude of 800–820m; the south paddock, with north and northwest aspects, varying from 790–810m, has chardonnay (1.2 ha), shiraz (1 ha) and cabernet sauvignon (3.5 ha). The home paddock is the most level, with a slight north aspect, and with 1.2 ha each of merlot and cabernet franc. The name, incidentally, derives from Lachlan Macquarie's exploration of the Blue Mountains in 1815. Exports to the US and Denmark.

▼▼▼▼ **Solitary Shiraz 2004** Peppery/spicy/leafy/minty cool-grown characters; well-made, not over-extracted, and the oak in balance. Screwcap. 13° alc. **RATING** 89 **DRINK** 2010 $ 25
Lost & Found Shiraz Cabernets Merlot 2005 Bright purple-red; attractive raspberry, redcurrant and blackberry mix; light- to medium-bodied, and without any green characters whatsoever. Screwcap. 13° alc. **RATING** 89 **DRINK** 2010 $ 16
Fontana Cabernet Sauvignon Cabernet Franc Merlot 2004 Savoury, leafy, briary aromas attesting to the cool climate, but balanced by a core of cassis/blackcurrant fruit. Screwcap. 14° alc. **RATING** 89 **DRINK** 2010 $ 25

Windance Wines NR

Lot 12, Loc 589, Caves Road, Yallingup, WA 6282 **REGION** Margaret River
T (08) 9755 2293 **F** (08) 9755 2293 **WWW**.windance.com.au **OPEN** 7 days 10–5
WINEMAKER Janice McDonald, Damon Eastaugh, Harry Clegg **EST.** 1998 **CASES** 4200
Drew and Rosemary Brent-White own this family business, situated 5 km south of Yallingup. A little over 6.5 ha of sauvignon blanc, shiraz, merlot and cabernet sauvignon have been established, incorporating sustainable land management and organic farming practices where possible. The wines are exclusively estate-grown.

Windarra NR

De Beyers Road, Pokolbin, NSW 2321 **REGION** Lower Hunter Valley
T (02) 4998 7648 **F** (02) 4998 7648 **OPEN** Tues–Sun 10–5
WINEMAKER Tom Andresen-Jung **EST.** 1985 **CASES** 2500
The Andresen family has 6 ha of semillon, chardonnay and shiraz. The exotic array of fortified wines are likely to come from further afield.

Windermere Wines NR

Lot 3, Watters Road, Ballandean, Qld 4382 **REGION** Granite Belt
T (07) 4684 1353 **F** (07) 4684 1353 **OPEN** 7 days 9.30–5
WINEMAKER Wayne Beecham, Kate Beecham **EST.** 1995 **CASES** 500
After spending 3 years travelling in Europe (1983–86), Wayne Beecham returned to Australia to take up a position with what was then Thomas Hardy Wines, specifically to establish the RhineCastle wine distribution in Qld. He studied wine marketing at Roseworthy while working for Hardys, but in 1993 he, wife Julie and daughter Kate decided to move to the Granite Belt to establish Windermere Wines from the ground up. His long service with Hardys stood him in good stead, landing him a cellar position at Hardys Tintara in the 1994 vintage, working with winemaker David O'Leary. In typical Australian fashion, Wayne Beecham says they decided on the Granite Belt because, 'if we were to succeed, we might as well do it in the toughest new region in the industry'.

Windowrie Estate

NR

Windowrie, Canowindra, NSW 2804 **REGION** Cowra
T (02) 6344 3234 **F** (02) 6344 3227 **WWW**.windowrie.com.au **OPEN** At the Mill, Vaux Street, Cowra
WINEMAKER John Holmes **EST.** 1988 **CASES** 70 000
Windowrie Estate was established in 1988 on a substantial grazing property at Canowindra, 30 km
north of Cowra and in the same viticultural region. A portion of the grapes from the 116-ha vineyard
are sold to other makers, but increasing quantities are being made for the Windowrie Estate and The
Mill labels; the Chardonnays have enjoyed show success. The cellar door is in a flour mill built in 1861
from local granite. It ceased operations in 1905 and lay unoccupied for 91 years until restored by the
O'Dea family. Exports to the UK, the US and other major markets.

Windows Margaret River

Location 775 Caves Road, Yallingup, WA 6282 (postal) **REGION** Margaret River
T (08) 9755 2719 **F** (08) 9755 2719 **OPEN** Not
WINEMAKER Christopher Davies, Barbara Davies **EST.** 1996 **CASES** 2500
Beginning in 1996, Len and Barbara Davies have progressively established 1.5 ha of cabernet sauvignon,
1 ha each of chenin blanc and shiraz, and 0.5 ha each of semillon and merlot. Prior to 2004 the grapes
were sold to other well known Margaret River wineries, but in that year the decision was taken to move
to winemaking. Since Barbara Davies is a qualified winemaker and works with her son Chris (as
assistant winemaker and vineyard manager) the decision wasn't too hard to make. What is more, it has
been rewarded with considerable show success for its consistently good, enticingly priced, wines.

ŸŸŸŸŸ **Cabernet Merlot 2004** Light- to medium-bodied; elegant, fresh and lively; fruit-driven
with cassis and berry flavours; fine, ripe tannins, good length. Gold medal Qantas WA
Wine Show '05. Screwcap. 14.1° alc. **RATING** 93 **DRINK** 2014 $ 15.95
Cabernet Sauvignon 2004 Bright colour; clean and fresh; very good cassis and
blackcurrant varietal fruit; good tannins and overall style; has length. Screwcap. 14.4° alc.
RATING 92 **DRINK** 2015 $ 15.95
Semillon 2005 Fresh, crisp, lively and firm; strangely, similar mouthfeel to Hunter Valley
semillon but with 3 degrees more alcohol, which it carries; grass, herb and a touch of citrus
are also varietal. Screwcap. 13.5° alc. **RATING** 90 **DRINK** 2010 $ 15.95

ŸŸŸŸ **Shiraz 2004** An attractive mix of red and black fruits, spice and oak; lively, light- to
medium-bodied, the extraordinary alcohol passing largely unnoticed; good length and
fine tannins. Screwcap. 16.3° alc. **RATING** 89 **DRINK** 2012 $ 15.95

ŸŸŸ **Chenin Blanc 2005 RATING** 83 $ 12.95

WindshakeR Ridge

★★★

PO Box 106, Karrinyup, WA 6921 **REGION** Swan District
T (08) 6241 4100 **F** (08) 9240 6220 **WWW**.windshaker.com.au **OPEN** Not
WINEMAKER Ryan Sudano **EST.** 2003 **CASES** 4000
The Moltoni family has owned a 2000-ha farming property for 3 generations. Robert Moltoni is the
driving force, establishing WindshakeR Ridge in 2003. The 25-ha vineyard (carnelian, semillon, shiraz
and verdelho) is 9 km north of the early settlement of Gingin, and looks out over the hills to the sea.
Moltoni is an accomplished poet, so much so that I cannot help but quote one of his poems, 'Easterlies
whistle through the gums; Crashing over silent ridges; Bathing vines in Namatjira Crimson;
WindshakeR, WindshakeR, WindshakeR; The ghost winds whisper down; Off the red plains to the sea.'

ŸŸŸŸŸ **Verdelho 2005** Light straw-green; clean, light- to medium-bodied stone fruit and a touch
of citrus; a long, dry finish. Cork. 14° alc. **RATING** 90 **DRINK** 2008 $ 13

ŸŸŸŸ **Chardonnay 2003** Well-made; abundant, sweet, peachy/tropical fruit; full and
flavoursome; has developed well; drink now. Cork. 14° alc. **RATING** 87 **DRINK** Now $ 13

ŸŸŸŸ **Shiraz 2004** Light-bodied, but well-enough balanced; sweet red fruits and light, savoury
tannins. Twin top. 14° alc. **RATING** 86 **DRINK** 2009

ŸŸŸ **Carnelian 2004 RATING** 83 $ 13

Windsors Edge NR

McDonalds Road, Pokolbin, NSW 2320 **REGION** Lower Hunter Valley
T (02) 4998 7737 **F** (02) 4998 7341 **WWW**.windsorsedge.com.au **OPEN** Fri–Mon 10–5, or by appt
WINEMAKER Tim Windsor, Jessie Windsor **EST.** 1996 **CASES** 1500
In 1995 Tim Windsor (a Charles Sturt winemaking graduate) and wife Jessie (an industrial chemist)
purchased the old Black Creek picnic racetrack at the northern end of McDonalds Road in Pokolbin.
The first vines were planted in 1996, and planting has continued: to date, 17 ha of shiraz, semillon,
chardonnay, tempranillo, tinta cao and touriga are in the ground.

Windy Creek Estate NR

27 Stock Road, Herne Hill, WA 6056 **REGION** Swan Valley
T (08) 9296 4210 **OPEN** Tues–Sun 11–5
WINEMAKER Tony Cobanov, Tony Roe **EST.** 1960 **CASES** 10 000
A substantial family-owned operation (previously known as Cobanov Wines) producing a mix of bulk
and bottled wine from 21 ha of estate grapes. Part of the annual production is sold as grapes to other
producers, including Houghton. Part is sold in bulk, part is sold in 2-litre flagons, and the remainder
in modestly priced bottles.

Windy Ridge Vineyard & Winery ★★★

Foster–Fish Creek Road, Foster, Vic 3960 **REGION** Gippsland
T (03) 5682 2035 **WWW**.windyridgewinery.com.au **OPEN** Holiday w'ends 10–5
WINEMAKER Graeme Wilson **EST.** 1978 **CASES** 300
The 2.6-ha Windy Ridge Vineyard was planted between 1978 and 1986, with the first vintage not
taking place until 1988. Winemaker Graeme Wilson favours prolonged maturation, part in stainless
steel and part in oak, before bottling his wines, typically giving the Pinot Noir 3 years and the
Cabernet 2 years.

YYYY **Upper Slope Pinot Noir 2004** Clear-cut varietal character; light- to medium-bodied but
long palate; red fruits and strong savoury/foresty characters; just gets away with low
alcohol. Cork. 12.1° alc. **RATING** 88 **DRINK** 2009 $ 30

YYYY **Pinot Noir 2003 RATING** 85 **DRINK** Now $ 30

wine by brad NR

PO Box 475, Margaret River, WA 6285 **REGION** Margaret River
T (08) 9757 2957 **F** (08) 9757 3701 **WWW**.winebybrad.com.au **OPEN** Not
WINEMAKER Brad Wehr, Clive Otto **EST.** 2003 **CASES** 2500
Brad Wehr says that wine by brad, 'is the result of a couple of influential winemakers and shadowy
ruffians deciding that there was something to be gained by putting together some pretty neat parcels
of wine from the region, creating their own label, and releasing it with minimal fuss'. This, therefore,
is another version of the virtual winery, with sales through the website.

WineTrust Estates NR

PO Box 541, Balgowlah, NSW 2093 **REGION** Warehouse
T (02) 9949 9250 **F** (02) 9907 8179 **WWW**.winetrustestates.com **OPEN** Not
WINEMAKER Various contract **EST.** 1999 **CASES** 32 000
Mark Arnold is the man behind WineTrust Estates, drawing on a lifetime of experience in wine
marketing. It is a virtual winery operation, drawing grapes from three states and five regions using
contract winemakers according to the grapes of origin. The top-of-the-range Picarus red wines come
from the Limestone Coast region.

Winewood   NR

Sundown Road, Ballandean, Qld 4382 **REGION** Granite Belt
T (07) 4684 1187 **F** (07) 4684 1187 **OPEN** W'ends & public hols 9–5
WINEMAKER Ian Davis **EST.** 1984 **CASES** 1000
A weekend and holiday activity for schoolteacher Ian Davis and town-planner wife Jeanette; the tiny winery is a model of neatness and precision planning. The use of marsanne with chardonnay and semillon shows an interesting change in direction. Has 4.5 ha of estate plantings, having added shiraz and viognier.

Winooka Park   NR

2161 Tarana Road, Gemalla, NSW 2795 **REGION** Central Ranges Zone
T (02) 6337 5534 **F** (02) 6337 5512 **OPEN** W'ends 11–4, or by appt
WINEMAKER Tony Marsh **EST.** 1991 **CASES** 300
Ruth and Tony Marsh run a part-time wine business, making the wine onsite from micro plantings (0.75 ha) of gewurztraminer, riesling, chardonnay, shiraz and cabernet sauvignon. The estate-grown grapes are supplemented by contract-grown fruit sourced from other Central Ranges areas at Meadow Flat, Oberon, Bathurst and Rylstone.

Winstead   ★★★★

75 Winstead Road, Bagdad, Tas 7030 **REGION** Southern Tasmania
T (03) 6268 6417 **F** (03) 6268 6417 **OPEN** By appt
WINEMAKER Neil Snare **EST.** 1989 **CASES** 350
The good news about Winstead is the outstanding quality of its extremely generous and rich Pinot Noirs, rivalling those of Freycinet for the abundance of their fruit flavour without any sacrifice of varietal character. The bad news is that production is so limited, with only 0.8 ha of pinot noir and 0.4 ha riesling being tended by fly-fishing devotee Neil Snare and wife Julieanne.

ŸŸŸŸŸ **Pinot Noir 2004** Ultra-controversial; supporters see it as stylish, with tangy, controlled stemmy inputs to a long and silky palate. Others disagree. **RATING** 92 **DRINK** 2009

ŸŸŸŸ **Riesling 2005 RATING** 85 **DRINK** 2009

Winya Wines   NR

145 Sandy Creek Road, Kilcoy, Qld 4515 (postal) **REGION** Queensland Zone
T (07) 5497 1504 **F** (07) 5497 1504 **WWW**.winyawines.com.au **OPEN** Not
WINEMAKER Craig Robinson (Contract) **EST.** 1997 **CASES** 350
Gary and Susanne Pratten have established 2 ha of merlot and malbec in the Somerset Valley area. The wines are made using contract-grown grapes until the estate vineyards come into production. Semillon, Chardonnay, Chardonnay Semillon, Shiraz, Merlot and Malbec are the dry table wines, with Winya White and Winya Red sweet alternatives.

Wirilda Creek   NR

RSD 91, McMurtrie Road, McLaren Vale, SA 5171 **REGION** McLaren Vale
T (08) 8323 9688 **F** (08) 8323 9260 **OPEN** 7 days 10–5
WINEMAKER Kerry Flanagan **EST.** 1993 **CASES** 1500
Wirilda Creek may be one of the newer arrivals in McLaren Vale but it offers the lot: wine, lunch every day (Pickers Platters reflecting local produce) and accommodation (4 rooms opening onto a private garden courtyard). Co-owner Kerry Flanagan (with partner Karen Shertock) has had great experience in the wine and hospitality industries: a Roseworthy graduate (1980), he has inter alia worked at Penfolds, Coriole and Wirra Wirra and also owned the famous Old Salopian Inn for a period. A little under 4 ha of McLaren Vale estate vineyards have now been joined by a little over 3 ha of vineyards at Antechamber Bay, Kangaroo Island. Exports to the US, Canada and Germany.

Wirra Wirra

★★★★★

McMurtie Road, McLaren Vale, SA 5171 **REGION** McLaren Vale
T(08) 8323 8414 **F**(08) 8323 8596 **WWW**.wirrawirra.com **OPEN** Mon–Sat 10–5,
Sun & public hols 11–5
WINEMAKER Samantha Connew, Alexia Roberts **EST.** 1969 **CASES** 120 000
Long respected for the consistency of its white wines, Wirra Wirra has now established an equally
formidable reputation for its reds. Right across the board, the wines are of exemplary character,
quality and style, The Angelus Cabernet Sauvignon and RSW Shiraz battling with each other for
supremacy. Long may the battle continue under the direction of the highly respected Tim James,
particularly in the wake of the death of the universally loved co-founder/owner Greg Trott in early
2005. Exports to all major markets.

▼▼▼▼▼ **Chook Block Shiraz 2002** Chock-full of regional dark chocolate; carries its alcohol with
grace; very, very long and concentrated black fruits; oak and tannin in restraint. Screwcap.
15° alc. **RATING** 97 **DRINK** 2022 **$** 100
RSW Shiraz 2003 A lush, layered array of black fruits and licorice; appealing texture and
length; great follow-up to '02. Cork. **RATING** 95 **DRINK** 2018 **$** 46
Adelaide Hills Chardonnay 2004 A very complex wine showing barrel ferment, wild
yeast and fortnightly stirring, yet retaining grace; a creamy mouthfeel to the nectarine and
apple fruit. Screwcap. 13° alc. **RATING** 94 **DRINK** 2009 **$** 26.50
Scrubby Rise Red 2004 Dense colour; archetypal regional mix of black fruits and bitter
chocolate; splendidly rich and complete, oozing flavour, and will be long lived. Sensational
value. Screwcap. 14.5° alc. **RATING** 94 **DRINK** 2014 **$** 15

▼▼▼▼▽ **Hand Picked Riesling 2005** Fine, floral fragrance; delicate apple, lime and a touch of
passionfruit; expands on the finish and aftertaste. From two Adelaide Hills Vineyards.
Screwcap. **RATING** 93 **DRINK** 2015 **$** 16.50
Church Block 2004 Good purple-red; bright, fresh red and black fruits with a touch of
chocolate; good length and tannin support; likewise French oak. Cabernet/Shiraz/Merlot.
Screwcap. 14.5° alc. **RATING** 92 **DRINK** 2012 **$** 20
Adelaide Hills Sauvignon Blanc 2005 Slightly smoky edges to the bouquet; delicate
pear, apple and gooseberry fruit supported by crunchy acidity. Screwcap. 13.5° alc.
RATING 90 **DRINK** Now **$** 20
Adelaide Hills Sauvignon Blanc Semillon Viognier 2005 Complex, rounded texture and
mouthfeel; well away from standard Sauvignon Blanc; good balance, food style; 10%
barrel-fermented. Screwcap. **RATING** 90 **DRINK** Now **$** 20
Mrs Wigley Rose 2005 Vibrant fuchsia; crisp and lively small red fruits; a long, virtually
dry, finish. Screwcap. 13.5° alc. **RATING** 90 **DRINK** Now **$** 18
Woodhenge McLaren Vale Shiraz 2003 Smooth, supple and round; fully ripe fruit
flavours have absorbed the oak; soft, ripe tannins. Quality cork. **RATING** 90 **DRINK** 2013
$ 29

▼▼▼▼ **Scrubby Rise 2005** Attractive mix of some tropical and more minerally notes, the 10%
barrel ferment component also aiding structure; good value; all-purpose wine. Sauvignon
Blanc/Semillon/Viognier. Screwcap. 13.5° alc. **RATING** 89 **DRINK** 2008 **$** 15
The Angelus Cabernet Sauvignon 2003 A potent, powerful wine with dark fruits,
blackcurrant, and uncharacteristically aggressive tannins; time in bottle will help. Cork.
14.5° alc. **RATING** 89 **DRINK** 2015 **$** 48
Scrubby Rise Red 2005 Deep purple colour; saturated with dark berry fruits, although
needs a touch more structure on the finish. Shiraz/Cabernet Sauvignon/Petit Verdot.
Screwcap. 14.5° alc. **RATING** 89 **DRINK** 2008 **$** 15

▼▼▼▽ **Sexton's Acre McLaren Vale Unwooded Chardonnay 2005** **RATING** 86 **DRINK** 2008 **$** 15

Wirruna Estate ★★★☆

RMB 5015A, Bethanga, Vic 3691 (postal) **REGION** North East Victoria Zone
T (02) 6040 4808 **F** (02) 6040 6046 **WWW**.wirrunawines.com **OPEN** Not
WINEMAKER John Woodhouse **EST.** 1997 **CASES** 1650
John and Sandra Woodhouse have established 1.5 ha of each of shiraz, durif and marsanne on the banks of Lake Hume. The varieties were chosen because of their compatibility with the hot, dry summers, while the Wirruna name is an Aboriginal word for the sunset depicted on the labels. Son-in-law Manfred Walch works as assistant winemaker during vintage, and John, Sandra and Manfred work on the property in a part-time capacity for most of the year. Picking, done over 3 weekends, is a family and friends affair.

ΨΨΨΨ **JW Family Reserve Shiraz 2002** Quite firm and fresh; medium-bodied spice and leather nuances; nicely balanced. Stained cork. **RATING** 88 **DRINK** 2008 $16
JW Family Reserve Marsanne 2004 Delicate blossom and talc aromas; crunchy acidity typical of the variety; all up, good varietal character, and will evolve very well with age. Screwcap. **RATING** 87 **DRINK** 2009 $16
JW Family Reserve Durif 2002 Medium- to full-bodied; spicy, savoury fruit; quite pronounced acidity from the cool vintage. Stained cork. **RATING** 87 **DRINK** 2008 $20

Wise Wine ★★★★☆

Lot 4 Eagle Bay Road, Dunsborough, WA 6281 **REGION** Margaret River
T (08) 9756 8627 **F** (08) 9756 8770 **WWW**.wisewine.com.au **OPEN** 7 days 10–5
WINEMAKER Amanda Kramer, Bruce Dukes (Consultant) **EST.** 1986 **CASES** 30 000
Wise Vineyards, headed by Perth entrepreneur Ron Wise, is going from strength to strength, with 18 ha at the Meelup Vineyard in Margaret River, 10 ha at the Donnybrook Vineyard in Geographe, and leases the Bramley and Bunkers Bay vineyards, with a total of almost 40 ha. Wine quality has taken a leap forward, with a number of excellent wines.

ΨΨΨΨΨ **Pemberton Reserve Chardonnay 2004** Great colour; a complex array of flavours; nectarine and light creamy/nutty nuances; long, balanced finish. Screwcap. 14° alc. **RATING** 94 **DRINK** 2012 $35

ΨΨΨΨΨ **Pemberton Unwooded Chardonnay 2005** Fine, elegant, intense and long grapefruit/nectarine; despite being unoaked, has considerable complexity; long finish. Screwcap. **RATING** 93 **DRINK** 2009 $17
The Bramley Cabernet Sauvignon 2003 Medium red-purple; a complex mix of spicy, cedary aromas and flavours wound through the blackcurrant and cassis fruit; good extract and balance. Screwcap. **RATING** 93 **DRINK** 2018 $40
Single Vineyard Donnybrook Chardonnay 2004 Glowing green-yellow; highly focused and intense nectarine, grapefruit and melon; excellent balance and length. Screwcap. 14° alc. **RATING** 92 **DRINK** 2011 $28
The Donnybrook 2003 Good colour; medium-bodied blackcurrant and cassis backed by attractive, cedary oak, good length and ripe tannins. Screwcap. **RATING** 92 **DRINK** 2015 $40
Margaret River Lot 80 Cabernet Sauvignon 2003 Pure cassis, mulberry and blackcurrant fruit drives the medium-bodied palate; easy access style. Screwcap. 13.5° alc. **RATING** 91 **DRINK** 2010 $28
Semillon Sauvignon Blanc 2005 Clean and correct; a light-bodied, fresh and lively herbaceous, passionfruit, apple mix. Screwcap. **RATING** 90 **DRINK** Now $17

ΨΨΨΨ **Single Vineyard Donnybrook Verdelho 2005** Fresh blossom aromas; a clean, light- to medium-bodied palate, but with drive and precision; good length. Screwcap. 13.5° alc. **RATING** 88 **DRINK** Now $24
Single Vineyard Cabernets Merlot 2003 Light-bodied; bright, fresh cassis and blackcurrant flavours; easy, early drinking lunch red. Screwcap. **RATING** 87 **DRINK** 2009 $20

ΨΨΨΨ **Margaret River Classic Red 2003** **RATING** 86 **DRINK** 2008 $17

Witchmount Estate ★★★★★

557 Leakes Road, Rockbank, Vic 3335 **REGION** Sunbury
T (03) 9747 1188 **F** (03) 9747 1066 **WWW**.witchmount.com.au **OPEN** Wed–Sun 10–5
WINEMAKER Tony Ramunno, Steve Goodwin **EST.** 1991 **CASES** 10 000
Gaye and Matt Ramunno operate Witchmount Estate in conjunction with its Italian restaurant and function rooms, which are open Wed–Sun for lunch and dinner. Over 20 ha of vines have been established since 1991: varieties include nebbiolo, barbera, tempranillo and the rare northern Italian white grape picolit. The quality of the wines is consistently good, the prices very modest. Exports to Canada.

▼▼▼▼▼ **Shiraz 2003** Elegant, supple and smooth; bordering on delicate, yet has terrific drive and length. **RATING** 94 **DRINK** 2013 $ 25

WJ Walker Wines NR

Burns Road, Lake Grace, WA 6353 **REGION** Central Western Australia Zone
T (08) 9865 1969 **OPEN** 7 days 10–4
WINEMAKER Porongurup Winery **EST.** 1998 **CASES** 1000
Lake Grace is 300 km due east of Bunbury, one of those isolated viticultural outposts which are appearing in many parts of Australia these days. There are 1.5 ha of shiraz and 0.5 ha of chardonnay.

Wolf Blass ★★★★★

Bilyara Vineyards, 97 Sturt Highway, Nuriootpa, SA 5355 **REGION** Barossa Valley
T (08) 8568 7300 **F** (08) 8568 7380 **WWW**.wolfblass.com.au **OPEN** Mon–Fri 9.15–5, w'ends & public hols 10–5
WINEMAKER Chris Hatcher (Chief), Caroline Dunn (Red), Kirsten Glaetzer (White) **EST.** 1966
CASES NFP
Although merged with Mildara and now under the giant umbrella of FWE, the brands (as expected) have been left largely intact. The white wines are particularly impressive, none more so than the Gold Label Riesling. After a short pause, the red wines have improved out of all recognition thanks to the sure touch (and top palate) of Caroline Dunn. All of this has occurred under the leadership of Chris Hatcher, who has harnessed the talents of the team and encouraged the changes in style. Exports to all major markets.

▼▼▼▼▼ **Platinum Label Adelaide Hills Shiraz 2002** Super-elegant, beautifully crafted, medium-bodied wine; black fruits, tannins and oak are seamlessly woven together; long, lingering finish; 50% Eden Valley/50% Barossa Valley. Screwcap. 14.5° alc. **RATING** 97 **DRINK** 2025 $ 199
Platinum Label Adelaide Hills Shiraz 2003 Dense, deep colour; medium- to full-bodied; gloriously rich and ripe blackberry fruit with bitter chocolate, spice, licorice and high-quality oak part of the team. Screwcap. **RATING** 96 **DRINK** 2023
Black Label Cabernet Sauvignon Shiraz 2002 Very good colour; medium-bodied; silky, sensual, supple texture; black fruits and licorice; seamless oak and tannins. Screwcap. **RATING** 96 **DRINK** 2017
Grey Label McLaren Vale Shiraz 2004 Deep, dense colour; archetypal McLaren Vale, bursting with blackberry and bitter chocolate fruit, but with lower alcohol and classy oak handling giving a great result for a great vintage. Screwcap. 14.5° alc. **RATING** 95 **DRINK** 2019
Gold Label Adelaide Hills Chardonnay 2005 Perfectly constructed and balanced; seamless stone fruit, melon and carefully controlled barrel ferment French oak; great line and length. Screwcap. 13.5° alc. **RATING** 94 **DRINK** 2010 $ 22
Gold Label Adelaide Hills Shiraz Viognier 2004 Typical, deep purple-red; ultra-fragrant and lifted aromas, and that supple, woven silk palate, a mark both of Blass and the viognier synergy with shiraz; delicious black fruits, chocolate and subliminal apricot. Screwcap. 14.5° alc. **RATING** 94 **DRINK** 2015
Gold Label Barossa Shiraz 2003 Seamlessly interwoven fruit and French/American oak; very good balance and structure; supple tannins, lovely finish. Top gold medal National Wine Show '05. Screwcap. **RATING** 94 **DRINK** 2015 $ 23

ᵀᵀᵀᵀᵀ **Gold Label Adelaide Hills Pinot Noir 2003** Ripe, dense fruit aromas in Adelaide Hills style; plenty of sweet fruit on the palate; good balance and length. Screwcap. **RATING** 93 **DRINK** 2009 $ 24

Grey Label Langhorne Creek Cabernet Sauvignon 2004 Very good colour; powerful blackcurrant fruit and touches of chocolate; varietal savoury tannins; sure oak. Screwcap. 14.5° alc. **RATING** 93 **DRINK** 2015

Gold Label Riesling 2005 Green-yellow; abundant lime and lemon aromas and flavours, but a little short of the necessary cleansing acidity. Screwcap. 12° alc. **RATING** 92 **DRINK** 2010 $ 24

ᵀᵀᵀᵀ **Eaglehawk Riesling 2005** Slightly four-square, but is flavoursome and has length to the tropical lime mix. Value plus. Screwcap. 12° alc. **RATING** 89 **DRINK** 2009 $ 9

Gold Label Mount Gambier Sauvignon Blanc 2005 Lemon, mineral and gooseberry aromas, the delicate palate fleshed out by subliminal residual sugar. Screwcap. 13° alc. **RATING** 89 **DRINK** Now $ 24

Gold Label Coonawarra Cabernet Sauvignon 2003 Light- to medium-bodied; clean blackcurrant, earth, spice and mint aromas and flavours; fine tannins and fair length; needs more punch. Screwcap. **RATING** 88 **DRINK** 2009 $ 23

Eaglehawk Chardonnay 2005 Clean, medium-bodied; gentle peach and a touch of citrus; good acidity and balance. Cork. 13.5° alc. **RATING** 87 **DRINK** 2008 $ 9

Eaglehawk Semillon Chardonnay 2005 Semillon drives the wine; tangy citrus and grass; invisible oak. Cork. 13° alc. **RATING** 87 **DRINK** 2009 $ 9

Red Label Classic Dry White 2005 Plenty of ripe fruit to support the touch of sweetness; a thoroughly amiable wine. Screwcap. 13° alc. **RATING** 87 **DRINK** Now $ 12

Yellow Label Merlot 2004 Fresh, lively juicy redcurrant and red cherry mix; nice mouthfeel and balance; good value. Cork. **RATING** 87 **DRINK** 2008 $ 14.50

ᵀᵀᵀᵀ **Red Label Semillon Sauvignon Blanc 2005** **RATING** 86 **DRINK** Now $ 12

Eaglehawk Rose 2005 **RATING** 86 **DRINK** Now

Eaglehawk Shiraz 2004 **RATING** 86 **DRINK** 2008

Eaglehawk Merlot 2004 **RATING** 86 **DRINK** Now $ 9

Red Label Cabernet Merlot 2004 **RATING** 86 **DRINK** Now $ 12

Yellow Label Cabernet Sauvignon 2003 **RATING** 86 **DRINK** Now $ 14.50

Red Label Chardonnay 2005 **RATING** 85 **DRINK** Now $ 12

Red Label Shiraz Cabernet 2004 **RATING** 85 **DRINK** Now $ 12

Eaglehawk Cabernet Sauvignon 2004 **RATING** 85 **DRINK** Now $ 9

Red Label Unwooded Chardonnay 2005 **RATING** 84 **DRINK** Now $ 12

Eaglehawk Shiraz Merlot Cabernet 2004 **RATING** 84 **DRINK** Now $ 9

Yellow Label Shiraz 2003 **RATING** 84 **DRINK** Now $ 14.50

Wolseley Wines ★★★☆

1790 Hendy Main Road, Moriac, Geelong, Vic 3240 **REGION** Geelong
T 0412 990 638 **WWW**.wolseleywines.com **OPEN** W'ends & public hols 11–6
WINEMAKER Will Wolseley **EST.** 1992 **CASES** 2500

Will Wolseley grew up in Somerset, England, and from an early age started making blackberry wine at home. He came to Australia in 1986 and enrolled in wine science at Charles Sturt University, gathering vintage experience at various wineries over the next 5 years. A 2-year search for an ideal vineyard site resulted in the acquisition of property on the gently sloping hills of Paraparap, just off the Great Ocean Road, inland from Bells Beach, Torquay. Here he established 6.5 ha of vineyard planted to pinot noir, cabernet sauvignon, chardonnay, shiraz, cabernet franc and semillon. Hail storms, frost and drought delayed the first commercial vintage until 1998, but the winery is now in full production. Uniquely, the winery runs on solar power.

ᵀᵀᵀᵀ **Geelong Chardonnay 2004** Green-gold; pronounced developed toasty barrel ferment aromas and flavours; yellow peach and melon fruit; a fraction short, but good value. Screwcap. 14.9° alc. **RATING** 89 **DRINK** 2008 $ 15

Geelong Cabernet Sauvignon 2003 Ripe, aromatic, but not jammy, blackcurrant fruit; medium-bodied; controlled oak and tannins. Screwcap. 14.1° alc. **RATING** 89 **DRINK** 2013 $ 25

ŢŢŢ♈ **Geelong Pinot Noir 8 2004** Firm, spicy forest floor mixed with plummy fruit; does not have the problems of the standard Pinot. Screwcap. 13.8° alc. **RATING** 86 **DRINK** Now $ 15

Geelong Pinot Noir 2004 RATING 84 **DRINK** Now $ 20

Wombat Forest ★★★

RMB 4060, Denver via Daylesford, Vic 3461 (postal) **REGION** Macedon Ranges
T (03) 5423 9331 **OPEN** Not
WINEMAKER Brendon Lawlor **EST.** 1997 **CASES** 300
Wombat Forest is jointly owned and operated by local couples Brendon and Deidre Lawlor, and David and Elizabeth Nikcevich. They personally planted the 1.2 ha of cabernet sauvignon and pinot noir between 1997 and 1999, and are ready to plant out the next stage. Pinot Noir, Cabernet Sauvignon and Sparkling (Pinot Noir) are the 3 wines.

ŢŢŢŢ **Cabernet Sauvignon 2003** Clean, light- to medium-bodied, fruit-driven, cassis/blackcurrant/mulberry/mint/leaf aromas and flavours all interwoven. Cork. 13° alc.
RATING 88 **DRINK** 2010

Wonbah Estate NR

302 Wonbah Road, Wonbah via Gin Gin, Qld 4671 **REGION** Queensland Coastal
T (07) 4156 3029 **F** (07) 4156 3035 **WWW**.wonbahwinery.com **OPEN** 7 days 9.30–4
WINEMAKER Bruce Humphery-Smith (Contract) **EST.** 1997 **CASES** 1500
The 5-ha vineyard, planted to shiraz, chardonnay, cabernet sauvignon, ruby cabernet, muscat and verdelho, is near Mt Perry, an hour's drive west of Bundaberg at the extreme northern end of the Burnett Valley, extending the viticultural map of Qld yet further. The 100-tonne winery is under the direction of the omnipresent Bruce Humphery-Smith, and the tasting room is in a restored slab hut dating from the turn of the 20th century. There are numerous tourist attractions around Mt Perry, not the least being the Boolboonda Tunnel, the largest self-supporting tunnel in the southern hemisphere, hand-hewn, and home to a colony of fairy bats.

Wonga Estate ★★★★

204 Jumping Creek Road, Wonga Park, Vic 3115 **REGION** Yarra Valley
T (03) 9722 2122 **F** (03) 9722 1715 **WWW**.wongaestate.com.au **OPEN** Mon–Sat 9–5, Sun 10–5 by appt
WINEMAKER Sergio Carlei (Consultant), Greg Roberts **EST.** 1997 **CASES** 650
Greg (formerly Grollo's national construction manager) and Jady Roberts began the development of their 1.8-ha vineyard in 1997, with a minor expansion in 2002. The clones of pinot noir and chardonnay were selected with the advice of Sandro Mosele (of Mornington Peninsula's Kooyong Estate) with continuing viticultural advice from Bill Christophersen (ex Coldstream Hills). The wines are made at the onsite micro-winery by Greg Roberts with the direction and assistance of Sergio Carlei. Since 2002 the range has been expanded with shiraz grown in the Colbinabbin area of Heathcote, open-fermented and basket-pressed. Foot-treading of whole bunches of pinot has also been successfully employed.

ŢŢŢŢ♈ **Yarra Valley Chardonnay 2004** Complex barrel ferment bouquet; clean, fresh melon and peach fruit; not particularly intense, but has good line and length. Diam. 13° alc.
RATING 90 **DRINK** 2011 $ 28

Wood Park ★★★☆

263 Kneebone Gap Road, Markwood, Vic 3678 **REGION** King Valley
T (03) 5727 3367 **F** (03) 5727 3682 **WWW**.woodparkwines.com.au **OPEN** At Milawa Cheese Factory
7 days 10–5
WINEMAKER John Stokes **EST.** 1989 **CASES** 9000
John Stokes planted the first vines at Wood Park in 1989 as part of a diversification program for his property at Bobinawarrah, in the hills of the Lower King Valley, east of Milawa. The vineyard is managed with minimal chemical use, winemaking a mix of modern and traditional techniques. In an unusual twist, Stokes acquires his chardonnay from cousin John Leviny, one of the King Valley pioneers, who has his vineyard at Meadow Creek. Exports to the US and other major markets.

ŸŸŸŸŸ **Cabernet Shiraz 2004** Good colour; ripe black fruits; supple texture, and good structure. 14° alc. **RATING** 90 **DRINK** 2014 $ 20

ŸŸŸŸ **Meadow Creek Chardonnay 2004** Traditional style; plenty of peachy fruit and unambiguous oak contribution from barrel ferment and maturation; part wild yeast. Screwcap. 13.5° alc. **RATING** 89 **DRINK** 2008 $ 22
Pinot Gris 2005 Powerful varietal character in flavour, texture and body; apple, pear and warm spice. Screwcap. 14° alc. **RATING** 88 **DRINK** Now $ 20
Kneebone's Gap Shiraz 2004 Notes of earth and spice to the light- to medium-bodied black cherry/blackberry fruit; fresh finish. Cork. 14° alc. **RATING** 87 **DRINK** 2010 $ 22

ŸŸŸŸ **Myrrhee Merlot 2004 RATING** 86 **DRINK** 2009 $ 18

🍇 Woodeneye Estate ★★★

PO Box 893, Irymple, Vic 3498 **REGION** Murray Darling
T 0419 518 846 **F** (03) 5024 6126 **WWW**.woodeneye.com.au **OPEN** Not
WINEMAKER Steve Glasson **EST.** 1990 **CASES** 750
Steve and Debi Glasson purchased their 12-ha vineyard at Irymple in October 1990. It was largely planted to sultana, and in 1992 they took the decision to remove all but 0.6 ha of 65-year-old grenache. They replanted the vineyard to chardonnay, cabernet sauvignon, shiraz and merlot, leading to the first vintage in 2003. In the meantime Steve Glasson had completed a winemaking course through La Trobe University at Bundoora, and made the wine in an insulated shed on the property. Construction of a new winery and cellar door on the property next door, which the Glassons also own, is underway, with completion planned for the 2007 vintage.

ŸŸŸŸ **Mildura Shiraz 2004** Bright red-purple; clean, medium-bodied wine with pleasant black fruit flavours, good structure and oak. Screwcap. 13.5° alc. **RATING** 88 **DRINK** 2008 $ 16.50
Mildura Cabernet Sauvignon 2004 Very ripe cassis/blackcurrant fruit verging on confit, yet restrained alcohol. Screwcap. 13.5° alc. **RATING** 87 **DRINK** 2008 $ 16.50

ŸŸŸŸ **Mildura Shiraz 2003 RATING** 84 **DRINK** Now $ 16.50

Woodlands ★★★★★

Cnr Caves Road/Metricup Road, Wilyabrup via Cowaramup, WA 6284 **REGION** Margaret River
T (08) 9755 6226 **F** (08) 9755 6236 **WWW**.woodlandswines.com **OPEN** 7 days 10.30–5
WINEMAKER Stuart Watson, David Watson **EST.** 1973 **CASES** 5500
The quality of the grapes, with a priceless core of 6.8 ha of 30+-year-old cabernet sauvignon, more recently joined by merlot, malbec, cabernet franc, pinot noir and chardonnay, has never been in doubt. Whatever the shortcomings of the 1990s, these days Woodlands is producing some spectacular wines in small quantities. The larger-volume Cabernet Sauvignon is also of very high quality. Some behind-the-scenes consultancy advice has played its part, and Woodlands is now a major player in the top echelon of Margaret River producers. Exports to the UK and Asia.

ŸŸŸŸŸ **Margaret Reserve Cabernet Merlot 2004** Good red-purple; pure and precise varietal characters; medium-bodied cassis and blackcurrant; fine tannins, quality oak on a long finish; lovely wine. Screwcap. 14° alc. **RATING** 95 **DRINK** 2019 $ 39
Reserve du Cave Malbec 2004 Very good colour; attractive juicy plum, raspberry and cherry confit, but with the structure usually lacking in Malbec, soft and fine tannins; 50 cases made. Quality cork. 13.5° alc. **RATING** 95 **DRINK** 2015 $ 65
Chloe Reserve Chardonnay 2004 Rich, complex and mouthfilling; ripe peach and melon fruit; good oak handling. Quality cork. 14° alc. **RATING** 94 **DRINK** 2009 $ 40
Cabernet Sauvignon Merlot 2004 Bright, clear, purple-red; a lovely medium-bodied mix of cassis, blackcurrant and black cherry; great balance, fine tannins; patience not required. Cork. **RATING** 94 **DRINK** 2009 $ 20
Ivy Kathleen Cabernet Sauvignon 2003 Excellent red-purple; medium- to full-bodied, clear-cut blackcurrant, cassis and mulberry fruit framed by positive tannins and classy oak. For release Dec '06. Cork. 14° alc. **RATING** 94 **DRINK** 2023 $ 79

Emilie May Cabernet Sauvignon 2002 Holding hue well; medium-bodied; classic cassis and blackcurrant, with fine, ripe tannins running through the length of the palate, and controlled French oak. Cork. 14° alc. **RATING** 94 **DRINK** 2015 $ 79

Reserve du Cave Cabernet Franc 2004 A powerful, savoury wine with black and red fruits; lingering finish; good acidity, low pH; 50 cases made. Quality cork. 13.5° alc. **RATING** 94 **DRINK** 2015 $ 65

TTTTY **Reserve du Cave Merlot 2004** Very good colour; medium-bodied, but intense olive, earth, cassis and blackcurrant; very well-judged oak; falters a fraction with the tannins, but this will likely be a passing phase. Cork. 13.5° alc. **RATING** 93 **DRINK** 2015 $ 65

Margaret River Chardonnay 2005 Elegant, restrained nectarine and white peach fruit; a long, light- to medium-bodied palate with controlled French oak barrel ferment, and good acidity; simply needs time. Screwcap. 13.5° alc. **RATING** 92 **DRINK** 2015 $ 20

Emily Special Reserve 2004 Typical Woodlands colour, hue and depth; a juicy mix of red and black fruits; fine tannins, and well-balanced and integrated oak. Cork. 13.5° alc. **RATING** 92 **DRINK** 2012 $ 25

Woodonga Hill   NR

Cowra Road, Young, NSW 2594 **REGION** Hilltops
T (02) 6382 2972 **F** (02) 6382 2972 **OPEN** 7 days 9–5
WINEMAKER Jill Lindsay **EST.** 1986 **CASES** 4000

Early problems with white wine quality appear to have been surmounted. The wines have won bronze and silver medals at regional wine shows in NSW and Canberra, and Jill Lindsay is also a contract-winemaker for other small producers.

Woodside Valley Estate   ★★★★★

PO Box 332, Greenwood, WA 6924 **REGION** Margaret River
T (08) 9345 4065 **F** (08) 9345 4541 **WWW**.woodsidevalleyestate.com.au **OPEN** Not
WINEMAKER Kevin McKay **EST.** 1998 **CASES** 500

Woodside Valley has been developed by a small syndicate of investors headed by Peter Woods. In 1998 they acquired 67 ha of land at Yallingup, and have now established 19 ha of chardonnay, sauvignon blanc, cabernet sauvignon, shiraz, malbec and merlot. The experienced Albert Haak is consultant viticulturist, and together with Peter Woods, took the unusual step of planting south-facing in preference to north-facing slopes. In doing so they indirectly followed in the footsteps of the French explorer Thomas Nicholas Baudin, who mounted a major scientific expedition to Australia on his ship The Geographe, and defied established views and tradition of the time in (correctly) asserting that the best passage for sailing ships travelling between Cape Leeuwin and Bass Strait was from west to east. Exports to the US and Japan.

TTTTT **Le Bas Margaret River Chardonnay 2004** Elegant and refined; a seamless fusion of nectarine, melon and French oak; excellent length and balance. Cork. **RATING** 94 **DRINK** 2009 $ 35

Baudin Margaret River Cabernet Sauvignon 2003 A very clean mix of ripe blackcurrant, cassis and mulberry fruit with sweet French oak; long finish. High-quality cork. **RATING** 94 **DRINK** 2018 $ 48

TTTTY **Bonnefoy Margaret River Shiraz 2003** Smoky, leathery, spicy aromas; black fruits, licorice and spice flavours to the medium-bodied palate; particularly good finish thanks to fine, ripe tannins. Quality cork. **RATING** 92 **DRINK** 2012 $ 48

Bissy Margaret River Merlot 2003 Clear-cut, no compromise, varietal character with green olive, spice, earth and bitter chocolate; fine tannins, quality oak and a long finish. High-quality cork. **RATING** 90 **DRINK** 2010 $ 45

WoodSmoke Estate

NR

Lot 2 Kemp Road, Pemberton, WA 6260 **REGION** Pemberton
T (08) 9776 0225 **F** (08) 9776 0225 **OPEN** By appt
WINEMAKER Julie White **EST.** 1992 **CASES** 1500
The former Jimlee Estate was acquired by the Liebeck family in 1998 and renamed WoodSmoke Estate. The original 2 ha of semillon, sauvignon blanc, cabernet franc and cabernet sauvignon were expanded with 2.5 ha of cabernet franc and merlot in 2000.

Woodstock

★★★☆

Douglas Gully Road, McLaren Flat, SA 5171 **REGION** McLaren Vale
T (08) 8383 0156 **F** (08) 8383 0437 **WWW**.woodstockwine.com.au **OPEN** Mon–Fri 9–5, w'ends, hols 12–5
WINEMAKER Scott Collett, Ben Glaetzer **EST.** 1974 **CASES** 20 000
One of the stalwarts of McLaren Vale, producing archetypal and invariably reliable full-bodied red wines, and spectacular botrytis sweet whites and high-quality (14-year-old) Tawny Port. Also offers a totally charming reception-cum-restaurant, which does a roaring trade with wedding receptions. Has supplemented its 22 ha of McLaren Vale vineyards with 10 ha at its Wirrega Vineyard, in the Limestone Coast Zone. Exports to the UK, Switzerland, Denmark, Canada, Hong Kong, China, Malaysia, Phillipines and Singapore.

ɣɣɣɣ **Shiraz 2002** Light- to medium-bodied; a mix of blackcurrant and cherry fruit; fine ripe tannins, the Langhorne Creek component characters dominant. McLaren Vale/Langhorne Creek/Limestone Coast. Screwcap. 14° alc. **RATING** 89 **DRINK** 2010 $ 20
Botrytis 2004 Fresh, vibrant, juicy tropical flavours with a twist of lemony acidity; cleverly balanced. Once a weird multi-varietal blend, now made from semillon. Screwcap. 11° alc. **RATING** 89 **DRINK** Now $ 17
Five Feet White 2005 A curious blend which, even more curiously, works quite well; aromas of lychee and musk, then a citrussy palate courtesy of Riesling. Viognier/Riesling. Screwcap. 13° alc. **RATING** 88 **DRINK** 2008 $ 16
Five Feet Red 2002 Unconvincing colour; a light- to medium-bodied mix of small berry fruits, chocolate, earth and spice; fine, soft, savoury tannins. Screwcap. 14° alc. **RATING** 88 **DRINK** 2009 $ 16

ɣɣɣɣ **McLaren Vale Rose 2005** Vibrant fuchsia purple-red; full-on cellar door style; raspberry coulis fruit and residual sugar sweetness. Screwcap. 13° alc. **RATING** 86 **DRINK** Now $ 15
Shiraz Cabernet 2001 **RATING** 86 **DRINK** 2008 $ 15

Woody Nook

NR

Metricup Road, Wilyabrup, WA 6280 **REGION** Margaret River
T (08) 9755 7547 **F** (08) 9755 7007 **WWW**.woodynook.com.au **OPEN** 7 days 10–4.30
WINEMAKER Neil Gallagher **EST.** 1982 **CASES** 5000
This improbably named and not terribly fashionable winery has produced some truly excellent wines over the years, featuring in such diverse competitions as Winewise, the Sheraton Wine Awards and the Qantas West Australian Wines Show. Cabernet Sauvignon has always been its strong point, but it has a habit of also bobbing up with excellent white wines in various guises. Since 2000 owned by Peter and Jane Bailey; Neil Gallagher continues as viticulturist, winemaker and minority shareholder. Exports to the UK, the US, Brazil, Hong Kong and Singapore.

Woolshed Wines

NR

380 Horseflat Lane, Mullamuddy via Mudgee, NSW 2850 **REGION** Mudgee
T (02) 6373 1299 **F** (02) 6373 1299 **OPEN** 7 days 10–5
WINEMAKER David Lowe (Contract) **EST.** 1999 **CASES** NA
Kay and Mick Burgoyne own and run the 8-ha vineyard formerly known as Valley View Estates, planted to chardonnay, cabernet, merlot, shiraz and muscat hamburg. The cellar door offers barbecues in a garden setting, and can cater for functions, concerts or festivals.

Woolybud ★★★

Playford Highway, Parndana, SA 5220 **REGION** Kangaroo Island
T (08) 8559 6031 **F** (08) 8559 6031 **OPEN** Not
WINEMAKER Dudley Partners **EST.** 1998 **CASES** 1000
The Denis family moved to their sheep-farming property, Agincourt, west of Parndana, in 1986. Like many others, the downturn in the wool industry caused them to look to diversify their farming activities, and this led to the planting of shiraz and cabernet sauvignon, and to the subsequent release of their Wollombi brand wines. The wines are available by mail order.

ΥΥΥΥ **Cabernet Sangiovese 2004** An interesting Super Tuscan blend; a savoury/spicy/cassis/cherry/blackcurrant mix comes together well; fine tannins. Screwcap. 13.5° alc. **RATING** 88 **DRINK** 2010 $16

ΥΥΥ **Rose 2005** **RATING** 84 **DRINK** Now $11

Woongarra Estate ★★★★☆

95 Hayseys Road, Narre Warren East, Vic 3804 **REGION** Port Phillip Zone
T (03) 9796 8886 **F** (03) 9796 8580 **WWW**.woongarrawinery.com.au **OPEN** Thurs–Sun 9–5 by appt
WINEMAKER Graeme Leith, Greg Dedman, Bruce Jones **EST.** 1992 **CASES** 2000
Dr Bruce Jones, and wife Mary, purchased their 16-ha property many years ago; it falls within the Yarra Ranges Shire Council's jurisdiction and is zoned 'Landscape', but because nearby Cardinia Creek does not flow into the Yarra River, it is not within the Yarra Valley wine region. In 1992 they planted 1 ha of sauvignon blanc, a small patch of shiraz and a few rows of semillon. Over 1 ha of sauvignon blanc and pinot noir followed in 1996 (mostly MV6, some French clone 114 and 115) with yet more 114 and 115 pinot noir in 2000, lifting total plantings to 3.2 ha of pinot noir, 1.4 ha of sauvignon blanc and a splash of the other two varieties. The white grapes have had various purchasers and contract makers; spectacular success has come with the Three Wise Men Pinot Noir, (a joint venture between Woongarra and Passing Clouds — see separate entry).

ΥΥΥΥΥ **Semillon 2002** An elegant but intense mix of lemon, citrus and a continuous streak of minerality; strong wine, still youthful. Made by Sergio Carlei. Cork. 12° alc. **RATING** 91 **DRINK** 2010 $13
Sauvignon Blanc Semillon 2005 Extremely flinty, minerally and intense, with some herb and citrus creeping through the minerally acidity; austere style. Screwcap. 12.5° alc. **RATING** 90 **DRINK** 2011 $13
2005 Woongarra Estate Yarra Ranges Sauvignon Blanc Semillon A crisp array of mineral/herb and grass through to more tropical fruit characters; good structure and balance. Bargain. Screwcap. **RATING** 90 **DRINK** 2008 $12.95

ΥΥΥΥ **Shiraz 2004** Good hue; light- to medium-bodied; spicy black cherry in typical cool-grown style; fine tannins and balanced oak; could surprise with age. Diam. **RATING** 89 **DRINK** 2012 $15

Woongooroo Estate NR

35 Doyles Road, Mount Archer, Kilcoy, Qld 4515 (postal) **REGION** Queensland Coastal
T (07) 5496 3529 **F** (07) 5496 3529 **WWW**.westatewine.com **OPEN** Not
WINEMAKER Golden Grove Estate (Sam Costanzo, Ray Costanzo) **EST.** 1997 **CASES** NFP
Woongooroo Estate was established by primary schoolteachers Phil and Gail Close, who planted a little over 3 ha of chardonnay, semillon, shiraz, cabernet franc, merlot and verdelho, together with a commercial olive grove. It is part of the a new, albeit unofficial, Qld wine region known as the Somerset Valleys Grape & Wine Producers Association, more generically falling within the Queensland Coastal Hinterland.

Word of Mouth Wines

Campbell's Corner, Pinnacle Road, Orange, NSW 2800 **REGION** Orange
T (02) 6362 3509 **F** (02) 6365 3517 **WWW**.wordofmouthwines.com.au
OPEN Fri–Sun & public hols 11–5
WINEMAKER David Lowe, Jane Wilson (Contract) **EST.** 1991 **CASES** 1500
Word of Mouth Wines acquired the former Donnington Vineyard in 2003, with its 10 ha of mature vineyards, planted (in descending order of size) to sauvignon blanc, chardonnay, merlot, cabernet sauvignon, pinot noir, riesling and pinot gris between 1991 and 1996. Since 1996 all the cabernet sauvignon, and most of the merlot, has been removed, with additional plantings of pinot gris, sauvignon blanc and chardonnay taking their place, along with viognier. Thus the focus is on white wines and pinot noir.

ȲȲȲȲȲ **Orange Sauvignon Blanc 2005** Spotlessly clean bouquet; has extremely good intensity to the complex gooseberry/tropical/grass fruit, driving through to a long, crisp finish. A worthy winner of several trophies at smaller wine shows. Screwcap. 14.5° alc. **RATING** 95 **DRINK** 2008 $ 20

ȲȲȲȲȲ **Orange Chardonnay 2004** Clean and fresh; nectarine, melon, fig and cashew; good balance, developing slowly. Screwcap. 14.4° alc. **RATING** 90 **DRINK** 2010 $ 20

ȲȲȲȲ **Orange Riesling 2005** Cleverly made; a lively passionfruit and citrus mix, good acidity and, on the aftertaste, the realisation of a touch of residual sugar. Screwcap. 13.4° alc. **RATING** 89 **DRINK** 2012 $ 20
Pinnacle Pinot Gris 2005 Pleasant, well-made, gentle tropical fruit, though lacks intensity. Screwcap. 14.4° alc. **RATING** 87 **DRINK** 2008 $ 23
Orange Pinot Noir 2004 Light-bodied; savoury/foresty/earthy nuances throughout; has varietal character, but needs more sweet fruit, notwithstanding the alcohol. Screwcap. 14.5° alc. **RATING** 87 **DRINK** Now $ 20

ȲȲȲȲ **Orange Merlot 2004** **RATING** 86 **DRINK** 2008 $ 24

Wordsworth Wines ★★★

Cnr South Western Highway/Thompson Road, Harvey, WA 6220 **REGION** Geographe
T (08) 9773 4576 **F** (08) 9733 4269 **WWW**.wordsworthwines.com.au **OPEN** 7 days 10–5
WINEMAKER Lamont's (Digby Leddin, Rachael Robinson), Western Range Wines (Ryan Sudano)
EST. 1997 **CASES** 5000
David Wordsworth has established a substantial business in a relatively short space of time: 27 ha of vines have been planted, with cabernet sauvignon (10 ha) and shiraz (5 ha) predominant, and lesser amounts of zinfandel, petit verdot, chardonnay, chenin blanc and verdelho. The winery features massive jarrah beams, wrought iron and antique furniture, and the tasting room seats 80 people. The wines have already had show success. Exports to the UK, the US and Singapore.

ȲȲȲȲ **Geographe Verdelho 2005** Has less reduction on the bouquet than the Chenin Blanc; attractive fruit salad flavours with bright, lemony acidity to close. Screwcap. 13.5° alc. **RATING** 87 **DRINK** 2008 $ 22

ȲȲȲȲ **Geographe Chenin Blanc 2005** **RATING** 84 **DRINK** Now $ 20

Wright Family Wines

'Misty Glen', 293 Deasey Road, Pokolbin, NSW 2320 **REGION** Lower Hunter Valley
T (02) 4998 7781 **F** (02) 4998 7768 **WWW**.mistyglen.com.au **OPEN** 7 days 10–4
WINEMAKER Contract **EST.** 1985 **CASES** 800
Jim and Carol Wright purchased their property in 1985, with a small existing vineyard in need of tender loving care. This was duly given, and the semillon, chardonnay and cabernet sauvignon revived. In 2000, 1.5 ha of shiraz was planted; 1.5 ha of chambourcin was added in 2002, lifting total plantings to 7.5 ha. Carol has been involved in the wine industry since the early 1970s, and is now helped by husband Jim (who retired from the coal mines in 2002), and by children and grandchildren. Wines are released under the Misty Glen label.

ΨΨΨΨ **Misty Glen Semillon 2005** An intense, rich, almost viscous wine, despite the relatively low alcohol; potent citrus/lime flavours; very long finish. Screwcap. 11.8° alc. **RATING** 93 **DRINK** 2015 $ 20

ΨΨΨΨ **Misty Glen Chardonnay 2005** A solid, peachy wine with strong vanilla oak, the saving grace is the balanced acidity on the finish. 12° alc. **RATING** 88 **DRINK** 2010 $ 20

ΨΨΨΨ **Misty Glen Cabernet Sauvignon 2004** Light-bodied; but a distinct skein of sweetness runs throughout — presumably deliberate. Would certainly ring the cellar door bell. Cork. 13.9° alc. **RATING** 86 **DRINK** 2011 $ 25
Misty Glen Chambourcin 2004 **RATING** 85 **DRINK** Now $ 20

Wright Robertson of Glencoe   NR

'Waratah Ridge', New England Highway, Glencoe, NSW 2365 **REGION** Northern Slopes Zone
T (02) 6733 3255 **F** (02) 6733 3220 **WWW**.wrightwine.com **OPEN** Mon–Fri 9–5, Sat 10–4
WINEMAKER Scott Wright **EST.** 1999 **CASES** 3000
Scott and Julie Wright began establishing their 4-ha vineyard (pinot noir, pinot gris, riesling, shiraz and cabernet sauvignon) in 1999, and now operate a winery making both their own wines and wines for 3 other producers. They also purchase grapes from other growers; an estate-grown Organic Syrah is the flagship wine.

Wroxton Wines   ★★★★

Flaxman's Valley Road, Angaston, SA 5353 **REGION** Eden Valley
T (08) 8565 3227 **F** (08) 8565 3312 **WWW**.wroxton.com.au **OPEN** By appt
WINEMAKER Stephen Henschke, Christian Canute (Contract) **EST.** 1995 **CASES** 60
Ian and Jo Zander are third-generation grapegrowers on the 200-ha Wroxton Grange property, which was established and named in 1845. The Zander family purchased the property in 1920, and planted their first vines; since 1973 an extensive planting program has seen the progressive establishment of riesling (15.4 ha), shiraz (10.5 ha), chardonnay (6.9 ha), semillon (2.5 ha) and traminer (2 ha). The vast majority of the grapes are sold; limited amounts are contract-made, primarily for consumption by guests at the B&B cottage or the self-contained suite in the large bluestone homestead (built around 1890). The two wines produced are Riesling and Shiraz.

ΨΨΨΨΨ **Single Vineyard Eden Valley Riesling 2005** Very good texture and structure; a minerally spine to lime juice and apple-accented fruit; long finish. Screwcap. 12.5° alc. **RATING** 93 **DRINK** 2015 $ 15

ΨΨΨΨ **Eden Valley Shiraz 2003** Light- to medium-bodied; savoury, earthy nuances with a contrast of slightly cooked fruit; some elements of sweet and sour. Cork. 15° alc. **RATING** 88 **DRINK** 2009 $ 18

Wyanga Park   ★★★

Baades Road, Lakes Entrance, Vic 3909 **REGION** Gippsland
T (03) 5155 1508 **F** (03) 5155 1443 **OPEN** 7 days 9–5
WINEMAKER Damien Twigg **EST.** 1970 **CASES** 3000
Offers a broad range of wines of diverse provenance directed at the tourist trade; one of the Chardonnays and the Cabernet Sauvignon are estate-grown. Winery cruises up the north arm of the Gippsland Lake to Wyanga Park are scheduled 4 days a week all year.

ΨΨΨΨ **Sauvignon Blanc 2004** Fresh and lively; grass, herb and mineral flavours, backed up by lemony acidity. Cork. 13.6° alc. **RATING** 88 **DRINK** Now $ 17
Traminer Riesling 2005 Strong spicy traminer lychee influence; at the driest end of the spectrum for a sweet wine class, but should develop very well. Cork. 13.2° alc. **RATING** 87 **DRINK** 2010 $ 15

ΨΨΨΨ **Estate Grown Chardonnay 2005** **RATING** 84 **DRINK** Now $ 19

Wyndham Estate ★★★★

700 Dalwood Road, Dalwood, NSW 2335 **REGION** Lower Hunter Valley
T (02) 4938 3444 **F** (02) 4938 3555 **WWW**.wyndhamestate.com **OPEN** 7 days 10–4.30 except public hols
WINEMAKER Sam Kurtz **EST.** 1828 **CASES** 1 million
This historic property is now merely a shopfront for the Wyndham Estate label. Winemaking was transferred from the Hunter to Mudgee (Poet's Corner) many years ago. The Bin wines often surprise with their quality, representing excellent value; the Show Reserve wines, likewise, can be very good. The wines come from various parts of South East Australia, sometimes specified, sometimes not.

ŸŸŸŸŸ **Show Reserve Shiraz 2003** Medium- to full-bodied; luscious, round black fruits; well-balanced and integrated French and American oak, sustained tannins. Not Hunter Valley. Gold medal Sydney Wine Show '06. Cork. 14.5° alc. **RATING** 93 **DRINK** 2013 $ 25
Show Reserve Cabernet Merlot 2001 Good colour; a medium- to full-bodied, rich and supple palate; good varietal expression and length, with fine, ripe tannins and classy oak. Deserves better than the ingenuous guff on the back and front labels. Cork. 14.5° alc. **RATING** 93 **DRINK** 2011 $ 25
Regional Selection Hunter Valley Semillon 2000 Light straw-green; still very restrained citrus, herb and grass; long, crunchy/minerally acidity dominates the palate. Cork. **RATING** 91 **DRINK** 2012 $ 30
Regional Selection Hunter Valley Shiraz 1999 Ultra-regional earthy style, literally shrieking its Hunter origin; the colour still good; nice red fruits, and powerful tannin still to soften and fully integrate. Cork. 13° alc. **RATING** 90 **DRINK** 2014 $ 30

ŸŸŸŸ **Bin 777 Semillon Sauvignon Blanc 2005** Gently fragrant and lively; crisp, lemony minerality; clean, long finish. Screwcap. **RATING** 89 **DRINK** Now $ 13.99
Regional Selection Hunter Valley Shiraz 2003 Bright colour; positive black and red fruits; fine, silky tannins, and balanced oak. Cork. **RATING** 89 **DRINK** 2010 $ 30
Bin 222 Chardonnay 2005 Lively, fresh citrus, melon and stone fruit; a light-bodied, fruit-driven style with good length. Screwcap. 13° alc. **RATING** 88 **DRINK** Now $ 14
Bin 444 Cabernet Sauvignon 2003 Fresh, direct black and red fruits on a light- to medium-bodied palate; balanced, savoury tannins. Cork. 14.5° alc. **RATING** 87 **DRINK** 2009 $ 14

ŸŸŸŸ **Bin 111 Verdelho 2005** Plenty of flavour: fruit salad plus hints of lemon and lime; good balance, better than many. Screwcap. 12° alc. **RATING** 86 **DRINK** Now $ 14
Bin 555 Shiraz 2003 **RATING** 86 **DRINK** Now $ 13.99
Bin 888 Cabernet Merlot 2003 Light- to medium-bodied spicy, blackcurrant fruit; neatly made commercial wine. Cork. 14° alc. **RATING** 86 **DRINK** 2008 $ 14
Bin 555 Sparkling Shiraz NV **RATING** 86 **DRINK** 2009 $ 14
Bin 333 Pinot Noir 2004 **RATING** 85 **DRINK** Now $ 14
Bin 222 Sparkling Chardonnay NV **RATING** 85 **DRINK** Now $ 14
Bin 999 Merlot 2004 **RATING** 84 **DRINK** Now $ 14

Wynns Coonawarra Estate ★★★★

Memorial Drive, Coonawarra, SA 5263 **REGION** Coonawarra
T (08) 8736 3266 **F** (08) 8736 3202 **WWW**.wynns.com.au **OPEN** 7 days 10–5
WINEMAKER Sue Hodder **EST.** 1897 **CASES** NFP
The large-scale production has not prevented Wynns from producing excellent wines covering the full price spectrum, from the bargain basement Riesling and Shiraz through to the deluxe John Riddoch Cabernet Sauvignon and Michael Shiraz. Even with steady price increases, Wynns offers extraordinary value for money. Good though that may be, there is even greater promise for the future; the vineyards are being rejuvenated by new trellising or replanting, and a regime directed to quality rather than quantity has been introduced, under the direction of Allen Jenkins. He is receiving enthusiastic support from the winemaking team headed by Sue Hodder. Exports to the UK, the US and other major markets.

ŸŸŸŸŸ **Chardonnay 2004** Light- to medium-bodied; very good fruit and oak balance and integration; melon and stone fruit plus spicy oak; clean finish, good acidity. Screwcap. **RATING** 90 **DRINK** 2010 $ 15.95

ŸŸŸŸ **Riesling 2005** Light floral and spice bouquet; a shy and delicate palate, but has length and balance, simply needing time to flower and garner higher points. Screwcap. **RATING** 89 **DRINK** 2013 $15.95

Shiraz 2004 Light- to medium-bodied; clean, fresh and unforced; mid-range red and black fruits; subtle oak; doesn't sing right now. Cork. **RATING** 89 **DRINK** 2010 $18.99

J Block Shiraz Cabernet 2004 Unconvincing colour, not entirely bright; a medium-bodied, elegant and restrained style; spice, earth and black fruits; fine tannins. Screwcap. **RATING** 89 **DRINK** 2014 $36

Wyuna Park ★★☆

105 Soho Road, Drysdale, Vic 3222 (postal) **REGION** Geelong
T (03) 5253 1348 **F** (03) 5253 2801 **OPEN** Not
WINEMAKER Bill Sawyer, Curlewis **EST.** 1998 **CASES** 150
Former professor of biochemistry and molecular biology at the University of Melbourne Bill Sawyer, and wife Diana, planted 1.6 ha of pinot noir and 0.4 ha of pinot gris between 1998 and 1999. The intention was to sell the grapes to other wineries, but in 2004 they could not resist the temptation to start making Pinot Noir at the estate. Bill Sawyer teaches biochemistry in the wine course at Dookie College, his winemaking at the estate putting theory into practice. The Pinot Gris is made by Rainer Breit at Curlewis. An unusual application of the pinot noir is partly as a saignee rose and partly as a fortified wine, although the main portion is made conventionally.

ŸŸŸŸ **Rose 2005** **RATING** 86 **DRINK** Now $15
Pinot Noir 2004 **RATING** 85 **DRINK** Now $18

Xabregas ★★★★★

Cnr Spencer Road/Hay River Road, Narrikup, WA 6326 **REGION** Mount Barker
T (08) 9321 2366 **F** (08) 9327 9393 **WWW**.xabregas.com.au **OPEN** By appt
WINEMAKER Dr Diane Miller, Greg Jones, Mike Garland (Contract) **EST.** 1996 **CASES** 12 000
In 1996 stockbrokers Terry Hogan and Eve Broadley, the major participants in the Spencer Wine Joint Venture, commenced a viticulture business which has now grown into 3 vineyards totalling 120 ha on sites 10 km south of Mount Barker. The varieties planted are riesling, chardonnay, sauvignon blanc, cabernet sauvignon, cabernet franc, merlot and shiraz. As well as being contract growers to Houghton, Howard Park and Forest Hill, and acting as contract managers to surrounding vineyards. The wines are modestly priced.

ŸŸŸŸŸ **Riesling 2005** Clean, pale straw-green; has good depth and total mouth-coating flavour; sweet lime juice; good acidity, dry finish. Screwcap. 12° alc. **RATING** 94 **DRINK** 2015 $14

Shiraz 2004 Very good colour; medium- to full-bodied; supple, round plum, blackberry and spice flavours; ripe tannins, positive quality oak. Trophy Best Shiraz Qantas Wine Show of WA '05. Cork. 14° alc. **RATING** 94 **DRINK** 2014 $14

ŸŸŸŸŸ **Show Reserve Chardonnay 2005** Light straw-green; a very elegant style with nectarine and white peach fruit; sophisticated barrel ferment inputs; good balance and length. Screwcap. 14° alc. **RATING** 93 **DRINK** 2012 $22

Cabernet Sauvignon 2004 Medium-bodied; ripe blackcurrant, mulberry and cassis fruit; soft tannins, good oak. Cork. 14° alc. **RATING** 90 **DRINK** 2014 $14

Xanadu Wines

Boodjidup Road, Margaret River, WA 6285 **REGION** Margaret River
T (08) 9757 2581 **F** (08) 9757 3389 **WWW**.xanaduwines.com **OPEN** 7 days 10–5
WINEMAKER Glenn Goodall **EST.** 1977 **CASES** 60 000
Xanadu fell prey to over-ambitious expansion and to the increasingly tight trading conditions in 2005 as wine surpluses hit hard. The assets were acquired by the Rathbone Group, completing the Yering Station/Mount Langi Ghiran/Parker Coonawarra Estate/Xanadu group. The prime assets were (and are) the 130 ha of vineyards and a winery to match. Exports to all major markets.

ƟƟƟƟƟ **Secession Semillon Sauvignon Blanc 2005** A delicate fresh bouquet, the palate likewise delicate, yet quite intense with passionfruit, green apple and snow pea flavours; very good line, and even better length. Screwcap. 12.5° alc. **RATING** 94 **DRINK** Now $14

ƟƟƟƟƟ **Margaret River Chardonnay 2004** Relatively light-bodied, but nicely focused, and — despite the oak — is fruit-driven. Whole bunch-pressed and 9 months on lees in oak. Good length. Screwcap. 13.5° alc. **RATING** 93 **DRINK** 2012 $25

ƟƟƟƟ **Frankland/Margaret River Shiraz 2004** Typical winery style, elegant and light- to medium-bodied, belying its alcohol; red fruits, spices and fine tannins. Screwcap. 15° alc. **RATING** 89 **DRINK** 2010 $25
Margaret River Cabernet Sauvignon 2004 Quite fragrant and distinctly spicy; cassis-accented fruit on the light- to medium-bodied palate; lean, but fine, tannins. Screwcap. 14.5° alc. **RATING** 89 **DRINK** 2010 $25
Secession Chardonnay 2004 A good, inevitably simple, unoaked style; clean, light-bodied melon and citrus fruit. Screwcap. 14° alc. **RATING** 87 **DRINK** 2009 $14

ƟƟƟ **Secession Shiraz Cabernet 2004 RATING** 83 $14

Yabby Lake Vineyard ★★★★★

1 Garden Street, South Yarra, Vic 3141 (postal) **REGION** Mornington Peninsula
T (03) 9251 5375 **F** (03) 9639 1540 **WWW**.yabbylake.com **OPEN** Not
WINEMAKER Tod Dexter, Larry McKenna **EST.** 1998 **CASES** NA
This high-profile wine business is owned by Robert and Mem Kirby (of Village Roadshow) who have been landowners in the Mornington Peninsula for decades. In 1998 they established Yabby Lake Vineyard, under the direction of vineyard manager Keith Harris; the vineyard is on a north-facing slope, capturing maximum sunshine while also receiving sea breezes. The main focus is the 21 ha of pinot noir, 10 ha of chardonnay and 5 ha of pinot gris; the 2 ha each of shiraz and merlot take a back seat. Tod Dexter (former long-term winemaker at Stonier) and Larry McKenna (ex Martinborough Vineyards and now the Escarpment in NZ) both have great experience.

ƟƟƟƟƟ **Mornington Peninsula Chardonnay 2004** Green-straw; restrained complexity to a sophisticated wine; melon, nectarine and cream on a very fine palate; high-quality oak. Cork. 13.5° alc. **RATING** 94 **DRINK** 2012 $38
Mornington Peninsula Pinot Noir 2004 An impressively rich and complex follow on to the '03; ripe plums and spice; excellent and oak support. Cork. 14.5° alc. **RATING** 94 **DRINK** 2012 $55

Yacca Paddock Vineyards ★★★★☆

PO Box 824, Kent Town, SA 5071 **REGION** Adelaide Hills
T (08) 8362 3397 **F** (08) 8363 3797 **WWW**.yaccapaddock.com **OPEN** Not
WINEMAKER Mr Riggs Wine Company **EST.** 2000 **CASES** 500
Filmmakers Kerry Heysen-Hicks and husband Scott Hicks have left little to chance in establishing Yacca Paddock Vineyards. The vineyards (22 ha) have been established under the direction of leading viticulturist Geoff Hardy, and the wines are made by equally illustrious winemaker Ben Riggs. The vineyard is at an altitude of 350 metres in the Adelaide Hills, and all of the vines are netted; grazing and guns alike are banned from the remaining 25 ha of bushland on the property, which is rapidly regenerating. In descending order of size the rainbow selection of varieties is chardonnay, pinot noir, tempranillo, merlot, cabernet sauvignon, riesling, sauvignon blanc, shiraz, arneis, dolcetto, tannat and durif.

ƟƟƟƟƟ **Adelaide Hills Shiraz Tannat 2003** Fragrant but intense and powerful; predominantly dark fruits; surprisingly silky palate; very impressive debut; 80% Shiraz/20% Tannat. Quality cork. **RATING** 92 **DRINK** 2013 $50
Adelaide Hills Dolcetto 2002 Elegant, light- to medium-bodied style; spicy, peppery, cedary mix with red cherry fruit and lemony acidity. Still youthful; good length. Cork. **RATING** 90 **DRINK** 2010 $25

Yaccaroo Wines NR

PO Box 201, Yankalilla, SA 5203 **REGION** Southern Fleurieu
T (08) 8558 3218 **OPEN** Not
WINEMAKER Justin Lane **EST.** 2004 **CASES** 250
Gavin and Julianne Schubert planted 2 ha of shiraz in 1998, followed by 2.2 ha of cabernet sauvignon in 1999. The original intention was to simply sell the grapes, but oversupply in the grape market has led to part of the production being made for the Yaccaroo wines.

Yackadale Wines NR

Fairview Road, Lucindale, SA 5272 **REGION** Limestone Coast Zone
T (08) 8766 2084 **F** (08) 8766 2058 **www**.las.sa.edu.au **OPEN** By appt
WINEMAKER Stuart Williams, Peter Friedricks **EST.** 1999 **CASES** 300
This is the venture of the Lucindale Area School, which has a vine-to-wine program. The school has 1.5 ha each of pinot noir and cabernet sauvignon, and the winery has been established in an old farmhouse adjacent to the vineyard. The students are involved in all aspects of viticulture and winemaking, including onsite chemical analysis, label design and bottling. Lucindale won the National Schools Wine Show in 2005 with a 2004 Cabernet Sauvignon, and is involved in various regional activities. The name, incidentally, is derived from the Yackadale Murray Grey cattle stud. The wines are sold through the school and selected local outlets.

Yaldara Wines ★★☆

Gomersal Road, Lyndoch, SA 5351 **REGION** Barossa Valley
T (08) 8524 4200 **F** (08) 8524 4678 **www**.yaldara.com.au **OPEN** 7 days 9–5
WINEMAKER Matt Tydeman **EST.** 1947 **CASES** 500 000
At the very end of 1999 Yaldara became part of the publicly listed Simeon Wines, the intention being that it (Yaldara) should become the quality flagship of the group. Despite much expenditure and the short-lived stay of at least one well known winemaker, the plan failed to deliver the expected benefits. In February 2002 McGuigan Wines made a reverse takeover for Simeon, and the various McGuigan brands will (presumably) fill the role intended for Yaldara.

TTTT **Duck's Flat Chenin Blanc Semillon Sauvignon Blanc 2004** RATING 84 DRINK Now

TTT **Duck's Flat Grenache Mataro Ruby Cabernet 2004** RATING 83

Yalumba ★★★★★

Eden Valley Road, Angaston, SA 5353 **REGION** Barossa Valley
T (08) 8561 3200 **F** (08) 8561 3393 **www**.yalumba.com **OPEN** Mon–Fri 8.30–5, Sat 10–5, Sun 12–5
WINEMAKER Brian Walsh, Alan Hoey, Louisa Rose, Peter Gambetta and others **EST.** 1849 **CASES** 900 000
Family-owned and run by Robert Hill Smith; much of its prosperity in the late 1980s and early 1990s turned on the great success of Angas Brut in export markets, but the company has always had a commitment to quality and shown great vision in its selection of vineyard sites, new varieties and brands. It has always been a serious player at the top end of full-bodied (and full-blooded) Australian reds, and was the pioneer in the use of screwcaps (for Pewsey Vale Riesling). While its 940 ha of estate vineyards are largely planted to mainstream varieties, it has taken marketing ownership of Viognier. Exports to all major markets.

TTTTT **The Virgilius Viognier 2004** Gentle peach and apricot aromas, then an ultra-complex and supple mouthfeel, with no impact whatsoever from the alcohol. A brilliant exercise in restrained power. Cork. 14.5° alc. RATING 96 DRINK 2010 $49.95
Octavius Shiraz 2001 Excellent black cherry and blackberry fruit, bright and still fresh; the oak in relative restraint; supple mouthfeel, flavour without excess alcohol. Cork. 13.5° alc. RATING 96 DRINK 2016 $89.95
Eden Valley Viognier 2004 Spotlessly clean; classic apricot, white peach and melon aromas and flavours; very good mouthfeel and texture. Enticing price. Gold medal Sydney Wine Show '06. Screwcap. 14.5° alc. RATING 94 DRINK Now $21.95
Octavius Shiraz 2002 Excellent hue; complex blackberry and plum fruit; spicy mocha oak and silky tannins; impressive length. Cork. RATING 94 DRINK Now $90

ŸŸŸŸŸ **Y Series Sauvignon Blanc 2005** Well-made; the clearest possible varietal character, with a mix of grass, herb, gooseberry and more tropical fruit; long, lemony finish. Screwcap. 11.5° alc. RATING 93 DRINK Now $ 12

Hand Picked Shiraz Viognier 2003 Good colour; a vibrant and fresh bouquet with Viognier lift; a very substantial wine in the mouth, with texture and structure from quite firm tannins. Cork. 14° alc. RATING 93 DRINK 2015 $ 28.95

Barossa Mourvedre Grenache Shiraz 2004 Very powerful dark fruits; slightly grainy tannins, and needing time. Gold medal National Wine Show '05. RATING 93 DRINK 2015 $ 29

Tricentenary Vines Barossa Valley Grenache 2003 Significantly more structure and authority than the Bush Vine; still juicy, but much more in the black fruit spectrum, and has structure. Cork. 14.5° alc. RATING 93 DRINK 2012

The Signature Cabernet Shiraz 2002 Bright red-purple; a medium-bodied, refined mix of black and red fruits; supple, fine tannins and a warm creche of vanilla oak around the fruit. Cork. RATING 93 DRINK 2015 $ 43

Wild Ferment Eden Valley Chardonnay 2005 Elegant stone fruit, citrus and melon; great mouthfeel, with a subliminal touch of oak. Screwcap. 14° alc. RATING 92 DRINK 2009 $ 18

Single Spur Adelaide Hills Chardonnay 2004 Tight, restrained mineral, stone fruit and cashew, with wild yeast influence. Screwcap. RATING 92 DRINK 2010 $ 23.95

Hand Picked Late Harvest Wrattonbully Viognier 2005 Texturally luscious to the point of honeyed viscosity; uncutuous apricot kernel/honey flavours; remarkable wine. Picked May 4. Cork. RATING 92 DRINK 2010 $ 25

Ringbolt Margaret River Cabernet Sauvignon 2003 Sweet blackcurrant cassis fruit; fine-grained, almost silky tannins; good oak and excellent length. Cork. 14° alc. RATING 91 DRINK 2010 $ 23

The Signature Cabernet Shiraz 2001 Smooth, supple, rounded fruit, integrated and balanced oak, and bottle age all shape what is a deliberate continuation of the style commenced 34 vintages previously. RATING 91 DRINK 2011 $ 42.95

Y Series Riesling 2005 Surprising power, texture and intensity; gentle tropical fruits; long finish. Screwcap. RATING 90 DRINK 2010 $ 11.95

ŸŸŸŸ **Eden Valley Semillon Sauvignon Blanc 2005** Spotless; light-bodied, elegant citrus/lemon blossom and fruit; grass, mineral and apple complete the roll; clean, fresh finish. Screwcap. 13.5° alc. RATING 89 DRINK 2008 $ 18

Y Series Pinot Grigio 2005 Spice, herb, apple and pear aromas; a relatively delicate but well-balanced palate. Screwcap. 14° alc. RATING 89 DRINK Now $ 12

Limited Release Sangiovese Rose 2005 Aromatic spice and cherry bouquet; a dry, but quite intense palate, with strawberry fruit; serious rose style. Screwcap. 13.5° alc. RATING 89 DRINK Now $ 12

Y Series Shiraz Viognier 2004 Fragrant and lifted in typical Shiraz Viognier style; a light-to medium-bodied wine with very pleasant, sweet red fruits. Great value. Twin top. RATING 89 DRINK 2008 $ 11.95

D Black Cuvee 1999 Still rich and relatively sweet after 5 years on lees; not easy to understand why the dosage is so high; certainly has plenty of flavour. 13.5° alc. RATING 89 DRINK Now $ 30

Oxford Landing Sauvignon Blanc 2005 Clear and clean varietal fruit in a tropical/passionfruit spectrum; crisp finish; remarkable for the region. Light but crisp, and well-balanced. Screwcap. RATING 88 DRINK Now $ 7.95

Y Series Viognier 2005 Honeysuckle, spice and citrus aromas; doesn't quite deliver on the palate, but good value nonetheless. Cork. RATING 88 DRINK Now $ 11.95

Barossa Valley Shiraz & Viognier 2003 Light- to medium-bodied; fresh, aromatic lift of viognier quite evident; likewise the apricot nuances on the palate; fine, distinctly savoury, tannins. Cork. RATING 88 DRINK 2009 $ 16.95

Bush Vine Grenache 2003 Light- to medium-bodied; soft, juicy, red berry fruit with a touch of confection common to most Barossa Valley grenaches; drink soon. RATING 88 DRINK Now

Christobel's Dry White 2005 Flavoursome, ripe tropical fruit; mouthfilling, with slight fruit sweetness; easy style. Sauvignon Blanc/Semillon. Screwcap. 14° alc. RATING 87 DRINK Now $ 14

Y Series Shiraz 2004 Good colour; attractive cherry and plum fruits; fine, ripe tannins provide texture and structure. Screwcap. 14° alc. **RATING** 87 **DRINK** 2009 $ 12

Galway Vintage Traditional Shiraz 2004 Light- to medium-bodied; nicely balanced savoury, spicy red fruits; indeed traditional, though helped by the vintage. Twin top. 14° alc. **RATING** 87 **DRINK** 2008 $ 14

Y Series Merlot 2004 Medium red-purple; uncompromising savoury herbal olive varietal fruit; the tannins and oak are quite sweet, however, and provide balance. Cork. 13.5° alc. **RATING** 87 **DRINK** 2009 $ 12

ΨΨΨΨ **Y Series Unwooded Chardonnay 2005** **RATING** 86 **DRINK** 2008 $ 12
Oxford Landing Chardonnay 2005 **RATING** 86 **DRINK** Now $ 8
Oxford Landing Shiraz 2004 **RATING** 86 **DRINK** Now $ 8
Y Series Cabernet Sauvignon 2004 **RATING** 85 **DRINK** 2009 $ 12
Oxford Landing Grenache Shiraz Mourvedre 2004 **RATING** 84 **DRINK** Now
Oxford Landing Merlot 2004 **RATING** 84 **DRINK** Now $ 8

ΨΨΨ **Oxford Landing Cabernet Sauvignon Shiraz 2004** **RATING** 83 $ 8

Yalumba The Menzies (Coonawarra)   ★★★★☆

Riddoch Highway, Coonawarra, SA 5263 **REGION** Coonawarra
T (08) 8737 3603 **F** (08) 8737 3604 **WWW**.yalumba.com **OPEN** 7 days 10–4.30
WINEMAKER Peter Gambetta **EST.** 2002 **CASES** 5000
Like many SA companies, Yalumba had been buying grapes from Coonawarra and elsewhere in the Limestone Coast Zone long before it became a landowner there. In 1993 it purchased the 20-ha vineyard which had provided the grapes previously purchased, and a year later added a nearby 16-ha block. Together, these vineyards now have 22 ha of cabernet sauvignon and 4 ha each of merlot and shiraz. The next step was the establishment of 82 ha of vineyard in the Wrattonbully region, led by 34 ha of cabernet sauvignon, the remainder equally split between shiraz and merlot. The third step was to build The Menzies Wine Room and Vineyard on the first property acquired — named Menzies Vineyard — and to offer the full range of Limestone Coast wines through this striking rammed-earth tasting and function centre.

ΨΨΨΨΨ **The Menzies Coonawarra Cabernet Sauvignon 2002** Good colour; fragrant red and black fruit aromas; medium-bodied, with vibrant blackcurrant and cassis fruit; lingering, fine ripe tannins. **RATING** 92 **DRINK** 2012 $ 43

Mawson's Bridge Block 7A Wrattonbully Sauvignon Blanc 2005 Tropical gooseberry and passionfruit aromas; very smooth and appealing; won't frighten the horses. Screwcap. 12° alc. **RATING** 90 **DRINK** Now $ 15

Smith & Hooper Cabernet Merlot 2003 Good colour; good balance, texture and structure; blackcurrant and cedar flavours; ripe tannins. Cork. **RATING** 90 **DRINK** 2009 $ 16.95

Mawson's Hill Block 3 Wrattonbully Cabernet Sauvignon 2004 Bright purple-red; medium-bodied blackcurrant and mulberry fruit, then slightly dusty tannins; good oak. Cork. 13.5° alc. **RATING** 90 **DRINK** 2012 $ 15

ΨΨΨΨ **Smith & Hooper Merlot 2003** Light- to medium-bodied; clear varietal earth and olive overtones; nicely integrated oak in balance with the fruit. Cork. 13.5° alc. **RATING** 89 **DRINK** 2010 $ 17

Yandoit Hill Vineyard   NR

Nevens Road, Yandoit Creek, Vic 3461 **REGION** Bendigo
T (03) 9379 1763 **F** (03) 9379 1763 **OPEN** By appt (special open days for mail list customers)
WINEMAKER Colin Mitchell **EST.** 1988 **CASES** 300
Colin and Rosa Mitchell commenced the development of Yandoit Hill with the first plantings in 1988 with merlot, and a little under a ha each of cabernet franc and cabernet sauvignon followed by 0.5 ha each of arneis (the first planting in Australia), and nebbiolo in 1995. The vineyard is situated 20 km north of Daylesford, roughly halfway from Ballarat to Bendigo and, although situated on the north-facing slope of Yandoit Hill, is in an uncompromisingly cool climate.

Yangarra Estate   ★★★★☆

Kangarilla Road, McLaren Vale, SA 5171 **REGION** McLaren Vale
T (08) 8383 7459 **F** (08) 8383 7518 **WWW**.yangarra.com **OPEN** By appt
WINEMAKER Peter Fraser **EST.** 2000 **CASES** 12 000
This is the Australian operation of Kendall-Jackson, one of the leading premium wine producers in California. In December 2000 Kendall-Jackson acquired the 172-ha Eringa Park vineyard from Normans Wines (97 ha are under vine, the oldest dating back to 1923). The renamed Yangarra Park is the estate base for the operation, which has, so it would seem, remained much smaller than originally envisaged by Jess Jackson. Exports to the US and Europe.

ΨΨΨΨ♀ **Shiraz 2004** Classic regional style; sumptuous, rich, black fruits in an envelope of dark chocolate; alcohol (for better or worse) part of the style. Screwcap. 15° alc. **RATING** 93 **DRINK** 2019 $ 28
       Old Vine Grenache 2004 Strong red-purple; sweet, luscious, juicy berry grenache varietal character; soft tannins and subtle oak. Screwcap. 15° alc. **RATING** 92 **DRINK** 2012 $ 28
       Chardonnay 2005 Smooth, attractive melon and white peach fruit; quite elegant, the oak inputs well controlled and balanced. Screwcap. 13.8° alc. **RATING** 90 **DRINK** Now $ 18

ΨΨΨΨ   **Rose 2005** A crossover between rose and light-bodied dry red, more in the latter camp; well-balanced and flavoursome. Grenache (70%)/Shiraz. Screwcap. 13.8° alc. **RATING** 89 **DRINK** 2008 $ 18
       Cadenzia 2004 Good colour; a super-ripe mix of plum, prune, chocolate and vanilla; overall, a touch too sweet. Grenache/Shiraz/Mourvedre. Screwcap. 15° alc. **RATING** 89 **DRINK** 2009 $ 28

Yanmah Ridge   NR

Yanmah Road, Manjimup, WA 6258 **REGION** Manjimup
T (08) 9772 1301 **F** (08) 9772 1501 **WWW**.yanmahridge.com.au **OPEN** By appt
WINEMAKER Peter Nicholas, John Wade (Consultant) **EST.** 1987 **CASES** 3500
Peter and Sallyann Nicholas have established 26 ha of vineyards on elevated, north-facing slopes, with semillon, sauvignon blanc, chardonnay, pinot noir, sangiovese, merlot, cabernet franc and cabernet sauvignon. The property was identified by Peter Nicholas in 1986 as 'the perfect location' after a study of grapegrowing regions in WA. The project was the last requirement for Nicholas to complete his winemaking degree at Roseworthy Agricultural College. Their viticulture is environmentally friendly, with no residual herbicides or chemical pesticides. A new winery was built in 2001, but the majority of the annual production is still sold (as grapes or wine) to other producers. Exports to England, Canada and Hong Kong.

Yarra Brook Estate   ★★★☆

Yarraview Road, Yarra Glen, Vic 3775 **REGION** Yarra Valley
T (03) 9763 7066 **F** (03) 9763 8757 **WWW**.yarrabrook.com.au **OPEN** By appt
WINEMAKER Timo Mayer, Charlie Brydon (Contract) **EST.** 1997 **CASES** 2000
Since 1997 Yarra Brook Estate has established 26 ha of vineyard, planted (in descending order) to pinot noir, chardonnay, cabernet sauvignon, sauvignon blanc, shiraz and merlot. While most of the grapes are sold to other producers, production under the Yarra Brook label has increased.

ΨΨΨΨ♀ **Sauvignon Blanc 2005** Pale green-straw; clean, aromatic blossom and passionfruit aromas, the same flavours (with a touch of grass) follow on the delicate but focused palate. Screwcap. 13.8° alc. **RATING** 91 **DRINK** Now $ 14

ΨΨΨ♀   **Pinot Noir 2004** Light- to medium purple-red; a melange of spice, plum and mint, not entirely ripe. Cork. 12.5° alc. **RATING** 86 **DRINK** 2008 $ 15

Yarra Burn

★★★★★

Settlement Road, Yarra Junction, Vic 3797 **REGION** Yarra Valley
T (03) 5967 1428 **F** (03) 5967 1146 **WWW**.yarraburn.com.au **OPEN** 7 days 10–5
WINEMAKER Mark O'Callaghan **EST.** 1975 **CASES** 15 000
Acquired by Hardys in 1995 and, for the time being, the headquarters of Hardys' very substantial Yarra Valley operations, the latter centring on the large production from its Hoddles Creek vineyards. The new brand direction has largely taken shape. Care needs to be taken in reading the back labels of the wines other than the Bastard Hill duo, for the majority are regional blends, albeit with a substantial Yarra Valley component. Exports to the UK and the US.

ΨΨΨΨΨ **Bastard Hill Chardonnay 2000** Complex and very intense; beautiful citrus, melon and white peach fruit; fastidious barrel ferment oak handling; aging superbly. Quality cork. **RATING** 96 **DRINK** 2010 $ 46
Shiraz Viognier 2003 Powerful wine, with silky red and black fruits, chocolate, plum and the viognier lift. Gold medal Sydney Wine Show '06. Cork. 13.7° alc. **RATING** 94 **DRINK** 2015 $ 19
Shiraz 2001 Clear bright colour; elegant red and black cherry and spice aromas and flavours; almost delicate, but totally delicious. Cork. **RATING** 94 **DRINK** 2015 $ 24.50
Yarra Valley Chardonnay Pinot Noir Pinot Meunier 2001 Fine mousse; high-toned grapefruit and spice aromas; fine, elegant and long palate; crystal bright and pure; great finish. **RATING** 94 **DRINK** 2011 $ 25

ΨΨΨΨΨ **Bastard Hill Pinot Noir 2003** A totally delicious array of cherry, strawberry and plum fruit aromas and flavours; silky and long; classic peacock's tail style; fine tannins. Minor brett issues. Cork. **RATING** 93 **DRINK** 2009 $ 50
Viognier 2005 Very rich and ripe, but not hot, fruit; layers of flavour ranging through apricot, musk and ginger; plenty of attitude. Screwcap. 14.2° alc. **RATING** 91 **DRINK** 2009 $ 19
Sauvignon Blanc Semillon 2003 Still very fresh; appealing tropical fruit and peach mix; excellent mid-palate; clean finish. Screwcap. **RATING** 90 **DRINK** Now $ 19.50
Chardonnay 2003 Very pale straw-green; complex barrel ferment aromas; elegant melon and citrus palate; initially light, builds through to the finish. Cork. **RATING** 90 **DRINK** Now $ 19.50
Pinot Gris 2004 Tight mineral, spice, apple and lemon aromas and flavours; bright, crisp finish; not alcoholic. Screwcap. 13° alc. **RATING** 90 **DRINK** Now $ 21.50
Viognier 2004 Spice, nectarine and apricot aromas; a delicate, fresh palate; good length and supple finish. Screwcap. **RATING** 90 **DRINK** Now $ 27.50

ΨΨΨΨ **Cabernet Sauvignon 2002** Light- to medium-bodied; fine, elegant savoury blackcurrant fruit and balanced tannins; just a little too light. Cork. **RATING** 89 **DRINK** 2008 $ 24.50
Pinot Gris 2005 Light-bodied; fresh citrus, pear and apple; good balance and length. Screwcap. 14.4° alc. **RATING** 88 **DRINK** 2009 $ 21

Yarra Edge

NR

PO Box 390, Yarra Glen, Vic 3775 **REGION** Yarra Valley
T (03) 9730 0100 **F** (03) 9739 0135 **WWW**.yering.com **OPEN** At Yering Station
WINEMAKER Tom Carson, Darren Rathbone **EST.** 1984 **CASES** 2000
Now leased to Yering Station, which makes the wines but continues to use the Yarra Edge brand for grapes from this estate. Tom Carson, Yering Station winemaker, was briefly winemaker/manager at Yarra Edge and knows the property intimately, so the rich style can be expected to continue. Exports to Hong Kong.

Yarra Ridge
★★★★

c/- Beringer Blass, GPO Box 753F, Melbourne Vic 3001 **REGION** Yarra Valley
T (03) 8626 3300 **WWW**.yarraridge.com.au **OPEN** Not
WINEMAKER Matt Steel **EST.** 1983 **CASES** 45 000
Now simply a brand owned by FWE, the winery having been sold to a partnership including Rob 'Sticks' Dolan. For the time being, Yarra Ridge wines will be made at Sticks, but they will presumably migrate to SA in due course.

ΥΥΥΥΥ **Unwooded Chardonnay 2004** Enjoyable tangy citrus and melon fruit; has good mouthfeel and length, well above the average for the style. Screwcap. 13° alc. **RATING** 90 **DRINK** 2009 $ 22
Shiraz 2004 Medium-bodied; spicy, savoury nuances to blackberry fruit; good oak management. Screwcap. 14.5° alc. **RATING** 90 **DRINK** 2011

ΥΥΥΥ **Pinot Noir 2004** Light- to medium-bodied; firm plum and black cherry fruit; not especially complex, but has a good finish. Screwcap. 13° alc. **RATING** 89 **DRINK** 2008
Pinot Noir Chardonnay 2001 Tangy lemon blossom and lemon rind aromas; crisp, delicate style, not particularly intense, but has fair length. **RATING** 89 **DRINK** Now $ 35
Shiraz 2003 Light- to medium-bodied; red and black fruits plus some cool climate spice; not particularly concentrated. Screwcap. **RATING** 89 **DRINK** 2010 $ 22
Merlot 2003 Olive, spice and blackcurrant aromas and flavours; good length and persistence. Screwcap. **RATING** 88 **DRINK** 2010 $ 22

ΥΥΥΥ **Pinot Noir 2003** **RATING** 86 **DRINK** Now $ 22

Yarra Track Wines
★★★☆

518 Old Healesville Road, Yarra Glen, Vic 3775 **REGION** Yarra Valley
T (03) 9730 1349 **F** (03) 9730 1910 **OPEN** 7 days 10–5.30
WINEMAKER MasterWineMakers **EST.** 1989 **CASES** 800
Jim and Diana Viggers began establishing their vineyard back in 1989; it now has 3.1 ha of chardonnay and 3.4 ha of pinot noir. The Viggers intend to increase wine production progressively, and sell part of the grape production in the meantime.

ΥΥΥΥΥ **Kane's Chardonnay 2005** Light straw-green; an elegant medium-bodied wine, with some creamy lees inputs, and typical Yarra Valley length to the white peach and melon fruit. Screwcap. 14.3° alc. **RATING** 92 **DRINK** 2010 $ 25

ΥΥΥΥ **Rose 2005** Pale, bright red-purple; neatly balanced, with enough residual sugar to keep the cellar door happy, yet leaving the wine fresh. Screwcap. 13.5° alc. **RATING** 86 **DRINK** Now $ 20

Yarra Vale
★★★☆

Paynes Road, Seville, Vic 3139 **REGION** Yarra Valley
T (03) 9735 1819 **F** (03) 9737 6565 **OPEN** Not
WINEMAKER Domenic Bucci **EST.** 1982 **CASES** 1500
This is the second time around for Domenic Bucci, who built the first stage of what is now Eyton-on-Yarra before being compelled to sell the business in the hard times of the early 1990s. He has established 2 ha of cabernet sauvignon and 0.5 ha of merlot, supplemented by chardonnay which is supplied in return for his winemaking services to the grower.

ΥΥΥΥΥ **Reserve Pinot Noir 2004** Good purple-red colour; clean and bright plum and cherry fruit; good structure, controlled tannins and balanced oak. Cork. 13.5° alc. **RATING** 91 **DRINK** 2010 $ 26
Reserve Shiraz 2004 Bright, light colour; light- to medium-bodied, smooth and supple red fruits; fine tannins, balanced oak. Cork. 14.8° alc. **RATING** 90 **DRINK** 2013 $ 33

♥♥♥♥ **Reserve Chardonnay 2004** A solid wine; ripe stone fruit and subtle oak, although the cork has done the wine no favours. Cork. 14° alc. **RATING** 87 **DRINK** Now $ 23

♥♥♥♡ **Sauvignon Blanc 2004 RATING** 86 **DRINK** Now $ 20
Cabernet Sauvignon 2002 RATING 86 **DRINK** 2010 $ 25

Yarra Valley Gateway Estate ★★★

669 Maroondah Highway, Coldstream, Vic 3770 **REGION** Yarra Valley
T (03) 9739 0568 **F** (03) 9739 0568 **WWW**.gatewayestate.com.au **OPEN** 7 days 9–5
WINEMAKER Matt Aldridge (Contract) **EST.** 1993 **CASES** 2150
Rod Spurling extended his successful hydroponic tomato-growing business by planting 5 ha of sauvignon blanc, chardonnay and pinot noir in 1993. This is part of the grouping of so-called Micro Masters in the Yarra Valley.

♥♥♥♥ **Spurling Hill Vineyard Sauvignon Blanc 2005** Clean, crisp and lively, flavour more in the mineral than fruit spectrum; pleasantly dry finish. Screwcap. **RATING** 88 **DRINK** Now $ 17
Spurling Farm Reserve Pinot Noir 2004 Good purple-red hue; light- to medium-bodied, with savoury/spicy/foresty nuances to the red fruit; a dry, foresty/earthy finish. Screwcap. 14° alc. **RATING** 88 **DRINK** 2009 $ 34

Yarra Yarra ★★★★☆

239 Hunts Lane, Steels Creek, Vic 3775 **REGION** Yarra Valley
T (03) 5965 2380 **F** (03) 5965 2086 **OPEN** By appt
WINEMAKER Ian Maclean **EST.** 1979 **CASES** NFP
Despite its small production, the wines of Yarra Yarra found their way onto a veritable who's who of Melbourne's best restaurants, encouraging Ian Maclean to increase the estate plantings from 2 ha to over 7 ha in 1996 and 1997. Demand for the beautifully crafted wines continued to exceed supply, so the Macleans have planted yet more vines and increased winery capacity. Exports to the UK and Singapore.

♥♥♥♥♥ **The Yarra Yarra 2003** Strong purple-red; cedary/earthy/savoury blackcurrant; medium-bodied, with fine-grained tannins and good oak. Cork. 13.5° alc. **RATING** 94 **DRINK** 2013 $ 65

♥♥♥♥♡ **Shiraz Viognier 2004** Medium red-purple; light- to medium-bodied; elegant, spicy, fresh red fruits with viognier lift, and not threatened by alcohol. Diam. 13.5° alc. **RATING** 92 **DRINK** 2012 $ 40
Cabernets 2003 Slightly less vivid hue; savoury/earthy/spicy/minty edges to cassis and blackcurrant fruit; fine tannins, long finish. Cork. 13° alc. **RATING** 92 **DRINK** 2013 $ 45
Sauvignon Blanc Semillon 2003 Glowing yellow-green, quite developed; a powerful, complex and rich white Bordeaux style; may be a bit less would have been better. Diam. 13° alc. **RATING** 90 **DRINK** 2009 $ 37

Yarra Yering ★★★★★

Briarty Road, Coldstream, Vic 3770 **REGION** Yarra Valley
T (03) 5964 9267 **F** (03) 5964 9239 **OPEN** Sat 10–5, Sun 2–5 while stocks last
WINEMAKER Bailey Carrodus, Mark Haisma **EST.** 1969 **CASES** 10 000
Dr Bailey Carrodus makes extremely powerful, occasionally idiosyncratic, wines from his 40-year-old, low-yielding unirrigated vineyards. Both red and white wines have an exceptional depth of flavour and richness, although my preference for what I believe to be his great red wines is well known. As he has expanded the size of his vineyards, so has the range of wines become ever more eclectic, none more so than the only Vintage Port being produced in the Yarra Valley. The wines are exported to the UK, US and other major markets.

♥♥♥♥♥ **Chardonnay 2003** Very good green-yellow; a complex, rich, textured wine with ripe nectarine fruit, seamless oak and very good acidity to close. Long finish. By far the best yet. Cork. 12.9° alc. **RATING** 94 **DRINK** 2010 $ 70

Underhill Shiraz 2003 Good colour; medium-bodied; smooth, supple black fruits and ripe tannins; integrated French oak; very good balance and length. Cork. 14° alc. **RATING** 94 **DRINK** 2015 $ 60

Dry Red No. 2 2003 Fragrant; more complex than the Underhill, but arguably not better; the viognier component assists the supple, smooth, medium-bodied palate. Sold out, this tasting note for interest. Cork. 13.5° alc. **RATING** 94 **DRINK** 2015 $ 65

Portsorts 2003 Deep, but not Portuguese, opacity of colour; layers of very complex fruit; anise, dried prune, blackberry, five-spice and puppy dogs tails; good fruit/spirit/sweetness balance; in fact, finishes quite dry. 21.5° alc. **RATING** 94 **DRINK** 2020 $ 70

ΨΨΨΨΨ **Dry Red No. 1 2003** Better colour than the New Vineyard, but does not have the depth of yesteryear; medium-bodied; complex flavour and texture, fresh and bright, but with a hard edge coming from the low alcohol and low pH. Cork. 12.5° alc. **RATING** 93 **DRINK** 2015 $ 60

New Vineyard Dry Red No. 1 2003 Medium-bodied; a lively assemblage of black and red fruits; very good mouthfeel, texture and length. Cork. 13° alc. **RATING** 93 **DRINK** 2015 $ 45

Sangiovese 2003 Colour development moving along; excellent satin-smooth texture and mouthfeel; a piquant cherry and strawberry mix; best to date under this label. Cork. 13.1° alc. **RATING** 93 **DRINK** 2012 $ 70

New Vineyard Shiraz 2003 Light- to medium-bodied; fresh, lively and long; cherry plum and spice; good acidity on the vibrant palate. Cork. 14.5° alc. **RATING** 91 **DRINK** 2013 $ 45

Pinot Noir 2003 Very deep colour; in archetypal Yarra Yering Pinot style; more density and structure than all the other top pinot noirs, but with less varietal character. The stuff of heroes. Cork. 13.6° alc. **RATING** 90 **DRINK** 2012 $ 70

ΨΨΨΨ **Merlot 2003** Light colour; light- to medium-bodied; savoury/earthy/olive/spice varietal character, but does not have enough structure or weight at its price point. Cork. 12.5° alc. **RATING** 89 **DRINK** 2010 $ 110

Yarrabank ★★★★★

38 Melba Highway, Yarra Glen, Vic 3775 **REGION** Yarra Valley
T (03) 9730 0100 **F** (03) 9739 0135 **WWW.**yering.com **OPEN** 7 days 10–5
WINEMAKER Michel Parisot, Tom Carson, Darren Rathbone **EST.** 1993 **CASES** 5000
The 1997 vintage saw the opening of the majestic new winery, established as part of a joint venture between the French Champagne house Devaux and Yering Station. Until 1997 the Yarrabank Cuvee Brut was made under Claude Thibaut's direction at Domaine Chandon, but thereafter the entire operation has been conducted at Yarrabank. There are now 4 ha of dedicated 'estate' vineyards at Yering Station; the balance of the intake comes from other growers in the Yarra Valley and southern Victoria. Wine quality has been quite outstanding, the wines having a delicacy unmatched by any other Australian sparkling wines. Exports to all major markets.

ΨΨΨΨΨ **Cuvee 2000** Excellent mousse, persistent and fine; pure mineral and apple woven through gentle yeast autolysis; exceptionally fine and long; great house style. **RATING** 95 **DRINK** 2010 $ 35

Cuvee 2001 Spicy, strawberry, nectarine fruit; long, elegant and fine; low dosage even though no malolactic fermentation; 4 years on yeast lees. 12.5° alc. **RATING** 94 **DRINK** 2010 $ 35

ΨΨΨΨΨ **Creme de Cuvee NV** Pale salmon-pink; rich and full in the mouth; moderately sweet à la Cuvee Riche of Domaine Chandon. **RATING** 92 **DRINK** Now $ 30

YarraLoch ★★★★★

36 Mary Street, St Kilda West, Vic 3182 (postal) **REGION** Yarra Valley
T (03) 8525 4275 **F** (03) 9534 7539 **WWW.**yarraloch.com.au **OPEN** Not
WINEMAKER Carlei Estate **EST.** 1998 **CASES** 3000
This is the ambitious project of successful investment banker Stephen Wood. He has taken the best possible advice, and has not hesitated to provide appropriate financial resources to a venture which has no exact parallel in the Yarra Valley or anywhere else in Australia. Twelve ha of vineyards may not

seem so unusual, but in fact he has assembled 3 entirely different sites, 70 km apart, each matched to the needs of the variety/varieties planted on that site. The 4.4 ha of pinot noir are on the Steep Hill Vineyard, with a northeast orientation, and a shaley rock and ironstone soil. The 4 ha of cabernet sauvignon have been planted on a vineyard at Kangaroo Ground, with a dry, steep northwest-facing site and abundant sun exposure in the warmest part of the day, ensuring full ripeness of the cabernet. Just over 3.5 ha of merlot, shiraz, chardonnay and viognier are planted at the Upper Plenty vineyard, 50 km from Kangaroo Ground. This has an average temperature 2° cooler and a ripening period 2–3 weeks later than the warmest parts of the Yarra Valley. Add the winemaking skills of Sergio Carlei, and some sophisticated (and beautiful) packaging, and you have a 3-star recipe for success.

ᵀᵀᵀᵀᵀ **Stephanie's Dream Yarra Valley Chardonnay 2004** An exceptionally elegant style; melon, nectarine and grapefruit interwoven with quality French oak and creamy lees characters; long finish. Diam. 13° alc. RATING 96 DRINK 2014 $40

Stephanie's Dream Yarra Valley Merlot 2004 Excellent purple-red; lively, intense medium-bodied palate; strong varietal expression through plum, blackcurrant and spice; excellent oak and extract. Diam. 14° alc. RATING 94 DRINK 2015 $40

ᵀᵀᵀᵀᵀ **Yarra Valley Cabernets 2004** Savoury, earthy Bordeaux style; super-fine tannins define the texture and, to a degree, the austere dark berry flavours; cries out for time. Cork. 14.5° alc. RATING 91 DRINK 2015 $25

Yarra Valley Pinot Noir 2003 Good colour; light- to medium-bodied; savoury, spicy plum flavours; tannins just a little bit powdery/dry; best with food. Diam. 14° alc. RATING 90 DRINK 2010 $25

Yarraman Estate   NR

Yarraman Road, Wybong, NSW 2333 REGION Upper Hunter Valley
T (02) 6547 8118 F (02) 6547 8039 WWW.yarramanestate.com OPEN 7 days 10–5
WINEMAKER Chris Mennie EST. 1958 CASES 55 000
This is the oldest winery and vineyard in the Upper Hunter, established in 1958 as Penfolds Wybong Estate; it was acquired by Rosemount in 1974, and retained until 1994. During 1999–2001 a new winery and storage area was built; after hitting financial turbulence it was acquired by a small group of Sydney businessmen. Board changes and subsequent strengthening of the management and winemaking team has seen a surge in exports to all major markets.

Yarrambat Estate   NR

45 Laurie Street, Yarrambat, Vic 3091 (postal) REGION Yarra Valley
T (03) 9717 3710 F (03) 9717 3712 WWW.yarrambatestate.com OPEN Not
WINEMAKER John Ellis (Contract) EST. 1995 CASES 1500
Ivan McQuilkin has a little over 2.6 ha of chardonnay, pinot noir, cabernet sauvignon and merlot on his vineyard in the northwestern corner of the Yarra Valley, not far from the Plenty River, which joins the Yarra River near Melbourne. He and Hayden Gregson run the vineyard (Ivan is responsible for the commercial aspects of the vineyard, Hayden for viticulture and wine production). It is very much an alternative occupation for McQuilkin, whose principal activity is as an international taxation consultant to expatriate employees. While the decision to make the wine was at least in part triggered by falling grape prices, hindsight proves it to have been a good one, because some of the wines have impressed. There are no cellar door sales; the conditions of the licence are that wine sales can only take place by mail order or over the internet.

Yarrawa Estate   NR

PO Box 6018, Kangaroo Valley, NSW 2577 REGION Shoalhaven Coast
T (02) 4465 1165 WWW.yarrawaestate.com OPEN Not
WINEMAKER Bevan Wilson EST. 1998 CASES 600
Susan and Mark Francis Foster established Yarrawa Estate in 1998, planting a wide variety of trees, table grapes and 2.5 ha of verdelho, chardonnay, chambourcin, merlot and cabernet sauvignon. The hillside vineyard has views across the Kangaroo Valley, with the Kangaroo River directly below. Finger board directions up the hill point the way for the first-time visitor. At the 2005 South Coast Wine Show Yarrawa Estate had the top-pointed Chambourcin (2004), following the success of the 2003.

Yarrawalla Wines

PO Box 17, Coldstream, Vic 3770 **REGION** Yarra Valley
T (03) 5964 9363 **F** (03) 5964 9363 **WWW**.yarrawallawines.com.au **OPEN** At 132 Auburn Road,
Hawthorn, Tues–Sat 12–6
WINEMAKER Dominique Portet **EST.** 1994 **CASES** 1500
A very prominent vineyard on Maddens Lane, with 23 ha of chardonnay, 13 ha of pinot noir and 7 ha
of sauvignon blanc. With the arrival of Dominique Portet (also on Maddens Lane), Yarrawalla has
ventured into winemaking under its own label, although the major part of the production continues
to be sold as grapes.

ΥΥΥΥΥ **Pinot Noir 2004** Good colour; supple, smooth, cherry, plum and spice; clear varietal
character; good balance and length. Screwcap. 14.5° alc. **RATING** 90 **DRINK** 2008 $ 16

ΥΥΥΥ **Sauvignon Blanc 2005** Well-made; attractive tropical passionfruit flavours; a relatively
soft finish, ready now. Screwcap. 13° alc. **RATING** 89 **DRINK** Now $ 14
Chardonnay 2004 Light- to medium-bodied; nectarine, melon and white peach; some
nutty/lees/oak notes; has Yarra Valley length, though not so much intensity. Screwcap.
14.5° alc. **RATING** 89 **DRINK** 2009 $ 16

Yarrowlumla Estates ★★★

1133 Bungendore Road, Bywong, NSW 2621 (postal) **REGION** Canberra District
T (02) 6236 9108 **F** (02) 6236 9508 **WWW**.yarrowlumla.com.au **OPEN** Not
WINEMAKER Lark Hill **EST.** 2004 **CASES** 500
In 2004 Martine and Stuart Gibson-Bode, together with Gary and Dianne Gibson (Stuart's parents)
purchased an existing 1.5 ha vineyard planted to chardonnay, sauvignon blanc, merlot and cabernet
sauvignon in 1997. The property is located in the hills above Bungendore, and the Aboriginal name
means 'where the cry comes back from the mountains' (echo).

ΥΥΥΥ **Merlot 2005** Light, bright colour; light-bodied, fresh, vibrant, small red fruits; a crossover
from rose, but overall effect good. Screwcap. 12.5° alc. **RATING** 87 **DRINK** 2008 $ 15

ΥΥΥΥ **Chardonnay Sauvignon Blanc 2005** Pleasant, light-bodied citrussy, minerally flavours;
fresh and lively thanks to low alcohol. Screwcap. 11.5° alc. **RATING** 86 **DRINK** 2008 $ 15

Yass Valley Wines NR

5 Crisps Lane, Murrumbateman, NSW 2582 **REGION** Canberra District
T (02) 6227 5592 **F** (02) 6227 5592 **OPEN** Wed–Sun & public hols 10–5, or by appt
WINEMAKER Michael Withers **EST.** 1978 **CASES** 1000
Michael Withers and Anne Hillier purchased Yass Valley in January 1991 and have subsequently
rehabilitated the existing run-down vineyards and extended the plantings. Mick Withers is a chemist
by profession and has completed a Wine Science degree at Charles Sturt University; Anne is a
registered psychologist and has completed a Viticulture diploma at Charles Sturt.

Yaxley Estate ★★★

31 Dransfield Road, Copping, Tas 7174 **REGION** Southern Tasmania
T (03) 6253 5222 **F** (03) 6253 5222 **OPEN** 7 days 10–6.30 by appt
WINEMAKER Hood Wines (Andrew Hood) **EST.** 1991 **CASES** 400
While Yaxley Estate was established back in 1991, it was not until 1998 that it offered each of the 4
wines from its vineyard plantings, which total just under 2 ha. Once again, it is the small batch
handling skills (and patience) of Andrew Hood that have made the venture possible.

ΥΥΥΥ **Pinot Gris 2005** Rich, big, layered flavour; ripe fruits into poached pear/peach. **RATING** 87
DRINK 2008 $ 25

ΥΥΥΥ **Pinot Noir 2004** **RATING** 84 **DRINK** Now $ 25

Yellowglen ★★★☆

Whites Road, Smythesdale, Vic 3351 **REGION** Ballarat
T (03) 5342 8617 **F** (03) 5333 7102 **WWW**.yellowglen.com.au **OPEN** Mon–Fri 10–5, w'ends 11–5
WINEMAKER Charles Hargrave **EST.** 1975 **CASES** 420 000
Just as the overall quality of Australian sparkling wine has improved out of all recognition over the past 15 years, so has that of Yellowglen. Initially the quality lift was apparent at the top end of the range; it now extends to the non-vintage commercial releases. The winemaking facility has closed.

TTTTY **Vintage Perle 2001** Elegant and refined style; tight and youthful mineral and citrus; breezy, dry finish;3 years on lees. Pinot Noir/Chardonnay/Pinot Meunier. **RATING** 92 **DRINK** 2008 $ 23

TTTT **Vintage Pinot Noir Chardonnay 2004** Tangy citrus and tangerine fruit, relatively dry finish. **RATING** 87 **DRINK** Now $ 16

TTTY **Cremant 2004** **RATING** 85 **DRINK** Now $ 16

TTT **Vintage Bella 2005** **RATING** 83 $ 16

Yellymong NR

Moulamein Road, Swan Hill, Vic 3585 **REGION** Swan Hill
T (03) 5032 2160 **F** (03) 5032 2160 **OPEN** By appt
WINEMAKER Allan Cooper **EST.** 2000 **CASES** 500
Gary and Jo Jeans have a tiny 0.4 ha of pinot gris, supplemented by purchases of other varieties from local growers, all of which are hand-picked. The Pinot Gris can be remarkably good given the (theoretically) unsuitable (too warm) climate.

Yengari Wines ★★★★

Lot 3 Wangaratta Road, Beechworth, Vic 3747 **REGION** Beechworth
T (03) 5833 9295 **F** (03) 5833 9296 **WWW**.yengari.com **OPEN** By appt
WINEMAKER Tony Lacy **EST.** 1998 **CASES** 2000
Tony Lacy and partner Trish Flores run an interesting grape and olive produce business. Painted candles coloured with wine lees, stationery tinted using the same colour bases, wine soap (shiraz, chardonnay and cabernet sauvignon) and water colour paints (shiraz from 100% sun-dried wine lees and chardonnay from sun-dried wine lees plus traces of natural water colour) are all produced and sold. Green Ant Wines is the separate venture of Tony Lacy, using contract-grown grapes from Rutherglen, Glenrowan, King Valley, Alpine Valley, Goulburn Valley and Nagambie.

TTTTY **Gravestein Reserve Shiraz Viognier 2002** Aromas of blackberry, spice, dried apricot and a dash of oak; a luscious, but not jammy, palate has an exotic mix of black fruits, spice and mocha, plus skilled use of French oak and tannin control. Cork. **RATING** 91 **DRINK** 2010 $ 32
Wendy's Paddock Single Vineyard Shiraz 2003 Vanilla, mocha, black cherry and soft spice aromas are followed by a palate with black cherry, blackberry and fine, silky, ripe tannins; nicely handled oak. Cork. **RATING** 90 **DRINK** 2011 $ 24

TTTT **Michael's Paddock Single Vineyard Cabernet Sauvignon 2003** Solid blackberry fruit, with slightly gamey edges to the aroma; plenty of flavour, structure and length. (From a Tallarook vineyard). Cork. **RATING** 89 **DRINK** 2013 $ 20
Barry's Paddock Single Vineyard Chardonnay 2004 Attractive peachy fruit runs through both the bouquet and palate; gentle oak is well-integrated, and the wine has the good mouthfeel which is such a feature of all of Tony Lacy's wines. Cork. **RATING** 88 **DRINK** 2008 $ 18

TTTY **Single Vineyard Coonawarra Cabernet Sauvignon 2004** **RATING** 86 **DRINK** 2009 $ 26

Yering Farm

St Huberts Road, Yering, Vic 3770 **REGION** Yarra Valley
T (03) 9739 0461 **F** (03) 9739 0467 **WWW.**yeringfarmwines.com **OPEN** 7 days 10–5
WINEMAKER Alan Johns **EST.** 1988 **CASES** 7000
Former East Doncaster orchardist Alan Johns acquired the 40-ha Yeringa Vineyard property in 1980; the property had originally been planted by the Deschamps family in the mid-19th century and known as Yeringa Cellars. The plantings now extend to 12 ha, the first wines being made by Alan Johns in 1992. Since that time all of the wines have been made onsite, and have enjoyed consistent show success over the years.

ΨΨΨΨ **Yarra Valley Pinot Noir 2004** Light, bright purple-red; clean, fresh cherry and strawberry fruit on a light- to medium-bodied, nicely balanced palate. Cork. **RATING** 89 **DRINK** 2009 **$** 45
Yarra Valley Pinot Noir 2003 Light- to medium-bodied; spicy, savoury aromas, the fruit profile more towards black fruits; fine tannins. Cork. **RATING** 89 **DRINK** Now **$** 28
Yarra Valley Merlot 2003 Clean, ripe, sweet red berry aromas and flavours; appropriate tannins and oak. Cork. **RATING** 89 **DRINK** 2010 **$** 25
Yarra Valley Cabernet Sauvignon 2003 Ripe, quite luscious, blackcurrant fruit; slightly simple structure. Cork. **RATING** 89 **DRINK** 2011 **$** 45
Yarra Valley Cabernet Sauvignon 2002 A light, savoury style, but does have good length and balance. Cork. **RATING** 88 **DRINK** 2010 **$** 25

Yering Range Vineyard

NR

14 McIntyre Lane, Coldstream, Vic 3770 **REGION** Yarra Valley
T (03) 9739 1172 **F** (03) 9739 1172 **OPEN** By appt
WINEMAKER Hanging Rock Winery **EST.** 1989 **CASES** 200
Yering Range has 2 ha of cabernet sauvignon under vine; part is sold and part is made under the Yering Range label.

Yering Station

38 Melba Highway, Yarra Glen, Vic 3775 **REGION** Yarra Valley
T (03) 9730 0100 **F** (03) 9739 0135 **WWW.**yering.com **OPEN** 7 days 10–5
WINEMAKER Tom Carson, Darren Rathbone, Caroline Mooney **EST.** 1988 **CASES** 60 000
The historic Yering Station (or at least the portion of the property on which the cellar door sales and vineyard are established) was purchased by the Rathbone family in January 1996 and is now the site of a joint venture with the French Champagne house Devaux. A spectacular and very large winery has been erected which handles the Yarrabank sparkling wines and the Yering Station and Yarra Edge table wines. It has immediately become one of the focal points of the Yarra Valley, particularly as the historic Chateau Yering, where luxury accommodation and fine dining are available, is next door. Yering Station's own restaurant is open every day for lunch, providing the best cuisine in the Valley. Since 2002, a sister company of Mount Langi Ghiran, now also owned by the Rathbone family. In 2004 Yering Station, via Tom Carson, was named International Winemaker of the Year by the International Wine & Spirit Competition in London. Exports to all major markets.

ΨΨΨΨΨ **Yarra Valley Chardonnay 2004** Graceful, silky smooth, sensuous mouthfeel; winemaker inputs with great balance; excellent line. 13° alc. **RATING** 95 **DRINK** 2014 **$** 20.50
MVR 2005 Fragrant and flowery blossom aromas; sweet apple, pear and apricot; vibrant acidity. Cork. **RATING** 94 **DRINK** Now **$** 23
Pinot Noir ED Rose 2005 Salmon-tinged; spicy strawberry and plum aromas; elegant but complex, with more length than any of the top-end roses. Screwcap. **RATING** 94 **DRINK** Now **$** 17.50
Yarra Valley Shiraz Viognier 2004 Typical bright purple-red; medium-bodied, lively, spicy/juicy berry fruit with sensitive oak and ripe tannins; one of the role models for this combination. Gold medal National Wine Show '05. Screwcap. 14° alc. **RATING** 94 **DRINK** 2016 **$** 23
Yarra Valley Cabernet Sauvignon 2003 Very good hue; a stylish, medium-bodied wine, with pure cabernet varietal fruit sensitively supported by French oak and fine, ripe tannins. Screwcap. **RATING** 94 **DRINK** 2018 **$** 23

ᵀᵀᵀᵀ♀ **Yarra Valley Chardonnay 2005** Clean, fragrant, fruit-driven style; spicy French oak merely a support system; long palate, fruit expanding on the finish. Screwcap. 13.5° alc. **RATING** 93 **DRINK** 2012 $ 20.50
Yarra Valley Pinot Noir 2004 Good hue; firm, fresh bright plum and black cherry fruit; still to unfurl its wings; simply needs time. Screwcap. 13.5° alc. **RATING** 92 **DRINK** 2013 $ 23

ᵀᵀᵀᵀ **Yarra Valley Nebbiolo 2004** Well-made, of course, but simply shows the limitations of the variety; a faintly spicy/savoury light-bodied dry red. Screwcap. 13° alc. **RATING** 88 **DRINK** 2009 $ 23

Yeringberg
★★★★★

Maroondah Highway, Coldstream, Vic 3770 **REGION** Yarra Valley
T (03) 9739 1453 **F** (03) 9739 0048 **OPEN** By appt
WINEMAKER Guill de Pury **EST.** 1863 **CASES** 1000
Makes wines for the new millennium from the low-yielding vines re-established on the heart of what was one of the most famous (and infinitely larger) vineyards of the 19th century. In the riper years, the red wines have a velvety generosity of flavour which is rarely encountered, yet never lose varietal character, while the Yeringberg Marsanne Roussanne takes students of history back to Yeringberg's fame in the 19th century. Exports to the UK, the US, Canada, Switzerland, Malaysia, Singapore and Hong Kong.

ᵀᵀᵀᵀᵀ **Chardonnay 2004** Super elegant, refined and balanced; melon, stone fruit and a hint of cashew, the oak a near-invisible web. Cork. 14° alc. **RATING** 94 **DRINK** 2011 $ 36
Marsanne Roussanne 2004 Clean, fresh, herb/spice/pear/green apple flavours; long, balanced palate and good acidity; 10 years minimum. Cork. 13.5° alc. **RATING** 94 **DRINK** 2014 $ 36
Pinot Noir 2003 Medium red-purple; clean, ripe plum aromas; the palate stacked with rich black cherry and plum; plenty of structure. Cork. 14° alc. **RATING** 94 **DRINK** 2010 $ 55
Dry Red 2003 Good colour; ripe blackcurrant/cassis fruit; while having much higher alcohol than normal, is not jammy nor shows dead fruit characters. Cork. 15° alc. **RATING** 94 **DRINK** 2019 $ 55

ᵀᵀᵀᵀ **Young Vines Shiraz 2003** Spicy blackberry aromas; a fresh, savoury palate; notwithstanding the alcohol, has some greenish notes. From new Yeringberg plantings, with a distinctly downplayed label. Cork. 15° alc. **RATING** 89 **DRINK** 2010 $ 25

Yerong Creek Estate
NR

'Barwon', Yerong Creek, NSW 2642 **REGION** Riverina
T (02) 6920 3569 **F** (02) 6920 3503 **WWW**.yerongcreekestate.com.au **OPEN** 7 days 10–5
WINEMAKER Cofield Wines **EST.** 1996 **CASES** NA
Robert and Julie Yates have a long-established sheep and wheat property. Like so many others, they thought some diversification would be a good idea, and planted 5 ha in 1996. In December 1997 a bushfire devastated the vineyard, destroying virtually all the vines, the irrigation system and endposts. With the help of family and friends they started again, this time with 2 ha planted to chardonnay and shiraz. Life in the bush can be tough.

Yilgarnia
★★★★

6634 Redmond West Road, Redmond, WA 6327 **REGION** Denmark
T (08) 9845 3031 **F** (08) 9845 3031 **WWW**.yilgarnia.com.au **OPEN** By appt
WINEMAKER Harewood Estate (James Kellie) **EST.** 1997 **CASES** 2000
Melbourne-educated Peter Buxton travelled across the Nullarbor and settled on a bush block of 405 acres on the Hay River, 6 km north of Wilson Inlet. That was over 40 years ago, and for the first 10 years Buxton worked for the WA Department of Agriculture in Albany. While there, he surveyed several of the early vineyards in WA, and recognised the potential of his family's property. Today there are 10 ha of vines in bearing, with another 6 ha planted in 2002 and 2003. All the vineyard plantings (8 varieties in all) are on north-facing blocks, the geological history of which stretches back 2 billion years.

ΤΤΤΤ℣ **Denmark Merlot 2004** Light- to medium-bodied; but strongly varietal, showing all the best points of merlot; sweet redcurrant fruit with multi-spice and black olive nuances. Screwcap. 14.5° alc. **RATING** 93 **DRINK** 2012 $ 21

Denmark Unwooded Chardonnay 2005 Fresh nectarine and citrus mix; good balance and length; a reliably excellent example of unwooded chardonnay. Gold medal Qantas WA Wine Show '05. Screwcap. 14.5° alc. **RATING** 91 **DRINK** 2009 $ 16

ΤΤΤΤ **Denmark Rose 2005** Bright, strong colour; spiced cherry and plum aromas, and abundant flavour in the same spectrum. Screwcap. 12.5° alc. **RATING** 88 **DRINK** Now $ 15

Denmark Classic White 2005 Plenty of fruit flavour ranging through tropical to lemon/citrus; good acidity lengthens the palate. Sauvignon Blanc/Chardonnay/Semillon. Screwcap. 13.5° alc. **RATING** 87 **DRINK** Now $ 15

Denmark Sparkling Shiraz NV Very rich with lots of red fruits and some spice; the dosage is too high, although time will partially fix this. A blend of 4 vintages in the base wine. 14.5° alc. **RATING** 87 **DRINK** 2012 $ 34

ΤΤΤ℣ **Denmark Cabernet Sauvignon 2003** Light colour; shows its low alcohol, with a mix of leaf, mint and sweet berry fruit; obviously struggled for ripeness. Screwcap. 12° alc. **RATING** 86 **DRINK** 2008 $ 19

Remembrance Methode Champenoise 2004 **RATING** 86 **DRINK** Now $ 34

Yokain Vineyard Estate   NR

Worsley Back Road, Allanson, WA 6225 (postal) **REGION** Geographe
T (08) 9725 3397 **F** (08) 9725 3397 **WWW**.yokain.com.au **OPEN** Not
WINEMAKER Siobhan Lynch **EST.** 1998 **CASES** 1000
David and Julie Gardiner began the establishment of their 17-ha vineyard in 1998, with all but 2 ha planted in that year. Verdelho, chardonnay, semillon, shiraz, cabernet sauvignon, merlot and cabernet franc are in production; the 2000 plantings of riesling and zinfandel produced their first grapes in 2003.

Yrsa's Vineyard   ★★★★☆

105 Tucks Road, Main Ridge, Vic 3928 **REGION** Mornington Peninsula
T (03) 5989 6500 **F** (03) 5989 6501 **WWW**.yrsasvineyard.com **OPEN** By appt
WINEMAKER Craig McLeod, Judy Gifford (Contract) **EST.** 1994 **CASES** 1500
Yrsa's Vineyard is named after the lady from whom Steven and Marianne Stern acquired the property. She, in turn, was named after Queen Yrsa of Sweden, born in 565AD, whose story is told in the Norse sagas. Well-known patent and trademark attorney Steven Stern (whose particular area of expertise is in the wine and liquor business) and wife Marianne have established around 2.5 ha each of pinot noir and chardonnay, and initially marketed the wines only in the UK.

ΤΤΤΤΤ **Ursa Major Mornington Peninsula Pinot Noir 2004** Powerful, sweet, round and spicy mouthfilling fruit; very ripe and very long, supported by appropriate tannins. Cork. 13.9° alc. **RATING** 94 **DRINK** 2011 $ 28

ΤΤΤΤ℣ **Ursa Major Mornington Peninsula Chardonnay 2004** Ripe, rich, sweet and supple stone fruit; has considerable intensity, comprehensively swallowing the barrel ferment oak. Made from Dijon clones. Cork. 13.8° alc. **RATING** 92 **DRINK** 2011 $ 28

Zanella Estate   ★★★★

Burnets Road, Traralgon, Vic 3844 **REGION** Gippsland
T (03) 5174 0557 **F** (03) 5174 0557 **OPEN** 7 days
WINEMAKER Ettore Zanella **EST.** 1996 **CASES** NA
Ettorre Zanella has established 1.5 ha of chardonnay, cabernet sauvignon, merlot and shiraz and makes the wine onsite (very competently).

ΤΤΤΤ℣ **Shiraz 2003** Deep colour; a solid, medium-bodied wine with a mix of licorice, blackberry and dark chocolate; powerful, lingering finish. **RATING** 92 **DRINK** 2013 $ 26

Zappacosta Estate Wines

NR

301 Kidman Way, Hanwood, NSW 2680 **REGION** Riverina
T (02) 6963 0278 **F** (02) 6963 0278 **OPEN** 7 days 10–5 by appt
WINEMAKER Dino Zappacosta **EST.** 1956 **CASES** 70 000
Zappacosta Estate, briefly known as Hanwood Village Wines, is primarily a bulk winemaker and supplier to others. Small amounts of Shiraz under the Zappacosta Estate label are made from time to time.

Zarephath Wines

 ★★★★☆

Moorialup Road, East Porongurup, WA 6324 **REGION** Porongurup
T (08) 9853 1152 **F** (08) 9853 1151 **WWW**.zarephathwines.com **OPEN** Mon–Sat 10–5, Sun 12–4
WINEMAKER Robert Diletti **EST.** 1994 **CASES** 3000
The 9-ha Zarephath vineyard is owned and operated by Brothers and Sisters of The Christ Circle, a Benedictine community. They say the most outstanding feature of the location is the feeling of peace and tranquility which permeates the site, something I can well believe on the basis of numerous visits to the Porongurups. Exports to the UK and NZ.

♟♟♟♟♟ **Chardonnay 2004** Light straw-green; vibrant and intense grapefruit and stone fruit, with a lovely streak of minerally acidity and quality oak. Screwcap. 13.5° alc. **RATING** 94 **DRINK** 2011 $ 23

♟♟♟♟♟ **Little Brother Late Harvest Riesling 2004** Aromatic lemon and lime blossom aromas; lovely balance and length, with many of the characters of Mosel Kabinett, residual sugar balanced by acidity; will age beautifully. Screwcap. 11° alc. **RATING** 92 **DRINK** 2014 $ 16
Shiraz 2003 Medium-bodied; bright, fresh red cherry, spice and plum fruits; fine, ripe tannins; subtle oak, good finish. Screwcap. **RATING** 90 **DRINK** 2012 $ 22

♟♟♟♟ **Little Brother Cabernet Merlot 2004** Lively, juicy red berries and blackcurrant; fruit-driven brasserie style. Screwcap. 13.5° alc. **RATING** 89 **DRINK** 2009 $ 16

♟♟♟♟ **Riesling 2005** Somewhat angular style, with grainy acidity, strange given the region. Screwcap. 13° alc. **RATING** 86 **DRINK** 2009 $ 19
Pinot Noir 2004 A pretty wine, but very light-bodied, crossover to rose. Serve chilled in summer. Screwcap. 13.5° alc. **RATING** 86 **DRINK** Now $ 25

Zema Estate

 ★★★★☆

Riddoch Highway, Coonawarra, SA 5263 **REGION** Coonawarra
T (08) 8736 3219 **F** (08) 8736 3280 **WWW**.zema.com.au **OPEN** 7 days 9–5
WINEMAKER Greg Clayfield **EST.** 1982 **CASES** 20 000
Zema is one of the last outposts of hand-pruning in Coonawarra, with members of the Zema family tending a 60-ha vineyard progressively planted since 1982 in the heart of Coonawarra's terra rossa soil. Winemaking practices are straightforward; if ever there was an example of great wines being made in the vineyard, this is it. The extremely popular and equally talented former Lindemans winemaker Greg Clayfield has joined the team, replacing long-term winemaker Tom Simons. Exports to all major markets.

♟♟♟♟♟ **Shiraz 2003** Medium-bodied; smooth, gently ripe and supple blackberry fruit; good tannin and oak management. Cork. **RATING** 91 **DRINK** 2013 $ 26
Shiraz 2004 Medium-bodied, savoury/spicy/earthy blackberry fruit; some tannin support, and good oak contributes positively. Cork. 14.5° alc. **RATING** 90 **DRINK** 2014 $ 26
Merlot 2004 A medium-bodied array of cassis, raspberry and mulberry fruit; controlled French oak, balanced tannins. Screwcap. 13.5° alc. **RATING** 90 **DRINK** 2014 $ 30
Cabernet Sauvignon 2003 Medium purple-red; sweet, juicy blackcurrant fruit with fine tannins and confident oak handling. Cork. 13.5° alc. **RATING** 90 **DRINK** 2013 $ 26
Cluny 2003 An attractive medium-bodied blend of red and black fruits; fine, sweet tannins, and the usual controlled oak. Business as usual. Screwcap. 13° alc. **RATING** 90 **DRINK** 2014 $ 26

Ziebarth Wines

NR

Foleys Road, Goodger, Qld 4610 **REGION** South Burnett
T (07) 4162 3089 **F** (07) 4162 3084 **WWW**.ziebarthwines.com.au **OPEN** Thurs–Sun & public hols 10–5 or by appt
WINEMAKER Crane Winery **EST.** 1998 **CASES** 650
The 4-ha vineyard (with 1 ha each of semillon, cabernet sauvignon, merlot and chardonnay, and 0.25 ha of chambourcin) is a minor diversification on a beef cattle property set on the edge of the Stuart Range (and which enjoys superb views). It is a small family operation which aims to provide a wine experience for visitors.

Zig Zag Road

201 Zig Zag Road, Drummond, Vic 3461 **REGION** Macedon Ranges
T (03) 5423 9390 **F** (03) 5423 9390 **OPEN** W'ends & public hols 10–6, or by appt
WINEMAKER Alan Stevens, Eric Bellchambers **EST.** 1972 **CASES** 300
Alan Stevens and Deb Orton purchased the vineyard in 1988 when it was 16 years old, having been established by Roger Aldridge. The dry-grown vines produce relatively low yields, and until 1996 the grapes were sold to Hanging Rock Winery. In 1996 the decision was taken to manage the property on a full-time basis, and to make the wine onsite, using 0.25 ha each of riesling, merlot and pinot noir, and 1 ha each of shiraz and cabernet sauvignon.

TTTT **Riesling 2004** Rich and powerful, with both depth and a core of minerality, finishing with brisk acidity. 12.2° alc. **RATING** 89 **DRINK** 2010 $18

TTTY **Cabernet Merlot 2003** **RATING** 86 **DRINK** 2008 $25

Zilzie Wines

Lot 66 Kulkyne Way, Karadoc via Red Cliffs, Vic 3496 **REGION** Murray Darling
T (03) 5025 8100 **F** (03) 5025 8116 **WWW**.zilziewines.com **OPEN** Not
WINEMAKER Bob Shields, Leigh Sparrow **EST.** 1999 **CASES** NFP
The Forbes family has been farming Zilzie Estate since 1911; it is currently run by Ian and Ros Forbes, and their sons Steven and Andrew. A diverse range of farming activities now include grapegrowing with 250 ha of vineyards. Having established a position as a dominant supplier of grapes to Southcorp, Zilzie formed a wine company in 1999 and built a winery in 2000. It has a capacity of 16 000 tonnes, but is designed so that modules can be added to take it to 50 000 tonnes. The business includes contract storage, contract processing, contract winemaking, bulk wine production and bottled and branded wines. National distribution through Rutherglen Wine & Spirit Company Limited; exports to the UK, the US, Canada, NZ, Singapore and Thailand.

TTTT **Buloke Sauvignon Blanc 2005** Clean, attractive, ripe tropical fruit bolstered by some residual sugar; maintains balance. Screwcap. **RATING** 87 **DRINK** Now $9.99

TTTY **Buloke Reserve Merlot 2004** **RATING** 86 **DRINK** Now $11
Buloke Reserve Cabernet Merlot 2004 **RATING** 86 **DRINK** 2008 $11
Buloke Reserve Shiraz 2004 **RATING** 85 **DRINK** Now $11
Cabernet Merlot Petit Verdot 2003 **RATING** 85 **DRINK** 2008 $14.99

Zonte's Footstep

NR

Wellington Road/PO Box 53, Langhorne Creek, SA 5255 **REGION** Langhorne Creek
T (08) 8537 3334 **F** (08) 8537 3231 **WWW**.zontesfootstep.com.au **OPEN** Not
WINEMAKER Ben Riggs **EST.** 1997 **CASES** 50 000
The 215-ha vineyard of Zonte's Footstep dates back to 1997 when a group of old school mates banded together to purchase the land and established the vineyard under the direction of viticulturist Geoff Hardy and longterm vigneron John Pargeter. Obviously enough, a large percentage of the grapes are sold to others, a small part skilfully made by Ben Riggs. While it is not clear who Zonte was, the footprint on the label is that of Diprotodon or giant wombat, which inhabited the southeastern corner of South Australia for more than 20 million years until becoming extinct 10–20 000 years ago. The wine quality is as good as the prices are modest.

Acknowledgments

This book would not be possible without the co-operation and goodwill of the vast majority of the 2176 wineries which inhabit its pages, and in particular those who provided almost 6000 wines for tasting (the remaining notes came from wine shows or similar events). To them my thanks, and to a few my sincere apologies as well. An unprecedented number of wines were sent to me in January, February and even March (I should gently point out there was a January 20 deadline) and in the outcome, some 500–600 wines remained untasted. While most of those arrived well after the deadline, despite our best endeavours a few submitted prior or close to the deadline got caught in the tsunami. All these wines have since been tasted, and the notes will appear in next year's edition.

Speaking of which, the new owners of the Coldstream sub-post office, Chris and Bev, never lost the smile on their faces, even when hidden behind mountains of wine boxes. When it became apparent that it was physically impossible to even briefly house the incoming parcels, Australia Post — which provides a countryside delivery service infinitely better than any of the commercial freight companies — arranged for a dedicated delivery van to bring the wines direct to the Coldstream Hills winery (where I do the tastings) each day until the tsunami abated.

Next, my stewards Marcus Hutson and Kate Fleming worked day after day after day unpacking, sorting and cataloguing the wines, pouring them and dealing with all the housekeeping which goes on in the wake of the tastings.

Saving the best till last, my PA, Paula, ably assisted by Beth, whose job it was to enter the wines in the database and keep track of all new wineries, somehow kept the production timetable more or less on track. When it was delayed by 10 days, the staunch HarperCollins team, headed by Ali Orman, responded by helping rather than complaining, and so we all got over the line with the minimum of pain.

Index